# AutoCAD Electrical 2022 for Engineers and Designers

**_Sham Tickoo_**
_Professor_
_Purdue University Northwest_
_Hammond, Indiana, USA_

_Contributing Authors_
**_Arti Deshpande_**
_Tickoo Institute of Emerging Technologies(TIET)_

**_Tickoo Institute of Emerging Technologies (TIET)_**
**_Gurugram, India_**

**_CADCIM Technologies_**
**_Indiana, USA_**

ISBN: 978-93-91392-55-0
***(For distribution in Saarc countries only)***



## Limits of Liability and Disclaimer of Warranty



## Distributors

**COMPUTER BOOK CENTRE**
12, Shrungar Shopping Centre
M.G. Road
BENGALURU–560001
Ph: 25587923/25584641

**DECCAN AGENCIES**
4-3-329, Bank Street
HYDERABAD-500195
Ph: 24756967/24756400

**MICRO MEDIA**
Shop No. 5, Mahendra Chambers
150 DN Rd. Next to Capital Cinema
V.T (C.S.T.) Station
MUMBAI-400001

**BPB BOOK CENTRE**
376 Old Lajpat Rai Market
DELHI-110006
Ph: 23861747

**INFOTECH**
G-2, Sidhartha Building, 96 Nehru Place
NEW DELHI-110019
Ph: 26438245

**BPB PUBLICATIONS**
20, Ansari Road, Darya Ganj
New Delhi-110002
Ph: 23254990/23254991

Published by Manish Jain for BPB Publications, 20 Ansari Road, Darya Ganj
New Delhi-110002 and Printed by Repro India Pvt. Ltd., Mumbai

## DEDICATION

*To teachers, who make it possible to disseminate knowledge*
*to enlighten the young and curious minds*
*of our future generations*

*To students, who are dedicated to learning new technologies*
*and making the world a better place to live in*

## THANKS

*To employees of CADCIM Technologies and*
*Tickoo Institute of Emerging Technologies (TIET)*
*for their valuable help*

This page is intentionally left blank

# Table of Contents

## Chapter 2: Working with Projects and Drawings



## Chapter 3: Working with Wires

## Chapter 4: Creating Ladders



## Chapter 5: Schematic Components

## Chapter 6: Schematic Editing

## Chapter 7: Connectors, Point-to-Point Wiring Diagrams, and Circuits

## Chapter 8: Panel Layouts

## Chapter 9: Schematic and Panel Reports

## Chapter 10: PLC Modules

## Chapter 11: Terminals

## Chapter 12: Settings, Configurations, Templates, and Plotting



## Chapter 13: Creating Symbols

## PROJECT AVAILABLE FOR FREE DOWNLOAD

In this textbook, one project has been given for free download. You can download this project from our website *www.cadcim.com*. To download this project, follow the given path: *Textbooks > CAD/CAM > AutoCAD Electrical > AutoCAD Electrical 2022 for Electrical Control Designers > Chapters for Free Download* and then select the project name from the **Chapters for Free Download** drop-down. Click the **Download** button to download the project in the PDF format.

# Preface

## AutoCAD Electrical 2022

AutoCAD Electrical, a product of Autodesk, Inc., is one of the world's leading application designed specifically to create and modify electrical control systems. This software incorporates the functionality of AutoCAD along with a complete set of electrical CAD features. In addition, its comprehensive symbol libraries and tools help you automate electrical engineering tasks and save your time and effort considerably, thereby providing you more time for innovation.

Prior to the introduction of this software, the electrical control designers had to rely on generic software applications requiring manual layout of electrical schematics that were often prone to design errors and user could not share design information using these applications. However, with the introduction of AutoCAD Electrical, the chances of error have reduced considerably, thereby enabling you to design 2D industrial controls faster and accurately. Moreover, AutoCAD Electrical 2022 is used to automate various control engineering tasks such as building circuits, numbering wires, creating bill of materials, and many more.

The **AutoCAD Electrical 2022 for Engineers and Designers** textbook has been written to assist the engineering students and the practicing designers who are new to AutoCAD Electrical. Using this textbook, the readers can learn the application of basic tools required for creating professional electrical-control drawings with the help of AutoCAD Electrical. Keeping in view the varied requirements of the users, this textbook covers a wide range of tools and features such as schematic drawings, Circuit Builder, panel drawings, parametric and nonparametric PLC modules, stand-alone PLC I/O points, ladder diagrams, point-to-point wiring diagrams, report generation, creation of symbols, and so on. This will help the readers to create electrical drawings easily and effectively. In this edition, the author has added new tutorials on the **Convert Ladder** and **Insert Wblocked Circuit** tools to help the users practice the tools learnt.

The salient features of this textbook are as follows:

- **Tutorial Approach**
  The author has adopted the tutorial point-of-view and the learn-by-doing theme in this textbook. This approach guides the users through the process of creating and managing electrical control drawings. Also, two projects have been added to enable the users to apply the skills learned in the text. In addition, there are about 26 exercises added in the textbook for the users to practice. Note that all tutorials and exercises in this textbook are based on the NFPA(US) standard.

- **Tips and Notes**
  Additional information related to various topics is provided to the users in the form of tips and notes.

- **Learning Objectives**
  The first page of every chapter summarizes the topics covered in that chapter.

- **Self-Evaluation Test, Review Questions, and Exercises**
  Every chapter ends with a Self-Evaluation Test so that the users can assess their knowledge of each chapter. The answers to Self-Evaluation Test are given at the end of the chapter. Also, Review Questions and Exercises are given at the end of each chapter and they can be used by the instructors as test questions and exercises.

- **Heavily Illustrated Text**
  The text in this book is heavily illustrated with the help of around 900 line diagrams and screen captures.

## Symbols Used in the Textbook

**Note**
The author has provided additional information related to various topics in the form of notes.

**Tip**
The author has provided special information to the users in the form of tips.

The author has provided this symbol next to the new topics as well as new tutorials added in this edition of the textbook.

This symbol indicates that the command or tool being discussed is enhanced in the current release.

## Naming Conventions Used in the Textbook

### Tool

If you click on an item in a toolbar or a panel of the Ribbon and a command is invoked to create/edit an object or perform some action, then that item is termed as Tool.

For example:
**To Create**: **Line** tool, **Circle** tool, **Extrude** tool
**To Edit**: **Fillet** tool, **Array** tool, **Stretch** tool
**Action**: **Zoom** tool, **Move** tool, **Copy** tool

If you click on an item in a toolbar or a panel of the Ribbon and a dialog box is invoked wherein you can set the properties to create/edit an object, then that item is also termed as **tool**, refer to Figure 1.

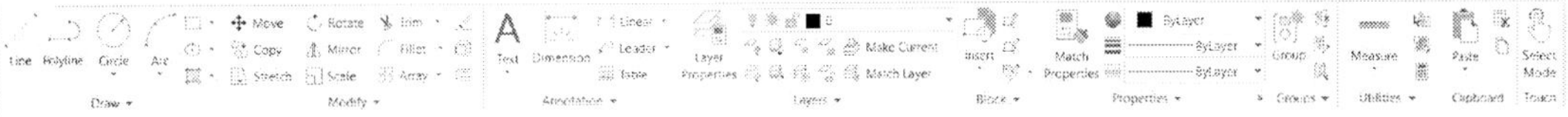


*Figure 1 Various tools in the Ribbon*

For example:
**To Create**: **Define Attributes** tool, **Create** tool, **Insert** tool
**To Edit**: **Edit Attributes** tool, **Block Editor** tool

## Button

If you click on an item in a Application Status Bar and the display of the corresponding object is toggled on/off, then that item is termed as Button. For example, **Grid** button, **Snap** button, **Ortho** button, **Properties** button, and so on, refer to Figure 2. The item in a dialog box that has a 3D shape like a button is also termed as Button. For example, **OK** button, **Cancel** button, **Apply** button, and so on, refer to Figure 3.

*Figure 2 Various buttons displayed in the Status Bar*

## Dialog Box

In this textbook, different terms are used for referring to the components of a dialog box, refer to Figure 3 for the terminology used.

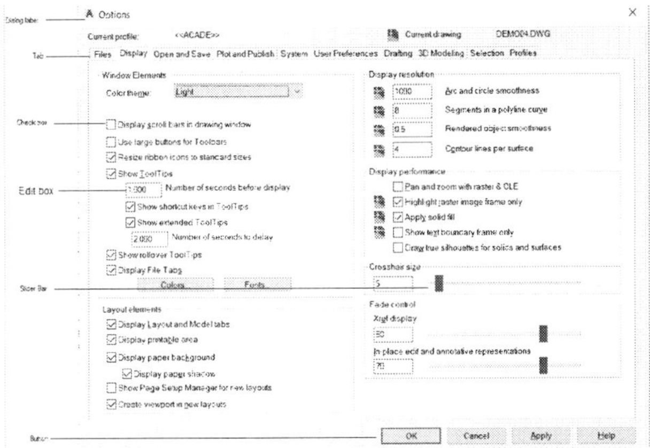


*Figure 3 The components in a dialog box*

## Drop-down

A drop-down is the one in which a set of common tools are grouped together for creating an object. You can identify a drop-down with a down arrow on it. These drop-downs are given a name based on the tools grouped in them. For example, **Edit Components** drop-down, **Modify Wires** drop-down, and so on, refer to Figure 4.

## Drop-down List

A drop-down list is the one in which a set of options are grouped together. You can set various parameters using these options. You can identify a drop-down list with a down arrow on it. To know the name of a drop-down list, move the cursor over it; its name will be displayed as a tool tip. For example, **Lineweight** drop-down list, **Linetype** drop-down list, **Object Color** drop-down list, and so on; refer to Figure 5.

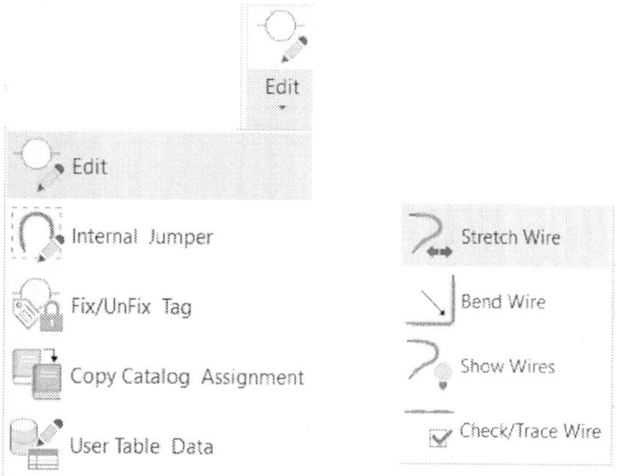


*Figure 4 The **Edit Components** and **Modify Wires** drop-downs*

## Options

Options are the items that are available in shortcut menu, drop-down list, Command Prompt, **Properties** panel, and so on. For example, choose the **Properties** option from the shortcut menu displayed on right-clicking on the active project, refer to Figure 6.

### Tools and Options in Menu Bar

A menu bar consists of both tools and options. As mentioned earlier, the term **tool** is used to create/edit something or perform some action. For example, in Figure 7, the item **Insert Wire** has been used to create a wire, therefore it will be referred as **Insert Wire** tool.

Similarly, an option in the menu bar is the one that is used to set some parameters. For example, in Figure 8, the item **Zip Project** has been used to zip a project, therefore, it will be referred as an option.

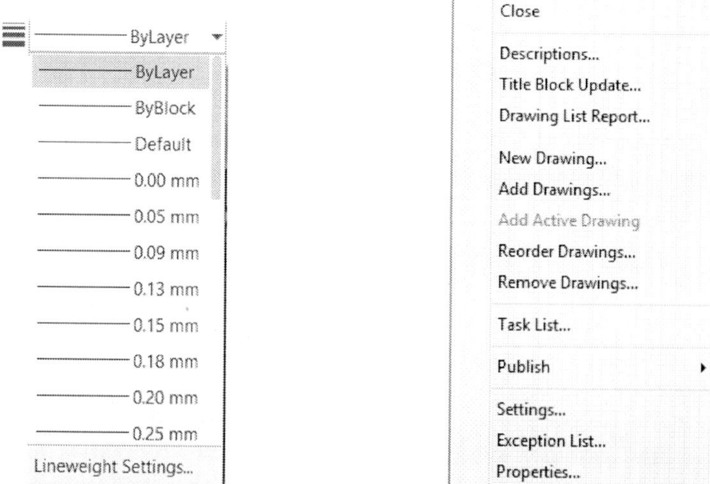


*Figure 5 The **LineWeight** drop-down list*

*Figure 6 Options in the shortcut menu*

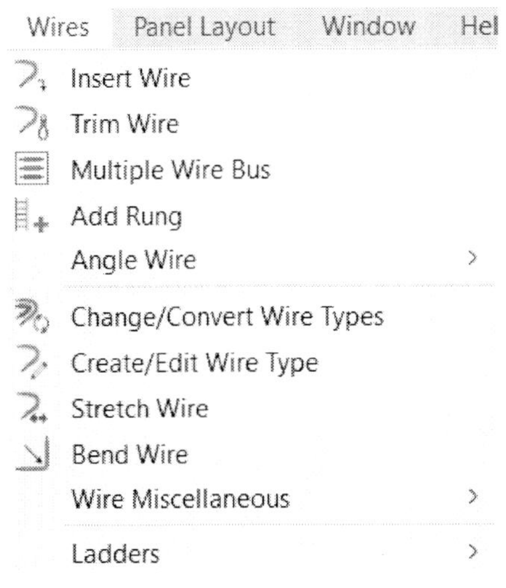


***Figure 7** Tools in the menu bar*

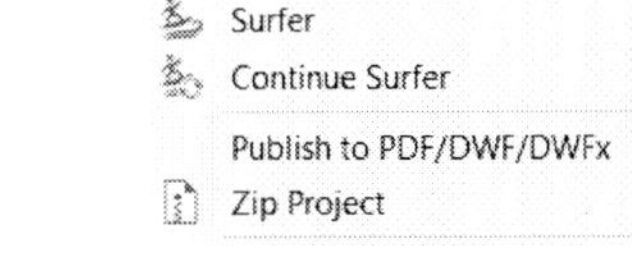


***Figure 8** Options in the menu bar*

## Formatting Conventions Used in the Textbook

Please refer to the following list for the formatting conventions used in this textbook.

- Command names are capitalized and bold. Example: The **MOVE** command

- A key icon appears when you have to respond by pressing the ENTER or the RETURN key. 

- Command sequences are indented. The responses are indicated in boldface. The directions are indicated in italics and the comments are enclosed in parentheses.

  Command: **MOVE**
  Select object: **G**
  Enter group name: *Enter a group name (the group name is group1)*

- The methods of invoking a tool/option from the **Ribbon**, **Menu Bar**, **Quick Access toolbar**, **Tool Palettes**, **Application menu**, toolbars, Status Bar, and Command prompt are enclosed in a shaded box.

| | |
|---|---|
| **Ribbon:** | Draw > Line |
| **Toolbar:** | Draw > Line |
| **Menu:** | Draw > Line |
| **Command:** | LINE or L |

## Free Companion Website

It has been our constant endeavor to provide you the best textbooks and services at affordable price. In this endeavor, we have come out with a Free Companion website that will facilitate the process of teaching and learning of AutoCAD Electrical 2022. If you purchase this textbook, you will get access to the files on the Companion website.

The following resources are available in the website:

- **Technical Support**
  You can get online technical support by contacting ***techsupport@cadcim.com***.

- **Instructor Guide**
  Solutions to all review questions and exercises in the textbook are provided in this guide.

- **Drawing Files**
  The drawing files used in illustration, tutorials, and exercises are available for free download.

If you face any problem in accessing these files, please contact the publisher at ***sales@cadcim.com*** or the author at ***stickoo@pnw.edu*** or ***tickoo525@gmail.com***.

## Video Courses

CADCIM offers video courses in CAD, CAE Simulation, BIM, Civil/GIS, and Animation domains on various e-Learning/Video platforms. To enroll for the video courses, please visit the CADCIM website using the following link: *https://www.cadcim.com/video-courses*

### Stay Connected

You can now stay connected with us through Facebook and Twitter to get the latest information about our textbooks, videos, and teaching/learning resources. To stay informed of such updates, follow us on Facebook ***(www.facebook.com/cadcim)*** and Twitter (***@cadcimtech***). You can also subscribe to our YouTube channel ***(www.youtube.com/cadcimtech)*** to get the information about our latest video tutorials.

# Chapter 1

## Introduction to AutoCAD Electrical 2022

### Learning Objectives

***After completing this chapter, you will be able to:***

- *Install and configure AutoCAD Electrical 2022*
- *Start AutoCAD Electrical*
- *Understand components of the initial AutoCAD Electrical screen*
- *Invoke AutoCAD Electrical commands*
- *Use various commands to save a file*
- *Exit AutoCAD Electrical*
- *Create and manage workspaces*
- *Use various options in AutoCAD Electrical help*

# INTRODUCTION

AutoCAD Electrical is a purpose-built controls design software. This software is used to create electrical schematic drawings and panel drawings. AutoCAD Electrical contains various schematic and panel symbols. These symbols, which are mostly the AutoCAD blocks with attributes, carry the intelligence of AutoCAD Electrical drawings. The standard symbol libraries such as JIC, IEC, JIS, and GB, which contain these symbols also get installed with the installation of AutoCAD Electrical. Besides all tools of AutoCAD software, AutoCAD Electrical also contains other electrical tools. You can use these tools for designing control systems speedily, economically, and accurately. As AutoCAD Electrical is compatible with AutoCAD, it is recommended to use the AutoCAD Electrical tools instead of AutoCAD tools when designing electrical circuits. However, AutoCAD Electrical drawings can be edited by using AutoCAD LT or AutoCAD. The all-inclusive symbol libraries and mechanized tasks help in increasing productivity and removing errors, and in providing exact information to the users.

# GETTING STARTED WITH AutoCAD Electrical 2022

You can start AutoCAD Electrical by double-clicking on its shortcut icon on the desktop of your computer. You can also load AutoCAD Electrical from the Windows taskbar by using the **Start** button at the bottom left corner of the screen (default position). To do so, choose the **Start** button to display a menu. Next, choose **AutoCAD Electrical 2022 - English > AutoCAD Electrical 2022 - English**, as shown in Figure 1-1; the AutoCAD Electrical 2022 interface is displayed with the **Start** tab chosen by default. In this tab, you need to choose the **New** button to create a new drawing or you can choose the **Open** button to open an existing drawing.

# AutoCAD Electrical INTERFACE COMPONENTS

Enhanced

There are various components in the interface of AutoCAD Electrical including the drawing area, **Command window**, **Ribbon**, **Application Menu**, **menu bar**, **Tool Palettes**, **PROJECT MANAGER**, **Model** and **Layout** tabs, Application Status Bar, several toolbars, and so on, refer to Figure 1-2. A title bar containing AutoCAD Electrical symbol and the current drawing name is displayed on top of the screen. Also, the screen has the standard window buttons such as close, minimize, and maximize on the top right corner. These buttons have the same functions as in any other standard window.

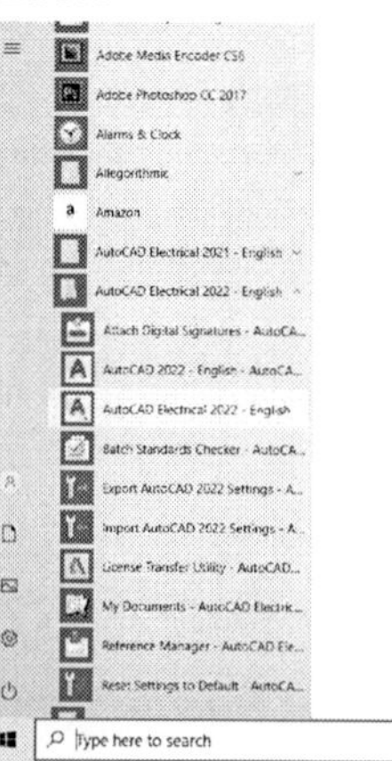


***Figure 1-1*** *Starting AutoCAD Electrical 2022*

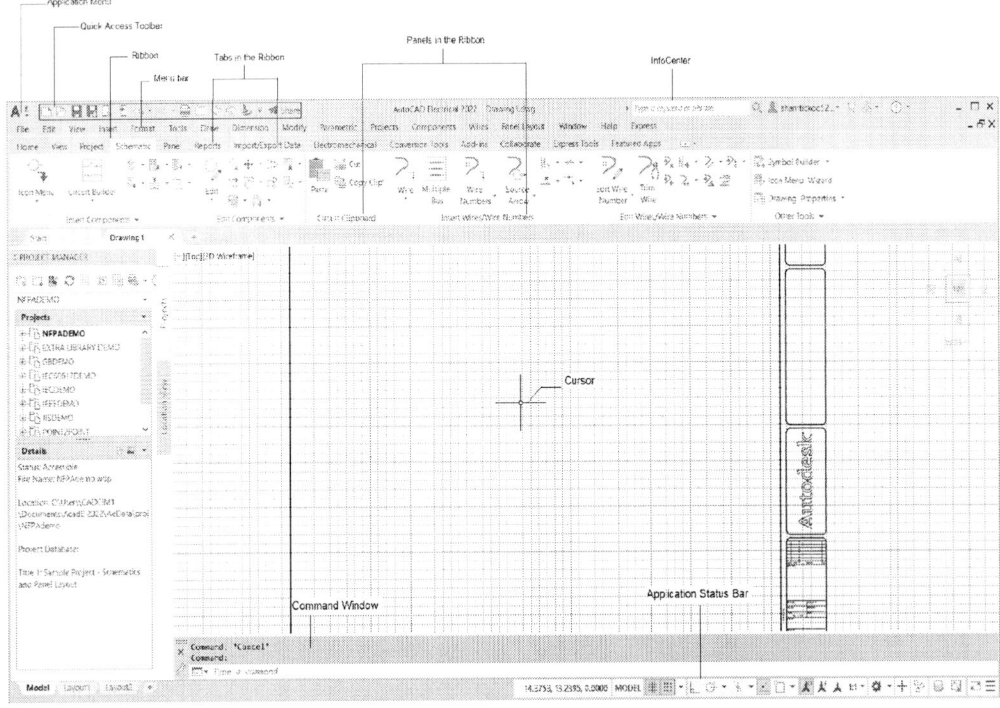


*Figure 1-2 AutoCAD Electrical interface components*

## Start Tab

The **Start** tab remains open by default in the initial interface of AutoCAD Electrical 2022. It displays the commonly used options used in AutoCAD Electrical, refer to Figure 1-3. These options are briefly explained next.

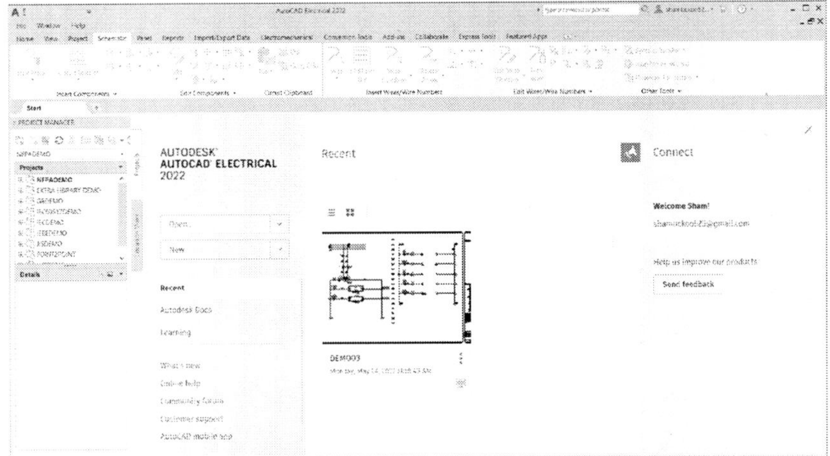


*Figure 1-3 The **Start** tab in AutoCAD Electrical 2022 interface*

### Open/New

Choose the **Open** button to open an existing file and choose the **New** button to start a new work from a blank slate or template.

### Autodesk Docs

Using **Autodesk Docs,** you can open or save files to the drives connected to your system. Note that you need to have **Desktop Connector** installed to access the connected drives on **Autodesk Docs**.

### Desktop Connector

**Desktop Connector** is a desktop service that integrates an Autodesk data management source (or data source) with your desktop folder and file structure for easy file management. The files in the data source are replicated in a connected drive. You can manage files in the data source through the connected drive just as you would do in any other folder on your machine. Note that changes that you make in the connected drive will be automatically uploaded to the data source.

### Recent

When you choose this option, all files you recently worked on are displayed in the **Recent** area.

### Learning

When you click on the **Learning** option, the **Learning** page will be displayed. The **Learning** page provides tools to help you learn AutoCAD Electrical, explore the product, learn new or improve existing skills, discover what has changed in the product, or receive relevant notifications. It also contains the **Tips**, **Videos**, and **Online Resources** sections which can help you learn more about the software.

## Drawing Area

The drawing area covers the major portion of the screen. In this area, you can draw objects and use commands. To draw objects, you need to define the coordinate points that can be selected by using the pointing device. The position of the pointing device is represented on the screen by the cursor. There is a coordinate system icon at the lower left corner of the drawing area.

**Tip**

*You can hide all screen components such as toolbars,* ***PROJECT MANAGER****, and* ***Ribbon*** *displayed on the screen by pressing the CTRL+0 keys or by choosing the* ***Clean Screen*** *option from the* ***View*** *menu. To turn on the display of the above mentioned screen components again, press the CTRL+0 keys. Note that the 0 key on the numeric keypad of the keyboard cannot be used for the* ***Clear Screen*** *option.*

## Command Window

The command window at the bottom of the drawing area has the Command prompt where you can enter the required commands. It also displays subsequent prompt sequences and messages. You can change the size of the window and also view all the previously used commands by placing the cursor on the top edge (double line bar known as the grab bar) and then dragging it. You can also press the F2 key to display **AutoCAD Text Window** which displays the previously used commands and prompts.

## AutoCorrect the Command Name

If you type a wrong command name at the Command prompt, a suggestion list with most relevant commands will be displayed, refer to Figure 1-4. You can invoke the desired command by selecting the respective option from this list.

## AutoComplete the Command Name

When you start typing a command name at the Command prompt, the complete name of the command will be displayed automatically. Also, a list of corresponding commands will be displayed, as shown in Figure 1-5. The commands that have not been used for a long time will be grouped in folders at the bottom of the list.

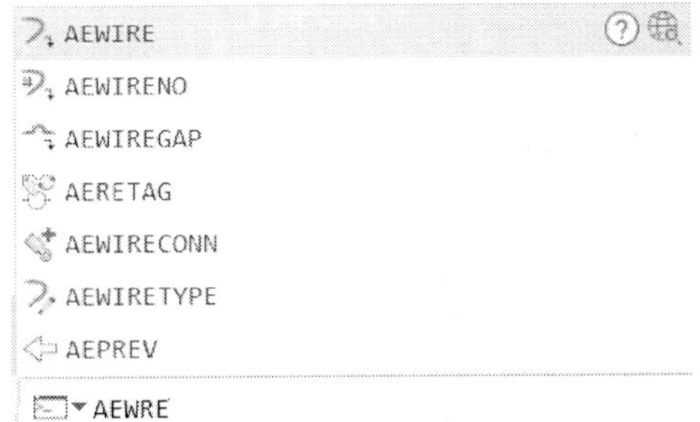


***Figure 1-4** Suggestion list with relevant commands*

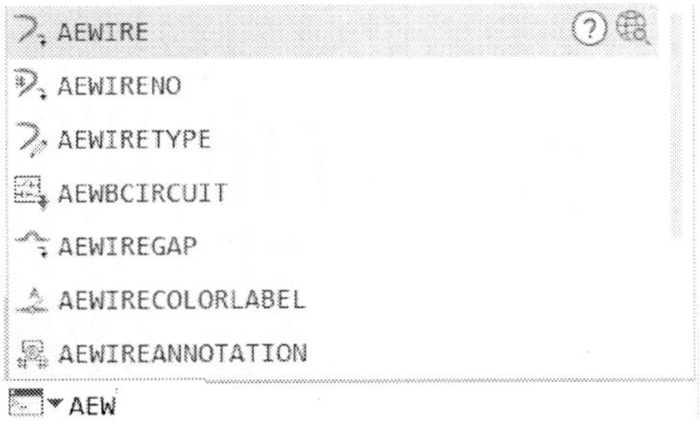

***Figure 1-5** Command line displaying complete command name*

## Internet Search

You can get more information about a command by using the **Search in Help** and **Search on Internet** buttons available adjacent to the command name in the Command line, refer to Figure 1-6. If you choose the **Search in Help** button, the **AutoCAD Electrical 2022 - Help** window will be displayed. In this window, you can find information about the command. By using the **Search on Internet** button, you can find information about the command on the internet.

## Input Search Options

In AutoCAD Electrical, you can enable or disable the functions such as AutoComplete and AutoCorrect by using the options available in the **Input Search Options** dialog box. To invoke this dialog box, right-click on the Command prompt; a shortcut menu will be displayed. Next, choose **Input Search Options** from the shortcut menu; the **Input Search Options** dialog box will be displayed, refer to Figure 1-7. Now, you can enable or disable the required functions by using this dialog box.

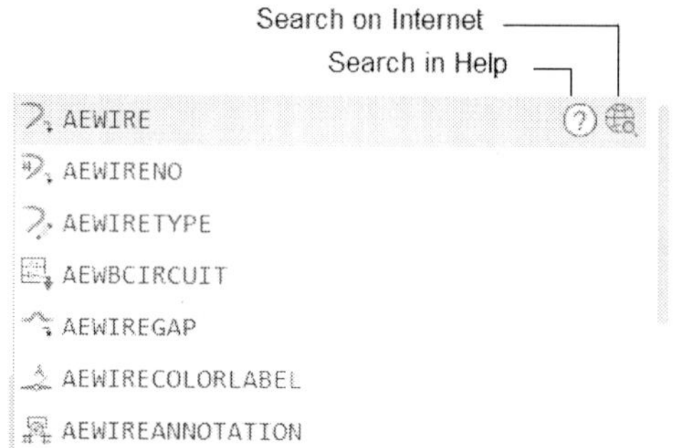


*Figure 1-6 The* ***Search in Help*** *and* ***Search on Internet*** *buttons displayed in the suggestion list*

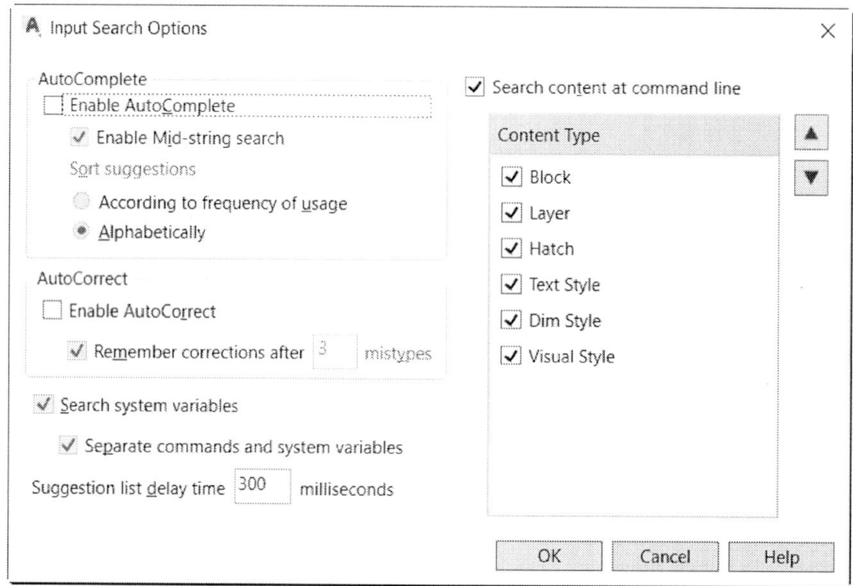


*Figure 1-7 The* ***Input Search Options*** *dialog box*

## Application Status Bar

The Application Status Bar is displayed at the bottom of the screen, refer to Figure 1-8. It contains some useful information and buttons that help in changing the status of some AutoCAD and AutoCAD Electrical functions easily. You can toggle between on and off states of most of these buttons by choosing them. Some of these buttons are not available by default. To display/hide buttons in the Application Status Bar, choose the **Customization** button at the extreme bottom right corner of the Application Status Bar; a flyout will be displayed. Next, choose the desired options from this flyout. The most commonly used buttons in the Application Status Bar are discussed next.

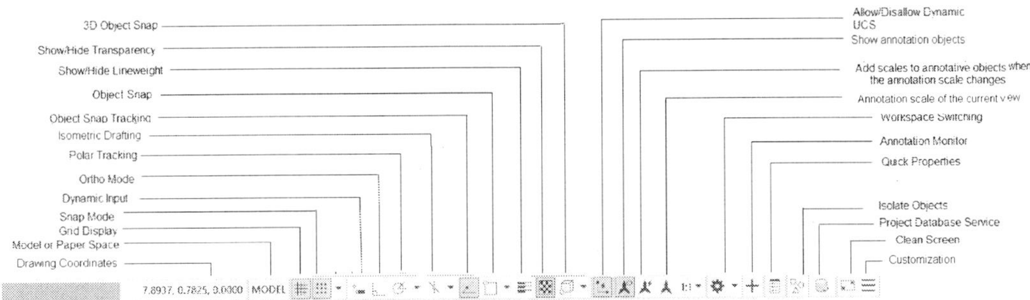


*Figure 1-8 The Application Status Bar*

## Drawing Coordinates

The coordinate information is displayed on the left corner of the Application Status Bar. You can choose the **Coordinates** option from the flyout that is displayed on choosing the **Customization** button to turn the coordinate display on and off.

## Snap Mode

The snap mode allows you to move the cursor in fixed increments. If the snap mode is on, the **Snap Mode** button will be chosen in the Application Status Bar; otherwise, it will be deactivated. You can also use the F9 function key as a toggle key to turn the snap off or on.

## Grid Display

The grid lines are used as reference lines to draw objects in AutoCAD Electrical. Choose the **Grid Display** button to display the grid lines on the screen. The F7 function key can be used to turn the grid display on or off.

## Ortho Mode

If the **Ortho Mode** button is chosen in the Application Status Bar, you can draw lines at right angles only. You can use the F8 function key to turn the ortho mode on or off.

## Polar Tracking

If you turn the polar tracking on, the movement of the cursor will be restricted along a path based on the angle set in the polar angle settings. Choosing the **Polar Tracking** button in the Application Status Bar turns the polar tracking on or off. You can also use the F10 function key to turn the polar tracking on or off. Note that turning the polar tracking on automatically turns off the ortho mode.

## Object Snap

The **Object Snap** button is a toggle button and is used to turn object snap on or off. You can also use the F3 function key to turn the object snap on or off.

## 3D Object Snap

The **3D Object Snap** button is a toggle button and is used to turn 3D object snap on or off. You can also use the F4 function key to turn the 3D object snap on or off.

## Object Snap Tracking

This button is used to turn the object snap tracking on or off. You can also use the F11 function key to turn the object snap tracking on or off.

## Dynamic UCS

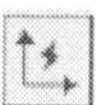
This button enables you to use the dynamic UCS. You can also use the F6 function key or CTRL + D keys to turn the dynamic UCS on or off.

## Dynamic Input

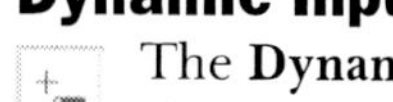
The **Dynamic Input** button is used to turn the **Dynamic Input** mode on or off. You can also use the F12 function key to turn this mode on or off. Turning it on facilitates the heads-up design approach because all commands, prompts, and dimensional inputs will now be displayed in the drawing area and you do not need to look at the Command prompt all the time. This saves the design time and also increases the efficiency of the user. If the **Dynamic Input** mode is turned on, you can enter commands through the **Pointer Input** boxes, and numerical values through the **Dimensional Input** boxes. Also, you can select the command options with the help of **Dynamic Prompt** options in the graphics window.

## Show/Hide Lineweight

This button is used to turn the display of lineweights on or off in the drawing. If this button is not chosen, the display of lineweight will be turned off.

## Transparency

This button is used to turn on or off the transparency of layers and objects.

## Quick Properties

If you select a sketched entity and choose the **Quick Properties** button in the Application Status Bar, the properties of the selected entity will be displayed in a panel.

## Model or Paper Space

MODEL This button is used to toggle between model space and paper space. The model space is used to work in a drawing area. Paper space is used to prepare your drawing for printing.

## Show annotation objects

This button is used to control the visibility of the annotative objects that do not support the current annotation scale in the drawing area.

## Add Scales to annotative objects when the annotative scale changes

This button, if chosen, automatically adds all the annotation scales that are set current to all the annotative objects present in the drawing.

## Annotation Scale of the current view

This button controls the size and display of the annotative objects in the model space.

## Workspace Switching

When you choose the **Workspace Switching** button, a flyout is displayed. This flyout contains predefined workspaces and options such as **Workspace Settings**, **Customize**, and so on. The options in this flyout will be discussed later in detail.

## Customization

The **Customization** button is available at the lower right corner of the Application Status Bar and is used to add or remove buttons from the Application Status Bar.

# Navigation Bar

In AutoCAD Electrical, the navigation tools are grouped together and are available in the drawing area, as shown in Figure 1-9. The tools in the **Navigation Bar** are discussed next.

## Full Navigation Wheel

The **Full Navigation Wheel** has a set of navigation tools that can be used for panning, zooming, and so on.

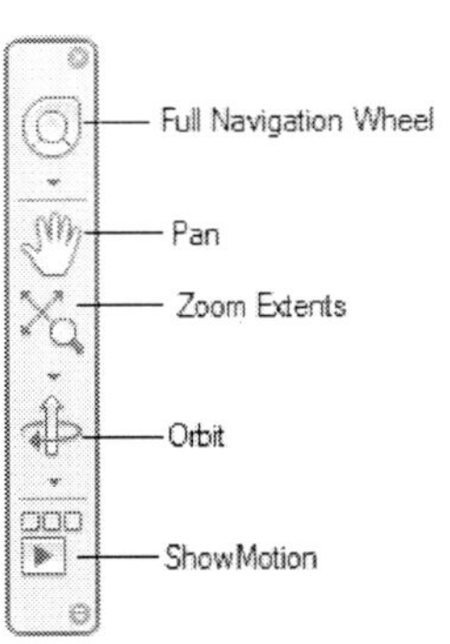


***Figure 1-9** Tools in the **Navigation Bar***

## Pan

This tool allows you to view the portion of the drawing that is outside the current display area. To do so, choose this button in the Application Status Bar, press and hold the left mouse button and then drag the drawing area. Press ESC to exit this command.

## Zoom Extents

Choose one of the tools from the group to zoom the view of the drawing on the screen as per your requirement without affecting the actual size of the objects.

## Orbit

This set of tools is used to rotate the view in 3D space.

## ShowMotion

Choose this button to capture different views in a sequence and animate them when required.

## Project Database Service

The Project Database Service (PDS) updates the scratch project database automatically. It is also used to save all non-AutoCAD Electrical attributes from block files into the project. Also, if the drawing files of a project are not found in the respective folder, an error message will be displayed in the **Project Database Service** message box.

## Units

Decimal

This button is used to display and control the units of drawing. It has a flyout that displays all the unit systems available for drawing.

## Lock UI

This button is used to dock/undock the toolbars, panels, and windows.

## Clean Screen

The **Clean Screen** button is located at the lower right corner of the screen. When you choose this button, all displayed toolbars, except the command window, Application Status Bar, and menu bar, disappear and the expanded view of the drawing is displayed. The expanded view of the drawing area can also be displayed by choosing **View > Clean Screen** from the **Menu Bar** or by using the CTRL+0 keys. Choose the **Clean Screen** button again to restore the previous display state.

# INVOKING COMMANDS IN AutoCAD Electrical

When AutoCAD Electrical is started, you can invoke AutoCAD Electrical commands to perform any operation. For example, to draw a wire, first you need to invoke the **AEWIRE** command and then define the start point and endpoint of the wire. Similarly, if you want to trim wires, you must invoke the **AETRIM** command and then select wires for trimming. AutoCAD Electrical provides the following options to invoke a command:

| | | | |
|---|---|---|---|
| **Keyboard** | **Ribbon** | **Application Menu** | **Toolbar** |
| **Marking Menu** | **Shortcut menu** | **Menu Bar** | **Tool Palettes** |

## Keyboard

You can invoke any AutoCAD Electrical command from the keyboard by entering the name of the command at the Command prompt and then pressing the ENTER key. If the **Dynamic Input** mode is on and the cursor is in the drawing area, by default the command will be entered through the **Pointer Input** box. The **Pointer Input** box is a small box displayed on the right of the cursor, as shown in Figure 1-10.

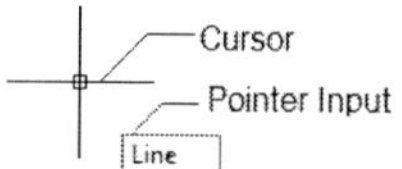


*Figure 1-10 The **Pointer Input** box displayed*

However, if the cursor is currently placed on any toolbar or menu bar, or if the **Dynamic Input** mode is turned off, the command will be entered through the Command prompt. Before you enter a command, the Command prompt is displayed as the last line in the command window area. If it is not displayed, you must cancel the existing command by pressing the ESC key. The following example shows how to invoke the **AEWIRE** command using the keyboard:

Command: **AEWIRE** Enter

## Ribbon

Most of the commands used for creating, modifying, and annotating components are available in the **Ribbon**, as shown in Figure 1-11.

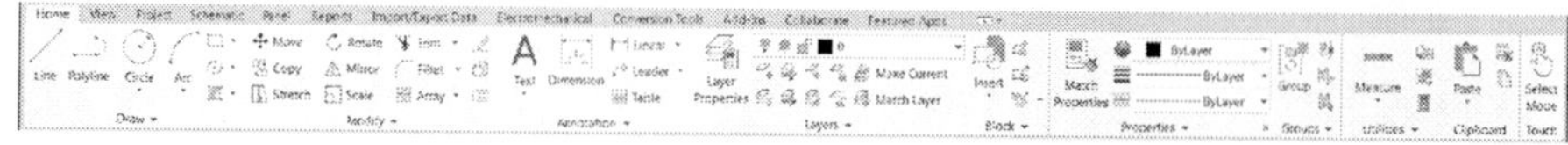

*Figure 1-11 The **Ribbon** for the **ACADE & 2D Drafting & Annotation** workspace*

When you start AutoCAD Electrical session for the first time, by default the **Ribbon** is displayed horizontally below the **Quick Access Toolbar**. The **Ribbon** consists of various tabs. These tabs have different panels, which in turn, have tools arranged in rows. Some of the panels and tools have a small black down arrow. This indicates that the corresponding panels and tools have some more buttons in the form of drop-down. Click on this down arrow to access the hidden tools. If you choose a tool from the drop-down, the corresponding command will be invoked and the tool chosen will be displayed in the panel. For example, to move components using the **Move Component** option, click on the down arrow next to the **Scoot** tool in the **Edit Components** panel of the **Schematic** tab; a drop-down will be displayed. Choose the **Move Component** tool from the drop-down and move components. Choose the down arrow to expand the panel. You will notice that a push pin is available at the left end of the panel. Click on the push pin to keep the panel in the expanded state.

You can reorder panels in a tab. To do so, press and hold the left mouse button on the panel to be moved and then drag it to the required position. To undock the **Ribbon**, right-click on the blank space in the **Ribbon** and choose the **Undock** option from the shortcut menu displayed. You can move, resize, anchor, and auto-hide the **Ribbon** using the shortcut menu that will be displayed when you right-click on the heading strip. To anchor the floating **Ribbon** vertically to the left or right of the drawing area, right-click on its heading strip; a shortcut menu will be displayed. Choose the corresponding option from this shortcut menu. The **Auto-hide** toggle button on the right of the **Express Tools** tab will hide the **Ribbon** into the heading strip and will display it only when you move the cursor over this strip.

You can customize the display of tabs and panels in the **Ribbon**. To do so, right-click on any one of the buttons in the **Ribbon**; a shortcut menu will be displayed. On moving the cursor over one of the options in the shortcut menu, a cascading menu will be displayed with a tick mark before all options indicating that the corresponding tab or panel will be displayed in the **Ribbon**. Select/clear the appropriate option to display/hide a particular tab or panel.

## Application Menu

You can invoke various commands from the **Application Menu**. To do so, choose the **Application** button available at the top left corner of the AutoCAD Electrical window; the **Application Menu** will be displayed, refer to Figure 1-12.

You can search for a command using the search field on the top of the **Application Menu**. To search for a command, enter the complete or partial name of the command in the search field; a list displaying all possible commands will be displayed. If you click on a command from the list, the corresponding command will get activated.

By default, the **Recent Documents** button is chosen in the **Application Menu**. As a result, the recently opened drawings will be listed. If you have opened multiple drawing files, choose the **Open Documents** button; the documents that are opened will be listed in the **Application Menu**. To set the preferences of the file, choose the **Options** button available at the bottom of the **Application Menu**. To exit AutoCAD Electrical, choose the **Exit AutoCAD Electrical** button next to the **Options** button.

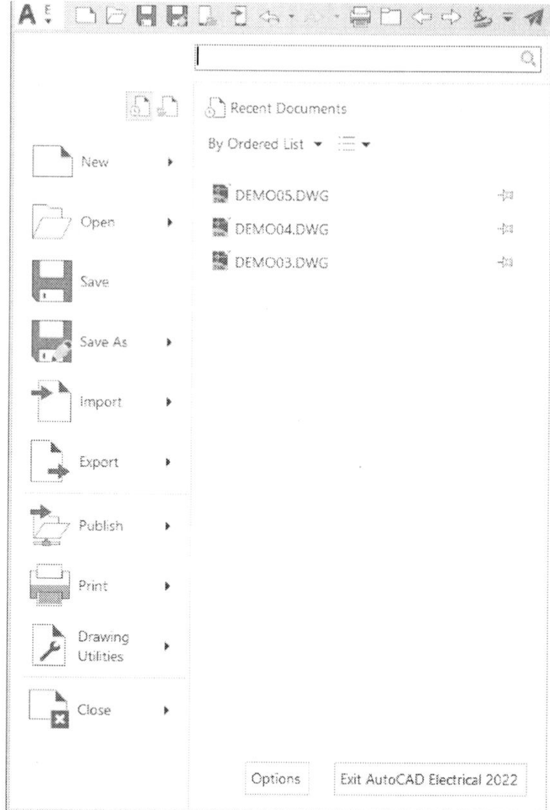


*Figure 1-12 The Application Menu*

## Menu Bar

You can also select commands from the menu bar. Menu bar is not displayed by default. To invoke the menu bar, choose the down arrow in the **Quick Access Toolbar**; a flyout will be displayed. Choose the **Show Menu Bar** option from the flyout; the menu bar will be displayed. As you move the cursor over the menu bar, different titles will be highlighted. You can choose the desired item from the menu bar by clicking on it. Once the item is chosen, the corresponding menu will be displayed directly under the title. Some of the menu items display an arrow on their right indicating that they have a cascading menu. The cascading menu provides various options to execute AutoCAD Electrical commands. You can display the cascading menu by choosing the menu item or by moving the arrow pointer to the right of that item. You can then choose any item from the cascading menu by clicking on it. For example, to insert a ladder, choose **Wires** from the menu bar and then choose the **Ladders** option; a cascading menu will be displayed, as shown in Figure 1-13. From the cascading menu, choose the **Insert Ladder** option.

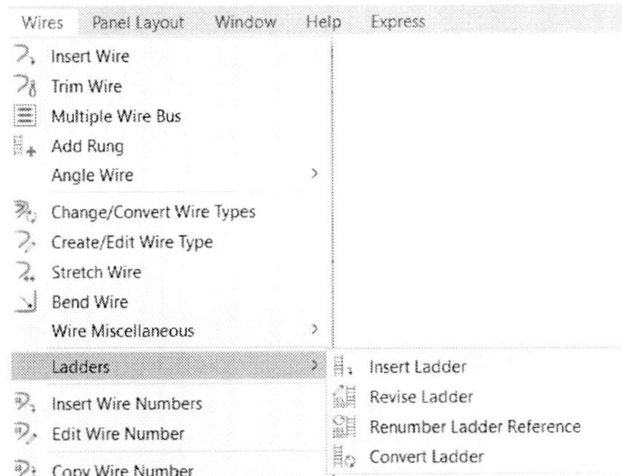


*Figure 1-13 The cascading menu*

# Toolbar

Toolbars are not displayed by default. To display a toolbar, first invoke the menu bar and then choose **Tools > Toolbars > ELECTRICAL** from it; the list of toolbars will be displayed. Select the required toolbar. In a toolbar, a set of tools representing various AutoCAD Electrical commands are grouped together. When you move the cursor over a tool in a toolbar, the tool will be lifted. The tooltip (name of the tool) and a brief description related to that tool will also be displayed below the tool. Once you locate the desired tool, the command associated with it can be invoked by choosing it. For example, you can invoke the **AEWIRE** command by choosing the **Insert Wire** tool from the **ACE:Main Electrical** toolbar.

Some of the tools in a toolbar have a small triangular arrow at its lower right corner. This arrow indicates that the tool has a flyout attached to it. If you hold cursor on the triangular arrow button, a flyout containing the options for the command will be displayed, as shown in Figure 1-14. Choose the desired option from the toolbar; a command will be displayed in the command window. The **ACE:Main Electrical** and **ACE:Panel Layout** toolbars are shown in Figures 1-15 and 1-16, respectively.

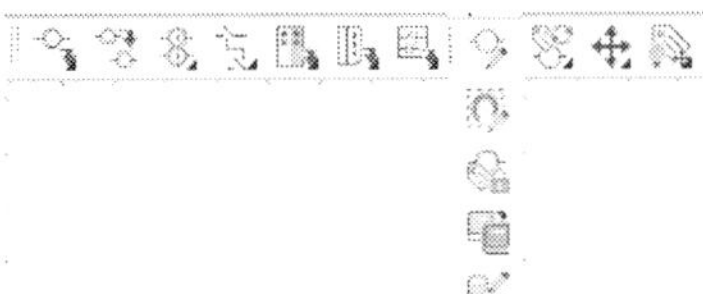

*Figure 1-14 The flyout*

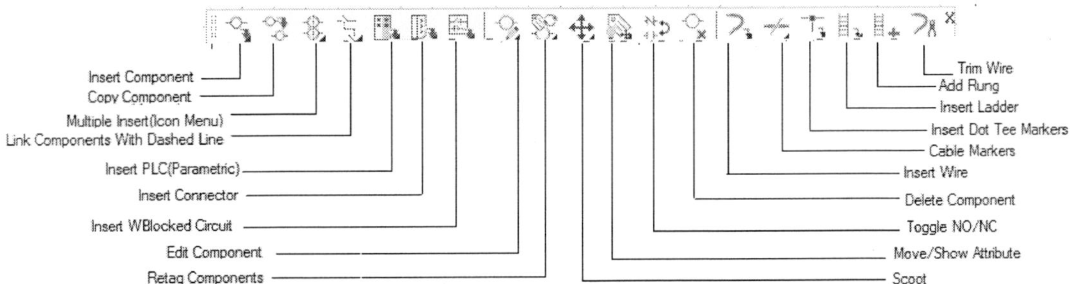


*Figure 1-15 The **ACE:Main Electrical** toolbar*

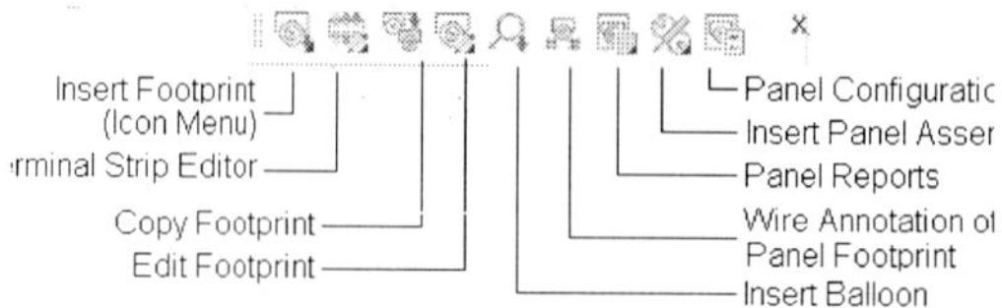


*Figure 1-16 The **ACE:Panel Layout** toolbar*

## Moving and Resizing Toolbars

Toolbars can be moved anywhere on the screen by placing the cursor on the strip and then dragging it to the desired location. You must hold the cursor down while dragging. While moving toolbars, you can dock them to the top or sides of the screen by dropping them in the docking area. You can prevent docking toolbars, as and when needed, by holding the CTRL key while moving the toolbar to a desired location. You can also change the size of toolbars by placing the cursor anywhere on the border of the toolbar where it takes the shape of a double-sided arrow, as shown in Figure 1-17, and then pulling it in the required direction, as shown in Figure 1-18. You can also customize toolbars to meet your requirements.

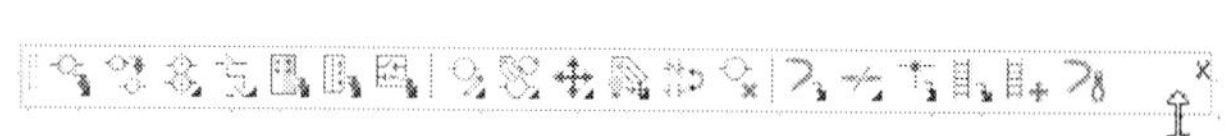

*Figure 1-17 Resizing the **ACE:Main Electrical** toolbar*

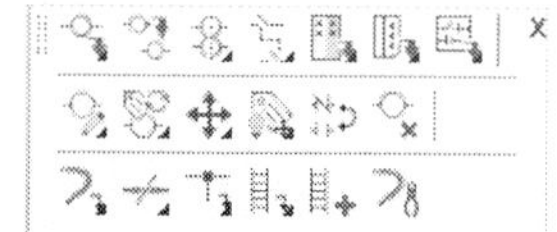

*Figure 1-18 The **ACE:Main Electrical** toolbar resized*

# Marking Menu

AutoCAD Electrical provides you with marking menus which are displayed on right-clicking on an AutoCAD Electrical Object. By using the marking menus, you can easily invoke the commands, if the toolbar is not displayed in the drawing area. These marking menus are context-sensitive, which means that the commands or tools in this menu will be displayed based on the object selected. Figure 1-19 shows a marking menu that is displayed on right-clicking on a component and Figure 1-20 shows a marking menu that is displayed on right-clicking on a wire. Figure 1-21 shows a marking menu that is displayed on right-clicking on a footprint. There are two basic modes for command selection: Menu mode and Mark mode. These modes are discussed next.

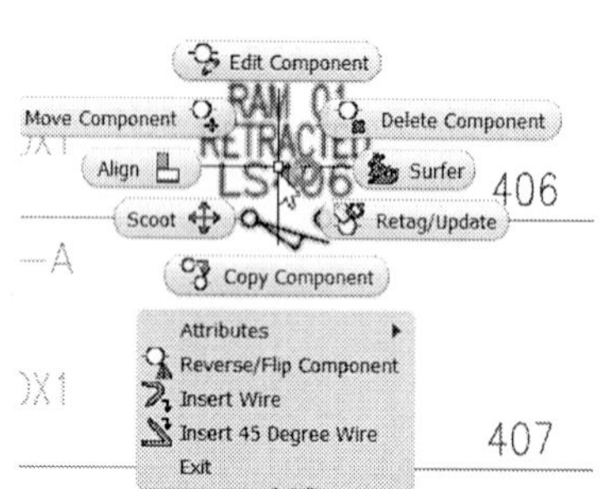


*Figure 1-19 The marking menu displayed on right-clicking on a component*

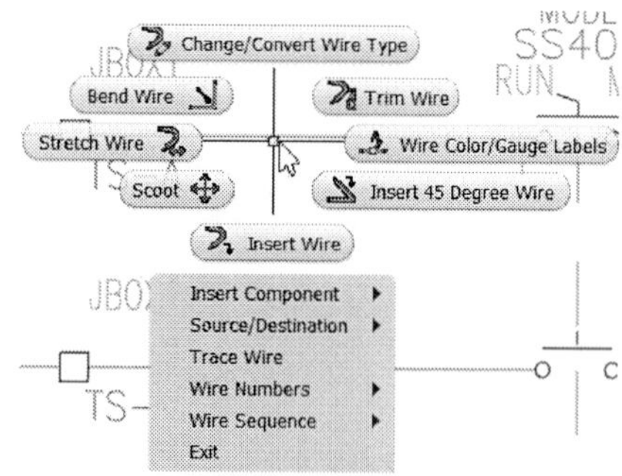


*Figure 1-20 The marking menu displayed on right-clicking on a wire*

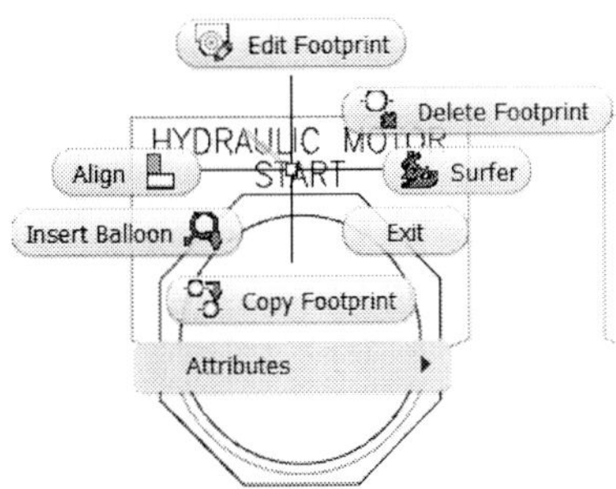


*Figure 1-21 The marking menu displayed on right-clicking on a footprint*

### Menu Mode

You can invoke the Menu mode by right-clicking on an object. When you invoke this mode, a marking menu will be displayed, showing the commands related to that object. Move the cursor over the command to be executed and click on it; the selected command will be executed. To exit the marking menu, click at the center of the menu or click anywhere outside the menu. If you press the ESC key, the command in progress will be cancelled.

### Mark Mode

Mark mode is similar to Menu mode. The only difference between them is that in this mode, you need to immediately move the cursor along the direction of the desired command after right-clicking on the component. On doing so, a rubber band line connected with the cursor is displayed. Release the mouse button on the command to be executed.

## Shortcut Menu

If you right-click in the drawing area, the AutoCAD shortcut menu will be displayed. This shortcut menu contains the commonly used commands of Windows and an option to select the previously invoked commands again, as shown in Figure 1-22. If you right-click in the drawing area while a command is active, a shortcut menu will be displayed containing the options of that particular command. Figure 1-23 shows the shortcut menu displayed while the **AEWIRE** command is active.

When you right-click on the command window, a shortcut menu will be displayed. This shortcut menu displays the six most recently used commands and some of the window options like **Copy** and **Paste**, as shown in Figure 1-24.

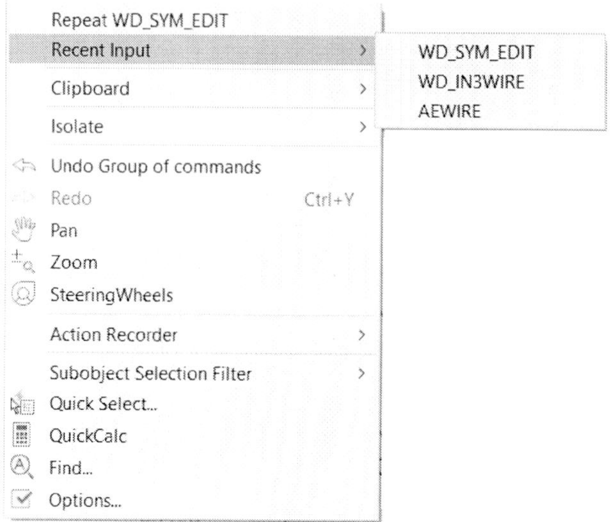


***Figure 1-22*** *The shortcut menu showing the recently used commands*

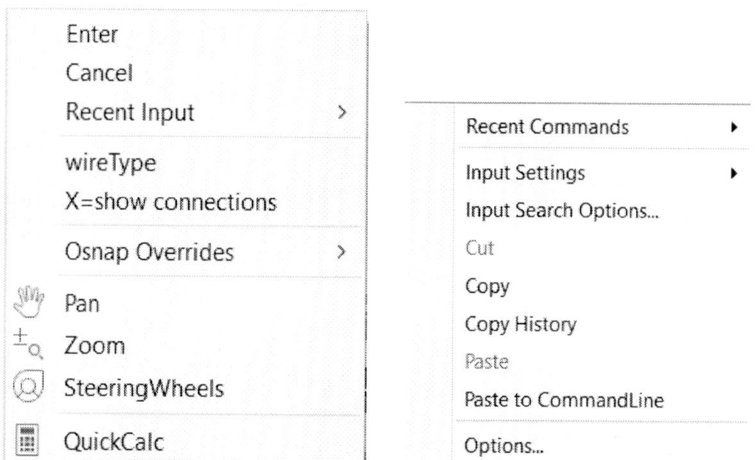


***Figure 1-23*** *The shortcut menu displayed on right-clicking in the drawing area with the **AEWIRE** command active*

***Figure 1-24*** *Command window shortcut menu*

The commands and their prompt entries are displayed in the History window (previous command lines not visible) and can be selected, copied, and pasted in the command line using the shortcut menu. As you press the up arrow key, the previously entered commands will be displayed in the command window. Once the desired command is displayed at the Command prompt, you can execute it by simply pressing the ENTER key.

When you right-click in the coordinate display area of the Status Bar, a shortcut menu will be displayed. This shortcut menu contains options to modify the display of coordinates, refer to Figure 1-25. You can also right-click on any of the toolbars to display a shortcut menu from where you can choose any toolbar to be displayed.

## Tool Palettes

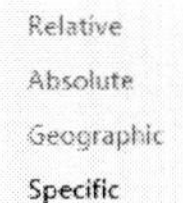


*Figure 1-25 The shortcut menu displayed*

The **Tool Palettes**, as shown in Figure 1-26, is an easy and convenient way of placing components in the current drawing. By default, the **Tool Palettes** is not displayed. To invoke the **Tool Palettes**, choose **Tools > Palettes > Tool Palettes** from the menu bar or choose the CTRL+3 keys to display the **Tool Palettes** as a window on the left of the drawing area. You can resize the **Tool Palettes** by using the resizing cursor that is displayed when you place the cursor on the top or bottom of the **Tool Palettes**. The **Tool Palettes** contains different commands for inserting components in Imperial and Metric units. When you move the **Tool Palettes** in the drawing area and right-click on its title bar, a shortcut menu is displayed, as shown in Figure 1-27. Using this shortcut menu, you can turn on or off the **Tool Palettes**. Also, you can move, change size, close, auto-hide, and dock the **Tool Palettes**. Also, you can create new palette, rename it, and customize palettes and commands by choosing the desired option from the shortcut menu.

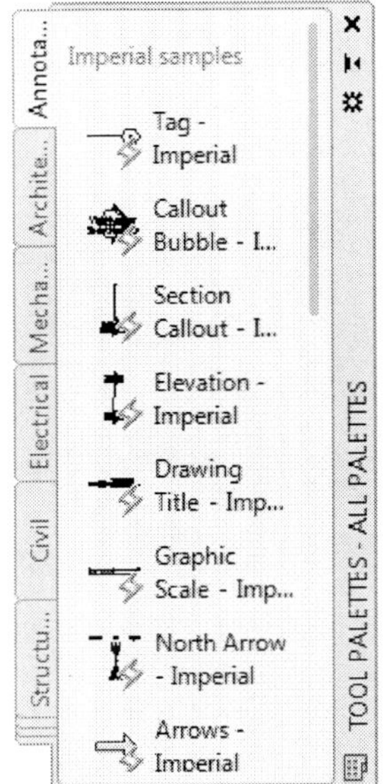


*Figure 1-26 The **Tool Palettes***

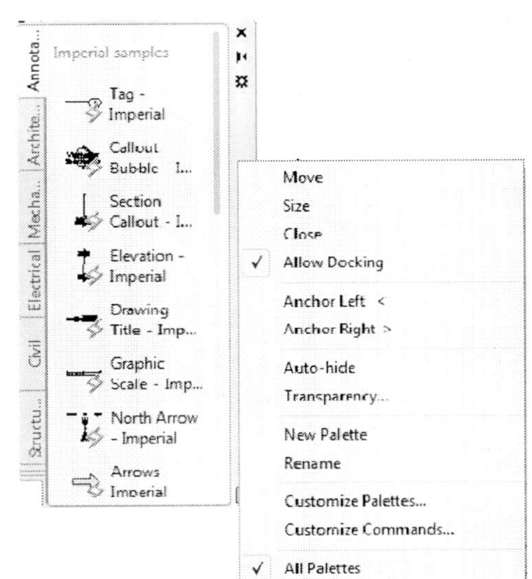


*Figure 1-27 Shortcut menu displayed on right-clicking on the title bar of the **Tool Palettes***

## File Tabs

The **File Tabs** button is available in the **Interface** panel of the **View** tab. It is used to toggle the display of the File tab bar which displays all opened files. You can easily switch between multiple opened drawings by clicking on them.

**Note**

*The **View** tab is not displayed by default in the AutoCAD Electrical interface. To display it, right-click on the **Ribbon**; a shortcut menu will be displayed. Next, choose **Show Tabs > View** from the shortcut menu.*

You can also create a new drawing file by clicking on the (+) sign available at the end of the file tabs. Figure 1-28 shows the **File Tabs** button chosen in the **Ribbon** and the File tab bar displayed at the bottom of the **Ribbon**.

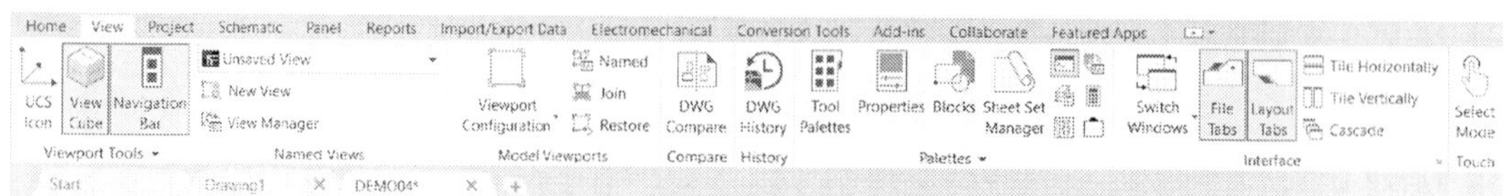

*Figure 1-28 The* ***File Tabs*** *button chosen in the* ***Ribbon*** *and File tab bar displayed at the bottom of the* ***Ribbon***

In the File tab bar, all the added tabs get arranged in a sequence in which the respective drawings are created. You can change the sequence of the tabs in the File tab bar by using the left mouse button. To do so, press and hold the left mouse button on any tab and drag it to the desired location. If a large number of files are opened, some of the files will not be visible in the File tab bar and therefore an overflow symbol will be displayed on the right end of the File tab bar, refer to Figure 1-29. To open a tab which is not visible in the File tab bar, click on the overflow symbol; the names of all the tabs will be displayed in a flyout, refer to Figure 1-29. Also, when you move the cursor on a tab name, previews of the Model and Layouts will be displayed, refer to Figure 1-29. You can open the desired environment by clicking on its preview.

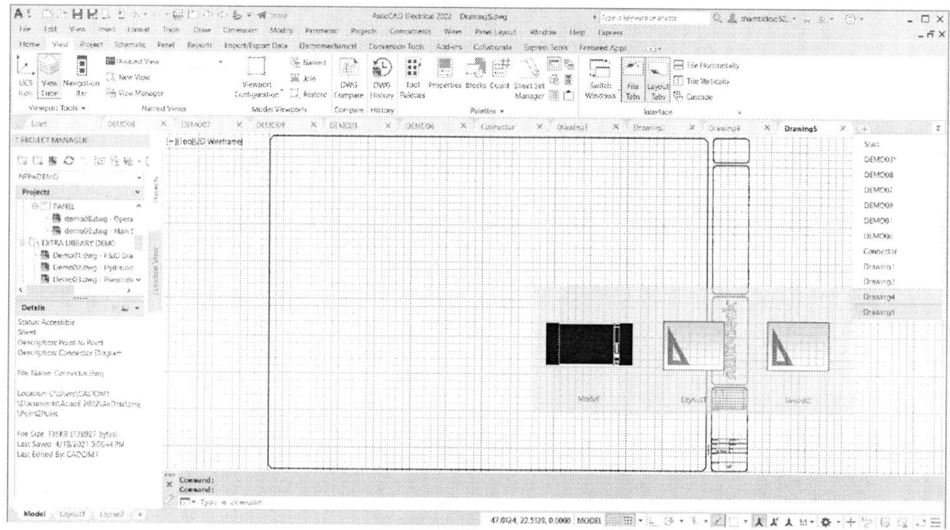

***Figure 1-29*** *Flyout with file tab names and preview of their respective drawings*

If you move the cursor over a file tab, the preview of the model and layout will be displayed. When you move the cursor over any preview in the file tab, the corresponding preview will be displayed in an enlarged form in the drawing area, refer to Figure 1-30.

There are two buttons available on the top of the preview window: **Plot** and **Publish**. By using **Plot**, you can plot the drawing and by using **Publish**, you can publish the drawing. When you right-click on a file tab, a shortcut menu containing various options such as **New**, **Open**, **Save**, **Save As**, **Close**, and so on will be displayed, refer to Figure 1-31. You can choose the option from the shortcut menu as per your requirement.

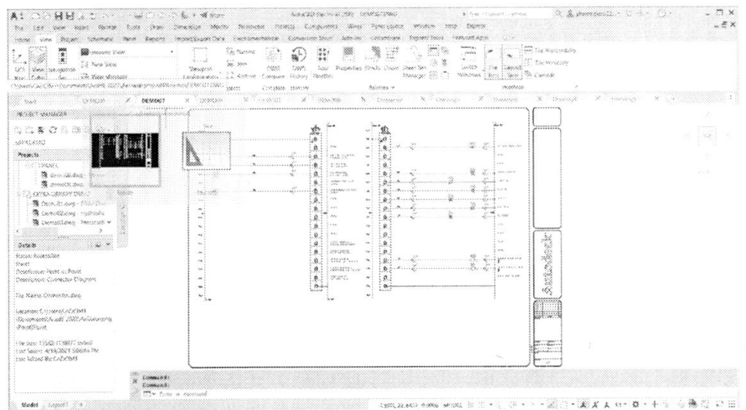

*Figure 1-30 Previews of model and layout*

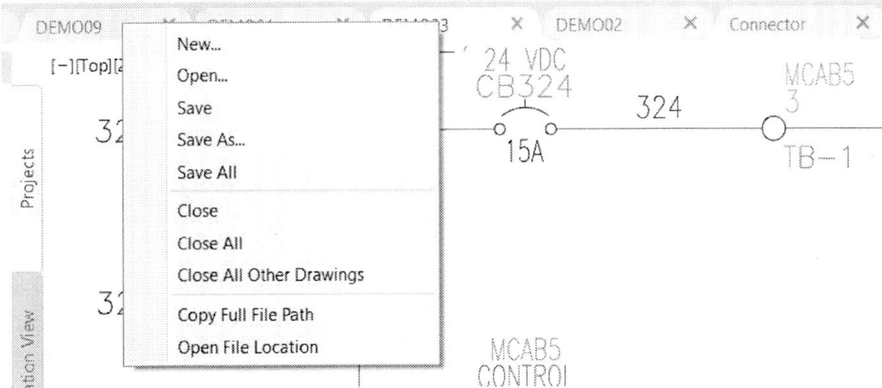


***Figure 1-31** Shortcut menu displayed on right-clicking on the File tab bar*

There are two icons displayed on the file tab: Asterisk and Lock. The Asterisk icon indicates that the file is modified but not saved. The Lock icon indicates that the file is locked and the changes cannot be saved with the original file name, although you can use the **SaveAs** tool to create another copy.

To open a drawing as a locked file, first choose the **Open** option from the shortcut menu displayed on right-clicking over the file tab; the **Select File** dialog box will be displayed. Select the desired file and then select the **Open Read-Only** option from the **Open** drop-down list. On doing so, the file will be opened as a locked file in the drawing area. You can also open the file as a locked file by using the **Open** button from the **Quick Access Bar**.

# PROJECT MANAGER

The **PROJECT MANAGER** is used to create new projects, add new drawings to a project, re-order drawing files, access the existing projects, or modify the existing information in a project, refer to Figure 1-32. By default, the **PROJECT MANAGER** is opened and docked on the left of your screen. The **PROJECT MANAGER** displays a list of projects. Using the **PROJECT MANAGER**, you can open, activate, edit, and close projects. The **PROJECT MANAGER** is discussed in detail in Chapter 2.

# COMPONENTS OF AutoCAD Electrical DIALOG BOXES

In AutoCAD Electrical, there are certain commands, which when invoked, display a dialog box. When you choose an item with ellipses [...] from the menu bar, a dialog box will be displayed. For example, when you choose **Options** from the **Tools** menu, the **Options** dialog box will be displayed.

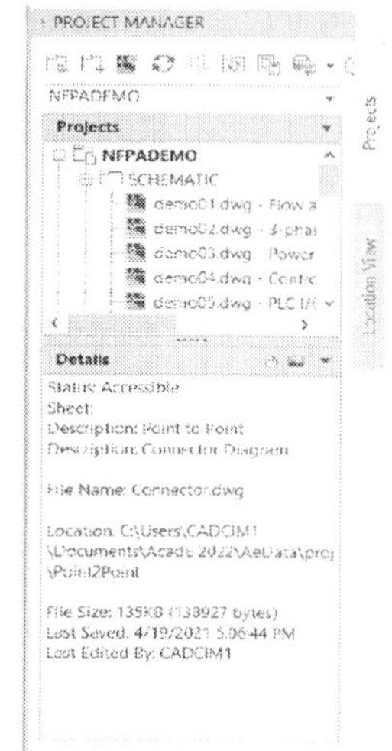


*Figure 1-32 The **PROJECT MANAGER***

A dialog box contains a number of parts like dialog label, radio buttons, text or edit boxes, check boxes, slider bars, image boxes, and command buttons. These components are also referred to as tiles. Some of the components of a dialog box are shown in Figure 1-33.

The title bar displays the name of the dialog box. The tabs specify various sections with a group of related options under them. The check boxes are toggle buttons for making a particular option available or unavailable. The drop-down list displays an item and an arrow on the right which when selected displays a list of items to choose from. You can also select a radio button to activate the option corresponding to it. Only one radio button can be selected at a time. The text box is an area where you can enter a text like a file name. It is also called an edit box because you can make any change to the text entered. In some dialog boxes, there is the **[...]** button, which displays another related dialog box. There are certain command buttons (**OK**, **Cancel**, **Help**) at the bottom of the dialog box. The dialog box has a **Help** button for getting help on various features of the dialog box.

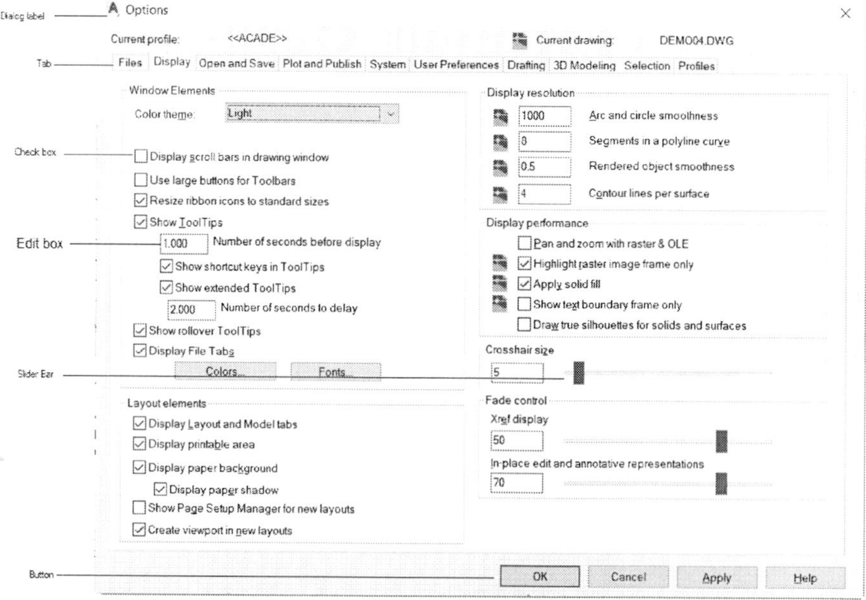


*Figure 1-33 Components of a dialog box*

## SAVING THE WORK

**Application Menu:** SAVE, SAVEAS
**Toolbar:** Quick Access Toolbar > Save
**Menu:** File > Save or Save As
**Command:** QSAVE, SAVEAS, SAVE

In AutoCAD Electrical, you need to save your work before you exit from the drawing editor or turn off the system. Also, it is recommended that you save your drawings after regular time intervals, so that in the event of a power failure or an editing error, all work done by you is not lost and only the unsaved part is affected.

AutoCAD Electrical has provided the **QSAVE**, **SAVEAS**, and **SAVE** commands that allow you to save your work on the hard disk of a computer. These commands allow you to save your drawing by writing it to a permanent storage device such as a hard drive, or a diskette in any removable drive.

When you choose **Save** from the **Quick Access Toolbar** or **Application Menu**, the **QSAVE** command is invoked. If the current drawing is unnamed and you save the drawing for the first time in the present session, the **QSAVE** command will prompt you to enter the file name in the **Save Drawing As** dialog box. You can enter a name for the drawing and then choose the **Save** button. If you have saved a drawing file once and then edited it, you can use the **QSAVE** command to save it. This allows you to do a quick save.

When you invoke the **SAVEAS** command, the **Save Drawing As** dialog box will be displayed, refer to Figure 1-34. Even if the drawing has been saved with a file name, this command provides you with an option to save it with a different file name. In addition to saving the drawing, it allows you to set a new name for the drawing, which is displayed in the title bar.

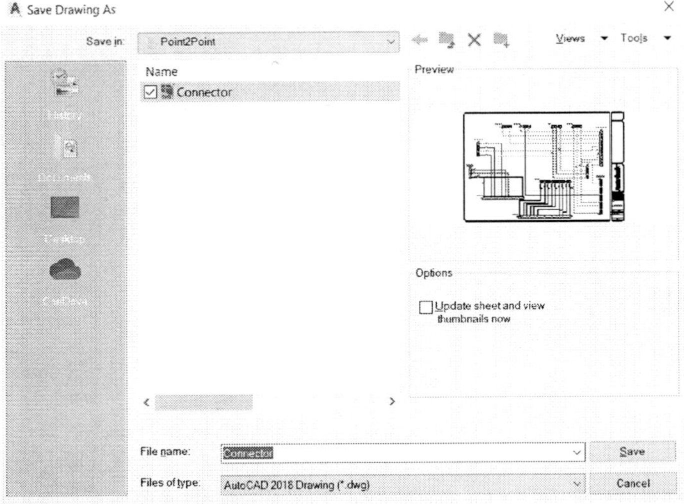


*Figure 1-34 The **Save Drawing As** dialog box*

This command is used when you want to save a previously saved drawing under a different file name. You can also use this command when you make certain changes to a template and want to save the changed template drawing without changing the original template.

The **SAVE** command is the most rarely used command and can be invoked only from the command line by entering **SAVE** at the Command prompt. This command is similar to the **SAVEAS** command and displays the **Save Drawing As** dialog box when invoked. With this command, you can save a previously saved drawing under a different file name.

## Save Drawing As Dialog Box

The **Save Drawing As** dialog box displays the information related to drawing files on your system. Various options in this dialog box are described next.

### Places List

A column of icons is displayed on the left in the dialog box. These icons contain shortcuts to the folders that are frequently used. You can quickly save your drawings in one of these folders. The **History** folder displays the list of the most recently saved drawings. The **FTP** folder displays the list of various FTP sites available for saving a drawing. By default, no FTP sites are shown in the dialog box. To add a FTP site to the dialog box, choose the **Tools** button at the upper-right corner of the dialog box to display a shortcut menu and select **Add/Modify FTP Locations**. The **Desktop** folder displays the list of contents on the desktop. The **Buzzsaw** icons connect you to their respective pages on a Web.

### File name

To save your work, enter the name of the drawing in the **File name** edit box by typing the file name or selecting it from the drop-down list.

### Files of type

The **Files of type** drop-down list, as shown in Figure 1-35, is used to specify a drawing format in which you want to save a file. For example, to save a file as an AutoCAD 2004 drawing file, select **AutoCAD 2004/LT 2004 Drawing (*.dwg)** from this drop-down list.

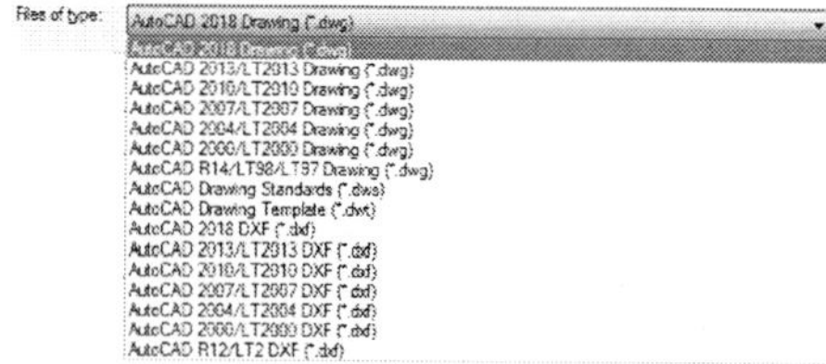


*Figure 1-35 The **Files of type** drop-down list*

### Save in

The active project is listed in the **Save in** drop-down list. AutoCAD Electrical initially saves the drawing in the folder of the active project. But if you want to save the drawing in a different folder, you need to specify the path.

## Views

*Figure 1-36 The Views flyout*

The options in the **Views** flyout are used to specify how the list of files will be displayed in the **Save Drawing As** dialog box, refer to Figure 1-36. These options are discussed next.

### List, Details, and Thumbnails Options

The **Files** list box displays the drawing files of a project. If you choose the **Details** option, it will display the detailed information about files (size, type, date, and time of modification) in the **Files** list box. In the detailed information, if you click on the **Name** label, the files will be listed with names in alphabetical order. If you again click on the **Name** label, the files will be listed in the reversed order. Similarly, if you click on the **Size** label, the files will be listed according to their size in ascending order. Double-clicking on the **Size** label will list the files in descending order of their size. Similarly, you can click on the **Type** label or the **Modified** label to list the files accordingly. If you choose the **List** option from the **Views** flyout, all files in the current folder will be listed in the **File** list box.

**Tip**

*The file name you enter to save a drawing should match its contents. This helps you to remember drawing details and makes it easier to refer to them later. Also, the file name can be 255 characters long and can contain spaces and punctuation marks.*

## Create New Folder

If you choose the **Create New Folder** button, AutoCAD Electrical will create a new folder with the name **New Folder**. The new folder is displayed in the **File** list box. You can accept the name or change it as per your requirement. Alternatively, press ALT+5 to create a new folder.

## Up one level

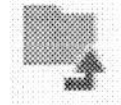

The **Up one level** button is used to display the folders that are up by one level. Alternatively, press ALT+2 to display the folder.

## Tools

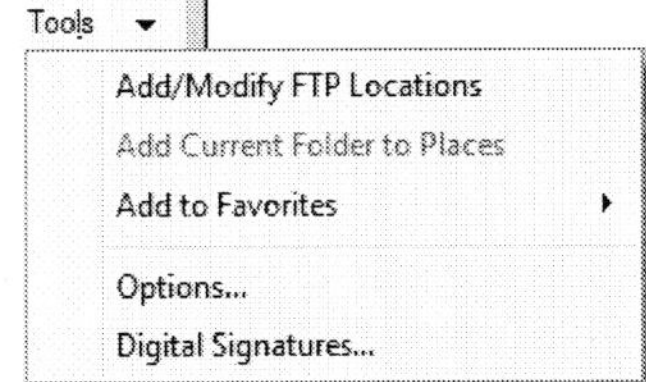


*Figure 1-37 The **Tools** flyout*

The **Tools** flyout has an option for adding or modifying the FTP sites, refer to Figure 1-37. These sites can then be browsed from the FTP shortcut in the **Places** list. The **Add Current Folder to Places** and **Add to Favorites** options are used to add the folder displayed in the **Save in** edit box to the **Places** list or to the **Favorites** folder.

The **Options** button, when chosen, displays the **Saveas Options** dialog box where you can save the proxy images of custom objects. This dialog box has the **DWG Options** and **DXF Options** tabs. The **Display Signatures** button displays the **Security Options** dialog box that is used to configure the security options of a drawing.

# AUTO SAVE

AutoCAD Electrical allows you to save your work automatically at specific intervals. To change the time intervals, you can enter the interval's duration in minutes in the **Minutes between saves** text box in the **File Safety Precautions** area of the **Options** dialog box (**Open and Save** tab). This dialog box can be invoked from the **Tools** menu. Depending on the power supply, hardware, and type of drawings, you should decide on an appropriate time and assign it to this variable. AutoCAD Electrical saves the drawing with the file extension *.sv$*. You can also change the time interval by using the **SAVETIME** system variable.

**Tip**

*Although the automatic save option saves your drawing after a certain time interval, you should not completely depend on it because the procedure for converting the sv$ file into a drawing file is cumbersome. Therefore, it is recommended that you save your files regularly by using the **QSAVE** or **SAVEAS** command.*

# CREATING BACKUP FILES

If a drawing file already exists and you use the **SAVE** or **SAVEAS** command to update the current drawing, AutoCAD Electrical will create a backup file. AutoCAD Electrical takes the previous copy of the drawing and changes it from a file type *.dwg* to *.bak*, and the updated drawing is saved as a drawing file with the *.dwg* extension. For example, if the name of a drawing is *myproj.dwg*, AutoCAD Electrical will change the name to *myproj.bak* and save the current drawing as *myproj.dwg*.

## Using the Drawing Recovery Manager to Recover Files

The automatically saved files can also be retrieved using the **Drawing Recovery Manager**. If the system crashes accidently and the automatic save operation is performed on a drawing, the **Drawing Recovery** dialog box will be displayed when AutoCAD Electrical is run the next time, as shown in Figure 1-38.

The dialog box informs you that the program unexpectedly failed and you can open the most suitable file from the backup files created by AutoCAD Electrical. To open the most suitable file among the backup files, choose the **Close** button from the **Drawing Recovery** dialog box; the **Drawing Recovery Manager** will be displayed on the left of the drawing area, as shown in Figure 1-39. The **Backup Files** rollout lists the original files, backup files, and automatically saved files. Select the required file; the preview of the file will be displayed in the **Preview** rollout. Also, the information corresponding to the selected file will be displayed in the **Details** rollout. To open the backup file, double-click on its name in the **Backup Files** rollout. Alternatively, right-click on the file name, and then choose **Open** from the shortcut menu. It is recommended that you save the backup file at the desired location before you start working on it.

# CLOSING A DRAWING

You can close the current drawing file without actually quitting AutoCAD Electrical by using the **CLOSE** command. If multiple drawing files are opened, choose **Close > All Drawings** from the **Application Menu**; the drawings will be closed. If you have not saved the drawing after making the last change to it and you invoke the **CLOSE** command, AutoCAD Electrical will display a dialog box that allows you to save the drawing before closing it. This box provides you with an option to discard the current drawing or the changes made to it. It also provides you with an option to cancel the command. After closing the drawing, you are still in AutoCAD Electrical from where you can open a new or an already saved drawing file. You can also use the close button (**X**) to close the drawing.

**Note**

*You can close a drawing even if a command is active.*

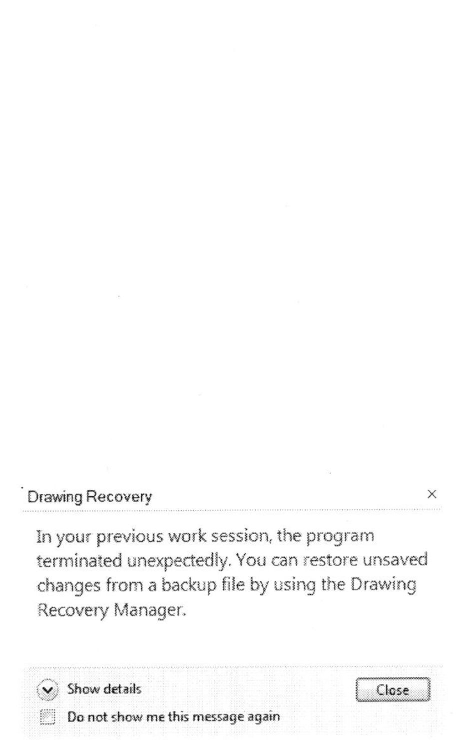

***Figure 1-38** The **Drawing Recovery** dialog box*

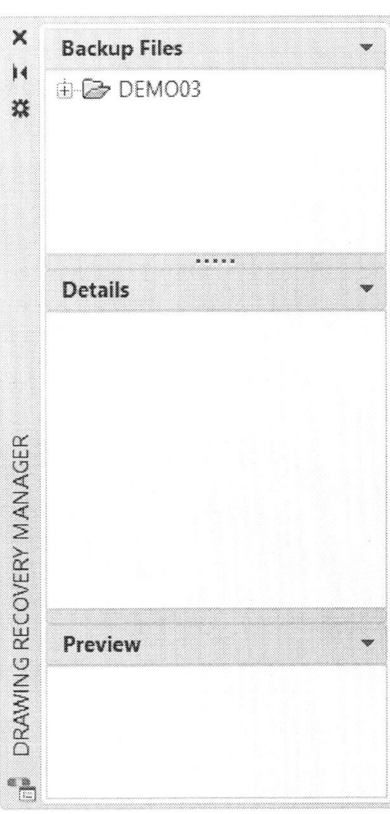


***Figure 1-39** The **Drawing Recovery Manager***

## QUITTING AutoCAD Electrical

You can exit the AutoCAD Electrical program by using the **EXIT** or **QUIT** command. Even if you have an active command, you can choose **Exit AutoCAD Electrical** from the **Application Menu** to quit the AutoCAD Electrical program. In case the drawing has not been saved, the **AutoCAD** message box will be displayed. Note that if you choose **No** in this message box, all changes made in the current drawings, till they were last saved, will be lost. You can also use the close button (**X**) of the main AutoCAD Electrical window (present in the title bar) to end the AutoCAD Electrical session.

**Tip**

*You can open the* ***Drawing Recovery Manager*** *again by choosing* ***Drawing Utilities > Open the Drawing Recovery Manager*** *from the* ***Application Menu*** *or by entering DRAWINGRECOVERY at the Command prompt.*

# DYNAMIC INPUT MODE

As mentioned earlier, turning the **Dynamic Input** mode on allows you to enter commands through the pointer input and dimensions using the dimensional input. When this mode is turned on, all prompts will be available at the tooltip as dynamic prompts. The settings for the **Dynamic Input** mode are made through the **Dynamic Input** tab of the **Drafting Settings** dialog box. To invoke the **Drafting Settings** dialog box, right-click on the **Dynamic Input** button in the Status Bar; a shortcut menu will be displayed. Choose the **Dynamic Input Settings** option from the shortcut menu; the **Drafting Settings** dialog box will be displayed, as shown in Figure 1-40. Alternatively, enter **DSETTINGS** at the Command prompt to display the **Drawing Settings** dialog box. The options in the **Dynamic Input** tab of the **Drafting Settings** dialog box are discussed next.

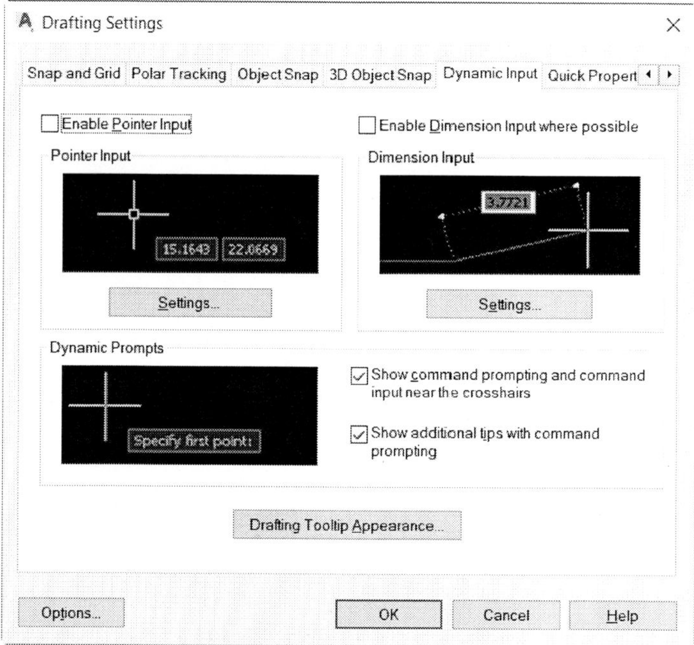


***Figure 1-40** The* ***Dynamic Input*** *tab of the* ***Drafting Settings*** *dialog box*

## Enable Pointer Input

With the **Enable Pointer Input** check box selected, you can enter commands through the pointer input. Figure 1-41 shows the **AEWIRE** command entered through the pointer input. If this check box is cleared, the **Dynamic Input** will be turned off and the commands will be entered through the Command prompt in a way similar to the old releases of AutoCAD Electrical.

On choosing the **Settings** button from the **Pointer Input** area, the **Pointer Input Settings** dialog box will be displayed, as shown in Figure 1-42. The radio buttons in the **Format** area of this dialog box are used to set the default settings for specifying other points, after specifying the first point. By default, the **Polar format** and **Relative coordinates** radio buttons are selected. As a result, coordinates will be specified in the polar form, with respect to the relative coordinates system. You can select the **Cartesian format** radio button to enter coordinates in the cartesian form. Likewise, if you select the **Absolute coordinates** radio button, numerical entries will be measured with respect to the absolute coordinate system.

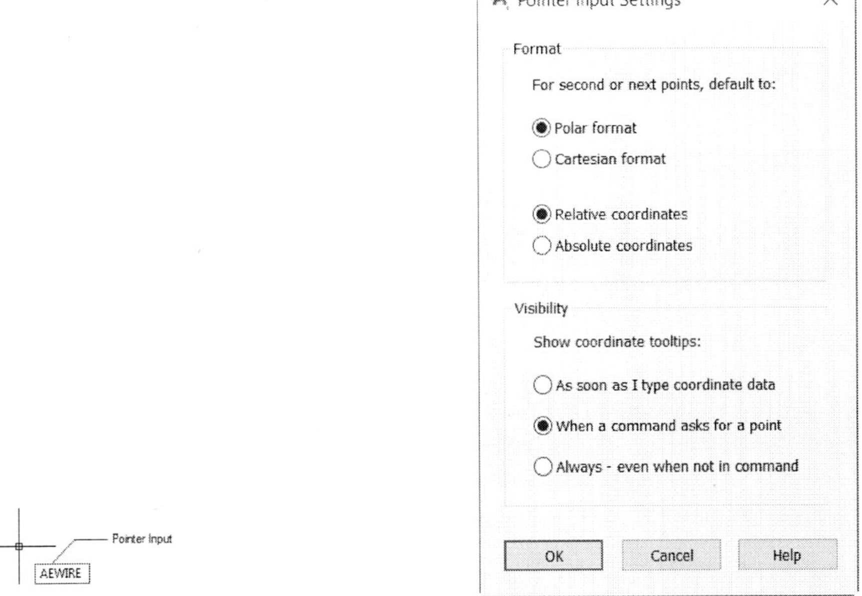


***Figure 1-41*** *Entering a command using the pointer input*

***Figure 1-42*** *The* ***Pointer Input Settings*** *dialog box*

The **Visibility** area in the **Pointer Input Settings** dialog box is used to set the visibility of tool tips of coordinates. By default, the **When a command ask for a point** radio button is selected. You can select the other radio buttons to modify this display.

# CREATING AND MANAGING WORKSPACES

A workspace is defined as a customized arrangement of toolbars, menus, and window palettes in the AutoCAD Electrical environment. Workspaces are required when you need to customize the AutoCAD Electrical environment for a specific use, in which you need only a certain set of toolbars and menus. For such requirements, you can create your own workspaces in which only the specified toolbars, menus, and palettes will be available. By default, the **ACADE & 2D Drafting & Annotation** workspace is set as the current workspace when you start AutoCAD Electrical. You can choose any other predefined workspace from the shortcut menu that will be displayed on choosing the **Workspace Switching** button in the Status Bar or by choosing the required workspace from **Tools > Workspaces** in the menu bar. You can also choose the workspace using the **Workspaces** toolbar.

## Creating a New Workspace

To create a new workspace, invoke the toolbars and window palettes that you want to display in the new workspace. Next, choose **Tools > Workspaces > Save Current As** from the menu bar; the **Save Workspace** dialog box will be displayed, as shown in Figure 1-43. Enter the name of the new workspace in the **Name** edit box and choose the **Save** button from the dialog box.

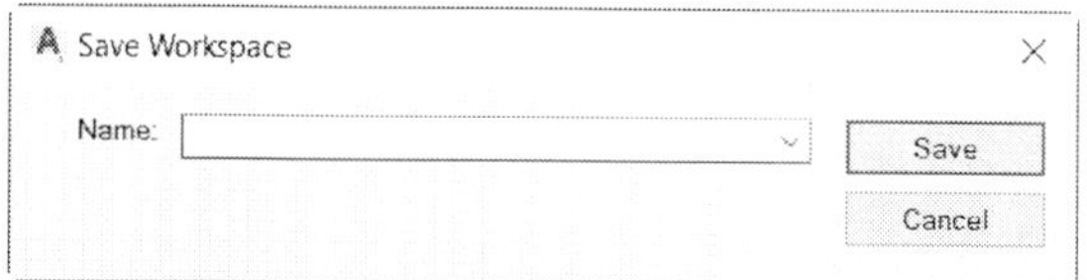


*Figure 1-43 The **Save Workspace** dialog box*

The new workspace will now be the current workspace in the shortcut menu that is displayed on choosing the **Workspace Switching** button on the Status Bar. Likewise, you can create workspaces as per your requirement and can switch from one workspace to the other by selecting the required name of the workspace from the drop-down list in the **Workspaces** toolbar.

## Modifying Workspace Settings

AutoCAD Electrical allows you to modify workspace settings. To do so, choose the **Workspace Switching** button from the Status Bar; a flyout will be displayed. Choose the **Workspace Settings** option from the flyout; the **Workspace Settings** dialog box will be displayed, as shown in Figure 1-44. All workspaces that are created are listed in the **My Workspace** drop-down list. You can make any of the workspaces as My Workspace by selecting it in the **My Workspace** drop-down list. You can also choose the **My Workspace** tool from the **Workspace Switching** toolbar to change the current workspace to the one that was set as **My Workspace** in the **Workspace Settings** dialog box. The other options in this toolbar are discussed next.

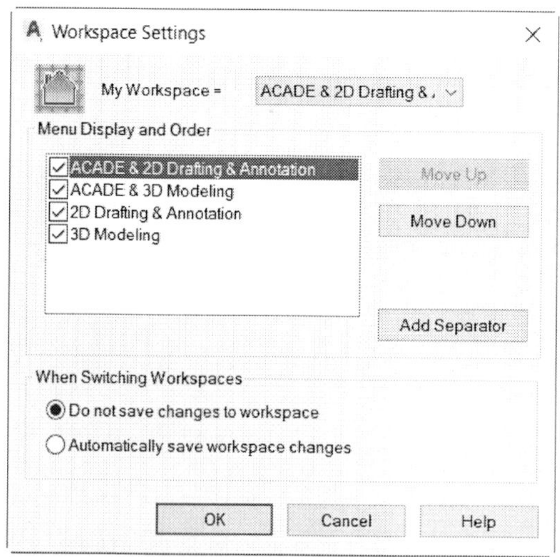


*Figure 1-44 The **Workspace Settings** dialog box*

### Menu Display and Order Area

The options in this area are used to set the order of the display of workspaces in the drop-down list of the **Workspaces** toolbar. By default, workspaces are listed in the sequence of their creation.

To change the order, select the workspace and choose the **Move Up** or **Move Down** button. You can also add a separator between workspaces by choosing the **Add Separator** button. A separator is a line that is placed between two workspaces in the shortcut menu that is displayed on choosing the **Workspace Switching** tool in the Status Bar.

### When Switching Workspaces Area

By default, the **Do not save changes to workspace** radio button is selected in this area. As a result, while switching workspaces, the changes made in the current workspace will not be saved. If you select the **Automatically save workspace changes** radio button, the changes made in the current workspace will automatically be saved when you switch to the other workspace.

## WD_M BLOCK

Most of the settings of a drawing used by AutoCAD Electrical are saved in a smart block on the drawing, called WD_M.dwg. Every drawing of AutoCAD Electrical should consist of non-visible WD_M block to make the drawing compatible with AutoCAD Electrical. The drawing should consist of only one copy of WD_M block. The WD_M.dwg block is situated in the default symbol library. The WD_M.dwg consists of various attributes that define layer names, default settings, and so on. If the WD_M block is not present in the existing or new drawing and if you want to insert any electrical component or want to edit drawing properties, then the **Alert** message box will be displayed, as shown in Figure 1-45. Choose the **OK** button in this message box to insert the WD_M block at 0,0 location. By default, the **Force this drawing's configuration settings to match the project settings** check box is selected. As a result, the drawing settings will be matched to the project settings.

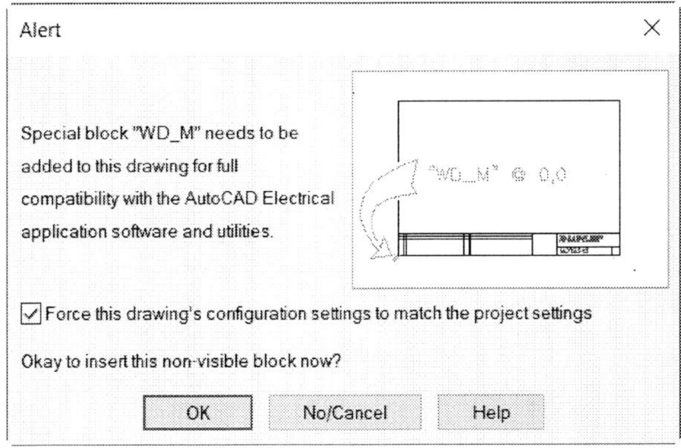


***Figure 1-45** The **Alert** message box*

**Note**

*For inserting panel layout symbols in the drawing, you need to insert the WD_PNLM block, which will be discussed in Chapter 8.*

## AutoCAD Electrical HELP

You can get online help and documentation about the working of AutoCAD Electrical 2022 commands from the **Help** menu in the menu bar, refer to Figure 1-46. You can access the **Help** menu for a particular tool. To do so, place the cursor on the particular tool and then press the

F1 key; the **AutoCAD Electrical 2022 - Help** window will be displayed. This window displays the detailed description related to that particular tool. The menu bar also contains InfoCenter bar, as shown in Figure 1-47. This bar helps you search information by using certain keywords. The options in the **Help** menu and the **InfoCenter** bar are discussed next.

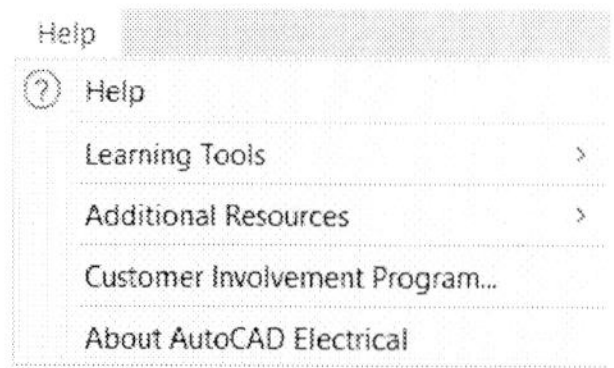


*Figure 1-46 The **Help** menu*

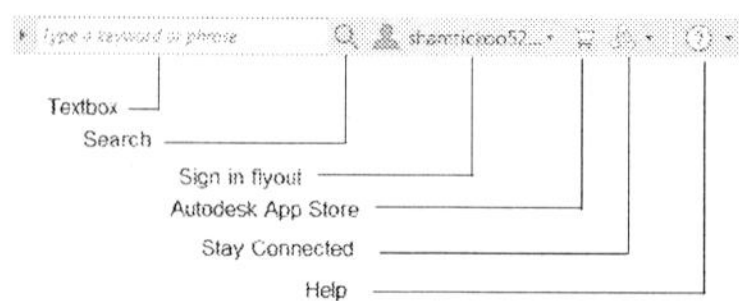


*Figure 1-47 The **InfoCenter** bar*

# Help Menu

## Electrical Help Topics

On choosing the **Help** option, the **AutoCAD Electrical 2022 - Help** window will be displayed. Figure 1-48 shows partial view of the **AutoCAD Electrical 2022 - Help** window.

*Figure 1-48 Partial view of the **AutoCAD Electrical 2022 - Help** window*

You can use this window to access help on different topics and commands. If you are in the middle of a command and require help regarding it, choose the **Help** button to display information about that particular command in the dialog box.

In this window, you can choose the **Help Home** button to explore new features in AutoCAD Electrical 2022. Also, you can browse videos, tutorials, and documentation for beginners and advanced users in the **Essential Skills Videos** and **Resources** sections. You can download sample files and offline help database from the **Downloads** section. You can also connect to other users of Autodesk community and discussion groups using the **Connect** section.

Click on the + sign at the left of these sections to display the list of topics under them. Next, select a topic from the list; contents of the selected topic will be displayed at the right side of the **AutoCAD Electrical 2022 - Help** window.

#### Search Field

When you type any word in the Search edit box and then choose the **Search** button, a list of topics related to the typed word will be displayed below the **Search** button. You can select the desired topic from the list; the information related to that topic will be displayed in the **AutoCAD Electrical 2022 - Help** window.

### Learning Resources

Choose **Help > Learning Tools > Learning Resources** from the menu bar; the **AutoCAD Electrical 2022 - Help** window will be displayed. Using this window, you can access information about topics such as user interface, AutoCAD Electrical Quick Reference Guide, AutoCAD Electrical 2022 Toolset New Feature Summary, and so on. When you choose a topic, the description of the feature improvements will be displayed in a window.

### Additional Resources

This utility connects you to the **Support Knowledge Base**, **Online Training Resources, Online Developer Center**, **Developer Help**, **API Help**, and **Autodesk User Group International** web pages. The **Developer Help** option provides a detailed help on customizing AutoCAD Electrical in a separate window. You can click on any link on the right of this window.

### About AutoCAD Electrical

This option gives you information about the Release, Serial number, Licensed to, and also the legal description about AutoCAD Electrical.

## InfoCenter Bar

### InfoCenter

**InfoCenter** is an easy way to get the desired help documentation. Enter the keywords to be searched in the textbox and choose the **Search** button; the result will be displayed as a link in the **AutoCAD Electrical 2022 - Help** window, refer to Figure 1-49. To display the required information in this window, click on any one of the search topics from the list, the information related to the search topic will be displayed at the right of the window.

### Autodesk App Store

Autodesk App Store helps you to download various applications for AutoCAD Electrical, get connected to the AutoCAD network, share information and designs, and so on. On choosing the **Autodesk App Store** button from the InfoCenter bar, the **AUTODESK APP STORE** window will be opened, refer to Figure 1-50.

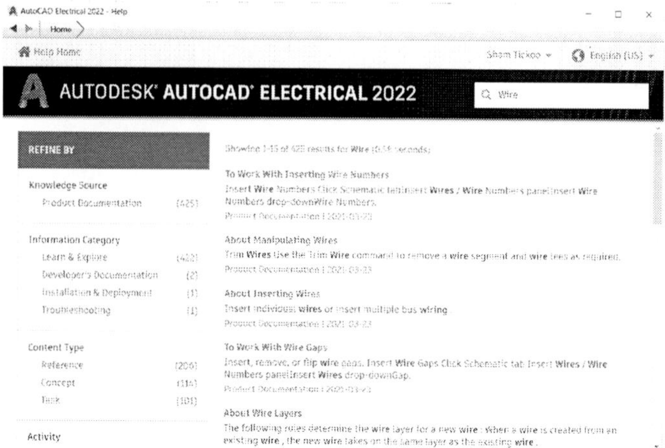

*Figure 1-49 The search results displayed using* ***InfoCenter***

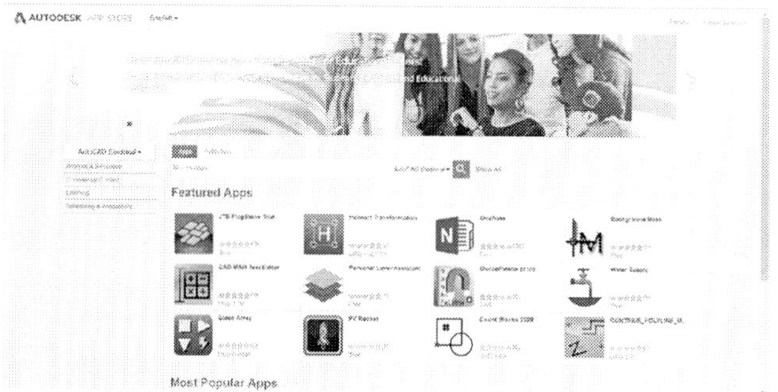

*Figure 1-50 The* ***AUTODESK APP STORE*** *window*

You can download various Autodesk apps from this page. Some of them are free of cost. You can also search for the apps by entering the name of the app in the **Search Apps** text box. You can download the AutoCAD apps from the **Featured Apps** panel of the **Featured Apps** tab in the **Ribbon**, refer to Figure 1-51. To download the AutoCAD apps, choose the required apps from the **Featured Apps** panel of the **Feature Apps** tab; the default browser will open with the icons of the apps to be downloaded. Now, you can download the app.

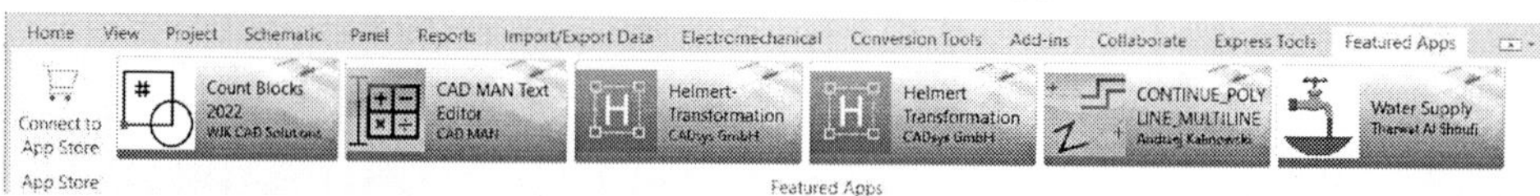


*Figure 1-51 The* ***Featured Apps*** *panel of the* ***Feature Apps*** *tab in the* ***Ribbon***

You can also download apps other than the apps available in the **Featured Apps** panel. To do so, choose the **Connect to App Store** button from the **App Store** panel of the **Featured Apps** tab; the **AUTODESK APP STORE** window will be displayed, refer to Figure 1-57. Next, choose **Show All** from the **AUTODESK APP STORE** window. Now, you can download the required apps from the window. You can also search apps by entering the name of the required app in the **Search Apps** text box. Some of the apps are paid and some of them are free to download.

The downloaded and installed apps will be available in the **Add-Ins** tab. You can choose the required app to work with and can manage it by choosing the **Exchange App Manager** button available in the **App Manager** panel of the **Add-Ins** tab. To manage the app, choose the **App Manager** button from the **App Manager** panel in the **Add-ins** tab; the **Autodesk App Manager** dialog box with all the installed apps will be displayed. To manage a particular app, right-click on it; a shortcut menu will be displayed, as shown in Figure 1-52.

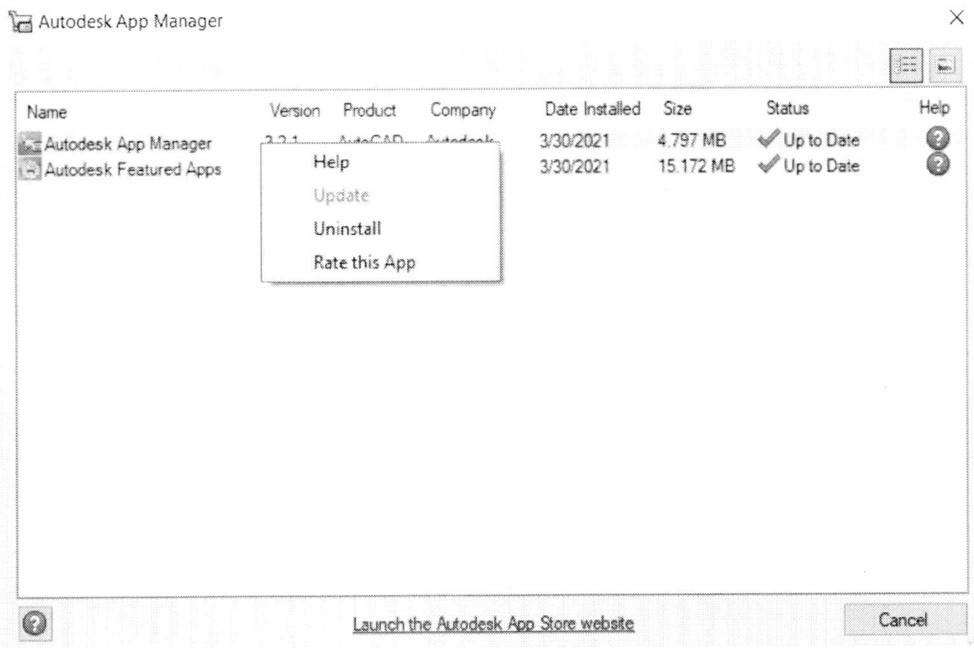


*Figure 1-52 The **Autodesk App Manager** dialog box*

Now, you can choose the required option to manage the app.

## Stay Connected

When you choose this button, a flyout is displayed, as shown in Figure 1-53. The options in this flyout provide you quick access to the subscription center and social media.

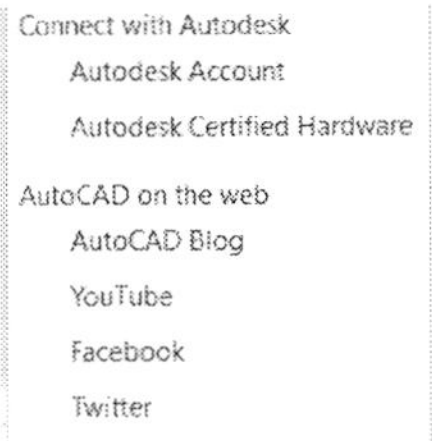


*Figure 1-53 The flyout displayed*

# SAVE TO WEB & MOBILE

**Application Menu:** Save As > Drawing to AutoCAD Web & Mobile
**Quick Access Toolbar:** Save to Web & Mobile **Command:** SAVETOWEBMOBILE

Using the **Save to Web & Mobile** tool, you can save copy of your drawings in your Autodesk web & mobile account from any remote location in the world using any device such as desktop or mobile having internet access. You can access this tool from the **Quick Access Toolbar** or **Application Menu**. When you choose this tool for the first time, you will be prompted to install the Save to AutoCAD Web and Mobile Plug-in. Choose the **Save to Web & Mobile** tool from the **Quick Access Toolbar**; the **Save in AutoCAD Web & Mobile** dialog box will be displayed, refer to Figure 1-54.

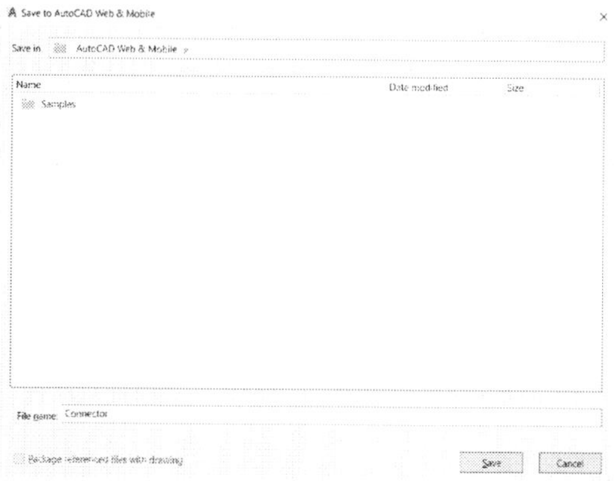


*Figure 1-54 The **Save in AutoCAD Web & Mobile** dialog box*

Enter the name of the file to be saved in the **File name** edit box. Next, choose the **Save** button.

**Note**

*1. The name of the saved files appear in the **Name** column of the list box available in the **Save in AutoCAD Web & Mobile Cloud Files** dialog box when you invoke this dialog box again.*

*2. You need to first sign in to your Autodesk account to use this tool. If you are not signed in and choose this tool, the Autodesk sign-in window will appear and will prompt you to sign in first.*

*3. The drawing files saved in your web and mobile account are saved to the cloud and utilise the cloud space. You can save them to your device by using the **Save As** tool.*

*4. You can also share the saved files with any of the co-workers or clients across the world. They can review or edit the drawing files depending upon the permissions you grant them.*

After saving the file to your web and mobile account, you can access it from anywhere across the world using any device (mobile, tablet, etc) having Wi-fi or internet connection.

**Note**

*You can access the saved web and mobile files using the **Open from Web & Mobile** tool available in the **Quick Access Toolbar**.*

# ADDITIONAL HELP RESOURCES

1. You can get help for a command by pressing the F1 key. On doing so, the **AutoCAD Electrical 2022 - Help** window containing information about the command will be displayed. You can exit the dialog box and continue working with the command.

2. You can get help about a dialog box by choosing the **Help** button in that dialog box.

3. Autodesk has provided several resources that can be used to seek assistance for your AutoCAD Electrical questions. The following is a list of some of the resources:

   a. Autodesk website: *https://www.autodesk.com*
   b. AutoCAD Electrical Technical Assistance website: *https://knowledge.autodesk.com*
   c. AutoCAD Electrical Discussion Groups website

4. CADCIM Technologies provides technical support for the study material discussed in our textbooks. Send us an email at *techsupport@cadcim.com* to seek technical assistance.

**Note**
*For the printing purpose, this textbook will follow the white background.*

## Self-Evaluation Test

**Answer the following questions and then compare them to those given at the end of this chapter:**

1. Which of the following combinations of keys should be pressed to turn the display of the **Tool Palettes** window on or off?

   (a) CTRL+3 (b) CTRL+0
   (c) CTRL+5 (d) CTRL+2

2. If WD_M block is not present in a drawing and you insert a component in it, then the __________ message box will be displayed.

3. The __________ option in the **Workspace Switching** flyout is used to save the current workspace settings as a new workspace.

4. You can use the __________ command to close the current drawing file without actually quitting AutoCAD Electrical.

5. You can retrieve the automatically saved files by using the __________.

6. The __________ button in the Application Status Bar is used to display the expanded view of the drawing.

7. You can press the F3 key to display the **AutoCAD Electrical** text window that displays previously used commands and prompts. (T/F)

8. You cannot create a new drawing using the **PROJECT MANAGER**. (T/F)

9. AutoCAD Electrical marking menu will be displayed when you right-click on the AutoCAD Electrical object such as component, wire, and so on. (T/F)

10. You can press the F1 key to display the **AutoCAD Electrical 2022 - Help** window. (T/F)

## Review Questions

**Answer the following questions:**

1. Which of the following combinations of keys needs to be pressed to toggle display of all toolbars displayed on the screen?

   (a) CTRL+3 (b) CTRL+0
   (c) CTRL+5 (d) CTRL+2

2. Which of the following commands is used to exit the AutoCAD Electrical program?

   (a) **QUIT** (b) **END**
   (c) **CLOSE** (d) **EXIT**

3. Which of the following commands is invoked when you choose **Save** from the **File** menu or choose the **Save** button in the **Quick Access Toolbar**?

   (a) **SAVE** (b) **LSAVE**
   (c) **QSAVE** (d) **SAVEAS**

4. The __________ button is used to add or remove buttons in the Application Status Bar.

5. The __________ button is used to toggle the display of the File tab bar which displays all opened files.

6. The __________ contains different commands for inserting components in Imperial and Metric units.

7. The shortcut menu invoked by right-clicking in the command window displays the most recently used commands and some of the window options such as **Copy**, **Paste**, and so on. (T/F)

8. The F12 function key is used to toggle the **Dynamic Input** mode. (T/F)

### Answers to Self-Evaluation Test

**1.** CTRL+3, **2.** **Alert**, **3.** **Save Current As**, **4.** **CLOSE**, **5.** **Drawing Recovery Manager**, **6.** **Clean Screen**, **7.** F, **8.** F, **9.** T, **10.** T

# Chapter 2

# Working with Projects and Drawings

## Learning Objectives

**After completing this chapter, you will be able to:**

- *Create new projects and drawings*
- *Edit the properties of projects and drawings*
- *Add drawing descriptions*
- *Open existing projects*
- *Activate and close projects*
- *Add existing and new drawings to the current project*
- *Group the drawings of a project*
- *Rename, replace, and remove drawings from projects*
- *Assign description to a drawing*
- *Open project drawings*
- *Copy existing projects*
- *Understand the working of the PROJECT MANAGER*

# INTRODUCTION

AutoCAD Electrical is a project-based software in which wiring diagrams related to each other are grouped under a project. A project is a set of electrical wiring diagrams that form a project file *<project_name>.wdp*. Each project is defined by an ASCII text file with *.wdp* extension. These project files contain a list of project information such as project settings, project or drawing properties, names and descriptions of drawing files, symbol library paths, and so on. You can have an unlimited number of projects. However, only one project can be active at a time. The list of these projects is displayed in the **PROJECT MANAGER**.

# PROJECT MANAGER

| | |
|---|---|
| **Ribbon:** | Project > Project Tools > Manager |
| **Toolbar:** | ACE:Main Electrical 2 > Project Manager or ACE:Project > Project Manager |
| **Menu:** | Projects > Project > Project Manager |
| **Command:** | AEPROJECT |

The **PROJECT MANAGER** is used to create new projects, open existing projects, add new drawings to a project, re-order drawing files, access existing projects, and modify existing information in a project. By default, the **PROJECT MANAGER** is displayed and docked on the left of the screen, refer to Figure 2-1. If the **PROJECT MANAGER** is not displayed by default, choose the **Manager** tool from the **Project Tools** panel of the **Project** tab; the **PROJECT MANAGER** will be displayed.

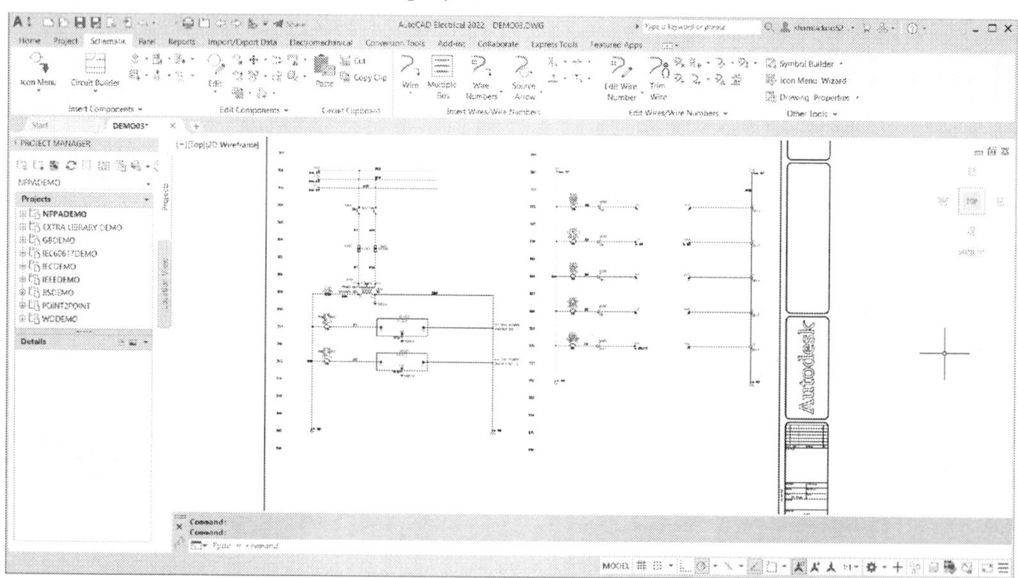


*Figure 2-1 AutoCAD Electrical screen with the* ***PROJECT MANAGER***

Alternatively, choose the **Project Manager** tool from the **ACE:Main Electrical 2** toolbar to display the **PROJECT MANAGER**. The **PROJECT MANAGER** is similar to other AutoCAD Electrical tool palettes. You can dock the **PROJECT MANAGER** at a specific location on the screen. Also, if you do not want to use the project tools, you can hide the **PROJECT MANAGER**.

The **PROJECT MANAGER** is divided into two tabs: **Projects** and **Location View**. The options in both these tabs are discussed in detail in this chapter.

## Projects TAB

In the **PROJECT MANAGER**, the **Projects** tab is chosen by default, refer to Figure 2-1. When you double-click on the title bar of the **PROJECT MANAGER**, it gets undocked and is displayed separately on the screen, refer to Figure 2-2. When you right-click on the title bar of the undocked **PROJECT MANAGER**, a shortcut menu is displayed, as shown in Figure 2-3. You can change the appearance, location, and display settings of the **PROJECT MANAGER** by choosing the respective options from the shortcut menu.

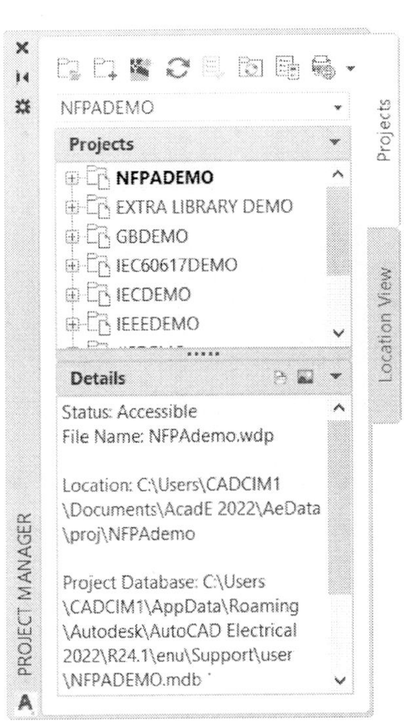


*Figure 2-2 The undocked* ***PROJECT MANAGER***

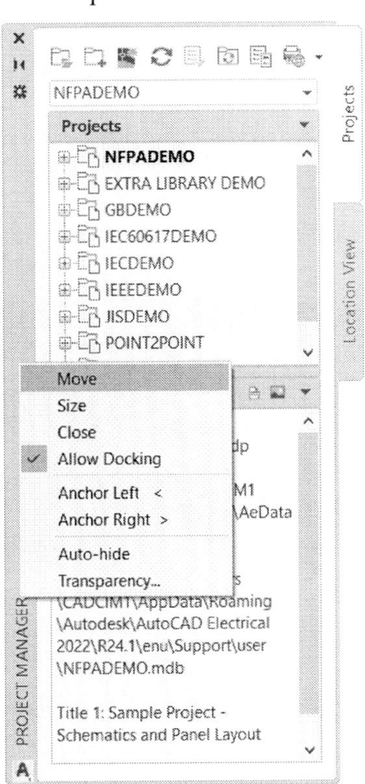


*Figure 2-3 The shortcut menu displayed by right-clicking on the title bar of the* ***PROJECT MANAGER***

When you double-click on a project name in the **Projects** rollout, a list of drawings associated with the project will be displayed. Also, the details of the selected project will be displayed in the **Details** rollout of the **PROJECT MANAGER**, as shown in Figure 2-4. The name of the active project will appear in bold text in the **Projects** rollout of the **PROJECT MANAGER**.

In AutoCAD Electrical 2022, five new projects are added in the Project Manager based on various drafting standards. Names of these projects are **IECDEMO**, **JISDEMO**, **GBDEMO**, **IEC60617DEMO**, and **IEEEDEMO**. These projects are based on respective symbol libraries. For example, in the **IECDEMO** project, the drawings are based on IEC symbol library whereas in the **IEEEDEMO** project, the drawings are based on IEEE symbol library. Detailed information about various drafting standards is provided later in this chapter.

When you right-click on a drawing name, a shortcut menu will be displayed. You can use the options in this shortcut menu to open, close, copy, remove, replace, rename, or access other editing options to modify the drawing file. These options are discussed in detail later in the chapter. You can open a drawing file by double-clicking on it in the **PROJECT MANAGER** and the corresponding drawing file name will appear in bold text in the **Projects** rollout of the **PROJECT MANAGER**.

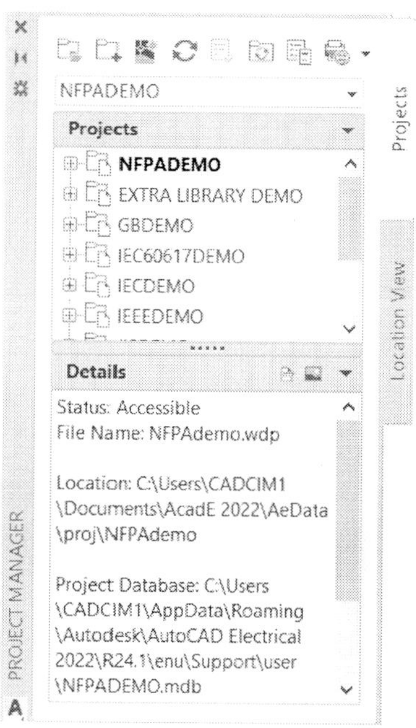


*Figure 2-4 The **PROJECT MANAGER** displaying the **Details** rollout*

**Note**

*You cannot create two projects with the same name in the **PROJECT MANAGER**. Moreover by using the **PROJECT MANAGER**, you can switch to different projects and change their settings.*

## Opening a Project

You can open an existing project by using the **Open Project** button from the **PROJECT MANAGER**. On doing so, the **Select Project File** dialog box will be displayed. Next, select the existing project from this dialog box and choose the **Open** button; the selected project's name will be automatically displayed in the **Projects** rollout in bold text and it will become an active project.

In the **Select Project File** dialog box, by default, the **nfpaDemo** folder is displayed in the **Look in** drop-down list, refer to Figure 2-5. You can customize this folder. To customize the default folder, open the windows explorer. Next, navigate to the location *c:\Users\User Name\Documents\AcadE 2022\AeData* and open the *wd.env* file in Notepad. Now, scroll down in the file and go to the line highlighted in blue, refer to Figure 2-6. In this line, remove the '*' symbol available at the start of the line. Also, select the text 'x:/some path/' and enter the desired path; the selected text is replaced by the desired path, refer to Figure 2-7. Next, save the *wd.env* file.

**Note**

*If you put any extra space at the start, in between, or at the end, the desired path will not change.*

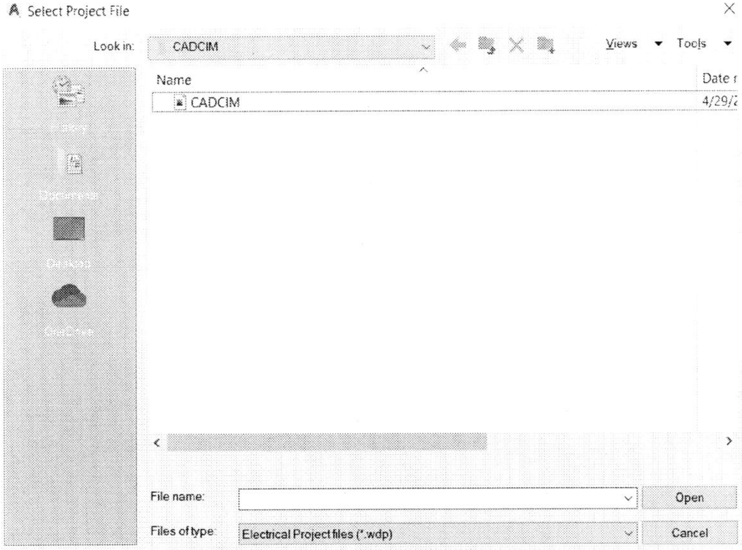


***Figure 2-5** The **Select Project File** dialog box*

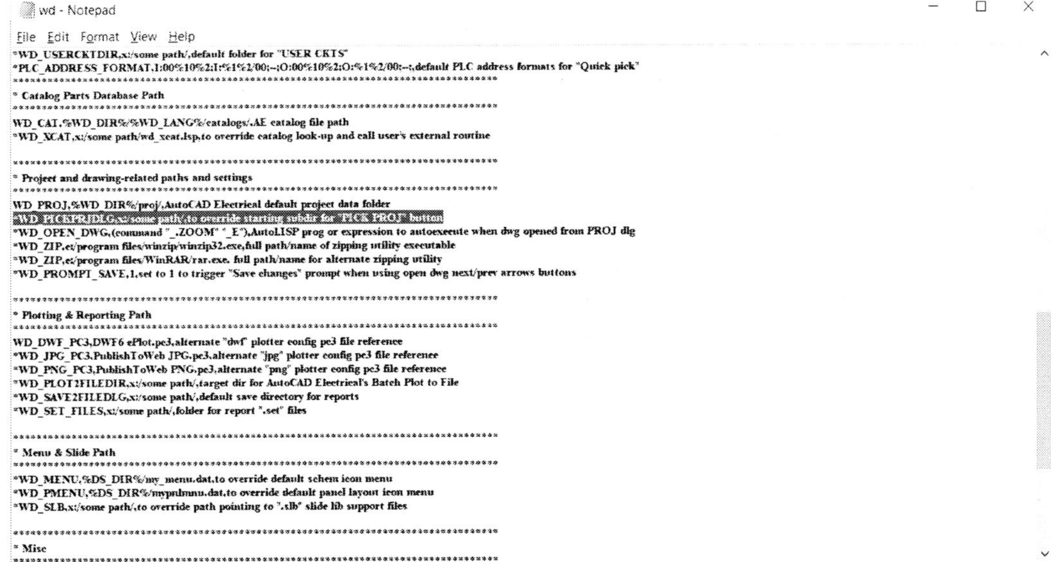


***Figure 2-6** The line highlighted in the wd.env file*

Now, choose the **Open Project** button from the **PROJECT MANAGER**; the modified **Select Project File** dialog box will be displayed, as shown in Figure 2-8. You will notice that the name of the folder is changed.

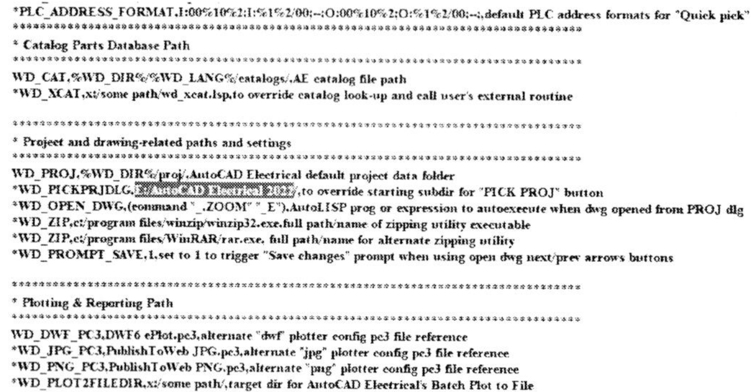

```
*PLC_ADDRESS_FORMAT,I:00%10%2:I:%1%2/00;--;O:00%10%2;O:%1%2/00;--;,default PLC address formats for "Quick pick"
********************************************************************************
* Catalog Parts Database Path
********************************************************************************
WD_CAT,%WD_DIR%/%WD_LANG%/catalogs/,AE catalog file path
*WD_XCAT,x:/some path/wd_xcat.lsp,to override catalog look-up and call user's external routine

********************************************************************************
* Project and drawing-related paths and settings
********************************************************************************
WD_PROJ,%WD_DIR%/proj/,AutoCAD Electrical default project data folder
*WD_PICKPRJDLG,E:/AutoCAD Electrical 2022/,to override starting subdir for "PICK PROJ" button
*WD_OPEN_DWG,(command "_.ZOOM" "_E"),AutoLISP prog or expression to autoexecute when dwg opened from PROJ dlg
*WD_ZIP,c:/program files/winzip/winzip32.exe,full path/name of zipping utility executable
*WD_ZIP,c:/program files/WinRAR/rar.exe, full path/name for alternate zipping utility
*WD_PROMPT_SAVE,1,set to 1 to trigger "Save changes" prompt when using open dwg next/prev arrows buttons

********************************************************************************
* Plotting & Reporting Path
********************************************************************************
WD_DWF_PC3,DWF6 ePlot.pc3,alternate "dwf" plotter config pc3 file reference
*WD_JPG_PC3,PublishToWeb JPG.pc3,alternate "jpg" plotter config pc3 file reference
*WD_PNG_PC3,PublishToWeb PNG.pc3,alternate "png" plotter config pc3 file reference
*WD_PLOT2FILEDIR,x:/some path/,target dir for AutoCAD Electrical's Batch Plot to File
```

*Figure 2-7 The selected text replaced by the desired path*

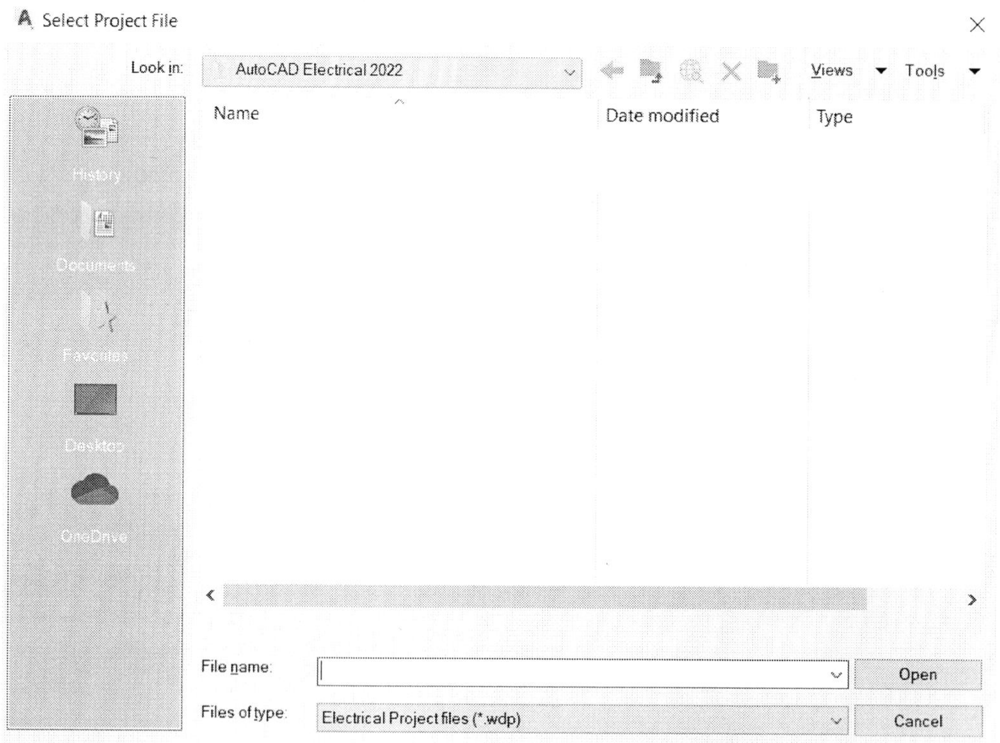


*Figure 2-8 Modified **Select Project File** dialog box*

# Creating a New Project

**Command:** ACENEWPROJECT

You can create a new project by choosing the **New Project** button from the **PROJECT MANAGER**. On doing so, the **Create New Project** dialog box will be displayed, as shown in Figure 2-9. Alternatively, use the **ACENEWPROJECT** command to create a new project. Different options in the **Create New Project** dialog box are discussed next.

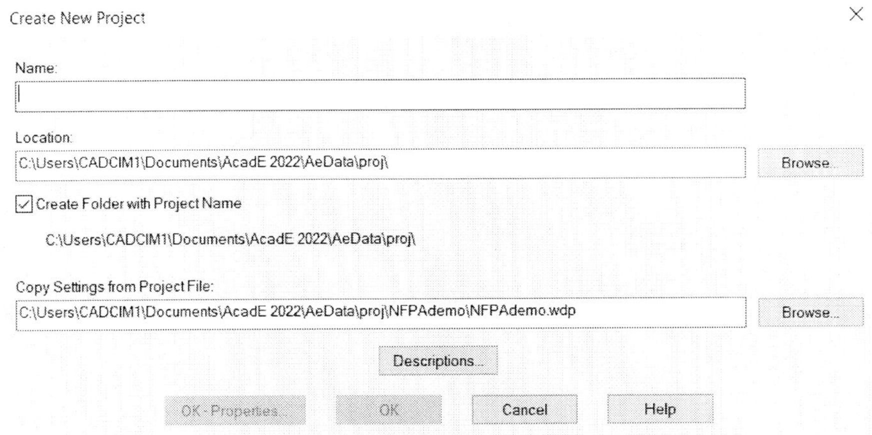


***Figure 2-9** The **Create New Project** dialog box*

## Name

The **Name** edit box is used to enter a name for the project. On doing so, the *.wdp* extension will be automatically added to the file name and displayed under the **Create Folder with Project Name** check box.

## Location

The **Location** edit box is used to specify the location for saving the project. You can also choose the **Browse** button on the right of the **Location** edit box to specify the location for saving the project file *(.wdp file)*. By default, *C:\Users\User Name\Documents\AcadE 2022\AeData\proj* is displayed in the **Location** edit box, refer to Figure 2-9.

## Create Folder with Project Name

The **Create Folder with Project Name** check box is selected by default in this dialog box. As a result, a folder with a name identical to the project name will be created. Also, the new project will be saved in that folder. The path of the folder will be the same as that defined in the **Location** edit box. If you clear the **Create Folder with Project Name** check box, a separate folder will not be created for the project.

## Copy Settings from Project File

You can also copy the settings from an existing project and apply it to a new project. To copy the settings from the existing project file, specify the name and location of the existing project file in the **Copy Settings from Project File** edit box. Alternatively, choose the **Browse** button on the right of this edit box; the **Select Project File** dialog box will be displayed. Select an existing project file and then choose the **Open** button; the settings of the specified project will be applied to the new project and the location of the specified project will be displayed in the **Copy Settings from Project File** edit box. By default, *C:\Users\User Name\Documents\AcadE 2022\AeData\proj\NFPAdemo\NFPAdemo.wdp* is displayed in the **Copy Settings from Project File** edit box.

## Descriptions

The **Descriptions** button is used to add a description to the project. Choose the **Descriptions** button; the **Project Description** dialog box will be displayed, as shown in Figure 2-10. In this dialog box, you can enter a description of the new project up to 12 lines per page. If you want to add more than 12 descriptions, click on the **>** button at the bottom of this dialog box. To include the description in the reports, select the **in reports** check box on the right of each description line. Note that the descriptions thus added will be included in the report headers of the report file and the title blocks of the drawing. Now, choose the **OK** button from this dialog box to save the changes made and exit the dialog box. The concept of report generation, title blocks, and **Project Description** dialog box is discussed in detail in the later chapters.

## OK

The **OK** button of the **Create New Project** dialog box will be activated only if you enter the name of the project in the **Name** edit box. Choose the **OK** button; the project that you created will be added to the current project lists in the **PROJECT MANAGER**. Also, it will become an active project and its name will appear in bold text in the **PROJECT MANAGER**.

## OK-Properties

The **OK-Properties** button will be activated only if you enter the project name in the **Name** edit box. Choose the **OK-Properties** button; a new project will be created and the **Project Properties** dialog box will be displayed. This dialog box is used to modify project settings, components, wire numbering, cross-references, styles, and drawing formats. All information defined in the **Project Properties** dialog box is saved to the project definition file (*.wdp*) as project and drawing defaults. Next, choose the **OK** button from this dialog box to exit from it. The options in the **Project Properties** dialog box are discussed later.

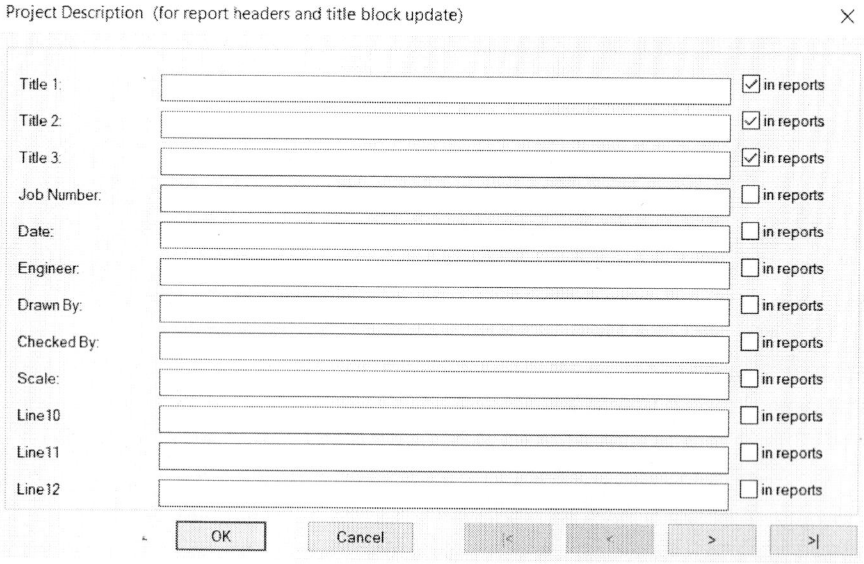

*Figure 2-10 The **Project Description** dialog box*

**Note**

*You can also create a new project by right-clicking inside the **Projects** rollout and then choosing the **New Project** option from the shortcut menu displayed or by selecting the **New Project** option from the Project selection drop-down list in the **PROJECT MANAGER**. You will learn more about it later in this chapter.*

# Working with Drawings

In the previous topic, you learned to create new projects using the **PROJECT MANAGER**. Now, you will learn to create new drawings within an active project.

You can add any number of drawings to your project at any time. A project file can have drawings located in different directories. But, it is recommended that you save your drawings and project file (*.wdp*) in the same folder. When you create a new drawing, an invisible smart block, WD_M, will automatically be added to your drawing at location 0,0. The WD_M block defines drawing settings. These settings may be different from the project settings. Thus, you can have different settings for different drawings in a single project. Also, each AutoCAD Electrical drawing should contain only one copy of invisible WD_M block. If multiple WD_M blocks are present in the drawing, the settings may not be stored and read consistently. Also, note that the drawing to be created will automatically get added to the active project.

## Creating a New Drawing

**Command:** ACENEWDRAWING

The **New Drawing** button is used to create a new drawing file. To do so, choose the **New Drawing** button from the **PROJECT MANAGER**; the **Create New Drawing** dialog box will be displayed, as shown in Figure 2-11.

Alternatively, invoke this dialog box by using the **ACENEWDRAWING** command or by right-clicking on the **Projects** rollout of the **PROJECT MANAGER** and then choosing the **New Drawing** option from the shortcut menu displayed. The different areas and options in this dialog box are discussed next.

### Drawing File Area

The options in the **Drawing File** area are used to specify the name of a drawing file, the template file to be used in the drawing, the location to save the drawing, and the description for the new drawing file. The options in this area are discussed next.

**Name:** Enter a name for the new drawing in the **Name** edit box; the *.dwg* extension will automatically be added to the drawing name. Note that the **OK** and **OK - Properties** buttons will be activated only after entering the name of the new drawing in this edit box.

**Template:** This edit box is used to specify the path and name of a template drawing (*.dwt*) for creating a drawing file. Alternatively, you can choose the **Browse** button; the **Select template** dialog box will be displayed. Select the template drawing from this dialog box and choose the **Open** button; the location of the template drawing will be displayed in the **Template** edit box.

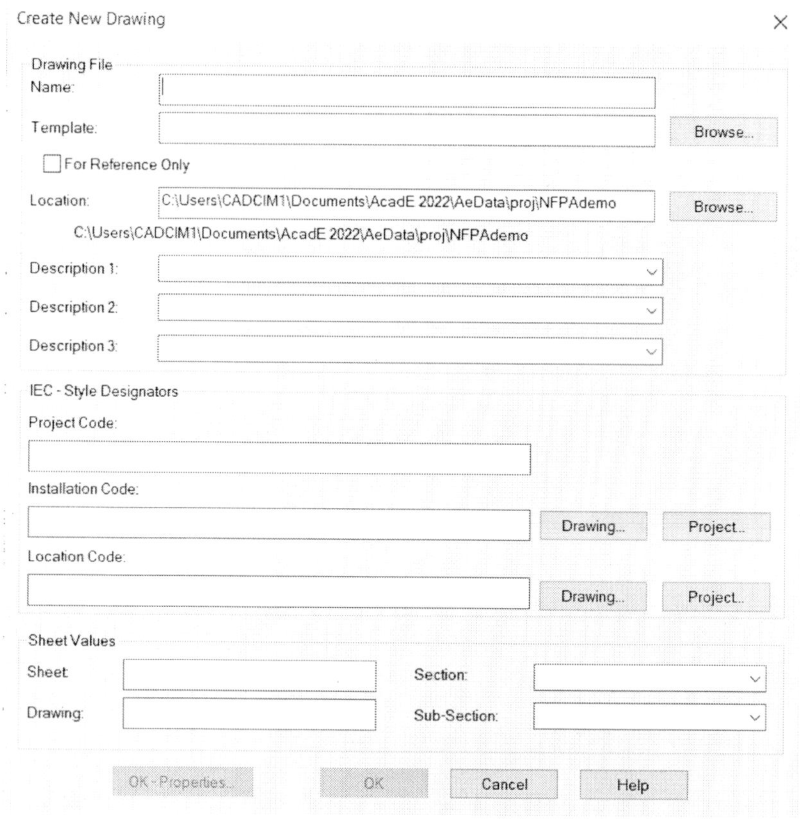

*Figure 2-11 The **Create New Drawing** dialog box*

**Note**

*After specifying the template in the **Template** edit box, next time when you create a new drawing, the template entered previously will automatically get displayed in the **Template** edit box. If this edit box is left blank, AutoCAD Electrical will use the default acad.dwt file.*

**For Reference Only:** The reference drawings are used for coversheets, terminal plans, and other non-electrical layouts in a project. These drawings save the processing time of AutoCAD Electrical functions. To create a reference drawing, you need to select the **For Reference Only** check box. On doing so, the reference drawing will be included in the project-wide plotting and title block update operations. All other electrical smart functions such as cross-referencing, automatic tagging, reporting, and so on will be non-functional. By default, the **For Reference Only** check box is cleared.

**Note**

*The color of the reference drawing icon displayed on the left of the drawing name in the **PROJECT MANAGER** is gray.*

**Location:** The **Location** edit box is used to specify the location of a new drawing. The directory of the active project file is specified by default in the **Location** edit box. Alternatively, choose the **Browse** button on its right to specify different location for the new drawing. If you leave the **Location** edit box blank, the drawing file will be created at the same location as that of the active project. Note that you cannot create duplicate drawings at the same location.

**Description 1-3:** The **Description 1**, **Description 2**, and **Description 3** edit boxes are used to enter description for a drawing. In these edit boxes, you can enter up to 3 description lines for a drawing file. You can also specify the description for a drawing by selecting it from the description drop-down lists. But this is possible only if you have entered description in the earlier drawings. The description thus entered will be displayed in the title block updates and custom drawing properties.

### OK

The **OK** button will be activated only if you enter a drawing file name in the **Name** edit box. When you choose the **OK** button, the new drawing gets automatically added at the bottom of the list in the active project and it appears in bold text. To view the drawing file, expand the active project by double-clicking on the project name.

### OK - Properties

The **OK - Properties** button will be activated only if you enter a drawing name in the **Name** edit box of the **Drawing File** area. Choose the **OK - Properties** button; a drawing file will be created at the specified location and also the **Drawing Properties** dialog box will be displayed, as shown in Figure 2-12.

This dialog box is used to define settings and options for a drawing. The options in the **Drawing Properties** dialog box will be discussed in the later chapters. The changes that you make using this dialog box will be saved as attribute values on the drawing's invisible WD_M block. Choose the **OK** button from the **Drawing Properties** dialog box; the drawing will be created and will appear in bold text at the bottom of the project list of the active project in the **PROJECT MANAGER**.

**Note**

*Mentioning information in the **Description** edit boxes, the **IEC-Style Designators** area, the **Sheet values** area as well as choosing the **OK - Properties** button is optional. You can also edit any of these fields later in the **Drawing Properties** dialog box.*

**Tip**

*The IEC style designators are widely used when you are using the IEC drafting standard. You must be aware of the drafting standards used in AutoCAD Electrical. The software has been designed to use seven International Drafting Standards which are listed below:*

*1. Joint Industrial Council ---- JIC1/JIC125 (USA)*
*2. International Electrotechnical Commission ---- IEC2/IEC 60617 (Europe, UK)*
*3. Japanese International Standard ---- JIS2 (Japan)*
*4. Guobiao Standard ---- GB2 (Chinese)*
*5. Australian Standard ---- AS2 (Australia)*
*6. Institute of Electrical and Electronics Engineers Standard ---- IEEE 315/315A*
*7. National Fire Protection Association Standard ---- NFPA (USA)*

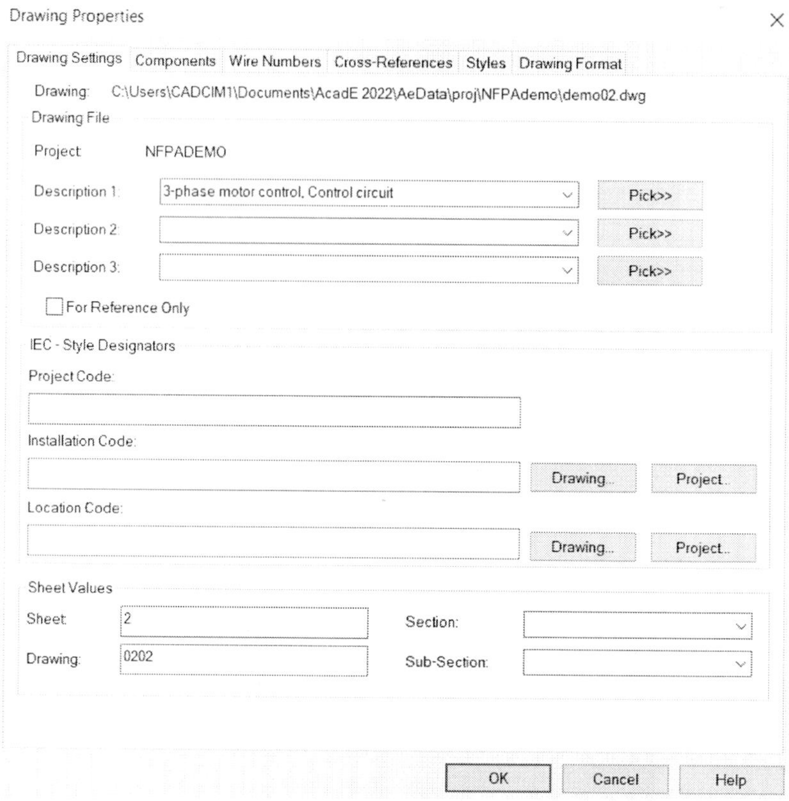

*Figure 2-12 The **Drawing Properties** dialog box*

## Adding a New Drawing to the Inactive Project

You can add a new drawing to the inactive project using the **PROJECT MANAGER**. To do so, choose the **New Drawing** button from the **PROJECT MANAGER**; the **Create New Drawing** dialog box will be displayed. Enter the required information in this dialog box, as explained earlier and then choose the **OK** button; a new drawing will be created. Also, this drawing will be automatically added to the active project and will appear in bold text at the end of the Project Drawing list. Next, to add this drawing to an inactive project, right-click on the inactive project name and choose the **Add Active Drawing** option from the shortcut menu displayed; the **Apply Project Defaults to Drawing Settings** message box will be displayed, as shown in Figure 2-13.

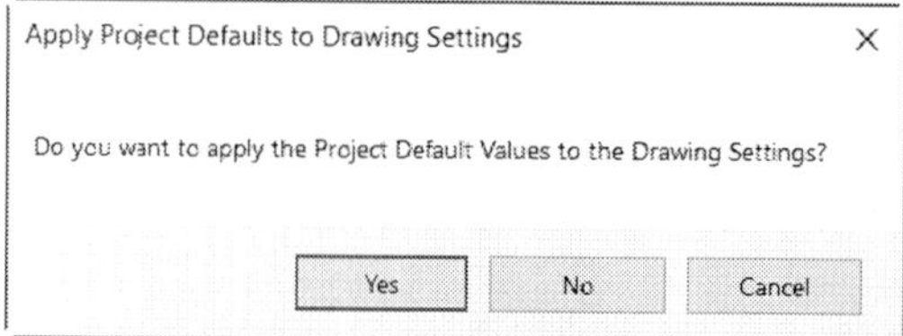


*Figure 2-13 The **Apply Project Defaults to Drawing Settings** message box*

Choose the **Yes** button from the **Apply Project Defaults to Drawing Settings** message box; the default values of the project will be added to the WD_M block definition of the newly added drawing. If you choose the **No** button, the new drawing will retain its existing settings. Choose the **Cancel** button to exit the command.

**Note**

*You can have a single drawing in multiple projects.*

## Adding Existing Drawings to the Current Project

You can also add the existing drawings to the current project. To do so, right-click on the project name in the Projects rollout of the **PROJECT MANAGER**; a shortcut menu will be displayed, as shown in Figure 2-14. Choose the **Add Drawings** option from the shortcut menu; the **Select Files to Add** dialog box will be displayed, as shown in Figure 2-15. In this dialog box, select the desired project folder from the **Look in** drop-down list and then select drawings to be added to the project. Next, choose the **Add** button; the **Apply Project Defaults to Drawing Settings** message box will be displayed, refer to Figure 2-13.

If you choose the **Yes** button, the default values of the project will be added to the WD_M block definition of the newly added drawing. But if you choose the **No** button, the new drawing will retain its existing settings. Also, the selected drawings will be added to your project and will appear at the end of the Project Drawing list.

**Note**

*You can select multiple drawing files at a time from the **Select Files to Add** dialog box by pressing the SHIFT or CTRL key.*

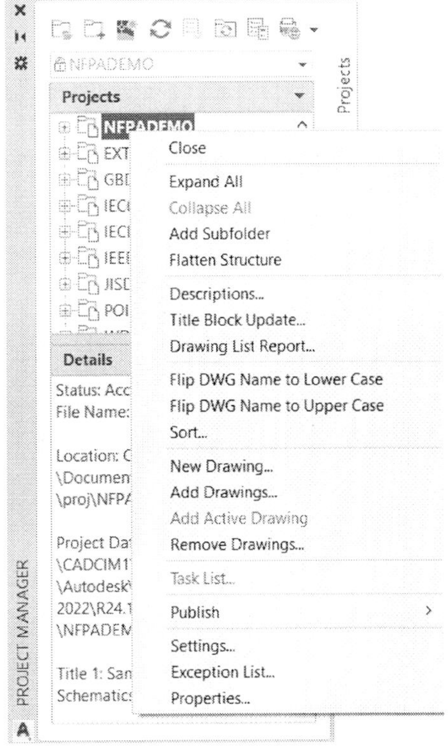


*Figure 2-14 The shortcut menu displayed by right-clicking on the active project name in the **PROJECT MANAGER***

# Working with Project Drawings

You can group drawings, remove drawings, assign description to drawings, preview drawings, configure the drawing list display, and so on by using the **PROJECT MANAGER**. Also, you can access the existing project and modify its related information using the **PROJECT MANAGER**.

## Grouping Drawings within a Project

You can group the drawings in a project in two ways: grouping using section/subsection and grouping using subfolders. These methods are discussed next.

### Grouping Drawings Using Section/ Subsection

You can create a group of drawings within a project list by assigning the section and sub-section codes to each drawing. To do so, expand the project by double-clicking on its name, if it is not already expanded; the drawings in that project will be displayed. Next, right-click on the drawing file; a shortcut menu will be displayed. Choose **Properties > Drawing Properties** from the shortcut menu; the **Drawing Properties** dialog box will be displayed, refer to Figure 2-12. In this dialog box, the **Drawing Settings** tab is chosen by default. Enter the required section and sub-section codes for the drawing in the **Sheet Values** area and choose the **OK** button; the section and sub-section codes will get assigned to the drawing file. Similarly, you can repeat the same procedure for each drawing that you want to group together, but ensure that the same section and sub-section codes are assigned to all of them.

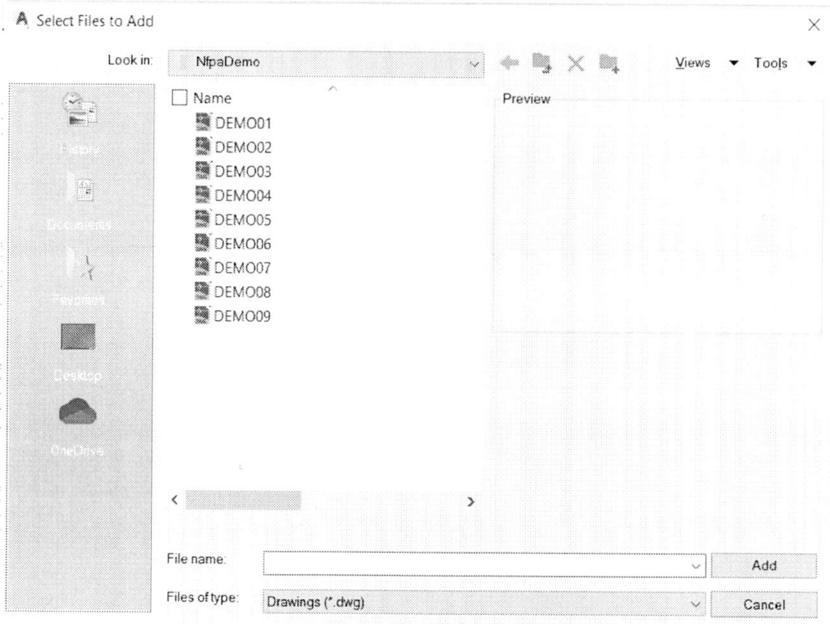


*Figure 2-15 The **Select Files to Add** dialog box*

## Grouping Drawings Using Subfolders

You can create subfolders within a project to organize the drawings. To create a subfolder, right-click on the project; a shortcut menu will be displayed. Choose **Add Subfolder** from it; a subfolder with the name **NEW FOLDER** will be created at the bottom of the drawing list. Rename it with a suitable name. Now, you can drag and drop the drawings available in the project into the subfolder. When you right-click on the subfolder; a shortcut menu will be displayed. The options in the shortcut menu are used to create and add drawings, rename the subfolder, and so on. You can add any number of subfolders in a project. Also, you can add subfolders within a subfolder.

You can also remove all the subfolders from an active project. To do so, right-click on an active project and choose **Flatten Structure** from the shortcut menu displayed; the **Flatten Project Structure** message box will be displayed warning you that if the process of flattening is continued, you will not be able to revert back the changes again. Note that when you use this option only subfolders are removed and the drawings are retained in the project.

After creating a group of drawings and subfolders, the project-wide tagging, cross-referencing, and reporting functions can be performed on the whole project or a part of the drawing set, using the section, sub-section coding, and subfolders.

## Changing the Order of Drawings in a Project

In the Project Drawing list, the drawings created are arranged in the same sequence as they are processed by AutoCAD Electrical during the project-wide tagging and cross-referencing operations. However, you can change the order of the drawings present in a project by dragging and dropping the drawings at the required place in a sequence. You can also reorder the drawings by moving them between two subfolders of a project. Note that you cannot reorder the drawings by moving them between two projects. You can press the CTRL or SHIFT key to select multiple drawings.

You can also sort the drawings in a project to change their order. To do so, right-click on the project name and choose the **Sort** option from the shortcut menu displayed. If the project contains subfolder(s), the **Sort Options** message box will be displayed showing four different combinations of options to sort the drawings in the project folder and its subfolder(s), refer to Figure 2-16. Choose one of these options as per your requirement; the **Sort** dialog box will be displayed, as shown in Figure 2-17.

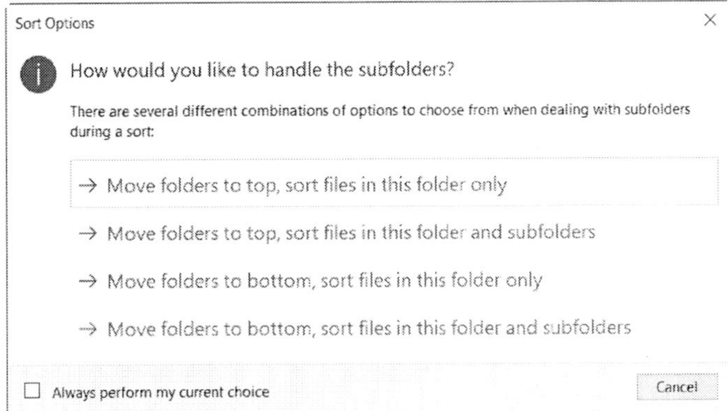


***Figure 2-16** The **Sort Options** message box*

You can sort out the drawings in different ways depending upon the options selected from the **Sort** dialog box. You can select the required option from the **Primary sort**, **Secondary sort**, **Third sort**, and **Fourth sort** drop-down lists. These drop-down lists include **REF** (reference status), **SEC** (section code), **SUBSEC** (sub-section), and **FILEPATHANDNAME** (file path and name) options.

Some projects do not contain subfolder(s). If you right-click on such a project and choose the **Sort** option from the shortcut menu displayed; the **Sort** dialog box will be displayed, refer to Figure 2-17.

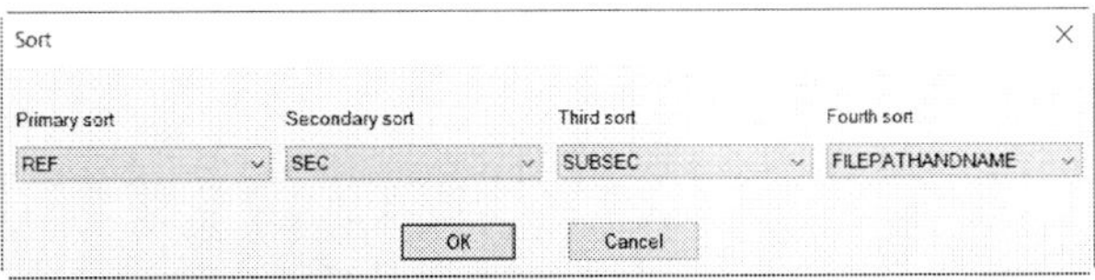


***Figure 2-17** The **Sort** dialog box*

After setting the required parameters, choose the **OK** button from the **Sort** dialog box; the dialog box is closed and the drawing displayed in the list will be arranged according to the options selected from the drop-down lists.

## Removing a Drawing from a Project

You can remove a drawing from a project using two methods. These methods are discussed next.

### First Method

Right-click on the drawing name in the **PROJECT MANAGER**; a shortcut menu will be displayed. Choose the **Remove** option from the shortcut menu; the **PROJECT MANAGER - Remove Files** message box will be displayed. Choose the **Yes** button from the message box; the drawing will be removed from the project, but it will not be deleted from the folder where it is stored.

### Second Method

Right-click on a project name; a shortcut menu will be displayed. Next, choose the **Remove Drawings** option from the shortcut menu; the **Select Drawings to Process** dialog box will be displayed, as shown in Figure 2-18. The options in this dialog box are discussed next.

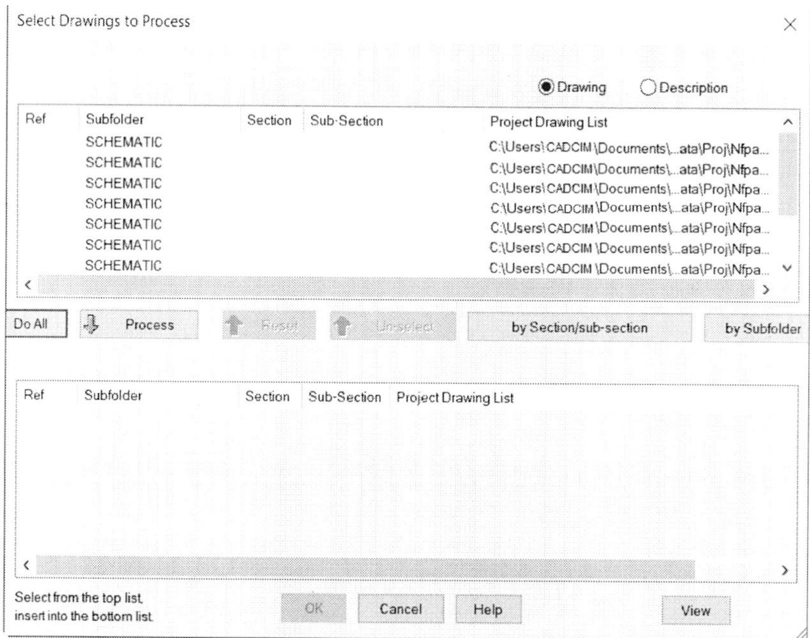


*Figure 2-18 The **Select Drawings to Process** dialog box*

**Drawing:** The **Drawing** radio button is used to display the path and the name of all drawings in a project. This radio button is selected by default.

**Description:** Select the **Description** radio button; the description of all drawings will be displayed in the top list of the **Select Drawings to Process** dialog box. Remember that the description will be displayed only if you have entered the description in the **Description**

**1/2/3** edit boxes in the **Create New Drawing** dialog box or in the **Description 1/2/3** edit boxes of the **Drawing Settings** tab in the **Drawing Properties** dialog box.

**Do All:** Choose the **Do All** button to transfer all drawings from the top list to the bottom list of the **Select Drawings to Process** dialog box.

**Process:** The **Process** button will be activated only if you select a drawing(s) from the top list. This button is used to transfer the selected drawing from the top list to the bottom list. To do so, select a drawing(s) and then choose the **Process** button; the selected drawing(s) will be transferred from the top list to the bottom list of the **Select Drawings to Process** dialog box. You can use the SHIFT or CTRL key to select more than one drawing at a time.

**Reset:** The **Reset** button will be activated only if you have transferred drawing(s) from the top list to the bottom list. Choose the **Reset** button to reset the drawings to their original positions in the dialog box.

**Un-select:** The **Un-select** button will be activated only if you select drawing(s) from the bottom list. The **Un-select** button is used to transfer drawing from the bottom list to the top list. To do so, select a drawing(s) from the bottom list and then choose the **Un-select** button; the drawings will be moved from the bottom list to the top list. You can unselect multiple drawings at a time by using the SHIFT or CTRL key.

**by Section/sub-section:** The **by Section/sub-section** button is used to select the drawings that have been grouped by specifying their sections and sub-sections. To do so, choose the **by Section/sub-section** button from the **Select Drawings to Process** dialog box; the **Select Drawings by Section/sub-section** dialog box will be displayed. Specify the section and sub-section codes in the **Section** and **Sub-section** edit boxes, respectively. Alternatively, select the section and sub-section codes from the **Section** and **Sub-section** drop-down lists, respectively. Next, choose the **OK** button from the **Select Drawings by Section/sub-section** dialog box; the corresponding drawing(s) will be transferred from the top list to the bottom list. Note that the **Section** and **Sub-section** drop-down lists display the section and sub-section codes only if you have entered the section and sub-section values in the **Sheet Values** area of the **Create New Drawing** dialog box or in the **Drawing Settings** tab of the **Drawing Properties** dialog box.

**by Subfolder:** The **by Subfolder** button is used to select the drawings that have been grouped in subfolders. To do so, choose the **by Subfolder** button from the **Select Drawings to Process** dialog box; the **Select Drawings by Subfolder** dialog box will be displayed. Select the subfolder(s) from this dialog box and choose the **OK** button; the drawings from the selected subfolder(s) will be transferred from the top list to the bottom list. Note that the **Select Drawings by Subfolder** dialog box displays the subfolders only if you have added subfolders in the project.

After selecting drawings from the **Select Drawings to Process** dialog box, choose the **OK** button; the **Remove Drawing(s) from Project List** message box will be displayed. In this message box, choose the **OK** button; the selected drawings will be removed from the project list. Note that the drawings will instantly be removed from the project list, but they will not be deleted permanently from the folder where they are stored.

## Assigning a Description to a Drawing

You can assign a three-line description to each drawing listed in your project. To do so, right-click on the name of a drawing in the project; a shortcut menu will be displayed. Next, choose **Properties > Drawing Properties** from the shortcut menu; the **Drawing Properties** dialog box will be displayed.

By default, the **Drawing Settings** tab is chosen in the **Drawing Properties** dialog box. Enter a description for the drawing in the **Description 1/2/3** edit boxes. You can also select the predefined description for your drawing from the **Description** drop-down list, refer to Figure 2-19. Note that the predefined description will be available only if you have entered the description for any of the drawings of a project. This figure shows the predefined descriptions listed in the **Description 1** drop-down list of the **Drawing Properties** dialog box. Next, choose the **OK** button; the drawing file will be updated and the changes will be saved.

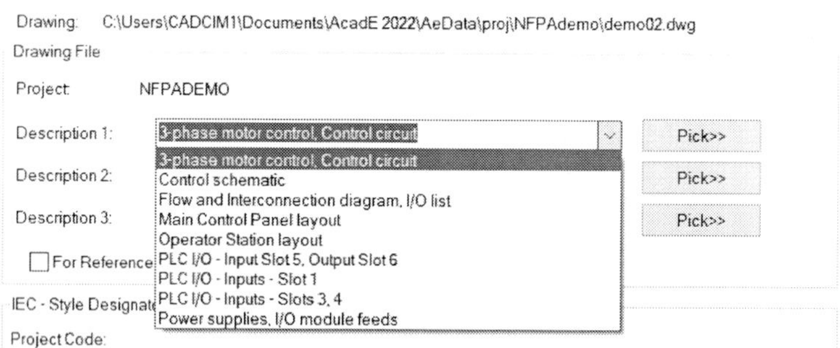


***Figure 2-19*** *Partial view of the* ***Drawing Properties*** *dialog box displaying predefined description*

**Note**

*The description specified in the* ***Description 1****,* ***Description 2****, and* ***Description 3*** *edit boxes of the* ***Create New Drawing*** *or* ***Drawing Properties*** *dialog box can be linked to the attribute in the title block for automatic update and will be discussed in the later chapters.*

After adding description to a drawing, you can preview the description in the **Details** rollout of the **PROJECT MANAGER**. These drawing details give a unique identity to the drawings based on users requirement and helps users to search a particular drawing among multiple drawings in a project file.

## Switching between the Drawings of an Active Project

| | |
|---|---|
| **Ribbon:** | Project > Other Tools > Previous DWG |
| | Project > Other Tools > Next DWG |
| **Toolbar:** | ACE:Main Electrical 2 > Previous Project Drawing |
| | ACE:Main Electrical 2 > Next Project Drawing |
| | ACE:Quick Pick > Previous Project Drawing |
| | ACE:Quick Pick > Next Project Drawing |
| **Command:** | AEPREV and AENEXT |

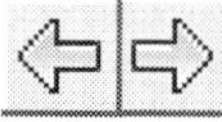

The **Previous DWG** and **Next DWG** tools are used to open the previous and next drawings of an active project. Using these tools, you can view and switch between various drawings of a project. To do so, open any drawing of the active project and then choose the **Previous DWG** or **Next DWG** tool from the **Other Tools** panel of the **Project** tab. Alternatively, you can choose the **Previous Project Drawing** or **Next Project Drawing** tool from the **ACE:Main Electrical 2** or the **ACE:Quick Pick** toolbar. On doing so, the currently opened drawing will be closed and all changes made to it will be saved. Also, the requested drawing will open. The currently opened drawing will appear in bold text in the project list.

**Tip**

*To open all drawings of an active project in a new window without closing the original drawing window, hold the SHIFT key while choosing the* ***Previous Project Drawing*** *or the* ***Next Project Drawing*** *button.*

**Note**

1. *You cannot view and switch among the drawings that are not associated with the active project.*
2. *You can use the* ***PROJECT MANAGER*** *to preview the drawings easily using the* ***Preview*** *button.*
3. *If you move among various drawings using the up and down arrow keys, the selected drawing will not open.*

## Configuring the Drawing List Display

The **Drawing List Display Configuration** button is used to configure the information related to various drawings in the **Projects** rollout of the **PROJECT MANAGER**. This button is used to display the required information such as drawing number, description, and so on. By default, only the name of the drawing is displayed in the **Projects** rollout of the **PROJECT MANAGER**, as shown in Figure 2-20. Choose the **Drawing List Display Configuration** button from the **PROJECT MANAGER**; the **Drawing List Display Configuration** dialog box will be displayed, as shown in Figure 2-21. The options in this dialog box are discussed next.

### Display Options Area

The **Display Options** area displays the predefined values that can be associated to a drawing.

### Current Display Order

The **Current Display Order** area lists the order in which the required display options will be displayed in the **Projects** rollout in the **PROJECT MANAGER**. The **File Name** option is displayed by default in this area. You can add other display options in this area by selecting them from the **Display Options** area and then choose >> button.

### >>

The >> button is used to move only the selected display option from the **Display Options** area to the **Current Display Order** area.

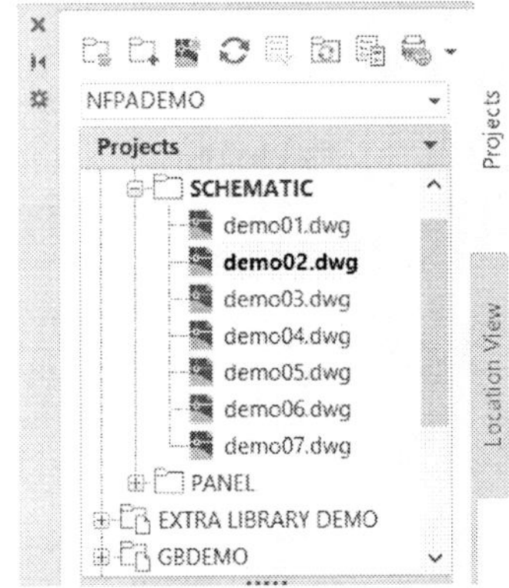


*Figure 2-20 Partial view of the* ***PROJECT MANAGER*** *displaying the drawing files of the project*

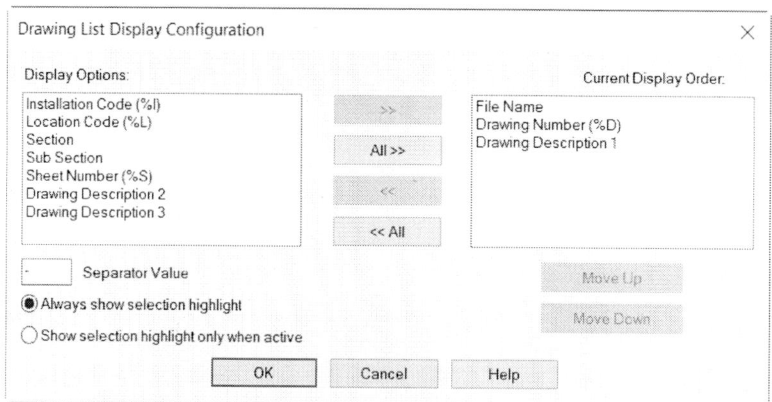


*Figure 2-21 The **Drawing List Display Configuration** dialog box*

## All>>

The **All>>** button is used to move all display options from the **Display Options** area to the **Current Display Order** area.

## <<

The **<<** button is used to move only the selected display option from the **Current Display Order** area to the **Display Options** area.

## <<All

The **<<All** button is used to move all display options from the **Current Display Order** area to the **Display Options** area.

## Separator Value

The **Separator Value** edit box is used to specify the character to be used as a separator between the values in the listing. You can enter a character in the **Separator Value** edit box or use the default character (-) in this edit box.

## Move Up

Choose the **Move Up** button to move the selected display option one step up in the **Current Display Order** area.

## Move Down

Choose the **Move Down** button to move the selected display option one step down in the **Current Display Order** area.

Choose the **OK** button in the **Drawing List Display Configuration** dialog box; the entire information related to drawings will be displayed in the **Projects** rollout, refer to Figure 2-22.

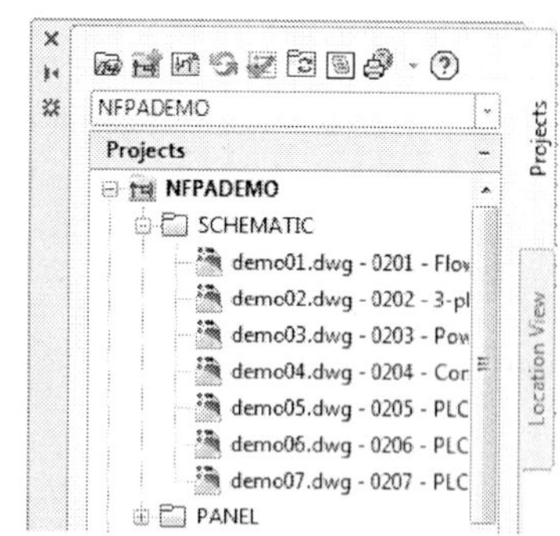


*Figure 2-22 Partial view of the **PROJECT MANAGER** displaying the drawing information*

**Note**

*The drawing options are displayed in the **Current Display Order** area in a particular sequence. The same sequence is followed for their display in the **Projects** rollout of the **PROJECT MANAGER**. If you want to change the sequence, choose the **Move Up** or **Move Down** button.*

## Copying a Project

| | |
|---|---|
| **Ribbon:** | Project > Project Tools > Copy |
| **Toolbar:** | ACE:Main Electrical 2 > Project Manager drop-down > Copy Project or ACE:Project > Copy Project |
| **Menu:** | Projects > Project > Copy Project |
| **Command:** | AECOPYPROJECT |

The **Copy** tool is used to copy the entire project as well as copy the drawings present within that project. To do so, choose the **Copy** tool from the **Project Tools** panel of the **Project** tab; the **Copy Project: Step 1 - Select Existing Project to Copy** wizard will be displayed, as shown in Figure 2-23.

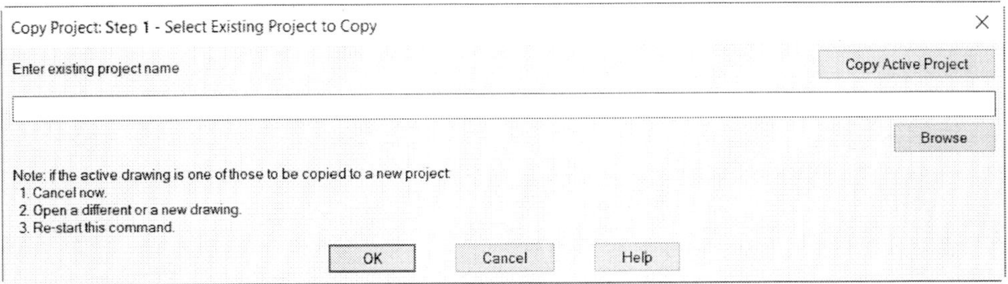


*Figure 2-23 The **Copy Project: Step 1 - Select Existing Project to Copy** wizard*

**Note**

*Before copying drawings to a new project, you need to close all drawings of that project.*

Next, enter the name and path of the existing project in the **Enter existing project name** edit box. Alternatively, choose the **Browse** button from this dialog box to select the existing project; the **Select existing project to copy** dialog box will be displayed. Next, double-click on the project folder that you want to copy. Select the project's *.wdp* file and choose the **Open** button; the name and path of the existing project will be displayed in the **Enter existing project name** edit box. You can also choose the **Copy Active Project** button available in this dialog box to copy the currently active project.

Choose the **OK** button; the **Copy Project: Step 2 - Select path and name for new project** wizard will be displayed, as shown in Figure 2-24. Enter a name for the new project in the **File name** edit box and select the path for the new project from the **Save in** drop-down list. By default, the *.wdp* extension will be displayed in the **Save as type** edit box. Next, choose the **Save** button; the **Select Drawings to Process** dialog box will be displayed, as shown in Figure 2-25.

Select the drawing files that you want to copy in the project from the top list of this dialog box. Next, choose the **Process** button; the selected drawings will be transferred from the top list of the **Select Drawings to Process** dialog box to the bottom list. The other options in the **Select**

**Drawings to Process** dialog box have already been discussed. Choose the **OK** button from the **Select Drawings to Process** dialog box; the **Copy Project: Step 4 -- Enter Base Path for Project Drawings** wizard will be displayed, refer to Figure 2-26.

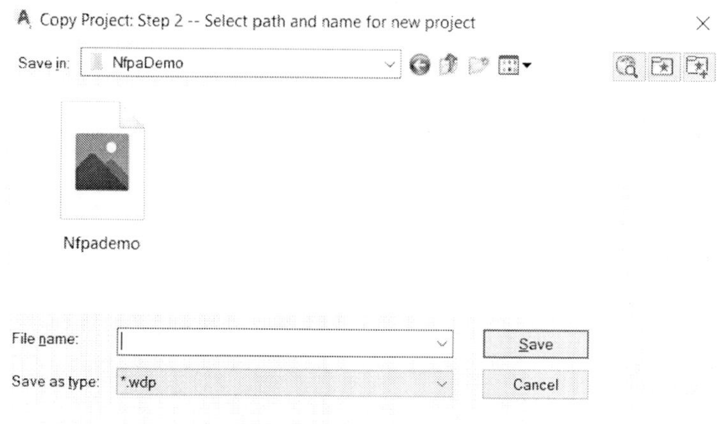


*Figure 2-24 The **Copy Project: Step 2 - Select path and name for new project** wizard*

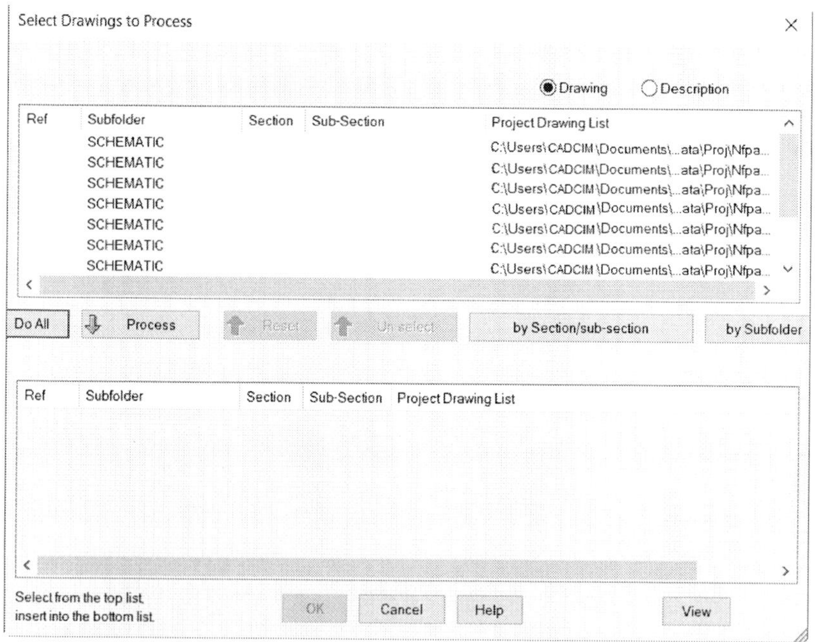


*Figure 2-25 The **Select Drawings to Process** dialog box*

**Note**

*In case, there is no drawing file in the project to be copied, then the **Select Drawings to Process** dialog box will not be displayed and the **AutoCAD Message** message box will be displayed. Choose the **OK** button in this message box; the **Copy Project: Step 4 -- Enter Base Path for Project Drawings** wizard will be displayed.*

Copy Project: Step 4 -- Enter Base Path for Project Drawings

C:\Users\CADCIM1\Documents\Acade 2022\AeData\Proj\New folder\

Browse

The base path above will be substituted for this path in the existing project:
c:\users\cadcim1\documents\acade 2022\aedata\proj\nfpademo\

Copies of the drawings will be copied to this new path.
If the directory path does not exist, it will be created.

Select Project-Related Files to be Copied

Title Block Setup (.wdt)
Project Line Labels (.wdl)
Component Description Defaults (.wdd)
Catalog Lookup Database (cat.mdb)
Footprint Lookup Database (lookup.mdb)
Family Code Mapping (wd_fam.dat)
Wire Color/Gauge Label (.wdw)
Schematic Lookup Database (schematic_lookup.mdb)
Location Codes (.loc)
Installation Codes (.inst)
Ratings Defaults (.wdr)
Component Tagging (.wdx)
Spreadsheet PLC I/O Utility Settings (.wdi)
RSLogix Import Mapping (.wdf)
User Defined Attributes (.wda)
Terminal Audit Filter (.wdn)

OK
Cancel

*Figure 2-26 The* ***Copy Project: Step 4 -- Enter Base Path for Project Drawings*** *wizard*

In this dialog box, enter the directory path where the new project will be saved. The directory path will be created, if it does not exist. In the **Select Project-Related Files to be Copied** area, you can specify the project related files that need to be copied to the project that you want to create. Note that the project related files to be copied will be activated in the **Select Project-Related Files to be Copied** area. To copy these files, select the check boxes on the left of the respective files and then choose the **OK** button; the **Copy Project: Step 5 -- Adjust new drawing file names** wizard will be displayed, as shown in Figure 2-27.

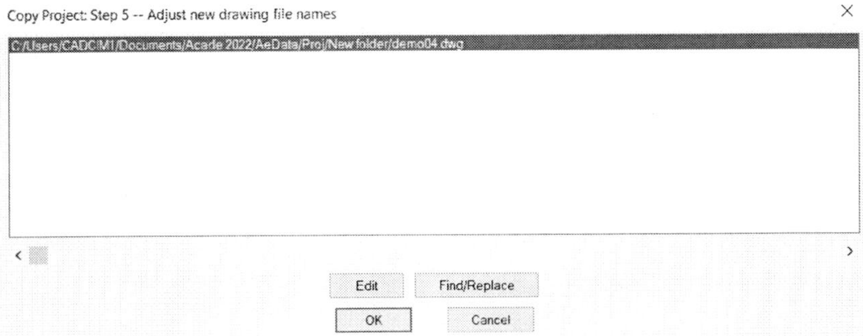


*Figure 2-27 The* ***Copy Project: Step 5 -- Adjust new drawing file names*** *wizard*

Choose the **Edit** button in this wizard to edit the file name and path of the selected drawing, if needed. Similarly, choose the **Find/Replace** button to find or replace a drawing file name and its path. Next, choose the **OK** button; the name of the new project will be displayed at the top in the **Projects** rollout in bold text and will become the active project.

## Deleting a Project

**Ribbon:** Project > Project Tools> Delete
**Menu:** Projects > Project > Delete Project
**Command:** AEDELETEPROJECT

The **Delete** tool or the **AEDELETEPROJECT** command is used to delete an existing project and its drawings permanently. To do so, choose the **Delete** tool from

the **Project Tools** panel of the **Project** tab; the **Select Existing Project to Delete** dialog box will be displayed, as shown in Figure 2-28.

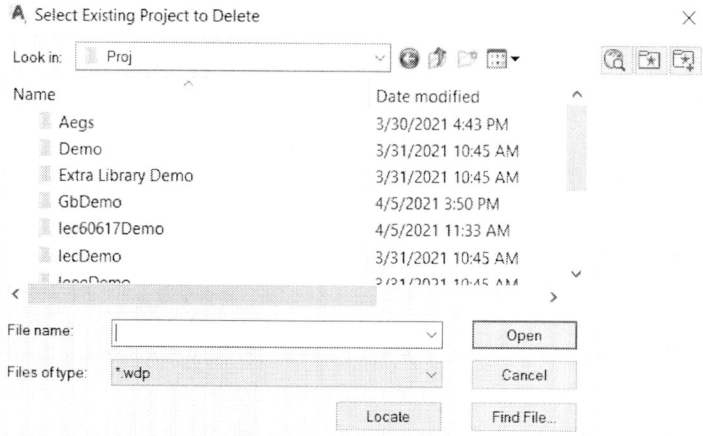


*Figure 2-28 The **Select Existing Project to Delete** dialog box*

Enter the name of the project file to be deleted in the **File name** edit box. Alternatively, select a project name from the list displayed in the **Select Existing Project to Delete** dialog box. Next, double-click on the name of the project folder, if it exists. Select the project definition file(*.wdp*) and choose the **Open** button; the **Project File Delete Utility** dialog box will be displayed, as shown in Figure 2-29. The options in this dialog box are discussed next.

## Delete ".wdp" project list file

The **Delete ".wdp" project list file** check box is used to permanently delete the selected project file with *.wdp* extension.

## Delete project's AutoCAD drawing files

The **Delete project's AutoCAD drawing files** check box is used to delete only the drawing files of a project. Note that this check box will be activated only if the related project consists of drawing files.

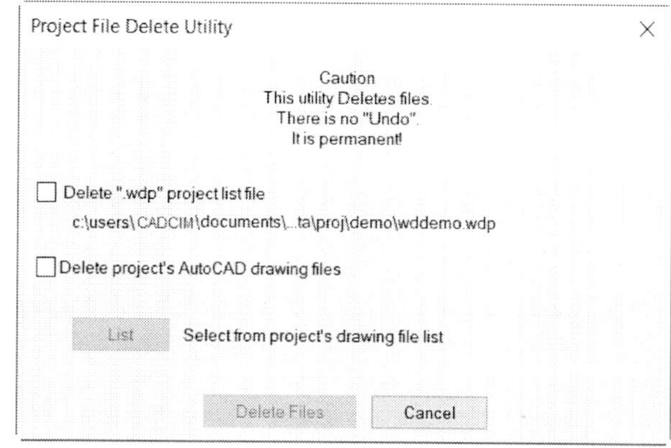


*Figure 2-29 The **Project File Delete Utility** dialog box*

## List

The **List** button will be activated only if you select the **Delete project's AutoCAD drawing files** check box. Choose the **List** button; the **Select Drawings to Process** dialog box will be displayed, refer to Figure 2-25. Select the drawings to be deleted from the drawing file list of the project. Next, choose the **OK** button from the **Select Drawings to Process** dialog box; the **Project File Delete Utility** dialog box will be displayed again. Choose the **Delete Files** button from the **Project File Delete Utility** dialog box; the selected files will be deleted permanently, and you cannot retrieve them.

## Other Options in the PROJECT MANAGER

As discussed earlier, the **PROJECT MANAGER** lists the drawing files associated with each project. You can change the settings of a project by using the **PROJECT MANAGER**, refer to Figure 2-30. The major tools and rollouts in the **PROJECT MANAGER** have already been discussed. The remaining ones are discussed next.

1. Buttons
2. Project selection drop-down list
3. Projects rollout
4. Project Drawing list
5. Details/Preview rollout

### Buttons

There are several buttons available in the **PROJECT MANAGER** such as **Refresh**, **Publish/Plot**, and so on, see Figure 2-31. These buttons are discussed next.

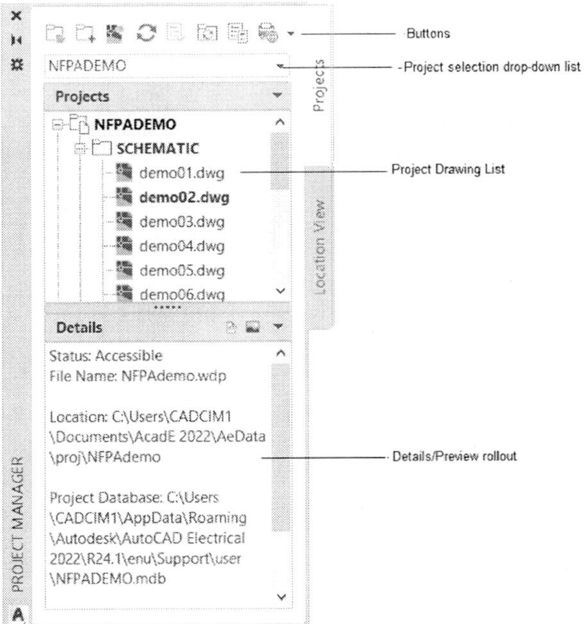


*Figure 2-30 Various components of the **PROJECT MANAGER***

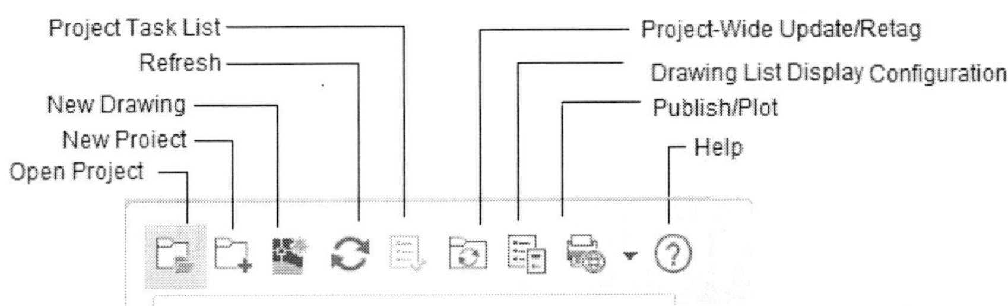


*Figure 2-31 Various buttons in the **PROJECT MANAGER***

### Refresh

The **Refresh** button is used to freshen the drawing list present in the **PROJECT MANAGER**.

### Project task List

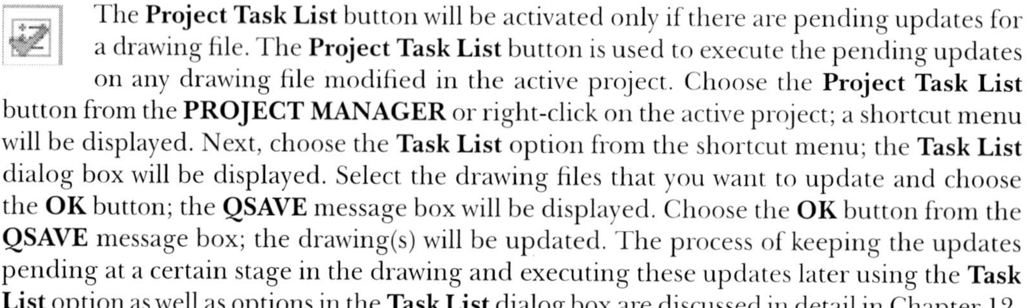

The **Project Task List** button will be activated only if there are pending updates for a drawing file. The **Project Task List** button is used to execute the pending updates on any drawing file modified in the active project. Choose the **Project Task List** button from the **PROJECT MANAGER** or right-click on the active project; a shortcut menu will be displayed. Next, choose the **Task List** option from the shortcut menu; the **Task List** dialog box will be displayed. Select the drawing files that you want to update and choose the **OK** button; the **QSAVE** message box will be displayed. Choose the **OK** button from the **QSAVE** message box; the drawing(s) will be updated. The process of keeping the updates pending at a certain stage in the drawing and executing these updates later using the **Task List** option as well as options in the **Task List** dialog box are discussed in detail in Chapter 12.

### Project-Wide Update/Retag

The **Project-Wide Update/Retag** button is used to update the related line reference numbers, device tagging, cross-reference text, and signal reference updates on the selected drawing files in an active project. Choose the **Project-Wide Update/Retag** button from the **PROJECT MANAGER**; the **Project-Wide Update or Retag** dialog box will be displayed. Specify the required options in this dialog box and choose the **OK** button; the **Select Drawings to Process** dialog box will be displayed. Now, select the drawings that you want to process and choose the **Process** button. Next, choose the **OK** button; the selected drawings will be updated. The options in the **Project-Wide Update or Retag** dialog box will be discussed in detail in Chapter 6. You can also use the **(WD_BUMP)** command to invoke the **Project-Wide Update or Retag** dialog box.

### Publish / Plot

Choose the **Publish / Plot** button from the **Project Manager**; the **Publish/Plot** drop-down will be displayed, as shown in Figure 2-32. The options in the drop-down of the **Publish / Plot** button are used to plot active drawings, publish the drawings of the active project to web, DWF, PDF, DWFx and zip the active project. Choose the **Plot Project** option from the drop-down to batch plot one or more drawings in the active project. The Plotting of drawings will be discussed in detail in Chapter 12.

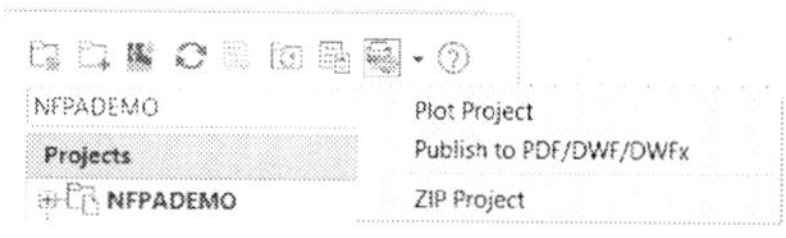


***Figure 2-32** The drop-down displayed on choosing the **Publish / Plot** button*

### Help

When you choose the **Help** button from the **PROJECT MANAGER**, the **AutoCAD Electrical 2022 - Help** window will be displayed. Alternatively, choose **Help** from the **Help** menu to display the **AutoCAD Electrical 2022 - Help** window. This window helps you understand different options, commands, and tools of AutoCAD Electrical.

**Note**

*If you press F1 or use the **HELP** command, it will also display the **AutoCAD Electrical 2022 - Help** window.*

## Project selection Drop-down List

The Project selection drop-down list is available at the top of the **PROJECT MANAGER**, as shown in Figure 2-33, and it consists of names of all open projects and following options:

1. Recent
2. New Project
3. Open Project

You cannot close any open project using the Project selection drop-down list. The other options in this drop-down list are discussed next.

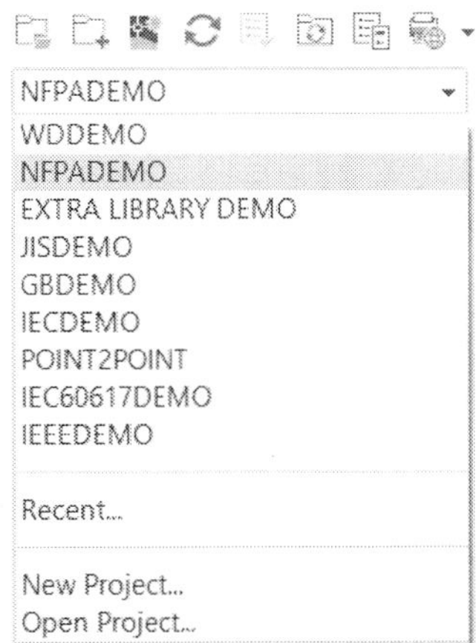


*Figure 2-33 The **PROJECT MANAGER** displaying the Project selection drop-down list*

### Recent

When you select the **Recent** option from the Project selection drop-down list, the **Recent Projects** dialog box will be displayed. In this dialog box, you can view the recently opened projects, view the drawings of the selected project, remove the selected project, and find the drawings from the recent projects list displayed in the **Recent Projects** dialog box.

### New Project

The **New Project** option is used to create a new project. To do so, select the **New Project** option from the Project selection drop-down list; the **Create New Project** dialog box will be displayed. The options in this dialog box have already been discussed. Specify the required options and choose the **OK** button; the new project will be created and will appear in bold text on the top of the list in the **Projects** rollout. Also, the newly created project will automatically become an active project.

### Open Project

The **Open Project** option is used to open an existing project. To do so, select the **Open Project** option from the Project selection drop-down list; the **Select Project File** dialog box will be displayed. Next, select the required project from this dialog box and choose the **Open** button; the selected project's name will automatically be displayed in the **Projects** rollout in bold text and the project will become an active project.

## Projects Rollout

The **Projects** rollout displays a list of all opened projects. You can open as many projects as you want, but only one project can be active at a time. The active project appears in bold text and is always displayed at the top of the list in the **Projects** rollout. When you right-click on the name of the active project or on the project that is in bold text, a shortcut menu will be displayed, as shown in Figure 2-34. The options in the shortcut menu are discussed next.

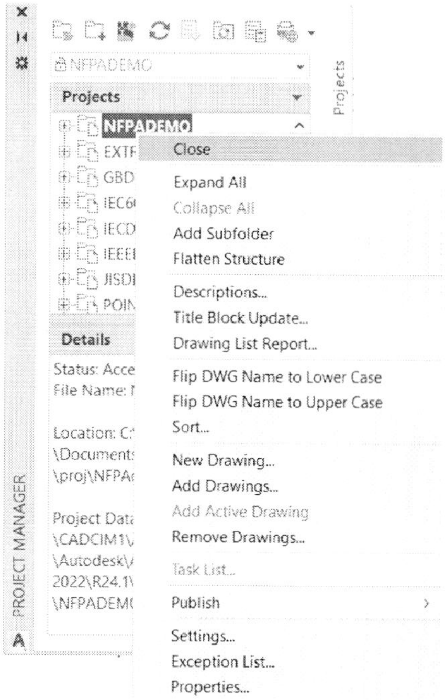

*Figure 2-34 The shortcut menu displayed by right-clicking on the active project in the* ***PROJECT MANAGER***

### Close

The **Close** option is used to remove the project which is displayed in the **Projects** rollout.

### Expand All

The **Expand All** option is used to expand a project and subfolder(s) in a project, if any.

### Collapse All

The **Collapse All** option is used to collapse a project and subfolder(s) in a project, if any.

### Add Subfolder

The **Add Subfolder** option is used to add a subfolder to a project.

### Flatten Structure

The **Flatten Structure** option is used to remove subfolder(s) from the project to get a flat drawing list in a project.

### Descriptions

The **Descriptions** option is used to edit the description of an existing project. It is also used to add description to a new project. To do so, choose the **Descriptions** option from the shortcut menu; the **Project Description** dialog box will be displayed, refer to Figure 2-10.

As the **Project Description** dialog box displays unlimited lines, you can enter the description as per your requirement. The information that you enter in these lines can be re-used in the Component, Bill of Material, and Wire reports that are generated for the project or mapped to title block of the drawing. Select the **in reports** check box from the **Project Description** dialog box to include the project description line information in report headers and title blocks, which will be discussed in detail in the later chapters.

### Title Block Update

The **Title Block Update** option is used to update the information of the title block for the entire project drawing set or for the active drawing. To update the title block information, right-click on the active project; a shortcut menu is displayed. Choose the **Title Block Update** option from the shortcut menu; the **Update Title Block** dialog box will be displayed, as shown in Figure 2-35. The options in this dialog box will be discussed in detail in Chapter 12. You can also update a title block by using the **WD_TB** command.

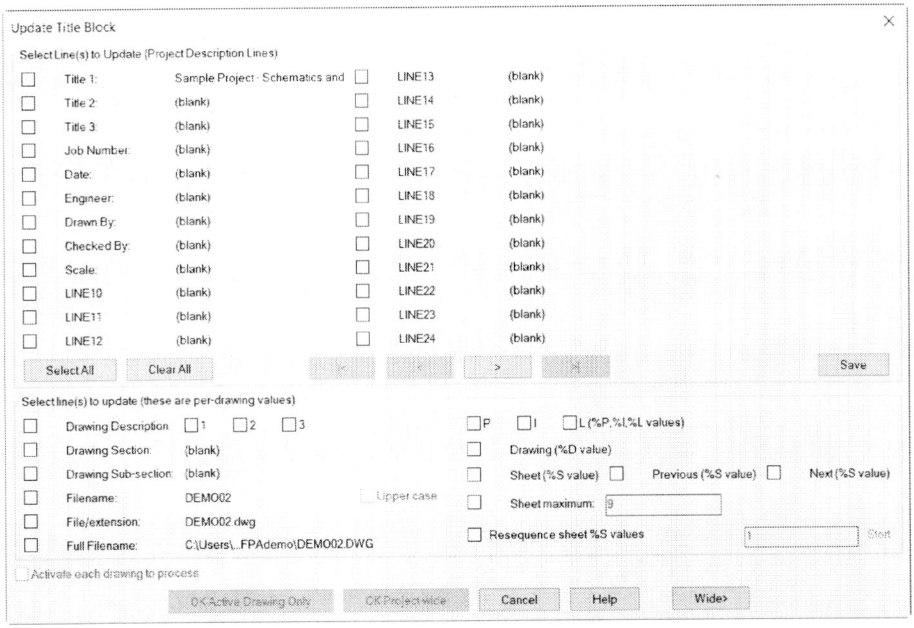

*Figure 2-35 The **Update Title Block** dialog box*

## Drawing List Report

The **Drawing List Report** option is used to generate a report that lists the project drawing information of title block such as file names, file date, time, sheet number, drawing descriptions, sections, and so on. To generate a report, choose the **Drawing List Report** option from the shortcut menu or use the **WD_DWGLST_PROJ** command; the **Drawing List Report** dialog box will be displayed. The options in this dialog box are used to extract the new drawing list report, display previous drawing list report, and select format file for report. You will learn more about the generation of reports in Chapter 9.

## Task List

The **Task List** option will be activated only if an active project has pending updates on any drawing file which is present within the active project and has been modified. Choose the **Task List** option from the shortcut menu; the **Task List** dialog box will be displayed. The options in the **Task List** dialog box will be discussed in Chapter 12.

## Publish

When you right-click on an active project and move the cursor to the **Publish** option of the shortcut menu, a cascading menu will be displayed, as shown in Figure 2-36. This cascading menu consists of various options such as **Plot Project**, **Publish To PDF/DWF/DWFx**, and **Zip Project**. Choose the **Plot Project** option to plot one or more drawings in the active project. The **Publish To PDF/DWF/DWFx**, and **Zip Project** options are used to publish the project to pdf, dwf, dwfx and to create the zipped file of a project, respectively.

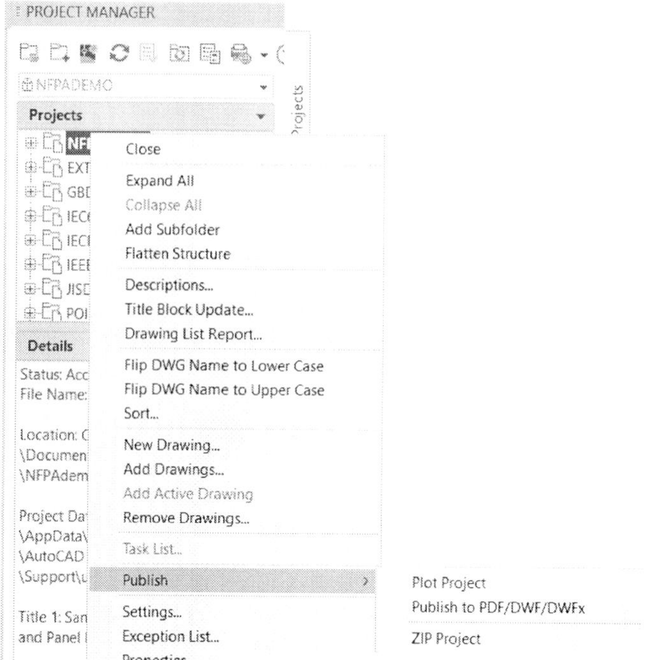


*Figure 2-36 Cascading menu displayed on selecting the* ***Publish*** *option*

### Settings

When you choose the **Settings** option from the shortcut menu, the **Current Settings** dialog box is displayed. This dialog box displays settings of a project and information about AutoCAD Electrical environment.

### Exception List

When you choose the **Exception List** option from the shortcut menu, the **Properties Exception List** dialog box is displayed, as shown in Figure 2-37. This dialog box displays the list of drawing files that possess the properties different from the project definition file (*.*WDP*). Figure 2-38 shows the **Properties Exception List** dialog box that will be displayed if the settings of all drawing files of a project match with the settings of the project definition file. Also, this dialog box displays that there are no exceptions.

**Note**

*You can view the difference between drawing properties and project defaults. To do so, choose* ***Settings Compare*** *from the* ***Projects*** *menu or choose the* ***Settings Compare*** *button from the* ***Drawing Properties*** *drop-down in the* ***ACE:Main Electrical 2*** *toolbar; the* ***Compare Drawing and Project Settings*** *dialog box will be displayed. This dialog box is used to compare the drawing and project default settings.*

### Properties

On choosing the **Properties** option from the shortcut menu, the **Project Properties** dialog box will be displayed, as shown in Figure 2-39. You can use this dialog box to edit and modify the properties for project settings, components, wire numbers, cross-references, styles, and drawing format. The editing of project properties will be discussed in detail in Chapter 12.

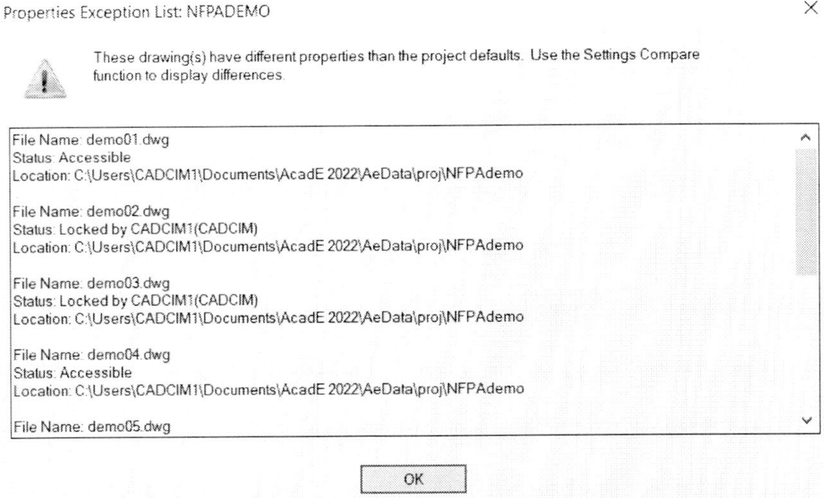


*Figure 2-37 The **Properties Exception List** dialog box*

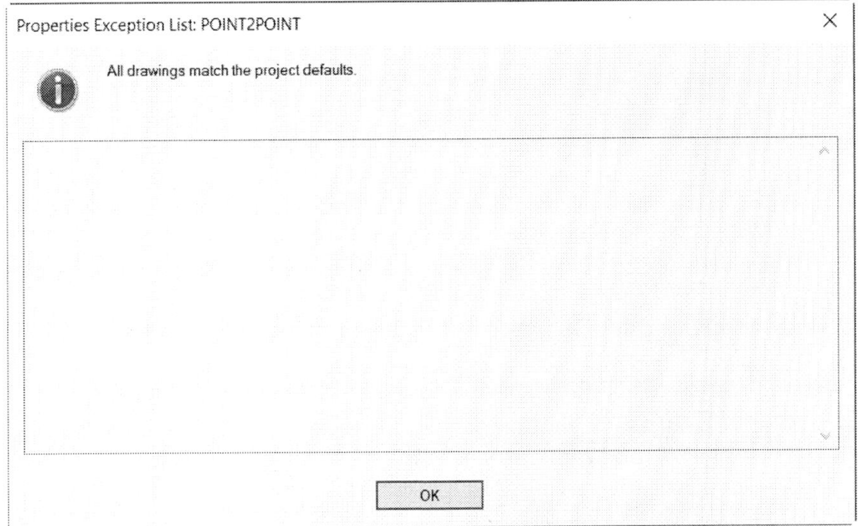


*Figure 2-38 The **Properties Exception List** dialog box*

**Note**

*The options discussed above will be displayed if you right-click on an active project in the **Projects** rollout. But if you right-click on an inactive project, a shortcut menu with the **Activate** option will be displayed, as shown in Figure 2-40. If you choose this option from the shortcut menu, the selected project will become active and will be displayed at the top of the projects list in bold text.*

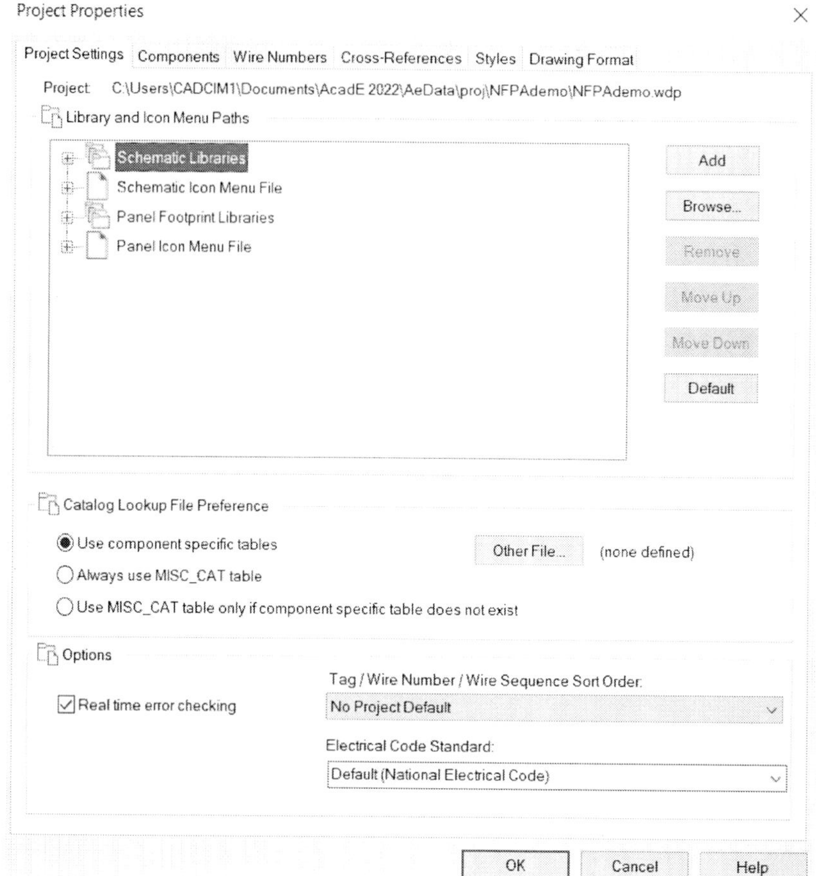


*Figure 2-39 The **Project Properties** dialog box*

## Project Drawing List

The Project Drawing list displays the drawings available in a project. If you double-click on a project name in the **Projects** rollout of the **PROJECT MANAGER**, the drawings associated with that project will be displayed. Right-click on a drawing file name; the editing options will be displayed, as shown in Figure 2-41. Using these options, you can open, close, remove, rename, and replace a drawing file. You can also edit the properties of a drawing by choosing **Drawing Properties** from the shortcut menu, refer to Figure 2-41. The options in this shortcut menu are discussed next.

**Note**

*You can convert a drawing file into a reference drawing. To do so, right-click on the drawing name and choose **Properties > Drawing Properties** from the shortcut menu; the **Drawing Properties** dialog box will be displayed. Select the **For Reference Only** check box from the **Drawing Settings** tab; the drawing file will be converted into a reference drawing. However, its extension (.dwg) will remain the same.*

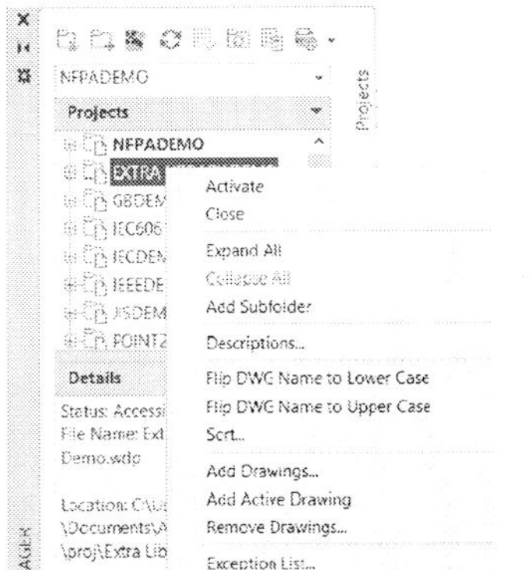

*Figure 2-40 The shortcut menu displaying the **Activate** option*

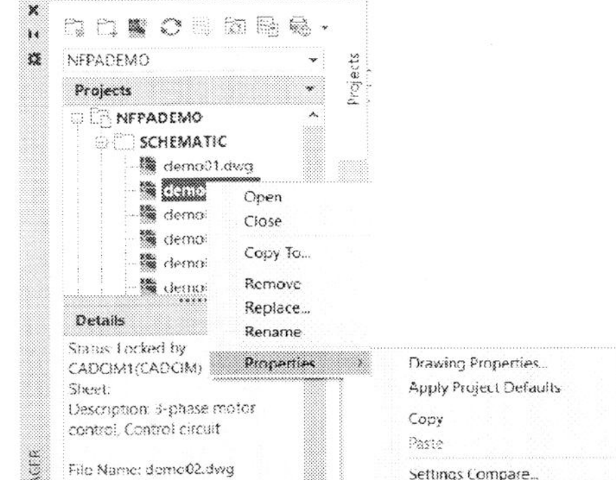

*Figure 2-41 The editing options available in the shortcut menu*

### Open

On choosing the **Open** option from the shortcut menu, the selected drawing will open in a new window and its name will appear in bold text in the Project Drawing list. Alternatively, you can select a drawing file name and press ENTER to open the corresponding drawing. You can also open a drawing file by double-clicking on it. The **OPEN** command is also used to open a drawing file.

### Close

Choose the **Close** option from the shortcut menu to close the current drawing file. This option will be available only if the drawing file is open. You can also close a drawing file by using the **CLOSE** command.

### Copy To

The **Copy To** option is used to copy the selected drawing to the same or another open project. To do so, choose the **Copy To** option from the shortcut menu; the **Copy To** dialog box will be displayed, as shown in Figure 2-42. Next, from the **Save in** drop-down list, select the location where you want to copy the drawings. If you want to change the name of the drawing file, enter the drawing file name in the **File name** edit box. Next, select the project name from the **Project** drop-down list. Choose the **Save** button; the **Apply Project Defaults to Drawing Settings** message box will be displayed. Choose the **Yes** button in the message box to apply the project default values to the newly added drawing's WD_M block definition; the selected drawing(s) will be copied to the specified project. If you want the new drawing to retain its existing settings, choose the **No** button.

### Remove

Choose the **Remove** option from the shortcut menu to remove the selected drawing from the current project. This option does not remove the drawings permanently.

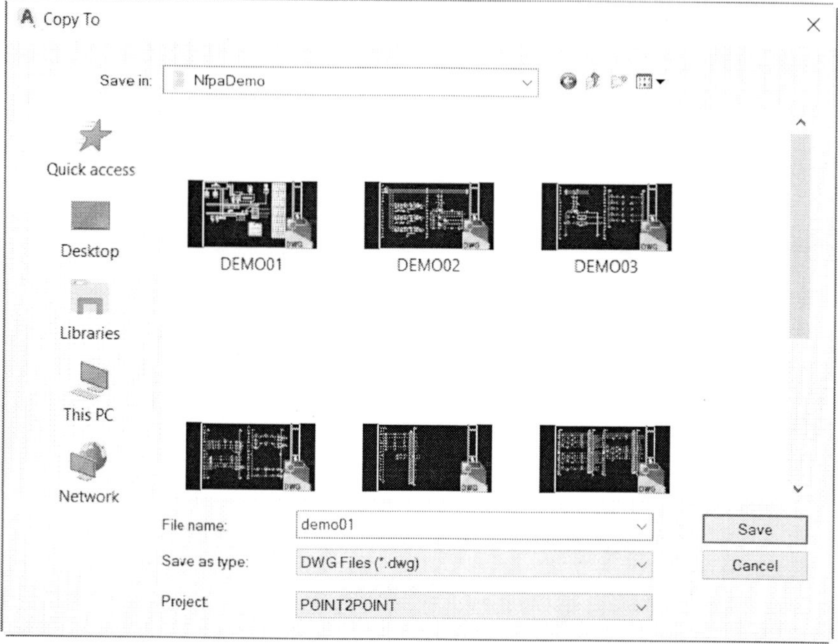


*Figure 2-42 The **Copy To** dialog box*

## Replace

The **Replace** option is used to replace the selected drawing with the desired one. To do so, choose the **Replace** option from the shortcut menu; the **Select Replacement Drawing** dialog box will be displayed, as shown in Figure 2-43. Next, select the drawing file and choose the **Select** button; the **Apply Project Defaults to Drawing Settings** message box will be displayed, refer to Figure 2-13. Choose the **Yes** button to apply the project default values to the newly added drawing's WD_M block definition. If you want the new drawing to retain its existing settings, choose the **No** button; the drawing file will get replaced with the selected drawings. This drawing will be displayed in the Project Drawing list. Also, note that if the drawing is already present in the project, it will display the message that drawing is already present in the project.

## Rename

The **Rename** option is used to rename the selected drawing. To do so, choose the **Rename** option from the Project Drawing list; the name of the selected drawing will be replaced by an edit box. Enter a new name in the edit box to rename the drawing.

## Drawing Properties

The **Drawing Properties** option is used to change the drawing settings, component tag format, wire number format, cross-reference format, styles, and drawing format. Also, you can edit, assign, and remove the section and sub-section codes of a drawing. To do so, choose **Properties > Drawing Properties** from the shortcut menu; the **Drawing Properties** dialog box will be displayed. In the **Drawing Properties** dialog box, you can assign descriptions to the drawing files. Note that each individual drawing can have its own drawing settings for designing purpose.

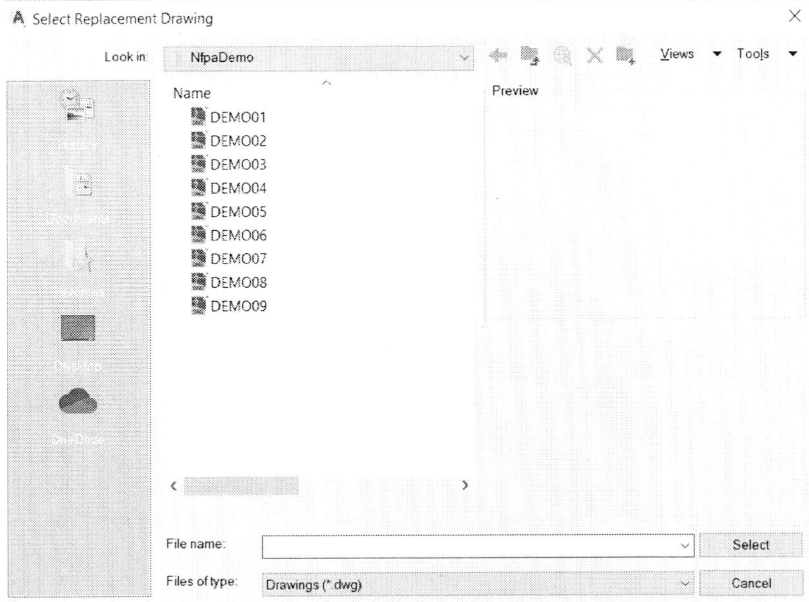


*Figure 2-43 The **Select Replacement Drawing** dialog box*

### Apply Project Defaults

Choose the **Apply Project Defaults** option from the shortcut menu to apply the project default settings of the project to the new drawing files, if it was not done while creating the drawing files.

### Copy

You can copy drawing settings and options from one drawing to one or more drawings by choosing the **Copy** option from the shortcut menu.

**Note**

*The drawing-specific information that is displayed in the **Drawing Settings** tab of the **Drawing Properties** dialog box cannot be copied from one drawing to another, refer to Figure 2-12.*

### Paste

Choose the **Paste** option from the shortcut menu to apply the copied drawing settings as well as other options from one drawing to other selected drawing(s).

### Settings Compare

The **Settings Compare** option is used to compare the drawing with its project settings. To do so, choose the **Settings Compare** option from the shortcut menu; the **Compare Drawing and Project Settings** dialog box will be displayed, as shown in Figure 2-44. This dialog box displays the differences between the drawing settings and their associated default values in the project definition file (*.wdp*). See Figure 2-44, where ***demo01.dwg*** is the drawing name and ***NFPADEMO*** is the project name.

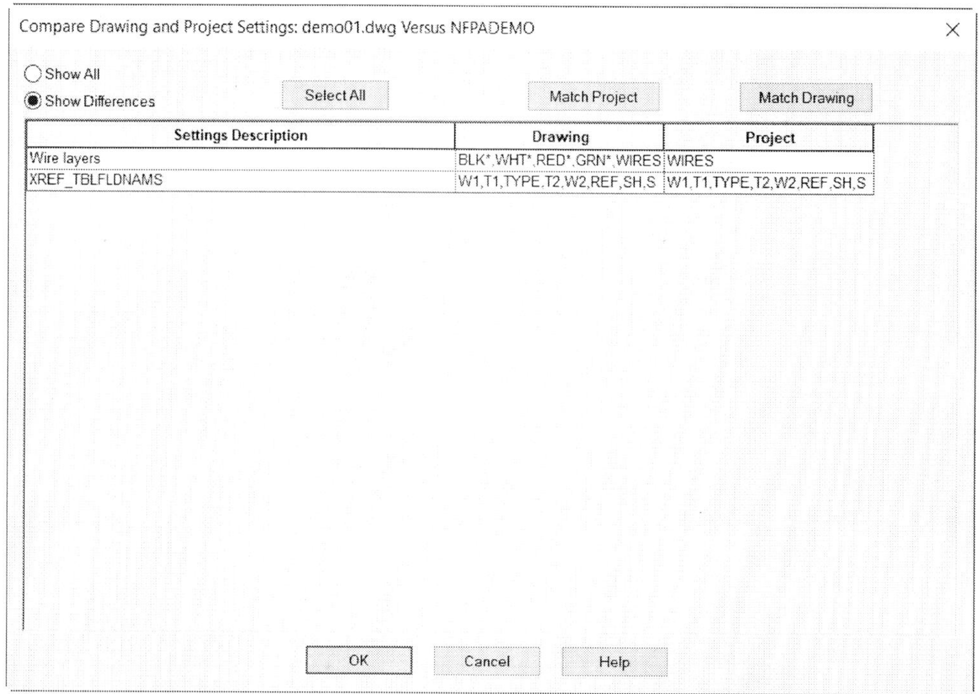


*Figure 2-44 The **Compare Drawing and Project Settings** dialog box*

## Details/Preview Rollout

The **Details/Preview** rollout displays the details of the selected project or drawing as well as the preview of the selected drawing. The **Details** and **Preview** rollouts shown in Figure 2-45 and Figure 2-46 respectively are discussed next.

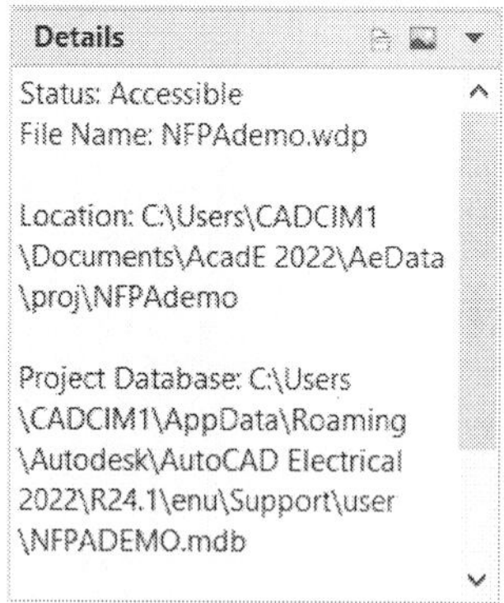


*Figure 2-45 The **PROJECT MANAGER** displaying the **Details** rollout*

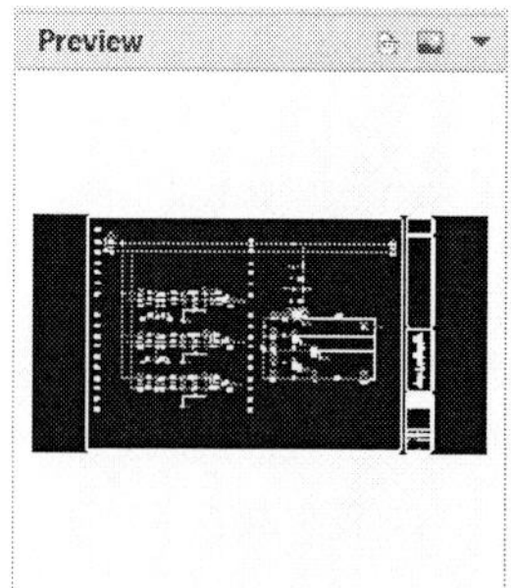


*Figure 2-46 The **PROJECT MANAGER** displaying the **Preview** rollout*

### Details

The **Details** button is used to view details of the selected project and drawing. To do so, select a project or drawing from the **Projects** rollout and then choose the **Details** button from the **Details/Preview** rollout in the **PROJECT MANAGER**; details of the selected project or drawing will be displayed in the **Details** rollout. Whenever you select a drawing file, its details get updated and remain visible till you select a new drawing file. The information that will be displayed in the **Details** rollout includes status, description if added, file name, file location, file size, date when the file was last saved, the name of the user who modified the file last, and so on, refer to Figure 2-45.

**Note**

*You can switch/move from one drawing to another by using the up and down arrow keys.*

### Preview

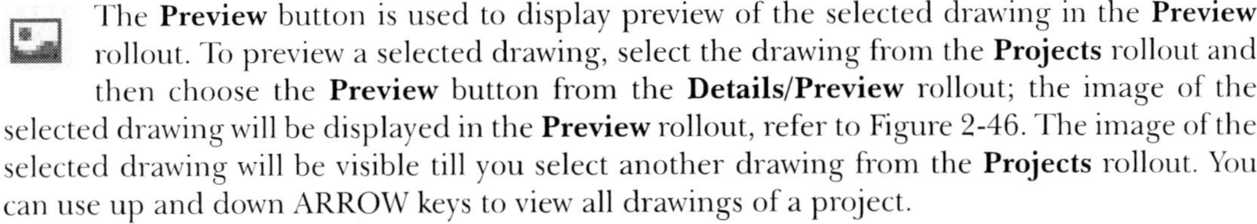

The **Preview** button is used to display preview of the selected drawing in the **Preview** rollout. To preview a selected drawing, select the drawing from the **Projects** rollout and then choose the **Preview** button from the **Details/Preview** rollout; the image of the selected drawing will be displayed in the **Preview** rollout, refer to Figure 2-46. The image of the selected drawing will be visible till you select another drawing from the **Projects** rollout. You can use up and down ARROW keys to view all drawings of a project.

**Note**

*As discussed in the previous section, you can use the **PROJECT MANAGER** to preview drawings. When you scroll through the drawings in the **PROJECT MANAGER** using the up and down ARROW keys, the preview or the details of the drawing get displayed in the **PROJECT MANAGER**.*

## Location View TAB

The options in the **Location View** tab of the **PROJECT MANAGER** are used to display and filter the components based on the installation and location codes, display details and connections of the components, and so on. Figure 2-47 shows the **PROJECT MANAGER** with the **Location View** tab chosen. The options in this tab are discussed next.

### Filter by Installation and Location

This button is used to filter components in the Component Tree as per the installation and location codes. When you click on the down arrow of this button, a flyout is displayed, refer to Figure 2-48. This flyout consists of various combinations of installation and location codes available in the active project as options. You can click on any of these options to view or hide components in the Component Tree based on the requirement.

### Refresh Tree for Local Changes

This button is used to refresh the Component Tree, the **Details** pane, and the **Connections** pane based on the changes made in the current session.

### Search Field

This field is used to specify the search text such as component name, installation code, or location code.

### Go

This button is used to search the text entered in the **Search field**.

*Figure 2-47 The **PROJECT MANAGER** with the **Location View** tab chosen*

*Figure 2-48 Flyout displayed on choosing the **Filter by Installation and Location** button*

## Component Tree

The Component Tree displays a list of all the components available in the active project. It has various nodes. The main node is the active project node. When you expand this node, a node representing installation code will be displayed. When you expand this node, all location code nodes will be listed as separate nodes. You need to expand these nodes to view the components with these installation/location codes as separate nodes. This list also includes PLC modules, connectors, cable markers, and terminals. You need to expand these component nodes in the Component Tree to view pin information of the components, refer to Figure 2-49. When you hover the cursor over a component, the detailed information about the component such as catalog information, assembly code, description is displayed, refer to Figure 2-50.

You will notice that there are different icons on the left of each component. The significance of these icons is explained in Table 2-1.

To expand or collapse all the nodes in the Component Tree, right-click on any of the installation or location nodes and choose the respective option from the shortcut menu displayed, refer to Figure 2-51.

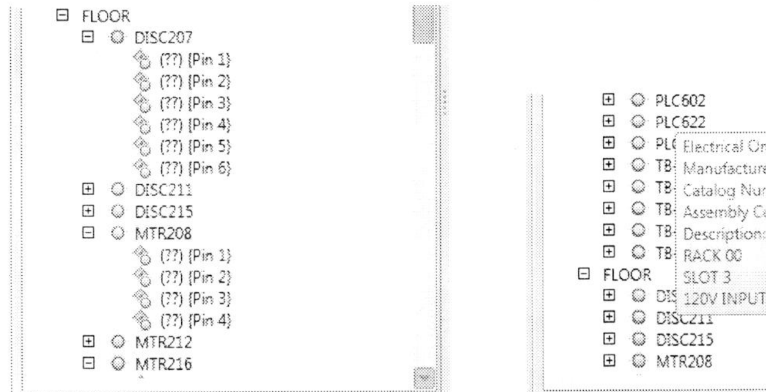


*Figure 2-49 The pin information of the components*

*Figure 2-50 The detailed information of the component*

*Table 2-1 The significance of icons*

| Icon | Significance |
|---|---|
| 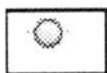 | AutoCAD Electrical component not linked to an Inventor component |
| 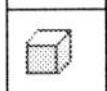 | Inventor component not linked to an AutoCAD Electrical component |
| 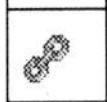 | Linked AutoCAD Electrical and Inventor components with no mismatches in data |
| 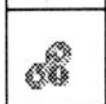 | Linked AutoCAD Electrical and Inventor components with some mismatch between the data |
| 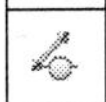 | AutoCAD Electrical cable not linked to Inventor cable |
| 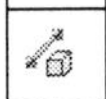 | Inventor cable not linked to AutoCAD Electrical cable |
| 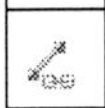 | Linked AutoCAD Electrical and Inventor Cable with no mismatches in data |
| 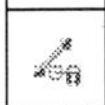 | Linked AutoCAD Electrical Inventor cable with some mismatch between the data |

When you right-click on an individual component node, a shortcut menu will be displayed, refer to Figure 2-52. Choose the **Surf** option; the **Surf** dialog box will be displayed. In this dialog box, related references of the component are displayed. The options in this dialog box are discussed in detail in Chapter 6.

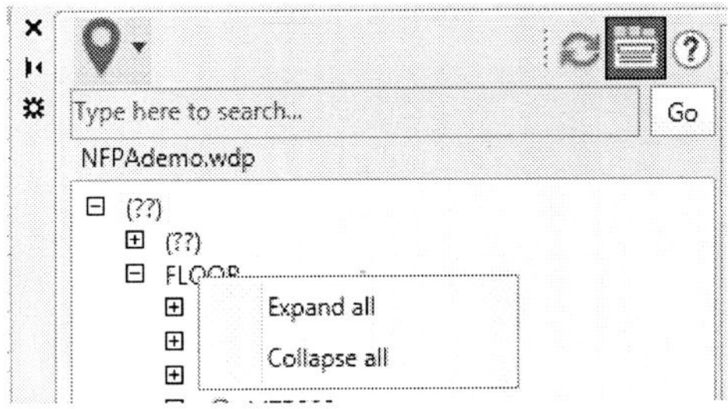


*Figure 2-51 The shortcut menu displayed on right-clicking on an installation/location node*

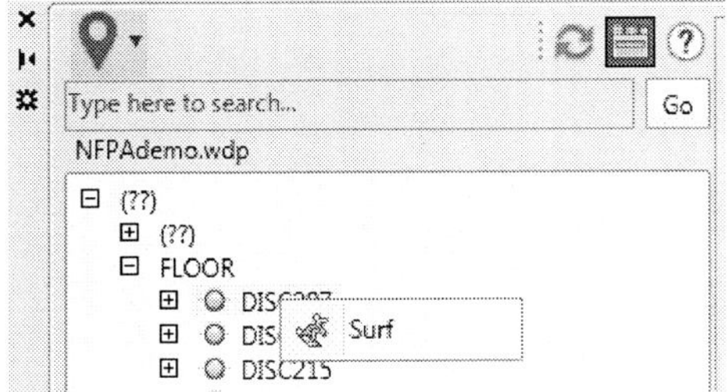


*Figure 2-52 The shortcut menu displayed on right-clicking on a component node*

## Display Details and Connections

This button is used to expand the **PROJECT MANAGER** with two additional tabs: **Details** and **Connections**. These two tabs are discussed next.

## Details Tab

When you choose this tab, the **Details** pane is displayed. Choose the installation or location node in the **PROJECT MANAGER**; a list of components in this node will be displayed in a grid in the **Details** pane, refer to Figure 2-53. You need to scroll horizontally in the pane or increase the size of the pane by stretching it horizontally to view all the columns in the grid. If you select an individual component node in the **PROJECT MANAGER**, the tabular information of only that component will be displayed in a grid.

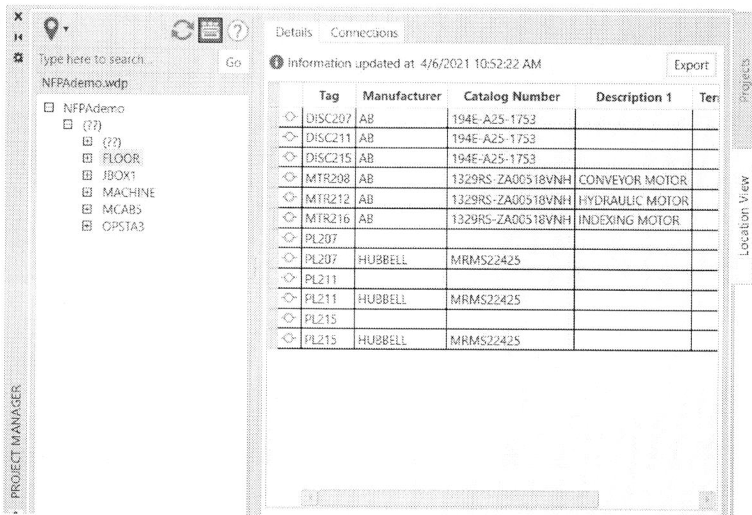

*Figure 2-53 The **Details** pane with tabular information*

If you right-click on the column name of the grid, a shortcut menu will be displayed, refer to Figure 2-54. The options in this shortcut menu are used to add or remove columns from the **Details** pane and to restore default number of columns. Similarly, if you right-click on the cell(s) or row(s) in the grid, a shortcut menu will be displayed, refer to Figure 2-55. This shortcut menu consists of two options: **Copy** and **Surf**. The **Surf** option is already discussed in the Component Tree. The **Copy** option will be activated only when you select cell(s) or row(s) in the grid. Using this option, you can copy the content of the selected cell(s) or row(s).

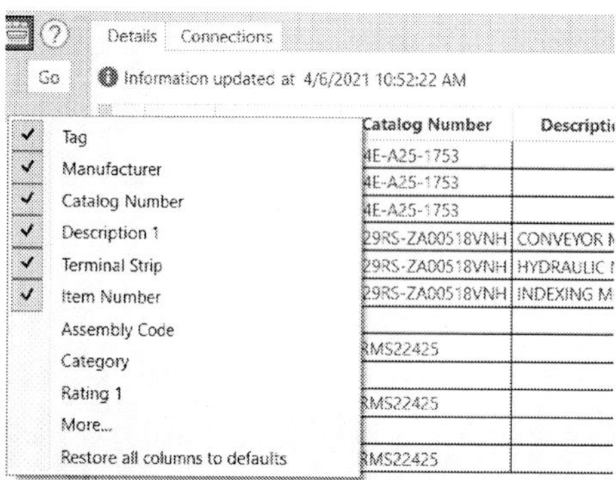

*Figure 2-54 The shortcut menu displayed on right-clicking on the column name*

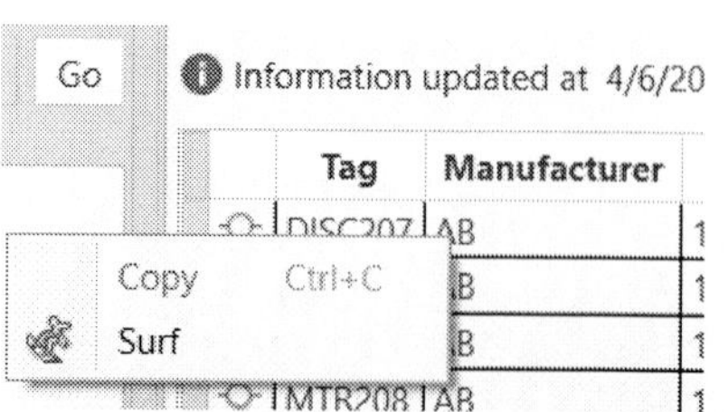

*Figure 2-55 The shortcut menu displayed on right-clicking on the cell(s) or row(s) in the grid*

The **Export** button located at the top right corner of the **Details** pane is used to export the data in the grid to .xls or .csv file. Note that in the export process only the data that is currently displayed in the grid will be exported.

## Connections Tab

When you choose this tab, the **Connections** pane is displayed. Choose the installation or location node in the **PROJECT MANAGER**; information about wiring of the components in this node will be displayed in a grid in the **Connections** pane, refer to Figure 2-56. You need to scroll horizontally in the pane or increase the size of the pane by stretching it horizontally to view all the columns in the grid. If you select an individual component node in the **PROJECT MANAGER**, the information regarding that component will only be displayed in the grid.

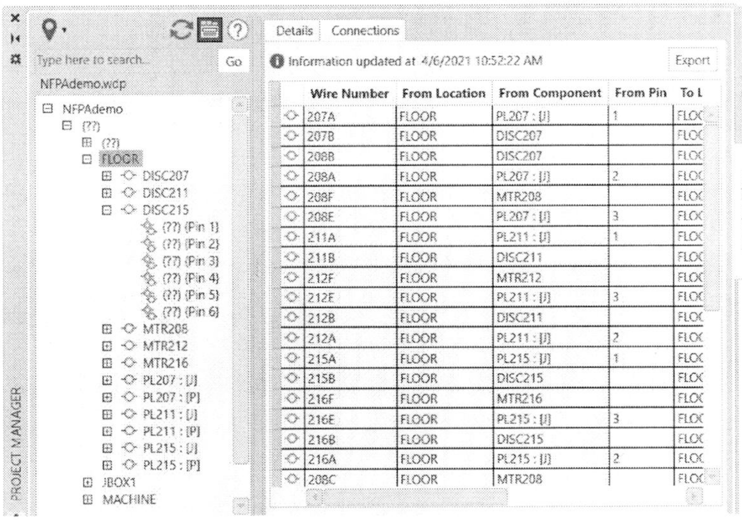

***Figure 2-56** The **Connections** pane with tabular information*

If you right-click on the column name in the grid, a shortcut menu will be displayed, refer to Figure 2-57. The options in this shortcut menu are used to add or remove columns from the **Connections** pane and to restore default number of columns. Similarly, if you right-click on the cell(s) or row(s) of the grid, a shortcut menu will be displayed, refer to Figure 2-58. This shortcut menu consists of two options: **Copy** and **Surf**. The **Surf** option is already discussed in the Component Tree. The **Copy** option will be activated only when you select cell(s) or row(s) in the grid. Using this option, you can copy the content from the selected cell(s) or row(s).

The **Export** button located at the top right corner of the **Connections** pane is used to export the data in the grid to *.xls* or *.csv* file. Note that in the export process only the data that is currently displayed in the grid will be exported.

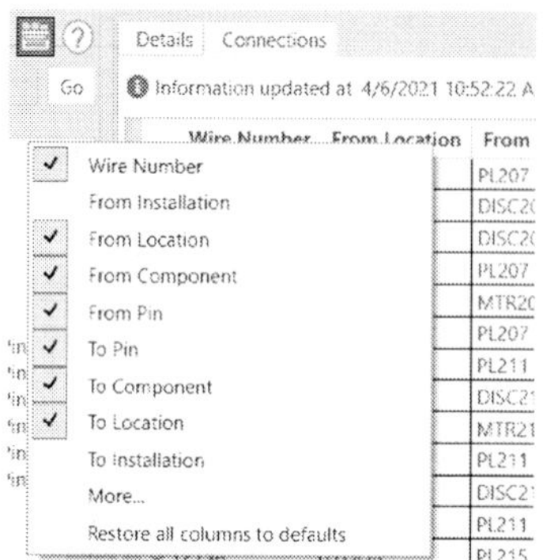


*Figure 2-57 The shortcut menu displayed on right-clicking on the column names*

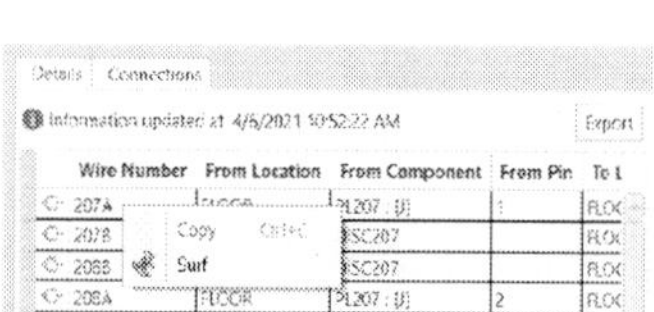


*Figure 2-58 The shortcut menu displayed on right-clicking on the cell(s) or row(s) of the grid*

**Note**

*1. If the project you are working is an electromechanical project and you are linking it with Autodesk Inventor, some additional buttons will be available in the **PROJECT MANAGER** such as **Filter the view by link status**, **Refresh the data from Inventor**, and so on. Also, some additional shortcut menu options will be available for the grid.*

*2. You can link AutoCAD Electrical component to the Inventor part or vice-versa. To do so, right-click on Inventor part or AutoCAD Electrical part and choose **Assign to Existing in Component Tree** from the shortcut menu displayed. The selected components will be linked with some differences. You need to resolve these differences using the **Details** and **Connections** pane in the **Location View** tab.*

*3. To insert connector from the **Location View** tab in the Inventor assembly of the electromechanical project, right-click on a node or a connector and then choose **Insert Connector (From List)** from the shortcut menu displayed.*

# TUTORIALS

## Tutorial 1

In this tutorial, you will create a new project and add project description to it, refer to Figure 2-59. You will also create a new drawing in the project. **(Expected time: 10 min)**

The following steps are required to complete this tutorial:

a. Create a new project.
b. Open the CADCIM project.
c. Create a new drawing.

### Creating a New Project

1. Start AutoCAD Electrical 2022 by choosing **Start > All Programs** (or **Programs**, if you are working with Windows XP Classic appearance mode) **> Autodesk > AutoCAD Electrical 2022 > AutoCAD Electrical 2022**(Windows 7). Alternatively, double-click on the

shortcut icon of AutoCAD Electrical 2022 on the desktop of your computer to start AutoCAD Electrical 2022.

2. In the AutoCAD Electrical 2022 interface, choose the **New** button in the **Start** tab. The **PROJECT MANAGER** is displayed by default on the left of the screen. If it is not displayed, choose the **Manager** tool from the **Project Tools** panel of the **Project** tab. Alternatively, choose the **Project Manager** tool from the **ACE:Main Electrical 2** toolbar to display the **PROJECT MANAGER**.

3. In the **PROJECT MANAGER**, make sure the **Projects** tab is chosen. Next, choose the **New Project** button; the **Create New Project** dialog box is displayed, as shown in Figure 2-60.

4. Enter **CADCIM** in the **Name** edit box.

5. Choose the **Browse** button; the **Browse For Folder** dialog box is displayed. By default, the **Proj** folder is selected in this dialog box. Choose the **OK** button; the location of the project is automatically displayed in the **Location** edit box.

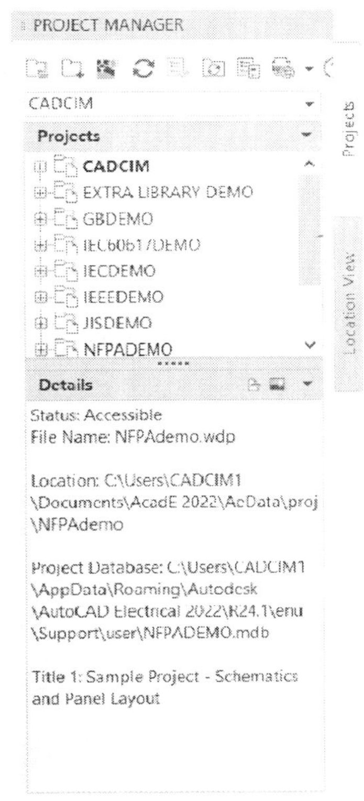


*Figure 2-59 The **PROJECT MANAGER** displaying the **CADCIM** project and its description*

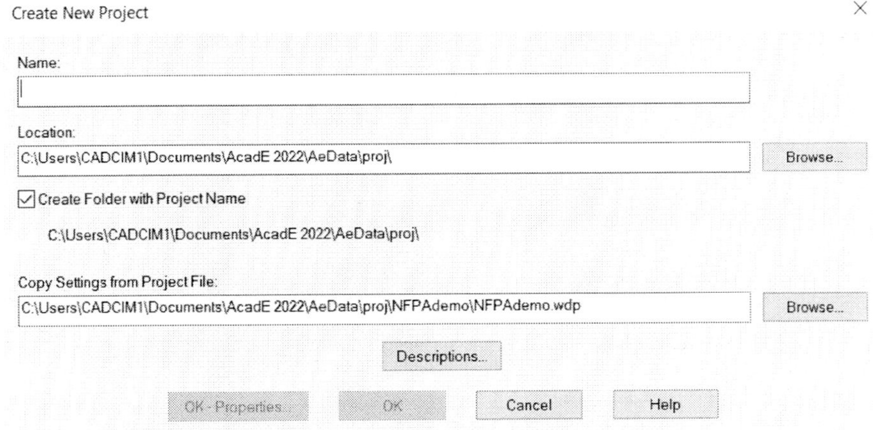


*Figure 2-60 The **Create New Project** dialog box*

6. Select the **Create Folder with Project Name** check box, if not selected.

7. By default, the name and path of the existing project is displayed in the **Copy Settings from Project File** edit box as *C:\Users\User Name\Documents\AcadE 2022\AeData\proj\NFPAdemo\NFPAdemo.wdp*. If it is not displayed, choose the **Browse** button; the **Select Project File** dialog box is displayed. Select the ***NFPADemo*** folder and then select the **NFPAdemo.wdp** project file.

   Next, choose the **Open** button; the path and name of the existing project is displayed in the **Copy Settings from Project File** edit box.

8. Choose the **Descriptions** button from the **Create New Project** dialog box; the **Project Description** dialog box is displayed.

9. Enter the following information in the **Project Description** dialog box, as shown in Figure 2-61.

   LINE1= CADCIM
   LINE2= AutoCAD Electrical
   LINE3= Sample Project
   LINE4= 1
   LINE5= 07/04/2021
   LINE6= Sham
   LINE7= John
   LINE8= Crystal
   LINE9= 1.00

   Next, select the **in reports** check box corresponding to each of these lines to include this description in the reports, refer to Figure 2-61.

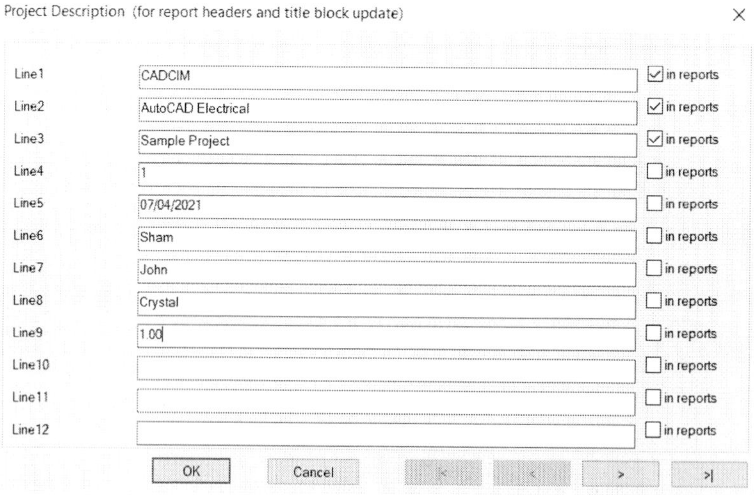

***Figure 2-61** The **Project Description** dialog box*

**Note**

*The information that you enter in the description lines of the **Project Description** dialog box will be displayed at a particular location in the title block of the drawing files of the **CADCIM** project, as shown in Figure 2-62. The title blocks will be discussed in detail in Chapter 12.*

10. Choose the **OK** button from the **Project Description** dialog box to save the changes made in this dialog box.

11. Choose the **OK** button from the **Create New Project** dialog box. You will notice that the **CADCIM** project appears in bold text at the top of the project list displayed in the **PROJECT MANAGER**, refer to Figure 2-63.

12. Next, select the **CADCIM** project from the **PROJECT MANAGER**.

13. Choose the **Details** button from the **Details/Preview** rollout. You will notice that the project description/information entered in the first nine lines of the **Project Description** dialog box is displayed in the **Details/Preview** area, as shown in Figure 2-63.

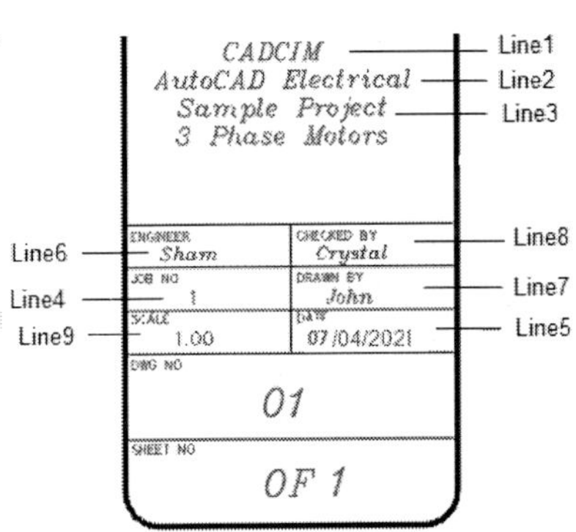


*Figure 2-62 The title block showing the description entered in the **Project Description** dialog box*

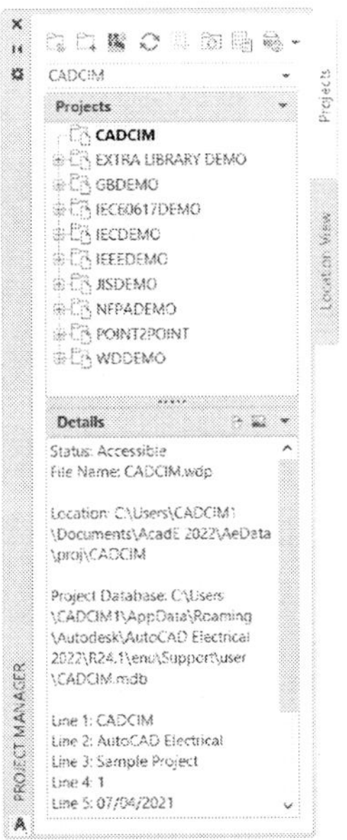


*Figure 2-63 The **PROJECT MANAGER** displaying the **CADCIM** project and its description*

**Note**

*1. It is recommended to save all the tutorials in the forthcoming chapters in the **CADCIM** project.*

*2. If the **CADCIM** project is not displayed in the **Projects** rollout of the **PROJECT MANAGER**, select the **Open Project** option from the Project selection drop-down list; the **Select Project File** dialog box is displayed. Select the **Proj** folder from the **Look in** drop-down list and then double-click on the **CADCIM** folder name. Next, select the **CADCIM** file and choose the **Open** button; the **CADCIM** project is displayed in the **Projects** rollout and it becomes the active project.*

## Creating a New Drawing

1. In the **PROJECT MANAGER**, choose the **New Drawing** button; the **Create New Drawing** dialog box is displayed, as shown in Figure 2-64.

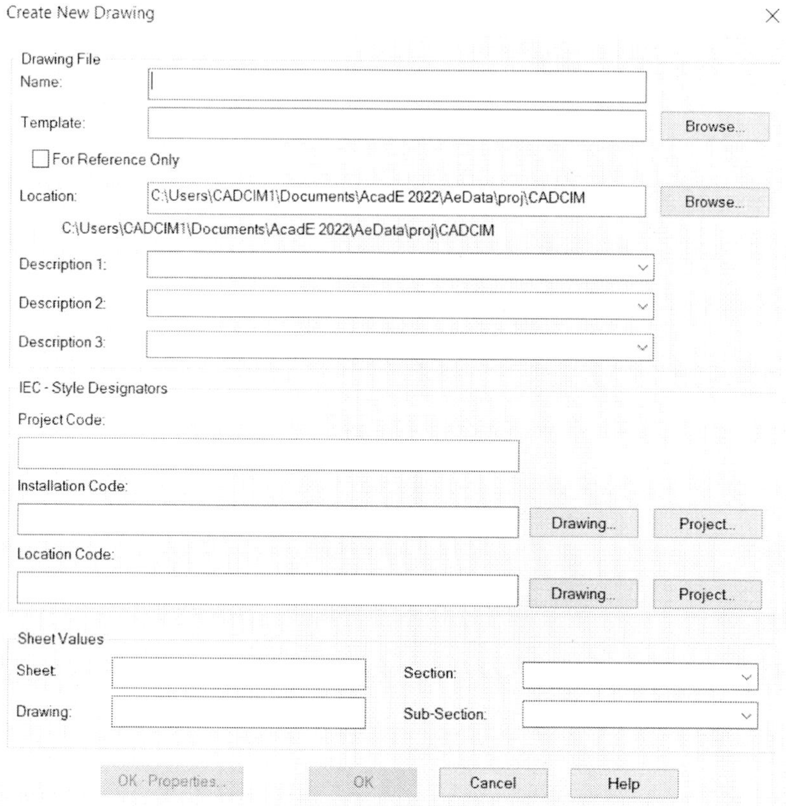


*Figure 2-64 The **Create New Drawing** dialog box*

2. Enter **C02_tut01** in the **Name** edit box. Next, choose the **Browse** button; the **Select template** dialog box is displayed. In this dialog box, select **ACAD_ELECTRICAL.dwt** from the list displayed and then choose the **Open** button; the name and path of the template is displayed in the **Template** edit box.

3. Clear the **For Reference Only** check box, if it is selected. Next, choose the **Browse** button available on the right of the **Location** edit box; the **Browse For Folder** dialog box is displayed. By default, the **CADCIM** project is selected. Choose the **OK** button; the location of the drawing is automatically displayed in the **Location** edit box.

4. Enter **3 Phase Motors** in the **Description 1** edit box.

5. Enter **Motor Control Circuit** in the **Description 2** edit box and enter **01** in the **Drawing** edit box of the **Sheet Values** area.

6. Choose the **OK** button from the **Create New Drawing** dialog box; you will notice that the drawing that you created gets added to the active project. To view the drawing that you created, double-click on **CADCIM** in the **PROJECT MANAGER**; the drawing list is displayed and the drawing *C02_tut01.dwg* appears in bold text in the **PROJECT MANAGER**. In this case, the active project is **CADCIM** and therefore, the drawing gets added to this project. Click on the drawing; the details and the preview of the drawing are displayed in the **PROJECT MANAGER**, as shown in Figures 2-65 and 2-66.

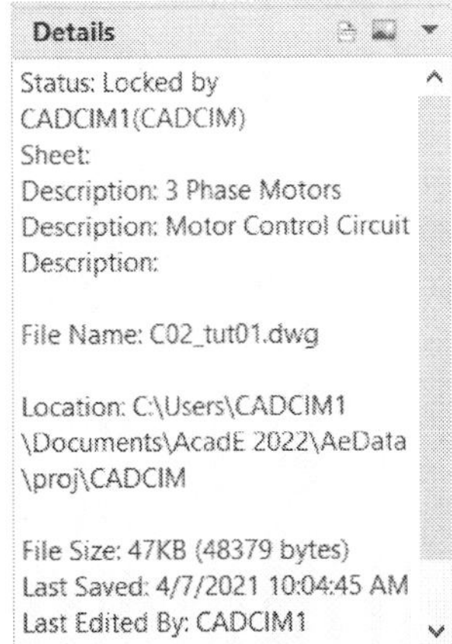


*Figure 2-65 The **Details** rollout displaying the description of C02_tut01.dwg*

*Figure 2-66 The **Preview** area displaying the preview of C02_tut01.dwg*

## Tutorial 2

In this tutorial, you will add and remove drawings from the **CADCIM** project and replace the drawings of the **POINT2POINT** project with the **CADCIM** project that you created in Tutorial 1 of this chapter. **(Expected time: 15 min)**

The following steps are required to complete this tutorial:

a. Add drawings from the existing project.
b. Remove the drawing.
c. Replace the drawing.

### Adding Drawings from the Existing Project

1. Right-click on the **CADCIM** project; a shortcut menu is displayed. Choose the **Add Drawings** option from the shortcut menu; the **Select Files to Add** dialog box is displayed.

2. In this dialog box, select the *c:\Users\User Name\Documents\AcadE 2022\AeData\proj* folder from the **Look in** drop-down list; a list of all the projects saved in this folder is displayed. Next, double-click on the **NfpaDemo** folder from the **Select Files to Add** dialog box; the drawings present in this folder are displayed.

3. Press SHIFT/CTRL and select the *DEMO01, DEMO02, DEMO03, DEMO04,* and *DEMO05* drawings. Next, choose the **Add** button; the **Apply Project Defaults to Drawing Settings** message box is displayed.

4. Choose the **Yes** button from this message box; the selected drawings are added to the **CADCIM** project, as shown in Figure 2-67.

## Removing the Drawing

1. Right-click on the *DEMO01.dwg* drawing and then choose the **Remove** option from the shortcut menu displayed; the **PROJECT - Manager Remove Files** message box is displayed. Choose the **Yes** button in this message box; the *DEMO01.dwg* drawing is removed from the drawing list, see Figure 2-68.

*Figure 2-67 The **PROJECT MANAGER** displaying the **CADCIM** project with the drawings added to it*

## Replacing the Drawing

1. To replace the *DEMO02*.dwg drawing of the **CADCIM** project with the *Connector.dwg* of the **POINT2POINT** project, right-click on the *DEMO02.dwg* drawing; a shortcut menu is displayed. Choose the **Replace** option from the shortcut menu; the **Select Replacement Drawing** dialog box is displayed.

2. Select the **Proj** folder from the **Look in** drop-down list. Next, double-click on the **Point2Point** folder; the *Connector.dwg* drawing is displayed in the **Select Replacement Drawing** dialog box.

3. Select the *Connector.dwg* drawing from this dialog box and choose the **Select** button; the **Apply Project Defaults to Drawing Settings** message box is displayed. Next, choose the **Yes** button; the *DEMO02.dwg* is replaced with the *Connector.dwg* drawing in the **CADCIM** project, as shown in Figure 2-69.

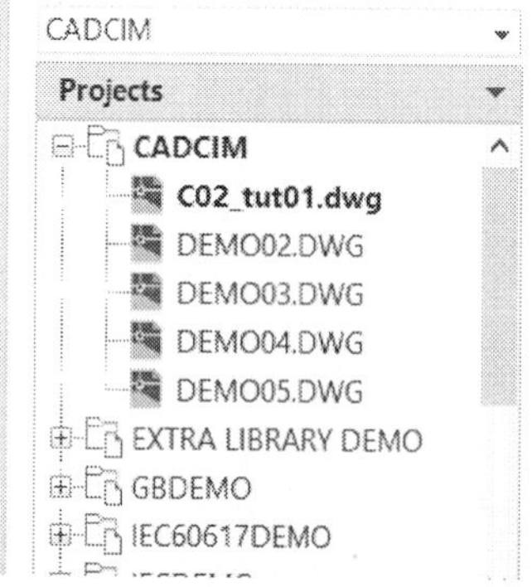


*Figure 2-68 The **PROJECT MANAGER** displaying the **CADCIM** project after removing the DEMO01.dwg drawing*

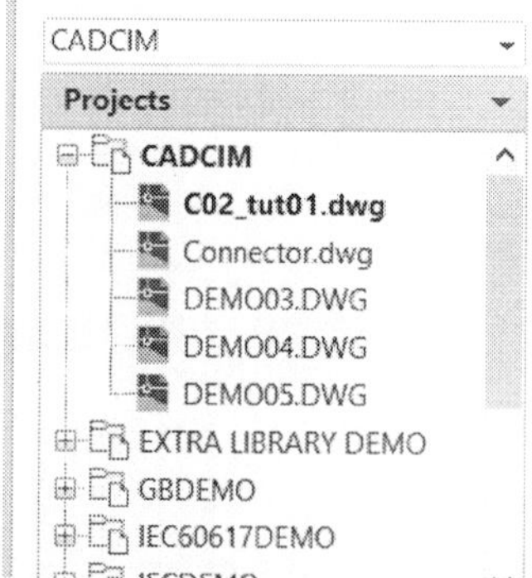


*Figure 2-69 The **PROJECT MANAGER** displaying the **CADCIM** project with the DEMO02.dwg drawing replaced by the Connector.dwg drawing*

# Tutorial 3

In this tutorial, you will create a subfolder within a **CADCIM** project and configure the drawing list display for the **CADCIM** project. **(Expected time: 15 min)**

The following steps are required to complete this tutorial:

a. Create a subfolder.
b. Configure the drawing list display.

## Creating a Subfolder

In this section, you will create a subfolder in the **CADCIM** project that is created in Tutorial 1.

1. Make sure that the **CADCIM** project is activated in the **PROJECT MANAGER**. Next, right-click on it; a shortcut menu is displayed.

2. Choose the **Add Subfolder** option from the shortcut menu; a subfolder with the name **NEW FOLDER** is created within the **CADCIM** project. Rename it as *TUTORIALS*.

3. Drag and drop the *C02_tut01.dwg* drawing created in Tutorial 1 on the *TUTORIALS* subfolder; the *C02_tut01.dwg* drawing is moved to the *TUTORIALS* subfolder, refer to Figure 2-70.

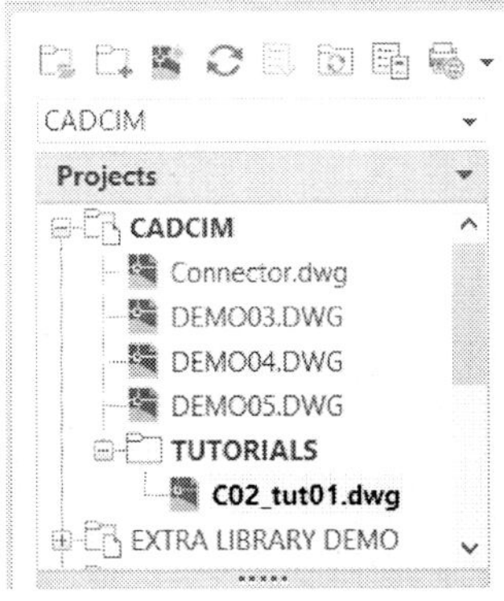


***Figure 2-70*** *The C02_tut01.dwg moved to the TUTORIALS subfolder*

**Note**

*1. In AutoCAD electrical, all projects and its subfolders names are displayed in uppercase.*

*2. You can collapse the* ***CADCIM*** *project by right-clicking on its name and choosing the* ***Collapse All*** *option from the shortcut menu displayed.*

## Configuring the Drawing List Display

1. Choose the **Drawing List Display Configuration** button from the **PROJECT MANAGER**; the **Drawing List Display Configuration** dialog box is displayed. You will notice that only the **File Name** is displayed in the **Current Display Order** area.

2. Select **Drawing Number(%D)** from the **Display Options** area and then choose the **>>** button; **Drawing Number(%D)** is moved to the **Current Display Order** area. Similarly, select **Drawing Description 1** from the **Display Options** area and choose the **>>** button; **Drawing Description 1** is moved to the **Current Display Order** area. Next, choose the **OK** button to close the **Drawing List Display Configuration** dialog box.

   You will notice that drawing numbers are added to the first four drawings in the **CADCIM** project and description is added to the *C02_tut01.dwg*.

## Tutorial 4

In this tutorial, you will copy an existing project with the name **Copy_Point2Point** and add three drawings into it. Next, you will find the list of drawings that have different settings. You will also compare and match the settings of one of the added drawings with the copied project.

**(Expected time: 15 min)**

The following steps are required to complete this tutorial:

a. Copy the **Point2Point** project.
b. Add the drawings.
c. Find the Exception list and compare the settings.

### Copying the Point2Point Project

1. Choose the **Copy** tool from the **Project Tools** panel of the **Project** tab; the **Copy Project: Step 1 - Select Existing Project to Copy** dialog box is displayed, as shown in Figure 2-71.

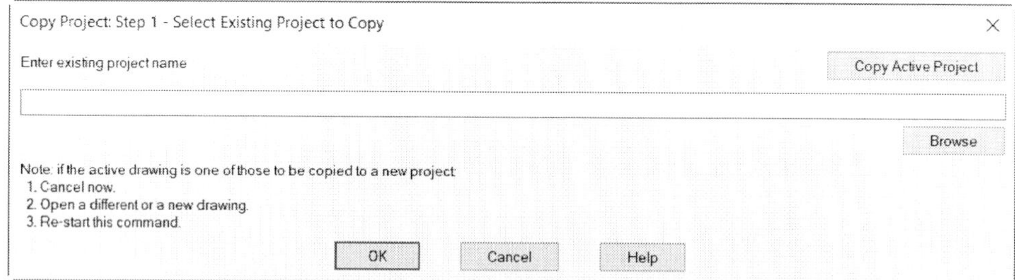


*Figure 2-71 The **Copy Project Step 1 - Select Existing Project to Copy** dialog box*

2. Choose **Browse** from this dialog box; the **Select existing project to copy** dialog box is displayed. In this dialog box, select the *c:\Users\User Name\Documents\AcadE 2022\AeData\proj* folder and then double-click on the **Point2Point** folder and then select **Point2Point.wdp** file displayed, refer to Figure 2-72. Next, choose the **Open** button; path of the *Point2Point.wdp* file is displayed in the edit box of the **Copy Project: Step 1 - Select Existing Project to Copy** dialog box.

3. Now, choose **OK** from this dialog box; the **Copy Project: Step 2 -- Select path and name for new project** dialog box is displayed. Choose the **Up One Level** button from this dialog box and then choose the **Create New Folder** button; the **New Folder** is added to the **Proj** folder. Next, rename the new folder as *Copy_Point2Point*.

4. Double-click on the **Copy_Point2Point** folder in the **Copy Project: Step 2 -- Select path and name for new project** dialog box and then enter **Copy_Point2Point** in the **File name** text box, refer to Figure 2-73.

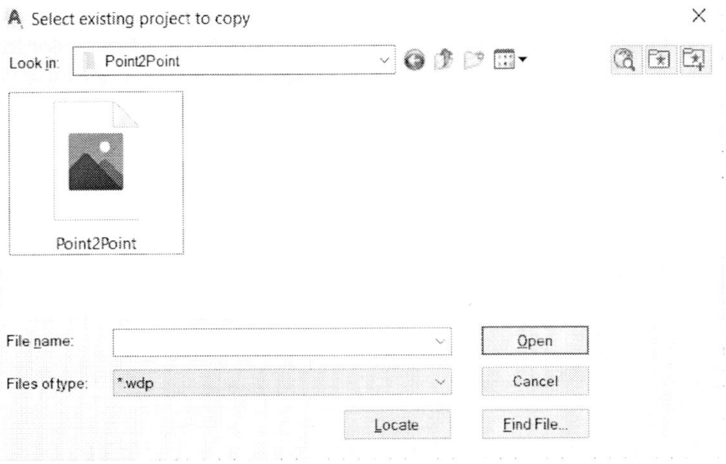

*Figure 2-72 The **Select existing project to copy** dialog box*

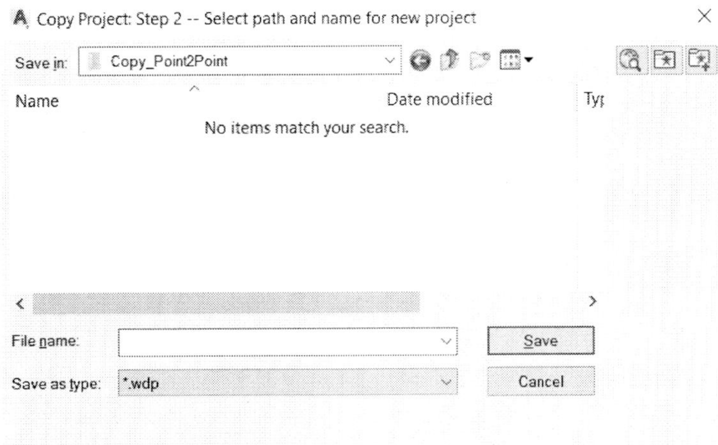


*Figure 2-73 The **Copy Project: Step 2 -- Select path and name for new project** dialog box*

5. Now, choose the **Save** button; the **Select Drawings to Process** dialog box is displayed, as shown in Figure 2-74. In this dialog box, choose the **Do All** button and then the **OK** button; the **Copy Project: Step 4 -- Enter Base Path for Project Drawings** dialog box is displayed.

6. In this dialog box, the edit box located at the top displays default path for the project drawings. Choose **OK** from this dialog box; the **Copy Project: Step 5 -- Adjust new drawing file names** dialog box is displayed, as shown in Figure 2-75.

7. Choose **OK** from this dialog box; the **Copy_Point2Point** project is added to the **Projects** rollout of the **PROJECT MANAGER**. Also, the drawings in the **Copy_Point2Point** project get saved in its project folder and this project becomes an active project.

**Note**

*To change the name of drawings in the copied project, select drawings one by one in the* ***Copy Project: Step 5 -- Adjust new drawing file names*** *dialog box and then choose* ***Edit****.*

## Adding the Drawings

1. Right-click on the **Copy_Point2Point** project in the **PROJECT MANAGER**; a shortcut menu is displayed. Choose the **Add Drawings** option from the shortcut menu; the **Select Files to Add** dialog box is displayed.

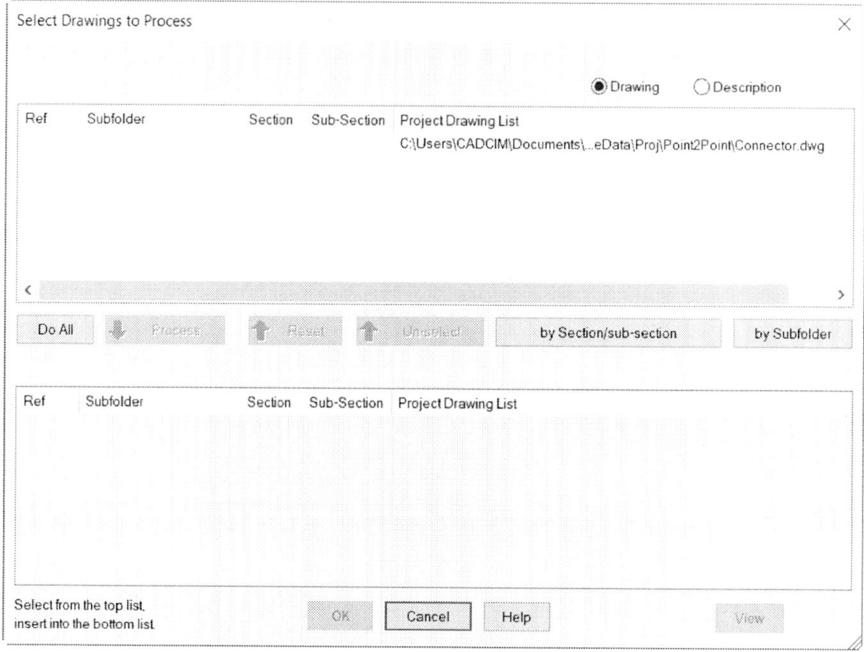


*Figure 2-74 The* ***Select Drawings to Process*** *dialog box*

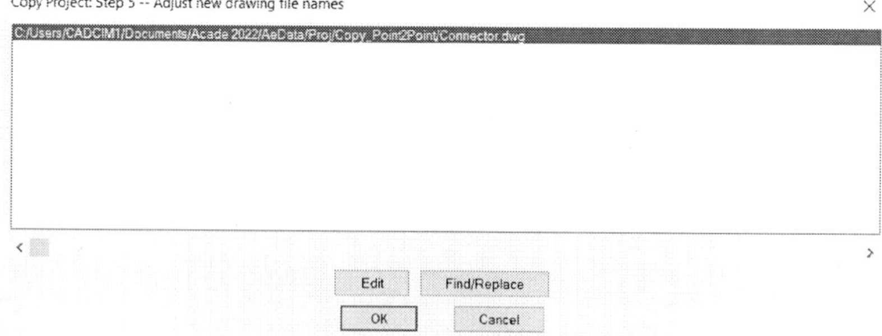


*Figure 2-75 The* ***Copy Project: Step 5 -- Adjust new drawing file names*** *dialog box*

2. In this dialog box, choose the **Up one level** button; the **Proj** folder is displayed in the **Look in** drop-down list. Next, double-click on the **NfpaDemo** folder; the drawings present in this folder are displayed. Press SHIFT/CTRL and select the *DEMO07, DEMO08,* and *DEMO09* drawings.

3. Choose the **Add** button; the **Apply Project Defaults to Drawing Settings** message box is displayed.

4. Choose the **No** button from this message box; the selected drawings are added to the **Copy_Point2Point** project, as shown in Figure 2-76. If the drawings are not displayed in the **Copy_Point2Point** project, choose **Refresh** from the **PROJECT MANAGER**.

## Finding the Exception List and Comparing the Settings

1. Right-click on the **Copy_Point2Point** project and choose **Exception List** from the shortcut menu displayed; the **Properties Exception List: COPY_POINT2POINT** dialog box is displayed, as shown in Figure 2-77. This dialog box lists the drawings which have different properties than the project default properties.

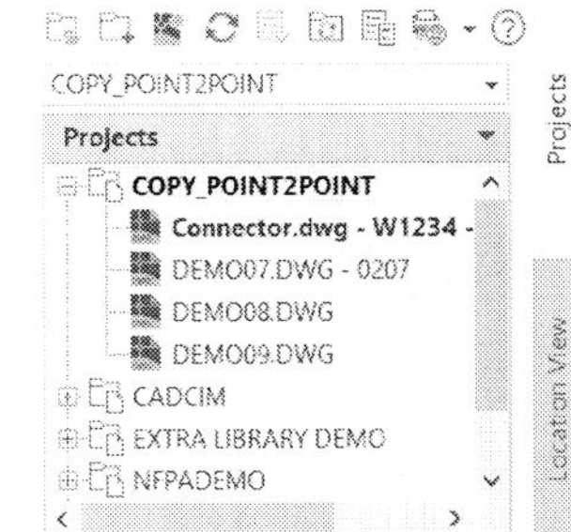


*Figure 2-76 The **Copy_Point2Point** project with the drawings added to it*

2. Select the **Connector.dwg** from **Copy_Point2Point** in the **Projects** rollout and right-click; a shortcut menu is displayed. Choose **Properties** from the shortcut menu; a cascading menu is displayed. Choose **Settings Compare** from the cascading menu; the **Compare Drawing and Project Settings: Connector.dwg Versus COPY_POINT2POINT** dialog box is displayed, as shown in Figure 2-78.

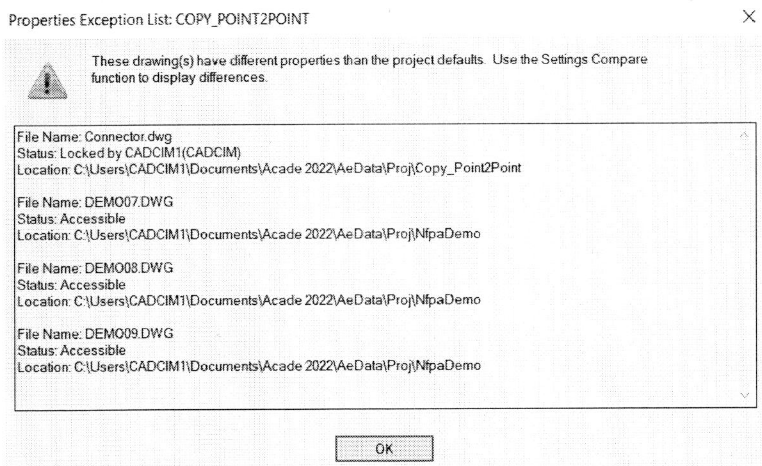


*Figure 2-77 The **Properties Exception List: COPY_POINT2POINT** dialog box*

You will notice that this dialog box displays the number of drawing settings that are different from its project. First entry in this dialog box indicates that component tags of the *Connector.dwg* are reference based and component tags of the **Copy_Point2Point** project are sequential in order.

3. Select the first entry and choose the **Match Drawing** button from the **Compare Drawing and Project Settings: Connector Versus COPY_POINT2POINT** dialog box. Next, choose **OK**; the component tag settings of the project are matched with the *Connector.dwg* file. To

confirm this, repeat step 2. You will notice that component tag settings are not displayed any more in the list.

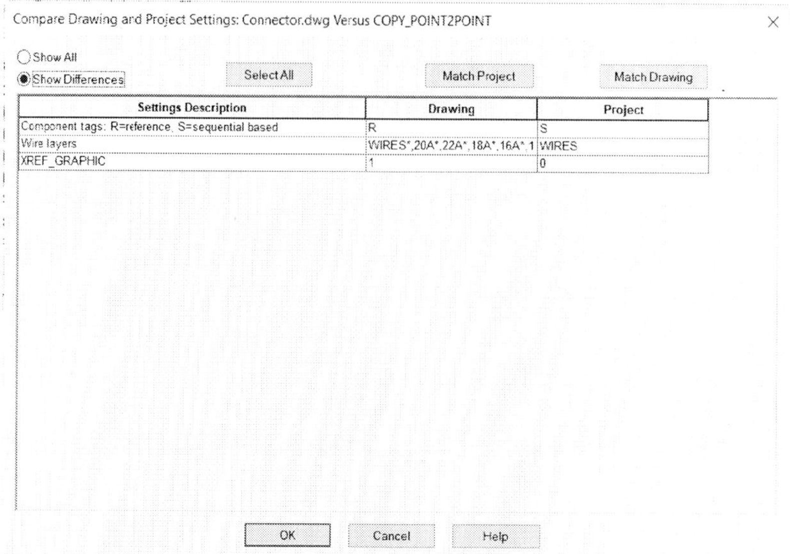


*Figure 2-78 The **Compare Drawing and Project Settings: DEMO007.DWG Versus COPY_POINT2POINT** dialog box*

## Tutorial 5

In this tutorial, you will surf a component and extract component information and connection details of the **CADCIM** project to an external file using the **Location View** tab in the **PROJECT MANAGER**. **(Expected time: 15 min)**

The following steps are required to complete this tutorial:

a. Surf the component.
b. Extract component information.
c. Extract connection details.

### Surfing the Component

1. Make sure the **CADCIM** project is activated. Choose the **Location View** tab from the **PROJECT MANAGER**. Next, choose the **CADCIM** node from the **PROJECT MANAGER**. Next, choose the **Display Details and Connections** button; the **PROJECT MANAGER** is expanded with the **Details** tab activated, as shown in Figure 2-79.

   You will notice that the component information is displayed in the **Details** pane in the grid.

2. Scroll down in the **PROJECT MANAGER** and select **LS406** from the **Tag** column. Next, right-click on it; a shortcut menu is displayed, as shown in Figure 2-80.

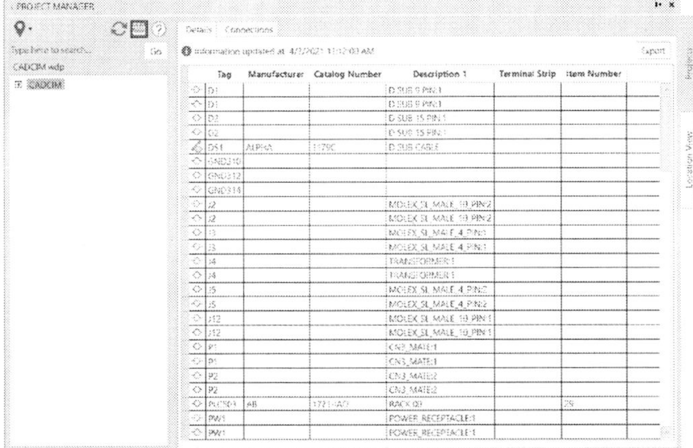

*Figure 2-79 Expanded **PROJECT MANAGER***

3. Choose **Surf** from the shortcut menu; the **Surf** dialog box is displayed, as shown in Figure 2-81. Choose **Go To** from the **Surf** dialog box; the *demo004.dwg* file is opened with **LS406** zoomed in.

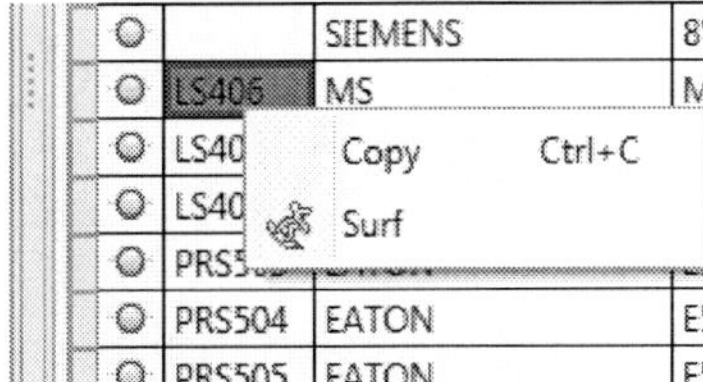


*Figure 2-80 Shortcut menu displayed*

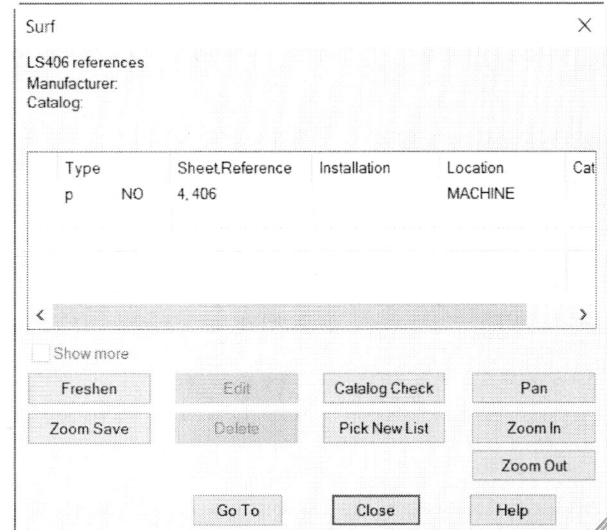


*Figure 2-81 The **Surf** dialog box*

**Note**

*The options in the **Surf** dialog box are discussed in detail in Chapter 6.*

## Extracting the Component Information

1. Right-click on the **Tag** column in the grid; a shortcut menu is displayed. Choose **More** from this shortcut menu; the **Columns to display** dialog box is displayed.

2. Scroll down in the **Columns to display** dialog box and select the **Category**, **Rating1**, **Location** and **Terminal Number** check boxes, as shown in Figure 2-82. Next, choose **OK**; the **Category**,

Rating1, Location and Terminal Number columns are added to the grid in the Details tab.

3. Choose **Export** from the **PROJECT MANAGER**; the **Save As** dialog box is displayed. Browse to *c:\Users\User Name\Documents\AcadE 2022\AeData\proj\CADCIM* and choose **Save**; the *ComponentDetails.csv* file is saved at the specified location.

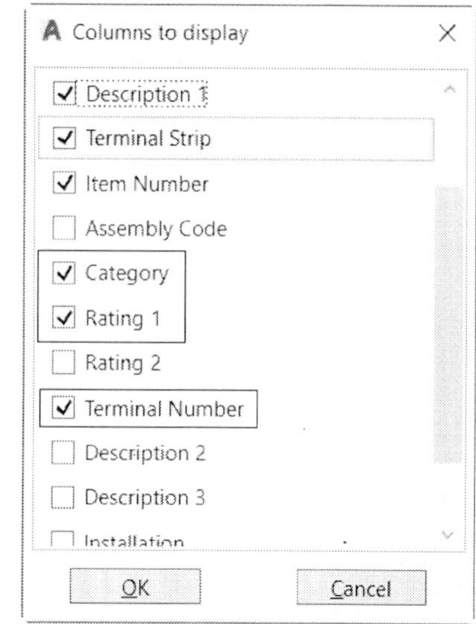


*Figure 2-82 The* ***Columns to display*** *dialog box*

## Extracting the Connection Details

1. Choose the **Connections** tab in the **PROJECT MANAGER**; the **PROJECT MANAGER** is modified with connection details of the **CADCIM** project displayed in the grid.

2. Right-click on the **Wire Number** column in the grid; a shortcut menu is displayed. Choose **More** from this shortcut menu; the **Columns to display** dialog box is displayed.

3. Scroll down in the **Columns to display** dialog box and select the **Wire Type**, **Wire Color**, and **Wire Gauge** check boxes. Next, choose **OK**; the **Wire Type**, **Wire Color**, and **Wire Gauge** columns are added to the grid in the **Connections** tab.

4. Choose **Export** from the **PROJECT MANAGER**; the **Save As** dialog box is displayed. Navigate to *c:\Users\User Name\Documents\AcadE 2022\AeData\proj\CADCIM* and choose **Save**; the *ConnectionDetails.csv* file is saved at the specified location.

## Self-Evaluation Test

**Answer the following questions and then compare them to those given at the end of this chapter:**

1. Which of the following buttons in the **PROJECT MANAGER** is used to execute the pending updates?

   (a) **New Project** (b) **Refresh**
   (c) **Project Task List** (d) **Surfer**

2. The __________ option is used to plot all drawings of a project or a specified group of drawings.

3. The __________ option is used to create copies of an existing project with all the drawings and related files.

4. The __________ dialog box is used to edit the properties of a drawing.

5. Choose the __________ button to preview a selected drawing.

6. You can add up to __________ lines of description per page for each drawing in a project.

7. A project file is an ASCII text file. (T/F)

8. The **PROJECT MANAGER** is used to manage the project files only. (T/F)

9. A project file always consists of drawings placed in a single directory. (T/F)

10. You can switch between sequential drawings in an active project. (T/F)

## Review Questions

**Answer the following questions:**

1. Which of the following buttons is used to change the appearance of a drawing list displayed in the **PROJECT MANAGER**?

   (a) **Plot Project** (b) **Project Task List**
   (c) **Move Up** (d) **Drawing List Display Configuration**

2. Which of the following options is used to add existing drawing(s) to a project?

   (a) **Descriptions** (b) **Add Active Drawing**
   (c) **Add Drawings** (d) **Title Block Update**

3. The **Remove Drawings** option is used both for removing and deleting a drawing file. (T/F)

4. You can close only the non-active projects. (T/F)

5. Projects can be closed by using the Project selection drop-down list. (T/F)

# EXERCISES

## Exercise 1

Create a new project with the project name **NEW_PROJECT** and add appropriate description to it. **(Expected time: 10 min)**

**Note**

*It is recommended to save all exercises of the forthcoming chapters in the* ***NEW_PROJECT*** *project.*

## Exercise 2

Create a new drawing with the name *C02_exer02.dwg* in the project created in Exercise 1 and add appropriate description to it. **(Expected time: 10 min)**

## Exercise 3

Using the **Copy** button, create a new project with the name **COPY_PROJECT** containing the drawings and settings of any existing project. **(Expected time: 10 min)**

## Answers to Self-Evaluation Test

**1.** C, **2. Plot Project**, **3. Copy Project**, **4. Drawing Properties**, **5. Preview**, **6.** three, **7.** T, **8.** F, **9.** F, **10.** T

# Chapter 3

# Working with Wires

## Learning Objectives

***After completing this chapter, you will be able to:***

- *Insert different types of wires*
- *Modify inserted wires*
- *Create wire layers*
- *Create and manage wire types and their properties*
- *Insert, erase, hide, fix, and reposition wire numbers*
- *Insert special wire numbering*
- *Insert in-line wire markers*
- *Understand the source and destination signal arrows*
- *Insert cable markers in wires*
- *Show the source and destination markers on wires*
- *Check line entities on non-wire layers*
- *Show and edit wire sequences*
- *Manipulate wire gaps*

# INTRODUCTION

In this chapter, you will learn in detail about the types of wire and wire layers. Also, you will learn how to insert wires in a drawing, modify wires using commands such as trim, stretch, create different wire types in drawings, insert in-line wire markers in wires, insert wire numbers in wires and reposition them, and troubleshoot wires. Later in this chapter, you will learn how to check, repair, trace wire gaps and pointers, and manipulate wire gaps. You will also learn about the source and destination signal arrows in this chapter.

# WIRES

A wire is a stretched out strand of drawn metal and is usually cylindrical in shape. They are used to carry electricity and telecommunication signals. The standard size of a wire is determined by wire gauge.

Wires are AutoCAD lines when they are placed on an AutoCAD Electrical defined wire layer. By default, the WIRES wire layer is present in a drawing. In AutoCAD Electrical, you can create as many wire layers as you want. You can also assign wire numbers to the wires that will be included in various wire connection reports. Two wire segments or a wire segment and a component are said to be connected if they fall within a trap distance of any part of the other wire segment or component. If more than one wires are connected together, it forms a wire network. In the next section, you will learn about the types of wires and the insertion of wires in drawings.

## Inserting Wires into a Drawing

In this section, you will learn about different types of wires and will also learn to insert them in a drawing. You can insert wire segments on a wire layer horizontally, vertically, or angled at 22.5, 45, or 67.5 degrees.

### Inserting Single Wire

| | |
|---|---|
| **Ribbon:** | Schematic > Insert Wires/Wire Numbers > Wire drop-down > Wire |
| **Toolbar:** | ACE:Main Electrical > Insert Wire<br>or ACE:Wires > Insert Wire |
| **Menu:** | Wires > Insert Wire |
| **Command:** | AEWIRE |

The **Wire** tool is used to insert wires. To insert a wire, choose the **Wire** tool from the **Insert Wires/Wire Numbers** panel of the **Schematic** tab; you will be prompted to specify the start point of the wire. You can either select a point using the pointing device or enter its coordinates at the Command prompt. After the start point of the wire is selected, AutoCAD Electrical will prompt you to enter the endpoint of the wire. Specify the endpoint where you want to terminate the wire; a wire will be drawn between the two specified points. You can specify the endpoint horizontally or vertically by entering H or V at the Command prompt. At this point, you may continue to select points or exit the **Wire** tool by pressing ESC or pressing the ENTER key twice. The command sequence that is displayed when you invoke the **Wire** tool is given next.

Choose the **Wire** tool
Current wiretype: "WIRES"

Specify wire start or [wireType/X=show connections]: *Specify the wire start point or enter an option (the options are discussed next).*

Specify wire end or [V=start Vertical H=start Horizontal TAB: Collision off Continue]: Enter.
Specify wire start or [Scoot/wireType/X=show connections]: *Press ESC to exit the command.*

The options in the above command sequence are discussed next.

### wireType

Once you invoke the **Wire** tool, the command window will display the current wire type that is being used. You can change the wire type by entering '**T**' at the Command prompt. To do so, enter **T** at the "*Specify wire start or [wireType/X=show connections]*" prompt and press ENTER; the **Set Wire Type** dialog box will be displayed, as shown in Figure 3-1. This dialog box is used to set wire types for new wires. The **Set Wire Type** dialog box displays the wire types that are used in the active drawing. This dialog box consists of various columns such as **Used**, **Wire Color**, **Size**, **Layer Name**, **Wire Numbering**, **USER1**, and **USER2**.

Set Wire Type

| | Used | Wire Color | Size | Layer Name | Wire Numbering | USER1 | USER2 | USE |
|---|---|---|---|---|---|---|---|---|
| 1 | X | BLK | 10AWG | BLK_10AWG | Yes | | | |
| 2 | X | BLK | 14AWG | BLK_14AWG | Yes | | | |
| 3 | X | | | GRN | Yes | | | |
| 4 | X | RED | 18AWG | RED_18AWG | Yes | | | |
| 5 | X | WHT | 16AWG | WHT_16AWG | Yes | | | |
| 6 | | | | | | | | |

OK Cancel Help

***Figure 3-1*** *The* ***Set Wire Type*** *dialog box*

These columns provide information about layer name, user-defined properties, and wire properties namely color, size, and so on. These columns also indicate whether wire numbers will be included in the wires of a selected wire layer or not. The columns in the **Set Wire Type** dialog box are discussed later in this chapter. Note that the properties of wire types are controlled through layers. Next, select a wire type from the **Layer Name** column; the **OK** button will be activated. Choose the **OK** button; the wire type of the wire will get automatically changed to the wire type selected in the **Set Wire Type** dialog box and will appear at the "***Current wiretype***" prompt. Now, you can continue inserting the specified wire type.

**Note**

*The list of wire types will only be displayed in the* ***Set Wire Type*** *dialog box if you have already defined wire types in your drawing. The procedure of defining wire types is discussed later in this chapter.*

**X=show connections**

If you enter **X** at the Command prompt and press ENTER, the wire connection points in a drawing will be displayed. Also, green cross marks (X) will be displayed at the location of the wire connection points of the components. Note that these green cross marks (X) will only be displayed if there are components in a drawing. Select the component from the drawing; the wire will be drawn to the nearest connection point. You will learn about inserting components into a drawing in the later chapters. Choose **Redraw** from the **View** menu to remove these green cross marks (X) from wire connection points.

**V=start Vertical/H=start Horizontal/Continue**

If you enter **V** at the Command prompt, a wire will be drawn vertically and if you enter **H** at the Command prompt, a wire will be drawn horizontally. Similarly, if you enter **Continue** or **C** at the Command prompt, the command will continue until you press ENTER.

**Scoot/wireType/X=show connections**

This Command prompt is displayed when you press ENTER after specifying the endpoint of the wire. Enter **S** at the Command prompt; the cursor will change into a selection box on the screen and you will be prompted to select the component, wire, or wire number. Select the wire, wire number, or component from your drawing to move them as per your requirement. The **Scoot** tool is discussed in detail in the later chapters.

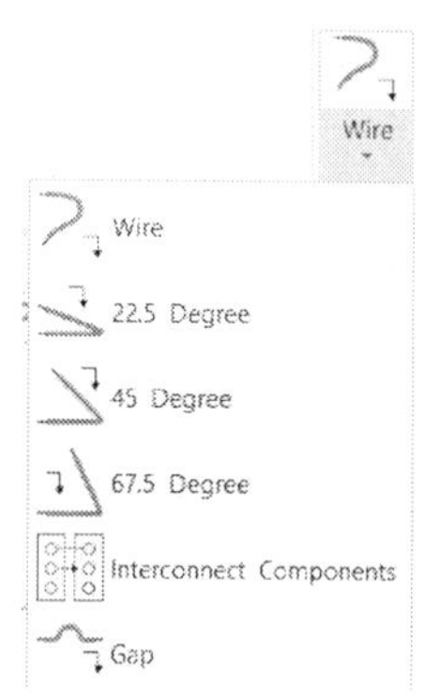


*Figure 3-2 The **Wire** drop-down for inserting different types of angled wires*

## Inserting Wires at Angles

You can also insert wires at certain angles. To do so, click on the down arrow on the **Wire** tool from the **Insert Wires/Wire Numbers** panel of the **Schematic** tab; the **Wire** drop-down will be displayed, as shown in Figure 3-2. The three options, namely **22.5 Degree**, **45 Degree**, and **67.5 Degree** are discussed next.

### Inserting a 22.5 Degree Wire

| | |
|---|---|
| **Ribbon:** | Schematic > Insert Wires/Wire Numbers > Wire drop-down> 22.5 Degree |
| **Toolbar:** | ACE:Main Electrical > Insert Wire > Insert 22.5 Degree Wire<br>or ACE:Wires > Insert 22.5 Degree Wire |
| **Menu:** | Wires > Angle Wire > Insert 22.5 Degree Wire |
| **Command:** | AE225WIRE |

The **22.5 Degree** tool is used to insert a wire at an angle of 22.5 degrees. To do so, choose the **22.5 Degree** tool from the **Wire** drop-down in the **Insert Wires/Wire Numbers** panel of the **Schematic** tab; you will be prompted to select a component or the branch for the 22.5 degree wire. You can specify a point by using the pointing device or entering its coordinates at the Command prompt. After the start point of the wire is selected, you will be prompted to specify the endpoint of the wire. Specify the endpoint where you want to terminate the wire; a wire will be drawn between the two specified points. At this point, you may continue selecting points or exit the **22.5 Degree** tool by pressing ESC. The command sequence that is displayed when you invoke the **22.5 Degree** tool is given next.

Choose the **22.5 Degree** tool
Current wiretype: "WIRES"
Select component or branch for 22.5 degree WIRE [T=wiretype, X=show connections]: *Select the component or branch for 22.5 degree angle wire.*
Specify wire end or [Continue]: *Specify the endpoint of the wire or enter Continue/C to continue the wire.*
Specify wire end or [Continue]: Enter
Select component for 22.5 degree wire [N=ninety degrees, T=wiretype, X=show connections]: *Press ESC to exit the command.*

In the above command sequence, if you enter '**T**' at the Command prompt, the **Set Wire Type** dialog box will be displayed that has been discussed earlier. If you enter '**X**' at the Command prompt, the wire connection points will be displayed in the drawing. Similarly, if you enter **C** or **Continue** at the Command prompt, it will continue the command until you press ESC. The 22.5 degree wire is shown in Figure 3-3.

## Inserting a 45 Degree Wire

| | |
|---|---|
| **Ribbon:** | Schematic > Insert Wires/Wire Numbers > Wire drop-down> 45 Degree |
| **Toolbar:** | ACE:Main Electrical > Insert Wire > Insert 45 Degree Wire or ACE:Wires > Insert 45 Degree Wire |
| **Menu:** | Wires > Angle Wire > Insert 45 Degree Wire |
| **Command:** | AE45WIRE |

The **45 Degree** tool is used to insert wires at an angle of 45 degrees. To do so, choose the **45 Degree** tool from the **Wire** drop-down in the **Insert Wires/Wire Numbers** panel of the **Schematic** tab; you will be prompted to select a component or the branch for the 45 degree wire. You can either specify a point using the pointing device or enter its coordinates. After the start point of the wire is selected, you will be prompted to enter the endpoint of wire. Specify the endpoint; a 45 degree wire will be drawn between two points, refer to Figure 3-3. At this point, you may continue selecting points or terminate the **45 Degree** tool by pressing ESC.

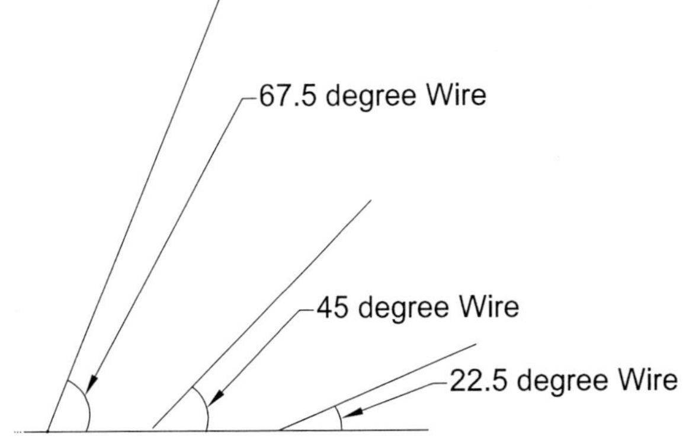


***Figure 3-3*** *Type of angled wires*

The command sequence that is displayed when you invoke the **45 Degree** tool is given next.

Choose the **45 Degree** tool
Current wiretype: "WIRES"
Select component or branch for 45 degree WIRE [T=wiretype, X=show connections]: *Select the component or branch for 45 degree angled wire.*
Specify wire end or [Continue]: *Specify the endpoint of the wire or enter Continue/C to continue the wire.*
Specify wire end or [Continue]: Enter
Select component for 45 degree wire [N=ninety degrees, T=wiretype, X=show connections]: *Press ESC to exit the command.*

## Inserting a 67.5 Degree Wire

| | |
|---|---|
| **Ribbon:** | Schematic > Insert Wires/Wire Numbers > Wire drop-down> 67.5 Degree |
| **Toolbar:** | ACE:Main Electrical > Insert Wire > Insert 67.5 Degree Wire or ACE:Wires > Insert 67.5 Degree Wire |
| **Menu:** | Wires > Angle Wire > Insert 67.5 Degree Wire |
| **Command:** | AE675WIRE |

The **67.5 Degree** tool is used to draw a wire at an angle of 67.5 degrees. To do so, choose the **67.5 Degree** tool from the **Wire** drop-down in the **Insert Wires/Wire Numbers** panel of the **Schematic** tab; you will be prompted to select the component or the branch for 67.5 degree wire. Either specify a point using the pointing device or enter its coordinates. After the start point of the wire is selected, you will be prompted to specify the endpoint of the wire. Specify the endpoint; the 67.5 degree wire will be drawn between the specified points, refer to Figure 3-3. At this point, you may continue selecting points or terminate the **67.5 Degree** tool by pressing ESC. The command sequence that is displayed when you invoke the **67.5 Degree** tool is given next.

Choose the **67.5 Degree** tool
Current wiretype: "WIRES"
Select component or branch for 67.5 degree WIRE [T=wiretype, X=show connections]: *Select the component or branch for 67.5 degree angled wire.*
Specify wire end or [Continue]: *Specify the endpoint of the wire or enter Continue/C to continue the wire.*
Specify wire end or [Continue]: Enter
Select component for 67.5 degree wire [N=ninety degrees, T=wiretype, X=show connections]: *Press ESC to exit the command.*

## Inserting Multiple Bus Wiring

| | |
|---|---|
| **Ribbon:** | Schematic > Insert Wires/Wire Numbers > Multiple Bus |
| **Toolbar:** | ACE:Main Electrical > Insert Wire > Multiple Wire Bus or ACE:Wires >Multiple Wire Bus |
| **Menu:** | Wires > Multiple Wire Bus |
| **Command:** | AEMULTIBUS |

The **Multiple Bus** tool is used to draw multiple wire bus. This tool is very useful when you want to create 3-phase circuits, point-to-point wiring diagrams, and so on. To draw multiple wire bus, choose the **Multiple Bus** tool from the **Insert Wires/Wire Numbers** panel of the **Schematic** tab; the **Multiple Wire Bus** dialog box will be displayed, as shown in Figure 3-4. Different areas and options in this dialog box are discussed next.

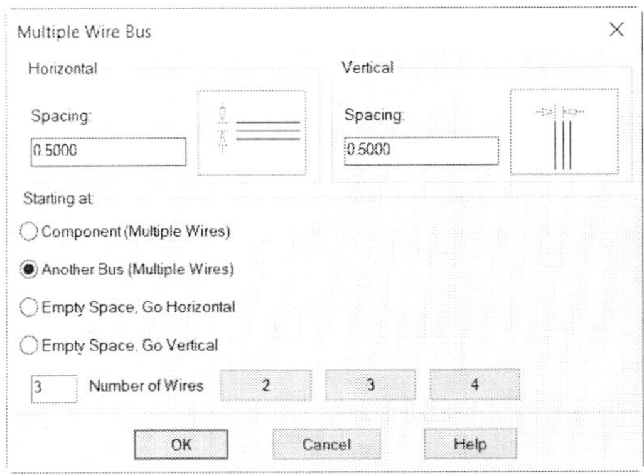


*Figure 3-4 The* ***Multiple Wire Bus*** *dialog box*

## Horizontal Area

Specify the horizontal spacing between two adjacent wires of a bus in the **Spacing** edit box of the **Horizontal** area. By default, 0.5000 is displayed in this edit box.

## Vertical Area

Specify the vertical spacing between two adjacent wires of a bus in the **Spacing** edit box of the **Vertical** area. By default, 0.5000 is displayed in this edit box.

## Starting at Area

This area is used to specify the start point of the wire. The options in this area are discussed next.

### Component (Multiple Wires)

The **Component (Multiple Wires)** radio button is used to start bus wires at wire connection points of the component. Note that you can select the connection points of a component using the window selection method. After selecting this radio button, the **Number of Wires** edit box will not be available.

The command sequence for the **AEMULTIBUS** command on selecting the **Component (Multiple Wires)** radio button is given next.

Command: **AEMULTIBUS**
Window select starting wire connection points: *Select the component's connection points using the window selection method.*

to (T=wiretype)(Continue/Flip):

Enter **C** at the Command prompt to continue the command and enter **F** to flip wires at right angles.

### Another Bus (Multiple Wires)

The **Another Bus (Multiple Wires)** radio button is used to start branching off the bus from the existing bus or set of wires. By default, the **Another Bus (Multiple Wires)** radio button is selected. Choose the **OK** button from the **Multiple Wire Bus** dialog box; you will be prompted to select the existing wire for starting the multiple phase bus connection. Select the existing wire; the first wire of the new bus will get attached to the pick point in an existing wire and the remaining wires of the new bus will get connected to the underlying wires as you move cursor slowly across them. Also, note that if the number of wires you are inserting exceeds the number of existing wires to make intersections, extra wires will be created on the first existing wire.

The command sequence for the **AEMULTIBUS** command on selecting the **Another Bus [Multiple Wires]** radio button is given next.

Command: **AEMULTIBUS**
Select existing wire to begin multi-phase bus connection: *Select the existing wire to begin the multi-phase bus connection.*

To terminate the command, press ESC.

### Empty Space, Go Horizontal

The **Empty Space, Go Horizontal** radio button is used to start a horizontal bus in the empty space. To do so, select the **Empty Space, Go Horizontal** radio button and choose the **OK** button from the **Multiple Wire Bus** dialog box; you will be prompted to specify the start point for the first phase. Specify the start point in the empty space; you will be prompted to specify the endpoint. Move the cursor as per your requirement; the horizontal multiple wire bus will be inserted into the drawing. Next, press ESC to exit the command.

The command sequence for the **AEMULTIBUS** command on selecting the **Empty Space, Go Horizontal** radio button is given next.

Command: **AEMULTIBUS**
Starting point for 1st phase or [wiretype(T)]: *Specify the starting point for 1st phase.*

### Empty Space, Go Vertical

Select the **Empty Space, Go Vertical** radio button to start the vertical bus from the point you specify in the empty space.

The command sequence for the **AEMULTIBUS** command on selecting the **Empty Space, Go Vertical** radio button is given next.

Command: **AEMULTIBUS**
Starting point for 1st phase or [wiretype(T)]: *Specify the starting point for 1st phase.*

### Number of Wires

The **Number of Wires** edit box is used to specify the number of wires that you want to insert into the drawing. To do so, enter the number of wires in the **Number of Wires** edit box. Alternatively, choose the **2**, **3**, or **4** button adjacent to the **Number of Wires** edit box to easily select the most commonly used quantities of multiple wires: 2, 3, or 4. For example, if you enter **3** in the **Number of Wires** edit box, a 3-Phase bus wiring will be created. Note that if you select the **Component (Multiple Wires)** radio button, this edit box will not be available.

# MODIFYING WIRES

You can modify wires by using the **Trim Wire** and **Stretch Wire** tools that are discussed next.

## Trimming a Wire

| | |
|---|---|
| **Ribbon:** | Schematic > Edit Wires/Wire Numbers > Trim Wire |
| **Toolbar:** | ACE:Main Electrical > Trim Wire |
| **Menu:** | Wires > Trim Wire |
| **Command:** | AETRIM |

The **Trim Wire** tool is used to erase the specified portion of a wire segment and wire tees. You can use this tool to trim multiple wires by selecting a single wire and drawing a fence through wires. To do so, choose the **Trim Wire** tool from the **Edit Wires/Wire Numbers** panel of the **Schematic** tab; the selection box will appear on the screen and you will be prompted to select the wire to trim. Select the wire segment to remove it from the drawing. Next, press ENTER or ESC to terminate the tool. Alternatively, click on the blank space in the drawing area to exit the tool. The command sequence that is displayed when you invoke the **Trim Wire** tool is given next.

Choose the **Trim Wire** tool
Fence/Crossing/Zext/<Select wire to TRIM>: *Select wire to trim or enter any of the options.*
Fence/Crossing/Zext/Undo/<Select wire to TRIM>: Enter

When you enter **AETRIM** at the Command prompt, the selection box will appear and you will be prompted to select the wire. Select the wire to be removed. Alternatively, you can enter the options that are discussed next.

### Fence

The **Fence** option is used to remove multiple wires at a time. If you enter **F** at the "**Fence/Crossing/Zext/<Select wire to TRIM>**" prompt and then press ENTER, you will be prompted to specify the first fence point. Specify the first point; you will be prompted to specify the second point and so on. Press ENTER to remove the wires that cut the fence from drawing and exit the **Trim** tool.

### Crossing

The **Crossing** option is used to remove the portion of multiple wires. If you enter **C** at the "**Fence/Crossing/Zext/<Select wire to TRIM>** prompt" and press ENTER, you will be prompted to specify the first corner point. Specify the first corner point; you will be prompted to specify the opposite corner. Specify the opposite corner; all wires selected by the crossing window will be trimmed.

### Zext

The **Zext** option is used when you want to see all wires in a drawing. When you enter **Z** at the Command prompt, AutoCAD Electrical zooms to the extent to display all wires drawn in a drawing.

Figure 3-5 shows wires before and after trimming.

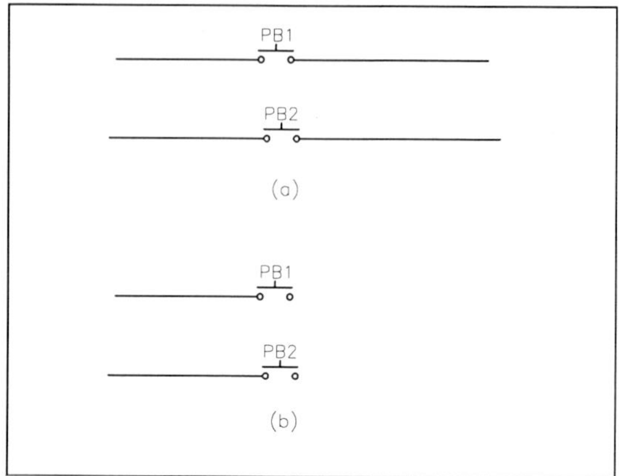


***Figure 3-5*** *(a) Wires before trimming and (b) wires after trimming*

**Note**

*Wires can also be removed from the drawing by using the AutoCAD **ERASE** command. However, using this command, the wire number information associated with the component and wire connection dots will not be removed. Therefore, it is recommended to use AutoCAD Electrical commands instead of AutoCAD commands.*

## Stretching Wires

| | |
|---|---|
| **Ribbon:** | Schematic > Edit Wires/Wire Numbers > Modify Wires drop-down > Stretch Wire |
| **Toolbar:** | ACE:Main Electrical > Insert Wire > Stretch Wire or ACE:Wires > Stretch Wire |
| **Menu:** | Wires > Stretch Wire |
| **Command:** | AESTRETCTWIRE |

The **Stretch Wire** tool is used to stretch a wire to connect it to another wire or to a component. To do so, choose the **Stretch Wire** tool from the **Modify Wire** drop-down in the **Edit Wires/ Wire Numbers** panel of the **Schematic** tab, as shown in Figure 3-6; the cursor will change into a selection box on the screen and you will be prompted to select the end of wire. Select the end of the wire that you want to connect to another wire or to a component. Next, press ESC or ENTER to exit the tool. The Command sequence that is displayed when you invoke the **Stretch Wire** tool is given next.

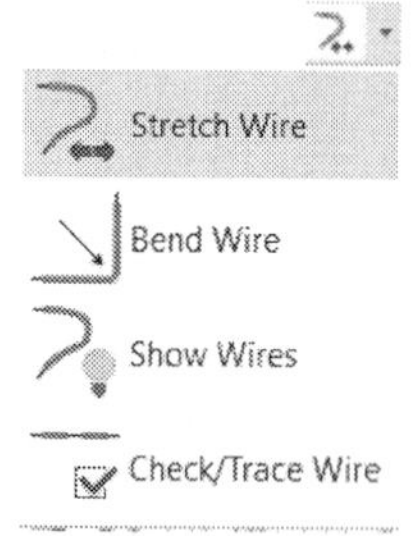


***Figure 3-6*** *The **Modify Wire** drop-down*

Choose the **Stretch Wire** tool
Stretch Wire
Select end of wire to stretch or ESC to exit: *Select the end of the wire to stretch.*
Select end of wire to stretch or ESC to exit: Press ESC or Enter to exit.

Figure 3-7 shows the wire and the component before and after stretching.

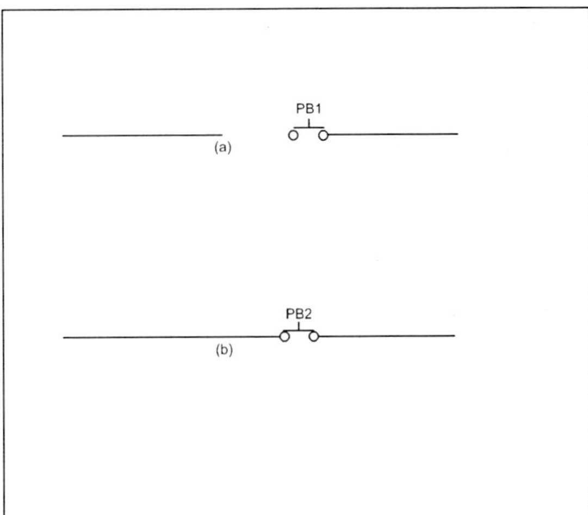


***Figure 3-7*** *(a) Wires before stretching and (b) wires after stretching*

**Note**

*You can use the **Stretch Wire** tool only if a drawing consists of a component or a bounding wire up to which the selected wire will be stretched.*

# WORKING WITH WIRE TYPES

AutoCAD Electrical software package comes with a standard wire type created in the WIRES layer. You can also create new wire types and modify their properties according to your requirement. You can define the new wire type in an existing wire layer or create a new layer. These wire layers control the properties of wire types such as color, line type, line weight, and so on. These wire types manage layers for wires and components automatically. A drawing can have unlimited number of wire types.

The wire type for a new wire can be determined by the following ways:

1. The wire layer of the new wire will be the same if the new wire is drawn from an existing wire. In other words, the current layer and the wire type of the new wire will be ignored.

2. The new wire is drawn on the **WIRES** layer if the drawing does not have any wire layer.

3. When the start point of a wire is in empty space and the endpoint is existing wire, the new wire takes on the wire layer of the ending wire. Therefore, the current layer and the current wire type will be ignored.

4. When the start point of a wire is in the empty space and the endpoint is the connection point of the component or vice versa, then the new wire will be drawn on the current wire layer and wire type.

5. When the start point of the new wire is the existing wire and endpoint is another existing wire, then the new wire will be drawn on the wire layer of the start wire.

AutoCAD Electrical defines the format for a wire layer. The typical way of naming a wire layer is as follows: (%C_%S) is the wire naming format, wherein %C is the color of the wire and %S is the gauge (size) of the wire. For example, BLK_2.00mm², RED_16AWG, and so on. The setting of wire types for new wires using the **Set Wire Type** dialog box will be discussed later in this chapter. In this section, you will learn how to edit existing wire types, create and change wire types, and convert lines into wires.

## Creating Wire Types

| | |
|---|---|
| **Ribbon:** | Schematic > Edit Wires/Wire Numbers > Modify Wire Type drop-down > Create/Edit Wire Type |
| **Toolbar:** | ACE:Main Electrical > Insert Wire > Create/Edit Wire Type or ACE:Wires > Create/Edit Wire Type |
| **Menu:** | Wires > Create/Edit Wire Type |
| **Command:** | AEWIRETYPE |

The **Create/Edit Wire Type** tool is used to create new wire types, edit existing wire types, configure wire types, and manage wire types. To create a wire type, choose the **Create/Edit Wire Type** tool from the **Modify Wire Type** drop-down in the **Edit Wires/Wire Numbers** panel of the **Schematic** tab, as shown in Figure 3-8; the **Create/Edit Wire Type** dialog box will be displayed, as shown in Figure 3-9.

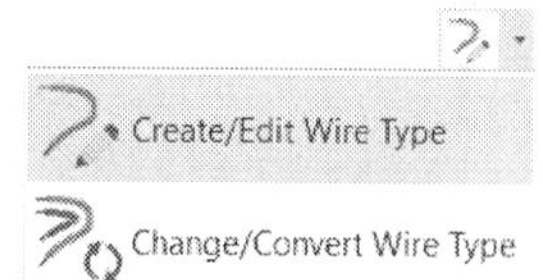


*Figure 3-8 The **Modify Wire Type** drop-down*

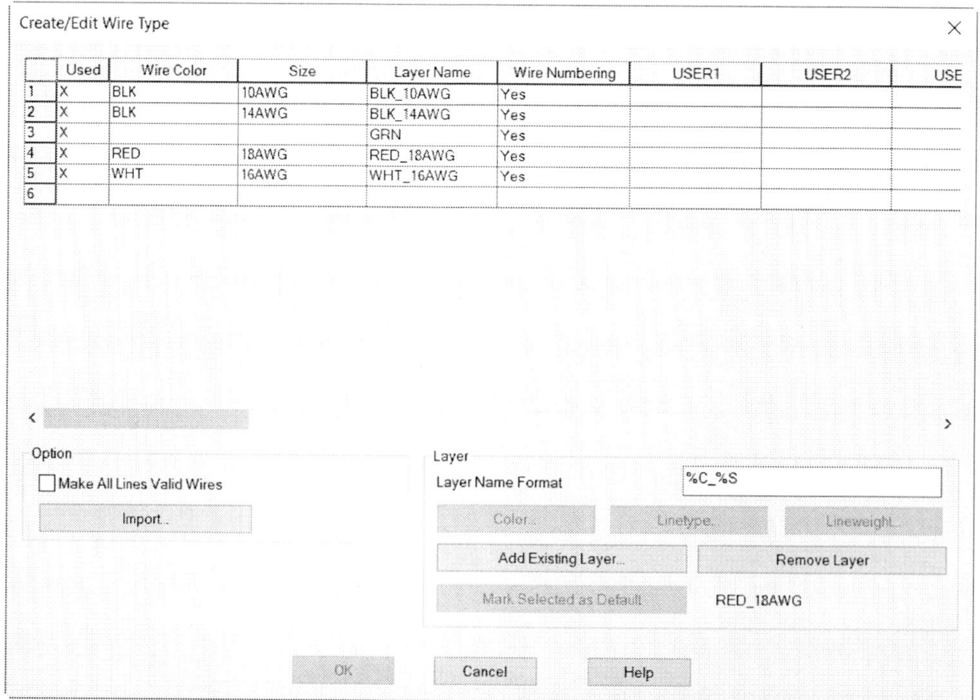


*Figure 3-9 The **Create/Edit Wire Type** dialog box*

This dialog box displays the list of wire types used in the active drawing and the list of layer names. It also displays the properties of wires such as color, size, and user-defined properties of wire in different columns of the grid area. This dialog box can also be used to specify whether the wire numbers should be assigned to the wires of a selected wire layer or not. Different areas and options in this dialog box are discussed next.

## Used Column

The **Used** column displays the currently used wire types in a drawing. If 'X' is displayed in the **Used** column, it indicates that the wire type is used in the current drawing. A blank value in this column indicates that the drawing consists of layer name but currently no wires are drawn on that layer.

## Wire Color Column

The **Wire Color** column displays the wire color of a wire type. You can enter a wire color for the wire type such as BLK for Black, BLU for Blue, GRN for Green, and so on in this column. You can edit and delete the contents of the **Wire Color** column at any time. The replaceable parameter for wire color is %C. If you specify this replaceable parameter in the **Layer Name Format** edit box, the color specified in the **Wire Color** column will automatically be added to the wire layer name.

**Tip**

*The **Create/Edit Wire Type** dialog box is similar to AutoCAD's **Layers Properties Manager** dialog box. You can also create new layers using the AutoCAD **Layers Properties Manager** dialog box which can be set as wire type layers in the **Create/Edit Wire Type** dialog box. But the layers created in the **Create/Edit Wire Type** dialog box will be automatically marked as wire type layers. So it is recommended to create wire layers using the **Create/Edit Wire Type** tool.*

## Size Column

The **Size** column displays the size of a wire type. In this column, you can enter the size of a wire. For example, the value 10 in this column implies that 10 is the gauge/size of the wire. You can edit and delete the contents of the **Size** column at any time. The replaceable parameter for size is %S. If you specify this replaceable parameter in the **Layer Name Format** edit box, the size specified in the **Size** column will automatically be added to the wire layer name.

**Note**

*When you right-click on any row of the **Wire Color** or **Size** column, a shortcut menu will be displayed. In the shortcut menu, various options are activated such as **Copy**, **Cut**, **Paste**, and **Delete Layer** except the **Rename Layer** option. You will also notice that the **Delete Layer** option is not available for the default layer.*

## Layer Name Column

The **Layer Name** column displays the layer name of a wire type. After specifying the wire color in the **Wire Color** column and the size in the **Size** column, the layer name is created and displayed in the **Layer Name** column automatically. The format of the layer name depends on the format specified in the **Layer Name Format** edit box of the **Layer** area. For example, if you enter **BLU** in the **Wire Color** column and **14** in the **Size** column and if the format of the layer name is %C_%S in the **Layer Name Format** edit box, BLU_14 will be displayed in the **Layer Name** column automatically. You can also enter a layer name in the **Layer Name** column manually. When you right-click on any row of the **Layer Name** column, a shortcut menu will be displayed. The options in the shortcut menu are used to copy and paste the layer name but you cannot cut the layer name as the **Cut** option is not activated in the shortcut menu. You can rename a layer name by choosing the **Rename Layer** option from the shortcut menu and also delete the entire layer by choosing the **Delete Layer** option from the shortcut menu, except the default layer. Unlike other columns, you cannot edit and delete the contents of the **Layer Name** column by using the left-click. By default, the name of the **WIRES** layer is displayed for the blank drawing in the **Layer Name** column of the **Create/Edit Wire Type** dialog box.

## Wire Numbering Column

In the **Wire Numbering** column, you can specify whether to assign wire numbers to the wires of a particular wire layer or not. When you click on any row of this column, the cell changes into a drop-down list. Select the **Yes** option from the drop-down list to assign wire numbers to the wires of the selected wire layer. If you select the **No** option from the drop-down list, the wire numbers will not be inserted into the wires of that particular wire layer. If non-fixed wire numbers have already been inserted in the wires of a wire network and you select the **No** option from the drop-down list, the inserted wire numbers will not be removed from wires. To remove wire numbers, you can use the **Delete Wire Numbers** tool, which is discussed later in this chapter.

## USER1-USER5 Columns

The **USER1-USER5** columns display the user-defined properties. The replaceable parameters %1 - %5 are assigned to these columns. Enter the wire type label in these columns, that is, **USER1 - USER5**. The headings of these columns can be changed. The process to do so is discussed in detail later in this chapter.

## USER6-USER20 Columns

The **USER6-USER20** columns display the user-defined properties. The replaceable parameters are not assigned to these columns. The headings of these columns can be changed. The process to do so is discussed next.

**Note**

*1. You can rename the headings of the **USER1-USER20** columns. To do so, right-click on the project name in the **PROJECT MANAGER**; a shortcut menu will be displayed. Next, choose the **Properties** option from the shortcut menu; the **Project Properties** dialog box will be displayed. In this dialog box, choose the **Wire Numbers** tab. In the **Wire Type** area of the **Wire Numbers** tab, choose the **Rename User Columns** button; the **Rename User Columns** dialog box will be displayed. Next, specify a new column name in the **Column Title** column and then choose the **OK** button; the headings of the columns will be changed. You cannot rename headings of the **Color**, **Size**, and **Layer Name** columns but all data corresponding to these columns can be copied, cut, and pasted on another column.*

*2. Multiple rows of the **Create/Edit Wire Type** dialog box can be selected by pressing CTRL or SHIFT. Alternatively, select a row and then drag the cursor across the rows that you want to select.*

*3. You can move the selected wire type anywhere within a grid. To do so, select the wire type row and then place your cursor on the selected row, which is below the left side of the* ***Used*** *column. Next, drag it to the required position.*

## Layer Area

The **Layer** area is used to define the format of layer name, color, linetype, and lineweight. The options in this area are also used to add an existing layer, remove a layer, and set a selected layer as default. The options in this area are discussed next.

### Layer Name Format

The **Layer Name Format** edit box is used to define a layer name. By default, (%C_%S) is displayed in this edit box. If you enter the color name in the **Wire Color** column and then size of the wire in the **Size** column, the layer name will get filled automatically in the **Layer Name** column. %C is the replaceable parameter for the wire color, %S is the replaceable parameter for the wire size, and %1 to %5 are the replaceable parameters for user 1 to user 5. Note that special characters such as <, >, /, \, :, ; and so on cannot be included in the layer name.

### Color

The **Color** button is used to set the color for a wire layer. This button will be available only if you select the layer name from the list displayed in the **Create/Edit Wire Type** dialog box. Choose the **Color** button; the **Select Color** dialog box will be displayed, as shown in Figure 3-10. In this dialog box, select the desired color and then choose the **OK** button; the selected color will be assigned to the selected layer. The number of colors is determined by your graphics card and monitor. Most of the color systems support eight or more colors. If your computer allows it, you can choose a color number between 0 and 255 (256 colors).

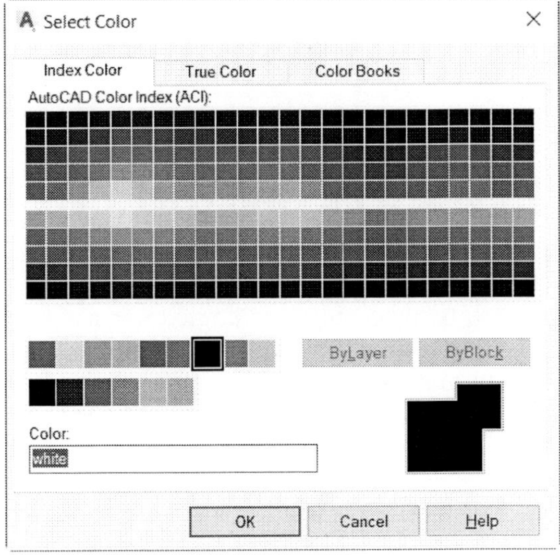


***Figure 3-10*** *The* ***Select Color*** *dialog box*

The first seven standard colors are given next:

| Color number | Color name | Color number | Color name |
|---|---|---|---|
| 1 | Red | 5 | Blue |
| 2 | Yellow | 6 | Magenta |
| 3 | Green | 7 | White |
| 4 | Cyan | | |

## Linetype

The **Linetype** button is used to set the linetype for a wire layer. This button will be available only if you select the layer name from the list displayed in the **Create/Edit Wire Type** dialog box. Choose the **Linetype** button; the **Select Linetype** dialog box will be displayed, as shown in Figure 3-11. This dialog box displays the linetypes that are defined and currently loaded in the drawing file. Select the desired linetype and then choose the **OK** button; the selected linetype will be assigned to the layer selected initially.

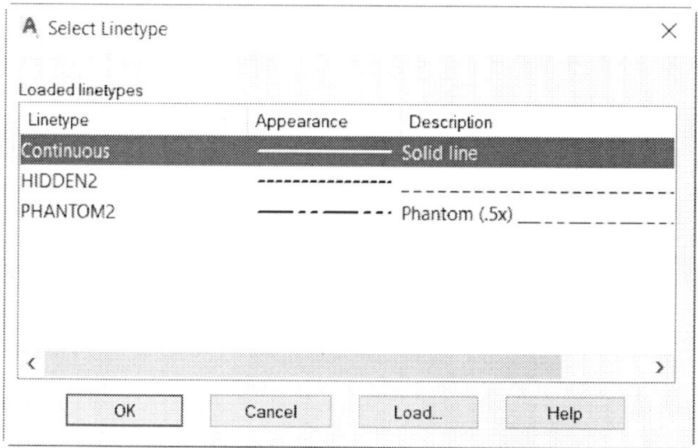


*Figure 3-11 The **Select Linetype** dialog box*

You can also load other linetypes and then assign them to layers. To load linetypes, choose the **Load** button from the **Select Linetype** dialog box; the **Load or Reload Linetypes** dialog box will be displayed, as shown in Figure 3-12. This dialog box displays all linetypes in the *acad.lin* file. In this dialog box, you can select single linetype or a number of linetypes by pressing and holding the SHIFT or CTRL key. If you right-click in the **Available Linetypes** area of the **Load or Reload Linetypes** dialog box, a shortcut menu will be displayed. You can use this shortcut menu to select or deselect all linetypes. Select the required linetype from this dialog box. Next, choose the **OK** button from this dialog box; the selected linetypes will be loaded and displayed in the **Select Linetype** dialog box. Now, select the desired linetype and choose the **OK** button from this dialog box; the linetype will be assigned to the selected wire layer.

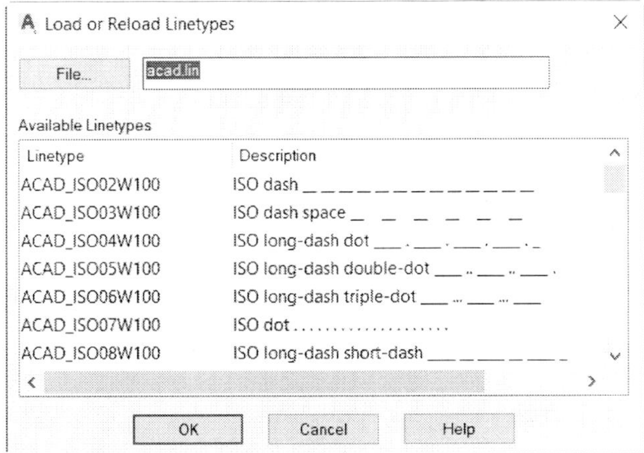


*Figure 3-12 The **Load or Reload Linetypes** dialog box*

**Note**

*By default, linetypes in the acad.lin file are displayed in the **Load or Reload Linetypes** dialog box. You can select linetypes from the acadiso.lin or acade.lin file by choosing the **File** button from this dialog box and then opening the acadiso.lin or acade.lin file from the **Select Linetype File** dialog box.*

*If you want special line types for constructing point-to-point diagrams, you need to load special line types from the acade.lin file from the **Select Linetype File** dialog box.*

### Lineweight

The **Lineweight** button will be activated only if you select a layer name from the list displayed in the **Create/Edit Wire Type** dialog box. The **Lineweight** button is used to give thickness to wires in a layer. This thickness is displayed on the screen if the display of the lineweight is on. If the display is off, you need to choose the **Show/Hide Line weight** button from the status bar.

To assign lineweight to a layer, select the layer and then choose the **Lineweight** button from the **Create/Edit Wire Type** dialog box; the **Lineweight** dialog box will be displayed, as shown in Figure 3-13. Select a lineweight from the **Lineweight** dialog box. Next, choose **OK** to return to the **Create/Edit Wire Type** dialog box. On doing so, the selected lineweight will be assigned to the wire layer that has been selected from the **Create/Edit Wire Type** dialog box.

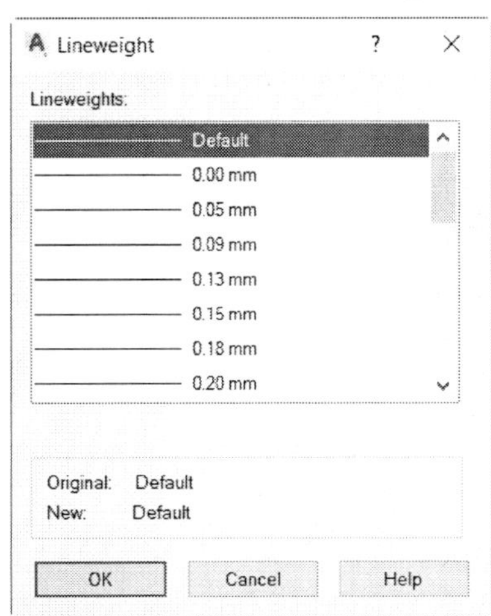


*Figure 3-13 The **Lineweight** dialog box*

### Add Existing Layer

The **Add Existing Layer** button is used to add an existing layer to the wire type selected from the **Create/Edit Wire Type** dialog box. To do so, choose the **Add Existing Layer** button from the **Layer** area; the **Layers for Line "Wires"** dialog box will be displayed, as shown in Figure 3-14.

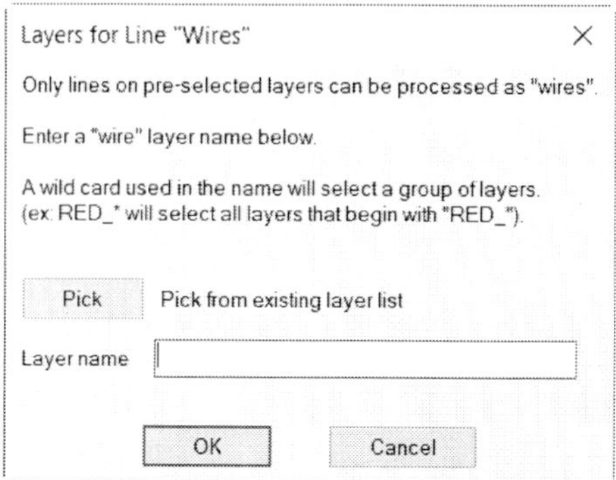


*Figure 3-14 The* ***Layers for Line "Wires"*** *dialog box*

Next, enter the name of the new layer in the **Layer name** edit box. Alternatively, choose the **Pick** button from the **Layers for Line "Wires"** dialog box; the **Select Layer for WIRES** dialog box will be displayed, as shown in Figure 3-15. In this dialog box, select the layer name from the list displayed. Choose the **OK** button twice to return to the **Create/Edit Wire Type** dialog box. The new wire layer will be created and displayed in this dialog box. You will also notice that the name of the new layer will be displayed at the bottom of the list displayed in the **Layer Name** column.

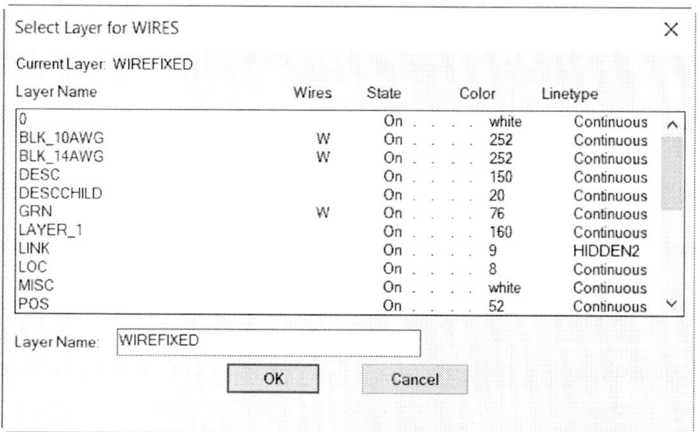


*Figure 3-15 The* ***Select Layer for WIRES*** *dialog box*

## Remove Layer

The **Remove Layer** button will be available only if you select the layer name other than the default layer name from the list displayed in the **Create/Edit Wire Type** dialog box. The **Remove Layer** button is used to remove the selected layer name from the **Create/Edit Wire Type** dialog box.

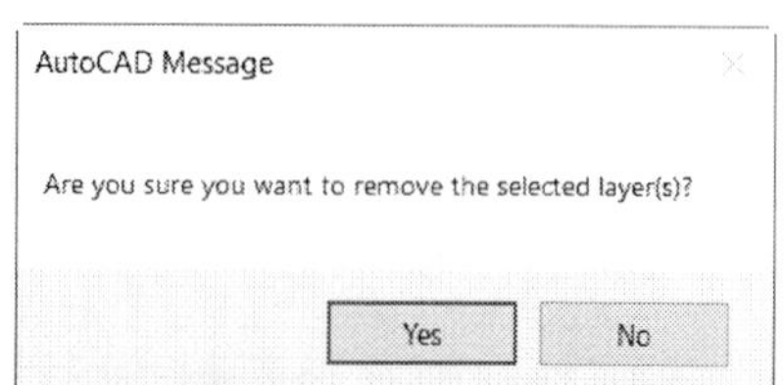


*Figure 3-16 The* ***AutoCAD Message*** *message box*

To do so, choose the **Remove Layer** button; the **AutoCAD Message** message box will be displayed, as shown in Figure 3-16. Choose **Yes** from this message box to remove the selected layer name from the **Layer Name** column. Choose **No** to retain the selected layer name in the **Layer Name** column. Note that the layer removed from the **Create/Edit Wire Type** dialog box will remain in the drawing as an AutoCAD line layer but not as a valid wire layer.

**Note**

*If a drawing consists of multiple layers of one color, then the* ***Remove Layer*** *button will be available only if you select all the layers of that particular color.*

### Mark Selected as Default

This button will be available only if you select the layer name from the list displayed in the **Create/Edit Wire Type** dialog box. The **Mark Selected as Default** button is used to make the selected wire layer as default. On choosing this button, the selected layer will become the default layer for new wire layers and the name of the layer will be displayed adjacent to this button.

## Option Area

The **Option** area is used to change all layers of a drawing to a valid wire layer and to import the wire types from an existing drawing into current drawing. The options in this area are discussed next.

### Make All Lines Valid Wires

The **Make All Lines Valid Wires** check box is used to convert each layer of a drawing into a valid wire layer. To do so, select this check box; you will notice that the grid area and options in the **Layer** area are not available. Also, all layers are removed from the grid area after choosing the **OK** button from the **Create/Edit Wire Type** dialog box. Note that all layers will be converted into wire layers that can be viewed in the **Change/Convert Wire Type** dialog box. The options in this dialog box will be discussed in the next section. By default, this check box is cleared.

### Import

The **Import** button is used to import wire types from an existing drawing into the current drawing. When you choose the **Import** button, the **Wire Type Import - Select Master Drawing** dialog box is displayed. Next, choose the required drawing from where you want to import the wire type and then choose the **Open** button; the **Import Wire Types** dialog box will be displayed. The **Wire Color** and **Size** columns are also available in the **Import Wire Types** dialog box. As a result, users can know the wire color and size of the imported wire types. In this dialog box, select the **Overwrite any Wire Numbering and USERn differences** check box in the **Import options if wire type already exists** area if you want to change the wire number setting and all USER values for the existing wire type to match the imported wire type. Then, select the **Update any layer color and linetype differences** check box if the color and linetype settings for the existing wire layer are to be changed to match the imported wire layer. Next, choose the **OK** button in this dialog box; the selected wire types with the defined settings will be imported and displayed in the **Create/Edit Wire Type** dialog box.

Select a wire type from the grid area of the **Create/Edit Wire Type** dialog box; the **OK** button will be activated. Next, choose the **OK** button; the selected wire type will be created and the name of the wire layer and properties will be saved in the drawing file.

**Note**

*You cannot leave the **Layer Name** column blank. The name of the layer created should be unique and it should not contain special characters such as / \ " : ; ? * | , = ' > <.*

*Whenever you enter any wire type data in the last row of the grid area in the **Create/Edit Wire Type** dialog box and then click anywhere in the grid area, a row is automatically added to the grid area.*

## Changing and Converting Wire Types

| | |
|---|---|
| **Ribbon:** | Schematic > Edit Wires/Wire Numbers > Modify Wire Type drop-down > Change/Convert Wire Type |
| **Toolbar:** | ACE:Main Electrical > Insert Wire > Change/Convert Wire Type or ACE:Wires > Change/Convert Wire Type |
| **Menu:** | Wires > Change/Convert Wire Types |
| **Command:** | AECONVERTWIRETYPE |

The **Change/Convert Wire Type** tool is used to change the wire type of existing wires. This tool is also used to convert lines into wires. To change the wire type of existing wires, choose the **Change/Convert Wire Type** tool from the **Modify Wire Type** drop-down in the **Edit Wires/Wire Numbers** panel of the **Schematic** tab; the **Change/Convert Wire Type** dialog box will be displayed, as shown in Figure 3-17. This dialog box displays all valid wire type layers present in a drawing. Most of the options in this dialog box are same as those in the **Create/Edit Wire Type** dialog box. The remaining options are discussed next.

**Note**

*You cannot edit the **Used, Wire Color, Size, Layer Name, Wire Numbering**, and **USER1-USER20** columns.*

### Pick <

The **Pick <** button is used to select a wire or a line from an active drawing. To select a wire, choose the **Pick <** button; the cursor will change into a selection box. Also, you will be prompted to select a wire or a line from the drawing area. If you select a wire, the **Change/Convert Wire Type** dialog box will be displayed again and you will notice that the selected wire type layer is displayed in blue color in the **Change/Convert Wire Type** dialog box. If you select a line from the drawing area, the **AutoCAD Message** message box will be displayed, as shown in Figure 3-18, prompting you to create a valid wire type layer in the **Create/Edit Wire Type** dialog box. Choose the **OK** button from the **AutoCAD Message** message box; the **Change/Convert Wire Type** dialog box will be displayed again.

### Change/Convert Area

The **Change/Convert** area will be available only if you select a wire type from the list displayed or if you choose the **Pick <** button. This area consists of the following check boxes:

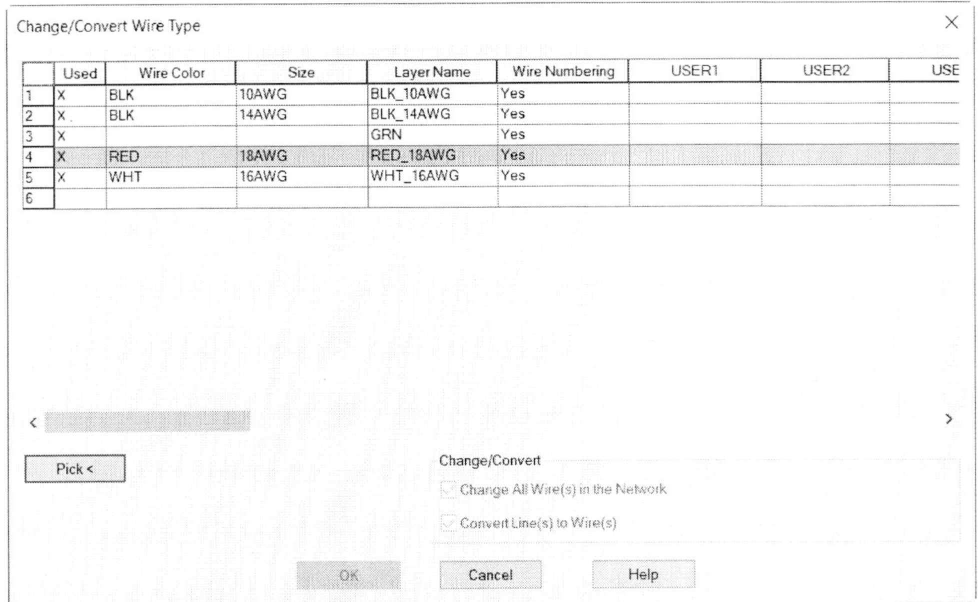


*Figure 3-17 The **Change/Convert Wire Type** dialog box*

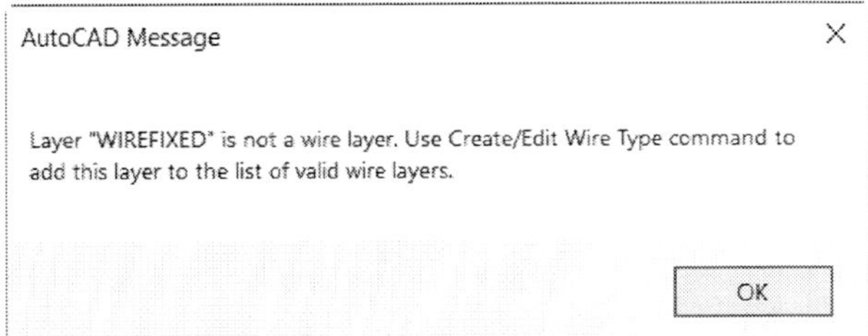


*Figure 3-18 The **AutoCAD Message** message box*

### Change All Wire(s) in the Network

The **Change All Wire(s) in the Network** check box is used to change all wires in the wire network into the selected wire type. By default, this check box is selected. If you clear this check box, only the single wire that you select will be changed to the selected wire type.

### Convert Line(s) to Wire(s)

The **Convert Line(s) to Wire(s)** check box is used to convert the selected line(s) to wire(s). It implies that the layer property of a line will get converted to the selected wire type layer. This check box is selected by default. If you clear this check box, the selected lines will not be converted into wires.

Select a wire type from the list displayed in the **Change/Convert Wire Type** dialog box; the **OK** button will become available. Next, choose the **OK** button; the cursor will change to the selection box and you will be prompted to select objects. Select wires and lines (if any) and press ENTER; the selected wires and lines (if found) will automatically be changed or converted to the wire type that you have selected from the **Change/Convert Wire Type** dialog box. Note that the row of the default wire type is highlighted in gray and the row of the selected wire type is highlighted in blue.

**Note**

*1. You can change the wire type by entering 'T' at the Command prompt during wire insertion.*

*2. You can also change/convert the wire type by right-clicking on the existing wire in the drawing and then choosing the **Change/Convert Wire Type** option from the marking menu.*

## Setting Wire Types

You can change the wire type while inserting wire into a drawing. To do so, choose the **Wire** tool from the **Insert Wires/Wire Numbers** panel of the **Schematic** tab; you will be prompted to specify the wire start. Enter **T** at the Command prompt and press ENTER; the **Set Wire Type** dialog box will be displayed, as shown in Figure 3-19. The options in this dialog box which were not discussed earlier are discussed next.

Set Wire Type

| | Used | Wire Color | Size | Layer Name | Wire Numbering | USER1 | USER2 | USE |
|---|---|---|---|---|---|---|---|---|
| 1 | X | BLK | 10AWG | BLK_10AWG | Yes | | | |
| 2 | X | BLK | 14AWG | BLK_14AWG | Yes | | | |
| 3 | X | | | GRN | Yes | | | |
| 4 | X | RED | 18AWG | RED_18AWG | Yes | | | |
| 5 | X | WHT | 16AWG | WHT_16AWG | Yes | | | |
| 6 | | | | | | | | |

OK Cancel Help

***Figure 3-19** The **Set Wire Type** dialog box*

### Used Column

The **Used** column displays the layers or the wire types that are already used in a drawing. If the **Used** column is blank, it indicates that the drawing consists of the layer name but currently no wires are found on that layer. However, if 'X' is displayed in the **Used** column, it indicates that the particular wire type is currently used in the drawing.

### USER1-USER20 Columns

The **USER1 -USER20** columns are user-defined columns. These user-defined columns are project-specific and you can rename the headings of these columns any time as discussed earlier. By default, the WIRES layer name is displayed and selected in the **Set Wire Type** dialog box. Note that the row of the default wire type will be highlighted in gray color. Select the wire type; the **OK** button will be activated. Choose the **OK** button; the selected wire type will become the current wire type and the wires that you insert will be created with the current wire type unless and until the wire type has been changed again.

**Note**

*The **Wire Color**, **Size**, and **Layer Name** columns of the **Set Wire Type** dialog box cannot be renamed.*

# WORKING WITH WIRE NUMBERS

Wire number is an attribute that is attached to an invisible block in a drawing. This invisible block is inserted with a wire and the wire number attribute is displayed near the wire. The location of the wire number attribute depends on the location style that you have selected. The distance of the wire number from the wire is determined by the attribute spacing within the wire number. Also, AutoCAD Electrical assigns different wire number types to wires depending on the layer of the wire. So, you can assign different colors to each of these layers of wire numbers.

A wire number can be placed above, left, below, or right with respect to wires or in-line with the wire. One wire number is assigned for each wire network. In this section, you will learn about different types of wire numbers, how to insert wire numbers in the drawing, and various editing tools of wire numbers.

## Types of Wire Number

There are four types of wire numbers. These are discussed next.

1. Normal
2. Fixed
3. Extra
4. Terminal/signal

In the normal type of wire number, the wire numbers are updated automatically when you use the **Wire Numbers** tool. This is the default type for inserting wire numbers.

In the fixed type of wire number, the wire numbers do not update automatically on using the **Wire Numbers** tool. These wire numbers are fixed, however, the wire numbers of this type can be edited manually.

In the extra type of wire numbers, the extra copies of normal or fixed wire number are assigned to a given wire network. Note that either a normal or a fixed wire number can be assigned to a single wire network. It is not possible to assign both wire numbers to a single wire network at the same time. Also, the wire network may contain many extra copies of the wire number that can be inserted at different locations in the wire network.

In the terminal/signal type of wire numbers, the wire numbers are assigned to terminals and signal arrows.

## Inserting Wire Numbers

| | |
|---|---|
| **Ribbon:** | Schematic > Insert Wires/Wire Numbers > Insert Wire Numbers drop-down > Wire Numbers |
| **Toolbar:** | ACE:Main Electrical 2 > Insert Wire Numbers > Insert Wire Numbers or ACE:Insert Wire Numbers > Insert Wire Numbers |
| **Menu:** | Wires > Insert Wire Numbers |
| **Command:** | AEWIRENO |

The **Wire Numbers** tool is used to assign wire numbers to wires in a drawing. To assign wire numbers to wires, choose the **Wire Numbers** tool from the **Insert Wire numbers** drop-down in the **Insert Wires/Wire Numbers** panel of the **Schematic** tab, as shown in Figure 3-20; the **Wire Tagging** dialog box will be displayed, refer to Figure 3-21. Using this dialog box, you can assign wire numbers to individual wires, wires in a single drawing, or wires of a whole project. Different areas and options in this dialog box are discussed next.

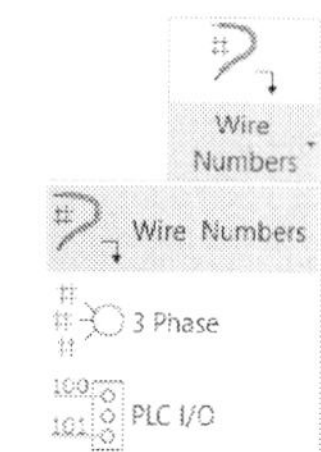


***Figure 3-20** The **Insert Wire numbers** drop-down*

### To do Area

In the **To do** area, you can assign wire numbers to the wires that do not have wire number or assign wire numbers to all wires. The options in this area are discussed next.

#### Tag new/un-numbered only

Select the **Tag new/un-numbered only** radio button to assign a wire number to a new wire or a wire having no wire number.

#### Tag/retag all

The **Tag/retag all** radio button is used to assign the wire number to all wires, including the wires that have wire number. This radio button is selected by default.

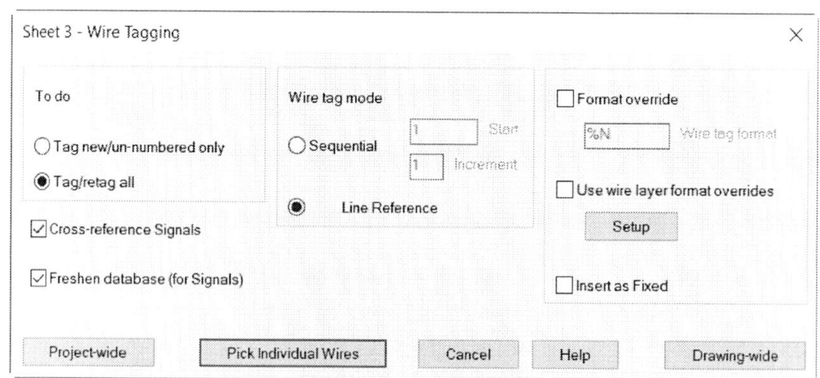


***Figure 3-21** The **Wire Tagging** dialog box*

**Note**

*If a drawing has sheet number specified to it and if you choose the **Wire Numbers** tool, the name of the **Wire Tagging** dialog box will become **Sheet: XX - Wire Taggingr** dialog box where XX stands for the sheet number.*

## Cross-reference Signals

The **Cross-reference Signals** check box is used to update the cross-reference text of the wire signal source and destination symbols. This check box is selected by default.

## Freshen database (for Signals)

The **Freshen database (for Signals)** check box is used to update the database for the wire signal source and destination symbols. This check box is selected by default.

## Wire tag mode Area

The **Wire tag mode** area is used to define the sequential and line reference settings of a drawing. The **Sequential** radio button is used to assign wire numbers to wires sequentially. To do so, select the **Sequential** radio button from this area; the **Start** edit box will be activated. Enter the starting value for the wire number in the **Start** edit box. By default, 1 is displayed in the **Start** and **Increment** edit boxes. However, you can change the default values displayed in the **Start** and **Increment** edit boxes in the **Wire Numbers** tab of the **Drawing Properties** or **Project Properties** dialog box. When you change the value in these edit boxes, the default value automatically gets changed in the **Start** and **Increment** edit boxes in the **Wire tag mode** area of the **Wire Tagging** dialog box.

The **Line Reference** radio button is used to assign wire numbers to the wires based on the reference number of the ladder. By default, this radio button is selected.

## Format override

In AutoCAD Electrical, the replaceable parameters that are used to define a default wire number tag format are as follows:

1. %S -Drawing's sheet number
2. %D -Drawing number
3. %N -Sequential or reference-based number applied to the component
4. %X -Suffix character position for the reference-based tagging (not present = end of tag)
5. %P -IEC-style project code (default for drawing)
6. %I -IEC-style "installation" code (default for drawing)
7. %L -IEC-style "location" code (default for drawing)

The **Format override** check box is used to override the default format of the wire number defined in the **Drawing Properties** dialog box. To do so, select the **Format override** check box; the **Wire tag format** edit box will become available. Enter the wire tag format for the wire numbers in this edit box. By default, the **Format override** check box is cleared and %N is displayed in the **Wire tag format** edit box. You can change the default tag format using the **Drawing Properties** dialog box.

## Use wire layer format overrides

The **Use wire layer format overrides** check box is used to override the default wire number format for the wire layers that are assigned in the **Layers** area of the **Drawing Format** tab in the **Drawing Properties** dialog box. Select the **Use wire layer format overrides** check box to override the default wire number format. To define the format for a wire layer, choose the **Setup** button; the **Assign Wire Numbering Formats by Wire Layer** dialog box will be displayed, as shown in Figure 3-22. This dialog box displays the wire layer, format for the wire number, starting wire sequence (%N), and suffix list for the wire number. Using this dialog box, you can specify new format for wire numbers.

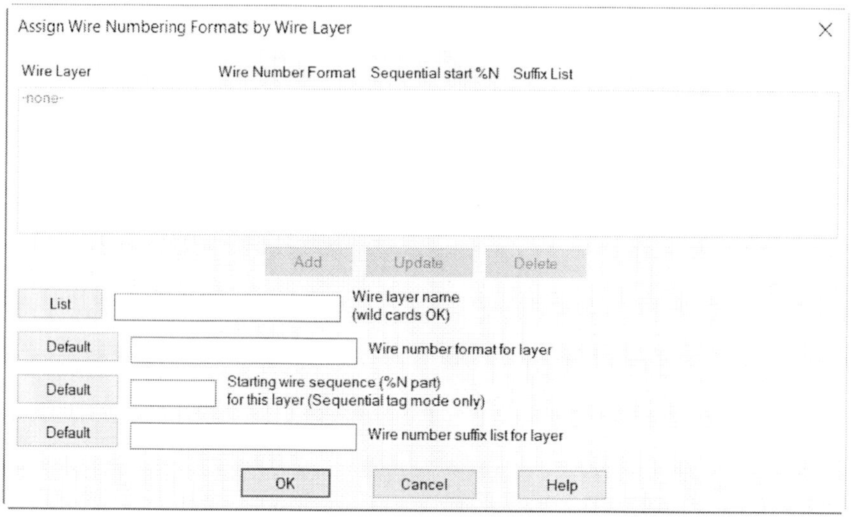

*Figure 3-22 The **Assign Wire Numbering Formats by Wire Layer** dialog box*

Enter the name of the layer in the **Wire layer name** edit box. Alternatively, choose the **List** button; the **Select Wire Layer** dialog box will be displayed, as shown in Figure 3-23. This dialog box displays the predefined wire layers. Select the wire layer from the list displayed and choose **OK**; the selected layer name of the wire will be displayed in the **Wire layer name** edit box of the **Assign Wire Numbering Formats by Wire Layer** dialog box. Note that the name of wire layer can consist of wild cards.

Specify the wire number format for the wire layer in the **Wire number format for layer** edit box. Alternatively, choose the **Default** button located on the left of this edit box; the default value of the wire number format, %N, will be displayed in the **Wire number format for layer** edit box.

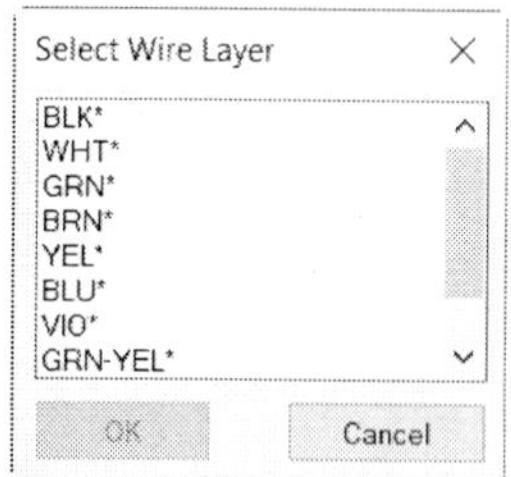


*Figure 3-23 The **Select Wire Layer** dialog box*

Specify the starting wire number for the wire layer in the **Starting wire sequence (%N part)** edit box. Alternatively, choose the **Default** button, the default value 1 will be displayed in this edit box. Note that this edit box can be used only if you have selected the **sequential** radio button from the **Wire tag mode** area of the **Wire Tagging** dialog box.

Specify a unique wire number suffix in the **Wire number suffix list for layer** edit box. Alternatively, choose the **Default** button, which is located on the left of this edit box to specify the default value of the wire numbering in the **Wire number suffix list for layer** edit box.

After specifying values in any of the edit boxes discussed above, the **Add** button will be activated. This button is used to add a new format for the specified wire layer. To do so, choose the **Add** button; the wire layer format will be added to the list displayed in the **Assign Wire Numbering Formats by Wire Layer** dialog box.

The **Update** button is used to update the changes made in the wire layer format. This button will be activated only after you add the wire layer format. Select the wire layer format from the list displayed in the **Assign Wire Numbering Formats by Wire Layer** dialog box and then choose the **Update** button; the selected wire layer format will get updated.

The **Delete** button will be available only after you select the wire layer format from the list displayed. To delete a wire layer format, choose the **Delete** button; the selected wire layer format will be deleted from the list.

Now, choose the **OK** button from the **Assign Wire Numbering Formats by Wire Layer** dialog box to save the changes made in this dialog box and to return to the **Wire Tagging** dialog box.

## Insert as Fixed

If you select the **Insert as Fixed** check box, all wire numbers inserted in the drawing will be fixed. This implies that wire numbers will not be updated if wire numbers are retagged later.

## Project-wide

The **Project-wide** button is used to assign or update wire numbers to the wires of the entire project. To do so, choose the **Project-wide** button from the **Wire Tagging** dialog box; the **Wire Tagging (Project-wide)** dialog box will be displayed, as shown in Figure 3-24. The options in this dialog box are the same as that of the **Wire Tagging** dialog box discussed earlier.

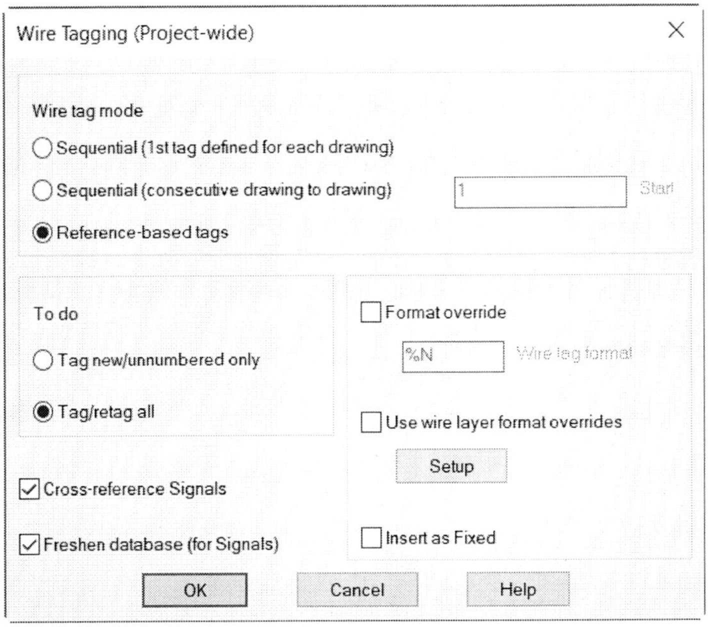

*Figure 3-24 The **Wire Tagging (Project-wide)** dialog box*

### Wire tag mode Area

In the **Wire tag mode** area, you can define the sequential or line reference settings for a drawing. The radio buttons in this area are discussed next.

If you select the **Sequential (1st tag defined for each drawing)** radio button, the wire number will start with the number specified in the **Wire Number Format** area of the **Wire Numbers** tab in the **Drawing Properties** dialog box.

If you select the **Sequential (consecutive drawing to drawing)** radio button, the edit box on the right of this radio button will become available. In this edit box, you can specify the starting number for the wire number. In the consecutive drawings, the wire number will increment automatically. Note that the settings that you have defined for wire numbers in the **Drawing Properties** dialog box will be ignored.

The **Reference-based tags** radio button is used to assign wire numbers to wires based on the reference number of the ladder. By default, this radio button is selected.

Specify the required options in the **Wire Tagging (Project-wide)** dialog box and choose the **OK** button; the **Select Drawings to Process** dialog box will be displayed. Select the drawings that you want to process and choose the **Process** button from the **Select Drawings to Process** dialog box; the selected drawings in the list will be moved from the top to the bottom of this dialog box. Next, choose the **OK** button from the **Select Drawings to Process** dialog box; the **QSAVE** message box will be displayed. Choose the **OK** button from the **QSAVE** message box; the active drawing will be saved and the selected drawings will get updated accordingly. If you choose the **No** button from the **QSAVE** message box, the selected drawings will get updated without saving the active drawing. If you choose the **Always QSAVE** button from the **QSAVE** message box, AutoCAD Electrical will save the active drawing for that session without displaying the **QSAVE** message box again. Choose the **Cancel** button in the **QSAVE** message box to exit the command.

**Note**

*After choosing the **OK** button in the **Select Drawings to Process** dialog box, the **QSAVE** message box will be displayed only if you have made changes in the active drawing and have not saved them.*

## Pick Individual Wires

The **Pick Individual Wires** button is used to assign or update wire numbers to the selected wires of the active drawing. To do so, choose the **Pick Individual Wires** button from the **Wire Tagging** dialog box; you will be prompted to select objects. Select individual wires from the drawing and press ENTER; the wire number will get assigned to the selected wires of the drawing.

## Drawing-wide

The **Drawing-wide** button is used to assign or update wire numbers in the active drawing. To do so, choose the **Drawing-wide** button from the **Wire Tagging** dialog box; the wire numbers will be assigned or updated in the active drawing.

## Copying Wire Numbers

| | |
|---|---|
| **Ribbon:** | Schematic > Edit Wires/Wire Numbers > Copy Wire Number drop-down> Copy Wire Number |
| **Toolbar:** | ACE:Main Electrical 2 > Copy Wire Number or ACE:Copy Wire Number > Copy Wire Number |
| **Menu:** | Wires > Copy Wire Number |
| **Command:** | AECOPYWIRENO |

The **Copy Wire Number** tool is used to copy and insert the already inserted wire number into the wire. You can use this tool to place an extra copy of the wire number anywhere in a wire network. To do so, choose the **Copy Wire Number** tool from the **Copy Wire Number** drop-down in the **Edit Wires/Wire Numbers** panel of the **Schematic** tab, as shown in Figure 3-25; the cursor will change into a selection box on the screen and you will be prompted to select wire for the extra wire number copy. Select the wire whose wire number you want to copy; the copied wire number will be displayed at the selected location. Next, press ENTER or ESC to exit the command.

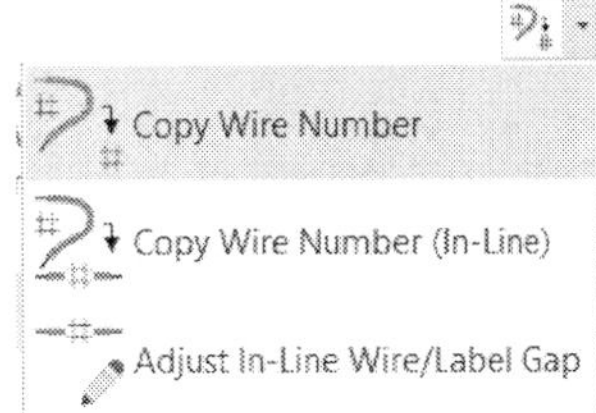


*Figure 3-25 The **Copy Wire Number** drop-down*

Note that the copied wire numbers follow the main wire number attribute of the network. If you update or modify the wire number in the network, the copies of the wire number will also get updated.

**Note**

*The copied wire numbers are created on their own layer. The layer of the copied wire numbers is WIRECOPY. You can define the layer for the wire number in the **Define Layers** dialog box, which is discussed in the later chapters. To invoke the **Define Layers** dialog box, choose the **Drawing Format** tab in the **Drawing Properties** dialog box. Next, choose the **Define** button from the **Layers** area of the **Drawing Properties** dialog box; the **Define Layers** dialog box will be displayed.*

## Positioning Wire Numbers In-line with a Wire

| | |
|---|---|
| **Ribbon:** | Schematic > Edit Wires/Wire Numbers > Copy Wire Number drop-down> Copy Wire Number (In-Line) |
| **Toolbar:** | ACE:Main Electrical 2 > Copy Wire Number > Copy Wire Number (In-Line) or ACE:Copy Wire Number > Copy Wire Number (In-Line) |
| **Menu:** | Wires > Copy Wire Number (In-Line) |
| **Command:** | AECOPYWIRENOIL |

The **Copy Wire Number (In-Line)** tool is used to place wire number in-line with a wire. To do so, choose the **Copy Wire Number (In-Line)** tool from the **Copy Wire Number** drop-down in the **Edit Wires/Wire Numbers** panel of the **Schematic** tab; you will be prompted to specify the insertion point for the in-line wire number. Next, specify the insertion point where you want to locate the wire number; the **Edit Wire Numbers/Attributes** dialog box will be displayed.

However, if the wire number has already been assigned to the wire and you choose the **Copy Wire Number (In-Line)** tool, the wire number will be inserted in-line directly with the wire, without displaying the **Insert wire number** dialog box. Enter the wire number in the **Wire number** edit box of this dialog box and choose the **OK** button; the wire number will get automatically inserted in-line with the wire. The command will continue until you press ESC.

**Note**

*You can use the **Adjust In-Line Wire/Label Gap** tool from the **Copy Wire Number** drop-down to adjust the gap between the wire and the wire number text.*

## Deleting Wire Numbers

| | |
|---|---|
| **Ribbon:** | Schematic > Edit Wires/Wire Numbers > Delete Wire Numbers |
| **Toolbar:** | ACE:Main Electrical 2 > Delete Wire Numbers |
| **Menu:** | Wires > Delete Wire Numbers |
| **Command:** | AEERASEWIRENUM |

The **Delete Wire Numbers** tool is used to delete wire number. Using this tool, you can delete the main wire number of the wire network as well as delete the copies of the wire number. To delete the wire number, choose the **Delete Wire Numbers** tool from the **Edit Wires/Wire Numbers** panel of the **Schematic** tab; the cursor will change into a selection box and you will be prompted to select objects. Select the wire numbers to be deleted and press ENTER; the selected wire numbers will be deleted automatically.

**Note**

*A wire network can have a wire number as well as the copies of the wire number. If you want to delete the main wire number along with all its copies, choose the **Delete Wire Numbers** tool from the **Edit Wires/Wire Numbers** panel of the **Schematic** tab. Then, select the wire network's main wire number; the main wire number and all copied wire numbers will be deleted. If you need to delete only a copy of the wire number, then choose the **Delete Wire Numbers** tool from the **Edit Wires/Wire Numbers** panel of the **Schematic** tab and select the copy that you need to delete; the selected copy of the wire number will be deleted, keeping the other wire numbers intact.*

**Tip**

*If you want to delete the wire numbers of the entire project or the active drawing, choose the **Utilities** tool from the **Project Tools** panel of the **Project** tab or choose **Projects > Project-Wide Utilities** from the menu bar; the **Project-Wide Utilities** dialog box will be displayed. Next, select the **Remove all wire numbers** radio button from the **Wire Numbers** area and choose the **OK** button; the **Batch Process Drawings** dialog box will be displayed. Specify whether you want to delete the wire numbers of the entire project or of the active drawing in the **Process** area of the **Batch Process Drawings** dialog box. By default, the **Project** radio button is selected. Choose the **OK** button; the **Select Drawings to Process** dialog box will be displayed. Select the drawings that you need to process and choose the **Process** button from this dialog box. Next, choose the **OK** button; the wire numbers of the specified drawings will be deleted.*

## Editing Wire Numbers

| | |
|---|---|
| **Ribbon:** | Schematic > Edit Wires/Wire Numbers > Edit Wire Number drop-down > Edit Wire Number |
| **Toolbar:** | ACE:Main Electrical 2 > Edit Wire Number or ACE:Edit Wire Numbers > Edit Wire Number |
| **Menu:** | Wires > Edit Wire Number |
| **Command:** | AEEDITWIRENO |

The **Edit Wire Number** tool is used to edit an existing wire number and assign a new wire number to the wires that do not have wire numbers. To edit an existing wire number, choose the **Edit Wire Number** tool from the **Edit Wire Number** drop-down in the **Edit Wires/Wire Numbers** panel of the **Schematic** tab, as shown in Figure 3-26; the cursor will change into a selection box and you will be prompted to select the wire or the component. Select the wire number or the wire; the **Edit Wire Number/Attributes** dialog box will be displayed, as shown in Figure 3-27. Using the options in this dialog box, you can modify, fix, and unfix the wire number and add/edit attributes in it. The options in this dialog box are discussed next.

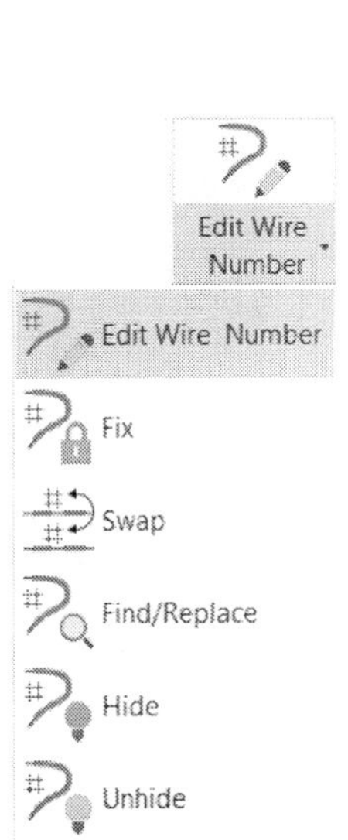


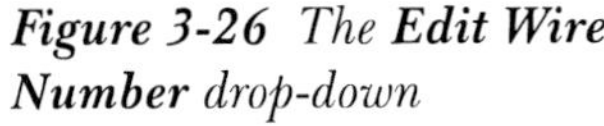

*Figure 3-26 The* ***Edit Wire Number*** *drop-down*

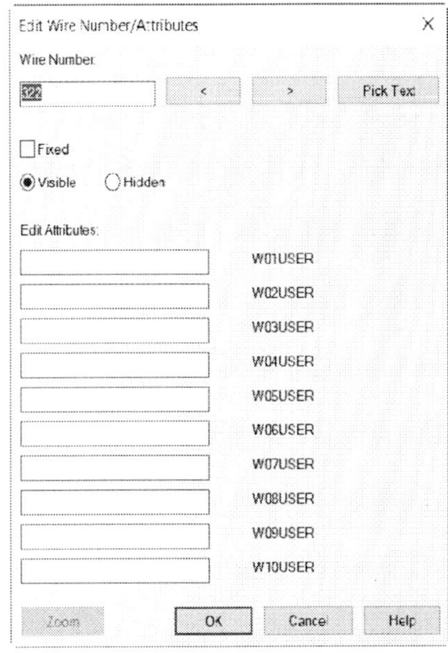


*Figure 3-27 The* ***Edit Wire Number/Attributes*** *dialog box*

You can specify a new value for the wire number in the **Wire Number** edit box. Alternatively, you can choose the **Pick Text** button to select the existing text from the drawing. You can increase or decrease the specified wire number value by choosing the **<** or **>** button. By default, the wire number of the selected wire is displayed in the **Wire Number** edit box.

In the **Wire Number** edit box, if you enter the wire number that is already present in the drawing and then choose the **OK** button, the **Duplicate Wire Number** dialog box will be displayed, as shown in Figure 3-28. In this dialog box, you can specify either a new wire number for the wire or use the duplicated wire number. You can select the **Do not display this real time alert for**

**this AutoCAD Electrical session** check box to change the wire number even if it is duplicated without displaying the **Duplicate Wire Number** dialog box. Alternatively, you can define the settings in the **Project Properties** dialog box, so that if you insert the duplicated wire numbers in the drawing, the **Duplicate Wire Number** dialog box will not be displayed. To define settings in the **Project Properties** dialog box, right-click on the project name and choose the **Properties** option from the shortcut menu; the **Project Properties** dialog box will be displayed. Clear the **Real time error checking** check box in the **Project Settings** tab and choose the **OK** button; the duplicated wire numbers will be displayed in the drawing without displaying the **Duplicate Wire Number** dialog box for that AutoCAD Electrical session.

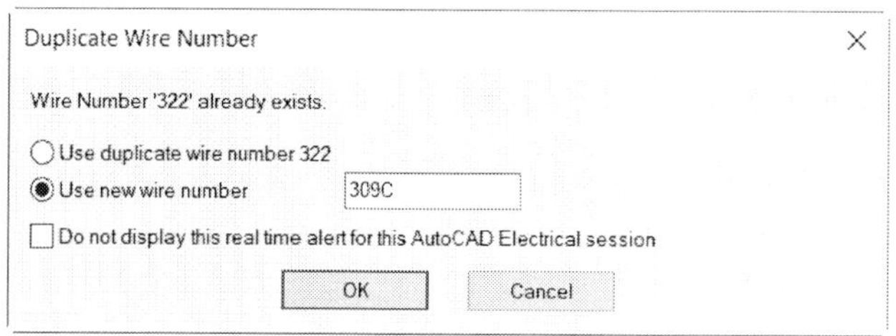


*Figure 3-28 The **Duplicate Wire Number** dialog box*

The **Fixed** check box is used to fix wire number, so that the wire number does not get updated when you use the **Insert Wire Numbers** tool to update wire numbers.

The **Visible** radio button is selected by default and is used to display the wire numbers on a drawing.

Select the **Hidden** radio button to hide the wire number on the drawing. The hidden wire numbers will be included in the wire reports, which will be discussed in the later chapters.

The **Zoom** button will be available only if wires or wire numbers travel off the screen. This button is used to restore the previous screen view.

Specify the required information in the **Edit Wire Number/Attributes** dialog box and choose the **OK** button; the selected wire number will be modified accordingly and you will be prompted to select another wire number. Select the wire number and modify them as per your requirement or press ENTER to exit the command.

If a wire number doesn't exist on the selected wire and you choose the **Edit Wire Number** tool from the **Edit Wires/Wire Numbers** panel of the **Schematic** tab, you will be prompted to select the wire. Select the wire that does not have the wire number; the **Edit Wire Number/Attributes** dialog box will be displayed. Specify the wire number in the **Wire Number** edit box and choose the **OK** button; the wire number will be assigned to the selected wire.

## Fixing Wire Numbers

| | |
|---|---|
| **Ribbon:** | Schematic > Edit Wires/Wire Numbers > Edit Wire Number drop-down > Fix |
| **Toolbar:** | ACE:Main Electrical 2 > Edit Wire Number > Fix Wire Numbers or ACE:Edit Wire Numbers > Fix Wire Numbers |
| **Menu:** | Wires > Wire Numbers Miscellaneous > Fix Wire Numbers |
| **Command:** | AEFIXWIRENO |

The **Fix** tool is used to lock wire numbers in a drawing to their current values. To do so, choose the **Fix** tool from the **Edit wire Number** drop-down in the **Edit Wires/Wire Numbers** panel of the **Schematic** tab; the cursor will change into a selection box and you will be prompted to select objects. Select the wire numbers that you want to lock and press ENTER; the wire numbers will be fixed and moved to the WIREFIXED layer automatically. Note that if you update wire numbers, the fixed wire numbers will not be updated.

> **Tip**
> *If you want to fix or unfix the wire numbers of the entire project or of the active drawing, choose the* ***Project-Wide Utilities*** *tool from the* ***ACE:Main Electrical 2*** *toolbar or choose* ***Projects > Project-Wide Utilities*** *from the menu bar; the* ***Project-Wide Utilities*** *dialog box will be displayed. Next, select the* ***Set all wire numbers to fixed*** *radio button from the* ***Wire Numbers*** *area to fix wire numbers and select the* ***Set all wire numbers to normal*** *radio button to unfix wire numbers. The fixed wire numbers will be moved to the WIREFIXED layer and the unfixed wire numbers will be moved to the WIRENO layer.*

## Hiding Wire Numbers

| | |
|---|---|
| **Ribbon:** | Schematic > Edit Wires/Wire Numbers > Edit Wire Number drop-down> Hide |
| **Toolbar:** | ACE:Main Electrical 2 > Edit Wire Number > Hide Wire Numbers or ACE:Edit Wire Numbers > Hide Wire Numbers |
| **Menu:** | Wires > Wire Numbers Miscellaneous >Hide Wire Numbers |
| **Command:** | AEHIDEWIRENO |

The **Hide** tool is used to hide a selected wire number. Also, this tool is used to change the attribute layer of the selected wire number to the WIRENO_HIDE layer (frozen layer). To hide the wire number, choose the **Hide** tool from the **Edit wire Number** drop-down in the **Edit Wires/Wire Numbers** panel of the **Schematic** tab; the cursor will change to a selection box on the screen and you will be prompted to select the wire number. Select the wire number; the wire number will be automatically moved to a special hidden layer and will become invisible. Next, press ENTER to exit the command. Note that the name of the new hidden layer is similar to that of the wire number layer name with the difference that "*_HIDE*" suffix will be added to the name of the new hidden layer. For example, if the name of the wire number text layer is *WIRENO,* the name of the hide layer will be "*WIRENO_HIDE*".

> **Tip**
> *You can also hide multiple wire numbers at a time. To do so, enter* ***W*** *at the Command prompt after choosing the* ***Hide*** *tool; you will be prompted to select wire number to hide. Select the wire number using the crossing window and then press ENTER; the wire numbers will be hidden.*

## Unhiding Wire Numbers

| | |
|---|---|
| **Ribbon:** | Schematic > Edit Wires/Wire Numbers > Edit Wire Number drop-down > Unhide |
| **Toolbar:** | ACE:Main Electrical 2 > Edit Wire Number > Unhide Wire Numbers or ACE:Edit Wire Numbers > Unhide Wire Numbers |
| **Menu:** | Wires > Wire Numbers Miscellaneous > Unhide Wire Numbers |
| **Command:** | AESHOWWIRENO |

The **Unhide** tool is used to make the hidden wire numbers visible. To do so, choose the **Unhide** tool from the **Edit Wire Number** drop-down in the **Edit Wires/Wire Numbers** panel of the **Schematic** tab; the cursor will change into a selection box and you will be prompted to select the wire or the wire number to unhide the wire number. Select the wire number or the wire with which the hidden wire number is linked; the wire number will be visible automatically.

## Swapping Wire Numbers

| | |
|---|---|
| **Ribbon:** | Schematic > Edit Wires/Wire Numbers > Edit Wire Number drop-down > Swap |
| **Toolbar:** | ACE:Main Electrical 2 > Edit Wire Number > Swap Wire Numbers or ACE:Edit Wire Numbers > Swap Wire Numbers |
| **Menu:** | Wires > Swap Wire Numbers |
| **Command:** | AESWAPWIRENO |

The **Swap** tool is used to interchange the position of wire numbers between two wire networks. To do so, choose the **Swap** tool from the **Edit Wire Number** drop-down in the **Edit Wires/Wire Numbers** panel of the **Schematic** tab; the cursor will change into a selection box and you will be prompted to select the first wire or the wire number. Next, select the first wire or the wire number; you will be prompted to select the second wire or the wire number. Select the second wire or the wire number; the wire numbers will interchange their positions. Press ENTER or ESC to exit the command.

## Finding/Replacing Wire Numbers

| | |
|---|---|
| **Ribbon:** | Schematic > Edit Wires/Wire Numbers > Edit Wire Number drop-down> Find/Replace |
| **Toolbar:** | ACE:Main Electrical 2 > Edit Wire Numbers > Find/Replace Wire Numbers or ACE:Edit Wire Numbers > Find/Replace Wire Numbers |
| **Menu:** | Wires > Wire Numbers Miscellaneous > Find/Replace Wire Numbers |
| **Command:** | AEFINDWIRENO |

The **Find/Replace** tool is used to find the required wire number and replace it with the specified wire number value. Using this tool, you can find the required wire number within the project or in the current drawing. To do so, choose the **Find/Replace** tool from the **Edit Wire Number** drop-down in the **Edit Wires/Wire Numbers** panel of the **Schematic** tab; the **Find/Replace Wire Numbers** dialog box will be displayed, as shown in Figure 3-29. This dialog box has three sets of **Find/Replace** edit boxes. As a result, you can find as well as replace three wire numbers at a time. In the **Find** edit box, enter the value of the wire number text that you want to search and in the **Replace** edit box, enter the wire number text with which you want to replace the found value. The options in this dialog box are discussed next.

Find/Replace Wire Numbers
Fill in up to three sets of find/replace wire number text.
Mode:
All,exact match
Part,substring match
First occurrence only
Find
Replace
Find
Replace
Find
Replace
Go Cancel Help

*Figure 3-29 The **Find/Replace Wire Numbers** dialog box*

## All,exact match

If you select the **All,exact match** radio button, the wire number text will be replaced, only if the entire text value matches the find value.

## Part,substring match

The **Part,substring match** radio button is selected by default. As a result, it will replace the text, if any part of the text value matches the find value.

## First occurrence only

The **First occurrence only** check box is used to replace only the first occurrence of the text value. This check box will be activated only when you select the **Part,substring match** radio button.

## Go

Choose the **Go** button; the modified **Find/Replace Wire Numbers** dialog box will be displayed, as shown in Figure 3-30. The options in this dialog box are used to specify whether to find and replace wire numbers in the entire project, in the active drawing, or in the selected wire numbers of the active drawing.

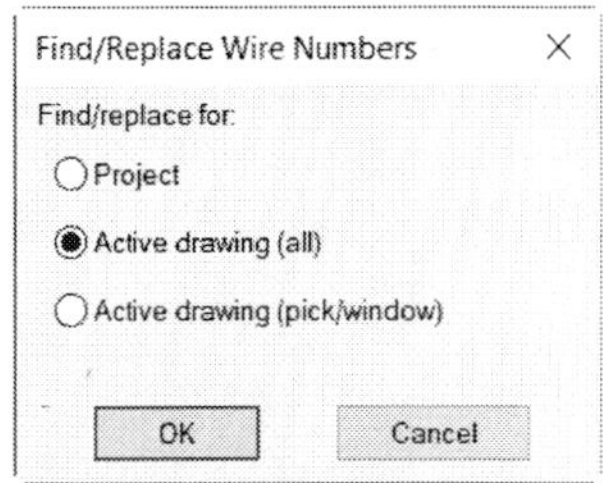


*Figure 3-30 The modified **Find/Replace Wire Numbers** dialog box*

The **Project** radio button is selected to process the entire project. By default, the **Active drawing (all)** radio button is selected. As a result, the active drawing will be processed.

If you select the **Active drawing (pick/window)** radio button, you will be able to pick the wire number text that will be replaced by the specified wire number text.

Choose the **OK** button; the old wire numbers will be replaced by the specified new wire numbers.

# Moving a Wire Number

| | |
|---|---|
| **Ribbon:** | Schematic > Edit Wires/Wire Numbers > Move Wire Number |
| **Toolbar:** | ACE:Main Electrical 2 > Move Wire Number |
| **Menu:** | Wires > Move Wire Number |
| **Command:** | AEMOVEWIRENO |

The **Move Wire Number** tool is used to move an existing wire number to a specific location on the same wire network. To do so, choose the **Move Wire Number** tool from the **Edit**

**Wires/Wire Numbers** panel of the **Schematic** tab; the cursor will change into a selection box and you will be prompted to specify a new wire number location on the wire. Select the wire segment where you want the wire number to be moved; the wire number will automatically be moved to the specified location. Next, press ENTER or right-click on the screen to exit the command.

## Scooting a Wire Number

| | |
|---|---|
| **Ribbon:** | Schematic > Edit Components > Modify Components drop-down > Scoot |
| **Toolbar:** | ACE:Main Electrical > Scoot or ACE:Scoot > Scoot |
| **Menu:** | Components > Scoot |
| **Command:** | AESCOOT |

The **Scoot** tool is used to slide a selected wire number on the same wire to the specified location. To do so, choose the **Scoot** tool from the **Modify Components** drop-down in the **Edit Components** panel of the **Schematic** tab, as shown in Figure 3-31; the cursor will change into a selection box and you will be prompted to select the wire number. Select the wire number; a rectangle drawn in temporary graphics will be displayed, which indicates the selected wire number. Next, specify the location where you want to place the wire number; the wire number will move on the same wire to the specified location. Next, press ENTER to exit the command. You can also scoot the entire wire, components, ladder bus, rungs, and so on.

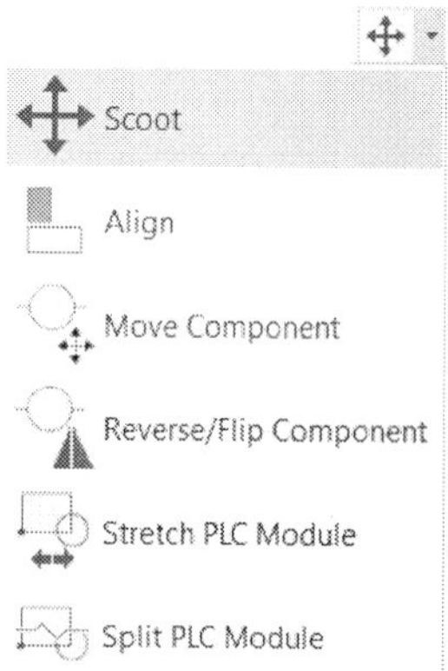


*Figure 3-31 The **Modify Components** drop-down*

## Flipping a Wire Number

| | |
|---|---|
| **Ribbon:** | Schematic > Edit Wires/Wire Numbers > Flip Wire Number |
| **Toolbar:** | ACE:Main Electrical 2 > Flip Wire Number |
| **Menu:** | Wires > Flip Wire Number |
| **Command:** | AEFLIPWIRENO |

The **Flip Wire Number** tool is used to flip or reverse the direction of a selected wire number about the wire. To do so, choose the **Flip Wire Number** tool from the **Edit Wires/Wire Numbers** panel of the **Schematic** tab; the cursor will change into a selection box and you will be prompted to select the wire number to mirror. Next, select the wire number; the wire number will be flipped. Now, press ENTER to exit the command.

## Toggling the Wire Number Position

| | |
|---|---|
| **Ribbon:** | Schematic > Edit Wires/Wire Numbers > Toggle Wire Number In-line |
| **Toolbar:** | ACE:Main Electrical 2 > Toggle Wire Number In-line |
| **Menu:** | Wires > Toggle Wire Number In-line |
| **Command:** | AETOGGLEWIRENO |

The **Toggle Wire Number In-line** tool is used to move the selected wire number from right, left, top, or bottom to in-line with wire and vice-versa. To do so, choose the

**Toggle Wire Number In-line** tool from the **Edit Wires/Wire Numbers** panel of the **Schematic** tab; the cursor will change into a selection box and you will be prompted to select the wire number to toggle. Next, select the wire number whose position you want to change; the wire number will be toggled. Right-click or press ENTER to exit the command. You can also select the wire itself to toggle the wire number.

**Note**

*1. If you choose the **Toggle Wire Number In-line** tool and then select the in-line wire number; the wire number will be moved either above or below the wire. The placement of the wire number above or below the wire depends on the settings defined in the **Wire Numbers** tab of the **Drawing Properties** dialog box.*

*2. If the length of the wire is too short to accommodate with in-line wire number, it will remain above or below the line wire number.*

## Repositioning the Wire Number Text with the Attached Leader

| | |
|---|---|
| **Ribbon:** | Schematic > Insert Wires/Wire Numbers > Wire Number Leader drop-down > Wire Number Leader |
| **Toolbar:** | ACE:Main Electrical 2 > Wire Number Leader or ACE:Wire Leaders > Wire Number Leader |
| **Menu:** | Wires > Wire Number Leader |
| **Command:** | AEWIRENOLEADER |

The **Wire Number Leader** tool is used to reposition the wire number text with an attached leader. You can add the wire leader to every wire number or to a selected wire number, if the space for the normal positioning of the wire number is not available. To relocate the wire number, choose the **Wire Number Leader** tool from the **Wire Number Leader** drop-down in the **Insert Wires/Wire Numbers** panel of the **Schematic** tab, as shown in Figure 3-32; you will be prompted to select the wire number for the leader. Select the wire number text; you will be prompted to specify distance for the wire leader. Now, drag the cursor and click to specify a new position for the wire number for the leader. Next, right-click or press ENTER to position the wire number along with the leader. Press ENTER to exit the command.

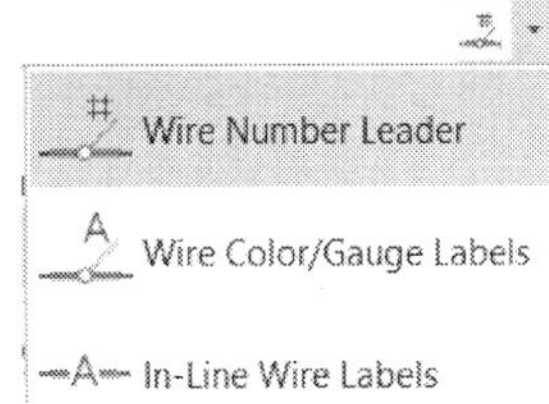


***Figure 3-32** The **Wire Number Leader** drop-down*

To remove the leader from the wire number, enter '**C**' at the Command prompt. Enter '**S**' at the Command prompt to scoot component, wire, and wire number. Press ENTER to exit the command.

**Tip**

*You can move the wire number without the use of a leader using the **Move/Show Attribute** tool. You can rotate a wire number at 90 degrees using the **Rotate Attribute** tool. These tools are discussed in Chapter 6 in detail.*

## INSERTING IN-LINE WIRE MARKERS

| | |
|---|---|
| **Ribbon:** | Schematic > Insert Wires/Wire Numbers > Wire Number Leader drop-down > In-Line Wire Labels |
| **Toolbar:** | ACE:Main Electrical 2 > Wire Number Leader > In-Line Wire Labels or ACE:Wire Leaders > In-Line Wire Labels |
| **Menu:** | Wires > Wire Numbers Miscellaneous > In-Line Wire Labels |
| **Command:** | AEINLINEWIRE |

Markers are used to identify conductor color or signal name. These markers can be inserted in-line to any wire. Also, these markers are for reference and are not considered for wire numbering and reports. To insert an in-line marker, choose the **In-Line Wire Labels** tool from the **Wire Number Leader** drop-down in the **Insert Wires/Wire Numbers** panel of the **Schematic** tab; the **Insert Component** dialog box will be displayed, as shown in Figure 3-33. This dialog box displays a list of predefined in-line markers and user-defined markers. The options in this dialog box are discussed in detail in Chapter 5.

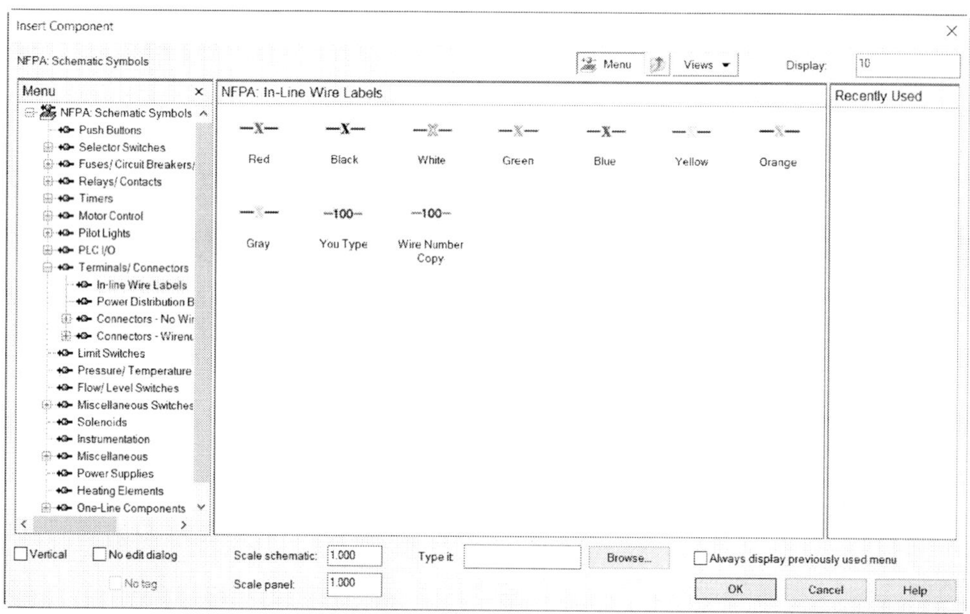


*Figure 3-33 The **Insert Component** dialog box*

Select a marker from the **NFPA: In-Line Wire Labels** area of the **Insert Component** dialog box; the dialog box will disappear and the cursor will change into a cross hair. Also, you will be prompted to specify the insertion point for the in-line marker. Now, specify the insertion point for the in-line marker; the marker will be inserted in between the wire. This command will continue until you press ESC. Alternatively, right-click on the screen and choose the **Cancel** option from the shortcut menu to cancel the command.

You can also create and insert user-defined markers. To do so, select the **You Type** in-line wire marker from the **NFPA: In-Line Wire Labels** area; you will be prompted to specify the insertion point for the marker. Next, specify the insertion point for the marker; the **Edit Attribute - COLOR** dialog box will be displayed, as shown in Figure 3-34. In this dialog box, enter the attribute value in the edit box. You can also increase or decrease the already specified attribute value by choosing the **<** or **>** button displayed on the right of the **Edit Attribute-COLOR** dialog box. Alternatively, you can choose the **Pick** button to select a similar attribute value from the drawing that has been specified earlier. Next, choose the **OK** button; the attribute value of the in-line marker will be inserted into your drawing.

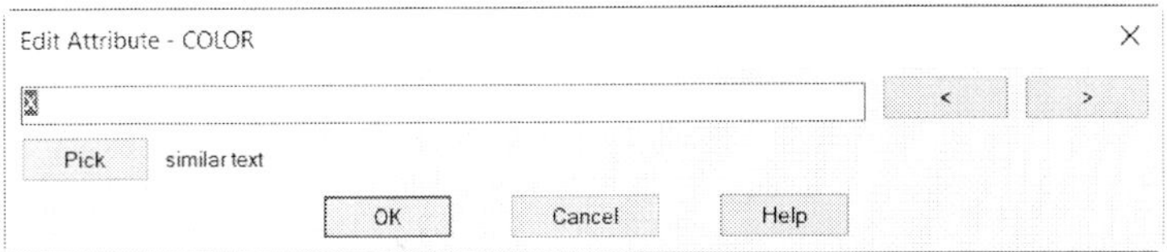


*Figure 3-34 The **Edit Attribute - COLOR** dialog box*

You can also insert the wire number as in-line marker. To do so, select the **Wire Number Copy** label from the **NFPA:In-Line Wire Labels** area; you will be prompted to specify the insertion point for the in-line marker. Specify the insertion point; the **Edit Wire Number/Attributes** dialog box will be displayed, refer to Figure 3-35. In this dialog box, enter wire number for the wire if it is not already assigned; wire number will be displayed as in-line wire marker. If you do not specify wire number for the wire in the **Edit Wire Number/Attributes** dialog box and if it does not have wire number, *"wn"* will get inserted into the wire.

This command will continue until you press ESC. Figure 3-36 shows wires with in-line markers and wire numbers.

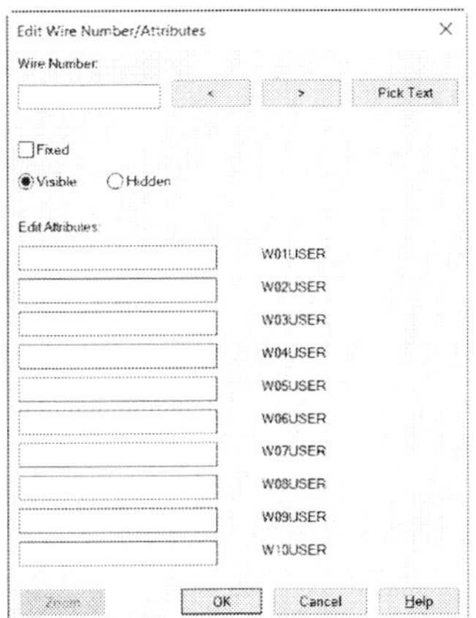


*Figure 3-35 The **Edit Wire Number/Attributes** dialog box*

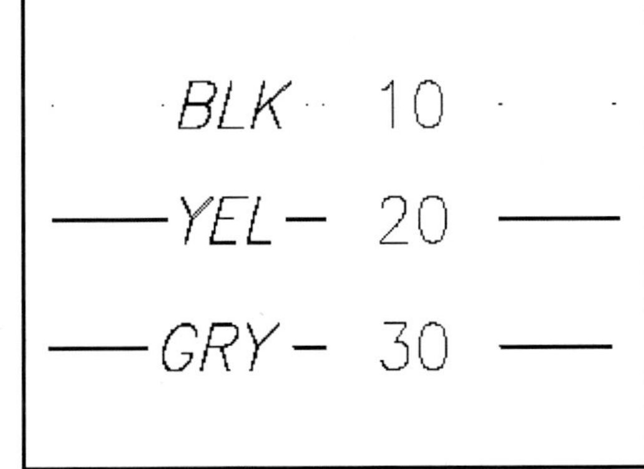


*Figure 3-36 Wires with in-line markers and wire numbers*

**Note**

*1. If a wire number has already been assigned to a wire and you select the **Wire Number Copy** label from the **NFPA:In-Line Wire Labels** area of the **Insert Component** dialog box, you will be prompted to specify the insertion point for the in-line marker. Specify the insertion point; the assigned wire number will get inserted in-line to the selected wire.*

*2. If the label is too wide, you can reduce its size by using the* ***Squeeze Attribute/Text*** *tool. To do so, choose the* ***Squeeze Attribute/Text*** *tool from the* ***Modify Attributes*** *drop-down in the* ***Edit Components*** *panel of the* ***Schematic*** *tab; you will be prompted to select the text or attribute to be squeezed. Next, select the text or attribute; the size of the text or the attribute will be reduced by 0.05. Press ENTER to exit the command. You will learn more about modifying the attributes in detail in Chapter 6.*

*3. You can also use the* ***Adjust In-Line Wire/Label Gap*** *tool from the* ***Copy Wire Number*** *drop-down to adjust the gap width of the label. To do so, choose the* ***Adjust In-Line Wire/Label Gap*** *tool from the* ***Edit Wires/Wire Numbers*** *panel of the* ***Schematic*** *tab; you will be prompted to select the in-line label. Next, select the in-line label; the gap width of the label will be adjusted automatically. Press ENTER to exit the command.*

*4. If the label is too narrow, you can stretch it by choosing the* ***Stretch Attribute/Text*** *tool from the* ***Modify Attributes*** *drop-down of the* ***Edit Components*** *panel of the* ***Schematic*** *tab.*

## Inserting Wire Color/Gauge Labels in a Drawing

| | |
|---|---|
| **Ribbon:** | Schematic > Insert Wires/Wire Numbers > Wire Number Leader drop-down > Wire Color/Gauge Labels |
| **Toolbar:** | ACE:Main Electrical 2 > Wire Number Leader > Wire Color/Gauge Labels or ACE:Wire Leaders > Wire Color/Gauge Labels |
| **Menu:** | Wires > Wire Numbers Miscellaneous > Wire Color/Gauge Labels |
| **Command:** | AEWIRECOLORLABEL |

The **Wire Color/Gauge Labels** tool is used to insert wire color/gauge labels to a wire with or without a leader. To insert wire color/gauge labels, choose the **Wire Color/Gauge Labels** tool from the **Wire Number Leader** drop-down in the **Insert Wires/Wire Numbers** panel of the **Schematic** tab; the **Insert Wire Color/Gauge Labels** dialog box will be displayed. In this dialog box, choose the **Setup** button to change the text size, arrow size and style, and leader gap size of the label. Choose the **Auto Placement** button; you will be prompted to select objects. Next, select the wires for which you want to add wire color/gauge labels and press ENTER; the **Color/gauge text for XX** dialog box will be displayed. You can edit the text string in this dialog box and choose **OK**; the wire color/gauge labels will be added and placed automatically on selected wires. Choose the **Manual** button in the **With leader** area if wire color/gauge labels are to be placed manually with a leader. Choose the **Manual** button in the **No leader** area if wire color/gauge labels are to be placed manually without a leader.

## Inserting the Special Wire Numbering in a Drawing

| | |
|---|---|
| **Ribbon:** | Schematic > Insert Wires/Wire Numbers > Insert Wire Numbers drop-down > 3 Phase |
| **Toolbar:** | ACE:Main Electrical 2 > Insert Wire Numbers > 3 Phase Wire Numbers or ACE:Insert Wire Numbers > 3 Phase Wire Numbers |
| **Menu:** | Wires > Wire Numbers Miscellaneous > 3 Phase Wire Numbers |
| **Command:** | AE3PHASEWIRENO |

The **3 Phase** tool is used to insert special wire numbers into the 3 phase bus and motor circuits. Using this tool, you can speed up the work of inserting wire numbers into the

3 phase circuits. To insert special wire numbers, choose the **3 Phase** tool from the **Insert Wire Numbers** drop-down in the **Insert Wire Numbers** panel of the **Schematic** tab, refer to Figure 3-37; the **3 Phase Wire Numbering** dialog box will be displayed, as shown in Figure 3-38. The options in this dialog box are discussed next.

## Prefix Area

The **Prefix** area is used to specify prefix value for wire numbers. To do so, enter the prefix value for wire numbers in the edit box of this area. Alternatively, choose the **List** button to select a pre-defined value for the prefix value.

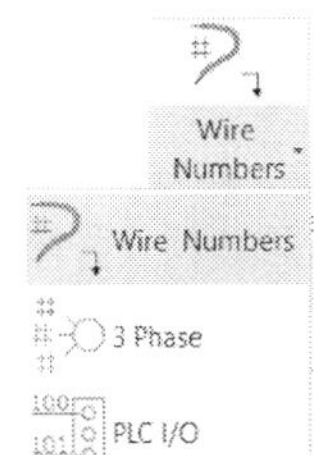


*Figure 3-37 The **Insert Wire Numbers** drop-down*

## Base Area

In the **Base** area, enter the starting number for the base of wire numbers in the edit box. Alternatively, choose the **Pick** button to select an existing wire number attribute value from the active drawing. Also, you can increase or decrease the base of the wire number by choosing the **>** or **<** button.

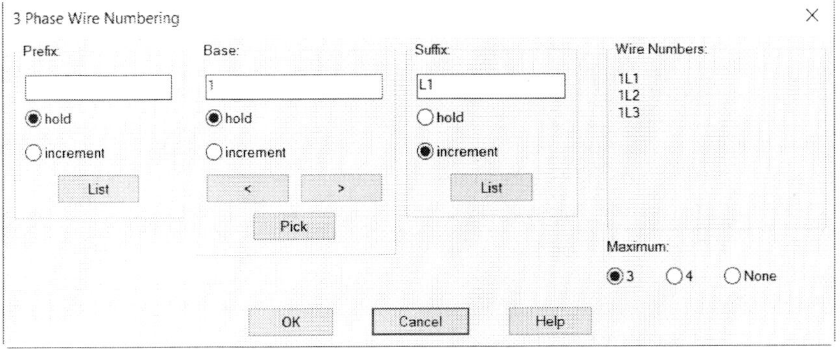


*Figure 3-38 The **3 Phase Wire Numbering** dialog box*

## Suffix Area

In the **Suffix** area, enter the suffix value for wire numbers in the edit box. Alternatively, choose the **List** button to select a pre-defined value for the suffix value.

## hold and increment

The **hold** and **increment** radio buttons are used to hold and increment the prefix value, base value, and suffix value for all wire numbers of a drawing. By default, the **hold** radio button is selected from the **Prefix** and **Base** areas and the **increment** radio button is selected from the **Suffix** area.

## Wire Numbers Area

The **Wire Numbers** area displays the preview of the wire numbers specified in the edit boxes of the **Prefix**, **Base**, and **Suffix** areas.

### Maximum Area

The **Maximum** area consists of radio buttons: **3**, **4**, and **None**. Depending upon the radio button selected, the preview of the values specified in the **Prefix**, **Base**, and **Suffix** areas get automatically updated in the **Wire Numbers** area. By default, the **3** radio button is selected.

# ADDING SOURCE AND DESTINATION SIGNAL ARROWS

AutoCAD Electrical uses the named source and destination signal codes for connecting wire networks within a drawing or between drawings. The source and destination arrows are used to carry wire's signal to a different area of the current drawing or across multiple drawings. Also, you will be able to designate the same wire in different areas of a drawing. In this section, you will learn how to insert source and destination signal arrows in drawings. You will also learn how to link source and destination signal arrows.

## Adding Source Signal Arrows

| | |
|---|---|
| **Ribbon:** | Schematic > Insert Wires/Wire Numbers > Signal Arrows drop-down > Source Arrow |
| **Toolbar:** | ACE:Main Electrical 2 > Source Signal Arrow or ACE:Signals > Source Signal Arrow |
| **Menu:** | Wires > Signal References > Source Signal Arrow |
| **Command:** | AESOURCE |

The **Source Arrow** tool is used to insert a source signal arrow into a wire. This tool is used to label a wire that specifies where the wire is coming from. To do so, choose the **Source Arrow** tool from the **Signal Arrows** drop-down in the **Insert Wires/Wire Numbers** panel of the **Schematic** tab, as shown in Figure 3-39; you will be prompted to select the endpoint of the wire for source. Next, select the endpoint of the wire; the **Signal - Source Code** dialog box will be displayed, as shown in Figure 3-40. Different options in this dialog box are discussed next.

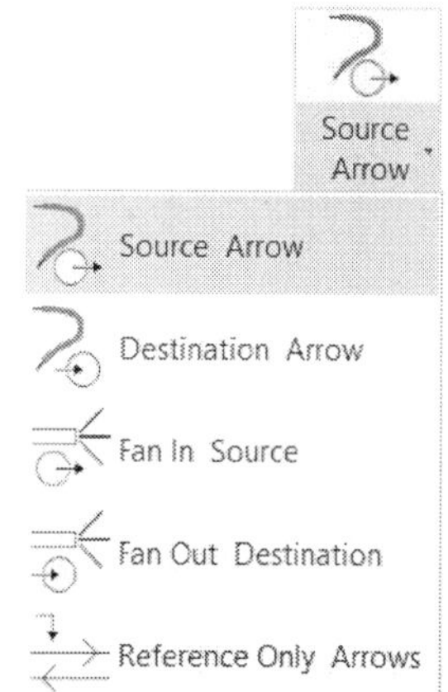

*Figure 3-39 The **Signal Arrows** drop-down*

**Note**

*When you select a wire that already has a source arrow or has no free end, the **Signal Arrow** message box will be displayed, as shown in Figure 3-41, and you will be prompted to add a branch to the existing network. Choose the **OK** button from this message box; a branch will be added to the existing network and the **Signal - Source Code** dialog box will be displayed, refer to Figure 3-40.*

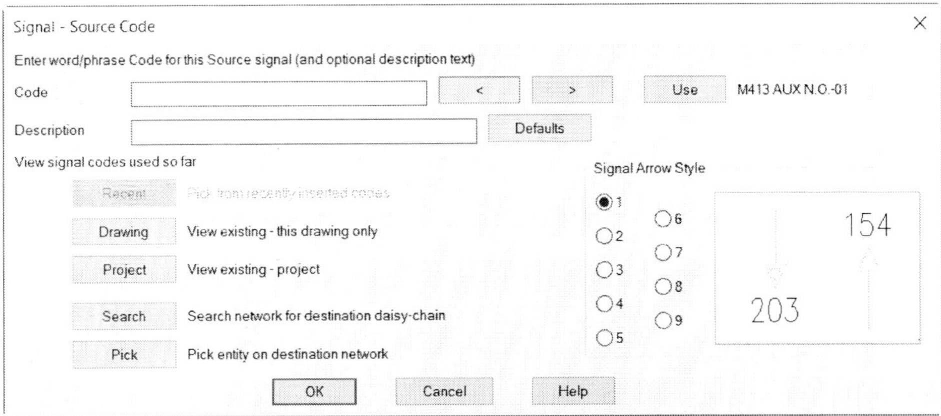


*Figure 3-40 The **Signal - Source Code** dialog box*

## Code

Specify the code for source signal in the **Code** edit box. This code is used to link the source wire network to the destination wire network. You can also choose the **Use** button on the right of this edit box to use the value displayed on the right of the **Use** button. Also, you can choose the **<** or **>** button to increment or decrement the last digit of the code. The code to be specified in the **Code** edit box should be maximum of 32 characters. This code can be a unique number, word, or phrase.

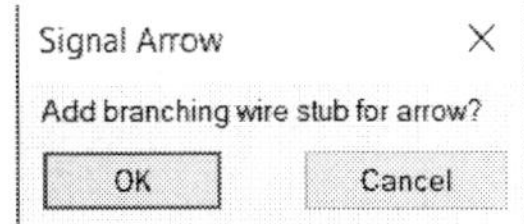


*Figure 3-41 The **Signal Arrow** message box*

## Description

The **Description** edit box is used to enter description for the source signal. Alternatively, you can choose the **Defaults** button to select the predefined description.

## Recent

The **Recent** button will be activated only if you have inserted source/destination signals recently in the drawing. This button is used to select source signal from a list of recently inserted codes. To do so, choose the **Recent** button; the **Signal Source/Destination codes -- Recent** dialog box will be displayed. Select the code from the list of recently inserted codes and choose the **OK** button; the specified code will be displayed in the **Code** edit box.

## Drawing

Choose the **Drawing** button; the **Signal codes -- this Drawing - Source and Destination** dialog box will be displayed. This dialog box displays a list of all source and destination codes used in the active drawing. Select a signal code from this dialog box and choose the **OK** button; the name of the signal code will be displayed in the **Code** edit box.

## Project

Choose the **Project** button; the **Signal codes -- Project - wide Destination** dialog box will be displayed. This dialog box displays the source and destination codes used in the active project. Select the signal code from this dialog box and choose the **OK** button; the name of the signal code will be displayed in the **Code** edit box.

## Search

The **Search** button is used to search for the selected wire network to find linked destination arrows. If a destination arrow is found, its signal code will be used for the new source arrow.

## Pick

The **Pick** button is used to select an existing wire network for searching destination arrows. To do so, choose the **Pick** button; you will be prompted to select a wire or an arrow on the source/destination network. Next, select the wire or the arrow; the name of the selected signal code will be used for the new source arrow.

## Signal Arrow Style Area

In the **Signal Arrow Style** area, you can select the signal arrow style for the source arrow. The first four styles are the pre-defined styles and the last five styles are the user-defined styles.

**Note**

*If at the time of insertion of source signal arrow, an existing destination signal code is selected as a destination from the drawing other than the active drawing, the destination signal arrow will be automatically updated.*

After specifying the required options in the **Signal - Source Code** dialog box, choose the **OK** button in this dialog box to insert the source arrow into the drawing; the **Source/Destination Signal Arrows** dialog box will be displayed, as shown in Figure 3-42.

Choose the **OK** button from this dialog box to insert the destination arrow in the same drawing. But note that the destination wire network should be in the same network. If the destination wire network is in a different drawing, first you need to insert the destination arrow in a different drawing using the **Destination Arrow** tool. Figure 3-43 shows the source signal arrow and the destination signal arrow.

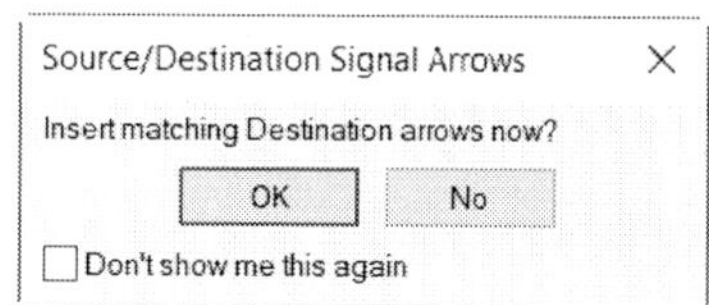


***Figure 3-42*** *The* ***Source/Destination Signal Arrows*** *dialog box*

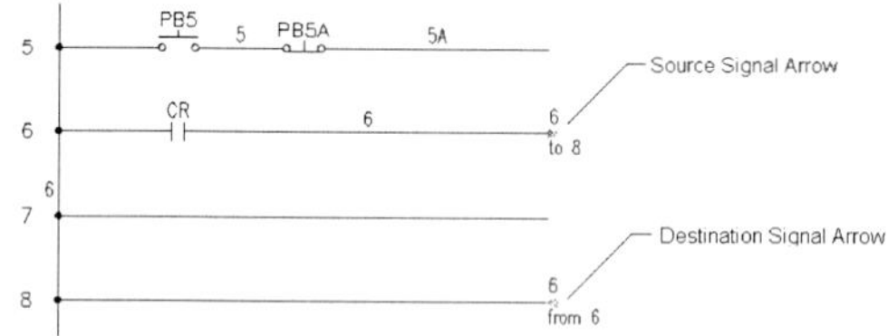


***Figure 3-43*** *The source signal arrow and the destination signal arrow*

**Note**

*1. A signal source code can be linked to multiple destination arrows, whereas a destination arrow can be linked to only one source code.*

*2. If wire numbers have not been added to the wire network, '???' will be displayed on the source and destination arrows.*

## Adding Destination Signal Arrows

| | |
|---|---|
| **Ribbon:** | Schematic > Insert Wires/Wire Numbers > Signal Arrows drop-down > Destination Arrow |
| **Toolbar:** | ACE:Main Electrical 2 > Destination Signal Arrow or ACE:Signals > Destination Signal Arrow |
| **Menu:** | Wires > Signal References > Destination Signal Arrow |
| **Command:** | AEDESTINATION |

The **Destination Arrow** tool is used to insert a destination signal arrow into a wire. The destination signal arrow indicates the origin of a wire number. The wire number of the source and the reference number, where the source arrow is located will be displayed with the destination arrow. To add the destination signal arrow, choose the **Destination Arrow** tool from the **Signal Arrows** drop-down in the **Insert Wires/Wire Numbers** panel of the **Schematic** tab, refer to Figure 3-39; you will be prompted to select the end of the wire for destination. Next, select the end of the wire on the schematic on which you want to show the continuity of the network; the **Insert Destination Code** dialog box will be displayed, as shown in Figure 3-44.

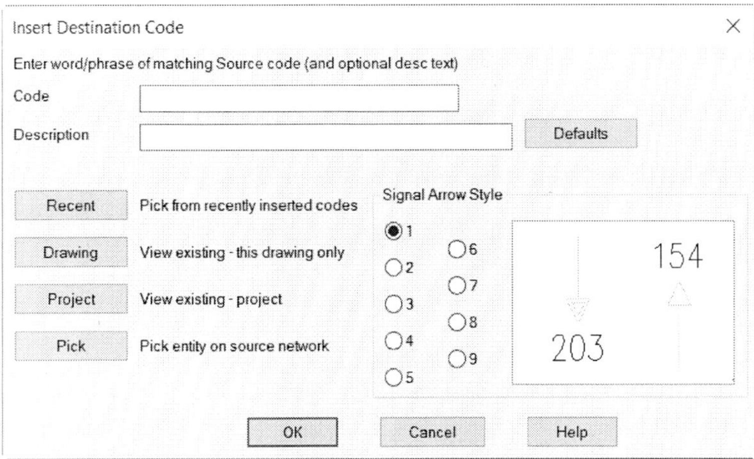


*Figure 3-44 The **Insert Destination Code** dialog box*

In this dialog box, you need to enter the text code that links the source and destination arrows. The options in this dialog box are the same as those of the **Signal Source Code** dialog box. In the former case, you need to enter the information about source signal arrows, whereas in the latter case, you need to enter the information of destination signal arrows. Specify the required information in the **Insert Destination Code** dialog box and choose the **OK** button; the destination arrow will be inserted into the drawing.

**Note**

*If you select the wire for which the destination signal arrow has already been inserted in the drawing and you choose the **Destination Arrow** tool from the **Insert Wires/Wire Numbers** panel of the **Schematic** tab; the **Destination "From" Arrow (Existing)** dialog box will be displayed. Using this dialog box, you can insert a destination arrow into the drawing at any time.*

# INSERTING CABLE MARKERS

**Ribbon:** Schematic > Insert Wires/Wire Numbers > Cable Markers
**Toolbar:** ACE:Main Electrical > Cable Markers
or ACE:Cable Markers > Cable Markers
**Menu:** Wires > Cables > Cable Markers
**Command:** AECABLEMARKER

In AutoCAD Electrical, there is no separate option for creating cables in a drawing. Therefore, to represent a cable in a drawing, you need to attach a cable marker to the existing wire. Cable markers are AutoCAD blocks and have similar attributes as that of schematic components. Cable markers act like any other parent or child component that carries attribute information such as tag, manufacturer, and catalog data. The first marker that you insert will be the parent and the other one will be the child. The conductor color values are carried on the RATING1 attribute of the cable marker. To insert a cable marker, choose the **Cable Markers** tool from the **Insert Wires/Wire Numbers** panel of the **Schematic** tab; the **Insert Component** dialog box will be displayed, as shown in Figure 3-45. The options in this dialog box will be discussed in detail in Chapter 5. Next, select the cable marker to insert from the **NFPA: Cable Markers** area of the **Insert Component** dialog box; you will be prompted to specify the insertion point for the cable marker. Next, specify the insertion point for the cable marker; the **Insert / Edit Cable Marker (Parent wire)** dialog box will be displayed, as shown in Figure 3-46.

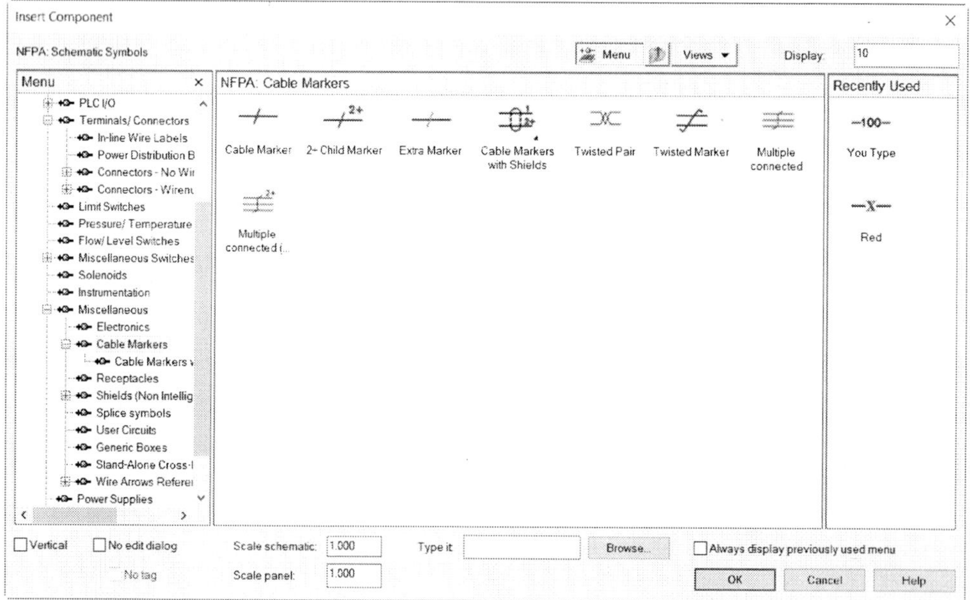


*Figure 3-45 The **Insert Component** dialog box*

Enter the tag of the cable in the **Cable Tag** edit box. Specify the catalog data, description, installation, and location codes in this dialog box. Also, specify the wire color in the **Wire Color/ ID** area. Next, choose the **OK** button from the **Insert / Edit Cable Marker (Parent wire)** dialog box; the **Insert Some Child Components?** dialog box will be displayed, as shown in Figure 3-47.

You can use this dialog box to insert the child cable marker in the drawing. By default, all options in this dialog box are selected. As a result, the attribute information on the child marker will be hidden. Choose the **Close** button in the **Insert Some Child Components?** dialog box, if you do not want to insert the child marker. If you want to insert the child cable marker in the drawing, choose the **OK Insert Child** button from the **Insert Some Child Components?** dialog box; you will be prompted to specify the insertion point. Next, specify the insertion point for the child marker; the **Insert / Edit Cable Marker (2nd + wire of cable)** dialog box will be displayed. Alternatively, choose the **2+ Child Marker** from the **Insert Component** dialog box; the **Insert / Edit Cable Marker (2nd + wire of cable)** dialog box will be displayed. Next, specify the required information in this dialog box and choose the **OK** button; the child cable marker will be inserted into the drawing and you will be prompted to specify the insertion point for the next child marker. Next, press ESC to exit the command. Figure 3-48 shows the parent and child cable markers inserted in wires.

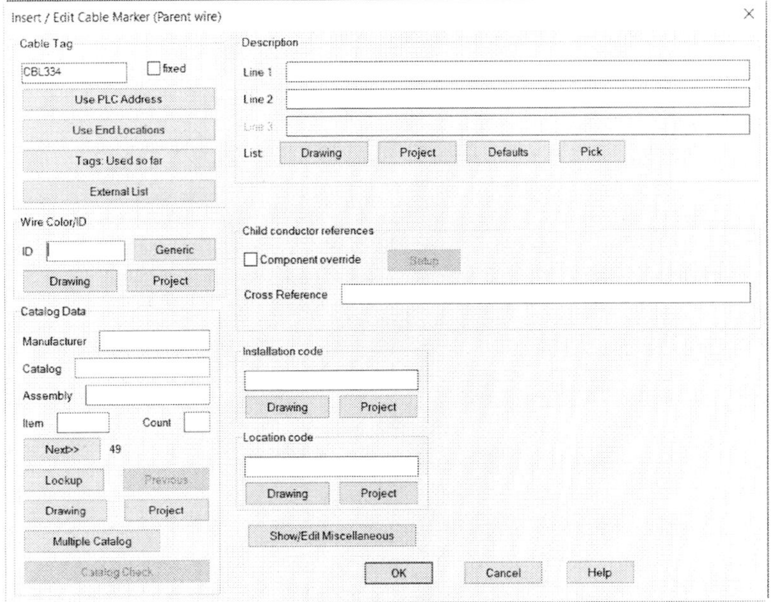


*Figure 3-46 The **Insert / Edit Cable Marker (Parent wire)** dialog box*

*Figure 3-47 The **Insert Some Child Components?** dialog box*

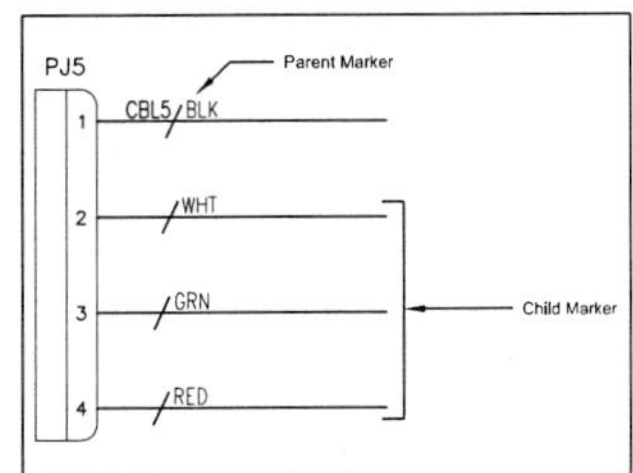


*Figure 3-48 The parent and child cable markers inserted into wires*

## Showing Source and Destination Markers on Cable Wires

Sometimes, you may need to show the individual wires of a cable at each end where they connect and the wires coming together to form a single line cable in between the ends. In such cases, you can use the **Fan In/Out Source** and **Fan In/Out Destination** tools. In this section, you will learn how the fan in/out source and fan in/out destination markers are inserted into a drawing. Figure 3-49 shows these markers. In the next section, you will learn about the use of the **Fan In/Out - Single Line Layer** tool to change a wire layer.

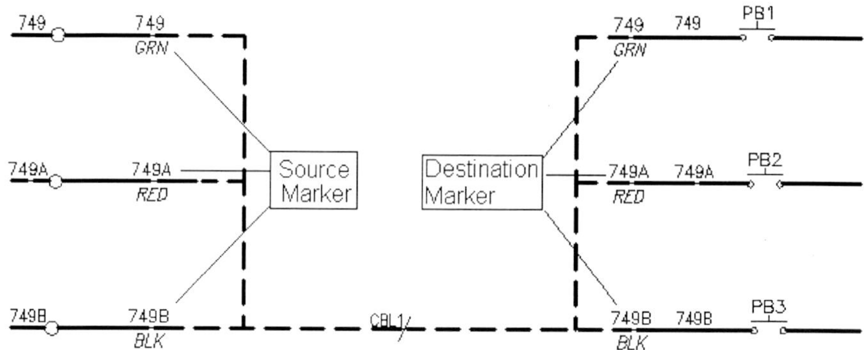


*Figure 3-49 The fan in/out source and destination markers inserted in the drawing*

### Adding Source Markers

| | |
|---|---|
| **Ribbon:** | Schematic > Insert Wires/Wire Numbers > Signal Arrows drop-down > Fan In Source |
| **Toolbar:** | ACE:Main Electrical 2 > Source Signal Arrow > Fan In/Out Source or ACE:Signals > Fan In/Out Source |
| **Menu:** | Wires > Signal References > Fan In/Out Source |
| **Command:** | AEFANINSRC |

The **Fan In Source** tool is used to insert an in-line fan in/out source marker into a drawing. After inserting a source marker, the wires coming out of the marker will get changed to a defined layer. To insert a source marker into the drawing, choose the **Fan In Source** tool from the **Signal Arrows** drop-down in the **Insert Wires/Wire Numbers** panel of the **Schematic** tab; the **Fan-In / Fan-Out Signal Source** dialog box will be displayed, as shown in Figure 3-50. After selecting the style for the source marker from the **Source marker style** list and the orientation for the source marker from the **Wire connection orientation** area in the **Fan-In / Fan-Out Signal Source** dialog box, you will be prompted to select insertion point for the fan in/out source marker on the wire. Specify the insertion point; the **Signal-Source Code** dialog box will be displayed.

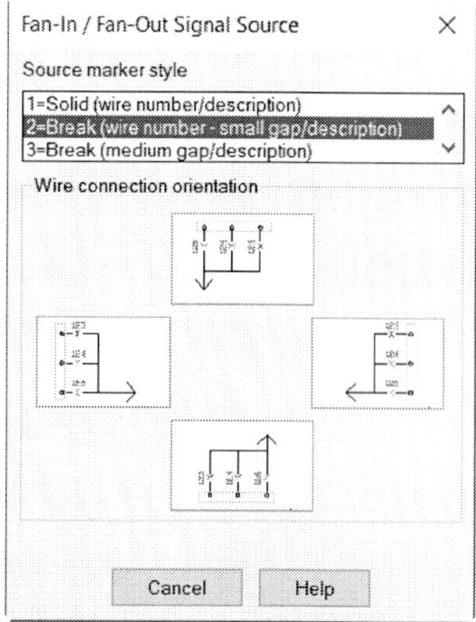


*Figure 3-50 The **Fan-In / Fan-Out Signal Source** dialog box*

The options in the **Signal-Source Code** dialog box have already been discussed. Next, specify the required options in this dialog box and choose the **OK** button; the **Source/Destination Signal markers (for Fan In/Out)** dialog box will be displayed, as shown in Figure 3-51. The options in this dialog box are used to insert the matching destination marker while inserting the source markers. These options are discussed next.

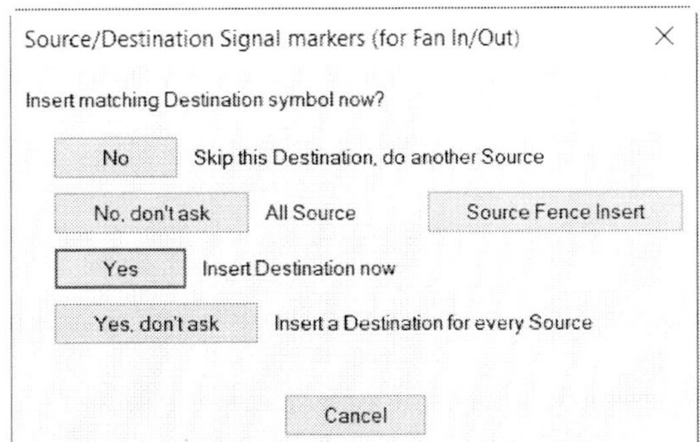


*Figure 3-51 The* ***Source/Destination Signal markers (for Fan In/Out)*** *dialog box*

The **No** button, if chosen, will not insert the matching destination marker after the source marker is inserted.

The **No, don't ask** button, if chosen, will not ask for inserting the matching destination marker, after each source is inserted.

Choose the **Yes** button to insert the matching destination marker after the source marker is inserted.

Choose the **Yes, don't ask** button to insert the matching destination markers automatically for each source. In this case, AutoCAD Electrical will not ask for permission.

The **Source Fence Insert** button is used to create a fence for inserting the destination marker in the specified fence. Now, choose the **No** button from the **Source/Destination Signal markers (for Fan In/Out)** dialog box; you will be prompted to specify the insertion point for the fan in/out next source. This command will continue until you press ESC. Also, you will notice that the wires going out from the marker will be changed into a defined layer.

## Adding Destination Markers

| | |
|---|---|
| **Ribbon:** | Schematic > Insert Wires/Wire Numbers > Signal Arrows drop-down> Fan Out Destination |
| **Toolbar:** | ACE:Main Electrical 2 > Source Signal Arrow > Fan In/Out Destination or ACE:Signals > Fan In/Out Destination |
| **Menu:** | Wires > Signal References > Fan In/Out Destination |
| **Command:** | AEFANINDEST |

The **Fan Out Destination** tool is used to insert in-line fan in/out destination markers on wires of a cable. After inserting a destination marker, the wires going into the marker will get changed to a defined layer.

To insert a destination marker in the drawing, choose the **Fan Out Destination** tool from the **Signal Arrows** drop-down in the **Insert Wires/Wire Numbers** panel of the **Schematic** tab; the **Fan-In / Fan-Out Signal Destination** dialog box will be displayed, as shown in Figure 3-52. After selecting the style for the destination marker from the **Destination marker style** list and the orientation for the destination marker from the **Wire connection orientation** area, you will be prompted to specify the insertion point for the fan in/out destination marker. Next, specify the insertion point for the fan in/out destination marker; the destination marker will be added. If the destination marker is already there, the **Destination "From" Arrow (Existing)** dialog box will be displayed, as shown in Figure 3-53. The options in this dialog box have already been discussed earlier.

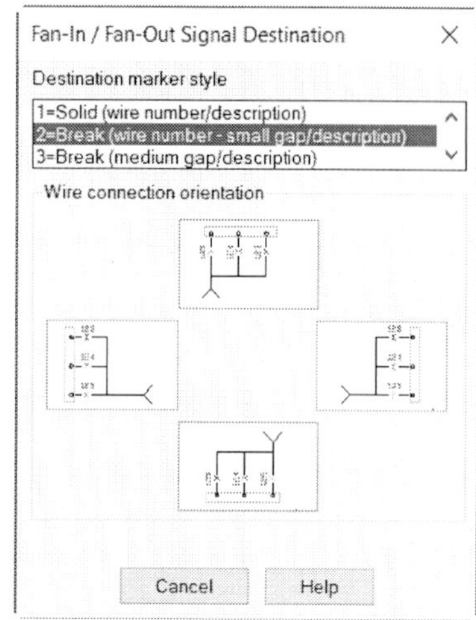


*Figure 3-52 The **Fan-In / Fan-Out Signal Destination** dialog box*

**Note**

*If you select the **Erase this destination arrow** check box in the **Destination "From" Arrow (Existing)** dialog box, the **Code** and **Reference** edit boxes as well as the **Recent**, **Drawing**, **Project**, and **Pick** buttons will not be available. Also, the destination marker that you insert will be erased keeping a gap between the two wires.*

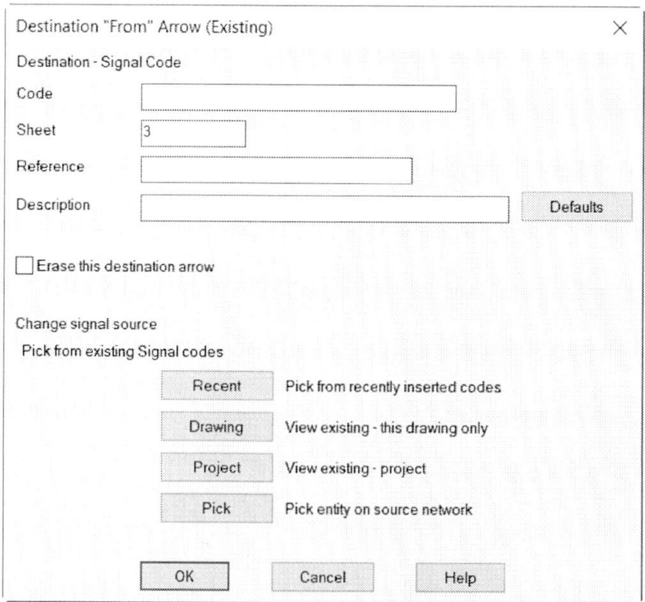


*Figure 3-53 The **Destination "From" Arrow (Existing)** dialog box*

Now, choose the **OK** button from the **Destination "From" Arrow (Existing)** dialog box; the fan in/out destination markers will be inserted into the wire. This command will continue until you press ESC.

**Note**

*You can set the style and the layer of a marker for a selected drawing using the* ***Drawing Properties*** *dialog box. To do so, select the required drawing from the* ***PROJECT MANAGER*** *and right-click on it; a shortcut menu will be displayed. Choose* ***Properties > Drawing Properties*** *from the shortcut menu; the* ***Drawing Properties*** *dialog box will be displayed. In this dialog box, choose the* ***Styles*** *tab and set the marker style and layer in the* ***Fan-In/Out Marker Style*** *area. The options in the* ***Drawing Properties*** *dialog box are discussed in detail in the later chapters.*

## Defining Fan-In/Out Layers

| | |
|---|---|
| **Ribbon:** | Schematic > Edit Wires/Wire Numbers > Fan In/Out - Single Line Layer |
| **Toolbar:** | ACE:Main Electrical 2 > Source Signal Arrow > Fan In/Out - Single Line Layer or ACE:Signals > Fan In/Out - Single Line Layer |
| **Menu:** | Wires > Signal References > Fan In/Out - Single Line Layer |
| **Command:** | AEFANIN |

The **Fan In/Out - Single Line Layer** tool is used to change or define a layer or a set of layers for the wires coming out from fan in/out source marker and the wires going into a destination marker. To change or define a fan in/out layer, choose the **Fan In/Out - Single Line Layer** tool from the **Edit Wires/Wire Numbers** panel of the **Schematic** tab; the **Fan-In/Out Single-line Layer** dialog box will be displayed, as shown in Figure 3-54. The different areas and options in this dialog box are discussed next.

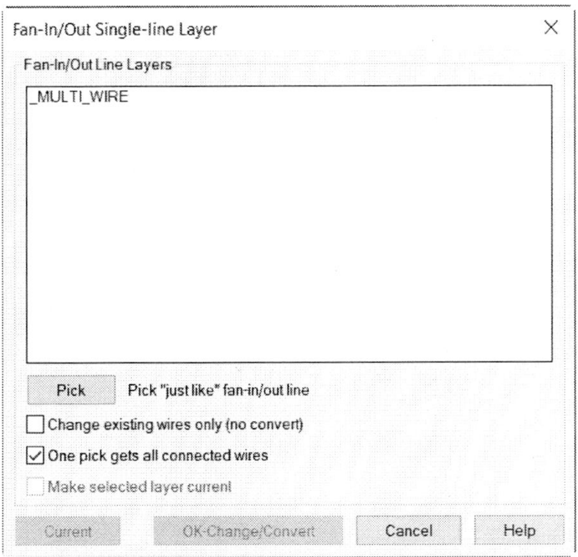


***Figure 3-54*** *The* ***Fan-In/Out Single-line Layer*** *dialog box*

### Fan-In/Out Line Layers Area

The **Fan-In/Out Line Layers** area is used to display a list of layers that has already been assigned as fan in/out layers in the **Drawing Properties** dialog box. The **Drawing Properties** dialog box will be discussed in detail in the later chapters.

### Pick

The **Pick** button is used to select similar fan in/out lines from a drawing and add the selected fan in/out lines layer to the **Fan-In/Out Line Layers** area. To select similar fan in/out lines from drawing and add them to the **Fan-In/Out Line Layers** area, choose the **Pick** button; you will be prompted to select objects. Now, select the wire(s); the **Layer** message box will be displayed. Choose the **OK** button from the **Layer** message box to add the selected wire layer to the valid layer list in the **Fan-In/Out Line Layers** area.

### Change existing wires only (no convert)

The **Change existing wires only (no convert)** check box is used to change the layers of the existing fan in/out wires. By default, this check box is cleared. As a result, any selected lines will get converted into the fan in/out layer.

### One pick gets all connected wires

The **One pick gets all connected wires** check box is used to change all wires in the current network to the selected fan in/out line layer associated with the selected wire network. By default, this check box is selected. Now, if you clear this check box, only the selected wires will get changed to the selected fan in/out line layer associated with the selected wire network.

### Make selected layer current

The **Make selected layer current** check box will be activated only when you select a fan in/out line layer from the **Fan-In/Out Line Layers** area. Select this check box; the selected layer will be set as the current layer. Alternatively, choose the **Current** button from the **Fan-In/Out Single-line Layer** dialog box to make the selected layer as the current layer. After specifying the desired settings in the **Fan-In/Out Single-line Layer** dialog box, select the desired layer from the **Fan-In/Out Line Layers** area in this dialog box and choose the **OK-Change/Convert** button to save the changes and exit the dialog box.

# TROUBLESHOOTING WIRES

The troubleshooting of wires can be done in different ways. Some of them are discussed next.

1. Bending of wires at right angles.
2. Checking line entities.

## Bending Wires at Right Angle

| | |
|---|---|
| **Ribbon:** | Schematic > Edit Wires/Wire Numbers > Modify Wire drop-down > Bend Wire |
| **Toolbar:** | ACE:Main Electrical > Insert Wire > Bend Wire or ACE:Wires > Bend Wire |
| **Menu:** | Wires > Bend Wire |
| **Command:** | AEBENDWIRE |

The **Bend Wire** tool is used to bend wires at right angle. This tool is also used to modify wire without disturbing the original wire connections between components. To bend a wire, choose the **Bend Wire** tool from the **Modify Wire** drop-down in the **Edit Wires/ Wire Numbers** panel of the **Schematic** tab, as shown in Figure 3-55; the cursor will change into a selection box and you will be prompted to select the first wire. Select the first wire; you will be prompted to select the second wire. Select the second wire that is perpendicular to the first wire; the wire will bend at right angle. The **AEBENDWIRE** command will continue until you press ESC or right-click on the screen. Figure 3-56 shows the wire before and after bending.

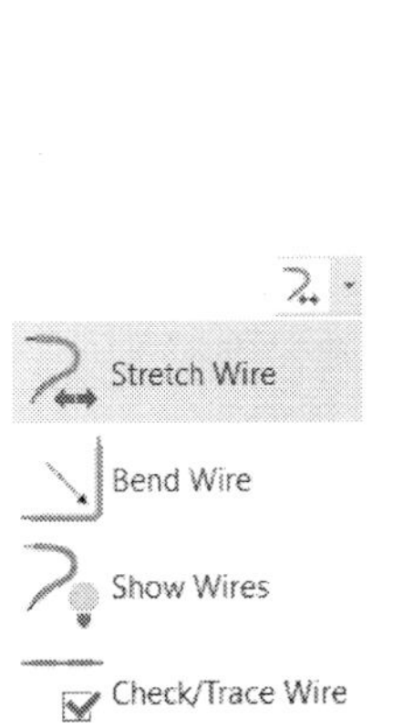


***Figure 3-55** The **Modify Wire** drop-down*

(a) (b)

***Figure 3-56** (a) Wire before bending (b) Wire after bending*

## Checking Line Entities

| | |
|---|---|
| **Ribbon:** | Schematic > Edit Wires/Wire Numbers > Modify Wire drop-down > Show Wires |
| **Toolbar:** | ACE:Main Electrical > Insert Wire > Show Wires or ACE:Wires > Show Wires |
| **Menu:** | Wires > Wire Miscellaneous > Show Wires |
| **Command:** | AESHOWWIRE |

The **Show Wires** tool is used to highlight lines (wires) in bright red color, which are found on a valid AutoCAD Electrical wire layer. This tool is also used to trace wire numbers and find out whether these wire numbers are on a valid wire layer or not. Additionally, this tool is used to check whether an entity is a wire or not. To check whether these wires or wire numbers are on valid wire layer or not, choose the **Show Wires** tool from the **Modify Wire** drop-down in the **Edit Wires/Wire Numbers** panel of the **Schematic** tab, refer to Figure 3-55; the **Show Wires and Wire Number Pointers** dialog box will be displayed, as shown in Figure 3-57. The options in this dialog box are discussed next.

### Show wires (lines on wire layers)

If you select the **Show wires (lines on wire layers)** check box, the lines (wires) on wire layers will be highlighted in bright red color. Note that they will be highlighted in bright red color only if you select the **Yes** option in the **Wire Numbering** column of the **Create/Edit Wire Type** dialog box. However, if you select the **No** option in the **Wire Numbering** column of the **Create/Edit Wire Type** dialog box, the lines (wires) on wire layers will be highlighted in magenta color. By default, this check box is selected.

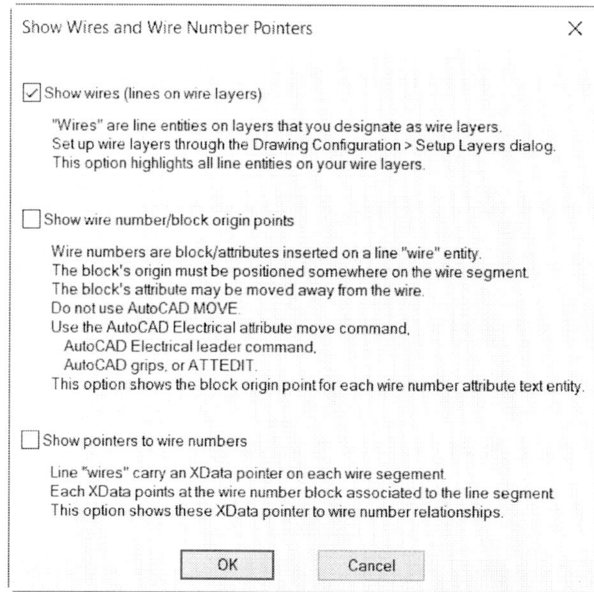


*Figure 3-57 The **Show Wires and Wire Number Pointers** dialog box*

### Show wire number/block origin points

If you select the **Show wire number/block origin points** check box, the block origin points for each wire number attribute text entity will be highlighted. Note that the origin of the block must be present on the wire segment.

### Show pointers to wire numbers

Lines (wires) contain an XData pointer on each wire segment. Each XData points at the wire number block is associated with the line segment. The XData also called as the extended entity data is the invisible information added to a block or even to a specific attribute. If you select the **Show pointers to wire numbers** check box, the XData pointer to wire number relationships will be highlighted.

After selecting the desired check boxes, choose the **OK** button from the **Show Wires and Wire Number Pointers** dialog box; the **Drawing Audit** message box will be displayed. This message box displays information about the lines on normal wire layers and the lines on no wire numbering layers. Choose the **OK** button in this message box; the wires, wire numbers, or pointers to wire numbers will be highlighted. You can choose **View > Redraw** from the menu bar to remove highlights.

# CHECKING, REPAIRING, AND TRACING WIRES AND GAP POINTERS

In this section, you will learn various ways of checking, repairing, and tracing of wires and gap pointers.

## Checking and Repairing Gap Pointers

| | |
|---|---|
| **Ribbon:** | Schematic> Edit Wires/Wire Numbers > Modify Wire Gap drop-down > Check/Repair Gap Pointers |
| **Toolbar:** | ACE:Main Electrical > Insert Wire > Check/Repair Gap Pointers or ACE:Wires > Check/Repair Gap Pointers |
| **Menu:** | Wires > Wire Numbers Miscellaneous > Check/Repair Gap Pointers |
| **Command:** | AEGAPPOINTER |

The **Check/Repair Gap Pointers** tool is used to add or repair Xdata pointers on wire segments. This tool is also used to verify Xdata pointers on both sides of a wire gap/loop. It also checks for their validity. If the Xdata pointers on both sides of a wire gap/loop are not valid, pointers will be created accordingly.

To add or repair Xdata pointers on wire segments, choose the **Check/Repair Gap Pointers** tool from the **Modify Wire Gap** drop-down in the **Edit Wires/Wire Numbers** panel of the **Schematic** tab, as shown in Figure 3-58; the cursor will change into a selection box and you will be prompted to select the wire segment. Select the wire segment; you will be prompted to select the other wire segment. Next, select the wire segment; the gap data is added, as required in wires. The command will continue until you press ENTER.

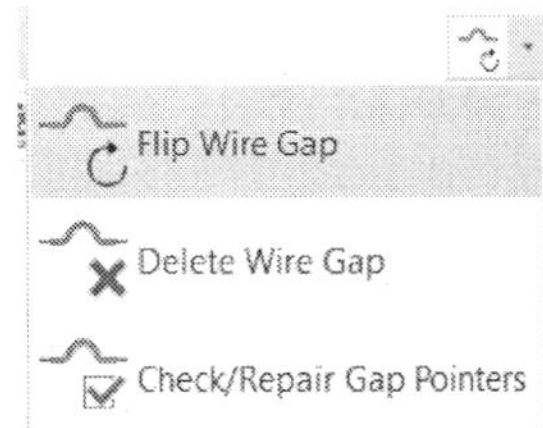


*Figure 3-58 The **Modify Wire Gap** drop-down*

## Checking/Tracing a Wire

| | |
|---|---|
| **Ribbon:** | Schematic > Edit Wires/Wire Numbers> Modify Wire drop-down > Check/Trace Wire |
| **Toolbar:** | ACE:Main Electrical > Insert Wire > Check/Trace Wire or ACE:Wires > Check/Trace Wire |
| **Menu:** | Wires > Wire Miscellaneous > Check/Trace Wire |
| **Command:** | AETRACEWIRE |

The **Check/Trace Wire** tool is used to check and highlight the wires of a wire network. Also, this tool is used to solve the problem related to shorted or unconnected wires. To check the wire, choose the **Check/Trace Wire** tool from the **Edit Wires/Wire Numbers** panel of the **Schematic** tab, refer to Figure 3-55; the cursor will change into a selection box and you will be prompted to select the wire segment. Select the wire segment and then press SPACEBAR to select the rest of the wires of the wire network. Once all wires of the wire network are selected, you will be prompted to select the wire segment again. Press ENTER to exit the command. The command sequence for checking/tracing the wire segment is as follows:

Choose the **Check/Trace Wire** tool
Check/Trace Wire Network
Select wire segment: *Select the wire segment for checking/tracing.*
Connected wire segment endpoints: *Shows the connected wire segment endpoints.*
Pan/Zoom/All segments/Quit/<Space=single step>: *Type **P** /**Z** /**A** /**Q** or press SPACEBAR.*

If you enter **A** at the **Pan/Zoom/All segments/Quit/<Space=single step>** prompt, all segments of the wire will be highlighted simultaneously. Alternatively, if you want to step through wire by wire, press SPACEBAR.

If you want to pan or zoom the selected wire, enter **P** or **Z** at the Command prompt; the connected wire segments endpoints will be displayed at the Command prompt. To exit the command, enter **Q** at the Command prompt.

**Note**

*To check errors in a drawing or in a project, choose the **DWG Audit** tool from the **Schematic** panel of the **Reports** tab; the **Drawing Audit** dialog box will be displayed. The options in this dialog box will be discussed in Chapter 6.*

# SHOWING AND EDITING WIRE SEQUENCES

In this section, you will learn about showing and editing wire sequences.

## Showing Wire Sequence

| | |
|---|---|
| **Ribbon:** | Schematic > Edit Wires/Wire Numbers > Wire Sequence drop-down > Show Wire Sequence |
| **Menu:** | Wires > Wire Miscellaneous > Show Wire Sequence |

The **Show Wire Sequence** tool is used to show the wire sequence for the selected wire network. To show the wire sequence, choose the **Show Wire Sequence** tool from the **Wire Sequence** drop-down in the **Edit Wires/Wire Numbers** panel of the **Schematic** tab, as shown in Figure 3-59; you will be prompted to select the wire network. Select a wire segment of the wire network; the connection for the first wire segment of a sequence will be shown by green arrows on the drawing. Also, you will be prompted to press SPACEBAR to show the connection for the next wire segment of a sequence. Press the SPACEBAR key to see the next wire segment connection of a sequence. If the selected wire network is spread across multiple drawings, the **(wire connection X of Y)** dialog box will be displayed (**X** represents current wire segment number and **Y** represents the total number of wire segments of a sequence), refer to Figure 3-60. This dialog box displays the drawing number, the sheet number of the drawing, the component to which the next wire segment is connected, and the location code. To show wire sequence continuously one by one, click on the **Next** button in this dialog box or press **Cancel** to terminate command. Once all the wire segments of a sequence are displayed, you will be prompted to press SPACEBAR to quit the command or press 1 to repeat the command.

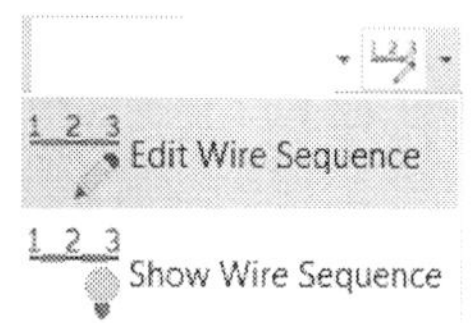


***Figure 3-59** The **Wire Sequence** drop-down*

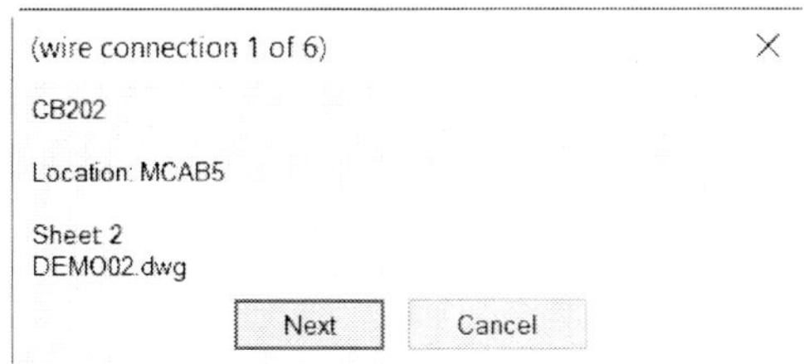


*Figure 3-60 The (wire connection 1 of 6) dialog box*

**Note**

*To activate the **Show Wire Sequence** tool, you can also right-click on the wire segment of the wire network; a marking menu will be displayed. Next, choose **Wire Sequence > Show Wire Sequence** from the marking menu.*

## Editing Wire Sequence

| | |
|---|---|
| **Ribbon:** | Schematic > Edit Wires/Wire Numbers > Wire Sequence drop-down > Edit Wire Sequence |
| **Menu:** | Wires > Wire Miscellaneous > Edit Wire Sequence |

The **Edit Wire Sequence** tool is used to edit the wire sequence for the selected wire network. To edit the wire sequence, choose the **Edit Wire Sequence** tool from the **Wire Sequence** drop-down in the **Edit Wires/Wire Numbers** panel of the **Schematic** tab, refer to Figure 3-59; you will be prompted to select the wire network. Select a wire segment of the wire network; the **Edit Wire Connection Sequence** dialog box will be displayed, refer to Figure 3-61. Note that the list displayed in this dialog box will vary as per the wire network selected. The options in this dialog box are used to edit the wire connection sequence.

The '*' symbol at the start of an entry in the list of this dialog box indicates that the corresponding wire segment is in the drawing other than the active drawing. Similarly, the 't' symbol at the start of an entry indicates that the corresponding wire segment is connected to a terminal.

To change a wire sequence, select a row from the list of wire sequences in the **Edit Wire Connection Sequence** dialog box and choose the **Move Up** or **Move Down** button to move the selected row up or down, respectively. You can also choose the **Pick Mode** button to actually pick the wire segments in the drawing for changing the wire sequence. You can use the **Sort Location** button to sort the list in this dialog box according to the installation and location values.

To connect additional component(s) to a terminal in a sequence, select the terminal and component(s) in the list; the **Add v** button will be activated. Next, choose the **Add v** button; the selected entries will be displayed in the **Direct-to-Terminal Secondary Sequences** list. The **Move Up** and **Move Down** button located below the **Add v** button are activated if you select more than one component to connect to terminal. These buttons will be used to change the sequence of components connected to the terminal. Choose **Reset** to remove the sequence from the **Direct-to-Terminal Secondary Sequences** list. The radio buttons in the **Connection** area are used to define whether the component is connected to the internal or external side of the connector, or is undefined.

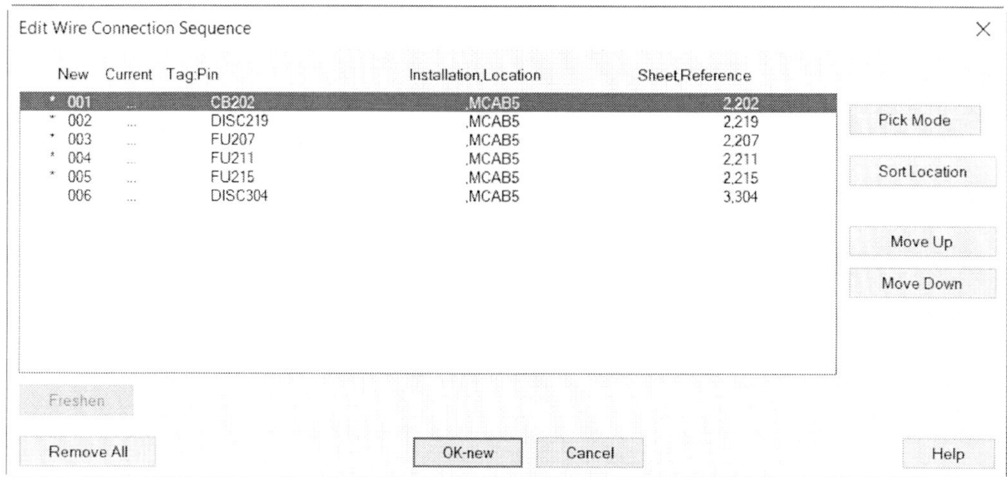


*Figure 3-61 The* ***Edit Wire Connection Sequence*** *dialog box*

The **Freshen** button is used to update the wire connectivity database for outdated files. The **Remove All** button is used to remove the wire connection override information from the wire network. After performing necessary changes, choose **OK-new** to modify the wire sequence and to update the component wire connection and terminal symbols information, if any.

# MANIPULATING WIRE GAPS

In this section, you will learn about various methods of manipulating wire gaps.

## Inserting Wire Gaps

| | |
|---|---|
| **Ribbon:** | Schematic > Insert Wires/Wire Numbers > Wire drop-down > Gap |
| **Toolbar:** | ACE:Main Electrical > Insert Wire >Insert Wire Gap or ACE:Wires > Insert Wire Gap |
| **Menu:** | Wires > Wire Miscellaneous > Insert Wire Gap |
| **Command:** | AEWIREGAP |

When wires cross each other, a gap is created between wires automatically. This wire gap can be set in the **Wiring Style** area of the **Styles** tab of the **Drawing Properties** dialog box. Sometimes, you may need to insert gap between the crossing wires manually. To insert wire gaps manually, first you need to set the options in the **Drawing Properties** dialog box. To do so, right-click on the selected drawing; a shortcut menu will be displayed. Choose **Properties > Drawing Properties** from the shortcut menu; the **Drawing Properties** dialog box will be displayed. Next, choose the **Styles** tab from this dialog box; the options in this tab will be displayed. Next, select the **Loop** option

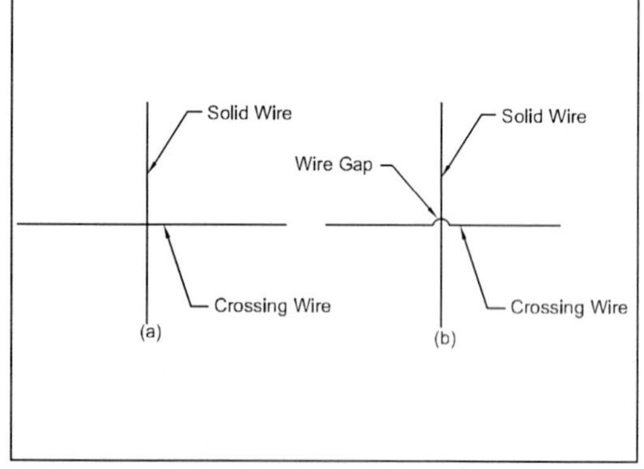


*Figure 3-62 The solid and crossing wires (a) before inserting the wire gap and (b) after inserting the wire gap*

from the **Wire Cross** drop-down list in the **Wiring Style** area and then choose the **OK** button from the **Drawing Properties** dialog box to exit this dialog box. To insert a gap between wires, choose the **Gap** tool from the **Wire** drop-down of the **Insert Wires/Wire Numbers** panel of the **Schematic** tab; the cursor will change into a selection box and you will be prompted to select the wire to remain solid. Select the wire; you will be prompted to select the crossing wire. Next, select the crossing wire; a gap between the wires will be inserted. Press ESC to exit the command. Figure 3-62 shows the wires before and after inserting the wire gap in between the solid and crossing wires.

## Removing Wire Gaps

| | |
|---|---|
| **Ribbon:** | Schematic> Edit Wires/Wire Numbers > Modify Wire Gap drop-down > Delete Wire Gap |
| **Toolbar:** | ACE:Main Electrical >Insert Wire > Delete Wire Gap or ACE:Wires > Delete Wire Gap |
| **Menu:** | Wires > Wire Miscellaneous > Delete Wire Gap |
| **Command:** | AEERASEWIREGAP |

The **Delete Wire Gap** tool is used to remove gap between the existing crossing wires. To do so, first you need to set the options in the **Drawing Properties** dialog box. To do so, right-click on the selected drawing; a shortcut menu will be displayed. Choose **Properties > Drawing Properties** from the shortcut menu; the **Drawing Properties** dialog box will be displayed. Choose the **Styles** tab in this dialog box. Next, select the **Solid** option from the **Wire Cross** drop-down list in the **Wiring Style** area and then choose the **OK** button from the **Drawing Properties** dialog box to exit this dialog box. To bridge the gap between wires, choose the **Delete Wire Gap** tool from the **Edit Wires/Wire Numbers** panel of the **Schematic** tab; the cursor will change into a selection box and you will be prompted to select objects. Select the wire segments where gap is not required and press ENTER; the gap between the wire segments will be removed.

## Flipping Wire Gaps/Loops

| | |
|---|---|
| **Ribbon:** | Schematic> Edit Wires/Wire Numbers > Modify Wire Gap drop-down > Flip Wire Gap |
| **Toolbar:** | ACE:Main Electrical > Insert Wire > Flip Wire Gap or ACE:Wires > Flip Wire Gap |
| **Menu:** | Wires > Wire Miscellaneous > Flip Wire Gap |
| **Command:** | AEFLIPWIREGAP |

The **Flip Wire Gap** tool is used to interchange the gap or loop between wires. To interchange the gap or loop, choose the **Flip Wire Gap** tool from the **Edit Wires/Wire Numbers** panel of the **Schematic** tab;the cursor will change into a selection box and you will be prompted to select the gap or the gapped wire. Select the gapped wire; you will notice that the gaps or the loops between the wires are interchanged. It implies that the gapped or the looped wire will become solid and the crossing wires will become gapped or looped. This command will continue until you press ENTER. Figure 3-63 shows the wires before and after flipping the wire gaps between them.

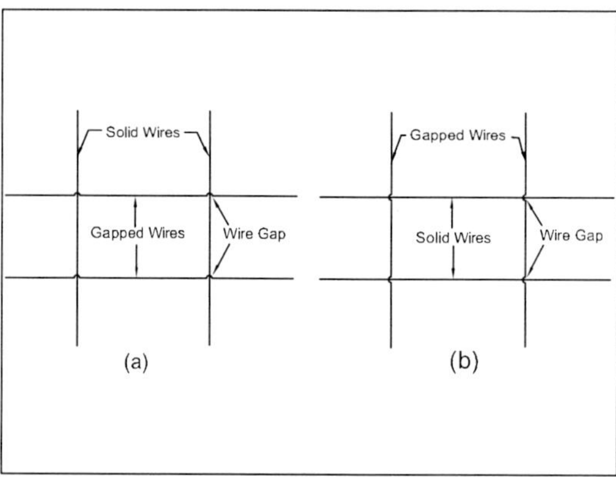


***Figure 3-63** The wires (a) before flipping the wire gap and (b) after flipping the wire gap*

If you enter **W** at the Command prompt, you will be prompted to select wires. You can select multiple wires by using a crossing window and then press ENTER. On doing so, the **Select to Gap Horizontal or Vertical Wires** dialog box will be displayed, as shown in Figure 3-64. The options in this dialog box are discussed next.

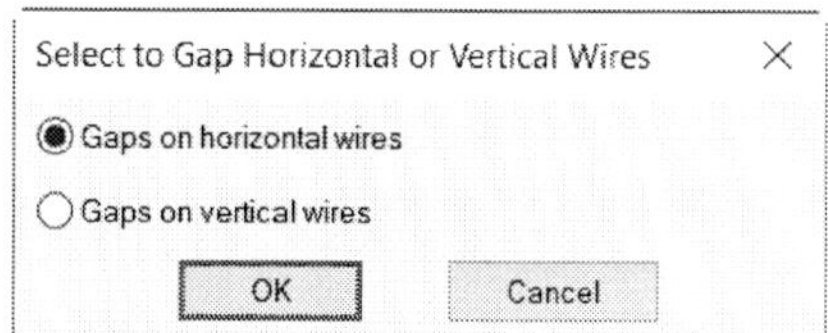


***Figure 3-64** The **Select to Gap Horizontal or Vertical Wires** dialog box*

The **Gaps on horizontal wires** radio button is selected by default and is used to flip gaps or loops on horizontal wires. Choose the **OK** button from the **Select to Gap Horizontal or Vertical Wires** dialog box; the gaps or loops will be flipped to horizontal wires. Select the **Gaps on vertical wires** radio button to flip gaps or loops on vertical wires and choose the **OK** button; the gaps or loops will be flipped on vertical wires.

# TUTORIALS

## Tutorial 1

In this tutorial, you will insert wire numbers into the *DEMO05.dwg* drawing file, as shown in Figure 3-65. Next, you will add wire to this drawing and use the **Trim Wire** tool to trim the wire. Also, you will use the **Delete Wire Numbers** tool to delete a wire number.

**(Expected time: 15 min)**

The following steps are required to complete this tutorial:

a. Open the drawing.
b. Save the drawing.

c. Add the drawing to the **CADCIM** project list.
d. Insert the wire.
e. Trim the wire.
f. Delete the wire number.
g. Save the drawing file.

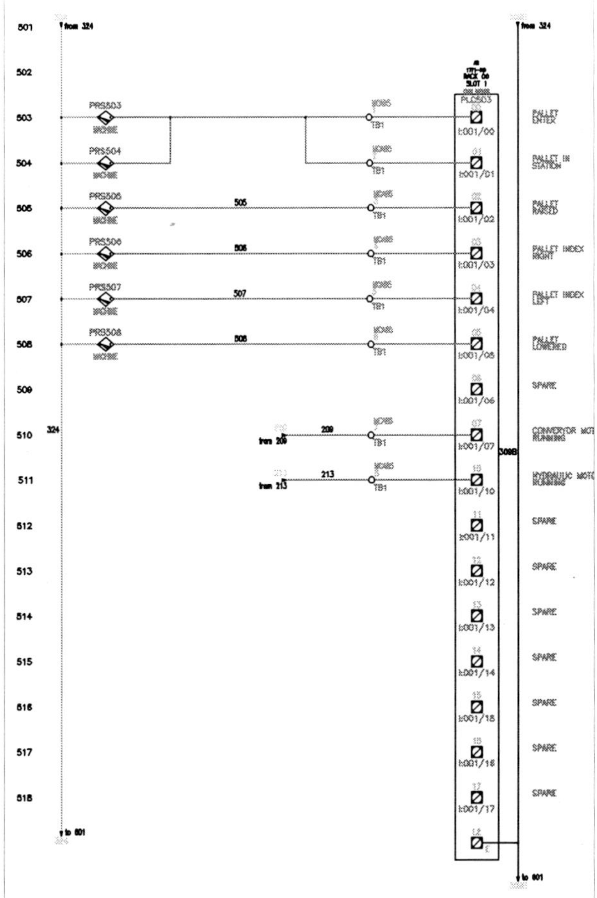


*Figure 3-65 Ladder diagram for Tutorial 1*

## Opening the Drawing

1. Make sure the **CADCIM** project is activated. If it is not already activated, right-click on the **CADCIM** project; a shortcut menu is displayed. Choose the **Activate** option from it.

2. Double-click on the drawing *DEMO05.dwg* to open it.

## Saving the Drawing

1. Save the drawing *DEMO05.dwg* with the name *C03_tut01.dwg*. To do so, choose **Save As > Drawing** from the **Application Menu** or choose **File > Save As** from the menu bar; the **Save Drawing As** dialog box is displayed.

**Note**

*If the **Save Drawing As** dialog box is not displayed, press ESC and enter **FILEDIA** at the Command promp; you are prompted to enter a new value for FILEDIA. Next, enter **1** at the Command prompt. Now, choose **Save As > Drawing** from the **Application Menu**; the **Save Drawing As** dialog box is displayed.*

2. Next, choose **Documents > Acade 2022 > AeData > Proj > CADCIM** and then enter **C03_tut01** in the **File name** edit box.

   By default, **AutoCAD 2018 Drawing (*.dwg)** is displayed in the **Files of type** drop-down list.

3. Choose the **Save** button from the **Save Drawing As** dialog box; the *C03_tut01.dwg* file is saved.

## Adding the Drawing to the CADCIM Project List

1. Right-click on the **CADCIM** project; a shortcut menu is displayed. Choose the **Add Active Drawing** option from the shortcut menu; the **Apply Project Defaults to Drawing Settings** message box is displayed. Choose the **Yes** button; the *C03_tut01.dwg* is added to the **CADCIM** project.

2. Drag and drop the *C03_tut01.dwg* drawing on the *TUTORIALS* subfolder; the *C03_tut01.dwg* drawing is moved to the *TUTORIALS* subfolder.

**Note**

*While adding the C03_tut01.dwg drawing file to the **CADCIM** project if the **Update Terminal Associations** message box is displayed, choose the **Yes** button in it; the C03_tut01.dwg is added to the **CADCIM** project.*

3. Next, choose **Save** from the **Application Menu** to save the drawing.

## Inserting the Wire

1. Choose the **Wire** tool from **Schematic > Insert Wires/Wire Numbers > Wire** drop-down; you are prompted to specify the start point of the wire. Specify the start point of the wire on the left of wire number 503, refer to Figure 3-66; you are prompted to specify the end point of the wire. Now, specify the endpoint of the wire on the left of wire number 504; you are again prompted to specify the start point of the wire. Next, specify the start point on the right of wire number 503; you are prompted to specify the endpoint of the wire. Specify the endpoint of the wire on the right of wire number 504; the wires are inserted in the drawing, as shown in Figure 3-66.

2. Press ENTER to exit the command.

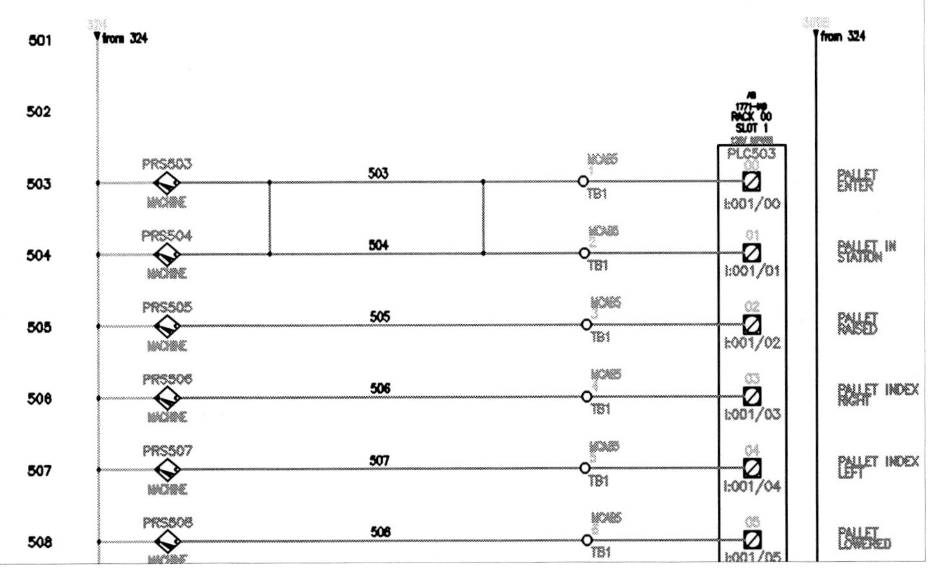

*Figure 3-66 Wires inserted in the drawing*

## Trimming the Wire

1. Choose the **Trim Wire** tool from the **Edit Wires/Wire Numbers** panel of the **Schematic** tab; you are prompted to select the wire. Select the middle wire of rung 504 that makes a short circuit between rung 503 and rung 504; the wire is trimmed, as shown in Figure 3-67.

2. Next, press ENTER to exit the command.

## Deleting the Wire Number

1. Choose the **Delete Wire Numbers** tool from the **Edit Wires/Wire Numbers** panel of the **Schematic** tab; you are prompted to select objects. Select the wire number 503 of rung 503 and then press ENTER; the wire number 503 is deleted, as shown in Figure 3-68.

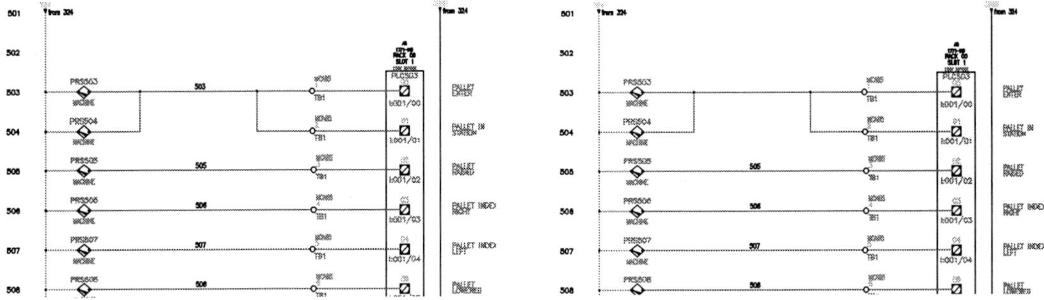

*Figure 3-67 Ladder after trimming the middle portion of rung 504*

*Figure 3-68 Ladder after deleting the wire number of rung 503*

## Saving the Drawing File

1. Choose **Save** from the **Application Menu** to save the *C03_tut01.dwg* drawing file.

**Note**

*It is recommended to save all tutorials in the forthcoming chapters in the TUTORIALS subfolder of the* ***CADCIM*** *project.*

## Tutorial 2

In this tutorial, you will use the *C03_tut01.dwg* drawing file and create a wire type using the **Create/Edit Wire Type** tool and then change the wire type of another wire to the wire type that you have created using the **Change/Convert Wire Type** tool, as shown in Figure 3-69.

**(Expected time: 10 min)**

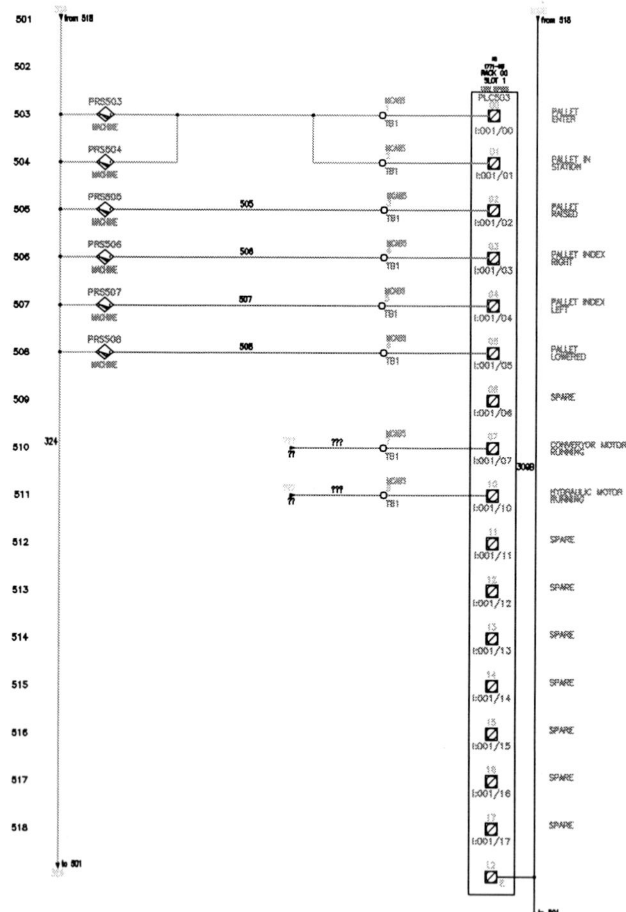


*Figure 3-69 Ladder diagram for Tutorial 2*

The following steps are required to complete this tutorial:

a. Open, save, and add the drawing to the **CADCIM** project list.
d. Create the wire type.
c. Change the wire type.
d. Save the drawing.

## Opening, Saving, and Adding the Drawing to the CADCIM Project List

1. Make sure the **CADCIM** project is activated. Double-click on the *C03_tut01.dwg* drawing to open it. You can also download this file from *www.cadcim.com*. The path of the file is as follows:

   *Textbooks > CAD/CAM > AutoCAD Electrical > AutoCAD Electrical 2022 for Electrical Control Designers*

2. Choose **Save As > Drawing** from the **Application Menu**; the **Save Drawing As** dialog box is displayed. Next, browse to **Documents > Acade 2022 > AeData > Proj > CADCIM** in the **Save in** drop-down list and then enter **C03_tut02** in the **File name** edit box.

   By default, **AutoCAD 2018 Drawing (*.dwg)** is displayed in the **Files of type** drop-down list.

3. Choose the **Save** button in the **Save Drawing As** dialog box; the *C03_tut02.dwg* is saved.

4. Right-click on the **CADCIM** project; a shortcut menu is displayed. Choose the **Add Active Drawing** option from the shortcut menu; the **Apply Project Defaults to Drawing Settings** message box is displayed. Choose the **Yes** button in the message box; the *C03_tut02.dwg* is added to the **CADCIM** project drawing list.

**Note**
*While adding the C03_tut02.dwg drawing file to the **CADCIM** project if the **Update Terminal Associations** message box is displayed, choose the **Yes** button from it; the C03_tut02.dwg is added to the **CADCIM** project.*

5. Move the drawing *C03_tut02.dwg* to the *TUTORIALS* subfolder as discussed earlier. Next, choose **Save** from the **Application Menu** to save the drawing.

## Creating the Wire Type

1. Choose the **Create/Edit Wire Type** tool from **Schematic > Edit Wires/Wire Numbers > Modify Wire Type** drop-down; the **Create/Edit Wire Type** dialog box is displayed, as shown in Figure 3-70.

2. Click in the **Wire Color** column of the blank cell of the **Create/Edit Wire Type** dialog box. Next, enter **GRN** in the selected cell of the **Wire Color** column.

3. Next, enter **14AWG** in the selected cell of the **Size** column and press ENTER; **GRN_14AWG** is displayed in the **Layer Name** column. Also, **Yes** is displayed in the **Wire Numbering** column, as shown in Figure 3-71.

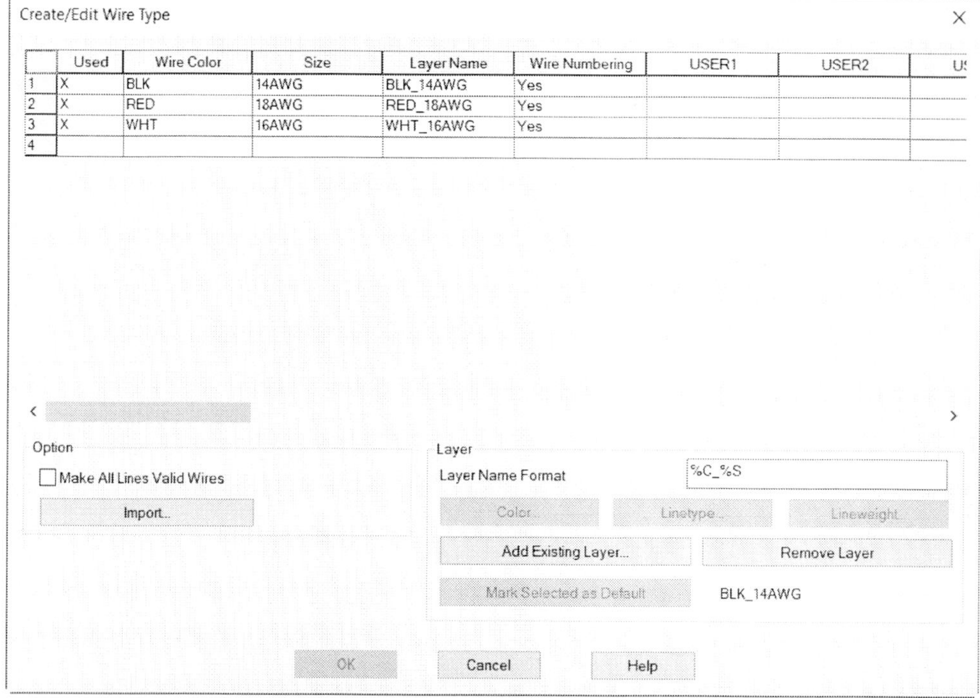


*Figure 3-70 The **Create/Edit Wire Type** dialog box*

Create/Edit Wire Type

| | Used | Wire Color | Size | Layer Name | Wire Numbering | USER1 | USER2 | USE |
|---|---|---|---|---|---|---|---|---|
| 1 | X | BLK | 14AWG | BLK_14AWG | Yes | | | |
| 2 | X | RED | 18AWG | RED_18AWG | Yes | | | |
| 3 | X | WHT | 16AWG | WHT_16AWG | Yes | | | |
| 4 | | GRN | 14 AWG | GRN_14 AWG | Yes | | | |

*Figure 3-71 The **Create/Edit Wire Type** dialog box showing the wire type that you have created*

4. Next, choose the **Color** button from the **Layer** area of the **Create/Edit Wire Type** dialog box; the **Select Color** dialog box is displayed. In this dialog box, select the green color and choose the **OK** button to return to the **Create/Edit Wire Type** dialog box.

5. Choose the **OK** button from the **Create/Edit Wire Type** dialog box; the wire type is created.

## Changing the Wire Type

1. To change the wire type of the selected wire to the wire type you have created, right-click on the wire between PRS503 and TB1 of rung 503; a marking menu is displayed. Choose the **Change/Convert Wire Type** option from the marking menu; the **Change/Convert Wire Type** dialog box is displayed. Select the row where GRN is displayed under the **Wire Color** column and choose the **OK** button; the wire type and the color of the selected wire is changed to green color (GRN_14AWG wire type). Next, press ENTER to exit the command.

## Saving the Drawing

1. Choose **Save** from the **Application Menu** to save the *C03_tut02.dwg* drawing file.

# Tutorial 3

In this tutorial, you will use the *C03_tut02.dwg* drawing file and insert a wire number and fix all wire numbers in it. You will also insert wire color/gauge labels, as shown in Figure 3-72.

**(Expected time: 15 min)**

The following steps are required to complete this tutorial:

a. Open, save, and add the drawing to the **CADCIM** project list.
b. Insert a wire number and fix all wire numbers.
c. Insert wire/color gauge labels.
d. Show wires and pointers to wire numbers.
e. Save the drawing.

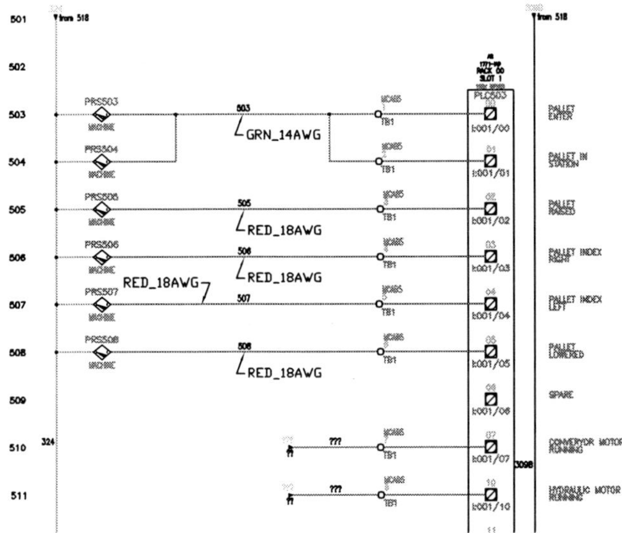


*Figure 3-72 Ladder diagram for Tutorial 3*

## Opening, Saving, and Adding the Drawing to the CADCIM Project List

1. Open the *C03_tut02.dwg* file and then save it with the name *C03_tut03.dwg*.

   You can also download this file from *www.cadcim.com*. The path of the file is as follows:

   *Textbooks > CAD/CAM > AutoCAD Electrical > AutoCAD Electrical 2022 for Electrical Control Designers*

2. Add the *c03_tut03.dwg* file to the *TUTORIALS* subfolder of the **CADCIM** project as discussed in Tutorial 2. Next, choose **Save** from the **Application Menu** to save the drawing.

## Inserting a Wire Number and Fixing All Wire Numbers

1. Choose the **Wire Numbers** tool from **Schematic > Insert Wires/Wire Numbers > Wire Numbers** drop-down; the **Sheet 5 - Wire Tagging** dialog box is displayed. 

2. In this dialog box, choose the **Pick Individual Wires** button; you are prompted to select objects. Select the middle wire of the rung 503 and press ENTER; the wire number 503 is inserted into the wire.

   Next, you need to fix the wire numbers in the drawing.

3. Choose the **Fix** tool from **Schematic > Edit Wires/Wire Numbers > Edit Wire Number** drop-down; you are prompted to select objects. Select the wire numbers 503, 505, 506, 507, and 508. Next, press ENTER; the selected wire numbers are fixed. Note that these wire numbers will not be updated at the time of retagging.

**Note**

*To unfix the fixed wire numbers, choose the* ***Edit Wire Number*** *tool from the* ***Schematic > Edit Wires/Wire Numbers > Edit Wire Number*** *drop-down; you are prompted to select the wire number. Select the wire number; the* ***Edit Wire Number/Attributes*** *dialog box is displayed. In this dialog box, clear the* ***Fixed*** *check box and choose* ***OK****; the selected wire number is unfixed.*

## Inserting Wire Color/Gauge Labels

1. Choose the **Wire Color/Gauge Labels** tool from **Schematic > Insert Wires/Wire Numbers > Wire Number Leader** drop-down; the **Insert Wire Color/Gauge Labels** dialog box is displayed.

2. In this dialog box, choose the **Auto Placement** button in the **With leader** area; you are prompted to select objects. Select the wires of rung 503, 505, 506, 507, and 508. Next, press ENTER; the **Color/gauge text for GRN_14AWG** dialog box is displayed. Choose **OK**; the **Color/gauge text for RED_14AWG** dialog box is displayed. Again, choose **OK**; the wire color/gauge labels are inserted for the selected wires, refer to Figure 3-72.

## Showing Wires and Pointers to Wire Numbers

1. Choose the **Show Wire** tool from the **Modify Wire** drop-down in the **Edit Wires/Wire Numbers** panel of the **Schemtic** tab; the **Show Wires and Wire Number Pointers** dialog box is displayed.

2. Make sure the **Show wires (Lines on wire layers)** check box is selected. Next, choose **OK**; the **Drawing Audit** message box is displayed. Choose **OK** in this message box.

   The **Drawing Audit** message box specifies that all wires in this drawing are on wire layers and are highlighted in red color.

3. Again, choose the **Show Wire** tool from the **Modify Wire** drop-down in the **Edit Wires/Wire Numbers** panel of the **Schematic** tab; the **Show Wires and Wire Number Pointers** dialog box is displayed.

4. Clear the **Show wires (Lines on wire layers)** check box and select the **Show pointers to wire numbers** check box and choose **OK**; the drawing is modified with pointers pointing to corresponding wire numbers.

## Saving the Drawing

1. Choose **Save** from the **Application Menu** to save the *C03_tut03.dwg* drawing file.

# Tutorial 4

In this tutorial, you will open the *C03_tut03.dwg* drawing file and use the **Show Wire Sequence** tool to trace the wire sequence of one of the wire networks in this drawing. Next, you will edit the wire sequence of this wire network using the **Edit Wire Sequence** tool.

**(Expected time: 15 min)**

The following steps are required to complete this tutorial:

a. Open, save, and add the drawing to the **CADCIM** project list.
b. Trace the wire sequence.
c. Edit the wire sequence.
d. Save the drawing.

## Opening, Saving, and Adding the Active Drawing to the CADCIM Project List

1. Open the *C03_tut03.dwg* file and then save it with the name *C03_tut04.dwg*.

   You can also download this file from *www.cadcim.com*. The path of the file is as follows:

   *Textbooks > CAD/CAM > AutoCAD Electrical > AutoCAD Electrical 2022 for Electrical Control Designers*

2. Add the *c03_tut04.dwg* file to the *TUTORIALS* subfolder of the **CADCIM** project as discussed in Tutorial 2. Next, choose **Save** from the **Application Menu** to save the drawing.

## Tracing the Wire Sequence

1. Select the wire network, as shown in Figure 3-73.

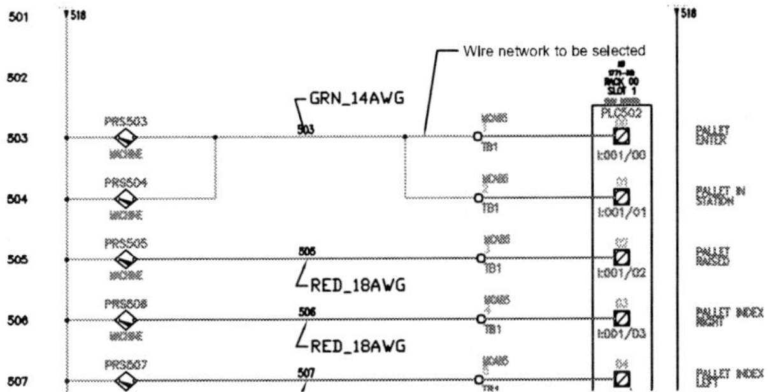


*Figure 3-73 Selected wire network*

2. Right-click on the selected wire and choose **Wire Sequence > Show Wire Sequence** from the marking menu, as shown in Figure 3-74; Green arrows are displayed between **PRS503** and **PRS504** representing the start of the wire sequence, refer to Figure 3-75. Also, Command Prompt notifies that first wire out of the three wires in the network is displayed and you are prompted to press SPACEBAR to see the next wire in the sequence.

3. Press SPACEBAR; the next wire sequence is shown by green arrows connecting **PRS504** with pin number 1 of **TB1** terminal strip along with the first sequence in grey arrows.

4. Press SPACEBAR again; green arrows are shown in between the pin number 1 of **TB1** and pin number 2 of **TB1** along with last two sequences in grey arrows. Figure 3-76 shows the complete wire connection sequence of the selected wire network. Next, you are prompted to press SPACEBAR again.

5. Press SPACEBAR. Now, you are prompted to press SPACEBAR to quit the command or press 1 to repeat the command. Press SPACEBAR to end the command.

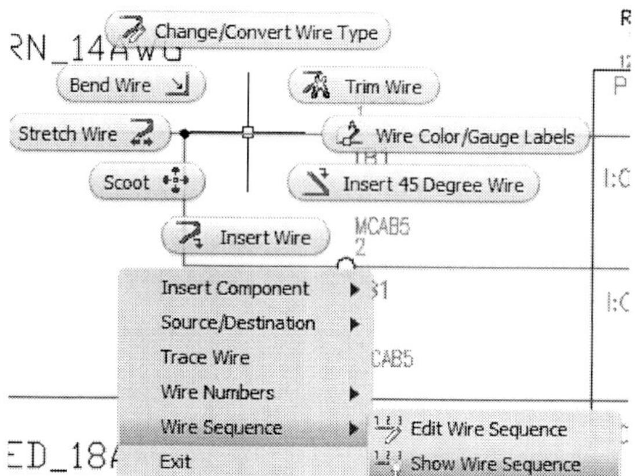


*Figure 3-74 Choosing **Show Wire Sequence** from the marking menu*

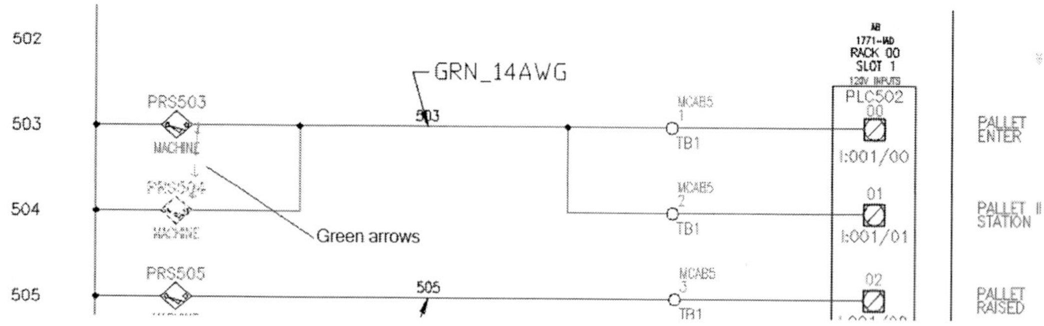


*Figure 3-75 Green arrows representing the start of the wire sequence*

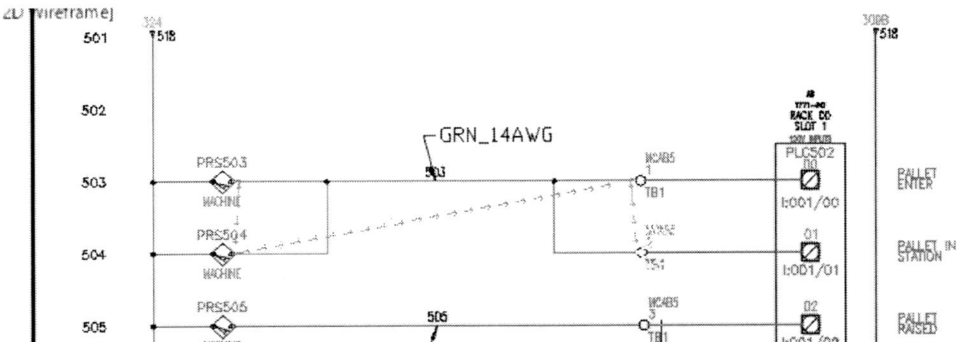


*Figure 3-76 Complete wire connection sequence of the selected wire network*

## Editing the Wire Sequence

1. Choose the **Edit Wire Sequence** tool from the **Wire Sequence** drop-down in the **Edit Wires/ Wire Numbers** panel of the **Schematic** tab; you are prompted to select wire network to process.

2. Select the same wire network that was selected earlier, refer to Figure 3-73; the **Edit Wire Connection Sequence** dialog box is displayed, as shown in Figure 3-77.

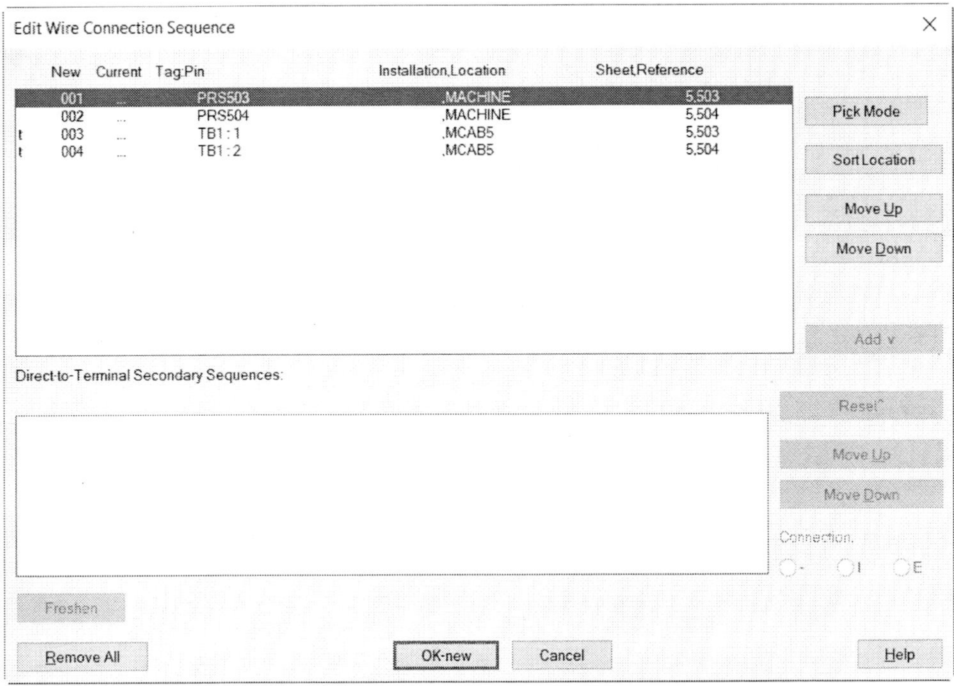


*Figure 3-77 The **Edit Wire Connection Sequence** dialog box*

3. Select the last row in the **Edit Wire Connection Sequence** dialog box and then choose **Move Up**; the last two rows get interchanged, as shown in Figure 3-78. Now, choose **OK-new**; the wire connection sequence is edited.

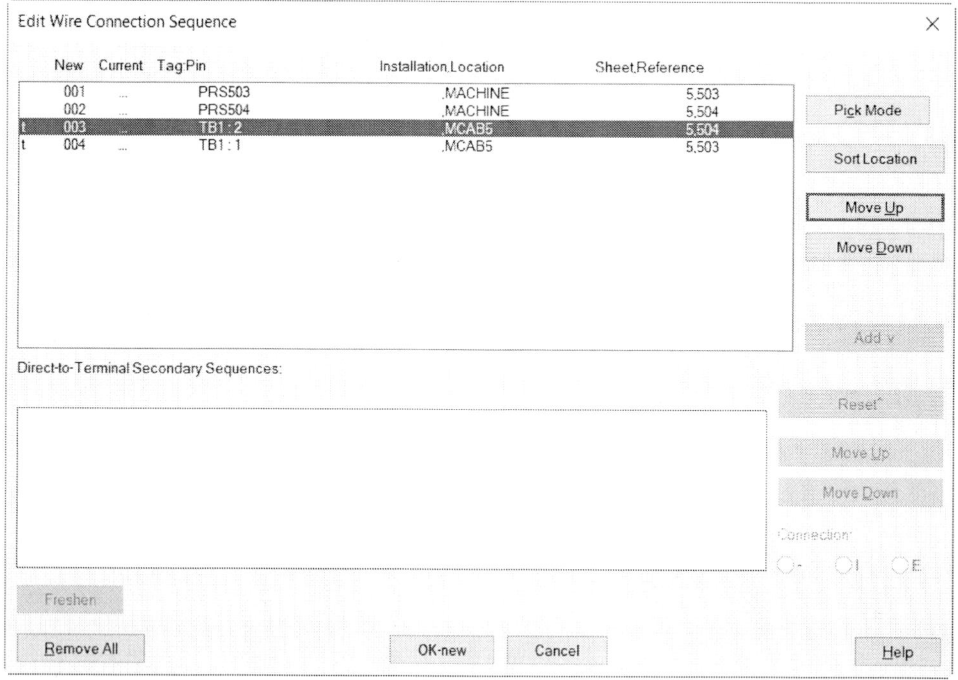


*Figure 3-78 The last two rows interchanged*

4. To see the edited wire connection sequence, use the **Show Wire Sequence** tool again. You will notice that the wire connection sequence is edited, as shown in Figure 3-79.

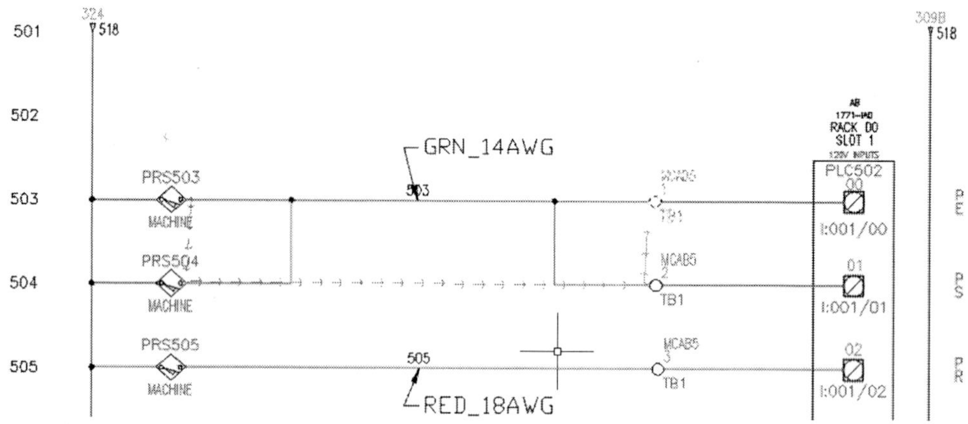


*Figure 3-79 Edited wire connection sequence*

## Saving the Drawing

1. Choose **Save** from the **Application Menu** to save the *C03_tut04.dwg* drawing file.

## Self-Evaluation Test

**Answer the following questions and then compare them to those given at the end of this chapter:**

1. Which of the following commands is used to create a wire type?

   (a) **AESOURCE** (b) **AEWIRETYPE**
   (c) **AEATTSHOW** (d) **AECONVERTWIRETYPE**

2. The __________ tool is used to stretch a wire until it meets another wire or a component.

3. Wire layer names for drawings are set in the __________ dialog box.

4. The __________ tool is used to bend wires at right angle.

5. The __________ tool is used to insert a source signal arrow into a wire.

6. The __________ tool is used to insert wire color/gauge labels into a wire.

7. When lines are placed on an AutoCAD Electrical defined wire layer, AutoCAD Electrical treats AutoCAD line entities as wires. (T/F)

8. The **Multiple Bus** tool is used to create multiple phase bus wiring. (T/F)

9. The **Trim Wire** tool is used to trim wires as well as the components inserted in it. (T/F)

10. You can define a limited number of wire layers in AutoCAD Electrical. (T/F)

## Review Questions

**Answer the following questions:**

1. Which of the following dialog boxes is similar to the **AutoCAD Layer Properties Manager** dialog box?

   (a) **Multiple Bus** (b) **Set Wire Type**
   (c) **Change/Convert Wire Type** (d) **Create/Edit Wire Type**

2. Which of the following tools is used to move a wire number to a different wire in the same wire network?

   (a) **Scoot** (b) **Move Wire Number**
   (c) **Copy Wire Number** (d) None of these

3. Which of the following commands is used to insert wire numbers?

   (a) **AEWIRE** (b) **AEWIREGAP**
   (c) **AEWIRENO** (d) **AECOPYWIRENO**

4. Which of the following tools is used to move the wire number from right, left, top, or bottom to in-line with wire and vice-versa?

   (a) **Wire Number Leader** (b) **Swap Wire Numbers**
   (c) **Move/Show Attribute** (d) **Toggle Wire Number (In-line)**

5. You can automatically add wire numbers to each wire network in your project drawings. (T/F)

6. A wire number is an attribute that is attached to an invisible block. (T/F)

7. You can insert an in-line marker into any wire. (T/F)

8. The **Create/Edit Wire type** tool is used only for creating the wire type. (T/F)

9. If there is no wire layer in a drawing, a new wire will be drawn in the **WIRES** layer. (T/F)

10. The **Set Wire Type** dialog box is used to set a wire type for new wires only. (T/F)

# EXERCISE

## Exercise 1

In this exercise, you will open the drawing *DEMO04.DWG* from the **CADCIM** project and add it to the **NEW_PROJECT** project and then you will save it with the name *C03_exer01.dwg* in this project, refer to Figure 3-80. Then, you will create a new wire type with the name BLU_16AWG and convert the wire type of the wire in between CR406 and TS-B which are located on rung 411 to the BLU_16AWG. You will also make the wire numbers of the rungs 411, 412, and 413 as fixed by using the **Edit Wire Number** tool. **(Expected time: 20 min)**

**Note**

*It is recommended to save all exercises of the forthcoming chapters in the **NEW_PROJECT** project.*

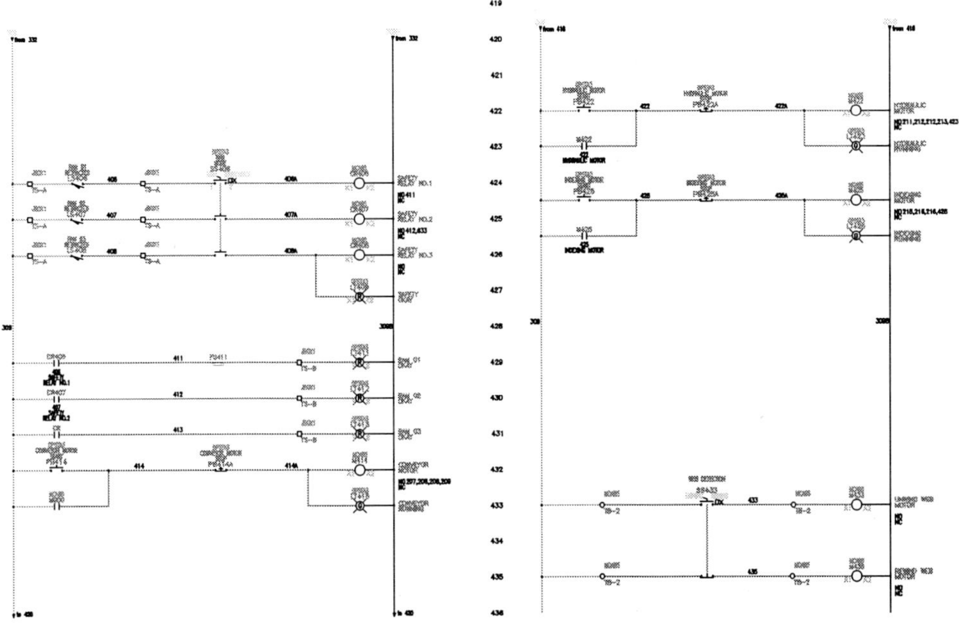

***Figure 3-80*** *Ladder diagram for Exercise 1*

## Answers to Self-Evaluation Test

**1.** b, **2. Stretch Wire**, **3. Create/Edit Wire Type**, **4. Bend Wire**, **5. Source Arrow**, **6. Wire Color/ Gauge Labels**, **7.** T, **8.** T, **9.** F, **10.** F

# Chapter 4

# Creating Ladders

## Learning Objectives

**After completing this chapter, you will be able to:**

- *Create ladders*
- *Insert a new ladder in the drawing*
- *Modify an existing ladder*
- *Understand the format referencing of ladders*

# INTRODUCTION

In this chapter, you will learn about ladders and their multiple parameters such as rung spacing, number of rungs, width of ladder, ladder reference numbers, and so on. You will also learn to insert single or three phase ladders (horizontal/vertical), add and remove rungs, revise a ladder, and so on.

# LADDERS

A collection of wires joined together to form a ladder-like matrix is called a ladder. The wires that are outside the ladder are called bus and the wires that are inside the ladder are called rungs. Usually, three phase ladders are created only with bus wires. Ladders are the base of schematic drawings. These schematic drawings are called ladder diagrams because they resemble the shape of a ladder. These diagrams are used to describe the logic connections of electrical control systems. Moreover, these diagrams are the specialized schematics that are commonly used to represent industrial control logic systems. The ladder diagrams have two vertical rails called bus (supply power) and several rungs (horizontal lines) that represent control circuits.

You can create the ladder type circuits easily by using the **Insert Ladder** and **Add Rung** tools. However, ladders and ladder rungs are wires and can also be created by using the **Wire** tool.

You can insert any number of ladders into a drawing anytime, provided the ladders do not overlap each other.

Ladders are of two types: vertical and horizontal. You can configure ladders using the **Project Properties** dialog box. To invoke the **Project Properties** dialog box, right-click on the active project; a shortcut menu will be displayed. Choose the **Properties** option from the shortcut menu; the **Project Properties** dialog box will be displayed. In this dialog box, choose the **Drawing Format** tab. Now, from the **Ladder Defaults** area, select the required type of the ladder. Figure 4-1 shows a ladder and its components.

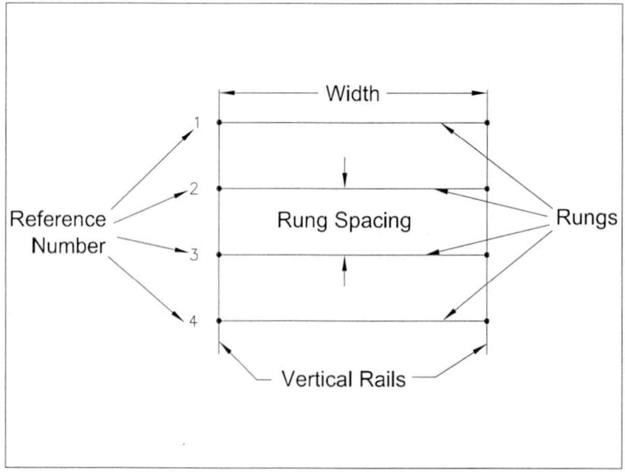


***Figure 4-1*** *Ladder and its components*

## Inserting a New Ladder

| | |
|---|---|
| **Ribbon:** | Schematic > Insert Wires/Wire Numbers > Insert Ladder drop-down >Insert Ladder |
| **Toolbar:** | ACE:Main Electrical > Insert Ladder or ACE:Ladders > Insert Ladder |
| **Menu:** | Wires > Ladders > Insert Ladder |
| **Command:** | AELADDER |

The **Insert Ladder** tool is used to insert a ladder along with rungs and reference numbers. You can insert a number of ladders in a drawing. To insert a ladder in a drawing, choose the **Insert Ladder** tool from the **Insert Ladder** drop-down in the **Insert Wires/Wire Numbers** panel of the **Schematic** tab, as shown in Figure 4-2; the **Insert Ladder** dialog box will be displayed, as shown in Figure 4-3. The areas and options in this dialog box are discussed next.

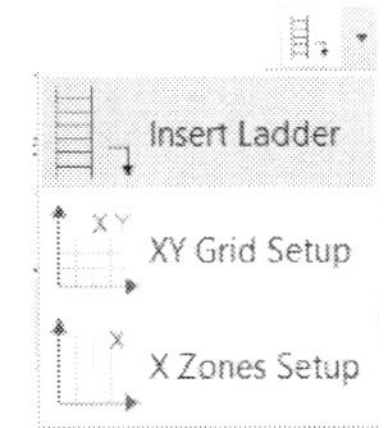


*Figure 4-2 The **Insert Ladder** drop-down*

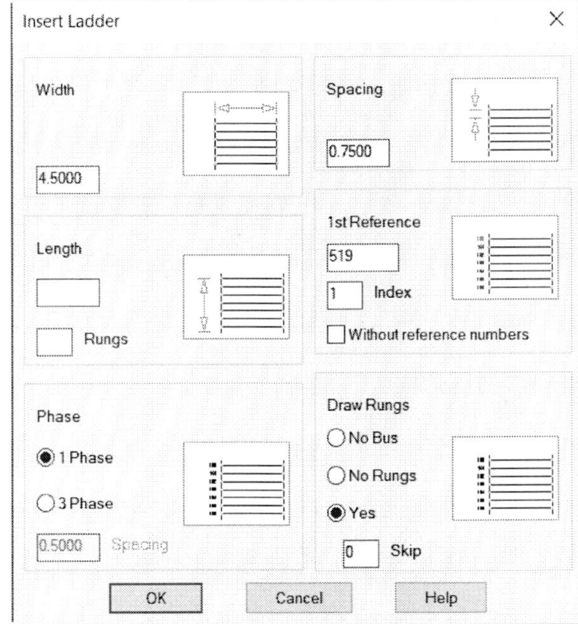


*Figure 4-3 The **Insert Ladder** dialog box*

**Note**

*If a drawing has sheet number specified to it and the ladder is being inserted into it, the name of the **Insert Ladder** dialog box will be **Sheet: XX - Insert Ladder** dialog box where XX stands for the sheet number.*

### Width

Enter the width of the ladder in the **Width** edit box. By default, 4.5000 (for NFPA drafting standard in inches) or 400 (for IEC drafting standard in mm) is displayed in this edit box.

## Spacing
Enter the value for spacing between two horizontal rungs of a ladder in the **Spacing** edit box. By default, the value in this edit box is 0.7500 (for NFPA drafting standard in inches) or 40 (for IEC drafting standard in mm).

## Length
You can enter the length of a ladder in the **Length** edit box to calculate the number of rungs automatically.

## Rungs
You can enter the number of rungs in the **Rungs** edit box. However, if you have already entered the length of a ladder in the **Length** edit box, the value of rungs will be calculated automatically and will be displayed in the **Rungs** edit box.

## 1st Reference
This edit box is used to specify the first line reference for a ladder. To do so, enter the 1st reference number for the ladder in the **1st Reference** edit box.

**Note**
*You can erase a particular line reference number from a ladder by using the AutoCAD* ***ERASE*** *command. But make sure not to erase the topmost line reference number because it is the MLR (master ladder reference) block of the ladder that carries the ladder's intelligence.*

## Index
The index value is used to increment the line reference number of a ladder. Enter the required index value in the **Index** edit box to increment the line reference number of a ladder. By default,1 is displayed in this edit box.

## Without reference numbers
If you select the **Without reference numbers** check box, the ladder will not show any line reference number. By default, this check box is cleared.

## Phase
The **Phase** area is used to specify the phase of a ladder. The options in the **Phase** area are discussed next.

### 1 Phase
By default, the **1 Phase** radio button is selected and is used to create a single-phase ladder. Note that the **Spacing** edit box in the **Phase** area will not be active if this radio button is selected.

### 3 Phase
Select the **3 Phase** radio button to create three-phase ladders. You will notice that when you select the **3 Phase** radio button, the **Width** and **Draw Rungs** areas will not be activated in the dialog box, as shown in Figure 4-4.

## Draw Rungs

The **Draw Rungs** area will be activated only if you select the **1 Phase** radio button from the **Phase** area. This area is used to specify how to draw rungs. The options in the **Draw Rungs** area are discussed next.

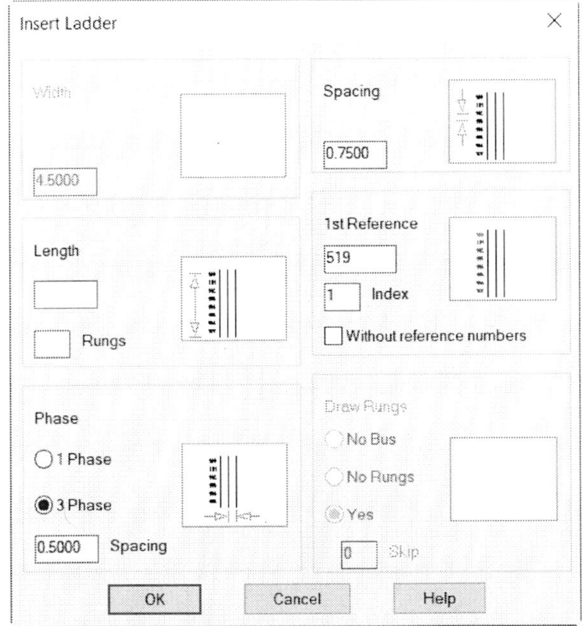


*Figure 4-4 The **Insert Ladder** dialog box with the **3 Phase** radio button selected*

### No Bus

Select the **No Bus** radio button to draw line reference numbers only, refer to Figure 4-5(a). You will also notice that the **Width** area will not be activated on selecting this radio button.

### No Rungs

The **No Rungs** radio button is selected to insert vertical rails and reference numbers of a ladder without rungs into a drawing, refer to Figure 4-5(b).

### Yes

The **Yes** radio button is selected by default and is used to insert rungs, reference numbers, and vertical bus automatically into a drawing, refer to Figure 4-5(c).

### Skip

The **Skip** edit box is used to specify the number of rungs to be skipped. For example, if you enter **1** in this edit box, then the rungs will be added at alternate line reference numbers. Similarly, if you enter **6** in this edit box, six rungs will be skipped between any two consecutive rungs drawn, as shown in Figure 4-6.

After specifying the desired settings in the **Insert Ladder** dialog box, choose the **OK** button; you will be prompted to specify the start position of the first rung. Specify the starting point of the first rung; the ladder will get inserted into your drawing provided you have entered the number of rungs in the **Rungs** edit box or the length of the ladder in the **Length** edit box.

Now, if you want to insert the ladder into your drawing manually, leave the **Rungs** and **Length** edit boxes blank. Choose the **OK** button; you will be prompted to specify the start position of the first rung. Specify the start position of the first rung; you will be prompted to specify the approximate position of the last reference number. Specify the approximate position of the last reference number by moving the cursor downward, and then click on the screen again; the ladder will get inserted into your drawing. The prompt sequence that will follow when you insert a ladder manually is given next:

Choose the **Insert Ladder** tool
Insert Ladder
Current wiretype: "WIRES"
Specify start position of first rung or [wireType]: *Specify the start position of the first rung of a ladder.*

Specify approximate position of the last reference number (Z=zoom down, R=realtime pan): *Specify the approximate position of the last reference number of the ladder, enter 'Z' to Zoom down, 'R' for Realtime Pan, or press ESC to exit the command.*

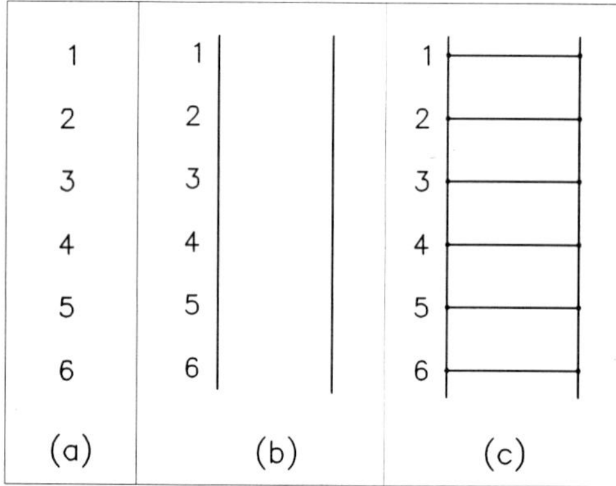


*Figure 4-5 The ladder created by selecting (a) the **No Bus** radio button (b) the **No Rungs** radio button, and (c) the **Yes** radio button from the **Draw Rungs** area*

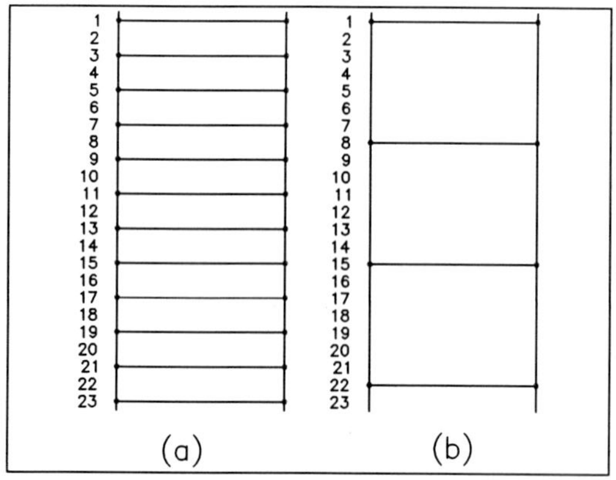


*Figure 4-6 The ladder with 18 Rungs with (a) Skip = **1** and (b) Skip = **6***

**Tip**

*The ladders are inserted into the default wire type till you change the wire type. To change the wire type, choose the **Insert Ladder** tool from the **Insert Wires/Wire Numbers** panel of the **Schematic** tab; the **Insert Ladder** dialog box will be displayed. Specify the required options and choose the **OK** button. Next, enter **T** at the Command prompt; the **Set Wire Type** dialog box will be displayed. Using this dialog box, you can change the wire type of the ladder. This dialog box has already been discussed in Chapter 3.*

**Note**

*You can use the **MOVE** command of AutoCAD to move the ladder. However, while doing so, make sure that you move the entire ladder including the very first line reference number (the MLR block insert). After doing so, choose the **Revise Ladder** tool from the **Edit Wires/Wire Numbers** panel of the **Schematic** tab; the **Modify Line Reference Numbers** dialog box will be displayed. Next, choose the **Cancel** button from this dialog box to reread and update its internal ladder location list.*

# MODIFYING AN EXISTING LADDER

At times, you may need to modify an existing ladder. You can add or delete rungs, change the size of the ladder, reposition it, convert line reference numbers, renumber ladder reference, and so on. To do so, you need to use the ladder modification tools such as **Revise Ladder**, **Convert Ladder**, and so on. The existing ladder can be modified by using different methods which are discussed next.

## Renumbering an Existing Ladder

| | |
|---|---|
| **Ribbon:** | Schematic > Edit Wires/Wire Numbers > Modify Ladder drop-down > Revise Ladder |
| **Toolbar:** | ACE:Main Electrical > Insert Ladder > Revise Ladder or ACE:Ladders |
| **Menu:** | Wires > Ladders > Revise Ladder |
| **Command:** | AEREVISELADDER |

The **Revise Ladder** tool is used to modify the spacing between line reference numbers. You can also use this tool to renumber the line reference numbers of ladders.

To modify a ladder, choose the **Revise Ladder** tool from the **Modify Ladder** drop-down in the **Edit Wires/Wire Numbers** panel of the **Schematic** tab, refer to Figure 4-7; the **Modify Line Reference Numbers** dialog box will be displayed, as shown in Figure 4-8. The different options in this dialog box are discussed next.

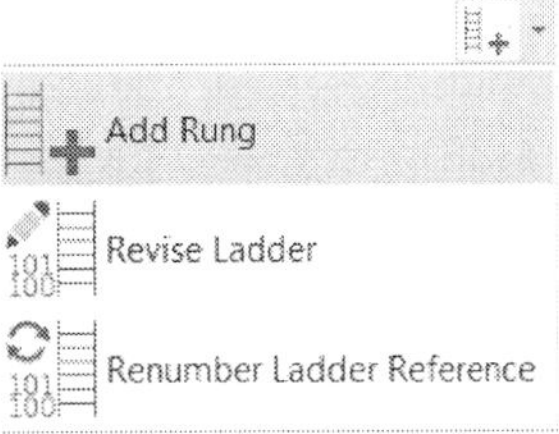


*Figure 4-7 The **Modify Ladder** drop-down*

### Rung Spacing

The **Rung Spacing** edit box is used to change the spacing between the line reference numbers of a ladder. The change in spacing between the line reference numbers will be in proportion to the value specified in this edit box.

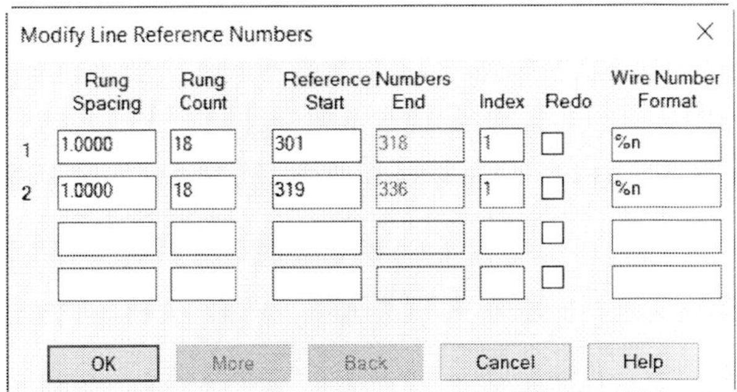


*Figure 4-8 The **Modify Line Reference Numbers** dialog box*

### Rung Count

The **Rung Count** edit box is used to change the number of reference numbers specified for each ladder. To do so, enter the desired number of reference numbers in the **Rung Count** edit box.

## Reference Numbers Start

The **Reference Numbers Start** edit box is used to specify the starting reference number for the ladder.

## Reference Numbers End

The **Reference Numbers End** edit box shows the reference number of the endpoint of the ladder based on the value in the **Rung Count** edit box and the **Reference Numbers Start** edit box.

## Index

The **Index** edit box is used to change the index value specified in the **Insert Ladder** dialog box. The index is the number by which the line reference numbering is incremented. By default, the index value in this edit box is 1.

## Redo

Select the **Redo** check box to refresh the line reference numbering.

## Wire Number Format

In the **Wire Number Format** edit box, specify the format of the wire number in the ladder. By default, %N is displayed in this edit box.

## More

The **More** button will be activated only if the number of ladders inserted in the drawing is more than four. Choose this button to display the succeeding set of ladders present in the drawing.

## Back

The **Back** button will be activated only if the number of ladders inserted in the drawing is more than four. Choose this button to display the previous set of ladders present in the drawing.

Choose the **OK** button to save the changes made in the **Modify Line Reference Numbers** dialog box.

**Note**

*On updating the ladder's reference numbers, the existing components or wire numbers do not get updated. To update the existing components, choose the* ***Retag Components*** *tool from the* ***Edit Components*** *panel of the* ***Schematic*** *tab; the* ***Retag Components*** *dialog box will be displayed. Specify the required options in this dialog box and choose the* ***OK*** *button; the component tags will be updated to match the new line reference number.*

*To update the wire numbers, choose the* ***Wire Numbers*** *tool from the* ***Insert Wires/Wire Numbers*** *panel of the* ***Schematic*** *tab; the* ***Wire Tagging*** *dialog box will be displayed. This dialog box has already been explained in the previous chapter. In this dialog box, select the* ***Tag/retag all*** *radio button from the* ***To do*** *area to update the wire numbers.*

## Changing the Size of a Ladder

In this section, you will learn how to shorten, lengthen, widen, or compress an existing ladder using the **Revise Ladder** tool.

### Lengthening or Shortening a Ladder

| | |
|---|---|
| **Ribbon:** | Schematic > Edit Wires/Wire Numbers > Modify Ladder drop-down > Revise Ladder |
| **Toolbar:** | ACE:Main Electrical > Insert Ladder > Revise Ladder or ACE:Ladders > Revise Ladder |
| **Menu:** | Wires > Ladders > Revise Ladder |
| **Command:** | AEREVISELADDER |

To lengthen or shorten a ladder, first you need to revise the ladder and then drag it. To do so, you need to follow two steps. These steps are discussed next.

Choose the **Revise Ladder** tool from the **Modify Ladder** drop-down in the **Edit Wires/Wire Numbers** panel of the **Schematic** tab; the **Modify Line Reference Numbers** dialog box will be displayed, refer to Figure 4-8. In this dialog box, specify the required value in the **Rung Count** edit box to match appropriate ladder length. Choose the **OK** button; the reference number of the ladder will change accordingly.

To lengthen or shorten a ladder, choose the **Stretch** tool from the **Modify** panel of the **Home** tab; the cursor will change to the selection box and you will be prompted to select the objects to stretch by using a crossing lasso. Next, select the vertical rails of a ladder, as shown in Figure 4-9 and then press ENTER; you will be prompted to specify the base point. Specify the base point or displacement and then click on the screen; the length of the ladder will change accordingly. Note that if you move the cursor downward, the length of the ladder will increase and if you move the cursor upward, the length of the ladder will decrease.

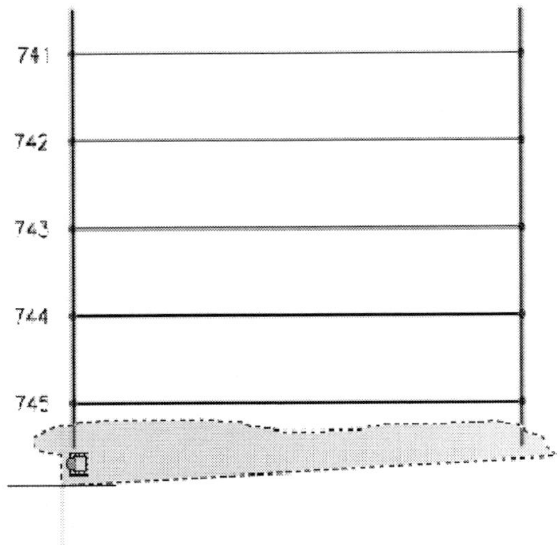


***Figure 4-9** Selecting the ladder by using the crossing lasso*

## Widening or Compressing a Ladder

| | |
|---|---|
| **Ribbon:** | Schematic > Edit Components > Modify Components drop-down > Scoot |
| **Toolbar:** | ACE:Main Electrical > Scoot<br>or ACE:Scoot > Scoot |
| **Menu:** | Components > Scoot |
| **Command:** | AESCOOT |

To widen or compress a ladder, choose the **Scoot** tool from the **Modify Components** drop-down in the **Edit Components** panel of the **Schematic** tab, as shown in Figure 4-10; the cursor will change into a selection box and you will be prompted to select the component, wire, or wire number.

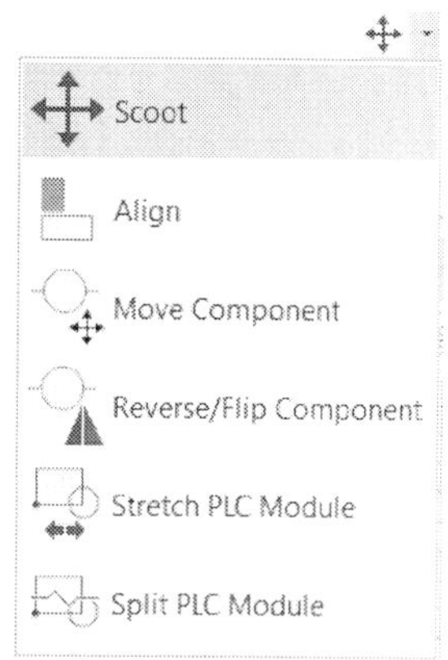


***Figure 4-10** The **Modify Components** drop-down*

Select the vertical rail of the ladder; the temporary rectangular graphics will be displayed. Move the cursor in the drawing according to your requirement and click on the screen. Next, press ENTER to exit the command. You can push in or pull out the vertical rail. If you push in the vertical rail, the ladder will be compressed and if you pull out the vertical rail, the ladder will be widened. Note that the ladder reference numbers cannot be moved when you use the **AESCOOT** command on vertical rails.

In case you want to align the components that are attached with ladders, choose the **Align** tool from the **Edit Components** panel of the **Schematic** tab; the components will be aligned. The alignment of components is discussed in detail in Chapter 6.

**Note**

*You can also use the **Scoot** tool to move rungs.*

## Repositioning a Ladder

As discussed earlier, you can change the position of an existing ladder on your drawing by using the **MOVE** command of AutoCAD. But make sure you select the entire ladder while repositioning it. To do so, choose the **Move** tool from the **Modify** panel of the **Home** tab; you will be prompted to select the objects. Select the ladder using a crossing window and press ENTER; you will be prompted to specify the base point for the ladder. Specify the base point or displacement for the ladder; the ladder will be moved to the specified location.

After moving the ladder to the desired location, you need to update the new location of the ladder in AutoCAD Electrical internal ladder location list. To do so, choose the **Revise Ladder** tool from the **Edit Wires/Wire Numbers** panel of the **Schematic** tab; the **Modify Line Reference Numbers** dialog box will be displayed, refer to Figure 4-8. Choose the **Cancel** button to force AutoCAD Electrical to reread and update its internal ladder location list.

## Changing the Rung Spacing

| | |
|---|---|
| **Ribbon:** | Schematic > Edit Wires/Wire Numbers > Modify Ladder drop-down > Revise Ladder |
| **Toolbar:** | ACE:Main Electrical > Insert Ladder > Revise Ladder or ACE:Ladders > Revise Ladder |
| **Menu:** | Wires > Ladders > Revise Ladder |
| **Command:** | AEREVISELADDER |

To change the rung spacing of an existing ladder, first you need to revise the ladder and then move rungs to their new locations. To revise the ladder, choose the **Revise Ladder** tool from the **Modify Ladder** drop-down in the **Edit Wires/Wire Numbers** panel of the **Schematic** tab, refer to Figure 4-7; the **Modify Line Reference Numbers** dialog box will be displayed, refer to Figure 4-8. Specify a new rung spacing value in the **Rung Spacing** edit box and then the new rung count value in the **Rung Count** edit box to change the length of the ladder. Choose the **OK** button from this dialog box; the ladder will be modified according to the specified values.

Now, to move rungs to a new location, choose the **Scoot** tool from the **Edit Components** panel of the **Schematic** tab. Alternatively, use the **STRETCH** command of AutoCAD to move the existing rungs to a new rung location. The **Scoot** tool is discussed in detail in Chapter 6.

## Adding Rungs

| | |
|---|---|
| **Ribbon:** | Schematic > Edit Wires/Wire Numbers > Modify Ladder drop-down >Add Rung |
| **Toolbar:** | ACE:Main Electrical > Add Rung |
| **Menu:** | Wires > Add Rung |
| **Command:** | AERUNG |

The **Add Rung** tool is used to add rungs between the vertical rails of a ladder having extra line reference numbers than the number of rungs in the ladder. To add rungs to a ladder, choose the **Add Rung** tool from the **Modify Ladder** drop-down in the **Edit Wires/Wire Numbers** panel of the **Schematic** tab, refer to Figure 4-7; you will be prompted to add the rung passing through the specified location. You can specify the insertion point or enter **T** at the Command Prompt. If you specify the insertion point anywhere in the blank space between the vertical bus wires, the rung will be added between the vertical rails. If you enter **T** at the Command Prompt, the **Set Wire Type** dialog box will be displayed. This dialog has already been discussed in the previous chapter. You can select a new wire type in this dialog box and the selected wire type will become the current wire type and you can continue inserting the rungs in the ladder with the changed wire type. This command will continue till you press ESC or ENTER.

The command sequence that will follow is given below.

Choose the **Add Rung** tool
Current wiretype: "**WIRES**"
Add rung passing through this location or [wiretype]: *Specify the insertion point for the rung or press ENTER to exit the command.*

In the above command sequence, the **Current wiretype** Command prompt shows the current wiretype. By default "**WIRES**" is selected and displayed in the Command prompt.

**Note**

*While adding a new rung to the ladder, if some schematic symbols are encountered in between the rungs, then AutoCAD Electrical will break the rungs across the symbols and get connected to the vertical rails.*

## Converting Line Reference Numbers

| | |
|---|---|
| **Ribbon:** | Conversion Tools > Tools > Convert Ladder |
| **Toolbar:** | ACE:Conversion Tools > Convert Ladder |
| **Menu:** | Wires > Ladders > Convert Ladder<br>or Projects > Conversion Tools > Convert Drawing > Convert Ladder |
| **Command:** | AE2LADDER |

The **Convert Ladder** tool is used to convert normal ladder reference text or numbers to AutoCAD Electrical intelligent ladder reference number. If you have existing non-AutoCAD Electrical drawing, this tool can be used to create AutoCAD Electrical intelligent drawing. To convert ladder reference, choose the **Convert Ladder** tool from the **Tools** panel of the **Conversion Tools** tab; the cursor will change into a selection box. Select the non-intelligent line reference number and press ENTER; the **Modify Line Reference Numbers** dialog box will be displayed, refer to Figure 4-8. Next, specify the required values in this dialog box and choose the **OK** button; you will notice that the existing ladder information has been updated.

## Renumbering the Ladder Line Reference

| | |
|---|---|
| **Ribbon:** | Schematic > Edit Wires/Wire Numbers ><br>Modify Ladder drop-down > Renumber Ladder Reference |
| **Toolbar:** | ACE:Main Electrical > Insert Ladder > Renumber Ladder Reference<br>or ACE:Ladders > Renumber Ladder Reference |
| **Menu:** | Wires > Ladders > Renumber Ladder Reference |
| **Command:** | AERENUMBERLADDER |

The **Renumber Ladder Reference** tool is used to renumber the line reference number of ladders within a project. To do so, choose the **Renumber Ladder Reference** tool from the **Modify Ladder** drop-down in the **Edit Wires/Wire Numbers** panel of the **Schematic** tab; the **Renumber Ladders** dialog box will be displayed, as shown in Figure 4-11. The options in this dialog box are discussed next.

Enter the first line reference number for the first ladder of the first drawing in the **1st drawing, 1st ladder, 1st line reference number** edit box. The **Use next sequential reference** radio button is selected by default. As a result, it will increment the first ladder reference of the second drawing and the following drawings by 1.

If you select the **Skip, drawing to drawing count =** radio button, the edit box on its right will be activated. In this edit box, you can enter the value that you want to skip for the top line reference number of the next drawing. For example, consider that there are two drawings, Dwg1.dwg and

Dwg2.dwg in a project and these drawings contain one ladder each with 10 rungs. Now, if you enter **100** in the **1st drawing, 1st ladder, 1st line reference number** edit box in the **Renumber Ladders** dialog box and **20** in the **Skip, drawing to drawing count =** edit box, the top line reference number of the ladder of Dwg1.dwg will be **100** and the top line reference number of the ladder in Dwg 2.dwg will be **130**.

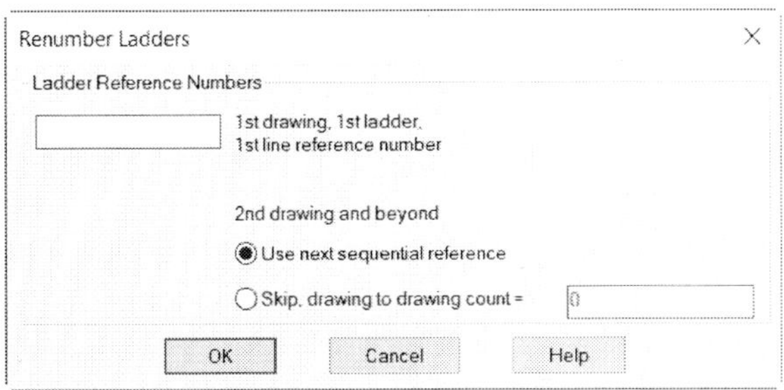


*Figure 4-11 The **Renumber Ladders** dialog box*

After entering the required parameters, choose the **OK** button; the **Select Drawings to Process** dialog box will be displayed. Select the drawing that you want to process and choose the **Process** button; the drawings will be transferred from the top list to the bottom list of the dialog box. Choose the **OK** button from the **Select Drawings to Process** dialog box; the line reference numbers of the ladder in the selected drawings will be changed according to the specified values.

# CHANGING THE REFERENCE NUMBERING STYLE OF A LADDER

You can change the referencing style of a ladder to be inserted into the drawing. To do so, right-click on the drawing in the **PROJECT MANAGER**; a shortcut menu will be displayed. Choose **Properties > Drawing Properties** from the shortcut menu; the **Drawing Properties** dialog box will be displayed. Next, choose the **Drawing Format** tab. By default, the **Reference Numbers** radio button is selected in the **Format Referencing** area of this dialog box. On choosing the **Setup** button in this area, the **Line Reference Numbers** dialog box will be displayed, as shown in Figure 4-12.

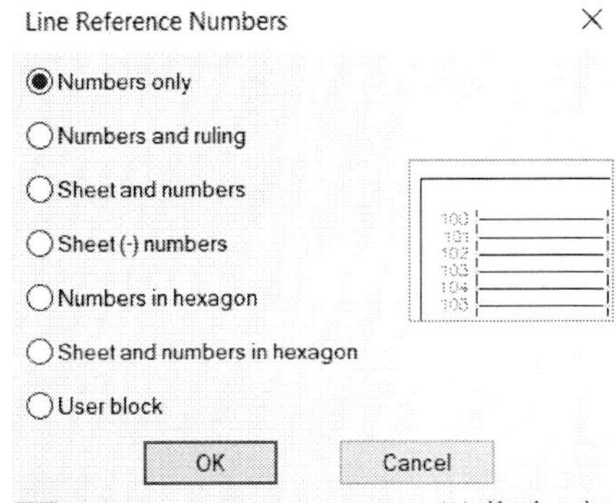


*Figure 4-12 The **Line Reference Numbers** dialog box*

By default, the **Numbers only** radio button is selected. As a result, reference numbers will be displayed along with the ladder inserted. Select the required radio button in this dialog box; the style of line reference numbers will change accordingly. Choose the **OK** button in the **Line Reference Numbers** dialog box to save the changes made and exit the dialog box. Also, choose **OK** in the **Drawing Properties** dialog box to exit the dialog box.

# INSERTING X GRID LABELS

| | |
|---|---|
| **Ribbon:** | Schematic > Insert Wires/Wire Numbers > Insert Ladder drop-down > X Zones Setup |
| **Toolbar:** | ACE:Main Electrical > Insert Ladder > X Zone or ACE:Ladders > X Zone |
| **Command:** | AEXZONE |

The **X Zones Setup** tool is used to insert X grid labels into the ladders of a drawing, which use X zone for format referencing. To insert X grid labels into ladders, choose the **X Zones Setup** tool from the **Insert Ladder** drop-down in the **Insert Wires/Wire Numbers** panel of the **Schematic** tab; the **X Zones Setup** dialog will be displayed. Note that this dialog box will be displayed only if you select the **X Zones** radio button in the **Drawing Format** tab of the **Drawing Properties** dialog box. If this radio button is not selected, the **AutoCAD Message** message box will be displayed, as shown in Figure 4-13, indicating that the drawing is not configured for X Zones.

Alternatively, you can invoke the **X Zones Setup** dialog box by selecting the **X Zones** radio button in the **Drawing Format** tab of the **Drawing Properties** or the **Project Properties** dialog box and then choosing the **Setup** button. The options in the **X Zones Setup** dialog box, as shown in Figure 4-14, are discussed next.

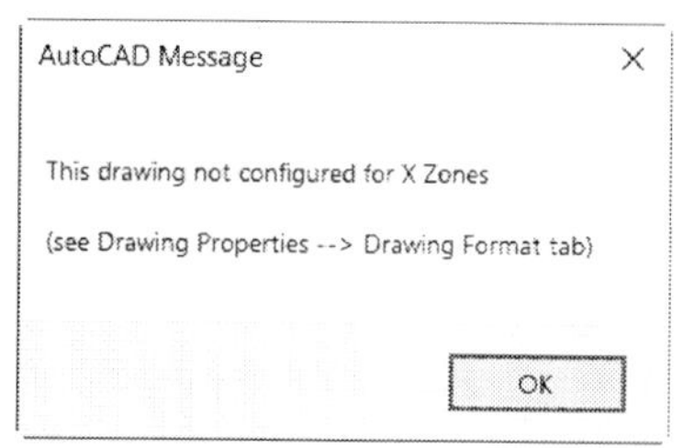


***Figure 4-13** The **AutoCAD Message** message box*

## Origin Area

The **Origin** area is used to specify the origin of the X Zone grid of a ladder. The options in this area are discussed next.

### X

Enter the X coordinate for the origin of the X Zone grid in the **X** edit box.

### Y

Enter the Y coordinate for the origin of the X Zone grid in the **Y** edit box.

### Pick>>

If you choose the **Pick>>** button, you will be prompted to specify the origin of the drawing. Specify the origin for the X zone near the upper left corner of the drawing. You will notice that the X and Y coordinates of the origin of the X zone grid will be displayed in the **X** and **Y** edit boxes of the **X Zones Setup** dialog box. Once you specify the values in these edit boxes, the **Insert zone labels** check box will be activated.

## Spacing Area

Enter horizontal spacing between grid columns in the **Horizontal** edit box of the **Spacing** area. By default, 2.0 is displayed in this edit box.

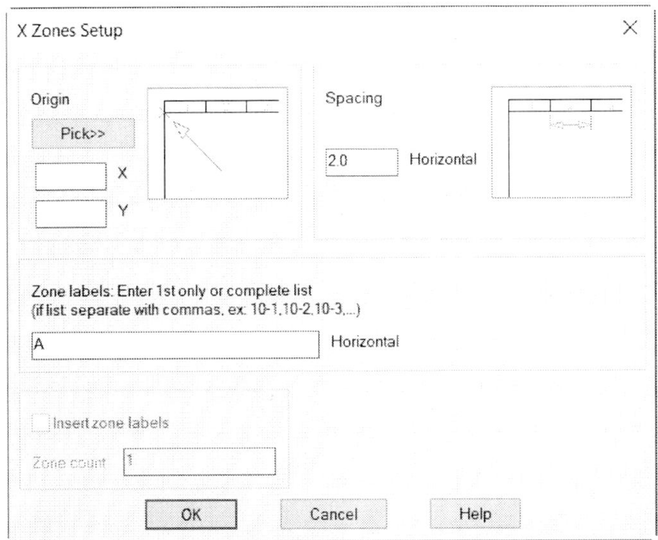


*Figure 4-14 The **X Zones Setup** dialog box*

## Zone labels Area

The **Zone labels** area is used to specify labels for grid columns. In the **Horizontal** edit box, you can enter the first value for zone or specify the complete list, but make sure you use comma for separating the list. By default, A is displayed in the **Horizontal** edit box of the **Zone labels** area.

## Insert zone labels

The **Insert zone labels** check box will get activated only if you enter the values in the **X** and **Y** edit boxes. If you select this check box, the **Zone count** edit box will be activated. The **Insert zone labels** check box is used to insert grid labels into your drawing. The **Zone count** edit box is used to specify column counts for the X zone grid of the ladder. Figure 4-15 shows the zone labels and zone spacing.

After specifying the desired settings in the **X Zones Setup** dialog box, choose the **OK** button; the X zone grid labels will be inserted into your drawing, as shown in Figure 4-16.

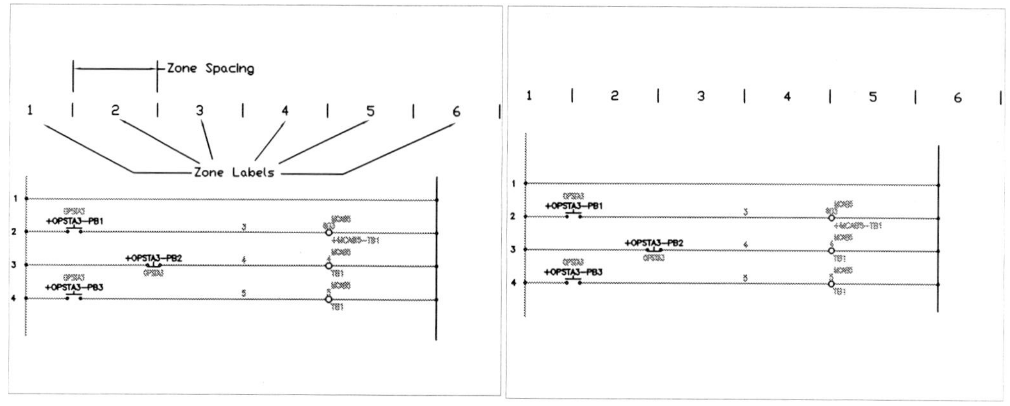


*Figure 4-15 Zone labels and zone spacing* *Figure 4-16 The ladder with X Zone grid labels*

# INSERTING X-Y GRID LABELS

**Ribbon:** Schematic > Insert Wires/Wire Numbers > Insert Ladder drop-down > XY Grid Setup
**Toolbar:** ACE:Main Electrical > Insert Ladder > XY Grid or ACE:Ladders > XY Grid
**Command:** AEXYGRID

The **XY Grid Setup** tool is used to insert X-Y grid labels into the ladders of drawings, which use XY grid for format referencing. To do so, choose the **XY Grid Setup** tool from the **Insert Ladder** drop-down in the **Insert Wires/Wire Numbers** panel of the **Schematic** tab; the **X-Y Grid Setup** dialog box will be displayed.

Note that this dialog box will be displayed only if you select the **X-Y Grid** radio button in the **Drawing Format** tab of the **Drawing Properties** dialog box. If this radio button is not selected, the **AutoCAD Message** message box will be displayed, as shown in Figure 4-17, indicating that the drawing is not configured for X-Y Grid.

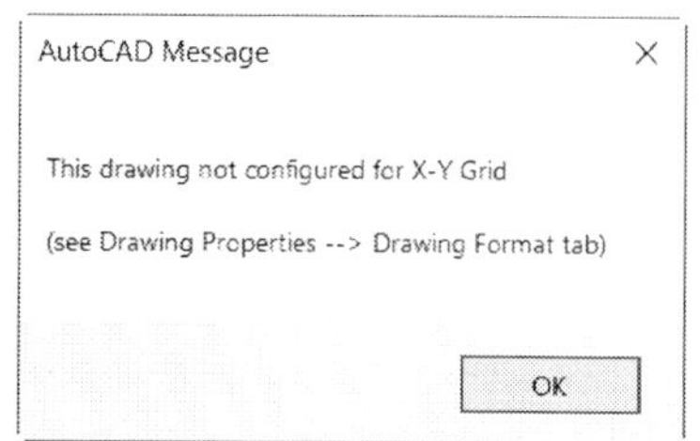


*Figure 4-17 The* ***AutoCAD Message*** *message box*

Alternatively, you can display the **X-Y Grid Setup** dialog box by selecting the **X-Y Grid** radio button in the **Drawing Format** tab of the **Drawing Properties** or the **Project Properties** dialog box and then choosing the **Setup** button. The options in the **X-Y Grid Setup** dialog box, as shown in Figure 4-18, are discussed next.

## Origin Area

The **Origin** area is used to specify the origin for the X-Y grid of a ladder. The options in this area are discussed next.

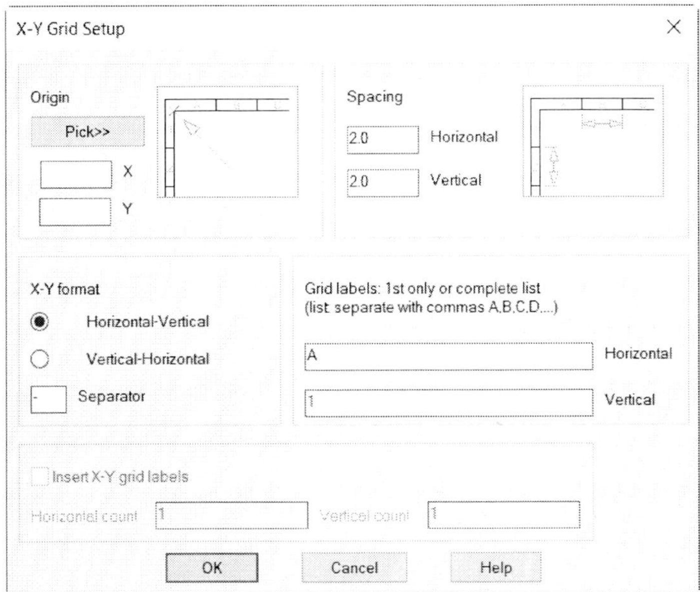


*Figure 4-18 The **X-Y Grid Setup** dialog box*

**X**

Enter the X coordinate for the origin of the X-Y grid in the **X** edit box.

**Y**

Enter the Y coordinate for the origin of the X-Y grid in the **Y** edit box.

**Pick>>**

Choose the **Pick** button; you will be prompted to specify the origin of the drawing. Specify the origin for the X-Y zone near the upper left corner of the drawing; you will notice that the X-coordinates and Y-coordinates of the origin will be displayed in the **X** and **Y** edit boxes, respectively. Once you specify values in these edit boxes, the **Insert X-Y grid labels** check box will be activated.

## Spacing Area

In the **Spacing** area, you can specify the horizontal and vertical spacing between grid columns in the **Horizontal** and **Vertical** edit boxes, respectively.

## X-Y format Area

The **X-Y format** area is used to specify the format for the X-Y grid, which helps in determining the %N part of the component tag. The **X-Y format** area consists of the **Horizontal-Vertical** and **Vertical-Horizontal** radio buttons.

The **Horizontal-Vertical** radio button is selected by default, which indicates that the horizontal values of the grid will be used as the first part and the vertical values will be used as the second part of the tag. If you select the **Vertical-Horizontal** radio button, the vertical values will be used as the first part and the horizontal values will be used as the second part of the tag. Specify the separator for these tags in the **Separator** edit box.

### Grid labels Area

The **Grid labels** area is used to specify labels for grid columns. Enter horizontal value for grid columns in the **Horizontal** edit box and vertical value for grid columns in the **Vertical** edit box. You can enter the first value for the grid column or the complete list separated by a separator such as comma, hyphen, and so on in the **Horizontal** and **Vertical** edit boxes.

### Insert X-Y grid labels

Select the **Insert X-Y grid labels** check box to insert grid labels into the drawing. The **Insert X-Y grid labels** check box will get activated only if you enter the values in the **X** and **Y** edit boxes. On selecting this check box, the **Horizontal count** and **Vertical count** edit boxes available below this check box will be activated. You can then enter the horizontal count and the vertical count in the **Horizontal count** and **Vertical count** edit boxes, respectively.

After specifying the desired settings in the **X-Y Grid Setup** dialog box, choose the **OK** button from the **X-Y Grid Setup** dialog box to insert the X-Y grid in the drawing and exit the dialog box. Figure 4-19 shows the ladder with X-Y grid setup.

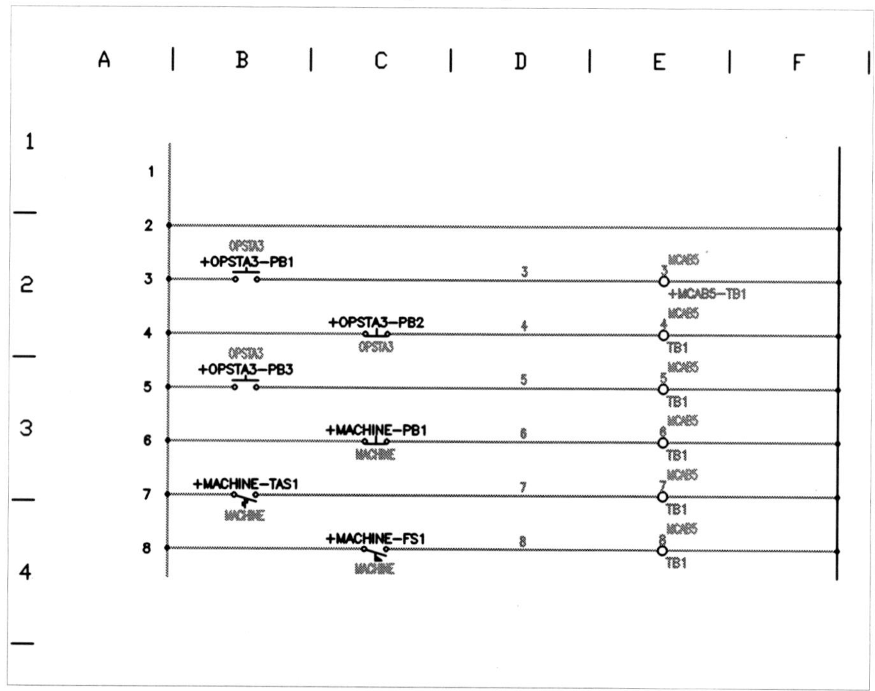


***Figure 4-19** The ladder with X-Y grid setup*

# TUTORIALS

## Tutorial 1

In this tutorial, you will insert a ladder into the drawing that was created in Tutorial 1 of Chapter 2 and then modify it by trimming rungs. You will also add wires between rungs, as shown in Figure 4-20. **(Expected time: 15 min)**

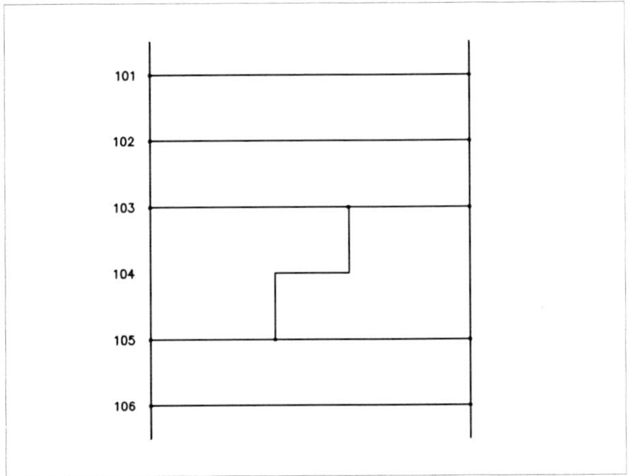


***Figure 4-20*** *The ladder diagram for Tutorial 1*

The following steps are required to complete this tutorial:

a. Open, save, and add the drawing to the **CADCIM** project drawing list.
b. Insert the ladder into the drawing.
c. Trim ladder rungs.
d. Add wires to the ladder.
e. Save the drawing file.

## Opening, Saving, and Adding the Drawing to the CADCIM Project list

1. Open the *C02_tut01.dwg* file and then save it with the name *C04_tut01.dwg*.

   You can also download this file from *www.cadcim.com*. The path of the file is as follows:

   *Textbooks > CAD/CAM > AutoCAD Electrical > AutoCAD Electrical 2022 for Electrical Control Designers*

2. Right-click on the *TUTORIALS* subfolder of the **CADCIM** project; a shortcut menu is displayed. Next, choose the **Add Active Drawing** option from the shortcut menu; the **Apply Project Defaults to Drawing Settings** message box is displayed. Choose the **Yes** button from this message box; *C04_tut01.dwg* is added in the *TUTORIALS* subfolder of the **CADCIM** project at the bottom of the drawing list. Next, choose **Save** from the **Application Menu** to save the drawing.

## Inserting the Ladder into the Drawing

1. To insert the ladder into the drawing, choose the **Insert Ladder** tool from **Schematic> Insert Wires/Wire Numbers > Insert Ladder** drop-down; the **Insert Ladder** dialog box is displayed, refer to Figure 4-21. By default, the **1 Phase** radio button is selected in the **Phase** area. If it is not selected, then select it.

2. Enter **5.0** in the **Width** edit box of the **Width** area.

3. Enter **1.0** in the **Spacing** edit box of the **Spacing** area.

4. Enter **101** in the **1st Reference** edit box. Also, make sure 1 is entered in the **Index** edit box.

   Make sure the **Without reference numbers** check box is clear.

5. Enter **6** in the **Rungs** edit box and click in the **Length** edit box of the **Insert Ladder** dialog box; the length of the ladder is automatically calculated and the value **5.5000** is displayed in the **Length** edit box. The **Yes** radio button is selected by default in the **Draw Rungs** area.

6. Make sure **0** is entered in the **Skip** edit box of the **Draw Rungs** area.

7. Choose the **OK** button; you are prompted to specify the start position of the first rung. Specify the start position as **7,14** at the Command prompt and press ENTER; the ladder is inserted into the drawing, as shown in Figure 4-22.

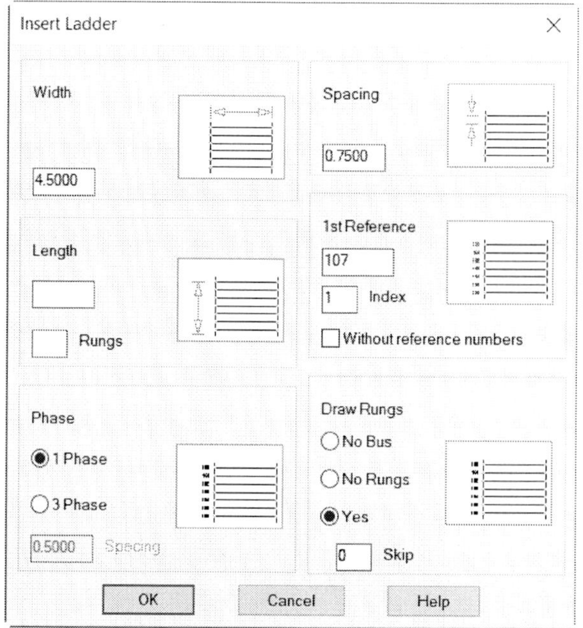


***Figure 4-21** The **Insert Ladder** dialog box*

## Trimming Ladder Rung

1. Choose the **Trim Wire** tool from the **Edit Wires/Wire Numbers** panel of the **Schematic** tab; a selection box is displayed and you are prompted to select a wire to trim. Select the rung **104**; the rung is trimmed from the ladder, as shown in Figure 4-23.

2. Press ENTER to exit the command.

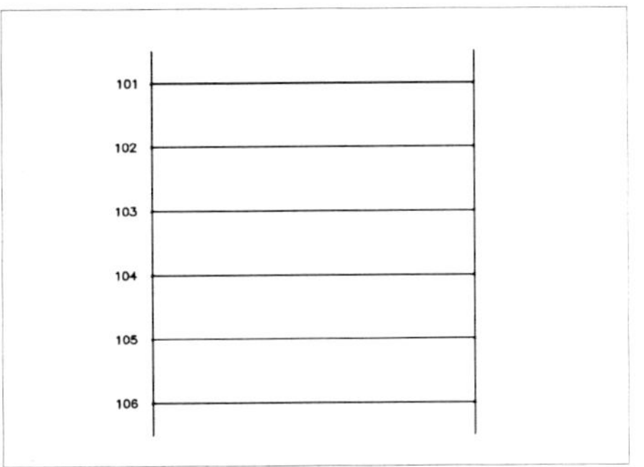


*Figure 4-22 The ladder inserted into the drawing*

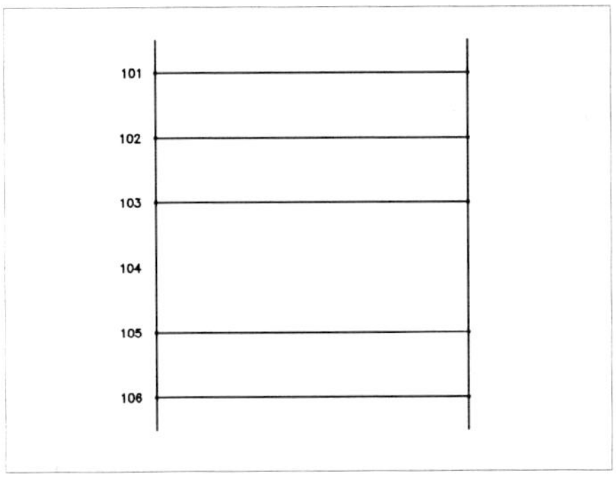

*Figure 4-23 The ladder with trimmed rung*

## Adding Wires to the Ladder

1. Choose the **Wire** tool from the **Insert Wires/Wire Numbers** panel of the **Schematic** tab; you are prompted to specify the start point of the wire. Add the wire to the ladder at the locations shown in Figure 4-24.

2. Press ENTER to exit the command.

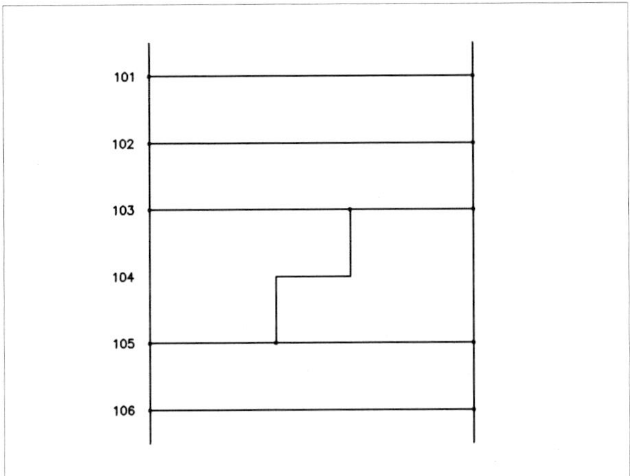


*Figure 4-24 The ladder with the wire added*

## Saving the Drawing File

1. Choose **Save** from the **Application Menu** to save the *C04_tut01.dwg* drawing file.

**Note**

*It is recommended that you save all tutorials given in the forthcoming chapters in the TUTORIALS subfolder of the* ***CADCIM*** *project.*

## Tutorial 2

In this tutorial, you will stretch and revise the ladder that you have created in Tutorial 1 of this chapter. Also, you will add rungs to the ladder, as shown in Figure 4-25.

**(Expected time: 10 min)**

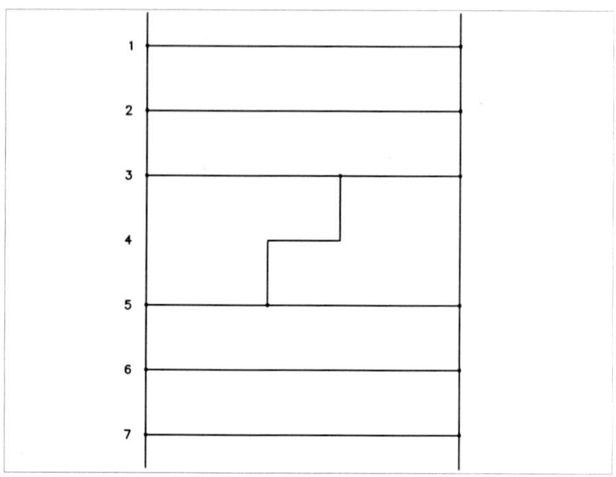


***Figure 4-25*** *The ladder diagram for Tutorial 2*

The following steps are required to complete this tutorial:

a. Open, save, and add the drawing to the **CADCIM** project drawing list.
b. Stretch the ladder.
c. Revise the ladder.
d. Add rungs to the ladder.
e. Save the drawing file.

### Opening, Saving, and Adding the Drawing to the CADCIM Project list

1. Open the *C04_tut01.dwg* file and then save it with the name *C04_tut02.dwg*.

   You can also download this file from *www.cadcim.com*. The path of the file is as follows:

   *Textbooks > CAD/CAM > AutoCAD Electrical > AutoCAD Electrical 2022 for Electrical Control Designers*

2. Right-click on the *TUTORIALS* subfolder of the **CADCIM** project; a shortcut menu is displayed. Next, choose the **Add Active Drawing** option from the shortcut menu; the **Apply Project Defaults to Drawing Settings** message box is displayed. Choose the **Yes** button from this message box; *C04_tut02.dwg* is added in the *TUTORIALS* subfolder of the **CADCIM** project at the bottom of the drawing list. Next, choose **Save** from the **Application Menu** to save the drawing.

## Stretching the Ladder

1. Choose the **Stretch** tool from the **Modify** panel of the **Home** tab. Select the ladder by using the crossing lasso from right to left, as shown in Figure 4-26 and press ENTER. Make sure you select only the vertical bus of the ladder.

2. Specify the base point by selecting the lower end of the vertical bus. Now, move the cursor vertically down and click to stretch the vertical bus, refer to Figure 4-27.

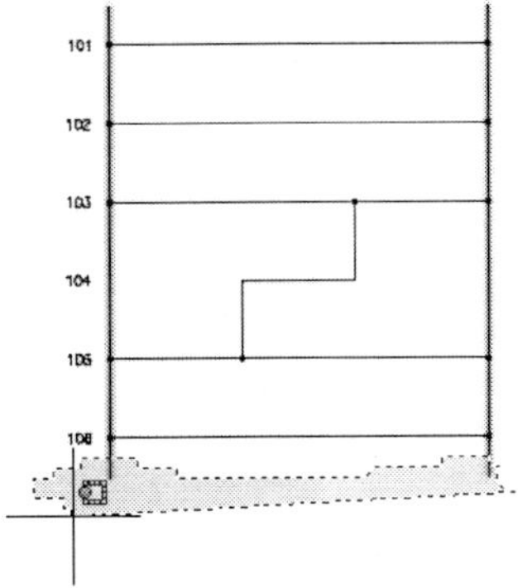


*Figure 4-26 Selecting the ladder by using the crossing lasso*

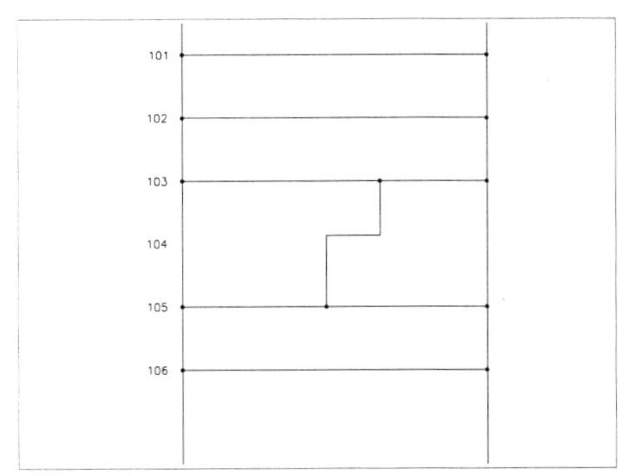


*Figure 4-27 The stretched ladder*

## Revising the Ladder

1. After stretching the ladder, you need to revise it. To do so, choose the **Revise Ladder** tool from **Schematic > Edit Wires/Wire Numbers > Modify Ladder** drop-down; the **Modify Line Reference Numbers** dialog box is displayed, as shown in Figure 4-28. 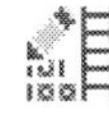

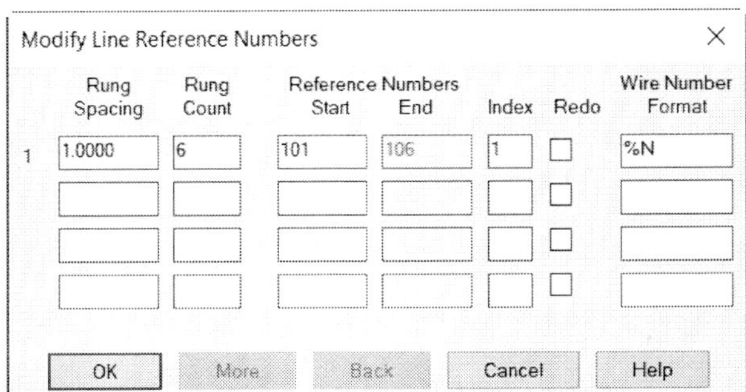


*Figure 4-28 The **Modify Line Reference Numbers** dialog box*

Since you entered **1.0000** in the **Spacing** edit box of the **Insert Ladder** dialog box while creating the ladder, the space between rungs in the **Rung Spacing** edit box is displayed as 1.0000.

2. Enter **7** and **1** in the **Rung Count** and **Reference Numbers Start** edit boxes, respectively. Also, make sure 1 is displayed in the **Index** edit box.

3. Once you enter the values in the **Rung Spacing**, **Rung Count**, and **Reference Numbers Start** edit boxes, the **Redo** check box is selected automatically. If it is not selected, select it manually.

By default, %N is displayed in the **Wire Number Format** edit box. Do not change it.

4. Choose the **OK** button; the new reference numbers are assigned to the ladder, refer to Figure 4-29.

## Adding Rungs to the Ladder

1. Choose the **Add Rung** tool from **Schematic > Edit Wires/Wire Numbers > Modify Ladder** drop-down; you are prompted to specify the location for the rung.

2. Click in the area between the vertical buses, under the rung **6**; a rung is added below the rung 6, as shown in Figure 4-30.

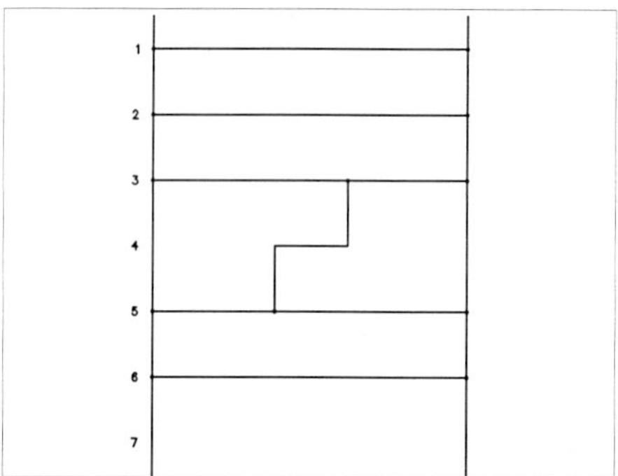


*Figure 4-29 The modified ladder*

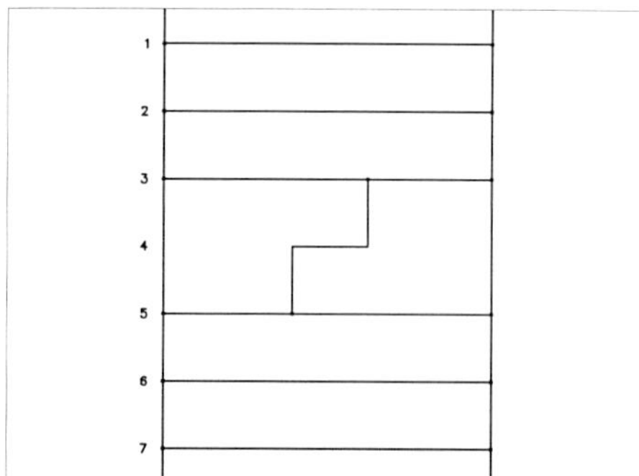


*Figure 4-30 A rung added to the ladder*

3. Press ENTER to exit the command.

## Saving the Drawing

1. Choose **Save** from the **Application Menu** to save the *C04_tut02.dwg* drawing file.

# Tutorial 3

In this tutorial, you will insert a three-phase ladder and also add a three-phase wire bus to the drawing, as shown in Figure 4-31. **(Expected time: 15 min)**

The following steps are required to complete this tutorial:

a. Create a new drawing *C04_tut03.dwg*.
b. Insert a three-phase ladder into the drawing.
c. Insert a three-phase wire bus.
d. Save the drawing file.

## Creating a New Drawing

1. Create a new drawing with the name *C04_tut03.dwg* in the *TUTORIALS* subfolder of the **CADCIM** project. Refer to Tutorial 1 of Chapter 2 for the method of creating the drawing.

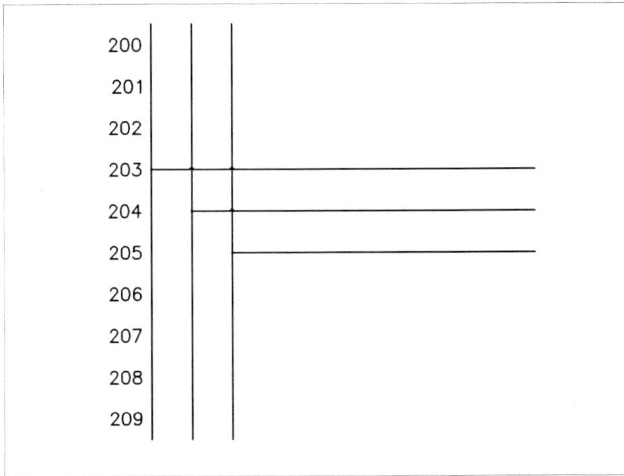


*Figure 4-31 Three-phase ladder and three-phase wire bus*

## Inserting the Three-Phase Ladder into the Drawing

1. Choose the **Insert Ladder** tool from **Schematic > Insert Wires/Wire Numbers > Insert Ladder** drop-down; the **Insert Ladder** dialog box is displayed.

2. In this dialog box, select the **3 Phase** radio button from the **Phase** area.

3. Enter **1** in the **Spacing** edit box of the **Phase** area.

4. Enter **1** in the **Spacing** edit box of the **Spacing** area.

5. Enter **200** in the **1st Reference** edit box to specify the beginning of the line reference for the ladder. Next, enter **1** in the **Index** edit box and enter **10** in the **Rungs** edit box.

6. Choose **OK**; you are prompted to specify the start position of the first rung. Enter **8, 15** at the Command prompt and press ENTER; the ladder is inserted into your drawing, as shown in Figure 4-32.

## Inserting the Three-Phase Wire Bus into the Drawing

1. Choose the **Multiple Bus** tool from the **Insert Wires/Wire Numbers** panel of the **Schematic** tab; the **Multiple Wire Bus** dialog box is displayed, as shown in Figure 4-33.

2. Enter **1** in both the **Spacing** edit box of the **Horizontal** and **Vertical** areas.

   In this dialog box, by default, the **Another Bus (Multiple Wires)** radio button is selected in the **Starting at** area and the value **3** is displayed in the **Number of Wires** edit box.

3. Choose the **OK** button; a selection box appears on the screen. Select the start point on the first (extreme left) vertical bus at reference 203. Move the cursor to the right up to the desired length and specify the endpoint in the drawing area. Next, click on the screen.

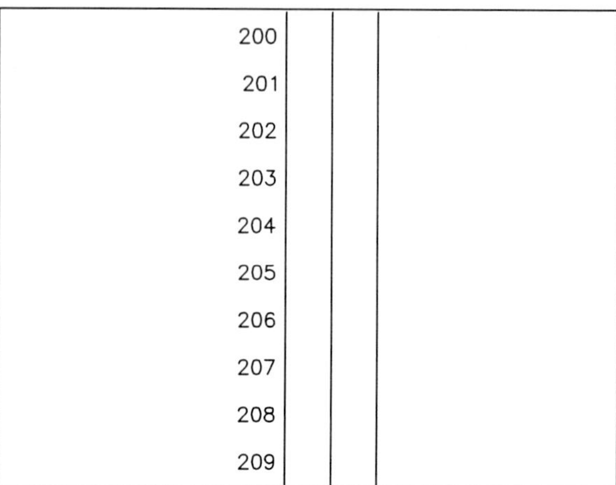


***Figure 4-32** Three-phase ladder*

4. Right-click on the screen or press ENTER to exit the command. The ladder with three-phase wire bus is shown in Figure 4-34.

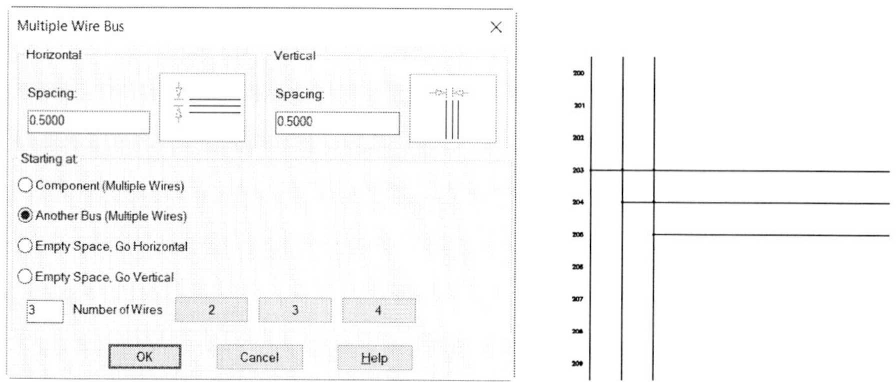


***Figure 4-33** The **Multiple Wire Bus** dialog box*

***Figure 4-34** The ladder with three-phase wire bus*

## Saving the Drawing

1. Choose **Save** from the **Application Menu** to save the *C04_tut03.dwg* drawing file.

## Tutorial 4

In this tutorial, you will set the format for reference numbers of a ladder and then insert a ladder into the drawing. Next, you will insert another ladder and insert X-Y grid labels into the drawing, refer to Figure 4-35. **(Expected time: 15 min)**

The following steps are required to complete this tutorial:

a. Create a new drawing.
b. Set format for reference numbers.

c. Insert a ladder into the drawing.
d. Insert X-Y grid labels into the drawing.
e. Renumber ladder line reference numbers.
f. Save the drawing file.

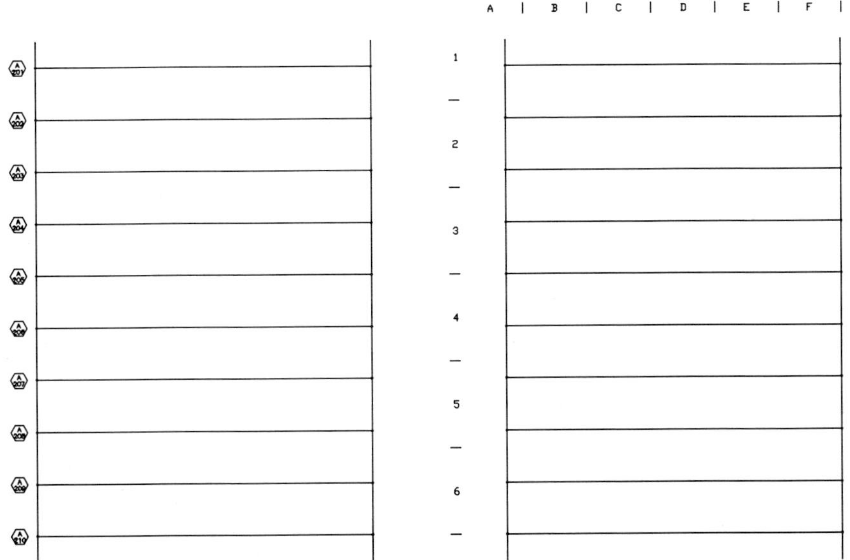


*Figure 4-35 The ladder diagram for Tutorial 4*

## Creating a New Drawing

1. Create a new drawing with the name *C04_tut04.dwg* in the *TUTORIALS* subfolder of the **CADCIM** project. Refer to Tutorial 1 of Chapter 2 for the method of creating the drawing.

## Setting the Format for Reference Numbers

1. Right-click on *C04_tut04.dwg* in the **PROJECT MANAGER**; a shortcut menu is displayed. Choose **Properties > Drawing Properties** from it, as shown in Figure 4-36; the **Drawing Properties** dialog box is displayed.

2. Make sure the **Drawing Settings** tab is chosen and then enter **A** in the **Sheet** edit box of the **Sheet Values** area. Now, choose the **Drawing Format** tab.

3. Make sure the **Reference Numbers** radio button is selected in the **Format Referencing** area and then choose the **Setup** button, refer to Figure 4-37; the **Line Reference Numbers** dialog box is displayed, as shown in Figure 4-38.

4. In this dialog box, select the **Sheet and numbers in hexagon** check box and choose the **OK** button to close the dialog box. Next, close the **Drawing Properties** dialog box. The format for reference numbers of the ladder is set.

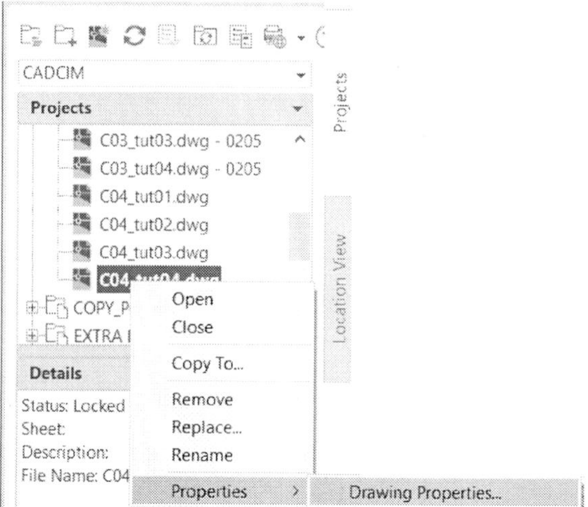


*Figure 4-36 Choosing* ***Drawing Properties*** *from the shortcut menu*

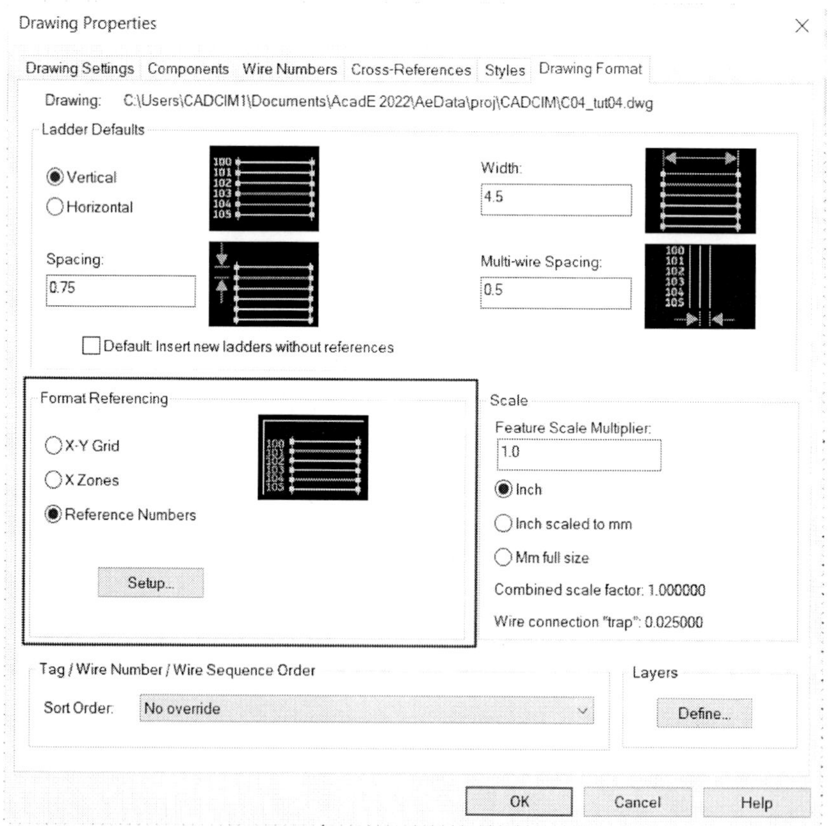


*Figure 4-37 The* ***Drawing Properties*** *dialog box*

## Inserting a Ladder into the Drawing

1. Choose the **Insert Ladder** tool from **Schematic > Insert Wires/Wire Numbers > Insert Ladder** drop-down; the **Sheet: A-Insert Ladder** dialog box is displayed.

Make sure the **1 Phase** radio button is selected in the **Phase** area.

2. Enter **10** in the **Width** edit box of the **Width** area. Next, enter **1.5** in the **Spacing** edit box of the **Spacing** area.

3. Enter **201** in the **1st Reference** edit box. Make sure 1 is displayed in the **Index** edit box and the **Without reference numbers** check box is clear.

4. Enter **10** in the **Rungs** edit box and click in the **Length** edit box of the **Sheet: A-Insert Ladder** dialog box; the length of the ladder is automatically calculated and is displayed as **14.25**. Make sure the **Yes** radio button is selected in the **Draw Rungs** area.

5. Enter **0** in the **Skip** edit box of the **Draw Rungs** area. Next, choose the **OK** button; you are prompted to specify the start position of the first rung. Specify the start position as **5,17.5** at the Command prompt and press ENTER; the ladder is inserted into the drawing, as shown in Figure 4-39.

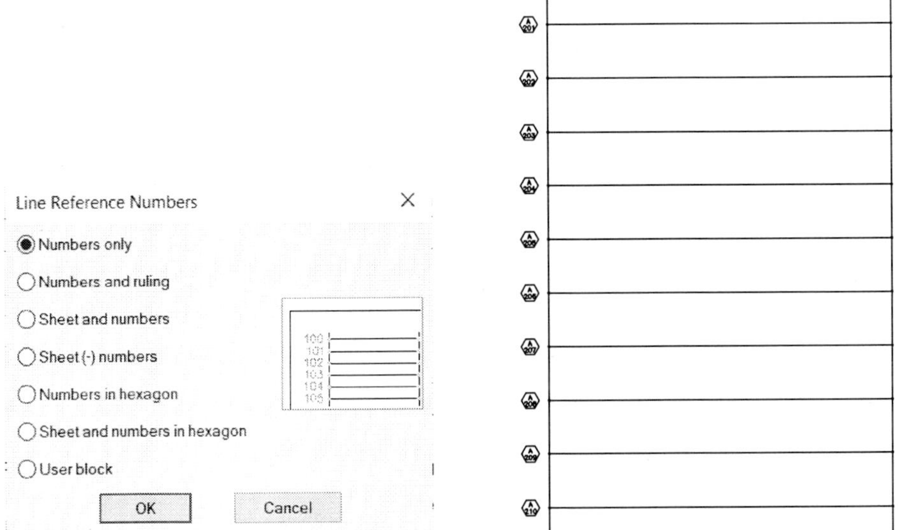


*Figure 4-38 The **Line Reference Numbers** dialog box*

*Figure 4-39 The inserted ladder*

## Inserting X-Y Grid Labels

1. Right-click on *C04_tut04.dwg* in the **PROJECT MANAGER**; a shortcut menu is displayed. Choose **Properties > Drawing Properties** from it; the **Drawing Properties** dialog box is displayed.

2. In this dialog box, choose the **Drawing Format** tab. Next, select the **X-Y Grid** radio button in the **Format Referencing** area and then choose the **OK** button to close the dialog box.

3. Choose the **Insert Ladder** tool from **Schematic > Insert Wires/Wire Numbers > Insert Ladder** drop-down; the **Sheet: A - Insert Ladder** dialog box is displayed. Make sure the **1 Phase** radio button is selected in the **Phase** area.

4. Enter **10** in the **Width** edit box of the **Width** area. Next, enter **1.5** in the **Spacing** edit box of the **Spacing** area.

5. Enter **10** in the **Rungs** edit box and click in the **Length** edit box of the **Sheet:A - Insert Ladder** dialog box; the length of the ladder is automatically calculated and is displayed as **14.25**. Make sure the **Yes** radio button is selected in the **Draw Rungs** area.

6. Enter **0** in the **Skip** edit box of the **Draw Rungs** area. Next, choose the **OK** button; you are prompted to specify the start position of the first rung. Specify the start position as **19,17.5** at the Command prompt and press ENTER; the ladder is inserted into the drawing.

7. Choose the **XY Grid Setup** tool from **Schematic > Insert Wires/Wire Numbers > Insert Ladder** drop-down; the **X-Y Grid Setup** dialog box is displayed.

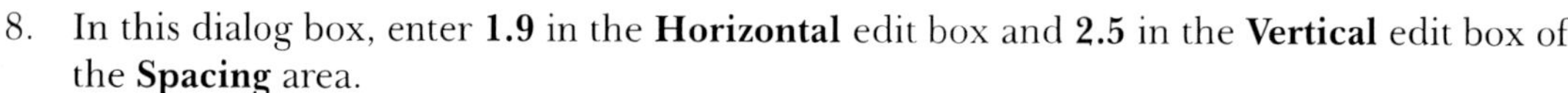

8. In this dialog box, enter **1.9** in the **Horizontal** edit box and **2.5** in the **Vertical** edit box of the **Spacing** area.

9. Enter **A,B,C,D,E,F** in the **Horizontal** edit box and **1,2,3,4,5,6** in the **Vertical** edit box of the **Grid Labels** area.

10. Enter **17.625** in the **X** edit box and **19** in the **Y** edit box of the **Origin** area. Next, select the **Insert X-Y Grid labels** check box at the bottom of the dialog box, refer to Figure 4-40. Now, choose the **OK** button to close the dialog box; the X-Y grid labels are inserted into the drawing, as shown in Figure 4-41.

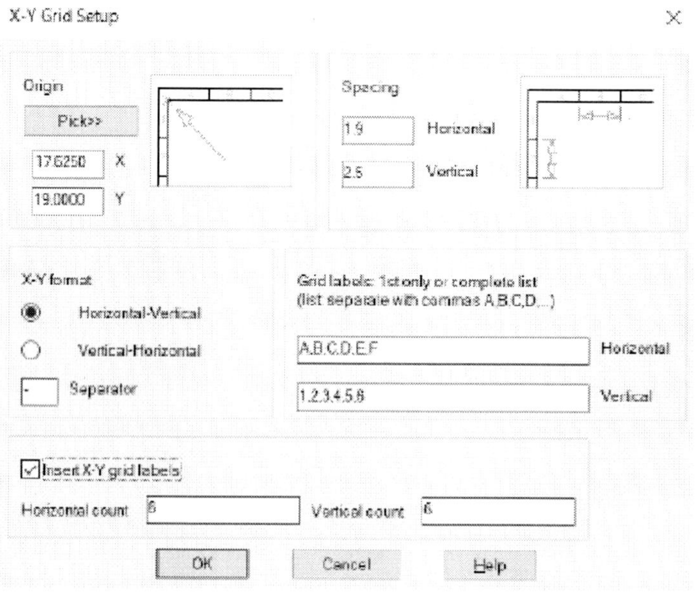


*Figure 4-40 The **X-Y Grid Setup** dialog box*

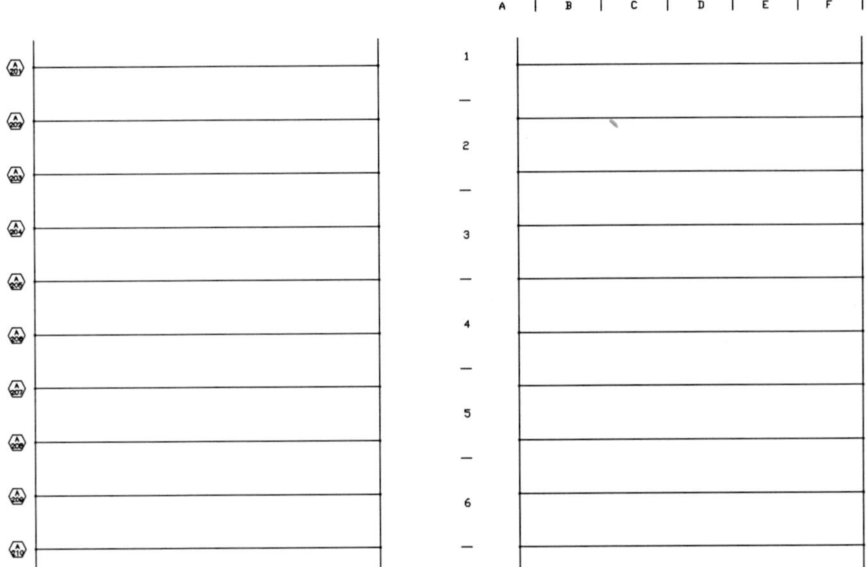


*Figure 4-41 The X-Y grid labels*

## Renumbering Ladder Line Reference Numbers

1. Choose the **Renumber Ladder Reference** tool from **Schematic > Edit Wires/Wire Numbers > Modify Ladder** drop-down; the **Renumber Ladders** dialog box is displayed.

2. In this dialog box, enter **401** in the **1st drawing, 1st ladder, 1st line reference number** edit box. Also, make sure the **Use next sequential reference** radio button is selected. Next, choose **OK**; the **Select Drawings to Process** dialog box is displayed.

3. In this dialog box, select all the drawings of Chapter 4(*C04_tut01.dwg, C04_tut02.dwg, C04_tut03.dwg,* and *C04_tut04.dwg)* and choose the **Process** button; the selected drawings are transferred from the top list to the bottom list. Next, choose **OK**; the line reference numbers for all the ladders are changed.

   You may open the above mentioned drawings one by one to see the change in line reference numbers.

## Saving the Drawing

1. Choose **Save** from the **Application Menu** to save the drawing file, *C04_tut04.dwg*.

# Tutorial 5

In this tutorial, you will convert the ladder that is created using the **Line** tool to an AutoCAD Electrical Intelligent ladder. **(Expected time: 15 min)**

The following steps are required to complete this tutorial:

a. Create a new drawing.
b. Create ladder using the **Line** and **Single Line Text** tools.
c. Convert the ladder into AutoCAD Electrical intelligent ladder.
d. Save the drawing file.

## Creating a New Drawing

1. Create a new drawing with the name *C04_tut05.dwg* in the *TUTORIALS* subfolder of the **CADCIM** project. Refer to Tutorial 1 of Chapter 2 for the method of creating the drawing.

## Creating Ladder using the Line and Single Line Text Tools

1. Choose the **Line** tool from the **Draw** panel of the **Home** tab and create a ladder, as shown in Figure 4-42. Make sure that there is a distance of 1 unit in between the rungs of the ladder.

2. Choose the **Single Line** tool from the **Text** drop-down in the **Annotation** panel of the **Home** tab. Next, insert the text at the left of the first rung of the ladder, refer to Figure 4-43.

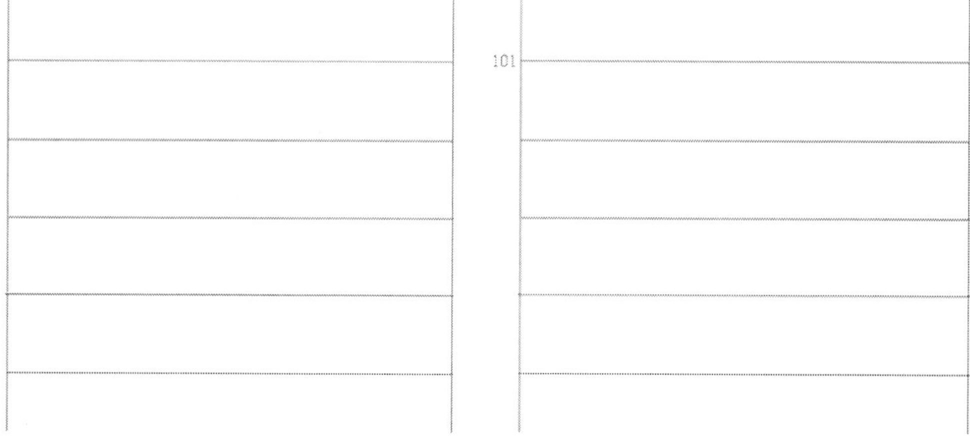


***Figure 4-42** Ladder created* ***Figure 4-43** Single line text created*

3. Choose the **Revise Ladder** tool from the **Modify Ladder** drop-down in the **Edit Wires/ Wire Numbers** panel of the **Schematic** tab; the AutoCAD message box is displayed which informs that the drawing has no smart ladders in it. Choose the **OK** button in this message box. This implies that the drawing does not have an AutoCAD Electrical intelligent ladder.

## Converting Ladder into AutoCAD Electrical Intelligent Ladder

1. Choose the **Convert Ladder** tool from the **Tools** panel of the **Conversion Tools** tab; you are prompted to select first ladder reference text object.

2. Select the '**101**' text in the drawing and press ENTER; the **Modify Line Reference Numbers** dialog box is displayed. Note that 101 is displayed in the **Reference Start** edit box of this dialog box.

3. Change the value in the **Rung Spacing** edit box to **1** and also change the value in the **Rung count** edit box to **5** in the first row of the **Modify Line Reference Numbers** dialog box. These values are changed so that the distance between the rungs of the ladder sets to 1 and also the number of rungs sets to 5.

4. Choose the **OK** button in this dialog box. Notice that now the line reference numbers for the remaining rungs of the ladder are displayed in the drawing, refer to Figure 4-44.

***Figure 4-44*** *Line reference numbers displayed*

In the following step you need to check whether this ladder is converted to AutoCAD Electrical intelligent ladder or not.

5. Choose the **Revise Ladder** tool from the **Modify Ladder** drop-down in the **Edit Wires/Wire Numbers** panel of the **Schematic** tab; the **Modify Line Reference Numbers** dialog box is displayed. Note that the ladder is displayed in this dialog box which implies that now it is an AutoCAD Electrical intelligent ladder.

### Saving the Drawing

1. Choose **Save** from the **Application Menu** to save the drawing file, *C04_tut05.dwg*.

## Self-Evaluation Test

**Answer the following questions and then compare them to those given at the end of this chapter:**

1. Which of the following tools is used to move the rungs of a ladder?

   (a) **Add Rung** (b) **Scoot**
   (c) **Move** (d) **Revise Ladder**

2. The **More** and **Back** buttons in the **Modify Line Reference Numbers** dialog box will be activated only if you insert __________ ladders into the drawing.

3. The __________ tool is used to add rungs to a ladder.

4. The __________ of the ladder will be automatically calculated once you enter the values for rungs, reference start, and index values in respective edit boxes.

5. Rungs can be added only if you choose the **Add Rung** tool from the **ACE:Main Electrical** toolbar and click in the blank space between the __________ rails.

6. To create a three-phase ladder, select the __________ radio button from the **Phase** area in the **Insert Ladder** dialog box.

7. Ladder diagrams are used to describe the logic of electrical control systems. (T/F)

8. The uppermost line reference number is the MLR block of the ladder and it carries the intelligence of the ladder. (T/F)

9. You can insert only a limited number of ladders into a drawing. (T/F)

10. If you update a ladder reference, the existing components and the wire numbers will be automatically updated. (T/F)

## Review Questions

**Answer the following questions:**

1. Which of the following tools is used to adjust the line reference number along the side of the ladder?

   (a) **Convert Ladder** (b) **Renumber Ladder Reference**
   (c) **Revise Ladder** (d) **Insert Ladder**

2. Which of the following options in the **Modify Line Reference Numbers** dialog box is used to control the distance between reference numbers?

   (a) **Rung Count** (b) **Reference Start**
   (c) **Index** (d) **Rung Spacing**

3. Which of the following features can be controlled while inserting a ladder?

   (a) Width (b) Reference Numbers
   (c) Spacing (d) All of these

4. Which of the following tools is used to insert wires between the rails of a ladder?

(a) **Revise Ladder** (b) **Add Rung**
(c) **Insert Ladder** (d) None of these

5. The line references cannot be modified. (T/F)

6. The vertical three-phase components are inserted from top to bottom. (T/F)

7. The **Index** edit box of the **Modify Line Reference Numbers** dialog box is used to display the increment between reference numbers. (T/F)

8. The **XY Grid Setup** tool is used to insert the X-Y grid labels into the drawing. (T/F)

9. The **STRETCH** command of AutoCAD is used only to stretch the ladder and not for shortening it. (T/F)

10. The **Revise Ladder** tool is used to shorten, lengthen, compress, and widen a ladder. (T/F)

# EXERCISES

## Exercise 1

Create a new drawing with the name *C04_exer01.dwg* in the **NEW_PROJECT** project and insert a ladder with 10 rungs starting with reference number 100, spacing between rungs = 0.5, and width = 6. You also need to add a wire between rungs 100 and 101, as shown in Figure 4-45. Trim the rung 104 and the middle portion of the rung 101 using the **Trim Wire** tool.

**(Expected time: 10 min)**

## Exercise 2

Create a new drawing with the name *C04_exer02.dwg* in the **NEW_PROJECT** project and insert a ladder with 12 rungs starting with reference number 500, spacing between rungs = 1, and width = 6. You also need to add a rung below the rung 12, as shown in Figure 4-46.

**(Expected time: 10 min)**

**Note**

*It is recommended to save all exercises of the forthcoming chapters in the* ***NEW_PROJECT*** *project.*

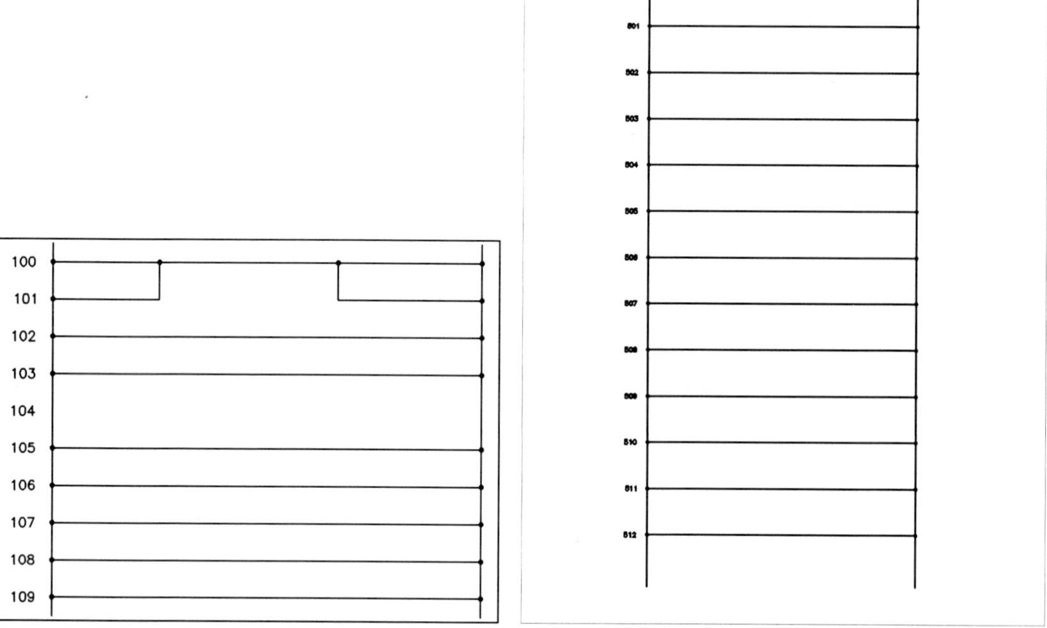


***Figure 4-45*** *Ladder diagram for Exercise 1*

***Figure 4-46*** *Ladder diagram for Exercise 2*

## Answers to Self-Evaluation Test

**1.** b, **2.** More than four, **3. Add Rung**, **4.** length, **5.** vertical, **6. 3 Phase**, **7.** T, **8.** T, **9.** F, **10.** F

# Chapter 5

# Schematic Components

## Learning Objectives

**After completing this chapter, you will be able to:**

- *Insert schematic components*
- *Annotate and edit schematic symbols*
- *Assign catalog part number to components*
- *Create parent-child relationship between components*
- *Swap or update blocks*
- *Insert components from the equipment, panel, and user defined lists*
- *Add a new record in the Schematic Component or Circuit dialog box*
- *Edit an existing record in the Schematic or Circuit dialog box*

# INTRODUCTION

In AutoCAD Electrical, schematic components are AutoCAD blocks with attributes such as TAG1, TAG2, DESC, RATING, LOC, INST, and so on. These components consist of visible attributes such as component tags, descriptions, pin numbers, and so on and invisible attributes such as manufacturer information, wire connection points, and so on. In this chapter, you will learn how to insert and edit schematic components such as push buttons, selector switches, and relays. You will also learn how to insert components from the equipment, panel, and catalog lists. Also, you will learn how to use AutoCAD Electrical tools to break wires, assign component tags, and cross reference to the related components while inserting components. Finally, this chapter describes how these tools can be used to specify the catalog information, component descriptions, and location codes.

# INSERTING SCHEMATIC COMPONENTS USING ICON MENU

| | |
|---|---|
| **Ribbon:** | Schematic > Insert Components > Icon Menu drop-down > Icon Menu |
| **Toolbar:** | ACE:Main Electrical > Insert Component<br>or ACE:Insert Component > Insert Component |
| **Menu:** | Components > Insert Component<br>or Components > Multiple Insert > Multiple Insert (Icon Menu) |
| **Command:** | AECOMPONENT |

You can insert components into a drawing by selecting a component from the icon menu. To insert a component, choose the **Icon Menu** tool from the **Icon Menu** drop-down in the **Insert Components** panel of the **Schematic** tab, refer to Figure 5-1. On doing so, the **Insert Component** dialog box will be displayed, as shown in Figure 5-2. Different areas and options available in this dialog box are discussed next.

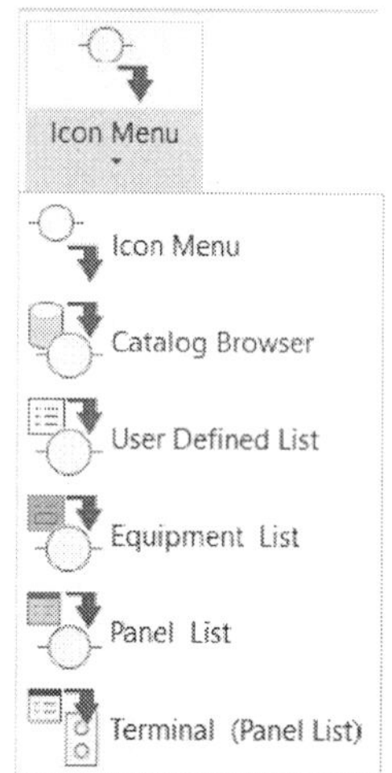

***Figure 5-1** The **Icon Menu** drop-down*

**Note**

*In order to use the **Insert Component** tool, the invisible WD_M block should be inserted into the drawing. The process of inserting a block into a drawing has been discussed in Chapter 1.*

## Menu Area

The **Menu** area located on the left in the **Insert Component** dialog box corresponds to the icons of the **NFPA: Schematic Symbols** area on the right of the dialog box. The **Menu** area displays the hierarchical structure of components. The first entry in this area, **Push Buttons**, corresponds to the icon of a push button and will be shown in the first row of the first column in the **NFPA: Schematic Symbols** area. Similarly, the tenth entry in the **Menu** area, **Limit Switches**, corresponds to the tenth icon in the **NFPA: Schematic Symbols** area and will be located in the second row and the fourth column of the **Insert Component** dialog box. You can expand the symbols by clicking on their respective nodes. For example, if you want to expand the **Selector**

**Switches** node from the **Menu** area, click on the (+) sign of the **Selector Switches** node in the **Menu** area; the **Illuminated Selector Switches** node will be displayed.

## NFPA: Schematic Symbols Area

The **NFPA: Schematic Symbols** area is displayed in the middle of the **Insert Component** dialog box. This area displays symbols and submenu icons corresponding to the menu or submenu selected in the **Menu** area that is located on the left in the **Insert Component** dialog box. When you select an icon, its submenu is displayed. You can choose the desired icon displayed in this area or select a component from the list displayed on the left in the **Insert Component** dialog box, refer to Figure 5-2.

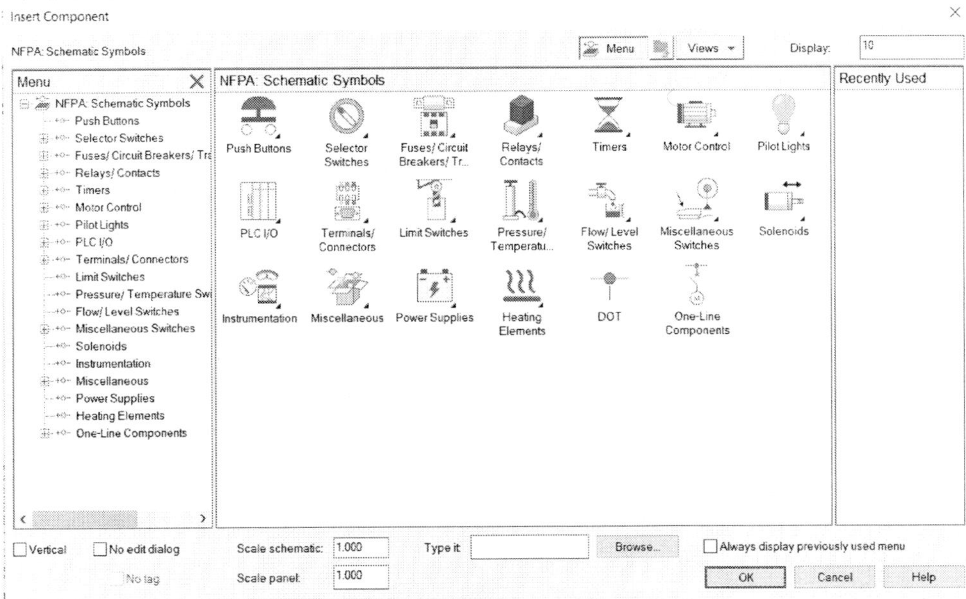


*Figure 5-2 The **Insert Component** dialog box*

## Menu

The **Menu** toggle button located at the top in the **Insert Component** dialog box is used to toggle the **Menu** area. By default, this toggle button is chosen. As a result, the **Menu** area is displayed on the left in the **Insert Component** dialog box, refer to Figure 5-2. If you choose the **Menu** toggle button again, the **Menu** area will be hidden and only the **NFPA: Schematic Symbols** area will be displayed, as shown in Figure 5-3.

## Up one level

The **Up one level** button will not be available until you select any of the icons displayed in the **NFPA: Schematic Symbols** area or select a component from the **Menu** area. If you choose the **Up one level** button, then the component symbols that are one level before the current menu in the **Menu** area will be displayed in the **NFPA: Schematic Symbols** area.

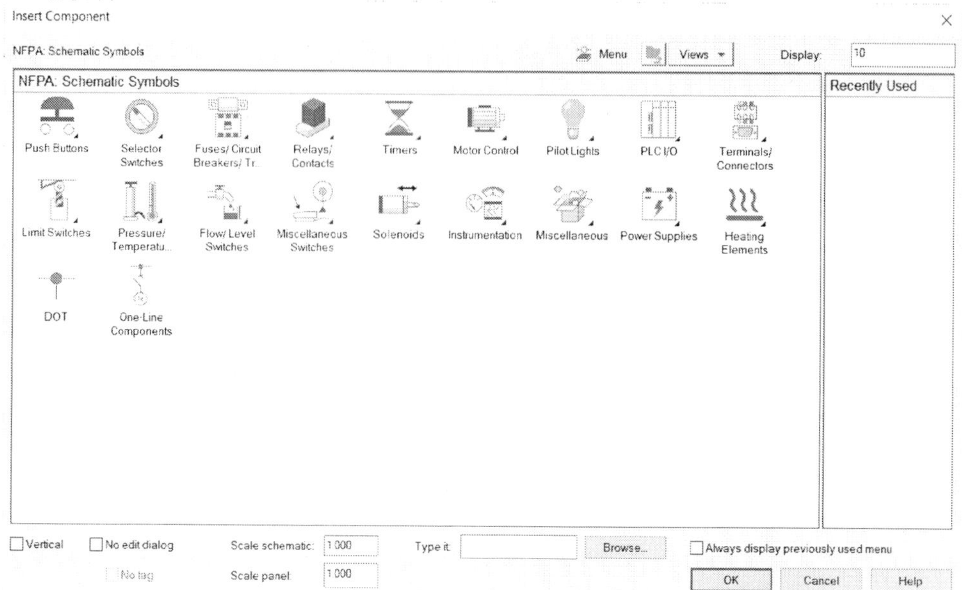


*Figure 5-3 The **Insert Component** dialog box displayed on choosing the **Menu** toggle button*

## Views

The **Views** button is used to change the display of the **NFPA: Schematic Symbols** and **Recently Used** areas. When you choose the **Views** button, a drop-down is displayed, as shown in Figure 5-4. This drop-down consists of the **Icon with text**, **Icon only**, and **List view** options. If you choose an option from the drop-down, a tick mark will be displayed next to that option.

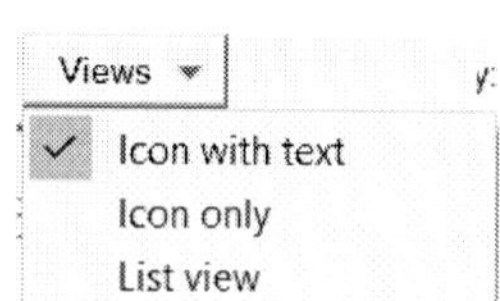


*Figure 5-4 The **Views** drop-down*

By default, the **Icon with text** option is chosen in the drop-down. As a result, icons along with their name are displayed in the **NFPA: Schematic Symbols** and **Recently Used** areas.

If you choose the **Icon only** option from the drop-down, then the **NFPA: Schematic Symbols** and the **Recently Used** areas will display only icons.

If you choose the **List view** option from the drop-down, then the icons along with their names will be displayed in the list form in the **NFPA: Schematic Symbols** and **Recently Used** areas.

## Recently Used Area

The **Recently Used** area displays the components that have been inserted in a drawing during the current AutoCAD Electrical session. After a component has been inserted in the drawing, the name of the component and the icon will be displayed in this area based on the option chosen from the **Views** drop-down. Note that the most recently used component is displayed on the top of the list. The total number of icons displayed in this area depend on the value specified in the **Display** edit box, which is located on the right of the **Views** button.

## Display

The **Display** edit box is used to specify the number of icons to be displayed in the **Recently Used** area. By default, 10 is displayed in this edit box.

## Vertical

If you select the **Vertical** check box, then the components will be inserted vertically in the drawing. By default, this check box is clear. As a result, the components will be inserted horizontally in the drawing. Select the **Vertical** check box to change the orientation of the components from horizontal to vertical. Note that if the **Vertical** check box is selected and you insert the component on the horizontal ladder, then the component will automatically be inserted horizontally.

## No edit dialog

By default, the **No edit dialog** check box is clear. On selecting this check box, the **No tag** check box will be activated in the dialog box. The **No edit dialog** check box is used to insert component without displaying the **Insert / Edit Component** dialog box. You can add details to a component later by choosing the **Edit** tool from the **Edit Components** panel of the **Schematic** tab. The **Insert / Edit Component** dialog box is discussed later in this chapter.

## No tag

By default, the **No tag** check box is clear. Select the **No tag** check box to insert a component without a component tag. You can add component details later by choosing the **Edit** tool from the **Edit Components** panel of the **Schematic** tab.

## Scale schematic

The **Scale schematic** edit box is used to specify the scale at which a component block is inserted into the schematic drawing. By default, 1.000 is displayed in this edit box. However, you can change the default value displayed in the **Scale schematic** edit box. To do so, choose the **Drawing Properties** tool from the **Other Tools** panel of the **Schematic** tab; the **Drawing Properties** dialog box will be displayed. In this dialog box, choose the **Drawing Format** tab and specify the value in the **Feature Scale Multiplier** edit box of the **Scale** area, refer to Figure 5-5.

## Scale panel

The **Scale panel** edit box is used to specify the scale at which the footprint is inserted into the panel drawing. By default, 1.000 is displayed in this edit box.

## Type it

You can also insert a component into a drawing by entering the block name of the component in the **Type it** edit box. Alternatively, you can use the **Browse** button to insert the component.

## Always display previously used menu

Select the **Always display previously used menu** check box to display the components of a previously opened menu each time you invoke the **Insert Component** dialog box. By default, this check box is clear.

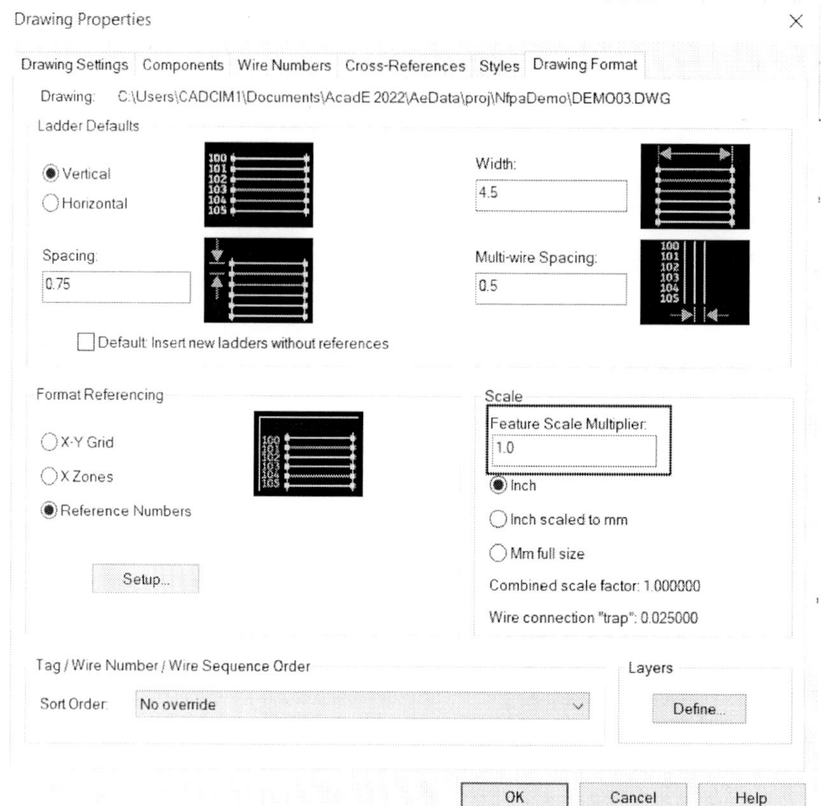


*Figure 5-5 The* ***Drawing Properties*** *dialog box*

To insert a component into your drawing, select a component from the list displayed in the **Menu** area; the **NFPA: Schematic Symbols** area will be changed according to the component selected and the area will be populated with various symbols of the selected icon. For example, if you select **Push Buttons** from the **Menu** area or the **Push Buttons** icon (first row, first column) from the **NFPA: Schematic Symbols** area, you will notice that the **NFPA: Schematic Symbols** area is changed to the **NFPA: Push Buttons** area, displaying various symbols of push buttons, as shown in Figure 5-6.

Select the symbol to be inserted; the symbol will appear on the cursor as a reference. The horizontal symbol will appear on the cursor by default and you will be prompted to specify the insertion point for the component. Next, specify the insertion point for the component; the **Insert / Edit Component** dialog box will be displayed. Specify the details of the component in this dialog box and choose the **OK** button; the component will be inserted into your drawing. The options in the **Insert / Edit Component** dialog box are discussed later in this chapter. Note that when you insert a symbol, the underlying wire breaks and then reconnects again. It happens only when you place the component directly on the wire or close to it within a trap distance.

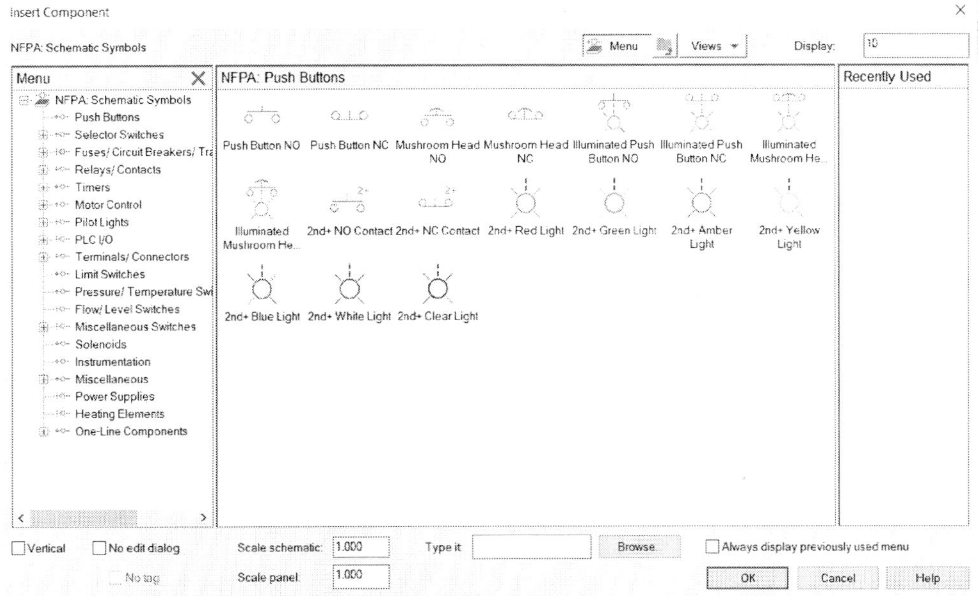


*Figure 5-6 The **Insert Component** dialog box displaying the **NFPA: Push Buttons** area*

**Note**

*1. If you select a vertical wire, AutoCAD Electrical will automatically insert a vertically oriented symbol.*

*2. You can insert multiple components at a time. To do so, choose the **Multiple Insert (Icon Menu)** tool from the **Multiple Insert** drop-down in the **Insert Components** panel of the **Schematic** tab, refer to Figure 5-7. You can also insert the copies of a selected component. To do so, choose the **Multiple Insert (Pick Master)** tool from the **Multiple Insert** drop-down in the **Insert Components** panel of the **Schematic** tab.*

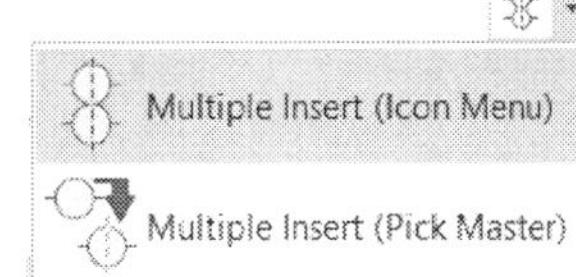


*Figure 5-7 The **Multiple Insert** drop-down*

# INSERTING COMPONENTS USING Catalog Browser

| | |
|---|---|
| **Ribbon:** | Schematic > Insert Components > Icon Menu drop-down > Catalog Browser |
| **Command:** | AECATALOGOPEN |

You can insert components into a drawing by using the **Catalog Browser** dialog box. To do so, choose the **Catalog Browser** tool from the **Icon Menu** drop-down in the **Insert Components** panel of the **Schematic** tab, refer to Figure 5-1. On doing so, the **Catalog Browser** dialog box will be displayed, refer to Figure 5-8.

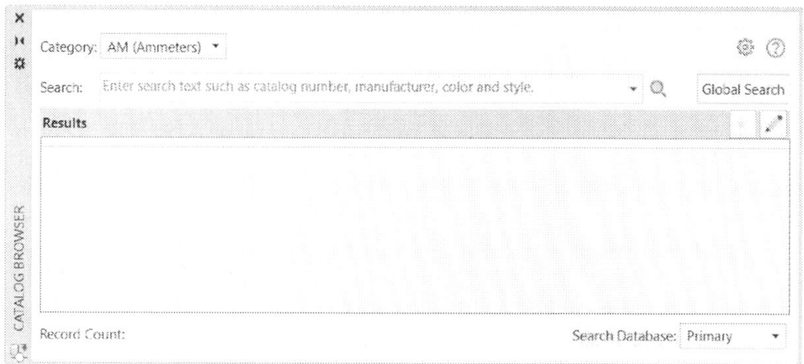


*Figure 5-8 The **Catalog Browser** dialog box*

**Note**

*The **Catalog Browser** dialog box is used in three modes as follows:*

*1. Insertion mode - In this mode, you can insert schematic components into a drawing.*
*2. Lookup mode - In this mode, you can assign a catalog value to a component.*
*3. Edit mode - In this mode, you can edit the catalog database.*
*The method of assigning the catalog information to a component and editing the catalog database in the Lookup mode and Edit mode, respectively, is discussed in detail later in this chapter. In the next section, the method of inserting components is discussed.*

## Category

From the **Category** drop-down list, you can select the category of the component to be inserted in the drawing area. For example, to insert a push button switch, select the **PB (Push buttons)** option from the drop-down list.

## Search

The **Search** field is used to search the required entries from the database based on the keywords mentioned in it. The following criteria are used to search the entries:

1. If the keywords are specified in quotes, for example "400V", the resulting entries will have the exact keywords in any column of the dialog box.

2. If the keywords are specified with OR in between them, the resulting entries will have either of the specified keywords in any of its columns.

3. If the keywords are specified as plain text, the resulting entries will have all the keywords in any of its columns but not necessarily together.

Note that as you enter the keywords in the **Search** field, the name of the manufacturer and the previous searches that are matching with the keywords are displayed in its drop-down list.

Also, when you enter the keywords in the **Search** field, you need to choose the **Search** button at the right of the **Search** field to display the entries from the specified category table as per the keywords mentioned.

## Database Grid

The Database grid displays the resulting entries as per the keywords mentioned in the **Search** field. There are a number of columns in this grid. If you click on any of these columns headers, the entries will be sorted in ascending or descending order. If you right-click on any of these column titles, a shortcut menu will be displayed, as shown in Figure 5-9. The options in the shortcut menu are discussed next.

### Column label list

All the columns displayed in the Database grid are available as options in the shortcut menu. If you click on the tick mark corresponding to any of the columns in the shortcut menu, that column will be removed from the Database grid.

### More

When you choose the **More** option, the **Columns to display** dialog box will be displayed, refer to Figure 5-10.

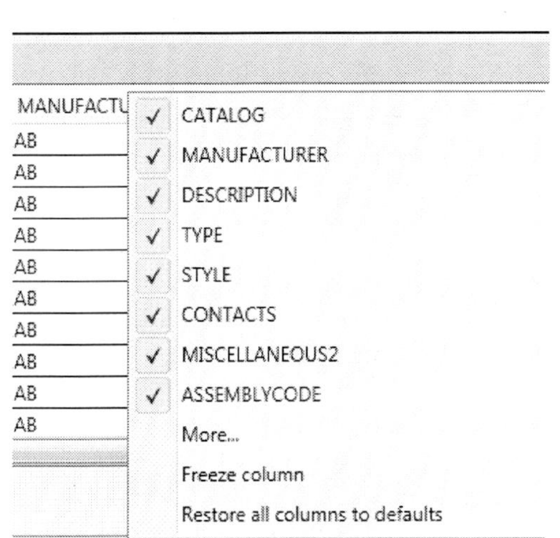


*Figure 5-9 The shortcut menu displayed*

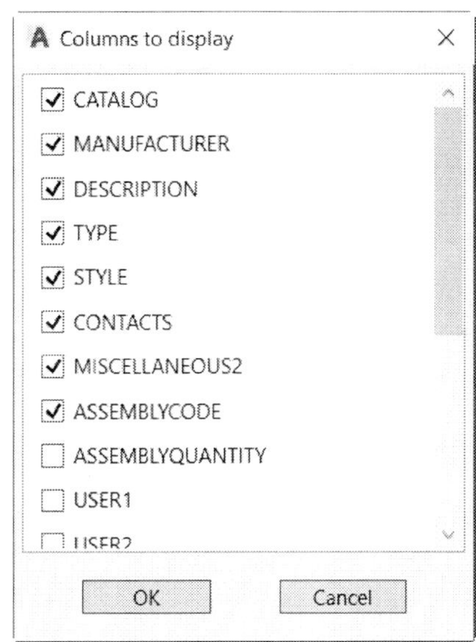


*Figure 5-10 The **Columns to display** dialog box*

This dialog box displays the names of the columns that can be displayed in the Database grid. To display a column in the Database grid, you need to select the corresponding check box.

### Freeze Column

You can choose the **Freeze column** option from the shortcut menu to freeze the selected column. Once the column is frozen, it will be visible even if you scroll the Database grid to the extreme left or extreme right.

## Restore all columns to defaults

Choose the **Restore all columns to defaults** option to undo the changes made to the column(s) such as size change, display order change, or visibility mode.

When you click (or right-click) on an entry in any of the columns of the Database grid, a flyout will be displayed, refer to Figure 5-11. The options in this flyout depend on the type of entry selected. These options are discussed next.

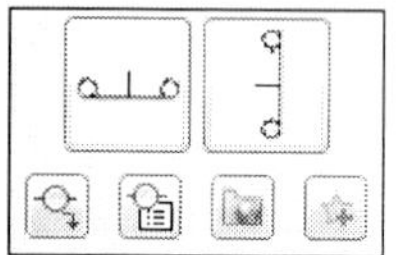

*Figure 5-11* *The flyout displayed*

The symbol image(s) associated with the selected entry are available at the top of the flyout. Note that the symbol image(s) will vary depending on the type of selected entry. Also, there will be no symbol image available for some of the entries. To insert a symbol image, click on it; you will be prompted to specify the insertion point. Also, the symbol image will get attached to the cursor. When you click at a desired location, the symbol image will be inserted at that location. Also, the **Insert/Edit Component** dialog box will be displayed. The options in the **Insert / Edit Component** dialog box are discussed later in this chapter.

This option is used to insert the component from the icon menu. When you choose this option, the **Insert Component** dialog box will be displayed. The options in this dialog box and the procedure to insert the component using the icon menu is discussed in the previous section.

If you choose this option, the **Bill Of Material Check** dialog box will be displayed, refer to Figure 5-12. This dialog box shows the details of the selected entry and the subassembly items, if any.

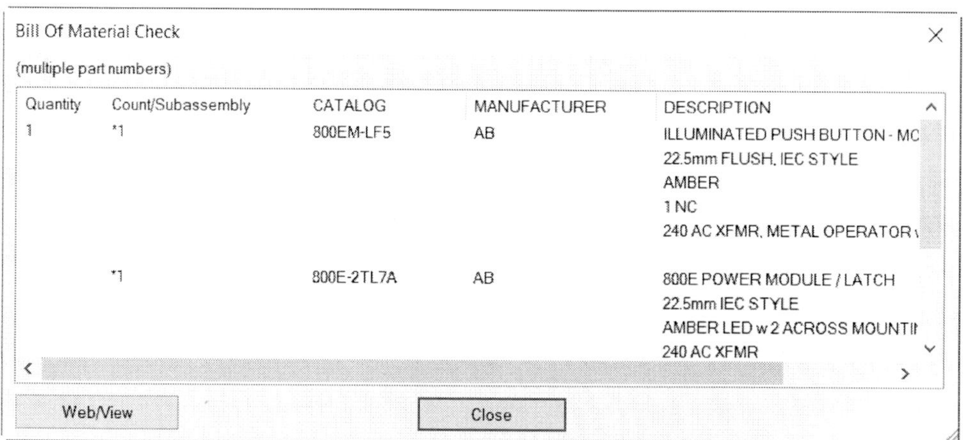


*Figure 5-12* *The* ***Bill Of Material Check*** *dialog box*

This option is used to retrieve additional information about the component. When you choose this option, the default internet browser window will be displayed. In this window, you can find more information about the component such as pictures and specifications.

 This option is used to add the selected entry to the Favorites list for the selected category. Note that this option is available in the flyout only if the selected entry is not in the Favorites list.

 This option is used to delete the selected entry from the Favorites list for the selected category. Note that this option is available in the flyout only if the selected entry is included in the Favorites list.

## Global Search

The **Global Search** button is used to search a keyword mentioned in the **Search** field from all the category tables of the catalog database. When you enter the keywords in the **Search** field and choose the **Global Search** button, the **Catalog Global Search** dialog box will be displayed, refer to Figure 5-13. In this dialog box, a list is displayed at the left side. In this table list, two columns are there. The first column specifies the number of entries for the table whereas the second column specifies the name of the category table. At the right of the list, catalog record list is there. In this list, details of each catalog record are specified in various columns. When you select any cell from the table list, catalog record list at its right is updated accordingly.

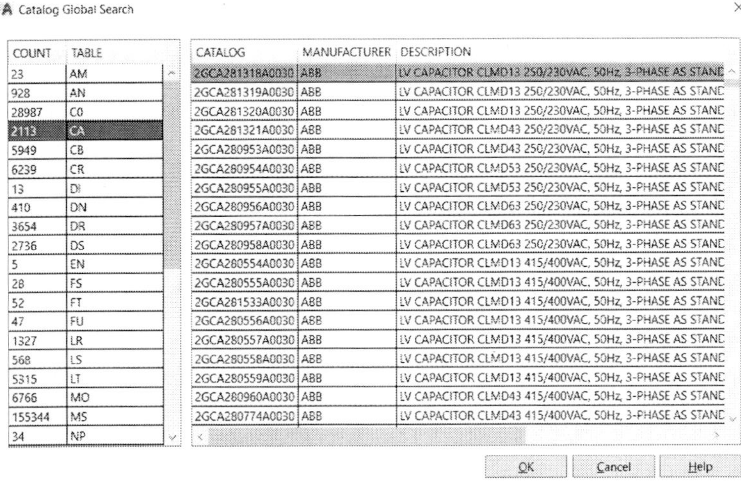

*Figure 5-13 The **Catalog Global Search** dialog box*

## Favorites List

 This button is used to display the Favorites list for the selected category. This button is activated only if one or more entries from the selected category are added to the Favorites list.

## Edits catalog database

 This button enables the **Catalog Browser** dialog box to switch from the Insertion mode to the Edit mode. The method of editing the catalog database is discussed later in the chapter in detail.

## Search Database

The **Search Database** drop-down list is available at the bottom in the **Catalog Browser** dialog box. It provides two options, **Primary** and **Secondary** for selecting a catalog database. The **Primary** option is selected by default and displays the default catalog database. The **Secondary** option will be activated if you have specified the secondary file for the catalog database. To activate this option, choose the **Other File** button in the **Project Setting** tab of the **Project Properties** dialog box and then specify the secondary file.

## Configure your Database

The **Configure your Database** button is available at the upper right corner of the **Catalog Browser** dialog box. It is used to configure the catalog database. To configure the database, choose the **Configure your Database** button; the **Configure Database** dialog box will be displayed, as shown in Figure 5-14. In this dialog box, you need to select the **Microsoft Access** or **Microsoft SQL Server** radio button to select the data source for configuring the database.

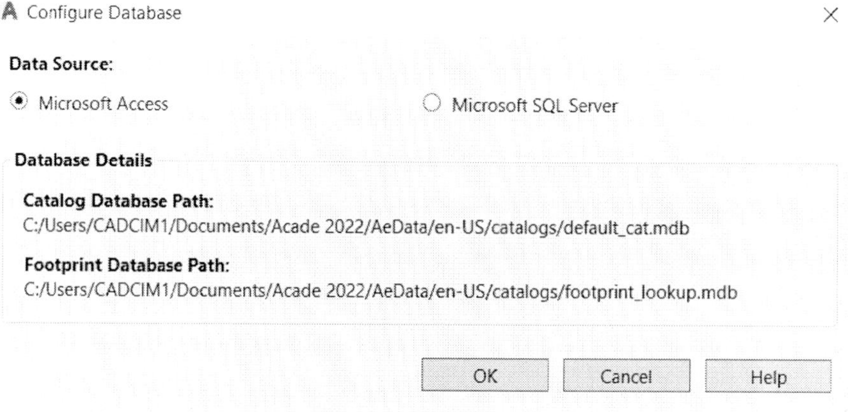


*Figure 5-14 The **Configure Database** dialog box*

If your database is in **Microsoft Access**, select the **Microsoft Access** radio button. You will notice that the locations of the catalog database and footprint database are displayed in the **Database Details** area, refer to Figure 5-14. Next, choose **OK** to configure the database.

If your database is in **Microsoft SQL Server**, select the **Microsoft SQL Server** radio button; the modified **Configure Database** dialog box is displayed, as shown in Figure 5-15.

In this dialog box, choose the browse button located next to the **SQL Server Link** edit box to select the server for connection from the **Select Server Instance** dialog box. Select Windows authentication or SQL Server authentication by selecting the respective radio button in the **Server Details** area. Also, select catalog database and footprint database from the **Database Details** area. Next, choose **Connect** and then **OK** to connect and configure the database.

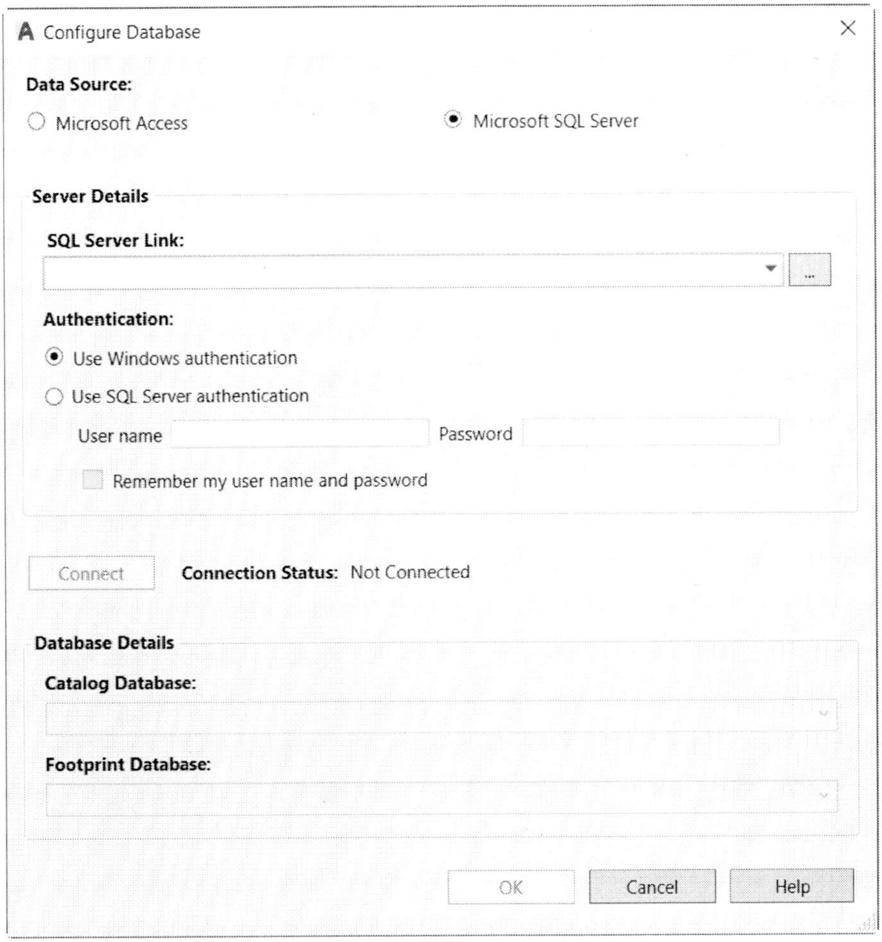

Configure Database

Data Source:

Microsoft Access

Microsoft SQL Server

Server Details

SQL Server Link:

Authentication:

Use Windows authentication

Use SQL Server authentication

User name Password

Remember my user name and password

Connect Connection Status: Not Connected

Database Details

Catalog Database:

Footprint Database:

OK Cancel Help

***Figure 5-15** The modified **Configure Database** dialog box*

# ANNOTATING AND EDITING THE SYMBOLS

**Ribbon:** Schematic > Edit Components >Edit Components drop-down > Edit<br>
**Toolbar:** ACE:Main Electrical > Edit Component<br>
or ACE:Edit Component > Edit Component<br>
**Menu:** Components > Edit Component<br>
**Command:** AEEDITCOMPONENT

You can enter the details while inserting components. However, you can also change or edit these details after inserting a component. To do so, choose the **Edit** tool from the **Edit Components** drop-down in the **Edit Components** panel of the **Schematic** tab, as shown in Figure 5-16; you will be prompted to select the component. Select the component; the **Insert / Edit Component** dialog box will be displayed, as shown in Figure 5-17. Different options in this dialog box are discussed next.

## Component Tag Area

In the **Component Tag** area, you can specify a tag for component or edit an existing tag. If the tag you entered in the edit box is already present in the project, then the **Duplicate Component** dialog box will be displayed. This dialog box alerts you about the duplication of the component tag. In this dialog box, first choose the required option and then choose the **OK** button; the component tag will be displayed in the edit box of the **Component Tag** area of the **Insert / Edit Component** dialog box.

*Figure 5-16 The **Edit Components** drop-down*

If you select the **fixed** check box in this area, then the component tag will not be updated during automatic retagging. By default, this check box is clear. Note that the component tag should be unique. The options in the **Component Tag** area are used to search the existing tag entries and are discussed next.

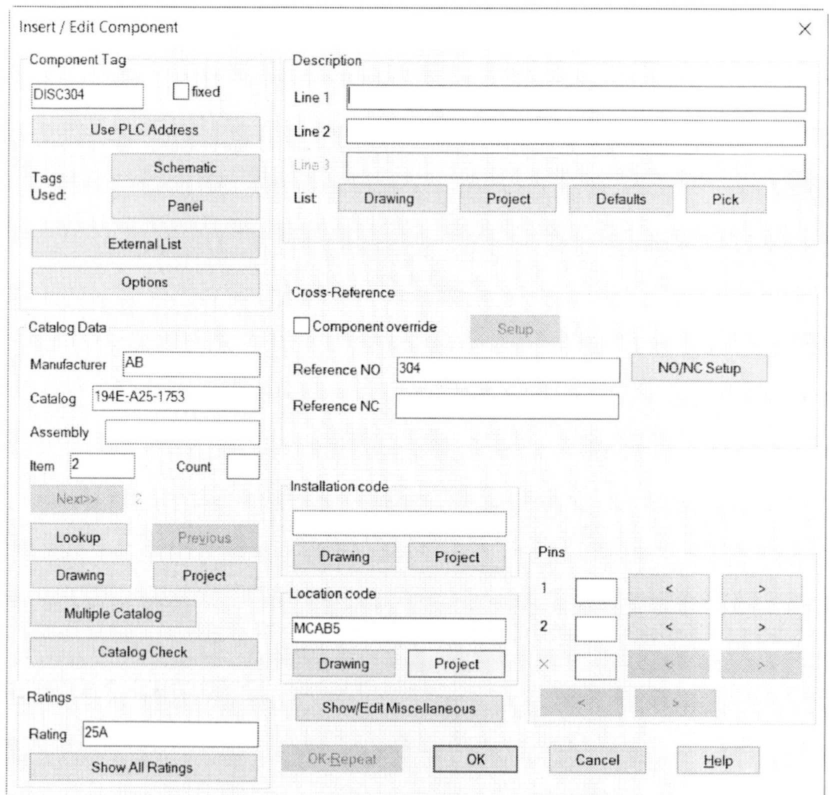


*Figure 5-17 The **Insert / Edit Component** dialog box*

**Note**

*The component tags are based on the settings of the drawing. These settings can be defined in the **Component TAG Format** area of the **Components** tab in the **Drawing Properties** dialog box.*

### Use PLC Address

If you choose the **Use PLC Address** button in the **Component Tag** area, then AutoCAD Electrical will start searching for a nearby PLC I/O address that is connected to the wire. If the PLC I/O address is found, AutoCAD Electrical uses this address in the **Component Tag** edit box as the component tag. If the PLC I/O address is not found, then the **Connected PLC Address Not Found** dialog box will be displayed. In this dialog box, you can select the address text by choosing the **Drawing**, **Project**, or **Manual Pick** button.

### Schematic

The **Schematic** button is used to select the schematic tags for the new component. To select a tag for the component, choose the **Schematic** button; the **XX Tags in Use** dialog box will be displayed. Note that **XX** stands for the family name. This dialog box displays the tags that are present in the active project. Select a tag from the list displayed in the **XX Tags in Use** dialog box. You can either copy or increment the selected tag for the new component using the **Copy Tag** and **Calculate Next** buttons, respectively. By default, only the tags of the parent or stand-alone references are displayed in the **Tags in Use** dialog box. However, you can select the required options from the **Tags in Use** dialog box to include child references, all components for all families, all panel components, and one-line components.

### Panel

The **Panel** button is used to select panel tags for the new component. To select a tag, choose the **Panel** button; the **Panel Tag List** dialog box will be displayed. Select the tag from the dialog box that you want to copy for the new component. Note that if there is no panel component present in the drawing then no panel tags will be displayed in the **Panel Tag List** dialog box.

### External List

The **External List** button is used to select the component tag from the external list. To select a component tag, choose the **External List** button; the **Select External Tag List file name** dialog box will be displayed. Select the file and then choose the **Open** button; the **File** dialog box will be displayed. Select the component name from the **File** dialog box and then choose the **OK** button; the **Component Annotation from External File** dialog box will be displayed. In this dialog box, modify the information in the **Tag** edit box as per your requirement and then choose the **OK** button; the tag name will be displayed in the edit box of the **Component Tag** area.

### Options

The **Options** button is used to override the default tag format of a drawing. To do so, choose the **Options** button from the **Component Tag** area; the **Option: Tag Format "Family" Override** dialog box will be displayed, as shown in Figure 5-18. Enter a value in the **Tag override format** edit box. Next, choose the **OK** button in this dialog box to change the format of the tag specified in the edit box of the **Component Tag** area of the **Insert / Edit Component** dialog box.

## Catalog Data Area

The **Catalog Data** area is used to specify the catalog and manufacturer information for the component. The catalog and manufacturer information are used in reports. This will be discussed in detail in Chapter 9. The catalog data is stored in the Microsoft Access database file. By default, the catalog data is saved in the *default_cat.mdb* file. The listing of similar components in a drawing or project can be done with their catalog assignments. The options in this area are discussed next.

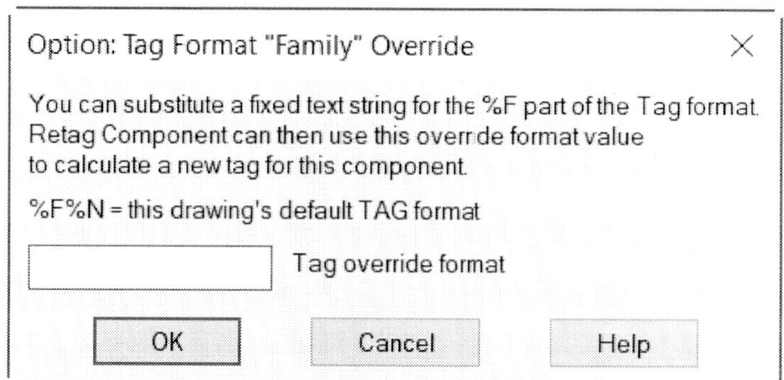


*Figure 5-18 The **Option: Tag Format "Family" Override** dialog box*

## Manufacturer

This edit box is used to specify the manufacturer code for the component. To do so, enter the manufacturer code in the **Manufacturer** edit box. Alternatively, choose the **Lookup** button; the **Catalog Browser** dialog box will be displayed. You can select the required manufacturer code from this dialog box. The **Catalog Browser** dialog box is discussed later in this chapter.

## Catalog

This edit box is used to specify the catalog number for the component. To do so, enter the catalog number in the **Catalog** edit box or choose the **Lookup** button and select the catalog number from the **Catalog Browser** dialog box.

## Assembly

The assembly code is used to link multiple part catalog values together. Enter the assembly code of the component in the **Assembly** edit box.

## Item

The **Item** edit box is used to specify the unique identifier for each component. Specify the tag value in the **Item** edit box.

## Count

The **Count** edit box is used to specify the quantity of the catalog part number.

## Lookup

When you choose the **Lookup** button, the **Catalog Browser** dialog box will be displayed. This dialog box displays the information that has been extracted from the catalog database of the component. Select the manufacturer and catalog values from the **Catalog Browser** dialog box and choose the **OK** button; the manufacturer and the catalog values will be displayed in the **Manufacturer** and **Catalog** edit boxes of the **Insert / Edit Component** dialog box. The options in the **Catalog Browser** dialog box are discussed later in this chapter.

## Drawing

The **Drawing** button is used to search the catalog data of similar components in the current drawing. To search the catalog data, choose the **Drawing** button; the **catalog values (this drawing)** dialog box will be displayed. This dialog box displays the catalog information of similar components used in the current drawing. Select the catalog value from the **catalog values (this drawing)** dialog box and choose the **OK** button; the values will be displayed in the **Manufacturer** and **Catalog** edit boxes of the **Insert / Edit Component** dialog box.

The **Catalog Check** button in the **catalog values (this drawing)** dialog box is used to check the catalog information. To check the catalog information, select the catalog value in this dialog box and then choose the **Catalog Check** button; the **Bill of Material Check** dialog box will be displayed. This dialog box displays the bill of material for the selected component.

## Project

The **Project** button is used to search the catalog data of similar components in the active project, another projects, or external file (.txt or .csv file). To search the catalog data, choose the **Project** button; the **Find: Catalog Assignments** dialog box will be displayed, as shown in Figure 5-19. In this dialog box, you can specify whether to search the catalog data in the active project, other project, or external file. The options in this dialog box are discussed next.

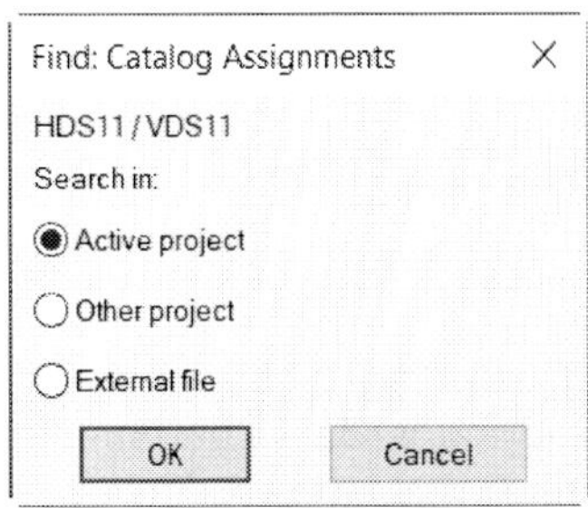


*Figure 5-19 The **Find: Catalog Assignments** dialog box*

### Active project

The **Active project** radio button is used to search the catalog data of similar components in the active project. By default, this radio button is selected. Choose the **OK** button in the **Find: Catalog Assignments** dialog box; the **QSAVE** message box will be displayed. Choose the **OK** button in the **QSAVE** message box; the **catalog values (this project)** dialog box will be displayed. Select the catalog data from the list displayed in this dialog box and choose the **OK** button; the catalog information will be displayed in the **Catalog Data** area of the **Insert / Edit Component** dialog box.

**Note**

*The **QSAVE** message box will be displayed only if you have made changes in the current drawing and have not saved them. Otherwise, the **catalog values (this project)** dialog box will be displayed directly.*

### Other project

The **Other project** radio button is used to search the catalog data of similar components in the other projects. To do so, select the **Other project** radio button and then choose the **OK** button; the **Recent Projects** dialog box will be displayed. Select the project from the list displayed in this dialog box and choose the **OK** button; the **catalog values** dialog box will be displayed. Select the catalog data from the list displayed in this dialog box and choose the **OK** button; the catalog information will be displayed in the **Catalog Data** area of the **Insert / Edit Component** dialog box.

### External file

The **External file** radio button is used to search the catalog data in external files. The extension of these external files is *.txt* or *.csv*. To search the catalog data in the external files, select the **External file** radio button and then choose the **OK** button; the **Select External Catalog List file name** dialog box will be displayed. Select the required catalog file and choose the **Open** button; a dialog box will be displayed. The title bar of this dialog box displays the name and path of the external file. Select the required catalog values in this dialog box; the **Catalog Assignment from External File** dialog box will be displayed. Specify the manufacturer, catalog, and assembly codes in this dialog box and choose the **OK** button; the values will be displayed in the **Catalog Data** area of the **Insert / Edit Component** dialog box.

## Multiple Catalog

The **Multiple Catalog** button is used to insert extra catalog part numbers into the selected component or to edit these catalog part numbers. To insert an extra catalog part number, choose the **Multiple Catalog** button; the **Multiple Bill of Material Information** dialog box will be displayed. In this dialog box, specify the required values and then choose the **OK** button; the extra catalog part numbers will be added to the component. This dialog box can be used to assign 99 part numbers to the component.

## Catalog Check

The **Catalog Check** button is used to check the catalog information of the selected component. To do so, choose the **Catalog Check** button; the **Bill Of Material Check** dialog box will be displayed. This dialog box displays how the catalog data of the selected component will appear in the Bill of Material report.

# Ratings Area

The **Ratings** area is used to specify the rating value of a component. This area will be activated only if a component has rating attributes. To specify rating attribute, enter a value in the **Rating** edit box. Alternatively, choose the **Show All Ratings** button; the **View/Edit Rating Value** dialog box will be displayed, as shown in Figure 5-20. Enter a rating value in the edit box. You can also specify the rating value by choosing the **Defaults** button. On doing so, the **RATINGs defaults** dialog box showing the default rating values will be displayed. Select a rating value and choose the **OK** button; the value will be displayed in the edit box of the **View/Edit Rating Value** dialog box. Next, choose the **OK** button in this dialog box; the rating value will be displayed in the **Rating** edit box of the **Ratings** area.

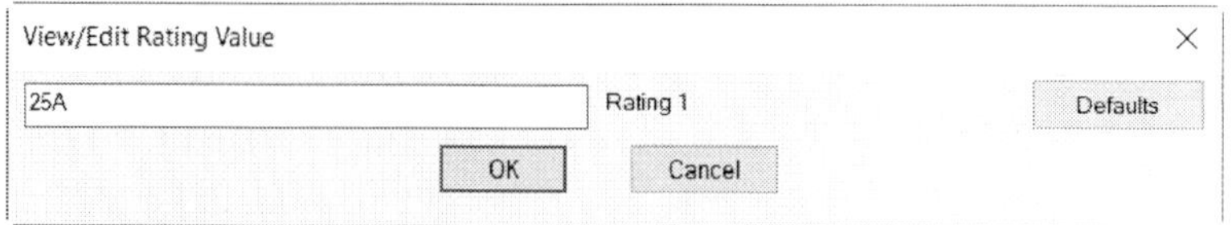


*Figure 5-20 The **View/Edit Rating Value** dialog box*

# Description Area

The **Description** area is used to specify the description for the component. You can enter upto three lines of description in the **Line 1**, **Line 2**, and **Line 3** edit boxes in the **Description** area. Different options in this area are discussed next.

**Note**

*When you enter a description for a component in the **Description** area, by default, the description will be entered in the capital letters (upper case). To change the description to lower case, right-click on the active project name; a shortcut menu will be displayed. Choose the **Properties** option from the shortcut menu; the **Project Properties** dialog box will be displayed. Next, choose the **Components** tab from this dialog box, clear the **Description text upper case** check box in the **Component Options** area, and then choose the **OK** button in the **Project Properties** dialog box; the description text will change to lower case.*

### Drawing

Choose the **Drawing** button to select a description used in the active drawing. To select a description found in the active drawing, choose the **Drawing** button; the **Description pick list - Drawing** dialog box will be displayed. This dialog box displays a list of descriptions used in the active drawing. Select the description and choose the **OK** button in this dialog box; the description will be displayed in the description lines of the **Description** area.

### Project

Choose the **Project** button to select a description used in the active project. To select a description found in the active project, choose the **Project** button; the **Description pick list - Project** dialog box will be displayed. This dialog box displays a list of descriptions used in the active project. Select the required description from this dialog box and choose the **OK** button; the description will be displayed in the description lines of the **Description** area.

### Defaults

When you choose the **Defaults** button, the **Descriptions (general)** dialog box will be displayed. This dialog box displays a list of default descriptions. This list is based on *wd_desc.wdd* ASCII text file, which will be discussed in Chapter 12. Select the description from the ASCII text file displayed and choose the **OK** button; the description will be displayed in the **Description** area of the **Insert / Edit Component** dialog box.

### Pick

The **Pick** button is used to select the description for a component from the current drawing. To do so, choose the **Pick** button; the **Insert / Edit Component** dialog box will disappear and you will be prompted to select the component for description text capture. Next, select the component from the current drawing; the **Insert / Edit Component** dialog box will appear again and the description of the selected component will be displayed in the **Description** area of this dialog box.

## Cross-Reference Area

The **Cross-Reference** area is used to display the references of a component. This area also displays the groups of components that carry the same TAG text string value. Note that you can also cross-reference components of different families, if they have the same TAG1/TAG2/TAG_*/TAG attributes. The options in this area are discussed next.

## Component override

Select the **Component override** check box to change the cross-reference format, which has been defined in the **Cross-References** tab of the **Drawing Properties** dialog box. Also, when you select this check box, the **Setup** button will be activated.

## Setup

The **Setup** button will be activated only when you select the **Component override** check box. This button is used to edit the cross-reference settings of a component. To edit these settings, choose the **Setup** button; the **Cross-Reference Component Override** dialog box will be displayed, as shown in Figure 5-21. Specify the options in this dialog box as per your requirement and then choose the **OK** button to return to the **Insert / Edit Component** dialog box.

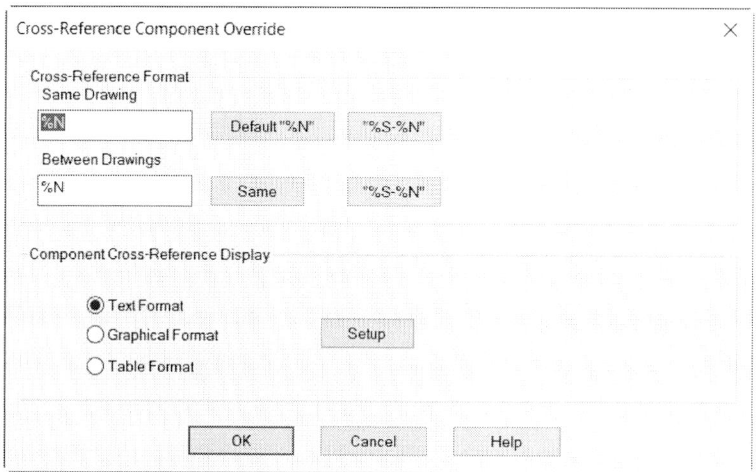


*Figure 5-21 The **Cross-Reference Component Override** dialog box*

## Reference NO / Reference NC

The **Reference NO** and **Reference NC** edit boxes will be activated only if the components have the NO/NC contacts. Enter the cross-reference information for the normally open contact in the **Reference NO** edit box and the normally closed contact in the **Reference NC** edit box. Note that the cross-reference information of the child contacts of the symbol are stored in the XREFNO and XREFNC attributes. Also, when you insert a child contact in the drawing, the XREFNO and XREFNC attributes will be updated automatically. You can also edit the information manually.

## NO/NC Setup

The **NO/NC Setup** button is used to create the pin list assignments for a component. If you choose the **NO/NC Setup** button, the **Maximum NO/NC counts and/or allowed Pin numbers** dialog box will be displayed, as shown in Figure 5-22.

Enter the required values in the **Maximum NO contact count**, **Maximum NC contact count**, **Maximum convertible NO/NC**, and **Maximum undefined type "4"** edit boxes. Alternatively, you can fill the values of these options by clicking on the appropriate arrow button located on the right of these edit boxes. Also, you can increase or decrease the values displayed in the edit boxes using these arrow buttons. Next, these values are copied to the parent component automatically from the pin list database information (if it is available) when a matching catalog number is selected. You can also edit the information manually.

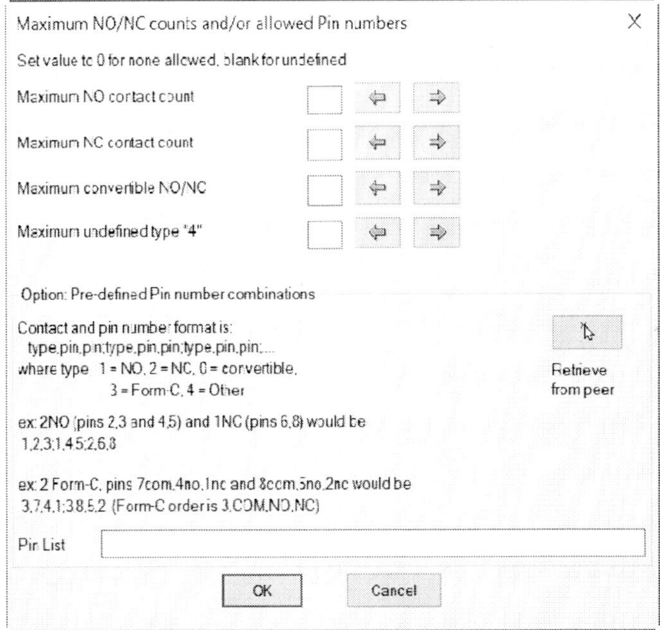


*Figure 5-22 The* ***Maximum NO/NC counts and/or allowed Pin numbers*** *dialog box*

## Installation code and Location code Areas

The installation and location codes are used to specify the physical location of a component. The **Installation code** area of the **Insert / Edit Component** dialog box is shown in Figure 5-23. Specify the installation code in the edit box in this area.

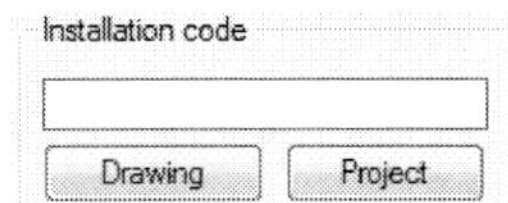


*Figure 5-23 The* ***Installation code*** *area*

Alternatively, you can choose the **Drawing** button to select the installation code found in the current drawing from the **Installation (this drawing)** dialog box or choose the **Project** button to select the installation codes from the **All Installations - Project** dialog box.

This dialog box displays the installation codes that are found in the active project. You can also select installation code from the external file by selecting the **Include external list** check box in the **All Installations - Project** dialog box. Select the installation code from the list displayed and then choose the **OK** button; the code will be displayed in the edit box of the **Installation code** area.

The **Location code** area of the **Insert / Edit Component** dialog box is shown in Figure 5-24. Specify the location code in the **Location code** edit box. Alternatively, choose the **Drawing** button to select the location code found in the current drawing or choose the **Project** button to select the location codes found in the

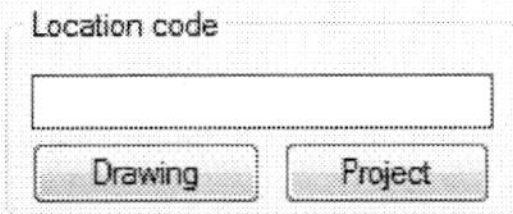


*Figure 5-24 The* ***Location code*** *area*

active project. Select the location code from the list displayed and choose the **OK** button; the code will be displayed in the edit box of the **Location code** area.

**Note**

*If a drawing or project does not contain the installation or location codes then the **Installation (this drawing)** or the **Location (this drawing)** dialog box and the **All Installations - Project** or the **All Locations - Project** dialog box will not display the list of codes.*

## Show/Edit Miscellaneous

The **Show/Edit Miscellaneous** button in the **Insert / Edit Component** dialog box is used to edit or view non standard AutoCAD Electrical attributes. If you choose this button, the **Edit Miscellaneous and Non-AutoCAD Electrical Attributes** dialog box will be displayed, as shown in Figure 5-25. This dialog box displays the attributes that are assigned to the component but are not predefined AutoCAD Electrical attributes.

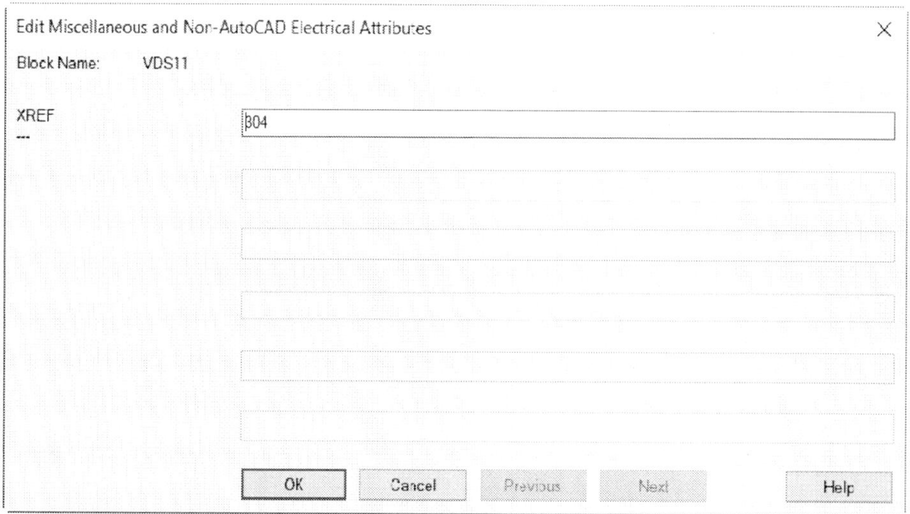


*Figure 5-25 The **Edit Miscellaneous and Non-AutoCAD Electrical Attributes** dialog box*

**Note**

*If the component does not have non-AutoCAD Electrical attributes, the **AutoCAD Electrical Message** message box with "**-none-**" text will be displayed on choosing the **Show/Edit Miscellaneous** button.*

## Pins Area

The **Pins** area, as shown in Figure 5-26, is used to assign pin numbers to a component. To do so, specify the pin numbers for the component in the **1** and **2** edit boxes. Alternatively, choose the arrow buttons located beside these edit boxes to enter the values. Choose the **<** or **>** button to increase or decrease the values in the edit boxes. Note that the number of pins in this area depend on the selected component.

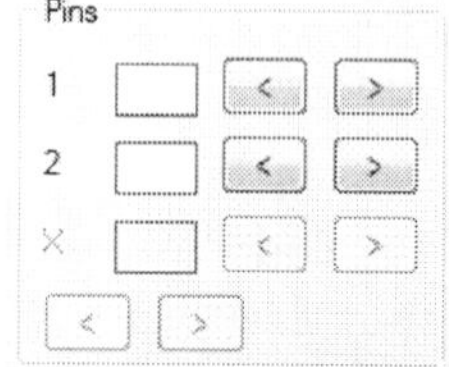


*Figure 5-26 The **Pins** area*

In case of a parametric connector, the arrow buttons will not be available in the **Pins** area, but the **List** button will be available. The **List** button is used for editing pins of already inserted connector. On choosing the **List** button, the **Connector Pin Numbers In Use** dialog box will be displayed. This dialog box displays the information of the pins of an already inserted connector. Specify the options in this dialog box. Next, choose the **OK** button to save the changes and return to the **Insert / Edit Component** dialog box.

### Switch Positions Area

The **Switch Positions** area will be available only when you select a selector switch to edit. In this area, you can mark the positions of selector switches.

The **OK-Repeat** button will be activated in the **Insert / Edit Component** dialog box only when a new component is inserted in the drawing. This button will not be activated while you edit a component. The **OK-Repeat** button is used to insert the same component again. When you choose the **OK-Repeat** button, you will be prompted to specify the insertion point for the new component. Once the component is inserted, you will be prompted again to specify the insertion point for another component that is same as the first component. Specify the insertion point; the **Insert / Edit Component** dialog box will be displayed again. Note that all the attributes that you entered for the previous component will be copied to the **Insert / Edit Component** dialog box for the current symbol.

Choose the **OK** button from the **Insert / Edit Component** dialog box to complete the editing or insertion of the selected component. The **OK** button will be activated while editing or inserting the component in the drawing.

## ASSIGNING CATALOG INFORMATION AND EDITING THE CATALOG DATABASE

You can assign catalog information to a component using the **Catalog Browser** dialog box. The **Lookup** button in the **Catalog Data** area of the **Insert / Edit Component** dialog box is used to assign the catalog information from the **Catalog Browser** dialog box to a component. To assign catalog information, choose the **Edit** tool from the **Edit Components** panel of the **Schematic** tab; you will be prompted to select the component. Next, select the component; the **Insert / Edit Component** dialog box will be displayed. Choose the **Lookup** button from the **Catalog Data** area of this dialog box; the **Catalog Browser** dialog box will be displayed in the Lookup mode, refer to Figure 5-27. This dialog box displays the catalog database of the components from where you can select the manufacturer or catalog values. The **Category** drop-down list displays the category of the selected component. Select the entry from the Database grid of the dialog box. You can also search for the required catalog information by using the **Search** field. After selecting the required entry, choose the **OK** button from the **Catalog Browser** dialog box; the selected catalog information will be displayed in the **Manufacturer** and the **Catalog** edit boxes of the **Insert/Edit Component** dialog box.

To edit the catalog database available in the **Catalog Browser** dialog box, choose the **Edit catalog database** button; the **Catalog Browser** dialog box will switch to Edit mode. Also, the name of the dialog box will change to **Catalog Browser - Edit Mode** dialog box and the color of the Database grid will change to yellow, refer to Figure 5-28. The options in this dialog box are discussed next.

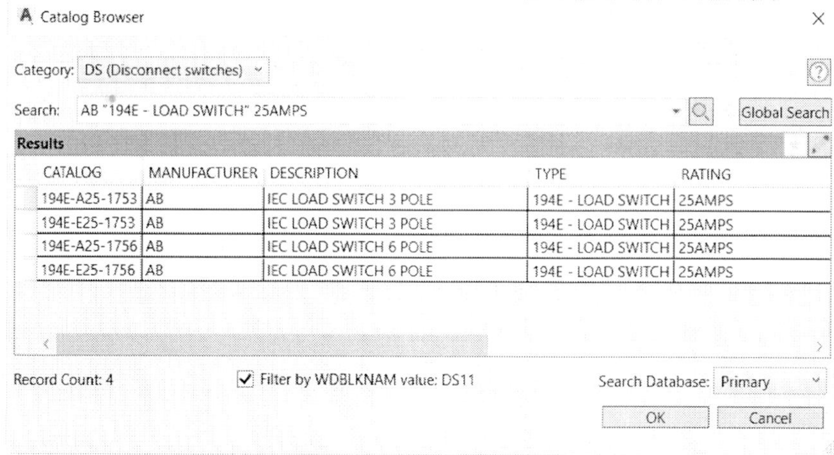


*Figure 5-27 The **Catalog Browser** dialog box*

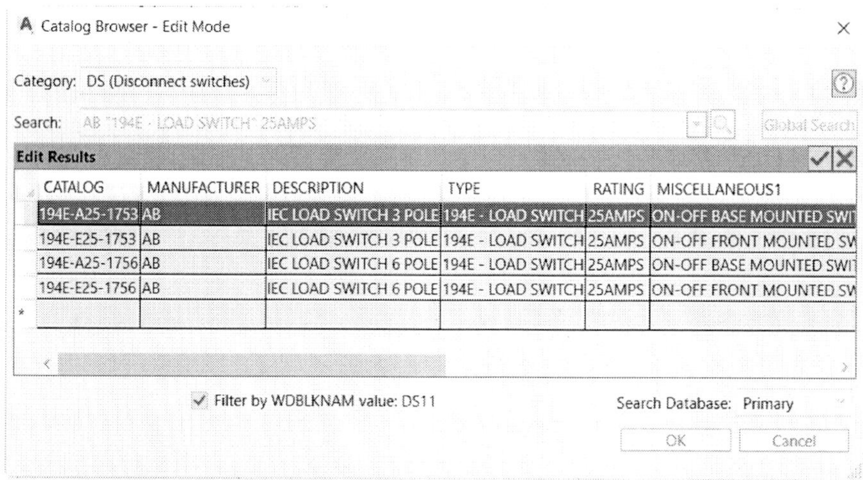


*Figure 5-28 The **Catalog Browser - Edit Mode** dialog box*

The **Category** drop-down list, the **Search** field, the **Filter by WDBLKNAM value: XX** check box, and the **Search Database** drop-down list will be deactivated in the Edit mode. When you right-click on any of the cells of a column in the Database grid, a shortcut menu will be displayed, as shown in Figure 5-29. The options in this shortcut menu are used to edit the selected entry in the Database grid.

The **Cut** option is used to cut the content of the selected cell. The **Copy** option is used to copy the content of the selected cell. The **Paste** option is used to paste the cut or copied content of the cell to another cell.

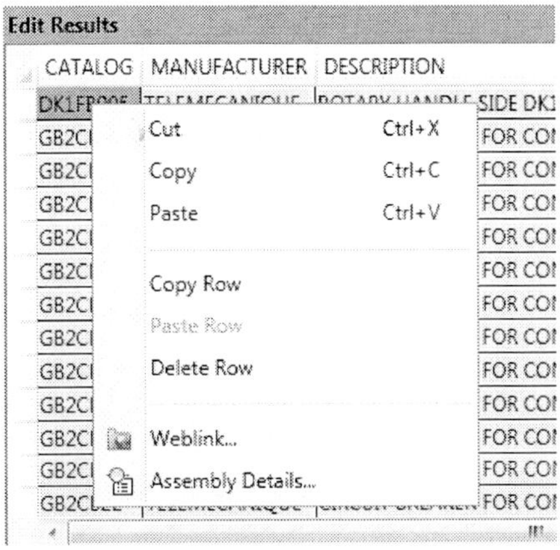

The **Copy Row** option is used to copy the selected row (entry) from the Database grid. The **Paste Row** option is used to paste the copied row to another row in the Database grid. The **Delete Row** option is used to delete the selected row from the Database grid.

The **Weblink** option is used to retrieve more information about the component. When you choose this option, the **Microsoft Internet Explorer** window will be displayed. In this window, you can find more information about the component such as pictures and specifications.

*Figure 5-29 The shortcut menu displayed*

When you choose the **Assembly Details** option, the **Bill Of Material Check** dialog box will be displayed, refer to Figure 5-12. This dialog box is used to show the details of the selected entry and subassembly items, if any.

You can also click in any cell of the Database grid and change the content by simply entering the desired text.

After editing the Database as explained above, if you choose the **Accept changes** button, the changes will be reflected in the **Catalog Browser - Edit Mode** dialog box and it will also exit from the Edit mode. If you want to cancel any changes made in the database, choose the **Cancel changes** button.

# CREATING A PROJECT SPECIFIC CATALOG DATABASE

**Ribbon:** Project > Other Tools > Create Project-Specific Catalog Database
**Menu:** Projects > Extras > Create Project-Specific Catalog Database
**Command:** AECREATEPROJCATALOG

When you install AutoCAD Electrical, the catalog information in the **Catalog Browser** dialog box is stored in a default Microsoft Access Database file. The extension of the file is *.mdb*. This file contains a huge sample vendor data. When you create a new project, a part of this sample data is used in the project. You can create a project specific catalog database which contains entries only for the components used in the project. You can send this project specific catalog database file to the client. This file is much smaller in size than the default catalog database file.

To create a project specific catalog database, activate the project for which you want to create it. Next, choose the **Create Project-Specific Catalog Database** tool from the **Other Tools** panel of the **Project** tab; the **Create Project-Specific Catalog Database** dialog box will be displayed, as shown in Figure 5-30. The options in this dialog box are discussed next.

## Project

The name of the active project will be displayed next to the project option.

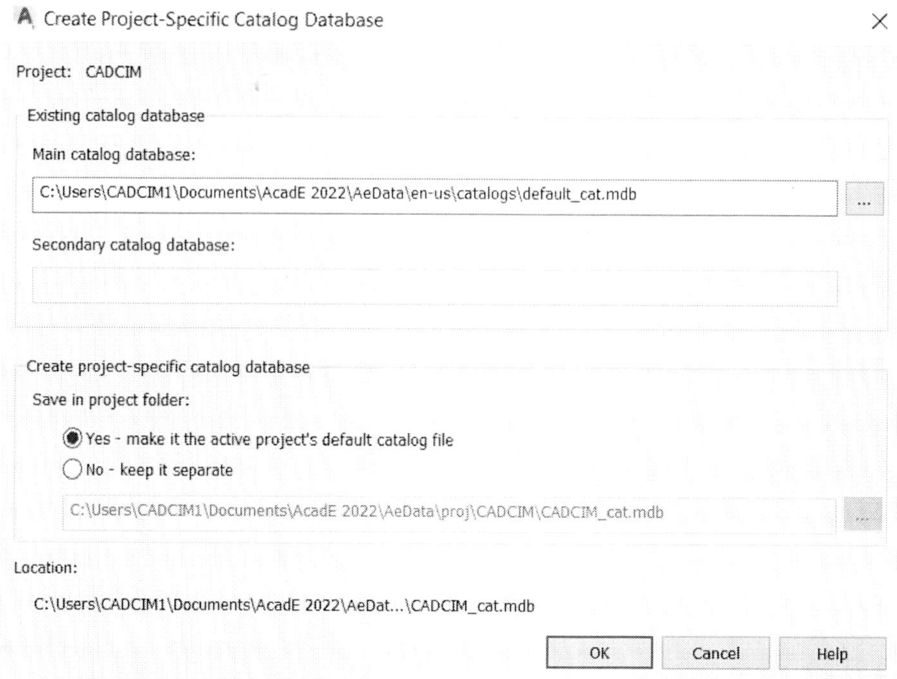


*Figure 5-30 The **Create Project-Specific Catalog Database** dialog box*

## Existing catalog database Area

The options in this area are used to specify the name and path of the main catalog database and the secondary catalog file. The options in this area are discussed next.

### Main catalog database

The **Main catalog database** edit box is used to specify the path and name of the main catalog file assigned to the active project. You can also choose the **Browse** button to select the file other than the default one.

### Secondary catalog database

The **Secondary catalog file** edit box is used to display the path and name of the secondary file, if you have specified the secondary option for catalog database. You can specify the secondary option by choosing the **Other File** button in the **Project Setting** tab of the **Project Properties** dialog box and specify the secondary file. You cannot change the path and name of the secondary file in this dialog box.

## Create project-specific catalog database Area

The options in this area are discussed next.

### Yes-make it the active project's default catalog file

By default, this radio button is selected. If you select this radio button, the project specific catalog file will be created and saved at the location specified in the edit box. The edit box is located at the bottom of the **Create project-specific catalog database** area. Also, it is the default catalog file for the active project. As a result, only the entries related to the active project will be displayed in it.

### No, keep it separate

If you select this radio button, the project specific catalog file will be created and saved at the location specified in the edit box below it. If you specify the same location that is displayed in the edit box by default, the project specific catalog database will become the default catalog file for the active project. Specify the location other than the default one to keep the project specific catalog database as a separate database.

### Location

It specifies the location of the project specific catalog database.

## CREATING PARENT-CHILD RELATIONSHIPS

| | |
|---|---|
| **Ribbon:** | Schematic > Insert Components > Icon Menu drop-down > Icon Menu |
| **Toolbar:** | ACE:Main Electrical > Insert Component drop-down > Insert Component or ACE:Insert Component > Insert Component |
| **Menu:** | Components > Insert Component |
| **Command:** | AECOMPONENT |

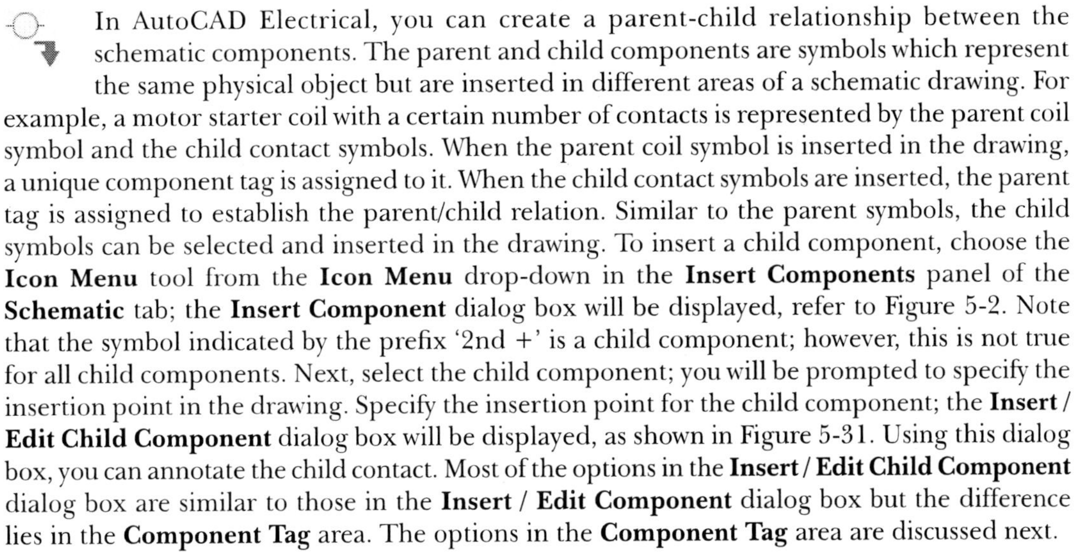

In AutoCAD Electrical, you can create a parent-child relationship between the schematic components. The parent and child components are symbols which represent the same physical object but are inserted in different areas of a schematic drawing. For example, a motor starter coil with a certain number of contacts is represented by the parent coil symbol and the child contact symbols. When the parent coil symbol is inserted in the drawing, a unique component tag is assigned to it. When the child contact symbols are inserted, the parent tag is assigned to establish the parent/child relation. Similar to the parent symbols, the child symbols can be selected and inserted in the drawing. To insert a child component, choose the **Icon Menu** tool from the **Icon Menu** drop-down in the **Insert Components** panel of the **Schematic** tab; the **Insert Component** dialog box will be displayed, refer to Figure 5-2. Note that the symbol indicated by the prefix '2nd +' is a child component; however, this is not true for all child components. Next, select the child component; you will be prompted to specify the insertion point in the drawing. Specify the insertion point for the child component; the **Insert / Edit Child Component** dialog box will be displayed, as shown in Figure 5-31. Using this dialog box, you can annotate the child contact. Most of the options in the **Insert / Edit Child Component** dialog box are similar to those in the **Insert / Edit Component** dialog box but the difference lies in the **Component Tag** area. The options in the **Component Tag** area are discussed next.

**Note**

*The* ***Catalog Data*** *area is not available in the* ***Insert / Edit Child Component*** *dialog box as the catalog data is stored in the parent component only.*

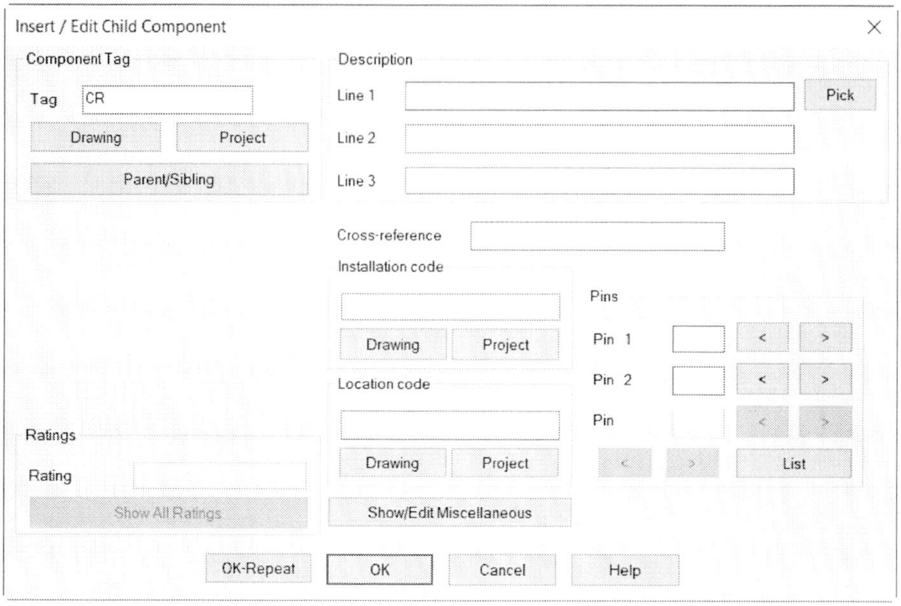

Insert / Edit Child Component

| Component Tag | | Description | |
|---|---|---|---|
| Tag | CR | Line 1 | Pick |
| Drawing | Project | Line 2 | |
| Parent/Sibling | | Line 3 | |

Cross-reference

Installation code: Drawing | Project

Location code: Drawing | Project

Pins: Pin 1 < > ; Pin 2 < > ; Pin < > ; < > List

Ratings: Rating; Show All Ratings

Show/Edit Miscellaneous

OK-Repeat | OK | Cancel | Help

*Figure 5-31 The **Insert / Edit Child Component** dialog box*

# Component Tag Area

The **Component Tag** area is used to build the parent-child relationship between components. After you have inserted the child component, the component tag will be displayed in the **Tag** edit box by default. You can also specify the component tag in the **Tag** edit box manually. Note that the tag is assigned to the child component based on the parent component to which it is linked. You can select the component tag by using the options discussed next.

## Drawing

The **Drawing** button is used to search the parent component tag of similar components in the current drawing. To do so, choose the **Drawing** button; the **Active Drawing list for FAMILY ="XX"** dialog box will be displayed, refer to Figure 5-32. Note that **XX** stands for the family name. The options in this dialog box are discussed next.

If you select the **Show all components for all families** check box at the bottom of this dialog box, the name of the **Active Drawing list for FAMILY** dialog box will be modified to the **Component List (this drawing only)** dialog box, as shown in Figure 5-33. In this dialog box, one additional column **Family** will be added to the list. By default, the **Show all components for all families** check box is clear.

Next, select the parent symbol from the list displayed. Note that only those parents will be displayed in the list that belong to the same family. Next, choose the **OK** button; you will return to the **Insert / Edit Child Component** dialog box. Notice that the component tag is displayed in the **Tag** edit box.

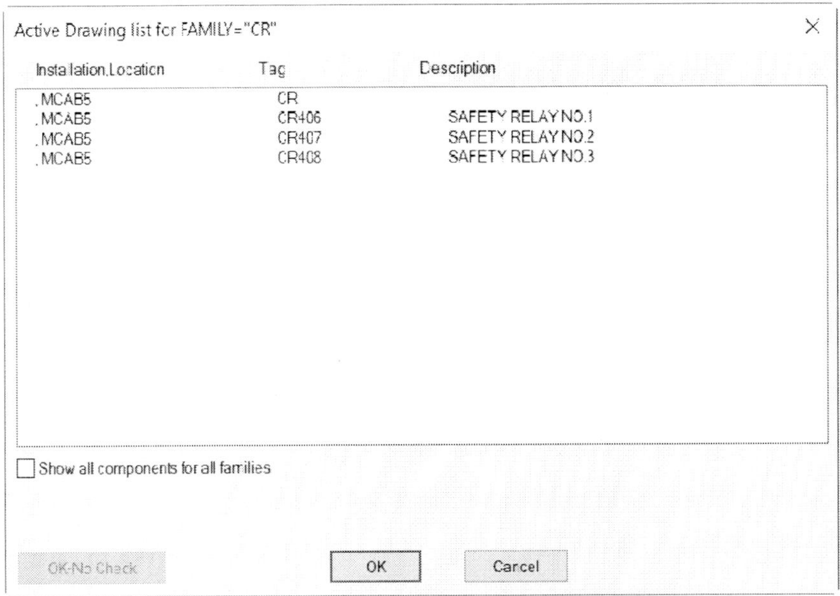

Active Drawing list for FAMILY="CR"

| Installation.Location | Tag | Description |
|---|---|---|
| .MCAB5 | CR | |
| .MCAB5 | CR406 | SAFETY RELAY NO.1 |
| .MCAB5 | CR407 | SAFETY RELAY NO.2 |
| .MCAB5 | CR408 | SAFETY RELAY NO.3 |

☐ Show all components for all families

OK-No Check | OK | Cancel

*Figure 5-32 The **Active Drawing list for FAMILY="CR"** dialog box*

Component List (this drawing only)

| Family | Installation.Location | Tag | Description |
|---|---|---|---|
| LS | .MACHINE | LS406 | RAM 01 RETRACTED |
| LS | .MACHINE | LS407 | RAM 02 RETRACTED |
| LS | .MACHINE | LS408 | RAM 03 RETRACTED |
| CR | .MCAB5 | CR | |
| CR | .MCAB5 | CR406 | SAFETY RELAY NO.1 |
| CR | .MCAB5 | CR407 | SAFETY RELAY NO.2 |
| CR | .MCAB5 | CR408 | SAFETY RELAY NO.3 |
| M | .MCAB5 | M414 | CONVEYOR MOTOR |
| M | .MCAB5 | M422 | HYDRAULIC MOTOR |
| M | .MCAB5 | M422 | HYDRAULIC MOTOR |
| M | .MCAB5 | M425 | INDEXING MOTOR |
| M | .MCAB5 | M425 | INDEXING MOTOR |
| M | .MCAB5 | M433 | UNWIND WEB MOTOR |
| M | .MCAB5 | M435 | REWIND WEB MOTOR |
| M | .MCAB5 | M900 | |
| LT | .OPSTA3 | LT409 | SAFETY OKAY |
| LT | .OPSTA3 | LT411 | RAM 01 OKAY |
| LT | .OPSTA3 | LT412 | RAM 02 OKAY |

☑ Show all components for all families

OK-No Check | OK | Cancel

*Figure 5-33 The **Component List (this drawing only)** dialog box*

## Project

The **Project** button is used to search the parent component tag of similar components in the active project. To do so, choose the **Project** button from the **Insert / Edit Child Component** dialog box; the **Complete Project list for FAMILY="XX"** dialog box will be displayed, as shown in Figure 5-34. This dialog box displays the parent symbols that belong to the same family type and are present within the active project. The options in this dialog box are discussed next.

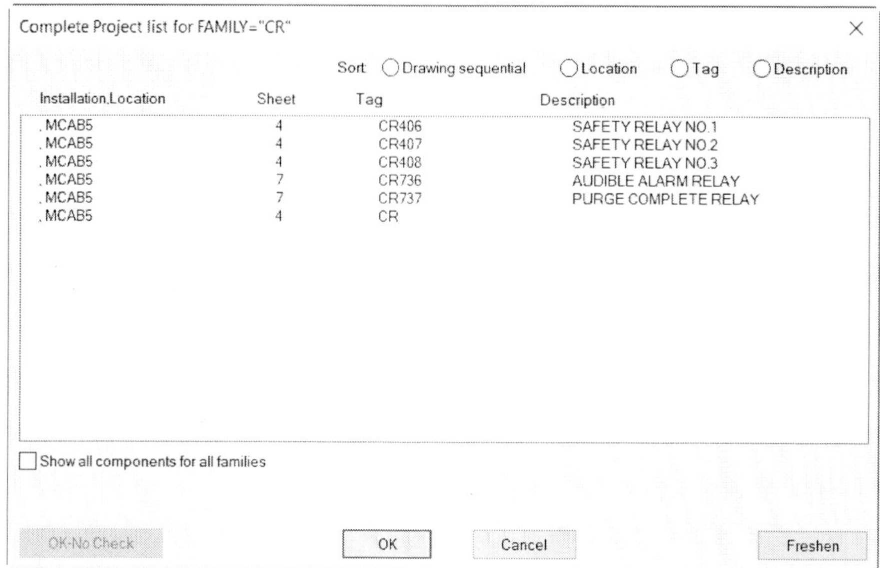


*Figure 5-34 The **Complete Project list for FAMILY="CR"** dialog box*

If you select the **Show all components for all families** check box, the **Component Project list for FAMILY** dialog box will be displayed with an additional **Family** column added in the list. By default, this check box is clear.

If the **QSAVE** message box is displayed after selecting the **Show all components for all families** check box, then choose the **OK** button in this dialog box, refer to Figure 5-35.

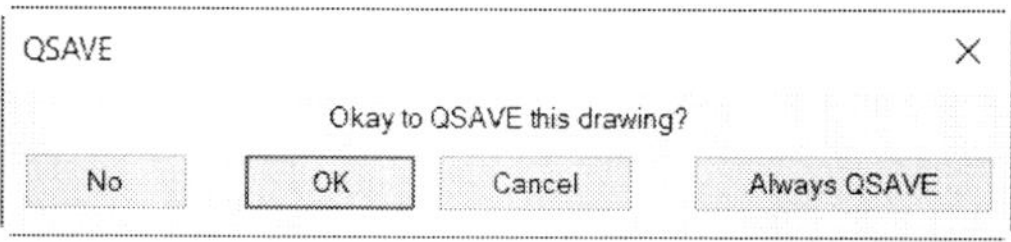


*Figure 5-35 The **QSAVE** message box*

The radio buttons on the right of the **Sort** option are used to sort the component tags.

Now, select the parent symbol from the list of all parent symbols of the same family type in the project; the manufacturer, catalog, and assembly codes will appear under the **Show all components for all families** check box. Choose the **OK** button in the **Complete Project list for FAMILY** dialog box; the information of the selected parent symbol will be displayed in the **Tag** edit box of the **Component Tag** area in the **Insert / Edit Child Component** dialog box.

## Parent/Sibling

The **Parent/Sibling** button is used to select the parent component or sibling component in the current drawing. To do so, choose the **Parent/Sibling** button in the **Component Tag** area; you will be prompted to select the component. Next, select the parent symbol or the sibling of the parent within the current drawing. Once you have selected the parent symbol, the attribute values of the parent symbol will be copied in the **Insert / Edit Child Component** dialog box and the information will automatically get transferred to the child contact.

Choose the **OK** button in the **Insert / Edit Child Component** dialog box to save the changes and exit the dialog box.

**Note**

*You can edit child component attributes independently anytime.*

# INSERTING COMPONENTS FROM THE EQUIPMENT LIST

**Ribbon:** Schematic > Insert Components > Icon Menu drop-down > Equipment List
**Toolbar:** ACE:Main Electrical > Insert Component drop-down > Insert Component (User Defined List) > Insert Component (Equipment List) or ACE:Insert Component > Insert Component (User Defined list) > Insert Component (Equipment List)
**Menu:** Components > Insert Component (Lists) > Insert Component (Equipment List)
**Command:** AECOMPONENTEQ

The **Equipment List** tool is used to insert schematic component from the equipment list. Using this tool, you can find and insert appropriate schematic symbol from *schematic_lookup.mdb*. To insert a schematic component from the equipment list, choose the **Equipment List** tool from the **Icon Menu** drop-down in the **Insert Components** panel of the **Schematic** tab. Alternatively, you can invoke the **Insert Component (Equipment List)** tool from the **ACE:Main Electrical** toolbar, as shown in Figure 5-36; the **Select Equipment List Spreadsheet File** dialog box will be displayed, as shown in Figure 5-37.

*Figure 5-36 The **Insert Component (Equipment List)** tool in the **ACE:Main Electrical** toolbar*

**Note**

*You can insert either a single or multiple schematic components from the equipment list.*

Select the spreadsheet file from the **Select Equipment List Spreadsheet File** dialog box and choose the **Open** button; the **Table Edit** dialog box will be displayed, as shown in Figure 5-38. This dialog box will be displayed only if multiple sheets/tables of the equipment list are found in the data file. Next, select the table to be edited from the **Table Edit** dialog box and choose **OK**; the **Settings** dialog box will be displayed, as shown in Figure 5-39. Note that if the equipment list does not have multiple sheets or tables and you choose the **Open** button from the **Select Equipment List Spreadsheet File** dialog box, then the **Settings** dialog box will be displayed. The options in the **Settings** dialog box are discussed next.

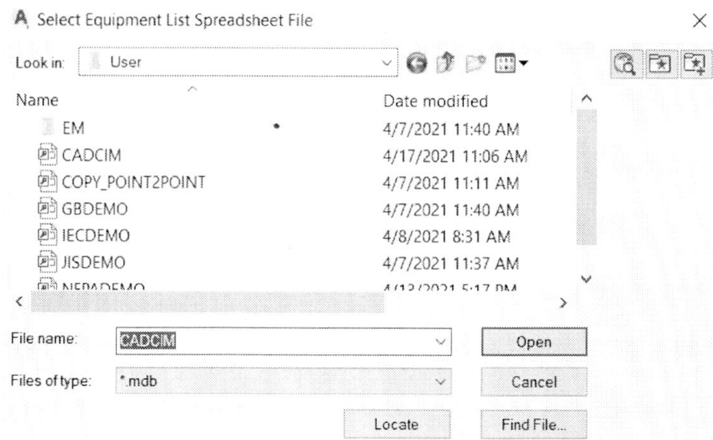

*Figure 5-37 The **Select Equipment List Spreadsheet File** dialog box*

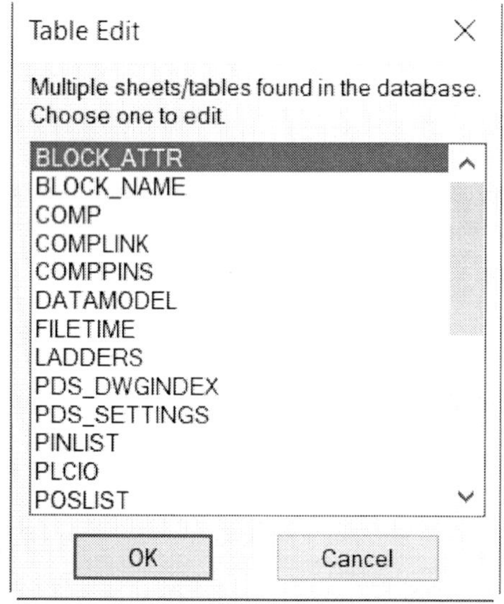

*Figure 5-38 The **Table Edit** dialog box*

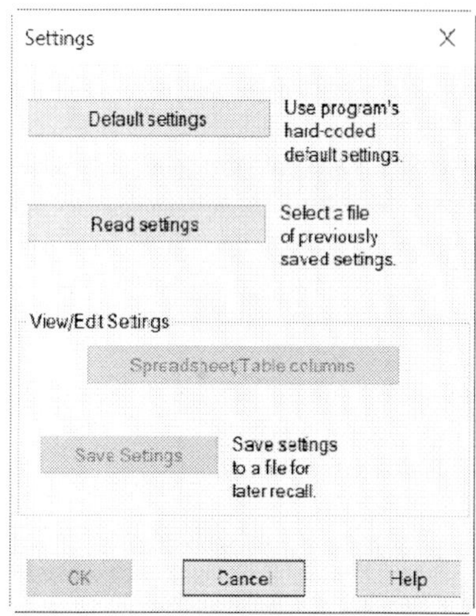

*Figure 5-39 The **Settings** dialog box*

**Tip**

*In the **Select Equipment List Spreadsheet File** dialog box, you can open the .csv, .xls, and .mdb files.*

## Default settings

When you choose the **Default settings** button from the **Settings** dialog box, the options in the **View/Edit Settings** area will be activated. Using this button, you will be able to use the AutoCAD Electrical default settings for reading the format of the database file.

## Read settings

The **Read settings** button is used to select and use the settings of the previously saved database file. The extension of the previously saved file is *.wde*.

## View/Edit Settings Area

The options in the **View/Edit Settings** area will be activated only when you choose the **Default settings** button. These options are used to change the mapping of the data file information to electrical categories and to save the settings to the file for later use. The options in this area are discussed next.

### Spreadsheet/Table columns

The **Spreadsheet/Table columns** button will be activated when you choose the **Default settings** button from the **Settings** dialog box. This button is used to define the order of data in the selected equipment list file. Also, you can modify the settings of a selected equipment list file. To define the order of data, choose the **Spreadsheet/Table columns** button from the **View/Edit Settings** area; the **Equipment List Spreadsheet Settings** dialog box will be displayed, as shown in Figure 5-40.

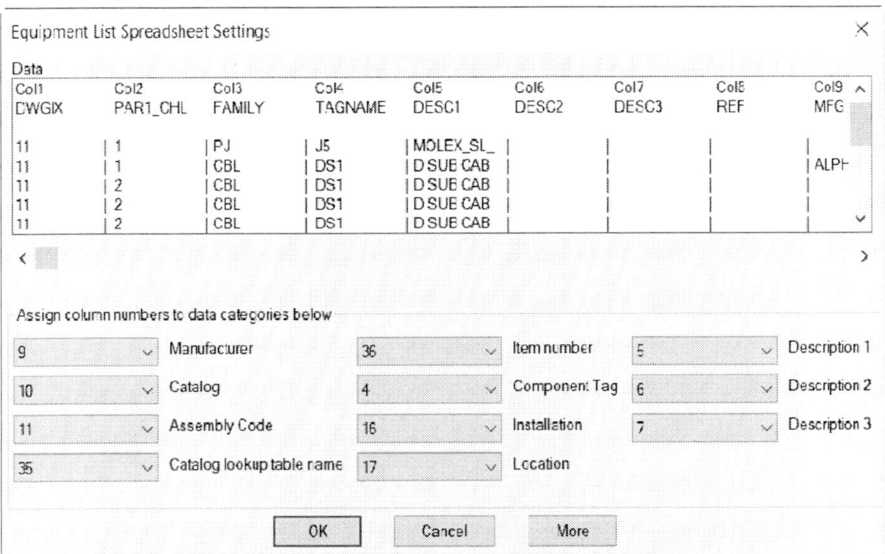


*Figure 5-40 The* ***Equipment List Spreadsheet Settings*** *dialog box*

In this dialog box, you can assign column numbers to data categories such as **Manufacturer**, **Catalog**, **Assembly Code**, and so on. After specifying the options in this dialog box, choose the **OK** button to return to the **Settings** dialog box.

### Save Settings

The **Save Settings** button will be activated only if you choose the **Default settings** button. This button is used to save the settings to the file so that it can be used later. To save the settings to a file, choose the **Save Settings** button; the **Save Settings** dialog box will be displayed. Enter the name of the file in the **File name** edit box. Next, choose the **Save** button; the column information will be saved in *.wde* format.

Now, choose the **OK** button in the **Settings** dialog box; the **Schematic equipment in** dialog box will be displayed, as shown in Figure 5-41. The options in this dialog box are discussed next.

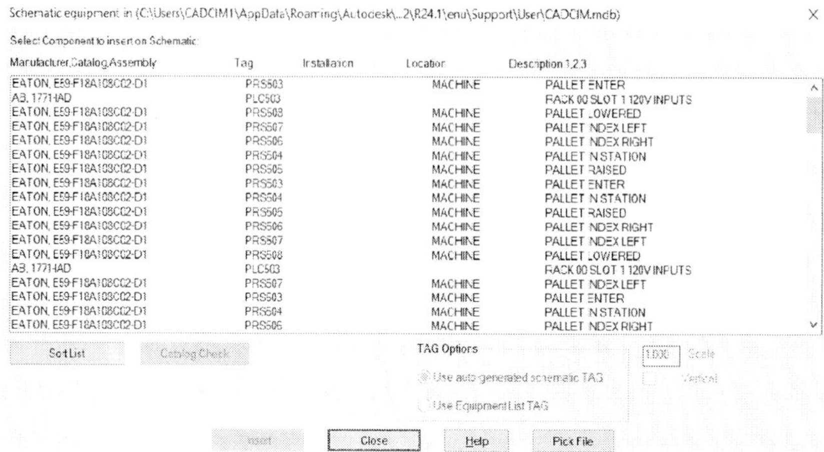


*Figure 5-41 The **Schematic equipment in** dialog box*

## Sort List

The **Sort List** button is used to sort out the list of components. To do so, choose this button; the **Sort** dialog box will be displayed, as shown in Figure 5-42. You can sort out the list of components displayed using the four levels of sort criteria: **Primary sort**, **Secondary sort**, **Third sort**, and **Fourth sort**. Select the required option from the drop-down list of these four levels of sort criteria to sort out the components and then choose the **OK** button to return to the **Schematic equipment in** dialog box.

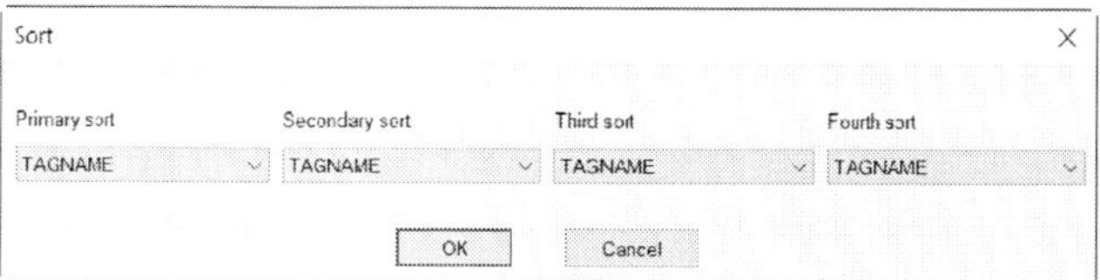


*Figure 5-42 The **Sort** dialog box*

## Catalog Check

The **Catalog Check** button will be activated only if the selected component contains the catalog data. This button is used to check the bill of material of a selected component.

## TAG Options Area

The options in the **TAG Options** area will be activated only after you select a component tag from the **Schematic equipment in** dialog box. The options in this area are used to specify whether to use auto-generated or the equipment list tag. The options in this area are discussed next.

### Use auto-generated schematic TAG

The **Use auto-generated schematic TAG** radio button is used to modify the schematic component tag based on the settings that you have defined in the **Drawing Properties** dialog box. By default, this radio button is selected.

### Use Equipment List TAG
The **Use Equipment List TAG** radio button is used to specify the component tag to be used as listed in the equipment list. Note that the tag used is set to be fixed in the schematic drawing.

### Scale
The **Scale** edit box will be activated only after you select the component from the equipment list displayed. Specify the insertion scale of the block in the **Scale** edit box. By default, 1.000 is displayed in this edit box.

### Vertical
The **Vertical** check box will be activated only after you select a component from the equipment list displayed. If you select the **Vertical** check box, the default drawing orientation will be changed. By default, this check box is clear.

### Pick File
The **Pick File** button is used to reselect the component list file for an existing extracted equipment list. Also, this button is used to select a new equipment list database file from the current project's database.

### Insert
The **Insert** button will be activated only after you have selected a component from the list displayed. This button is used to find and insert a selected schematic component. To insert the selected component, choose the **Insert** button; the **Insert** dialog box will be displayed, as shown in Figure 5-43. This dialog box displays the block name of the selected component with a short description of each block name. The options in the **Insert** dialog box are discussed next.

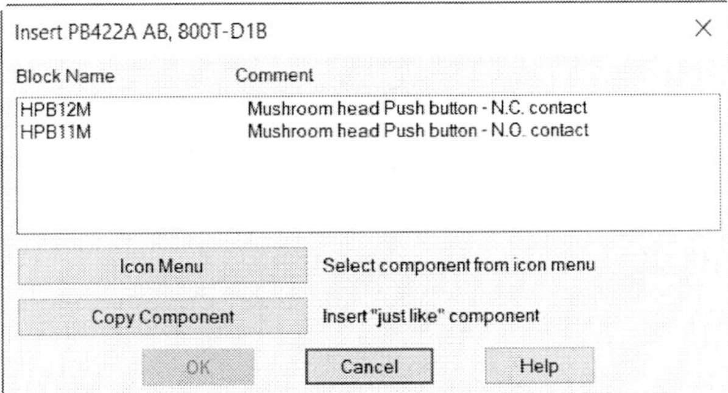


*Figure 5-43 The* ***Insert*** *dialog box*

### Icon Menu
The **Icon Menu** button is used to select and insert component from the **Insert Component** dialog box. Choose the **Icon Menu** button; the **Insert Component** dialog box will be displayed. Next, insert the component by following the procedure discussed earlier.

### Copy Component
The **Copy Component** button is used to copy a selected component and then insert it into the drawing. To do so, choose the **Copy Component** button; you will be prompted to select

the component to be copied. Next, select the component and insert the copied component by following the procedure discussed earlier for inserting the component. The component will be inserted and the **Schematic equipment in** dialog box will be displayed again.

The **OK** button of the **Insert** dialog box will be activated only if you select the block name from the list displayed. Choose the **OK** button; you will be prompted to specify the insertion point for the block. Specify the insertion point; the **Insert/Edit Component** dialog box will be displayed. Enter the required information in this dialog box and choose the **OK** button from the **Insert/Edit Component** dialog box; the **Schematic equipment in** dialog box will be displayed again. Choose the **Close** button to exit from this dialog box.

## INSERTING COMPONENTS FROM THE USER DEFINED LIST

| | |
|---|---|
| **Ribbon:** | Schematic > Insert Components > Icon Menu drop-down > User Defined List |
| **Toolbar:** | ACE: Main Electrical > Insert Component > Insert Component drop-down<br>ACE: Insert Component >Insert Component (User Defined List)<br>> Insert Component (User Defined List) |
| **Menu:** | Components > Insert Component (Lists) > Insert Component (User Defined List) |
| **Command:** | AECOMPONENTCAT |

The **User Defined List** tool is used to insert a schematic symbol from a user-defined pick list. The data displayed in the pick list is stored in a database in *.mdb* format with the file name as *wd_picklist.mdb*. The location of this file is *C:\users\user name\documents\acade 2022\aedata\en-us\catalogs*. From the pick list, you can select the catalog number or the component description to be inserted into the drawing. You can edit, add, or delete the pick list data any time. To insert a schematic component from a user defined list, choose the **User Defined List** tool from the **Icon Menu** drop-down in the **Insert Components** panel of the **Schematic** tab; the **Schematic Component or Circuit** dialog box will be displayed, as shown in Figure 5-44. Different options in this dialog box are discussed next.

### Sort by

The **Sort by** drop-down list is used to sort the list displayed in the **Schematic Component or Circuit** dialog box. To sort the list, select an option from the **Sort by** drop-down list; the list displayed will be sorted out accordingly. You can sort out the list by selecting the **Description**, **Catalog**, or **Manufacturer** option. By default, the **Description** option is selected in this drop-down list.

### Add

The **Add** button is used to create a new record of a schematic symbol. To do so, choose the **Add** button; the **Add record** dialog box will be displayed. The options in this dialog box are discussed later in this chapter. Specify the options as per your requirement in this dialog box and choose the **OK** button; a new record will be added to the pick list.

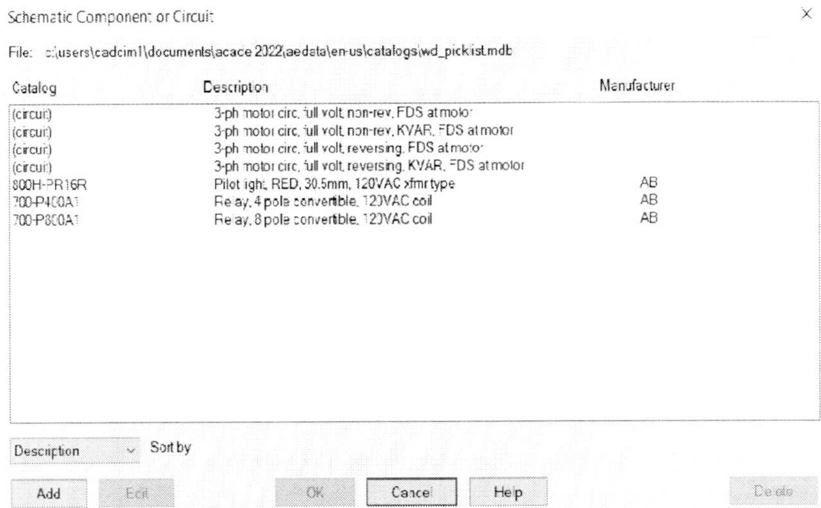


*Figure 5-44 The* ***Schematic Component or Circuit*** *dialog box*

## Edit

The **Edit** button will be activated only when a component is selected from the list. This button is used to modify an existing record. To modify a record, select the component from the list and choose the **Edit** button; the **Edit Record** dialog box will be displayed. The options in this dialog box are the same as in the **Add record** dialog box, and are discussed later in this chapter. Using this dialog box, you can modify the information of the component.

## Delete

The **Delete** button will be activated only after you select a component from the list displayed. This button is used to delete the selected component. To delete a component, choose the **Delete** button; the **Delete Pick List Entry** dialog box will be displayed. Choose the **OK** button; the selected record will be deleted. Choose the **Cancel** button to retain the existing record.

The **OK** button in the **Schematic Component or Circuit** dialog box will be activated only if you select a component or a circuit from the list displayed. Now, select the component in the **Schematic Component or Circuit** dialog box and then choose the **OK** button; the component along with the cursor will be displayed and you will be prompted to specify the insertion point for the component. Next, specify the insertion point for the component; the **Insert / Edit Component** dialog box will be displayed. Enter the required information in this dialog box and choose the **OK** button; the component will be inserted into the drawing.

**Note**

*If you select a circuit from the* ***Schematic Component or Circuit*** *dialog box and choose the* ***OK*** *button, the* ***Circuit Scale*** *dialog box will be displayed. The options in the* ***Circuit Scale*** *dialog box will be discussed in the Chapter 7. Specify the options in this dialog box as per your requirement. Choose the* ***OK*** *button in the* ***Circuit Scale*** *dialog box; you will be prompted to specify the insertion point for the circuit. Next, specify the insertion point for the circuit; the circuit will be inserted into the drawing.*

## Adding a New Record in the Schematic Component or Circuit Dialog Box

You can add a record using the **Schematic Component or Circuit** dialog box. To invoke this dialog box, choose the **User Defined List** tool from the **Icon Menu** drop-down in the **Insert Components** panel of the **Schematic** tab; the **Schematic Component or Circuit** dialog box will be displayed, refer to Figure 5-44. To add a new record in this dialog box, choose the **Add** button in this dialog box; the **Add record** dialog box will be displayed, as shown in Figure 5-45. Different options and areas in this dialog box are discussed next.

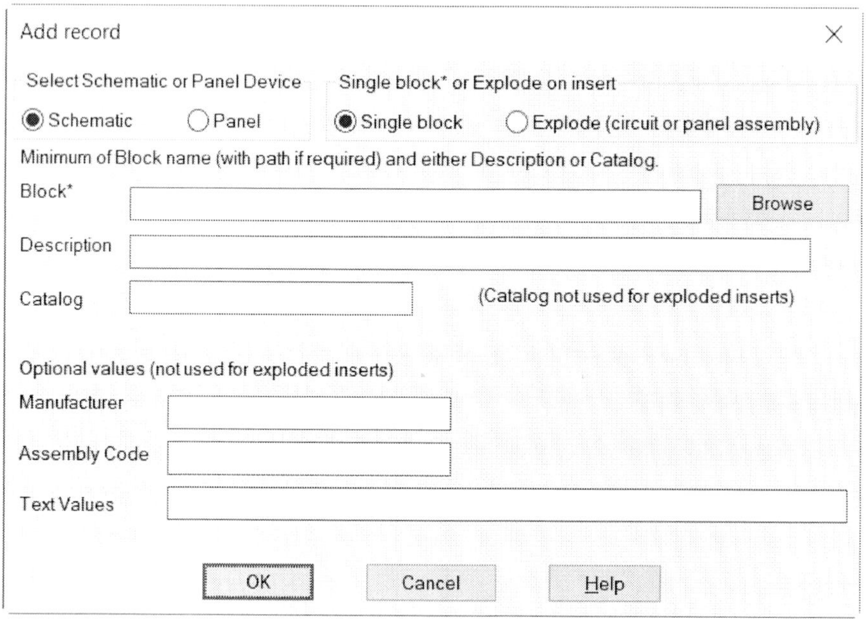

*Figure 5-45 The **Add record** dialog box*

### Select Schematic or Panel Device Area

In this area, you need to specify whether the component or circuit is schematic type or panel type. By default, the **Schematic** radio button is selected. As a result, record will be added for the Schematic device/circuit. If you select the **Panel** radio button, the record will be added for the **Panel** device/circuit.

### Single block* or Explode on insert Area

In this area, you need to specify whether to insert a component or a circuit as a block or exploded when inserted in the drawing. The options in this area are discussed next.

The **Single block** radio button is selected by default. It is used to insert component as a single block.

Select the **Explode (circuit or panel assembly)** radio button in the **Add record** dialog box; the component or the circuit will be exploded while inserting it. Also, you will notice that the **Block*** edit box of the **Minimum of Block name (with path if required) and either Description or Catalog** area is changed to the **Circuit** edit box or the **Assembly** edit box depending upon the radio button selected in the **Select Schematic or Panel Device** area, as shown in Figures 5-46 and 5-47, respectively.

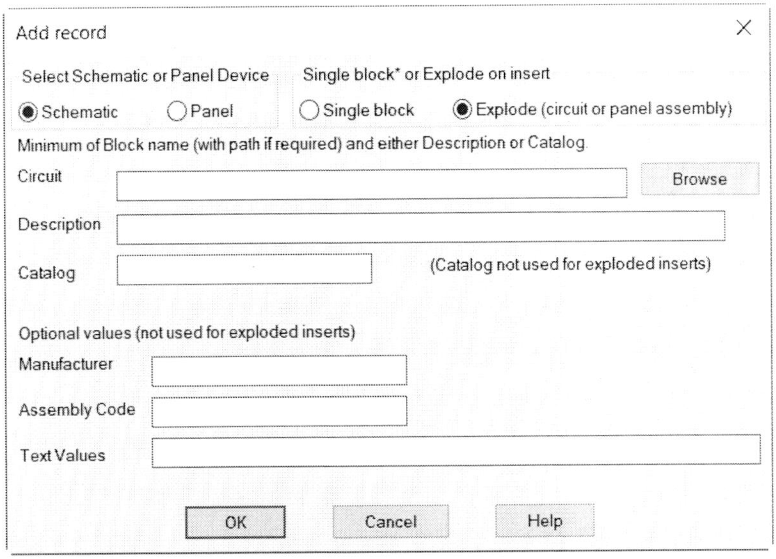

***Figure 5-46*** *The* ***Add record*** *dialog box with the* ***Schematic*** *and* ***Explode (circuit or panel assembly)*** *radio buttons selected*

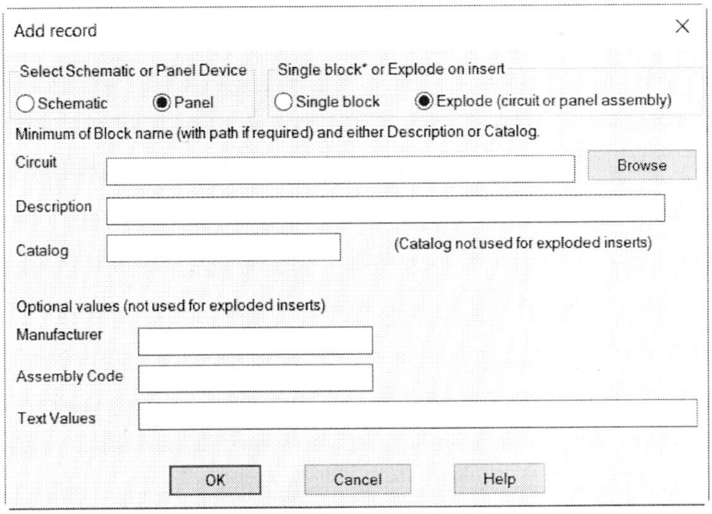

***Figure 5-47*** *The* ***Add record*** *dialog box with the* ***Panel*** *and* ***Explode (circuit or panel assembly)*** *radio buttons selected*

## Minimum of Block name (with path if required) and either Description or Catalog Area

In the **Minimum of Block name (with path if required) and either Description or Catalog** area, you can provide the name, description, and the catalog information of the block. The options in this area are discussed next.

### Block*/Assembly/Circuit drawing

Enter the name and path of the block in the **Block*** edit box. Alternatively, choose the **Browse** button to insert the name of the block; the **Select Schematic component or circuit** dialog box will be displayed. Select the drawing file and then choose the **Open** button in this dialog box; the name and path of that drawing file will be automatically displayed in the **Block*** edit box. Also, if you select the **Explode (circuit or panel assembly)** radio button from the **Single block* or Explode on insert** area, the **Block*** edit box will be changed to the **Circuit drawing** edit box or the **Assembly** edit box, refer to Figures 5-46 and 5-47.

### Description

Enter the description for the component or the circuit in the **Description** edit box. This description is just for reference, it will not be retrieved in reports. This is discussed in the later chapters.

### Catalog

Enter the catalog value in the **Catalog** edit box. The catalog value is not used for the exploded inserts. You can also enter wildcards in this edit box. Wild cards are used in the catalog number column in order to reduce the number of entries in the lookup file. Wild card characters include:
* = match any characters
? = match any single character
# = match any single numeric digit
@ = match any single alphabetic character

## Optional Values (not used for exploded inserts) Area

The options in the **Optional Values (not used for exploded inserts)** area are not used for the exploded inserts. The edit boxes in this area are used to specify the manufacturer and assembly codes and the text values of the component.

After specifying all values, choose the **OK** button in the **Add record** dialog box; the component or circuit will automatically be added to the list displayed in the **Schematic Component or Circuit** dialog box.

**Note**

*If you select a component or a circuit from the list displayed in the* ***Schematic Component or Circuit*** *dialog box and then choose the* ***Add*** *button, the* ***Add New Record--Prefill with Defaults*** *message box will be displayed, as shown in Figure 5-48. Choose the* ***OK*** *button to prefill the new record with values from the selected entry. If you choose the* ***No*** *button, you will have to enter the data for the component manually as discussed earlier.*

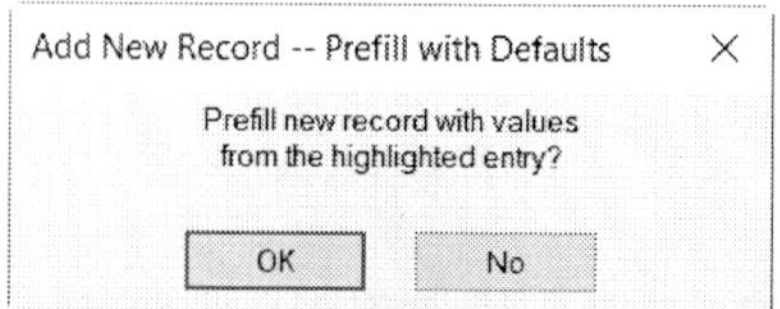


***Figure 5-48*** *The* ***Add New Record--Prefill with Defaults*** *message box*

## Editing an Existing Record in the Schematic Component or Circuit Dialog Box

You can edit an existing record in the **Schematic Component or Circuit** dialog box. To edit an existing record of the schematic component in the component list, select a component or a circuit from this dialog box; the **Edit** button will be activated. Choose this button; the **Edit Record** dialog box will be displayed, as shown in Figure 5-49. The options in this dialog box are the same as that in the **Add record** dialog box, which has already been discussed in the previous topic.

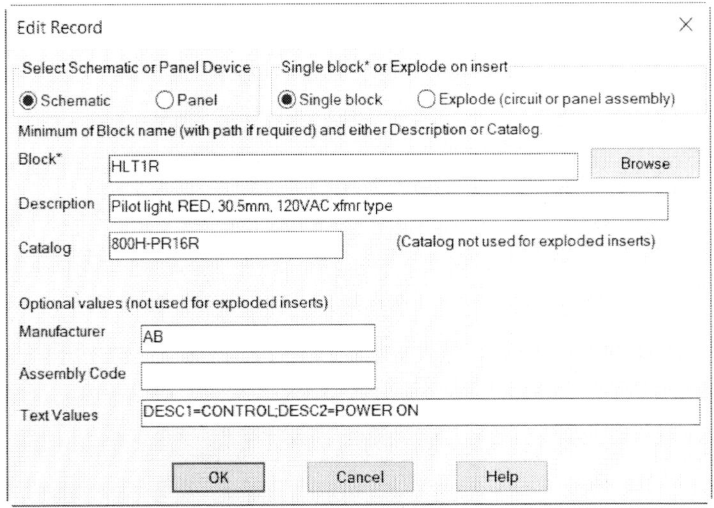


*Figure 5-49 The **Edit Record** dialog box*

Make necessary changes in the **Edit Record** dialog box and then choose the **OK** button; you will notice that the modified component or the circuit name is displayed in the **Schematic Component or Circuit** dialog box.

# INSERTING COMPONENTS FROM PANEL LISTS

| | |
|---|---|
| **Ribbon:** | Schematic > Insert Components > Icon Menu drop-down > Panel List |
| **Toolbar:** | ACE:Main Electrical > Insert Component > Insert Component drop-down > Insert Component (Panel List)<br>or ACE:Insert Component > Insert Component drop-down > Insert Component (Panel List) |
| **Menu:** | Components > Insert Component (Panel List) |
| **Command:** | AECOMPONENTPNL |

The **Insert Component (Panel List)** tool is used to insert a schematic component from a panel component list. Also, this tool is used to create a list of all panel components by extracting the component information from the selected panel layout drawings. To insert a schematic component from a panel list, choose the **Panel List** tool from the **Icon Menu** drop-down in the **Insert Components** panel of the **Schematic** tab; the **Panel Layout List--> Schematic Components Insert** dialog box will be displayed, as shown in Figure 5-50. Different options in this dialog box are discussed next.

**Note**

*You will learn about the panel components (footprints) in detail in Chapter 8.*

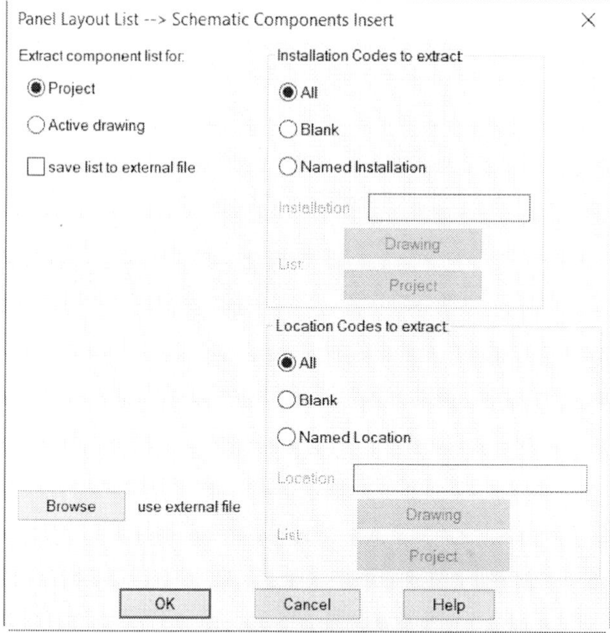


*Figure 5-50 The* ***Panel Layout List --> Schematic Components Insert*** *dialog box*

## Extract component list for Area

The options in this area are discussed next.

### Project

The **Project** radio button is selected by default and is used to extract the component list data from the active project.

### Active drawing

Select the **Active drawing** radio button to extract the component list data from the active drawing. Note that this radio button is inactive if there are no schematic components in the active drawing.

### save list to external file

Select the **save list to external file** check box to create a comma-delimited file of the panel component data. If you want to create a comma-delimited file of the panel components from the entire project, you need to select the **Project** radio button and the **save list to external file** check box. Next, choose the **OK** button; the **Select Drawings to Process** dialog box will be displayed. Select the drawings and choose the **Process** button; the drawings will be transferred from the top list to the bottom list. Next, choose the **OK** button in the **Select Drawings to Process** dialog box; the **Select file for Panel Layout --> Schematic list** dialog box will be displayed. The name of the extracted file will be the same as that of the project name. By default, project name will be displayed in the **File name** edit box and *.wd3* extension will be displayed in the **Save as type** drop-down list. You can open the file in the comma-delimited "CSV" format and the data will be displayed in the spreadsheet format. You can edit the data and save it. Further, you can save the external file in the *.csv* format.

**Note**
*In the comma-delimited file format, data values are separated by commas. This format is generally used for transferring data from one application to another because most database systems are able to import and export comma-delimited data. In this format, each column value is separated by a comma and each row starts with a new line. The values written in comma-delimited format are also called comma-separated values (CSV).*

### Browse

The **Browse** button is used to create a spreadsheet listing from the panel component list of the previous project. Choose this button; the **Select component list file** dialog box will be displayed. Select the file and choose the **Open** button to open the spreadsheet file from the panel component list.

## Installation Codes to extract Area

The options in this area are used to extract information about the components that have installation code. These options are discussed next.

The **All** radio button is selected by default and is used to extract information about panel components that have installation values.

Select the **Blank** radio button, if you do not want to extract information about components with specific installation values.

If you select the **Named Installation** radio button, the **Installation** edit box will be activated. Enter the name of the installation code in the **Installation** edit box. Alternatively, you can choose the **Drawing** button to use the installation code that are used in the previous drawing or choose the **Project** button to use the installation code of a project.

## Location Codes to extract Area

The **Location Codes to extract** area is used to extract information about the components that have location codes. The options in this area are similar to those discussed in the **Installation Codes to extract** area.

Once you have specified the settings, choose the **OK** button; the **Select Drawings to Process** dialog box will be displayed. Specify the required drawings using this dialog box and choose the **OK** button; the **Panel Components** dialog box will be displayed, as shown in Figure 5-51. This dialog box displays the list of panel components extracted from the selected drawings that you need to insert in the schematic drawings. The options in this dialog box are discussed next.

**Note**
*If you select the **Active drawing** radio button from the **Panel Layout List —> Schematic Components Insert** dialog box and choose the **OK** button, the **Panel Components** dialog box will be displayed directly without displaying the **Select Drawing to Process** dialog box.*

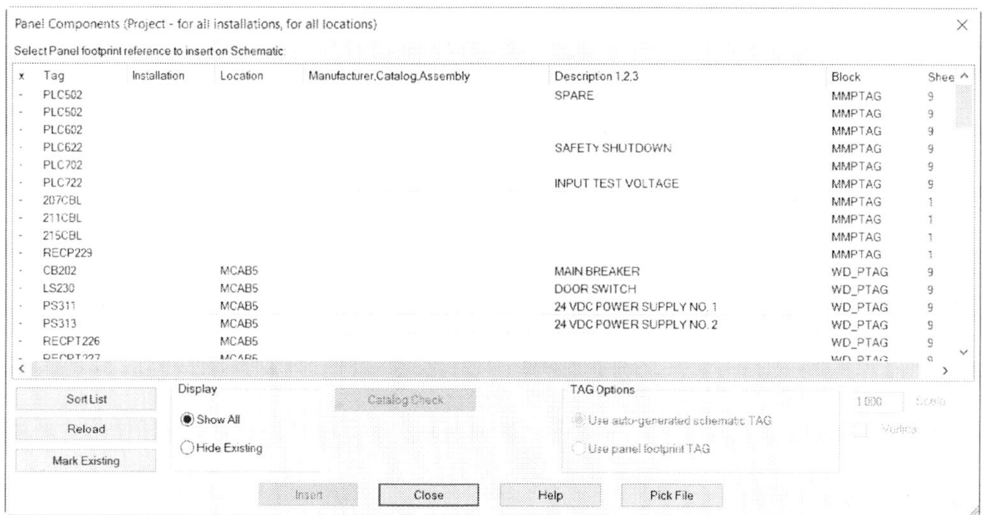

*Figure 5-51 The* ***Panel Components*** *dialog box*

## Sort List

The **Sort List** button is used to categorize the list of panel components displayed. Choose this button; the **Sort Fields** dialog box will be displayed. There are four levels of sort criteria such as **Primary sort**, **Secondary sort**, **Third sort**, and **Fourth sort** that can be used to categorize components. Select an option from each of the drop-down list of these four levels of sort criteria to sort out the displayed components.

## Reload

The **Reload** button is used to re-extract the panel component data from a project, active drawing, or saved external file. Choose this button; the **Panel Layout List —> Schematic Components Insert** dialog box will be displayed again, refer to Figure 5-50. The options in this dialog box have already been discussed.

## Mark Existing

If a listed panel component tag already has its schematic component inserted in the drawing and if there is an exact match on catalog and manufacturer values between these components, then on choosing the **Mark Existing** button, an 'x' will be displayed in the **x** column of the **Panel Components** dialog box. Similarly, if the tags match and there is a mismatch on catalog and manufacturer values between these components, an 'o' will be displayed in the **x** column. Note that the marked components such as 'x' or 'o' cannot be inserted multiple times. The **Insert** button will be activated only if '-' is placed in the **x** column.

## Display Area

The options in the **Display** area are used to control the display of the panel data. These options are discussed next.

### Show All

The **Show All** radio button is selected by default and is used to display entire extracted panel data.

### Hide Existing

Select the **Hide Existing** radio button to hide the existing panel data. In other words, after selecting this radio button, the components that have already been inserted in the schematic drawing will be hidden.

**Tip**

*It is recommended that you use the **Hide Existing** option to avoid inserting multiple panel components (footprints) for the same component.*

## Catalog Check

The **Catalog Check** button will be activated only if the selected component contains the catalog data. This button is used to check the Bill of Material of the selected component.

## TAG Options Area

The options in the **TAG Options** area are used to specify the tag settings for the drawing. These options are discussed next.

### Use auto-generated schematic TAG

The **Use auto-generated schematic TAG** radio button is selected by default. It is used to modify the schematic component tag based on the settings defined in the **Drawing Properties** dialog box.

### Use panel footprint TAG

Select the **Use panel footprint TAG** radio button to use the tag defined for the panel footprint. These tags are fixed, therefore they cannot be updated when the components are retagged.

## Scale

The **Scale** edit box is used to specify the insertion scale for the block. This edit box will be activated only if you select the component that has not been inserted. By default, 1.000 is displayed in this edit box.

## Vertical

The **Vertical** check box will be activated only if you select the component that has not been inserted. If you select the **Vertical** check box, the default drawing orientation will be changed.

## Pick File

The **Pick File** button is used to reselect the panel component list file.

## Insert

The **Insert** button will be activated only if you select a panel component that has not been inserted. To insert the component, select it from the list displayed and then choose the **Insert** button; the **Insert** dialog box will be displayed. Note that this dialog box will only be displayed if you have selected a single component from the panel list. The options in this dialog box have been already discussed. Next, select the component and choose the **OK** button from the **Insert** dialog box; you will be prompted to specify the insertion point. Specify the insertion point for the component; the **Insert / Edit Component** dialog box will be displayed. Enter the desired information and choose the **OK** button; the **Panel Components** dialog box will be displayed again. You can also insert multiple components at a time. To do so, select multiple components by pressing CTRL or SHIFT for insertion from the panel list displayed in the **Panel Components** dialog box. Next, choose the **Insert** button; the **Spacing for Insertion** dialog box will be displayed, as shown in Figure 5-52. The options in this dialog box are discussed next.

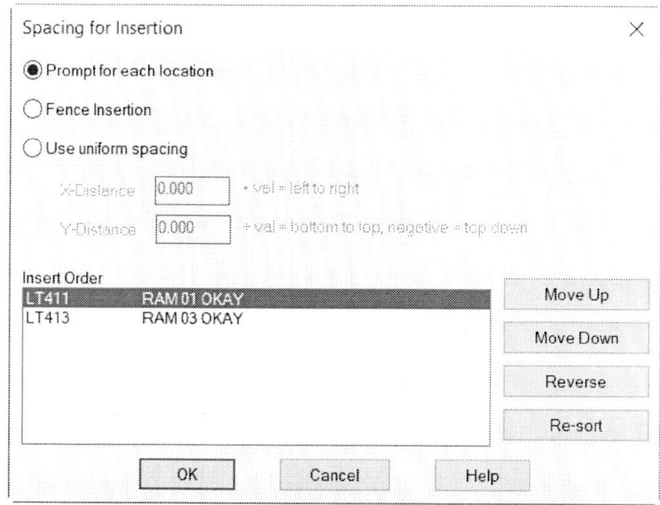


*Figure 5-52 The **Spacing for Insertion** dialog box*

## Prompt for each location

The **Prompt for each location** radio button is selected by default and is used to specify the location for each component.

## Fence Insertion

The **Fence Insertion** radio button is used to specify the location for the selected components. The components are selected by creating a fence around the required components. When you select the **Fence Insertion** radio button and choose **OK**, you will be prompted to select the fence from point. Select the components by clicking at different locations. Once you are done with creating the fence lines, press ENTER to exit the command and return to the **Insert** dialog box.

## Use uniform spacing

The **Use uniform spacing** radio button is used to specify the location of the first component. To do so, select this radio button; the **X-Distance** and **Y-Distance** edit boxes will be activated. These edit boxes are discussed next.

### X-Distance and Y-Distance

Enter the values in the **X-Distance** and **Y-Distance** edit boxes to calculate the insertion coordinates for the remaining components. If you enter a negative value in the **X-Distance** edit box, the component will be inserted toward the left of the first component. If you enter a negative value in the **Y-Distance** edit box, the components will be inserted from top to bottom.

**Note**

*The **X-Distance** and **Y-Distance** edit boxes do not specify the insertion co-ordinates for the first component, they are rather applied only after you insert the first component. In other words, the co-ordinates or the values that are specified in the **X-Distance** and **Y-Distance** edit boxes will apply for the components that you insert after the first component.*

## Insert Order Area

The **Insert Order** area displays the order in which components will be inserted into a drawing.

## Move Up

Choose the **Move Up** button to move the selected component one step up in the **Insert Order** area.

## Move Down

Choose the **Move Down** button to move the selected component one step down in the **Insert Order** area.

## Reverse

Choose the **Reverse** button to reverse the order of all components available in the **Insert Order** area in descending order.

## Re-sort

Choose the **Re-sort** button to re-sort all components available in the **Insert Order** area in ascending order.

When you choose the **OK** button in the **Spacing for Insertion** dialog box; the **Insert** dialog box will be displayed. Select the block name and then choose the **OK** button in the **Insert** dialog box; you will be prompted to specify the insertion point for the component. Next, specify the insertion point for the component; the **Insert / Edit Component** dialog box will be displayed. Enter the information as per your requirement in this dialog box and choose the **OK** button; the **Insert** dialog box will be displayed again.

Select the component to be inserted in the drawing again and choose the **OK** button; the component will be inserted. If you choose the **Cancel** button, you will return to the **Panel Components** dialog box. Note that the selection of components in the **Insert** dialog box will continue until all components displayed in this dialog box have been inserted in the drawing. To insert more components, repeat the above process. To exit the command, choose the **Close** button in the **Panel Components** dialog box; the **Update other drawings?** message box will be displayed, as shown in Figure 5-53.

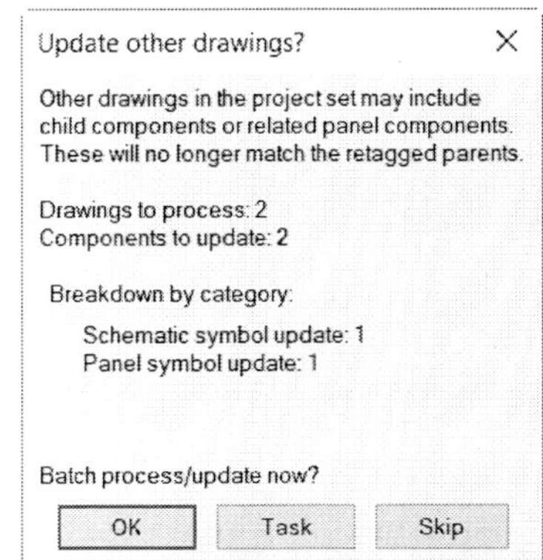


*Figure 5-53 The **Update other drawings?** message box*

Choose the **OK** button to update the drawings immediately. If you choose the **Task** button, the drawings will not get updated at that time but the changes will get saved in the project task list.

The changes in the drawing can be updated later by using the **Project Task List** button of the **PROJECT MANAGER**. If you choose the **Skip** button, no drawing will get updated.

## SWAPPING AND UPDATING BLOCKS

| | |
|---|---|
| **Ribbon:** | Schematic > Edit Components > Swap/Update Block |
| **Toolbar:** | ACE:Main Electrical > Insert Component > Swap/Update Block or ACE:Insert Component > Swap/Update Block |
| **Menu:** | Components> Component Miscellaneous > Swap/Update Block |
| **Command:** | AESWAPBLOCK |

The **Swap/Update Block** tool is used to replace or update a block in a drawing. Also, this tool is used to update drawings if the library has been changed. To replace or update a block, choose the **Swap/Update Block** tool from the **Edit Components** panel of the **Schematic** tab; the **Swap Block / Update Block / Library Swap** dialog box will be displayed, as shown in Figure 5-54. Different areas and options in this dialog box are discussed next.

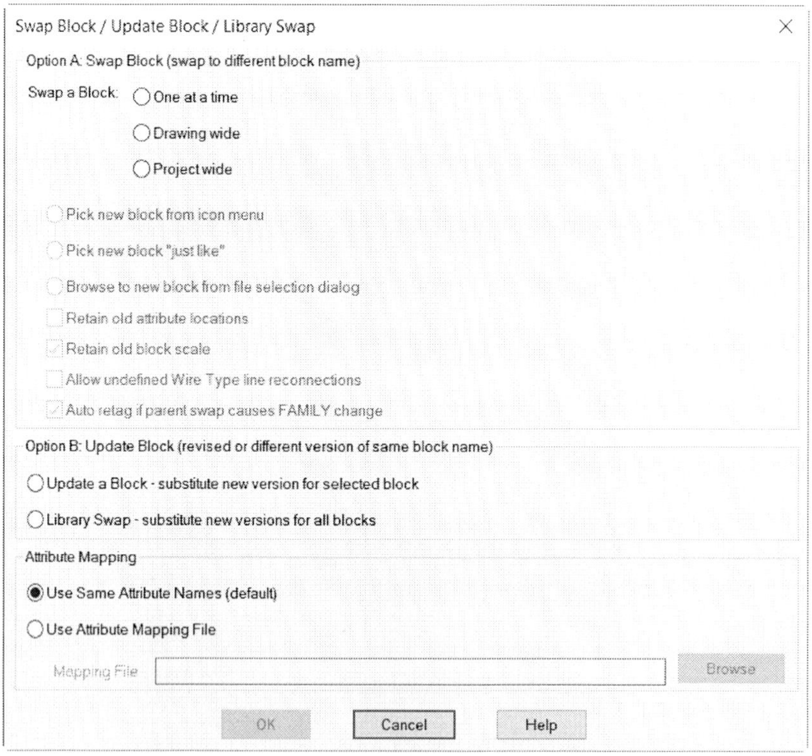

*Figure 5-54 The* ***Swap Block / Update Block / Library Swap*** *dialog box*

In this dialog box, only one area out of the **Option A: Swap Block (swap to different block name)** and **Option B: Update Block (revised or different version of same block name)** areas can be used at a time. These areas are discussed next.

**Note**

*When you use the **Swap/Update Block** tool, the attribute values, wire connections, attribute positions, and so on will be retained during the swapping process.*

## Option A: Swap Block (swap to different block name) Area

The options in this area are used to exchange a block with a block of a different name and are discussed next. This area will be activated only when you select any of the radio buttons present within this area.

### One at a time

The **One at a time** radio button is used to interchange one block with another block at a time.

### Drawing wide

The **Drawing wide** radio button is used to interchange one block with another block within the entire drawing.

### Project wide

The **Project wide** radio button is used to interchange one block with another block within the entire project. Select any of the radio buttons in the **Option A: Swap Block (swap to different block name)** area; the radio buttons and the check boxes below the **Project wide** radio button will be activated. These check boxes and radio buttons are discussed next.

### Pick new block from icon menu

This radio button is used to select a new block from the **Insert Component** dialog box.

### Pick new block "just like"

This radio button is used to select the new block that is same as the original block. Select this radio button and then choose **OK**; you will prompted to select the "just like" component to be used as master. Next, select the component to be used as the master component; you will be prompted to select the component to swap out. Next, select the component to swap out; the selected component will be swapped with the master component.

### Browse to new block from file selection dialog

This radio button is used to select a new block from the **Select Block to use as master** dialog box. The new block will replace the existing block in the drawing and open the required block using this dialog box; you will be prompted to select component to swap out. Select the component to be swapped with other component; the old component will be swapped with the new component selected from the **Select Block to use as master** dialog box. Press ENTER to exit the command.

### Retain old attribute locations

This check box is used to retain the attribute locations of the original block when you insert a new block.

### Retain old block scale

This check box is selected by default and is used to retain the scale value of the original block when you insert a new block.

### Allow undefined Wire Type line reconnections

Select this check box to include non-wire lines for reconnection when the new block is swapped. These lines are displayed in the **Wire From/To** and **Cable From/To** reports. By default, this check box is clear, which implies that the non-wire lines are excluded and do not appear in the reports.

### Auto retag if parent swap causes FAMILY change

By default, this check box is selected. As a result, components are retagged automatically if the family code of the component changes on swapping.

If you clear this check box, then the tag will remain unchanged even if it does not match with the family code of the new component.

**Note**

*While swapping the components if the family type of the component gets changed, the catalog assignment values will be lost.*

## Option B: Update Block (revised or different version of same block name) Area

This area is used to replace the blocks with the updated version of the same block in the drawing database. Also, this area is used to modify the library blocks. The radio buttons in this area are discussed next.

### Update a Block - substitute new version for selected block

This radio button is used to update a selected block with an updated version of the same block. To do so, select the **Update a Block** radio button; the **OK** button will be activated. Choose the **OK** button; you will be prompted to select the block to be updated. Select the block; the **Select a substitute.dwg file for block** dialog box and the **Update Block - New block's path\filename** dialog box will be displayed. Select the required file from the **Select a substitute.dwg file for block** dialog box and choose the **Open** button. Figure 5-55 shows the **Update Block - New block's path\filename** dialog box. Different options in the **Update Block - New block's path\filename** dialog box are discussed next.

#### Path\filename of new block

Enter the path\filename for the new block in the **Path\filename of new block** edit box. Alternatively, choose the **Browse** button to select the path for the new block; the **Select a substitute .dwg file for block** dialog box will be displayed. Select the drawing file and then choose the **Open** button; the path and file name of that drawing file will be displayed automatically in the **Path\filename of new block** edit box.

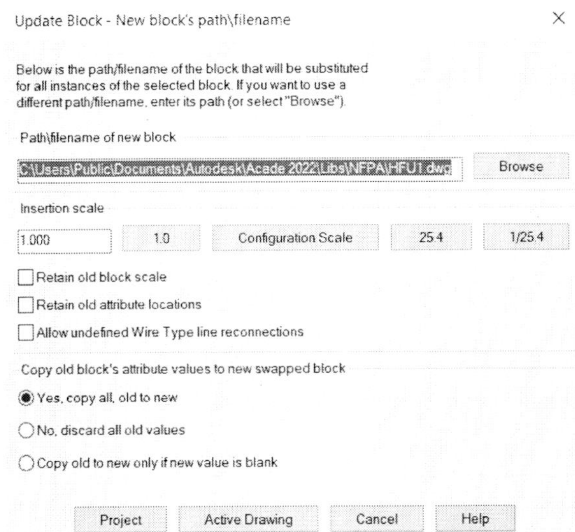


*Figure 5-55 The **Update Block - New block's path\filename** dialog box*

## Insertion scale Area

Specify the insertion scale in the edit box of the **Insertion scale** area. This scale is used for inserting new block. By default, 1.000 is displayed in this edit box. If you choose the **25.4** button, then 25.4 will appear in the edit box.

If you choose the **Configuration Scale** button, then the value that you have defined in the **Scale** area of the **Drawing Format** tab of the **Drawing Properties** dialog box will be displayed in the edit box. For example, if you have entered 2 in the **Feature Scale Multiplier** edit box of the **Scale** area in the **Drawing Format** tab of the **Drawing Properties** dialog box, then 2 will be displayed in the edit box.

Similarly, if you choose the **25.4** or **1/25.4** button, the corresponding values will be displayed in the edit box.

## Retain old block scale

If you select the **Retain old block scale** check box, the scale value of the old block will be retained. The other buttons in this area will get deactivated.

## Retain old attribute locations

Select the **Retain old attribute locations** check box to retain the attribute locations of the original block.

## Copy old block's attributes values to new swapped block Area

The **Copy old block's attributes values to new swapped block** area is used to specify whether to copy the attribute value of the old blocks to the new blocks or not. The options in this area are discussed next.

### Yes, copy all, old to new

By default, the **Yes, copy all, old to new** radio button is selected. As a result, the attribute values are copied to the new block.

**No, discard all old values**
The **No, discard all old values** radio button is used to discard all old attribute values.

**Copy old to new only if new value is blank**
The **Copy old to new if new value is blank** radio button is used to copy the old attribute value only if the new value is blank.

#### Project
When you choose the **Project** button, the **Select Drawings to Process** dialog box will be displayed. Using this button, you can swap the block of all drawings with the required block. When you choose the **OK** button, the **QSAVE** message box will be displayed. Choose the **OK** button; the drawings will get updated project wide. Also, the component that you have selected from the **Update Block** dialog box will get replaced with the component that you have selected from your drawing.

#### Active Drawing
When you choose the **Active Drawing** button, the old block will be replaced with the new block in the active drawing.

### Library Swap - substitute new versions for all blocks
The **Library Swap - substitute new versions for all blocks** radio button is used to replace all blocks in a library with the updated version of the same block in the active drawing or project. The **Library Swap - substitute new versions for all blocks** option is similar to the **Update a Block - substitute new version for selected block** option. However, if the **Library Swap - substitute new versions for all blocks** radio button is selected, then all blocks in a drawing will be swapped with the block that belongs to a library file. To swap the library, select the **Library Swap - substitute new versions for all blocks** radio button from the **Option B: Update Block (revised or different version of same block name)** area and choose the **OK** button; the **Library Swap -- All Drawing** dialog box will be displayed, as shown in Figure 5-56.

Most of the options in this dialog box have already been discussed. The remaining options are discussed next.

#### Path to new block library
Specify the path for the symbol library in the **Path to new block library** edit box. Alternatively, choose the **Browse** button; the **Browse For Folder** dialog box will be displayed. Next, select the library and choose **OK**; the path of the library will be displayed in the **Path to new block library** edit box. By default, *C:\users\public\documents\autodesk\acade 2022\libs\NFPA* is displayed in this edit box.

### Pick
The **Pick** button is used to select the block that you need to replace using the library file.

**Note**
*If a block exists in the drawing but does not exist in the block library, it will not get changed. Also, the name of the block that you want to swap must match exactly.*

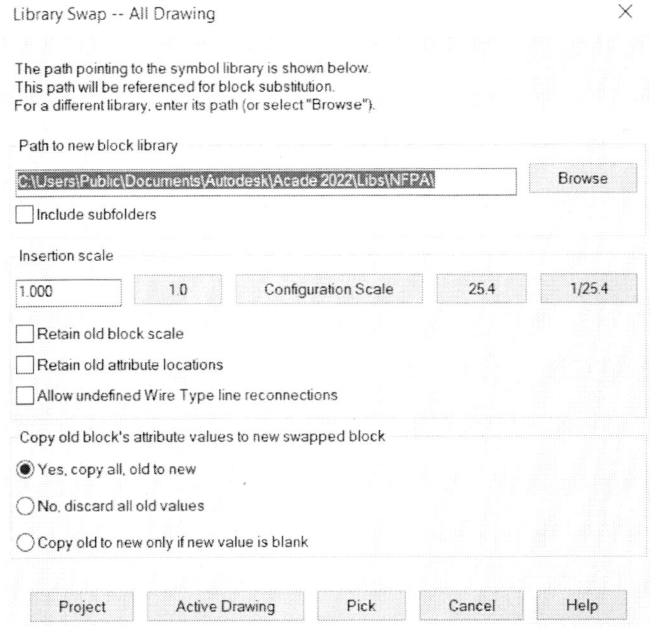


*Figure 5-56 The **Library Swap -- All Drawing** dialog box*

## Attribute Mapping Area

The block can be swapped or updated using the options available in the **Option A: Swap Block** and **Option B: Update Block** areas but you may need to map the attribute values to different attribute names. To do so, you can use an attribute mapping file. You can use the *.xls*, *.csv*, or *.txt* file formats. The **Attribute Mapping** area consists of the **Use Same Attribute Names (default)** and **Use Attribute Mapping File** radio buttons. These radio buttons are discussed next.

### Use Same Attribute Names (default)

By default, the **Use Same Attribute Names (default)** radio button is selected. As a result, attribute names of the original blocks are used while mapping them on the new block.

### Use Attribute Mapping File

The **Use Attribute Mapping File** radio button, if selected, uses a mapping file to map the attribute names of the old block to the attribute names of the new block. After selecting the **Use Attribute Mapping File** radio button, the **Mapping File** edit box will be activated. You can enter the mapping file in this edit box. Alternatively, choose the **Browse** button; the **Select Attribute Mapping File** dialog box will be displayed. Next, select the file and choose the **Open** button; the name and path of the mapping file will be displayed in the **Mapping File** edit box.

The **OK** button in the **Swap Block / Update Block / Library Swap** dialog box will be activated only if you select any one of the options from the **Option A: Swap Block (swap to different block name)** or **Option B: Update Block (revised or different version of same block name)** areas. Choose this button after specifying the settings.

# TUTORIALS

## Tutorial 1

In this tutorial, you will insert a ladder with four rungs into the drawing and then insert push buttons, relays, and pilot lights from the **Insert Component** dialog box. Also, you will add a description to components, as shown in Figure 5-57. **(Expected time: 20 min)**

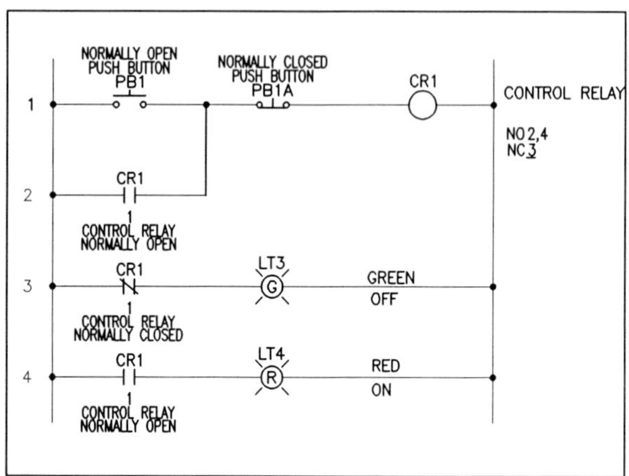


***Figure 5-57** Ladder and components inserted in it*

The following steps are required to complete this tutorial:

a. Create a new drawing.
b. Insert ladder into the drawing.
c. Insert components and add descriptions to components.
d. Add the wire.
e. Trim the rung of the ladder.
f. Save the drawing file.

### Creating a New Drawing

1. Open the **PROJECT MANAGER**, if it is not already displayed.

2. Activate the **CADCIM** Project.

3. Choose the **New Drawing** button in the **PROJECT MANAGER**; the **Create New Drawing** dialog box is displayed. Enter **C05_tut01** in the **Name** edit box of the **Drawing File** area.

4. Next, choose the **Browse** button on the right of the **Template** edit box; the **Select template** dialog box is displayed. Select the **ACAD_ELECTRICAL** template from this dialog box and choose the **Open** button; the path and location of the template file is displayed in the **Template** edit box.

5. Enter **Schematic Components** in the **Description 1** edit box.

6. Choose the **OK** button; the *C05_tut01.dwg* is created in the **CADCIM** project and displayed at the bottom of the drawing list in it.

7. Move the *C05_tut01.dwg* to the *TUTORIALS* subfolder as discussed earlier.

## Inserting Ladder into the Drawing

1. Choose the **Insert Ladder** tool from **Schematic > Insert Wires/Wire Numbers > Insert Ladder** drop-down; the **Insert Ladder** dialog box is displayed.

2. Set the following parameters in the **Insert Ladder** dialog box:

   Width: **5.0**
   1st Reference: **1**
   **1 Phase**: Select this radio button
   Spacing: **1.0**
   Rungs: **4**
   **Yes**: Select this radio button

   After setting these parameters, click in the **Length** edit box; the length of the ladder is automatically calculated and is displayed in this edit box.

3. Choose the **OK** button; you are prompted to specify the start position of the first rung. Enter **10, 15** at the Command prompt and press ENTER; the ladder is inserted in the drawing, as shown in Figure 5-58.

4. Zoom in the drawing.

***Figure 5-58** The ladder inserted in the drawing*

## Inserting Components and Adding Description to Components

1. Choose the **Icon Menu** tool from **Schematic > Insert Components > Icon Menu** drop-down; the **Insert Component** dialog box is displayed, as shown in Figure 5-59.

2. Select the **Push Buttons** icon from the **NFPA: Schematic Symbols** area displayed on the right in the **Insert Component** dialog box; the **NFPA: Schematic Symbols** area is replaced by the **NFPA: Push Buttons** area.

3. Select **Push Button NO** from the **NFPA: Push Buttons** area. You will notice that the component attached with the cursor is displayed. Also, you are prompted to specify the

insertion point for the push button. Next, place the push button at the extreme left of the rung 1; the **Insert / Edit Component** dialog box is displayed.

The PB1 is displayed in the edit box of the **Component Tag** area. Do not change the value.

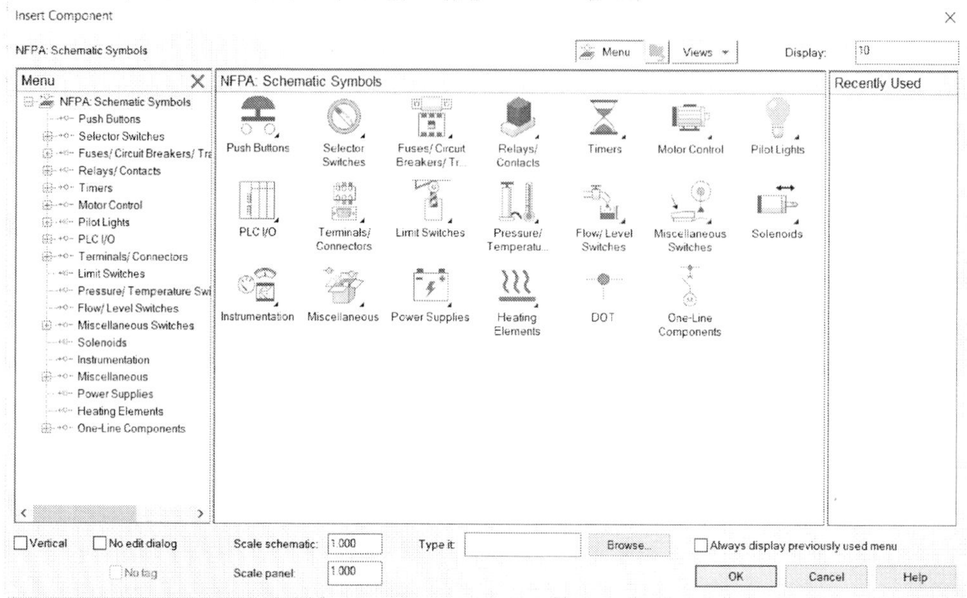


*Figure 5-59 The **Insert Component** dialog box*

4. Enter **NORMALLY OPEN** and **PUSH BUTTON** in the **Line 1** and **Line 2** edit boxes of the **Description** area, respectively.

5. Choose the **OK** button from the **Insert / Edit Component** dialog box; the PB1 component is inserted in the drawing.

6. Again, choose the **Icon Menu** tool from **Schematic > Insert Components > Icon Menu** drop-down; the **Insert Component** dialog box is displayed.

7. Select the **Push Buttons** icon from the **NFPA: Schematic Symbols** area displayed on the right in the **Insert Component** dialog box; the **NFPA: Schematic Symbols** area is modified to the **NFPA: Push Buttons** area, displaying various types of push buttons.

8. Select the **Push Button NC** component; you will notice that the component attached with the cursor is displayed. Also, you are prompted to specify the insertion point for the push button. Next, place the push button to the right of PB1 on the rung 1, refer to Figure 5-57; the **Insert / Edit Component** dialog box is displayed. PB1A is displayed in the edit box of the **Component Tag** area. Do not change this value.

9. Enter **NORMALLY CLOSED** and **PUSH BUTTON** in the **Line 1** and **Line 2** edit boxes in the **Description** area, respectively.

10. Choose the **OK** button from the **Insert / Edit Component** dialog box; the PB1A symbol is inserted in the drawing.

11. Repeat Step 1. Select the **Relays / Contacts** icon displayed in the **NFPA: Schematic Symbols** area of the **Insert Component** dialog box; the **NFPA: Relays and Contacts** area is displayed.

12. Select **Relay Coil** that is located in the first row and the first column in the **NFPA: Relays and Contacts** area of the **Insert Component** dialog box; you are prompted to specify the insertion point. Next, place the relay to the right of the PB1A push button on rung1; the **Insert / Edit Component** dialog box is displayed.

    CR1 is displayed in the edit box of the **Component Tag** area. Do not change this value.

13. Enter **CONTROL RELAY** in the **Line 1** edit box of the **Description** area.

14. Choose the **OK** button in the **Insert / Edit Component** dialog box; the component is inserted into rung 1 of the ladder.

15. Repeat Step1. Select the **Relays/Contacts** icon from the **Insert Component** dialog box; the **NFPA: Relays and Contacts** area is displayed.

16. Select **Relay NO Contact** from the **NFPA: Relays and Contacts** area; you are prompted to specify the insertion point for the symbol. Place **Relay NO Contact** at the extreme left of rung 2; the **Insert / Edit Child Component** dialog box is displayed.

17. In this dialog box, choose the **Drawing** button from the **Component Tag** area; the **Active Drawing list for FAMILY = "CR"** dialog box is displayed. Select **CR1** from this dialog box and choose the **OK** button; **CR1** is displayed in the **Tag** edit box.

18. Enter **CONTROL RELAY** in the **Line 1** edit box of the **Description** area, if it is not displayed already.

19. Enter **NORMALLY OPEN** in the **Line 2** edit box of the **Description** area.

20. Choose the **OK** button from the **Insert / Edit Child Component** dialog box; CR1 is inserted in the drawing in rung 2.

21. Repeat Step 1. Select the **Relays/Contacts** icon from the **NFPA: Schematic Symbols** area in the **Insert Component** dialog box; the **NFPA: Relays and Contacts** area is displayed.

22. Select the **Relay NC Contact** symbol; you are prompted to specify the insertion point. Place the symbol on the left of rung 3; the **Insert / Edit Child Component** dialog box is displayed.

23. In this dialog box, choose the **Drawing** button from the **Component Tag** area; the **Active Drawing list for FAMILY = "CR"** dialog box is displayed. In this dialog box, select the first tag entry, CR1, whose description is CONTROL RELAY and then choose the **OK** button; CR1 is displayed in the **Tag** edit box and CONTROL RELAY is displayed in the **Line 1** edit box of the **Description** area in the **Insert / Edit Child Component** dialog box.

24. Next, enter **NORMALLY CLOSED** in the **Line 2** edit box of the **Description** area.

25. Choose the **OK** button in the **Insert / Edit Child Component** dialog box; CR1 is inserted on rung 3 in the drawing.

26. Repeat Step 1. Next, select the **Pilot Lights** icon from the **NFPA: Schematic Symbols** area; the **NFPA: Schematic Symbols** area is modified to the **NFPA: Pilot Lights** area. Next, select the **Green Standard** symbol that is located on the first row and the second column; you are prompted to specify the insertion point. Place the symbol on the right of the **Relay NC Contact** symbol on the rung 3; the **Insert / Edit Component** dialog box is displayed. By default, LT3 is displayed in the edit box of the **Component Tag** area. Do not change this value.

27. Enter **GREEN** and **OFF** in the **Line 1** and **Line 2** edit boxes of the **Description** area, respectively.

28. Choose **OK** from the **Insert / Edit Component** dialog box; the LT3 symbol is inserted on rung 3.

29. Similarly, place CR1 (Relay NO Contact) with the description CONTROL RELAY and NORMALLY OPEN at extreme left of rung 4.

30. Insert the Pilot light **(Red Standard)** from the **Insert Component** dialog box with the description RED and ON to the right of CR1 on rung 4. Figure 5-60 shows the ladder with the following components inserted in it:

    (a) PB1, (b) PB1A, (c) CR1 and its contacts, (d) LT3 and (e) LT4

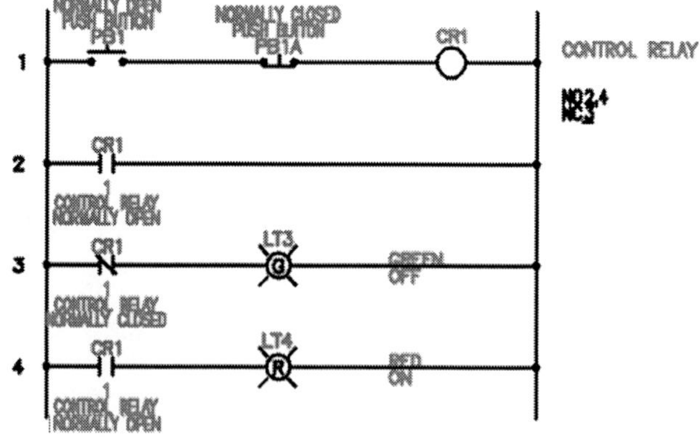


*Figure 5-60 The ladder and components*

**Note**

*In order to check the cross-reference fields of the relay coil (CR1) inserted on rung 1, choose the **Edit** tool from the **Edit Components** panel of the **Schematic** tab; you are prompted to select component. Next, select CR1 that is located on rung 1; the **Insert / Edit Component** dialog box is displayed. In this dialog box, the **Cross-Reference** area displays the number of NO and NC contacts used along with this relay coil.*

## Adding the Wire

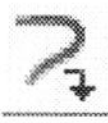

1. Choose the **Wire** tool from **Schematic > Insert Wires/Wire Numbers > Wire** drop-down; you are prompted to specify the start point of the wire.

2. Click in the middle of PB1 and PB1A of rung 1 and drag the cursor downward and click on rung 2; a wire is drawn between rung 1 and rung 2 and these rungs are joined, as shown in Figure 5-61. Press ESC to exit the command.

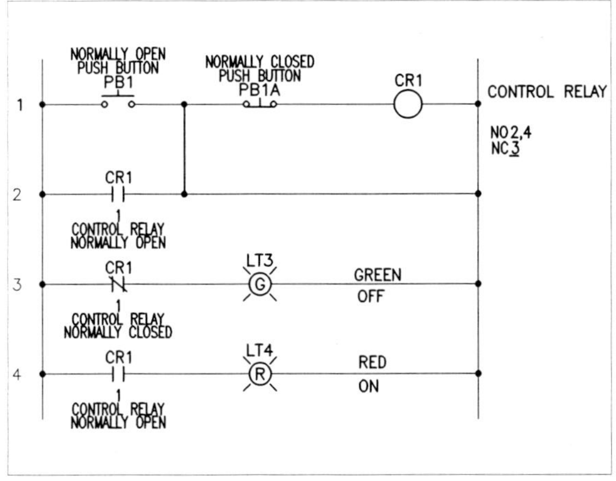


*Figure 5-61 Wire inserted between rung 1 and rung 2*

## Trimming the Rung

1. Choose the **Trim Wire** tool from the **Edit Wires/Wire Numbers** panel of the **Schematic** tab; you are prompted to select the wire. Select the right portion of rung 2; the selected portion is removed, as shown in Figure 5-62.

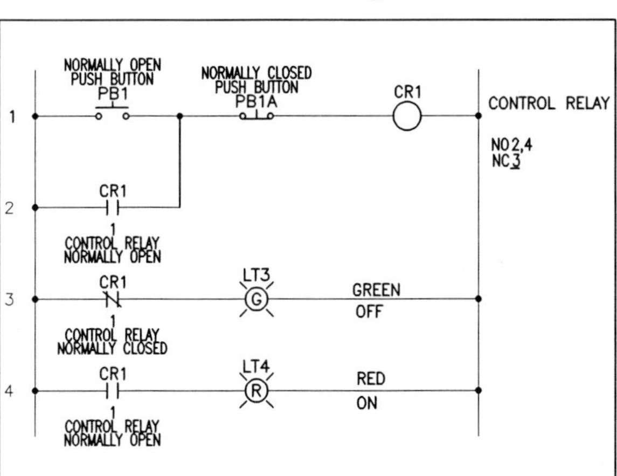


*Figure 5-62 The ladder with the half portion of rung 2 trimmed*

2. Press ESC to exit the command.

## Saving the Drawing File

1. Choose **Save** from the **Application Menu** to save the *C05_tut01.dwg* drawing file.

# Tutorial 2

In this tutorial, you will open the *C05_tut01.dwg* file of Tutorial 1 of this chapter. Next, you will edit the component PB1 and add the catalog information to this component. **(Expected time: 15 min)**

The following steps are required to complete this tutorial:

a. Open, save, and add the drawing to the **CADCIM** project.
b. Edit the component.
c. Save the drawing file.

## Opening, Saving, and Adding the Drawing to the CADCIM Project

1. Open *C05_tut01.dwg* drawing file. Save it with the name *C05_tut02.dwg*. Add it to the **CADCIM** project list, as discussed in the earlier chapters.

## Editing the Component

1. Choose the **Edit** tool from **Schematic > Edit Components > Edit Components** drop-down; you are prompted to select the component to be edited. Select the PB1 push button; the **Insert/Edit Component** dialog box is displayed.

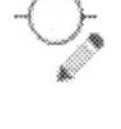

2. Choose the **Lookup** button in the **Catalog Data** area; the **Catalog Browser** dialog box is displayed, as shown in Figure 5-63.

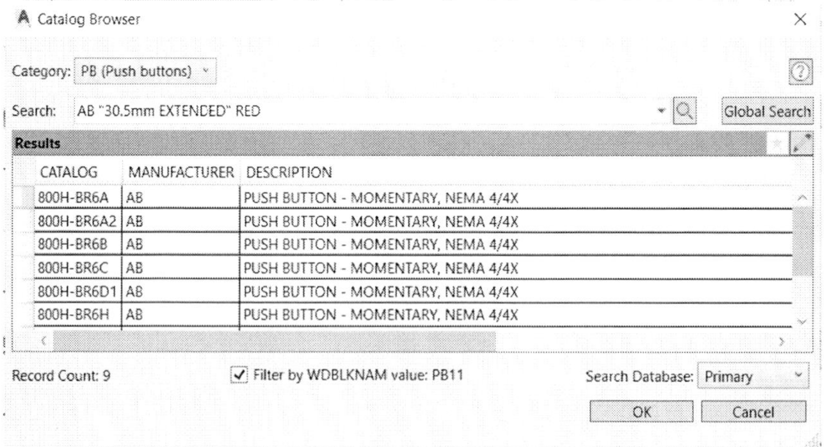


*Figure 5-63 The **Catalog Browser** dialog box*

3. Select **800H-BR6A** from the **Catalog Browser** dialog box.

   Make sure **AB**, **30.5mm EXTENDED**, and **RED** are selected in the **MANUFACTURER**, **TYPE**, and **STYLE** columns, respectively.

4. Choose the **OK** button in the **Catalog Browser** dialog box; AB and 800H-BR6A are displayed in the **Manufacturer** and **Catalog** edit boxes in the **Catalog Data** area of the **Insert / Edit Component** dialog box.

5. Choose the **OK** button in the **Insert / Edit Component** dialog box to add the catalog data to the component PB1; the **Update other drawings?** message box is displayed. Choose the **OK** button in this message box; the **QSAVE** message box is displayed. Choose the **OK** button in this message box to save the changes in the drawing.

### Saving the Drawing File

1. Choose **File > Save** from the menu bar to save the *C05_tut02.dwg* drawing file.

## Tutorial 3

In this tutorial, you will use the **Swap/Update Block** tool to swap a PB1A block with a limit switch LS1 that you have inserted in the drawing of Tutorial 1 of this chapter, as shown in Figure 5-64. **(Expected time: 15 min)**

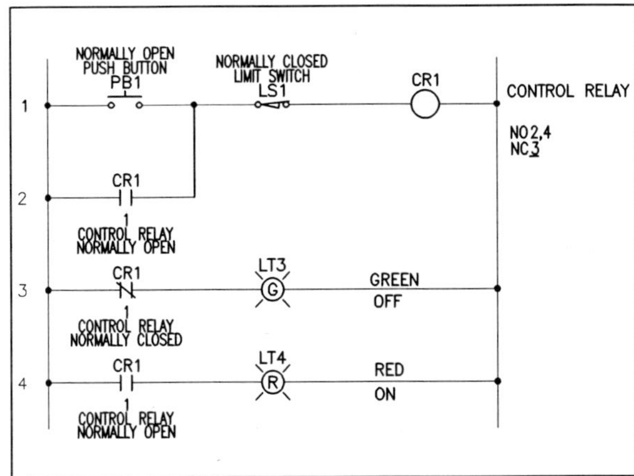


***Figure 5-64** The push button PB1A swapped with the limit switch LS1*

The following steps are required to complete this tutorial:

a. Open, save, and add the drawing to the **CADCIM** project.
b. Swap the block.
c. Save the drawing file.

### Opening, Saving, and Adding the Drawing to the CADCIM Project

1. Open *C05_tut01.dwg* drawing file. Save it with the name *C05_tut03.dwg*. Add it to the **CADCIM** project list, as discussed in the earlier chapters.

### Swapping the Block

1. Choose the **Swap/Update Block** tool from the **Edit Components** panel of the **Schematic** tab; the **Swap Block / Update Block / Library Swap** dialog box is displayed, as shown in Figure 5-65.

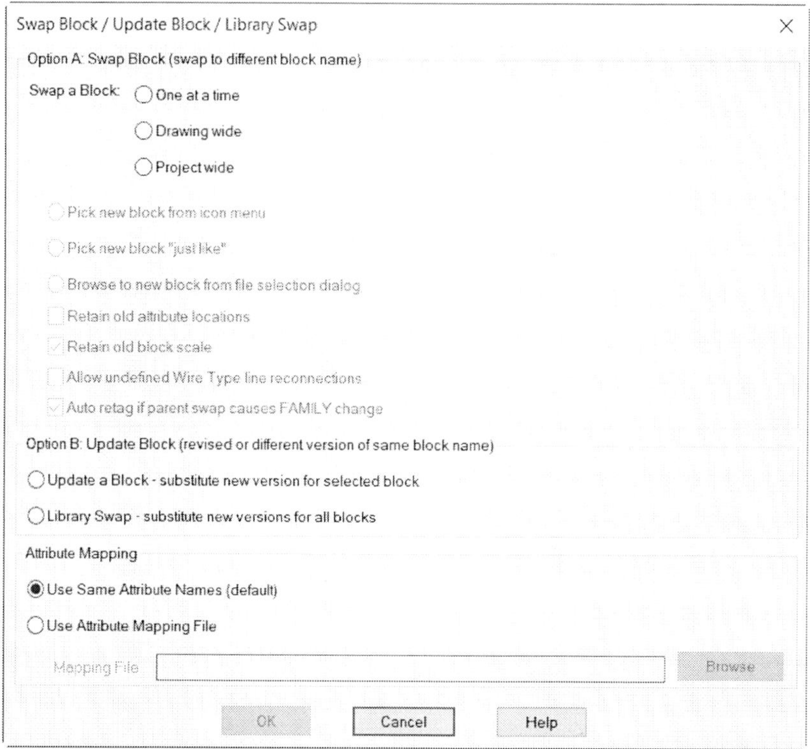


*Figure 5-65 The* ***Swap Block / Update Block / Library Swap*** *dialog box*

2. Select the **One at a time** radio button in the **Option A: Swap Block (swap to different block name)** area; the other options in this area are activated.

3. Select the **Retain old block scale** and **Auto retag if parent swap causes FAMILY change** check boxes in the **Option A: Swap Block (swap to different block name)** area, if they are not selected.

4. Clear the **Allow undefined Wire Type line reconnections** check box, if it is selected.

5. Select the **Pick new block from icon menu** radio button from the **Option A: Swap Block (swap to different block name)** area; the **OK** button is activated. Next, choose the **OK** button; the **Insert Component** dialog box is displayed.

6. Next, select the **Limit Switches** icon from the **NFPA: Schematic Symbols** area; a list of limit switches is displayed in the **NFPA: Limit Switches** area.

7. Select **Limit Switch, NC**; you are prompted to select the component to swap out. Next, select the PB1A push button that you have placed on rung 1; the push button is swapped with LS1. Now, press ENTER to exit the command.

8. To enter description for the limit switch, choose the **Edit** tool from **Schematic > Edit Components > Edit Components** drop-down; you are prompted to select the component. Select LS1; the **Insert / Edit Component** dialog box is displayed.

9. Enter **LIMIT SWITCH** in the **Line 2** edit box of the **Description** area in the **Insert / Edit Component** dialog box.

10. Choose the **OK** button; the description is displayed on top of the component. Figure 5-66 shows the push button swapped with the limit switch.

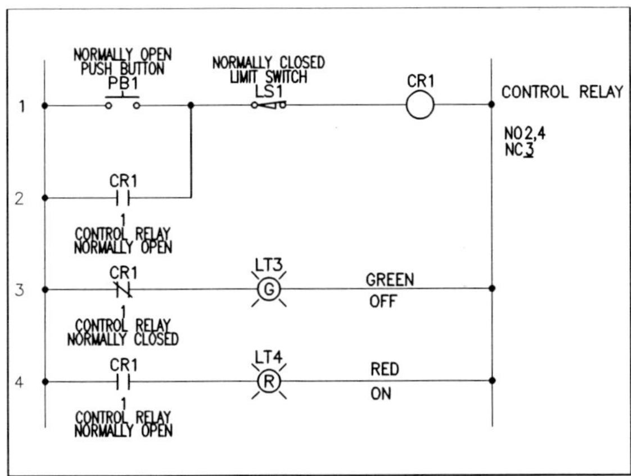


*Figure 5-66 The push button (PB1A) swapped with the limit switch (LS1)*

## Saving the Drawing File

1. Choose **Save** from the **Application Menu** to save the *C05_tut03.dwg* drawing file.

---

# Tutorial 4

In this tutorial, you will change the symbol library setting from NFPA to JIC 125. Also, you will swap a limit switch LS1 of the **NFPA** library with a proximity switch PRS1 from the **JIC 125** library, as shown in Figure 5-67. **(Expected time: 20 min)**

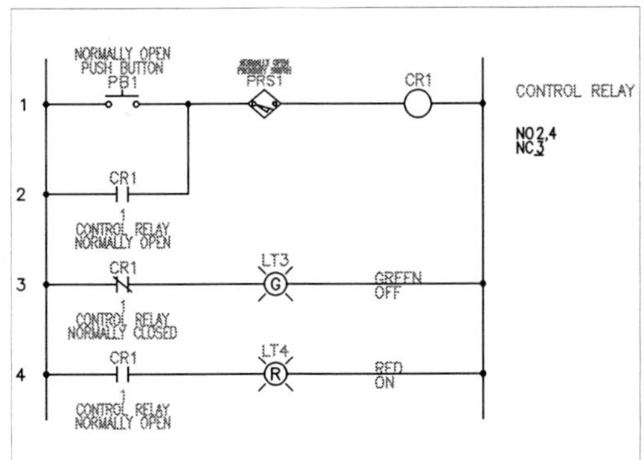


*Figure 5-67 The limit switch LS1 of the* ***NFPA*** *library changed to the proximity switch PRS1 of the* ***JIC 125*** *library*

The following steps are required to complete this tutorial:

a. Open, save, and add the drawing to the **CADCIM** project.
b. Change the library.

c. Swap the component.
d. Create project specific catalog database.
e. Save the drawing file.

## Opening, Saving, and Adding the Drawing to the CADCIM Project

1. Open *C05_tut03.dwg* drawing file. Save it with the name *C05_tut04.dwg*. Add it to the **CADCIM** project list, as discussed in the earlier chapters.

## Changing the Library

1. By default, the schematic library *C:/Users/Public/Documents/Autodesk/Acade 2022/Libs/NFPA/* is selected in the **Library and Icon Menu Paths** area of the **Project Properties** dialog box. To change the library **NFPA** to **JIC 125**, right-click on the **CADCIM** project displayed in the **Projects** rollout of the **PROJECT MANAGER**; a shortcut menu is displayed. Choose the **Properties** option from the shortcut menu; the **Project Properties** dialog box is displayed.

2. Click on the (+) sign of the **Schematic Libraries** in the **Library and Icon Menu Paths** area in the **Project Properties** dialog box; a list of schematic libraries is displayed, as shown in Figure 5-68.

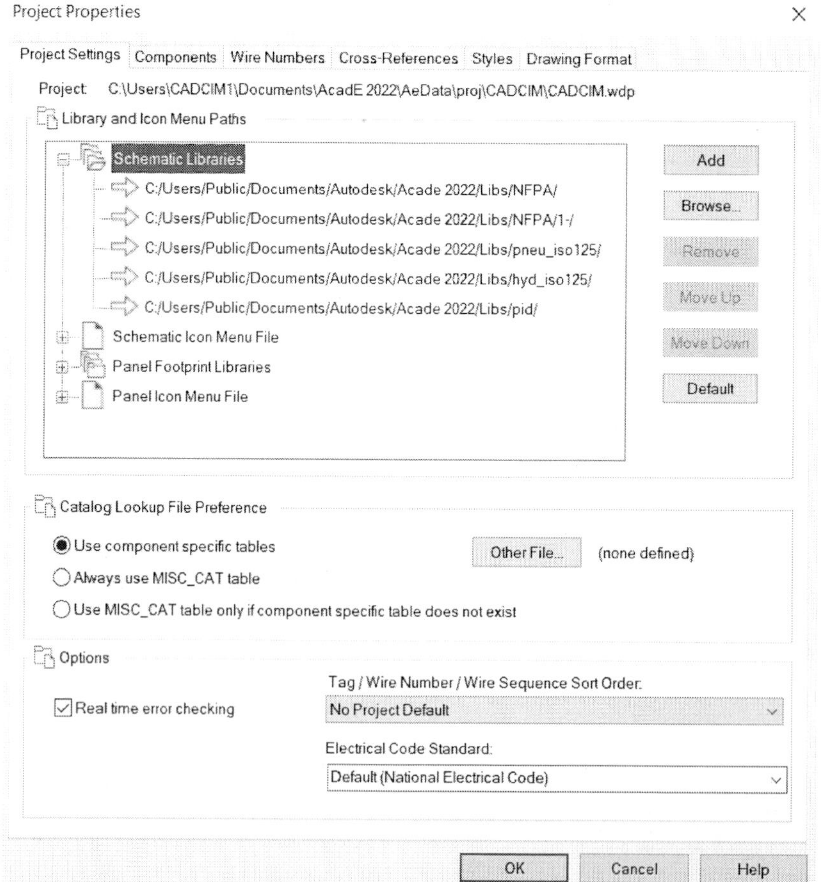


*Figure 5-68 The **Project Properties** dialog box*

3. Next, select *C:/Users/Public/Documents/Autodesk/Acade 2022/Libs/NFPA/* and then choose the **Browse** button; the **Browse For Folder** dialog box is displayed.

4. Next, select the *jic125* folder and choose the **OK** button; the path *C:/Users/Public/Documents/Autodesk/Acade 2022/Libs/jic 125* is displayed under the **Schematic Libraries**.

5. Click on the (+) sign of the **Schematic Icon Menu File** in the **Library and Icon Menu Paths** area and double-click on the path *ACE_NFPA_MENU.DAT;* the **Select ".dat" AutoCAD Electrical icon menu file** dialog box is displayed. Select **ACE_JIC_MENU.DAT** from this dialog box and choose **Open**; the icon menu file is changed from *NFPA* to *JIC*.

6. Choose the **OK** button in the **Project Properties** dialog box. In this way, you can change the library from **NFPA** to **JIC 125**.

## Swapping the Component

1. Choose the **Swap/Update Block** tool from the **Edit Components** panel of the **Schematic** tab; the **Swap Block / Update Block / Library Swap** dialog box is displayed.

2. Next, select the **One at a time** radio button from the **Option A: Swap Block** area; the other options in the **Option A: Swap Block** area become activated.

3. Select the **Pick new block from icon menu** radio button from the **Option A: Swap Block** area and choose the **OK** button; the **Insert Component** dialog box is displayed.

4. Select the **Miscellaneous Switches** icon from the **Insert Component** dialog box in the **JIC: Schematic Symbols** area; the **JIC: Schematic Symbols** area is modified to the **JIC: Other Switch Types** area.

5. Select **Proximity Switch NO** from the **JIC: Other Switch Types** area; you are prompted to select the component to swap. Select the LS1 component; the limit switch LS1 is modified to the proximity switch PRS1. Press ENTER to exit the command.

6. Now, right-click on the PRS1; a marking menu is displayed. Choose the **Edit Component** option from the marking menu; the **Insert / Edit Component** dialog box is displayed. Enter **NORMALLY OPEN** in the **Line 1** edit box and then **PROXIMITY SWITCH** in the **Line 2** edit box of the **Description** area. Next, choose the **OK** button in the **Insert / Edit Component** dialog box; the description of PRS1 is changed, as shown in Figure 5-69.

7. Revert to the *NFPA* schematic library and the *NFPA* icon menu file in the **Project Properties** dialog box as done earlier.

## Creating Project Specific Catalog Database

1. Choose the **Create Project Specific Catalog Database** tool from the **Other Tools** panel of the **Project** tab; the **Create Project-Specific Catalog Database** dialog box is displayed. In this dialog box, select the **No - keep it separate** radio button; the edit box and the browse button below it is activated.

If you select the **Yes - make it the active project default catalog file** radio button, the project specific catalog database file will be the default project catalog file.

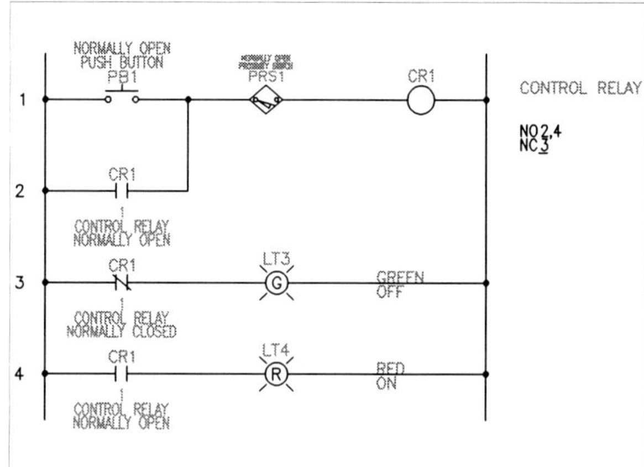


***Figure 5-69*** *Limit switch LS1 swapped to proximity switch PRS1*

2. Choose the browse button; the **Save** dialog box is displayed. In this dialog box, specify the location in the **Look in** drop-down list. Note that the location you specify should be other than the default location specified in the edit box, refer to Figure 5-70. Next, enter **CADCIM** in the **File name** edit box and then choose the **Open** button to close the **Save** dialog box; the specified location is displayed in the edit box located below the **No - keep it separate** radio button. Now, choose the **OK** button in the **Create Project-Specific Catalog Database** dialog box; the *CADCIM.mdb* file is created at the specified location.

Create Project-Specific Catalog Database

Project: CADCIM

Existing catalog database

Main catalog database:

C:\Users\CADCIM1\Documents\AcadE 2022\AeData\en-us\catalogs\default_cat.mdb

Secondary catalog database:

Create project-specific catalog database

Save in project folder:

Yes - make it the active project's default catalog file

No - keep it separate

C:\Users\CADCIM1\Desktop\CADCIM.mdb

Location:

C:\Users\CADCIM1\Desktop\CADCIM.mdb

OK Cancel Help

***Figure 5-70*** *The* ***Create Project-Specific Catalog Database*** *dialog box*

## Saving the Drawing File

1. Choose **Save** from the **Application Menu** to save the drawing file.

# Self-Evaluation Test

**Answer the following questions and then compare them to those given at the end of this chapter:**

1. Which of the following commands is used to insert a component into a drawing?

   (a) **AECOMPONENT** (b) **AEEDITCOMPONENT**
   (c) **AEPLCP** (d) **AECOPYCOMP**

2. When you select a child component from the **Insert Component** dialog box, the __________ dialog box is displayed after specifying the insertion point of the component.

3. The __________ tool is used to create a list of all panel components by extracting component information directly from the selected panel layout drawings.

4. The __________ tool is used to replace one block instance with another block.

5. The __________ button in the **Panel Components** dialog box is used to reopen the **Panel Layout List —> Schematic Components Insert** dialog box which enables you to re-extract data or select a saved external file to use.

6. When you choose the **Add** button in the **Schematic Component or Circuit** dialog box, the __________ dialog box is displayed.

7. The **Recently Used** area on the right in the **Insert Component** dialog box displays the components inserted during the current editing session. (T/F)

8. The **OK-Repeat** button in the **Insert / Edit Component** dialog box is used to insert another component similar to the one inserted into the drawing. (T/F)

9. If you select the **fixed** check box in the **Component Tag** area of the **Insert/Edit Component** dialog box, the component tag will not update during the automatic retag operations. (T/F)

10. The **Catalog Browser** dialog box, in its Lookup mode, displays the database table that matches the family type of the inserted component. (T/F)

## Review Questions

**Answer the following questions:**

1. Which of the following dialog boxes is displayed when you choose the **Icon Menu** tool?

   (a) **Insert Component** (b) **Schematic Component or Circuit**
   (c) **Select component list file** (d) **Insert / Edit Component**

2. Which of the following dialog boxes will be displayed if you choose the **Catalog Check** button in the **Catalog Browser** dialog box?

   (a) **Find: Catalog Assignments** (b) **Cross-Reference Component Override**
   (c) **Settings** (d) **Bill Of Material Check**

3. Which one of the following tools, if chosen, displays the **Swap Block/Update Block/Library Swap** dialog box?

   (a) **Insert Component** (b) **Swap/Update Block**
   (c) **Edit Component** (d) **Insert Component (Catalog List)**

4. To insert multiple components at a time, choose the __________ tool from the **Insert Components** panel of the **Schematic** tab.

5. You cannot select multiple components from the **Panel Components** dialog box. (T/F)

6. The process of inserting a child component is similar to that of inserting a parent component. (T/F)

7. You will not be able to edit the component, once you insert it into a drawing. (T/F)

8. The **Component Override** check box in the **Insert/Edit Component** dialog box is used to change the cross reference formatting for the component and override the settings in the **Drawing Properties** dialog box. (T/F)

9. If the **Ratings** area in the **Insert/Edit Component** dialog box is not activated, then it implies that the component being edited does not have the rating attributes. (T/F)

10. The **Catalog Check** button, if chosen, only performs the Bill of Material check but does not display the result. (T/F)

# EXERCISES

## Exercise 1

Create a new drawing with the name *C05_exer01.dwg* in the **NEW_PROJECT** project and insert a ladder with the following specifications: Width = 5; Spacing = 1.000; Rungs = 12, and 1st Reference = 1. Also, you will insert components into the ladder, as shown in Figure 5-71. Use the **Wire** tool to add wires and the **Trim Wire** tool to trim wires. Figure 5-71 shows the complete ladder diagram for Exercise 1. **(Expected time: 25 min)**

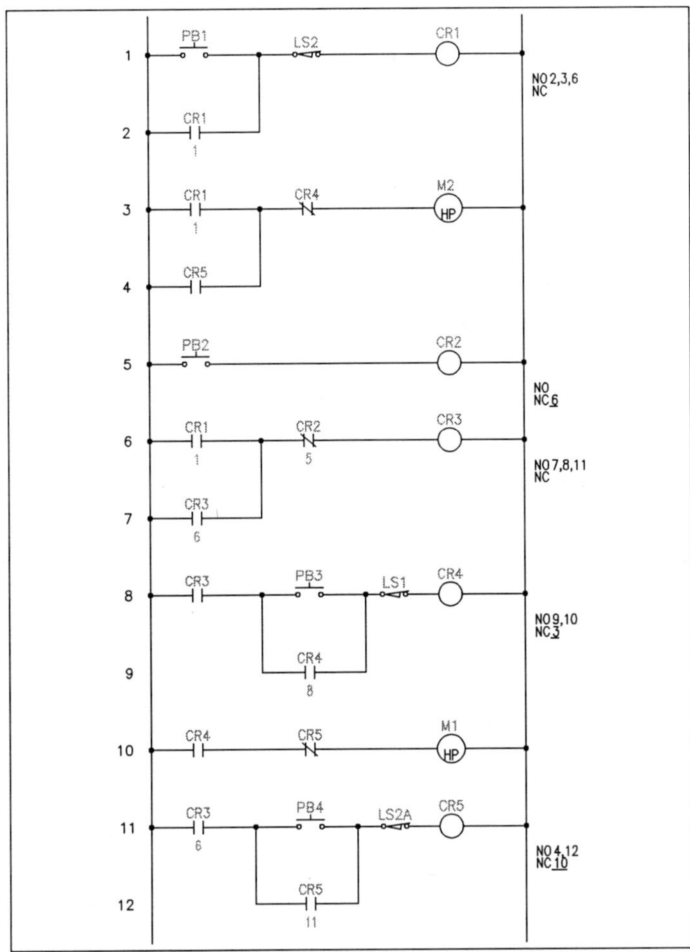


*Figure 5-71 Ladder with components inserted for Exercise 1*

## Exercise 2

In this exercise, you will change the symbol library setting from NFPA to JIC 125. Next, you will swap a limit switch LS1 of the **NFPA** library with a toggle switch NO TG8 of the **JIC 125** library and switch LS2A with a proximity switch PRS11, as shown in Figure 5-72. Also, you will create a project specific catalog database for the NEW_PROJECT project.

**(Expected time: 20 min)**

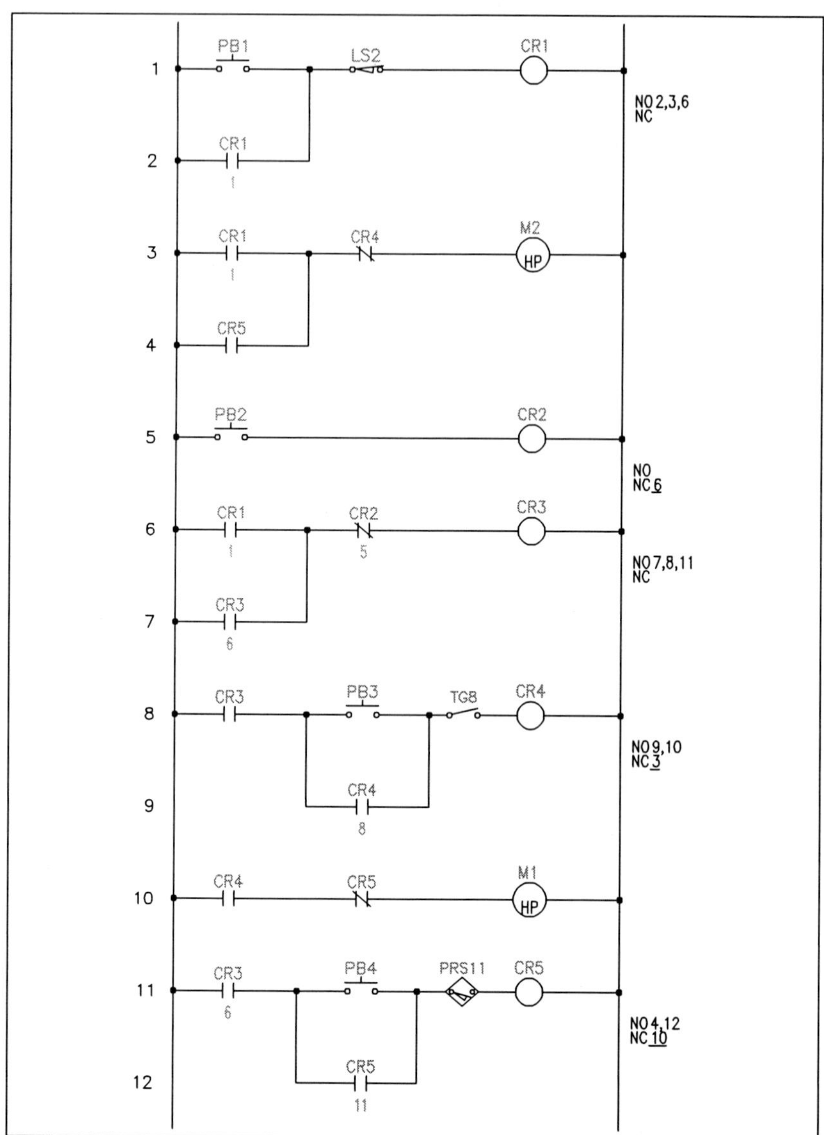


*Figure 5-72 Ladder diagram for Exercise 2*

## Answers to Self-Evaluation Test

**1.** a, **2. Insert / Edit Child Component**, **3. Panel List**, **4. Swap/Update Block**, **5. Reload**, **6. Add record**, **7.** T, **8.** T, **9.** T, **10.** T

# Chapter 6

# Schematic Editing

## Learning Objectives

***After completing this chapter, you will be able to:***

- *Use basic schematic editing commands*
- *Update components from catalog database*
- *Update a schematic component from a one-line component*
- *Toggle between the normally open and normally closed contacts and vice-versa*
- *Copy the catalog assignment and location values from one component to multiple components*
- *Use auditing tools to find out errors in the project and rectify them*
- *Retag the drawings*
- *Use the tools for editing attributes*

# INTRODUCTION

In this chapter, you will learn about different tools that are used to create or modify electrical schematic drawings. You can edit, move, copy, and align components in your drawing. These tools are very important as they provide extra functionalities to electrical schematic drawings. Also, later in this chapter, you will learn about surfing of components, auditing tools, editing tools of attributes, and retagging of drawings.

# CHANGING THE COMPONENT LOCATION WITH SCOOT TOOL

| | |
|---|---|
| **Ribbon:** | Schematic > Edit Components > Modify Components drop-down > Scoot |
| **Toolbar:** | ACE:Main Electrical > Scoot or ACE:Scoot > Scoot |
| **Menu:** | Components > Scoot |
| **Command:** | AESCOOT |

The **Scoot** tool is used to move objects such as components, terminals, PLC I/O modules, signal arrows, wire segments, wires with wire crossing-loops, ladder rungs, ladder buses, and so on in the drawing. The **Scoot** tool is similar to the AutoCAD **Move** tool. However, the **Scoot** tool has intelligence about electrical objects, which enables you to reposition electrical objects. Also, this tool is used to reconnect wires after repositioning the components. To scoot components, choose the **Scoot** tool from the **Modify Components** drop-down in the **Edit Components** panel of the **Schematic** tab, as shown in Figure 6-1; you will be prompted to select component, wire, or wire number for scoot. Select the component to scoot along with its connected wire; a temporary graphic indicating that you have selected the component will be displayed. Next, move the cursor to a place where you want to locate the component; the selected object will move in the orthogonal direction to the specified location.

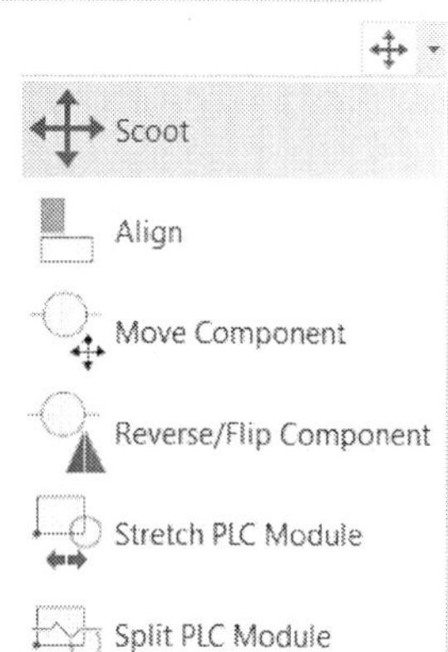


***Figure 6-1** The **Modify Components** drop-down*

Also, the wires will be reconnected after you scoot the components, the components will be updated, and the existing wire numbers will be recentered. Next, press ESC or click on the screen to exit the command.

Figures 6-2(a) and 6-2(b) show the components and wires before and after scooting.

If you move components to a location that requires component updates, the **Component(s) Moved** dialog box will be displayed, as shown in Figure 6-3. The options in this dialog box are discussed next.

## OK to Retag

Choose the **OK to Retag** button to retag the components automatically. Now, if the moved component is linked to other components in the current drawing, the **AutoCAD** message box will be displayed, as shown in Figure 6-4. Choose the **OK** button to update the related component in the drawing.

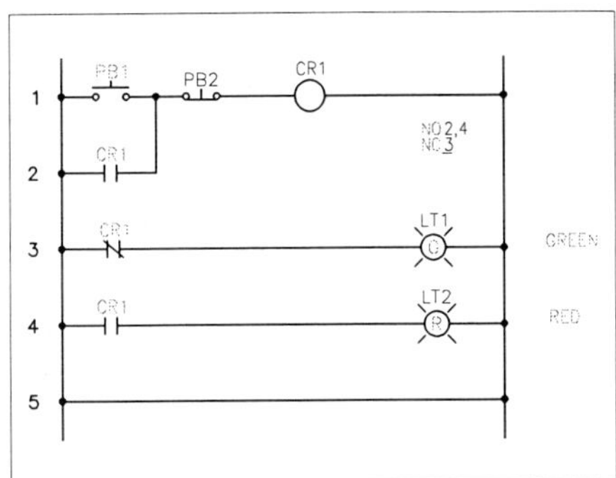


*Figure 6-2(a)* *Components and wires before scooting*

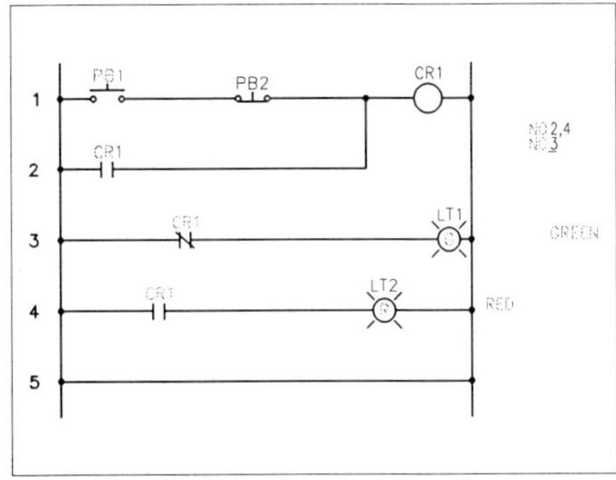


*Figure 6-2(b)* *Components and wires after scooting*

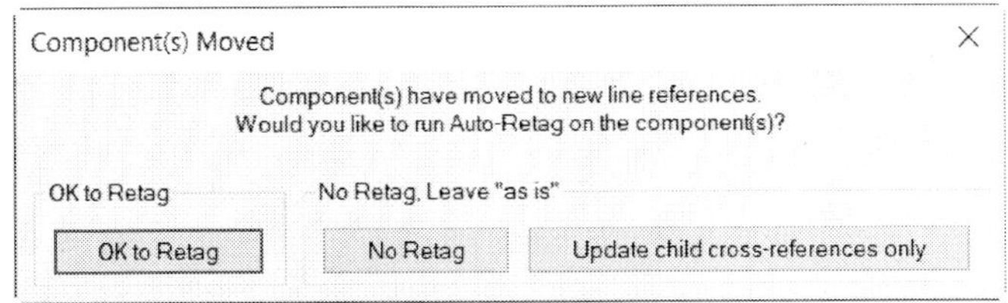


***Figure 6-3*** *The* ***Component(s) Moved*** *dialog box*

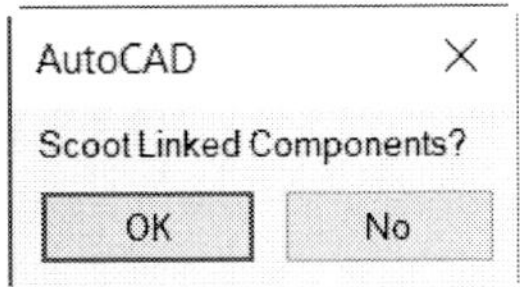


***Figure 6-4*** *The* ***AutoCAD*** *message box*

Also, if the component that you have moved consists of child components or related panel components in the other drawings of the active project, the **Update other drawings?** message box will be displayed, as shown in Figure 6-5. Choose the **OK** button from the **Update other drawings?** message box to batch process or update the other drawings of a project.

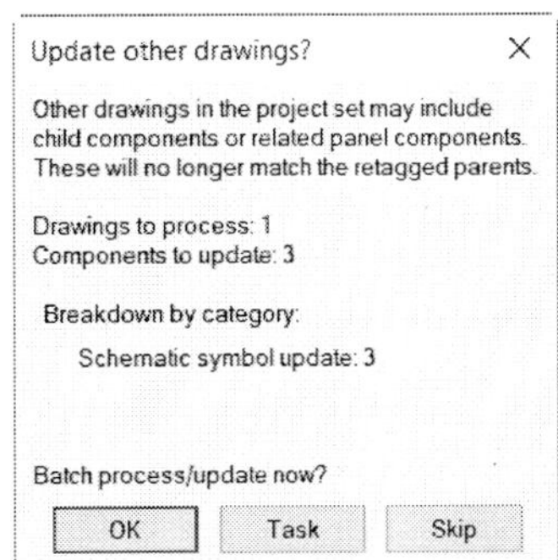


***Figure 6-5*** *The* ***Update other drawings?*** *message box*

Choose the **Task** button to save all modifications in the task list to be run later. The task list is maintained inside the project task list database file (project_update.mdb). You can access this list by choosing the **Project Task List** button from the **PROJECT MANAGER**. Choose the **Skip** button to skip the batch process.

**Note**

*If the moved component does not have related components in the current drawing, the* ***Update other drawings?*** *message box will be displayed directly after choosing the* ***OK to Retag*** *button from the* ***Component(s) Moved*** *dialog box.*

*If the moved component has related components in the current drawing as well as in the other drawings of the project, the* ***Update other drawings*** *message box will be displayed after choosing the* ***Yes-Update*** *button in the* ***Update Related Component?*** *message box.*

## No Retag

If you do not want to retag a component, choose the **No Retag** button.

## Update child cross-references only

Choose the **Update child cross-references only** button to update only the child cross-references.

**Note**

*If you select a wire segment that contains components to scoot, the entire wire along with its components and bus will be scooted. If they move to a new line reference, you can auto-retag components by choosing the* ***OK to Retag*** *button from the* ***Component(s) Moved*** *dialog box.*

# CHANGING COMPONENT LOCATIONS USING THE MOVE COMPONENT TOOL

| | |
|---|---|
| **Menu:** | Schematic > Edit Components > Modify Components drop-down > Move Component |
| **Toolbar:** | ACE:Main Electrical > Scoot > Move Component or ACE:Scoot > Move Component |
| **Menu:** | Components > Move Component |
| **Command:** | AEMOVE |

The **Move Component** tool is used to move the selected component from its current location or wire location to the specified location. To do so, choose the **Move Component** tool from the **Modify Components** drop-down in the **Edit Components** panel of the **Schematic** tab, refer to Figure 6-1; you will be prompted to select a component to move. Select the component; you will be prompted to specify insertion point. Specify the insertion point for the component; the selected component will be moved to the specified location, the underlying wires will be reconnected, and the component tags will be updated automatically. Figures 6-6(a) and 6-6(b) show the components before and after they are moved.

If you move objects to a location that needs component updates, the **Component(s) Moved** dialog box will be displayed, refer to Figure 6-3. The options in this dialog box have been discussed earlier.

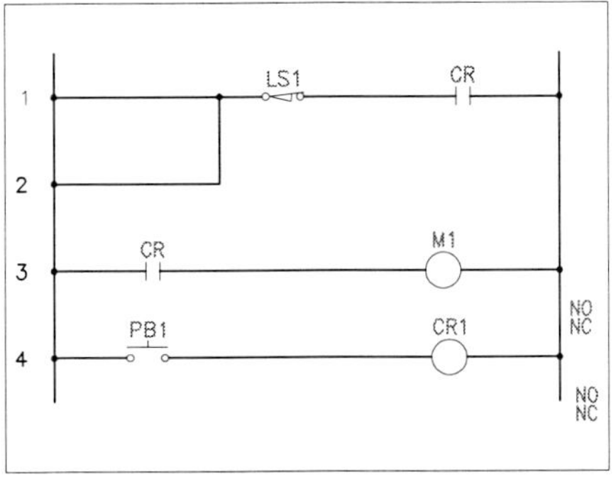


***Figure 6-6(a)*** *Components before using the* ***Move Component*** *tool*

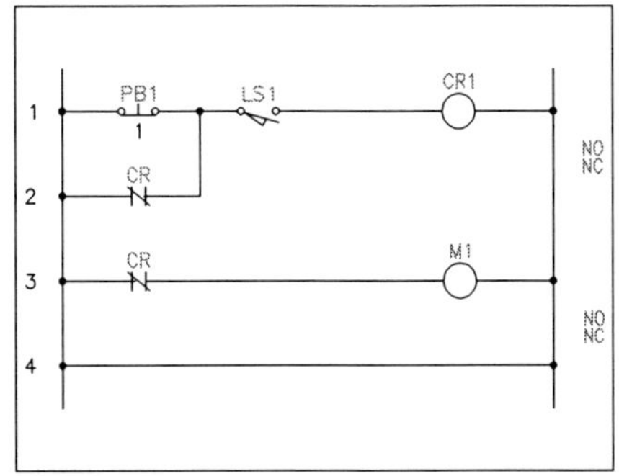


***Figure 6-6(b)*** *Components after using the* ***Move Component*** *tool*

## COPYING A COMPONENT

| | |
|---|---|
| **Ribbon:** | Schematic > Edit Components > Copy Component |
| **Toolbar:** | ACE:Main Electrical > Copy Component |
| **Menu:** | Components > Copy Component |
| **Command:** | AECOPYCOMP |

The **Copy Component** tool is used to copy the selected component and insert the copied component to the specified location in the drawing. To do so, choose the **Copy Component** tool from the **Edit Components** panel of the **Schematic** tab; you will be prompted to select the component to copy. Select the component to be copied; you will be prompted to specify the insertion point for the copied component. Specify the insertion point; the **Insert / Edit Component** dialog box will be displayed, as shown in Figure 6-7. The options in this dialog box have already been discussed in Chapter 5.

Next, enter the required values in this dialog box and choose the **OK** button; the values along with the copied component will be displayed in your drawing. If you do not change the values displayed in the **Insert / Edit Component** dialog box, the values of the original component will be transferred to the copied component. Also, the copied component will be retagged automatically and wire numbers will get updated accordingly.

**Note**

*1. If the selected component that you want to copy is a child component, the* ***Insert / Edit Child Component*** *dialog box will be displayed instead of the* ***Insert / Edit Component*** *dialog box.*

*2. You can also copy the components using the* ***COPY*** *command of AutoCAD, but in this case, the components will not get retagged and the wires will not get reconnected automatically.*

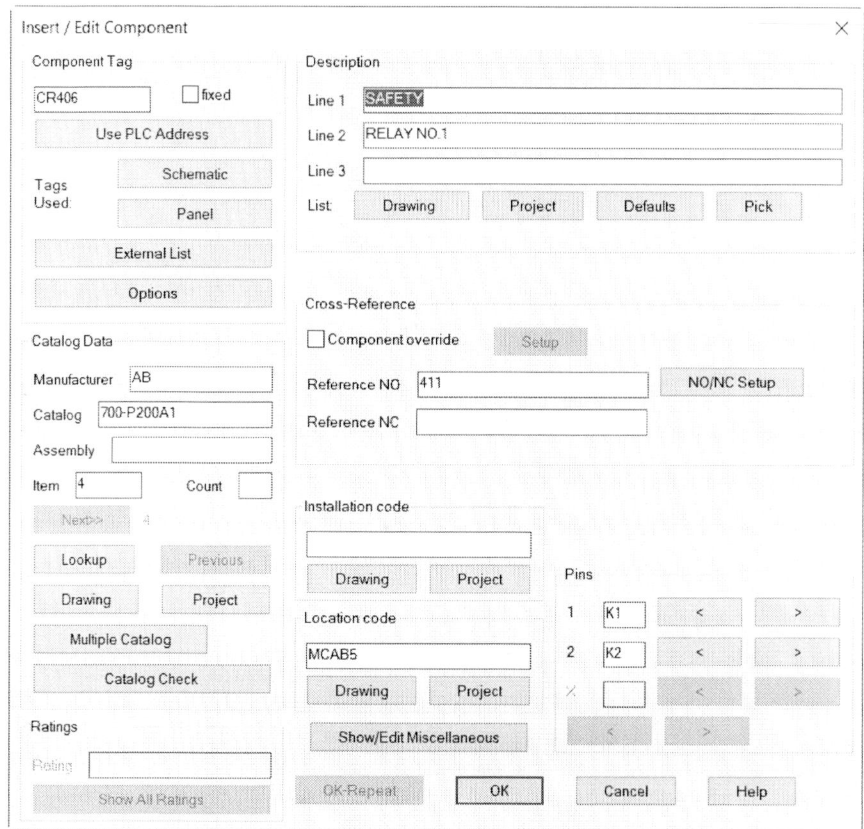


*Figure 6-7 The **Insert / Edit Component** dialog box*

# ALIGNING COMPONENTS

| | |
|---|---|
| **Ribbon:** | Schematic > Edit Components > Modify Components drop-down > Align |
| **Toolbar:** | ACE:Main Electrical > Scoot > Align or ACE:Scoot > Align |
| **Menu:** | Components > Align |
| **Command:** | AEALIGN |

The **Align** tool is used to line up components vertically or horizontally. To do so, choose the **Align** tool from the **Modify Components** drop-down in the **Edit Components** panel of the **Schematic** tab; you will be prompted to select the components to be aligned. Select the components; a temporary line passing through the center of the component will be displayed. This component is treated as the reference or master component with which you need to align the rest of the components that you select. Next, select the components to align with the master component and then press ENTER; all the selected components will be aligned to the master component.

Figure 6-8 (a) shows the components before alignment, Figure 6-8 (b) shows the master component along with a dashed line, and Figure 6-8 (c) shows the components after alignment.

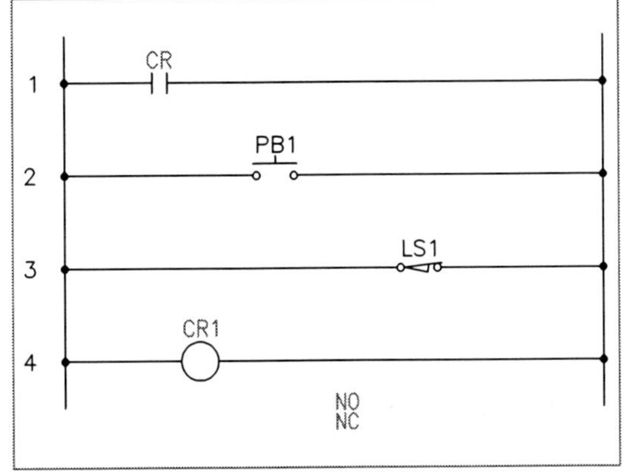


*Figure 6-8(a) Components before alignment*

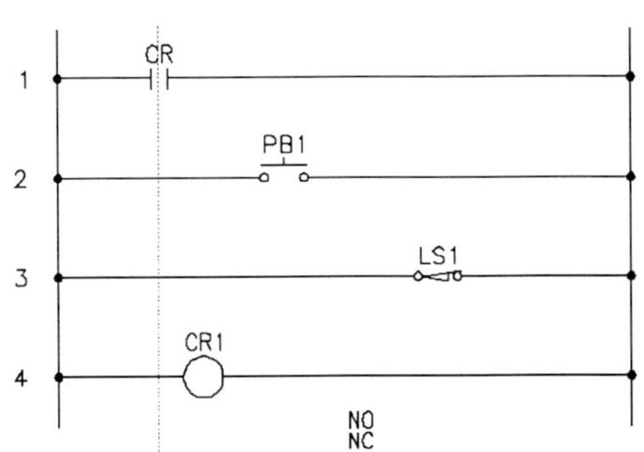


*Figure 6-8 (b) The master component along with a dashed line*

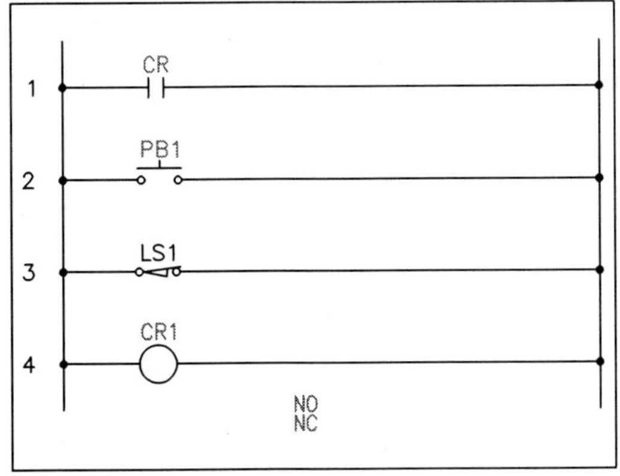


*Figure 6-8(c) Components after alignment*

# DELETING COMPONENTS

**Ribbon:** Schematic > Edit Components > Delete Component
**Toolbar:** ACE:Main Electrical > Delete Component
**Menu:** Components > Delete Component
**Command:** AEERASECOMP

The **Delete Component** tool is used to delete a component from the drawing. Also, after deleting the component, the wires get reconnected and the wire numbers get updated. To delete a component, choose the **Delete Component** tool from the **Edit Components** panel of the **Schematic** tab from the menu bar; you will be prompted to select components. Select the component(s) and press the ENTER key or right-click on the screen; the component(s) will be deleted.

If you select a parent component that has child contacts, the **Search for / Surf to Children?** dialog box will be displayed, as shown in Figure 6-9.

Choose the **No** button in the **Search for / Surf to Children?** dialog box to delete the component. If you choose the **OK** button, the **QSAVE** message box will be displayed, as shown in Figure 6-10.

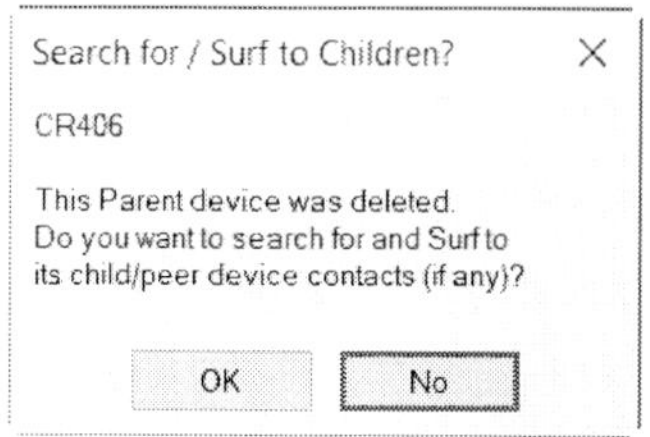


*Figure 6-9 The* ***Search for / Surf to Children?*** *dialog box*

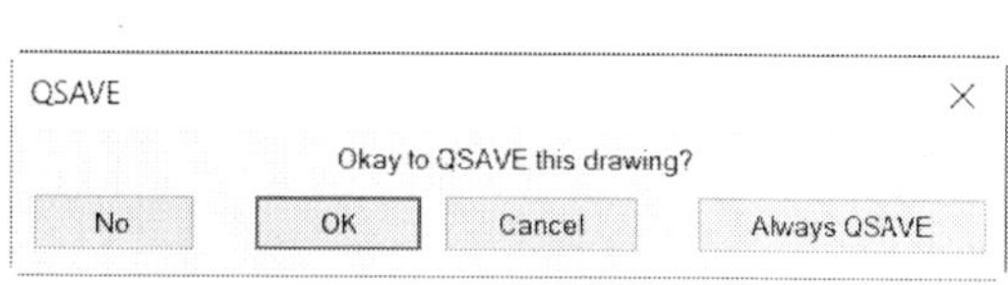


*Figure 6-10 The* ***QSAVE*** *message box*

Next, choose the **OK** button from the **QSAVE** message box; the active drawing will be saved. After choosing the **OK** button, the component will be deleted and the drawing will be updated. But if the selected component has its references in the current drawing and you choose the **OK** button in the **QSAVE** message box, the **Surf** dialog box will be displayed. The options in this dialog box are used to modify or delete the related components. The options in the **Surf** dialog box are discussed later in this chapter.

If you choose the **No** button from the **QSAVE** message box, the drawing will not be saved and the component will be deleted. But if the selected component has its references in the current drawing and you choose the **No** button in the **QSAVE** message box, the **Surf** dialog box will be displayed. The options in this dialog box are discussed in detail in the later section.

If you choose the **Always QSAVE** button, AutoCAD Electrical will save the active drawing for that session without displaying the **QSAVE** message box each time.

If you choose the **Cancel** button, the component will be deleted and the references of the component will not be displayed.

# UPDATING COMPONENTS FROM CATALOG DATABASE

| | |
|---|---|
| **Ribbon:** | Project > Other Tools > Component Update From Catalog |
| **Menu:** | Projects > Extras > Component Update From Catalog |
| **Command:** | AEUPDFROMCAT |

You have already learned in detail about assigning catalog values to a component from the catalog database in Chapter 5. If these values are changed later in the catalog database, you can update them using the **Component Update From Catalog** tool. You can create two reports using this feature: Error Exception Report and Components Updated From Catalog Report. To generate these reports, choose the **Component Update From Catalog** tool from the **Other Tools** panel of the **Project** tab; the **Component Update From Catalog** dialog box will be displayed, as shown in Figure 6-11. The options in this dialog box that are used to generate these two reports are discussed next.

## Update Components on Area

Select the **Project** radio button in this area and choose **OK**; the **Select Drawing to Process** dialog box will be displayed. Select the drawings for which you want updates for the component catalog values and choose the **Process** button; the selected drawings will be transferred from the top list to the bottom list of this dialog box. Next, choose **OK** from this dialog box; the **Error Exception Report** dialog box will be displayed, refer to Figure 6-12. This dialog box contains three columns: **Component**, **Location**, and **Comment** in which the list of exceptions, if any, are displayed for the selected drawings. It also includes all pinlist updates for surfing the child contacts. You can then manually update the child contacts per drawing. When you choose the **Components** button at the bottom left of this dialog box, the **Components Updated From Catalog Report** dialog box is displayed. This dialog box provides the details of the component name, its location, data updated, previous data, and current data per drawing, as shown in Figure 6-13.

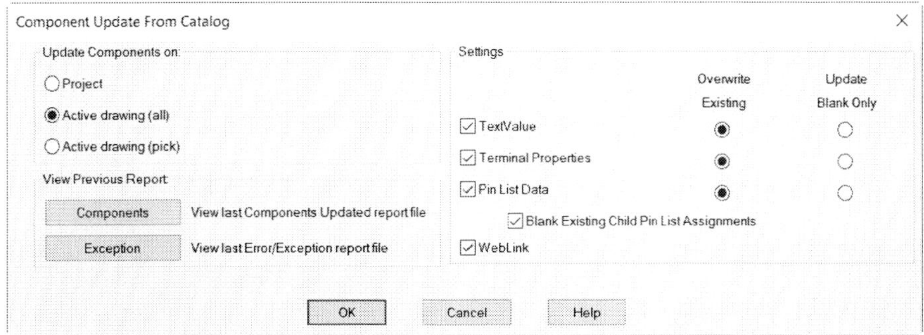


*Figure 6-11 The* ***Component Update From Catalog*** *dialog box*

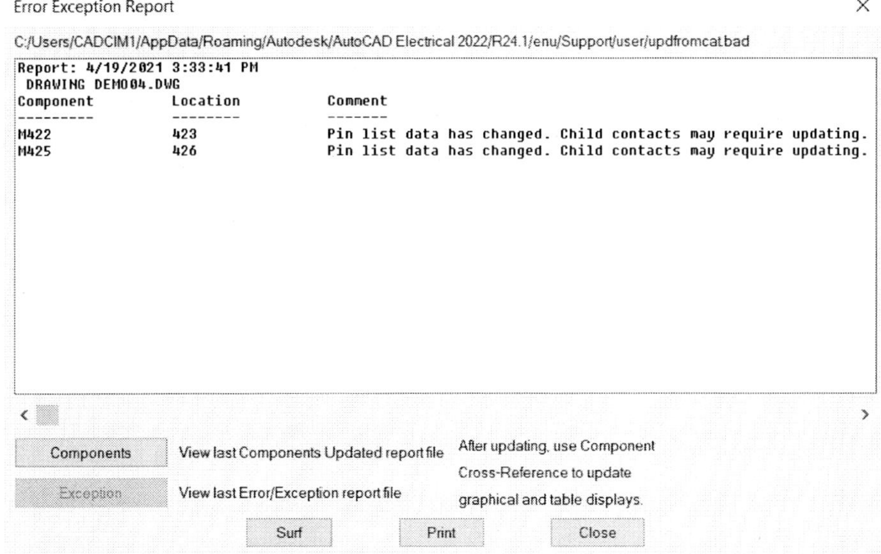


*Figure 6-12 The* ***Error Exception Report*** *dialog box*

Choose the **Surf** button; the **Surf** dialog box will be displayed. The options in this dialog box are discussed in detail in the later section. You can also print the data by choosing the **Print** button.

When you select the **Active drawing(all)** radio button and then choose **OK** in the **Component Update From Catalog** dialog box, an error exception report only for the active drawing is displayed in the **Error Exception Report** dialog box. Similarly, if you choose the **Components** button in this dialog box, the **Components Updated From Catalog Report** dialog box will be displayed. It provides the details of the component name, its location, data updated, previous data, and current data for the active drawing only.

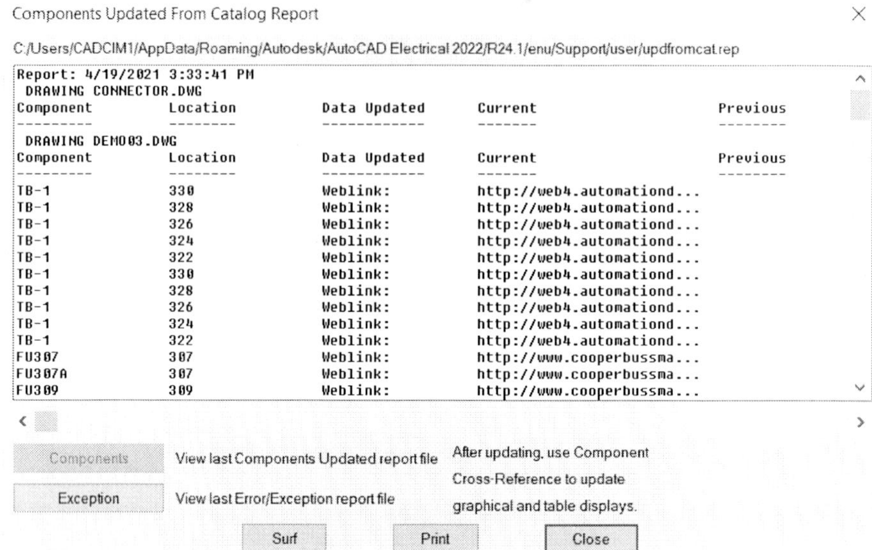


*Figure 6-13 The **Components Updated From Catalog Report** dialog box*

Select the **Active drawing(pick)** radio button if you want to get the error exception report and component updation report for a specific component.

## View Previous Report Area

In this area, choose the **Components** button to view the report of the component updates from the previous use of this feature. Similarly, choose the **Exception** button to view the previous exception report.

## Settings Area

The options in this area are discussed next.

### TextValue

By default, the **TextValue** check box is selected. As a result, the attribute values assigned by the current TextValue are updated in the catalog database for the catalog number. These values overwrite the existing values as the **Overwrite Existing** radio button next to this check box is selected by default. If you want to retain the existing values, you can select the **Update Blank Only** radio button.

### Terminal Properties

By default, the **Terminal Properties** check box is selected. As a result, the terminal properties are updated on the terminal to match the value in the catalog database for the assigned catalog number. Note that the related terminals on other drawings are also updated to keep consistency in all the terminals. If you want to retain the existing values, you can select the **Update Blank Only** radio button.

### Pin List Data

By default, the **Pin List Data** check box is selected. As a result, pinlist value on the schematic parent is updated so as to match the value in the catalog database for the assigned catalog number. If you want to retain the existing values, you can select the **Update Blank Only** radio button. Note that the child contact pins are not updated here. Make sure that the **Blank Existing Child Pin Assignments** radio button below this check box is selected so that the manual pin assignment becomes easier. Also, note that when you choose the **Surf** button in the **Error Exception Report** dialog box, the **Surf** dialog box is displayed. This dialog box provides the list of child contacts of the parents for which the pinlist data is updated.

### WebLink

If you select this check box, weblink value of the component is updated to match the value in the catalog database for the assigned catalog number.

## UPDATING A SCHEMATIC COMPONENT FROM A ONE-LINE COMPONENT

You can update a schematic component from a one-line component. In other words, you can copy information such as descriptions, catalog values, installation/location codes, and so on from a one-line component to a schematic component. To do so, choose the **Edit** tool from the **Edit Components** drop-down in the **Edit Components** panel of the **Schematic** tab and select the schematic component to be updated from the active drawing; the **Insert/Edit Component** dialog box will be displayed. In this dialog box, choose the **Schematic** button from the **Component Tag** area; the **XX Tags in Use** dialog box will be displayed. Note that **XX** stands for the schematic component to be updated. In this dialog box, select the **Show one-line components (1-*)** check box from the **Show** area; one-line components will be displayed along with the other components, refer to Figure 6-14.

Next, select the desired one-line component from the list. Also, select the check boxes in the **Copy** area based on the requirement and choose the **Copy Tag** button; the **Copy Tag** dialog box will be displayed, refer to Figure 6-15. Choose the **OK** button from this dialog box; the **Copy Tag** dialog box will disappear and the **Insert/Edit Component** dialog box will be displayed with the updated values of the schematic component. Choose the **OK** button in this dialog box to update the schematic component from a one-line component.

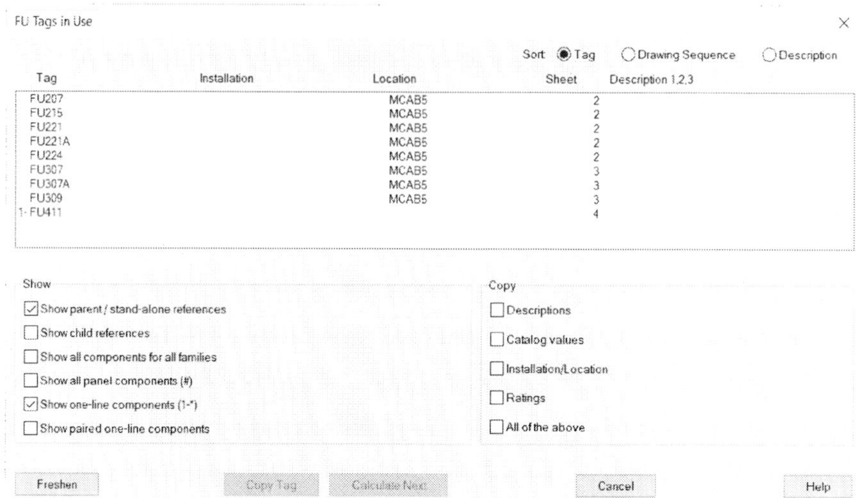


*Figure 6-14 The **FU Tags in Use** dialog box*

The **Show paired one-line components** check box is available in the **Show** area of the **XX Tags in Use** dialog box. You need to select this check box along with the **Show one-line components (1-*)** check box and the **Show parent / stand-alone references** check box to show pair of matching one-line components with schematic or panel component.

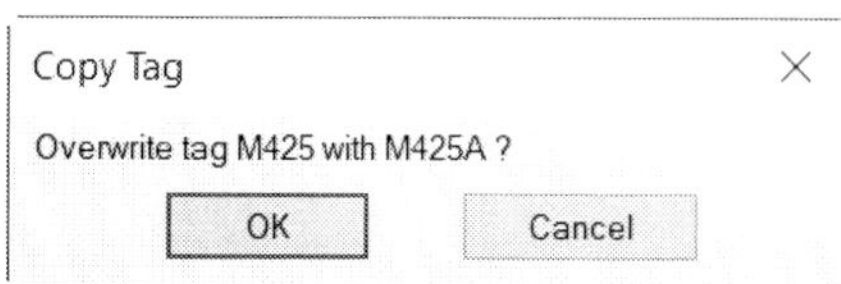


*Figure 6-15 The **Copy Tag** dialog box*

# SURFING A REFERENCE

| | |
|---|---|
| **Ribbon:** | Project > Other Tools > Surfer drop-down >Surfer |
| **Toolbar:** | ACE:Main Electrical 2 > Surfer or ACE:Surfer |
| **Menu:** | Projects > Surfer |
| **Command:** | AESURF |

The **Surfer** tool is used to search the related references of a component, wire number, terminal, cables, and signal. Using this tool, you can move from one reference to another across the drawings of a project. This tool is also used to search component tag, wire number, item number or catalog number. To search the related references of a component, choose the **Surfer** tool from the **Other Tools** panel of the **Project** tab; you will be prompted to select the tag for surfer trace. Select the component or the component tag; the **Surf** dialog box will be displayed, as shown in Figure 6-16.

This dialog box displays the name of component, manufacturer code, and catalog number of the selected component at the top. Different options in this dialog box are discussed next.

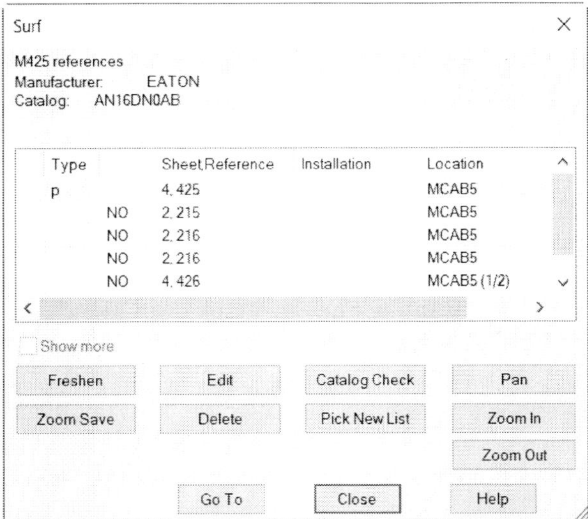


*Figure 6-16 The **Surf** dialog box*

## Type

Different codes for different type of symbols are displayed in the **Type** column. These codes are:

c - Component symbol
p - Parent symbol or one-line symbol. Note that in case of one-line symbol, '1-' will be displayed in the **Category** column in the **Surf** dialog box
t - Terminal symbol
w - Wire number
# - Panel symbol
#np - Panel nameplate
Dst - Destination arrow
Src - Source arrow

## Sheet,Reference

This column displays the sheet number and line reference number of the component.

## Installation

This column displays the installation value of the selected component.

## Location

This column displays the location value of the selected component.

## Category

The category of the selected component is displayed in the **Category** column such as '1-' in case of one-line symbols.

## Show more

The **Show more** check box will be activated only when you are in the IEC tagging mode, or if any non-installation/location matching references are not present. Select this check box to display extra non-installation/location matching reference if you are using the IEC tagging mode. By default, the **Show more** check box is clear. As a result, only the exact surf matches in the list will be displayed.

## Freshen

The **Freshen** button is used to refresh the **Surf** dialog box with the changes made in the active drawing. To refresh the **Surf** dialog box, select a reference from the list displayed and choose the **Freshen** button; the **QSAVE** message box will be displayed. Next, choose the **OK** button in the **QSAVE** message box to save the changes made in the drawing; the **Surf** dialog box will be displayed again. If you choose the **NO** button from the **QSAVE** message box, the active drawing will not be saved and the **Surf** dialog box will be displayed again.

## Edit

The **Edit** button is used to edit the selected reference. On choosing this button, the **Insert / Edit Component** dialog box will be displayed. Using this dialog box, you can edit references. The options in the **Insert / Edit Component** dialog box have been discussed in the earlier chapters.

## Catalog Check

The **Catalog Check** button will be activated only if the reference has catalog and manufacturer information added to it. This button is used to display the Bill of Material of the selected reference.

## Pan

The **Pan** button allows you to view the portion of the drawing that is outside the current display area.

**Note**

*When the **Tool Palettes** is docked, the **Pan** button does not work.*

## Zoom Save

The **Zoom Save** button is used to save the current zoom factor on the WD_M block of the drawing. To do so, choose the **Zoom Save** button; the Command prompt will display "**Surf zoom factor saved on WD_M block**".

## Zoom In

Choose the **Zoom In** button to double the size of the drawing.

## Zoom Out

Choose the **Zoom Out** button to decrease the size of the drawing by half.

## Pick New List

The **Pick New List** button is used to select a new component to surf.

## Go To

Choose the **Go To** button to go to the reference of the selected component. This button zooms the selected component. If the component is in a different drawing, the drawing that is opened will be saved and other drawing where the component is located will be opened and the selected component will be zoomed. Also note that when you select the reference from the list displayed and choose the **Go To** button, the selected reference will be zoomed and in the **Surf** dialog box, 'x' will be displayed in the left of the **Type** column.

## Close

Choose the **Close** button to close the **Surf** dialog box.

**Note**

*If you select the source or destination symbols in the drawing using the **Surfer** tool, then the **Surf** dialog box will look a little different. However, the options will remain the same.*

# TOGGLING BETWEEN NORMALLY OPEN AND NORMALLY CLOSED CONTACTS

| | |
|---|---|
| **Ribbon:** | Schematic > Edit Components > Toggle NO/NC |
| **Toolbar:** | ACE:Main Electrical > Toggle NO/NC |
| **Menu:** | Components > Toggle NO/NC |
| **Command:** | AETOGGLENONC |

The **Toggle NO/NC** tool is used to toggle contacts from normally open to normally closed and vice-versa. In other words, this tool is used to flip contacts from one state to another (open/closed). To toggle between contacts, choose the **Toggle NO/NC** tool from the **Edit Components** panel of the **Schematic** tab; you will be prompted to select the component to toggle NO/NC. Select the component; you will notice that if the component is normally open (NO), it will change to normally closed (NC) and vice versa. Also, the attribute information will be extracted from the selected component and the component data will be copied onto the replacement symbol. The command will continue till you press ENTER or right-click on the screen.

Figures 6-17 (a) and 6-17 (b) show the contacts of components before and after toggling.

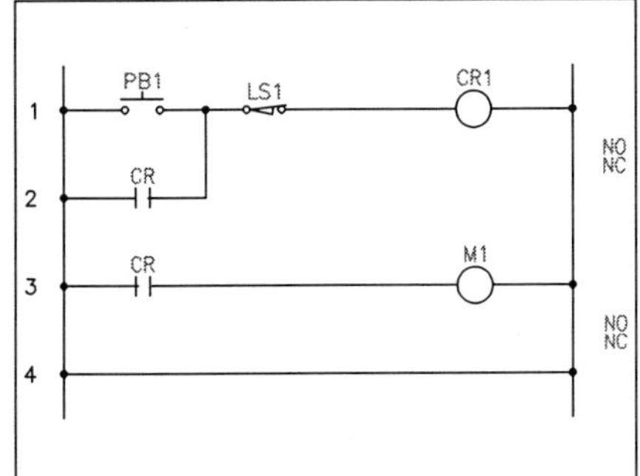


***Figure 6-17(a)*** *Contacts of components before toggling*

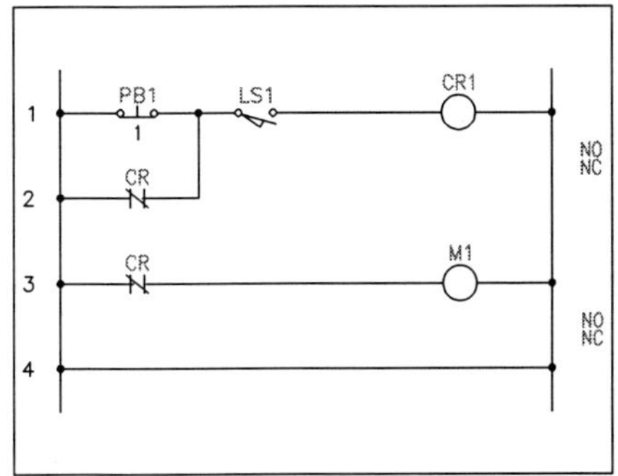


***Figure 6-17(b)*** *Contacts of components after toggling*

# COPYING THE CATALOG ASSIGNMENT

**Ribbon:** Schematic > Edit Component > Edit Components drop-down > Copy Catalog Assignment
**Toolbar:** ACE:Main Electrical > Edit Component > Copy Catalog Assignment or ACE:Edit Component > Copy Catalog Assignment
**Menu:** Components > Component Miscellaneous > Copy Catalog Assignment
**Command:** AECOPYCAT

The **Copy Catalog Assignment** tool is used to copy the catalog part numbers from one component to another. Also, this tool is used to insert or edit the catalog data of the selected component or footprint. This tool helps in assigning the same catalog information to multiple components. To copy manufacturer, catalog, assembly, and multiple catalog attributes from one component to other selected components, choose the **Copy Catalog Assignment** tool from the **Edit Components** drop-down in the **Edit Components** panel of the **Schematic** tab, as shown in Figure 6-18; you will be prompted to select the master component. Select the component to be treated as master component; the **Copy Catalog Assignment** dialog box will be displayed, as shown in Figure 6-19. This dialog box displays the catalog data of the selected component.

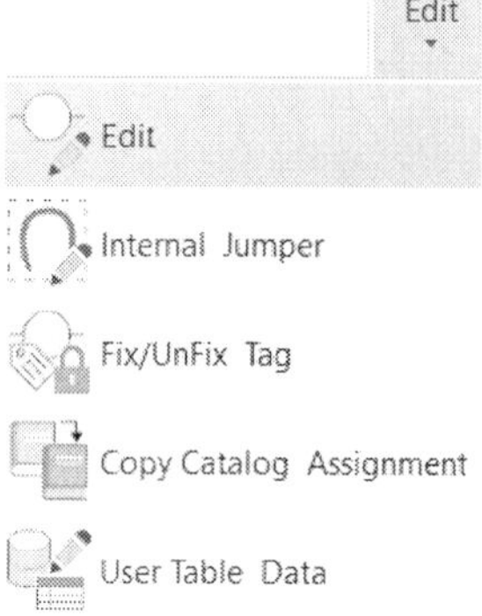


*Figure 6-18 The **Edit Components** drop-down*

**Note**

*If the catalog assignment is not assigned to the master component, the **Copy Catalog Assignment** dialog box will not display any catalog data. Also, if you want to modify the catalog assignment both for the master and child components, choose the **Catalog Lookup** button from the **Copy Catalog Assignment** dialog box. On doing so, the **Catalog Browser** dialog box will be displayed. Next, select the desired catalog information and then choose the **OK** button from this dialog box; the catalog data will be assigned to the selected component.*

Copy Catalog Assignment
Manufacturer BUSSMANN
Catalog FRS-R-5
Assembly
Catalog Lookup
Find: Drawing Only
Multiple Catalog
Catalog Check
Step 1: Select part number information. Select OK
Step 2: Select devices to copy to.
Note: child or related devices are not automatically updated. They must be included in the selection.
OK
Cancel

*Figure 6-19 The **Copy Catalog Assignment** dialog box*

The options in the **Copy Catalog Assignment** dialog box are discussed next.

## Manufacturer

In the **Manufacturer** edit box, the manufacturer data of the master component is displayed. You can edit the manufacturer data or enter new data by choosing the **Catalog Lookup** button, which is discussed later in this chapter.

## Catalog

The **Catalog** edit box displays the catalog data of the master component. If it is not displayed, you can enter it by choosing the **Catalog Lookup** button and then selecting the desired catalog.

## Assembly

The **Assembly** edit box is used to display the assembly code of the master component.

## Catalog Lookup

Choose the **Catalog Lookup** button from the **Copy Catalog Assignment** dialog box; the **Catalog Browser** dialog box will be displayed, which has been discussed in the previous chapters. Select the catalog information from the **Catalog Browser** dialog box for the master component and choose the **OK** button; the catalog information will be displayed in the **Manufacturer** and **Catalog** edit boxes.

## Find: Drawing Only

The **Find: Drawing Only** button is used to search the symbols of the same family block name within the active drawing. To do so, choose the **Find: Drawing Only** button from the **Copy Catalog Assignment** dialog box; the **xx catalog values (this drawing)** dialog box will be displayed. Note that **xx** stands for the family block name. This dialog box displays catalog information of the symbols of the same family type. Select the catalog values from this dialog box and choose **OK**; the values will be displayed in the **Manufacturer** and **Catalog** edit boxes of the **Copy Catalog Assignment** dialog box.

## Multiple Catalog

The **Multiple Catalog** button is used to add extra catalog information to the selected component. Also, this button is used to verify the catalog information. To add extra catalog information, choose the **Multiple Catalog** button; the **Multiple Bill of Material Information** dialog box will be displayed. In this dialog box, you can add extra catalog information. You can add up to 99 additional part numbers to any schematic or panel component. Specify the required options in this dialog box and then choose the **OK** button to return to the **Copy Catalog Assignment** dialog box; the extra catalog assignment will be displayed adjacent to the **Multiple Catalog** button.

## Catalog Check

The **Catalog Check** button is used to check for the catalog information of the selected component. To do so, choose the **Catalog Check** button; the **Bill Of Material Check** dialog box will be displayed. It displays the Bill Of Material of the master component.

After specifying the options in the **Copy Catalog Assignment** dialog box, choose the **OK** button; you will be prompted to pick the target component(s). Select the target component(s) and press ENTER; the catalog information will be copied to the target component(s). If the target component consists of catalog data different from the master component, the **Different symbol block names** dialog box will be displayed, as shown in Figure 6-20. If you choose the **OK** button, the **Caution: Existing Data on Target** dialog box will be displayed, as shown in Figure 6-21. Different options in this dialog box are discussed next.

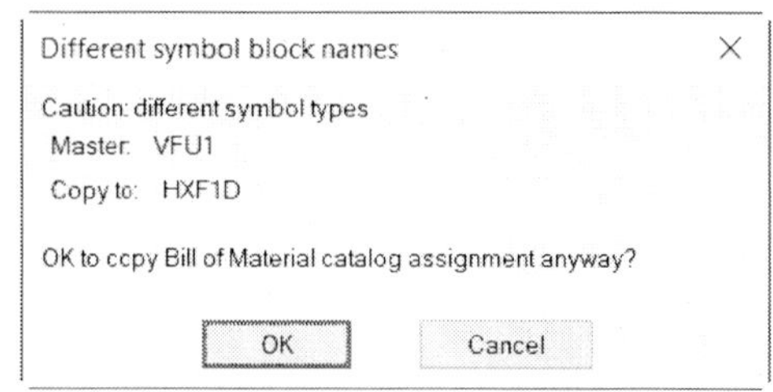


*Figure 6-20 The **Different symbol block names** dialog box*

The **Catalog Check** button is used to display the catalog information of the master and target component(s).

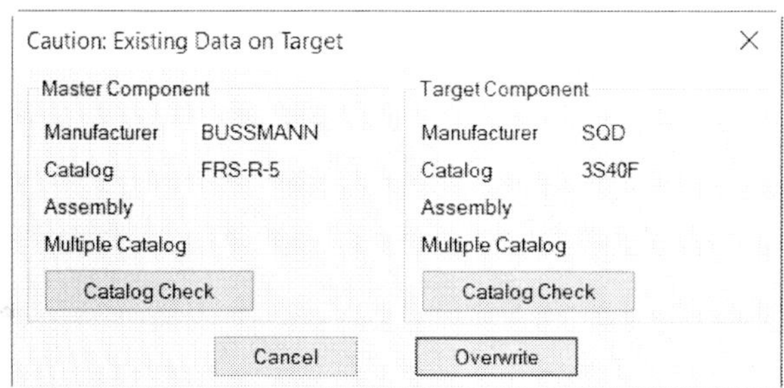


*Figure 6-21 The **Caution: Existing Data on Target** dialog box*

To overwrite the catalog information of the master component to the target component(s), choose the **Overwrite** button; the catalog information of the master component will be applied to the target component(s). But if the target component has its child contacts or references, then after choosing the **Overwrite** button, the **Update Related Components?** message box will be displayed. In this message box, choose the **Yes-Update** button; the related components will be updated. Choose the **Skip** button to skip the update of the related components.

# EDITING USER TABLE DATA RECORDS

| | |
|---|---|
| **Ribbon:** | Schematic > Edit Components > User Table Data |
| **Toolbar:** | ACE:Edit Component > Edit User Table Data |
| **Menu:** | Components > Component Miscellaneous > Edit User Table Data |
| **Command:** | AEUSERTABLE |

The **Edit User Table Data** tool is used to add user data records or edit the existing user data records in the user database table of the project database file. To add or edit the user table data, choose the **User Table Data** tool from the **Edit Components** drop-down in the **Edit Components** panel of the **Schematic** tab, refer to Figure 6-18; you will be prompted to select a component. Select the component; the **Edit User Table Data** dialog box will be displayed, as shown in Figure 6-22. If the user data records are available for the selected component, these records will be displayed in this dialog box. You can select the record to edit or delete it. To add a new record, choose the **Add New** button; the **Add New USER data record** dialog box will be displayed, as shown in Figure 6-23. In this dialog box, enter the new record information in the **Data** edit box and choose the **OK** button; the new record will be added to the user database table and it will also be displayed in the **Edit User Table Data** dialog box.

Edit User Table Data

Add/Edit/Remove free-form user data records attached to the selected block insert.
These records are stored in a USER database table in the project database file.

Select existing record to edit or "Add new" to create a new record.

Record Number Data (255 char max per record)

No existing USER data records found on this block insert.
Select "Add new" to add a new record.

Add New | Delete Record

Save Changes | Cancel | Wide> | Help

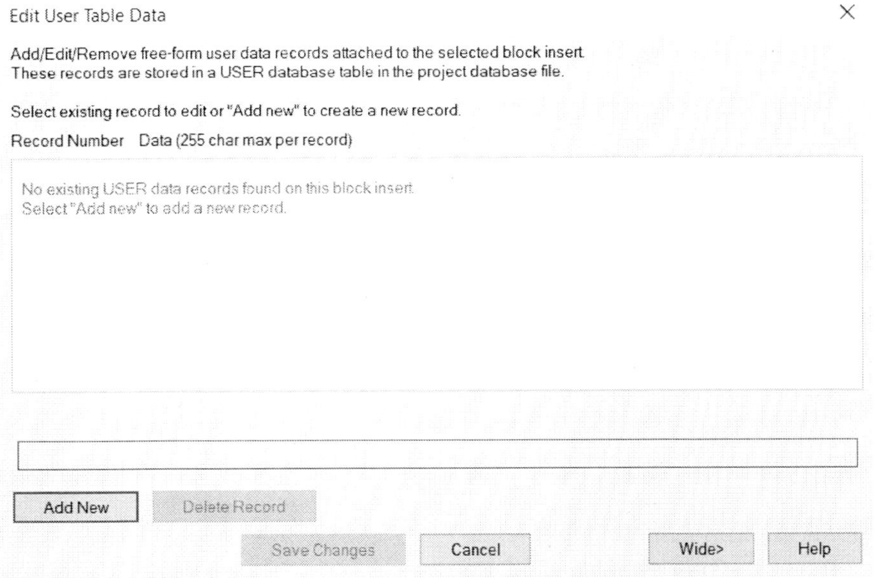

*Figure 6-22 The **Edit User Table Data** dialog box*

Add New USER data record

Enter record data in the edit box (255 characters max).
The record number is a three digit number between 000 and 199.
The next available number will pre-fill the Record number edit box.

Record Number 000

Data

OK | Cancel

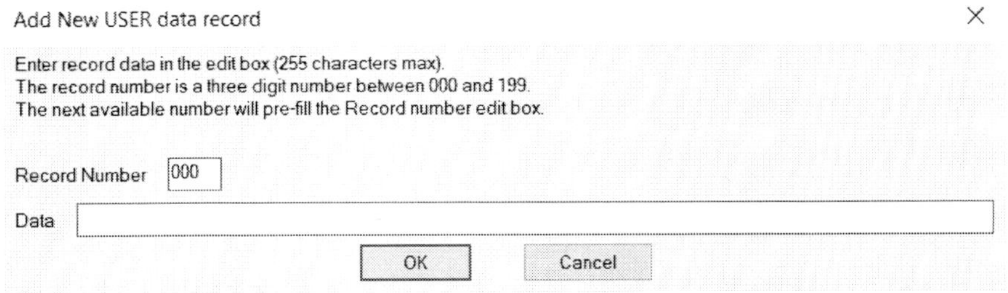

*Figure 6-23 The **Add New USER data record** dialog box*

# COPYING INSTALLATION/LOCATION CODE VALUES

| | |
|---|---|
| **Ribbon:** | Schematic > Edit Components > Copy Installation/Location Code Values |
| **Toolbar:** | ACE:Main Electrical 2 > Location Symbols drop-down> Copy Installation/Location Code Values or ACE:Location Symbols > Copy Installation/Location Code Values |
| **Menu:** | Components > Component Tagging > Copy Installation/Location Code Values |
| **Command:** | AECOPYINSTLOC |

The **Copy Installation/Location Code Values** tool is used to copy the installation and location code assignments from one component to another. To do so, choose the **Copy Installation/Location Code Values** tool from the **Edit Components** panel of the **Schematic** tab; the **Copy Installation/Location to Components** dialog box will be displayed, as shown in Figure 6-24. Different options in this dialog box are discussed next.

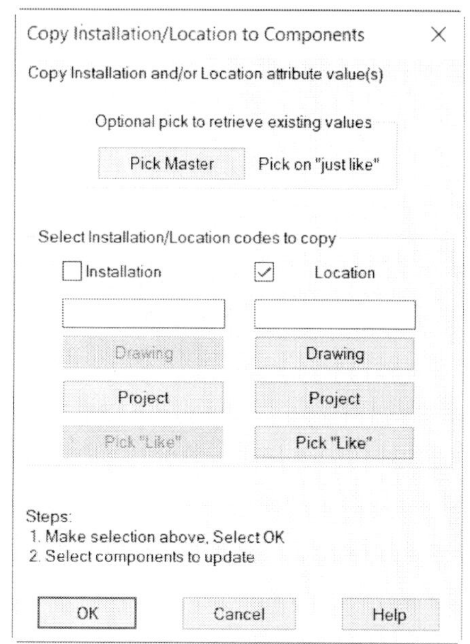


*Figure 6-24 The* ***Copy Installation/Location to Components*** *dialog box*

## Pick Master

The **Pick Master** button is used to select the master component from where the attributes will be copied. To select the master component, choose the **Pick Master** button; the **Copy Installation/Location to Components** dialog box will disappear and you will be prompted to select the master component to get the installation and location values. Select the component from the drawing; the **Copy Installation/Location to Components** dialog box will be displayed again with the installation and location values of the selected component.

## Select Installation/Location codes to copy Area

The options in this area are used to copy the installation and location codes on the selected component that you will select. These options are discussed next.

### Installation

Select the **Installation** check box; the edit box below this check box as well as the **Drawing** and the **Pick "Like"** buttons will be activated. Next, enter the installation code that you want to copy from the master component to the other components in the edit box.

### Drawing

The **Drawing** button is used to display the list of installation codes present in the active drawing.

### Project

The **Project** button is used to display the list of installation codes present in the active project.

### Pick "Like"

The **Pick "Like"** button is used to select the component from where installation values are copied.

### Location

The **Location** check box is selected by default. As a result, the edit box below this check box as well as the **Drawing**, **Project**, and **Pick "Like"** buttons are active. Enter the location code that you want to copy from the master component in the edit box below the **Location** check box.

### Drawing

The **Drawing** button is used to display the list of location codes present in the active drawing.

### Project

The **Project** button is used to display the list of location codes present in the active project.

### Pick "Like"

The **Pick "Like"** button is used to select the component from where the location values will be copied. To do so, choose the **Pick "Like"** button; you will be prompted to select the component to get the location code. Select the component; the location code will be displayed in the edit box, which is below the **Location** check box.

After specifying the required options in the **Copy Installation/Location to Components** dialog box, choose the **OK** button; you will be prompted to select components. Select the component(s) to copy the installation/location values and press ENTER; the installation/location values will be copied to the selected component.

**Note**

*AutoCAD Electrical does not show any warning if you overwrite existing installation and location codes.*

# AUDITING DRAWINGS

The auditing tools are used to check errors in the project. These tools help in troubleshooting and improving the accuracy of a drawing. There are two auditing tools: **Electrical Audit** and **Drawing Audit**. These tools are discussed next.

## Electrical Auditing

| | |
|---|---|
| **Ribbon:** | Reports > Schematic > Electrical Audit |
| **Toolbar:** | ACE:Main Electrical 2 > Schematic Reports > Electrical Audit<br>or ACE:Schematic Reports > Electrical Audit |
| **Menu:** | Projects > Reports > Electrical Audit |
| **Command:** | AEAUDIT |

The **Electrical Audit** tool is used to find out the problems that affect the drawings of a project. This tool can be used to correct some of the errors in drawings. To find errors, choose the **Electrical Audit** tool from the **Schematic** panel of the **Reports** tab; the **Electrical Audit** dialog box will be displayed, refer to Figure 6-25. The progress of the electrical audit will be displayed in the edit box. Once the audit is finished, the edit box will display the total number of errors that occurred in the active project. In this dialog box, the **Project** radio button is selected by default. As a result, the total number of errors found in the active project will be displayed in the edit box of the **Electrical Audit** dialog box. If you select the **Active Drawing** radio button, then the total number of errors found in the active drawing will be displayed in the edit box. This dialog box also displays the date and time of the electrical audit report.

The **Details** button is used to view errors as well as to expand or collapse the **Electrical Audit** dialog box. To view errors, choose the **Details** button; the **Electrical Audit** dialog box will expand and display detailed information about the errors found in the project, refer to Figure 6-26. If you choose this button again, the **Electrical Audit** dialog box will collapse, refer to Figure 6-25.

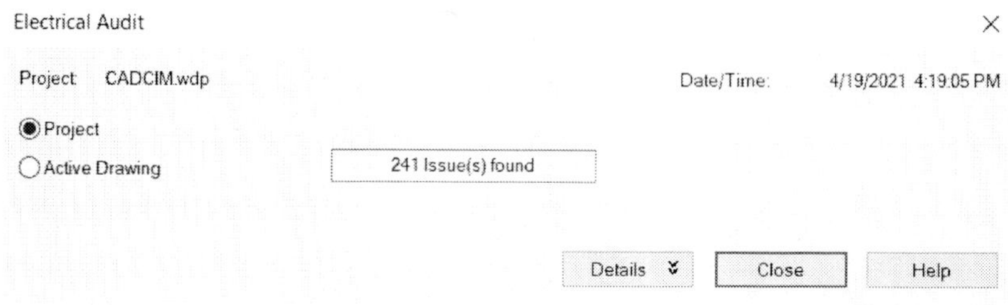


***Figure 6-25** The **Electrical Audit** dialog box*

***Figure 6-26** The expanded **Electrical Audit** dialog box displaying errors on choosing the **Details** button*

**Note**

*If the active drawing is not a part of the active project, then the **Active Drawing** radio button will not be activated in the **Electrical Audit** dialog box.*

*If errors are not found in a project or active drawing, then the **Details** button in the **Electrical Audit** dialog box will not be activated.*

The expanded **Electrical Audit** dialog box has ten different tabs. If the tab has a red circle and a white 'x', it means an error is present in that category. To view the errors present in a tab, choose the tab; the information about the errors will be displayed in the lower part of the **Electrical Audit** dialog box.

Different tabs and buttons in the **Electrical Audit** dialog box are discussed next.

## Wire - No Connection

By default, the **Wire - No Connection** tab is chosen in the **Electrical Audit** dialog box. This tab displays the disconnected wires that are found in the project. The report list below this tab consists of disconnected wire number, error message, drawing, and the location point where an error occurs. If the wire number record is not found in the drawings of a project, the **Wire Number** column will be blank.

## Wire Exception

The **Wire Exception** tab displays the missing or the duplicated wire numbers that are found in an active project.

## Cable Exception

The **Cable Exception** tab displays the duplicated cable and the wire ID's that are found in an active project.

## Component - No Catalog Number

The **Component - No Catalog Number** tab displays the components that have no catalog data.

## Component Duplication

The **Component Duplication** tab displays the duplicated schematic/panel components.

## Component - No Connection

The **Component - No Connection** tab displays the component connections with disconnected wires.

**Note**

*For a schematic component, the corresponding field in the **Category** column is blank.*

## Mixed Component Network

The **Mixed Component Network** tab displays components in a wire network that consists of components of different types such as one-line symbols, schematic symbols, and so on. To view the mixed components in a wire network, choose the **Mixed Component Network** tab; the report list will be displayed containing the tag name of the component (from/to), component type (from/to), error message, and the name of the drawing (from/to) where an error occurs.

## Terminal Duplication

The **Terminal Duplication** tab displays the duplicated schematic terminal numbers.

## Pin Exception

The **Pin Exception** tab displays the pin assignments of a component that has been duplicated.

## Contacts

The **Contacts** tab displays a child component without a parent.

## Recovery Tip

The **Recovery Tip** area at the bottom of the **Electrical Audit** dialog box displays the recovery tip to fix an error in the drawing.

## Mark as Ignored

The **Mark as Ignored** button will be activated when you select an error from the list. To mark the selected errror as 'Ignored, select the error and then choose the **Mark as Ignored** button; the status for this error will be changed to 'Ignored' in the **Status** column.

## Mark as Issue

The **Mark as Issue** button will be activated when you select the error from the list. To mark the errror as 'Issue', select the error and then choose the **Mark as Issue** button; the status for this error will be changed to 'Issue' in **Status** column.

## Hide Ignored Issue

The **Hide Ignored Issue** check box is used to remove the enries which are marked as 'Ignored' from the list.

## Go To

The **Go To** button takes you to an error location within the project and corrects the error. To go to an error location, select the error from the report list displayed in the **Electrical Audit** dialog box and then choose the **Go To** button. Alternatively, double-click on the error displayed in the **Electrical Audit** dialog box; the current drawing will be saved. Also, the drawing that contains the selected error will be opened and the selected component will be zoomed and highlighted. As the component gets highlighted, it is easier to identify the object with error. Now, you can edit the selected component without closing the **Electrical Audit** dialog box. To do so, right-click on the selected component in the drawing area; a marking menu will be displayed. Choose the required component editing option from the marking menu; the corresponding editing dialog box will be displayed. In this dialog box, specify the required options and then choose the **OK** button to exit the dialog box. Once you go through an error location, an 'x' will appear in the extreme left column of the **Electrical Audit** dialog box.

## Export Tab

The **Export Tab** button is used to save the errors in the active tab of the audit report to a text file.

## Export All

The **Export All** button is used to save the errors of all the tabs of the audit report to a text file.

## Print

The **Print** button is used to print an audit report. On choosing this button, the **Print** dialog box will be displayed, as shown in Figure 6-27. Select the name of the printer from the **Name** drop-down list and then choose the **OK** button; the audit report will be printed.

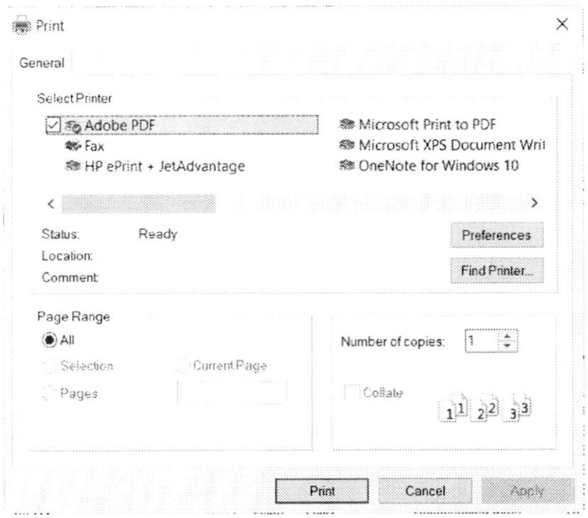


*Figure 6-27 The **Print** dialog box*

# Auditing a Drawing

| | |
|---|---|
| **Ribbon:** | Reports > Schematic > DWG Audit |
| **Toolbar:** | ACE:Main Electrical 2 > Schematic Reports > Drawing Audit<br>or ACE:Schematic Reports > Drawing Audit |
| **Menu:** | Projects > Reports > Drawing Audit |
| **Command:** | AEAUDITDWG |

The **DWG Audit** tool is used to find out the problems in wiring that affect the wire connectivity of a design. Using this tool, you can audit a single drawing or multiple drawings in a project. The auditing of a drawing is performed to check for wire gaps, wire number, color, zero length wires, gauge labels, and wire number floaters for errors, and so on. To find out errors in wires and to rectify them, choose the **DWG Audit** tool from the **Schematic** panel of the **Reports** tab; the **Drawing Audit** dialog box will be displayed, as shown in Figure 6-28. Different options in the **Drawing Audit** dialog box are discussed next.

The **Audit drawing or project** area consists of two radio buttons: **Active drawing** and **Project**. These radio buttons are discussed next.

## Auditing an Active Drawing

The **Active drawing** radio button is selected by default and is used to audit an active drawing only. Choose the **OK** button from the **Drawing Audit** dialog box; the modified **Drawing Audit** dialog box will be displayed, as shown in Figure 6-29. The options in the modified **Drawing Audit** dialog box are discussed next.

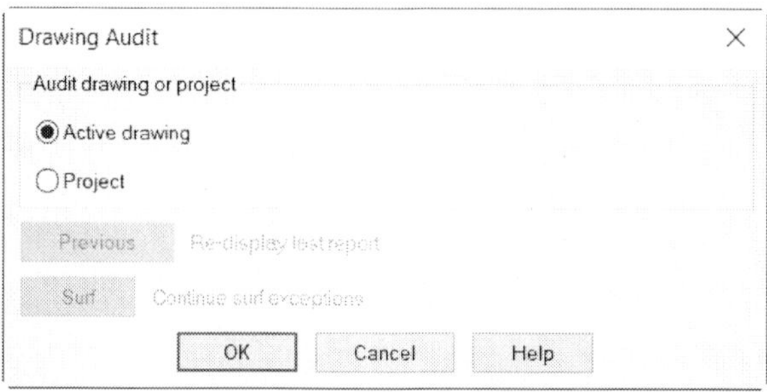


*Figure 6-28 The **Drawing Audit** dialog box*

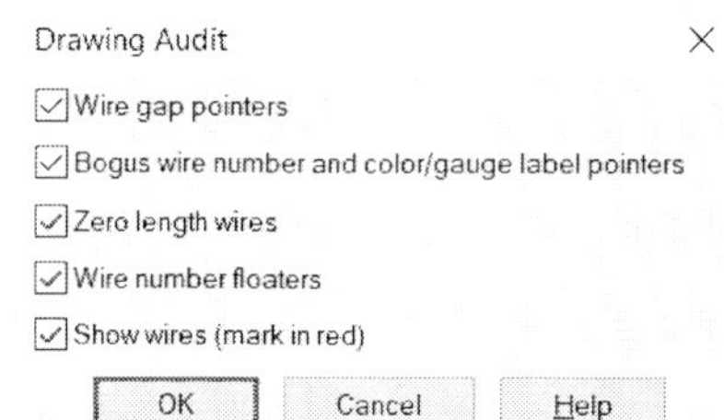


*Figure 6-29 The modified **Drawing Audit** dialog box*

#### Wire gap pointers

This check box is used to find out the problems related to the missing wires that were connected through gap pointers.

#### Bogus wire number and color/gauge label pointers

This check box is used to check for and clean up the wires that have non-existent wire numbers. Also, this check box is used to check for bad color/gauge label pointers.

#### Zero length wires

This check box is used to check and erase the zero length line entities present on a wire layer.

#### Wire number floaters

This check box is used to check and erase the wire numbers that are not linked to a wire network.

#### Show wires (mark in red)

This check box is used to display a red outline around each wire entity and magenta outline around the wires defined on the no wire numbering layers. This check box will be activated only if you select the **Active drawing** radio button from the **Drawing Audit** dialog box.

After specifying the options in the modified **Drawing Audit** dialog box, choose the **OK** button; the **Drawing Audit** message box will be displayed, as shown in Figure 6-30. Choose the **OK** button in this message box; the **Report: Audit for this drawing** dialog box will be displayed, as shown in Figure 6-31. You can save and print a report by choosing the **Save As** button and the **Print** button, respectively from this dialog box.

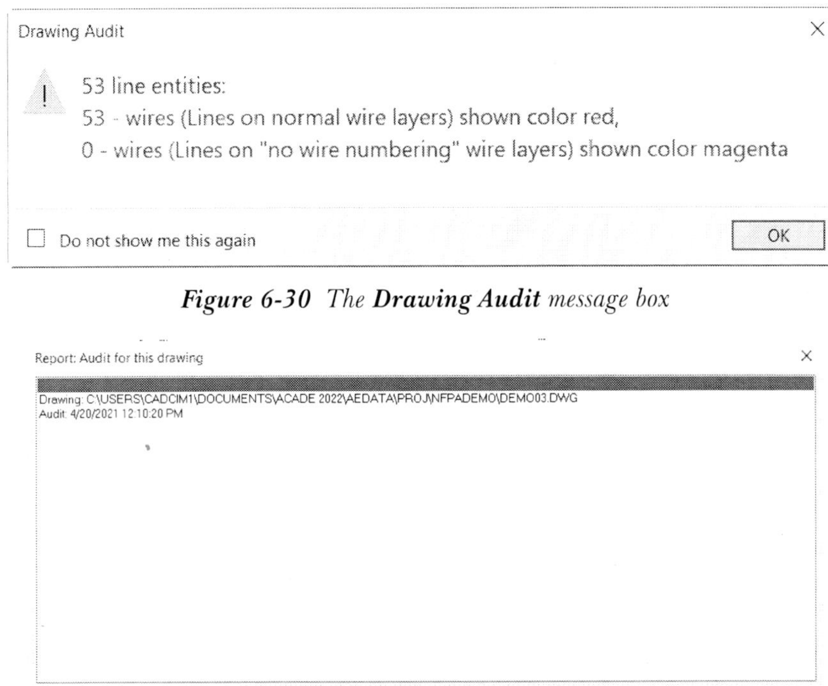


*Figure 6-30 The* ***Drawing Audit*** *message box*

*Figure 6-31 The* ***Report: Audit for this drawing*** *dialog box*

## Previous

The **Previous** button of the **Drawing Audit** dialog box is activated if you have already generated the audio report, and is used to display the previous audit report. To do so, choose the **Previous** button; the **Report: Audit** dialog box will be displayed. This dialog box re-displays the last run audit report.

## Auditing an Active Project

The **Project** radio button is used to audit an active project. To do so, select the **Project** radio button from the **Active drawing or project** area of the **Drawing Audit** dialog box, refer to Figure 6-28, and then choose the **OK** button from this dialog box; the modified **Drawing Audit** dialog box will be displayed, as shown in Figure 6-32. The options in the modified **Drawing Audit** dialog box have already been discussed.

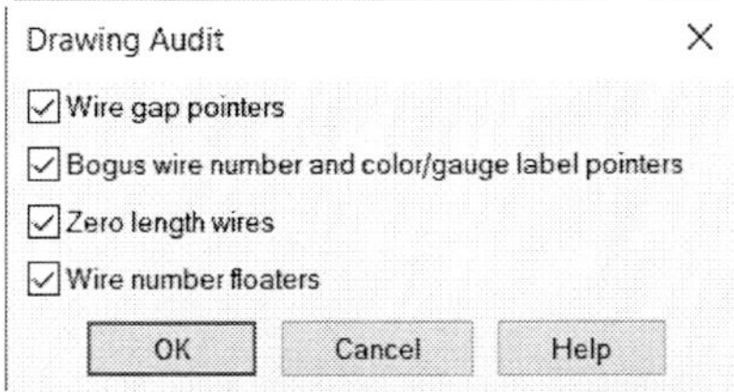


*Figure 6-32 The modified* ***Drawing Audit*** *dialog box*

Next, choose the **OK** button from the modified **Drawing Audit** dialog box; the **Select Drawings to Process** dialog box will be displayed, as shown in Figure 6-33. Select the drawings that you want to process and choose the **Process** button from this dialog box; the selected drawings will be moved from the top list to the bottom list. Next, choose the **OK** button in this dialog box; the **QSAVE** message box will be displayed, as shown in Figure 6-34. Next, choose the **OK** button in the **QSAVE** message box; the changes made in the current drawing will be saved and the auditing report of drawings will be displayed in the **Report: Audit** dialog box, as shown in Figure 6-35.

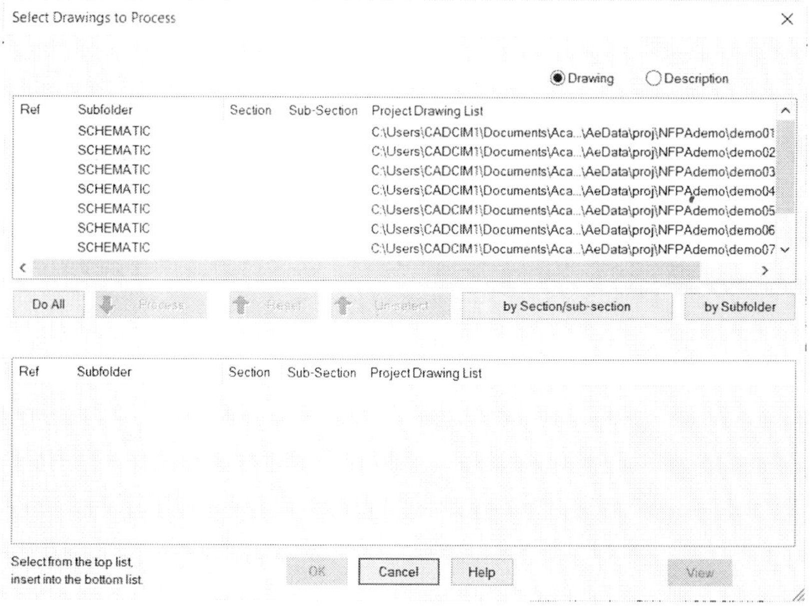

*Figure 6-33 The **Select Drawings to Process** dialog box*

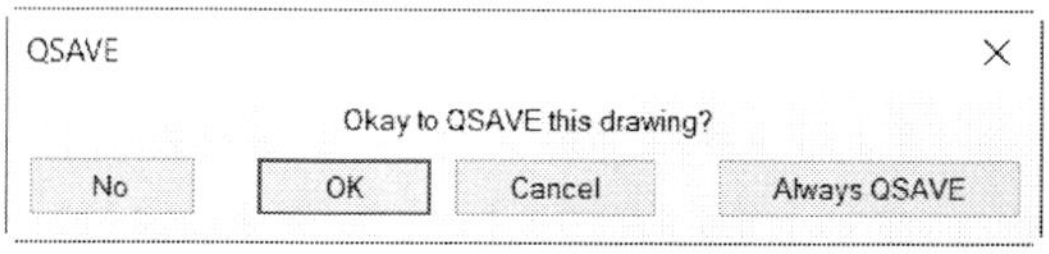

*Figure 6-34 The **QSAVE** message box*

*Figure 6-35 The **Report: Audit** dialog box*

**Note**

*The **QSAVE** message box will be displayed only if you have made any changes in the current drawing and have not saved them.*

# RETAGGING DRAWINGS

| | |
|---|---|
| **Ribbon:** | Project > Project Tools > Update/Retag |
| **Toolbar:** | ACE:Main Electrical 2 > Project Manager > Project-Wide Update/Retag |
| | ACE:Project > Project-Wide Update/Retag |
| **Menu:** | Projects > Project-Wide Update/Retag |
| **Command:** | AEPROJUPDATE |

The **Project-Wide Update/Retag** tool is used to update the selected drawings in a project. Also, this tool is used to retag components, update the cross-reference of component, retag wire numbers and signal references, and so on. To update or retag the drawings of a project, choose the **Update/Retag** tool from the **Project Tools** panel of the **Project** tab or choose **Projects > Project-Wide Update/Retag** from the menu bar; the **Project-Wide Update or Retag** dialog box will be displayed, as shown in Figure 6-36. Different options in this dialog box are discussed next.

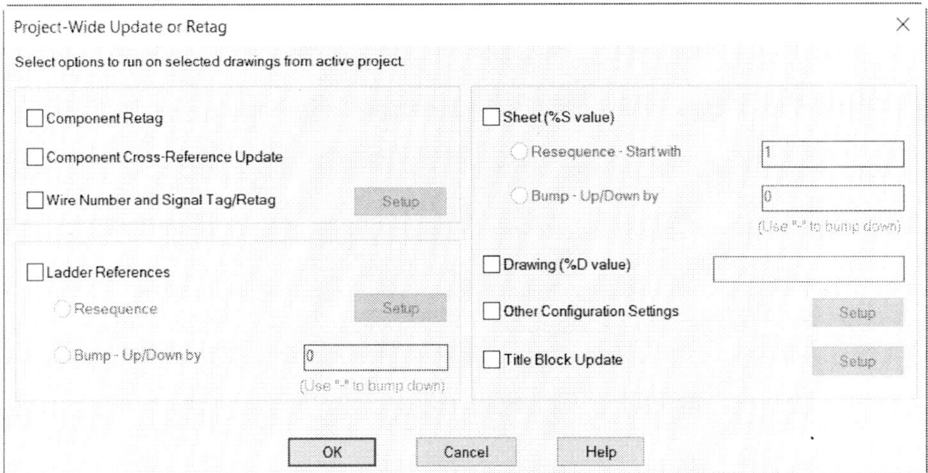


*Figure 6-36 The **Project-Wide Update or Retag** dialog box*

## Component Retag

The **Component Retag** check box is used to retag all non-fixed components of the selected drawings.

## Component Cross-Reference Update

The **Component Cross-Reference Update** check box is used to update the cross-reference of components of the selected drawings.

## Wire Number and Signal Tag/Retag

The **Wire Number and Signal Tag/Retag** check box is used to update signal symbols and the wire numbers that are not fixed. Select the **Wire Number and Signal Tag/Retag** check box; the **Setup** button will be activated. Using this button, you can insert or update wire numbers that are linked to wire networks. To do so, choose the **Setup** button; the **Wire Tagging (Project-wide)** dialog box will be displayed, as shown in Figure 6-37. The options in this dialog box have been discussed in Chapter 3. Specify the required options in this dialog box and then choose the **OK** button to return to the **Project-Wide Update or Retag** dialog box.

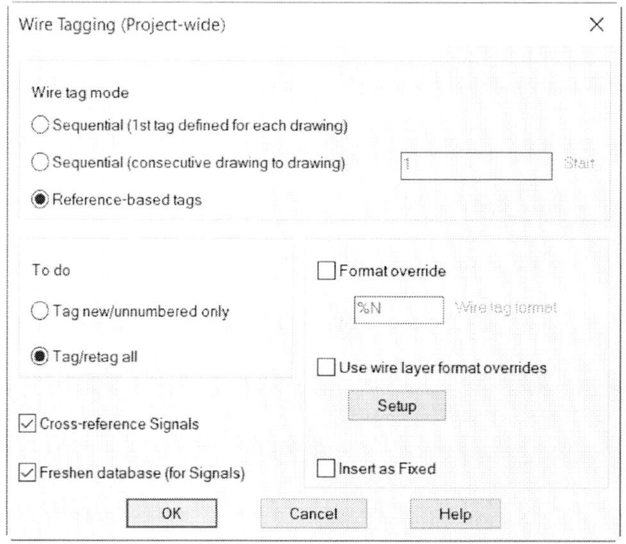


*Figure 6-37 The **Wire Tagging (Project-wide)** dialog box*

## Ladder References

The **Ladder References** check box is used to renumber the ladders sequentially. To renumber each ladder of drawings sequentially, select this check box; the options below the **Ladder References** check box will be activated. These options are discussed next.

### Resequence

The **Resequence** radio button is selected automatically when you select the **Ladder References** check box and is used to define the starting reference number for a ladder. Also, it is used to define the sequence of ladders in different drawings. The **Setup** button located on the right of the **Resequence** radio button is used to renumber ladder reference. To do so, choose the **Setup** button; the **Renumber Ladders** dialog box will be displayed, as shown in Figure 6-38. Using this dialog box, you can renumber the reference numbers of a ladder of the

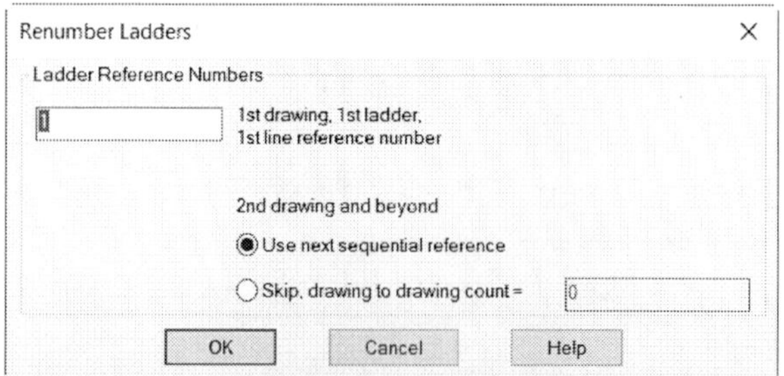


*Figure 6-38 The **Renumber Ladders** dialog box*

selected drawings in an active project. The options in this dialog box have already been discussed in detail in Chapter 4.

Specify the required options in this dialog box and choose the **OK** button to return to the **Project-Wide Update or Retag** dialog box.

### Bump-Up/Down by

The **Bump-Up/Down by** radio button is used to increase or decrease the existing ladder line reference numbers by a specified amount. To do so, select this radio button; the edit box on the right of this radio button will be activated. Specify a value in this edit box; the reference number of the ladder will change accordingly. Also, if you add drawings in the middle of a project, the ladder references will move up. However, if you remove drawings from the project, the ladder references will move down. If you enter a negative value in the edit box, the line reference number of the ladder will move down.

## Sheet (%S value)

If you select the **Sheet (%S value)** check box, the options below this check box will be activated. This check box is used to resequence the sheet value automatically in the successive drawings.

### Resequence - Start with

The **Resequence - Start with** radio button is selected by default and it enables you to enter a number to start resequencing.

### Bump - Up/Down by

Select the **Bump - Up/Down by** radio button; the edit box adjacent to this radio button will be activated. Next, enter the required value in the edit box; the current sheet value will move up or down by the specified value.

## Drawing (%D value)

The **Drawing (%D value)** check box is used to update drawing's %D (drawing name) parameter project-wide. Select this check box; the edit box adjacent to this check box will be activated.

## Other Configuration Settings

The **Other Configuration Settings** check box is used to update the drawing settings of the drawing related to component, cross-reference, wire numbers, and format project-wide. Select this check box; the **Setup** button will be activated. Choose the **Setup** button; the **Change Each Drawing's Settings -- Project-wide** dialog box will be displayed, as shown in Figure 6-39. The options in this dialog box are used to change the settings of the drawings. These options are discussed next.

### Component Tagging Settings

The **Component Tagging Settings** check box is used to specify the settings for the component tag. If you select the **Component Tagging Settings** check box, the **Sequential** radio button, the **Reference-based** radio button, and the **Format** edit box will be activated. Select the **Sequential** radio button for tagging the components sequentially. The **Reference-based** radio button is selected by default. As a result, the components are tagged based on reference of the ladder. Enter the format for component tagging in the **Format** edit box. By default, %F%N is displayed in this edit box.

### Cross-Reference Format*

The **Cross-Reference Format** check box is used to specify the format for cross-reference of the component. Select this check box; the **Format** edit box will be activated. Enter the format for cross-reference in the **Format** edit box. By default, %N is displayed in this edit box.

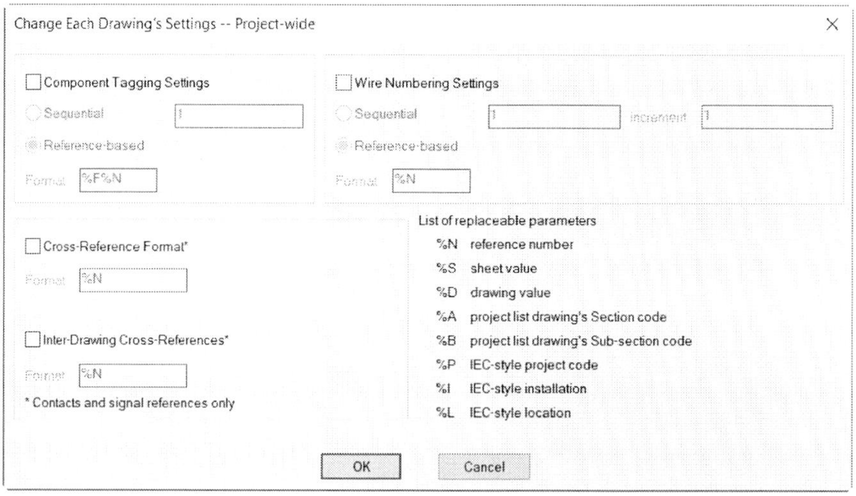

*Figure 6-39 The **Change Each Drawing's Settings -- Project-wide** dialog box*

### Inter-Drawing Cross-References*

The **Inter-Drawing Cross-Reference** check box is used to specify the format for the inter-drawing cross-references.

### Wire Numbering Settings

The **Wire Numbering Settings** check box is used to specify the settings for the wire numbers. Select this check box; the other options will be activated. These options are discussed next. Select the **Sequential** radio button for numbering the wires sequentially. You can enter the increment value in the **increment** edit box for wire numbering. Select the **Reference-based** radio button for numbering the wires based on reference number of the ladder. Enter the format of wire numbers in the **Format** edit box. By default, %N is displayed in this edit box.

## Title Block Update

Select the **Title Block Update** check box in the **Project-Wide Update or Retag** dialog box to update the title block information of the active drawing or the entire project. By selecting this check box, the **Setup** button next to this check box will be enabled. Choose the **Setup** button; the **Update Title Block** dialog box will be displayed. Using this dialog box, you can update the attributes of the title block. The options in this dialog box will be discussed in Chapter 12. Specify the required options in the **Update Title Block** dialog box and choose the **OK** button; you will return to the **Project-Wide Update or Retag** dialog box.

You can use any one of the options in the **Project-Wide Update or Retag** dialog box or use all of them simultaneously by selecting the options displayed in this dialog box. After selecting the options, choose the **OK** button from the **Project-Wide Update or Retag** dialog box; the **Select Drawings to Process** dialog box will be displayed. Select the required drawings and choose the **Process** button; the selected drawings will be displayed in the bottom list. Next, choose the **OK** button from this dialog box; the selected drawings will be processed and updated accordingly.

# USING TOOLS FOR EDITING ATTRIBUTES

In AutoCAD Electrical, there are a number of tools that can be used to modify attributes. These tools are used to modify the attributes of selected symbols but they are not used to modify the block. In this section, you will learn about different tools used for modifying attributes.

## Moving Attributes

**Ribbon:** Schematic > Edit Components > Modify Attributes drop-down > Move/Show Attribute
**Toolbar:** ACE:Main Electrical > Modify Attributes drop-down > Move/Show Attribute or ACE:Edit Attributes > Move/Show Attribute
**Menu:** Components > Attributes > Move/Show Attribute
**Command:** AEATTSHOW

The **Move/Show Attribute** tool is used to move attributes of a component. To do so, choose the **Move/Show Attribute** tool from the **Modify Attributes** drop-down in the **Edit Components** panel of the **Schematic** tab, as shown in Figure 6-40; you will be prompted to select the attribute to move or pick block graphics for list. Select the attributes that you want to move and press ENTER; you will be prompted to specify the base point of the attribute. Specify the base point for the attribute and press ENTER or click on the screen; you will be prompted again to select the attributes to move. Press ENTER to exit the command. If you enter 'W' at the Command prompt, you will be able to move multiple attributes at a time by selecting attributes using the crossing window.

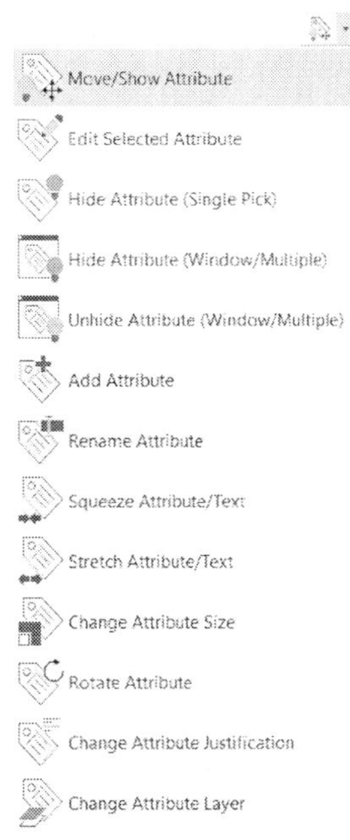


***Figure 6-40*** *The* ***Modify Attributes*** *drop-down*

## Editing Attributes

**Ribbon:** Schematic > Edit Components > Modify Attributes drop-down > Edit Selected Attribute
**Toolbar:** ACE:Main Electrical > Modify Attributes drop-down > Edit Selected Attribute or ACE:Edit Attributes > Edit Selected Attribute
**Menu:** Components > Attributes > Edit Selected Attribute
**Command:** AEEDITATT

The **Edit Selected Attribute** tool is used to edit the selected attribute. To do so, choose the **Edit Selected Attribute** tool from the **Edit Components** panel of the **Schematic** tab; you will be prompted to select an attribute. Select an attribute; the **Edit Attribute** dialog box will be displayed, refer to Figure 6-41.

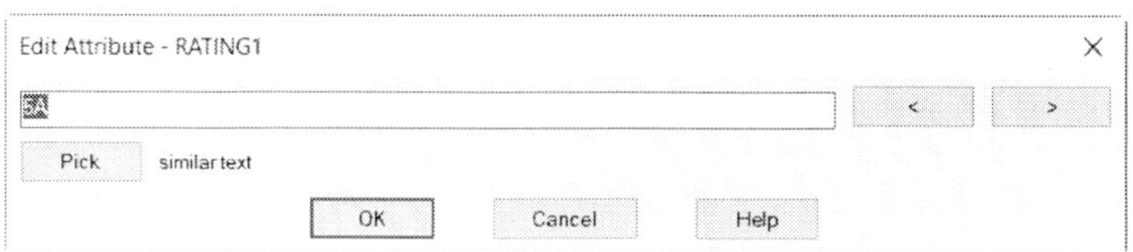


*Figure 6-41 The* ***Edit Attribute - Rating1*** *dialog box*

Enter the new name for the attribute in the edit box. Alternatively, choose the **Pick** button from the **Edit Attribute** dialog box for selecting the attribute from the current drawing. You can increase or decrease the selected attribute value by choosing the **>** and **<** buttons. Next, choose the **OK** button; the name of the selected attribute will be changed to the specified name. Press ENTER to exit the command. You can also edit components using the **Edit** tool. To do so, choose the **Edit** tool from the **Edit Components** panel of the **Schematic** tab; the **Insert / Edit Component** dialog box will be displayed. Specify the required description in the **Description** area of this dialog box and choose the **OK** button; the attribute of the component will be changed. Another method of editing the attribute of a component is by using the **Move/Show Attribute** tool. To edit the attribute text of a component, choose the **Move/Show Attribute** tool from the **Edit Components** panel of the **Schematic** tab; you will be prompted to select an attribute to move or pick on block graphics for list. Select the graphics of the block; the **SHOW / HIDE Attributes** dialog box will be displayed, as shown in Figure 6-42. Next, select the **Edit Attributes** check box located at the top right corner of this dialog box; the dialog box will be modified to the **EDIT Attributes** dialog box. Next, select the name of attribute from the list displayed in the **EDIT Attributes** dialog box; the **Edit Attribute** dialog box will be displayed. Specify the required options and choose the **OK** button in the **Edit Attribute** dialog box; the attribute value will be changed to the specified value.

## Hiding Attributes

| | |
|---|---|
| **Ribbon:** | Schematic > Edit Components > Modify Attributes drop-down > Hide Attribute (Single Pick) |
| **Toolbar:** | ACE:Main Electrical > Modify Attributes drop-down > Hide Attribute (Single Picks) or ACE:Edit Attributes > Hide Attribute (Single Picks) |
| **Menu:** | Components > Attributes > Hide/Unhide Attribute > Hide Attribute (Single Picks) |
| **Command:** | AEHIDEATT |

The **Hide Attribute (Single Pick)** tool is used to hide the selected attribute. To do so, choose the **Hide Attribute (Single Pick)** tool from the **Modify Attributes** drop-down in the **Edit Components** panel of the **Schematic** tab; you will be prompted to select the attribute to hide or pick on block graphics for list. Select the attribute to hide it. Press ENTER to exit the command. Note that if you select the graphics of a block, the **SHOW / HIDE Attributes** dialog box will be displayed, refer to Figure 6-42. The attributes that have an asterisk (*) displayed in the **Visible** column of the **SHOW / HIDE Attributes** dialog box are visible in the drawing. To make these attributes invisible in the drawing, select these attributes in the dialog box; the asterisk will disappear from the **Visible** column indicating that the attribute is now invisible in the drawing. Similarly, if you select the attribute in the dialog box which does not have an asterisk in the **Visible** column, the asterisk will appear in this column indicating that the attribute is now visible in the drawing.

You can hide multiple attributes at a time. To do so, enter 'W' at the Command prompt; you will be prompted to select the attributes. Select the attributes by using the crossing window and then press ENTER; the attributes will hide. Press ENTER to exit the command. You can also hide multiple attributes using the **Hide Attribute (Window/Multiple)** tool. To do so, choose the **Hide Attribute (Window/Multiple)** tool from the **Edit Components** panel of the **Schematic** tab; you will be prompted to select the attributes. Select the attribute and press ENTER; the **Flip Attribute to Invisible** dialog box will be displayed. Select the required attributes to flip to invisible and choose the **OK** button; the attributes will hide. Note that you can select multiple attributes from the **Flip Attribute to Invisible** dialog box by using the CTRL or SHIFT key.

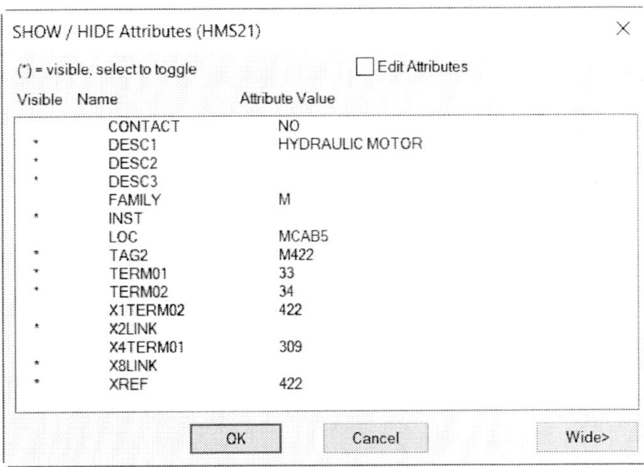


*Figure 6-42 The **SHOW / HIDE Attributes** dialog box*

## Unhiding Attributes

**Ribbon:** Schematic > Edit Components >Modify Attributes drop-down > Unhide Attribute (Window/Multiple)
**Menu:** Components > Attributes > Hide/Unhide Attribute > Unhide Attribute (Window/Multiple)
**Command:** AESHOWATTRIB

The **Unhide Attribute (Window/Multiple)** tool is used to unhide the hidden attributes. To do so, choose the **Unhide Attribute (Window/Multiple)** tool from the **Modify Attributes** drop-down in the **Edit Components** panel of the **Schematic** tab; you will be prompted to select objects. Select graphics of the symbol block and press ENTER; the **Flip Attributes to Visible** dialog box will be displayed. Select the attributes that you want to display and choose the **OK** button in the **Flip Attributes to Visible** dialog box; the attributes will be visible on the screen. Note that multiple attributes can be selected from the **Flip Attributes to Visible** dialog box by pressing CTRL or SHIFT. If you enter 'W' at the Command prompt, you will be prompted to specify the first corner. Specify the first corner; you will be prompted to specify the opposite corner. Specify the opposite corner and then press ENTER; the **Flip Attributes to Visible** dialog box will be displayed. Select one or more attributes and choose the **OK** button; the attributes will be flipped to visible.

## Adding Attributes

| | |
|---|---|
| **Ribbon:** | Schematic > Edit Components > Modify Attributes drop-down > Add Attribute |
| **Toolbar:** | ACE:Main Electrical > Modify Attributes drop-down > Add Attribute or ACE:Edit Attributes > Add Attribute |
| **Menu:** | Components > Attributes > Add Attribute |
| **Command:** | AEATTRIBUTE |

The **Add Attribute** tool is used to add a new attribute to the existing AutoCAD Electrical block. To do so, choose the **Add Attribute** tool from the **Modify Attributes** drop-down in the **Edit Components** panel of the **Schematic** tab; you will be prompted to select an object. Select the object; the **Add Attribute** dialog box will be displayed, as shown in Figure 6-43. The options in this dialog box are discussed next.

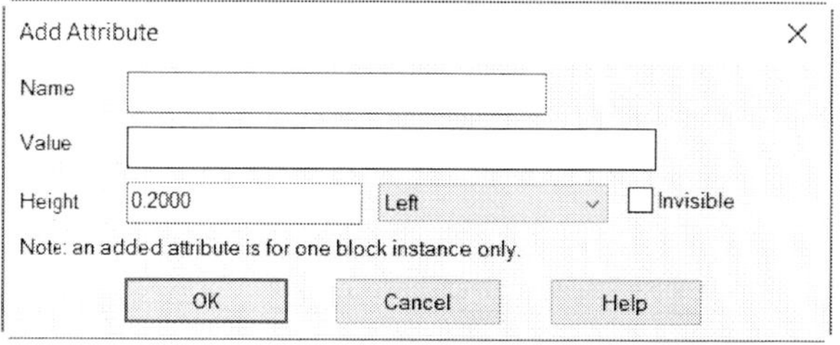


***Figure 6-43** The **Add Attribute** dialog box*

The **Name** edit box is used for identifying an attribute tag. Specify the name of the attribute in this edit box.

Specify a value for the attribute text in the **Value** edit box. The specified value will be displayed both in the drawing and reports.

Specify the height for the attribute value in the **Height** edit box. By default, 0.2000 is displayed in the **Height** edit box.

Select the justification for the attribute value from the drop-down list adjacent to the **Height** edit box. By default, Left is selected in the drop-down list.

Select the **Invisible** check box to make the attribute text invisible in the drawing. By default, this check box is clear.

Specify the required options in the **Add Attribute** dialog box and choose the **OK** button in this dialog box; you will be prompted to specify the location for attribute. By default, the first location point is already selected by AutoCAD Electrical and it is 0, 0. Next, specify the second location point and click on the screen; the attribute value will be inserted into the drawing.

## Squeezing an Attribute/Text

| | |
|---|---|
| **Ribbon:** | Schematic > Edit Components > Modify Attributes drop-down > Squeeze Attribute/Text |
| **Toolbar:** | ACE:Main Electrical > Modify Attributes drop-down> Squeeze Attribute/Text or ACE:Edit Attributes > Squeeze Attribute/Text |
| **Menu:** | Components > Attributes > Squeeze Attribute/Text |
| **Command:** | AEATTSQUEEZE |

The **Squeeze Attribute/Text** tool is used to reduce the attribute or text size to make it suitable for tight places. After each click on the attribute or text, the width of the attribute or text reduces by 5%. To squeeze the attribute or text size, choose the **Squeeze Attribute/Text** tool from the **Modify Attributes** drop-down in the **Edit Components** panel of the **Schematic** tab; you will be prompted to select the attribute or text to be squeezed. Select the attribute or text; you will be prompted again to select the attribute or text. Continue the selection till it is squeezed to a required size. Next, press ENTER to exit the command.

## Stretching an Attribute/Text

| | |
|---|---|
| **Ribbon:** | Schematic > Edit Components > Modify Attributes drop-down > Stretch Attribute/Text |
| **Toolbar:** | ACE:Main Electrical >Modify Attributes drop-down > Stretch Attribute/Text or ACE:Edit Attributes > Stretch Attribute/Text |
| **Menu:** | Components > Attributes > Stretch Attribute/Text |
| **Command:** | AEATTSTRETCH |

The **Stretch Attribute/Text** tool is used to expand the attribute or text size. After each click on the attribute or text, the width of the attribute or text increases by 5%. To stretch an attribute, choose the **Stretch Attribute/Text** tool from the **Modify Attributes** drop-down in the **Edit Components** panel of the **Schematic** tab; you will be prompted to select the attribute or text. Select the attribute or text; the attribute or text will be stretched. The command will continue till you press ENTER.

## Changing the Attribute Size

| | |
|---|---|
| **Ribbon:** | Schematic > Edit Components > Modify Attributes drop-down > Change Attribute Size |
| **Toolbar:** | ACE:Main Electrical >Modify Attributes drop-down > Change Attribute Size or ACE:Edit Attributes > Change Attribute Size |
| **Menu:** | Components > Attributes > Change Attribute Size |
| **Command:** | AEATTSIZE |

The **Change Attribute Size** tool is used to change the height and width of the attribute text that has already been inserted into the drawing. To change the text size of the attribute, choose the **Change Attribute Size** tool from the **Modify Attributes** drop-down in the **Edit Components** panel of the **Schematic** tab; the **Change Attribute Size** dialog box will be displayed, as shown in Figure 6-44. The options in this dialog box are discussed next.

Specify the size for the attribute in the **Size** edit box. Specify the width for the attribute in the **Width** edit box. Alternatively, choose the **Pick >>** button; you will be prompted to select the attribute. Select the required attribute; the **Change Attribute Size** dialog box will be displayed again and the values of the selected attribute size and width will be displayed in the **Size** and **Width** edit boxes. By default, the **Apply** check boxes are selected. As a result, the new size and width is applied to the attribute that you select. If you clear the **Apply** check boxes in the **Change Attribute Size** dialog box, the **Single**, **By Name**, and **Type It** buttons will not be activated.

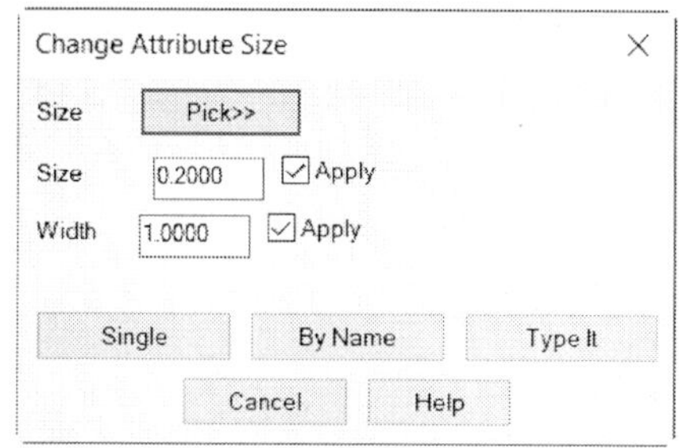


***Figure 6-44** The **Change Attribute Size** dialog box*

The **Single** button is used to select one attribute at a time. The **By Name** button is used to change the size and width of the same type of attributes. For example, if you select DESC2 attribute of a symbol, then the size and width of only DESC2 attribute of all the components present in the drawing will get changed. Choose the **By Name** button; you will be prompted to select the attribute/name. Select the attribute/name and press ENTER; the size and width of the attributes of same type will be changed according to the specified size and width. You can also select multiple attributes at a time. To do so, enter **W** at the Command prompt; you will be prompted to specify the first corner. Specify the first corner; you will be prompted to specify the opposite corner. Specify the opposite corner and then press ENTER; the size and width of the selected attributes will get changed according to the specified size. Also, if you enter **ALL** at the Command prompt, all attributes by the same name that are present in the drawing will be selected and changed to the new attribute size. Press ESC to exit the command.

The **Type It** button is used to specify the name of the attribute to be matched to the selected attributes. To do so, choose the **Type It** button; the **Enter Attribute Name** dialog box will be displayed. Enter the attribute name in the edit box that you want to match to the attributes that you will select. For example, DESC1 for description of the component, TAG1 for tag of the component, and so on. Next, choose the **OK** button in the **Enter Attribute Name** dialog box; you will be prompted to select blocks to process. Select the blocks and press ENTER; the size of attributes will be changed accordingly. Alternatively, select multiple attributes by window selection. Also, if you enter **ALL** at the Command prompt, all attributes present in the active drawing will be selected. Next, press ENTER to change the attributes to the new attribute size and width. Note that you can also enter wildcards in the edit box and include a series of attribute names to match by separating each attribute name using semi-colons.

If you do not enter any attribute name in the edit box of the **Enter Attribute Name** dialog box and choose **OK**, then it will again return to the **Change Attribute Size** dialog box. Choose the **Cancel** button to exit from this dialog box.

## Rotating an Attribute

**Ribbon:** Schematic > Edit Components > Modify Attributes drop-down > Rotate Attribute
**Toolbar:** ACE:Main Electrical > Modify Attributes drop-down > Rotate Attribute or ACE:Edit Attributes > Rotate Attribute
**Menu:** Components > Attributes > Rotate Attribute
**Command:** AEATTROTATE

The **Rotate Attribute** tool is used to rotate the selected attribute text by 90 degrees. To do so, choose the **Rotate Attribute** tool from the **Modify Attributes** drop-down in the **Edit Components** panel of the **Schematic** tab; you will be prompted to select the attribute text to rotate. Select the attribute text; the text will be rotated by 90 degrees in counterclockwise direction. Press ENTER to exit the command. Now, if you want to move the attribute text, enter '**M**' at the Command prompt and press ENTER; you will be prompted to specify the base point. Specify the base point and press ENTER; you will be prompted to specify the destination point. Specify the destination point and press ENTER; the attribute text will be moved to the specified location.

## Changing the Justification of an Attribute

**Ribbon:** Schematic > Edit Components > Modify Attributes drop-down > Change Attribute Justification
**Toolbar:** ACE:Main Electrical > Modify Attributes drop-down> Change Attribute Justification or ACE:Edit Attributes > Change Attribute Justification
**Menu:** Components > Attributes >Change Attribute Justification
**Command:** AEATTJUSTIFY

The **Change Attribute Justification** tool is used to change the justification of any attribute such as wire number text, component description text, and so on. To change the justification of an attribute, choose the **Change Attribute Justification** tool from the **Modify Attributes** drop-down in the **Edit Components** panel of the **Schematic** tab; the **Change Attribute/Text Justification** dialog box will be displayed, as shown in Figure 6-45. The options in this dialog box are discussed next.

Select the required justification for the attribute text from the **Select Justification** area in this dialog box; the **OK** button will be activated. Choose **OK**; you will be prompted to select the text or attribute to change the justification. Select the text or attribute; the justification of the attribute or text will be changed.

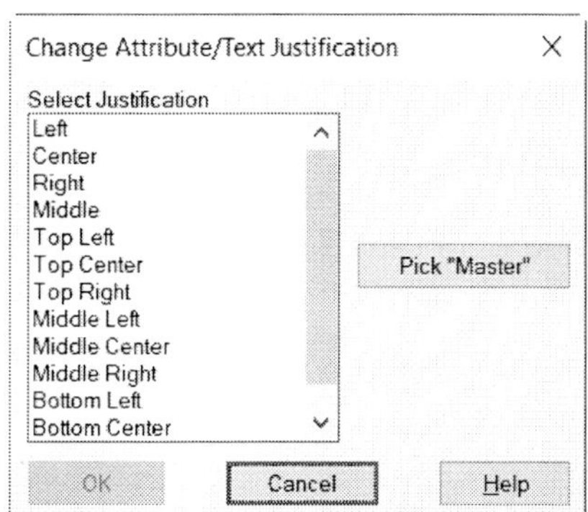


*Figure 6-45 The **Change Attribute/Text Justification** dialog box*

Alternatively, choose the **Pick Master** button; you will be prompted to select the master attribute or text that will be used for justification of other attributes or text. Next, select the attribute or text; the **Change Attribute/Text Justification** dialog box will be displayed on the screen again. Choose **OK**; you will be prompted to select the attribute or text for the change of justification. Select attributes or text and press ENTER; the justification of attributes or text will be changed. Alternatively, enter '**W**' at the Command prompt to select the attributes or text by using a crossing window. Press ENTER to exit the command.

## Changing an Attribute Layer

| | |
|---|---|
| **Ribbon:** | Schematic > Edit Components > Modify Attributes drop-down > Change Attribute Layer |
| **Toolbar:** | ACE:Main Electrical > Modify Attributes drop-down > Change Attribute Layer<br>or ACE:Edit Attributes > Change Attribute Layer |
| **Menu:** | Components > Attributes > Change Attribute Layer |
| **Command**: | AEATTLAYER |

The **Change Attribute Layer** tool is used to change the layer of the selected attribute. To do so, choose the **Change Attribute Layer** tool from the **Modify Attributes** drop-down in the **Edit Components** panel of the **Schematic** tab; the **Force Attribute/Text to a Different Layer** dialog box will be displayed, as shown in Figure 6-46.

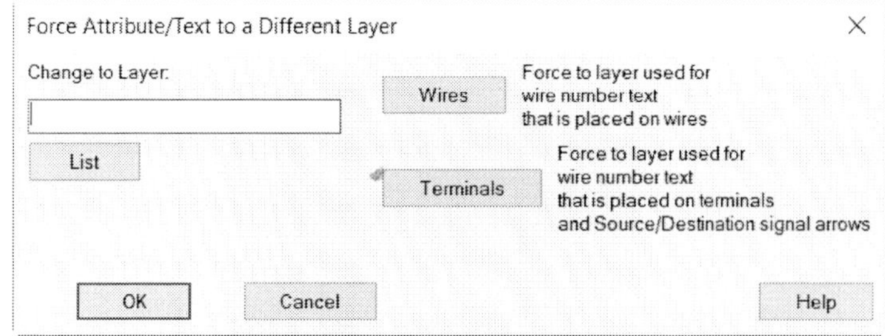


*Figure 6-46 The **Force Attribute/Text to a Different Layer** dialog box*

Enter the name of the target layer in the **Change to Layer** edit box. Alternatively, choose the **List** button; the **Layers in Drawing** dialog box will be displayed. Select the layer and choose the **OK** button; the name of the target layer will be displayed in the **Change to Layer** edit box.

If you choose the **Wires** button, the WIRENO will be displayed in the **Change to Layer** edit box. This button is used to change the layer of a selected attribute or text for the layer that has been used for wire number text placed on wires.

If you choose the **Terminals** button, the WIREREF will be displayed in the **Change to Layer** edit box. In this case, the layer of the attribute or text that you select will get changed to the layer that is used for wire number text placed on terminals and source/destination signal arrow.

**Note**

*The **Wires** and **Terminals** buttons in the **Force Attributes/Text to a Different Layer** dialog box will be activated only if the WIRES and TERMINALS layers are available in the active drawing respectively.*

After specifying the required options in the **Force Attribute/Text to a Different Layer** dialog box, choose the **OK** button in this dialog box; you will be prompted to select the attribute or text to move to layer. Select the attribute or text; the attribute or text layer will get changed to the layer that you have entered in the **Change to Layer** edit box. Press ENTER to exit the command.

# TUTORIALS

## Tutorial 1

In this tutorial, you will insert a ladder and its components into a drawing. Next, you will use the **Copy Component**, **Scoot**, **Move Component**, and **Delete Component** tools for copying, scooting, moving, and deleting the inserted components. refer to Figure 6-47. Also, you will hide the attributes of components. **(Expected time: 30 min)**

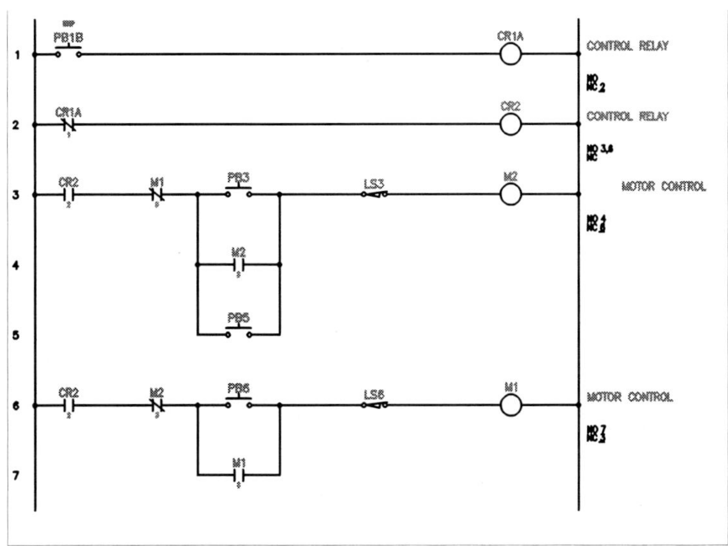


*Figure 6-47* *Ladder diagram for Tutorial 1*

The following steps are required to complete this tutorial:

a. Create a new drawing.
b. Insert ladder in the drawing.
c. Insert components and add descriptions.
d. Copy components.
e. Hide attributes.
f. Delete components.
g. Move components.
h. Add wires.
i. Scoot components.
j. Trim wires.
k. Align components.
l. Save the drawing file.

## Creating a New Drawing

1. Activate the **CADCIM** project, if it is not already active.

2. Choose the **New Drawing** button from the **PROJECT MANAGER**; the **Create New Drawing** dialog box is displayed. Enter **C06_tut01** in the **Name** edit box of the **Drawing File** area. Select the template as **ACAD_ELECTRICAL.dwt** and enter **Schematic Components** in the **Description 1** edit box.

3. Choose the **OK** button; the *C06_tut01.dwg* drawing is created in the **CADCIM** project and is displayed at the bottom of the drawing list in the **CADCIM** project. Next, move the *C06_tut01.dwg* to the *TUTORIALS* subfolder of the **CADCIM** project.

## Inserting Ladder into the Drawing

1. Choose the **Insert Ladder** tool from **Schematic > Insert Wires/Wire Numbers > Insert Ladder** drop-down; the **Insert Ladder** dialog box is displayed.

2. Set the following parameters in the **Insert Ladder** dialog box:

   Width: **8.000**
   1st Reference: **1**
   **1 Phase**: Select this radio button
   Spacing: **1.000**
   Rungs: **7**
   **Yes**: Select this radio button

3. After setting these parameters, click in the **Length** edit box; the length of the ladder is automatically calculated and displayed in this edit box. Also, make sure that 0 is displayed in the **Skip** edit box of the **Draw Rungs** area.

4. Choose the **OK** button; you are prompted to specify the start position of the first rung. Enter **11,18** at the Command prompt and press ENTER; the ladder is inserted into the drawing, as shown in Figure 6-48. Next, choose **View > Zoom > In** from the menu bar to zoom in the drawing.

***Figure 6-48*** *Ladder with 7 rungs*

## Inserting Components and Adding Descriptions

1. Choose the **Icon Menu** tool from **Schematic > Insert Components > Icon Menu** drop-down; the **Insert Component** dialog box is displayed.

2. Select the **Push Buttons** icon from the **NFPA: Schematic Symbols** area of the **Insert Component** dialog box; the **NFPA: Schematic Symbols** area is modified to the **NFPA: Push Buttons** area.

3. Select the **Push Button NO** icon from the **NFPA: Push Buttons** area; the cursor along with the component is displayed and you are prompted to specify the insertion point for the push button. Enter **11.5,18** at the Command prompt and press ENTER; the push button is placed at rung 1 and the **Insert / Edit Component** dialog box is displayed. By default, PB1B is displayed in the edit box of the **Component Tag** area.

4. Enter **STOP** in the **Line 1** edit box in the **Description** area.Next, choose the **OK** button from the **Insert / Edit Component** dialog box; the PB1B component is inserted into the drawing.

5. Repeat step 1. Select the **Relays/Contacts** icon displayed in the **NFPA: Schematic Symbols** area of the **Insert Component** dialog box; the **NFPA: Relays and Contacts** area is displayed.

6. Select the **Relay Coil** icon in the **NFPA: Relays and Contacts** area of the **Insert Component** dialog box; you are prompted to specify the insertion point. Enter **13,18** at the Command prompt and press ENTER; the **Insert / Edit Component** dialog box is displayed. By default, CR1A is displayed in the edit box of the **Component Tag** area.

7. Enter **CONTROL RELAY** in the **Line 1** edit box in the **Description** area. Next, choose the **OK** button from the **Insert / Edit Component** dialog box; the component CR1A gets added to rung 1 of the ladder.

8. Repeat Step 1. Select the **Relays/Contacts** icon displayed in the **Insert Component** dialog box; the **NFPA: Relays and Contacts** area is displayed.

9. Select the **Relay Coil** icon in the **NFPA: Relays and Contacts** area of the **Insert Component** dialog box; you are prompted to specify the insertion point. Enter **13.5,17** at the Command prompt and press ENTER. By default, CR2 is displayed in the edit box of the **Component Tag** area of the **Insert / Edit Component** dialog box.

10. Enter **CONTROL RELAY** in the **Line 1** edit box in the **Description** area. Next, choose the **OK** button from the **Insert / Edit Component** dialog box; the component CR2 gets added to rung 2 of the ladder.

11. Repeat Step 1. Select the **Relays/Contacts** icon and then select **Relay NC Contact** in the **NFPA: Relays and Contacts** area of the **Insert Component** dialog box; you are prompted to specify the insertion point. Enter **11.5,17** at the Command prompt and press ENTER; the **Insert / Edit Child Component** dialog box is displayed.

12. Choose the **Drawing** button from the **Component Tag** area of the **Insert / Edit Child Component** dialog box; the **Active Drawing list for FAMILY = "CR"** dialog box is displayed. Select **CR1A** from this dialog box and choose the **OK** button; the information is displayed in the **Insert / Edit Child Component** dialog box.

    By default, **CONTROL RELAY** is displayed in the **Line 1** edit box of the **Description** area.

13. Enter **NORMALLY CLOSED** in the **Line 2** edit box of the **Description** area. Next, choose the **OK** button in the **Insert / Edit Child Component** dialog box; the component CR1A is added to the ladder rung 2.

14. Repeat Step 1. Select the **Relays/Contacts** icon and then select **Relay NO Contact** in the **NFPA: Relays and Contacts** area; you are prompted to specify the insertion point. Enter **11.5,16** at the Command prompt and press ENTER; the **Insert / Edit Child Component** dialog box is displayed.

15. Choose the **Drawing** button from the **Component Tag** area of the **Insert / Edit Child Component** dialog box; the **Active Drawing list for FAMILY = "CR"** dialog box is displayed. Select **CR2** from this dialog box and choose the **OK** button; the information is displayed in the **Insert / Edit Child Component** dialog box.

16. Enter **NORMALLY OPEN** in the **Line 2** edit box of the **Description** area in the **Insert / Edit Child Component** dialog box and then choose the **OK** button from this dialog box; the CR2 control relay is inserted into the drawing in the rung 3.

17. Repeat step 1. Select the **Motor Control** icon from the **NFPA: Schematic Symbols** area in the **Insert Component** dialog box. Next, select **Motor Starter Coil** from the **NFPA: Motor Control** area; you are prompted to specify the insertion point for the component.

18. Enter **17.5,16** at the Command prompt and press ENTER; the **Insert / Edit Component** dialog box is displayed. Enter **M2** in the edit box of the **Component Tag** area. Also, enter its description as **MOTOR CONTROL** in the **Line 1** edit box of the **Description area** of the **Insert / Edit Component** dialog box. Choose the **OK** button from this dialog box; the **Motor Starter Coil** is inserted into rung 3 of the ladder.

**Note**

*You may need to move the attributes of the inserted components by using the* ***Move/Show Attribute*** *tool.*

Next, you need to insert **2nd + Starter Contact NO** in the rung 4.

19. Choose the **Motor Control** icon from the **Insert Component** dialog box and then select **2nd+Starter Contact NO** from the **NFPA: Motor Control** area; you are prompted to specify the insertion point.

20. Enter **11.5,15** at the Command prompt and press ENTER; the **Insert / Edit Child Component** dialog box is displayed. Choose the **Drawing** button from the **Component Tag**

area of the **Insert / Edit Child Component** dialog box; the **Active Drawing list for FAMILY = "M"** dialog box is displayed. Select **M2** from this dialog box and choose the **OK** button; the information is displayed in the **Insert / Edit Child Component** dialog box.

21. Enter **NORMALLY OPEN** in the **Line 2** edit box of the **Description** area in the **Insert / Edit Child Component** dialog box and then choose the **OK** button from this dialog box; the M2 starter contact is inserted into the drawing in the rung 4.

22. Repeat step 1. Select the **Motor Control** icon from the **NFPA: Schematic Symbols** area in the **Insert Component** dialog box. Next, select **Motor Starter Coil** from the **NFPA: Motor Control** area; you are prompted to specify the insertion point for the component.

23. Enter **18,13** at the Command prompt. Enter **M1** in the edit box of the **Component Tag** area. Also, enter its description as **MOTOR CONTROL** in the **Line 1** edit box of the **Description** area of the **Insert / Edit Component** dialog box. Choose the **OK** button from the **Insert / Edit Component** dialog box; the **Motor Starter Coil (M1)** is inserted into rung 6 of the ladder.

24. Again, repeat step 1. Select the **Motor Control** icon and then select **2nd+Starter Contact NC** from the **NFPA: Motor Control** area of the **Insert Component** dialog box; you are prompted to specify the insertion point for the component.

25. Enter **12.8,16** at the Command prompt and press ENTER; the **Insert / Edit Child Component** dialog box is displayed. Choose the **Drawing** button from the **Component Tag** area of the **Insert / Edit Child Component** dialog box; the **Active Drawing list for FAMILY = "M"** dialog box is displayed. Select **M1** from this dialog box and choose the **OK** button; the information is displayed in the **Insert / Edit Child Component** dialog box.

26. Enter **NORMALLY CLOSED** in the **Line 2** edit box of the **Description** area in the **Insert / Edit Child Component** dialog box and then choose the **OK** button from this dialog box; the Motor starter contact (M1) is inserted into the drawing in the rung 3.

    Next, you need to insert **Limit Switch, NC** in the rung 3.

27. Choose the **Limit Switches** icon from the **Insert Component** dialog box; the **NFPA: Limit Switches** area is displayed. Select **Limit Switch, NC** from this area; you are prompted to specify the insertion point.

28. Enter **16,16** at the Command prompt and press ENTER; the **Insert / Edit Component** dialog box is displayed. By default, **LS3** is displayed in the **Component Tag** edit box of the **Insert / Edit Component** dialog box. Also, enter **LIMIT SWITCH** and **NORMALLY CLOSED** in the **Line 1** and **Line 2** edit boxes, respectively in the **Description** area of the **Insert / Edit Component** dialog box. Choose the **OK** button; LS3 gets inserted into rung 3.

    Similarly, you need to insert **Limit Switch, NO** in the rung 1.

29. Choose the **Limit Switch, NO** from the **NFPA: Limit Switches** icon of the **Insert Component** dialog box; you are prompted to specify the insertion point.

30. Enter **18,18** at the Command prompt and press ENTER; the **Insert / Edit Component** dialog box is displayed. By default, LS1A is displayed in the edit box of the **Component Tag** area in this dialog box. Next, choose the **OK** button; LS1A is inserted into rung 1 of drawing. Figure 6-49 shows the ladder with components inserted in it.

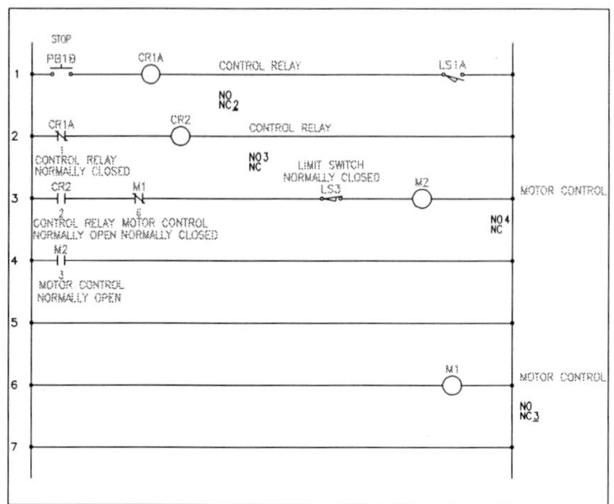


*Figure 6-49 Components inserted in the ladder*

31. Choose the **Move/Show Attribute** tool from **Schematic > Edit Components > Modify Attributes** drop-down; you are prompted to select the object. Select the **Motor Control** attribute of the **Motor Starter Coil** and press ENTER; you are prompted to specify the base point. Specify the base point at the left corner of the attribute and move the attribute, refer to Figure 6-49.

## Copying Components

1. Choose the **Copy Component** tool from the **Edit Components** panel of the **Schematic** tab; you are prompted to select a component to copy.

2. Select **PB1B** (push button) placed on rung 1; you are prompted to specify the insertion point for the copied component. Enter **14,16** at the Command prompt and press ENTER; the **Insert / Edit Component** dialog box is displayed.

3. By default, PB3 is displayed in the edit box of the **Component Tag** area. Enter **DOWN** in the **Line 1** edit box of the **Description** area of the **Insert / Edit Component** dialog box. Next, choose the **OK** button in this dialog box; the component PB3 gets inserted into rung 3.

4. Similarly, right-click on CR2 placed on rung 3 and choose the **Copy Component** option from the marking menu displayed; you are prompted to specify the insertion point. Enter **12,13** at the Command prompt and press ENTER; the **Insert / Edit Child Component** dialog box is displayed.

5. Choose the **Drawing** button from the **Component Tag** area of the **Insert / Edit Child Component** dialog box; the **Active Drawing list for FAMILY = "CR"** dialog box is displayed. Select CR2 (third entry) from this dialog box and choose the **OK** button; the information is displayed in the **Insert / Edit Child Component** dialog box.

By default, **CONTROL RELAY** is displayed in the **Line 1** edit box of the **Description** area and **NORMALLY OPEN** in the **Line 2** edit box of the **Description** area.

6. Choose the **OK** button in the **Insert / Edit Child Component** dialog box; the component CR2 is inserted into rung 6 of the drawing.

7. Right-click on PB1B that you have placed on rung 1 and choose the **Copy Component** option from the marking menu displayed; you are prompted to specify the insertion point. Enter **13,14** at the Command prompt and press ENTER; the **Insert / Edit Component** dialog box is displayed.

8. Remove description from the **Line 1** of the **Description** area in the **Insert / Edit Component** dialog box. Also, enter **PB5** in the edit box of the **Component Tag** area, if it is not displayed. Next, choose the **OK** button in this dialog box; the PB5 is inserted on rung 5. Right-click on **PB1B** and choose the **Copy Component** option from the marking menu displayed; you are prompted to specify the insertion point.

9. Enter **14,13** at the Command prompt and press ENTER; the **Insert / Edit Component** dialog box is displayed. In this dialog box, **PB6** is displayed by default in the edit box of the **Component Tag** area. Remove the description from the **Line 1** edit box of the **Description** area and choose the **OK** button; PB6 is inserted into rung 6 in the ladder.

10. Right-click on Motor control M2 that is on rung 4 and choose the **Copy Component** option from the marking menu displayed; you are prompted to specify the insertion point. Enter **12,12** at the Command prompt and press ENTER; the **Insert / Edit Child Component** dialog box is displayed.

11. Choose the **Drawing** button from the **Component Tag** area of the **Insert / Edit Child Component** dialog box; the **Active Drawing list for FAMILY = "M"** dialog box is displayed. Select **M1** (first entry) from this dialog box and choose the **OK** button; the information is displayed in the **Insert / Edit Child Component** dialog box.

12. Enter **NORMALLY OPEN** in the **Line 2** edit box of the **Description** area in the **Insert / Edit Child Component** dialog box and then choose the **OK** button from this dialog box; the Motor starter contact (M1) is inserted into the drawing in rung 7.

13. Similarly, select M1 from rung 3 and copy it to rung 6 at **15,13**. Choose the **Drawing** button from the **Component Tag** area of the **Insert / Edit Child Component** dialog box; the **Active Drawing list for FAMILY = "M"** dialog box is displayed. Select **M2** (fourth entry) from this dialog box and choose the **OK** button; the information is displayed in the **Insert / Edit Child Component** dialog box.

14. Enter **NORMALLY CLOSED** in the **Line 2** edit box of the **Description** area in the **Insert / Edit Child Component** dialog box and then choose the **OK** button from this dialog box; the M2 starter contact is inserted into the drawing in rung 6.

15. Next, select limit switch LS3 from 3rd rung and copy it at **15,15**. Again, select LS3 and copy it at **16,13**. You will notice that the limit switch is inserted in rung 4 and rung 6. Keep the values in the **Description** area intact. Figure 6-50 shows the copied components.

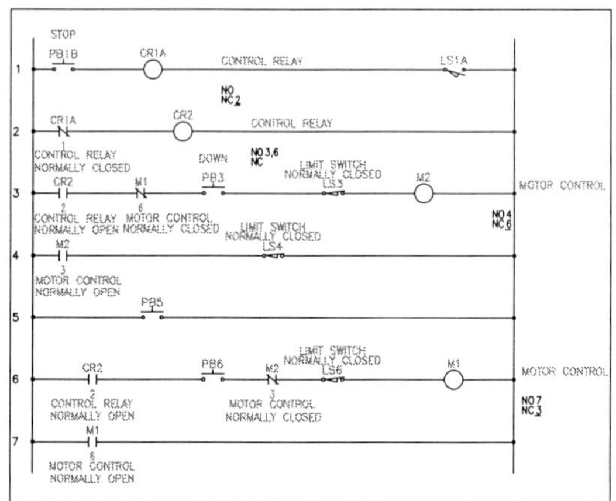


*Figure 6-50 The copied components*

## Hiding Attributes

1. Choose the **Hide Attribute (Single Pick)** tool from **Schematic > Edit Components > Modify Attributes** drop-down; you are prompted to select the attributes to hide.

2. Select the DESC1 and DESC2 attributes of the following components:

   CR1A placed on rung 2,
   CR2, M1, PB3, and LS3 placed on rung 3,
   M2 and LS4 placed on rung 4,
   CR2, M2, and LS6 placed on rung 6, and
   M1 placed on rung 7.

   On doing so, the description of the components is hidden.

3. Press ENTER to exit the command. Figure 6-51 shows the ladder and component with hidden attributes.

## Deleting Components

1. Choose the **Delete Component** tool from the **Edit Components** panel of the **Schematic** tab; you are prompted to select objects.

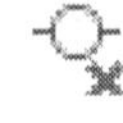

2. Select LS1A from rung 1 and LS4 from rung 4, and then press ENTER; the **Search for / Surf to Children?** dialog box is displayed. Choose the **No** button from this dialog box; components are deleted from the drawing, as shown in Figure 6-52.

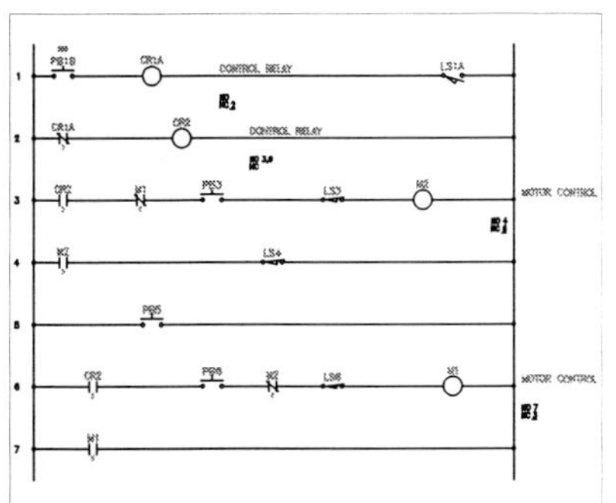

Figure 6-51 The ladder after hiding attributes

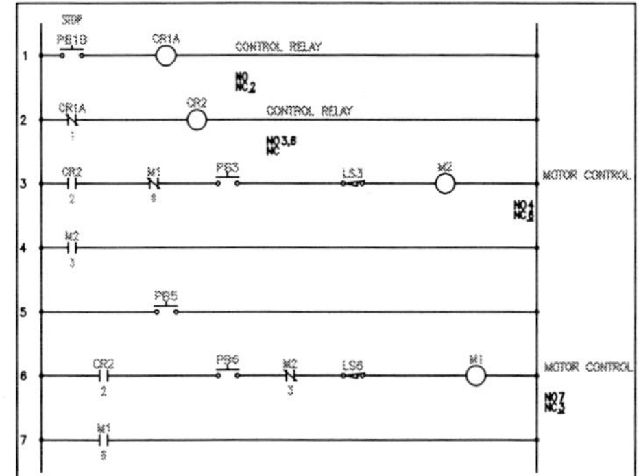


Figure 6-52 The ladder after deleting components

## Moving Components

1. Choose the **Move Component** tool from **Schematic > Edit Components > Modify Components** drop-down; you are prompted to select the component to move.

2. Select M2 from rung 6; you are prompted to specify the insertion point for the component.

3. Enter **13,13** at the Command prompt and press ENTER; M2 is moved to a new location in rung 6, as shown in Figure 6-53.

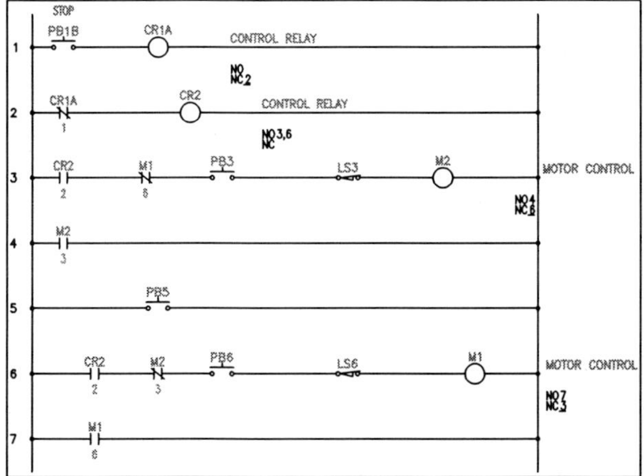


*Figure 6-53 M2 moved to a different location*

## Adding Wires

1. Choose the **Wire** tool from **Schematic > Insert Wires/Wire Numbers > Wire** drop-down; you are prompted to specify the starting point of the wire at the Command prompt.

2. Enter **13.4,16** at the Command prompt and press ENTER; you are prompted to specify the wire endpoint. Next, enter **13.4,15** and press ENTER; the wire is inserted between rung 3 and 4 on the left side of the PB3.

3. Enter **14.6,16** at the Command prompt and press ENTER; you are prompted to specify the wire endpoint. Next, enter **14.6,15** and press ENTER; the wire is inserted between rung 3 and 4 on the right side of the PB3.

4. Enter **13.4,15** at the Command prompt and press ENTER; you are prompted to specify the wire endpoint. Next, enter **13.4,14** and press ENTER; the wire is inserted between rung 4 and 5.

5. Enter **14.6,15** at the Command prompt and press ENTER; you are prompted to specify the wire endpoint. Next, enter **14.6,14** and press ENTER; the wire is inserted between rung 4 and 5.

6. Enter **13.4,13** at the Command prompt and press ENTER; you are prompted to specify the wire endpoint. Next, enter **13.4,12** and press ENTER; the wire is inserted between rung 6 and 7 on the left side of the PB6.

7. Enter **14.6,13** at the Command prompt and press ENTER; you are prompted to specify the wire endpoint. Next, enter **14.6,12** and press ENTER; the wire is inserted between rung 6 and 7 on the right side of the PB6. Now, press ENTER to exit the command. Figure 6-54 shows the wires inserted in the drawing.

## Scooting Components

1. Choose the **Scoot** tool from **Schematic > Edit Components > Modify Components** drop-down; you are prompted to select the component.

2. Select M2 from rung 4 and enter **14,15** at the Command prompt and then press ENTER; M2 is moved to a new location.

3. Select PB5 from rung 5 and enter **14,14** at the Command prompt and then press ENTER; PB5 is moved to a new location.

4. Select M1 from rung 7 and enter **14,12** at the Command prompt and then press ENTER; M1 is moved to a new location.

5. Press ENTER to exit the command. Figure 6-55 shows the schematic diagram after using the **Scoot** tool.

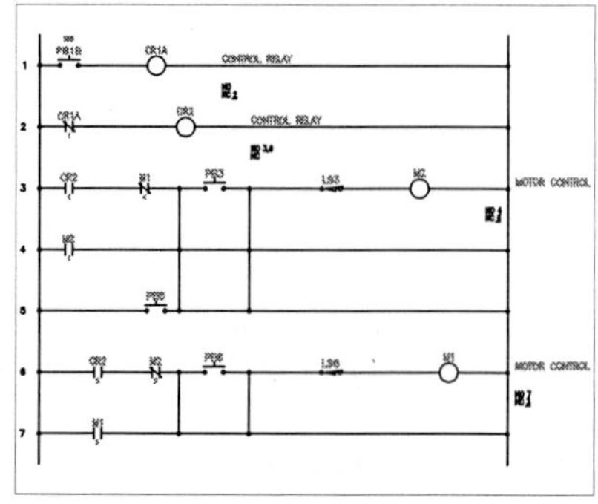


*Figure 6-54 Wires inserted in the ladder*

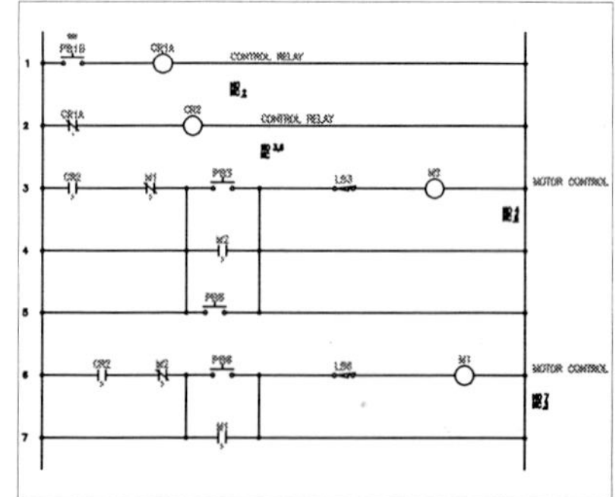


*Figure 6-55 The ladder after using the **Scoot** tool*

## Trimming Wires

1. Choose the **Trim Wire** tool from the **Edit Wires/Wire Numbers** panel of the **Schematic** tab; you are prompted to select the wire to trim.

2. Select the following wires to trim: right and left portions of rung 4, rung 5, and rung 7. Next, press ENTER to exit the command.

## Aligning Components

1. Choose the **Align** tool from **Schematic > Edit Components > Modify Components** drop-down; you are prompted to select the component to align horizontally or vertically.

2. Select PB1B on rung 1; an imaginary line passing through the center of PB1 is displayed and you are prompted to select objects.

3. Select CR1A placed on rung 2, CR2 placed on rung 3, and CR2 placed on rung 6 from the left of the ladder. Next, press ENTER; the components are aligned toward the left.

4. Repeat step1. Select M1 from rung 3; an imaginary line passing through the center of M1 is displayed and you are prompted to select objects. Next, select M2 placed on rung 6 and press ENTER; M1 placed on rung 3 and M2 placed on rung 6 are aligned.

5. Repeat step 1 and then select M1 placed on the right side of rung 6. Next, select M2 placed on rung 3, CR2 placed on rung 2, and CR1A placed on rung 1 and press ENTER; the selected components are aligned.

6. Repeat step 1 and then select PB3 from rung 3; you are prompted to select objects. Next, select M2 placed on rung 4, PB5, PB6, and M1 placed on rung 7 from the drawing and then press ENTER; the selected components are aligned. Figure 6-56 shows the aligned components.

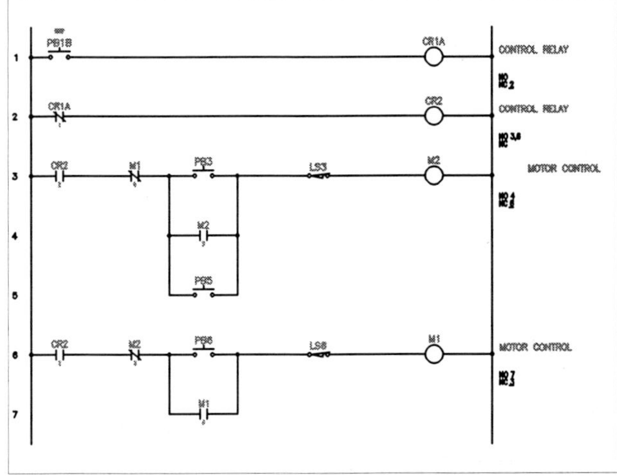


***Figure 6-56*** *The trimmed wires and the aligned components*

## Saving the Drawing File

1. Choose **Save** from the **Application Menu** to save the drawing file *C06_tut01.dwg*.

# Tutorial 2

In this tutorial, you will audit the *C06_tut01.dwg* drawing of the **CADCIM** project by using the **Electrical Audit** and **Drawing Audit** tools and add catalog data to a component in this drawing. You will also surf a component in the *demo004.dwg* drawing. **(Expected time: 20 min)**

The following steps are required to complete this tutorial:

a. Open the drawing.
b. Audit the drawing using the **DWG Audit** tool.
c. Audit the drawing using the **Electrical Audit** tool.
d. Surf the component.
e. Save the drawing file.

## Opening the Drawing

1. Right-click on *C06_tut01.dwg* drawing file of the **CADCIM** project in the **Projects** rollout of the **PROJECT MANAGER**; a shortcut menu is displayed. Choose the **Open** option from the shortcut menu; the drawing is opened.

## Auditing the Drawing using the DWG Audit Tool

1. Choose the **DWG Audit** tool from the **Schematic** panel of the **Reports** tab; the **Drawing Audit** dialog box is displayed.

2. Select the **Active drawing** radio button, if it is not selected by default. Next, choose the **OK** button; the modified **Drawing Audit** dialog box is displayed.

3. Choose the **OK** button in the modified **Drawing Audit** dialog box; the **Drawing Audit** message box is displayed.

4. Choose the **OK** button in the **Drawing Audit** message box; the **Report: Audit for this drawing** dialog box is displayed.

5. Choose the **Close** button from the **Report: Audit for this drawing** dialog box.

   The visual wire indicators in the diagram are shown in red color, refer to Figure 6-57.

6. Choose **View > Redraw** from the menu bar to eliminate the wire indicators.

## Auditing the Drawing Using the Electrical Audit Tool

1. Choose the **Electrical Audit** tool from the **Schematic** panel of the **Reports** tab: the **Electrical Audit** dialog box is displayed. 

2. Select the **Active Drawing** radio button from the **Electrical Audit** dialog box; the errors in the *C06_tut01.dwg* drawing file are displayed in the edit box located on the right of the **Active Drawing** radio button.

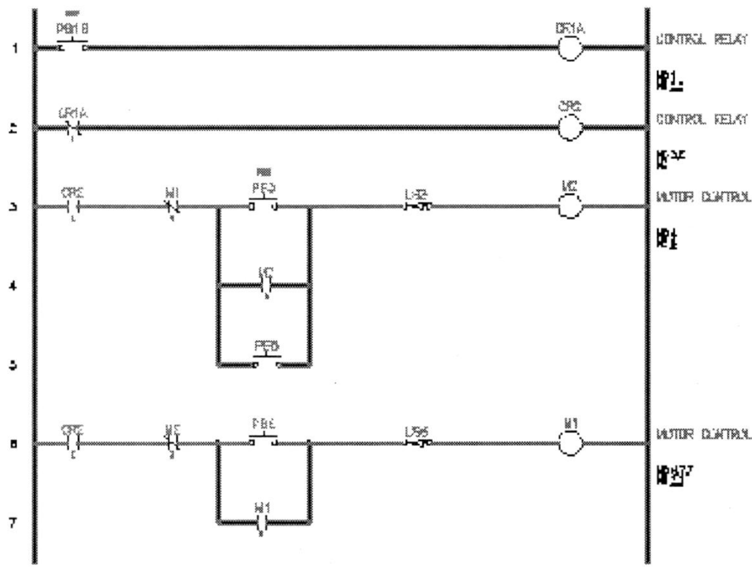


***Figure 6-57** Visual wire indicators indicating wires in the drawing*

3. Choose the **Details** button from the **Electrical Audit** dialog box to expand it.

4. Choose the **Component - No Catalog Number** tab from the **Electrical Audit** dialog box. Next, select the PB1B push button from the **Tag Name** column of this tab. Next, choose the **Go To** button; PB1B push button is zoomed in the drawing area.

**Note**
*After choosing the **Go To** button, if the **QSAVE** message box is displayed, choose the **OK** button in this message box to save the changes.*

5. Right-click on the PB1B component; a marking menu is displayed. Choose the **Edit Component** option from the marking menu; the **Insert / Edit Component** dialog box is displayed.

6. Choose the **Project** button from the **Catalog Data** area of the **Insert / Edit Component** dialog box; the **Find: Catalog Assignments** dialog box is displayed. Select the **Active Project** radio button, if it is not selected.

7 Choose the **OK** button from the **Find: Catalog Assignments** dialog box; the **HPB11 / VPB11 catalog values(this project)** dialog box is displayed.

**Note**
*If the **QSAVE** message box is displayed, choose the **OK** button in it to save the changes.*

8. Select the **800T-A2A** catalog number from the **Catalog Number** column and choose the **OK** button from the **HPB11 / VPB11 catalog values** dialog box; AB is displayed in the **Manufacturer** edit box and 800T-A2A is displayed in the **Catalog** edit box of the **Insert / Edit Component** dialog box.

9. Next, choose the **OK** button from the **Insert / Edit Component** dialog box to save the changes and exit this dialog box. Now, you can notice 'x' on the left of the PB1B in the **Electrical Audit** dialog box.

10. Choose the **Close** button from the **Electrical Audit** dialog box.

    In this manner, you can rectify the missing catalog number error from the drawing. Now, you need to check whether an error is rectified or not.

11. Choose the **Electrical Audit** tool from the **Schematic** panel of the **Reports** tab; the **Electrical Audit** dialog box is displayed. Choose the **Active Drawing** button to display the errors in the active drawing.

12. Choose the **Details** button to expand this dialog box. Next, choose the **Component - No Catalog Number** tab from the **Electrical Audit** dialog box.

    You will notice that the selected error is corrected and is not displayed in the **Electrical Audit** dialog box. In other words, PB1B is not displayed in the list.

13. Choose the **Close** button to exit the **Electrical Audit** dialog box.

## Surfing the Component

1. Add the *demo002.dwg* drawing from the **NFPADEMO** project to the **CADCIM** project as discussed in Chapter 2.

2. Make sure the **CADCIM** project is activated. Next, open the *demo004.dwg* drawing.

3. Choose the **Surfer** tool from the **Other Tools** panel of the **Project** tab; you are prompted to select tag for surfer trace. Select the **M422** tag corresponding to the ladder reference number 422; the **Surf** dialog box is displayed, as shown in Figure 6-58.

   Notice that the **Surf** dialog box displays all the five normally open contacts of M422 with manufacturer website link address.

4. Select the second entry in the **Surf** dialog box and choose **Go To**; the *demo002.dwg* drawing opens and shows the selected normally open contact zoomed in. Also, 'x' is displayed in the leftmost column of the selected entry to indicate the surfing. Now, close the **Surf** dialog box.

## Saving the Drawing File

1. Choose **Save** from the **Application Menu** to save the drawing file.

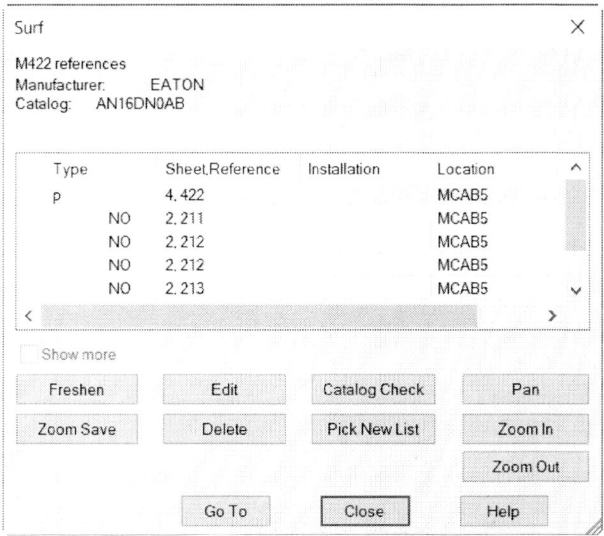


*Figure 6-58 The* ***Surf*** *dialog box*

## Tutorial 3

In this tutorial, you will create a schematic drawing. Next, you will add catalog data to one of the components and then copy it to other components. Also, you will add location data to one of the control relay and copy it to the rest of the control relays. **(Expected time: 40 min)**

The following steps are required to complete this tutorial:

a. Create a new drawing.
b. Insert the ladder.
c. Insert components in the ladder.
d. Copy the catalog data.
e. Enter the location data.
f. Save the drawing file.

### Creating a New Drawing

1. Choose the **New Drawing** button in the **PROJECT MANAGER**; the **Create New Drawing** dialog box is displayed. Enter **C06_tut03** in the **Name** edit box of the **Drawing File** area.

2. Choose the **Browse** button located on the right of the **Template** edit box; the **Select template** dialog box is displayed. Select the **ACAD_ELECTRICAL** template and choose the **Open** button; the location and path of the template file is displayed in the **Template** edit box.

3. Enter **Schematic Components** in the **Description 1** edit box. Next, choose the **OK** button in the **Create New Drawing** dialog box; the *C06_tut03.dwg* drawing is created and displayed at the bottom of the drawing list in the **CADCIM** project. Now, move *C06_tut03.dwg* to the *TUTORIALS* subfolder of the **CADCIM** project.

## Inserting the Ladder

1. Choose the **Insert Ladder** tool from **Schematic > Insert Wires/Wire Numbers > Insert Ladder** drop-down; the **Insert Ladder** dialog box is displayed.

2. Set the following parameters in the **Insert Ladder** dialog box:

   Width: **6.000** Spacing: **1.000**
   1st Reference: **101** Rungs: **7**

   Make sure that the **1Phase** radio button in the **Phase** area and the **Yes** radio button in the **Draw Rungs** area are selected. Do not change values in the rest of the edit boxes.

3. Click in the **Length** edit box; the length of the ladder is automatically calculated and displayed in the edit box. Next, choose the **OK** button; you are prompted to specify the start position of the first rung.

4. Enter **8,13** at the Command prompt and press ENTER; the ladder is inserted into the drawing. Next, choose **View > Zoom > Extents** from the menu bar; the drawing gets zoomed.

## Inserting Components in the Ladder

1. Choose the **Icon Menu** tool from **Schematic > Insert Components > Icon Menu** drop-down; the **Insert Component** dialog box is displayed.

2. Select the **Push Buttons** icon from the **NFPA: Schematic Symbols** area of the **Insert Component** dialog box. Next, select the **Push Button NO** icon in the **NFPA: Push Buttons** area; the cursor along with the component is displayed on the screen and you are prompted to specify the insertion point for the push button.

3. Enter **8.5,13** at the Command prompt and press ENTER; the push button is placed at rung 1 and the **Insert / Edit Component** dialog box is displayed. Next, make sure PB101 is displayed in the **Component Tag** edit box and enter **START** in the **Line1** of the **Description** area. Next, choose the **OK** button in the **Insert / Edit Component** dialog box. Similarly, insert other components as mentioned in Table 1.

***Table 1*** *Components to be inserted in the ladder*

| Rung Number | Component to be selected from the **Insert Component** dialog box | Insertion point to be specified at the Command prompt | Component tag values to be specified in the **Component Tag** edit box of the **Insert / Edit Component** dialog box, if it is not already displayed | Descriptions to be specified in the **Description** area of the **Insert / Edit Component** or **Insert / Edit child Component** dialog box |
|---|---|---|---|---|
| 101 | Limit Switch, NC | 9.5,13 | LS101 | UP |
| 101 | Relay Coil | 11.5,13 | CR101 | CONTROL RELAY |

| 102 | Relay NO Contact | 9,12 | CR101 | CONTROL RELAY |
|---|---|---|---|---|
| 103 | Relay NO Contact | 9,11 | CR101 | CONTROL RELAY |
| 103 | Relay NC Contact | 10.5,11 | CR 101 | CONTROL RELAY |
| 103 | 1 Phase Motor | 12.5,11 | MOT103 | DOWN MOTOR |
| 104 | Relay NO Contact | 9,10 | CR101 | CONTROL RELAY |
| 105 | Relay Coil | 11.5,9 | CR105 | CONTROL RELAY |
| 106 | Relay Coil | 11.5,8 | CR106 | CONTROL RELAY |
| 106 | Relay NC Contact | 10.5,8 | CR105 | CONTROL RELAY |
| 107 | Relay NO Contact | 9,7 | CR106 | CONTROL RELAY |

4. After entering description and other information in the **Insert / Edit Component** or **Insert / Edit Child Component** dialog box, choose the **OK** button; the components are inserted in the drawing, as shown in Figure 6-59.

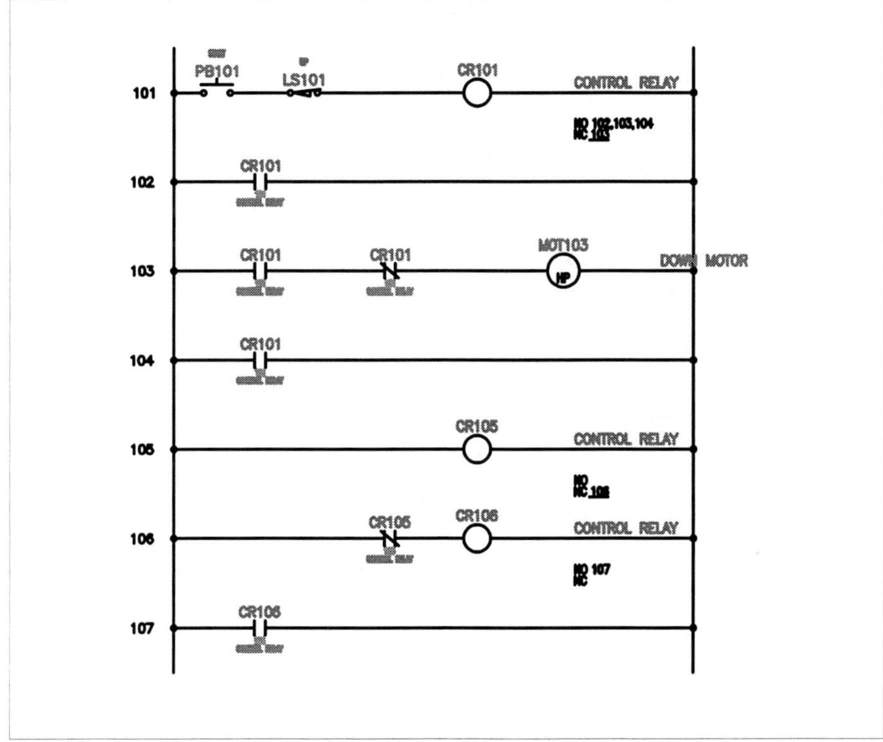


***Figure 6-59*** *Components inserted in the drawing*

## Copying the Catalog Data

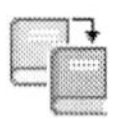

1. Choose the **Copy Catalog Assignment** tool from **Schematic > Edit Components > Edit Components** drop-down; you are prompted to select the master component.

2. Select CR101 placed on rung 101 as the master component; the **Copy Catalog Assignment** dialog box is displayed.

3. Choose the **Catalog Lookup** button; the **Catalog Browser** dialog box is displayed, as shown in Figure 6-60.

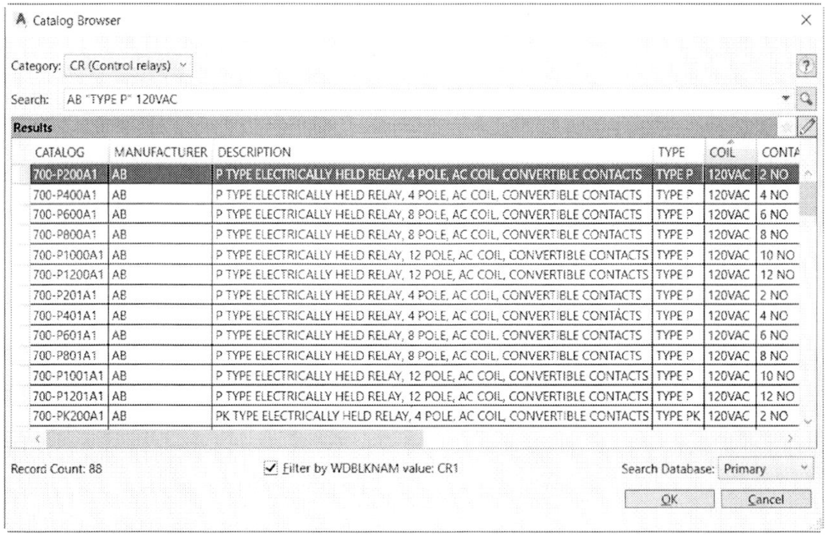


*Figure 6-60 The **Catalog Browser** dialog box*

4. Select the row which contains **700-P200A1** in its **Catalog** column and then choose the **OK** button; the **Copy Catalog Assignment** dialog box is displayed again. In this dialog box, **AB** is displayed in the **Manufacturer** edit box and **700-P200A1** is displayed in the **Catalog** edit box.

5. Choose the **OK** button from the **Copy Catalog Assignment** dialog box; you are prompted to select the target components.

6. Select CR105 and CR106 placed on rung 105 and rung 106, respectively and press ENTER; the **Update Related Components?** message box is displayed. Choose the **Skip** button; the catalog data is copied to the selected components.

**Note**

*Choose the **OK** button from the **QSAVE** message box, if it is displayed.*

You need to check the catalog data of CR105 and CR106.

7. Right-click on CR105 and CR106 one by one; a marking menu is displayed. Next, choose the **Edit Component** option; the **Insert / Edit Component** dialog box is displayed. You

will notice that the catalog data information is displayed in the **Catalog Data** area of the **Insert / Edit Component** dialog box. Choose the **OK** button in this dialog box; the **Assign Symbol to Catalog Number** message box is displayed. In this message box, select **Map symbol to catalog number**; the message box is closed.

## Entering the Location Data

1. Click on the down arrow given on the right of the **Edit Components** panel of the **Schematic** tab; a flyout will be displayed. Choose the **Copy Installation/Location Code Values** button from the flyout; the **Copy Installation/Location to Components** dialog box is displayed.

2. Make sure the **Location** check box is selected and then enter **MCAB5** in the **Location** edit box. Next, choose the **OK** button; you are prompted to select objects. Next, select CR105 and CR106 placed on rung 105 and rung 106, respectively, and then press ENTER; the **Update Related Components?** message box is displayed.

3. Choose the **Skip** button from the **Update Related Components?** message box; the location codes are assigned to the selected components. If the **QSAVE** message box is displayed, choose the **OK** button from it; the drawings get updated and MCAB5 is displayed on the CR105 and CR106, as shown in Figure 6-61.

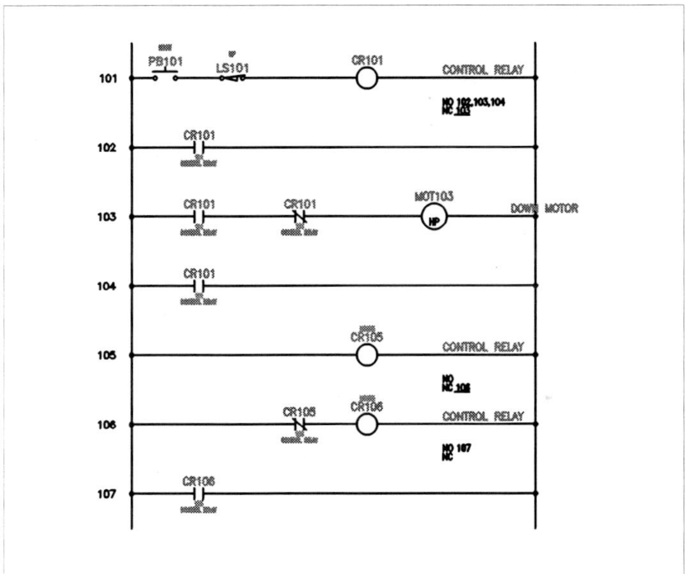


***Figure 6-61** The updated drawing*

## Saving the Drawing File

1. Choose **Save** from the **Application Menu** to save the drawing file.

## Tutorial 4

In this tutorial, you will update *C06_tut01.dwg* and *C06_tut03.dwg* drawing files using the **Project-Wide Update/Retag** tool. **(Expected time: 15 min)**

The following steps are required to complete this tutorial:

a. Open the drawings.
b. Update the drawings.
c. Save the drawing files.

### Opening, Saving, and Adding the Drawings to the CADCIM Project List

1. Open the *C06_tut01.dwg* and *C06_tut03.dwg* files.

   You can also download these files from *www.cadcim.com*. The path of the file is as follows:

   *Textbooks > CAD/CAM > AutoCAD Electrical > AutoCAD Electrical 2022 for Electrical Control Designers*

2. Save the *C06_tut01.dwg* file with the name *C06_tut01_update.dwg* file and *C06_tut03.dwg* file with the name *C06_tut03_update.dwg* file and add them to the **CADCIM** project list as done earlier.

### Updating the Drawings

In this section, you will use the **Update/Retag** tool to update ladder references, component tags, sheet numbers, and wire numbers of *C06_tut01_update.dwg* and *C06_tut03_update.dwg* drawing files.

1. Choose the **Update/Retag** tool from the **Project Tools** panel of the **Project** tab; the **Project-Wide Update or Retag** dialog box is displayed.

2. Select the **Component Retag** and **Wire Number and Signal Tag/Retag** check boxes. Next, choose the **Setup** button located next to the **Wire Number and Signal Tag/Retag** check box; the **Wire Tagging (Project-wide)**dialog box is displayed. Make sure the **Reference-based tags** and the **Tag/retag all** radio buttons are selected in this dialog box Also, select the **Insert as Fixed** check box.

3. Select the **Format override** check box and then enter **%N%S** in the edit box below it, refer to Figure 6-62. Next, choose the **OK** button from the **Wire Tagging (Project-wide)**dialog box to close it.

   Note that **%N** stands for reference number and **%S** stands for sheet value.

4. Select the **Ladder References** check box from the **Project-Wide Update or Retag** dialog box. Make sure that the **Resequence** radio button is selected and then choose the **Setup** button located next to it to renumber the ladder references; the **Renumber Ladders** dialog box is displayed.

5. Enter **60** in the edit box and make sure the **Use next sequential reference** radio button is selected, refer to Figure 6-63. Next, choose **OK** in the **Renumber Ladders** dialog box.

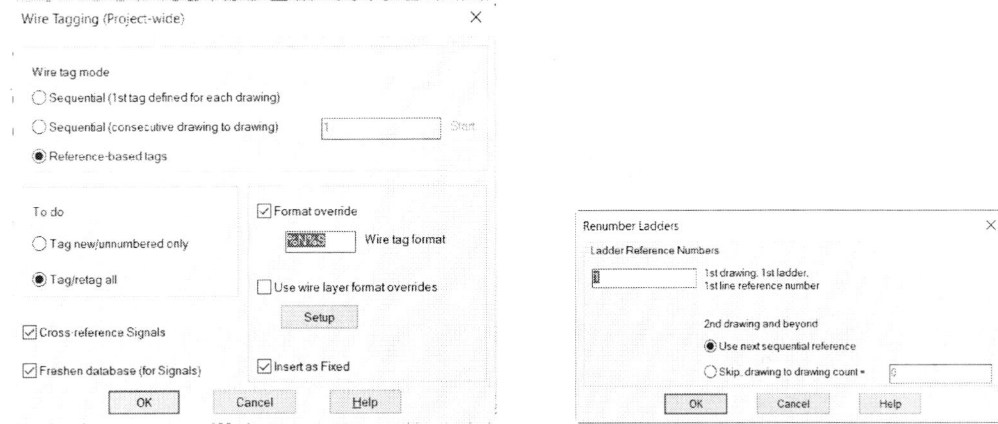


*Figure 6-62 The* ***Wire Tagging (Project-wide)*** *dialog box*

*Figure 6-63 The* ***Renumber Ladders*** *dialog box*

6. Select the **Sheet ( %S value)** check box from the **Project-Wide Update or Retag** dialog box. Make sure the **Resequence - Start with** radio button is selected and enter **01** in the edit box located next to it.

7. Choose **OK** from the **Project-Wide Update or Retag** dialog box; the **Select Drawings to Process** dialog box is displayed.

8. Select *C06_tut01_update.dwg* and *C06_tut03_update.dwg* drawing files from the upper part of the **Select Drawings to Process** dialog box and choose **Process**; the selected drawings files are transferred to the lower part of the dialog box. Next, choose **OK**; updation of the selected drawing files starts and the messages are displayed in the command prompt. Once the updation process is completed, you will notice change in the ladder reference numbers, component tags, and wire numbers of both the drawing files.

## Saving the Drawing File

1. Choose **Save** from the **Application Menu** to save the *C06_tut01_update.dwg* and *C06_tut03_update.dwg* drawing files.

---

# Self-Evaluation Test

**Answer the following questions and then compare them to those given at the end of this chapter:**

1. Which of the following commands is used to copy components?

(a) **AECOMPONENT** (b) **AECOPYCOMP**
(c) **AEWIRE** (d) **AEAUDIT**

2. The default format for component tagging is _________.

3. The _________ tool is used to change the text size and width of attributes.

4 The _________ tool is used to update or retag components.

5. The _________ tool is used to copy the selected components.

6. The _________ button of the **Electrical Auditing** dialog box is used to display the detailed information of the errors found in a project.

7. You can scoot a component in any direction. (T/F)

8. You can align components only vertically. (T/F)

9. The **Electrical Audit** tool is used to correct errors in a project. (T/F)

10. You cannot print an auditing report. (T/F)

## Review Questions

**Answer the following questions:**

1. Which of the following tabs of the **Electrical Audit** dialog box displays the missing or duplicated wire numbers in a project?

(a) **Cable Exception** (b) **Component - No Connection**
(c) **Wire Exception** (d) **Wire - No Connection**

2. Which of the following buttons is used to align components vertically or horizontally?

(a) **Move** (b) **Pick Master**
(c) **Scoot** (d) **Align**

3. Which of the following buttons is used to change the state of a normally open (NO) component to a normally closed (NC) and vice-versa?

(a) **Toggle NO/NC** (b) **Project-Wide Update/Retag**
(c) **Setup** (d) **Copy Component**

4. Which of the following check boxes should be selected to retag all non-fixed components of the drawing(s)?

(a) **Component Cross-Reference Update** (b) **Wire gap pointers**
(c) **Wire Number and Signal Tag/Retag** (d) **Component Retag**

5. When you choose the **Go To** button in the **Electrical Audit** dialog box, AutoCAD Electrical takes you to the error location in the project and rectify the error. (T/F)

6. If you select the **Title Block Update** check box, the title block information of only the active drawing will be updated. (T/F)

7. By choosing the **Move Component** button, you can reposition a selected component from its current location or wire location and insert it at a new location. (T/F)

8. The auditing tools find out errors in project drawings. (T/F)

9. The **Move/Show Attribute** tool is used to move attributes. (T/F)

# EXERCISES

## Exercise 1

In this exercise, you will create a new drawing named *C06_exer01.dwg* and insert a ladder with Width = 5, Spacing= 1, Rungs = 6, and 1st reference = 500. Also, you will insert components in the ladder, as shown in Figure 6-64. In addition, you will use the basic editing tools such as **Copy Component** and **Align Component** to copy and align the components, respectively. You will use the **Wire** tool to insert wire between rung 500 and rung 501 and the **Trim Wire** tool to trim the wire. **(Expected time: 25 min)**

## Exercise 2

In this exercise, you will audit the **NEW_PROJECT** project using the **DWG Audit** and **Electrical Audit** tools. Also, you will save the report on the desktop as *drawing_audit.txt* and *electrical_audit.txt*. **(Expected time: 15 min)**

## Exercise 3

In this exercise, you will open the *C06_exer01.dwg* drawing file and save it as *C06_exer03.dwg* in the **NEW_PROJECT** project. Next, you will change ladder references, component tags, and cross-references from reference-based to sequential using the **Update/Retag** tool, refer to Figure 6-65. **(Expected time: 20 min)**

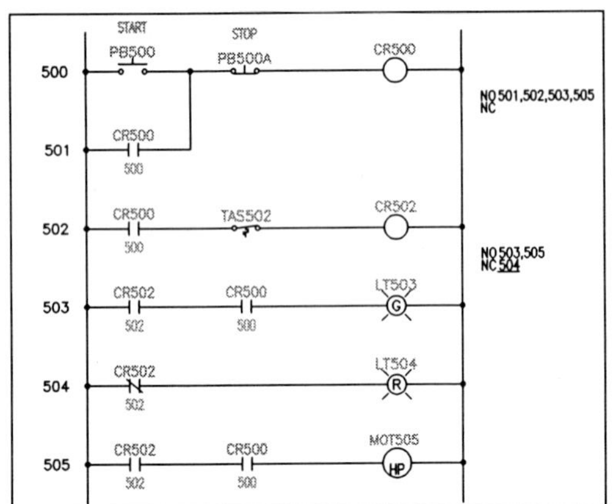


*Figure 6-64 Components inserted in the ladder*

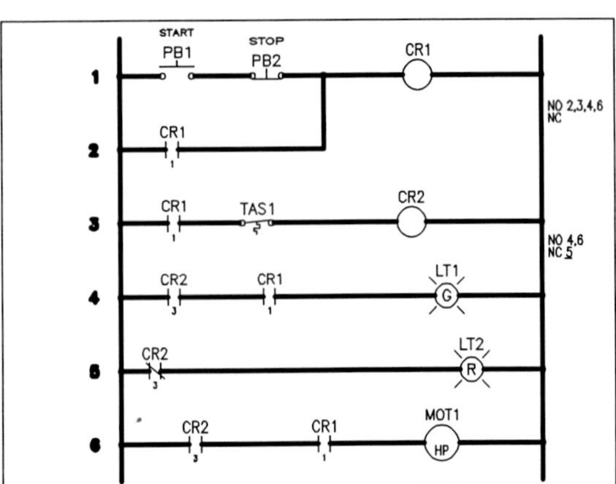


***Figure 6-65*** *References changed using the* ***Update/Retag*** *tool*

**Hint:** Enter **1** in the edit box on the right of the **Sequential** radio button in the **Change Each Drawing's Settings - Project-wide** dialog box.

## Answers to Self-Evaluation Test

1. b, 2. %F%N, 3. **Change Attribute Size**, 4. **Update/Retag**, 5. **Copy Compone[illegible]** 6. **Details**, 7. F, 8. F, 9. T, 10. F

# Chapter 7

# Connectors, Point-to-Point Wiring Diagrams, and Circuits

## Learning Objectives

**After completing this chapter, you will be able to:**

- *Insert connectors*
- *Edit the existing connector and connector pin numbers*
- *Insert splices*
- *Create and edit point-to-point wiring diagrams*
- *Insert wires and multiple wire bus*
- *Bend wires at right angle*
- *Create, insert, move, and copy circuits*
- *Save circuits using WBlock*
- *Insert WBlock circuits*
- *Build a circuit using the Circuit Builder tool*
- *Add multiple-phase ladders and wires*
- *Add three-phase symbol to a multiple-phase circuit*

# INTRODUCTION

An electrical connector is a conductive device that is used to join electrical circuits together. Typically, an electrical connector is used to connect a wire, or a group of wires at a single junction. It is designed in such a way that it separates wires easily. In AutoCAD Electrical, there are connector tools that enable you to easily place automatically built parametric connectors based on the information you specify.

In this chapter, you will learn to insert connectors in a drawing and use different connector tools to manage connector data, including pins and receptacles in the project drawings. Using these tools, you can quickly create custom connectors, add and remove pins, edit connectors for specific applications, and so on. Also, you will learn about the point-to-point wiring tools that help you in creating point-to-point wiring diagrams easily as opposed to ladder diagrams.

In the circuits section, you will learn to save repetitive circuits in a project as icons. This will help you reproduce drawings in very less time with great accuracy. These saved circuits are similar to blocks as these are also inserted as a single object.

# INSERTING CONNECTORS

| | |
|---|---|
| **Ribbon:** | Schematic > Insert Components > Insert Connector drop-down > Insert Connector |
| **Toolbar:** | ACE:Main Electrical > Insert Connector drop-down >Insert Connector or ACE:Insert Connector > Insert Connector |
| **Menu:** | Components > Insert Connector > Insert Connector |
| **Command:** | AECONNECTOR |

The **Insert Connector** tool is used to create a connector from the user-defined parameters. The connector created using this tool consists of plug, receptacle, pin numbers, and other attributes. The pin numbers are displayed on the plug side (round corners), receptacle side (square corners), or on both sides. A component tag is displayed above the connector. The connector with different components is shown in Figure 7-1.

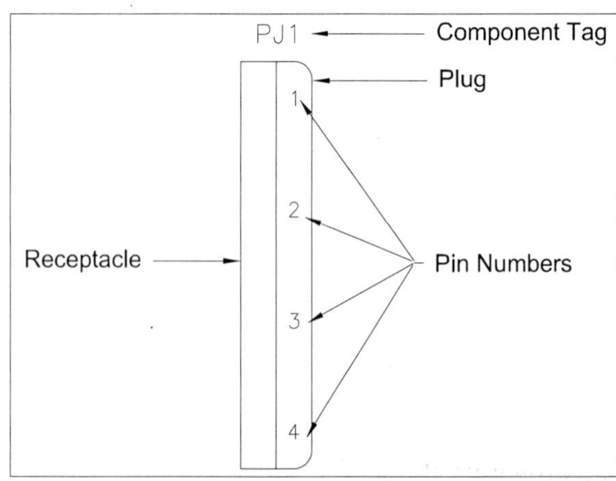


***Figure 7-1** The connector and its components*

To insert a connector in a drawing, choose the **Insert Connector** tool from the **Insert Connector** drop-down in the **Insert Components** panel of the **Schematic** tab, as shown in Figure 7-2; the **Insert Connector** dialog box will be displayed, as shown in Figure 7-3. In this dialog box, you can specify the parameters for inserting connectors. The areas and options in this dialog box are discussed next.

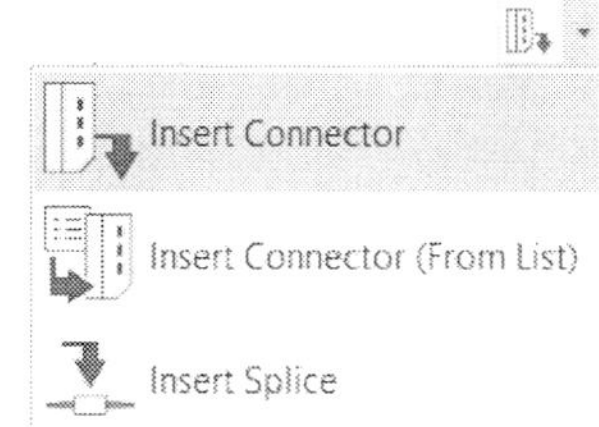


*Figure 7-2 The **Insert Connector** drop-down*

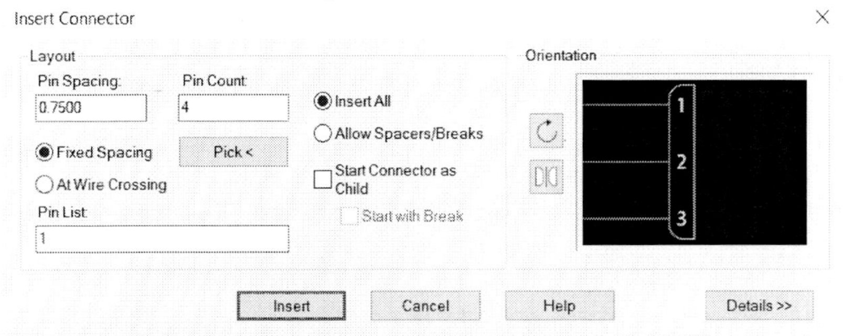


*Figure 7-3 The **Insert Connector** dialog box*

## Layout Area

The **Layout** area is used to specify the spacing between the pins, pin count, format for the pins, and so on. The options in this area are discussed next.

### Pin Spacing

This edit box is used to specify the spacing value between pins for the connector. By default, 0.7500 is displayed in this edit box.

### Pin Count

This edit box is used to specify the number of pins that you want to include in the connector.

### Pick <

The **Pick <** button is used to define the pin count for a connector by selecting two points from the drawing area. This is an alternative method to determine pin count for a new connector. To define a pin count, choose the **Pick <** button; the **Insert Connector** dialog box will close and you will be prompted to specify the first insertion point for the connector. Next, specify the first insertion point for the connector; you will be prompted to specify the second insertion point for the connector. Specify the second insertion point; the **Insert Connector** dialog box will be displayed again, with the pin count in the **Pin Count** edit box.

### Fixed Spacing

The **Fixed Spacing** radio button is used to maintain uniform spacing between pins. By default, the **Fixed Spacing** radio button is selected. As a result, a connector will be created within the specified pin spacing.

## At Wire Crossing

The **At Wire Crossing** radio button is used to adjust the spacing between the pins according to their intersection with the underlying wires. To adjust the spacing, select this radio button; the pins will automatically be placed at its intersection with the underlying wires. If wire crossings are not present, the default pin spacing will be used for rest of the pins.

## Pin List

The **Pin List** edit box is used to specify the format for pin numbers. To do so, specify the starting pin number or letter for the connector separated by commas in the **Pin List** edit box. By default, the specified pin value will be incremented by one character. You can also enter a specific pin list order in this edit box.

## Insert All

The **Insert All** radio button is used to insert a connector without any breaks or spacers.

## Allow Spacers/Breaks

The **Allow Spacers/Breaks** radio button is used to add spacers or breaks between the pins of a connector. To add spacers or breaks, select the **Allow Spacers/Breaks** radio button and then choose the **Insert** button from the **Insert Connector** dialog box; you will be prompted to specify the insertion point for the connector. Next, specify the insertion point; the **Custom Pin Spaces / Breaks** dialog box will be displayed, as shown in Figure 7-4. The options in this dialog box are discussed next.

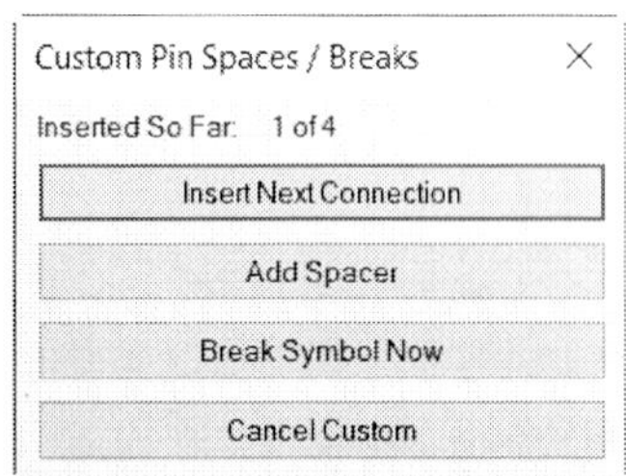


*Figure 7-4 The **Custom Pin Spaces / Breaks** dialog box*

### Insert Next Connection

Choose the **Insert Next Connection** tool; the next pin of the connector will be inserted without any space, as shown in Figure 7-5.

### Add Spacer

Choose the **Add Spacer** button to add space between the connector pins. Figure 7-6 shows the connector with space added between pins 1 and 2.

### Break Symbol Now

The **Break Symbol Now** button is used to break connector symbol at the current pin location. To break the connector symbol, choose the **Break Symbol Now** button; you will be prompted to specify the insertion point for the remaining connector. Specify the insertion point for the remaining part of the connector; the **Connector Layout** dialog box will be displayed, as shown in Figure 7-7. The options in this dialog box are same as those in the **Insert Connector** dialog box. Specify the required options in the **Connector Layout** dialog box and then choose the **OK** button; the **Custom Pin Spaces / Breaks** dialog box will be displayed again. To break the connector symbol again, you need to repeat the process discussed above. Figure 7-8 shows the connector after choosing the **Break Symbol Now** button.

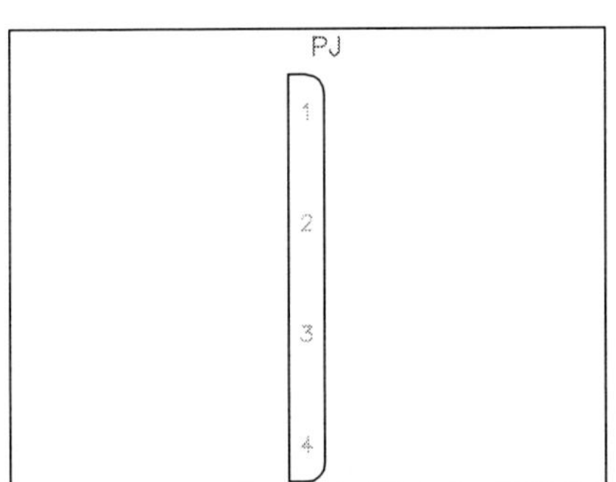


***Figure 7-5*** *Connector pins inserted without any space*

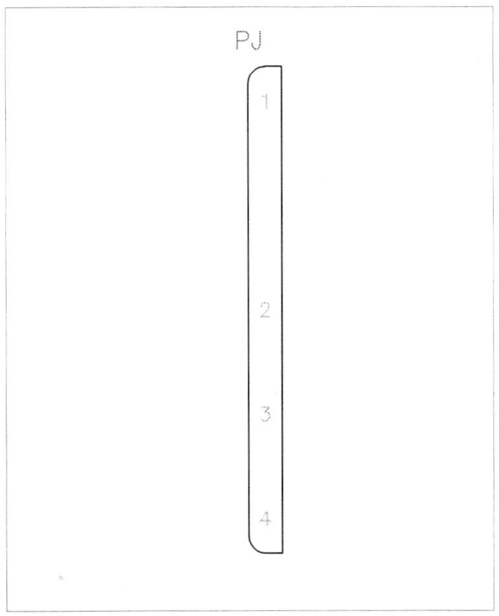


***Figure 7-6*** *The space added between the connector pins*

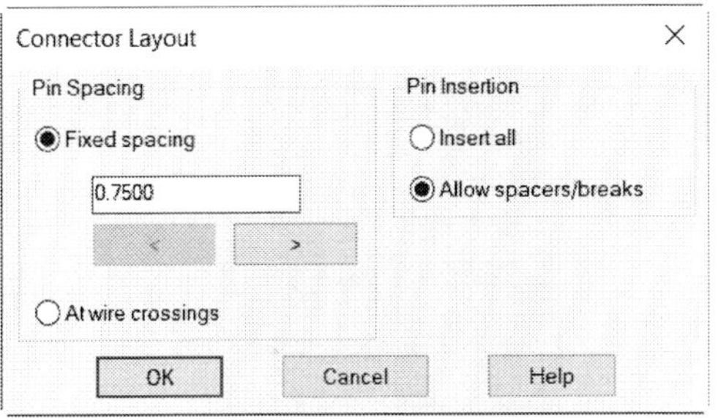


***Figure 7-7*** *The **Connector Layout** dialog box*

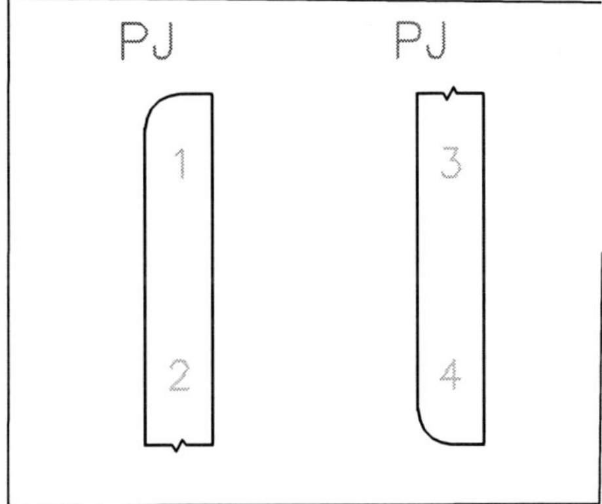


***Figure 7-8*** *The connector after choosing the **Break Symbol Now** button*

### Cancel Custom

The **Cancel Custom** button is used to insert the remaining pins in the connector without breaks or spacers. To insert the connector pins without any further prompts, choose the **Cancel Custom** button; the command will be cancelled and a connector will be inserted with the remaining pins without breaks or spacers.

## Start Connector as Child

The **Start Connector as Child** check box is used to insert a connector as child component. To insert a child of a parent connector, select this check box; the connector will be inserted as a child component. Also, the **Start with Break** check box will be activated. After the insertion of the connector, you need to correlate the connector to a parent connector. To link a child and parent connector, you need to define a common tag ID.

### Start with Break

The **Start with Break** check box is used to start the child connector symbol with a broken top, which indicates that it is a continuation of a different connector. By default, the **Start with Break** check box is cleared, which indicates that the child component has a round corner that can be set by entering the value in the **Radius** edit box of the **Size** area of the **Insert Connector** dialog box. Note that the **Size** area will be available on clicking the **Details** button of the **Insert Connector** dialog box.

## Orientation Area

The **Orientation** area, as shown in Figure 7-9, consists of the **Rotate** and **Flip** buttons. These buttons are used to change the orientation of a connector. In this area, you can preview the connector in the preview window. The options in this area are discussed next.

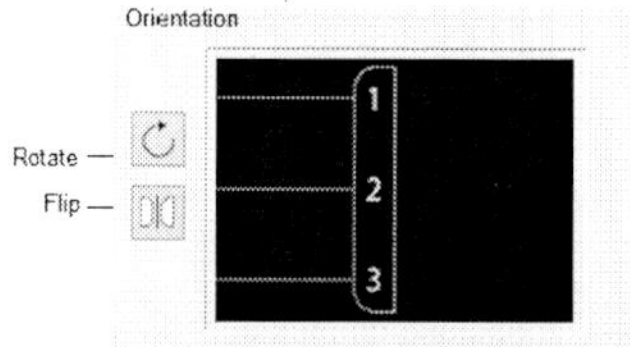


*Figure 7-9 The **Orientation** area showing the **Rotate** and **Flip** buttons and preview of a connector*

### Rotate

Choose the **Rotate** button to switch the orientation of a connector between the horizontal and vertical positions, as shown in Figures 7-10 and 7-11, respectively. You can view the orientation of a connector in the preview window of the **Orientation** area.

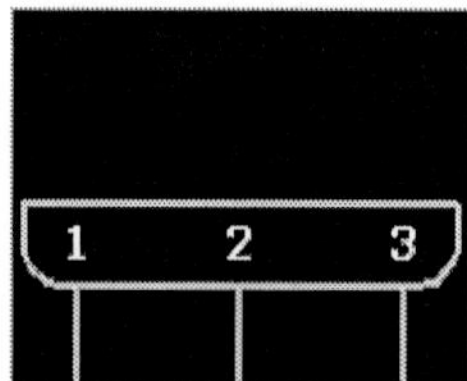

*Figure 7-10 The horizontal orientation*

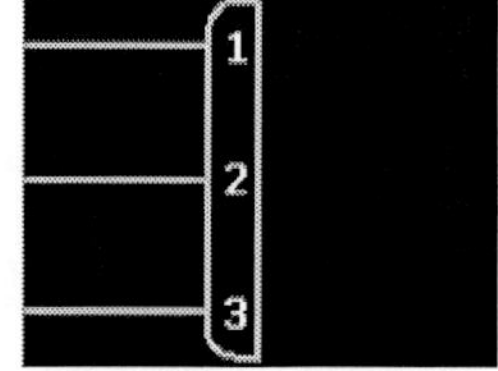


*Figure 7-11 The vertical orientation*

### Flip

Choose the **Flip** button to flip the connector.

## Details

The **Details** button is used to expand or collapse the **Insert Connector** dialog box. Choose the **Details>>** button to expand the **Insert Connector** dialog box. Figure 7-12 shows the expanded **Insert Connector** dialog box.

The options displayed after the expansion of the **Insert Connector** dialog box are discussed next.

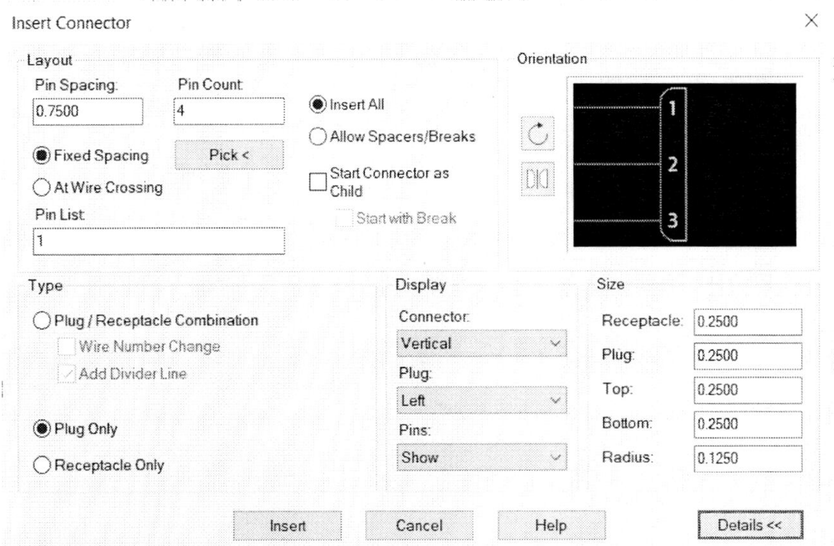


*Figure 7-12 The expanded **Insert Connector** dialog box after choosing the **Details** button*

## Type Area

The **Type** area is used to define the type of connector. The options in this area are discussed next.

### Plug/Receptacle Combination

The **Plug/Receptacle Combination** radio button is used to insert both the plug and receptacle sides of a connector.

#### Wire Number Change

Select the **Wire Number Change** check box to change the wire number through the connector symbol.

#### Add Divider Line

The **Add Divider Line** check box is used to add a divider line between the plug and receptacle of a connector. If you clear the **Add Divider Line** check box, no divider line will be added between the plug and receptacle of a connector, as shown in Figure 7-13.

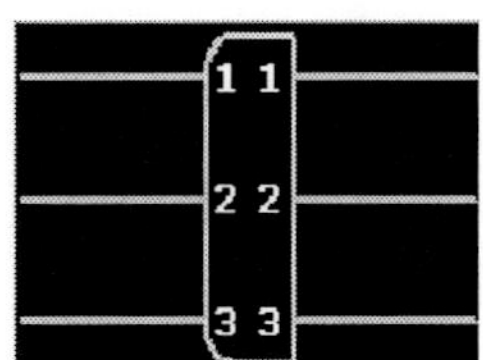


*Figure 7-13 The connector without the divider line*

### Plug Only

Select the **Plug Only** radio button to insert only the plug side of a connector, as shown in Figure 7-14.

### Receptacle Only

Select the **Receptacle Only** radio button to insert only the receptacle side of a connector, as shown in Figure 7-15.

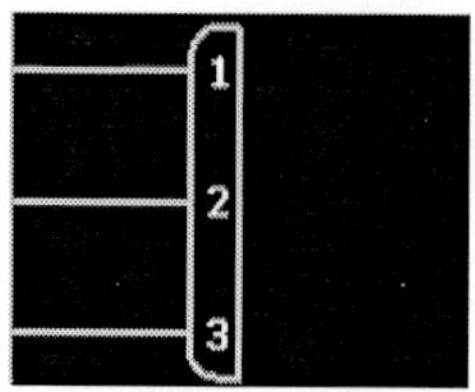


*Figure 7-14 The plug of a connector*

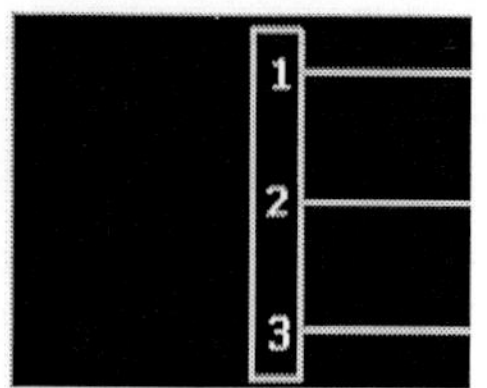


*Figure 7-15 The receptacle of a connector*

## Display Area

The **Display** area is used to define the placement of a connector. The options in this area are discussed next.

### Connector

The options in the **Connector** drop-down list are used to define the orientation of a connector. Using the options in this drop-down list, you can specify whether to insert the connector horizontally or vertically. To define the orientation of a connector, select an option from the **Connector** drop-down list. The options in this drop-down list work similar to the **Rotate** button in the **Orientation** area.

### Plug

The options in the **Plug** drop-down list are used to define the position of a plug. Note that the **Top** and **Bottom** options will be displayed in the **Plug** drop-down list only if you choose the **Rotate** button from the **Orientation** area and set it along the horizontal axis. The **Right** and **Left** options will be displayed in the **Plug** drop-down list only if you choose the **Rotate** button from the **Orientation** area and set it along the vertical axis. The options in the **Plug** drop-down list work similar to the **Flip** button in the **Orientation** area.

### Pins

The options in the **Pins** drop-down list are used to specify the position of pins of a connector. To specify the position of pins, select an option from the **Pins** drop-down list; the position of pins of the connector will be changed. You can make pin numbers visible on connector or hide them by selecting the required options from the **Pins** drop-down list. Note that the options in this drop-down list changes as per the options selected in the **Type** area.

## Size Area

The options in the **Size** area are used to define different parameters for building the outline of a connector. The different options in this area are discussed next.

### Receptacle

The **Receptacle** edit box is used to specify the width of the receptacle side of a connector. By default, 0.2500 is displayed in this edit box.

### Plug

The **Plug** edit box is used to specify the width of the plug side of a connector. By default, 0.2500 is displayed in this edit box.

### Top

The **Top** edit box is used to specify the distance from the top of a connector to the first pin of a connector. By default, 0.2500 is displayed in this edit box.

### Bottom

The **Bottom** edit box is used to specify the distance from the bottom of a connector to the last pin of a connector. By default, 0.2500 is displayed in this edit box.

### Radius

The **Radius** edit box is used to enter the radius for the rounded portion of the plug representation of a connector. If you leave this edit box blank, there will be no fillet in the corner of the plug. By default, 0.1250 is displayed in this edit box.

## Insert

The **Insert** button is used to insert a connector into the drawing.

After specifying required options, choose the **Insert** button and specify the insertion point; the connector will be inserted at the specified point and the **Insert / Edit Component** dialog box will be displayed. The options in this dialog box are discussed in the next section.

**Note**

1. *If you choose the* ***Insert*** *button without specifying the pin count in the* ***Pin Count*** *edit box, the* ***Pin count not defined*** *message box will be displayed informing that the connector cannot be inserted without defining the pin count.*

2. *Once the settings in the* ***Insert Connector*** *dialog box are changed they will remain the same throughout AutoCAD Electrical sessions until modified.*

# EDITING CONNECTOR

| | |
|---|---|
| **Ribbon:** | Schematic > Edit Components >Edit Components drop-down > Edit |
| **Toolbar:** | ACE:Main Electrical > Edit Component<br>or ACE:Edit Component > Edit Component |
| **Menu:** | Components > Edit Component |
| **Command:** | AEEDITCOMPONENT |

When you insert a connector in the drawing, the **Insert / Edit Component** dialog box will be displayed. You can also edit the connector at any time. To do so, choose the **Edit** tool from the **Edit Components** drop-down in the **Edit Components** panel of the **Schematic** tab; you will be prompted to select a component to edit. Select the connector to be edited; the **Insert / Edit Component** dialog box will be displayed, refer to Figure 7-16. Almost all options in this dialog box have been discussed in Chapter 5. The remaining options in this dialog box are discussed next.

The **Pins** area is used to assign pin numbers to the pins of a connector. To edit or assign pin numbers to a connector, choose the **List** button from the **Pins** area; the **Connector Pin Numbers In Use** dialog box will be displayed, as shown in Figure 7-17. This dialog box lists all pin numbers that have been assigned to the connectors. Select the connector pin number row that you want to modify; the options in the **Pin Numbers** and **Pin Descriptions** areas will be activated. The tag and pin count of the selected connector will be displayed on the upper left corner of the **Connector Pin Numbers In Use** dialog box. The options in this dialog box are discussed next.

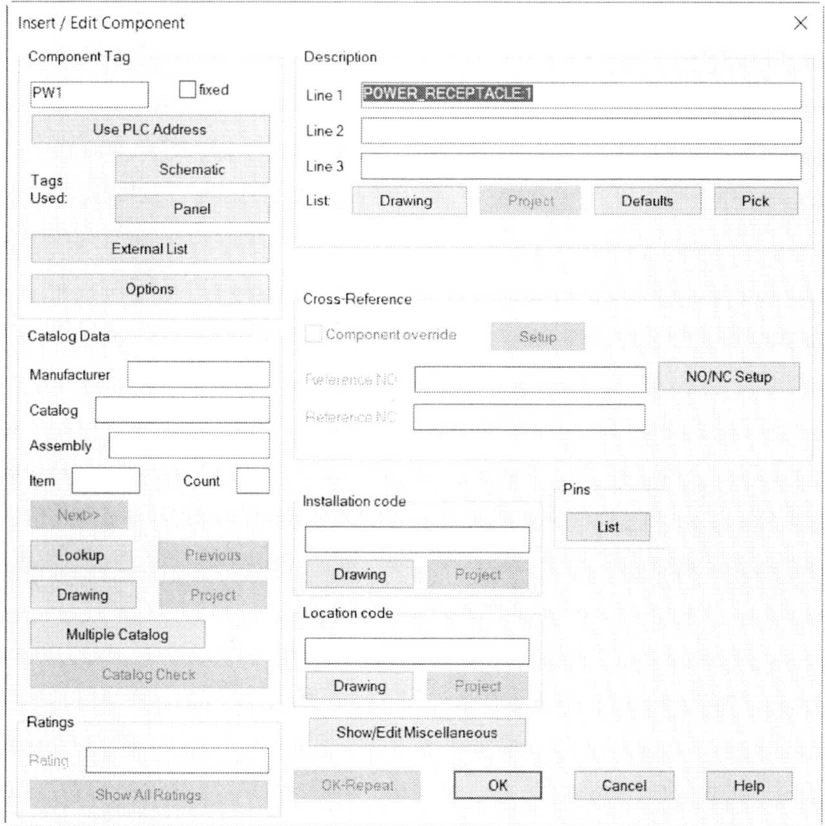


*Figure 7-16 The **Insert / Edit Component** dialog box*

## Pin List Area

The **Pin List** area displays all available pins that can be assigned to a connector.

## Sheet, Reference

The **Sheet**, **Reference** column of the **Connector Pin Numbers In Use** dialog box displays the sheet number and the reference line number of a connector.

## Plug

The **Plug** column displays the pin number of the plug. You can change the value of this column by entering a new value in the **Plug** edit box of the **Pin Numbers** area.

## Description

The **Description** column displays the description of the terminal, which is linked to a wire connection point. The first **Description** column displays the description of a plug and the second **Description** column displays the description of a receptacle. You can edit the description of both plug and receptacle by specifying new values in the **Plug** and **Receptacle** edit boxes of the **Pin Descriptions** area. The descriptions that you enter in these edit boxes are automatically displayed in the respective **Description** columns.

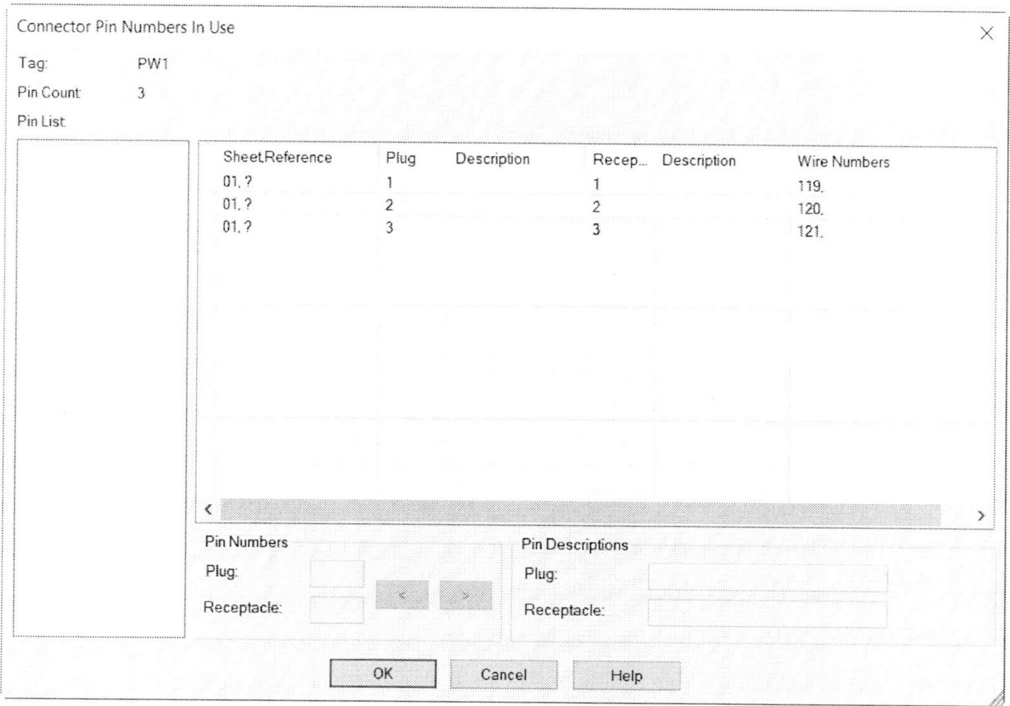


*Figure 7-17 The **Connector Pin Numbers In Use** dialog box*

## Receptacle

The **Receptacle** column displays the pin number of a receptacle. The value in this column changes automatically when you enter a new value in the **Receptacle** edit box of the **Pin Numbers** area.

## Wire Numbers

The **Wire Numbers** column displays the wire numbers associated to a connector.

## Pin Numbers Area

The **Pin Numbers** area will be activated only if you select a row from the list displayed. This area displays pin numbers of rows selected for plug and receptacle in the **Plug** and **Receptacle** edit boxes, respectively. You can enter the new value for plug and receptacle pin numbers in the **Plug** and **Receptacle** edit boxes. The values displayed in these edit boxes can be either incremented or decremented by choosing the respective arrow buttons located on the right of the **Plug** and

**Receptacle** edit boxes. The values specified in these edit boxes are displayed in the **Plug** and **Receptacle** columns.

## Pin Descriptions

The **Pin Descriptions** area will be available only if you select a row from the list displayed. You can enter description for plug and receptacle pin numbers in the **Plug** and **Receptacle** edit boxes and the specified description for both the plug and receptacle will be displayed in the **Description** columns. After specifying the required options, choose the **OK** button from **Connector Pin Numbers In Use** dialog box. Next, choose the **OK** button from the **Insert / Edit Component** dialog box to edit the pin numbers of the connector.

**Note**

*If you enter a new value or modify a value in the* ***Pin Numbers*** *area, the modified value will be automatically displayed in the* ***Pin List*** *area of the* ***Connector Pin Numbers In Use*** *dialog box.*

# INSERTING A CONNECTOR FROM THE LIST

| | |
|---|---|
| **Ribbon:** | Schematic > Insert Components > Insert Connector drop-down > Insert Connector (From List) |
| **Toolbar:** | ACE:Main Electrical > Insert Connector drop-down > Insert Connector from List<br>or ACE:Insert Connector > Insert Connector from List |
| **Menu:** | Components > Insert Connector > Insert Connector from List |
| **Command:** | AECONNECTORLIST |

The **Insert Connector (From List)** tool is used to import connector wiring information from an external report. To do so, choose the **Insert Connector (From List)** tool from the **Insert Components** panel of the **Schematic** tab; the **Autodesk Inventor Professional Import File Selection** dialog box will be displayed. In this dialog box, select the required file and then choose the **Open** button to import the data. Note that the file should be in *.xml*, *.xls*, *.mdb*, or *.csv* format.

# MODIFYING CONNECTORS

AutoCAD Electrical has various tools for modifying connectors and changing the orientation of connectors. Using these modifying tools, you can break, add, or remove the pins of a connector.

## Adding Pins to a Connector

| | |
|---|---|
| **Ribbon:** | Schematic > Edit Components > Modify Connectors drop-down > Add Connector Pins |
| **Toolbar:** | ACE:Main Electrical > Insert Connector drop-down > Add Connector Pins<br>or ACE:Insert Connector > Add Connector Pins |
| **Menu:** | Components > Insert Connector > Add Connector Pins |
| **Command:** | AECONNECTORPIN |

The **Add Connector Pins** tool is used to add additional pins to an existing connector. To do so, choose the **Add Connector Pins** tool from the **Modify Connectors** drop-down in the **Edit Components** panel of the **Schematic** tab, refer to Figure 7-18; you will be prompted to select a connector. After selecting a connector, you will be prompted to specify the insertion point for the new pin. Next, specify the insertion point; the next available pin number will be added to the connector and each pin will be added in line with the remaining connector pins. Also, you can manually specify the pin number for the connector as per your requirement. To specify the pin number for a connector manually, enter the pin number for the connector in the command prompt and then specify the insertion point.

The **AECONNECTORPIN** command will continue until you press ESC or ENTER. Alternatively, right-click on the screen and choose the **Enter** option from the shortcut menu to exit the command. Figure 7-19 shows the connector before and after adding the pins.

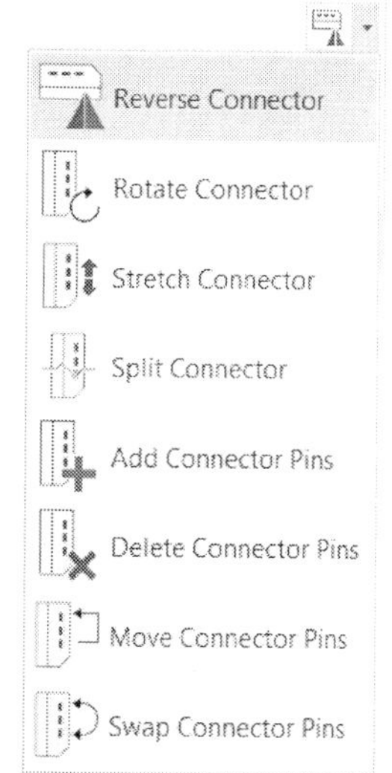


***Figure 7-18** The **Modify Connectors** drop-down*

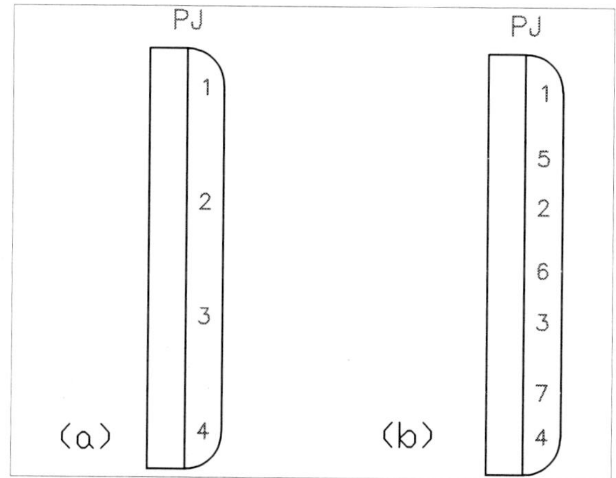


***Figure 7-19** The connector (a) before adding the pins (b) after adding the pins*

## Deleting a Connector Pin

**Ribbon:** Schematic > Edit Components > Modify Connectors drop-down> Delete Connector Pins
**Toolbar:** ACE:Main Electrical > Insert Connector drop-down > Delete Connector Pins or ACE:Insert Connector > Delete Connector Pins
**Menu:** Components > Insert Connector > Delete Connector Pins
**Command:** AEERASEPIN

The **Delete Connector Pins** tool is used to delete pins from a connector. To do so, choose the **Delete Connector Pins** tool from the **Modify Connectors** drop-down in the **Edit Components** panel of the **Schematic** tab, refer to Figure 7-18; you will be prompted to select a connector pin to delete. Select the connector pin; the pin number will be deleted from the connector. Next, press ENTER or ESC to exit the command or right-click on the screen to end the command.

## Moving a Connector Pin

| | |
|---|---|
| **Ribbon:** | Schematic > Edit Components > Modify Connectors drop-down > Move Connector Pins |
| **Toolbar:** | ACE:Main Electrical > Insert Connector drop-down > Move Connector Pins<br>ACE:Insert Connector > Move Connector Pins |
| **Menu:** | Components > Insert Connector > Move Connector Pins |
| **Command:** | AEMOVEPIN |

The **Move Connector Pins** tool is used to move pins within an existing connector. To do so, choose the **Move Connector Pins** tool from the **Modify Connectors** drop-down in the **Edit Components** panel of the **Schematic** tab; you will be prompted to select the connector pin to be moved. Select the connector pin; you will be prompted to specify a new location for the selected connector pin. Next, specify a new location for the pin; the connector pin will be moved to the specified location. Press ENTER or ESC to exit the command or right-click on the screen to terminate the command.

## Swapping Connector Pins

| | |
|---|---|
| **Ribbon:** | Schematic > Edit Components >Modify Connectors drop-down > Swap Connector Pins |
| **Toolbar:** | ACE:Main Electrical> Insert Connector drop-down > Swap Connector Pins<br>ACE:Insert Connector > Swap Connector Pins |
| **Menu:** | Components > Insert Connector > Swap Connector Pins |
| **Command:** | AESWAPPINS |

The **Swap Connector Pins** tool is used to interchange one set of connector pin numbers with another set on an existing connector or between different connectors on the drawing. Using this tool, you can swap the pin numbers of a connector without changing locations of pins. To swap pin numbers of a connector, choose the **Swap Connector Pins** tool from the **Modify Connectors** drop-down in the **Edit Components** panel of the **Schematic** tab; you will be prompted to select the connector pin to swap. Select the connector pin; a temporary graphics will be drawn around the selected pin number, which indicates that the pins have been included in the swap list and you will be prompted to select the connector pin to swap with. Next, select the connector pin to be swapped. The **AESWAPPINS** command will continue until you press ENTER or ESC. Alternatively, right-click on the screen to end the command. Figure 7-20 shows the connector before and after swapping the pins.

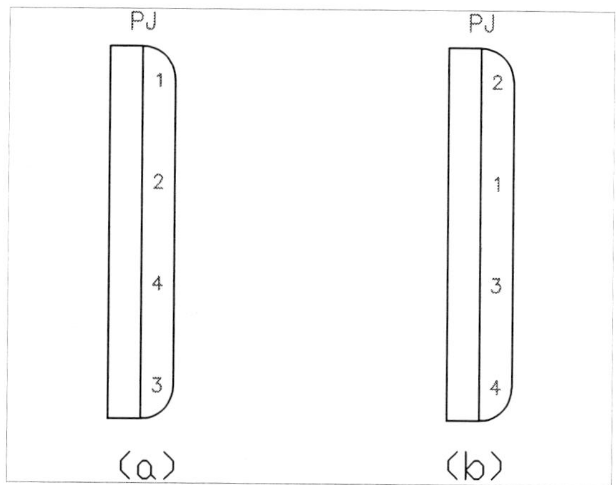


*Figure 7-20* *The connector (a) before swapping the pins (b) after swapping the pins*

## Reversing a Connector

| | |
|---|---|
| **Ribbon:** | Schematic > Edit Components > Modify Connectors drop-down > Reverse Connector |
| **Toolbar:** | ACE:Main Electrical > Insert Connector drop-down > Reverse Connector or ACE:Insert Connector > Reverse Connector |
| **Menu:** | Components > Insert Connector > Reverse Connector |
| **Command:** | AEREVERSE |

The **Reverse Connector** tool is used to reverse the direction of the connector about its horizontal or vertical axis. To reverse the direction of a connector, choose the **Reverse Connector** tool from the **Modify Connectors** drop-down in the **Edit Components** panel of the **Schematic** tab; you will be prompted to select a connector to reverse. Select the connector to be reversed; the direction of the connector will be reversed. The **AEREVERSE** command will continue until you press ENTER or ESC. Alternatively, right-click to exit the command. Figure 7-21 shows the connector before and after reversing its direction.

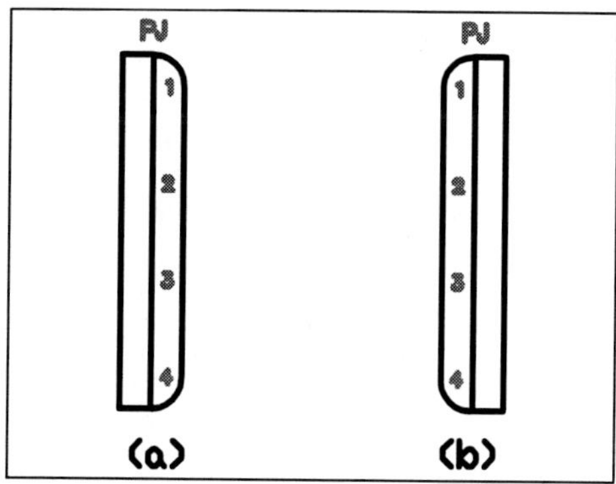


*Figure 7-21* *The connector (a) before reversing its direction (b) after reversing its direction*

**Note**

*If you reverse a receptacle connector that has no rounded corners, the appearance of graphics will remain unchanged, but the wire connection attributes will move to the other side of the connector.*

## Rotating a Connector

| | |
|---|---|
| **Ribbon:** | Schematic > Edit Components > Modify Connectors drop-down > Rotate Connector |
| **Toolbar:** | ACE:Main Electrical > Insert Connector drop-down >Rotate Connector or ACE:Insert Connector > Rotate Connector |
| **Menu:** | Components > Insert Connector > Rotate Connector |
| **Command:** | AEROTATE |

The **Rotate Connector** tool is used to rotate a connector by 90-degree in counterclockwise direction. To rotate a connector about its insertion point, choose the **Rotate Connector** tool from the **Modify Connectors** drop-down in the **Edit Components** panel of the **Schematic** tab; you will be prompted to select the connector to rotate. Next, select the connector; the selected connector will be rotated by 90-degree in counterclockwise direction. Keep on selecting the connector till the appropriate orientation of the connector is achieved. You can also change the orientation of attributes of a connector by entering **H** at the Command prompt. Press ENTER or ESC to exit the command. Alternatively, right-click on the screen and choose **Enter** from the shortcut menu to exit the command.

The following prompt sequence displays the use of the **Rotate Connector** tool for rotating the connector.

Choose the **Rotate Connector** tool
Current settings: Hold attribute orientation=Yes
Select connector to Rotate or [Hold]: *Select the connector that you want to rotate.*
Select connector to Rotate or [Hold]: *Enter **H** for holding attributes to their original orientation.*
Hold attributes at original orientation? [Yes/No]<Yes>: *Enter **Y** for holding the attribute at its original position.*
Hold attributes at original orientation? [Yes/No]<Yes>: *Enter **N** for rotating the attribute along with the original orientation of a connector.*
Current settings: Hold attribute orientation=No
Select connector to Rotate or [Hold]: *Select the connector again.*
Select connector to Rotate or [Hold]: Enter *to exit the command.*

The setting for holding attributes at original orientation of a connector is retained until you change it.

Figure 7-22 shows the connector with its original orientation and Figure 7-23 shows the connector with Hold = Yes and Hold = No.

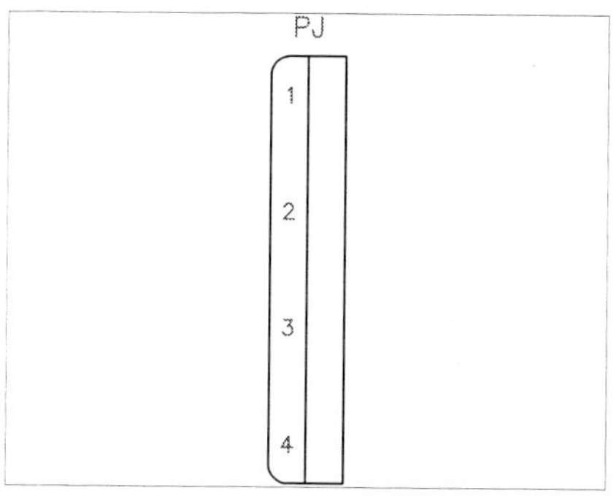


*Figure 7-22 The original orientation of a connector*

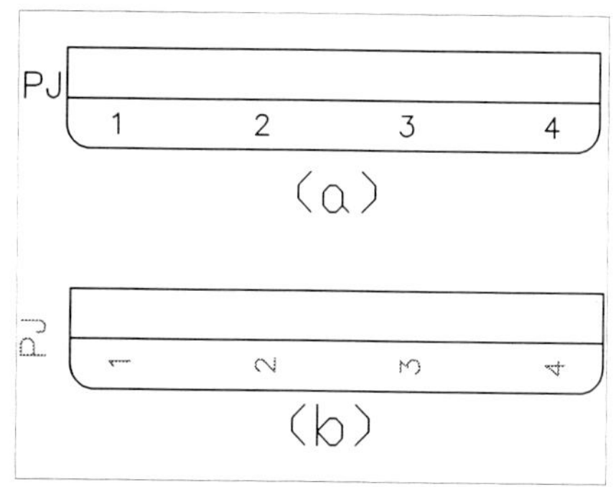


*Figure 7-23 The connector when (a) Hold = Yes and (b) Hold = No*

## Stretching a Connector

| | |
|---|---|
| **Ribbon:** | Schematic > Edit Components > Modify Connectors drop-down > Stretch Connector |
| **Toolbar:** | ACE:Main Electrical > Insert Connector drop-down > Stretch Connector or ACE:Insert Connector > Stretch Connector |
| **Menu:** | Components > Insert Connector > Stretch Connector |
| **Command:** | AESTRETCH |

The **Stretch Connector** tool is used to stretch a connector. Using this tool, you can increase or decrease the length of a connector. To stretch a connector, choose the **Stretch Connector** tool from the **Modify Connectors** drop-down in the **Edit Components** panel of the **Schematic** tab; you will be prompted to specify the end of the connector that you want to stretch. Next, select the end of the connector; a straight line along with the cursor will be displayed on the screen and you will be prompted to specify the second point of displacement. Specify the second point of displacement for the connector or drag the cursor downwards; the connector will be stretched. Figure 7-24 shows the connector while stretching and Figure 7-25 shows the connector after stretching.

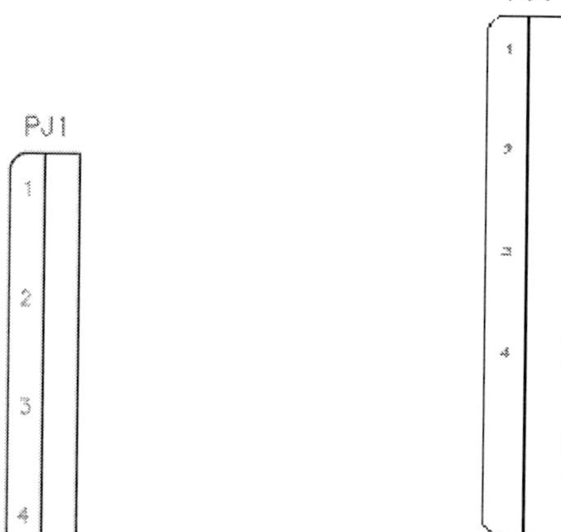


*Figure 7-24 The connector while stretching*

*Figure 7-25 The connector after stretching*

**Note**

*The **Stretch Connector** tool is used only to stretch a connector. This tool cannot relocate any of its pins. To relocate its pins, you can use the **Move Connector Pins** button, as explained earlier in this chapter.*

## Splitting a Connector

| | |
|---|---|
| **Ribbon:** | Schematic > Edit Components > Modify Connectors drop-down > Split Connector |
| **Toolbar:** | ACE:Main Electrical > Insert Connector drop-down > Split Connector or ACE:Insert Connector > Split Connector |
| **Menu:** | Components > Insert Connector > Split Connector |
| **Command:** | AESPLIT |

The **Split Connector** tool is used to split a connector into two separate parts such as parent and child or child and another child. Also, this tool is used to place a portion of a connector at a location other than the original one. To split a connector, choose the **Split Connector** tool from the **Modify Connectors** drop-down in the **Edit Components** panel of the **Schematic** tab; you will be prompted to select the connector block that you want to split. Select the connector block; you will be prompted to specify the split point of the connector. Next, specify the split point; the **Split Block** dialog box will be displayed, as shown in Figure 7-26. The options in this dialog box are discussed next.

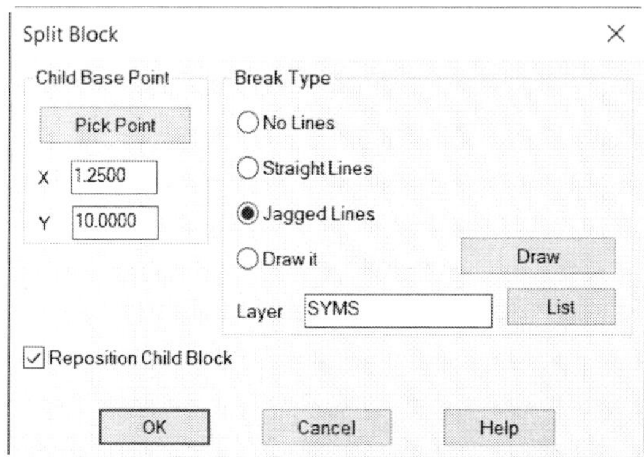


*Figure 7-26 The **Split Block** dialog box*

### Child Base Point Area

The **Child Base Point** area is used to specify the base point for the placement of the child symbol that is created when you split a connector. You can either specify the co-ordinates in the **X** and **Y** edit boxes or you can manually select the insertion point for the child part using the **Pick Point** button.

### Break Type Area

The **Break Type** area is used to specify the type of break for a connector. The options in this area are discussed next.

### No Lines

Select the **No Lines** radio button to break a connector without creating any line, as shown in Figure 7-27.

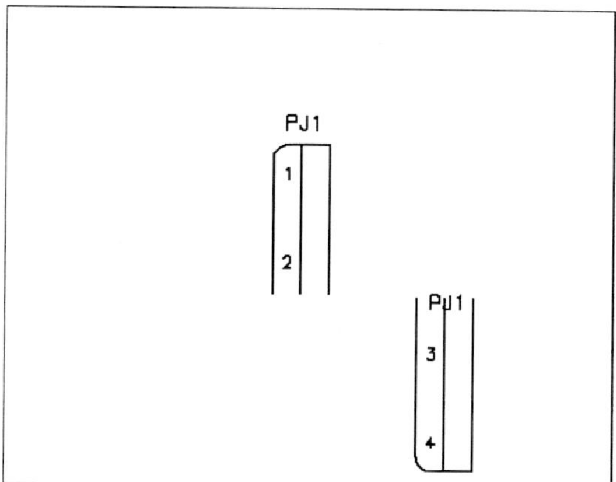


*Figure 7-27 The connector with the **No Lines** radio button selected*

### Straight Lines

Select the **Straight Lines** radio button; a straight line will be drawn where the connector breaks, as shown in Figure 7-28.

### Jagged Lines

By default, the **Jagged Lines** radio button is selected. As a result, jagged lines will be drawn where the connector breaks, as shown in Figure 7-29.

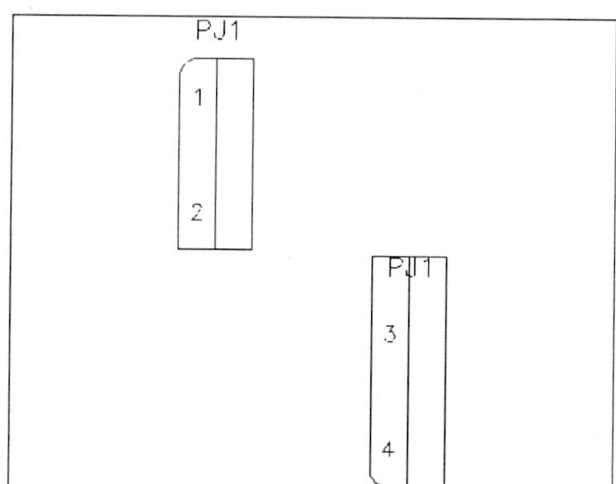


*Figure 7-28 The connector with the **Straight Lines** radio button selected*

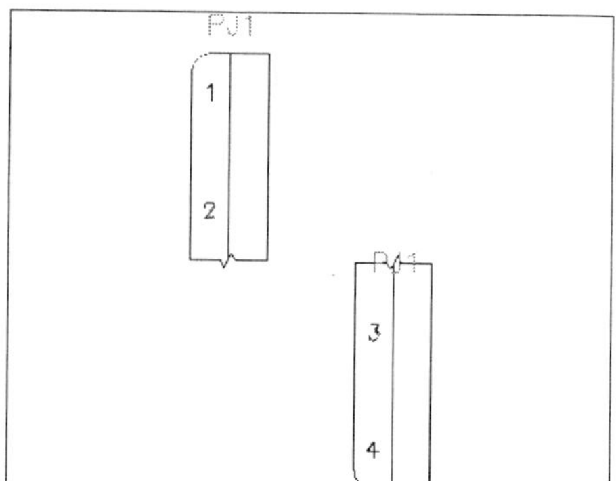


*Figure 7-29 Connector with the **Jagged Lines** radio button selected*

### Draw it

The **Draw it** radio button is used to draw a break type for a connector manually. The line drawn can be used for both the parent and the child components. To draw a break type manually, select the **Draw it** radio button; the **Split Block** dialog box will disappear and you will be prompted to draw break lines at the split point. Draw the break lines and press ENTER or right-click on the screen; the **Split Block** dialog box will appear again.

## Draw

The **Draw** button enables you to manually draw a break line at the split point. The line drawn can be used for both the parent and child components.

## Layer

This edit box is used to specify a layer for the child block. By default, SYMS is displayed in this edit box. Alternatively, choose the **List** button; the **Select Layer** dialog box will be displayed, as shown in Figure 7-30. This dialog box displays a list of existing layers. Select a layer from this dialog box; the selected layer will be displayed in the **Layer** edit box.

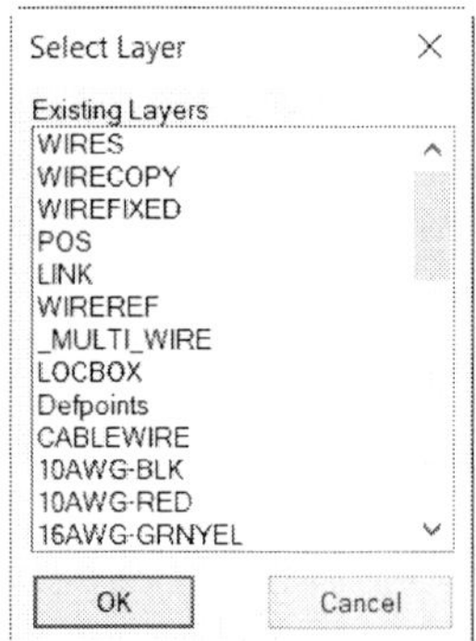


***Figure 7-30** The **Select Layer** dialog box*

## Reposition Child Block

The **Reposition Child Block** check box is used to move the child block to a new location. By default, this check box is selected. If you clear this check box, the connector will split and the parts of the connector will remain at their original position. Also, the break lines will be created between the two split parts of the connector, as shown in Figure 7-31.

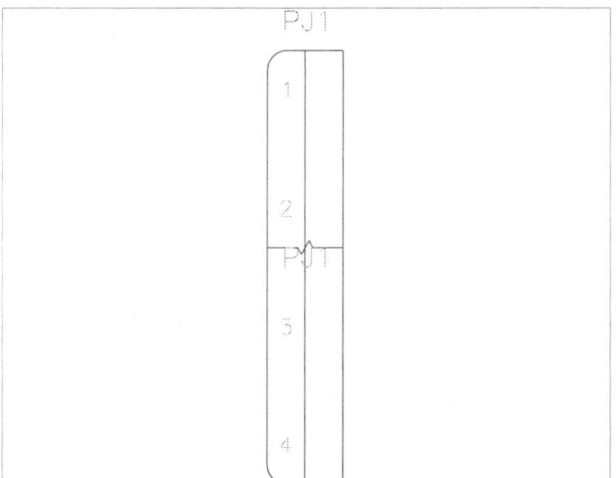


***Figure 7-31** The connector with the **Reposition Child Block** check box cleared*

The **OK** button will be activated only if you specify the X and Y coordinates in the **X** and **Y** edit boxes. Specify the required options in the **Split Block** dialog box and choose the **OK** button in this dialog box; you will be prompted to specify the insertion point for the child block. Specify the insertion point; the child block will be inserted into the drawing.

# USING POINT-TO-POINT WIRING DIAGRAMS

A point-to-point wiring diagram is the detailed diagram of each circuit installation showing all the wiring, connectors, terminal boards, and electrical or electronic components of the circuit. The diagrams also identify wires by wire numbers or color coding. Wiring diagrams are necessary to troubleshoot and repair electrical or electronic circuits.

Point-to-point wiring diagrams are used by a number of industries such as the automotive or airline industry to create control schematics. Most of the standard AutoCAD Electrical tools fully support this style of design. In addition to this, AutoCAD Electrical has a number of tools that offer functionality specifically for working with point-to-point design methods. In this section, you will learn to insert splices and wires in connectors.

## Inserting Splices

| | |
|---|---|
| **Ribbon:** | Schematic > Insert Components > Insert Connector drop-down > Insert Splice |
| **Toolbar:** | ACE:Main Electrical > Insert Connector drop-down > Insert Splice or ACE:Insert Connector > Insert Splice |
| **Menu:** | Components > Insert Connector > Insert Splice |
| **Command:** | AESPLICE |

The **Insert Splice** tool is used to connect one or more wires. To connect wires, choose the **Insert Splice** tool from the **Insert Connector** drop-down in the **Insert Components** panel of the **Schematic** tab, refer to Figure 7-2; the **Insert Component** dialog box will be displayed, as shown in Figure 7-32.

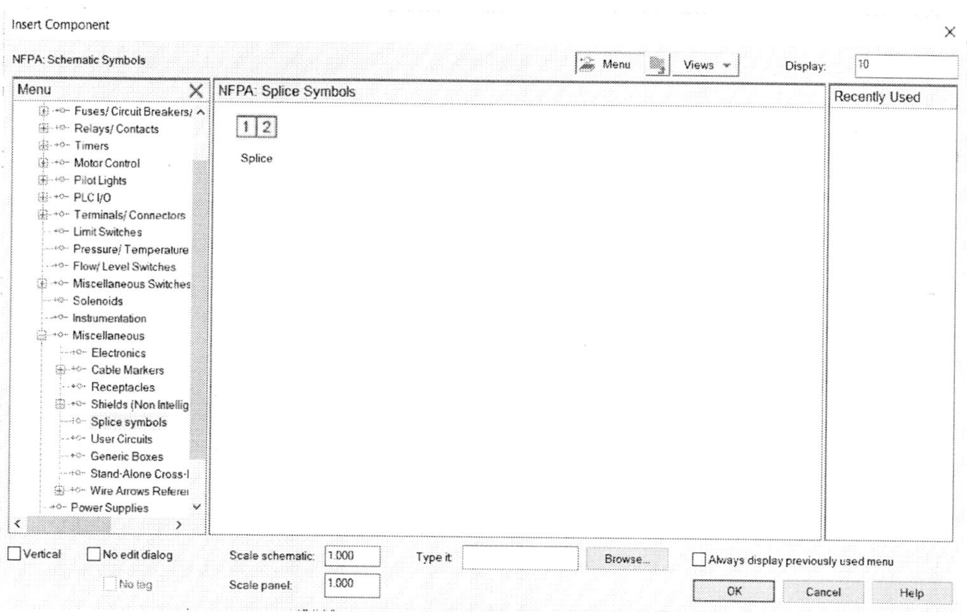


*Figure 7-32 The **Insert Component** dialog box*

Select the **Splice** symbol from the **NFPA: Splice Symbols** area of the **Insert Component** dialog box; the splice symbol along with the cursor will be displayed and you will be prompted to specify the insertion point for the symbol. Specify the insertion point; the **Insert / Edit Component** dialog will be displayed. The options in this dialog box have already been discussed in Chapter 5.

Next, specify the required options in this dialog box and choose the **OK** button; the splice will get inserted into the drawing, as shown in Figure 7-33.

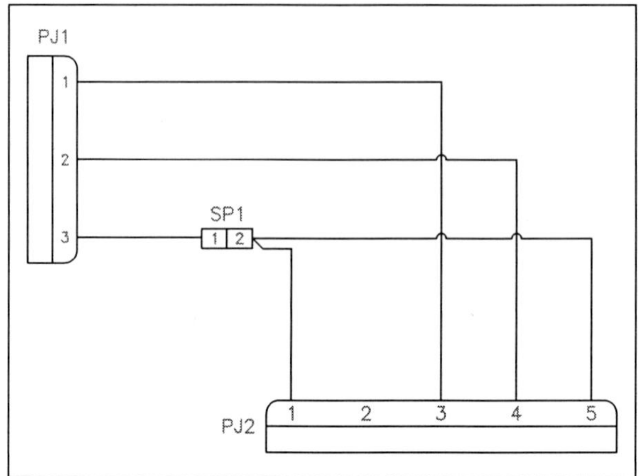


***Figure 7-33** The drawing after inserting connectors and splice*

**Note**

*If you insert splice on an existing wire, the wire will break up. Also, the wire numbers will change.*

## Inserting Wires into Connectors

**Ribbon:** Schematic > Insert Wires/Wire Numbers > Wire drop-down > Wire
**Toolbar:** ACE:Main Electrical > Insert Wire drop-down > Insert Wire or ACE:Wires > Insert Wire
**Menu:** Wires > Insert Wire
**Command:** AEWIRE

You have already learned about inserting wires in Chapter 3. Now, you will learn to insert wires into connectors. The **Wire** tool is used to insert wires into the drawing. To do so, choose the **Wire** tool from the **Wire** drop-down in the **Insert Wires/Wire Numbers** panel of the **Schematic** tab; AutoCAD Electrical prompts you to specify the starting point of the wire. Specify the start point; you will be prompted to specify the endpoint of the wire. Specify the endpoint; a wire will be inserted between the two entities. This prompt will continue until you press ENTER. The prompt sequence for this command is given next.

Choose the **Wire** tool
Current wiretype: "WIRES"
Specify wire start or [wireType/X=show connections]: *Specify the wire start point or enter an option (the options are discussed next).*
Specify wire end or [V= start Vertical H= start Horizontal TAB=Collision off/Continue]: *Specify wire endpoint/* Enter.
Specify wire start or [Scoot wireType X=show connections]: *Press ESC to exit the command.*

Figure 7-34 shows a connector after inserting a wire.

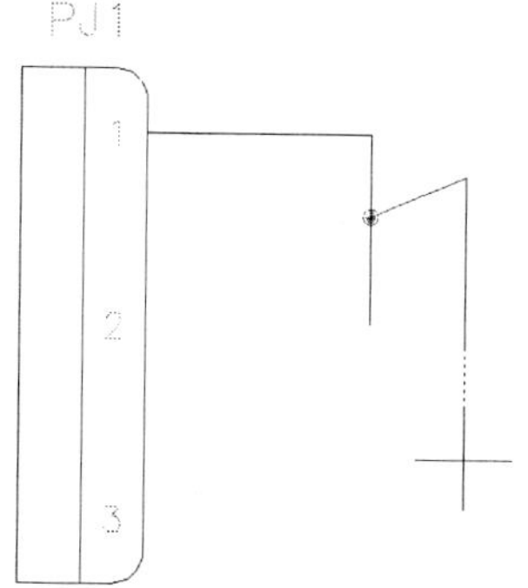


***Figure 7-34*** *Wire inserted in a connector*

## Inserting Multiple Wire Bus into Connectors

| | |
|---|---|
| **Ribbon:** | Schematic > Insert Wires/Wire Numbers >Multiple Bus |
| **Toolbar:** | ACE:Main Electrical > Insert Wire drop-down > Multiple Wire Bus or ACE:Wires > Multiple Wire Bus |
| **Menu:** | Wires > Multiple Wire Bus |
| **Command:** | AEMULTIBUS |

The **Multiple Bus** tool is used to insert multiple wire bus. To do so, choose the **Multiple Bus** tool from the **Insert Wires/Wire Numbers** panel of the **Schematic** tab; the **Multiple Wire Bus** dialog box will be displayed, as shown in Figure 7-35. The options in this dialog box have already been discussed in Chapter 3.

Next, select the **Component (Multiple Wires)** radio button and choose the **OK** button in this dialog box; you will be prompted to window select the starting wire connection points. Next, select the wire connection points of a connector by a crossing window and press ENTER; the wires will start from the connection point of a connector. Next, move the cursor as per your requirement and click on the screen; the wires will be drawn. Figure 7-36 shows the connector with a 3 wires bus inserted.

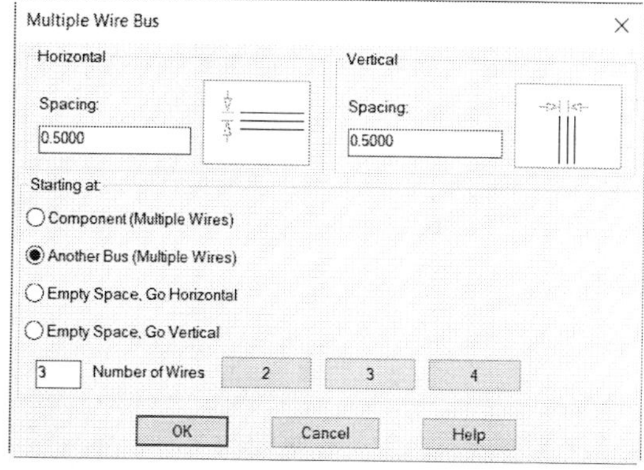


***Figure 7-35*** *The* ***Multiple Wire Bus*** *dialog box*

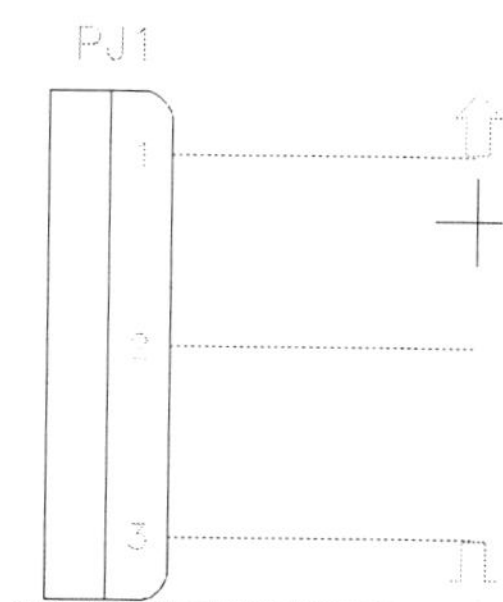


***Figure 7-36*** *The connector with a 3 wire bus inserted*

## Bending Wires at Right Angles

| | |
|---|---|
| **Ribbon:** | Schematic > Edit Wires/Wire Numbers >Modify Wire drop-down > Bend Wire |
| **Toolbar:** | ACE:Main Electrical > Insert Wire drop-down > Bend Wire<br>or ACE:Wires > Bend Wire |
| **Menu:** | Wires > Bend Wire |
| **Command:** | AEBENDWIRE |

The **Bend Wire** tool is used to bend a wire at right angle. To do so, choose the **Bend Wire** tool from the **Modify Wire** drop-down in the **Edit Wires/Wire Numbers** panel of the **Schematic** tab; a selection box will be displayed and you will be prompted to select the first wire. Select the wire that makes the right angle with the other wire; you will be prompted to select the second wire. Select the second wire; the additional wire segments are added to bend the wires at 90-degree. You can exit the **AEBENDWIRE** command by pressing ESC from the keyboard or by right-clicking on the screen. When a wire is defined at right angle, you can modify the wire and create a new right angle bend while maintaining the original wire connections to the components. Figure 7-37 shows the wires connected to the connector before and after bending.

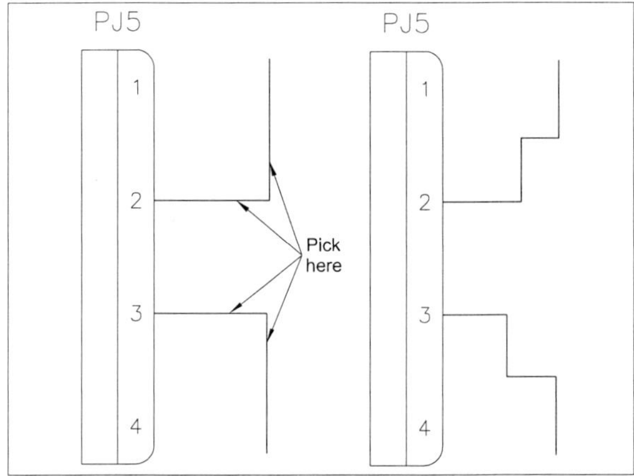


***Figure 7-37*** *The wires connected to the connector before and after bending*

**Note**

*The method to insert wires, multiple wire bus, and bend wires has already been discussed in Chapter 3.*

# WORKING WITH CIRCUITS

The route along which electricity flows is called electrical circuit. A circuit consists of wires, components, power supply, and so on.

In this section, you will learn to save circuits as symbols in icon menu file for repetitive use. Also, you will learn to copy the circuits, move the circuits, and so on.

## Saving Circuits to an Icon Menu

| | |
|---|---|
| **Ribbon:** | Schematic > Edit Components > Circuit drop-down > Save Circuit to Icon Menu |
| **Toolbar:** | ACE:Main Electrical > Circuit drop-down > Save Circuit to Icon Menu or ACE:Circuits > Save Circuit to Icon Menu |
| **Menu:** | Components > Save Circuit to Icon Menu |
| **Command:** | AESAVECIRCUIT |

You can save the selected portion of a circuit for future use. To save the selected portion of a circuit, choose the **Save Circuit to Icon Menu** tool from the **Circuit** drop-down in the **Edit Components** panel of the **Schematic** tab, as shown in Figure 7-38; the **Save Circuit to Icon Menu** dialog box will be displayed, as shown in Figure 7-39. The options in this dialog box are similar to those in the **Insert Component** dialog box. The rest of the options in this dialog box are discussed next.

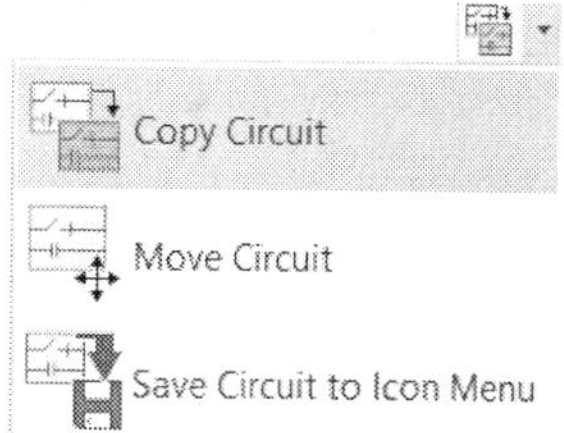


*Figure 7-38 The **Circuit** drop-down*

The options in the **Add** drop-down list are used to add component, command, new circuit, existing circuit, and submenu icon to the menu. To add a new circuit to icon menu, click on the **Add** drop-down list displayed at the upper right corner of the **Save Circuit to Icon Menu** dialog box; different options will be displayed. Next, select the **New Circuit** option from the drop-down list; the **Create New Circuit** dialog box will be displayed, as shown in Figure 7-40. The different areas and options in the **Create New Circuit** dialog box are discussed next.

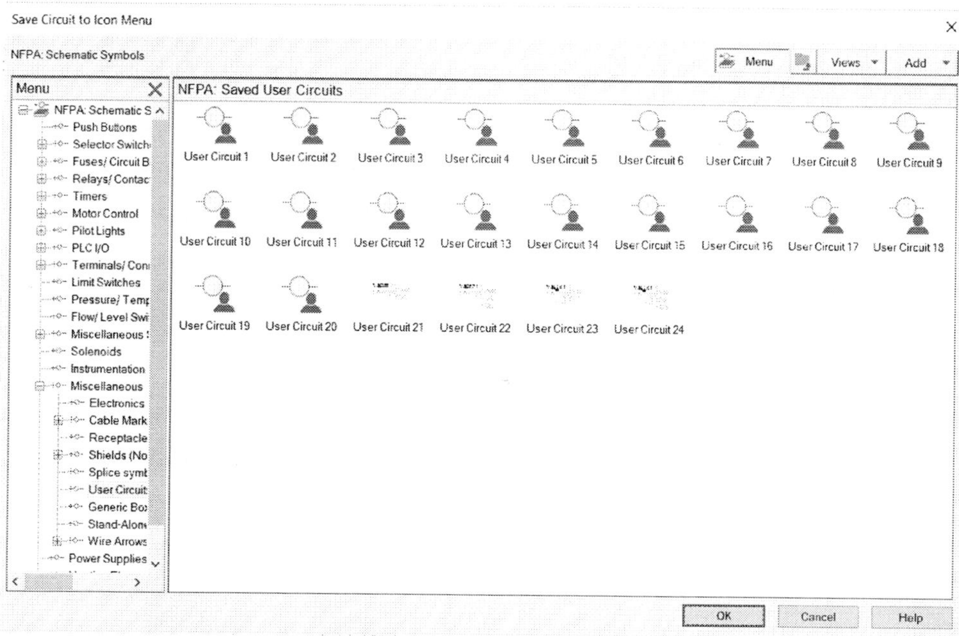


*Figure 7-39 The **Save Circuit to Icon Menu** dialog box*

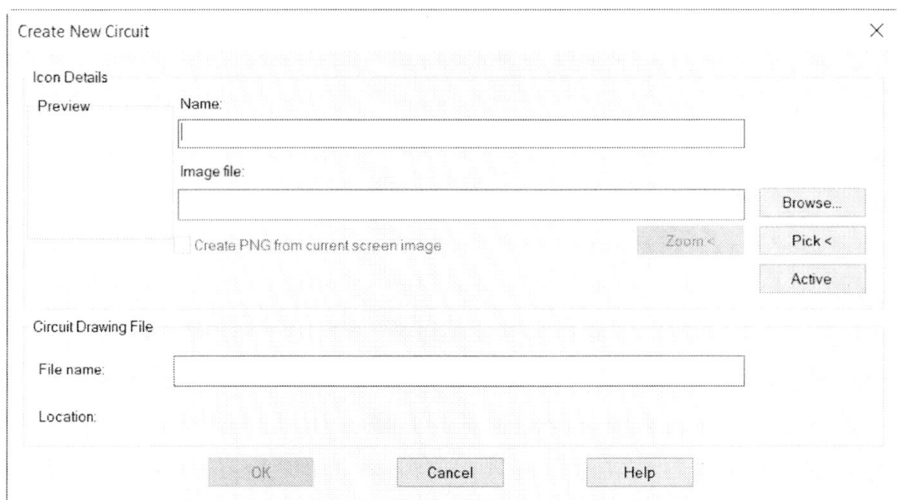


*Figure 7-40 The **Create New Circuit** dialog box*

## Icon Details Area

The **Icon Details** area is used to specify the name and image for the new icon. Also, this area displays the preview of an image. The options in the **Icon Details** area are discussed next.

### Name

Enter a name for the circuit in the **Name** edit box.

### Image file

The **Image file** edit box is used to specify the image file to be used for the new icon. You can enter the name of the image file in the **Image file** edit box manually. Alternatively, choose the **Browse** button; the **Select image file** dialog box will be displayed. In this dialog box, you can browse to the images saved in *.sld* or *.png* files format. Select the file from the **Select image file** dialog box and then choose the **Open** button; the file name will be displayed in the **Image file** edit box. Also, you can choose the **Pick <** button; the **Create New Circuit** dialog box will temporarily disappear and you will be prompted to select the block. After selecting the block, the **Create New Circuit** dialog box will be displayed again and the name of the block will be displayed in the **Image file** edit box.

You can also specify the active drawing name as an image file in the **Image file** edit box by choosing the **Active** button from the **Create New Circuit** dialog box. On choosing the **Active** button, the name of the image file will be displayed in the **Image file** edit box and the location of the image file will be displayed under the **Create PNG from current screen image** check box.

### Create PNG from current screen image

The **Create PNG from current screen image** check box is used to create the *.png* file from the current screen image. If you enter the name of the image file in the **Image file** edit box, the **Create PNG from current screen image** check box will be activated and get selected automatically. If you clear the **Create PNG from current screen image** check box, the **Zoom**

< button will be deactivated and there will not be any preview in the **Preview** area. Note that if you enter the full path of the image file in the **Image file** edit box, this check box will not be activated.

### Preview Area

The **Preview** area will be available only if you specify the image file in the **Image file** edit box. The preview of the selected drawing or block is displayed in this area.

## Circuit Drawing File Area

The **Circuit Drawing File** area is used to define the file name of the new circuit. Also, this area displays the location of the circuit drawing file that is being created.

### File name

Specify the file name for the circuit in the **File name** edit box.

### Location

If you enter the file name for a circuit in the **File name** edit box, the path and location of the circuit will be displayed on the right of the **Location** label in the **Circuit Drawing File** area.

After specifying the parameters in the **Icon Details** and **Circuit Drawing File** areas, the **OK** button will be activated. Choose the **OK** button; you will be prompted to specify the base point. Specify the base point in the drawing area; you will be prompted to select objects. Select individual objects or all objects at once using the crossing window and then press ENTER; the **Save Circuit to Icon Menu** dialog box will be displayed again. You will notice that the circuit is saved as an icon in the **NFPA: Saved User Circuits** area and the preview of the circuit in the form of icon is also displayed in the **Save Circuit to Icon Menu** dialog box. Next, choose the **OK** button to save the changes made in the **Save Circuit to Icon Menu** dialog box and exit from this dialog box.

**Tip**

*While selecting a circuit, you can choose* ***View > Zoom In*** *from the menu bar to zoom in the circuit.*

**Note**

*1. You can also save a circuit using the* ***Save Circuit to Icon Menu*** *dialog box. To do so, right-click in the* ***NFPA: Saved User Circuits*** *area of this dialog box; a shortcut menu will be displayed. Next, choose* ***Add icon > New circuit*** *from the shortcut menu; the* ***Create New Circuit*** *dialog box will be displayed. Specify the options as per your requirement to create a new circuit and then save it in the* ***Save Circuit to Icon Menu*** *dialog box.*

*2. You can also add existing circuits to the icon menu. To do so, choose the* ***Add circuit*** *option from the* ***Add*** *drop-down in the* ***Save Circuit To Icon Menu*** *dialog box; the* ***Add Existing Circuit*** *dialog box will be displayed. You can use this dialog box to add existing circuits to the* ***Save Circuit to Icon Menu*** *dialog box.*

## Inserting Saved Circuits

| | |
|---|---|
| **Ribbon:** | Schematics > Insert Components > Insert Circuit drop-down > Insert Saved Circuit |
| **Toolbar:** | ACE:Main Electrical > Circuit drop-down > Insert Saved Circuit or ACE:Circuits > Insert Saved Circuit |
| **Menu:** | Components > Insert Saved Circuit |
| **Command:** | AESAVEDCIRCUIT |

The **Insert Saved Circuit** tool is used to insert the circuit that you saved using the **Save Circuit to Icon Menu** tool. Similar to blocks, the saved circuits are inserted as single blocks. To insert a circuit, choose the **Insert Saved Circuit** tool from the **Insert Circuit** drop-down in the **Insert Components** panel of the **Schematic** tab, as shown in Figure 7-41; the **Insert Component** dialog box will be displayed, as shown in Figure 7-42.

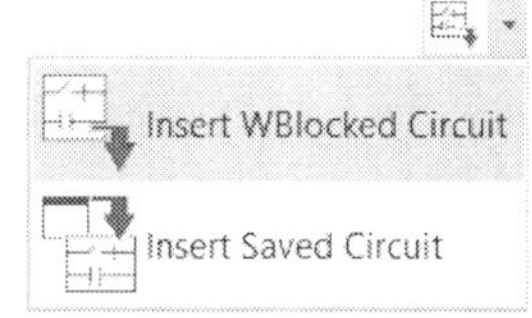


*Figure 7-41 The **Insert Circuit** drop-down*

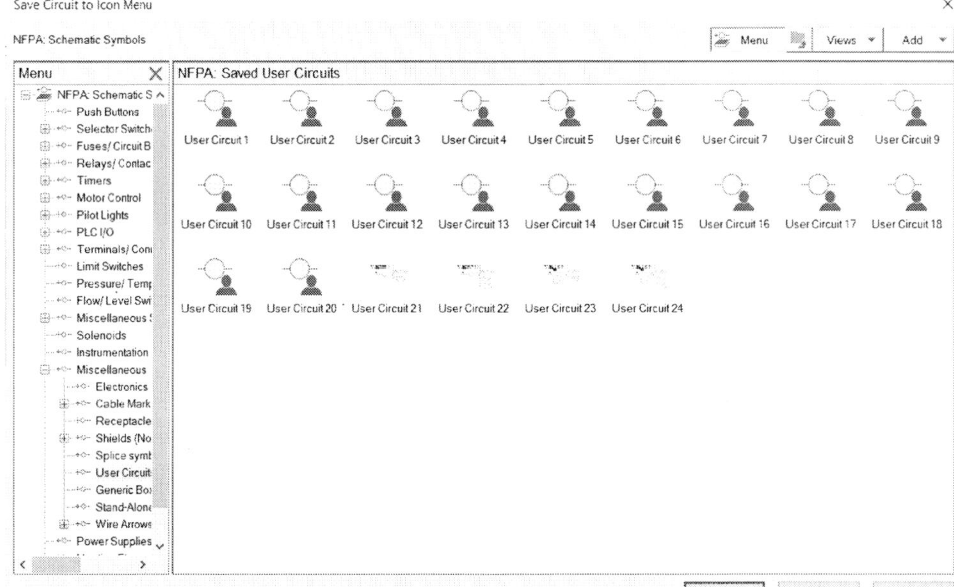


*Figure 7-42 The **Save Circuit to Icon Menu** dialog box*

Select a circuit from the **NFPA: Saved User Circuits** area of the **Insert Component** dialog box; the **Circuit Scale** dialog box will be displayed, as shown in Figure 7-43. The different options in this dialog box are discussed next.

### Custom scale

Specify the insertion scale of the circuit in the **Custom scale** edit box. By default, 1.0000 is displayed in this edit box. Alternatively, select the **1.0** radio button to display 1.000 in the **Custom scale** edit box.

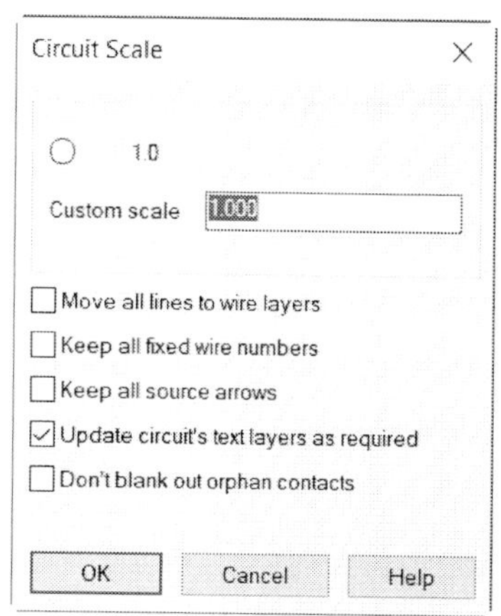


*Figure 7-43 The **Circuit Scale** dialog box*

### Move all lines to wire layers

Select the **Move all lines to Wire Layers** check box to move all nonlayer "0" line objects to a valid wire layer. By default, this check box is clear.

### Keep all fixed wire numbers

Select the **Keep all the fixed wire numbers** check box to retain all fixed wire numbers. By default, this check box is clear.

### Keep all source arrows

If you select the **Keep all source arrows** check box, the circuit source arrows will not be erased. By default, this check box is clear.

### Update circuit's text layers as required

By default, the **Update circuit's text layers as required** check box is selected. As a result, the circuit's text layers will be updated according to the drawing configuration settings of AutoCAD Electrical. If you clear this check box, the circuit's text layers will not be updated.

### Don't blank out orphan contacts

If you select the **Don't blank out orphan contacts** check box, the tag ID will not be changed for the contacts whose parents are not found. By default, this check box is clear.

After specifying the required options in the **Circuit Scale** dialog box, choose the **OK** button from this dialog box; you will be prompted to specify the insertion point for the saved circuit in your drawing. Next, specify the insertion point; the circuit will be inserted. Note that once the circuit is inserted, the components and cross-references in the circuit will also get updated.

**Note**

*If you enter 2, 3, or any digit other than 1 in the **Custom Scale** edit box and then choose the **OK** button in this dialog box, the size of the circuit will change accordingly. Also, note that when you choose the **Insert Saved Circuit** button next time, the options in the **Circuit Scale** dialog box will be slightly different, as shown in Figure 7-44. This dialog box displays the options when 2 is specified in the **Custom scale** edit box.*

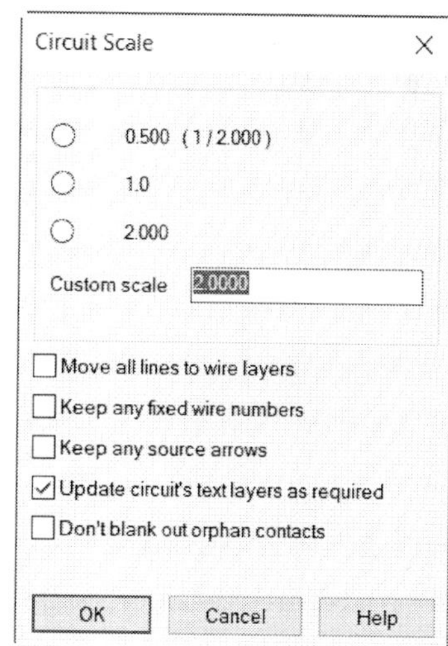


*Figure 7-44 The modified **Circuit Scale** dialog box*

## Moving Circuits

**Ribbon:** Schematics > Edit Components > Circuit drop-down> Move Circuit
**Toolbar:** ACE:Main Electrical > Circuit drop-down > Move Circuit
or ACE:Circuits > Move Circuit
**Menu:** Components > Move Circuit
**Command:** AEMOVECIRCUIT

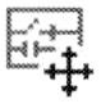

The **Move Circuit** tool is used to move a selected circuit from one location to the other in a drawing. The **AEMOVECIRCUIT** command is similar to AutoCAD **MOVE** command. To move a selected circuit, choose the **Move Circuit** tool from the **Circuit** drop-down in the **Edit Components** panel of the **Schematics** tab; you will be prompted to select objects. Select an individual object or a number of objects at a time from a drawing using the crossing window and then press ENTER; you will be prompted to specify the base point or the displacement. Specify the base point or the displacement; you will be prompted to specify the second point of displacement. Next, specify the second point of displacement or the new circuit location; the circuit will be moved to a specified location. After the circuit is moved, AutoCAD Electrical will start updating components and cross-references based on their new line reference locations. Also, the **Update Related Components?** message box will be displayed, if the components to be moved have related components in the current drawing, refer to Figure 7-45.

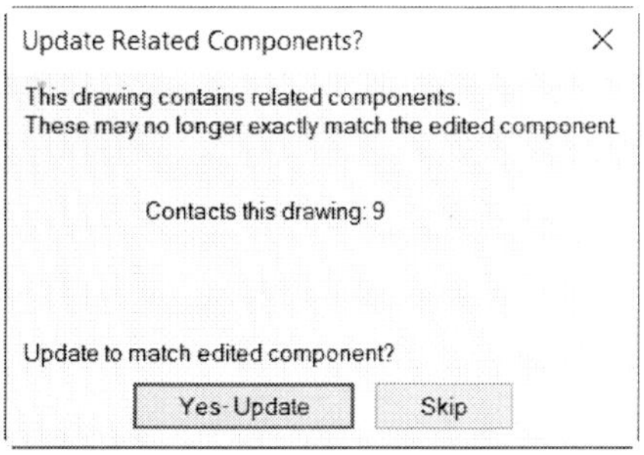

***Figure 7-45** The **Update Related Components?** message box*

If you choose the **Yes-Update** button in this message box, the edited component will be updated. Also, the **Update other drawings?** message box will be displayed, if the components to be moved have related components in other drawings, as shown in Figure 7-46. However, if you choose the **Skip** button, AutoCAD Electrical will skip the update process. Choose the **OK** button from the **Update other drawings?** message box; the drawings will get updated and the **QSAVE** message box will be displayed, as shown in Figure 7-47. Choose the **OK** button from the **QSAVE** message box to save the changes made while updating the drawings.

If you choose the **Task** button from the **Update other drawings?** message box, the components and cross-references of the drawings will not be updated at that time but will be saved in the project task list, which you can update later. To update the pending list, choose the **Project Task List** button from the **PROJECT MANAGER**; the **Task List** dialog box will be displayed. The options in this dialog box will be discussed in Chapter 12.

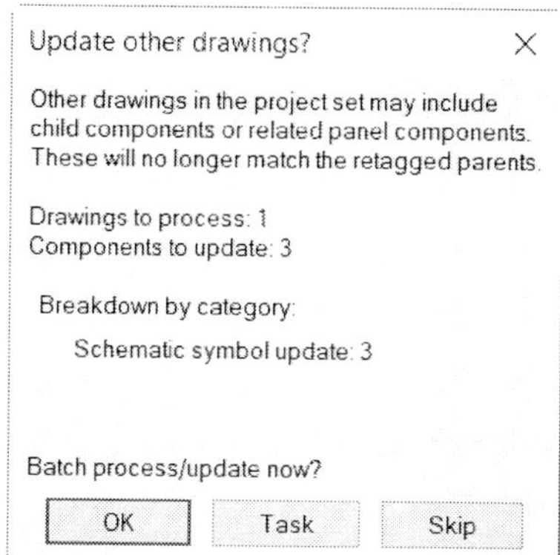


*Figure 7-46 The **Update other drawings?** message box*

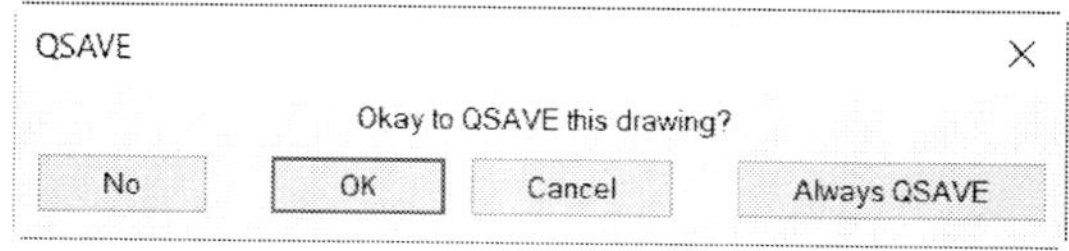


*Figure 7-47 The **QSAVE** message box*

**Note**

*If the circuit being moved does not have related components in the current drawing as well as in other drawings, the circuit will move to the specified location without displaying the **Update Related Components?** and **Update other drawings?** message boxes.*

*The **QSAVE** message box will be displayed only if you have made changes in the current drawing and have not saved it.*

## Copying Circuits

| | |
|---|---|
| **Ribbon:** | Schematic > Edit Components > Circuit drop-down > Copy Circuit |
| **Toolbar:** | ACE:Main Electrical > Circuit drop-down> Copy Circuit<br>or ACE:Circuits > Copy Circuit |
| **Menu:** | Components > Copy Circuit |
| **Command:** | AECOPYCIRCUIT |

The **Copy Circuit** tool is used to copy an existing circuit and then paste it to the specified location in the same drawing. Also, the copied components get automatically retagged according to the new line reference of the specified location. The **AECOPYCIRCUIT** command is similar to AutoCAD **COPY** command. To copy a circuit, choose the **Copy Circuit** tool from the **Circuit** drop-down in the **Edit Components** panel of the **Schematic** tab; you will be prompted to select the circuit to copy. Select the components and wires that you need to copy. You can select the components and wires one by one, or a number of components and wires at a time using the lasso. After selecting the objects, press ENTER; you will be prompted to specify the base point or the displacement. Next, specify the base point or displacement; you will be prompted to specify the second point of displacement. Next, specify the second point of displacement or the new circuit location point; the copied circuit will be inserted into the drawing. Also, you will be prompted to specify another location point where you want to insert same circuit. Press ENTER to exit the command. Note that if the copied circuit consists of terminals, fixed wire numbers, or component tags, the **Copy Circuit Options** dialog box will be displayed, as shown in Figure 7-48. This dialog box also consists of options to update or retain the terminal numbers of the terminal strip. Note that the options in the dialog box will change depending on the circuit you select to copy. The different areas and options in this dialog box are discussed next.

## Wire Numbers Area

The **Wire Numbers** area is used to specify whether to keep the wire number fixed or to remove the fixed wire numbers from the drawing. This area will be activated only if wire numbers are also included in the selection. The options in this area are discussed next.

Select the **Keep fixed wire numbers** radio button from the **Wire Numbers** area to keep the fixed wire numbers. Select the **Blank all** radio button to keep all wire numbers blank.

## Component Tags Area

The **Component Tags** area is used to specify whether to keep component tags fixed or to retag all component tags. The options in this area are discussed next.

Select the **Keep fixed component tags** radio button from the **Component Tags** area to keep component tags fixed. By default, the **Retag all** radio button is selected and is used to retag all components. Select the **Don't blank out orphan contacts** check box to retain all orphan contacts.

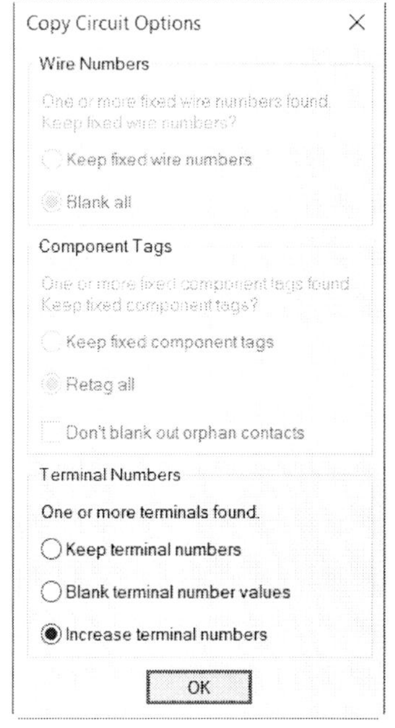


*Figure 7-48 The **Copy Circuit Options** dialog box*

## Terminal Numbers Area

The **Terminal Numbers** area is used to specify whether to keep the terminal numbers unchanged, keep them blank, or update them.

Select the **Keep terminal numbers** radio button to retain the terminal numbers of the copied circuit. Select the **Blank terminal number values** radio button to remove all terminal number values of the copied circuit. Select the **Increase terminal numbers** radio button to update the terminal numbers.

After specifying the required options, choose the **OK** button from the **Copy Circuit Options** dialog box; the circuit will be copied at the specified location. Note that if the circuit has source signal arrows then after choosing the **OK** button from the **Copy Circuit Options** dialog box, the **Copied Source Signal Arrow** dialog box will be displayed, as shown in Figure 7-49. Choose the **Keep Arrows** button to keep source arrows. If you do not want to keep the source arrows, choose the **Erase** button. After you choose the button from the **Copied Source Signal Arrow** dialog box, AutoCAD Electrical will start updating components and cross-references based on the drawing property settings.

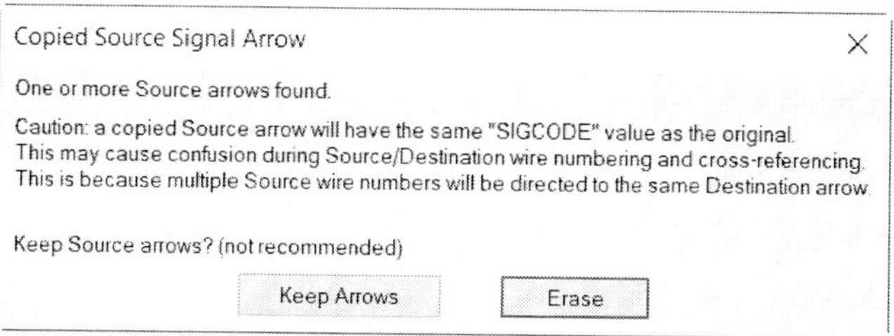


*Figure 7-49* *The* ***Copied Source Signal Arrow*** *dialog box*

**Note**

*1. If you want to make multiple copies of a selected circuit, enter '**M**' at the Command prompt after specifying the base point or the displacement.*

*2. If the circuit being copied does not have fixed wire numbers and component tags, the circuit will be copied at the specified location without displaying the* ***Copy Circuit Options*** *dialog box.*

## Saving Circuits by Using WBlock

**Command:** WBLOCK

You can save circuits as blocks using AutoCAD **WBLOCK** command. These saved blocks can be inserted later into any drawing file. Using this command, you can save unlimited number of circuits without using the **Save Circuit to Icon Menu** tool. When you enter the **WBLOCK** command at the Command prompt, the **Write Block** dialog box will be displayed, as shown in Figure 7-50. Choose the **Pick point** button from the **Base point** area; the dialog box will disappear temporarily. Next, specify the insertion base point that will be taken as the origin point of the block's coordinate system.

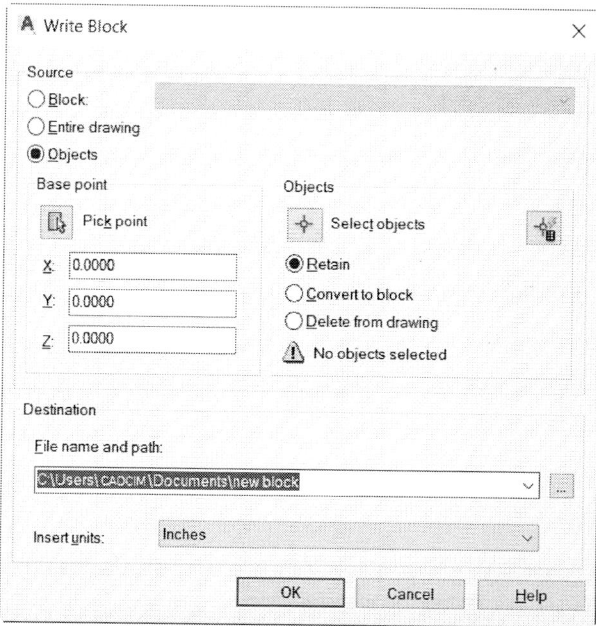


*Figure 7-50* *The* ***Write Block*** *dialog box*

After specifying the insertion base point, you need to select objects that will constitute a block. To do so, choose the **Select objects** button from the **Objects** area; the dialog box will disappear temporarily and a selection box will be displayed. You can select objects on the screen using any selection method. After completing the selection process, right-click or press the ENTER key to return to the dialog box. The number of objects selected is displayed at the bottom of the **Objects** area of the **Write Block** dialog box.

Next, enter the name and location in the **File name and path** edit box to save the circuit block. Alternatively, choose the **[...]** button on the right of the **File name and path** edit box; the **Browse for Drawing File** dialog box will be displayed. Next, specify the location for the drawing file in the **Browse for Drawing File** dialog box and enter the name of the file in the **File name** edit box. Then, choose the **Save** button from the **Browse for Drawing File** dialog box to return to the **Write Block** dialog box. By default, *C:\Users\User Name\Documents\new block* is displayed in the **File name and path** edit box. Choose the **OK** button from the **Write Block** dialog box; the circuit will be saved.

## Inserting the WBlocked Circuit

| | |
|---|---|
| **Ribbon:** | Schematic > Insert Components > Insert Circuit drop-down >Insert WBlocked Circuit |
| **Toolbar:** | ACE:Main Electrical > Insert Circuit drop-down >Insert WBlocked Circuit or ACE:Circuits > Insert WBlocked Circuit |
| **Menu:** | Components > Insert WBlocked Circuit |
| **Command:** | AEWBCIRCUIT |

The **Insert WBlocked Circuit** tool is used to insert a WBlocked circuit. To do so, choose the **Insert WBlocked Circuit** tool from the **Insert Circuit** drop-down in the **Insert Components** panel of the **Schematic** tab; the **Insert WBlocked Circuit** dialog box will be displayed, as shown in Figure 7-51. Select the required WBlock circuit from the list displayed to insert into the drawing. Next, choose the **Open** button; the **Circuit Scale** dialog box will be displayed, refer to Figure 7-43. Specify the required parameters in this dialog box and choose the **OK** button from the **Circuit Scale** dialog box; you will be prompted to specify the insertion point for the circuit. Specify the insertion point; the WBlocked circuit will be inserted into your drawing and components and cross-references in the circuit will get updated based on the drawing property settings.

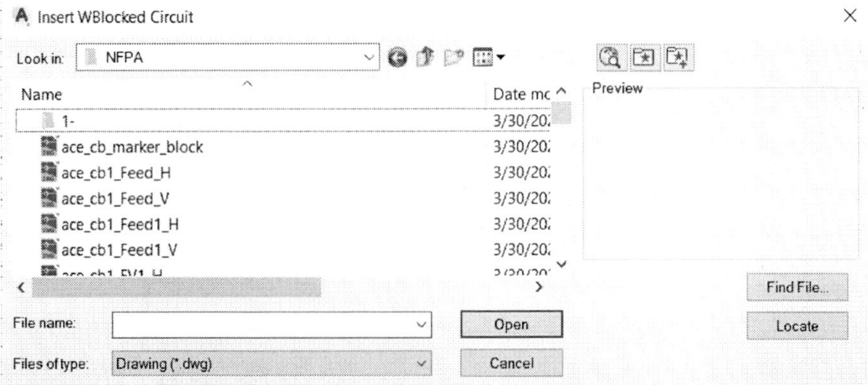


***Figure 7-51** The **Insert WBlocked Circuit** dialog box*

# BUILDING A CIRCUIT

| | |
|---|---|
| **Ribbon:** | Schematic > Insert Components > Circuit Builder drop-down > Circuit Builder |
| **Toolbar:** | ACE:Main Electrical > Insert Circuit drop-down >Circuit Builder or ACE:Circuits > Circuit Builder |
| **Menu:** | Components > Circuit Builder |
| **Command:** | AECIRCBUILDER |

You can build motor control circuits and power feed circuits using the **Circuit Builder** tool. The circuit built using this tool includes single phase, three phase, and one-line circuits. Using this tool, you can either insert a circuit or configure a circuit by using the list of available circuit categories. The procedure to insert a circuit using this tool is discussed next.

## Inserting a Circuit

Choose the **Circuit Builder** tool from the **Circuit Builder** drop-down in the **Insert Components** panel of the **Schematic** tab; the **Circuit Selection** dialog box will be displayed, as shown in Figure 7-52. The options and areas in this dialog box are discussed next.

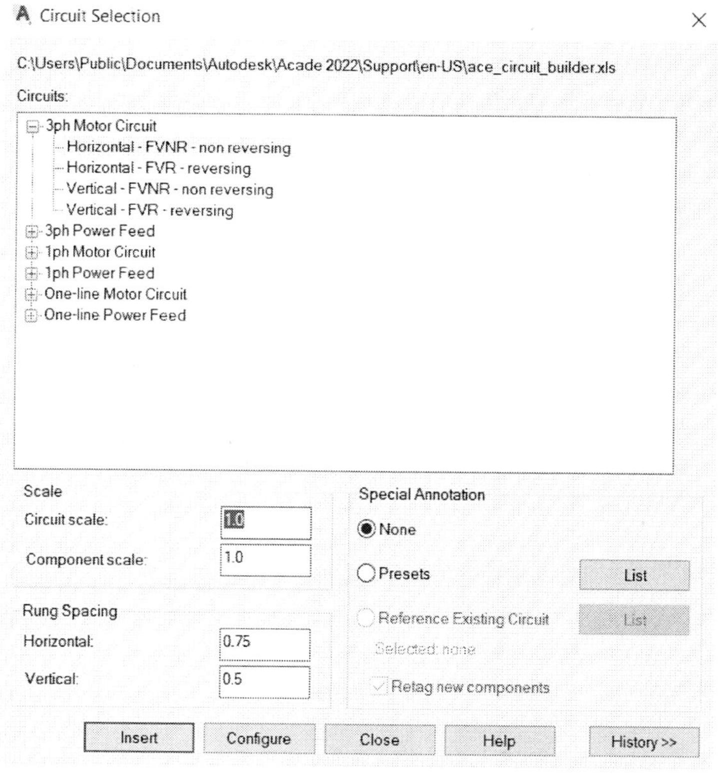

***Figure 7-52** The **Circuit Selection** dialog box*

**Note**

*The data displayed in the **Circuit Selection** dialog box is stored in the default circuit spreadsheet file, refer to Figure 7-53. The path for this file is C:\users\public\documents\autodesk\acade2022\support\ en-us\ace_circuit_builder.xls.*

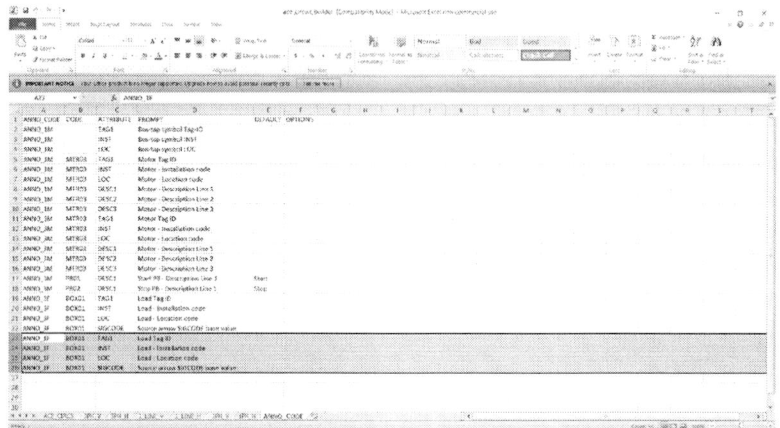

***Figure 7-53*** *The default circuit spreadsheet file*

## Circuits Area

The tree structure in this area is used to select a circuit category and circuit type available in the default circuit spreadsheet file. To do so, click on the + sign on the required circuit category; the circuit types of the selected category will be displayed. You need to select the required circuit type from the list.

## History >>

On choosing the **History >>** button located in the lower right of the **Circuit Selection** dialog box, the dialog box gets modified and the **History** area gets added to it, as shown in Figure 7-54.

## History Area

By default, this area is blank and a drop-down list is displayed with the **Default** option at the bottom of this area, refer to Figure 7-54. When you configure a circuit using the **Circuit Builder** tool, the name of the configured circuit is included as an option in this drop-down list. If you select this option from the drop-down list, the **History** area shows the circuit parameters of the configured circuit such as motor type, wire size, and so on, refer to Figure 7-55. You can use it as a reference to configure a new circuit. Note that this area is not activated if the **Reference Existing Circuit** radio button in the **Special Annotation** area is selected.

## Scale Area

The options in this area are discussed next.

### Circuit Scale

This edit box is used to specify the insertion scale value for the entire circuit.

### Component Scale

This edit box is used to specify the insertion scale value for individual circuit components.

## Rung Spacing Area

The options in this area are discussed next.

### Horizontal

This edit box is used to set 3-phase horizontal rung spacing for the circuit. By default, the horizontal ladder rung spacing value specified for the drawing in the **Drawing Format** tab of the **Drawing Properties** dialog box is displayed in this edit box.

### Vertical

This edit box is used to specify 3-phase vertical rung spacing value for the circuit. By default, the multi-wire spacing specified for the drawing in the **Drawing Format** tab of the **Drawing Properties** dialog box is displayed in this edit box.

## Special Annotation Area

The options in this area are used to apply annotation presets for the circuit. These options are discussed next.

### None

This radio button is used to ignore special annotation presets for the circuit.

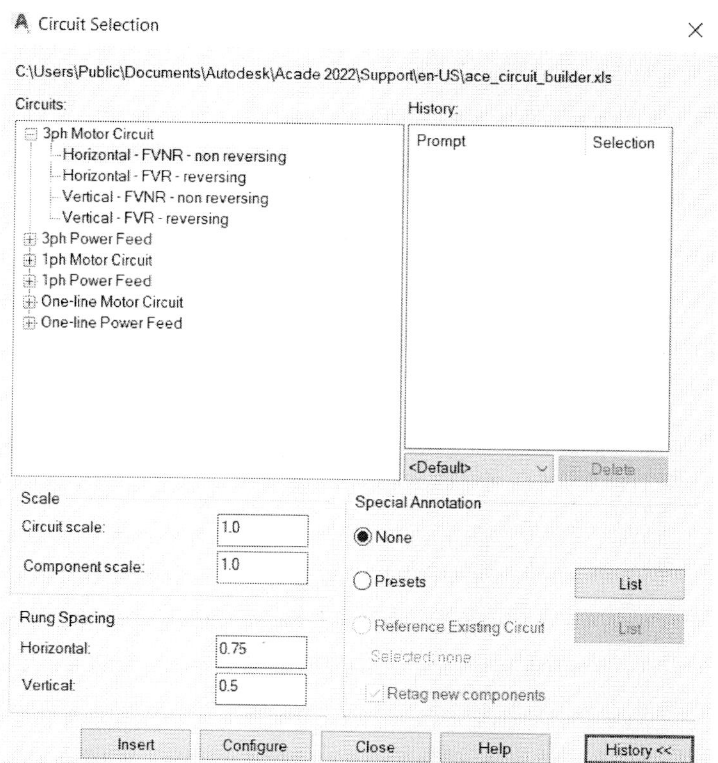


*Figure 7-54 The modified **Circuit Selection** dialog box*

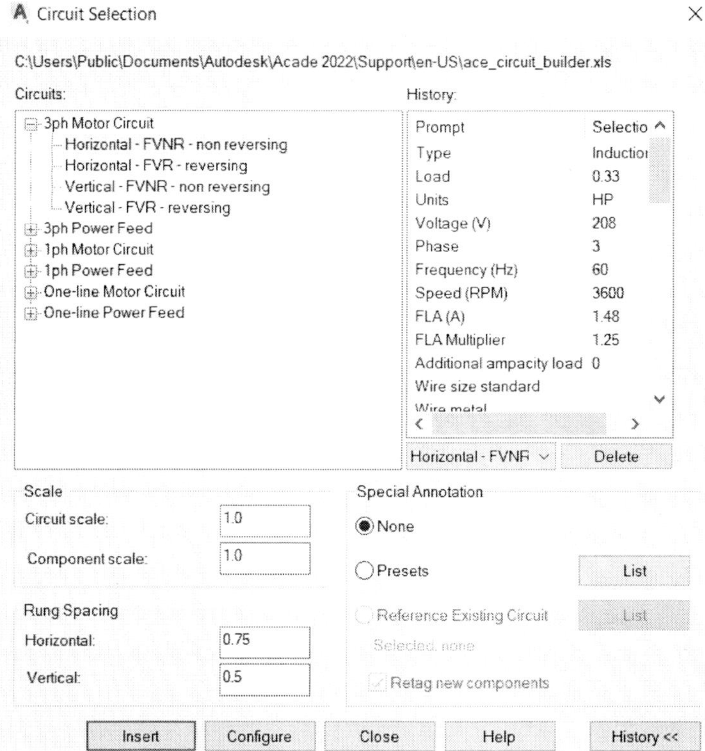


*Figure 7-55 The **Circuit Selection** dialog box with configured circuit parameters in the **History** area*

## Presets

Select this radio button if you want to use the annotation presets specified in the ANNO_CODE sheet of the default circuit spreadsheet file, refer to Figure 7-53. Choose the **List** button next to this radio button; the **Annotation Presets** dialog box will be displayed, as shown in Figure 7-56. This dialog box consists of component attribute presets available in the ANNO_CODE sheet of the default circuit spreadsheet file. Choose the options in this dialog box to apply the annotation presets for the circuit.

## Reference Existing Circuit

Select this radio button if you want to use annotation presets from the existing circuit. Note that this radio button is not activated if a circuit is selected from the drop-down list below the **History** area. This radio button and the **List** button located next to it will be activated if there is a circuit(s) built using the **Circuit Builder** tool in the current drawing. Choose the **List** button next to this radio button; the **Existing Circuits** dialog box will be displayed. You can choose the circuit from this dialog box as a reference circuit to apply annotation presets for the new circuit.

## Retag new components

This check box is activated only when the **Reference Existing Circuit** radio button is selected. This check box is selected to retag components in the new circuit.

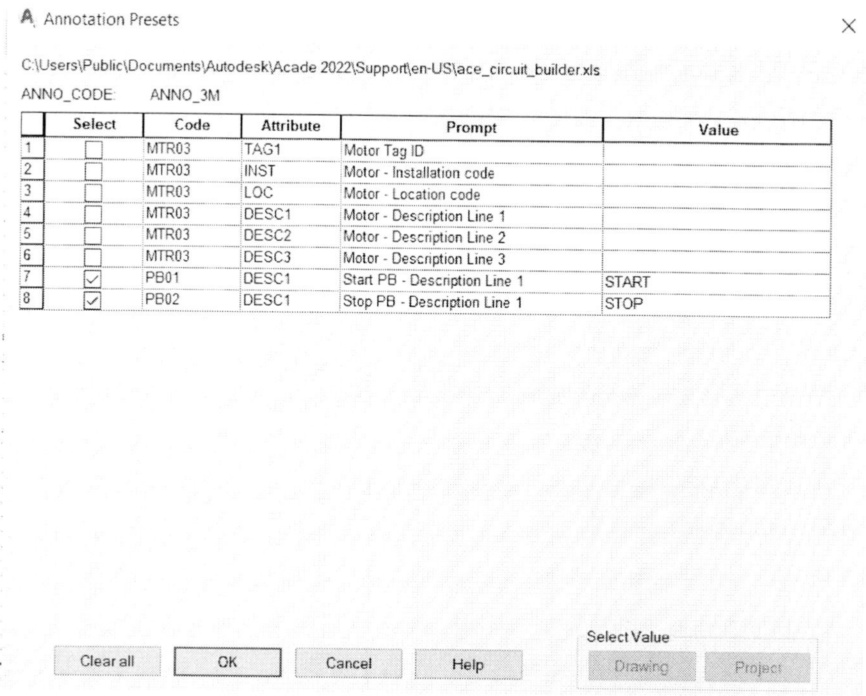


*Figure 7-56 The* ***Annotation Presets*** *dialog box*

### Insert

Choose the **Insert** button at the bottom of the **Circuit Selection** dialog box to insert a circuit using the settings specified in the **Circuit Selection** dialog box.

## Configuring a Circuit

If you need to configure a new circuit by modifying the circuit components in a reference circuit, select a reference circuit based on your requirement from the **Circuit Selection** dialog box, as discussed in the previous section, and then choose the **Configure** button from the **Circuit Selection** dialog box; you will be prompted to specify the insertion point for the circuit. Specify the insertion point for the circuit; the sketch of the circuit will be inserted with template drawing markers at the specified location and the **Circuit Configuration** dialog box will be displayed, refer to Figure 7-57. You can configure a new circuit by specifying the options in this dialog box as per your requirement. The options in this dialog box are discussed next.

### Circuit

The name of the circuit category selected in the **Circuit Selection** dialog box is displayed next to this option.

### Type

The circuit type selected in the **Circuit Selection** dialog box is displayed next to this option.

## Name

In this edit box, the name of the circuit to be configured is displayed. The name displayed is dependent on the reference circuit selected in the **Circuit Selection** dialog box. You can also enter the new name for the circuit in this edit box. Note that once the circuit is configured, the name in this edit box is added as an option in the drop-down list below the **History** area in the **Circuit Selection** dialog box.

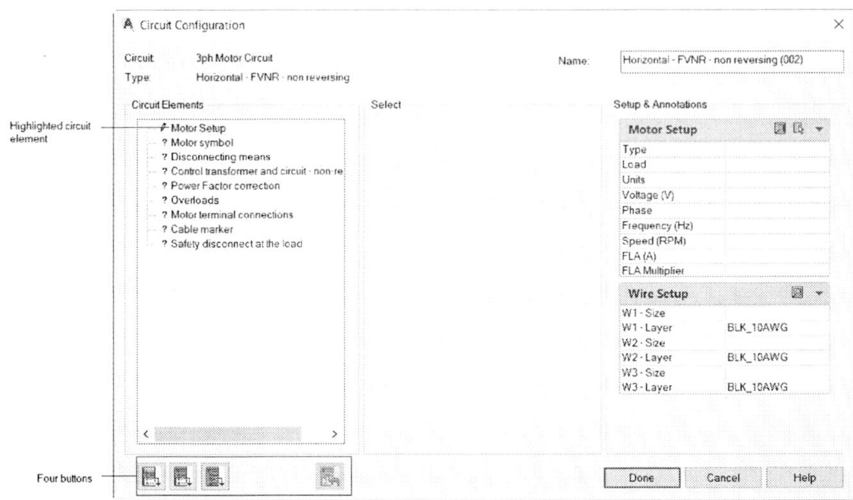


*Figure 7-57 The **Circuit Configuration** dialog box*

## Circuit Elements Area

The tree structure in this area consists of circuit elements of a reference circuit. Select the circuit elements one by one from this area and specify the parameters in the **Setup & Annotations** area to configure them based on your requirement.

## Select Area

This area displays drop-down list(s) with various options of the circuit element selected in the **Circuit Elements** area. Select the desired option from the drop-down list(s) based on your requirement.

## Setup & Annotations Area

This area displays various parameters and annotation values for the circuit element selected in the **Circuit Elements** area. If you select **Motor Setup** from the **Circuit Elements** area, the **Motor Setup** list box and the **Wire Setup** list box will be displayed with the related parameters in this area. You need to select a circuit element and enter the values for the respective parameters in this area based on the circuit configuration requirements. In case of some of the parameters, a drop-down list is available such as **Type**, **Load** for the **Motor Setup** circuit element. You can also select the options available in this drop-down list.

When you select **Motor Setup** from the **Circuit Elements** area, two buttons will be displayed on the right of the **Motor Setup** list box in the **Setup & Annotations** area, refer to Figure 7-57. Choose the first button; the **Select Motor** dialog box will be displayed, as shown in Figure 7-58. Select the desired options from **Type**, **Voltage(v)**, and **Frequency(Hz)** drop-down lists; the list of motors is displayed. Next, select one of the motors with predefined parameters from the list. Next, choose **OK** from this dialog box to return back to the **Circuit Configuration** dialog box. You will notice that all the parameters of the selected motor are displayed in the **Setup & Annotations** area. Choose the second button; the **Circuit Configuration** dialog box will be closed temporarily and you will be prompted to select motor symbol from the existing circuit. Select the motor symbol from the existing circuit; the **Circuit Configuration** dialog box will be displayed again.

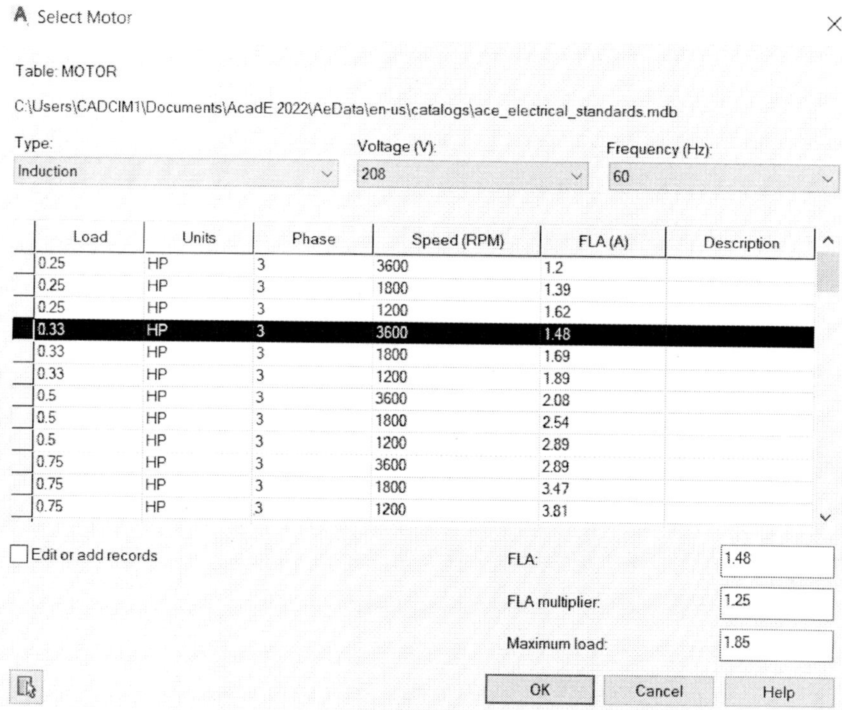


*Figure 7-58 The **Select Motor** dialog box*

Similarly, there is a button located next to the **Wire Setup** list box. Choose this button; the **Wire Size Lookup** dialog box will be displayed, as shown in Figure 7-59. You can select a wire size based on various parameters specified in this dialog box. After specifying the parameters, choose **OK** to return back to the **Circuit Configuration** dialog box.

For all the circuit elements in the **Circuit Elements** area, except the **Motor Setup**, a button is located on the right of the **Setup & Annotation** area. This button is used to select catalog data from the **Catalog Browser** dialog box for the selected circuit element.

There are four buttons available in the **Circuit Configuration** dialog box at the bottom of the **Circuit Elements** area, refer to Figure 7-57. The first button is used to insert only the highlighted circuit element from the **Circuit Elements** area. The second button is used to insert circuit elements upto the highlighted circuit including the highlighted one. The third button is used to insert all circuit elements from the **Circuit Elements** area. The fourth button is used to reverse the most recent insertion of circuit elements. Note that the fourth button will be activated only when you choose any one of the buttons from the first three buttons.

After specifying the options in the **Circuit Configuration** dialog box, choose the **Done** button; the configured circuit will be inserted at the specified location. Note that, if you have not specified the parameters for some of the circuit elements, the **Circuit Configuration: Done** message box will be displayed warning you about the template drawing markers that were not replaced by circuit elements. Choose **Yes** to **continue** or choose **No** to return to the **Circuit Configuration** dialog box.

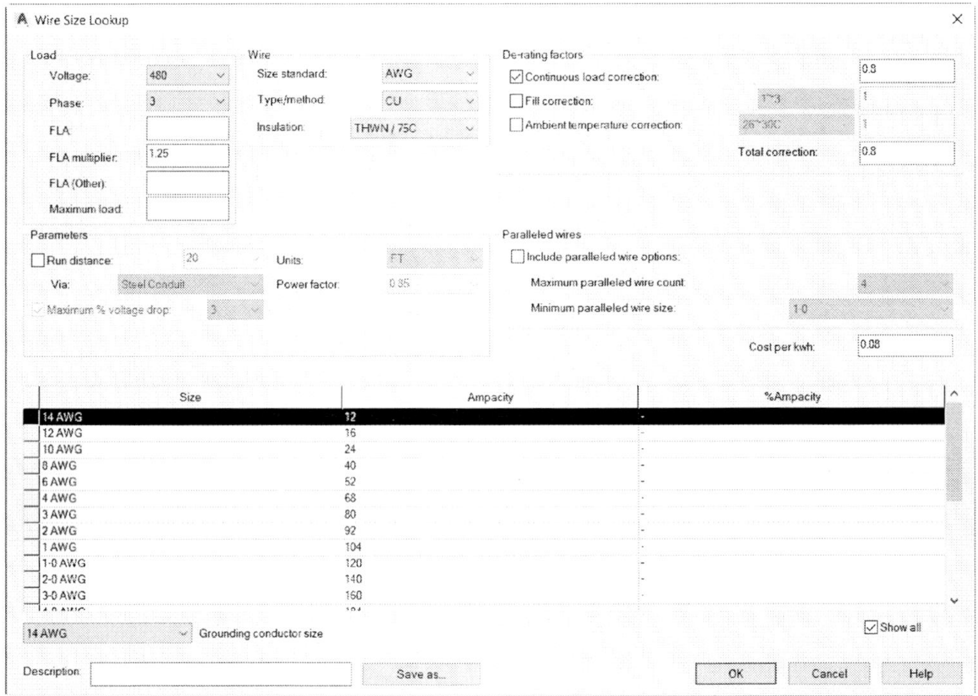


*Figure 7-59 The **Wire Size Lookup** dialog box*

# MULTIPLE PHASE CIRCUITS

The circuits that have multiple phase wires are called multiple phase circuits. You can use the **Multiple Bus** tool to draw multiple phase wires at a time. In this section, you will learn how to add multiple phase ladders and wires to a drawing, and three-phase symbols to a multiple-phase circuit.

## Adding Multiple Phase Ladders and Wires

To insert multiple phase ladder into a drawing, choose the **Insert Ladder** tool from the **Insert Wires/Wire Numbers** panel of the **Schematic** tab; the **Insert Ladder** dialog box will be displayed. Next, select the **3 Phase** radio button from the **Phase** area of this dialog box for creating the three phase ladder. After selecting the **3 Phase** radio button, the option in the **Width** and **Draw Rungs** areas will not be activated. Next, specify the options in the **Insert Ladder** dialog box as per your requirement and then choose the **OK** button; you will be prompted to specify the start position of first rung. Specify the start position of the first rung; the three phase ladder will get inserted into your drawing.

Now, to add multiple phase wire to an already inserted ladder, choose the **Multiple Bus** tool from the **Insert Wires/Wire Numbers** panel of the **Schematic** tab; the **Multiple Wire Bus** dialog box will be displayed.

The options in this dialog box have already been discussed in Chapter 3. Next, enter the horizontal and vertical spacing values in the **Spacing** edit boxes of the **Horizontal** and **Vertical** areas of the **Multiple Wire Bus** dialog box. Next, select the **Another Bus (Multiple Wires)** radio button to start the bus branching off from an existing bus or set of wires. The first wire of the new bus will attach to the pick point on an existing wire and the remaining wires of the new bus will connect to the underlying wires as you slowly move the cursor across them. Next, enter **3** in the **Number of Wires** edit box. Alternatively, choose the **3** button adjacent to the **Number of Wires** edit box and then choose the **OK** button from the **Multiple Wire Bus** dialog box; you will be prompted to select an existing wire to begin multi-phase bus connection. Select the required wire from the three phase ladder; the three phase wire will be inserted into the three phase ladder, refer to Figure 7-60. Press ENTER or ESC to exit the command.

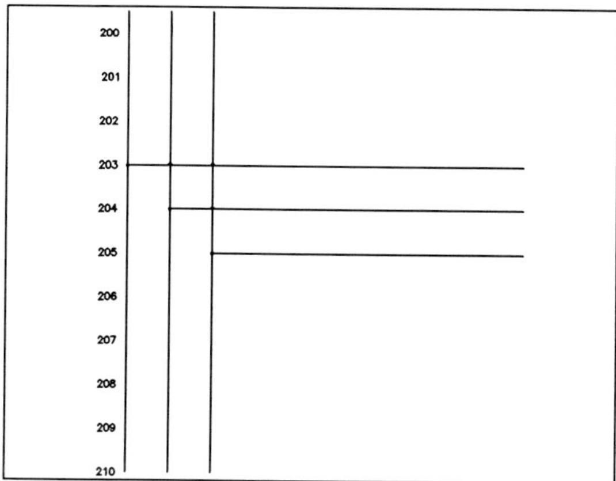


***Figure 7-60*** *Three phase bus wire inserted in three phase ladder*

## Adding Three-phase Symbols

The three-phase components are the AutoCAD blocks with attributes just like the single-phase components. The three-phase components are inserted into the drawing as parent components with two child components. All these components are inserted in a single operation. These components create a parent and child relationship and also create dashed link lines between components, as shown in Figure 7-61. To insert three-phase components into the drawing, choose the **Icon Menu** tool from the **Insert Components** panel of the **Schematic** tab; the **Insert Component** dialog box will be displayed. Select the three phase symbols such as **3 Phase Overloads**, **3Phase Starter Contacts NO**, **3 Pole Circuit Breaker**, and so on from the **NFPA:Motor Control** area in the **Insert Component** dialog box; you will be prompted to specify the insertion point. Specify the insertion point; the **Build Up or Down?** dialog box will be displayed if the symbol is inserted on horizontal wires and the **Build to Left or Right?** dialog box will be displayed if the symbol is inserted on vertical wires. Note that the horizontal three-phase components are inserted from top to bottom and the vertical three-phase components are inserted from left to right. Examples of three-phase symbols are 3 Pole Fuse with Tags, 3 Pole

Circuit Breaker, and so on. The insertion process of three-phase components is the same as that of single-phase components.

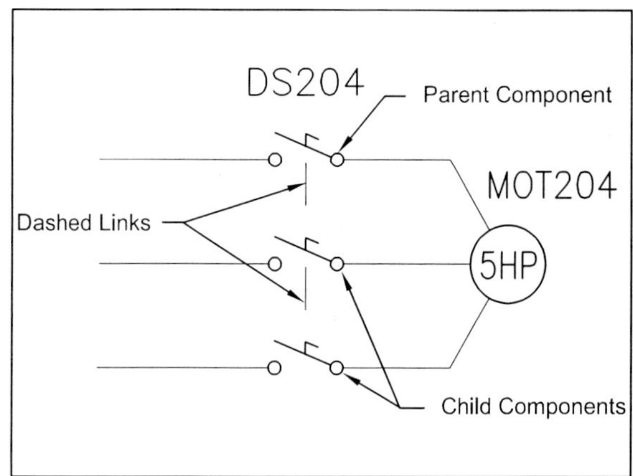


***Figure 7-61*** *The dashed link lines between the parent and child components*

# TUTORIALS

## Tutorial 1

In this tutorial, you will create a point-to-point wiring diagram, as shown in Figure 7-62.

**(Expected time: 25 min)**

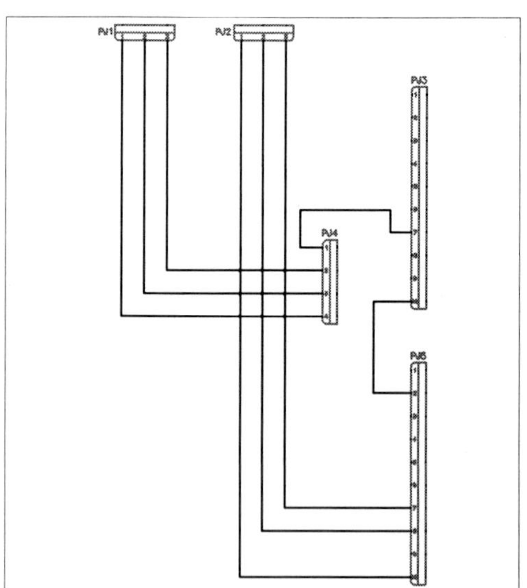

***Figure 7-62*** *The point-to-point wiring diagram*

The following steps are required to complete this tutorial:

a. Create a new drawing.
b. Insert connectors.
c. Copy connectors.

d. Insert the multiple wire bus.
e. Save the drawing.

## Creating a New Drawing

1. Activate the **CADCIM** project as discussed in the previous chapters.

2. Choose the **New Drawing** button from the **PROJECT MANAGER**; the **Create New Drawing** dialog box is displayed. Enter **C07_tut01** in the **Name** edit box of the **Drawing File** area. Select the **ACAD_ELECTRICAL.dwt** template and enter **Connector Diagram** in the **Description 1** edit box.

   Make sure the **For Reference Only** check box is cleared in the **Create New Drawing** dialog box and *C:\Users\User Name\Documents\AcadE 2022\AeData\Proj\CADCIM* is displayed in the **Location** edit box.

3. Choose the **OK** button from the **Create New Drawing** dialog box; the *C07_tut01.dwg* drawing is created in the **CADCIM** project and displayed at the bottom of the drawing list in the **CADCIM** project. Move the drawing *C07_tut01.dwg* to the *TUTORIALS* subfolder.

## Inserting Connectors

1. Choose the **Insert Connector** tool from **Schematic > Insert Components > Insert Connector** drop-down; the **Insert Connector** dialog box is displayed.

2. Choose the **Details** button from the **Insert Connector** dialog box and then set the following parameters to insert the three-pin connector:

   **Pin Spacing**: **0.7500**
   **Pin Count**: **3**
   **Pin List**: **1**

   Select the **Plug / Receptacle Combination** radio button and the **Add Divider Line** check box from the **Type** area and then select **Plug Side** from the **Pins** drop-down list in the **Display** area. Also, make sure the **Fixed Spacing** and **Insert All** radio buttons are selected from the **Layout** area. Keep rest of the values intact.

3. Choose the **Insert** button; you are prompted to specify the insertion point for the connector. Also, preview of the connector is displayed in dashed lines along with the cursor.

4. Enter **V** and then enter **10,19** at the Command prompt. Next, press ENTER; the **Insert / Edit Component** dialog box is displayed.

5. Enter **PJ1** in the edit box of the **Component Tag** area and then choose **OK**; the three-pin connector is inserted into the drawing horizontally and the **PJ1** is displayed on the left of the connector.

6. Choose the **Insert Connector** tool from **Schematic > Insert Components > Insert Connector** drop-down; the **Insert Connector** dialog box is displayed. Next, enter

**10** in the **Pin Count** edit box and keep the rest of the values intact in the **Insert Connector** dialog box.

7. Choose the **Insert** button; you are prompted to specify the insertion point. Also, the preview of the ten-pin connector is displayed along with the cursor. Enter **20,17** at the Command prompt and press ENTER; the **Insert / Edit Component** dialog box is displayed.

8. Enter **PJ3** in the edit box of the **Component Tag** area and choose **OK** from the **Insert / Edit Component** dialog box; the ten-pin connector is inserted into the drawing and **PJ3** is displayed on the top of the connector.

9. Similarly, you need to insert the four-pin connector into the drawing. To do so, enter **4** in the **Pin Count** edit box of the **Insert Connector** dialog box and keep the rest of the values intact.

10. Choose the **Insert** button; you are prompted to specify the insertion point. Enter **17,12** at the Command prompt and press ENTER; the **Insert / Edit Component** dialog box is displayed.

11. Enter **PJ4** in the **Component Tag** edit box and choose the **OK** button in the **Insert / Edit Component** dialog box; the four-pin connector is inserted into the drawing and **PJ4** is displayed on the top of the connector. Figure 7-63 shows the PJ1, PJ3, and PJ4 connectors.

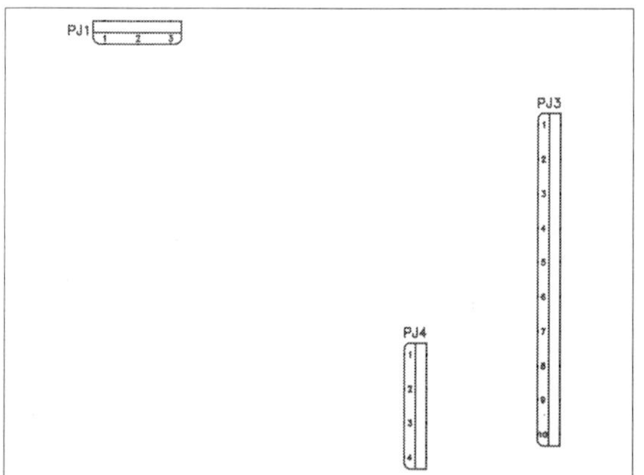


***Figure 7-63*** *The PJ1, PJ3, and PJ4 connectors*

## Copying Connectors

1. Choose the **Copy Component** tool from the **Edit Components** panel of the **Schematic** tab; you are prompted to select the component to be copied.

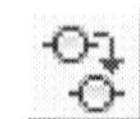

2. Select the three-pin connector PJ1; you are prompted to specify the insertion point for the connector.

3. Enter **14,19** at the Command prompt and press ENTER; the **Insert / Edit Component** dialog box is displayed.

4. In this dialog box, enter **PJ2** in the edit box of the **Component Tag** area and choose the **OK** button; the PJ2 connector is inserted into the drawing.

5. Right-click on the ten-pin connector PJ3; a marking menu is displayed. Choose the **Copy Component** option from the marking menu; you are prompted to specify the insertion point for the ten-pin connector.

6. Enter **20,8** at the Command prompt and press ENTER; the **Insert / Edit Component** dialog box is displayed.

7. Enter **PJ5** in the edit box of the **Component Tag** area of the **Insert / Edit Component** dialog box and choose the **OK** button; PJ5 is inserted in the drawing, as shown in Figure 7-64.

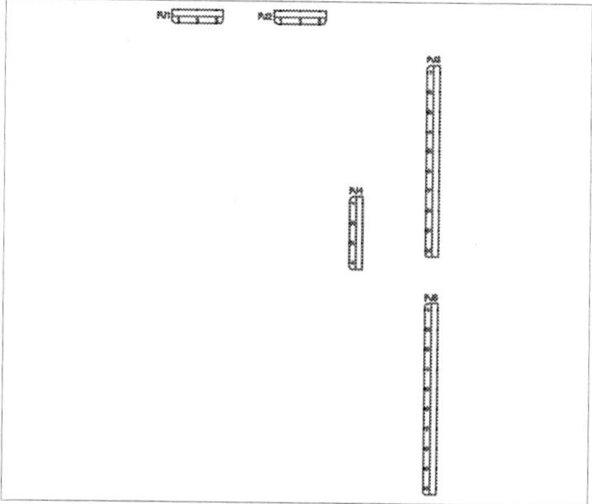

*Figure 7-64 The copied connectors inserted in the drawing*

## Inserting the Multiple Wire Bus

1. Choose the **Multiple Bus** tool from the **Insert Wires/Wire Numbers** panel of the **Schematic** tab; the **Multiple Wire Bus** dialog box is displayed, as shown in Figure 7-65.

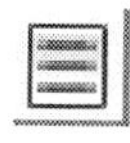

2. Set the following parameters in the **Multiple Wire Bus** dialog box:

Spacing (Horizontal area): **0.7500**
Spacing (Vertical area): **1.000**
Number of Wires: **3**
Component (Multiple Wires): Select this radio button

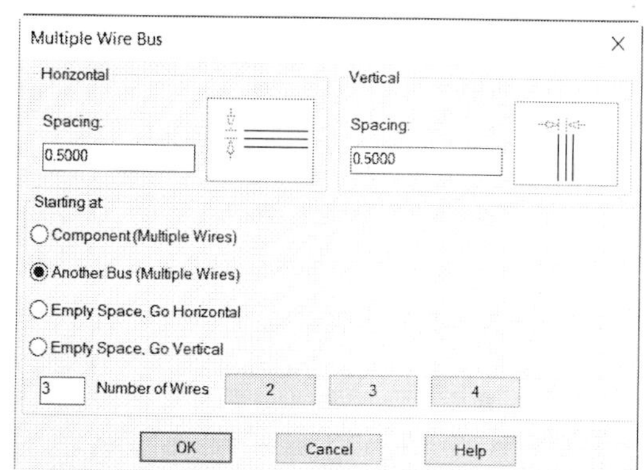


*Figure 7-65 The **Multiple Wire Bus** dialog box*

3. Choose the **OK** button; green crosses are displayed at the connection points of all connectors. Also, you are prompted to window-select the start wire connection points.

4. Select three green points of the PJ1 connector using a crossing window; red rhombus-shaped graphics are displayed at the green cross points.

5. Press ENTER and move the cursor downward and then toward the right.

6. Enter **F** at the Command prompt and then press ENTER; the wires are flipped.

7. Drag the cursor toward the right and join the cursor to the green connection points 2, 3, and 4 of the PJ4 connector and click on it. You will notice that wires are inserted between the PJ1 and PJ4 connectors.

8. Choose the **Multiple Bus** tool from the **Insert Wires/Wire Numbers** panel of the **Schematic** tab; the **Multiple Wire Bus** dialog box is displayed.

9. Enter **2** in the **Number of Wires** edit box. If this edit box is not available, then select any of the radio buttons in the **Starting at** area except the **Component (Multiple Wires)** radio button.

10. Select the **Component (Multiple Wires)** radio button.

11. Choose the **OK** button; you are prompted to window select the starting wire connection points. Also, the green cross connection points are displayed at the pin numbers of the connectors.

12. Window select the pin numbers 2 and 3 of PJ2; red rhombus-shaped graphics are displayed at the green cross points.

13. Press ENTER and move the cursor downward and then toward the right.

14. Enter **F** at the Command prompt and press ENTER.

15. Move the cursor toward the right and position it at the green connection points of pin numbers 7 and 8 of the PJ5 connector. Click at the pin number 7; a wire connecting PJ2 and PJ5 is created.

16. Choose the **Wire** tool from the **Schematic > Insert Wires/Wire Numbers > Wire** drop-down; you are prompted to specify the starting point of the wire.

17. Select the pin number 1 of the PJ2 connector and move the cursor downward. Now, move the cursor toward right to connect it to the pin number 10 of the PJ5 connector.

18. Select the pin number 2 of the PJ5 connector and move the cursor toward left and then move it upward.

19. Enter **C** at the Command prompt and press ENTER. Next, move the cursor toward right and click at the pin number 10 of PJ3.

20. Similarly, connect the wire between the pin number 1 of PJ4 and the pin number 7 of PJ3. Press ENTER to exit the command. Figure 7-66 shows point-to-point wiring diagram.

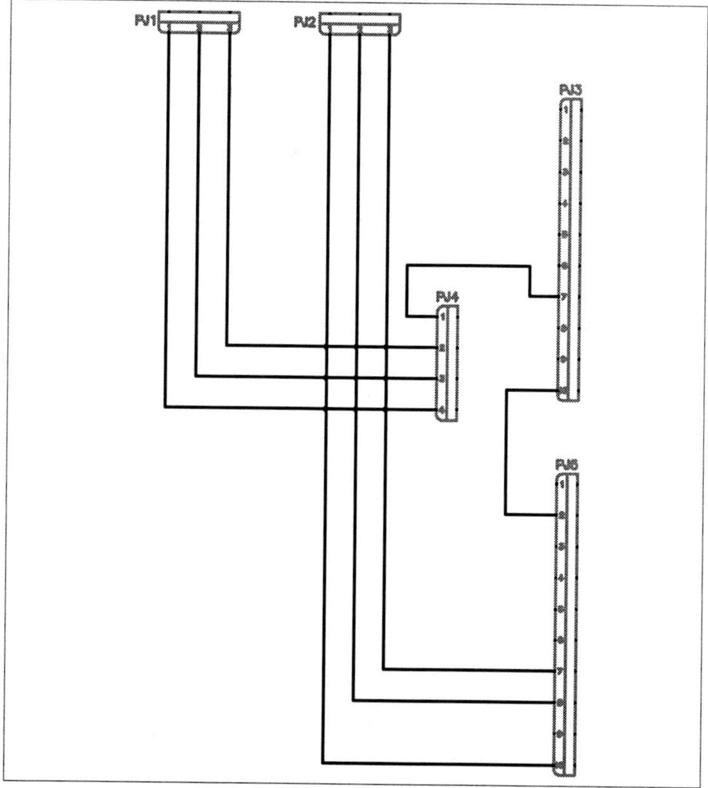


*Figure 7-66 The point-to-point wiring diagram*

## Saving the Drawing File

1. Choose **Save** from the **Application Menu** to save the drawing file.

## Tutorial 2

In this tutorial, you will create a point-to-point wiring diagram using connectors and a splice, as shown in Figure 7-67. **(Expected time: 20 min)**

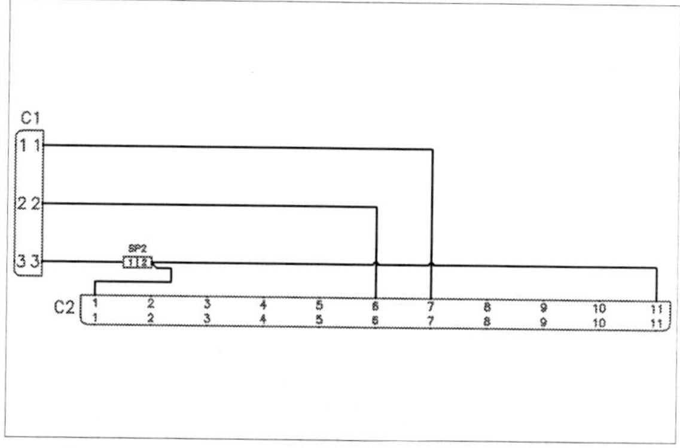


***Figure 7-67*** *The point-to-point wiring diagram with connectors and a splice*

The following steps are required to complete this tutorial:

a. Create a new drawing.
b. Insert connectors.
c. Insert wires.
d. Insert a splice.
e. Save the drawing.

## Creating a New Drawing

1. Choose the **New Drawing** button from the **PROJECT MANAGER**; the **Create New Drawing** dialog box is displayed. Enter **C07_tut02** in the **Name** edit box of the **Drawing File** area. Select the template as **ACAD_ELECTRICAL.dwt** and enter **Connector Diagram** in the **Description 1** edit box.

2. Choose the **OK** button from the **Create New Drawing** dialog box; *C07_tut02.dwg* drawing is created in the **CADCIM** project and displayed at the bottom of the drawing list in the **CADCIM** project. Move the drawing *C07_tut02.dwg* to the *TUTORIALS* subfolder.

## Inserting Connectors

1. Choose the **Insert Connector** tool from **Schematic > Insert Components > Connector** drop-down; the **Insert Connector** dialog box is displayed.

2. Choose the **Details** button from the **Insert Connector** dialog box and then set the following parameters to insert the three-pin connector:

   **Pin Spacing**: **1.000**
   **Pin Count**: **3**
   **Pin List**: **1**
   **Plug / Receptacle Combination:** Select this radio button
   **Both Sides**: Select this option from the **Pins** drop-down list in the **Display** area
   **Add Divider Line**: Clear this check box if it is selected
   Make sure the **Fixed Spacing** and **Insert All** radio buttons are selected. Keep the rest of the values intact.

3. Choose the **Insert** button from the **Insert Connector** dialog box; you are prompted to specify the insertion point for the connector.

4. Enter **4.5,7** at the Command prompt and press ENTER; the **Insert / Edit Component** dialog box is displayed.

5. Enter **C1** in the edit box of the **Component Tag** area and then choose the **OK** button; the three-pin connector is inserted into the drawing and C1 is displayed at the top of the connector, refer to Figure 7-68.

6. Similarly, you need to insert an eleven-pin connector. To do so, repeat step 1 and choose the **Details** button from the **Insert Connector** dialog box and then set the following parameters:

**Pin Spacing**: **1.000**
**Pin Count**: **11**
**Fixed Spacing**: Select this radio button
**Insert All**: Select this radio button
**Pin List**: **1**
**Both Sides**: Select this option from the **Pins** drop-down list in the **Display** area
**Add Divider Line**: Clear this check box if selected

Keep rest of the values intact.

7. Next, choose the **Insert** button; you are prompted to specify the insertion point for the connector.

8. Enter **V** and then **5.5,4** at the Command prompt and press ENTER; the **Insert / Edit Component** dialog box is displayed.

9. Enter **C2** in the edit box of the **Component Tag** area and then choose the **OK** button; the eleven-pin connector is inserted into the drawing and C2 is displayed at the top of the connector, refer to Figure 7-68.

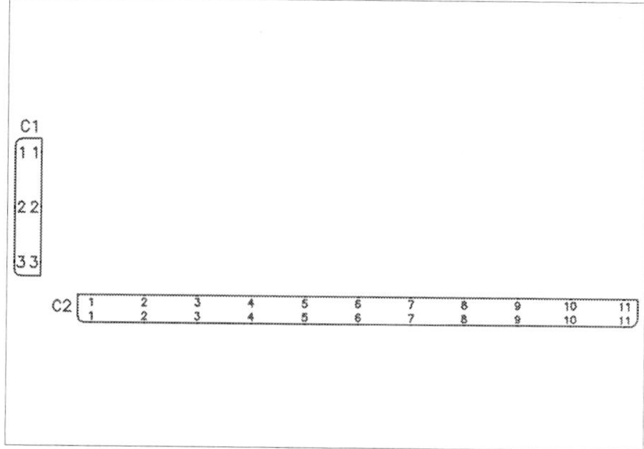


***Figure 7-68*** *The three-pin and eleven-pin connectors*

## Inserting Wires

1. Choose the **Multiple Bus** tool from the **Insert Wires/Wire Numbers** panel of the **Schematic** tab; the **Multiple Wire Bus** dialog box is displayed.

   Now, you need to connect the pin numbers 1 and 2 of the C1 connector to the pin numbers 6 and 7 of the C2 connector.

2. Set the following parameters in the **Multiple Wire Bus** dialog box:

   **Spacing (Horizontal** area): **1.000**
   **Spacing (Vertical** area): **1.000**
   **Number of Wires**: **2**
   Select the **Component (Multiple Wires)** radio button

3. Choose the **OK** button from the **Multiple Wire Bus** dialog box; you are prompted to window select the starting wire connection points.

4. Select the pin numbers 1 and 2 of the connector C1 using a crossing window and press ENTER; you are prompted to specify the wire end connection points. Move the cursor downward and connect the wires to the pin numbers 6 and 7 of the connector C2.

5. Next, choose the **Wire** tool from **Schematic > Insert Wires/Wire Numbers > Wire** drop-down; you are prompted to specify the starting point of the wire.

6. Select the pin number 3 of the connector C1 and move the cursor to the right and then join it to the pin number 11 of the connector C2. Figure 7-69 shows wires inserted between connectors C1 and C2.

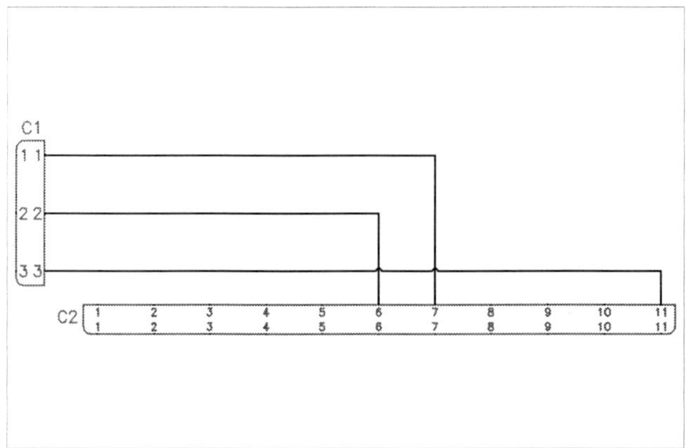


***Figure 7-69** Wire inserted between connectors C1 and C2*

## Inserting the Splice

1. Choose the **Insert Splice** tool from **Schematic > Insert Components > Insert Connector** drop-down; the **Insert Component** dialog box is displayed. 

2. Select the **Splice** symbol from the **NFPA: Splice Symbols** area of the **Insert Component** dialog box; the splice symbol along with the cursor is displayed. Also, you are prompted to specify the insertion point for the splice.

3. Next, enter **7,5** at the Command prompt and press ENTER; the splice is inserted into the wire between the pin number 3 of the connector C1 and the pin number 11 of the connector C2. Also, the **Insert / Edit Component** dialog box is displayed.

4. Next, enter **SP2** in the edit box of the **Component Tag** area of the **Insert / Edit Component** dialog box and then choose the **OK** button; **SP2** is displayed at the top of the inserted splice.

5. Choose the **Wire** tool from **Schematic > Insert Wires/Wire Numbers > Wire** drop-down; you are prompted to specify the starting point of the wire.

6. Next, select the point 2 of the splice SP2.

7. Move the cursor downward and connect it to the pin number 1 of the connector C2. Press ENTER to exit the command. Figure 7-70 shows the connector diagram with the splice inserted in it.

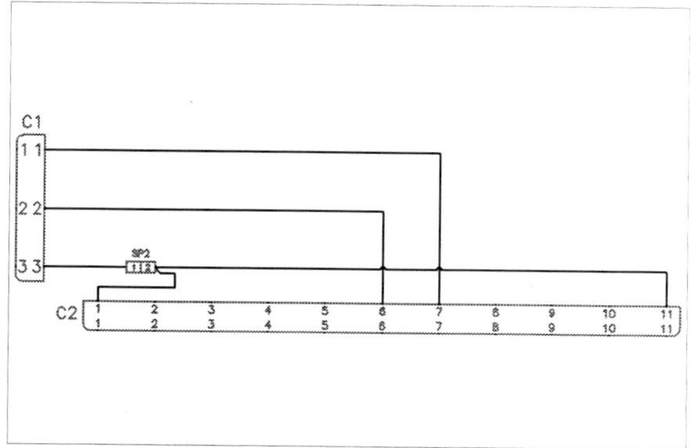


*Figure 7-70 The point-to-point wiring diagram with connectors and a splice*

## Saving the Drawing File

1. Choose **Save** from the **Application Menu** to save the drawing file.

# Tutorial 3

In this tutorial, you will insert a user-circuit into the drawing, copy the inserted circuit, and then save the circuit, as shown in Figure 7-71. **(Expected time: 15 min)**

The following steps are required to complete this tutorial:

a. Create a new drawing.
b. Insert a three-phase ladder into the drawing.
c. Insert the saved circuit into the drawing.
d. Copy the existing circuit.
e. Save the entire circuit in the **Save Circuit to Icon Menu** dialog box.
f. Save the drawing file.

## Creating a New Drawing

1. Create a drawing file with the name *C07_tut03.dwg* in the **CADCIM** project, as discussed in Tutorial 1 of this chapter.

## Inserting the Three-phase Ladder

1. Choose the **Insert Ladder** tool from **Schematic > Insert Wires/Wire Numbers > Insert Ladder** drop-down; the **Insert Ladder** dialog box is displayed.

2. Select the **3 Phase** radio button from the **Phase** area.

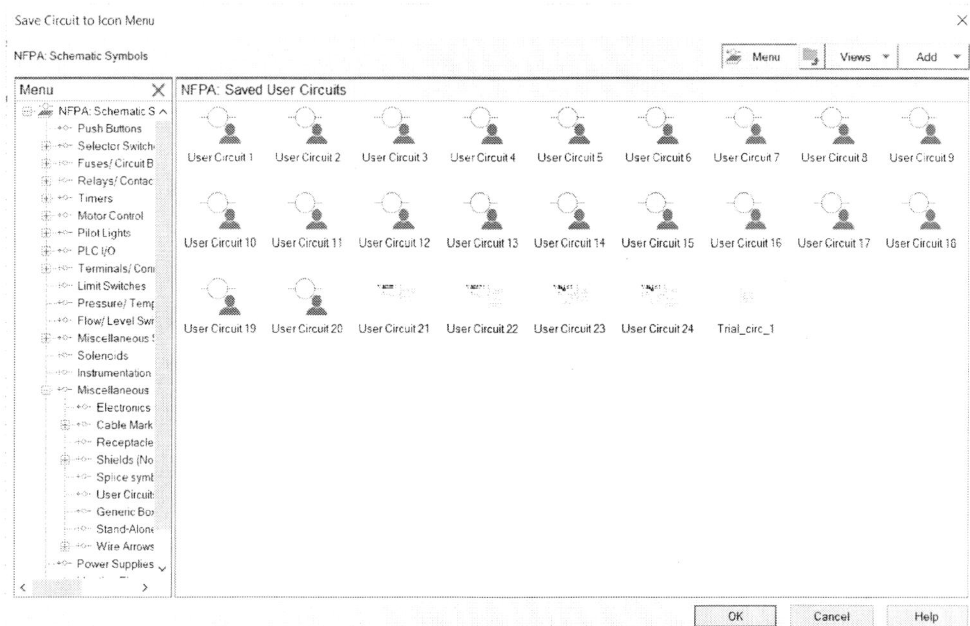


*Figure 7-71 The **Save Circuit to Icon Menu** dialog box showing the saved user-circuit*

3. Enter **0.5** in the **Spacing** edit box of the **Phase** area.

4. Enter **0.5** in the **Spacing** edit box at the top right corner of the **Insert Ladder** dialog box.

5. Enter **1** in the **1st Reference** edit box.

   By default, 1 is displayed in the **Index** edit box.

6. Clear the **Without reference numbers** check box, if it is selected.

7. Next, enter **16** in the **Rungs** edit box and click in the **Length** edit box; you will notice that the length of the ladder is automatically calculated and is displayed in this edit box.

8. Choose the **OK** button; the dialog box is closed and you are prompted to specify the start position of the first rung. Enter **3,18** at the Command prompt and press ENTER; the three-phase ladder is inserted into the drawing, as shown in Figure 7-72.

## Inserting the Saved Circuit

1. Choose the **Insert Saved Circuit** tool from **Schematic > Insert Components > Insert Circuit** drop-down; the **Insert Component** dialog box is displayed.

2. Click on **User Circuit 21**; the **Insert Component** dialog box is closed and the **Circuit Scale** dialog box is displayed. In this dialog box, make sure 1.000 is displayed in the **Custom scale** edit box and the **Update circuit's text layers as required** check box is selected.

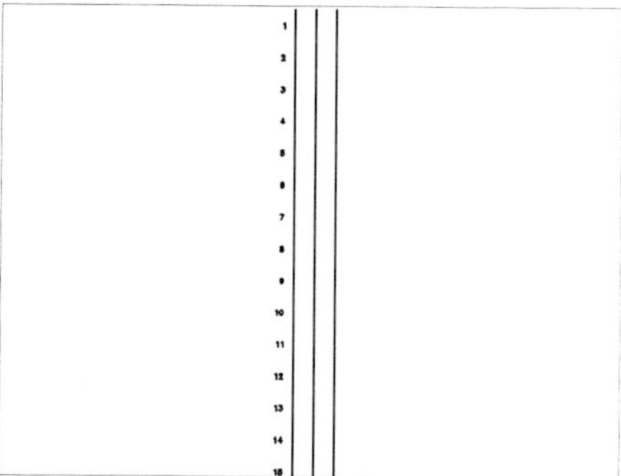

*Figure 7-72 The three-phase ladder*

3. Choose the **OK** button to close the **Circuit Scale** dialog box; you are prompted to specify the insertion point. Place the cursor on the extreme left vertical bus of the ladder at the reference number **1** and then click on the screen; the saved circuit is inserted into the drawing, as shown in Figure 7-73.

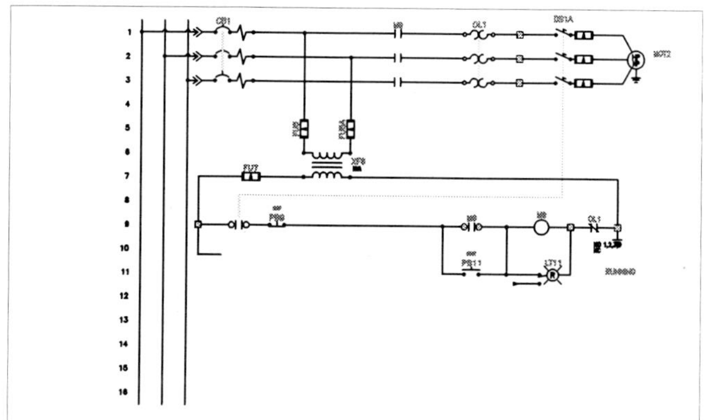

*Figure 7-73 The saved circuit inserted into the drawing*

## Copying the Circuit

1. Choose the **Copy Circuit** tool from **Schematic > Edit Components > Circuit** drop-down; you are prompted to select objects. Select the circuit that you have inserted in the previous steps by dragging the cursor from right to left.

   You need to be careful while selecting the circuit. Do not select the wire numbering of the ladder.

2. Press ENTER; you are prompted to specify the base point. Specify the base point on the extreme left of the ladder with the reference number 1 and then move the cursor downward. Next, place the circuit on the extreme left vertical bus of the ladder with the reference number 13, as shown in Figure 7-74. If the **Copy Circuit Options** dialog box is displayed, choose the **OK** button in this dialog box. Next, if the **Gapped wire pointer problem** message box is displayed, Choose the **OK** button in this message box.

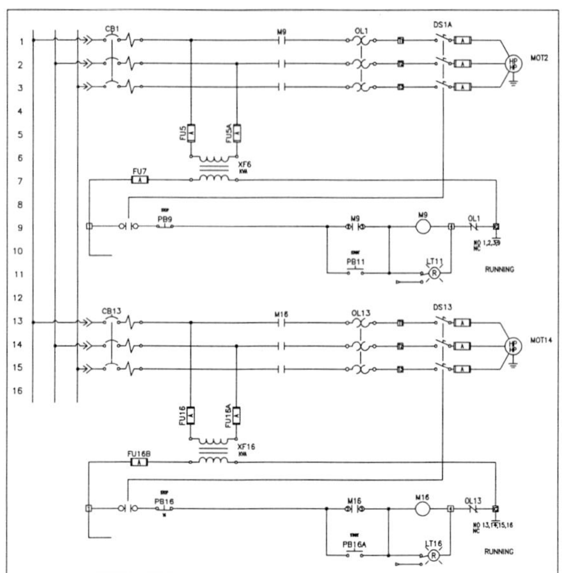


*Figure 7-74 The copied circuit*

## Saving the Circuit to Icon Menu

1. Choose the **Save Circuit to Icon Menu** tool from **Schematic > Edit Components > Circuit** drop-down; the **Save Circuit to Icon Menu** dialog box is displayed.

2. Click on the **Add** drop-down list located at the upper right corner of the **Save Circuit to Icon Menu** dialog box; different options are displayed. Select the **New Circuit** option from it; the **Create New Circuit** dialog box is displayed.

3. Enter **Trial _circ_1** in the **Name** edit box of the **Icon Details** area.

4. Choose the **Active** button; *C07_tut03* is displayed in the **Image file** edit box.

5. Select the **Create PNG from current screen image** check box, if it is not selected.

6. Enter **Trial_1** in the **File name** edit box of the **Circuit Drawing File** area.

7. Choose the **OK** button; the dialog box is closed and you are prompted to specify the base point. Specify the base point on the extreme left of the ladder with the reference number 1; you are prompted to select the objects. Next, select the whole circuit and press ENTER; the **Save Circuit to Icon Menu** dialog box is displayed again.

   You will notice that the circuit gets saved in the **Save Circuit to Icon Menu** dialog box, as shown in Figure 7-75.

8. Choose the **OK** button from the **Save Circuit to Icon Menu** dialog box to save the changes made and exit this dialog box.

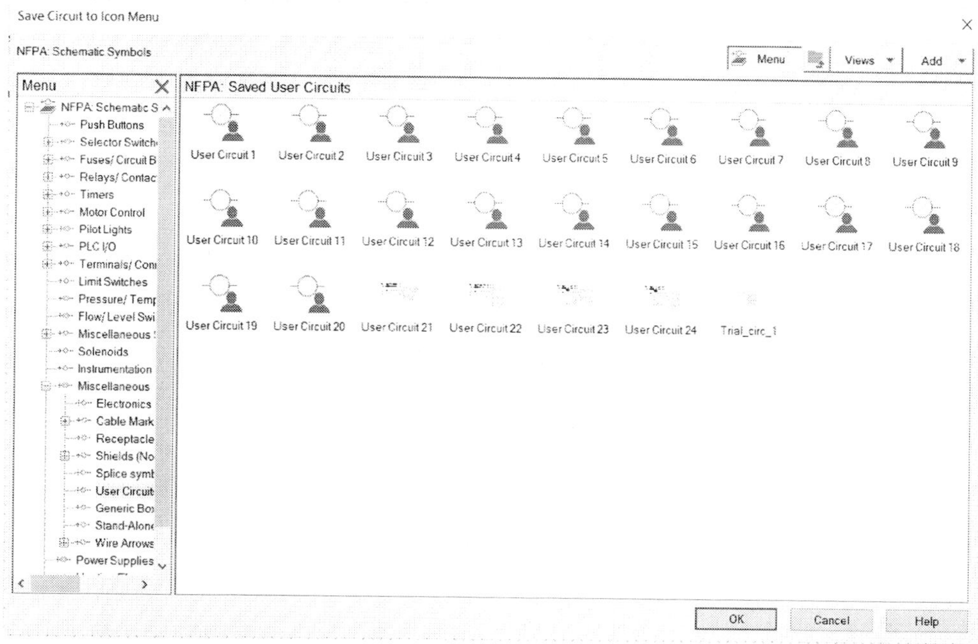


***Figure 7-75** The **Save Circuit to Icon Menu** dialog box showing the saved circuit*

## Saving the Drawing File

1. Choose **Save** from the **Application Menu** to save the drawing file.

## Tutorial 4

In this tutorial, you will configure a one-line motor circuit using the **Circuit Builder** tool, as shown in Figure 7-76. **(Expected time: 15 min)**

***Figure 7-76** The one-line motor circuit*

The following steps are required to complete this tutorial:

a. Create a new drawing.
b. Create a one-line motor circuit.
c. Save the drawing file.

### Creating a New Drawing

1. Create a drawing file with the name *C07_tut04.dwg* in the **CADCIM** project, as discussed in Tutorial 1 of this chapter.

### Creating a One-line Motor Circuit

1. Choose the **Circuit Builder** tool from **Schematic > Insert Components > Circuit Builder** drop-down; the **Circuit Selection** dialog box is displayed.

2. If the **History** area is not displayed, choose the **History >>** button at the bottom of the dialog box; the **History** area is displayed in it.

3. Click on the **+** sign at the left of the **One-line Motor Circuit** category; the circuit types related to this category are displayed below it, refer to Figure 7-77.

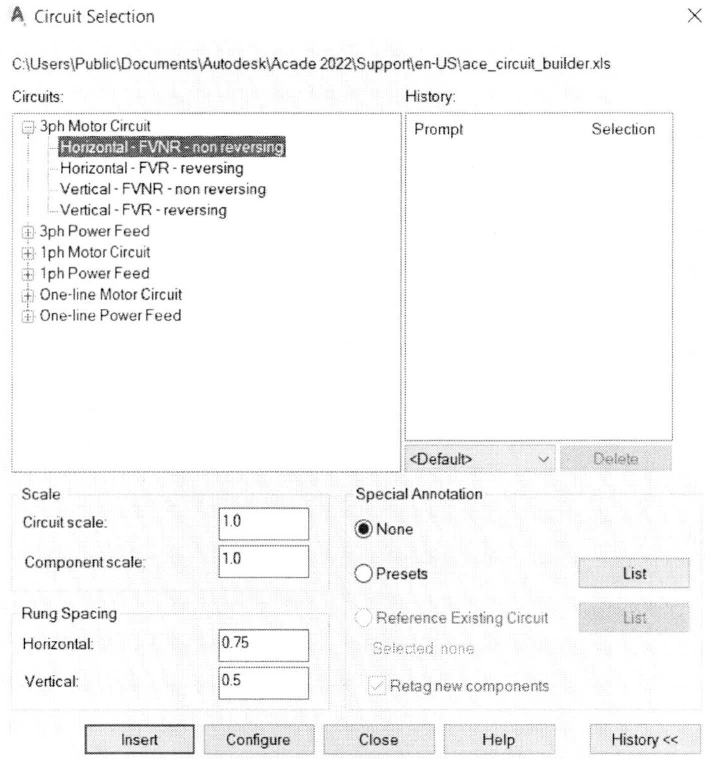


*Figure 7-77 The **Circuit Selection** dialog box*

4. Select **Horizontal - FVNR - non reversing** and choose the **Configure** button; the circuit template is displayed along with the cursor and you are prompted to specify the insertion point.

5. Place the cursor approximately at the middle of the drawing area; the template is inserted and the **Circuit Configuration** dialog box is displayed, as shown in Figure 7-78.

6. In this dialog box, make sure **Motor Setup** is selected in the **Circuit Elements** area. Next, choose the first button located at the right of the **Motor Setup** list box in the **Setup & Annotations** area; the **Select Motor** dialog box is displayed.

7. In this dialog box, make sure **Single Phase** is selected in the **Type** drop-down list, **208** is selected in the **Voltage (V)** drop-down list, and **60** is selected in the **Frequency (Hz)** drop-down list. Next, select the first entry from the table and choose the **OK** button to close the dialog box; the parameters for the selected motor are displayed in the **Setup & Annotations** area of the **Circuit Configuration** dialog box.

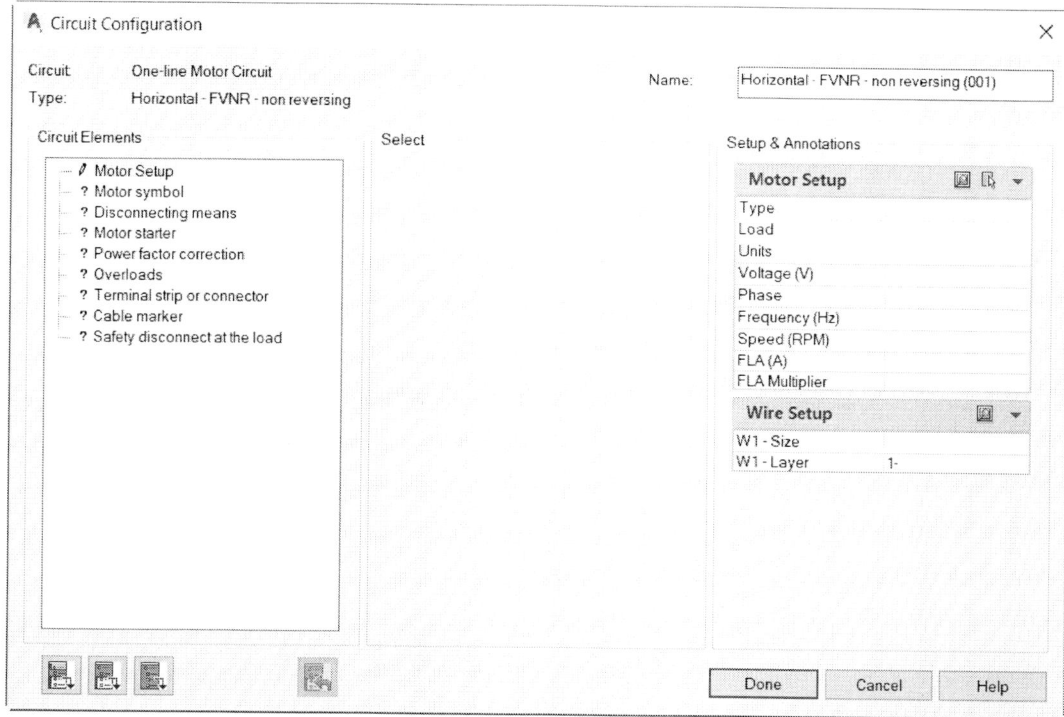


*Figure 7-78 The **Circuit Configuration** dialog box*

8. Select **Motor Symbol** from the **Circuit Elements** area and then select **None** in the **Motor** drop-down list of the **Select** area.

9. Select **Disconnecting means** from the **Circuit Elements** area. Next, select **Fuses** from the **Main Disconnect** drop-down list of the **Select** area; parameters for the fuse are displayed in the **Setup & Annotations** area.

10. Choose the button located at the right of the **Fuse** list box in the **Setup & Annotations** area; the **Catalog Browser** dialog box is displayed. 

11. Delete the text from the **Search** field of the dialog box, if any, and press ENTER; all the entries for fuses are displayed in the Database grid.

12. Select **1492-FB1C30-L** from the **Catalog** column in the **Catalog Browser** dialog box and choose the **OK** button in the dialog box; the parameters for the selected fuse are displayed in the **Setup & Annotations** area.

13. Select **Motor Starter** from the **Circuit Elements** area. Next, choose the button located at the right of the **Motor Stater** list box in the **Setup & Annotations** area; the **Catalog Browser** dialog box is displayed.

14. In this dialog box, delete the text from the **Search** field, if any, and press ENTER. Next, select **193-B1R6K** from the **Catalog** column in the **Catalog Browser** dialog box and choose

the **OK** button; the parameters for selected motor starter are displayed in the **Setup & Annotations** area.

**Note**

*You can use the **Search** field in the **Catalog Browser** dialog box to search the desired catalog information.*

15. Select **Overloads** from the **Circuit Elements** area. Next, choose the button located at the right of the **Overload Relay** list box in the **Setup & Annotations** area; the **Catalog Browser** dialog box is displayed.

16. In this dialog box, delete the text from the **Search** field and press ENTER. Next, select **193-A4R6D** from the **Catalog Browser** dialog box and choose the **OK** button in the dialog box; the parameters for the selected overload relay are displayed in the **Setup & Annotations** area.

17. Select **Safety disconnect at the load** from the **Circuit Elements** area. Next, choose the button located at the right of the **Disconnect Switch** list box in the **Setup & Annotations** area; the **Catalog Browser** dialog box is displayed.

18. Select **1494C-DRX661-A5** from the **Catalog Browser** dialog box and choose the **OK** button in the dialog box; the parameters for selected disconnect switch are displayed in the **Setup & Annotations** area.

19. Choose the **Insert all the circuit elements** button in the **Circuit Configuration** dialog box; one-line motor circuit is configured, as shown in Figure 7-79 and the **Circuit Configuration** dialog box is displayed again. Next, choose the **Done** button in this dialog box to exit the command.

***Figure 7-79** The one-line motor circuit*

**Note**

*You may change the component tags for the above circuit as discussed in the earlier chapters.*

## Saving the Drawing File

1. Choose **Save** from the **Application Menu** to save the drawing file.

# Tutorial 5

In this tutorial, you will insert a user-circuit into a drawing, save the circuit as a wblocked circuit, and then insert the wblocked circuit into another drawing, refer to Figure 7-80. **(Expected time: 15 min)**

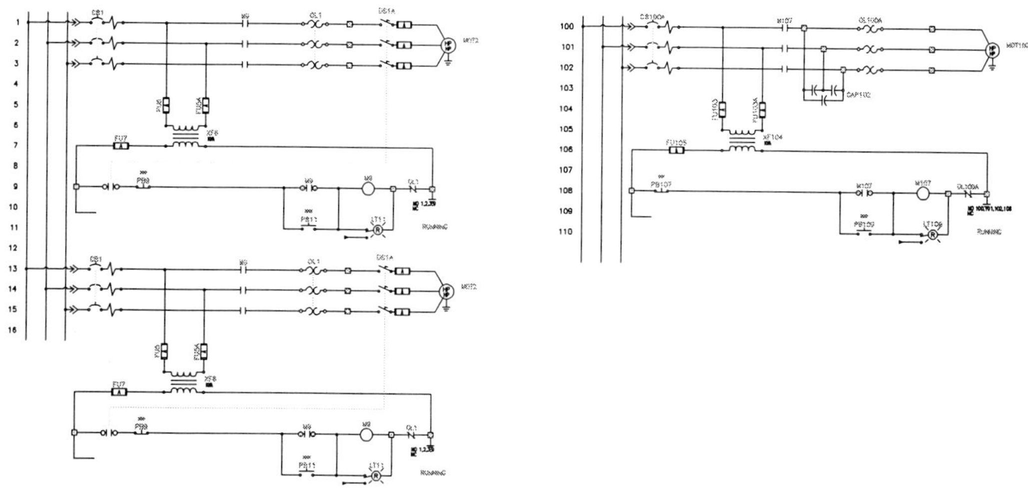

*Figure 7-80 Inserted wblocked circuit*

The following steps are required to complete this tutorial:

a. Create a new drawing.
b. Insert a three-phase ladder into the drawing.
c. Insert the saved circuit into the drawing.
d. Save the circuit as a wblocked circuit.
e. Insert the saved wblocked circuit.

## Creating a New Drawing

1. Create a drawing file with the name *C07_tut05.dwg* in the **CADCIM** project, as discussed in Tutorial 1 of this chapter.

## Inserting the Three-phase Ladder

1. Choose the **Insert Ladder** tool from **Schematic > Insert Wires/Wire Numbers > Insert Ladder** drop-down; the **Insert Ladder** dialog box is displayed.

2. Select the **3 Phase** radio button from the **Phase** area.

3. Enter **0.5** in the **Spacing** edit box of the **Phase** area.

4. Enter **0.5** in the **Spacing** edit box at the top right corner of the **Insert Ladder** dialog box.

5. Enter **100** in the **1st Reference** edit box.

   By default, 1 is displayed in the **Index** edit box.

6. Clear the **Without reference numbers** check box, if it is selected.

7. Next, enter **12** in the **Rungs** edit box and click in the **Length** edit box; you will notice that the length of the ladder is automatically calculated and is displayed in this edit box.

8. Choose the **OK** button; the dialog box is closed and you are prompted to specify the start position of the first rung. Enter **3,18** at the Command prompt and press ENTER; the three-phase ladder is inserted into the drawing.

## Inserting the Saved Circuit

1. Choose the **Insert Saved Circuit** tool from **Schematic > Insert Components > Insert Circuit** drop-down; the **Insert Component** dialog box is displayed.

2. Click on **User Circuit 22**; the **Insert Component** dialog box is closed and the **Circuit Scale** dialog box is displayed. In this dialog box, make sure 1.000 is displayed in the **Custom scale** edit box and the **Update circuit's text layers as required** check box is selected.

3. Choose the **OK** button to close the **Circuit Scale** dialog box; you are prompted to specify the insertion point. Place the cursor on the extreme left vertical bus of the ladder at the reference number **100** and then click on the screen; the saved circuit is inserted into the drawing, as shown in Figure 7-81.

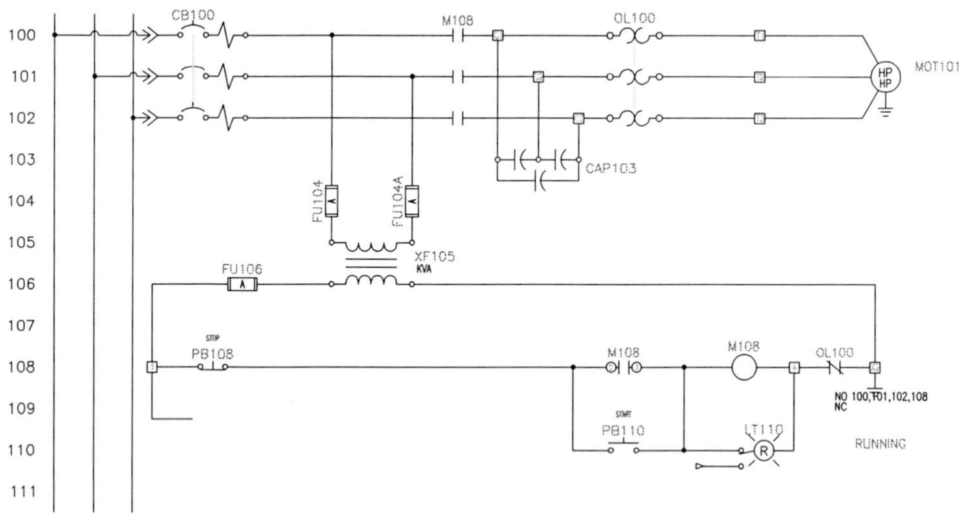


*Figure 7-81 Inserted saved circuit*

## Saving the Circuit as a Wblocked Circuit

1. Type **Wblock** at the Command Prompt and press ENTER; the **Write Block** dialog box is displayed. In this dialog box, choose the **Pick Point** button from the **Base point** area; you are prompted to specify the insertion base point.

2. Click on the extreme left of the ladder with the reference number 100; base point is specified and the **Write Block** dialog box is displayed again. Notice that the coordinates of the base point are displayed in the **X**, **Y**, and **Z** edit boxes of the **Base Point** area.

3. Choose the **Select Objects** button from the **Objects** area; you are prompted to select objects. Select the inserted circuit including the ladder and press ENTER; the **Write Block** dialog box is displayed again.

   Next, you need to specify location for the wblocked circuit.

4. In the **Destination** area, enter **C:\Users\CADCIM1\Documents\customblock** in the **File name and path** edit box and then choose the **OK** button; the selected objects are converted to a wblocked circuit and the circuit is saved at the specified location.

## Inserting the Saved Wblocked Circuit

1. Open the C07_tut03 drawing from the **CADCIM** project. Next, choose the **Insert Wblocked Circuit** tool from the **Insert Circuit** drop-down in the **Insert Components** panel of the **Schematic** tab; the **Insert WBlocked Circuit** dialog box is displayed, as shown in Figure 7-82.

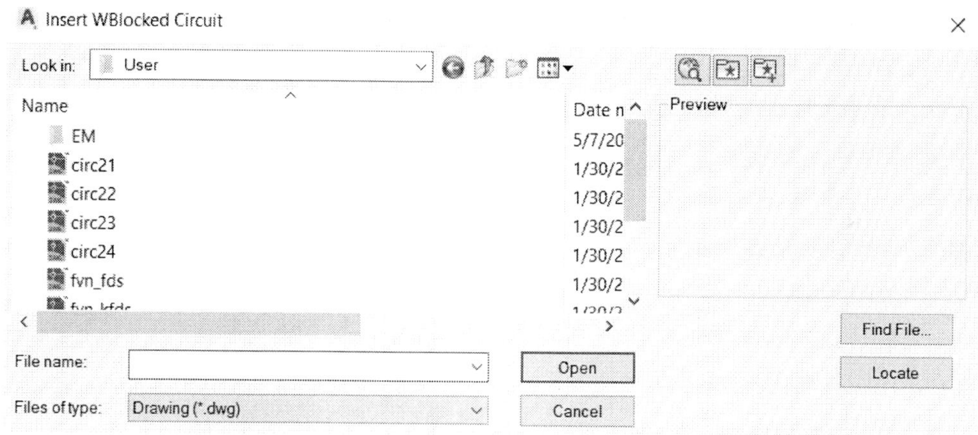


*Figure 7-82 The **Insert WBlocked Circuit** dialog box*

2. In this dialog box, navigate to the location where the wblocked circuit was saved. Next, select **customblock** from this dialog box and choose the **Open** button; the **Circuit Scale** dialog box is displayed. In this dialog box, make sure **1.000** is displayed in the **Custom scale** edit box and the **Update circuit's text layers as required** check box is selected.

3. Choose the **OK** button to close the **Circuit Scale** dialog box; you are prompted to specify the insertion point.

4. Enter **17,18** at the Command prompt and press ENTER; the saved wblocked circuit is inserted into the drawing, as shown in Figure 7-83.

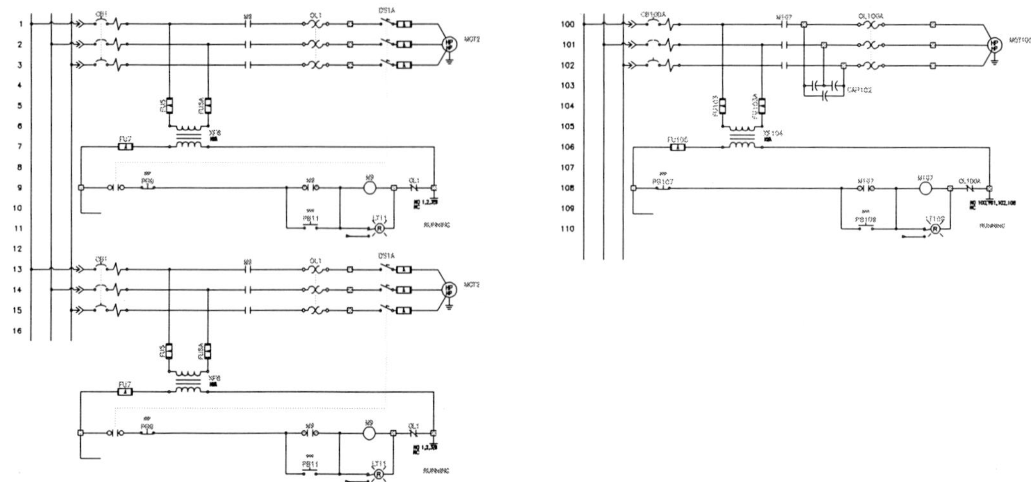

***Figure 7-83*** *Inserted wblocked circuit*

## Saving the Drawing File

1. Choose **Save** from the **Application Menu** to save the *C07_tut03.dwg* drawing file.

2. Also, save the *C07_tut05.dwg* drawing file.

## Self-Evaluation Test

**Answer the following questions and then compare them to those given at the end of this chapter:**

1. Which of the following commands is used to insert a connector?

   (a) **AECONNECTOR** (b) **AECONNECTORPIN**
   (c) **AEWIRE** (d) **AECONNECTORLIST**

2. When you choose the __________ tool, the connector is split into two separate parts.

3. The __________ and __________ buttons in the **Insert Connector** dialog box are used to change the orientation of a connector.

4. The __________ tool is used to increase the length of a connector.

5. The __________ tool is used to insert the WBlocked circuit in a drawing.

6. Connectors are used to connect a wire or a group of wires at a single junction. (T/F)

7. When you choose the **Rotate Connector** tool, the orientation of the connector switches between the horizontal and vertical positions. (T/F)

8. The **Insert Splice** tool is used to connect wires by inserting a splice. (T/F)

9. The **Swap Connector Pins** tool is used to swap pin numbers and pin locations. (T/F)

10. You can flip a connector by choosing the **Reverse Connector** tool. (T/F)

## Review Questions

**Answer the following questions:**

1. Which of the following options in the **Insert Connector** dialog box is used to display only the plug of a connector?

   (a) **Receptacle only** (b) **Plug only**
   (c) **Plug/Receptacle Combination** (d) **Insert All**

2. Which of the following buttons is used to expand the **Insert Connector** dialog box?

   (a) **Insert** (b) **Rotate**
   (c) **List** (d) **Details**

3. Which of the following tools is used to create a new circuit?

   (a) **Move Circuit** (b) **Copy Circuit**
   (c) **Insert Saved Circuit** (d) **Save Circuit to Icon Menu**

4. Which of the following radio buttons in the **Split Block** dialog box is used to draw straight lines at the end of the break of a connector?

   (a) **Draw it** (b) **Jagged Lines**
   (c) **Straight Lines** (d) **Allow Spacers/Breaks**

5. The point-to-point schematic wiring diagrams compared to schematic ladder diagrams are a closer representation of how a machine or control system is actually wired. (T/F)

6. The **Scoot** tool is used to move a connector along with wires. (T/F)

7. The **Description** column in the **Connector Pin Numbers In Use** dialog box displays the description of the plug only. (T/F)

8. You can insert multiple wires into a drawing by choosing the **Multiple Wire Bus** tool. (T/F)

9. A connector can be rotated in the clockwise direction by choosing the **Rotate Connector** tool. (T/F)

# EXERCISES

## Exercise 1

Create a connector diagram, as shown in Figure 7-84, and then delete the pins 7, 8, 9, 10, 11, and 14 using the **Delete Connector Pins** tool. Next, save the drawing as *C07_exer01.dwg*.

**(Expected time: 20 min)**

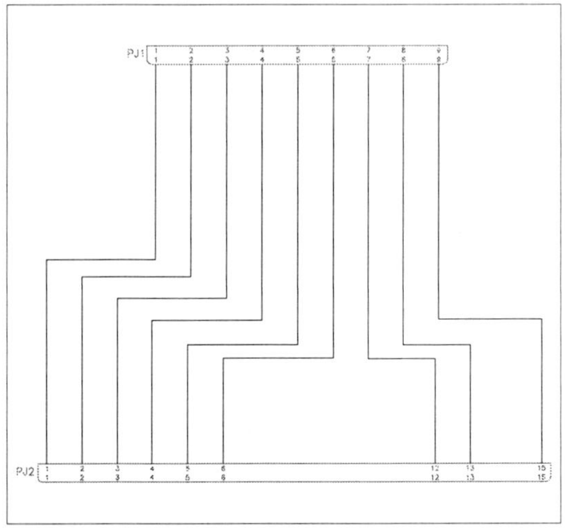


***Figure 7-84*** *The connector diagram for Exercise 1*

## Exercise 2

Create a three-phase ladder with the following parameters: Spacing = 1.000, Spacing = 0.5000 of the **Phase** area, Rungs = 20, and Reference number = 100. Next, insert a saved circuit **User Circuit 24** from the **NFPA: Saved User Circuits** area of the **Insert Component** dialog box at rung **100**. Then, copy this circuit and place it on the rung **110**, as shown in Figure 7-85. Save the circuit in the **Save Circuit to Icon Menu** dialog box with the name **Trial_circ_2**.

**(Expected time: 20 min)**

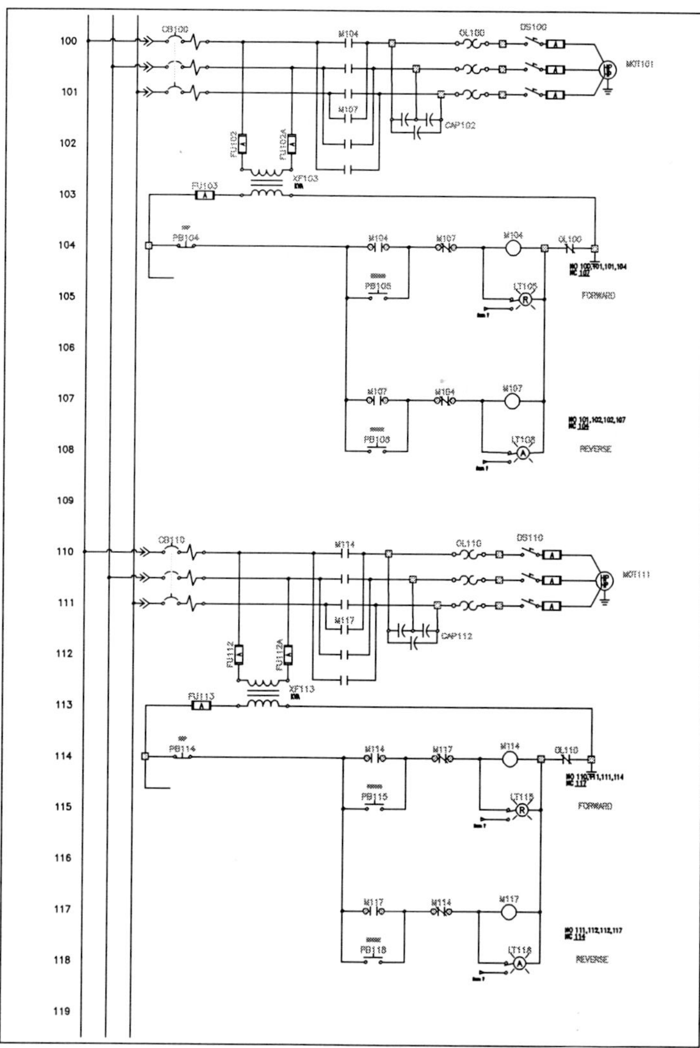


*Figure 7-85* *The circuit diagram for Exercise 2*

## Answers to Self-Evaluation Test

**1.** a, **2. Split Connector**, **3. Flip, Rotate**, **4. Stretch Connector**, **5. Insert WBlocked Circuit**, **6.** T, **7.** T, **8.** T, **9.** F, **10.** T

# Chapter 8

# Panel Layouts

## Learning Objectives

**After completing this chapter, you will be able to:**

- *Understand the WD_PNLM block file*
- *Create panel layouts from schematic list*
- *Annotate and edit a footprint*
- *Insert footprints from icon menu*
- *Add a new record of footprint to the footprint lookup table*
- *Insert footprints manually*
- *Insert footprints from user defined list, equipment list, and vendors menu*
- *Copy a footprint*
- *Set the panel drawing configuration and footprint layers*
- *Make an Xdata visible*
- *Insert balloons, nameplates, and DIN Rail into drawing*
- *Edit the footprint lookup database file*

# INTRODUCTION

AutoCAD Electrical provides different tools to create intelligent panel layout drawings. You can design panel layouts either by using the information of the schematic drawings or without using schematic drawings. You can use footprint symbols supplied by vendors in AutoCAD format with AutoCAD Electrical.

Using the panel layout tools, you can create intelligent mechanical or panel layout drawings. The following are the key features of panel layout drawings:

1. Due to the bi-directional capabilities of panel layout drawings, the panel drawings get updated automatically whenever the schematic wiring diagrams are updated and vice-versa.

2. You can extract wire number, information of wire color or gauge, and connection sequencing data directly from the schematics and annotate it on to the panel footprint.

3. You can use AutoCAD Electrical to extract various reports from the panel layout drawings such as Bill of Material reports, panel component reports, nameplate reports, wire connection reports, and so on.

In this chapter, you will learn about WD_PNLM block file. Also, you will learn how to insert footprints using the **Schematics list**, **Icon Menu**, **Manual**, **Equipment List**, **User Defined List**, and **Manufacturer Menu** tools. This chapter also explains annotating and editing of footprints. In addition to this, you will learn about setting panel drawing configuration, copy footprint, inserting nameplates, balloons, and DIN Rail in the panel layout drawings.

# THE WD_PNLM BLOCK FILE

Whenever you insert a panel component into a drawing for the first time using the **Icon Menu**, **Schematic List**, or **Manual** tools, AutoCAD Electrical first checks for the WD_PNLM block file in the drawing and reads configuration settings from the attributes that it contains. If the drawing file contains invisible WD_PNLM block, you can insert panel component into the drawing directly. But if the drawing file does not have invisible WD_PNLM block, the **Alert** dialog box will be displayed, as shown in Figure 8-1. Choose the **OK** button in the **Alert** dialog box to insert the WD_PNLM block file in the drawing. This file contains only attributes and no graphical information. A drawing is considered as a panel layout drawing if this block is present in the drawing. This block file is inserted automatically at the 0,0 location of every panel layout drawing.

**Note**

*The WD_M and WD_PNLM blocks can be inserted in the same drawing.*

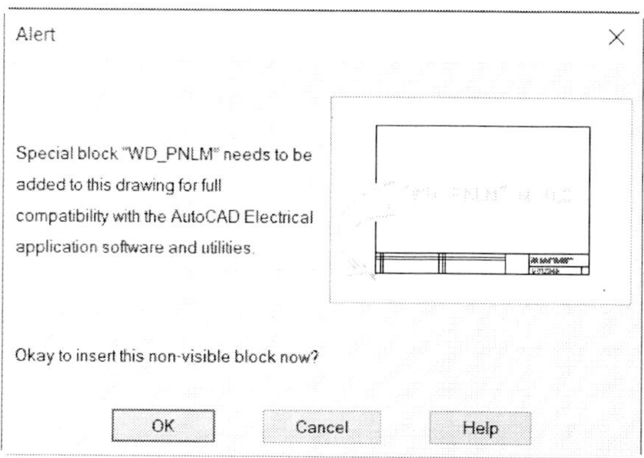


*Figure 8-1 The **Alert** dialog box showing the invisible WD_PNLM block*

## CREATING PANEL LAYOUTS FROM SCHEMATIC LIST

**Ribbon:** Panel > Insert Component Footprints > Insert Footprints drop-down > Schematic List
**Toolbar:** ACE:Panel Layout > Insert Footprint (Icon Menu) drop-down > Insert Footprint (Schematic List)
or ACE:Component Footprint > Insert Footprint (Schematic List)
**Menu:** Panel Layout > Insert Footprint (Schematic List)
**Command:** AEFOOTPRINTSCH

The **Schematic List** tool is used to insert panel footprints from the schematic component list. This list displays the names of the components that have already been inserted in the schematic drawings of an active project. Using this tool, you can link the panel footprint and schematic component. To insert a panel footprint from a schematic component list, choose the **Schematic List** tool from the **Insert Footprints** drop-down in the **Insert Component Footprints** panel of the **Panel** tab, refer to Figure 8-2; the **Schematic Components List --> Panel Layout Insert** dialog box will be displayed, as shown in Figure 8-3. Different areas and options in this dialog box are discussed next.

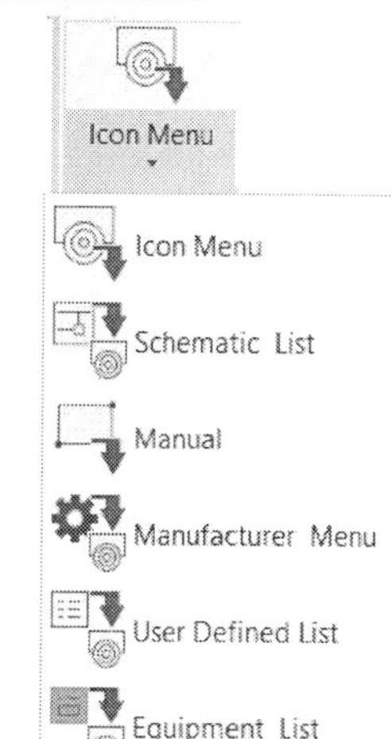


*Figure 8-2 The **Insert Footprints** drop-down*

**Note**

*1. If you are using the **Schematic List** tool for the first time in AutoCAD Electrical session, the **Schematic Components List --> Panel Layout Insert** dialog box will be displayed. Else, the **Schematic Components** dialog box will be displayed directly. The **Schematic Components** dialog box is discussed later in this chapter.*

*2. The one-line components are not extracted and displayed in the schematic component list.*

### Extract component list for Area

The **Extract component list for** area is used to extract component list data for active drawing or project. The options in this area are discussed next.

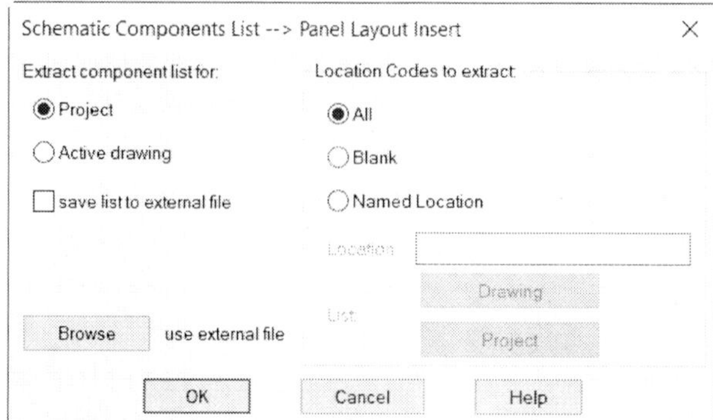


***Figure 8-3** The **Schematic Components List --> Panel Layout Insert** dialog box*

The **Project** radio button is selected by default and is used to extract component list from the entire active project. To extract component list from the project, select the **Project** radio button and then choose the **OK** button from the **Schematic Components List --> Panel Layout Insert** dialog box; the **Select Drawings to Process** dialog box will be displayed. The options in this dialog box have already been discussed in the previous chapters. Next, select the drawing or drawings that you want to process and choose the **Process** button; the selected drawing(s) will be displayed in the bottom list of the **Select Drawings to Process** dialog box. Next, choose the **OK** button from the **Select Drawings to Process** dialog box; the **Schematic Components (active project)** dialog box will be displayed. The options in this dialog box are discussed in the next section.

In case you extract component list from the entire project with the **save list to external file** check box selected in the **Schematic Components List --> Panel Layout Insert** dialog box and choose the **OK** button; the **Select Drawings to Process** dialog box will be displayed. Next, select the drawing or drawings that you want to process and choose the **Process** button; the selected drawing(s) will be displayed in the bottom list of the **Select Drawings to Process** dialog box. Next, choose the **OK** button from the **Select Drawings to Process** dialog box; the **Select file for Schematic – –> Panel Layout list** dialog box will be displayed. Using this dialog box, you can save component list to an external file. An external file can be saved in the comma delimited text files such as *.wd1* or *.csv*. Specify the file name in the **File name** edit box and choose the **Save** button; the **Schematic Components (active project)** dialog box will be displayed.

Select the **Active drawing** radio button from the **Schematic Components List – –> Panel Layout Insert** dialog box to extract component list from the active drawing. Next, choose **OK** from the **Schematic Components List --> Panel Layout Insert** dialog box; the **Schematic Components (active drawing)** dialog box will be displayed. Note that the **Schematic Components (active drawing)** dialog box will be displayed only if the active drawing has schematic components in it. If you select the **save list to external file** check box from the **Schematic Components List --> Panel Layout Insert** dialog box and choose the **OK** button in this dialog box, the **Select file for Schematic --> Panel Layout list** dialog box will be displayed after choosing the **OK** button in the **Select Drawings to Process** dialog box, as discussed earlier. In the **Select file for Schematic --> Panel Layout list** dialog box, specify a file name in the **File name** edit box and choose the **Save** button; the **Schematic Components (active drawing)** dialog box will be displayed.

## Browse

The **Browse** button is used to select the saved external schematic component list file.

## Location Codes to extract Area

The **Location Codes to extract** area is used to extract information for components that have location codes. This area contains three radio buttons: **All**, **Blank**, and **Named Location**. These radio buttons are discussed next.

### All

The **All** radio button is selected by default and is used to extract information for all components present in an active project.

### Blank

Select the **Blank** radio button to extract information for components without a location code.

### Named Location

The **Named Location** radio button is used to extract components information for the specified location code. To do so, select the **Named Location** radio button; the **Location** edit box as well as the **Drawing** and **Project** buttons will be activated. Enter the location code in the **Location** edit box. Alternatively, choose the **Drawing** or **Project** button from the **Location Codes to extract** area; the **All Locations** dialog box will be displayed. Select the location code used either in the active drawing or active project and then choose the **OK** button; the location code will be displayed in the **Location** edit box.

## Selecting Schematic Components for Inserting them into a Panel Drawing

You can select schematic components to insert them into a panel. To do so, select the **Project** radio button from the **Schematic Components List – – > Panel Layout Insert** dialog box and choose the **OK** button; the **Select Drawings to Process** dialog box will be displayed. Select the drawings that you want to process and choose the **Process** button; the selected drawings will be displayed in the bottom list of the **Select Drawings to Process** dialog box. Next, choose the **OK** button from this dialog box; the **Schematic Components (active project)** dialog box will be displayed, as shown in Figure 8-4. The options in this dialog box are discussed next.

**Note**

*1. If you select the **Active drawing** radio button from the **Extract component list for** area and choose the **OK** button from the **Schematic Components List --> Panel Layout Insert** dialog box; the **Schematic Components (active drawing)** dialog box will be displayed.*

*2. The options in the **Schematic Components (active project)** dialog box and the **Schematic Components (active drawing)** dialog box are same. If an active drawing does not have schematic data, a message will be displayed at the Command prompt indicating that no schematic data is found.*

*3. One-line components are not included in the list displayed in the **Schematic Components (active project)** dialog box.*

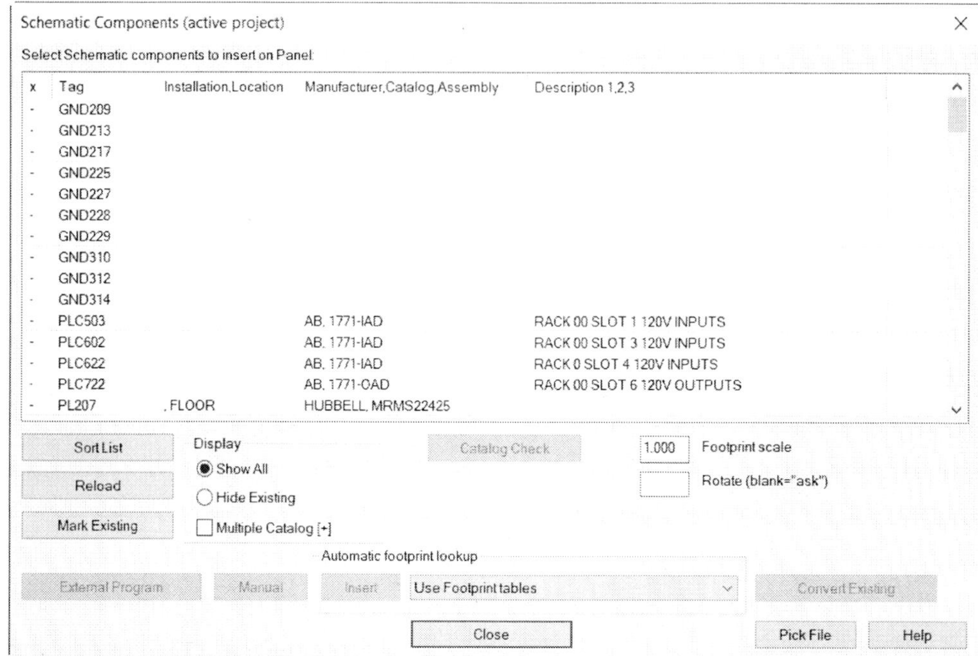


*Figure 8-4 The* ***Schematic Components (active project)*** *dialog box*

## Sort List

The **Sort List** button is used to sort out a list of schematic components. If you choose this button, the **Sort** dialog box will be displayed. You can use this dialog box to sort out the list of schematic components displayed in the **Schematic Components (active project)** dialog box using four levels of sorting criteria such as primary sort, secondary sort, third sort, and fourth sort. You can select any of these criteria options from the respective drop-down lists and then choose the **OK** button in this dialog box; the list displayed in the **Schematic Components (active project)** dialog box will be sorted accordingly.

The sorted list in the **Schematic Components (active project)** dialog box and the **Schematic Components (active drawing)** dialog box remain unchanged across sessions of AutoCAD Electrical.

## Reload

The **Reload** button is used to extract schematic component data again from the active project, active drawing or the saved external file. To extract the data again, choose the **Reload** button; the **Schematic Components List --> Panel Layout Insert** dialog box will be displayed again, refer to Figure 8-3.

## Mark Existing

The **Mark Existing** button is used to mark the schematic component whose footprints are already inserted on the panel layout. To mark the existing components, choose the **Mark Existing** button; an 'x' will be displayed in the **x** column indicating that the schematic component already has its footprint inserted on the panel layout. If the tag of the schematic component and footprint matches, but the catalog information does not match, an 'o' is displayed in the '**x**' column. This way, you can separate the existing and non-existing schematic components with existing and non-existing footprints. The marked components cannot be inserted multiple times. The **Insert** button will become available only if you select the schematic component where '-' is displayed in the **x** column and if the selected component has catalog data.

## Display Area

The **Display** area is used to control the display of schematic components. The options in this area are discussed next.

The **Show All** radio button is selected by default and is used to show all schematic components in the **Schematic Components (active project)** dialog box.

The **Hide Existing** radio button is used to hide the existing schematic components.

Select the **Multiple Catalog [+]** check box to display a list of main catalog numbers as well as multiple catalog numbers of components in the **Schematic Components (active project)** dialog box. Note that the multiple catalog numbers of a component will be displayed only if you have assigned multiple catalog numbers to it.

## Catalog Check

The **Catalog Check** button will be activated only if the selected schematic component has the catalog data. This button is used to execute the Bill of Material check.

## Footprint scale

The **Footprint scale** edit box is used to specify the insertion scale of the block. By default, 1.000 is displayed in this edit box.

## Rotate (blank = "ask")

The **Rotate (blank = "ask")** edit box is used to specify the rotation angle of a block.

## Convert Existing

The **Convert Existing** button is used to convert a dumb block into a smart AutoCAD Electrical footprint. This button will be activated only if you select a non-existing schematic component that is marked with '-' in the **x** column. To convert a block, select a component from the list displayed in this dialog box and choose the **Convert Existing** button; you will be prompted to select the object to be converted into the selected component. Also, the **Schematic Components (active project)** dialog box will disappear. Next, select the desired block to convert it into a smart AutoCAD Electrical footprint.

## Manual

The **Manual** button is used to insert footprint of the selected component. Using this button, you can insert the footprint of existing schematic components multiple times. This button will be activated only when you select a schematic component from the list displayed in the **Schematic Components (active project)** dialog box. When you choose the **Manual** button, the **Footprint** dialog box will be displayed. Specify the required options in the **Footprint** dialog box and choose the **OK** button; the footprint along with the cursor will be displayed and you will be prompted to specify location for the footprint. Next, specify the location; the footprint will be inserted into the drawing and the **Panel Layout - Component Insert/Edit** dialog box will be displayed. Specify the required options in this dialog box and choose the **OK** button in the **Panel Layout - Component Insert/Edit** dialog box; the **Schematic Components (active project)** dialog box will be displayed again.

## Pick File

The **Pick File** button is used to select an existing schematic extracted component list file or extract a new copy of schematic component data from an active project, active drawing or external file. When you choose this button, the **Schematic Components List --> Panel Layout Insert** dialog box will be displayed.

## Automatic footprint lookup Area

The options in the **Automatic footprint lookup** area are used to find and insert footprint of the schematic component selected in the **Schematic Components (active project)** dialog box.

The **Use Footprint tables** option in the drop-down list is used to search the footprint of the selected schematic component in the *footprint_lookup.mdb* file.

The **Use Wiring diagram tables** option in the drop-down list is used to search footprint for the selected schematic component in the wiring diagram table. This table matches the manufacturer code of a schematic component and attaches an '_WD' suffix to the footprint.

The **1st Wiring diagram table, 2nd Footprint table** option is used to search footprint for the selected schematic first in the wiring diagram table and then in the footprint lookup table.

The **Insert** button will be activated only if the selected schematic component has catalog data and if its footprint is not inserted into the drawing already. To insert the footprint of the selected schematic component into the drawing, choose the **Insert** button; you will be prompted to specify the location for the footprint. Next, specify the location for the footprint; you will be prompted to select the rotation. Next, select the rotation by moving the cursor horizontally or vertically and click on the screen; the **Panel Layout - Component Insert/Edit** dialog box will be displayed. Enter the required information in this dialog box. This dialog box will be explained later in this chapter. Choose the **OK** button from this dialog box; the **Schematic Components (active project)** dialog box will appear on the screen again. Next, choose the **Close** button to exit the **Schematic Components (active project)** dialog box.

**Note**

*If a footprint match is not found for the selected schematic component, then the **Footprint** dialog box will be displayed after choosing the **Insert** button in the **Schematic Components (active project)** dialog box. After choosing the **OK** button from the **Footprint** dialog box, the **Manufacturer/ Catalog --> Footprint not found** dialog box will be displayed.*

You can also insert multiple footprints in a single operation. To do so, press the SHIFT or CTRL key and select schematic components from the list displayed in the **Schematic Components (active project)** dialog box, and then choose the **Insert** button from this dialog box; the **Spacing for**

**Footprint Insertion** dialog box will be displayed, as shown in Figure 8-5. The options in this dialog box are discussed next.

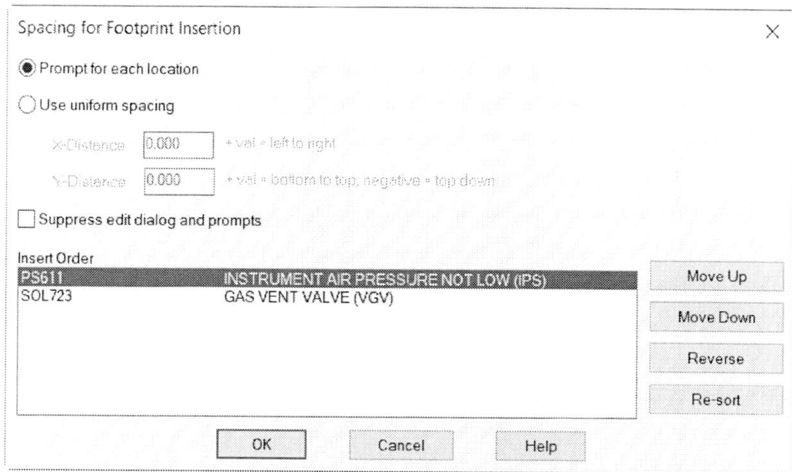


*Figure 8-5 The* ***Spacing for Footprint Insertion*** *dialog box*

## Prompt for each location

The **Prompt for each location** radio button is selected by default. As a result, you will be prompted to specify the insertion point for each component in a drawing.

## Use uniform spacing

Select the **Use uniform spacing** radio button to insert schematic components with uniform spacing between each component in a drawing. On selecting the **Use uniform spacing** radio button, the **X-Distance** and **Y-Distance** edit boxes will be activated. Enter the required values in these edit boxes; the rest of the components will be inserted into the drawing according to the values specified in these edit boxes. In other words, these values compute the insertion point for the remaining components.

## Suppress edit dialog and prompts

The **Suppress edit dialog and prompts** check box is clear by default. Select this check box to suppress the **Panel Layout - Component Insert/Edit** dialog box that is displayed after each footprint insertion. On selecting this check box, all values from the schematic component will be placed on the panel footprint automatically.

## Move Up

Choose the **Move Up** button to move the selected component one step up in the **Insert Order** area.

## Move Down

Choose the **Move Down** button to move the selected component one step down in the **Insert Order** area.

### Reverse

Choose the **Reverse** button to reverse order of all components available in the **Insert Order** area in the descending order.

### Re-sort

Choose the **Re-sort** button to sort all components available in the **Insert Order** area in the ascending order.

After specifying the required options in the **Spacing for Footprint Insertion** dialog box, choose the **OK** button from this dialog box; you will be prompted to specify the location for component. Specify the location; you will be prompted to select the rotation. Next, select the rotation in horizontal or vertical direction by moving the cursor horizontally or vertically and click on the screen; the **Panel Layout - Component Insert/Edit** dialog box will be displayed. Enter the required information in this dialog box and choose **OK**; a footprint will be inserted into the drawing and the above procedure will be repeated until all components present in the **Insert Order** area of the **Spacing for Footprint Insertion** dialog box are inserted. Once all components are inserted, the **Schematic Components (active project)** dialog box will be displayed again.

**Note**

*If the footprint match for the components displayed in the **Insert Order** area of the **Spacing for Footprint Insertion** dialog box is not found in the footprint_lookup.mdb file or in wiring diagram tables, the **Footprint** dialog box will be displayed after choosing the **OK** button in the **Spacing for Footprint Insertion** dialog box. The options in the **Footprint** dialog box are discussed later in this chapter.*

## ANNOTATING AND EDITING FOOTPRINTS

| | |
|---|---|
| **Ribbon:** | Panel > Edit Footprints > Edit |
| **Toolbar:** | ACE:Panel Layout > Edit Footprint<br>or ACE:Edit Footprint Component > Edit Footprint |
| **Menu:** | Panel Layout > Edit Footprint |
| **Command:** | AEEDITFOOTPRINT |

The **Edit** tool is used to edit a footprint. Using this tool, you can make changes in the selected footprint at any time. You can edit the values such as component tag, description, installation, location codes, catalog data, and so on. You may also need to update a footprint due to changes in catalog or assembly values. To edit a footprint, choose the **Edit** tool from the **Edit Footprints** panel of the **Panel** tab; you will be prompted to select panel layout component. Select the required component; the **Panel Layout - Component Insert/Edit** dialog box will be displayed, as shown in Figure 8-6. The different areas and options in this dialog box are discussed next.

### Item Number Area

In the **Item Number** area, you can assign an item number to a footprint. The options in this area are discussed next.

## Item Number

If an existing panel component is found with the catalog information similar to that of a new component, the same item number will be assigned to a new component and will automatically be displayed in the **Item Number** edit box. Alternatively, you can enter the item number manually in the **Item Number** edit box.

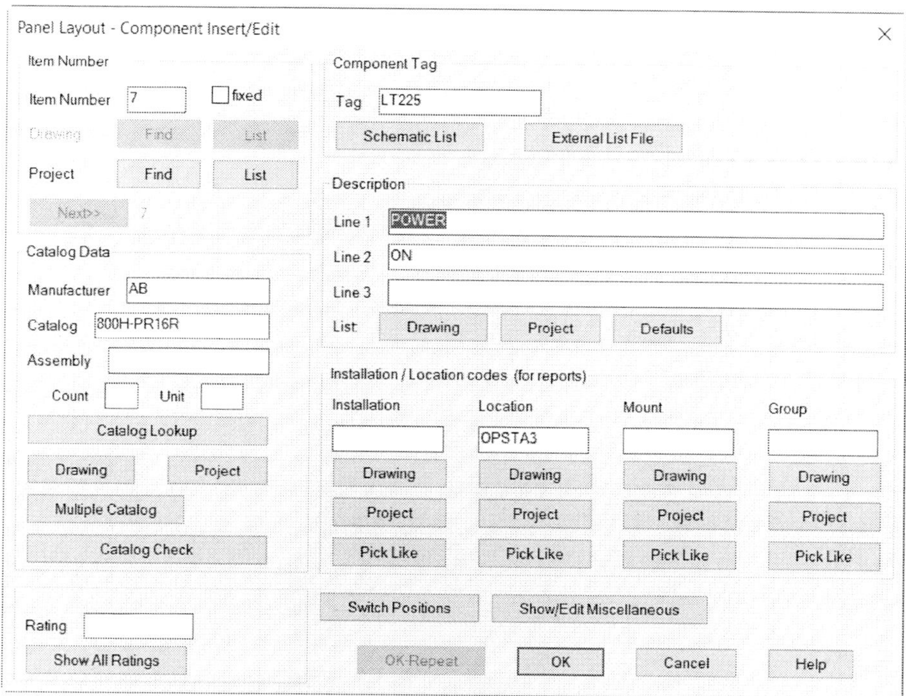


*Figure 8-6 The **Panel Layout - Component Insert/Edit** dialog box*

If you enter an item number that is already assigned to a different component part number, and choose the **OK** button, the **Duplicate Item Number** dialog box will be displayed, as shown in Figure 8-7. If you choose the **Overwrite - Use it anyway** button, the item number will be assigned to a component. Choose the **Cancel - Don't use it** button if you do not want to use the already assigned item number.

## Find

The **Find** button is used to find the item number that you have assigned to the catalog part number of the similar component in an active drawing or in an active project. If no other component that matches the catalog part number of the similar component is found, the **No Item Number Match for this Catalog Part Number** dialog box will be displayed. In this dialog box, you can specify the required options to display the item number in the **Item Number** edit box.

## List

The **List** button is used to display a list of item numbers found in an active drawing or project. To display a list of item numbers, choose the **List** button; the **ITEM numbers in use** dialog box will be displayed.

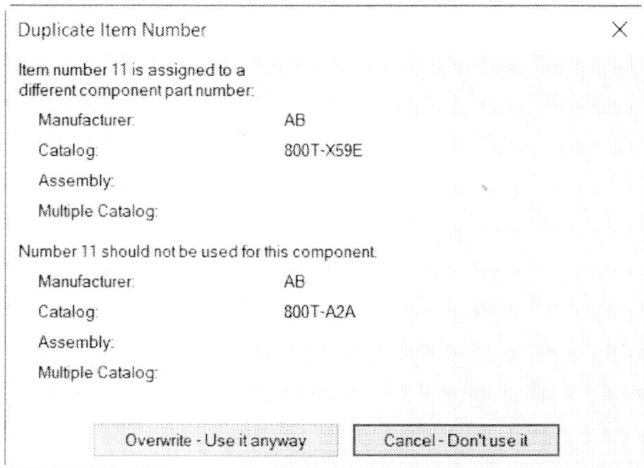


***Figure 8-7** The **Duplicate Item Number** dialog box*

### Next

Choose the **Next** button to find and assign the next available item number. The assigned item number is displayed on right of the **Next >>** button. Note that this button is activated when you are inserting a new panel component or editing the existing panel component for which item number is not assigned.

## Catalog Data Area

In the **Catalog Data** area, you can assign the catalog part number to a footprint. The options in this area are discussed next.

### Manufacturer

The **Manufacturer** edit box displays manufacturer number assigned to a footprint. In this edit box, you can either specify a new manufacturer number or edit the displayed manufacturer number.

### Catalog

The **Catalog** edit box displays the catalog number assigned to a footprint. In this edit box, you can either specify a new catalog number or edit the displayed catalog number.

### Assembly

Enter the **Assembly** code in the **Assembly** edit box. This code is used to link multiple part numbers together.

### Catalog Lookup

The **Catalog Lookup** button is used to select manufacturer or catalog values for a footprint from the catalog database of the component. This button has been discussed in the earlier chapters.

### Drawing

Choose the **Drawing** button; the **Family Components** dialog box will be displayed. This dialog box displays the part numbers that have been used for similar components in the current drawing.

Select the part number from this dialog box and choose the **OK** button; the part number will be displayed in the **Manufacturer**, **Catalog**, and **Assembly** edit boxes. Also, note that these values will be displayed in these edit boxes only if the component that you have selected from the **Family Components** dialog box has these values.

## Project

The **Project** button enables you to search for the part of numbers of similar components that have been used in the project. To do so, choose the **Project** button; the **Find: Catalog assignments** dialog box will be displayed, as shown in Figure 8-8. The options in the **Find: Catalog assignments** dialog box are discussed next.

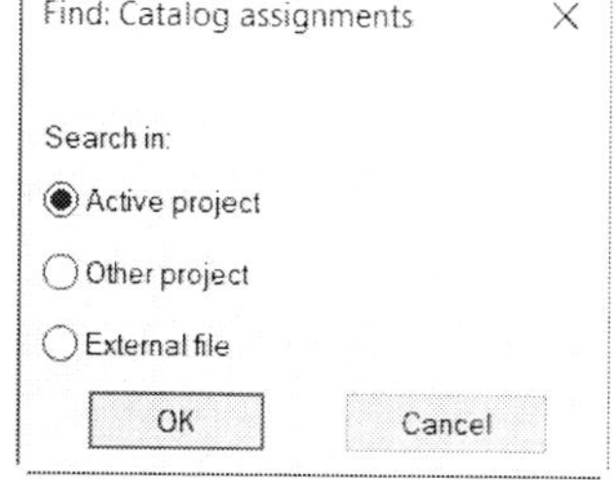


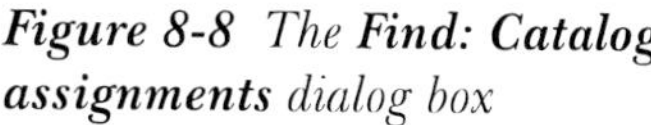

***Figure 8-8** The **Find: Catalog assignments** dialog box*

**Note**

*If you choose the **OK** button from the **Find: Catalog assignments** dialog box without saving the changes made in the active drawing, the **QSAVE** message box will be displayed. You can save the changes in the active drawing by choosing the **OK** button from this dialog box. Choose the **OK** button; the **catalog values (this project)** dialog box will be displayed.*

The **Active project** radio button is selected by default. As a result, part numbers of similar components in an active project will be displayed. Next, choose the **OK** button from the **Find: Catalog assignments** dialog box; the **catalog values (this project)** dialog box will be displayed. Select the required part number and then choose the **OK** button; manufacturer values, catalog values, and assembly values (if any) will be displayed in the **Manufacturer**, **Catalog**, and **Assembly** edit boxes of the **Panel Layout - Component Insert/Edit** dialog box.

Select the **Other project** radio button from the **Find: Catalog assignments** dialog box and then choose **OK**; the **Recent Projects** dialog box will be displayed. Select the path of the project from the **Recent Projects** dialog box and choose the **OK** button; the **catalog values** dialog box will be displayed. Select the required part number and choose the **OK** button; manufacturer values, catalog values, and assembly values (if any) will be displayed in the **Manufacturer**, **Catalog**, and **Assembly** edit boxes.

Select the **External file** radio button and choose **OK**; the **Select External Catalog List file name** dialog box will be displayed. Select the name of the catalog file and then choose the **Open** button; a dialog box listing the name of components will be displayed. Next, select a component from the dialog box displaying the name and path of the catalog file on its title bar; the **Catalog Assignment from External File** dialog box will be displayed, as shown in Figure 8-9.

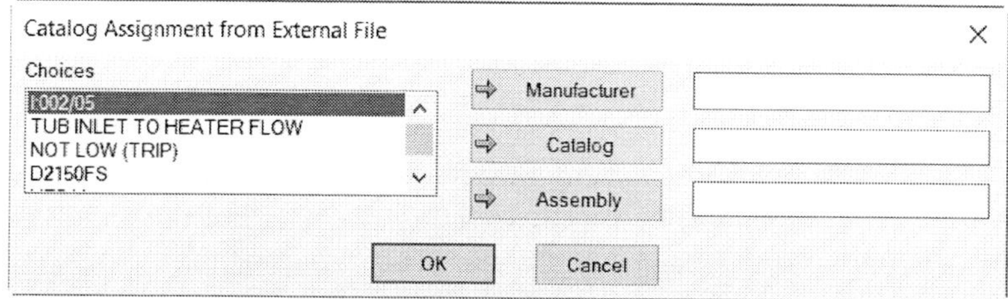


***Figure 8-9** The **Catalog Assignment from External File** dialog box*

Select the manufacturer, catalog, and assembly values from the **Choices** area and choose the **Manufacturer**, **Catalog**, and **Assembly** buttons respectively; the values will be displayed in the respective edit boxes in this dialog box. Next, choose the **OK** button in the **Catalog Assignment from External File** dialog box; the manufacturer, catalog, and assembly values will be displayed in the respective edit boxes in the **Panel Layout - Component Insert/Edit** dialog box.

### Catalog Check

Choose the **Catalog Check** button from the **Panel Layout - Component Insert/Edit** dialog box; the **Bill Of Material Check** dialog box will be displayed. This dialog box displays details of the selected item.

## Rating Area

The **Rating** area is used to specify the values for each rating attribute. This area will be activated only if the component being edited has rating attributes. This area consists of the **Rating** edit box and the **Show All Ratings** button. To specify a rating attribute, enter the rating of the attribute in the **Rating** edit box. Alternatively, choose the **Show All Ratings** button from the **Panel Layout - Component Insert/Edit** dialog box; the **View/Edit Rating Values** dialog box will be displayed. You can enter upto 12 rating attributes for a component in this dialog box. Next, choose the **OK** button from this dialog box; the rating value will be displayed in the **Rating** edit box.

## Component Tag Area

In the **Component Tag** area, you can assign or edit the tag of a footprint. The options in this area are discussed next.

### Tag

The tag of a component is displayed in the **Tag** edit box. You can enter a new tag for a component in this edit box or can edit an existing tag.

### Schematic List

Choose the **Schematic List** button; the **Schematic Tag List** dialog box will be displayed. Next, select the tag from the schematic tag list and choose **OK**; the component tag and its description will be displayed in the **Tag** edit box and in the **Description** area.

### External List File

Choose the **External List File** button; the **Select Component tag list file** dialog box will be displayed, as shown in Figure 8-10. Select the component tag list file and choose the **Open** button from the **Select Component tag list file** dialog box; the **File:** dialog box will be displayed. Next, select a tag for the component and choose the **OK** button from the **File:** dialog box; the **Component Annotation from External File** dialog box will be displayed, as shown in Figure 8-11. Next, select the component tag from the **Choices** area of this dialog box and choose the = button; the contents of the edit box located on the right of the **Component Annotation from External File** dialog box will be overwritten by the selected component tag. Similarly, choose the + button to append the selected component tag to the contents of the edit box. Enter the required information in this dialog box and then choose the **OK** button; the information will be displayed in the **Panel Layout - Component Insert/Edit** dialog box.

**Note**

*Once the **File:** dialog box is displayed, the settings for this session of AutoCAD Electrical will be saved. If you choose the **External List File** button again, the **File:** dialog box will be displayed directly without displaying the **Select Component tag list file** dialog box. To invoke the **Select Component tag list file** dialog box, you need to choose the **Pick File** button from the **File:** dialog box.*

Select Component tag list file
Look in: User
Name
Date m
EM 6/1/202
demoplc 1/21/2(
try2use 1/21/2(
File name:
Files of type: Text/Template/Extract File (*.txt)
Open
Cancel
Locate
Find File...

***Figure 8-10** The **Select Component tag list file** dialog box*

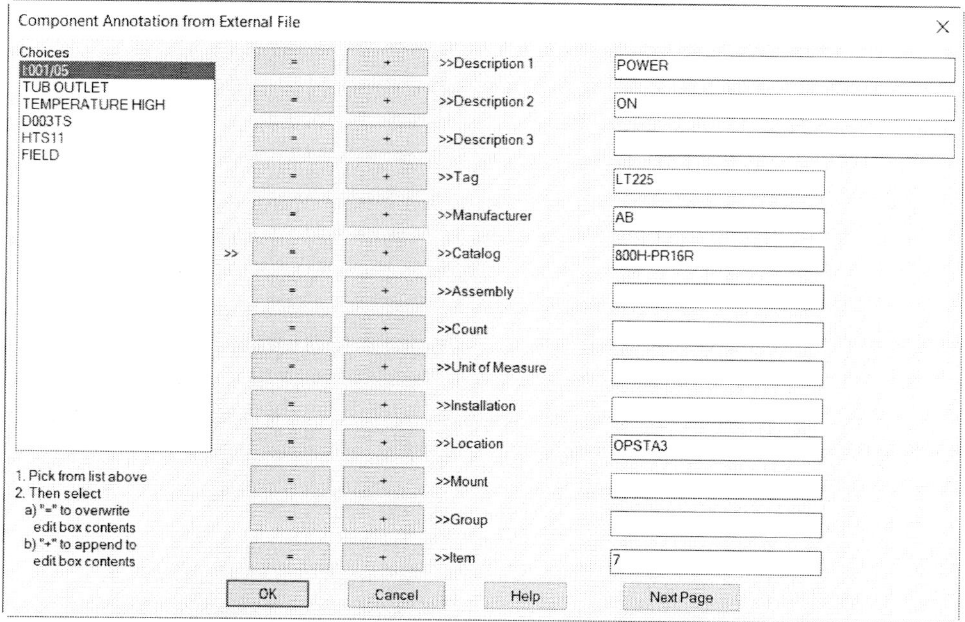


***Figure 8-11** The **Component Annotation from External File** dialog box*

## Description Area

The **Description** area of the **Panel Layout - Component Insert/Edit** dialog box is used to enter the description of the component. You can enter upto three lines of description attribute text in the **Description** area. This area has three edit boxes: **Line 1**, **Line 2**, and **Line 3** and three buttons: **Drawing**, **Project**, and **Defaults**. The options in this area are discussed next.

### Drawing

The **Drawing** button is used to display the list of descriptions of similar components found in the current drawing. To select a description from the current drawing, choose the **Drawing** button; the **Descriptions** dialog box will be displayed. This dialog box displays a list of descriptions that have been used in the current drawing. Next, select a description from the list displayed in the **Descriptions** dialog box and choose the **OK** button; the selected description will be displayed in the **Line 1**, **Line 2**, and **Line 3** edit boxes of the **Description** area. Also, note that if a component has only two description lines, the description will be displayed only in the **Line 1** and **Line 2** edit boxes.

### Project

The **Project** button is used to display a list of descriptions of similar components that have been used in the active project. To select a description from an active project, choose the **Project** button; the **Descriptions** dialog box will be displayed. Next, select a required description and choose the **OK** button; the description will be displayed in the **Line 1**, **Line 2**, and **Line 3** edit boxes of the **Description** area. Also, note that if a component has only two description lines, the description will be displayed only in the **Line 1** and **Line 2** edit boxes.

### Defaults

The **Defaults** button is used to display a list of standard descriptions. To select a default description, choose the **Defaults** button; the **Descriptions (general)** dialog box will be displayed. Select the description and choose the **OK** button; the selected description will be displayed in the **Description** area of the **Panel Layout - Component Insert/Edit** dialog box.

## Installation / Location codes (for reports) Area

The options in the **Installation / Location codes (for reports)** area are used to specify the installation, location, mount, and group codes for a component. Enter the installation, location, mount, and group codes in the **Installation, Location, Mount**, and **Group** edit boxes, respectively. Alternatively, you can specify these codes by choosing the **Drawing**, **Project**, and **Pick Like** buttons in this area.

## Switch Positions

Choose the **Switch Positions** button; the **Switch Positions** dialog box will be displayed. In this dialog box, you can label the position of a selector switch.

## Show/Edit Miscellaneous

Choose the **Show/Edit Miscellaneous** button; the **Edit Miscellaneous and Non-AutoCAD Electrical Attributes** dialog box will be displayed. In this dialog box, you can view or edit any non-AutoCAD Electrical attributes. Note that if non-AutoCAD Electrical attributes are not present, then after choosing the **Show/Edit Miscellaneous** button, the **AutoCAD Electrical Message** message box will be displayed.

After specifying the required options in the **Panel Layout - Component Insert/Edit** dialog box, choose the **OK** button in this dialog box to save the changes made and to exit this dialog box.

## INSERTING FOOTPRINTS FROM THE ICON MENU

| | |
|---|---|
| **Ribbon:** | Panel > Insert Component Footprints > Insert Footprints drop-down >Icon Menu |
| **Toolbar:** | ACE:Panel Layout > Insert Footprint drop-down > Insert Footprint (Icon Menu) or ACE:Component Footprint > Insert Footprint (Icon Menu) |
| **Menu:** | Panel Layout > Insert Footprint (Icon Menu) |
| **Command:** | AEFOOTPRINT |

You can insert footprints from the icon menu by using the **Icon Menu** tool. This tool is also used when you want to create panel drawings prior to schematic drawings. Also, this tool is used to insert some panel components that are not listed in schematic drawings such as nameplates, din rails, and so on. To insert a footprint from the icon menu into a panel layout drawing, choose the **Icon Menu** tool from the **Insert Component Footprints** panel of the **Panel** tab; the **Insert Footprint** dialog box will be displayed, as shown in Figure 8-12.

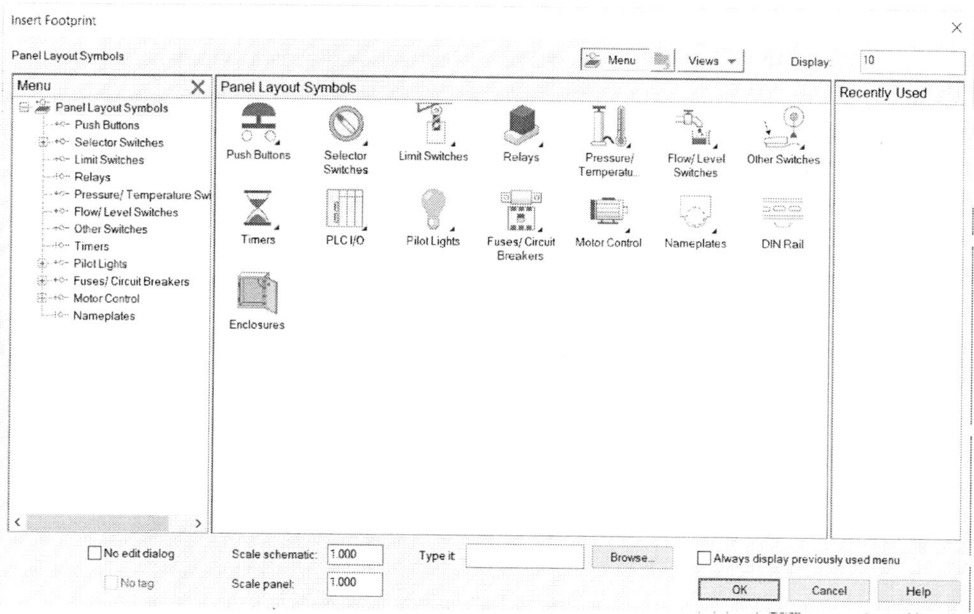


*Figure 8-12 The **Insert Footprint** dialog box*

The options and areas in this dialog box are similar to that in the **Insert Component** dialog box, which has already been discussed in Chapter 5. Next, select the required component from the list displayed on the left of the **Insert Footprint** dialog box or the icons shown on the right of the **Insert Footprint** dialog box; the **Panel Layout Symbols** area will get changed and various symbols of the selected icon will be displayed. For example, if you choose the **Push Buttons** from the **Menu** area or choose the **Push Buttons** icon (first row, first column) from the **Panel Layout Symbols** area, you will notice that the **Panel Layout Symbols** area is changed into the **Panel: Push Buttons** area, as shown in Figure 8-13. The dialog box displays different types of push buttons.

Next, select a symbol to insert from the **Insert Footprint** dialog box; the **Footprint** dialog box will be displayed, as shown in Figure 8-14. The different areas in this dialog box are discussed next.

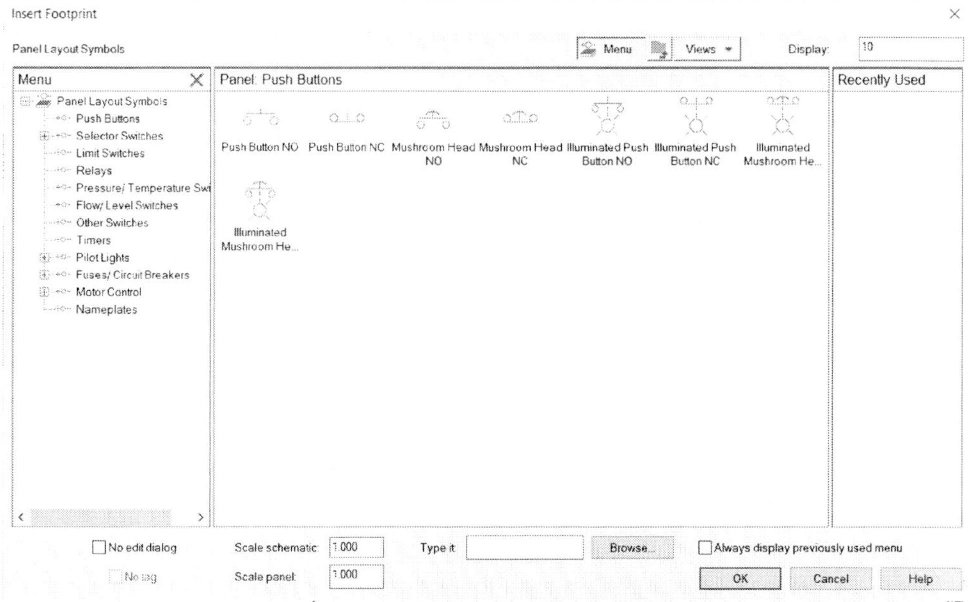


***Figure 8-13*** *The* ***Insert Footprint*** *dialog box showing the* ***Panel: Push Buttons*** *area*

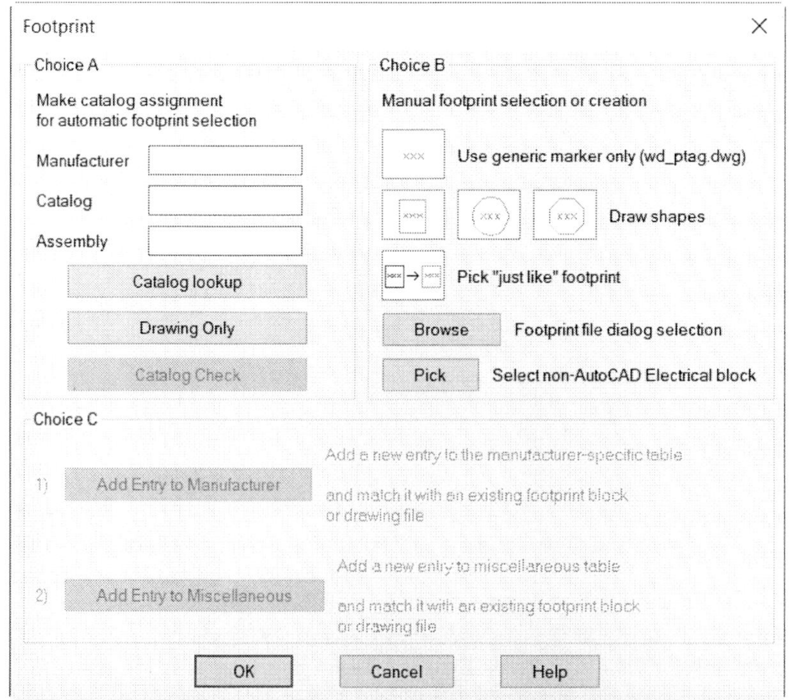


***Figure 8-14*** *The* ***Footprint*** *dialog box*

**Note**

*The **Footprint** dialog box will also be displayed if a footprint match for a selected schematic component is not found or if a catalog number is not assigned to a schematic component, as discussed in the previous topic.*

## Choice A Area

In the **Choice A** area, you can assign a new catalog number or edit an already displayed one. The options in this area are discussed next.

You can manually enter manufacturer, catalog number, and assembly values in the **Manufacturer**, **Catalog**, and **Assembly** edit boxes, respectively. Alternatively, choose the **Catalog lookup** button; the **Catalog Browser** dialog box will be displayed. Select a catalog number from this dialog box and choose the **OK** button; the catalog information will be displayed in the **Manufacturer**, **Catalog**, and **Assembly** edit boxes. You can also choose the **Drawing Only** button from this dialog box; the **catalog values (this drawing)** dialog box will be displayed. Select catalog values and choose the **OK** button from the **catalog values (this drawing)** dialog box to display values in the **Manufacturer**, **Catalog**, and **Assembly** edit boxes of the **Footprint** dialog box.

The **Catalog Check** button is used to display catalog information. This button will be activated only when the catalog information is available in both the **Manufacturer** and **Catalog** edit boxes.

## Choice B Area

The **Choice B** area in the **Footprint** dialog box is used to select or create footprints manually. The options in this area are discussed next.

### Use generic marker only

A generic marker is a block without graphical information. It contains attributes such as tag, description text, catalog information, and so on. To insert a generic marker into your drawing, select the graphical representation adjacent to the **Use generic marker only** field; you will be prompted to specify insertion point for the generic marker.

Next, specify the insertion point; you will be prompted to select the rotation. You can select rotation either in horizontal or vertical direction. To do so, move your cursor horizontally or vertically and then click on the screen; the **Panel Layout - Component Insert/Edit** dialog box will be displayed. The options in this dialog box have been discussed earlier. Next, specify the required information in this dialog box and choose the **OK** button; the generic marker will be inserted into the drawing. Figure 8-15 shows the example of a generic marker.

P_TAG1

GE

CR115B2

***Figure 8-15** A generic marker*

### Draw shapes

You can draw the shapes of footprints manually. Also, to represent a footprint, you can draw rectangle, circle, and polygon by selecting the graphical representation adjacent to the **Draw shapes** field. Select the required graphical representation of footprint adjacent to the **Draw shapes** field; you will be prompted to specify the position of the selected footprint. After specifying the position of the footprint, the **Panel Layout - Component Insert/Edit** dialog box will be displayed.

Enter the required information in this dialog box and choose the **OK** button; graphical representation selected from **Draw Shapes** of the **Choice B** area will be drawn and information in the form of xdata will be assigned to the footprint. For example, if you want to insert a footprint of rectangular shape, select graphical representation of a rectangle and then specify the two corners of the rectangle.

Similarly, if you want to insert a footprint of circular shape, select the circular graphical representation and specify the center point or radius of the circle.

### Pick "just like" footprint

Select the graphical representation adjacent to **Pick "just like" footprint** to create a new footprint shape similar to an existing footprint shape.

### Browse

The **Browse** button is used to select a footprint from footprint libraries for insertion.

### Pick

The **Pick** button is used to convert a non-AutoCAD Electrical block into a smart AutoCAD Electrical block.

**Note**

*If you select an AutoCAD Electrical block, then the **This block is already AutoCAD Electrical - smart** dialog box will be displayed. Choose the **Overwrite** button from this dialog box to overwrite the existing component data of the footprint block. Choose the **Cancel** button to exit this dialog box.*

## Choice C Area

The **Choice C** area will be activated only if the manufacturer and catalog numbers are specified in the **Choice A** area. This area is used to add a new footprint table to the footprint lookup database file. The options in this area are discussed next.

### Add Entry to Manufacturer

You can add a new entry in the footprint lookup table *'footprint_lookup.mdb'*. To do so, enter the manufacturer and catalog values in the **Choice A** area and then choose the **Add Entry to Manufacturer** button from the **Choice C** area; the **Add footprint record** dialog box will be displayed, as shown in Figure 8-16. Note that the table of the new record that you add in the footprint database will have the same name as that of the manufacturer of the component. The **Catalog Number** and **Assembly Code** edit boxes in this dialog box will be enabled only if you have created a new footprint lookup table using the **Footprint Database Editor** tool. These options will be discussed later in the chapter. Rest of the options in the **Add footprint record** dialog box are discussed next.

**Note**

*If the catalog part number of a component is already present in the footprint lookup table 'footprint_lookup.mdb' then after choosing the **Add Entry to Manufacturer** button, the **Manufacturer/Catalog ->Footprint found** dialog box will be displayed. In this dialog box, you can edit the existing record or choose the **Go Back** button to return to the **Footprint** dialog box.*

### Catalog Number

The **Catalog Number** edit box displays the catalog number of the record.

### Assembly Code

The **Assembly code** edit box displays the assembly code of the record.

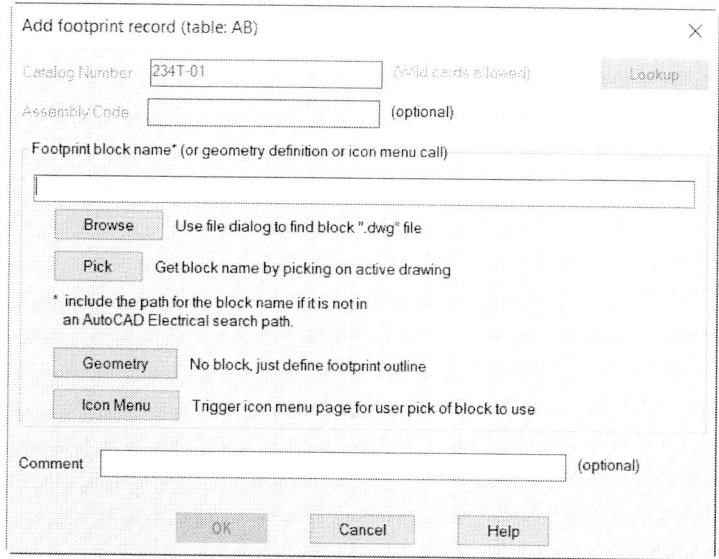


*Figure 8-16 The* ***Add footprint record (table: XX)*** *dialog box*

### Footprint block name* (or geometry definition or icon menu call) Area

The options in the **Footprint block name* (or geometry definition or icon menu call)** area are discussed next.

Enter the name of a block manually in the edit box that is located above the **Browse** button. The name of the block can be either symbol name or AutoLISP expression. Alternatively, choose the **Browse** button; the **Select Footprint Block** dialog box will be displayed. In this dialog box, select the folder and browse to the required block name, and then choose **Open**; the name and path of the block drawing file will be displayed in the edit box. You can also choose the **Pick** button to select the block name from an active drawing.

The **Geometry** button is used to define outline for the footprint. To do so, choose the **Geometry** button; the **Define Footprint Shape** dialog box will be displayed. This dialog box enables you to define the shape of a footprint. Specify the options in this dialog box and exit from the dialog box.

Choose the **Icon Menu** tool; the **Footprint Lookup: Icon Menu Page Trigger** dialog box will be displayed. Enter the icon menu file name in the **Icon menu file name** edit box. Alternatively, choose the **Browse** button from this dialog box to search for the required file name and then choose the **OK** button; the icon menu file name will be displayed in the edit box of the **Footprint block name* (or geometry definition or icon menu call)** area.

### Comment

The **Comment** edit box is used to enter a comment for the footprint record. The specified comment will be the reference for this file only and will not get extracted in any of the AutoCAD Electrical reports.

Once you enter the name of the footprint block in the edit box of the **Footprint block name* (or geometry definition or icon menu call)** area, the **OK** button will be activated. Choose the **OK** button; you will be prompted to select the location for the block drawing file. Next, specify the required location; you will be prompted to select the rotation angle. Select the rotation angle and press ENTER; the **Panel Layout - Component Insert/Edit** dialog box will be displayed. In this dialog box, enter the required information and choose the **OK** button; the footprint block will be inserted into the drawing. Note that the footprint block will be added to the footprint lookup file.

**Note**

*If the name of the footprint block specified in the edit box of the* ***Footprint block name* [or geometry definition or icon menu call]*** *area is not found then after choosing the* ***OK*** *button in the* ***Add footprint record*** *dialog box, the* ***AutoCAD Message*** *message box will be displayed. Choose the* ***OK*** *button in this message box to return to the* ***Add footprint record*** *dialog box.*

## Add Entry to Miscellaneous

The **Add Entry to Miscellaneous** button will become available only if the catalog values specified in the **Choice A** area do not exist in the footprint lookup file. This button is used to add a new record to the miscellaneous footprint lookup table (_PNLMISC). To add a new record, choose the **Add Entry to Miscellaneous** button from the **Footprint** dialog box; the **Add footprint record** dialog box will be displayed, refer to Figure 8-16. The options in this dialog box have been discussed earlier. After specifying the required options in this dialog box, choose the **OK** button from this dialog box; you will be prompted to specify the location and the rotation angle for the footprint. Specify the location and the rotation angle of the footprint to be inserted as discussed earlier. Note that the footprint block will be added to the _PNLMISC lookup file.

# INSERTING FOOTPRINTS MANUALLY

| | |
|---|---|
| **Ribbon:** | Panel > Insert Component Footprints >Insert Footprints drop-down > Manual |
| **Toolbar:** | ACE:Panel Layout > Insert Footprint drop-down > Insert Footprint (Manual) or ACE:Component Footprint > Insert Footprint (Manual) |
| **Menu:** | Panel Layout > Insert Footprint (Manual) |
| **Command:** | AEFOOTPRINTMAN |

You can insert footprints manually. To do so, choose the **Manual** tool from the **Insert Component Footprints** panel of the **Panel** tab, refer to Figure 8-2; the **Insert Component Footprint -- Manual** dialog box will be displayed, as shown in Figure 8-17. The options in this dialog box have been discussed earlier. Select the required footprint shape from this dialog box. Based on the selected footprint shape, you will be prompted to specify the position for the footprint. Specify the position; the **Panel Layout - Component Insert / Edit** dialog box will be displayed. Specify the required options in this dialog box and choose the **OK** button to insert the footprint into the drawing.

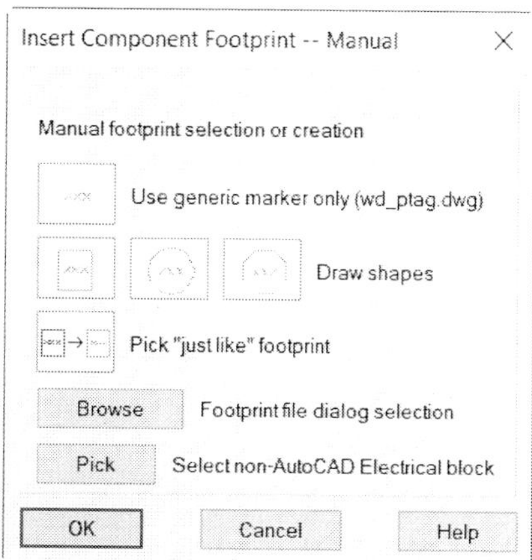


***Figure 8-17*** *The* ***Insert Component Footprint -- Manual*** *dialog box*

# INSERTING FOOTPRINTS FROM A USER DEFINED LIST

**Ribbon:** Panel > Insert Component Footprints > Insert Footprints drop-down > User Defined List
**Toolbar:** ACE:Panel Layout > Insert Footprint drop-down > Insert Footprint (User Defined List)
or ACE:Component Footprint > Insert Footprint (User Defined List)
or ACE:Insert Footprint (Lists) > Insert Footprint (User Defined List)
**Menu:** Panel Layout > Insert Footprint (Lists) > Insert Footprint (User Defined List)
**Command:** AEFOOTPRINTCAT

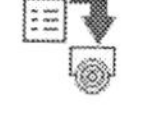

You can select catalog or description for footprints from a user-defined pick list. To insert a footprint from a user-defined pick list, choose the **User Defined List** tool from the **Insert Component Footprints** panel of the **Panel** tab; the **Panel footprint: Select and Insert by Catalog or Description Pick** dialog box will be displayed, as shown in Figure 8-18. This dialog box displays the catalog data saved in the *wd_picklist.mdb* database file. The options in this dialog box have already been discussed in Chapter 5. The procedure to insert footprints using the **User Defined List** tool is discussed next.

**Note**

*The options in the* ***Panel footprint: Select and Insert by Catalog or Description Pick*** *dialog box are the same as those of the* ***Schematic Component or Circuit*** *dialog box. The only difference is that a panel component is selected from the* ***Panel footprint: Select and Insert by Catalog or Description Pick*** *dialog box, whereas a schematic component is selected from the* ***Schematic Component or Circuit*** *dialog box.*

Select the required catalog number from the dialog box and choose the **OK** button; the **AutoCAD Message** message box will be displayed. Next, choose the **OK** button from this message box; the command ends and you cannot insert the footprint from the user defined list. To overcome this problem, you need to add a library path in the **Panel Footprint Libraries** library. The steps to add a new path to libraries is given in Tutorial 4 of this chapter.

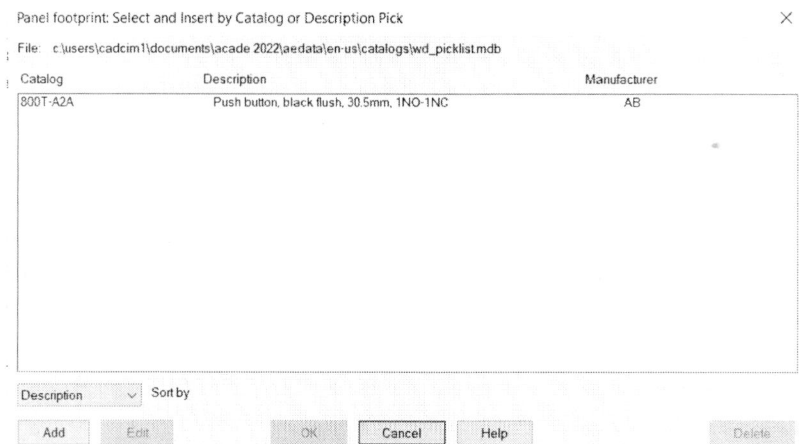


*Figure 8-18 The **Panel footprint: Select and Insert by Catalog or Description Pick** dialog box*

After adding a new path to library, choose the **User Defined List** tool again and then select the required catalog number from the **Panel Footprint: Select and Insert by Catalog or Description Pick** dialog box. Next, choose the **OK** button; you will be prompted to specify the location for footprint. Next, specify the location for footprint; you will be prompted to select the rotation. Select the rotation by moving the cursor in the horizontal or vertical direction and then press ENTER; the **Panel Layout - Component Insert/Edit** dialog box will be displayed. Enter the required information in this dialog box and choose the **OK** button; the footprint block will be inserted into the drawing.

**Note**

*The data displayed in the **Panel footprint: Select and Insert by Catalog or Description Pick** dialog box is saved in the wd_picklist.mdb access file. You can add data or edit this file by choosing the **Add** or **Edit** button or by using the **Microsoft Office Access**. Also, you can delete the data by choosing the **Delete** button from the **Panel footprint: Select and Insert by Catalog or Description Pick** dialog box.*

## INSERTING FOOTPRINTS FROM AN EQUIPMENT LIST

**Ribbon:** Panel > Insert Component Footprints > Insert Footprints drop-down > Equipment List

**Toolbar:** ACE:Panel Layout > Insert Footprint drop-down > Insert Footprint (User Defined List) > Insert Footprint (Equipment List) or ACE:Component Footprint > Insert Footprint (User Defined List) > Insert Footprint (Equipment List) or ACE:Insert Footprint (Lists) > Insert Footprint (Equipment List)

**Menu:** Panel Layout > Insert Footprint Lists > Insert Footprint (Equipment List)

**Command:** AEFOOTPRINTEQ

The **Equipment List** tool is used to extract data from the equipment list and also to find out appropriate panel symbol by searching in the *footprint_lookup.mdb* file. To extract a footprint from an equipment list and insert it into a drawing, choose the **Equipment List** tool from the **Insert Component Footprints** panel in the **Panel** tab; the **Select Equipment**

**List Spreadsheet File** dialog box will be displayed. Select the required file from the dialog box and choose the **Open** button; the **Table Edit** dialog box will be displayed, as shown in Figure 8-19. Select the table or sheet in this dialog box and then choose the **OK** button; the **Settings** dialog box will be displayed, as shown in Figure 8-20. The options in the **Settings** dialog box have already been discussed in Chapter 5.

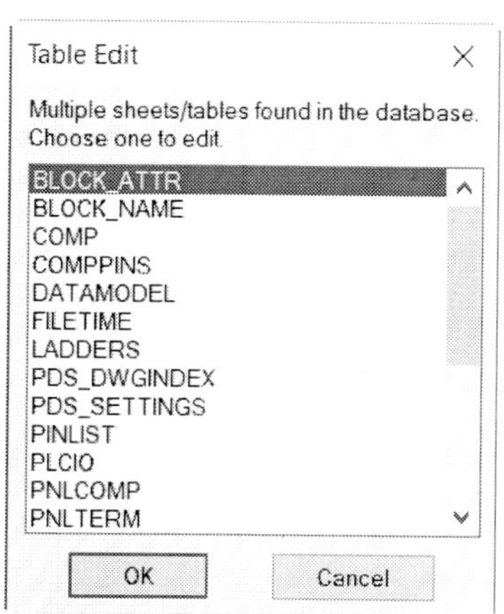


*Figure 8-19 The* ***Table Edit*** *dialog box*

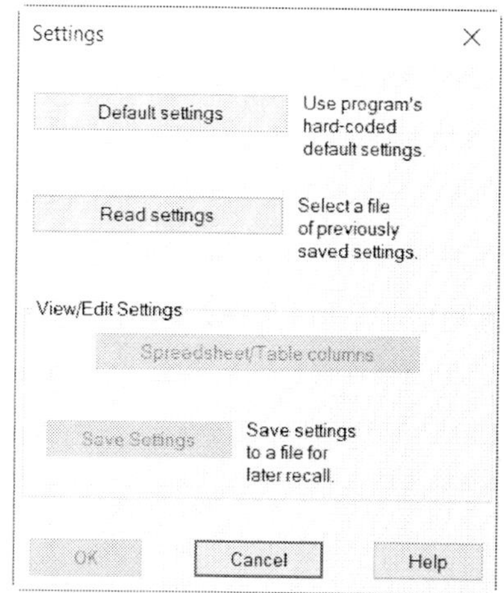


*Figure 8-20 The* ***Settings*** *dialog box*

The **OK** button in the **Settings** dialog box will be activated only if you choose the **Default settings** button. Choose the **Default settings** button and then choose the **OK** button; the **Panel equipment in** dialog box will be displayed, as shown in Figure 8-21. The options in the **Panel equipment in** dialog box are the same as that of the **Schematic Components** dialog box, refer to Figure 8-4.

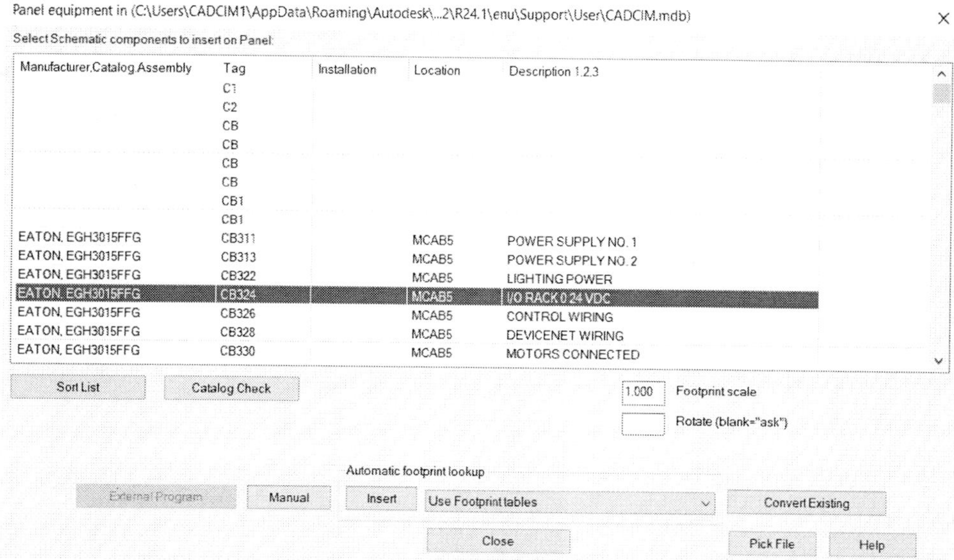


*Figure 8-21 The* ***Panel equipment in*** *dialog box*

Next, select the schematic component that you want to insert in the panel layout drawing; the **Insert** button will be activated. Choose the **Insert** button; you will be prompted to specify the location for footprint. Specify the location; you will be prompted to select the rotation. Select the rotation by moving the cursor in the horizontal or vertical direction and press ENTER; the **Panel Layout - Component Insert/Edit** dialog box will be displayed. Enter the required information in this dialog box and choose the **OK** button; the footprint will be inserted into the drawing and the **Panel equipment in** dialog box will be displayed again. To insert more footprints into the drawing, you need to repeat the steps discussed above. To exit the **Panel equipment in** dialog box and to save the changes made in this dialog box, choose the **Close** button. Note that if the child components or related panel components are present in other drawings of a project then after choosing the **Close** button in the **Panel equipment in** dialog box, the **Update other drawings?** message box will be displayed, as shown in Figure 8-22. Choose the **OK** button from this dialog box to update other drawings of a project; the **QSAVE** message box will be displayed. Next, choose the **OK** button in the **QSAVE** message box to save and update the drawings accordingly.

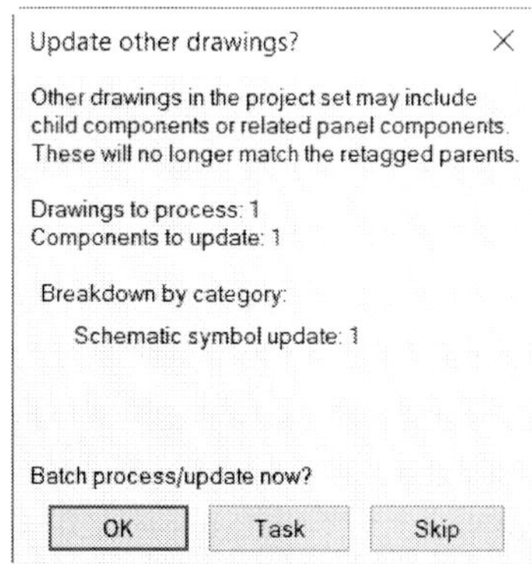


*Figure 8-22 The **Update other drawings?** message box*

## INSERTING FOOTPRINTS FROM VENDOR MENUS

| | |
|---|---|
| **Ribbon:** | Panel > Insert Component Footprints > Insert Footprints drop-down > Manufacturer Menu |
| **Toolbar:** | ACE:Panel Layout > Insert Footprint (Icon Menu)> Insert Footprint (Manufacturer Menu) or ACE:Component Footprint > Insert Footprint (Manufacturer Menu) |
| **Menu:** | Panel Layout > Insert Footprint (Manufacturer Menu) |
| **Command:** | AEFOOTPRINTMFG |

You can insert footprints by using the vendor menus. To do so, choose the **Manufacturer Menu** tool from the **Insert Component Footprints** panel of the **Panel** tab; the **Vendor Menu Selection - Icon Menu Files (*.pnl extension)** dialog box will be displayed, as shown in Figure 8-23.

In this dialog box, select the required vendor icon menu file and choose the **OK** button; the **Vendor Panel Footprint** dialog box will be displayed, as shown in Figure 8-24. The options in this dialog box, except the **Vendor Menu Select...** button, are similar to the options in the **Insert Footprint** dialog box. These options have been discussed earlier.

The **Vendor Menu Select...** button is used to select the vendor again from the **Vendor Menu Selection - Icon Menu Files (*.pnl extension)** dialog box.

Vendor Menu Selection - Icon Menu Files (*.pnl extension)

Vendor icon menu files found in AutoCAD Electrical support file search path

Allen-Bradley

Browse

OK Cancel Help

*Figure 8-23 The* ***Vendor Menu Selection - Icon Menu Files (*.pnl extension)*** *dialog box*

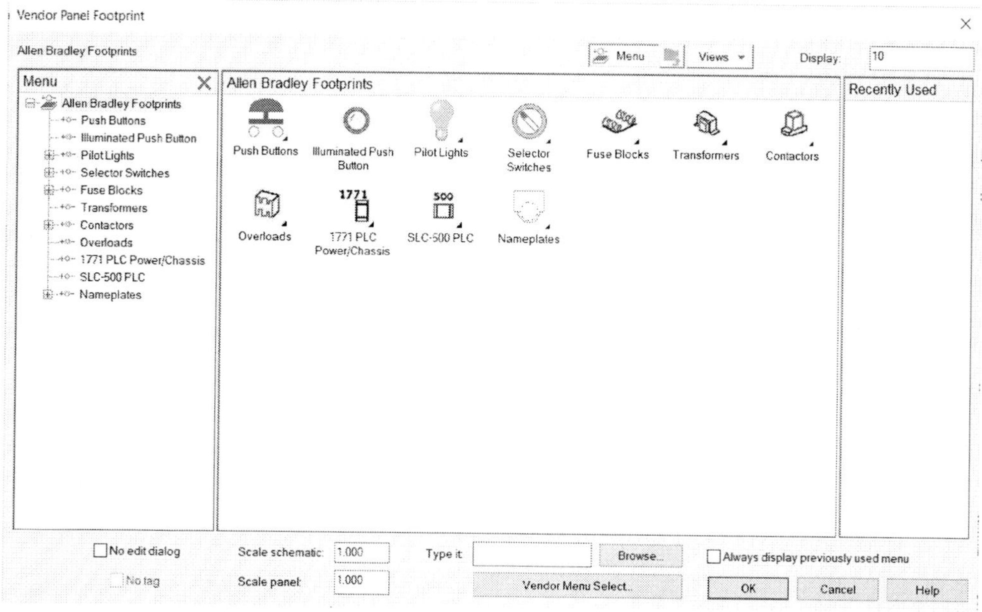


*Figure 8-24 The* ***Vendor Panel Footprint*** *dialog box*

**Note**

*If you choose the* ***Manufacturer Menu*** *tool the second time, the* ***Vendor Panel Footprint*** *dialog box will be displayed directly. This will happen only for the current session of AutoCAD Electrical. However, if you run the software again and if you select the same option, it will first display the* ***Vendor Menu Selection - Icon Menu Files (*.pnl extension)*** *dialog box and then the* ***Vendor Panel Footprint*** *dialog box.*

Next, select the required footprint icon from the **Vendor Panel Footprint** dialog box or select the name of the footprint displayed on the left of the dialog box; various types of selected icons will be displayed. Next, select the required footprint block; the footprint block along with the cursor will be displayed and you will be prompted to select the location. Next, select the location; the **Panel Layout - Component Insert/Edit** dialog box will be displayed. Enter the required information in this dialog box and choose the **OK** button; the footprint will be inserted into the drawing.

## COPYING A FOOTPRINT

| | |
|---|---|
| **Ribbon:** | Panel > Edit Footprints > Copy Footprint |
| **Toolbar:** | ACE:Panel Layout > Copy Footprint |
| **Menu:** | Panel Layout > Copy Footprint |
| **Command:** | AECOPYFOOTPRINT |

The **Copy Footprint** tool is used to copy a selected footprint in an active drawing. This tool copies a balloon and a nameplate associated with the selected footprint. To copy a selected footprint, choose the **Copy Footprint** tool from the **Edit Footprints** panel of the **Panel** tab; you will be prompted to select the component. Next, select the component and specify the location and press ENTER; the **Panel Layout - Component Insert/Edit** dialog box will be displayed. Enter the required information in this dialog box and choose the **OK** button; the copied footprint will be inserted into the drawing. Note that you can also use the **COPY** command of AutoCAD for copying a footprint but the balloon and nameplate associated with the footprint will not be copied.

## SETTING THE PANEL DRAWING CONFIGURATION

| | |
|---|---|
| **Ribbon:** | Panel > Other Tools > Panel Configuration drop-down > Configuration |
| **Toolbar:** | ACE:Panel Layout > Panel Configuration |
| **Menu:** | Panel Layout > Panel Configuration |
| **Command:** | AEPANELCONFIG |

The configuration settings of a panel drawing are saved as attribute values on *WD_PNLM* invisible block. This invisible block should be present in every panel drawing. You have already learnt about WD_PNLM invisible block in this chapter. The **Configuration** tool is used to set properties of a panel drawing in addition to the settings specified in the **Drawing Properties** dialog box. This tool is also used to define panel footprint drawing defaults such as balloon setup, footprint insertion scale, footprint layer setup, and so on. To define the panel drawing defaults, choose the **Configuration** tool from the **Panel Configuration** drop-down in the **Other Tools** panel of the **Panel** tab, as shown in Figure 8-25; the **Panel Drawing Configuration and Defaults** dialog box will be displayed, as shown in Figure 8-26.

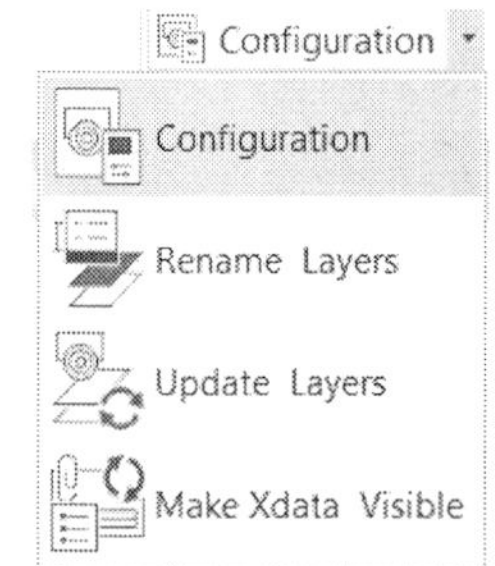


***Figure 8-25** The **Panel Configuration** drop-down*

Using this dialog box, you can define the starting item number, balloon configuration, footprint layers, default settings for panel drawing functions, and so on. The different areas and options in this dialog box are discussed next.

## Item numbering Area

In the **Item numbering** area, you can specify an item number for a footprint. An item number can be a number or a letter. Enter the first item number in the **Start** edit box for a footprint.

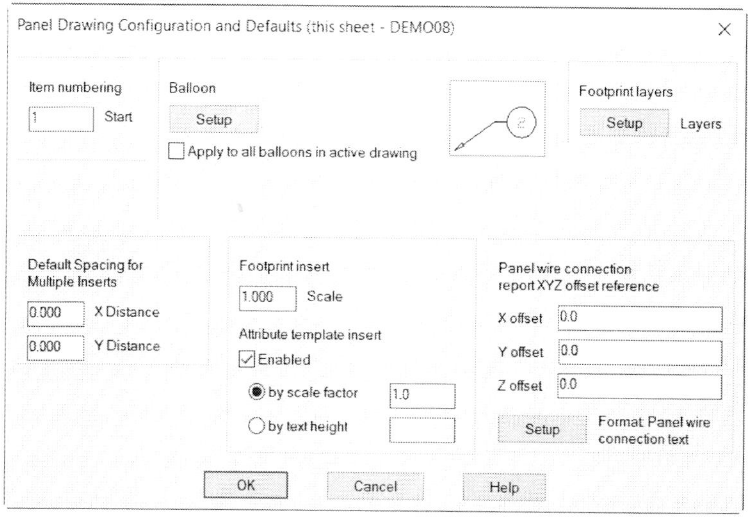


*Figure 8-26 The **Panel Drawing Configuration and Defaults** dialog box*

## Balloon Area

In the **Balloon** area, you can specify the type of balloon to be inserted into the drawing. You can insert different types of balloons such as circles, ellipse, polygon, or text only into a panel drawing. This area also shows the preview of a balloon. To define the type, size, margin, text size, and arrow type and size for a balloon, choose the **Setup** button in this area; the **Panel balloon setup** dialog box will be displayed, as shown in Figure 8-27. Different areas and options in this dialog box are discussed next.

### Balloon Area

The **Balloon** area displays the balloon type and balloon size. The options in this area are discussed next.

#### Circle

By default, the **Circle** and the **Diameter** radio buttons are selected in the **Balloon Type** and the **Balloon Size** columns, respectively. You can specify the diameter of the circular balloon in the edit box available on the right of the **Diameter** radio button. If you select the **Fit** radio button, the edit box adjacent to this radio button will be activated. Enter the fit margin value in the edit box. By default, 0.125 is displayed in this edit box. The size of the circle changes automatically according to the values specified in these edit boxes to fit the text and margin value.

#### Ellipse

Select the **Ellipse** radio button; the **Axis** and **Fit** radio buttons will be activated. To specify the axes of an ellipse, select the **Axis** radio button. Next, you need to enter horizontal and vertical values in the **Horizontal** and **Vertical** edit boxes. By default, 0.375 and 0.125 are displayed in the **Horizontal** and **Vertical** edit boxes, respectively. Select the **Fit** radio button; the edit box adjacent to this radio button will become available. Enter the fit margin value in the edit box. By default, 0.250 is displayed in this edit box.

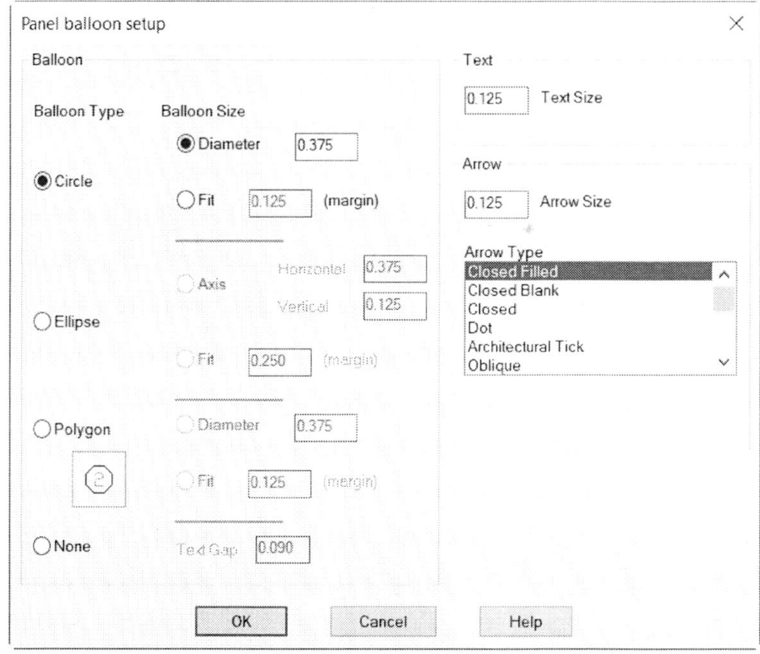


*Figure 8-27 The* ***Panel balloon setup*** *dialog box*

## Polygon

Select the **Polygon** radio button; the Polygon Shape symbol, the **Diameter** radio button, and the **Fit** radio button will be activated, refer to Figure 8-28.

To specify the shape of polygon, select the Polygon Shape symbol; the **Pick Polygon Shape** dialog box will be displayed, as shown in Figure 8-29.

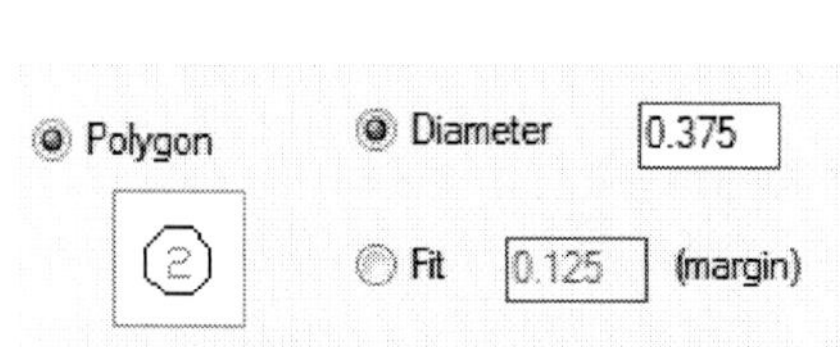


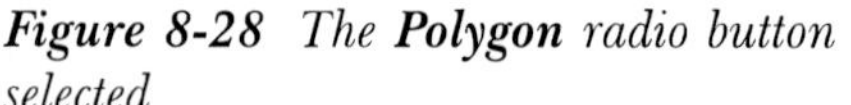

*Figure 8-28 The* ***Polygon*** *radio button selected*

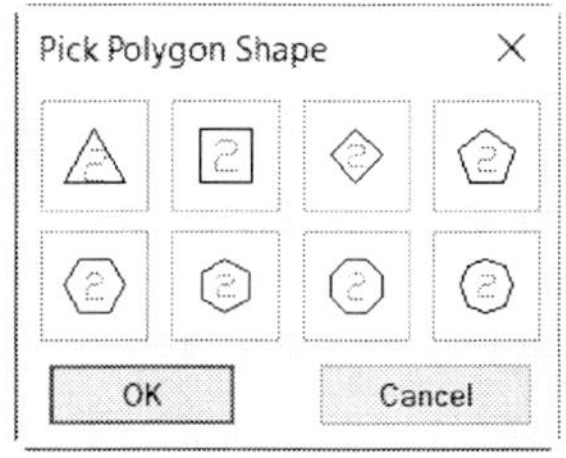


*Figure 8-29 The* ***Pick Polygon Shape*** *dialog box*

Select the required polygon symbol and choose the **OK** button; the selected polygon symbol will be displayed in place of the Polygon Shape symbol. By default, the **Diameter** radio button is selected and 0.375 is displayed in the edit box adjacent to it. Select the **Fit** radio button; the edit box adjacent to it will become available. Enter the required margin value in the edit box.

#### None

The **None** radio button is used to display only text. Select the **None** radio button; the **Text Gap** edit box will be available. By default, 0.090 is displayed in the **Text Gap** edit box. The value in this edit box determines the space between the end of a leader line and the text.

### Text Area

In the **Text** area, you can specify the text size of a balloon marker by entering the text size in the **Text Size** edit box.

### Arrow Area

In the **Arrow** area, you can specify the size and type of an arrowhead. This area consists of the **Arrow Size** edit box and the **Arrow Type** list box. Choose the required type of an arrowhead from the **Arrow Type** list box and then enter the size of an arrowhead in the **Arrow Size** edit box.

In order to add a user-defined arrowhead in the **Arrow Type** list box, choose the **User Arrow** option from this list box; the **Select Custom Arrow Block** dialog box will be displayed, as shown in Figure 8-30. Next, select the type of arrowhead from the **Select from Drawing Blocks** drop-down list and then choose the **OK** button; the arrowhead type will be added to the **Arrow Type** list box.

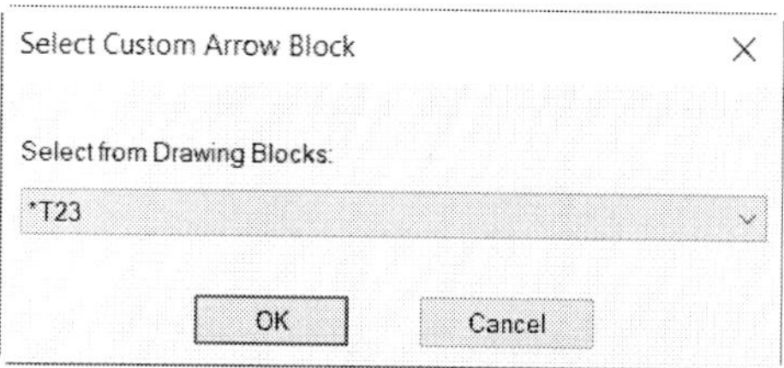


*Figure 8-30 The* ***Select Custom Arrow Block*** *dialog box*

After specifying the required options in the **Panel balloon setup** dialog box, choose the **OK** button from this dialog box to save the changes made in the **Panel balloon setup** dialog box and return to the **Panel Drawing Configuration and Defaults** dialog box.

## Apply to all balloons in active drawing

This check box is used to update all the balloons in the active drawing as per the settings in the **Panel balloon setup** dialog box.

## Footprint layers Area

In the **Footprint layers** area, you can set layers for the panel component, non-text graphics, and layers of nameplates. To set the layers, choose the **Setup** button; the **Panel Component Layers** dialog box will be displayed, as shown in Figure 8-31. The options in this dialog box are discussed next.

### Panel Component Layers (check box = freeze) Area

The **Panel Component Layers (check box = freeze)** area lists all the layers of panel component. You can change the layer name of a tag by entering a new name in the edit box located on the right of the corresponding panel layer component.

In case you do not want an attribute to be moved to a PNL layer, and if you want to place that attribute on layers other than "0" then select the **Ignore above for symbol's non-layer "0" entities** check box.

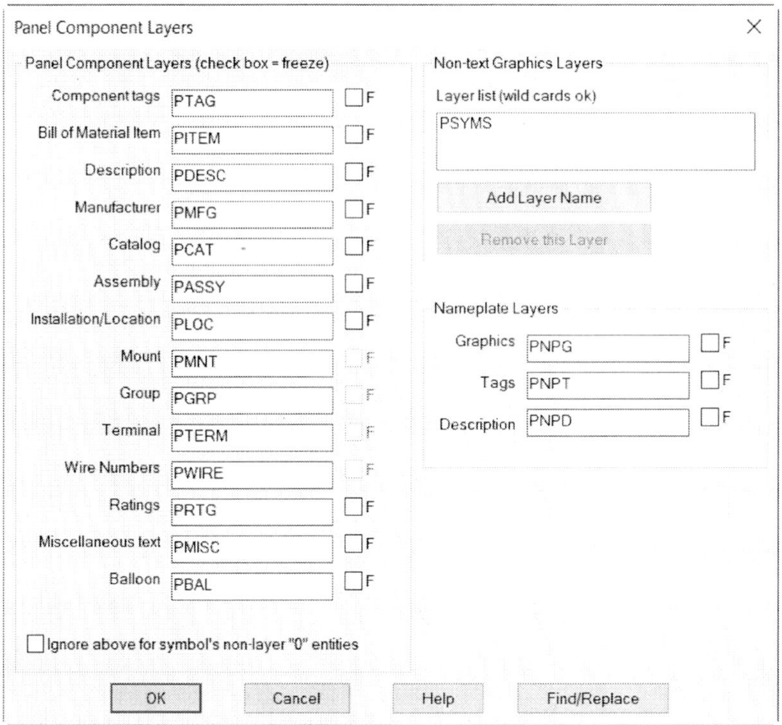

*Figure 8-31 The **Panel Component Layers** dialog box*

### F

The **F** check box will become available only if the panel component layer exists. Select the **F** check box to freeze or thaw the required layers.

## Non-text Graphics Layers Area

You can define layers for the footprint in the **Non-text Graphics Layers** area. When you insert a panel component into a drawing, the block will be inserted on the first layer that is present in the **Layer list (wild cards ok)** list. To add a layer to the **Layer list (wild cards ok)** list, choose the **Add Layer Name** button; the **Layers for Panel Component Graphics** dialog box will be displayed. In this dialog box, enter name for the new layer to be created. Alternatively, choose the **Pick** button from the **Layers for Panel Component Graphics** dialog box; the **Pick Layer for Components** dialog box will be displayed. Select the required layer for components from this dialog box and choose the **OK** button in this dialog box; the name of the layer will be displayed in the **Layer name** edit box of the **Layers for Panel Component Graphics** dialog box. Choose the **OK** button in this dialog box; the layer will be added to the **Layer list (wild cards ok)** list.

You can remove the layer from the **Layer list (wild cards ok)** list by selecting the layer name from the **Layer list (wild cards ok)** list and then choosing the **Remove this Layer** button from the **Non-text Graphics Layers** area.

### Nameplate Layers Area

The existing nameplate layers for graphics, tags, and description are listed in the **Nameplate Layers** area. You can place all nameplate objects on a single layer by using the same layer for all entries. This area consists of the **Graphics**, **Tags**, and **Description** edit boxes.

### Find/Replace

The **Find/Replace** button is used to find and replace names of the layers. To do so, choose the **Find/Replace** button; the **Find/Replace - Layer Names** dialog box will be displayed. Enter the layer name that you want to be replaced in the **Find** edit box and then enter the new layer name in the **Replace** edit box. Next, choose the **OK** button from the **Find/Replace - Layer Names** dialog box; the layer name will be replaced by the specified name.

After specifying the required options in the **Panel Component Layers** dialog box, choose the **OK** button from this dialog box to return to the **Panel Drawing Configuration and Defaults** dialog box.

## Default Spacing for Multiple Inserts Area

You can specify the spacing values for inserting multiple footprints in the **X Distance** and **Y Distance** edit boxes, respectively.

## Footprint insert Area

In the **Footprint insert** area, you can enter the scale for the footprint symbol in the **Scale** edit box. Also, you can define the scale of the attribute template when the footprint is inserted. By default, the **by scale factor** radio button is selected and **1.0** is displayed in the edit box. You can also select the **by text height** radio button to define the scale for text height. When you select the **by text height** radio button, the edit box that is adjacent to this radio button will be activated. You can change values in these edit boxes according to your requirement.

## Panel wire connection report XYZ offset reference Area

In this area, you can specify the X, Y, and Z offset values and format for the text added to a panel component by adding the information in the **X offset**, **Y offset**, and **Z offset** edit boxes. Choose **OK** to save changes and to exit the **Panel Drawing Configuration and Defaults** dialog box.

# MAKING THE XDATA VISIBLE

| | |
|---|---|
| **Ribbon:** | Panel > Other Tools > Panel Configuration drop-down > Make Xdata Visible |
| **Toolbar:** | ACE:Panel Layout > Edit Footprint > Make Xdata Visible<br>or ACE:Edit Footprint Component > Make Xdata Visible |
| **Menu:** | Panel Layout > Make Xdata Visible |
| **Command:** | AESHOWXDATA |

Xdata is also called extended entity data. For some functions, AutoCAD Electrical adds invisible data to a footprint block or even to specific attributes. This invisible data is called Xdata. The **Make Xdata Visible** tool is used for converting invisible Xdata into visible attribute, which is attached to a footprint block. To do so, choose the **Make Xdata Visible** tool from the **Panel Configuration** drop-down in the **Other Tools** panel of the **Panel** tab, refer to Figure 8-25; you will be prompted to select a footprint. Next, select the required footprint; the **Select Xdata to Change to a Block Attribute** dialog box will be displayed, as shown in Figure 8-32.

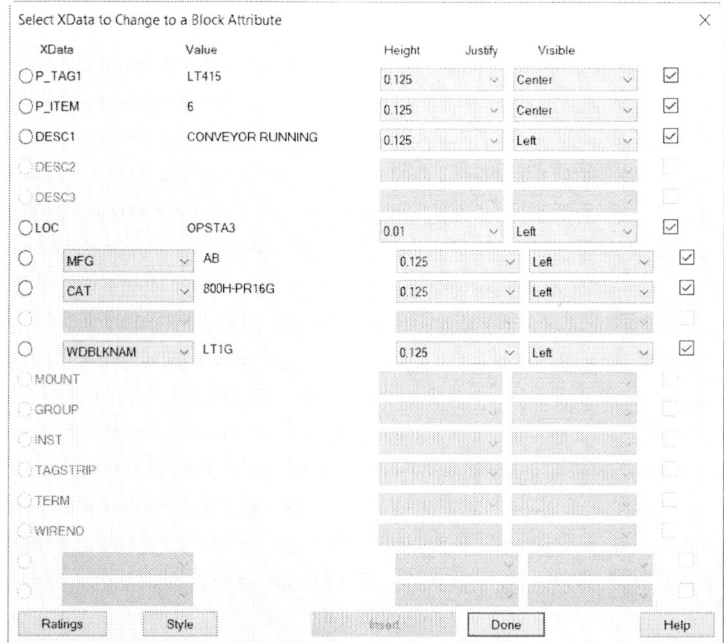


*Figure 8-32 The **Select Xdata to Change to a Block Attribute** dialog box*

Select Xdata such as P_ITEM, MFG, CAT, and so on from this dialog box and choose the **Insert** button; the **Select XData to Change to a Block Attribute** dialog box will disappear and you will be prompted to specify the location for attribute. Next, specify the location; the **Select XData to Change to a Block Attribute** dialog box will be displayed again. Repeat the above process for making the rest of XData visible on the footprint block. The options in the **Select XData to Change to a Block Attribute** dialog box are discussed next.

## XData

The **XData** column displays the XData attributes of a footprint.

## Value

The **Value** column displays the value of the XData attached to a footprint.

## Height

In the **Height** column, select the height for specific attribute value from the drop-down list. If you select the **-add-** option from the drop-down list, the **Add text height** dialog box will be displayed, as shown in Figure 8-33. In this dialog box, enter the height of text in the **New text height** edit box and choose the **OK** button; the new text height will be added to the drop-down list of a particular attribute.

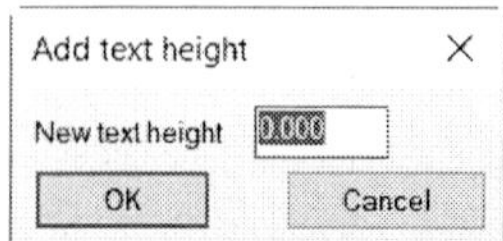


*Figure 8-33 The **Add text height** dialog box*

The same process can be repeated for the attributes where you want to add a text height.

## Justify

In the **Justify** column, select the required justification for the specific attribute value from the drop-down list.

## Visible

In the **Visible** column, select the check box to make a specific attribute value visible on the screen.

## Ratings

The **Ratings** button is used to set the values for rating attributes of a footprint.

## Style

The **Style** button is used to specify the text style, width factor, and line weight for attributes. To specify these parameters, choose the **Style** button; the **Text style and width factor for new attributes** dialog box will be displayed, as shown in Figure 8-34. The options in this dialog box are discussed next.

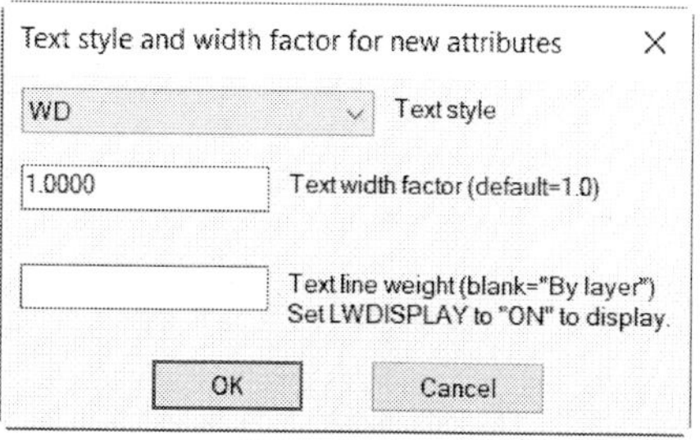


*Figure 8-34 The **Text style and width factor for new attributes** dialog box*

Select the required text style from the **Text style** drop-down list. By default, WD is selected in this drop-down list. Enter the required text width factor in the **Text width factor** edit box. You can enter the text line weight in the **Text line weight** edit box. By default, this edit box is blank, which indicates that the **By layer** text line weight will be applied to an attribute. After specifying the required options in the **Text style and width factor for new attributes** dialog box, choose the **OK** button in this dialog box to save the changes made and to return to the **Select XData to Change to a Block Attribute** dialog box.

## Insert

The **Insert** button will be activated only if you select the XData attribute value under the **XData** column. Choose the **Insert** button; you will be prompted to specify the location for the selected XData attribute value. Next, specify the location; the XData attribute value will be inserted into the footprint block, which has been discussed earlier.

## Done

Choose the **Done** button after finishing the insertion of XData attribute values into the footprint block.

**Note**

*After inserting an attribute value in a footprint block, the respective radio button will not be activated in the **Select XData to Change to a Block Attribute** dialog box. If you want to modify and add XData, choose the **Xdata Editor** tool from the **Other Tools** panel of the **Project** tab or choose **Projects > Extras > Xdata Editor** from the menu bar.*

# RENAMING PANEL LAYERS

**Ribbon:** Panel > Other Tools > Panel Configuration drop-down > Rename Layers
**Toolbar:** ACE:Panel Layout > Miscellaneous Panel Tools > Rename Panel Layers or ACE:Panel Miscellaneous > Rename Panel Layers
**Menu:** Panel Layout > Miscellaneous Panel Tools > Rename Panel Layers
**Command:** AERENAMEPANLELLAYER

You have already learned about defining footprint layer setup for panel drawings using the **Configuration** tool in the last section. You can rename existing panel layers in panel drawings using the **Rename Layers** tool. To do so, choose the **Rename Layers** tool from the **Panel Configuration** drop-down in the **Other Tools** panel of the **Panel** tab; the **Rename Panel Layers** dialog box will be displayed, as shown in Figure 8-35.

In this dialog box, choose the **Find/Replace** button to find and replace the desired panel layer names. Similarly, choose the **Edit** button to edit panel layer names.

**Note**

*If you rename the existing panel layers using the **RENAME** command of AutoCAD, the AutoCAD electrical layer assignment information available in the WD_PNLM block of the drawing is not updated.*

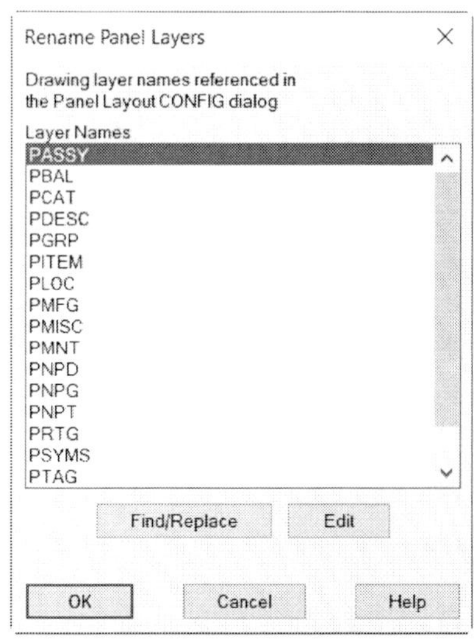


***Figure 8-35** The **Rename Panel Layers** dialog box*

# ADDING A BALLOON TO A COMPONENT

**Ribbon:** Panel > Insert Component Footprints > Balloon
**Toolbar:** ACE:Panel Layout > Insert Balloon
**Menu:** Panel Layout > Insert Balloon
**Command:** AEBALLOON

The **Balloon** tool is used to add balloon to an inserted footprint. The balloon is used to label the footprint. To insert a balloon into a footprint, choose the **Balloon** tool from the **Insert Component Footprints** panel of the **Panel** tab; you will be prompted to select a component for the balloon. Next, select the required component; you will be prompted to specify the starting point of leader or the insertion point of the balloon. Now, specify the insertion point of the balloon or starting point of the leader. Next, press ENTER if you want to insert a balloon without leader. Else, specify the endpoint of leader and then press ENTER; the balloon will be inserted into the footprint. Press ENTER to exit the command. Figure 8-36 shows the footprint with leader and balloon. The balloon displays the item number that you have assigned in the **Item Number** area of the **Panel Layout - Component Insert/Edit** dialog box. If you do not want to insert a leader along with the balloon, select the component and specify the start point of leader or insertion point of balloon and then press ENTER; the balloon will be inserted at the selected point. Figure 8-37 shows the footprint without leader and with balloon.

Note that if you change the item number that is assigned to a footprint, balloon labels will be updated automatically.

If you add a balloon to a footprint that does not have an item number assigned to it, then on choosing the **Balloon** tool from the **Insert Component Footprints** panel of the **Panel** tab, you will be prompted to select a component. Select the component; you will be prompted to specify the starting point of a leader or insertion point of a balloon. Specify the starting point of a balloon or a leader; you will be prompted to specify the end point of the leader. Specify the endpoint of the leader and then press ENTER; the **No Item Number Match for this Catalog Part Number** dialog box will be displayed, as shown in Figure 8-38. The options in this dialog box are discussed next.

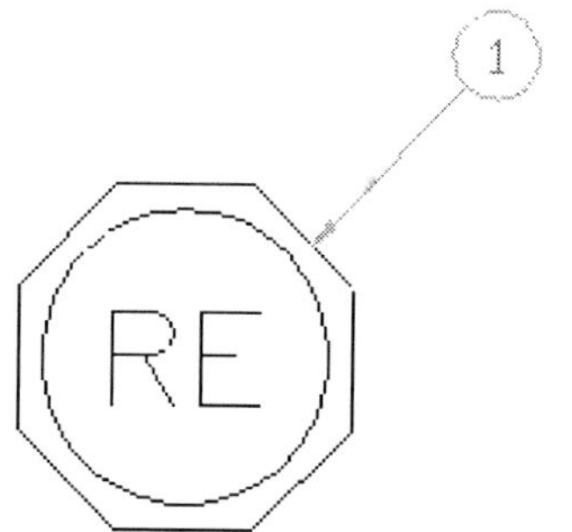


***Figure 8-36** Footprint with leader and balloon*

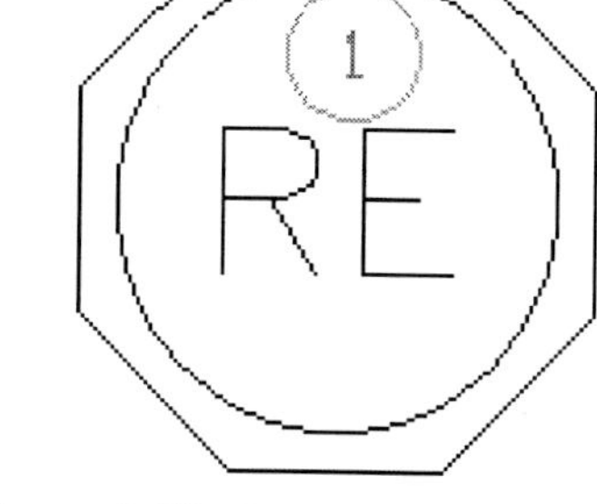


***Figure 8-37** Footprint without leader and with balloon*

No Item Number Match for this Catalog Part Number

No matching Item number found.
(no other component was found that has both an Item number assignment and a match on this component's catalog part number)

Component part number assignment

Manufacturer AB
Catalog 800T-J4B
Assembly code
Multiple Catalog (none)

Item:

List Drawing

List Project

Use Next>> 49

OK Cancel

***Figure 8-38** The **No Item Number Match for this Catalog Part Number** dialog box*

You can enter an item number for footprint in the **Item:** edit box. The **List** button is used to display the item numbers that have been used in the current drawing. To do so, choose the **List** button that is adjacent to **Drawing**; the **ITEM numbers in use : Drawing only** dialog box will be displayed, as shown in Figure 8-39. The list displayed in this dialog box is for reference only. You can also check for the Bill of Material by choosing the **Catalog Check** button from the **ITEM numbers in use : Drawing only** dialog box.

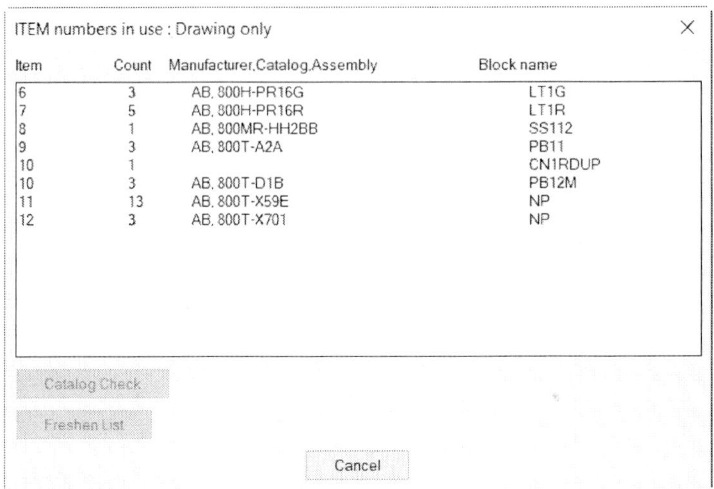


*Figure 8-39 The **ITEM numbers in use : Drawing only** dialog box*

Now, if you choose the **List** button that is adjacent to **Project**, the **ITEM numbers in use Project-wide** dialog box will be displayed, as shown in Figure 8-40. This dialog box displays a list of item numbers assigned to the footprints in the current project. This list is for reference only. Next, choose the **Catalog Check** button from this dialog box; the Bill of Material of the selected component will be displayed in the **Bill Of Material Check** dialog box.

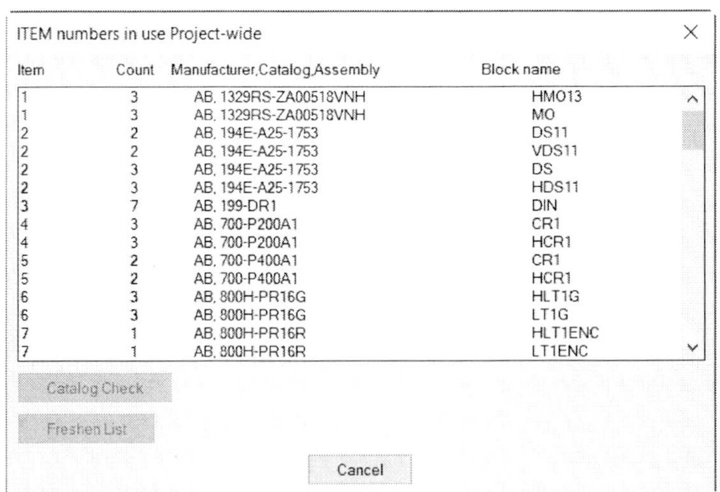


*Figure 8-40 The **ITEM numbers in use Project-wide** dialog box*

**Note**

*The **Catalog Check** button will be available only if a component has manufacturer and catalog information.*

The **Use Next >>** button is used to assign next available item number to a component.

After specifying the required options in the **No Item Number Match for this Catalog Part Number** dialog box, choose the **OK** button from this dialog box; the balloon is inserted into the footprint.

**Note**

*If you do not enter any item number in the* ***Item:*** *edit box and choose* ***OK*** *from the* ***No Item Number Match for this Catalog Part Number*** *dialog box, a balloon with '?' will be inserted into the footprint, as shown in Figure 8-41.*

*If you have already inserted a balloon into a footprint and chosen the* ***Balloon*** *tool from the* ***Insert Component Footprints*** *panel of the* ***Panel*** *tab, you will be prompted to select a component. Select the component; the* ***Existing Item Balloon*** *message box will be displayed, as shown in Figure 8-42. Choose the* ***OK*** *button from this message box to delete the existing balloon and to insert a new balloon into the footprint.*

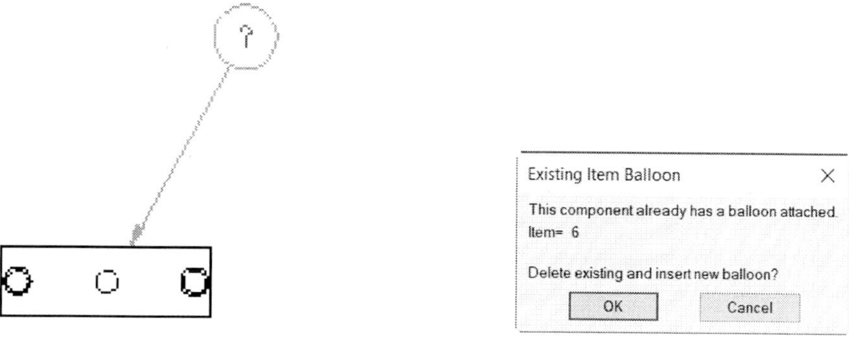


*Figure 8-41 A balloon without item number* *Figure 8-42 The* ***Existing Item Balloon*** *message box*

## ADDING MULTIPLE BALLOONS

You can also insert multiple balloons for a footprint. To do so, you need to follow the steps given next:

(a) Right-click on the active project; a shortcut menu will be displayed. Choose the **Properties** option from the shortcut menu; the **Project Properties** dialog box will be displayed.

(b) Choose the **Components** tab and then choose the **Item Numbering** button from the **Component Options** area of this dialog box; the **Item Numbering Setup** dialog box will be displayed.

(c) In this dialog box, by default, the **Accumulate Project Wide** radio button is selected in the **Item Numbering Mode** area. Next, select the **Per-Part Number Basis (excluding ASSYCODE Combination)** radio button from the **Item Assignments** area and then choose the **OK** button from this dialog box. Next, choose **OK** in the **Project Properties** dialog box.

(d) Choose the **Edit** tool from the **Edit Footprints** panel of the **Panel** tab or choose **Panel Layout > Edit Footprint** from the menu bar; you will be prompted to select a component. Select the required component from the panel drawing; the **Panel Layout - Component Insert/Edit** dialog box will be displayed.

(e) Choose the **Multiple Catalog** button from the **Catalog Data** area; the **Multiple Bill of Material Information** dialog box will be displayed.

(f) In the **Multiple Bill of Material Information** dialog box, select a number from the **Sequential Code** drop-down list and then choose the **Catalog Lookup** button from it; the **Catalog Browser** dialog box will be displayed. Next, choose the desired part number from it; the manufacturer and catalog values will be displayed in the **Manufacturer** and **Catalog** edit boxes, respectively. Repeat this process for all part numbers assigned to a footprint. Note that you can assign 99 extra part numbers to a footprint.

(g) Enter the required item number in the **Item Number** edit box and then choose the **OK** button in the **Multiple Bill of Material Information** dialog box; the number of extra part numbers specified in the **Multiple Bill of Material Information** dialog box will be displayed on the right of the **Multiple Catalog** button in the **Panel Layout - Component Insert/Edit** dialog box. Next, choose the **OK** button from the **Panel Layout - Component Insert/Edit** dialog box.

(h) Choose the **Balloon** tool from the **Insert Component Footprints** panel of the **Panel** tab; you will be prompted to select a component to which you want to add the balloon. Next, select the component; you will be prompted to specify the starting point of a leader or insertion point of the balloon. Specify the starting point of the balloon or the starting point of the leader; you will be prompted to specify the end point of the leader. Specify the endpoint of the leader.

(i) Enter **D** at the Command prompt; you will be prompted to specify the direction of balloons. Enter a character for the direction and press ENTER; multiple balloons will be inserted on the footprint in the specified direction, as shown in Figure 8-43.

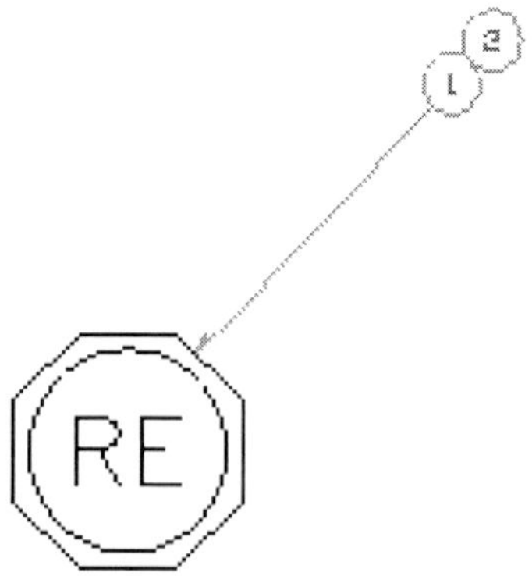


***Figure 8-43*** *Multiple balloons inserted on the footprint*

Note that if you do not specify the direction of balloons and press ENTER, the direction that was specified earlier (given in brackets in the Command prompt) will be set automatically.

# RESEQUENCING ITEM NUMBERS

**Ribbon:** Panel > Edit Footprints > Resequence Item Numbers
**Toolbar:** ACE:Panel Layout > Miscellaneous Panel Tools > Resequence Item Numbers
**Menu:** Panel Layout >Miscellaneous Panel Tools > Resequence Item Numbers
**Command:** AERESEQUENCE

You can resequence item numbers of the panel and schematic components using the **Resequence Item Numbers** tool. The order of resequencing the item numbers is panel components, schematic components with panel representation, and then schematic components with no panel representation. Note that the item number allotted to the schematic component with panel representation is same as the related panel component.

When you resequence the item numbers, the manufacturers across the active project get sorted and consequently the item numbers of the components with the same catalog numbers are synchronized in the project.

To resequence the item numbers, choose the **Resequence Item Numbers** tool from the **Edit Footprints** panel of the **Panel** tab; the **Resequence Item Numbers** dialog box will be displayed, as shown in Figure 8-44. The options in the **Resequence Item Numbers** dialog box are discussed next.

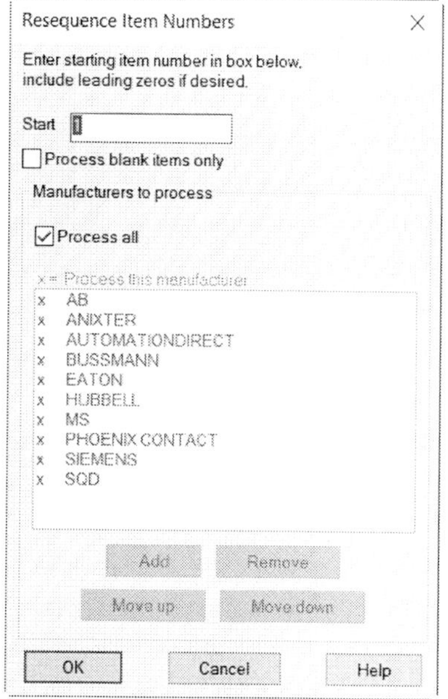


***Figure 8-44** The **Resequence Item Numbers** dialog box*

## Start

This edit box is used to specify the starting item number to be used for resequencing.

## Process blank items only

This check box is selected to assign item number only to the components which do not have item numbers assigned. By default, this check box is clear. As a result, the item numbers of all components will be resequenced and existing item numbers will be replaced.

## Manufacturers to Process Area

The options in this area are discussed next.

### Process All

This check box is selected by default and is used to resequence the item numbers of all manufacturers' component.

### Manufacturers to Process List box

This list box is used to select the manufacturers for which the item numbering resequencing is to be carried out. The 'x' symbol in front of the manufacturer indicates that the manufacturer is selected for resequencing.

### Add

This button is used to select the manufacturer from the Manufacturer to Process list box for item number resequencing. Note that this button is activated only if any of the manufacturer is deselected from this list box by using the **Remove** button next to it.

### Remove

This button is used to deselect the manufacturer from the Manufacturer to Process list box.

### Move Up, Move Down

The **Move Up** and **Move Down** buttons are used to change the order of the manufacturers in the **Manufacturers to Process** list box.

After specifying the required options, choose the **OK** button in the **Resequence Item Numbers** dialog box to resequence item numbers as per the options specified in this dialog box.

**Note**

*To revert back to the item number resequencing mode used in AutoCAD Electrical 2016 version, enter the system variable AEITEMRESEQUENCEMODE in the Command Prompt and then enter **0**.*

## INSERTING NAMEPLATES

Nameplates are special type of panel footprints that are inserted into a drawing as blocks. You can link nameplates to panel footprint components or can insert them as stand-alone components. A nameplate is child of a parent footprint component. The parent-child relationship between them is established by using invisible Xdata pointers. When a nameplate is linked to a parent footprint, it will extract description, location, and other information from the associated panel component. To insert a nameplate into a drawing, choose the **Icon Menu** tool from the **Insert Component Footprints** panel of the **Panel** tab; the **Insert Footprint** dialog box will be displayed, refer to Figure 8-13. Select the **Nameplates** icon from the **Panel Layout Symbols** area of the **Insert Footprint** dialog box; the **Panel: Nameplates** area with various types of nameplates will be displayed, refer to Figure 8-45.

Next, select the required nameplate from the **Panel: Nameplates** area; you will be prompted to select a component for inserting the nameplate. Select the component and press ENTER; the **Panel Layout - Nameplate Insert/Edit** dialog box will be displayed, refer to Figure 8-46. The options in this dialog box are similar to that of the **Panel Layout - Component Insert/Edit** dialog box. The only difference is that in the **Panel Layout - Nameplate Insert/Edit** dialog box, you need to enter data for nameplates, whereas in the **Panel Layout - Component Insert/Edit** dialog box, you need to enter data for footprint blocks. Next, enter the required information in the **Panel Layout - Nameplate Insert/Edit** dialog box and choose the **OK** button; a nameplate will be inserted into the selected component and it will be linked to the component, as shown in Figure 8-47.

You can insert a nameplate as a stand-alone component. In this case, you need to press ENTER without selecting the component. Specify the insertion point for the nameplate; you will be prompted to select the rotation. Select the rotation by moving the cursor in the horizontal or vertical direction and press ENTER; the **Panel Layout - Nameplate Insert/Edit** dialog box will be displayed, refer to Figure 8-46. Enter the required information in this dialog box and choose the **OK** button; the nameplate will be inserted into a drawing as a stand-alone component.

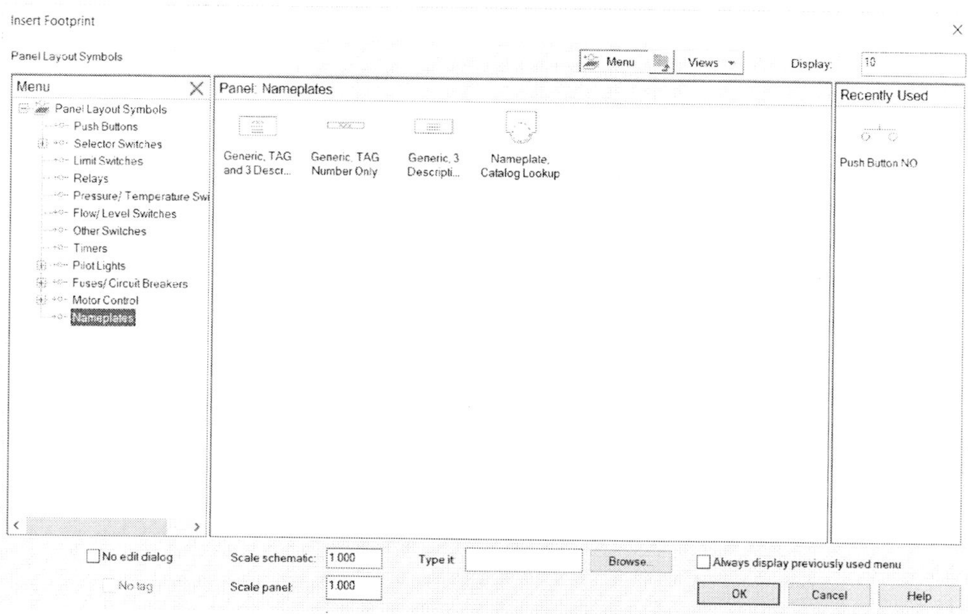


*Figure 8-45 The **Insert Footprint** dialog box with the **Panel: Nameplates** area*

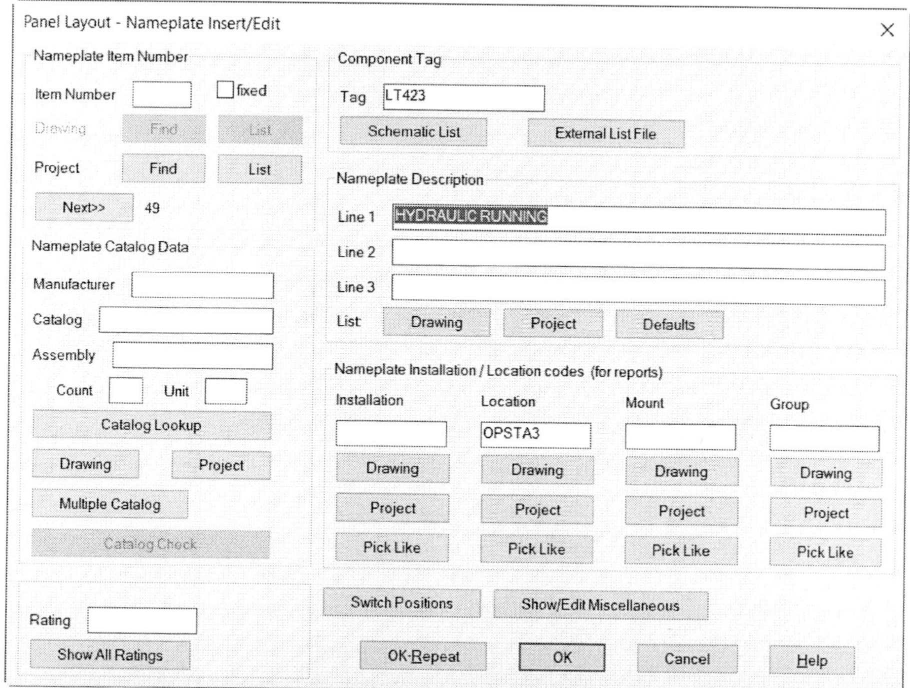


*Figure 8-46 The **Panel Layout - Nameplate Insert/Edit** dialog box*

A nameplate can be moved by using the **MOVE** command of AutoCAD. You can copy both the footprint and nameplate using the **Copy Footprint** tool.

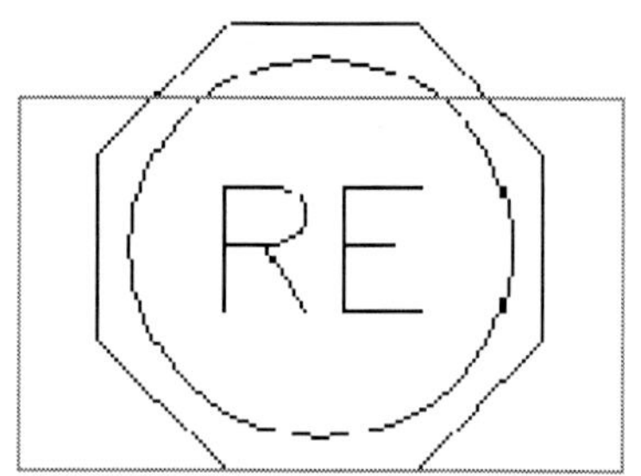


*Figure 8-47 The footprint with the nameplate inserted*

If you select the **Nameplate, Catalog Lookup** icon from the **Panel: Nameplates** area of the **Insert Footprint** dialog box; the **Nameplate** dialog box will be displayed, as shown in Figure 8-48. The options and areas in this dialog box are similar to that of the **Footprint** dialog box and have been discussed earlier. Choose the **Catalog lookup** button from the **Choice A** area; the **Catalog Browser** dialog box will be displayed. The options in this dialog box have been discussed earlier. Select a nameplate from the **Catalog Browser** dialog box and choose the **OK** button; the manufacturer and catalog values will be displayed in the **Manufacturer** and **Catalog** edit boxes of the **Choice A** area of the **Nameplate** dialog box. Next, choose **OK** from the **Nameplate** dialog box; you will be prompted to select a component. Select the required component and then press ENTER; the **Panel Layout - Nameplate Insert/Edit** dialog box will be displayed. Enter the required information in this dialog box and choose the **OK** button; the nameplate will be inserted into the selected component.

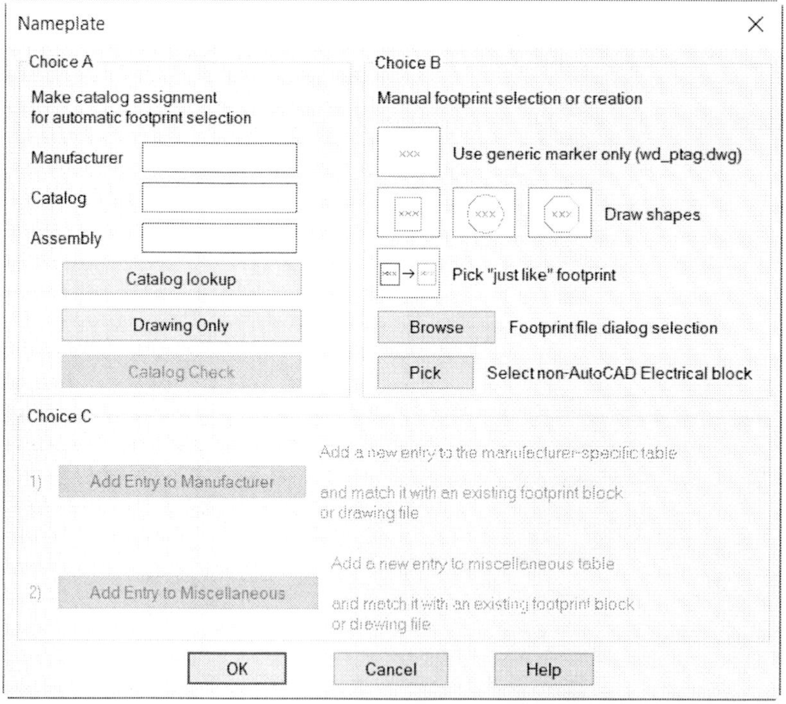

*Figure 8-48 The **Nameplate** dialog box*

You can also insert half round nameplate into a footprint. To do so, choose the **Catalog lookup** button from the **Choice A** area of the **Nameplate** dialog box; the **Catalog Browser** dialog box will be displayed. Select any Half Round part number from the **TYPE** column, as shown in Figure 8-49, and choose the **OK** button from the **Catalog Browser** dialog box; part number values will be displayed in the **Choice A** area. Next, choose **OK** from the **Nameplate** dialog box;

you will be prompted to select a component. Select the component and press ENTER; the **Panel Layout - Nameplate Insert/Edit** dialog box will be displayed. Enter the required information in this dialog box and choose the **OK** button; the half round nameplate will be inserted into the footprint, as shown in Figure 8-50.

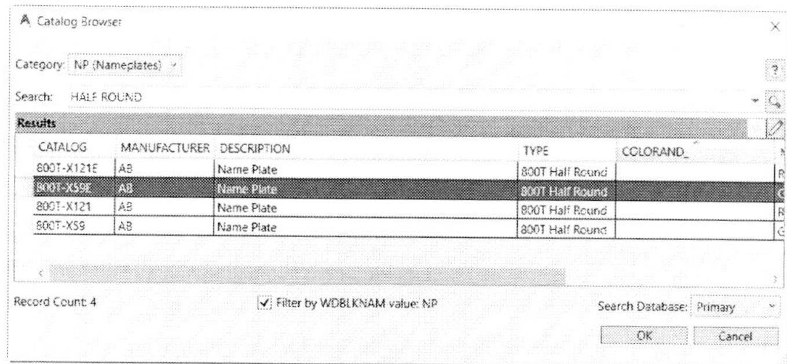


***Figure 8-49*** *The* ***Catalog Browser*** *dialog box showing the* ***800T Half Round*** *selected*

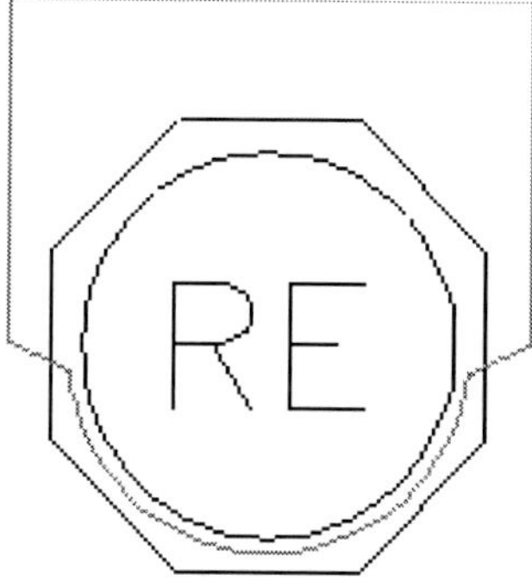


***Figure 8-50*** *The half round nameplate inserted into the footprint*

## INSERTING DIN RAIL

The DIN Rail is a standardized 35 mm wide metal track attached to the back of an electrical panel where devices can easily be clipped or removed. It is also known as top-hat rail because it has a hat-shaped cross-section. It is widely used for mounting circuit breakers and industrial control equipment inside the equipment racks. In a DIN Rail, it is very easy to snap-on and remove hardware devices while installing, maintaining, and replacing them. In addition to the popular 35 mm top-hat Rail (EN 50022, BS 5584), several other mounting rails have been standardized such as 15 mm wide top-hat Rail (EN 50045, BS 6273), 75 mm wide top-hat Rail (EN 50023, BS 5585), and G-type Rail (EN 50035, BS 5825). In this section, you will learn how the DIN Rail utility is used to create wire duct and DIN Rail objects in the panel layouts. Wire ducts and DIN Rails are frequently drawn as collection of parallel lines and equally spaced mounting holes. The DIN Rail utility simplifies the redundant tasks of creating these objects and groups them together as a single block for annotation purposes.

To insert a DIN Rail, choose the **Icon Menu** tool from the **Insert Component Footprints** panel of the **Panel** tab; the **Insert Footprint** dialog box will be displayed. Select the **DIN Rail** icon from the **Panel Layout Symbols** area of this dialog box; the **Din Rail** dialog box will be displayed, as shown in Figure 8-51. Various options and areas in this dialog box are discussed next.

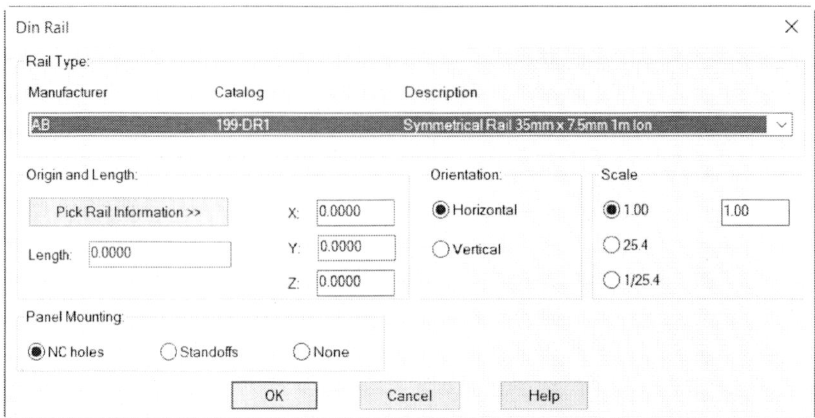


*Figure 8-51 The **Din Rail** dialog box*

## Rail Type Area

The drop-down list in the **Rail Type** area contains a list of various rail types. It displays the manufacturer, catalog, and description of various DIN Rail types. You can select the required rail type from the drop-down list. By default, AB, 199-DR1, and Symmetrical Rail 35mm x 7.5mm 1m lon is selected in this drop-down list. It consists of AB, AD, Newark, and PANDUIT rail types. By default, these rail types are saved in the *wddinrl.xls* file and the default location of this file is *C:\Users\User Name\Documents\Acade2022\AeData\ en-US\Catalogs*.

## Origin and Length Area

In this area, you can specify the origin and length of a component. To do so, enter the length of the rail in the **Length** edit box. Enter the X, Y, and Z co-ordinates in the **X**, **Y**, and **Z** edit boxes, respectively. Alternatively, to define the length and origin of a rail, choose the **Pick Rail Information >>** button in this area; the **Din Rail** dialog box will disappear and you will be prompted to specify an insertion point for the rail. Specify the insertion point for the rail; you will be prompted to specify the endpoint of the rail. Specify the endpoint of the rail and click on the screen; the **Din Rail** dialog box will appear again and the values will be displayed in the **Length**, **X**, **Y**, and **Z** edit boxes.

## Orientation Area

The **Orientation** area is used to specify the orientation for the DIN Rail. The **Horizontal** radio button in this area is selected by default and is used to insert the DIN Rail in the horizontal direction, as shown in Figure 8-52. If you select the **Vertical** radio button in this area, a DIN Rail will be inserted in the vertical direction, as shown in Figure 8-53.

## Scale Area

The **Scale** area is used to specify the scale for the DIN Rail. To do so, specify the scale for the DIN Rail in the edit box on the right of the **1.00** radio button. Alternatively, select the **1.00**, **25.4**, or **1/25.4** radio button to display the scale for the DIN Rail in the edit box.

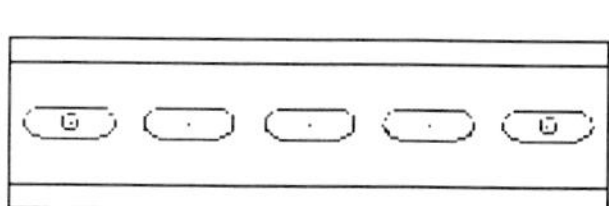

*Figure 8-52 The DIN Rail in the horizontal direction*

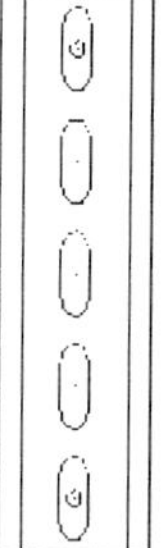

*Figure 8-53 The DIN Rail in the vertical direction*

## Panel Mounting Area

The radio buttons in the **Panel Mounting** area are used to specify the mounting options for a DIN Rail. The options in this area are discussed next.

The **NC holes** radio button in this area is selected by default. It mounts the rail at NC holes only, as shown in Figure 8-54. Select the **Standoffs** radio button to insert the rail at standoffs. Select the **None** radio button to insert the rail without NC holes and standoffs, refer to Figure 8-54.

After specifying the required options in the **Din Rail** dialog box, choose the **OK** button; the **Panel Layout - Component Insert/Edit** dialog box will be displayed. Enter the required information in this dialog box and choose the **OK** button; the DIN Rail will be inserted into the drawing.

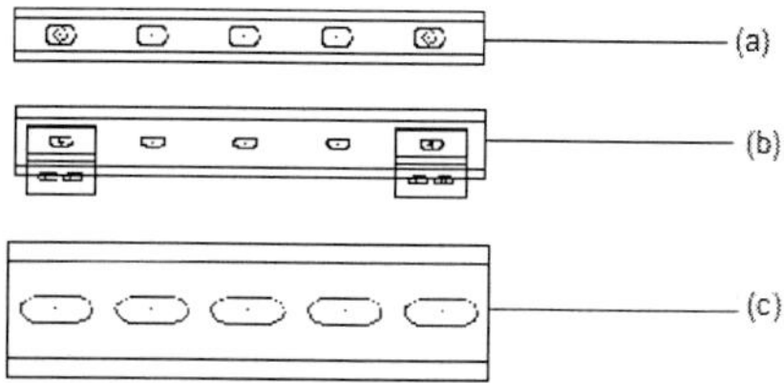


*Figure 8-54 The DIN Rail with the (a)* ***NC holes****, (b)* ***Standoffs****, and (c)* ***None*** *radio buttons selected*

**Note**

*1. If the* ***Length, X, Y,*** *and* ***Z*** *edit boxes are left blank, and you choose the* ***OK*** *button, the* ***AutoCAD Message*** *message box will be displayed, as shown in Figure 8-55. This message box informs you that more information is needed. Choose the* ***OK*** *button in this message box; the* ***Din Rail*** *dialog box will be displayed again.*

*2. If the length specified in the* ***Length*** *edit box for the DIN Rail is too short, and you choose the* ***OK*** *button, the* ***AutoCAD Message*** *message box will be displayed, as shown in Figure 8-56. This message box will inform you that the specified length is too short. Choose the* ***OK*** *button; the* ***Panel Layout - Component Insert/Edit*** *dialog box will be displayed. Enter the required information in this dialog box and choose the* ***OK*** *button; the DIN Rail will be inserted in the drawing. This condition is true for AB, AD, and Newark manufacturers and is not applicable to the PANDUIT manufacturer.*

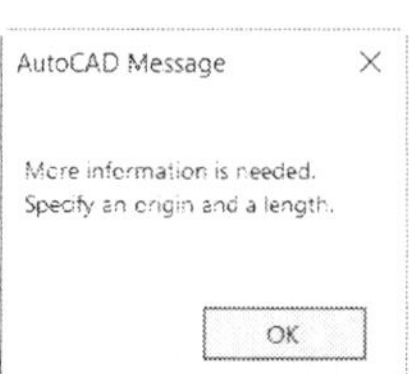


*Figure 8-55 The* ***AutoCAD Message*** *message box*

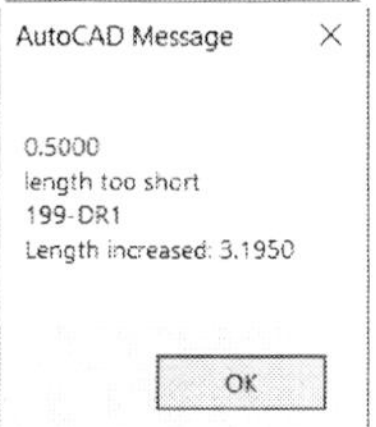


*Figure 8-56 The* ***AutoCAD Message*** *message box*

# EDITING THE PANEL FOOTPRINT LOOKUP DATABASE FILE

| | |
|---|---|
| **Ribbon:** | Panel > Other Tools > Footprint Database Editor |
| **Toolbar:** | ACE:Panel Layout > Miscellaneous Panel Tools > Footprint Database Editor |
| **Menu:** | Panel Layout > Database File Editor > Footprint Database Editor |
| **Command:** | AEFOOTPRINTDB |

The **Footprint Database Editor** tool is used to create a new footprint lookup table and to edit an existing footprint lookup table. The default location for the footprint lookup database file is *C:\Users\User Name\Documents\Acade 2022\AeData\en-US\Catalogs*. The name of the footprint database file is *footprint_lookup.mdb*. The footprint database file contains table for each manufacturer code and the footprint lookup table name must match the manufacturer code. To create or edit a footprint database file, choose the **Footprint Database Editor** tool from the **Other Tools** panel of the **Panel** tab; the **Panel Footprint Lookup Database Editor** dialog box will be displayed, as shown in Figure 8-57. The options in this dialog box are discussed next.

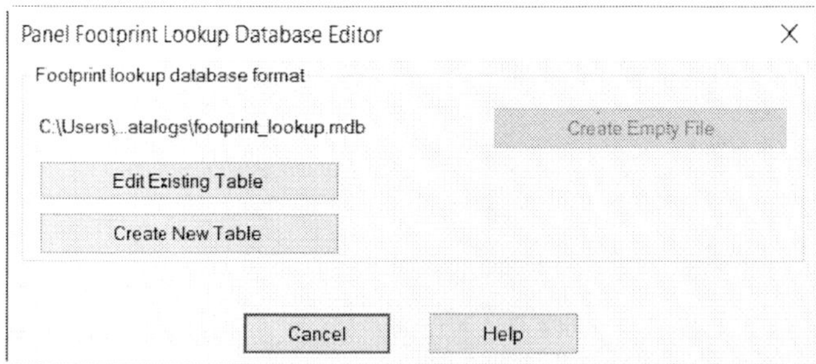


*Figure 8-57 The* ***Panel Footprint Lookup Database Editor*** *dialog box*

## Edit Existing Table

The **Edit Existing Table** button is used to edit an existing footprint lookup table. To do so, choose the **Edit Existing Table** button; the **Table Edit** dialog box will be displayed. Select the table that you want to edit and choose the **OK** button from the **Table Edit** dialog box; the **Footprint lookup** dialog box will be displayed. Next, select a part number from the list displayed; the **Edit Record** and **Delete** buttons will be activated. You can edit or add a record as per your requirement by choosing the **Edit Record** or **Add New** buttons, respectively. Next, choose the **OK/Save/Exit** button to save the record and to exit the **Footprint lookup** dialog box.

## Create New Table

The **Create New Table** button is used to create a new manufacturer footprint lookup table. To do so, choose the **Create New Table** button; the **Enter New Table Name to Create** dialog box will be displayed, as shown in Figure 8-58.

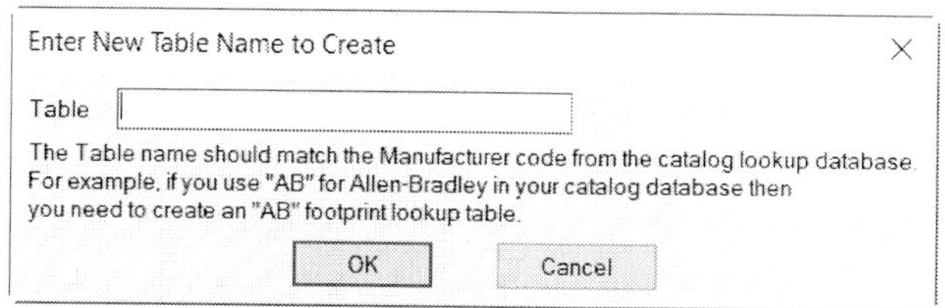


***Figure 8-58** The **Enter New Table Name to Create** dialog box*

Next, enter the table name in the **Table** edit box. Note that the table name should match the manufacturer code in the catalog lookup file. Next, choose the **OK** button from this dialog box; the **Footprint lookup** dialog box will be displayed. Choose the **Add New** button to add a new record; the **Add footprint record** dialog box will be displayed. The options in the **Add footprint record** dialog box have been discussed earlier. Enter the required information in the **Add footprint record** dialog box and choose the **OK** button; the details of this new footprint record will be displayed in the **Footprint lookup** dialog box. Now, you can edit this record by using different options in the **Footprint lookup** dialog box. Choose the **OK/Save/Exit** button to save the record and to exit this dialog box.

## Create Empty File

The **Create Empty File** button will be activated only if the default *Footprint_lookup.mdb* file does not exist in the assigned location. This button is used to create a blank footprint lookup file.

# TUTORIALS

## Tutorial 1

In this tutorial, you will extract schematic component list from the **CADCIM** project using the **Schematic List** tool. Next, you will insert components from the list in the panel drawings as footprints and then add nameplates to footprints. **(Expected time: 20 min)**

The following steps are required to complete this tutorial:

a. Create a new drawing.
b. Insert the footprint into the drawing using the **Schematic List** tool.
c. Insert nameplates.

### Creating a New Drawing

1. Activate the **CADCIM** project, if it is not already activated. Click on the *TUTORIALS* subfolder in it.

2. Choose the **New Drawing** button from the **PROJECT MANAGER**; the **Create New Drawing** dialog box is displayed. Enter **C08_tut01** in the **Name** edit box of the **Drawing File** area.

Select **ACAD_ELECTRICAL.dwt** as the template and enter **Panel Components** in the **Description 1** edit box.

3. Choose the **OK** button in the **Create New Drawing** dialog box; the *C08_tut01.dwg* is created in the *TUTORIALS* subfolder of the **CADCIM** project and displayed at the bottom of the drawing list in this subfolder.

## Inserting Footprints

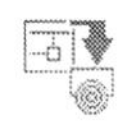

1. Choose the **Schematic List** tool from **Panel > Insert Component Footprints > Insert Footprints** drop-down; the **Alert** message box is displayed. Choose the **OK** button in this message box; a non-visible block is inserted into the drawing and the **Schematic Components List --> Panel Layout Insert** dialog box is displayed.

2. Select the **Project** radio button in the **Extract component list for:** area, if it is not already selected.

3. Select the **All** radio button in the **Location Codes to extract** area, if it is not already selected.

4. Choose the **OK** button from the **Schematic Components List --> Panel Layout Insert** dialog box; the **Select Drawings to Process** dialog box is displayed.

5. Choose the **Do All** button from the **Select Drawings to Process** dialog box; the drawings in the top list are transferred to the bottom list.

6. Choose the **OK** button from this dialog box; the **Schematic Components (active project)** dialog box is displayed.

7. Choose the **Sort List** button from the **Schematic Components (active project)** dialog box; the **Sort** dialog box is displayed. Select the **TAGNAME** option from the **Primary sort** drop-down list and choose the **OK** button; the list of schematic components is sorted out according to the tag name.

8. Scroll down the list displayed in the **Schematic Components (active project)** dialog box and search for **PB414A**, **PB422A**, and **PB425A**.

9. Press CTRL and click on rows one by one to select **PB414A**, **PB422A**, and **PB425A.**

10. Enter **0** in the **Rotate (blank = "ask")** edit box.

11. Choose the **Insert** button from the **Schematic Components (active project)** dialog box; the **Spacing for Footprint Insertion** dialog box is displayed.

12. Select the **Use uniform spacing** radio button; the **X-Distance** and **Y-Distance** edit boxes are activated.

13. Enter **0** in the **X-Distance** edit box, if it is not already displayed.

14. Enter **-3.5** in the **Y-Distance** edit box and select the **Suppress edit dialog and prompts** check box.

15. By default, **PB414A** is selected in the **Insert Order** area. Choose the **OK** button; you are prompted to specify the location for **PB414A**.

16. Enter **5,17** at the Command prompt and press ENTER; the footprints are inserted into the drawing and the **Schematic Components (active project)** dialog box appears again.

17. Choose the **Close** button from the **Schematic Components (active project)** dialog box to exit this dialog box. If the **Update other drawings** message box is displayed, choose the **Skip** button in this message box. Also, notice that the footprints of **PB414A**, **PB422A**, and **PB425A** are inserted into the drawing, as shown in Figure 8-59.

    Next, you need to move the attributes of following footprints: **PB414A**, **PB422A**, and **PB425A**.

18. Make sure the **Snap Mode** button is not chosen. Choose the **Move/Show Attribute** tool from **Schematic > Edit Components > Modify Attributes** drop-down; you are prompted to select an attribute to move. Next, select **GN** of **PB414A** and press ENTER; you are prompted to specify a base point.

19. Click on the screen near the **PB414A** component and move the cursor upward and then place the attribute **GN** on the top of **PB414A**, as shown in Figure 8-60.

***Figure 8-59*** *Footprints inserted into the drawing*

***Figure 8-60*** *Footprints after moving the attributes*

20. Similarly, move the attributes of the rest of footprints, refer to Figure 8-60. Press ENTER to exit the command.

## Inserting Nameplates

1. Choose the **Icon Menu** tool from **Panel > Insert Component Footprints > Insert Footprints** drop-down; the **Insert Footprint** dialog box is displayed.

2. Select the **Nameplates** icon from the **Panel Layout Symbols** area of the **Insert Footprint** dialog box; the **Panel: Nameplates** area is displayed.

3. Select the **Nameplate, Catalog Lookup** icon from the **Panel: Nameplates** area; the **Nameplate** dialog box is displayed.

4. Choose the **Catalog lookup** button from the **Choice A** area; the **Catalog Browser** dialog box is displayed.

5. Select the **800H-W100A** from the **CATALOG** column of the **Catalog Browser** dialog box, as shown in Figure 8-61.

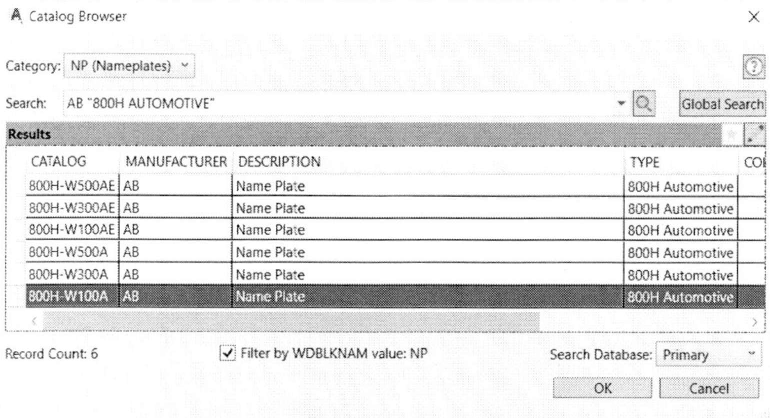


*Figure 8-61 Selecting **800H-W100A** from the **Catalog Browser** dialog box*

6. Choose **OK** from the **Catalog Browser** dialog box; the **Nameplate** dialog box appears again. Also, the manufacturer AB is displayed in the **Manufacturer** edit box and the 800H-W100A catalog is displayed in the **Catalog** edit box.

7. Choose **OK** from the **Nameplate** dialog box; you are prompted to select footprints. Select the footprints **PB414A**, **PB422A**, and **PB425A** from the drawing and press ENTER; the **Panel Layout - Nameplate Insert/Edit** dialog box is displayed. The description of the nameplate is displayed in the **Nameplate Description** area.

8. Choose **OK** from the **Panel Layout - Nameplate Insert/Edit** dialog box; the **Panel Layout - Nameplate Insert/Edit** dialog box is displayed again. Keep all the values intact and choose **OK**; the **Panel Layout - Nameplate Insert/Edit** dialog box is displayed again.

9. Choose **OK** from the **Panel Layout - Nameplate Insert/Edit** dialog box; nameplates are inserted into footprints, as shown in Figure 8-62.

***Figure 8-62*** *Nameplates inserted in footprints*

## Saving the Drawing File

1. Choose **Save** from the **Application Menu** to save the drawing file.

# Tutorial 2

In this tutorial, you will edit the footprints created in Tutorial 1 of this chapter and assign item numbers to them. Next, you will add balloons to footprints. **(Expected time: 15 min)**

The following steps are required to complete this tutorial:

a. Open, save, and add the drawing in the **CADCIM** project.
b. Edit the footprints and assign item numbers.
c. Insert balloons.
d. Save the drawing file.

## Opening, Saving, and Adding the Drawing in the CADCIM Project

1. Open the *C08_tut01.dwg* drawing file. Save it with the name *C08_tut02.dwg*. Add it to the **CADCIM** project list, as discussed in the earlier chapters.

## Editing Footprints and Assigning Item Numbers

1. Choose the **Edit** tool from the **Edit Footprints** panel of the **Panel** tab; you are prompted to select the component.

2. Select **PB414A**; the **Panel Layout - Component Insert/Edit** dialog box is displayed.

3. Enter **51** in the **Item Number** edit box of the **Item Number** area and choose the **OK** button; the **Update Related Components?** message box is displayed. Choose the **Yes-Update** button; the **Update other drawings?** message box is displayed. Choose **OK**; the **QSAVE** message box is displayed. Choose **OK**; the item number is assigned to the footprint.

**Note**

*If the **Mismatch Item Number Found** message box is displayed, choose the **OK** button.*

4. Similarly, assign **52** and **53** as item number to **PB422A** and **PB425A**, respectively.

## Inserting Balloons

1. Choose the **Balloon** tool from the **Insert Component Footprints** panel of the **Panel** tab; you are prompted to select the component for balloon.

2. Select **PB414A**; you are prompted to specify the start point of the leader or the balloon insert point.

3. Select the starting point of the leader for PB414A, as shown in Figure 8-63. Note that you can select any point at the edge of a footprint.

4. Make sure the **Ortho Mode** button is not chosen. Move the cursor toward right and click at the position shown in Figure 8-64, and then press ENTER; a balloon is inserted in PB414 and you are prompted to select a component for balloon.

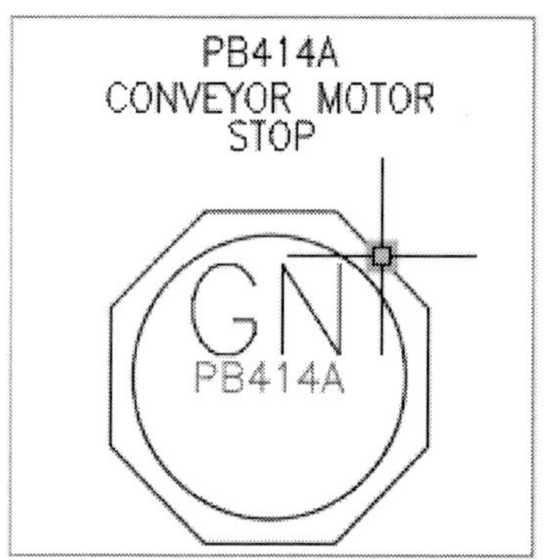


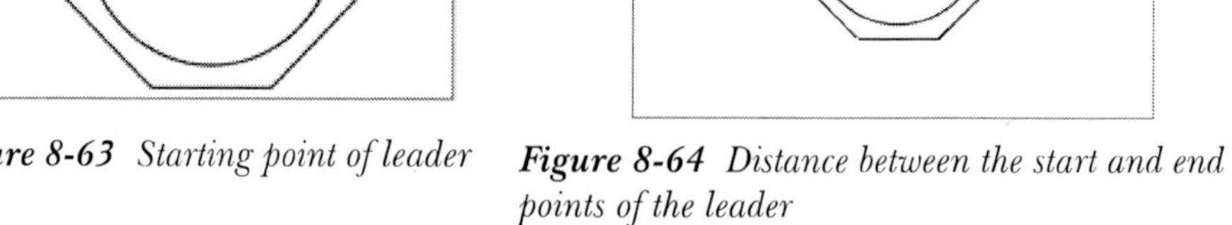

***Figure 8-63*** *Starting point of leader*

***Figure 8-64*** *Distance between the start and end points of the leader*

5. Select **PB422A** and repeat the above procedure for inserting balloon into it.

6. Select **PB425A** and repeat the above procedure for inserting balloon into it; the **Update Related Components?** message box is displayed. Choose the **Yes-Update** button; the **Update other drawings?** message box is displayed. Choose **OK**; the **QSAVE** message box is displayed. Choose **OK**; a balloon is inserted in PB425A.

7. Press ESC or ENTER to exit the command. Figure 8-65 shows footprints with the balloons inserted.

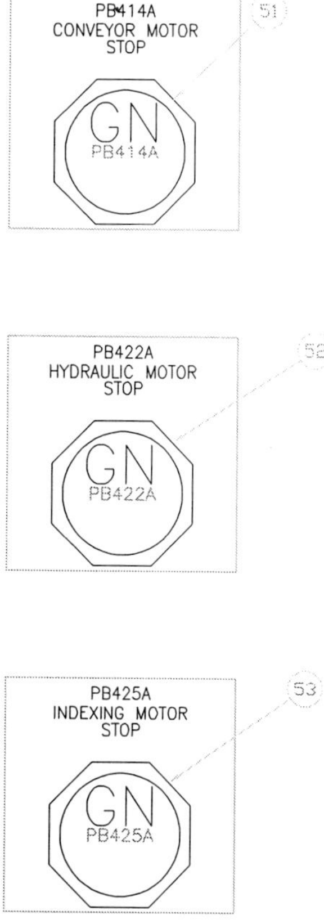


***Figure 8-65** Footprints with the balloons inserted*

## Saving the Drawing File

1. Choose **Save** from the **Application Menu** to save the drawing file.

# Tutorial 3

In this tutorial, you will insert a footprint manually in the drawing file, as shown in Figure 8-66, using the **Manual** tool. Also, you will make the Xdata of the footprint visible by using the **Make Xdata Visible** tool. **(Expected time: 10 min)**

The following steps are required to complete this tutorial:

a. Open, save, and add the drawing in the **CADCIM** project.
b. Insert the footprint manually using the **Manual** tool.
c. Make the Xdata of the footprint visible.
d. Save the drawing file.

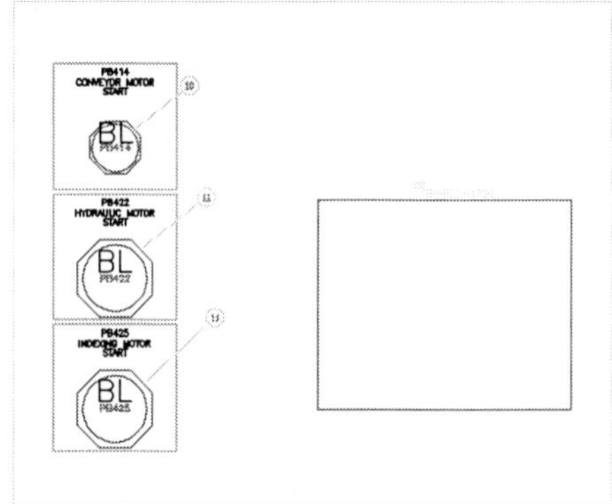

*Figure 8-66 The footprint inserted manually*

## Opening, Saving, and Adding the Drawing in the CADCIM Project

1. Open the *C08_tut02.dwg* drawing file. Save it with the name *C08_tut03.dwg*. Add it to the **CADCIM** project list, as discussed in the earlier chapters.

## Inserting the Footprint Manually

1. Choose the **Manual** tool from **Panel > Insert Component Footprints > Insert Footprints** drop-down; the **Insert Component Footprint -- Manual** dialog box is displayed.

2. Select the Rectangle symbol from **Draw shapes**; you are prompted to specify the first corner.

3. Next, enter **9,16** at the Command prompt and press ENTER; you are prompted to specify the opposite corner.

4. Enter **14,12** at the Command prompt and press ENTER; the **Panel Layout - Component Insert/Edit** dialog box is displayed.

5. In the **Catalog Data** area of this dialog box, enter **AB** in the **Manufacturer** edit box and **174E-E25-1756** in the **Catalog** edit box.

6. Choose **OK** from this dialog box; a footprint is inserted into the panel drawing, as shown in Figure 8-67.

## Making Xdata of the Footprint Visible

1. Choose the **Make Xdata Visible** tool from **Panel > Other Tools > Panel Configuration** drop-down; you are prompted to select a footprint.

2. Select the footprint that you created manually; the **Select XData to Change to a Block Attribute** dialog box is displayed.

3. Select the **MFG** radio button and choose the **Insert** button; you are prompted to specify the location for attribute (MFG).

4. Place the MFG attribute at the top of the footprint; the **Select XData to Change to a Block Attribute** dialog box is displayed again. Now, select the **CAT** radio button and choose the **Insert** button; you are prompted to specify the location for attribute (CAT).

5. Place the CAT attribute, as shown in Figure 8-68.

***Figure 8-67*** *The footprint inserted manually*

***Figure 8-68*** *Footprint with visible Xdata*

6. Choose the **Done** button from the **Select XData to Change to a Block Attribute** dialog box to exit the dialog box.

## Saving the Drawing File

1. Choose **Save** from the **Application Menu** to save the drawing file.

# Tutorial 4

In this tutorial, you will create a drawing and insert footprint in it using the **User Defined List** tool. Also, you will add a new library to the **Panel Footprint Libraries** library.

**(Expected time: 15 min)**

The following steps are required to complete this tutorial:

a. Create a new drawing.
b. Insert the footprint using the **User Defined List** tool.
c. Save the drawing file.

## Creating a New Drawing

1. Activate the **CADCIM** project. Next, click on the *TUTORIALS* subfolder in it.

2. Choose the **New Drawing** button from the **PROJECT MANAGER**; the **Create New Drawing** dialog box is displayed. Enter **C08_tut04** in the **Name** edit box of the **Drawing File** area. Select the template as **ACAD_ELECTRICAL.dwt** and enter **Panel Components** in the **Description 1** edit box.

3. Choose the **OK** button; the *C08_tut04.dwg* file is created in the *TUTORIALS* subfolder of the **CADCIM** project and displayed at the bottom of the drawing list in the **CADCIM** project.

## Inserting Footprints from a User Defined List and Adding Library to the Panel Footprint Libraries

1. Choose the **User Defined List** tool from the **Panel > Insert Component Footprints > Insert Footprints** drop-down; the **Panel footprint: Select and Insert by Catalog or Description Pick** dialog box is displayed.

2. Select **800T-A2A** catalog from this dialog box; the buttons in this dialog box are activated.

3. Choose **OK** from the **Panel footprint: Select and Insert by Catalog or Description Pick** dialog box; the **AutoCAD Message** message box is displayed, as shown in Figure 8-69. Choose the **OK** button from this message box; the command ends and you cannot insert the footprint from the user defined list. Now, to overcome this problem, you can add a library path in the **Panel Footprint Libraries** library. The procedure to add a new path to libraries is discussed next.

***Figure 8-69** The **AutoCAD Message** message box*

4. Right-click on the **CADCIM** project in the **Projects** rollout of the **PROJECT MANAGER**; a shortcut menu is displayed. Next, choose the **Properties** option from the shortcut menu; the **Project Properties** dialog box is displayed.

5. In this dialog box, the **Project Settings** tab is chosen by default. Expand the **Panel Footprint Libraries** node from the **Library and Icon Menu Paths** area; the name and path of the panel footprint library is displayed.

6. Select the *C:/Users/Public/Documents/Autodesk/Acade 2022/Libs/Panel/* Library and then choose the **Add** button located on the right of the **Library and Icon Menu Paths** area in the **Project**

**Properties** dialog box; an edit box is automatically added at the bottom of the selected library.

7. Enter **x`** in the blank edit box.

8. Choose the **OK** button in the **Project Properties** dialog box to save the changes made in this dialog box.

9. Choose the **User Defined List** tool from **Panel > Insert Component Footprints > Insert Footprints** drop-down; the **Panel footprint: Select and Insert by Catalog or Description Pick** dialog box is displayed.

10. Select the **800T-A2A** catalog from this dialog box and then choose the **OK** button; you are prompted to specify the location for AB/ABPB3.

11. Enter **15,20** at the Command prompt and press ENTER; you are prompted to select the rotation.

12. Enter **H** at the Command prompt for horizontal orientation and then press ENTER; you are prompted to specify the rotation angle.

13. Press ENTER to accept the default value 0 for the rotation; the **Panel Layout - Component Insert/Edit** dialog box is displayed.

14. Enter **PB1** in the **Tag** edit box of the **Component Tag** area.

15. Choose the **Defaults** button from the **Description** area; the **Descriptions (general)** dialog box is displayed.

16. In the **Descriptions (general)** dialog box, select **START** that is below the **Generic descriptions for PUSH BUTTONS** heading; buttons in this dialog box are activated.

17. Choose **OK** from the **Descriptions (general)** dialog box; the description is displayed in the **Line 1** edit box of the **Description** area.

18. Choose **OK** from the **Panel Layout - Component Insert/Edit** dialog box. If the **Update other drawings** message box is displayed, choose the **Skip** button in this message box. The footprint of the **Push Button (PB1)** is inserted into the drawing, as shown in Figure 8-70.

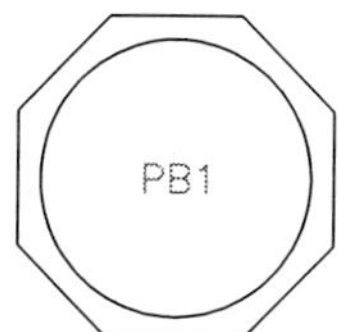


***Figure 8-70*** *Footprint inserted into the drawing*

## Saving the Drawing File

1. Choose **Save** from the **Application Menu** to save the drawing file.

# Tutorial 5

In this tutorial, you will add a new footprint record to the footprint user defined list database file (*wd_picklist.mdb*). **(Expected time: 15 min)**

The following steps are required to complete this tutorial:

a. Open, save, and add the drawing in the **CADCIM** project.
b. Add the new footprint record to footprint user defined list database using the **User Defined List** tool.
c. Save the drawing file.

## Opening, Saving, and Adding the Drawing in the CADCIM Project

1. Open *C08_tut04.dwg* drawing file. Save it with the name *C08_tut05.dwg*. Add it to the **CADCIM** project list, as discussed in the earlier chapters.

## Adding a New Footprint Record Using the User Defined List Tool

1. Choose the **User Defined List** tool from **Panel > Insert Component Footprints > Insert Footprints** drop-down; the **Panel footprint: Select and Insert by Catalog or Description Pick** dialog box is displayed.

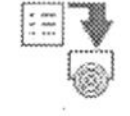

2. Select the catalog displayed in this dialog box, as shown in Figure 8-71.

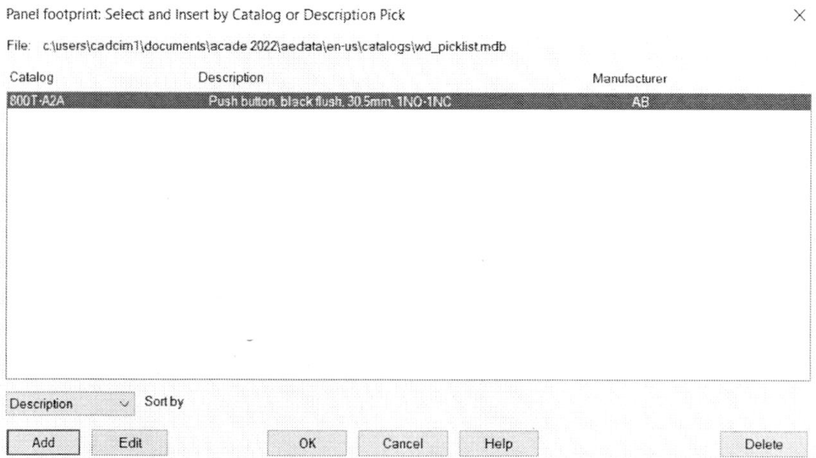


*Figure 8-71 Selecting the catalog in the* ***Panel footprint: Select and Insert by Catalog or Description Pick*** *dialog box*

3. Choose the **Add** button; the **Add New Record -- Prefill with Defaults** message box is displayed.

4. Choose **OK** from the **Add New Record -- Prefill with Defaults** message box; the data of the selected catalog is displayed in the **Add record** dialog box, as shown in Figure 8-72.

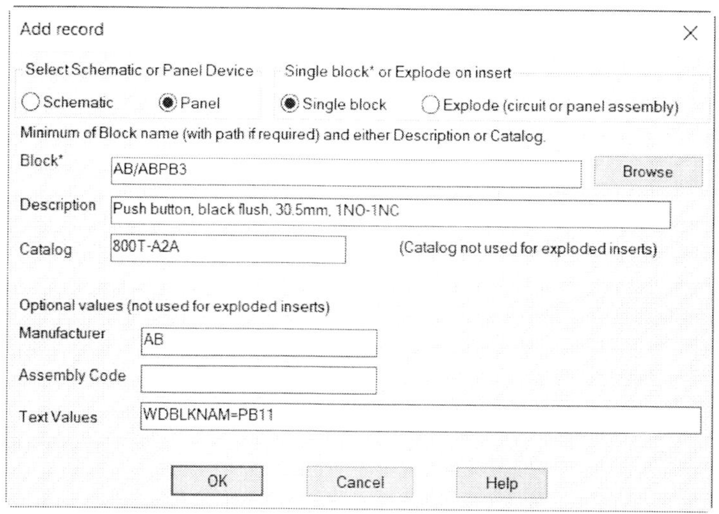


*Figure 8-72 The **Add record** dialog box*

5. Choose the **Browse** button located on the right of the **Block*** edit box; the **Select Panel footprint or footprint assembly** dialog box is displayed.

6. Browse **AB>PB-PUSH BUTTONS** in the **Look in** drop-down in the **Select Panel footprint or footprint assembly** dialog box.

7. Select **Abpb2c.dwg** from the **Select Panel footprint or footprint assembly** dialog box, refer to Figure 8-73 and choose the **Open** button; the name and path of the drawing file is displayed in the **Block*** edit box of the **Add record** dialog box.

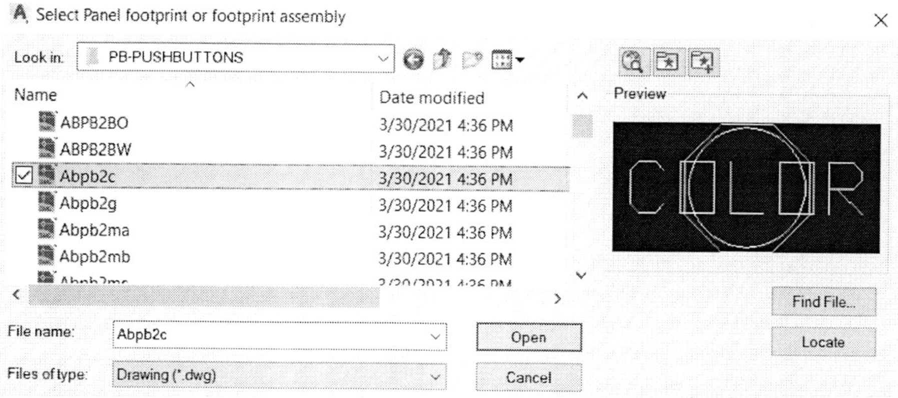


*Figure 8-73 The **Select Panel footprint or footprint assembly** dialog box*

8. In the **Description** edit box, delete **black flush** and enter **Yellow**.

9. Delete the existing catalog data from the **Catalog** edit box and then enter **440E-L10342** in it.

10. Choose **OK**; the new footprint record is displayed in the **Panel footprint: Select and Insert by Catalog or Description Pick** dialog box.

11. Choose the **Cancel** button from the **Panel footprint: Select and Insert by Catalog or Description Pick** dialog box to exit from it.

    The footprint record is automatically added to Microsoft Access Database file with the name *wd_picklist.mdb* file. To view this file, browse to *Documents > Acade 2022 > AeData > en_US > Catalogs > wd_picklist.*

    Figure 8-74 shows the *wd_picklist.mdb* file after adding the new footprint record.

PICKLIST

| DESCR | BLOCK | SCH_OR_PN | EXPLODE | CAT | MFG | ASSYCODE | TEXTVALS | RECNUM |
|---|---|---|---|---|---|---|---|---|
| 3-ph motor circ | FVN_FDS | S | Y | (circuit) | | | | 1 |
| 3-ph motor circ | FVN_KFDS | S | Y | (circuit) | | | | 2 |
| 3-ph motor circ | FVR_KFDS | S | N | (circuit) | | | | 3 |
| 3-ph motor circ | FVR_FDS | S | N | (circuit) | | | | 4 |
| Relay, 4 pole c | HCR1 | S | N | 700-P400A1 | AB | | | 5 |
| Relay, 8 pole c | HCR1 | S | N | 700-P800A1 | AB | | | 6 |
| Pilot light, RED | HLT1R | S | N | 800H-PR16R | AB | | DESC1=CONTROL;DES | 7 |
| Push button, b | AB/ABPB3 | P | N | 800T-A2A | AB | | WDBLKNAM=PB11 | 9 |
| Push button, y | C:\Users\Publi | P | N | 440E-L10342 | AB | | WDBLKNAM=PB11 | 11 |

***Figure 8-74*** *The wd_picklist database file after adding the new footprint record*

## Saving the Drawing File

1. Choose **Save** from the **Application Menu** to save the drawing file.

# Self-Evaluation Test

**Answer the following questions and then compare them to those given at the end of this chapter:**

1. Which of the following commands is used to insert a footprint?

   (a) **AEFOOTPRINT** (b) **AECOMPONENT**
   (c) **AEFOOTPRINTDB** (d) **AEEDITFOOTPRINT**

2. The _________ attribute is used to link the schematic symbol to a panel footprint.

3. The _________ tool is used to set the panel footprint drawing defaults.

4. The _________ tool is used to extract data from an equipment list.

5. The _________ tool is used to copy the footprint as well as the nameplate associated with it.

6. A balloon inserted into a footprint displays an _________ assigned to it.

7. The **Schematic List** tool is used to insert and annotate panel footprints by using the project's schematic component list. (T/F)

8. The **Edit** tool in the **Edit Footprints** panel is used to edit a footprint. (T/F)

9. The invisible data attached to a footprint block cannot be changed to a visible data. (T/F)

10. Item numbers are used in balloons only. (T/F)

## Review Questions

**Answer the following questions:**

1. Which of the following is a footprint database file?

   (a) wd_picklist (b) footprint_lookup.mdb
   (c) schematic_lookup (d) wd_lang1

2. Which of the following invisible blocks is used to store panel configuration settings as attributes?

   (a) wd_m.dwg (b) wd_mlrh.dwg
   (c) wd_pnlm.dwg (d) wd_mlrv.dwg

3. Which of the following tools is used to insert a footprint manually?

   (a) **Icon Menu** (b) **Schematic List**
   (c) **Manufacturer Menu** (d) **Manual**

4. Which of the following buttons is used to add a new entry to the footprint lookup database?

   (a) **Find** (b) **Browse**
   (c) **Add Entry to Manufacturer** (d) **Add Entry to Miscellaneous**

5. The panel drawing can have a number of wd_pnlm.dwg block files. (T/F)

6. The **Mark Existing** button in the **Schematic Components (active project)** dialog box is used to identify the components that have already been inserted into the panel drawings. (T/F)

7. The **COPY** command of AutoCAD is used to copy both footprint and nameplate. (T/F)

8. The **Panel Component Layers** dialog box is used to set layers for panel components. (T/F)

9. Nameplates cannot be inserted into a drawing as a stand-alone component. (T/F)

# EXERCISES

## Exercise 1

In this exercise, you will insert the footprints of Pilot Lights, as shown in Figure 8-75, by using the **Schematic List** tool. Also, you will make the Xdata attached to a footprint visible by using the **Make Xdata Visible** tool. Next, you will use the **Move/Show Attribute** tool to move the attributes such as LT409, LT411, LT412, and LT413, as shown in Figure 8-75.

**(Expected time: 20 min)**

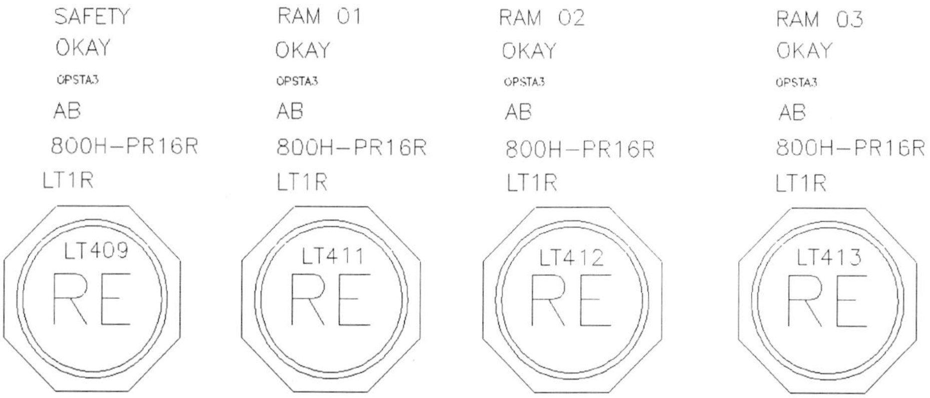

***Figure 8-75*** *The footprint of pilot lights inserted in the drawing using the* ***Schematic List*** *tool*

## Exercise 2

In this exercise, you will insert the following footprints: EATON, EGH3015FFG, CB311; AB, 700-P200A1, CR101; AB, 800T-D1B, PB414A by using the **Equipment List** tool into the drawing, as shown in Figure 8-76. Also, you will move attributes such as CB311 and PB414A using the **Move/Show Attribute** tool. **(Expected time: 20 min)**

**Hint:** Choose the **CADCIM** file from the **Select Equipment List Spreadsheet File** dialog box and **COMP** from the **Table Edit** dialog box.

## Exercise 3

In this exercise, you will create a Newark, TK2-48-AG, Snaptrak 3"X.75"DIN Rail, as shown in Figure 8-77. Also, in the **Din Rail** dialog box, enter **10** in the **Length** edit box, **9** in the **X** edit box, and **9** in the **Y** edit box. Make sure that you do not change the rest of the options. Next, enter **D1** in the **Tag** edit box of the **Panel Layout - Component Insert/Edit** dialog box.

**(Expected time: 15 min)**

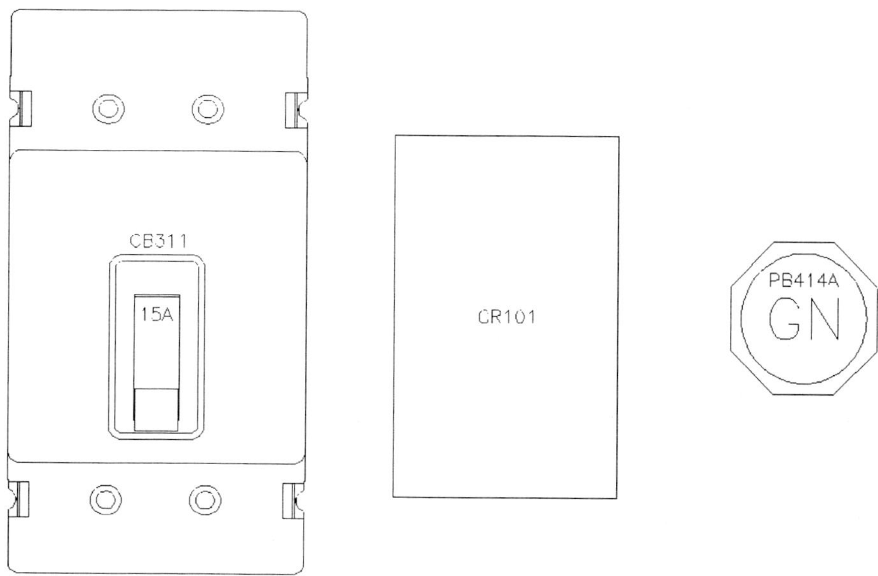


*Figure 8-76* *Footprints inserted into the drawing*

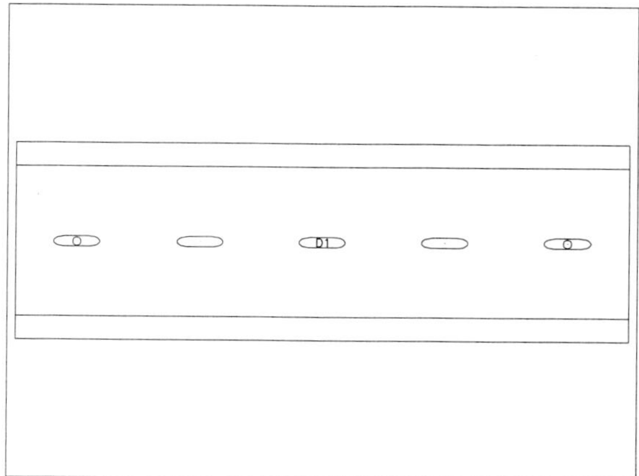

*Figure 8-77* *The Newark DIN Rail*

## Answers to Self-Evaluation Test

**1.** a, **2. Component Tag**, **3. Configuration**, **4. Insert Footprint Equipment List**, **5. Copy Footprint**, **6. item number**, **7.** T, **8.** T, **9.** F, **10.** F

# Chapter 9

# Schematic and Panel Reports

## Learning Objectives

**After completing this chapter, you will be able to:**

- *Generate schematic and panel reports*
- *Change the report format*
- *Place reports in a drawing*
- *Save reports to external files*
- *Plot reports*
- *Generate cumulative reports*
- *Set format files for a report*

# INTRODUCTION

In AutoCAD Electrical, you can manually or automatically run reports such as Bill of Materials, Wire From/To, Components, and so on. These reports consist of different fields of information and this information is as accurate as the information in your drawings. Moreover, more fields can be added to the report according to your requirement. Each report style is created with predefined categories and format. Every report can be customized to match your requirements such as adding or removing column headings, changing column order, and adding descriptive information.

AutoCAD Electrical extracts multiple fields from each report type. Using the reporting tools, you can save more time as you do not need to spend time in copying information from schematic drawings.

In this chapter, you will learn how to create reports with information extracted from the components inserted in the drawings. The formats of reports are flexible and are extracted from the information found in the drawings. Also, you will learn how to create schematic reports, panel reports, cumulative reports, edit reports, change the format of reports, save reports to external file, place report on the drawing, plot reports, and set format files for the report.

# GENERATING SCHEMATIC REPORTS

| | |
|---|---|
| **Ribbon:** | Reports > Schematic > Reports |
| **Toolbar:** | ACE:Main Electrical 2 > Schematic Reports drop-down > Schematic Reports |
| **Menu:** | Projects > Reports > Schematic Reports |
| **Command:** | AESCHEMATICREPORT |

In AutoCAD Electrical, you can run multiple schematic reports. To do so, choose the **Reports** tool from the **Schematic** panel of the **Reports** tab; the **Schematic Reports** dialog box will be displayed, as shown in Figure 9-1. The reports that can be extracted are displayed in the **Report Name** area of this dialog box and are discussed next.

## Bill of Material Reports

By default, the **Bill of Material** option is chosen in the **Report Name** area, refer to Figure 9-1. You can extract the bill of material of a schematic drawing at any time. It reports only those components that have catalog information. This report extracts component data directly from drawing files.

The different areas in the **Schematic Reports** dialog box when the **Bill of Material** option is chosen in the **Report Name** area are discussed next.

### Bill of Material Area

The **Project** radio button is selected by default in this area and is used to process the entire drawing within the project. Select the **Active drawing** radio button if you want to process the active drawing only.

**Note**

*The **Active drawing** radio button will be activated only if the active drawing is a part of an active project.*

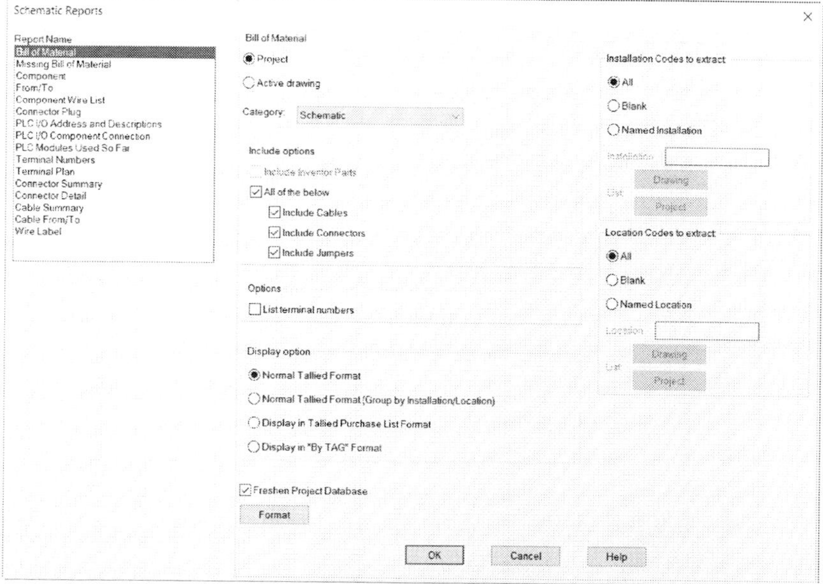


*Figure 9-1 The **Schematic Reports** dialog box*

## Category

To run the report, you can select the options such as **One-Line**, **One-Line bus-tap**, **Hydraulic**, and so on from the **Category** drop-down list. By default, **Schematic** is selected in the **Category** drop-down list.

## Include options Area

This area is used to include specified options in a report. If you select the **All of the below** check box, the **Include Cables**, **Include Connectors**, and **Include Jumpers** check boxes will also be selected. You can also use the individual check boxes to include or exclude any of these information in the report.

The **Include Inventor Parts** check box is activated if the active project is linked to an inventor assembly. If you select this check box, the electrical components in the inventor assembly will also be included in the report. Note that the linked electrical components that are displayed in inventor assembly as well as in AutoCAD electrical drawing will not be repeated in the report.

## Options Area

You can select the **List terminal numbers** check box in this area to list the tag-ID and combination of terminal numbers in a report.

## Display option Area

The options in the **Display option** area are used to set the format of a report. These options are discussed next.

### Normal Tallied Format

By default, the **Normal Tallied Format** radio button is selected. As a result, identical components or component assemblies are matched and displayed as single line items in a report.

### Normal Tallied Format (Group by Installation/Location)

If you select the **Normal Tallied Format (Group by Installation/Location)** radio button, the identical components or component assemblies that have same installation or location codes are matched and displayed as single line items in a report.

### Display in Tallied Purchase List Format

If you select the **Display in Tallied Purchase List Format** radio button, then each part will be displayed as a separate entry and will be tallied across all component types.

### Display in "By TAG" Format

If you select the **Display in "By TAG" Format** radio button, then all instances of the given component or terminal tag will be processed together and then reported as single entry in the report.

## Installation Codes to extract

The options in the **Installation Codes to extract** area are used to extract information of components based on the installation codes assigned to them. The options in this area are discussed next.

### All

The **All** radio button is selected by default in this area. It is used to process all components that carry part number values.

### Blank

If you select the **Blank** radio button, the components that do not have an installation code will be processed.

### Named Installation

If you select the **Named Installation** radio button, the **Installation** edit box, and the **Drawing** and **Project** buttons in the **List** area will be activated. This radio button is used to extract components' information for the specified installation code. To do so, enter the required installation code in the **Installation** edit box. Alternatively, choose the **Drawing** or **Project** button from the **List** area to select the installation code that is used in the active drawing or project. A report for multiple installation codes can also be created.

## Location Codes to extract

The options in the **Location Codes to extract** area are used to extract information about components based on the location codes assigned to them. The options in this area are same as those discussed in the **Installation Codes to extract** area.

## Freshen Project Database

By default, the **Freshen Project Database** check box is selected. As a result, the outdated drawing files get updated in the project database.

## Format

The **Format** button is used to change the format of the extracted data. To do so, choose the **Format** button; the **Report format settings file selection** dialog box will be displayed. In this dialog box, select the required format file and then choose the **OK** button; the name and path of the format file will be displayed on the right of the **Format** button.

**Note**

*The process to create format file for reports is discussed later in the chapter.*

After specifying the required options in the **Schematic Reports** dialog box, choose the **OK** button from this dialog box; the **Select Drawings to Process** dialog box will be displayed, as shown in Figure 9-2.

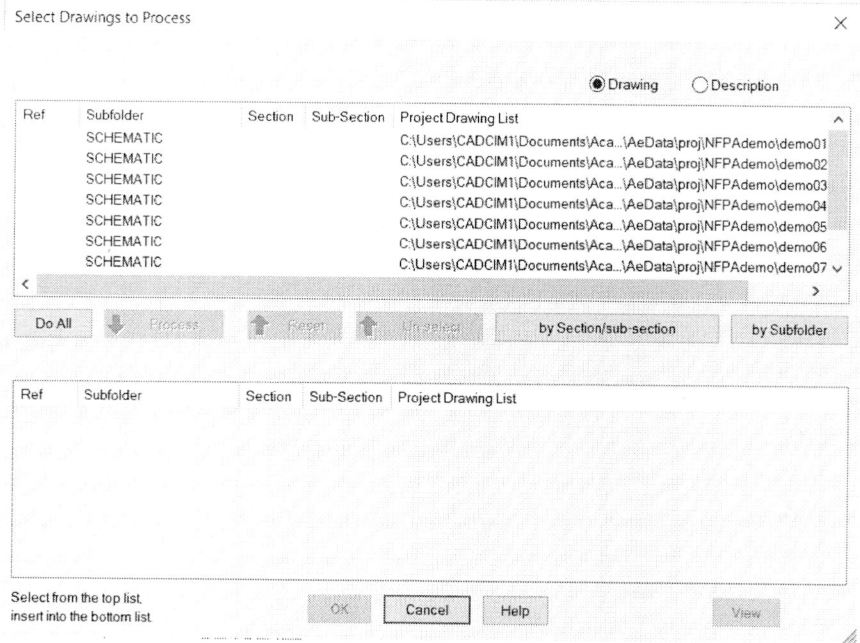


*Figure 9-2 The* ***Select Drawings to Process*** *dialog box*

In this dialog box, select the drawings to be processed and choose the **Process** button; the selected drawings will be transferred from the top list to the bottom list of the dialog box. Next, choose the **OK** button; the **Report Generator** dialog box will be displayed. This dialog box displays the result of report generation. The options in this dialog box will be discussed later in this chapter.

**Note**

*1. If you select the* ***Active drawing*** *radio button from the* ***Bill of Material*** *area of the* ***Schematic Reports*** *dialog box, the* ***Report Generator*** *dialog box will be displayed directly without the* ***Select Drawings to Process*** *dialog box being displayed.*

*2. If you have made any changes in the current drawing and have not saved them, then the* ***QSAVE*** *message box will be displayed after choosing the* ***OK*** *button from the* ***Select Drawings to Process*** *dialog box. Choose the* ***OK*** *button from the* ***QSAVE*** *message box to save the changes made in the current drawing; the* ***Report Generator*** *dialog box will be displayed.*

## Missing Bill of Material Reports

The **Missing Bill of Material** report displays a list of parent or stand-alone components that do not have catalog information. When you choose the **Missing Bill of Material** option from the **Report Name** area of the **Schematic Reports** dialog box, the **Schematic Reports** dialog box will be modified, as shown in Figure 9-3. The different areas and options in this dialog box are discussed next.

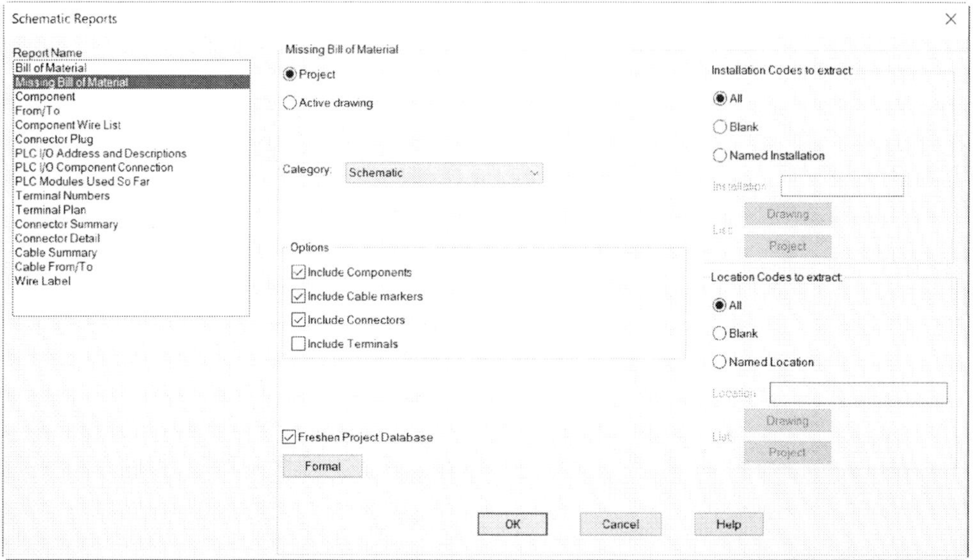


*Figure 9-3 The modified **Schematic Reports** dialog box after choosing the **Missing Bill of Material** option from the **Report Name** area*

### Missing Bill of Material Area

The **Missing Bill of Material** area is used to specify whether to process a project or an active drawing for generating a report.

### Options Area

This area is used to include the components, cable markers, connectors, and terminals in the report.

The other areas in this dialog box have already been discussed in the previous section.

## Component Reports

The **Component** report displays a list of component tag name, manufacturer name, catalog information, description text, and so on. When you choose the **Component** option from the **Report Name** area of the **Schematic Reports** dialog box, the **Schematic Reports** dialog box will be modified, as shown in Figure 9-4. In this type of report, the information extracted from the project or drawing consists of components that are present in the schematic drawings. Different areas of this dialog box are discussed next.

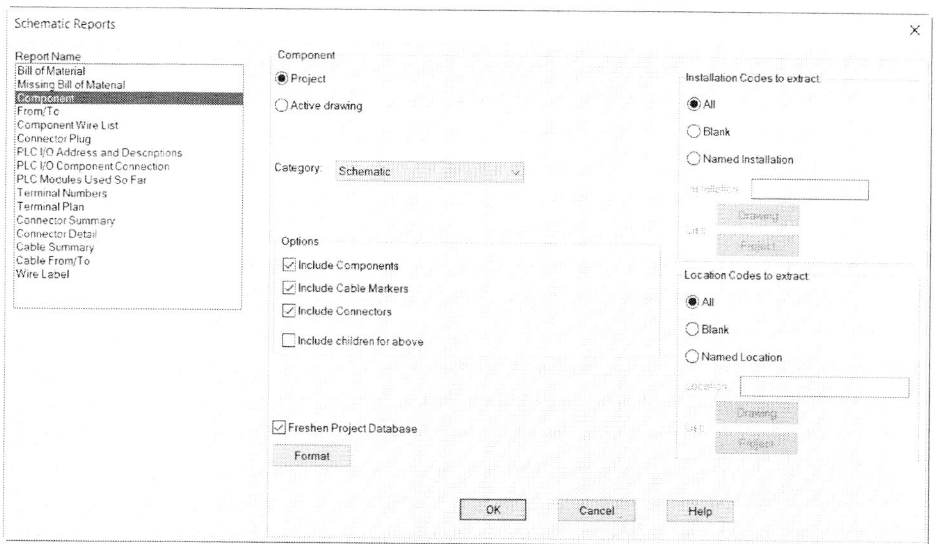


*Figure 9-4 The modified **Schematic Reports** dialog box after choosing the **Component** option from the **Report Name** area*

### Component Area

The **Component** area is used to specify whether to process the entire project or an active drawing for generating the report. The **Project** radio button in this area is selected by default and is used to process the entire project. Select the **Active drawing** radio button to process the active drawing only.

### Options Area

The **Options** area is used to include components, cable markers, connectors, and their child components in the report.

The other options in the **Schematic Reports** dialog box have already been discussed in the previous section.

## From/To Reports

The **From/To** report displays the information extracted from the components, location codes, terminal, and wire connection of a project. When you choose the **From/To** option from the **Report Name** area, the **Schematic Reports** dialog box will be modified, as shown in Figure 9-5. Different areas and options in this dialog box are discussed next.

### From/To Area

The **From/To** area is used to specify whether to process a project or an active drawing for generating a report. Select the **Project** radio button to process a project. The **Active drawing (all)** radio button is selected by default and is used to process the active drawing.

The **Active drawing (pick)** radio button is used to process the selected wires. To process the selected wires, select the **Active drawing (pick)** radio button and then choose the **OK** button from the **Schematic Reports** dialog box; a selection box will be displayed and you will be prompted to select wires. Next, select the wires that you want to process and press ENTER; the **Location Code Selection for From/To Reporting** dialog box will be displayed. Note that this dialog box will be displayed only if the location codes are available in the active project, active drawing, or for the components picked in the active drawing. The options in the **Location Code Selection for From/To Reporting** dialog box are discussed later in this chapter. You can move the location codes to the **Report From/To** area of the **Location Code Selection for From/To Reporting** dialog box by selecting them from the **Location codes** area present on both the left and right sides of this dialog box and then choosing the **OK** button; the **Report Generator** dialog box will be displayed. This dialog box displays the report of the selected wires.

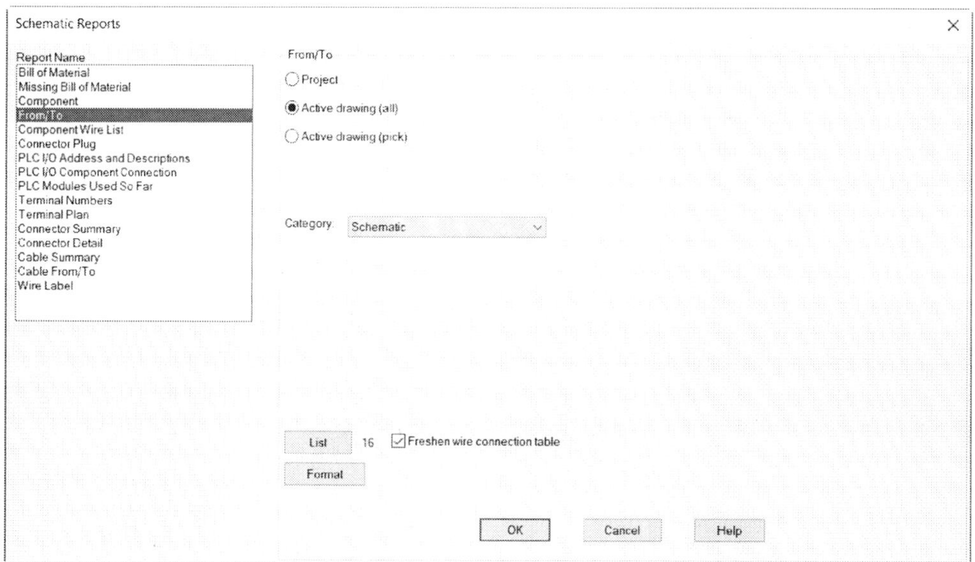


*Figure 9-5 The modified **Schematic Reports** dialog box after choosing the **From/To** option from the **Report Name** area*

## List

The **List** button in the **Schematic Reports** dialog box is used to display the outdated drawings. To view the outdated drawings, choose the **List** button; the **Drawing list: Wire connection processing - Freshen** dialog box will be displayed, refer to Figure 9-6. This dialog box displays the drawings that seem to be outdated with the project's wire connection table.

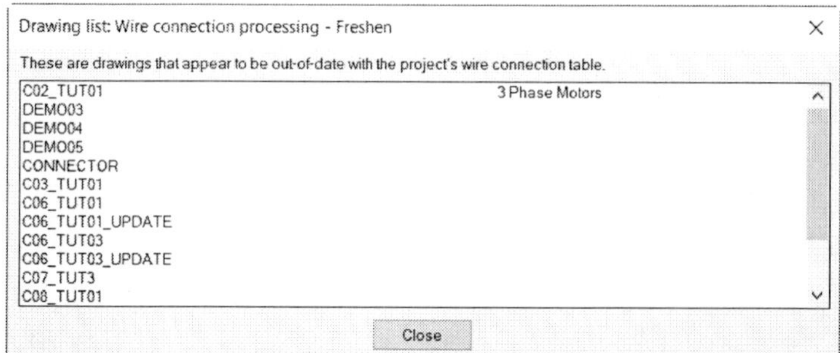


*Figure 9-6 The **Drawing list: Wire connection processing - Freshen** dialog box*

### Freshen wire connection table

The **Freshen wire connection table** check box is used to update the wire connection table of the outdated drawing files.

### Format

The **Format** button is used to change the format of the extracted information. To do so, choose the **Format** button; the **Report format settings file selection** dialog box will be displayed.

In this dialog box, select the report format settings file and then choose the **OK** button; the name and path of the format file will be displayed on the right of the **Format** button.

**Note**

*The procedure to create the report format settings file is discussed in detail later in this Chapter.*

After specifying the required options in the **Schematic Reports** dialog box, choose the **OK** button; the **Location Code Selection for From/To Reporting** dialog box will be displayed, refer to Figure 9-7. This dialog box displays a list of location codes from where you can select the locations "from" and "to" to display them in the report. Also, the location codes found in the entire project are displayed on either side of this dialog box. The different areas and options in the **Location Code Selection for From/To Reporting** dialog box are discussed next.

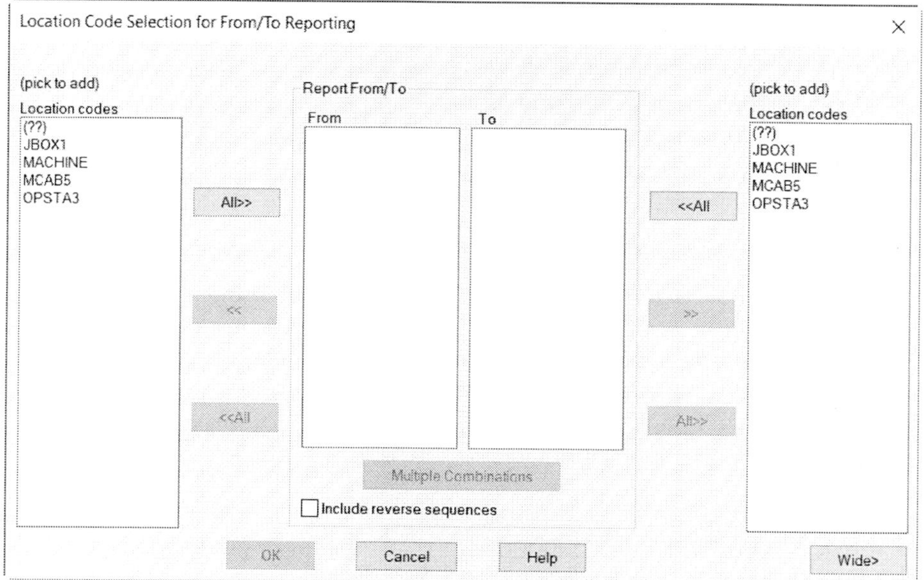


*Figure 9-7 The **Location Code Selection for From/To Reporting** dialog box*

**Note**

*If you have made changes in the current drawing and have not saved it, the **QSAVE** message box, as shown in Figure 9-8, will be displayed after choosing the **OK** button in the **Schematic Reports** dialog box.*

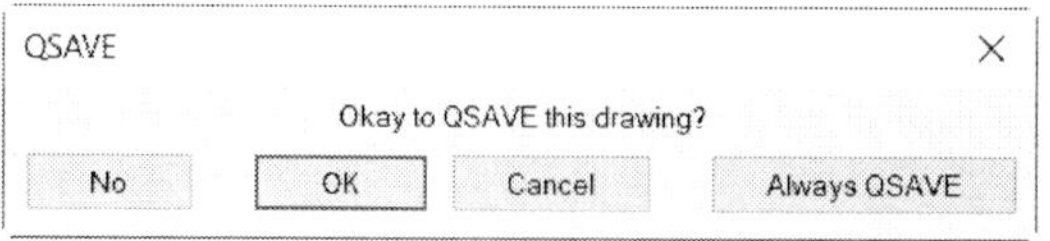


*Figure 9-8 The QSAVE message box*

### Location codes Area

The **Location codes** area displays all location codes found in the project, active drawing, or selected wires. The **Location codes** area is present on both the right and left sides of the **Location Code Selection for From/To Reporting** dialog box. When you select any of these location codes, the selected location code automatically moves to the **Report From/To** area of the dialog box. Choose the **All>>** or **All<<** button to move all location codes present in the **Location codes** area to the **Report From/To** area at a time. The '??' symbol in the **Location codes** area indicates that a component or a stand-alone terminal does not have location code assigned to it.

### Report From/To Area

The **Report From/To** area displays the location codes that are moved from the **Location codes** areas on the left and right sides of the dialog box. The list displayed in this area is used to generate the **Wire From/To** report. The **>>** or **<<** button is used to remove the selected location code from the **Report From/To** area.

### Multiple Combinations

The **Multiple Combinations** button will be activated only when the location codes are added in the **Report To/From** area. This button is used to process multiple from/to combination of location codes and combine them into a single report. To process multiple from/to combination of location codes, choose the **Multiple Combinations** button; the **Select Multiple From/To Location Combinations for report** dialog box will be displayed, as shown in Figure 9-9. This dialog box displays the link between the location codes of the From/To side. These From/To combinations of location codes are processed and then combined into a single report. The list displayed in this dialog box can be altered as per your requirement in the following ways:

By default, the **Eliminate combinations with any Location common to both From and To** check box is selected. As a result, the location codes, which are common to both From and To sides, will be eliminated. If you clear this check box, the location codes that are common to the From/To side will not be eliminated, as shown in Figure 9-10.

Select the number of location codes that you want to group together from the **From: number of Locations to group** and the **To: number of Locations to group** drop-down lists.

The **Remove Highlighted** button is used to remove the selected location code from the list displayed in the **Select Multiple From/To Location Combinations for report** dialog box.

When you choose the **Keep Highlighted Only** button, only the location code that you have selected from the list displayed in this dialog box will be retained. If you want the whole list to be displayed again, clear the **Eliminate combinations with any Location common to both From and To** check box.

Select Multiple From/To Location Combinations for report: (20 combinations total)

Each of the following From/To combinations will be processed and then combined into a single report.
Adjust list as required and then select OK.
(press SHIFT or CTRL key for multiple selection)
Note: "(??)" = blank Location

(??) ==> JBOX1
(??) ==> MACHINE
(??) ==> MCAB5
(??) ==> OPSTA3
JBOX1 ==> (??)
JBOX1 ==> MACHINE
JBOX1 ==> MCAB5
JBOX1 ==> OPSTA3
MACHINE ==> (??)
MACHINE ==> JBOX1
MACHINE ==> MCAB5
MACHINE ==> OPSTA3
MCAB5 ==> (??)

Eliminate combinations with any Location common to both From and To

1 From: number of Locations to group 1 To: number of Locations to group

Remove Highlighted Keep Highlighted Only

OK Cancel

*Figure 9-9 The **Select Multiple From/To Location Combinations for report** dialog box*

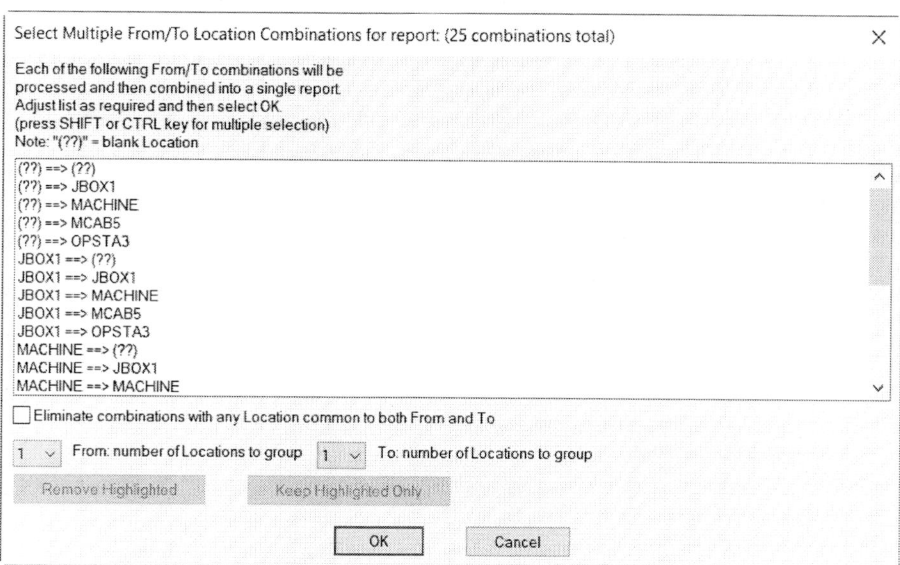


*Figure 9-10 The **Eliminate combinations with any Location common to both From and To** check box cleared*

Now, select the location codes from the **Select Multiple From/To Location Combinations for report** dialog box and choose the **OK** button; the **Report Generator** dialog box will be displayed. The options in the **Report Generator** dialog box will be discussed later in this chapter. Now, if you choose the **Close** button in the **Report Generator** dialog box, the **Location Code Selection for From/To Reporting** dialog box will be displayed again and you can select the location codes again.

**Note**

*1. You can select multiple location codes at a time from the* ***Select Multiple From/To Location Combinations for report*** *dialog box by pressing the SHIFT or CTRL key.*

*2. The* ***Report Generator*** *dialog box will also be displayed after choosing the* ***OK*** *button in the* ***Location Code Selection for From/To Reporting*** *dialog box.*

## Component Wire List Reports

The **Component Wire List** report displays the information extracted from the component wire connection. The report contains the wire number assigned to the connecting wire, the wire connection's terminal pin number (if present), the component's tag name and location code (if present), layer name of the connected wire, reference number of the component, and so on. When you choose the **Component Wire List** option from the **Report Name** area of the **Schematic Reports** dialog box, the respective options will be displayed in the **Schematic Reports** dialog box, refer to Figure 9-11. Different areas in this dialog box are discussed next.

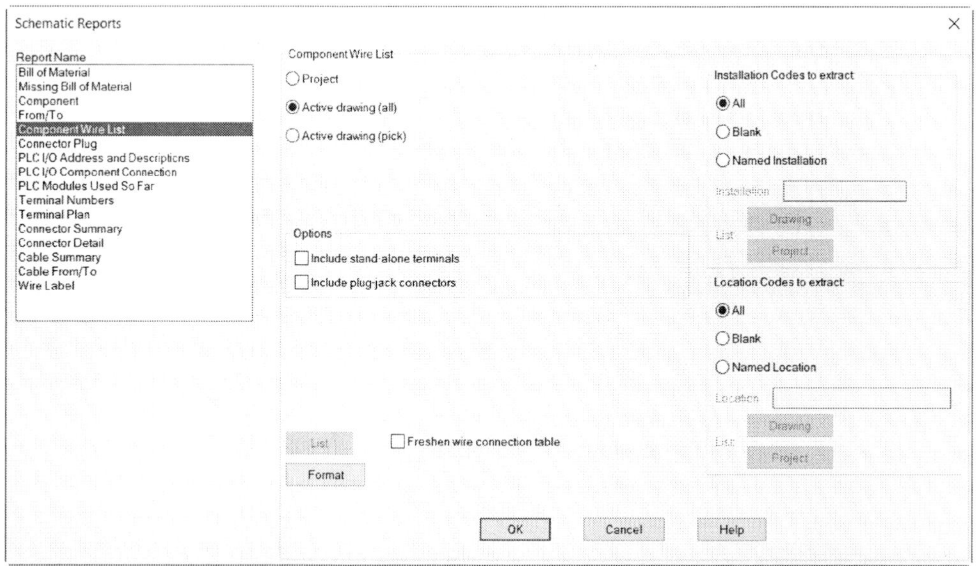


*Figure 9-11 The* ***Schematic Reports*** *dialog box after choosing the* ***Component Wire List*** *option from the* ***Report Name*** *area*

### Component Wire List Area

The **Component Wire List** area is used to specify whether to process the entire project, an active drawing, or selected components in the active drawing. Select the **Project** radio button to process the entire project. By default, the **Active drawing (all)** radio button is selected, which implies that the active drawing will be processed. Select the **Active drawing (pick)** radio button to pick individual components from the active drawing.

### Options Area

The **Options** area is used to specify whether to include stand-alone terminals and plug-jack connectors in the report or not. The options in the rest of the areas have already been discussed in the previous section.

Choose the **OK** button from the **Schematic Reports** dialog box; the **Report Generator** dialog box will be displayed. The options in this dialog box are discussed later in this chapter. Choose the **Close** button from the **Report Generator** dialog box to exit this dialog box.

## Connector Plug Reports

The **Connector Plug** report displays the information extracted from the plug/jack connection and pin charts. This report contains wire number, wire layer, cable, and so on. When you choose the **Connector Plug** option from the **Report Name** area of the **Schematic Reports** dialog box, the **Schematic Reports** dialog box will be modified, as shown in Figure 9-12. After specifying the desired settings in the **Connector Plug** area and selecting the **Project** radio button, choose the **OK** button from the **Schematic Reports** dialog box; the **Select Drawings to Process** dialog box will be displayed. Select the required drawings from this dialog box and choose **OK**; the **Report Generator** dialog box will be displayed.

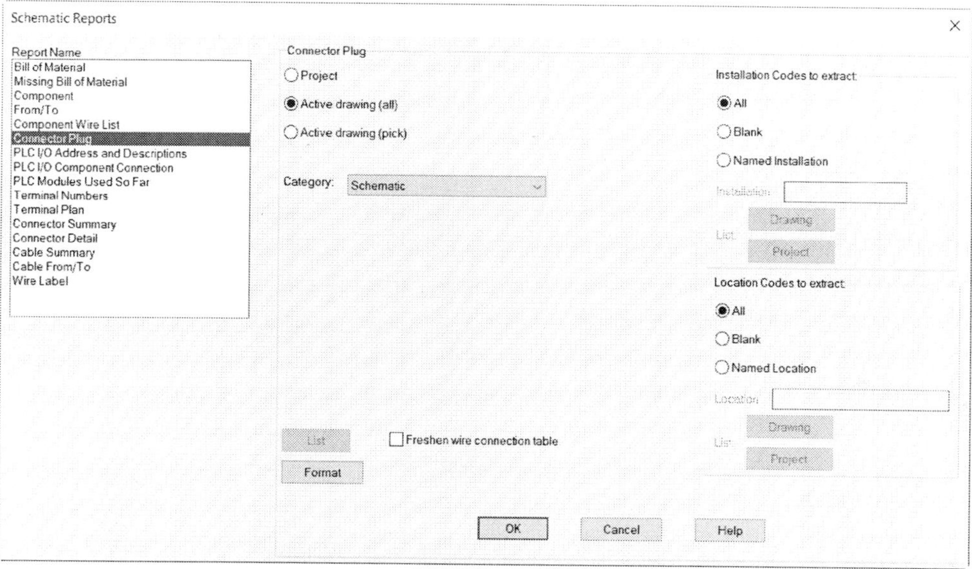


*Figure 9-12 The modified **Schematic Reports** dialog box after choosing the **Connector Plug** option from the **Report Name** area*

## PLC I/O Address and Descriptions Reports

The **PLC I/O Address and Descriptions** report displays the starting and ending I/O address numbers of each PLC module. Also, the report displays five lines of description text and the connected wire number for each I/O point. When you choose the **PLC I/O Address and Descriptions** option from the **Report Name** area of the **Schematic Reports** dialog box, the **Schematic Reports** dialog box is modified. After specifying the desired settings in the **PLC I/O Address and Descriptions** area and selecting the **Project** radio button, choose the **OK** button; the **Select Drawings to Process** dialog box will be displayed. Select the required drawings from this dialog box and choose **OK**; the **Report Generator** dialog box will be displayed.

## PLC I/O Component Connection Reports

The **PLC I/O Component Connection** report displays the information of components that are connected to PLC I/O points.

## PLC Modules Used So Far Reports

The **PLC Modules Used So Far** report displays the PLC I/O modules that have been used in the project. Also, this report displays the beginning and the end address of the PLC module.

## Terminal Numbers Reports

The **Terminal Numbers** report displays the information related to terminals such as terminal strip ID, terminal number, wire number associated with terminal, installation code, location code, and so on.

## Terminal Plan Reports

The **Terminal Plan** report displays the information related to wire number, location codes, terminal strip ID, wire layer name, and so on.

## Connector Summary Reports

The **Connector Summary** report displays the connector summary such as connector tag, pins used, maximum pins allowed, a list of repeated pin numbers used, and so on. This report can be run for the entire project or for a selected connector.

## Connector Detail Reports

The **Connector Detail** report displays connector details such as connector tag, terminal pin number, wire number, type of the connector, location code if present, catalog, and so on. You can run this report for the entire project or for a single connector.

## Cable Summary Reports

The **Cable Summary** report displays tags of cable marker, sheet number, manufacturer code, catalog, reference number, and so on. You need to run this report for the entire project.

## Cable From/To Reports

The **Cable From/To** report displays the parent cable tag of the conductor, wire number, pin number, location code, installation code, and so on. You can run this report for the entire project, active drawing, or selected cables.

## Wire Label Reports

The **Wire Label** report displays the list of wire labels and cable labels.

## Wire Signal and Stand-alone Reference Reports

| | |
|---|---|
| **Ribbon:** | Reports > Schematic > Signal Error/List |
| **Toolbar:** | ACE:Signals > Signal Error/List Report |
| **Menu:** | Wires > Signal References > Signal Error/List Report |
| **Command:** | AESIGNALERRORREPORT |

The **Signal Error/List** tool is used to generate two types of reports: the wire signal source/destination codes report and the stand-alone reference source/destination codes report.

To generate these reports, choose the **Signal Error/List** tool from the **Schematic** panel of the **Reports** tab; the **Wire Signal or Stand-Alone References Report** dialog box will be displayed, as shown in Figure 9-13. The options in this dialog box are discussed next.

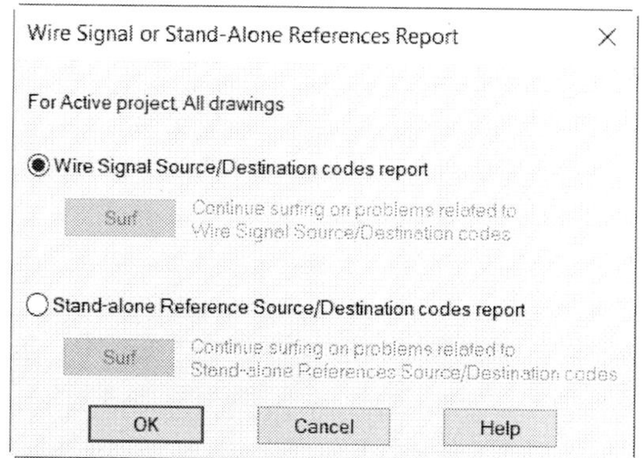


***Figure 9-13** The **Wire Signal or Stand-Alone References Report** dialog box*

### Wire Signal Source/Destination codes report

This radio button is selected by default. It is used to generate a report of the wire source/destination codes or generate a report for the exceptions found for the wire source/destination codes in the active project. Choose the **OK** button from the **Wire Signal or Stand-Alone References Report** dialog box; the **Wire Signal Report/Exceptions/Surf Exceptions** dialog box will be displayed, as shown in Figure 9-14. The options in this dialog box are discussed next.

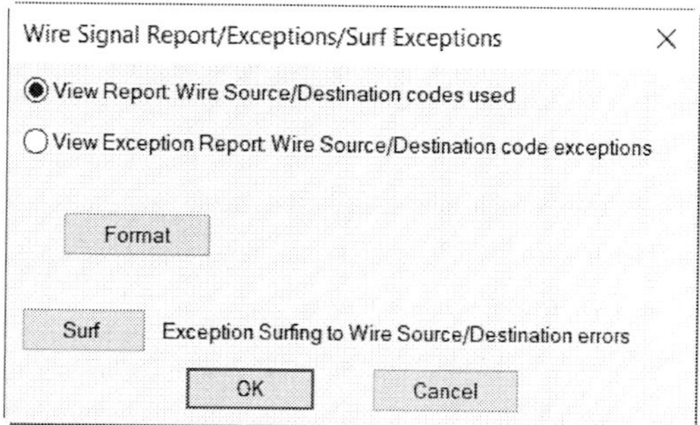


***Figure 9-14** The **Wire Signal Report/Exceptions/Surf Exceptions** dialog box*

#### View Report: Wire Source/Destination codes used

This radio button is selected to view the list of wire source/destination codes used in the active project in the form of a report. Choose **OK** in the **Wire Signal Report/Exceptions/ Surf Exceptions** dialog box; the **Report Generator** dialog box will be displayed with the list of wire source/destination codes used in the active project. The options in the **Report Generator** dialog box are discussed in the next section.

#### View Exception Report: Wire Source/Destination code exceptions

Select this radio button and then choose **OK** from the **Wire Signal Report/Exceptions/ Surf Exceptions** dialog box; the **Report Generator** dialog box will be displayed with the list of signal exceptions found for the active project such as destination not found, repeated source, and so on.

#### Format

If you choose the **Format** button in the dialog box, the **Report format settings file selection, report type=SIGREP** dialog box will be displayed. This dialog box displays a list of format files available, if any, for this type of report. You can choose the **Browse** button in this dialog box to browse to the list of other format files. You can also create new format files using the **Report Format File Setup** tool which is discussed later in the chapter.

#### Surf

If you choose the **Surf** button from the dialog box, the **Report Generator** dialog box will be displayed with the list of wire source/destination codes used in the active project. When you choose the **Close** button from this dialog box, the **Surf** dialog box will be displayed with the list of signal exceptions found for the active project. The options in this dialog box are used for surfing the problems related to the source/destination codes in the active project.

### Stand-alone Reference Source/Destination codes report

If you select this radio button and choose the **OK** button in the **Wire Signal or Stand-Alone References Report** dialog box, the **Stand-alone Reference Report/Exceptions/Surf Exceptions** dialog box will be displayed. Note that if there are no stand alone references in the active project, the **AutoCAD Message** message box will be displayed, informing you that no stand alone references are found. The options in this dialog box are similar to the options in the **Wire Signal Report/Exceptions/Surf Exceptions** dialog box discussed earlier. Using these options, you can generate a report for the stand-alone reference source/destination codes in the active project or generate a report for the exceptions found for the stand-alone reference source/ destination codes in the active project.

### Surf

The **Surf** button located below the **Wire Signal Source/ Destination codes report** radio button is used for surfing the problems related to the source/destination codes in the active project.

## Missing Catalog Data

**Ribbon:** Reports > Schematic > Missing Catalog Data
**Toolbar:** ACE:Schematic Reports > Show Missing Catalog Assignments
**Command:** AEMISSINGCATREPORT

The **Missing Catalog Data** tool is used to mark the components in the active drawing that do not have catalog data. To mark the components in the drawing that do not have catalog data, open the drawing and choose the **Missing Catalog Data** tool from the **Schematic** panel of the **Reports** tab; the **Show Missing Catalog Asssignments** dialog box will be displayed, as shown in Figure 9-15.

Show Missing Catalog Assignments

Show — Active drawing - show

Report — Drawing or project-wide

Cancel

*Figure 9-15 The* ***Show Missing Catalog Assignments*** *dialog box*

In this dialog box, if you choose the **Show** button, the dialog box will disappear and the diamond shaped temporary graphics will be displayed around the components for which catalog data is not available, refer to Figure 9-16. You can choose **View > Redraw** from the menu bar to remove graphics displayed.

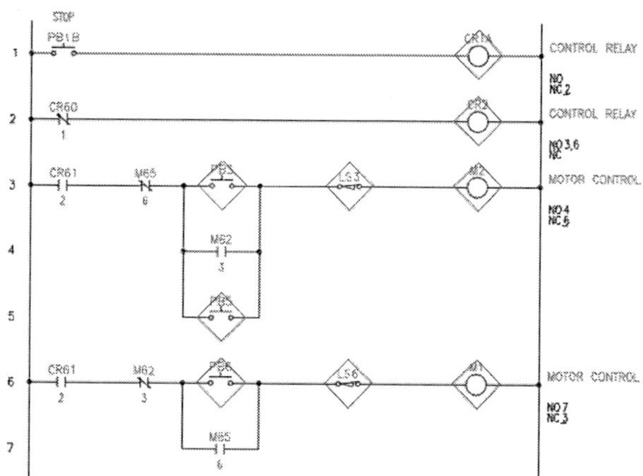


*Figure 9-16 Temporary graphics displayed*

If you choose the **Report** button, the **Schematic Reports** dialog box will be displayed with the **Missing Bill of Material** option selected in the **Report Name** area. The options in this dialog box are already discussed earlier in the chapter.

## Generating Component Cross-Reference Report

**Ribbon:** Schematic > Edit Components > Component Cross-Reference drop-down > Component Cross Reference
**Toolbar:** ACE:Cross-Reference > Component Cross Reference
**Menu:** Components > Cross-Reference > Component Cross Reference
**Command:** AEXREF

The **Component Cross-Reference** tool is used to display the cross-reference report on related parent and child contacts. To display the cross-reference report on related parent and child contacts, choose the **Component Cross Reference** tool from the **Component Cross-Reference** drop-down in the **Edit Components** panel of the **Schematic** tab, refer to Figure 9-17; the **Component Cross-Reference** dialog box will be displayed, as shown in Figure 9-18.

In this dialog box, by default, the **Active drawing (all)** radio button in the **Run Cross-reference on:** area is selected. Next, choose the **Cross-reference** button; the **Cross Reference Report** dialog box will be displayed that shows the cross-reference information of the components in the active drawing. If you want to check the cross-reference information of individual components, select the **Active Drawing (pick)** radio button and select the **Project** radio button if you want to check the cross-reference information of the components in the project. If you choose the **Exception** button, the **Error Exception Report** will be displayed that shows the list of parent components that do not have child contacts as well as the child contacts that do not have the parent component.

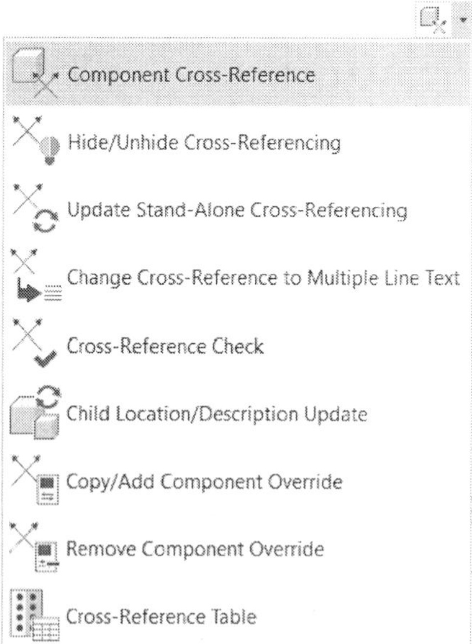


***Figure 9-17** The **Component Cross-Reference** drop-down*

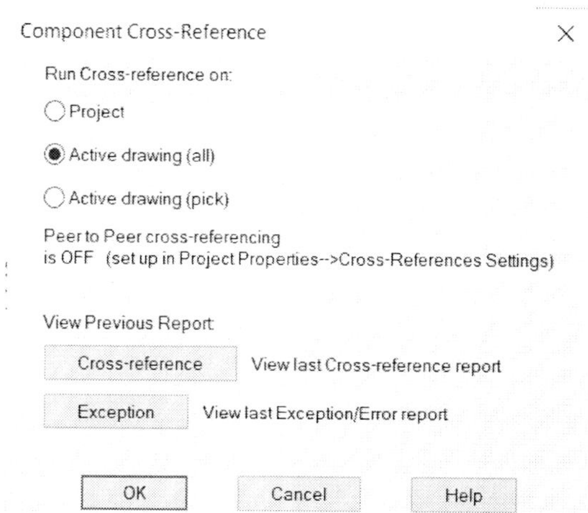


*Figure 9-18 The* ***Component Cross-Reference*** *dialog box*

# UNDERSTANDING THE Report Generator DIALOG BOX

The **Report Generator** dialog box displays the result of the report selected from the **Report Name** area of the **Schematic Reports** dialog box. The **Report Generator** dialog box shown in Figure 9-19 displays the report when the **Bill of Material** option is chosen in the **Report Name** area of the **Schematic Reports** dialog box, refer to Figure 9-1. Note that the options, which will be available in this dialog box, depend upon the options chosen in the **Report Name** area of the **Schematic Reports** dialog box. Using the **Report Generator** dialog box, you can change the format of a report, place report in a drawing, edit report, and save report to an external file. The different areas and options of the **Report Generator** dialog box are discussed next.

Report Generator

Project Bill Of Material for all locations (23 records)

| TAGS | QTY | SUB | CATALOG | MFG | DESCRIPTION |
|---|---|---|---|---|---|
| CB311 | 7 | | EGH3015FFG | EATON | |
| CB313 | | | | | |
| CB322 | | | | | |
| CB324 | | | | | |
| CB326 | | | | | |
| CB328 | | | | | |
| CB330 | | | | | |
| CR101 | 6 | | 700-P200A1 | AB | P TYPE ELECTRICALLY HELD RELAY, 4 POLE, AC COIL, CONVERTIBLE CONT |
| CR105 | | | | | TYPE P |
| CR106 | | | | | 120VAC |
| CR67 | | | | | 2 NO |
| CR71 | | | | | 115-120VAC 60Hz / 110VAC 50Hz COIL, RATING: 10A, OPEN TYPE RELAY |
| CR72 | | | | | |
| CR406 | 3 | | 700-P200A1 | AB | P TYPE ELECTRICALLY HELD RELAY, 4 POLE, AC COIL, CONVERTIBLE CONT |
| CR407 | | | | | TYPE P |
| CR408 | | | | | 120VAC |
| | | | | | 2 NO |

Header: Time/Date — Add — First section only; Title Line — Add — First section only; Project Lines — Add — First section only; Column Labels — Add — First section only

Breaks: Add page breaks; Special breaks; Installation/Location; Add Special break values to header

Squeeze 1 2 3; Add blanks between entries; Sort; User Post; Change Report Format

Edit Mode | Put on Drawing | Save to File | Print | Close | Help | Wide>

*Figure 9-19 The* ***Report Generator*** *dialog box*

## Header Area

The options in the **Header** area are used to add information to the report header. This area consists of the **Time/Date**, **Title Line**, **Project Lines**, and **Column Labels** options. Select the **Add** check box adjacent to these options to add the corresponding header information in the report. By default, the **Add** check box is clear. The **First section only** check box will be activated only if you select the **Add** check box adjacent to it and any of the check boxes from the **Breaks** area. Select the **First section only** check box to display the header information only at the top of the first section only.

## Breaks Area

The options in the **Breaks** area are used to add breaks in the report. In this area, you can select the options for page breaks or special breaks in a report. Also, you can break a report into sections based on the options that you will select. You can select only one check box at a time from this area. Select the **Add page breaks** check box to add breaks to a report. The **Special breaks** check box is used to add special breaks to the report. When you select the **Special breaks** check box, the drop-down list below this check box as well as the **Add Special break values to header** check box will be activated. Also, the report will be divided into different sections based on the special break that you select from the drop-down list. Select this check box; special break values will be added to the header of the report that depends on the option that you select from the drop-down list. Clear this check box to remove special break values from the header of the report.

## Squeeze

The **Squeeze** check box is used to reduce the width of the report that is listed in the **Report Generator** dialog box. By default, the **Squeeze** check box is selected. If you clear this check box, the width of the report will be increased. Three radio buttons are available adjacent to the **Squeeze** check box. Select the **1** radio button for the maximum squeezing of the report. Select the **3** radio button for minimum squeezing of the report. By default, the **2** radio button is selected. As a result, the report is moderately squeezed.

## Add blanks between entries

The **Add blanks between entries** check box is used to add a blank line between the entries of the report.

## Sort

The **Sort** button is used to sort the report. To do so, choose the **Sort** button; the **Sort** dialog box will be displayed, refer to Figure 9-20. Select the required options from the **Primary sort**, **Secondary sort**, **Third sort**, and **Fourth sort** drop-down lists and choose the **OK** button; the report will be sorted.

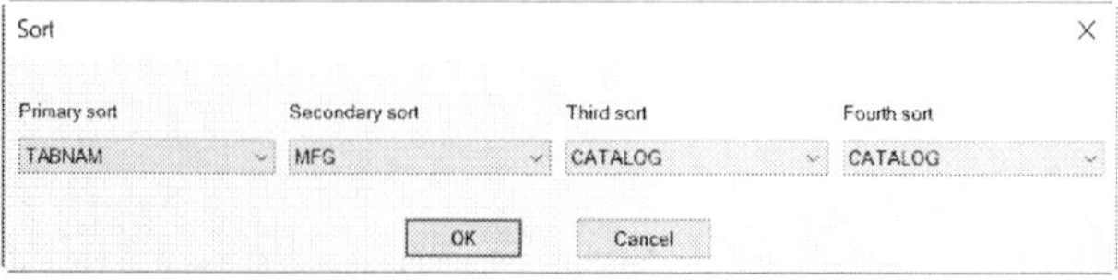


***Figure 9-20** The **Sort** dialog box*

**Note**

*The options in the **Primary sort**, **Secondary sort**, **Third sort**, and **Fourth sort** drop-down lists and other options of the **Sort** dialog box depend on the report name that you have chosen from the **Report Name** area of the **Schematic Reports** dialog box.*

## User Post

The **User Post** button is used to run an AutoLISP routine against the generated report and it returns the results to the **Report Generator** dialog box. To run an AutoLISP routine against the report, choose the **User Post** button; the **Report Data Post-processing Options** dialog box will be displayed, as shown in Figure 9-21.

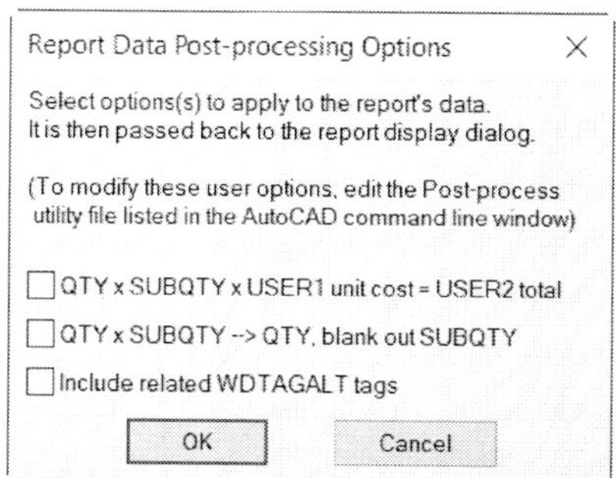


***Figure 9-21*** *The **Report Data Post-processing Options** dialog box*

When you select any of the check boxes in this dialog box and then choose the **OK** button, the LISP routine will be executed against the data and then the **Report Generator** dialog box will be displayed.

**Note**

*The options in the **Report Data Post-processing Options** dialog box depend on the option that you choose from the **Report Name** area of the **Schematic Reports** dialog box.*

## Change Report Format

The **Change Report Format** button is used to change data fields and their order in the report. Also, this button is used to change the field name or justification of columns in the report to match the column settings. To change the data fields and their order in the report, choose the **Change Report Format** button from the **Report Generator** dialog box; the **### Data Fields to Report** dialog box will be displayed, as shown in Figure 9-22. Note that the prefix of the **Data Fields to Report** dialog box will change according to the option selected from the **Report Name** area of the **Schematic Reports** dialog box. The dialog box shown in Figure 9-22 will be displayed when you select the **Bill of Material** option from the **Report Name** area of the **Schematic Reports** dialog box. The options in this dialog box are discussed later in this chapter.

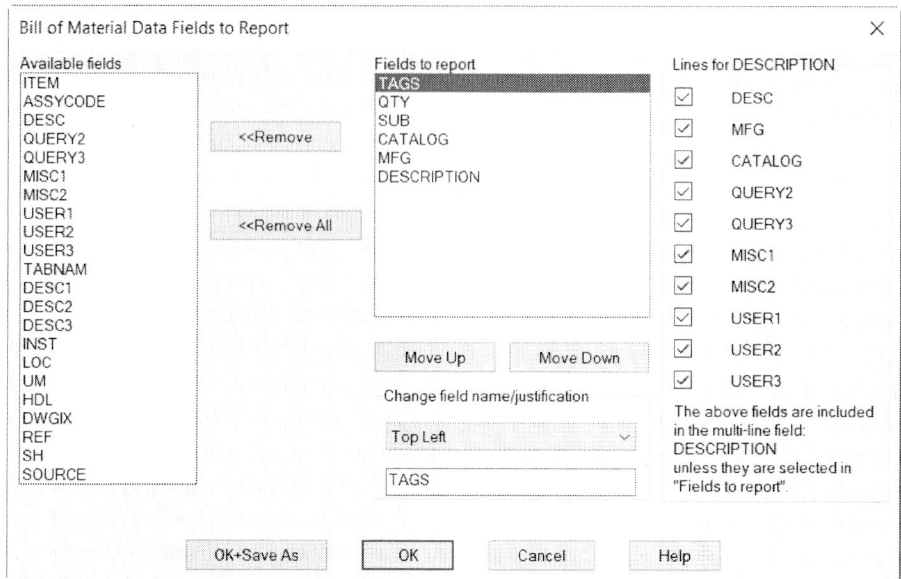


*Figure 9-22 The **Bill of Material Data Fields to Report** dialog box*

## Edit Mode

The **Edit Mode** button is used to edit a report before you insert it into the drawing. To do so, choose the **Edit Mode** button from the **Report Generator** dialog box; the **Edit Report** dialog box will be displayed. In this dialog box, you can edit, delete, and move the data up and down in the report. Also, you can add new lines above or below the selected line from the catalog lookup table in the report. Note that the options in this dialog box depend on the option chosen from the **Report Name** area of the **Schematic Reports** dialog box. The options in this dialog box are discussed later in this chapter.

## Put on Drawing

The **Put on Drawing** button is used to display a report in tabular form in a drawing. To do so, choose the **Put on Drawing** button; the **Table Generation Setup** dialog box will be displayed, as shown in Figure 9-23. Specify the required options in this dialog box and choose the **OK** button to place the table in the drawing. The options in this dialog box are discussed later in this chapter. Note that the **Put on Drawing** button will not be available if you choose the **Wire Label** option from the **Report Name** area of the **Schematic Reports** dialog box.

## Save to File

The **Save to File** button is used to save the report to a file. To do so, choose the **Save to File** button; the **Save Report to File** dialog box will be displayed, as shown in Figure 9-24. Using this dialog box, you can save report in multiple formats of output files such as ASCII, Excel, Access database, XML, and comma delimited. The options in this dialog box are discussed later in this chapter.

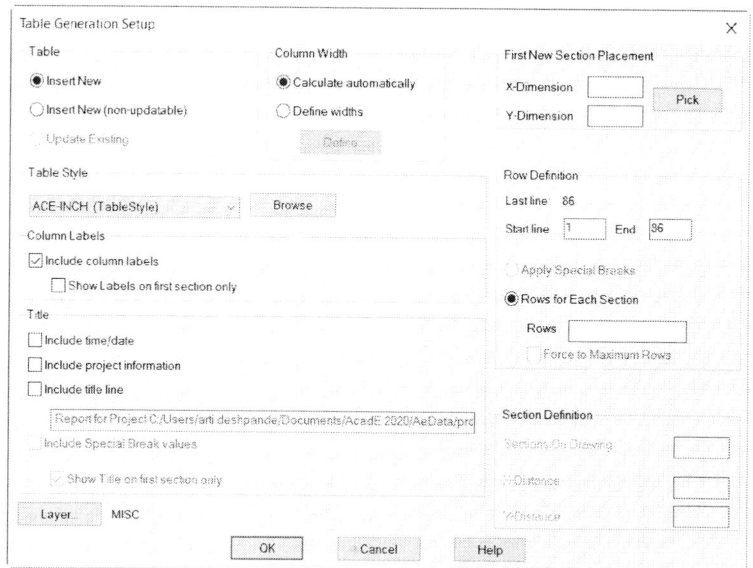


*Figure 9-23 The **Table Generation Setup** dialog box*

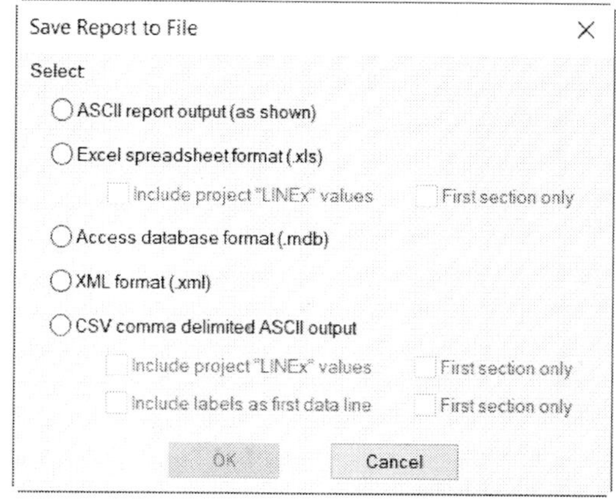


*Figure 9-24 The **Save Report to File** dialog box*

## Print

The **Print** button is used to print reports from the **Report Generator** dialog box. To do so, choose the **Print** button; the **Print** dialog box will be displayed. Specify the required settings of the printer in this dialog box and choose the **OK** button; the report will be printed.

## Wide>

The **Wide>** button is used to increase the width of the **Report Generator** dialog box.

## Surf

The **Surf** button will be available in the **Report Generator** dialog box only when you choose the **Missing Bill of Material** option from the **Report Name** area of the **Schematic Reports** dialog box. This button is used to trace the symbols that cause errors. To do so, choose the **Surf** button; the **Surf** dialog box will be displayed, as shown in Figure 9-25. The options in this dialog box have already been discussed in Chapter 6.

## Pin chart Area

The **Pin chart** area will be available in the **Report Generator** dialog box only when you choose the **Connector Plug** option from the **Report Name** area of the **Schematic Reports** dialog box. The options in this area are discussed next.

### on

The **on** radio button is used to set a chart for pin numbers. To do so, select the **on** radio button; the **Pin Chart** dialog box will be displayed, as shown in Figure 9-26. The information that you set in the **Pin Chart** dialog box will be displayed in the report. The options in this dialog box are discussed next.

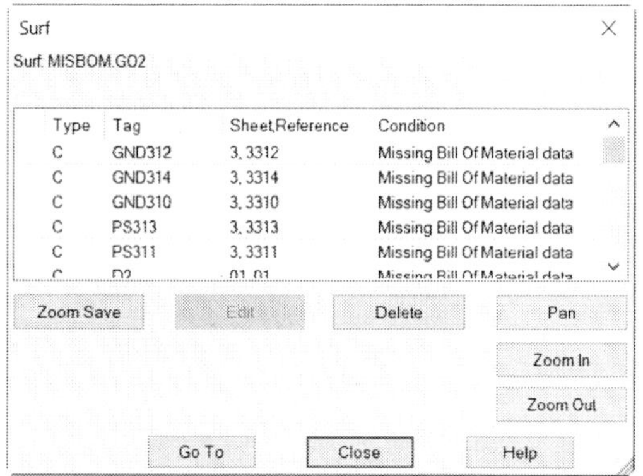


*Figure 9-25 The **Surf** dialog box*

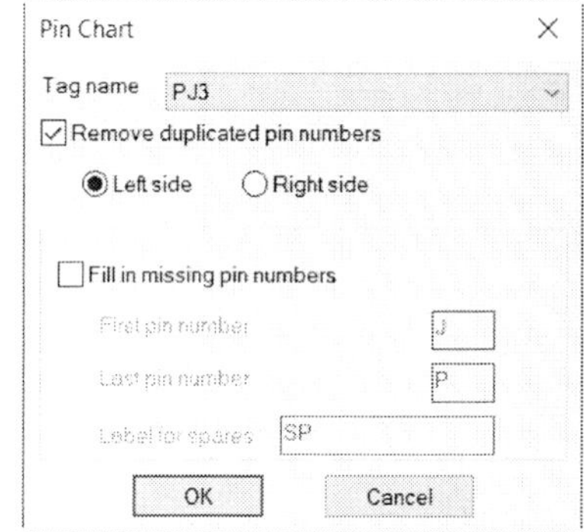


*Figure 9-26 The **Pin Chart** dialog box*

#### Tag name

Select the tag name of the required component from the **Tag name** drop-down list. The selected tag name will be displayed in the report.

#### Remove duplicated pin numbers

The **Remove duplicated pin numbers** check box is used to remove the duplicate pin number of the selected plug from the report. By default, this check box is selected. If you clear this check box, the **Left side** and **Right side** radio buttons will not be available.

By default, the **Left side** radio button is selected and is used to display the wiring information that is available on the left side of the pin symbol.

Select the **Right side** radio button to display the wiring information available on the right of the pin symbol.

#### Fill in missing pin numbers

Select the **Fill in missing pin numbers** check box to recognize the additional pin numbers that are not defined in the schematic drawing for spare pin connections. On selecting this check box, the **First pin number**, **Last pin number**, and **Label for spares** edit boxes will be activated. Enter the first and last pin numbers in the **First pin number** edit box and the **Last pin number** edit box, respectively.

Enter the required label for spares in the **Label for spares** edit box to display a text string under the **WIRENO** column in the report.

After specifying the required values in the **Pin Chart** dialog box, choose the **OK** button; the report displayed in the **Report Generator** dialog box will be changed accordingly.

### off

By default, the **off** radio button on the right of **Pin chart** in the **Report Generator** dialog box is selected. As a result, the **Pin Chart** dialog box will not be displayed and you will not be able to set a pin chart.

## Internal/External codes left/right

The **Internal/External codes left/right** check box will be available in the **Report Generator** dialog box only if you choose the **Terminal Plan** option from the **Report Name** area of the **Schematic Reports** dialog box. When you select this check box, the **E-left**, **I-left**, **E-right**, **I-right** radio buttons will be activated. "I" indicates internal codes and "E" indicates external codes on the wire connection. If you select any one of these radio buttons, all internal or external connections on the left or right side of the wire connection will be displayed in the **Report Generator** dialog box and the report displayed in this dialog box will be sorted accordingly.

## Plug/Male side, Jack/Female side, Show All

The **Plug/Male side**, **Jack/Female side**, and **Show All** radio buttons will be available in the **Report Generator** dialog box only if you select the **Connector Detail** option from the **Report Name** area of the **Schematic Reports** dialog box. The **Plug/Male side**, **Jack/Female side**, and **Show All** radio buttons are used to filter the report displayed in the **Report Generator** dialog box. Select the **Plug/Male side** radio button to display only the plug/male side of a connector in the report. Select the **Jack/Female side** radio button to display only the jack/female side of a connector in the report. Select the **Show All** radio button to display both the plug/male side and jack/female side of a connector in the report.

## Edit Wire Label and Edit Cable Label

The **Edit Wire Label** and **Edit Cable Label** buttons will be available in the **Report Generator** dialog box only if you choose the **Wire Label** option from the **Report Name** area of the **Schematic Reports** dialog box. These buttons are used to modify a report before inserting it into the drawing. Also, using these buttons, you can edit and delete lines, move data up and down in the report, and add new lines above or below the selected line from a catalog lookup table in the report. To edit a report, choose the **Edit Wire Label** or **Edit Cable Label** button; the **Edit Report** dialog box will be displayed. The options in this dialog box are discussed later in this chapter.

# CHANGING REPORT FORMATS

You can change the format of the report displayed in the **Report Generator** dialog box. The **Change Report Format** button in the **Report Generator** dialog box is used to change data fields and their order in the report. Also, by using this button, you can change the name of a field or the justification of the columns in the report. The column label justification changes to match the column setting. To change the format of a report, choose the **Change Report Format** button from the **Report Generator** dialog box; the **XXX Data Fields to Report** dialog box will be displayed, refer to Figure 9-27. Note that XXX stands for prefix to the name of the **Data Fields to Report** dialog box and will depend upon the option chosen from the **Report Name** area of the **Schematic Reports** dialog box. The different options and areas in this dialog box are discussed next.

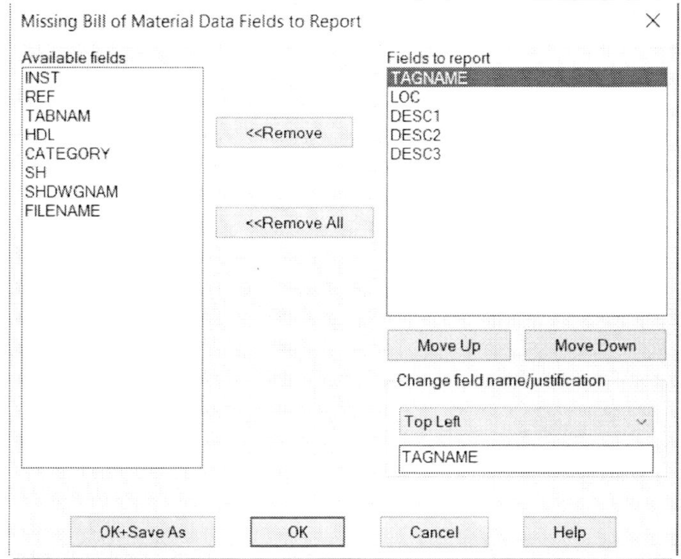


*Figure 9-27 The **Missing Bill of Material Data Fields to Report** dialog box*

## Available fields Area

The **Available fields** area consists of fields that are available for formatting a report. This area is used to list the user-defined attributes. When you select a field from this area, the field will automatically move to the **fields to report** area. You will learn about adding fields in this area using the **User Attributes** tool in the later section.

## Fields to report Area

The **Fields to report** area displays the list of fields to be displayed in the report.

### <<Remove

Choose the **<<Remove** button to remove the selected field from the **Fields to report** area.

### <<Remove All

Choose the **<<Remove All** button to remove all the fields from the **Fields to report** area.

## Move Up

Choose the **Move Up** button to move the selected field one step up in the **Fields to report** area.

## Move Down

Choose the **Move Down** button to move the selected field one step down in the **Fields to report** area.

## Change field name/justification Area

In the **Change field name/justification** area, you can change the field name as well as the justification of the fields. This area consists of the drop-down list that includes the justification styles and an edit box that is used for changing the name of the field.

Select the required option from the drop-down list to justify the fields of any column or a column label vertically and horizontally.

To rename the existing field name that is displayed in the **Fields to report** area, select the field name from the **Fields to report** area; the field will automatically be displayed in the edit box located below the drop-down list in the **Change field name/justification** area. Next, enter the new field name in the edit box; the selected field name will be changed in the **Fields to report** area. For example, if you select the MFG from the **Fields to report** area, the selected field name will automatically be displayed in the edit box located below the drop-down list of the **Change field name/justification** area. Now, enter **USER1** in the edit box and click on the **Fields to report** area; MFG in the **Fields to report** area will get changed to USER1. Also, the name of the check box displayed in the **Lines for DESCRIPTION** area will be changed. In this case, the check box of MFG will get changed to USER1.

## Lines for DESCRIPTION Area

The **Lines for DESCRIPTION** area will be available in the **Data Fields to Report** dialog box only when you choose the **Bill of Material** option from the **Report Name** area of the **Schematic Reports** dialog box. The **Lines for DESCRIPTION** area has the following check boxes: **DESC**, **MFG**, **CATALOG**, **QUERY2**, **QUERY3**, **MISC1**, **MISC2**, **USER1**, **USER2**, and **USER3**. These fields will be included in the multi-line field description of the report, only if they are present in the **Fields to report** area and the respective check boxes are selected. If you clear the check box present in the **Lines for DESCRIPTION** area, the respective field will not be included in the **Description** column of a report.

## OK

When you choose the **OK** button, the changes made in the **Data Fields to Report** dialog box are reflected in the report and the changes in the format are saved in the default format file *bom.set* that is saved in the user folder.

## Adding Fields Using the User Attributes Tool

**Ribbon:** Reports > Miscellaneous > User Attributes
**Toolbar:** ACE:Main Electrical 2 > Schematic Reports drop-down > User Defined Attribute List
**Menu:** Projects > Reports > User Defined Attribute List
**Command:** AEUDA

As discussed in the previous section, the **Available fields** area in the **Data Fields to Report** dialog box consists of fields that are available for formatting a report. You can increase the fields in this area by using the **User Attributes** tool. This tool is used to create a text file in which you can add user defined attribute fields. These fields can then be included in a report to enhance it using the options in the **Data Fields to Report** dialog box.

To add fields in the **Available Field** area, choose the **User Attributes** tool from the **Miscellaneous** panel of the **Reports** tab; the **User Defined Attribute List: unnamed.wda** dialog box will be displayed, as shown in Figure 9-28. Different columns and options in this dialog box are discussed next.

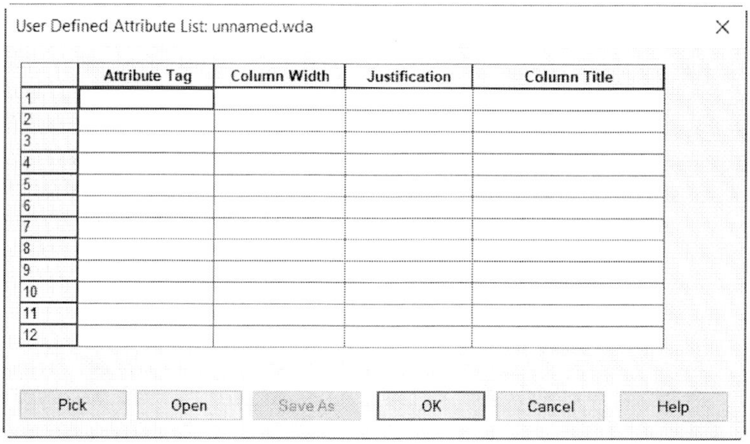

*Figure 9-28 The **User Defined Attribute List: unnamed.wda** dialog box*

### Attribute Tag Column

This column contains a number of cells where you can enter user-defined attributes one by one. If you right-click on a cell, a shortcut menu will be displayed with four options: **Pick**, **Cut**, **Copy**, and **Paste**. Choose the **Pick** option to pick an attribute from an active drawing. Similarly, choose the **Cut**, **Copy**, and **Paste** options to cut, copy, and paste the user-defined attributes from one cell to another in this column. Note that you need to enter an attribute in this column to activate other cells in the column such as **Column Width**, **Justification**, and **Column Title** in a row.

### Column Width Column

After you enter an attribute in the **Attribute Tag** column, enter the column width value in the respective cell of this column. If this column is left blank, the column width of the attribute will be restricted to 24 characters.

## Justification Column

After you enter an attribute in the **Attribute Tag** column, click on the **Justification** column; a drop-down list will be displayed. It consists of options such as, **Top Left**, **Top Center**, **Top Right**, and so on. Select the required option from it to justify the attribute in the report. If this column is left blank, by default, the **Top Left** option will be selected.

## Column Title Column

This column is used to enter a column title for an attribute. It acts as a header for the attribute field in the **Report Generator** dialog box. If you right-click on a cell, a shortcut menu will be displayed. It consists of three options: **Cut**, **Copy**, and **Paste**. These options are used to cut, copy, and paste the column titles from one cell to another.

## Pick

Choose this button to pick an attribute from the active drawing. Note that this button is activated only when any cell from the **Attribute Tag** column is selected.

## Open

Choose this button to open an existing user defined attribute list file. This file is opened in the **User Defined Attribute List: ###.wda** dialog box. Note that ### stands for the existing file name. You can then edit this file using the options discussed above.

## Save As

Choose this button to save the user defined attribute list file with the extension .wda. The default location to save this file is *C:\Users\User name\Documents\Acade 2022\AeData\Proj\ active project name.* Note that the attributes added in this dialog box will be added in the **Available fields** area of the **Data fields to Report** dialog box only when you save this file at the default location mentioned above with the same file name as that of the active project.

Next, generate a report as discussed earlier, refer to Figure 9-19. In the **Report Generator** dialog box, choose the **Change Report Format** button; the **Data Fields to Report** dialog box will be displayed. You will notice that the attributes added in the user-defined attribute list file are available in the **Available Fields** area of this dialog box.

# PLACING REPORTS IN THE DRAWING

After generating the desired report from the **Report Generator** dialog box, if you want to place the generated report in your drawing, choose the **Put on Drawing** button from the **Report Generator** dialog box; the **Table Generation Setup** dialog box will be displayed, refer to Figure 9-23. Different options in this dialog box are discussed next.

## Table Area

The **Table** area consists of three radio buttons: **Insert New**, **Insert New (non-updatable)**, and **Update Existing**. The **Insert New** radio button and the **Insert New (non-updatable)** radio button will be activated if a matching table is not already inserted into the drawing. The **Insert New (non-updatable)** radio button and the **Update Existing** radio button will be activated only if a matching table exists in the drawing. The options in this area are discussed next.

### Insert New

The **Insert New** radio button is used to insert a new table into the drawing.

### Insert New (non-updatable)

The **Insert New (non-updatable)** radio button is used to insert a non-updatable table. This table will not be recognized the next time a report is ready for insertion in the drawing.

### Update Existing

The **Update Existing** radio button is used to update an existing table with current information.

## Column Width Area

In the **Column Width** area, you can specify the method of calculating the width of columns. The options in this area are discussed next.

### Calculate automatically

By default, the **Calculate automatically** radio button is selected and calculates the width of a column automatically.

### Define widths

The **Define widths** radio button is used to define the width of a column manually. When you select this radio button, the **Define** button will become available. Choose the **Define** button; the **Column Widths** dialog box will be displayed, as shown in Figure 9-29. In this dialog box, select the required label from the list; the **Width** edit box and the **Update** button will become available. Also, the width of the selected label will be displayed in the **Width** edit box. Now, you can edit the width displayed in the **Width** edit box. To update this width in the list, choose the **Update** button. Next, choose the **OK** button to save the changes made in this dialog box and to return to the **Table Generation Setup** dialog box. Note that if the text string is longer than the column width, the text will wrap.

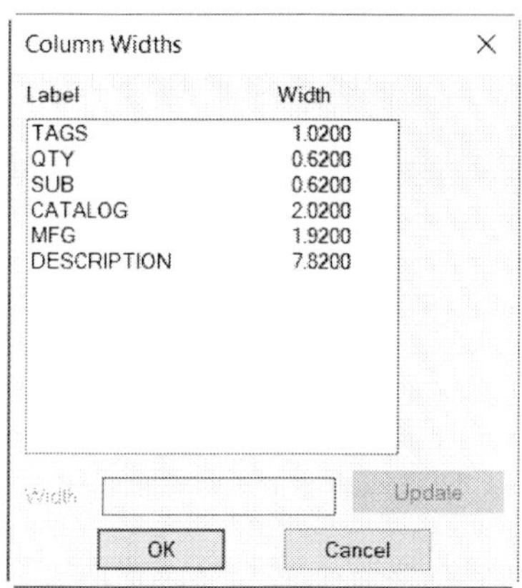


*Figure 9-29 The* ***Column Widths*** *dialog box*

## First New Section Placement Area

The **First New Section Placement** area is used to specify the location for placing table in the drawing by entering the X and Y coordinates in the **X-Dimension** and **Y-Dimension** edit boxes, respectively. Alternatively, you can choose the **Pick** button located next to these edit boxes to select the location for placing the table.

## Column Labels Area

The **Column Labels** area is used to specify whether to include column headings, text color of column headings, and labels only in the first section of the table. This area consists of the **Include column labels** check box and the **Show Labels on first section only** check box. In this area, the **Include column labels** check box is selected by default.

## Row Definition Area

The options in the **Row Definition** area are used to specify the start and end lines, number of rows in a table, number of rows for each section, special breaks in the table, and so on. The options in this area are discussed next.

### Apply Special Breaks

The **Apply Special Breaks** radio button is used to break the sections of a table according to the type of break such as manufacturer, installation/location, and so on selected in the **Report Generator** dialog box. This radio button will be activated only when you select the **Special breaks** check box from the **Report Generator** dialog box.

### Rows for Each Section

By default, the **Rows for Each Section** radio button is selected. As a result, the **Rows** edit box is active. Specify the maximum number of rows for each section of a table in the **Rows** edit box.

### Force to Maximum Rows

The **Force to Maximum Rows** check box will be activated only when you enter the number of rows in the **Rows** edit box. If you select the **Force to Maximum Rows** check box, blank lines will be added at the end of each section of the table until the number of rows become equal to the number of rows specified in the **Rows** edit box.

## Section Definition Area

The **Section Definition** area will be activated only when you enter the number of rows in the **Rows** edit box. In this area, you can specify the number of sections in the drawing as well as the X and Y distance between sections. If you enter **1** in the **Sections On Drawing** edit box, the **X-Distance** and **Y-Distance** edit boxes will not be activated.

### Sections On Drawing

In the **Sections On Drawing** edit box, you can specify the maximum number of sections of a table in a single drawing of a report. If this edit box is left blank, there will be unlimited number of sections in one drawing.

### X-Distance

In the **X Distance** edit box, you can specify the distance from the end of one table section to the beginning of the next table section in the x direction.

### Y-Distance

In the **Y-Distance** edit box, you can specify the distance from the end of one table section to the beginning of the next table section in the y direction.

## Title Area

In the **Title** area, you can specify whether to include time, date, project information, title line, special breaks, title color of the text, and so on in the title of a table. The options in this area are discussed next.

### Include time/date

Select the **Include time/date** check box to display time and date in a table. By default, this check box is clear.

### Include project information

Select the **Include project information** check box to display the project description lines above a table. Note that only the description lines that you have selected from the **Project Descriptions** dialog box will be displayed in the table. By default, this check box is clear.

**Note**

*The **Project Description** dialog box will be displayed if you right-click on the project name and choose the **Descriptions** option from the shortcut menu.*

### Include title line

Select the **Include title line** check box to display the title of the report above the table. On doing so, you can also modify the title of the default report by entering the text in the edit box next to this check box. By default, this check box is clear.

### Include Special Break values

The **Include Special Break values** check box will be activated only when you select the **Special breaks** check box from the **Report Generator** dialog box. The **Include Special Break values** check box is used to include the special breaks for the title line of each section of a table. By default, this check box is selected. As a result, special breaks for the title line of each section of a table will be displayed irrespective of whether the **Show Title on first section only** check box is selected. If you clear the **Include Special Break values** check box, no special breaks will be included in the table.

### Show Title on first section only

The **Show Title on first section only** check box is used to show the title only in the first section of a multi section table instead of all sections. By default, this check box is selected.

## Layer

The **Layer** button is used to specify a layer for the table on which a table will be created. To do so, choose the **Layer** button; the **Select Layer for Table** dialog box will be displayed, as shown in Figure 9-30. In this dialog box, the MISC layer name is selected by default and is displayed on the right of the **Layer** button. To change the default layer, select the layer name from the **Select Layer for Table** dialog box. Alternatively, enter the layer name in the **Layer Name** edit box and choose the **OK** button; the selected layer will be assigned to the table and layer name will be displayed on the right of the **Layer** button in the **Table Generation Setup** dialog box.

After specifying the required options in the **Table Generation Setup** dialog box, choose the **OK** button from this dialog box; you will be prompted to specify the insertion point for the table. Next, specify the insertion point for the table; the table will be inserted into the drawing. Following is the command sequence for inserting table into the drawing.

Specify the insertion point (Z=zoom down, R=realtime pan, S=object snap): *Enter Z to zoom out the table, Enter R for realtime pan, and enter S to use object snap mode.*

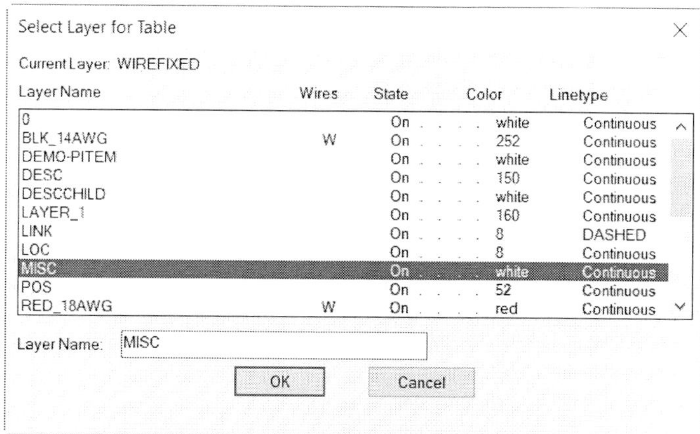


***Figure 9-30** The **Select Layer for Table** dialog box*

When you enter **Z** at the Command prompt, the table will zoom out.

When you enter **R** at the Command prompt, you can pan the table easily. To exit the realtime pan command, right-click and choose the **Exit** option.

When you enter **S** at the Command prompt, the table will use the object snap mode and you will be prompted to specify the insertion point for the table. Next, specify the insertion point; the table will be inserted in the drawing at the specified location. Also, the **Report Generator** dialog box will be displayed again.

## SAVING THE REPORT TO FILES

You can save the report to a file by using the **Save to File** button in the **Report Generator** dialog box. You can save reports in the following file formats: ASCII (*.rep*), Excel (*.xls*), Access (*.mdb*), XML (*.xml*), and CSV comma delimited (comma-separated value)(*.csv*). To save a report, choose the **Save to File** button from the **Report Generator** dialog box; the **Save Report to File** dialog box will be displayed, as shown in Figure 9-31. Next, select the radio button of the required format from the **Select** area; the **OK** button will be activated. Choose the **OK** button; the **Select file for report** dialog box will be displayed. Next, enter the file name in the **File name** edit box and specify the path or accept the default path and file name. The report type will automatically be displayed in the **Save as type** edit box. Next, choose the **Save** button to save the report; the **Optional Script File** dialog box will be displayed, as shown in Figure 9-32. In this dialog box, you can pass the report file to a script file, which will provide a link for post-processing the data or automatically pass it to another application. The options in the **Optional Script File** dialog box are discussed next.

**Note**

*The LINEx values can be included only in the Excel (.xls) and the CSV file formats by selecting the **Include project "LINEx" values** check box. In case of CSV file format, you can include the labels as the first data line by selecting the **Include labels as first data line** check box.*

Choose the **Close - No Script** button from the **Optional Script File** dialog box, if you do not want to pass the report file to a script file.

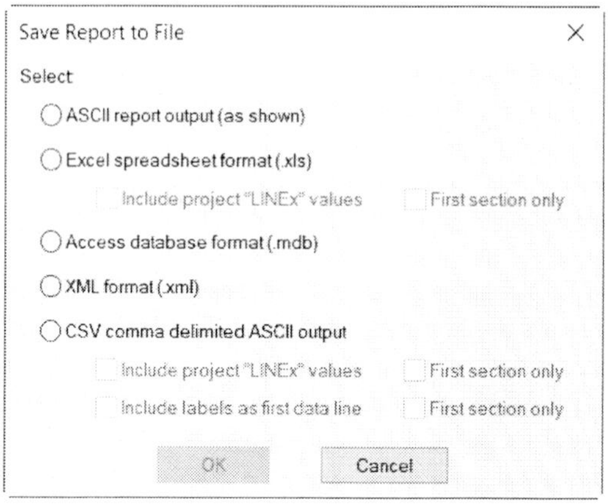

*Figure 9-31 The **Save Report to File** dialog box*

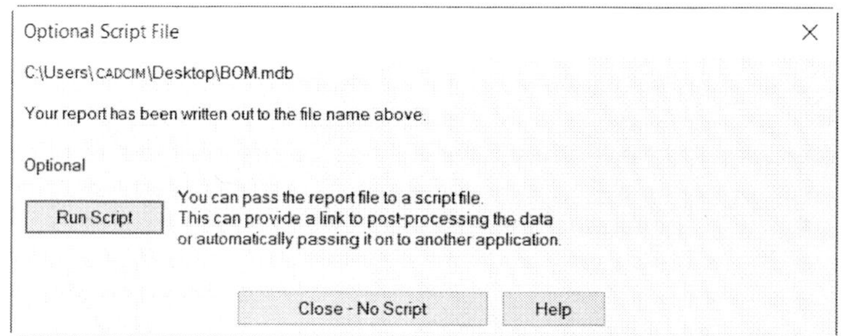


*Figure 9-32 The **Optional Script File** dialog box*

The **Run Script** button is used to pass the report file to a script file. To do so, choose the **Run Script** button; a dialog box containing the location and file name in the title bar will be displayed, as shown in Figure 9-33. Also, the report file is passed to a script file. As a result, the script file can be executed.

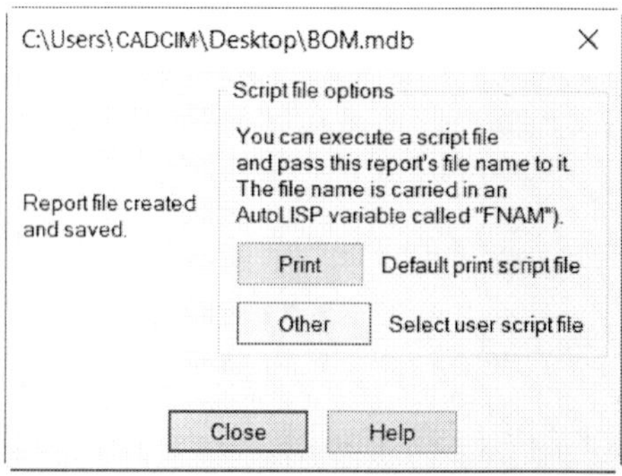


*Figure 9-33 The location and file name at the title bar of the dialog box*

Choose the **Print** button in this dialog box to print the default script file. When you choose the **Other** button, the **Select Script File** dialog box will be displayed, as shown in Figure 9-34. Select the script file and then choose the **Open** button; the script files will be opened.

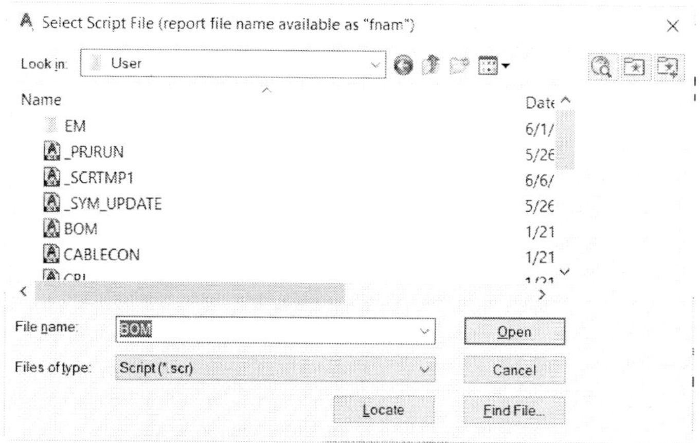


*Figure 9-34 The* ***Select Script File*** *dialog box*

Choose the **Close** button from the dialog box that has file name and location displayed at the title bar; you will return to the **Report Generator** dialog box.

# EDITING A REPORT

To edit a report before inserting it into the drawing, choose the **Edit Mode** button from the **Report Generator** dialog box; the **Edit Report** dialog box will be displayed, as shown in Figure 9-35. The options in this dialog box depend on the option chosen from the **Report Name** area of the **Schematic Reports** dialog box. The dialog box shown in Figure 9-35 will be displayed when you choose the **Missing Bill of Material** option from the **Report Name** area of the **Schematic Reports** dialog box.

**Note**

*When you choose the* ***Bill of Material*** *option from the* ***Report Name*** *area of the* ***Schematic Reports*** *dialog box, the* ***Add from Catalog*** *button will be available and the* ***Add New*** *button, the* ***Add Copy*** *button, the* ***Add as Subassembly item*** *check box, the* ***Move to Top*** *button, the* ***Move to Bottom*** *button, and the* ***Swap*** *button will not be available in the* ***Edit Report*** *dialog box.*

## New lines Area

In the **New lines** area, you can add new lines above or below the selected line or add them as subassembly of the selected line. The options in this area are discussed next.

### Add New

The **Add New** button is used to create a new line in the report.

### Add Copy

The **Add Copy** button is used to create the copy of the selected report line.

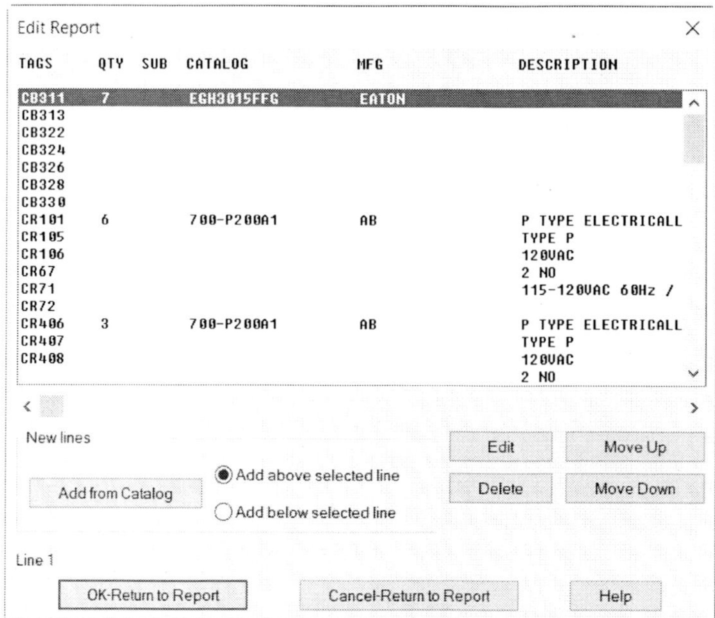

*Figure 9-35 The* ***Edit Report*** *dialog box*

## Add from Catalog

The **Add from Catalog** button will be available only when you choose the **Bill of Material** option from the **Report Name** area of the **Schematic Reports** dialog box. This button is used to add a catalog part from the Catalog Browser. To add a catalog part, choose the **Add from Catalog** button; the **Catalog Browser** dialog box will be displayed, refer to Figure 9-36. The options in the **Catalog Browser** dialog box have already been discussed in Chapter 5. Specify the required options in the **Catalog Browser** dialog box and then select the required catalog part number from the list displayed; the **OK** button will be activated. Choose the **OK** button; the selected catalog will be added to the list displayed in the **Edit Report** dialog box.

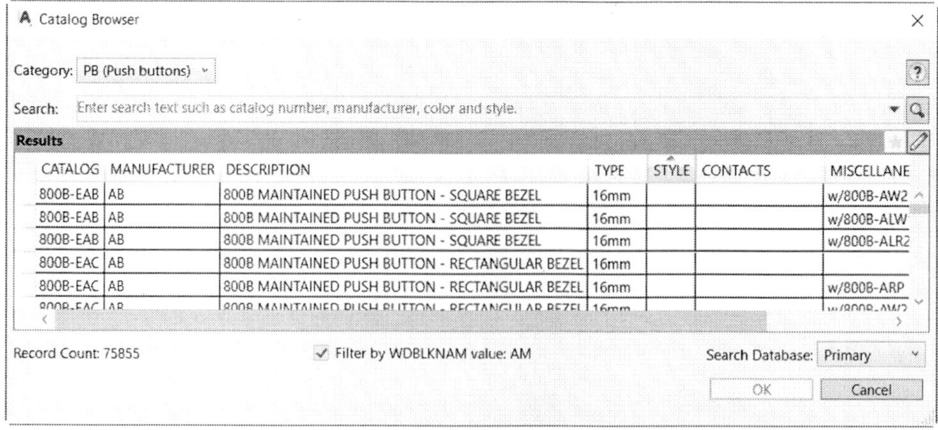

*Figure 9-36 The* ***Catalog Browser*** *dialog box*

## Add above selected line

The **Add above selected line** radio button is used to add the catalog part number above the line that you have selected from the list displayed in the **Edit Report** dialog box.

## Add below selected line

The **Add below selected line** radio button is used to add catalog part number below the line that you have selected from the list displayed in the **Edit Report** dialog box.

## Edit

The **Edit** button is used to edit the values of the selected line. On choosing this button, the **Edit Line x** dialog box will be displayed. In this dialog box, you can edit the values of the selected line and then choose the **OK** button to return to the **Edit Report** dialog box.

## Delete

The **Delete** button is used to delete the selected line(s). On choosing this button, the **Delete lines from report** message box will be displayed. Choose the **OK** button; the selected report line will be deleted. Note that you can select multiple lines by pressing CTRL or SHIFT.

## Move Up

Choose the **Move Up** button to move the selected line one step up.

## Move Down

Choose the **Move Down** button to move the selected line one step down.

## Move to Top

Choose the **Move to Top** button to move the selected line to the top of the report. Note that this button will not be available in the **Edit Report** dialog box if you choose the **Bill of Material** option from the **Report Name** area of the **Schematic Reports** dialog box.

## Move to Bottom

Choose the **Move to Bottom** button to move the selected line to the bottom of the report. This button will also not be available, if you choose the **Bill of Material** option from the **Report Name** area of the **Schematic Reports** dialog box.

## Swap

The **Swap** button is used to swap the description of the selected line. This button will not be available, if you choose the **Bill of Material** option from the **Report Name** area of the **Schematic Reports** dialog box.

## OK-Return to Report

Choose the **OK-Return to Report** button to retain the changes made in the **Edit Report** dialog box and to return to the **Report Generator** dialog box.

## Cancel-Return to Report

Choose the **Cancel-Return to Report** button to discard the changes made in the **Edit Report** dialog box and to return to the **Report Generator** dialog box.

# GENERATING PANEL REPORTS

| | |
|---|---|
| **Ribbon:** | Reports > Panel > Reports |
| **Toolbar:** | ACE:Panel Layout > Panel Reports or ACE:Panel Reports >Panel Reports |
| **Menu:** | Projects > Reports > Panel Reports |
| **Command:** | AEPANELREPORT |

Panel reports are similar to schematic reports, but they are limited to panel components, nameplates, and terminal footprint. Although schematic reports and panel reports are almost the same yet the difference lies between the two in component attributes. Schematic components use TAG1 as the attribute name, whereas panel footprints use P_TAG1 as the attribute name.

In AutoCAD Electrical, you can run multiple panel reports at a time. To run a panel report, choose the **Reports** tool from the **Panel** panel of the **Reports** tab; the **Panel Reports** dialog box will be displayed, as shown in Figure 9-37. In this dialog box, a list of reports is available in the **Report Name** area. You can extract the reports displayed in this area as per your requirement. The **Bill of Material** option in this area is chosen by default, as shown in Figure 9-37 and it is discussed next.

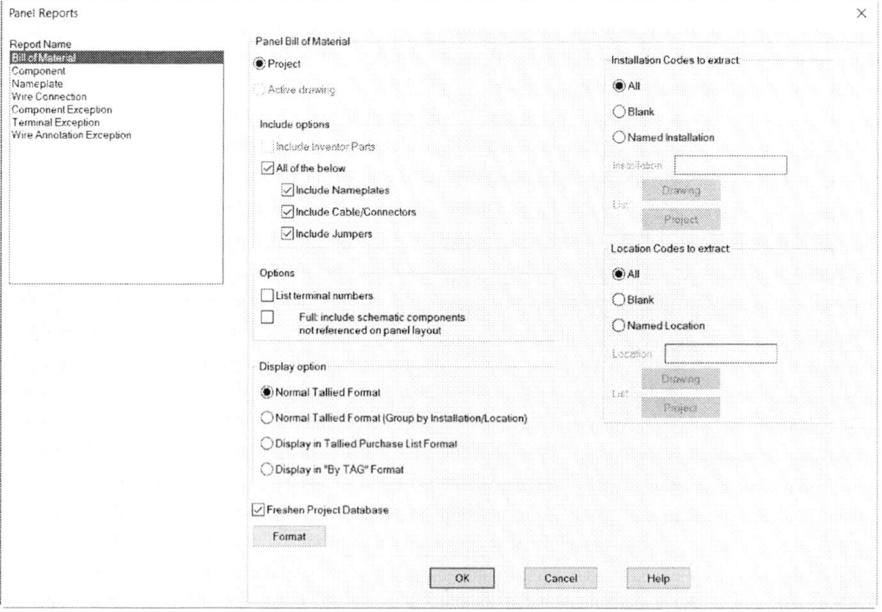


*Figure 9-37 The **Panel Reports** dialog box*

# Bill of Material Report

The **Bill of Material** report extracts information from panel components, terminal footprints, nameplates, and so on. The options displayed in the **Panel Reports** dialog box when the **Bill of Material** option is chosen are discussed next.

## Panel Bill of Material Area

In the **Panel Bill of Material** area, you can specify whether the report of the active project or active drawing is to be generated.

## Include options Area

This area is used to include the specified options in the report. The options in this area are discussed next.

### Include Nameplates

This check box is used to include the information about nameplate in the report.

### Include Cable/Connectors

This check box is used to include the cable/connectors information in the report.

### All of the below

The **All of the below** check box is used to include the information about nameplates, cable, connectors, and jumpers in the report.

### Include Jumpers

Select the **Include Jumpers** check box to include the information of jumpers in the report.

### Include Inventor Parts

The **Include Inventor Parts** check box is activated if the active project is linked to an inventor assembly. If you select this check box, the electrical components in the inventor assembly will also be included in the report. Note that the linked electrical components that are displayed in inventor assembly as well as in AutoCAD electrical drawing will not be repeated in the report.

## Options Area

This area is used to include the specified options in the report. The options in this area are discussed next.

### List terminal numbers

Select the **List terminal numbers** check box to list the tag ID of terminals and the combination of terminal numbers.

### Full: include schematic components not referenced on panel layout

The **Full: include schematic components not referenced on panel layout** check box is used to include the information of all schematic components that are not found on the panel layout in the report.

**Note**

*The options in the* ***Display option, Installation Codes to extract,*** *and* ***Location Codes to extract*** *areas as well as the* ***Freshen Project Database*** *check box and the* ***Format*** *button have been discussed earlier.*

Specify the required options in the **Panel Reports** dialog box and select the **Project** radio button, if it is not selected. Next, choose the **OK** button; the **Select Drawings to Process** dialog box will be displayed. In this dialog box, select the drawings to be processed and choose the **Process** button; the drawings will be transferred from the top list to the bottom list. Next, choose the **OK** button; the **Report Generator** dialog box will be displayed. The options in the **Report Generator** dialog box have been discussed earlier.

**Note**

*If you make changes in the current drawing and did not save it, then after choosing the* ***OK*** *button in the* ***Panel Reports*** *dialog box, the* ***QSAVE*** *message box will be displayed. Choose the* ***OK*** *button in this message box to save the current drawing; the* ***Report Generator*** *dialog box will be displayed.*

Now, to place the report table in the drawing, choose the **Put on Drawing** button from the **Report Generator** dialog box; the **Table Generation Setup** dialog box will be displayed. Specify the required settings in the **Table Generation Setup** dialog box and then choose the **OK** button from it; you will be prompted to specify the insertion point for the table. Next, specify the insertion point; the table will be inserted into the drawing. The options in the **Table Generation Setup** dialog box have been discussed earlier.

# GENERATING THE CUMULATIVE REPORT

| | |
|---|---|
| **Ribbon:** | Reports > Miscellaneous > Automatic Reports |
| **Toolbar:** | ACE:Main Electrical 2 > Schematic Reports > Automatic Report Selection or ACE:Schematic Reports > Automatic Report Selection |
| **Menu:** | Projects > Reports > Automatic Report Selection |
| **Command:** | AEAUTOREPORT |

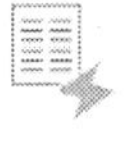

The **Automatic Reports** tool is used to generate multiple reports at a time. Also, this tool is used to run different reports at different stages. You can use this tool to automatically place the report tables on drawings or create a number of output files. To generate a report, choose the **Automatic Reports** tool from the **Miscellaneous** panel of the **Reports** tab; the **Automatic Report Selection** dialog box will be displayed, as shown in Figure 9-38. The options in this dialog box are discussed next.

## Report Name Area

The options in the **Report Name** area are used to select the type of report to be generated. This area contains a list of schematic and panel reports that are used for automatic generation of report. The **Schematic Report** area consists of options for generating schematic reports and the **Panel Report** area consists of options for generating panel reports.

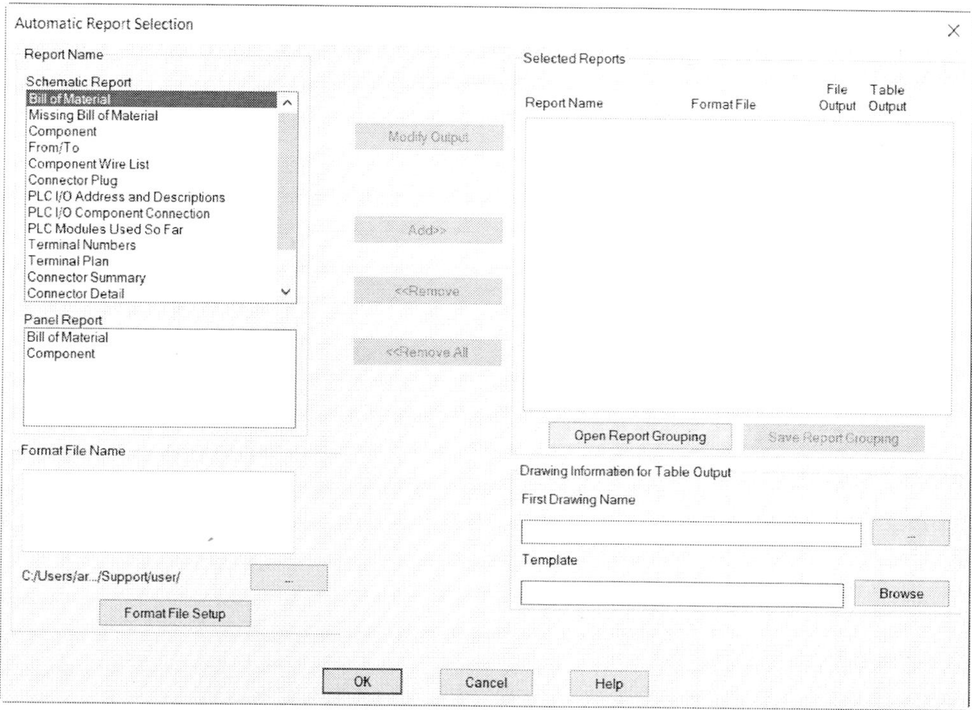


*Figure 9-38 The* ***Automatic Report Selection*** *dialog box*

## Format File Name Area

The **Format File Name** area displays a list of format files both for schematic and panel reports. The type of format file displayed in the **Format File Name** area depends on the type of report selected from the **Schematic Report** and **Panel Report** areas.

If a report type displayed in the **Schematic Report** or **Panel Report** area does not have a format file, choose the **Format File Setup** button from the **Format File Name** area; the **Report Format File Setup** dialog box will be displayed, as shown in Figure 9-39. Using this dialog box, you can create and save the format file for the selected report type. The options in the **Report Format File Setup** dialog box are discussed in the later section. Note that the path and location of the format file is displayed below the **Format File Name** area of the **Automatic Report Selection** dialog box. To change the directory of the format file displayed in the **Format File Name** area, choose the **Browse** button located on the right of the path and location of the format file in the **Automatic Report Selection** dialog box; the **Browse For Folder** dialog box will be displayed. Specify the name of the folder in the **Browse For Folder** dialog box. Next, choose the **OK** button in the **Browse For Folder** dialog box; the new path and location of the format file will be displayed in the **Format File Name** area.

## Add>>

The **Add>>** button is used to add the selected report name and format file to the **Selected Reports** area. This button will be activated only when the report name is selected from the **Report Name** area and its format file is selected from the **Format File Name** area at a time.

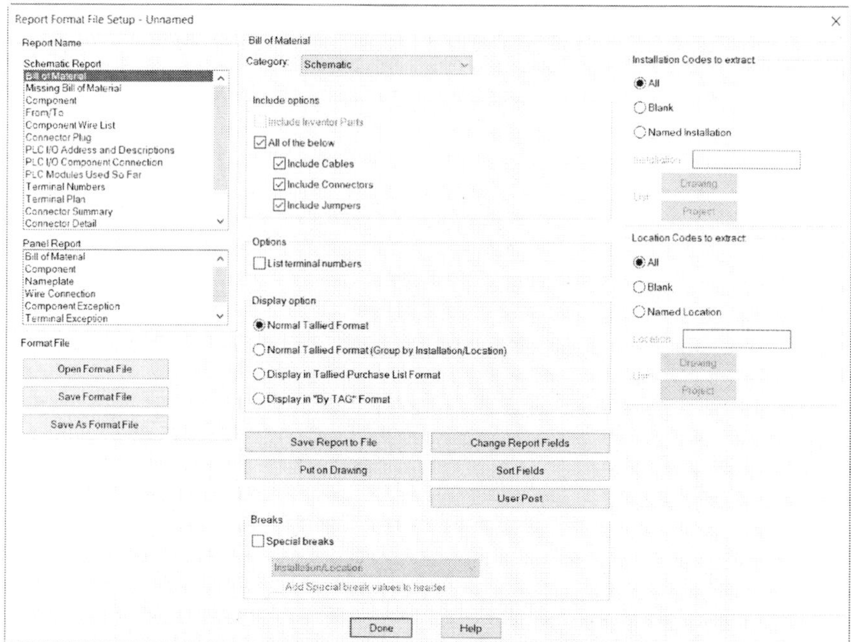


*Figure 9-39 The **Report Format File Setup** dialog box*

## <<Remove

This button is used to remove the selected report from the **Selected Reports** area.

## <<Remove All

This button is used to remove all reports from the **Selected Reports** area.

## Modify Output

The **Modify Output** button will be activated only if you choose the report name from the **Selected Reports** area. This button is used to change the type of output of the selected report name. To do so, choose the **Modify Output** button; the **Report Output Options** dialog box will be displayed. In this dialog box, you can specify whether to set report to the file output or to the table output. After specifying the type of output in the **Report Output Options** dialog box, choose the **OK** button; the output type will be changed in the **Selected Reports** area.

## Selected Reports Area

The **Selected Reports** area displays a list of reports that you want to generate. This area consists of report name, format file, file output, and table output. If 'x' is displayed under the **File Output** and **Table Output** columns, the portion will be considered for the automatic generation of report. If 'o' is displayed under the **File Output** and **Table Output** columns, the portion will not be considered for the automatic generation of report.

## Save Report Grouping

The **Save Report Grouping** button will be available only when a report file is displayed in the **Selected Reports** area. This button is used to save the file that consists of report name and format file. This saved file can be retrieved and used later to run the same group of reports on the active project or on any other project. To save a group of format files, choose the **Save Report Grouping** button; the **Enter name for Automatic Report Group file** dialog box will be displayed. In this dialog box, specify a name for the file in the **File name** edit box. By default, **.rgf* is displayed in the **Save as type** drop-down list. Next, choose the **Save** button from the **Enter name for Automatic Report Group file** dialog box to save the file and exit this dialog box.

## Open Report Grouping

The **Open Report Grouping** button is used to open the saved group file of report names and format files. On choosing the **Open Report Grouping** button, the **Enter name for Automatic Report Group file** dialog box will be displayed. In this dialog box, select the required file and choose the **Open** button; the grouped report file will be displayed in the **Selected Reports** area.

## Drawing Information for Table Output Area

In the **Drawing Information for Table Output** area, you can specify the name and location for the drawing file and the template to be used for creating the drawing files for reports. The options in this area are discussed next.

### First Drawing Name

Specify the file name and the location of the starting drawing file in the **First Drawing Name** edit box. Alternatively, choose the **Browse** button on the right of the **First Drawing Name** edit box; the **Enter Name for First Drawing** dialog box will be displayed. In this dialog box, enter the name of the drawing file in the **File name** edit box and choose the **Save** button; the location and name of the drawing file will be displayed in the **First Drawing Name** edit box of the **Drawing Information for Table Output** area. The drawing number will be incremented for any succeeding drawing files that you will create. If you enter only the name of the drawing file in the **First Drawing Name** edit box, the report drawing files will be created and saved in the active project automatically.

### Template

Specify the template drawing file to create the drawing files for reports in the **Template** edit box. Alternatively, you can choose the **Browse** button on the right of the **Template** edit box; the **Select Template** dialog box will be displayed. Next, select the template drawing file and choose the **Open** button; the file name and location of the template drawing file will be displayed in the **Template** edit box.

After specifying the required options in the **Automatic Report Selection** dialog box, choose the **OK** button; the report of the selected report names will be created. Note that the drawing file of the report will be added at the bottom of the project drawing list.

# SETTING THE FORMAT FILE FOR REPORTS

| | |
|---|---|
| **Ribbon:** | Reports > Miscellaneous > Report Format Setup |
| **Toolbar:** | ACE:Main Electrical 2 > Schematic Report > Report Format File Setup or ACE:Schematic Reports > Report Format File Setup |
| **Menu:** | Projects > Reports > Report Format File Setup |
| **Command:** | AEFORMATFILE |

The **Report Format File Setup** tool is used to create format files. This tool is also used to save the settings of a report to a file for later use. To do so, choose the **Report Format Setup** tool from the **Miscellaneous** panel of the **Reports** tab; the **Report Format File Setup** dialog box will be displayed, refer to Figure 9-39. The **Report Format File Setup** dialog box can also be invoked by choosing the **Format File Setup** button from the **Automatic Report Selection** dialog box as discussed in the previous section.

Using the **Report Format File Setup** dialog box, you can save the settings of a report to a text file with *.set* extension. You can use the report format files while generating reports using the **Reports** tool in the **Schematic** and **Panel** panel and **Automatic Reports** tool in the **Miscellaneous** panel. Most of the options in the **Report Format File Setup** dialog box are similar to that in the **Schematic Reports** and **Panel Reports** dialog boxes. The remaining options in the **Report Format File Setup** dialog box are discussed next.

**Note**

*The options in the **Report Format File Setup** dialog box will depend on the option you choose from the **Report Name** area of the **Report Format File Setup** dialog box.*

## Format File Area

In the **Format File** area, you can define the standards for a report before it is generated. By default, the path and location of the format file is *C:\Users\CADCIM\Appdata\Roaming\Autodesk\AutoCAD Electrical 2022\R24.1\enu\Support\User.* In this area, you can open a format file, save a format file, and so on. The options in this area are discussed next.

### Open Format File

The **Open Format File** button is used to open and edit the format files that are saved. To open and edit a format file, choose the **Open Format File** button from the **Format File** area; the **Report format settings file selection** dialog box will be displayed, as shown in Figure 9-40. Note that the type of format file and the title bar of the dialog box will depend on the option chosen from the **Report Name** area of the **Report Format File Setup** dialog box. Now, select the required format file from the **Report format settings file selection** dialog box. Alternatively, choose the **Browse** button from the **Report format settings file selection** dialog box to select the format file from the **Select *.set format file** dialog box. Next, choose the **Open** button from the **Select *.set format file** dialog box displayed; you will return to the **Report Format File Setup** dialog box.

### Save Format File

The **Save Format File** button is used to save the format file and its settings.

### Save As Format File

The **Save As Format File** button is used to save the settings of format file to a new format file.

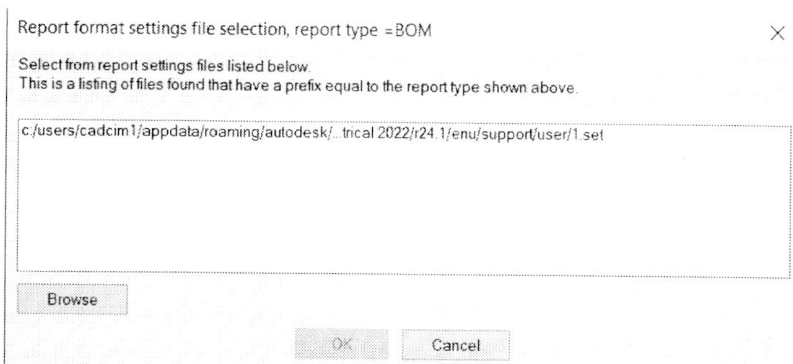


***Figure 9-40** The **Report format settings file selection** dialog box*

**Note**

*1. In the **Select *.set format file** dialog box, you need to select the .set file related to the option chosen from the **Report Name** area of the **Report Format File Setup** dialog box; otherwise **AutoCAD Message** message box will be displayed. This message box displays that the *.set file is not for the option chosen from the **Report Name** area of the **Report Format File Setup** dialog box.*
*2. The title bar of the **Select *.set format file** dialog box will change according to the option chosen from the **Report Name** area of the **Report Format File Setup** dialog box.*

## Save Report to File

The **Save Report to File** button is used to save the report to a file. You can save the report to the following format files: ASCII report, Comma-Delimited, Excel Spreadsheet, Access Database, and XML format. To save a report to a file, choose the **Save Report to File** button; the **Save Report to File** dialog box will be displayed, as shown in Figure 9-41. Select the required type of the output file from the **Save Report to File** dialog box and specify the other options in this dialog box. Note that most of the options in this dialog box have been discussed in the earlier sections. Next, choose the **OK** button from the **Save Report to File** dialog box to save the changes made and exit the **Save Report to File** dialog box.

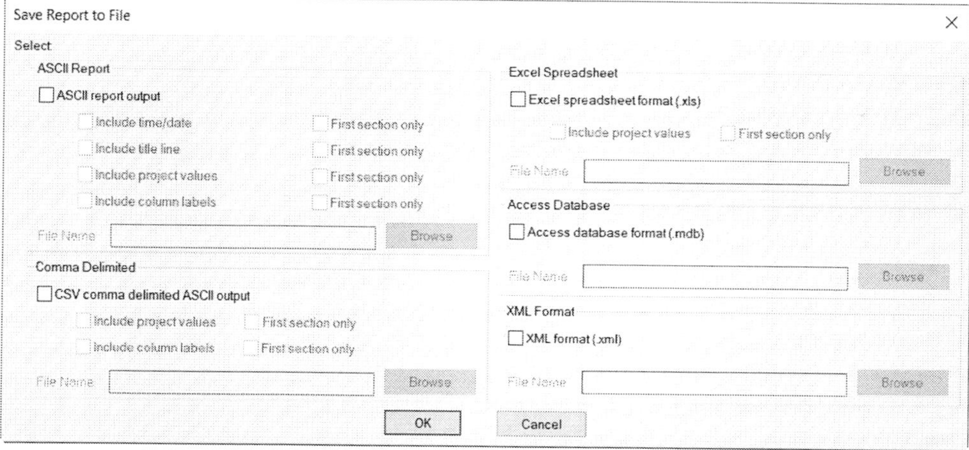


***Figure 9-41** The **Save Report to File** dialog box*

## Change Report Fields

The **Change Report Fields** button is used to change data fields and their order in the report. To do so, choose the **Change Report Fields** button; the **Data Fields to Report** dialog box will be displayed. The options in this dialog box have been discussed earlier. Next, specify the required options in this dialog box and then choose the **OK** button from the **Data Fields to Report** dialog box; the selected data fields will be included in a report. Note that the title bar of the **Data Fields to Report** dialog box will change according to the option that you have chosen from the **Report Name** area.

## Put on Drawing

The **Put on Drawing** button is used to insert the report into the drawing in the form of a table. On choosing this button, the **Table Generation Setup** dialog box will be displayed. The options in the **Table Generation Setup** dialog box have been discussed earlier. Next, specify the required options in this dialog box. Choose the **OK** button in this dialog box to save the changes made and to return to the **Report Format File Setup** dialog box.

## Sort Fields

The **Sort Fields** button is used to sort the order of fields in a report. To do so, choose the **Sort Fields** button; the **Sort** dialog box will be displayed. Select the required options from this dialog box and choose the **OK** button to return to the **Report Format File Setup** dialog box.

## Done

Choose the **Done** button; the **Save Report Format Changes?** message box will be displayed, as shown in Figure 9-42. In this message box, choose the **Yes** button to save the changes or choose the **No** button to discard the changes made in the **Report Format File Setup** dialog box.

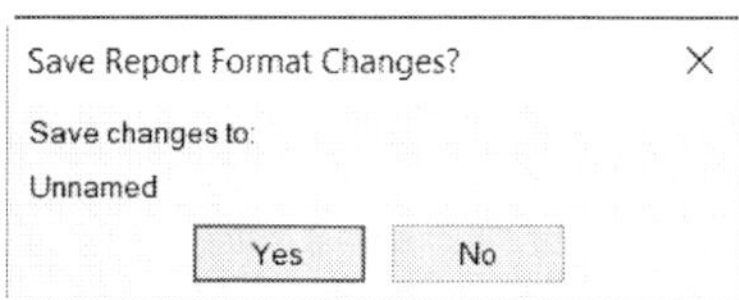


*Figure 9-42 The **Save Report Format Changes?** message box*

# TUTORIALS

## Tutorial 1

In this tutorial, you will generate a schematic Bill of Material report of the **CADCIM** project and then insert a table into the drawing. Also, you will generate a schematic Component report and save the report to the **Excel Spreadsheet** format file (.xls). **(Expected time: 20 min)**

The following steps are required to complete this tutorial:

a. Create a new drawing.
b. Generate a schematic Bill of Material report and place it in the drawing.
c. Add an attribute field in the schematic Bill of Material report.
d. Generate and save the component report.
e. Close the **Excel Spreadsheet** format file (.xls).
f. Save the drawing file.

## Creating a New Drawing

1. Activate the **CADCIM** project in the **PROJECT MANAGER**, if it is inactive.

2. Choose the **New Drawing** button from the **PROJECT MANAGER**; the **Create New Drawing** dialog box will be displayed. In this dialog box, enter **C09_tut01** in the **Name** edit box and **Schematic BOM** in the **Description 1** edit box. Choose the **OK** button; the *C09_tut01.dwg* file is created and displayed at the bottom of the drawing list in the **CADCIM** project. Next, move *C09_tut01.dwg* to the *TUTORIALS* subfolder of the **CADCIM** project.

## Generating the Schematic Bill of Material Report and Placing it in the Drawing

1. Choose the **Reports** tool from the **Schematic** panel of the **Reports** tab; the **Schematic Reports** dialog box is displayed, as shown in Figure 9-43.

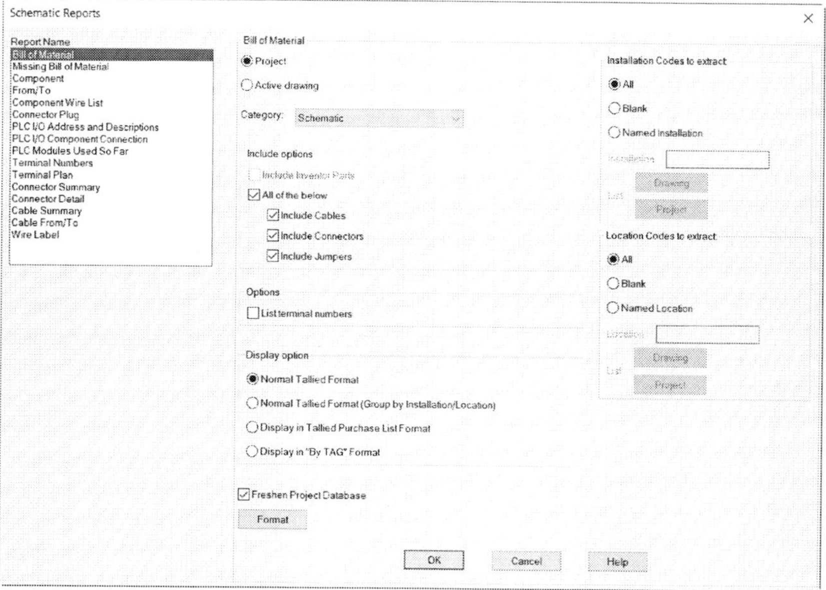


*Figure 9-43 The Schematic Reports dialog box*

2. Choose the **Bill of Material** option from the **Report Name** area, if it is not selected. Next, specify the required options in the **Schematic Reports** dialog box, refer to Figure 9-43.

3. Choose the **OK** button from the **Schematic Reports** dialog box; the **Select Drawings to Process** dialog box is displayed. Choose the **Do All** button from this dialog box; all the drawings from the top list of the dialog box are transferred to the bottom list. Next, choose the **OK** button from this dialog box; the **Report Generator** dialog box is displayed.

**Note**

*If the **QSAVE** message box is displayed, choose the **OK** button from it to display the **Report Generator** dialog box.*

4. Choose the **Put on Drawing** button from the **Report Generator** dialog box; the **Table Generation Setup** dialog box is displayed. Select the **Insert New** radio button from the **Table** area and the **Include column labels** check box from the **Column Labels** area, if not already selected. Retain rest of the default values in the dialog box.

5. Next, choose the **OK** button in the **Table Generation Setup** dialog box; you are prompted to specify the insertion point for the table. Click on the upper left corner of the title block; the Bill of Material report is inserted into the drawing and the **Report Generator** dialog box is displayed again. Choose the **Close** button in the **Report Generator** dialog box to exit.

6. Choose **View > Zoom > In** from the menu bar to zoom the table. The report is displayed in a tabular format, as shown in Figure 9-44. The zoomed view of the report in tabular format is shown in Figure 9-45.

| ITEM | TAGS | QTY | SUB | CATALOG | MFG | DESCRIPTION |
|---|---|---|---|---|---|---|
| | CB311<br>CB313<br>CB322<br>CB324<br>CB326<br>CB328<br>CB330 | 7 | | EGH3015FFG | EATON | CIRCUIT BREAKER – E125 FRAME<br>3-POLE CIRCUIT BREAKER<br>15AMPS<br>TYPE E125H, FIXED THERMAL & MAGNETIC TRIP<br>690VAC, 250VDC, 15AMPS |
| | CR101<br>CR105<br>CR106<br>CR396<br>CR397<br>CR398 | 6 | | 700–P200A1 | AB | P TYPE ELECTRICALLY HELD RELAY, 4 POLE, AC COIL, CONVERTIBLE CONTACTS<br>TYPE P<br>120VAC<br>2 NO<br>115–120VAC 60Hz / 110VAC 50Hz COIL, RATING: 10A, OPEN TYPE RELAY RAIL MOUNT |
| | DS304 | 1 | | 194E–A25–1753 | AB | IEC LOAD SWITCH 3 POLE<br>194E – LOAD SWITCH<br>25AMPS<br>ON–OFF BASE MOUNTED SWITCH (INCLUDES OPERATING SHAFT)<br>480VAC, 25AMPS |
| | FU309 | 1 | | FRS–R–15 | BUSSMANN | DUAL ELEMENT FUSE – CLASS RK5<br>TIME DELAY, CURRENT LIMITING<br>600VAC<br>15AMPS |
| | FU307<br>FU307A | 2 | | FRS–R–5 | BUSSMANN | DUAL ELEMENT FUSE – CLASS RK5<br>TIME DELAY, CURRENT LIMITING<br>600VAC<br>5AMPS |
| | LS396<br>LS397<br>LS398 | 3 | | MS–50L | MS | |
| | LT405<br>LT413<br>LT416 | 3 | | 800H–PR16G | AB | GREEN PILOT LIGHT – STANDARD, ROUND OILTIGHT<br>30.5mm<br>120VAC XFMR<br>PLASTIC LENS<br>CORROSION RESISTANT |
| | LT399<br>LT401<br>LT402<br>LT403 | 4 | | 800H–PR16R | AB | RED PILOT LIGHT – STANDARD, ROUND OILTIGHT<br>30.5mm<br>120VAC XFMR<br>PLASTIC LENS<br>CORROSION RESISTANT |
| | M404<br>M412<br>M415<br>M423<br>M425 | 5 | | AN16DN0AB | EATON | FULL VOLTAGE MOTOR STARTER NEMA SIZE 1<br>NON–REVERSING<br>27AMPS, 110/120VAC<br>3–POLE, 110/120 AC, 50/60HZ COIL<br>OPEN TYPE WITHOUT ENCLOSURE |
| | PB404 | 1 | *1 | 800EP–E2 | AB | PUSH BUTTON – MOMENTARY, IP66, NEMA 4/4X/13<br>22.5mm EXTENDED, IEC STYLE<br>BLACK<br>2 NO<br>PLASTIC OPERATOR w 2 ACROSS MTG |
| | | | *2 | 800E–2X10 | AB | 800E CONTACT BLOCK<br>22.5mm IEC STYLE<br>1 NO |
| | | | *1 | 800E–A2L | AB | 800E MOUNTING LATCH – 2 ACROSS<br>22.5mm IEC STYLE<br>2 ACROSS MOUNTING LATCH<br>2 ACROSS MOUNTING LATCH |
| | PB18<br>PB412<br>PB415 | 3 | | 800T–A2A | AB | PUSH BUTTON – MOMENTARY, NEMA 4/13<br>30.5mm FLUSH<br>BLACK<br>1 NO 1 NC |
| | PB404A<br>PB412A<br>PB415A | 3 | | 800T–D1B | AB | PUSH BUTTON – MUSHROOM, NEMA 4/13<br>30.5mm<br>GREEN<br>2 NO 2 NC |
| | PLC502 | 3 | | 1771–IAD | AB | 1771 PLC–5 DIGITAL AC/DC INPUT MODULE<br>1771<br>DISCRETE INPUT<br>79–138 VAC<br>16 POINT INPUT; GENERAL PURPOSE 120 VAC/DC |
| | PRS503<br>PRS504<br>PRS505<br>PRS506<br>PRS507<br>PRS508 | 18 | | E59–F18A108C02–D1 | EATON | IPROX PROGRAMMABLE INDUCTIVE PROXIMITY SENSOR<br>INDUCTIVE<br>6–48VDC<br>8MM SENS. RANGE, 3 WIRE, NO DEFAULT SETTING, 18MM DIA<br>STANDARD RANGE, SHIELDED, 2M CABLE |
| | SS396<br>SS423 | 2 | | 800MR–HH2BB | AB | SELECTOR SW – 2 POS MAINT, NEMA 13<br>22.5mm<br>BLACK KNOB<br>2 NO 2 NC<br>QUICK CONNECT TERMS |
| | TB–2 | 4 | | DN–T1/0 | AUTOMATIONDIRECT | TERMINAL BLOCK<br>FEED–THROUGH<br>140AMPS<br>GRAY, 14–1/0AWG<br>19pcs/ft (62/m) |
| | TB–1 | 10 | | DN–T10 | AUTOMATIONDIRECT | TERMINAL BLOCK<br>FEED–THROUGH<br>30AMPS<br>GRAY, 18–10AWG<br>50pcs/ft (168/m) |
| | TB1 | 12 | | 2770011 | PHOENIX CONTACT | 2LEVEL TERMINAL BLOCK – UKK 3<br>MULTI–LEVEL<br>32AMPS<br>GRAY, 0.2–2.5MM^2, 26–12 AWG<br>CLIPLINE – MODULAR SCREW TERMINAL BLOCK |
| | TS–A | 6 | | 8WA1 011–1BF22 | SIEMENS | 8WA1 SINGLE TERMINAL – SIZE 2.5<br>FEED–THROUGH<br>20AMPS<br>ORANGE, 600V, 22–12AWG<br>W/ SCREW CONNECTIONS ON BOTH SIDES, RAIL MOUNTED |
| | TS–B | 3 | | 8WA1 011–1BF24 | SIEMENS | 8WA1 SINGLE TERMINAL – SIZE 2.5<br>FEED–THROUGH<br>20AMPS<br>BLACK, 600V, 22–12AWG<br>W/ SCREW CONNECTIONS ON BOTH SIDES, RAIL MOUNTED |
| | DS1 | 1 | | 1179C | ALPHA | |
| | XF309 | 1 | | 3S40F | SQD | 1PH TRANSFORMER, CLASS 7400<br>DRY TRANSFORMER<br>3KVA<br>480V–120/240V, 60HZ<br>GENERAL PURPOSE TRANSFORMER, ENCLOSURE NEMA 3R |

***Figure 9-44*** *The Bill of Material report displayed in tabular format*

| ITEM | TAGS | QTY | SUB | CATALOG | MFG | DESCRIPTION |
|---|---|---|---|---|---|---|
| | CB311<br>CB313<br>CB322<br>CB324<br>CB326<br>CB328<br>CB330 | 7 | | EGH3015FFG | EATON | CIRCUIT BREAKER – E125 FRAME<br>3–POLE CIRCUIT BREAKER<br>15AMPS<br>TYPE E125H, FIXED THERMAL & MAGNETIC TRIP<br>690VAC, 250VDC, 15AMPS |
| | CR101<br>CR105<br>CR106<br>CR396<br>CR397<br>CR398 | 6 | | 700–P200A1 | AB | P TYPE ELECTRICALLY HELD RELAY, 4 POLE, AC COIL, CONVERTIBLE CONTACTS<br>TYPE P<br>120VAC<br>2 NO<br>115–120VAC 60Hz / 110VAC 50Hz COIL, RATING: 10A, OPEN TYPE RELAY RAIL MOUNT |
| | DS304 | 1 | | 194E–A25–1753 | AB | IEC LOAD SWITCH 3 POLE<br>194E – LOAD SWITCH<br>25AMPS<br>ON–OFF BASE MOUNTED SWITCH (INCLUDES OPERATING SHAFT)<br>480VAC, 25AMPS |
| | FU309 | 1 | | FRS–R–15 | BUSSMANN | DUAL ELEMENT FUSE – CLASS RK5<br>TIME DELAY, CURRENT LIMITING<br>600VAC<br>15AMPS |
| | FU307<br>FU307A | 2 | | FRS–R–5 | BUSSMANN | DUAL ELEMENT FUSE – CLASS RK5<br>TIME DELAY, CURRENT LIMITING<br>600VAC<br>5AMPS |
| | LS396<br>LS397<br>LS398 | 3 | | MS–50L | MS | |
| | LT405<br>LT413<br>LT416 | 3 | | 800H–PR16G | AB | GREEN PILOT LIGHT – STANDARD, ROUND OILTIGHT<br>30.5mm<br>120VAC XFMR<br>PLASTIC LENS<br>CORROSION RESISTANT |
| | LT399<br>LT401<br>LT402<br>LT403 | 4 | | 800H–PR16R | AB | RED PILOT LIGHT – STANDARD, ROUND OILTIGHT<br>30.5mm<br>120VAC XFMR<br>PLASTIC LENS<br>CORROSION RESISTANT |

*Figure 9-45 The Zoomed view (Partial) of the Bill of Material report*

## Adding an Attribute Field in the Schematic Bill of Material Report

1. Choose the **User Attributes** tool from the **Miscellaneous** panel of the **Reports** tab; the **User Defined Attribute List: unnamed.wda** dialog box is displayed, as shown in Figure 9-46.

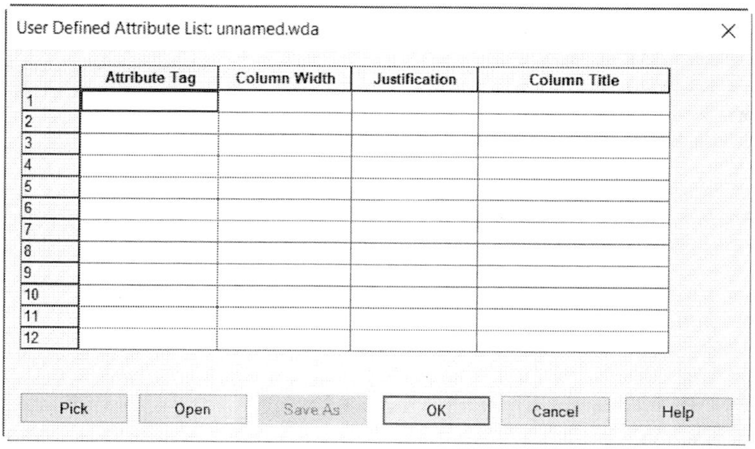

User Defined Attribute List: unnamed.wda

| | Attribute Tag | Column Width | Justification | Column Title |
|---|---|---|---|---|
| 1 | | | | |
| 2 | | | | |
| 3 | | | | |
| 4 | | | | |
| 5 | | | | |
| 6 | | | | |
| 7 | | | | |
| 8 | | | | |
| 9 | | | | |
| 10 | | | | |
| 11 | | | | |
| 12 | | | | |

Pick | Open | Save As | OK | Cancel | Help

*Figure 9-46 The **User Defined Attribute List: unnamed.wda** dialog box*

2. Enter **FAMILY** in the first cell of both the **Attribute Tag** and **Column Title** columns of this dialog box.

3. Click in the first cell of the **Justification** column; a drop-down list is displayed. Select the **Top Left** option from it.

   Even if you leave this option blank, by default the **Top Left** option will be selected.

   As the **Column Width** column of the **User Defined Attribute List: unnamed.wda** dialog box is left blank, column width for the attribute is restricted to 24 characters.

4. Choose the **Save As** button; the **Create File** dialog box is displayed. Browse to *C:\Users\User name\Documents\Acade 2022\AeData\Proj\CADCIM* from the **Save in** drop-down list and then make sure **CADCIM** is displayed in the **File Name** edit box. Next, choose **Save** from the dialog box; a **CADCIM** text file is created at the specified location with the *.wda* extension.

5. Choose the **OK** button in the **User Defined Attribute List: unnamed.wda** dialog box to close it. Next, choose the **Report Format Setup** tool from the **Miscellaneous** panel of the **Reports** tab; the **Report Format File Setup - Unnamed** dialog box is displayed. Make sure that the **Bill of Material** option is selected from the **Schematic Report** list in this dialog box.

6. Next, choose the **Change Report Fields** button from the **Report Format File Setup - Unnamed** dialog box; the **Bill of Material Data Fields to Report** dialog box is displayed. You will notice that the **Family** field is added to the **Available Fields** area of this dialog box.

7. Select **Family** from the **Available fields** area; it automatically moves to the **Fields to report** area.

**Note**

*You can change the order of fields in the **Field to report** area by using the **Move Up** and **Move Down** buttons available below it.*

8. Choose the **OK** button to close this dialog box. Next, choose the **Done** button from the **Report Format File Setup - Unnamed** dialog box to close it; the **Save Report Format Changes** message box is displayed. Choose the **Yes** button in the message box; the **Select Bill of Material *.set format file** dialog box is displayed. Now, specify the desired name and location in this dialog box to save the report format changes in the form of file and then choose the **Save** button to close the dialog box.

9. Choose the **Reports** tool from the **Schematic** panel of the **Reports** tab; the **Schematic Reports** dialog box is displayed. Choose the **Bill of Material** option from the **Report Name** area, if it is not already chosen.

10. Choose the **Format** button; the **Report format settings file selection, report type=BOM** dialog box is displayed. Click on the **Browse** button located at the bottom of the dialog box; the **Select BOM*.set format file** dialog box is displayed. In this dialog box, browse to the location that is specified in step 8 and select the saved format file. Next, choose the **Open** button; the name and location of the format file is displayed on the right of the **Format** button.

11. Choose the **OK** button from the **Schematic Reports** dialog box; the **Select Drawings to Process** dialog box is displayed. In this dialog box, choose the **Do All** button; all the drawings from the top list of the dialog box are transferred to the bottom list. Choose the **OK** button from this dialog box; the **QSAVE** message box is displayed. Choose the **OK** button from it; the **Report Generator** dialog box is displayed.

    You will notice that the **Family** attribute field is added in the **Report Generator** dialog box.

12. Choose the **Close** button in the **Report Generator** dialog box to close it.

## Generating and Saving the Component Report

1. Choose the **Reports** tool from the **Schematic** panel of the **Reports** tab; the **Schematic Reports** dialog box is displayed.

2. Choose the **Component** option from the **Report Name** area of this dialog box.

3. Accept the default values in this dialog box and choose the **OK** button in the **Schematic Reports** dialog box; the **Select Drawings to Process** dialog box is displayed.

4. Choose the **Do All** button from the **Select Drawings to Process** dialog box; all the drawings from the top list are transferred to the bottom list of this dialog box.

5. Choose the **OK** button from the **Select Drawings to Process** dialog box; the **Report Generator** dialog box is displayed.

**Note**

*If the **QSAVE** message box is displayed, choose the **OK** button from it to display the **Report Generator** dialog box.*

6. Choose the **Sort** button from the **Report Generator** dialog box; the **Sort** dialog box is displayed.

7. Select **TAGNAME** from the **Primary sort** drop-down list, **ITEM** from the **Secondary sort** drop-down list, and **MFG** from the **Third sort** drop-down list. Next, choose the **OK** button from the **Sort** dialog box; the report displayed in the **Report Generator** dialog box is sorted accordingly.

8. Choose the **Save to File** button from the **Report Generator** dialog box; the **Save Report to File** dialog box is displayed.

9. Select the **Excel spreadsheet format (.xls)** radio button and choose the **OK** button in this dialog box; the **Select file for report** dialog box is displayed.

10. Browse to *C:\Users\User Name\Documents\Acade 2022\AeData\Proj\CADCIM* from the **Save in** drop-down list and then enter **COMPONENT** in the **File name** edit box. By default, **. xls* is displayed in the **Save as type** edit box. Do not change this file extension.

11. Choose the **Save** button from the **Select file for report** dialog box; the **Optional Script File** dialog box is displayed.

12. Choose the **Close - No Script** button to return to the **Report Generator** dialog box.

13. Choose the **Close** button to exit the **Report Generator** dialog box.

14. Open the saved *COMPONENT.xls* file from *C:\Users\User Name\Documents\Acade 2022\AeData\Proj\CADCIM*. The excel file is shown in Figure 9-47.

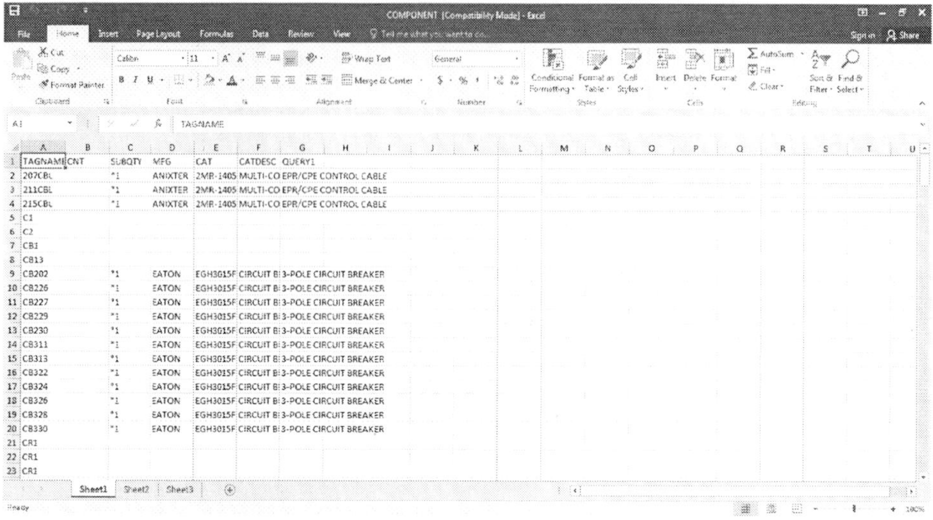

| | A | B | C | D | E | F | G |
|---|---|---|---|---|---|---|---|
| 1 | TAGNAME | CNT | SUBQTY | MFG | CAT | CATDESC | QUERY1 |
| 2 | 207CBL | | *1 | ANIXTER | 2MR-1405 | MULTI-CO | EPR/CPE CONTROL CABLE |
| 3 | 211CBL | | *1 | ANIXTER | 2MR-1405 | MULTI-CO | EPR/CPE CONTROL CABLE |
| 4 | 215CBL | | *1 | ANIXTER | 2MR-1405 | MULTI-CO | EPR/CPE CONTROL CABLE |
| 5 | C1 | | | | | | |
| 6 | C2 | | | | | | |
| 7 | CB1 | | | | | | |
| 8 | CB13 | | | | | | |
| 9 | CB202 | | *1 | EATON | EGH3015F | CIRCUIT B | 3-POLE CIRCUIT BREAKER |
| 10 | CB226 | | *1 | EATON | EGH3015F | CIRCUIT B | 3-POLE CIRCUIT BREAKER |
| 11 | CB227 | | *1 | EATON | EGH3015F | CIRCUIT B | 3-POLE CIRCUIT BREAKER |
| 12 | CB229 | | *1 | EATON | EGH3015F | CIRCUIT B | 3-POLE CIRCUIT BREAKER |
| 13 | CB230 | | *1 | EATON | EGH3015F | CIRCUIT B | 3-POLE CIRCUIT BREAKER |
| 14 | CB311 | | *1 | EATON | EGH3015F | CIRCUIT B | 3-POLE CIRCUIT BREAKER |
| 15 | CB313 | | *1 | EATON | EGH3015F | CIRCUIT B | 3-POLE CIRCUIT BREAKER |
| 16 | CB322 | | *1 | EATON | EGH3015F | CIRCUIT B | 3-POLE CIRCUIT BREAKER |
| 17 | CB324 | | *1 | EATON | EGH3015F | CIRCUIT B | 3-POLE CIRCUIT BREAKER |
| 18 | CB326 | | *1 | EATON | EGH3015F | CIRCUIT B | 3-POLE CIRCUIT BREAKER |
| 19 | CB328 | | *1 | EATON | EGH3015F | CIRCUIT B | 3-POLE CIRCUIT BREAKER |
| 20 | CB330 | | *1 | EATON | EGH3015F | CIRCUIT B | 3-POLE CIRCUIT BREAKER |
| 21 | CR1 | | | | | | |
| 22 | CR1 | | | | | | |
| 23 | CR1 | | | | | | |

***Figure 9-47*** *Component report saved in an Excel file*

## Closing the Excel Spreadsheet Format File

1. Choose **Close** from the **Office Button** or **File > Exit** from the menu bar to exit the **COMPONENT**.xls file.

## Saving the Drawing File

1. Choose **Save** from the **Application Menu** to save the drawing file *C09_tut01.dwg*.

2. Choose **Close > Current Drawing** from the **Application Menu** to close the drawing file.

# Tutorial 2

In this tutorial, you will generate the Panel Nameplate report for the **CADCIM** project and then place the report in a drawing in a tabular format. Also, you will generate the panel Component report and save it in an ASCII format file. **(Expected time: 20 min)**

The following steps are required to complete this tutorial:

a. Create a new drawing *C09_tut02.dwg* in the **CADCIM** project.
b. Generate the Panel Nameplate report.
c. Generate and save the Panel Component report.
d. Close the saved ASCII format file.
e. Save the drawing file.

## Creating a New Drawing

1. Activate the **CADCIM** project in the **PROJECT MANAGER**.

2. Choose the **New Drawing** button from the **PROJECT MANAGER**; the **Create New Drawing** dialog box will be displayed. In this dialog box, enter **C09_tut02** in the **Name** edit box and

**Panel Nameplate** in the **Description 1** edit box. Next, choose the **OK** button; the *C09_tut02.dwg* file is created and displayed at the bottom of the drawing list in the **CADCIM** project.

3. Move *C09_tut02.dwg* to the *TUTORIALS* subfolder of the **CADCIM** project.

## Generating the Panel Nameplate Report

1. Choose the **Reports** tool from the **Panel** panel of the **Reports** tab; the **Panel Reports** dialog box is displayed.

2. Choose the **Nameplate** option from the **Report Name** area.

3. Make sure the **Project** radio button is selected in the **Panel Nameplate** area.

   Make sure the **All** radio button is selected in the **Installation Codes to extract** and **Location Codes to extract** areas.

4. Choose the **OK** button in the **Panel Reports** dialog box; the **Select Drawings to Process** dialog box is displayed.

5. Choose the **Do All** button; all the drawings from the top list of the **Select Drawings to Process** dialog box are transferred to the bottom list of this dialog box.

**Note**

*After choosing the **OK** button in the **Select Drawings to Process** dialog box, if the **QSAVE** message box is displayed, choose the **OK** button in this message box to display the **Report Generator** dialog box.*

6. Choose the **OK** button in this dialog box; the **Report Generator** dialog box is displayed.

7. Choose the **Put on Drawing** button in the **Report Generator** dialog box; the **Table Generation Setup** dialog box is displayed. Accept all the default values in this dialog box and choose the **OK** button; you are prompted to specify the insertion point for the table.

8. Insert the table at the center of the title block; the **Report Generator** dialog box is displayed again. Choose the **Close** button to exit the **Report Generator** dialog box.

9. Choose **View > Zoom > In** from the menu bar to zoom the table. The report is displayed in a tabular format.

## Generating and Saving the Panel Component Report

1. Choose the **Reports** tool from the **Panel** panel of the **Reports** tab; the **Panel Reports** dialog box is displayed.

2. Choose the **Component** option from the **Report Name** area of the **Panel Reports** dialog box.

3. Select the **Project** radio button from the **Panel Component** area.

4. Choose the **OK** button in the **Panel Reports** dialog box; the **Select Drawings to Process** dialog box is displayed.

5. Choose the **Do All** button in the **Select Drawings to Process** dialog box; all the drawings are transferred from the top list to the bottom list.

6. Choose the **OK** button in the **Select Drawings to Process** dialog box; the **Report Generator** dialog box is displayed.

**Note**

*After choosing the **OK** button in the **Select Drawings to Process** dialog box, if the **QSAVE** message box is displayed, choose the **OK** button in this message box to display the **Report Generator** dialog box.*

7. Choose the **Save to File** button from the **Report Generator** dialog box to save the report; the **Save Report to File** dialog box is displayed.

8. Select the **ASCII report output (as shown)** radio button and choose the **OK** button in this dialog box; the **Select file for report** dialog box is displayed.

9. Browse to *C:\Users\User Name\Documents\Acade 2022\AeData\Proj\CADCIM* in the **Save in** drop-down list. By default, *. *rep* is displayed in the **Save as type** drop-down list and **PNLCOMP** is displayed in the **File name** edit box.

10. Choose the **Save** button; the **Optional Script File** dialog box is displayed.

11. Choose the **Close - No Script** button to return to the **Report Generator** dialog box.

12. Choose the **Close** button to exit the **Report Generator** dialog box.

13. Open the saved ASCII file *PNLCOMP.REP* from *C:\Users\User Name\Documents\Acade 2022\AeData\Proj\CADCIM* by using the Notepad file.

## Closing the ASCII Format File

1. Choose **File > Exit** from the menu bar to exit the *PNLCOMP.REP* file.

## Saving the Drawing File

1. Choose **Save** from the **Application Menu** to save the drawing file as *C09_tut02.dwg*.

# Tutorial 3

In this tutorial, you will create and save the format files for schematic components and panel components of the **CADCIM** project. Next, you will use the **Automatic Reports** tool to group the format files and generate the report. **(Expected time: 25 min)**

The following steps are required to complete this tutorial:

a. Create format file for schematic components.
b. Create format file for panel components.
c. Create group for automatic report generation.
d. Generate automatic report.

## Creating Format File for Schematic Components

In this section, you will create a format file for schematic components using the **Report Format Setup** tool.

1. Make sure the **CADCIM** project is activated and the *C09_tut02.dwg* file is open. Next, choose the **Report Format Setup** tool from the **Miscellaneous** panel of the **Reports** tab; the **Report Format File Setup - Unnamed** dialog box is displayed.

2. Choose the **Component** option from the **Schematic Report** area of this dialog box; the modified **Report Format File Setup-Unnamed** dialog box is displayed, as shown in Figure 9-48.

3. Choose the **Change Report Fields** button from the **Report Format File Setup-Unnamed** dialog box; the **Component Data Fields to Report** dialog box is displayed.

4. Choose the **FILENAME** option from the **Available fields** area; the **FILENAME** is shifted to the **Fields to report** area.

5. Make sure **FILENAME** is highlighted in the **Fields to report** area and then move it to the bottom using the **Move Down** button, as shown in Figure 9-49.

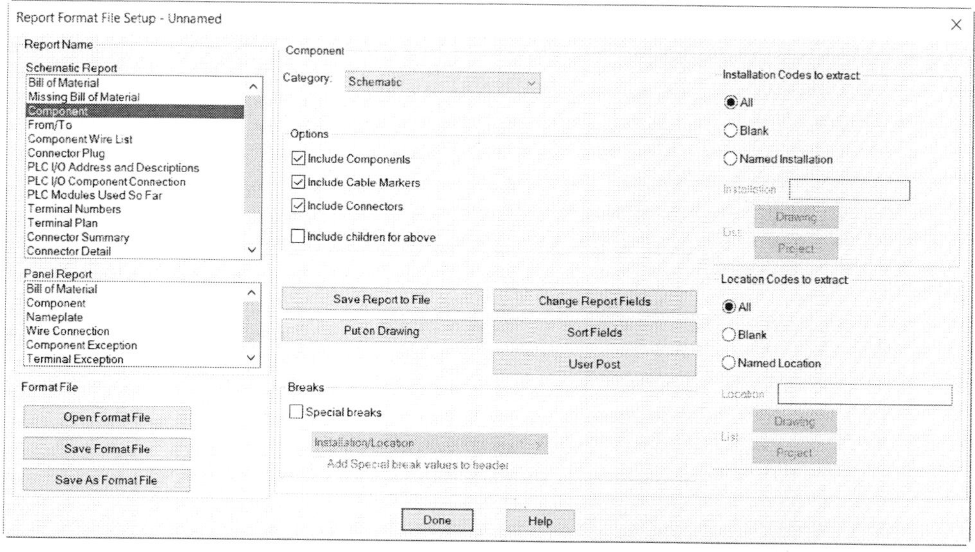


*Figure 9-48 The modified **Report Format File Setup - Unnamed** dialog box*

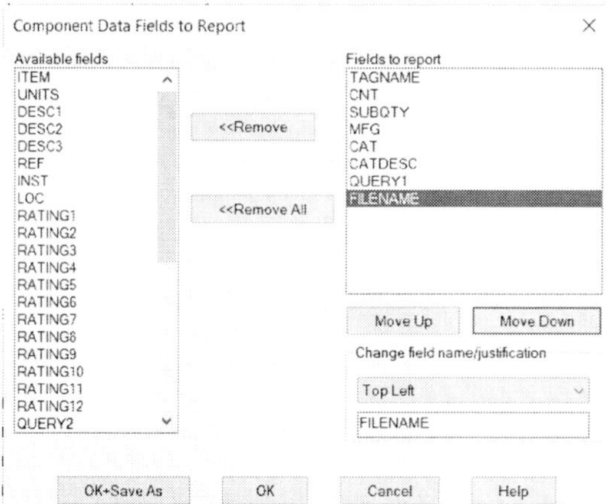


*Figure 9-49 The **FILENAME** option moved to the bottom in the **Fields to report** area*

6. Choose the **OK** button in the **Component Data Fields to Report** dialog box.

7. Choose the **Save Report to File** button from the **Report Format File Setup - Unnamed** dialog box; the **Save Report to File** dialog box is displayed.

8. Select the **Excel spreadsheet format [.xls]** check box from the **Excel Spreadsheet** area in the **Save Report to File** dialog box; the options below this check box are activated. Next, select the **Include project values** and **First section only** check boxes.

9. Choose the **Browse** button located at the right of the **File Name** edit box; the **Select file for report** dialog box is displayed. In this dialog box, specify the desired location in the **Save in** drop-down list.

10. Enter **Schematic Components_CADCIM** in the **File name** edit box and then choose the **Save** button from the **Select file for Report** dialog box; the path of the **Schematic Components_CADCIM** is displayed in the **File Name** edit box of the **Save Report to File** dialog box.

11. Choose the **OK** button from the **Save Report to File** dialog box; you return to the **Report Format File Setup - Unnamed** dialog box. Choose the **Save Format File** button from this dialog box; the **Select Component *.set format file** dialog box is displayed.

12. In this dialog box, enter **schematic components_format** in the **File name** edit box and then choose the **Save** button from the **Select Component *.set format file** dialog box.

## Creating Format File for Panel Components

In this section, you will create a format file for schematic components using the **Report Format Setup** tool.

1. Make sure the **Report Format File Setup - XX** dialog box is opened. Choose the **Component** option from the **Panel Report** area of this dialog box; the modified **Report Format File Setup-Unnamed** dialog box is displayed, as shown in Figure 9-50.

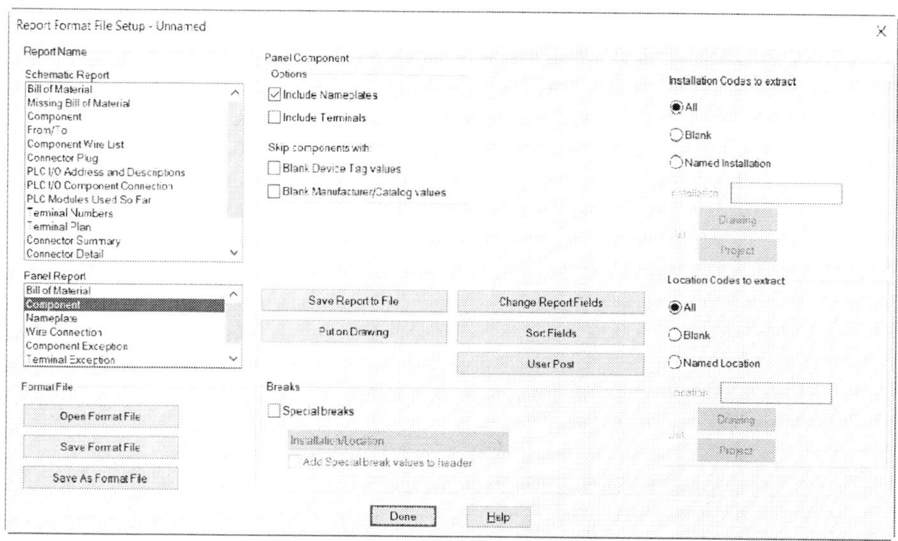


*Figure 9-50 The modified **Report Format File Setup - Unnamed** dialog box*

2. Choose the **Change Report Fields** button from the **Report Format File Setup-Unnamed** dialog box; the **Panel Component Data Fields to Report** dialog box is displayed.

3. Choose the **FILENAME** option from the **Available fields** area; it is shifted to the **Fields to report** area.

4. Make sure **FILENAME** is highlighted in the **Fields to report** area and then move it to the bottom using the **Move Down** button, as shown in Figure 9-51.

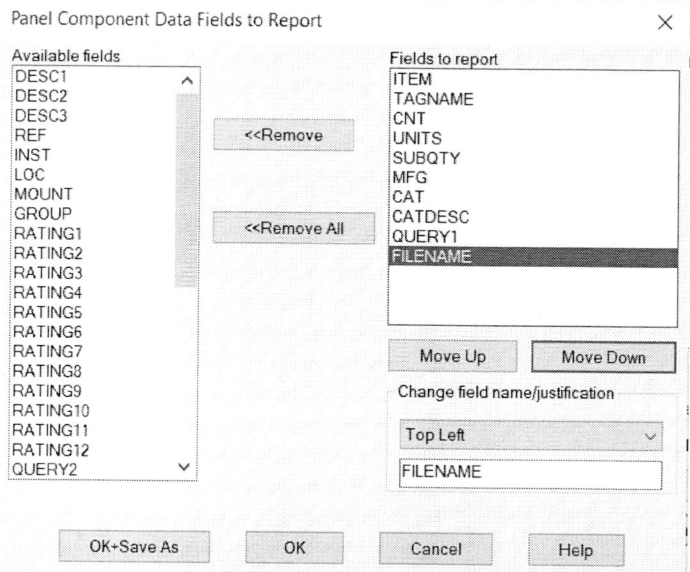


*Figure 9-51 **FILENAME** moved to the bottom in the **Fields to report** area*

5. Choose the **OK** button in the **Panel Component Data Fields to Report** dialog box; you will return to the **Report Format File Setup - XX** dialog box.

6. Choose the **Put on Drawing** button from the **Report Format File Setup - Unnamed** dialog box; the **Table Generation Setup** dialog box is displayed.

7. Select the **Include time/date**, **Include project information**, and **Include title line** check boxes from the **Title** area of this dialog box. Also, make sure that the **Insert New** radio button from the **Table** area, the **Calculate automatically** radio button from the **Column Width** area, and the **Rows for Each Section** check box from the **Row Definition** area are selected.

8. Choose the **Pick** button from the **First new Section Placement** area; you are prompted to specify the insertion point. Click on the upper left corner of the drawing area.

   Note that the table that will be generated in the automatic report generation process will have this point as its upper left corner.

9. Choose the **OK** button from the **Table Generation Setup** dialog box; you will return to the **Report Format File Setup - XX** dialog box.

10. Choose the **Save As Format File** button from this dialog box; the **Select Panel Component *.set format file** dialog box is displayed. In this dialog box, enter **panel components_format** in the **File name** edit box and then choose the **Save** button from the **Select Panel Component *.set format file** dialog box.

11. Choose the **Done** button from the **Report Format File Setup - Unnamed** dialog box.

## Creating Group for Automatic Report Generation

In this section, you will create group for generating automatic report of all the components.

1. Choose the **Automatic Reports** tool from the **Miscellaneous** panel of the **Reports** tab; the **Automatic Report Selection** dialog box is displayed.

2. Choose the **Component** option from the **Schematic Report** area of this dialog box; the modified **Automatic Report Selection** dialog box is displayed, as shown in Figure 9-52.

3. Select **schematic components_format.set** from the **Format File Name** area of this dialog box; the **Add>>** button is activated. Choose the **Add>>** button; a row is added to the **Selected Reports** area of the dialog box.

   You will notice that x is displayed in the **File Output** column of the added row. This is because the file output is selected in the *schematic components_format.set* format file.

4. Choose the **Component** option from the **Panel Report** area of this dialog box; the modified **Automatic Report Selection** dialog box is displayed.

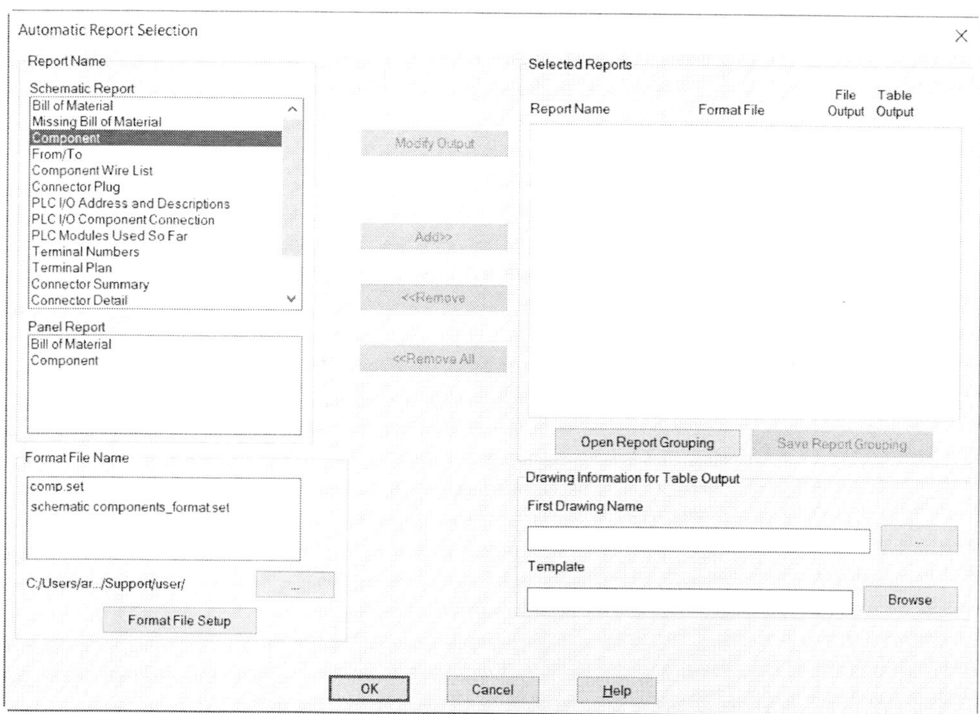


*Figure 9-52 The modified **Automatic Report Selection** dialog box*

5. Select **panel components_format.set** from the **Format File Name** area of this dialog box; the **Add>>** button is activated. Choose the **Add>>** button; a row is added to the **Selected Reports** area of the dialog box, as shown in Figure 9-53.

   You will notice that x is displayed in the **Table Output** column of the added row. This is because the table output is selected in the *panel components_format.set* format file.

6. Choose the **Save Report Grouping** button located below the **Selected Reports** area of the dialog box; the **Enter name for Automatic Report Group file** dialog box is displayed, as shown in Figure 9-54.

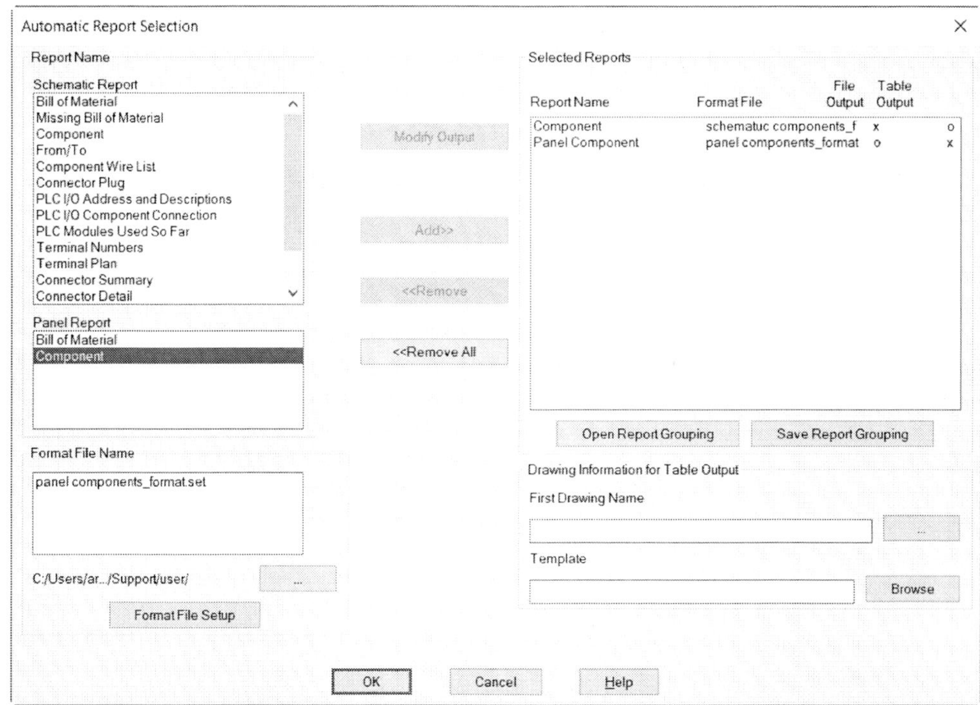

*Figure 9-53 The modified* ***Automatic Report Selection*** *dialog box*

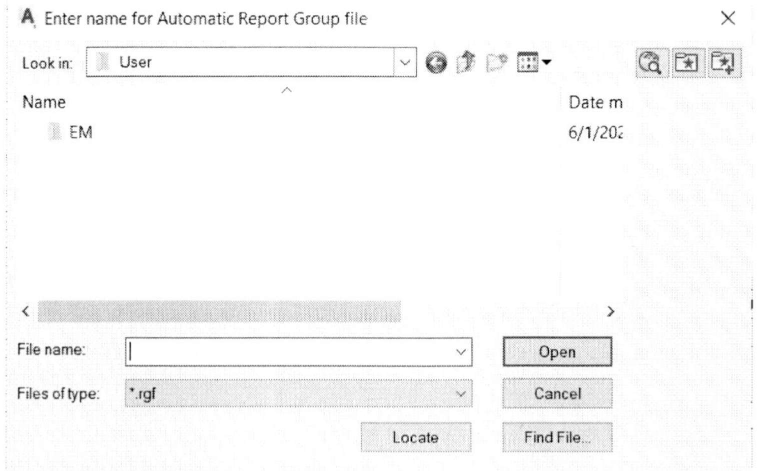

*Figure 9-54 The* ***Enter name for Automatic Report Group file*** *dialog box*

7. In this dialog box, enter **Schematic & Panel Components** in the **File name** edit box and then choose the **Save** button; the *Schematic & Panel Components.rgf* file is created at the default location.

**Note**

*For generating automatic report of schematic and panel components of other projects, choose the **Open Report Grouping** button from the **Automatic Report Selection** dialog box and then select the **Schematic & Panel Components.rgf** file from the **Enter name for Automatic Report Group file** dialog box.*

## Generating Automatic Report

In this section, you will generate the automatic report of schematic and panel components.

1. Make sure the **Automatic Report Selection** dialog box is opened. Choose the Browse button located on the left of the **First Drawing Name** edit box; the **Enter Name for First Drawing** dialog box is displayed.

2. In this dialog box, make sure that CADCIM is displayed in the **Save in** drop-down list. Also, enter **PANEL COMPONENTS** in the **File name** edit box and then choose the **Save** button; the path of the file is displayed in the **First drawing name** edit box.

3. Now, you need to specify the template in the **Template** edit box, To do so, choose the **Browse** button; the **Select template** dialog box is displayed. In this dialog box, select **ACAD_ELECTRICAL.dwt** from the list displayed and then choose the **Open** button; the name and path of the template is displayed in the **Template** edit box.

4. Choose the **OK** button from the **Automatic Report Selection** dialog box; the automatic report for schematic as well as panel components is generated at the specified location.

**Note**

*If the **QSAVE** message box is displayed, choose the **OK** button from this message box.*

5. Open the windows explorer and browse to the location where you have saved the *Schematic Components_CADCIM.xls* file. Next, open this file, refer to Figure 9-55.

6. Open the ***PANEL COMPONENTS*.dwg** file created in the **CADCIM** project during the automatic report generation process. You will notice that panel components are listed in the table; refer to Figure 9-56.

7. Choose **Close > Current Drawing** from the **Application Menu** to close the the *C09_tut03.dwg* file.

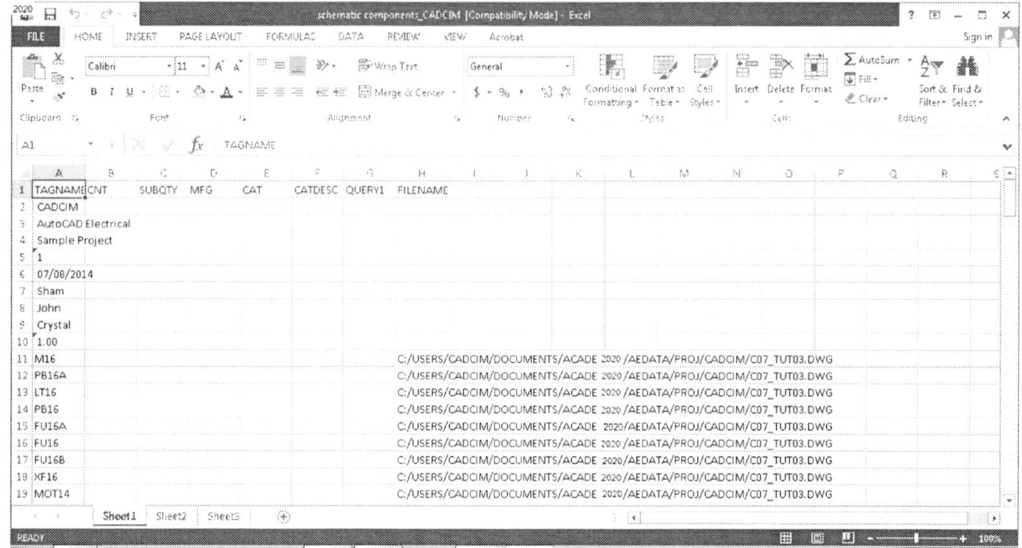

Figure 9-55 The Schematic Components_CADCIM file

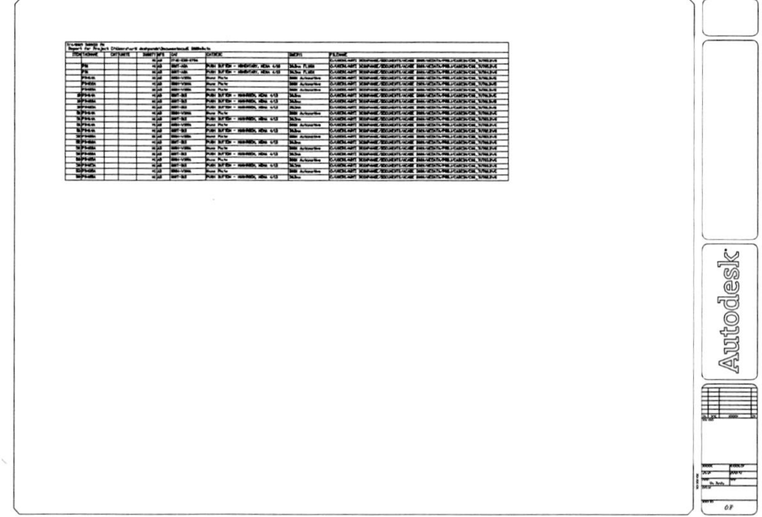

Figure 9-56 The list of panel components

## Self-Evaluation Test

**Answer the following questions and then compare them to those given at the end of this chapter:**

1. Which of the following commands is used to create schematic reports?

(a) **AESCHEMATICREPORT** (b) **AEAUDIT**
(c) **AEPANELREPORT** (d) **AEAUDITDWG**

2. The __________ dialog box is used to change the report format and to export the report to the drawing or to an external file.

3. When you choose the **Put on Drawing** button from the **Report Generator** dialog box, the __________ dialog box is displayed.

4. Choose the __________ button in the **Table Generation Setup** dialog box to display the **Select Layer for Table** dialog box.

5. When you choose the **Sort** button from the **Report Generator** dialog box, the __________ dialog box will be displayed.

6. If you choose the __________ report from the **Report Name** area of the **Schematic Reports** dialog box, then the report of the component wire connection will be extracted and displayed in the **Report Generator** dialog box.

7. You can create reports with the information extracted from the components inserted in your drawing. (T/F)

8. Schematic components and panel footprints use the same attribute name. (T/F)

9. The **Panel Reports** tool is used to create and specify the panel-based reports. (T/F)

10. The **Report Generator** dialog box displays the results of the selected report name. (T/F)

## Review Questions

**Answer the following questions:**

1. Which of the following buttons in the **Report Generator** dialog box is used to modify a report?

   (a) **Surf** (b) **User Post**
   (c) **Sort** (d) **Edit Mode**

2. Which one of the following file types is used to save the extracted reports?

   (a) **Adobe PageMaker** (b) **ASCII**
   (c) **MS-Word** (d) **PowerPoint**

3. Which of the following commands is used to create panel reports?

   (a) **AESCHEMATICREPORT** (b) **AEAUDIT**
   (c) **AEPANELREPORT** (d) **AEAUDITDWG**

4. Which of the following report options is used to provide the report of error checking between the schematic terminals and panel layout terminals?

(a) **Nameplate** report (b) **Wire connection** report
(c) **Terminal Exception** report (d) **Component Exception** report

5. The **Wire Annotation Exception** report lists the wires that do not contain annotation information regarding its source or destination. (T/F)

6. The **Panel Bill of Material** report displays the report of panel components and nameplates only. (T/F)

7. The **Component** report of the schematic component provides the project-wide report of all the components found in that wiring diagram set. (T/F)

8. You can change the order of data fields in the **Data Field to Report** dialog box. (T/F)

9. In AutoCAD Electrical, the report generation of schematic drawings is a time consuming process. (T/F)

10. When you select the **Wire From/To** report name from the **Report Name** area of the **Schematic Reports** dialog box, then only the component and terminal information are extracted from every drawing in the project. (T/F)

# EXERCISES

## Exercise 1

In this exercise, you will create a new drawing as *C09_exer01.dwg* and then generate the schematic Missing Bill of Material report of the **NEW_PROJECT** project. Next, you will save the report to the Access database (.mdb) as *missing_bom*. Also, you will generate a Panel Bill of Material report of the **NEW_PROJECT** project and place it on *C09_exer01.dwg* drawing.
**(Expected time: 20 min)**

## Exercise 2

In this exercise, you will use the **Report Format Setup** tool for creating format files for the schematic Bill of Material and panel Bill of Material and then save them as *bom.set* and *panel_bom.set* respectively, in the **NEW_PROJECT** project. Also, you will save the schematic Bill of Material report and panel Bill of Material report to a file in the **Excel Spreadsheet (.xls)** format as *bom.xls* and *panel_bom.xls*, respectively. Next, you will use the **Automatic Reports** tool to group the format files and for generating the reports. **(Expected time: 30 min)**

### Answers to Self-Evaluation Test

**1.** a, **2. Report Generator**, **3. Table Generation Setup**, **4. Layer**, **5. Sort**, **6. Component Wire List**, **7. T**, **8. F**, **9. T**, **10. T**

# Chapter 10

# PLC Modules

## Learning Objectives

**After completing this chapter, you will be able to:**

- *Insert parametric and nonparametric PLC modules*
- *Edit parametric and nonparametric PLC modules*
- *Insert individual PLC I/O points*
- *Create and modify the parametric PLC modules*
- *Create PLC I/O wiring diagrams using the spreadsheet data*
- *Map the spreadsheet information*
- *Modify and save the new setting configuration*
- *Tag components and wire numbers based on PLC I/O address*

# INTRODUCTION

A programmable logic controller (PLC) or programmable controller is a digital computer that is used to automatically regulate the industrial process. For example, you can use programmable logic controller to control machinery on assembly lines of a factory. This controller is designed to meet a range of industrial activities such as multiple inputs and output arrangements, extended temperature ranges, providing resistance to vibration, and so on. The programs designed to regulate the machine operation are usually stored in a battery-backed or non-volatile memory. A PLC is an instance of a real time system because output results are needed to be produced in response to input conditions within a time-bound period, else it will result in an unintended operation. Over the years, the functionality of PLC has evolved to accommodate sequential relay control, motion control, process control, distributed control systems, and networking. In PLC, microprocessor controlled interface is inbuilt and is designed to control or monitor some other I/O functions. Being an industrial computer control system, it always monitors the state of input devices and makes decisions on the basis of custom program for controlling the state of devices connected as outputs.

In this chapter, you will learn how to use PLC I/O module functions, insert parametric and nonparametric PLC modules, and create custom PLC I/O modules.

# INSERTING PARAMETRIC PLC MODULES

| | |
|---|---|
| **Ribbon:** | Schematic > Insert Components > Insert PLC drop-down > Insert PLC (Parametric) |
| **Toolbar:** | ACE:Main Electrical > Insert PLC (Parametric) or ACE:Insert PLC > Insert PLC (Parametric) |
| **Menu:** | Components > Insert PLC Modules > Insert PLC (Parametric) |
| **Command:** | AEPLCP |

AutoCAD Electrical can generate PLC I/O modules in different graphical styles through parametric generation technique on demand. These modules are generated by a database file and a library of symbol blocks. PLC I/O modules can be inserted as independent symbols. PLC modules behave like other schematic components. These modules are AutoCAD blocks containing attributes for connection points, tagging, and so on.

To insert a PLC module, choose the **Insert PLC (Parametric)** tool from the **Insert PLC** drop-down in the **Insert Components** panel of the **Schematic** tab, as shown in Figure 10-1; the **PLC Parametric Selection** dialog box will be displayed, as shown in Figure 10-2. Using this dialog box, you can select the PLC module and its graphics that you want to insert in a drawing. The different options and areas in this dialog box are discussed next.

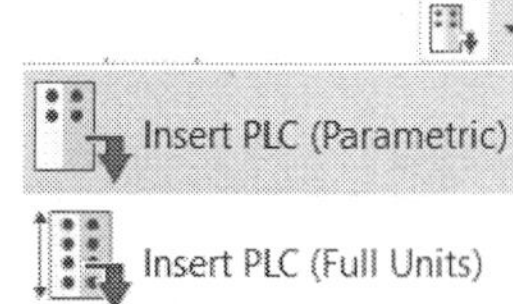


***Figure 10-1** The **Insert PLC** drop-down*

## Manufacturer Catalog Tree

The Manufacturer Catalog tree, shown in Figure 10-3, displays a list of PLC modules. This list can be filtered by selecting the manufacturer, series, and type of PLC. The data displayed in the Manufacturer Catalog tree is stored in the *ACE_PLC.mdb* database file.

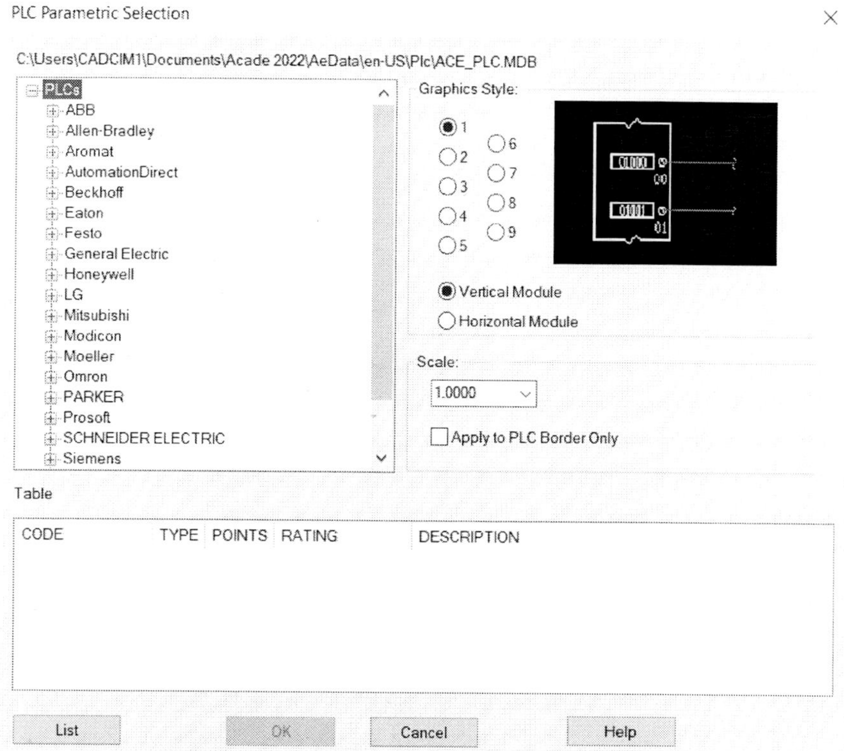


*Figure 10-2 The **PLC Parametric Selection** dialog box*

You can select a PLC module from the Manufacturer Catalog tree. To do so, click on the + sign on the required manufacturers module; PLC modules of the selected manufacturer will be displayed. Select the required module from the module list; the detailed information of the selected module will be displayed at the lower part of the **PLC Parametric Selection** dialog box, as shown in Figure 10-4.

## Graphics Style Area

The **Graphics Style** area displays the graphical styles of a PLC module. This area consists of five (1-5) pre-defined PLC styles and four (6-9) user-defined PLC styles. With the user-defined styles, you can add style for PLC of your choice. When you select a style number, the preview of that style will be displayed in the preview window of the **Graphics Style** area.

You can insert a PLC module into a drawing vertically or horizontally by selecting the **Vertical Module** or **Horizontal Module** radio button from the **Graphics Style** area.

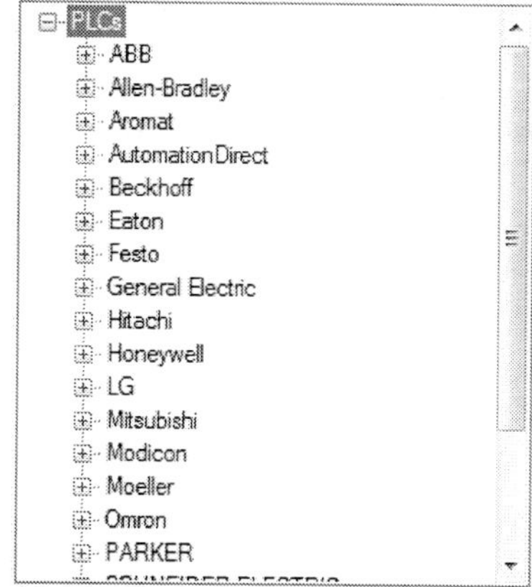


*Figure 10-3 The Manufacturer Catalog tree*

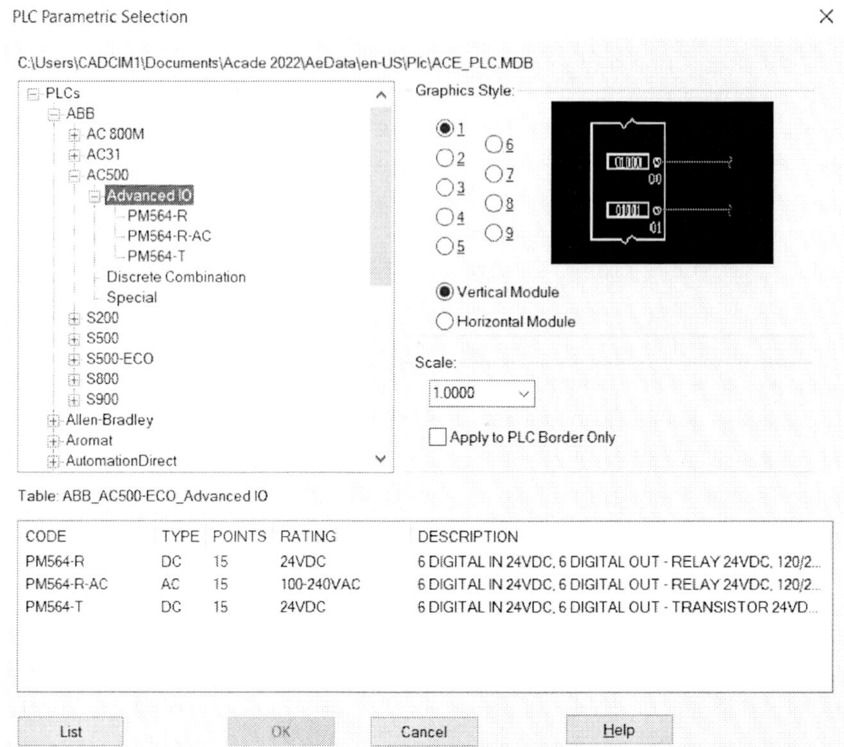


*Figure 10-4 The* ***PLC Parametric Selection*** *dialog box displaying the details of the selected module*

## Scale Area

In the **Scale** area, you can specify the scale for a PLC module. To do so, select the **Apply to PLC Border Only** check box from the **Scale** area to apply the scale only to the border of PLC module on insertion. By default, this check box is clear.

## List

The **List** button is used to display the report of the selected module. To do so, choose the **List** button; the **Report Generator** dialog box will be displayed. The options in the **Report Generator** dialog box have been discussed in Chapter 9.

After selecting the required module, graphics style, and scale, choose the **OK** button from the **PLC Parametric Selection** dialog box; the outline of the module will be displayed with an 'X' at the wire connection point of the topmost I/O point and you will be prompted to specify the insertion point for the PLC module. Specify the insertion point; the **Module Layout** dialog box will be displayed, as shown in Figure 10-5. The different areas and options in this dialog box are discussed next.

### Spacing Area

The edit box in the **Spacing** area is used to specify the spacing between the I/O points of a module. By default, the spacing value in this edit box will be the same as that of the spacing of the underlying rungs of a ladder. To override the spacing value, you need to enter a new value in the edit box in the **Spacing** area. To increment or decrement a value in the edit box, choose the arrow buttons below the edit box in the **Spacing** area.

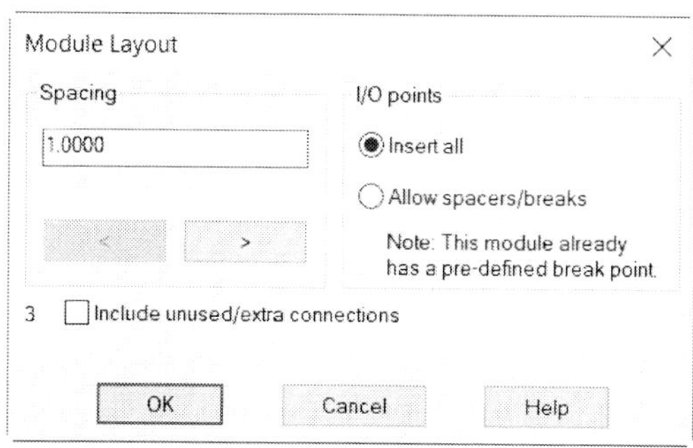


*Figure 10-5 The **Module Layout** dialog box*

## I/O points Area

The **I/O points** area is used to specify whether to break a module into numerous parts or insert all I/O points of a PLC module in a single operation without breaks. The **I/O points** area consists of the following radio buttons:

### Insert all

The **Insert all** radio button is selected by default and is used to insert a module in a single operation without any break.

### Allow spacers/breaks

Select the **Allow spacers/breaks** radio button to break a module into many parts.

## Include unused/extra connections

The **Include unused/extra connections** check box is used to include all unused and extra connections into the PLC module.

After specifying the required options in the **Module Layout** dialog box, choose the **OK** button from this dialog box; the **I/O Point** dialog box will be displayed, as shown in Figure 10-6. In this dialog box, enter the required rack and slot values in the **RACK** and **SLOT** edit boxes, respectively. Choose the arrow buttons on the left of these edit boxes to increment or decrement the values in the **RACK** and **SLOT** edit boxes.

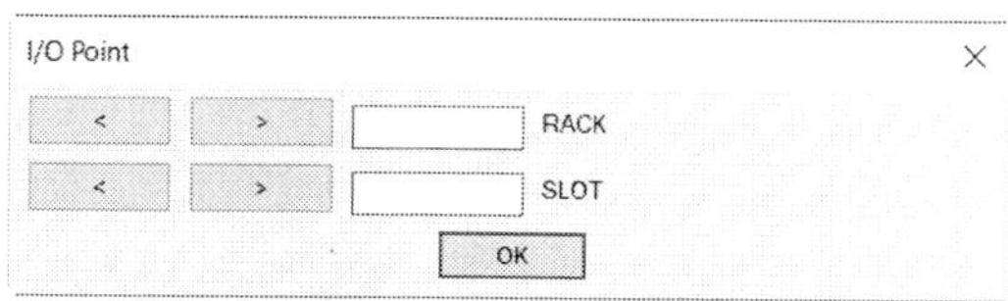


*Figure 10-6 The **I/O Point** dialog box*

**Note**

*The options in the **I/O Point** dialog box depend on the PLC module selected from the **PLC Parametric Selection** dialog box.*

After specifying the required values in the **I/O Point** dialog box, choose the **OK** button from this dialog box; the **I/O Address** dialog box will be displayed, as shown in Figure 10-7. Using this dialog box, you can specify the address for the first I/O point.

The values in the **Quick picks** drop-down list are based on the values that you have specified in the **I/O Point** dialog box in the **RACK** and **SLOT** edit boxes. Select the required value from the **Quick picks** drop-down list; the value will be displayed in the **Beginning address** edit box. Alternatively, enter the required value for the first I/O address of a PLC module in the

**Beginning address** edit box. Note that the other I/O points of a module will be incremented based on the value specified in the **Beginning address** edit box.

To view the information of the selected PLC module, choose the **List** button in the **I/O Address** dialog box; the **Report Generator** dialog box will be displayed.

After specifying the required options in the **I/O Address** dialog box, choose the **OK** button in this dialog box; the selected PLC module will be inserted into the drawing.

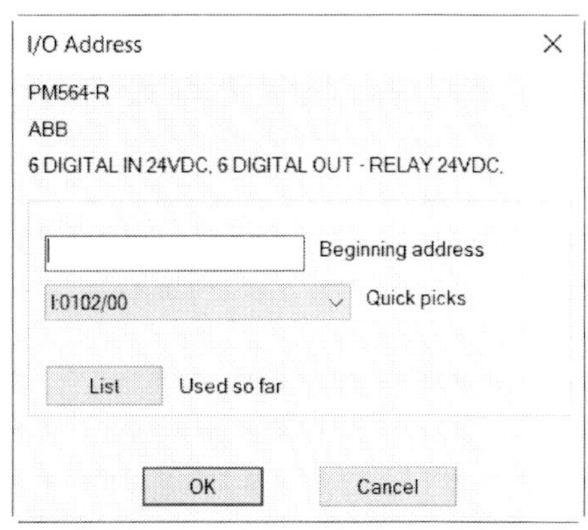


*Figure 10-7 The **I/O Address** dialog box*

## Inserting Spacers and Breaks

If the module does not fit into a single ladder, you can break the module and continue inserting the module in other area of the same drawing or in another drawing. Also, you can add spacers for skipping I/O point of a module. To break a module or add a spacer, select the **Allow spacers/breaks** radio button from the **I/O points** area of the **Module Layout** dialog box and then choose the **OK** button; the **I/O Point** dialog box will be displayed. This dialog box has been discussed earlier. In this dialog box, specify the required options and then choose the **OK** button; the **Custom Breaks/Spacing** dialog box will be displayed, as shown in Figure 10-8.

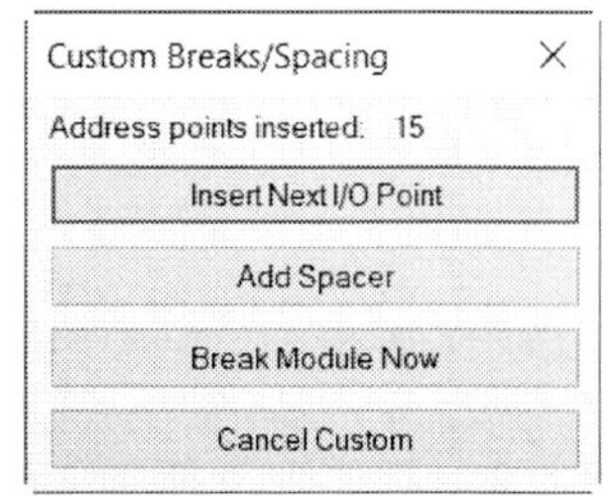


*Figure 10-8 The **Custom Breaks/Spacing** dialog box*

The options in the **Custom Breaks/Spacing** dialog box are discussed next.

### Insert Next I/O Point

Choose the **Insert Next I/O Point** button; the next I/O point of a PLC module will be inserted without spaces on rung of a ladder. Figure 10-9 shows the PLC module inserted into a ladder after choosing the **Insert Next I/O Point** button.

### Add Spacer

To add spaces into a module, choose the **Add Spacer** button; a cross mark will be displayed in the drawing indicating that a space is added in the PLC module. Note that an I/O address will not be inserted at this point. Figure 10-10 shows the PLC module after the **Add Spacer** button is chosen.

### Break Module Now

The **Break Module Now** button is used to break a module at the current I/O point as many times as you need. To break a module, choose the **Break Module Now** button from the **Custom Breaks/Spacing** dialog box; you will be prompted to specify the insertion point for the required PLC module. Specify the insertion point; the **Module Layout** dialog box will be displayed again. Specify the required options in this dialog box and choose the **OK** button; the **Custom Breaks/Spacing** dialog box will be displayed again. Notice that the module will break at this point.

Figure 10-11 shows the PLC module after choosing the **Break Module Now** button from the **Custom Breaks/Spacing** dialog box.

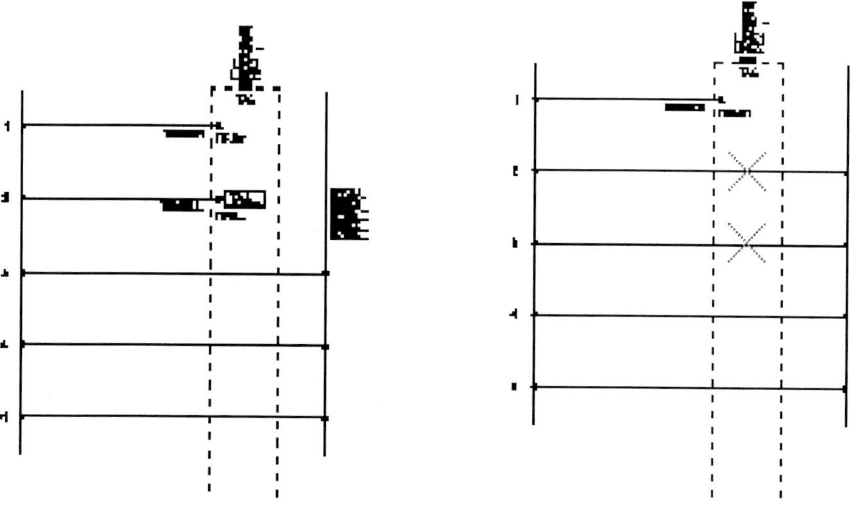

*Figure 10-9 The PLC module after choosing the* ***Insert Next I/O Point*** *button*

*Figure 10-10 The PLC module after choosing the* ***Add Spacer*** *button*

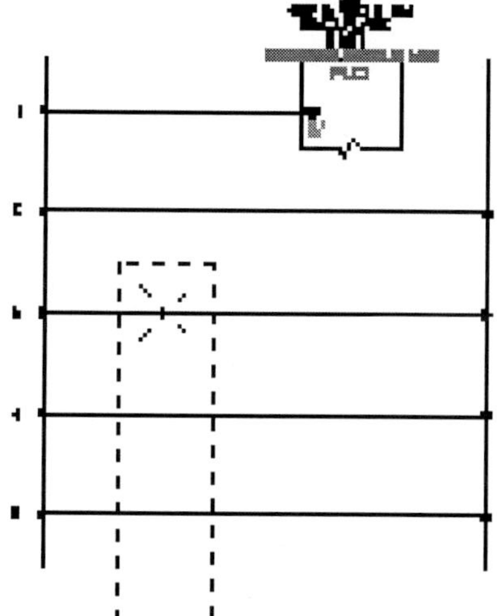

*Figure 10-11 The PLC module after choosing the* ***Break Module Now*** *button*

## Cancel Custom

The **Cancel Custom** button is used to insert the remaining I/O points in a PLC module without any breaks or spacers.

Now, if you want to stop the insertion process to move to a different drawing or to execute a command, then you must first break the module. To do so, select the **Allow spacers/breaks** radio button in the **Module Layout** dialog box and then choose **OK**; the **I/O Point** dialog box will be displayed. Enter the required information in this dialog box and choose **OK**; the **I/O Addresses** dialog box will be displayed. Choose **OK** from this dialog box; the **Custom Breaks/Spacing** dialog box will be displayed. In this dialog box, choose the **Break Module Now** button; you will be prompted to specify the insertion point for the module. Next, press ESC to cancel the insertion of the module; the **Data Saved** message box will be displayed, as shown in Figure 10-12. The **Data Saved** message box informs you that the remaining part of the module has been saved. Note that AutoCAD Electrical will save this information for the current session only. Choose the **OK** button from the **Data Saved** message box. Now, you can execute any number of commands or operations before you continue inserting the PLC module.

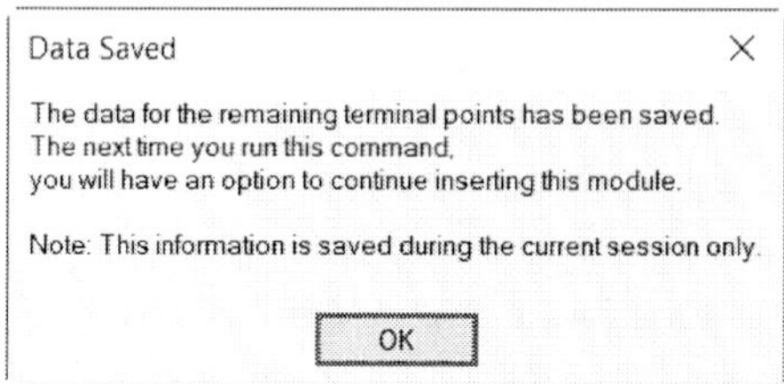


*Figure 10-12 The **Data Saved** message box*

Now, if you choose the **Insert PLC (Parametric)** tool from the **Insert Components** panel of the **Schematic** tab, the **Continue "Broken" Module** dialog box will be displayed, as shown in Figure 10-13. The options in this dialog box are discussed next.

### Continue Module

The **Continue Module** button is used to continue the previously broken module.

### Start New Module

The **Start New Module** button is used to start a new module and discard the remainder of the broken module's data.

### Cancel

Choose the **Cancel** button to exit the **Continue "Broken" Module** dialog box. After choosing this button, the broken module's data is saved. You can insert the broken module later.

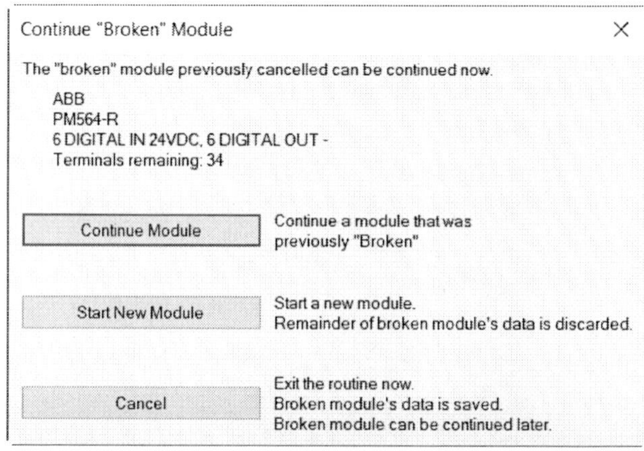


*Figure 10-13 The **Continue "Broken" Module** dialog box*

**Note**

*If you choose the **Start New Module** button or exit AutoCAD Electrical, you will lose the saved data.*

## INSERTING NONPARAMETRIC PLC MODULES

| | |
|---|---|
| **Ribbon:** | Schematic > Insert Components > Insert PLC drop-down > Insert PLC (Full Units) |
| **Toolbar:** | ACE:Main Electrical > Insert PLC (Parametric) > Insert PLC (Full Units) or ACE:Insert PLC > Insert PLC (Full Units) |
| **Menu:** | Components > Insert PLC Modules > Insert PLC (Full Units) |
| **Command:** | AEPLC |

The **Insert PLC (Full Units)** tool is used to insert a PLC module into a drawing as a single unit. If you insert a PLC module into a drawing using this tool, the underlying rungs of a ladder will break and then reconnect. Using this tool, you can insert PLC I/O points as a complete PLC module or as independent symbols into the drawing. To insert a PLC module, choose the **Insert PLC (Full Units)** tool from the **Insert Components** panel of the **Schematic** tab; the **Insert Component** dialog box will be displayed, as shown in Figure 10-14.

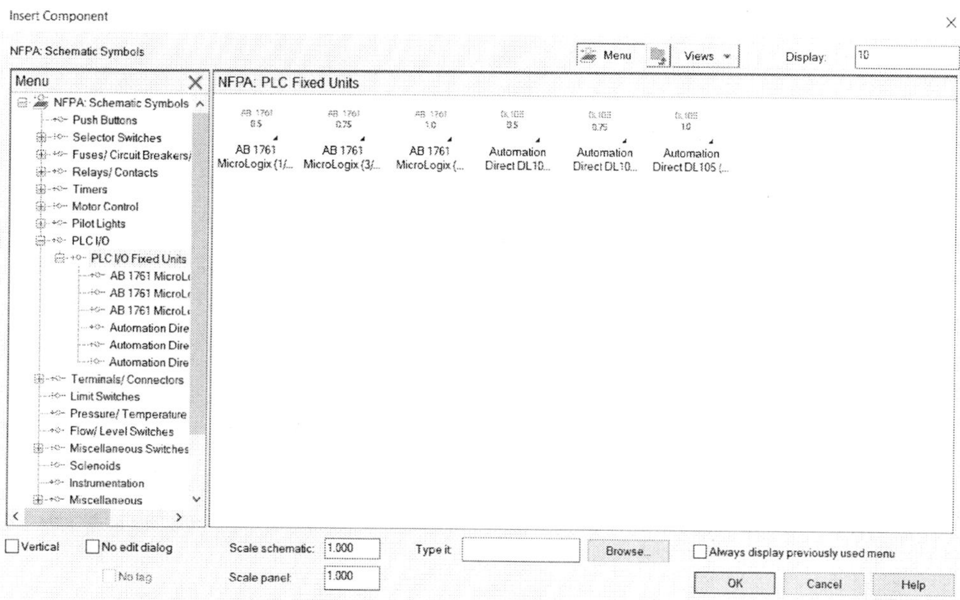


*Figure 10-14 The **Insert Component** dialog box*

In this dialog box, the nonparametric PLC modules are displayed in the **NFPA: PLC Fixed Units** area. Now, select the required module from the **NFPA : PLC Fixed Units** area; the **Insert Component** dialog box will disappear and you will be prompted to specify the insertion point for the PLC module. Next, specify the insertion point; the **Edit PLC Module** dialog box will be displayed. The options in this dialog box will be discussed in detail in the next section. Enter the required values in this dialog box and choose the **OK** button; the complete PLC module will be inserted into the drawing. Figure 10-15 shows a complete nonparametric PLC module.

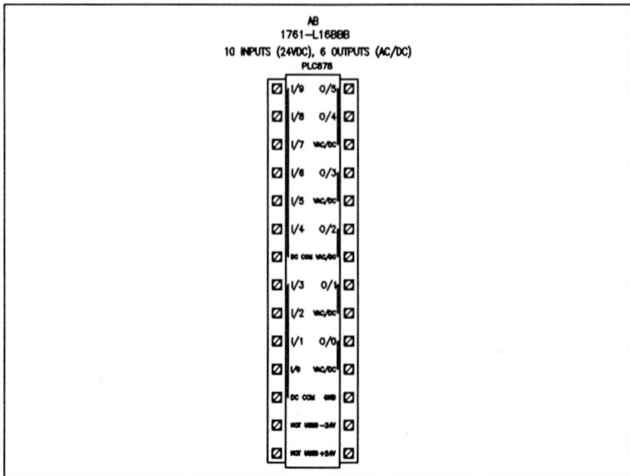


*Figure 10-15 A complete nonparametric PLC module*

# EDITING A PLC MODULE

| | |
|---|---|
| **Ribbon:** | Schematic > Edit Components > Edit Components drop-down > Edit |
| **Toolbar:** | ACE:Main Electrical > Edit Component<br>or ACE:Edit Component > Edit Component |
| **Menu:** | Components > Edit Component |
| **Command:** | AEEDITCOMPONENT |

You can edit a PLC module inserted into the drawing. To do so, choose the **Edit** tool from the **Edit Components** panel of the **Schematic** tab; you will be prompted to select a component. Select the required PLC module from the drawing; the **Edit PLC Module** dialog box will be displayed, as shown in Figure 10-16. In the **Edit PLC Module** dialog box, you can edit the I/O point description, installation/location codes, catalog data, and so on.

The areas and options in this dialog box are discussed next.

## Addressing Area

The **Addressing** area is used to specify first I/O address of a PLC module. The options in this area are discussed next.

### First address

The **First address** edit box is used to specify the first I/O address for a PLC module. Alternatively, select the available I/O address displayed in the **First address** list box. After specifying first I/O address in the **First address** edit box, you will notice that the selected I/O address will be displayed in the **Address** edit box of the **I/O Point Description** area automatically.

### Drawing

The **Drawing** button is used to select the first I/O address of a PLC module from the active drawing. To do so, choose the **Drawing** button; the **PLC I/O Point List (this drawing)** dialog box will be displayed. This dialog box displays the list of PLC I/O addresses that have been used in the current drawing. You can select first I/O address from the list displayed.

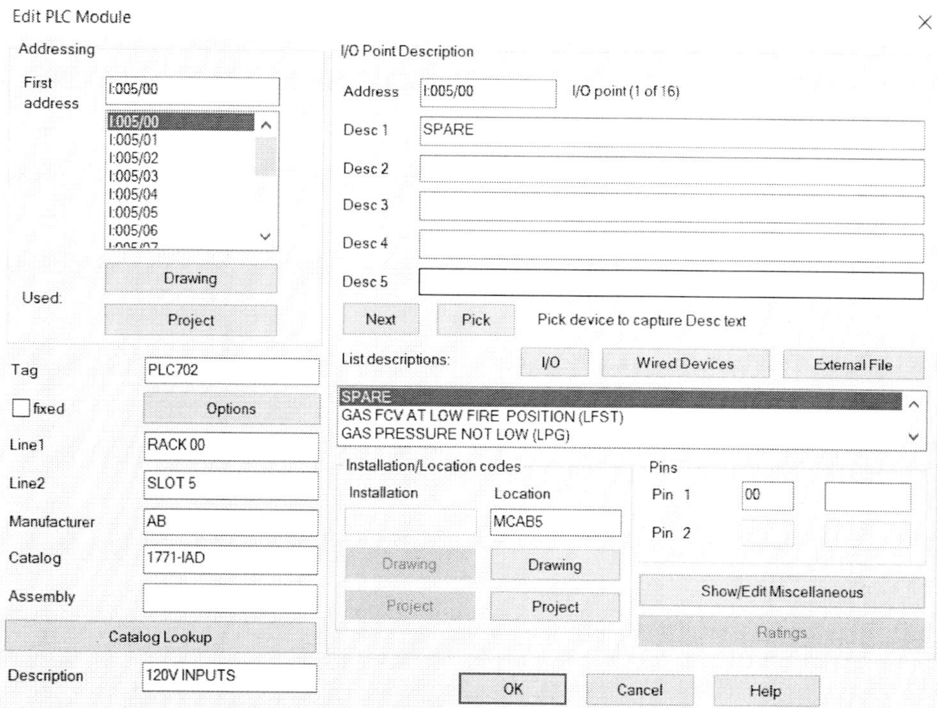


*Figure 10-16 The **Edit PLC Module** dialog box*

## Project

On choosing this button, the **PLC I/O Points Used** dialog box will be displayed. This dialog box lists the addresses used in the active project. You can select I/O point address from this list. Also, you will notice that if the selected I/O address has the first address and I/O point descriptions, the values in the **First address** and **Address** edit boxes will be changed automatically.

### Note

*When you specify the first I/O point address manually in the **First address** edit box of the **Addressing** area and click on any other option in the **Edit PLC Module** dialog box, the **I/O Addressing** dialog box will be displayed. Choose the required option in this dialog box. On doing so, if the **AutoCAD Message** message box is displayed informing you that all the address values were not resequenced, choose the **OK** button in the **AutoCAD Message** message box, refer to Figure 10-17. To resequence remaining addresses, you need to do it manually.*

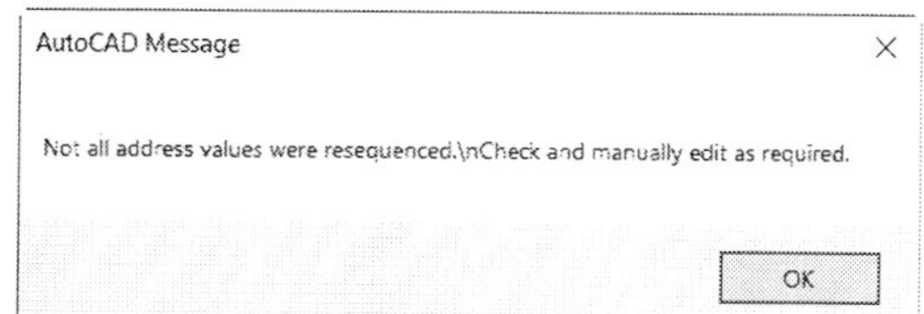


*Figure 10-17 The **AutoCAD Message** message box*

## Tag

The **Tag** edit box is used to display the tag name of a PLC module.

### fixed

If you select the **fixed** check box, the component tag will not be updated during automatic retagging. By default, this check box is cleared.

### Options

When you click on the **Options** button, the **Option:Tag Format "Family" Override** dialog box is displayed. Using this dialog box, you can replace a fixed text string for the %F part of the tag format.

### Line1 and Line2

The **Line1** and **Line2** edit boxes are used to specify additional description for a PLC module.

### Manufacturer

The **Manufacturer** edit box is used to specify the manufacturer number of an I/O point of a PLC module.

### Catalog

The **Catalog** edit box is used to specify the catalog value of the I/O point of a PLC module.

### Assembly

The **Assembly** edit box is used to specify the assembly code for the I/O point of a PLC module. This code is used to associate multiple part numbers together.

### Catalog Lookup

This button is used to specify the catalog, manufacturer, and assembly code information for a PLC module.

### Description

The **Description** edit box displays the description of a module. You can edit this description.

### I/O Point Description Area

The **I/O Point Description** area is used to specify the address and description of I/O points of a PLC module.

#### Next

When you choose the **Next** button from the **I/O Point Description** area, the next value in the **First address** drop-down list will be displayed in the **Address** edit box. Also, the I/O address will be changed in the **List descriptions** drop-down list, which is located below the **Next** button.

#### Pick

The **Pick** button is used to select description for a module from the current drawing.

#### I/O

The **I/O** button is used to display a list of I/O point descriptions.

## Wired Devices

The **Wired Devices** button is used to display the list of descriptions of the wired devices connected to the I/O module.

## External File

The **External File** button is used to select description for I/O point of a PLC module from an external file. To select description from an external file, choose the **External File** button; the **Select External I/O listing file name** dialog box will be displayed, as shown in Figure 10-18. In this dialog box, select the required file and choose **Open**; the **Select PLC annotation for I/O address** dialog box will be displayed. Next, select the required description from the **Select PLC annotation for I/O address** dialog box and choose **OK**; the **I/O Point annotation for address** dialog box will be displayed. Now, in this dialog box you can add and edit a description as per your requirement. Next, choose the **OK** button from the **I/O Point annotation for address** dialog box; the description will be displayed in the **I/O Point Description** area of the **Edit PLC Module** dialog box.

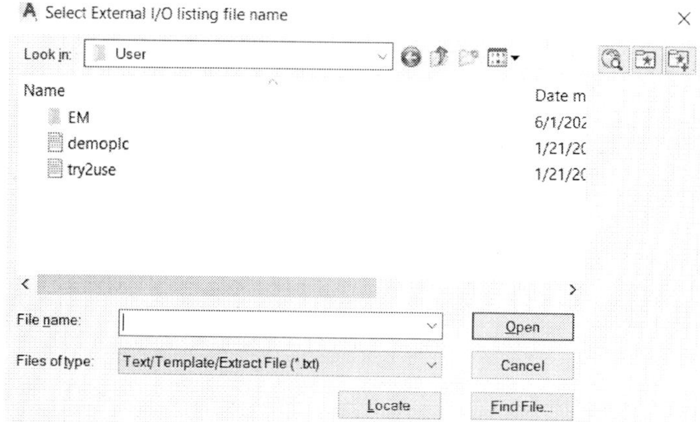


***Figure 10-18** The **Select External I/O listing file name** dialog box*

**Note**

*To select a file other than the default file, choose the **Pick File** button from the **Select PLC annotation for I/O address** dialog box; the **Select External I/O listing file name** dialog box will be displayed again.*

## List descriptions

The **List descriptions** area displays the list of descriptions assigned to I/O point of a module.

# Installation/Location codes Area

The options in the **Installation/Location codes** area are used to specify the installation and location codes for a PLC module. You can specify the installation and location codes in the **Installation** and **Location** edit boxes manually. Alternatively, you can choose the **Drawing** or the **Project** button from the **Installation/Location codes** area to select the installation and location codes that have been used in the current drawing or in the current project.

## Pins Area

The options in the **Pins** area are used to assign pin numbers to terminals of a PLC module.

### Pin 1 and Pin 2

The **Pin 1** and **Pin 2** edit boxes are used to specify the pin numbers for the selected I/O point of a PLC module.

### Show/Edit Miscellaneous

The **Show/Edit Miscellaneous** button is used to view or edit miscellaneous and non-AutoCAD Electrical attributes.

### Ratings

The **Ratings** button will be activated only when a PLC module consists of rating attributes. Choose the **Ratings** button to specify values for each rating attribute. You can enter up to 12 rating attributes on a module.

After specifying the required options in the **Edit PLC Module** dialog box, choose the **OK** button from this dialog box to save the changes made.

# STRETCHING PLC MODULES

| | |
|---|---|
| **Ribbon:** | Schematic > Edit Components > Modify Components drop-down > Stretch PLC Module |
| **Toolbar:** | ACE:Main Electrical > Modify Components drop-down > PLC Module or ACE:Scoot > Stretch PLC Module |
| **Menu:** | Components > Component Miscellaneous > Stretch PLC Module |
| **Command:** | AESTRETCHPLC |

You can stretch a PLC module inserted into the drawing. To do so, choose the **Stretch PLC Module** tool from the **Modify Components** drop-down in the **Edit Components** panel of the **Schematic** tab, refer to Figure 10-19; you will be prompted to select objects. Select one end of the required PLC module from where you want to stretch the PLC module and then select the other end of the PLC module. Next, select the base point of displacement and then select the second base point of displacement; the selected PLC module will be stretched between the two selected base points.

# SPLITTING PLC MODULES

| | |
|---|---|
| **Ribbon:** | Schematic > Edit Components > Modify Components drop-down > Split PLC Module |
| **Toolbar:** | ACE:Main Electrical > Modify Components drop-down > Split PLC Module or ACE:Scoot > Split PLC Module |
| **Menu:** | Components > Component Miscellaneous > Split PLC Module |
| **Command:** | AESPLITPLC |

You can split a PLC module inserted into the drawing. To do so, choose the **Split PLC Module** tool from the **Modify Components** drop-down in the **Edit Components** panel of the **Schematic** tab, refer to Figure 10-19; you will be prompted to the select block to be split.

Select the PLC module to be split. Next, select the point on the PLC where you want to split it. On doing so, the **Split Block** dialog box will be displayed, as shown in Figure 10-20. In this dialog box, the **X** and **Y** edit boxes in the **Child Base Point** area display coordinates of the PLC module from where you want to split the PLC module. You can specify the type of break for a PLC by selecting one of the radio buttons in the **Break type** area. Select the **Reposition Child Block** check box, if you want to reposition the splitted part of the PLC to the other location. After specifying the desired options, choose the **OK** button in the **Split Block** dialog box to split the selected PLC.

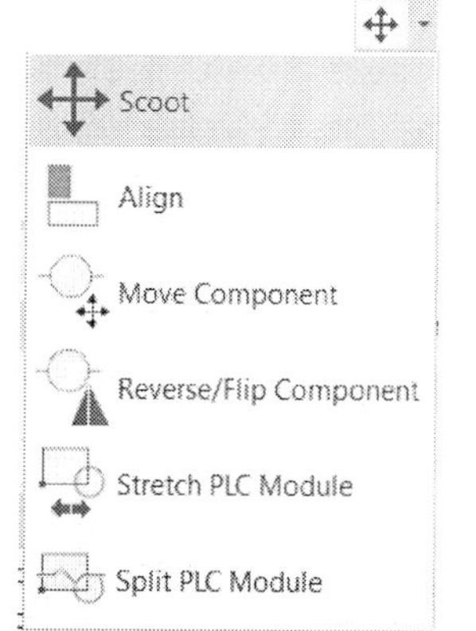


***Figure 10-19** The **Modify Components** drop-down*

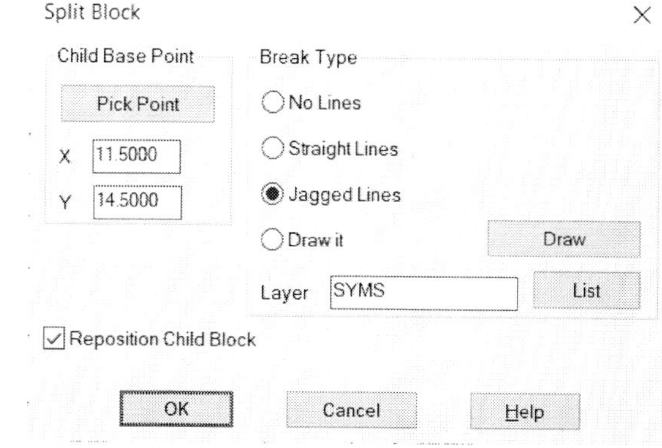


***Figure 10-20** The **Split Block** dialog box*

# INSERTING INDIVIDUAL PLC I/O POINTS

You can insert individual PLC I/O points into a drawing. These PLC I/O points are parent or child schematic symbols. To insert individual PLC I/O points into a drawing, choose the **Icon Menu** tool from the **Insert Components** panel of the **Schematic** tab; the **Insert Component** dialog box will be displayed. Select the **PLC I/O** icon displayed in the **NFPA: Schematic Symbols** area of this dialog box; the **NFPA: PLC I/O** area will be displayed, as shown in Figure 10-21. This area displays the parent and child symbols of a PLC module.

The symbols with prefix 1$^{st}$ Point are the parent symbols and with 2$^{nd+}$ are the child symbols. Select the desired symbol from the **NFPA: PLC I/O** area of the **Insert Component** dialog box; you will be prompted to specify the insertion point. Specify the insertion point; the **Edit PLC I/O Point** dialog box will be displayed, as shown in Figure 10-22. In this dialog box, specify the I/O address, catalog information, and so on for a parent symbol. After specifying the required options in the **Edit PLC I/O Point** dialog box, choose the **OK** button; the PLC symbol will be inserted into a drawing. Figure 10-23 shows individual PLC I/O points inserted into a ladder. Note that you cannot assign catalog information to a child symbol. Therefore, in case of child PLC symbols, you have to link child symbol to a parent symbol. To link a child symbol, choose the **Parent/Sibling** button from the **Edit PLC I/O Point** dialog box; you will be prompted to select PLC I/O point or module. Select a PLC module; the child PLC module will be linked to the parent PLC module. Note that if you select the first icon in the **NFPA: PLC I/O** area which is **PLC I/O Modules**, then the **PLC Parametric Selection** dialog box will be displayed. Now, you can follow the procedure for inserting the Parametric PLC Module or click **Cancel** to exit the dialog box.

**Note**

*If you insert a child PLC symbol into a drawing, then the* ***Manufacturer****,* ***Catalog****, and* ***Assembly*** *edit boxes will not be activated in the* ***Edit PLC I/O Point*** *dialog box.*

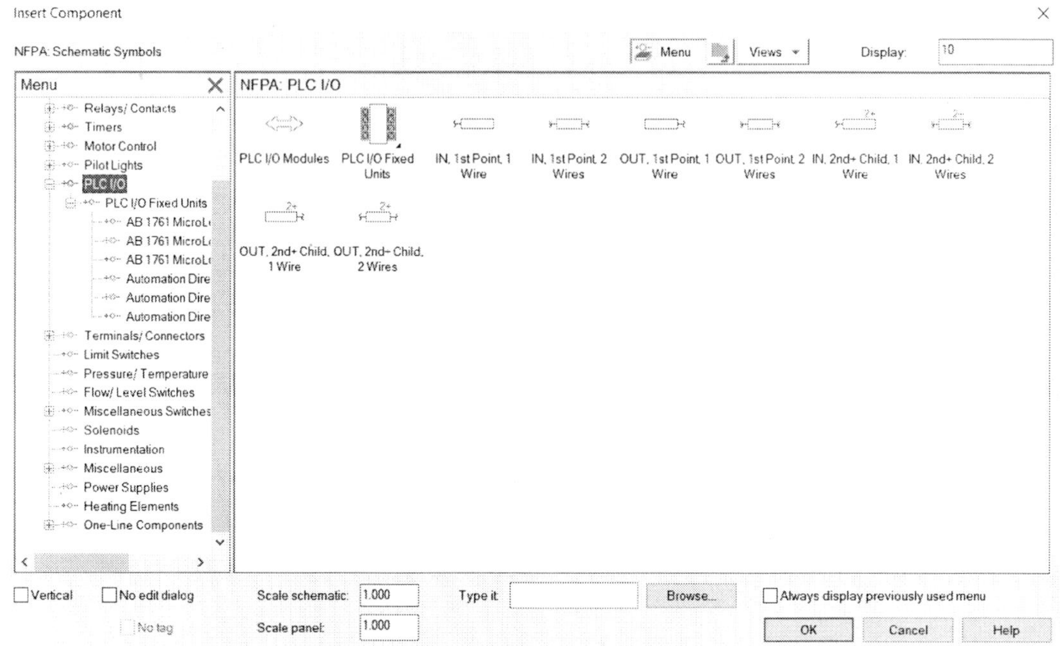


*Figure 10-21* *The* ***NFPA: PLC I/O*** *area of the* ***Insert Component*** *dialog box*

*Figure 10-22* *The* ***Edit PLC I/O Point*** *dialog box*

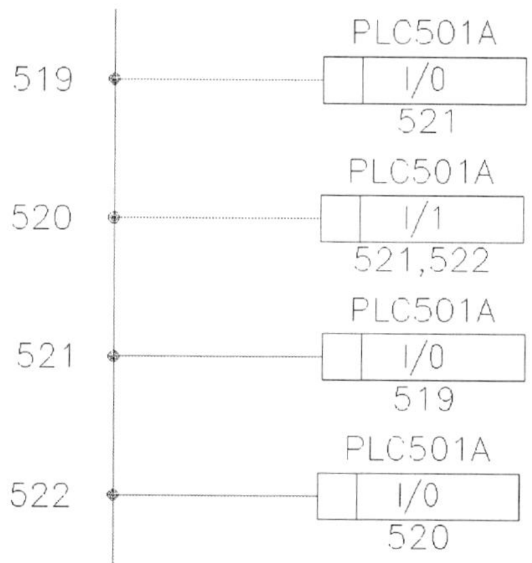


***Figure 10-23*** *Individual PLC I/O points inserted into a ladder*

# CREATING AND MODIFYING PARAMETRIC PLC MODULES

| | |
|---|---|
| **Ribbon:** | Schematic > Other Tools > Database Editors drop-down > PLC Database File Editor |
| **Toolbar:** | ACE:Main Electrical > Insert PLC (Parametric) > PLC Database File Editor or ACE:Insert PLC > PLC Database File Editor |
| **Menu:** | Components > Insert PLC Modules > PLC Database File Editor |
| **Command:** | AEPLCDB |

You can create as well as modify parametric PLC modules by using the **PLC Database File Editor** tool. This tool is also used to edit and modify the PLC database file *ACE_PLC.MDB*. To create a PLC module, choose the **PLC Database File Editor** tool from the **Other Tools** panel of the **Schematic** tab; the **PLC Database File Editor** dialog box will be displayed, refer to Figure 10-24. The options in the **PLC Database File Editor** dialog box are discussed next.

## PLC Module Selection List

The PLC Module Selection List, shown in Figure 10-25, displays the expanded tree view of PLC data files present in the PLC database. The list consists of manufacturer, series, type, and part number categories. If you right-click on a category shown in Figure 10-24, a shortcut menu will be displayed. Using the options in the shortcut menu, you can cut, copy, delete, paste, rename, create new module, and so on. The options in the shortcut menu are discussed next.

### New Manufacturer

When you right-click on the PLC branch of the tree structure, a shortcut menu will be displayed. Choose the **New Manufacturer** option from the shortcut menu; a blank edit box will be displayed at the end of the PLC Module Selection List. Next, enter the name of the manufacturer in this edit box and click outside this edit box; a new manufacturer for PLC module will be created. The manufacturer will appear in an alphabetical order in the PLC Module Selection List after choosing the **Done** button in the **PLC Database File Editor** dialog box.

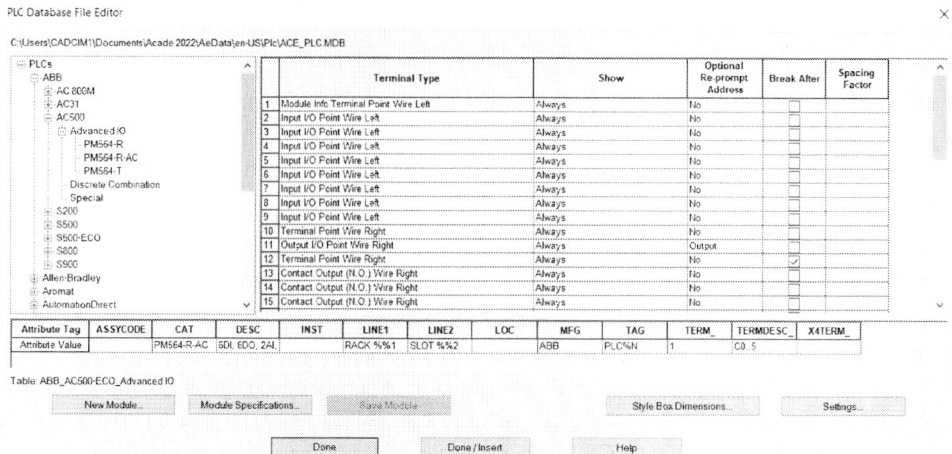

*Figure 10-24 The* ***PLC Database File Editor*** *dialog box*

## New Series

The **New Series** option will be displayed when you right-click on the manufacturer branch of the PLC tree structure. On choosing the **New Series** option from the shortcut menu, a blank edit box will be displayed at the end of the manufacturer series. Enter the required series in the blank edit box. Once you choose the **Done** button in this dialog box, the new series will get arranged in alphabetical order in the PLC Module Selection List.

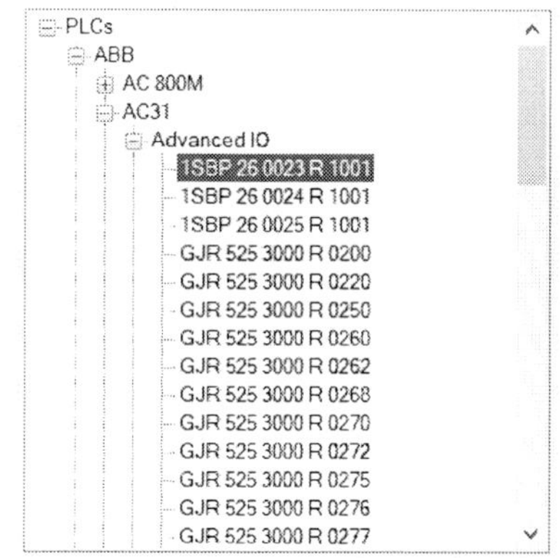

***Figure 10-25*** *The PLC Module Selection List*

## New Type

The **New Type** option will be displayed when you right-click on the series branch of the tree structure. On choosing the **New Type** option from the shortcut menu, a blank edit box will be displayed at the end of the selected series. Enter the required type in the blank edit box; the new type will get arranged in alphabetical order in the PLC Module Selection List.

## New Module

The **New Module** option will be displayed only when you right-click on the type or module branches of the tree structure. To create a new PLC module, choose the **New Module** option from the shortcut menu; the **New Module** dialog box will be displayed. Options in this dialog box are discussed later in the chapter. Enter the required information in this dialog box and choose the **OK** button; a new module will be created and displayed at the end of the respective manufacturer, series, and type. The module will then get arranged in the alphabetical order in the PLC Module Selection List.

## Paste Module

The **Paste Module** option will be displayed only when you right-click on the type branch of the PLC tree structure. This option will become available after cutting or copying a PLC module in the module branch of the tree PLC structure. To paste a PLC module, choose the **Paste Module** option from the shortcut menu; the copied PLC module will be pasted into the highlighted PLC type.

**Note**

*If you paste a PLC module part number to a PLC type that already has a module with the same name, the* ***AutoCAD*** *message box will be displayed. This message box prompts you to specify a new code. Choose the* ***OK*** *button from the* ***AutoCAD*** *message box; the* ***New Module Code*** *dialog box will be displayed. In this dialog box, enter a name for the new module code and choose* ***OK****; a new module code will be displayed at the end of the PLC type of the tree PLC structure.*

### Delete

Choose the **Delete** option from the shortcut menu to delete the entire PLC module, manufacturer, series, or type from the PLC Module Selection List and the PLC database file *ACE_PLC.MDB*.

### Rename

Choose the **Rename** option from the shortcut menu to rename the PLC module's type, manufacturer, or series in the tree structure. Note that the name of PLC manufacturer, series, or type should not be repeated in the same branch of the tree structure.

### Cut

The **Cut** option will be displayed only after you right-click on the module branch of the tree structure. Choose the **Cut** option from the shortcut menu to cut the selected module code from the tree structure.

### Copy

The **Copy** option will be available only after you right-click on the module branch of the tree structure. Choose the **Copy** option from the shortcut menu to copy the selected module code from the tree structure and then paste it in the same or new PLC type category.

## Terminal Grid Area

When you select a module from the PLC Module Selection List, the information related to the module will be displayed in the **Terminal Grid** area, as shown in Figure 10-26. The options in the **Terminal Grid** area are discussed next.

| | Terminal Type | Show | Optional Re-prompt | Break After | Spacing Factor |
|---|---|---|---|---|---|
| 1 | Module Info Input I/O Point Wire Left | Always | No | | |
| 2 | Input I/O Point Wire Left | Always | No | | |
| 3 | Input I/O Point Wire Left | Always | No | | |
| 4 | Input I/O Point Wire Left | Always | No | | |
| 5 | Input I/O Point Wire Left | Always | No | | |
| 6 | Input I/O Point Wire Left | Always | No | | |
| 7 | Input I/O Point Wire Left | Always | No | | |
| 8 | Input I/O Point Wire Left | Always | No | | |
| 9 | Input I/O Point Wire Left | Always | No | | |

*Figure 10-26 The* ***Terminal Grid*** *area*

## Terminal Type

The **Terminal Type** column is used to specify the type of the terminal. If you click on any cell of this column, the cell will be changed to a drop-down list. You can select the required type of terminal from the drop-down list.

## Show

The options in the **Show** column are used to display the unused terminal. If you click on any cell of this column, the cell will be changed to a drop-down list. This drop-down list consists of **Always**, **When Excluding Unused**, and **When Including Unused** options.

## Optional Re-prompt

The options in the **Optional Re-prompt** column are used to prompt you to specify new beginning address for the I/O points of a PLC module. When you click on any cell of this column, it will change to a drop-down list. The options displayed in the drop-down list are **No**, **Input**, and **Output**.

## Break After

Select the **Break After** check box to break a module with the corresponding terminal type selected in the **Terminal Grid** area.

## Spacing Factor

The **Spacing Factor** column is used to override the current rung spacing for I/O point with the specified spacing factor.

When you right-click on a column or a cell of the **Terminal Grid** area, a shortcut menu will be displayed. The options of the shortcut menu are used to edit, insert, and delete the terminals. You can edit multiple rows of the **Terminal Grid** area at a time. The options in this shortcut menu are discussed next.

## Edit Terminal

The **Edit Terminal** option is used to edit the selected terminal. To do so, right-click in the **Terminal Grid** area; a shortcut menu will be displayed. Choose the **Edit Terminal** option from the shortcut menu; the **Select Terminal Information** dialog box will be displayed, as shown in Figure 10-27. Next, select the desired category and type of a terminal from this dialog box and choose **OK**; the selected category and its type will be displayed in the selected cell or column in the **Terminal Grid** area of the **PLC Database File Editor** dialog box.

## Insert Terminal Before

Choose the **Insert Terminal Before** option from the shortcut menu; a terminal will be inserted before the selected row in the **Terminal Grid** area.

## Insert Terminal After

Choose the **Insert Terminal After** option from the shortcut menu; a terminal will be inserted after the selected row in the **Terminal Grid** area.

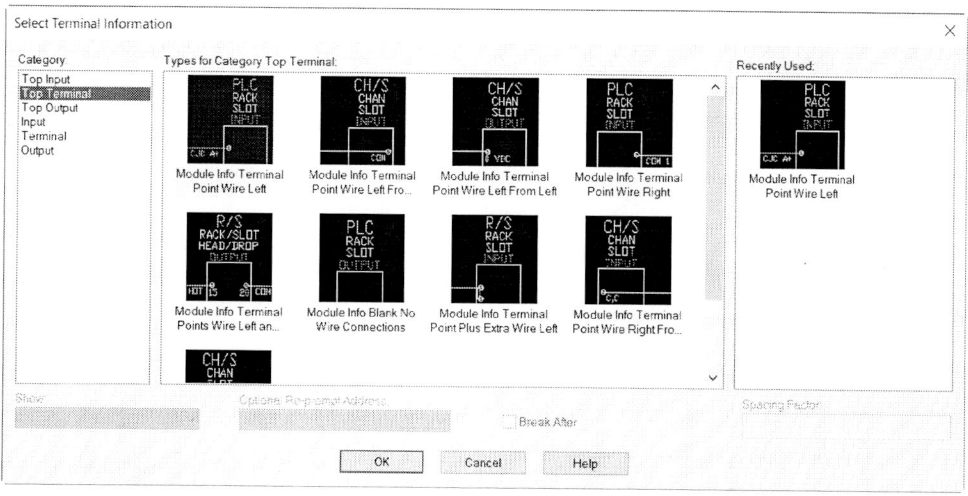


*Figure 10-27 The **Select Terminal Information** dialog box*

## Delete Terminal

Choose the **Delete Terminal** option from the shortcut menu; the selected terminal row will be deleted from the **Terminal Grid** area.

# Terminal Attributes Area

The **Terminal Attributes** area, as shown in Figure 10-28, displays the attribute values associated with the selected terminal.

| Attribute Tag | ASSYCODE | CAT | DESC | DESCA_ | DESCB_ | DESCC_ | DESCD_ | DESCE_ | INST | LINE1 | LINE2 | LOC | MFG |
|---|---|---|---|---|---|---|---|---|---|---|---|---|---|
| Attribute Value | 200-TB3 | 200-IE8 | 8-PT ANALO | | | | | | | MODULE % | SLOT %%2 | | ABB |

Table: ABB_s200_analog_input

*Figure 10-28 The **Terminal Attributes** area*

# New Module

The **New Module** button is used to create a new PLC module. To do so, choose the **New Module** button from the **PLC Database File Editor** dialog box; the **New Module** dialog box will be displayed, as shown in Figure 10-29. The options in this dialog box are discussed next.

## Manufacturer

The **Manufacturer** edit box is used to enter manufacturer name. You can enter it manually or you can select a pre-defined manufacturer name for a new module by clicking on the arrow displayed on the right of the **Manufacturer** edit box.

## Series

The **Series** edit box is used to specify a series for a new module. To do so, enter the series name in the **Series** edit box. Alternatively, you can select a pre-defined series name by clicking on the arrow displayed on the right of the **Series** edit box.

## Series Type

The **Series Type** edit box is used to specify type of series for a new module. To do so, enter the series type in the **Series Type** edit box. Alternatively, you can select a pre-defined series type by clicking on the arrow displayed on the right of the **Series Type** edit box.

## Code

The **Code** edit box is used to specify code (catalog number) for a new module.

## Description

The **Description** edit box is used to specify the description for a PLC module.

## Module Type

The **Module Type** edit box is used to specify the type of a PLC module.

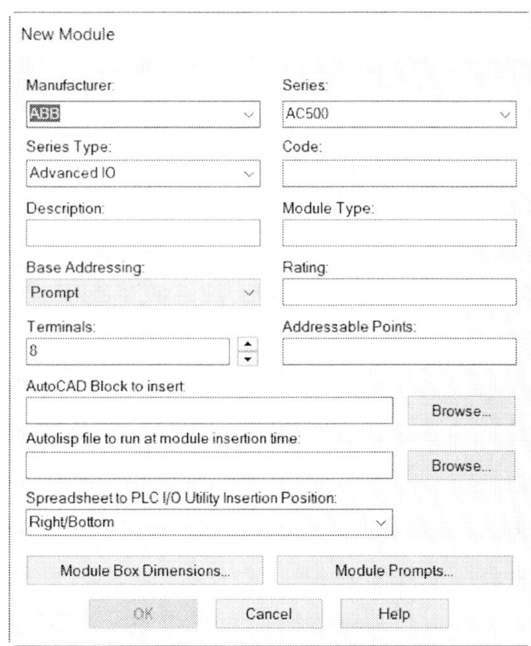


*Figure 10-29 The* ***New Module*** *dialog box*

## Base Addressing

The **Base Addressing** drop-down list contains different options to select various types of addressing. You can select the **Octal**, **Decimal**, **Hexadecimal**, and **Prompt** options from this drop-down list.

## Rating

The **Rating** edit box is used to specify the power rating value for a PLC module.

## Terminals

The **Terminals** spinner is used to specify the total number of terminals of a PLC module. You can increment or decrement the specified value by clicking the arrow buttons on right of the **Terminals** edit box.

## Addressable Points

The **Addressable Points** edit box is used to specify the total number of addressable points on a PLC module.

## AutoCAD Block to insert

The **AutoCAD Block to insert** edit box is used to insert AutoCAD block after the last I/O point of a PLC module. You can specify the AutoCAD block to be inserted by entering its name in this edit box or by using the **Browse** button.

## Autolisp file to run at module insertion time

The **Autolisp file to run at module insertion time** edit box is used to specify the AutoCAD lisp routine to be run after the PLC module is inserted into a drawing.

## Module Box Dimensions

The **Module Box Dimensions** button is used to define the dimensions for outer box of a PLC module. To do so, choose the **Module Box Dimensions** button from the **New Module** dialog box; the **Module Box Dimensions** dialog box will be displayed, as shown in Figure 10-30. Specify the required options in this dialog box for outer box dimensions of the module. If you leave the edit boxes blank, the default style box dimensions will be used. If you need to set color for the box lines, then enter **COLOR**<colorname> in the **Line Properties** edit box and if you need to set the line type for the box lines, enter **LTYPE**<linetypename> in the **Line Properties** edit box. Choose the **OK** button in the **Module Box Dimensions** dialog box to return to the **New Module** dialog box.

## Module Prompts

The **Module Prompts** button in the **New Module** dialog box is used to define prompts for a module that will be used at the time of insertion of a module in a drawing. To define prompts for a module, choose the **Module Prompts** button from the **New Module** dialog box; the **Prompts at Module Insertion Time** dialog box will be displayed, as shown in Figure 10-31. In this dialog box, you can define nine prompts which will be used at the time of insertion of a module. To create the custom prompt, select the required prompt from the **Prompt Number** area and enter the prompt text in the **New Prompt Text** edit box and then choose the **Change** button, which is on the right of the **New Prompt Text** edit box; the prompt text will be displayed in the **Prompt Text** area. To delete the required text in the **Prompt Text** area, select the text from this area and then choose the **Remove Selected Prompt** button. Next, choose **OK** to save the changes made in this dialog box and to return to the **New Module** dialog box.

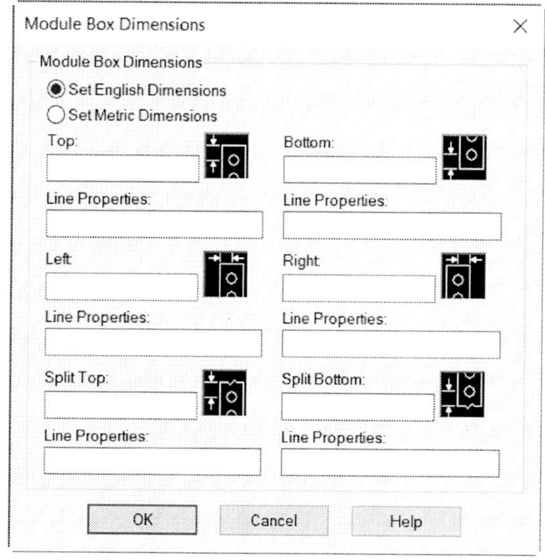


*Figure 10-30 The* ***Module Box Dimensions*** *dialog box*

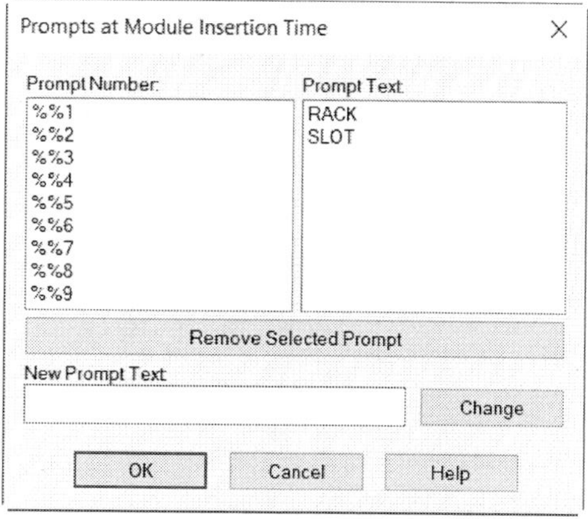


*Figure 10-31 The* ***Prompts at Module Insertion Time*** *dialog box*

After specifying the required options in the **New Module** dialog box, choose the **OK** button in this dialog box; a new module will be created and added to the PLC Module Selection List.

## Module Specifications

The **Module Specifications** button is used to edit the specifications of an existing PLC module. To do so, choose the **Module Specifications** button from the **PLC Database File Editor** dialog box; the **Module Specifications** dialog box will be displayed, as shown in Figure 10-32. The options in the **Module Specifications** dialog box are similar to the options in the **New Module** dialog box, which have already been discussed. Specify the required options in the **Module Specifications** dialog box and choose the **OK** button to save the changes made and to return to the **PLC Database File Editor** dialog box.

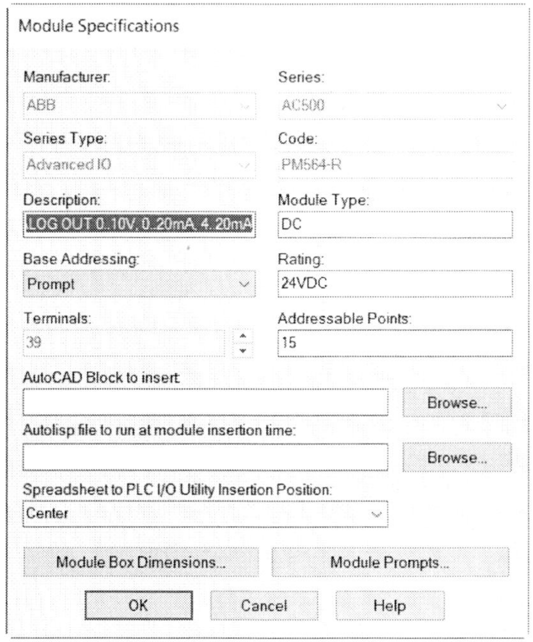


*Figure 10-32 The **Module Specifications** dialog box*

## Style Box Dimensions

The **Style Box Dimensions** button is used to define the dimensions of a module box for a specific graphic style. To define the dimensions of a module box, choose the **Style Box Dimensions** button from the **PLC Database File Editor** dialog box; the **Style Box Dimensions** dialog box will be displayed, as shown in Figure 10-33. The options in this dialog box are similar to that in the **Module Box Dimensions** dialog box and have already been discussed.

## Settings

The **Settings** button is used to add or edit the symbols available for building a module. To add or edit the symbols, choose the **Settings** button from the **PLC Database File Editor** dialog box; the **Terminal Block Settings** dialog box will be displayed, as shown in Figure 10-34. The options in this dialog box are discussed next.

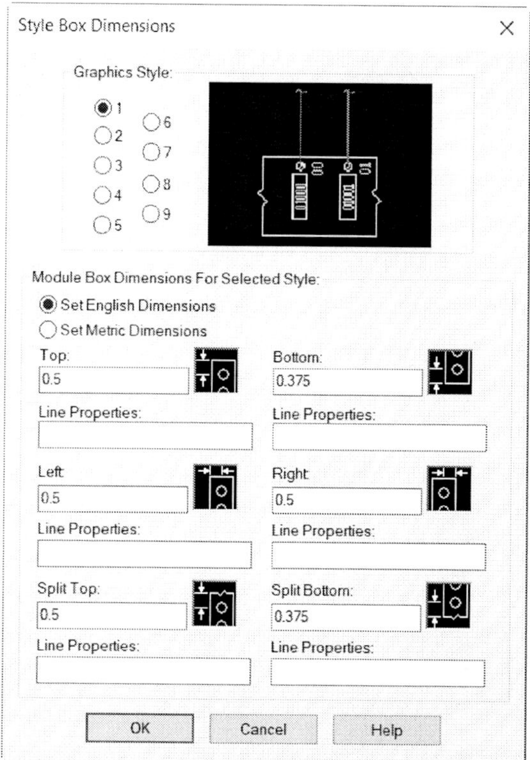


*Figure 10-33 The **Style Box Dimensions** dialog box*

## Block File Name

The **Block File Name** column displays the block file name of a terminal of a PLC module. Enter the file name of the terminal block in the required cell of the **Block File Name** column by clicking on it. Alternatively, select the block file name cell and then choose the **Browse** button from the **Terminal Block Settings** dialog box; the **Select File** dialog box will be displayed. Select the drawing file and choose the **Open** button; the file name will be displayed in the selected cell of the **Block File Name** column.

## Category

The **Category** column is used to define the category for the terminal of a PLC module. When you click on any cell in the **Category** column, the cell will change into a drop-down list. You can specify the required category in the respective cell of the **Category** column manually or select a category from the drop-down list. By default, the **Top Terminal**, **Top Input**, **Top Output**, **Input**, **Terminal**, and **Output** options are available in the drop-down list.

## Unique Description

The **Unique Description** column is used to enter a description for a terminal. By default, the description for a terminal is displayed under the **Unique Description** column of the **Terminal Block Settings** dialog box. You can edit this description by clicking on the respective cell and entering a new description.

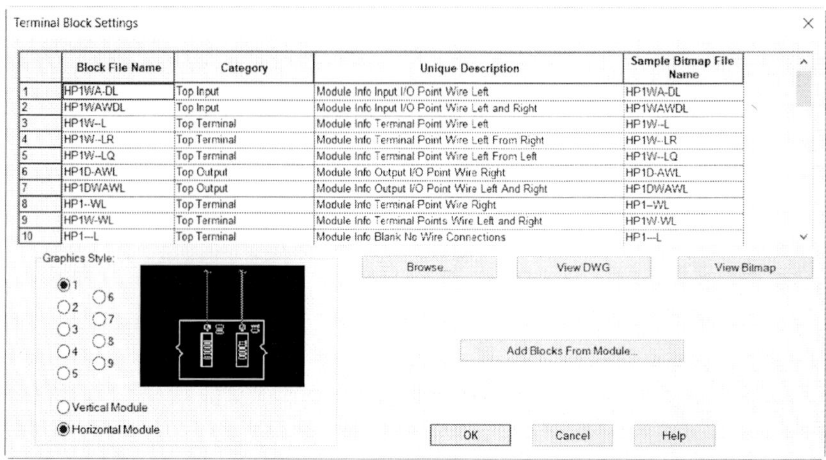

*Figure 10-34 The* ***Terminal Block Settings*** *dialog box*

## Sample Bitmap File

The **Sample Bitmap File** column is used to specify a bitmap file for a terminal. You can specify the bitmap file manually or by clicking on the required cell in the **Sample Bitmap File** column and choosing the **Browse** button.

### Note

*1. You can add a terminal to a list. To do so, click on any column of the last row; a blank row is added to the bottom of the list. Next, enter the required information in this blank row.*
*2. The* ***Browse*** *button is available only when you select any cell of the* ***Block File Name*** *column or the* ***Sample Bitmap File*** *column.*

## View DWG

The **View DWG** button is used to view an AutoCAD drawing of the selected terminal. To view an AutoCAD drawing, choose the **View DWG** button from the **Terminal Block Settings** dialog box; the **Terminal Block Preview** dialog box will be displayed. In this dialog box, you can zoom or pan a drawing to view the attributes of a terminal. After you have seen the preview of the drawing, choose the **Done** button to exit the **Terminal Block Preview** dialog box.

## View Bitmap

The **View Bitmap** button is used to view a bitmap file of the selected terminal. To view a bitmap file, choose the **View Bitmap** button from the **Terminal Block Settings** dialog box; the **Terminal Sample** dialog box will be displayed. In this dialog box, you can see the preview of the selected terminal. Once the preview of the selected terminal has been displayed, choose the **Done** button to exit the **Terminal Sample** dialog box.

## Add Blocks From Module

The **Add Blocks From Module** button is used to specify the module from which the terminal block will be added. To specify the module, choose the **Add Blocks From Module** button from the **Terminal Block Settings** dialog box; the **PLC Selection** dialog box will be displayed. Select the required module from the tree structure and choose the **OK** button from this dialog box to return to the **Terminal Block Settings** dialog box.

After specifying the required options in the **Terminal Block Settings** dialog box, choose the **OK** button in this dialog box to return to the **PLC Database File Editor** dialog box.

**Note**

*When you right-click on any of the columns in the **Terminal Block Settings** dialog box, a shortcut menu will be displayed. This shortcut menu has options such as **New Row**, **Delete Row**, and so on.*

After specifying the options in the **PLC Database File Editor** dialog box, choose the **Done** button to save the changes made and close the dialog box.

Now, to insert the PLC, choose the **Done / Insert** button from the **PLC Database File Editor** dialog box; the **PLC Parametric Selection** dialog box will be displayed. Select the required module and then choose the **OK** button from the **PLC Parametric Selection** dialog box. Next, follow the steps described earlier in the chapter to insert the PLC module.

# CREATING PLC I/O WIRING DIAGRAMS

| | |
|---|---|
| **Ribbon:** | Import/Export Data > Import > PLC I/O Utility |
| **Toolbar:** | ACE:Main Electrical > Insert PLC (Parametric) > Spreadsheet to PLC I/O Utility |
| **Menu:** | Components > Insert PLC Modules > Spreadsheet to PLC I/O Utility |
| **Command:** | AESS2PLC |

The **PLC I/O Utility** tool is used to create a set of PLC I/O wiring diagrams directly from the spreadsheet data. Using this tool, you can generate multiple drawings quickly. To create a drawing using spreadsheet data, choose the **PLC I/O Utility** tool from the **Import** panel of the **Import/Export Data** tab; the **Select PLC I/O Spreadsheet Output File** dialog box will be displayed, as shown in Figure 10-35. The PLC I/O spreadsheet output file will be available in the *.xls*, *.csv*, and *.mdb* formats. Select the required file from this dialog box and choose the **Open** button; the **Spreadsheet to PLC I/O Utility** dialog box will be displayed, as shown in Figure 10-36. The options in this dialog box are discussed next.

## Settings

The **Settings** edit box is used to specify the settings for creating the PLC I/O wiring diagrams. Enter the name of the file(.wdi) in the **Settings** edit box. Alternatively, use the **Browse** button to specify the settings of the PLC I/O wiring diagram.

## Setup

When you choose the **Setup** button, the **Spreadsheet to PLC I/O Utility Setup** dialog box is displayed. The options in this dialog box are used to modify and save a new setting configuration. These options are discussed in the later section.

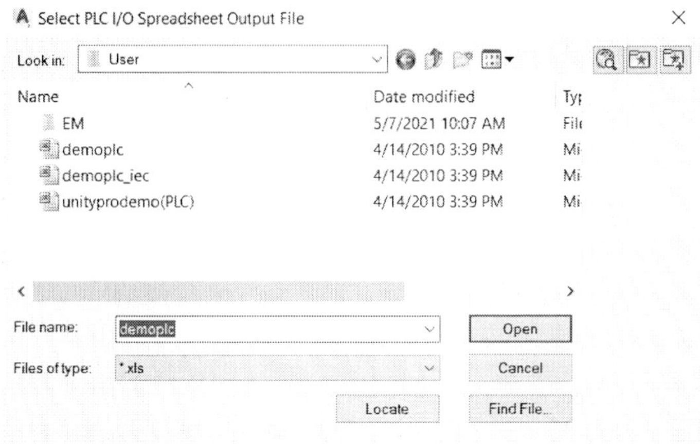

*Figure 10-35* The **Select PLC I/O Spreadsheet Output File** *dialog box*

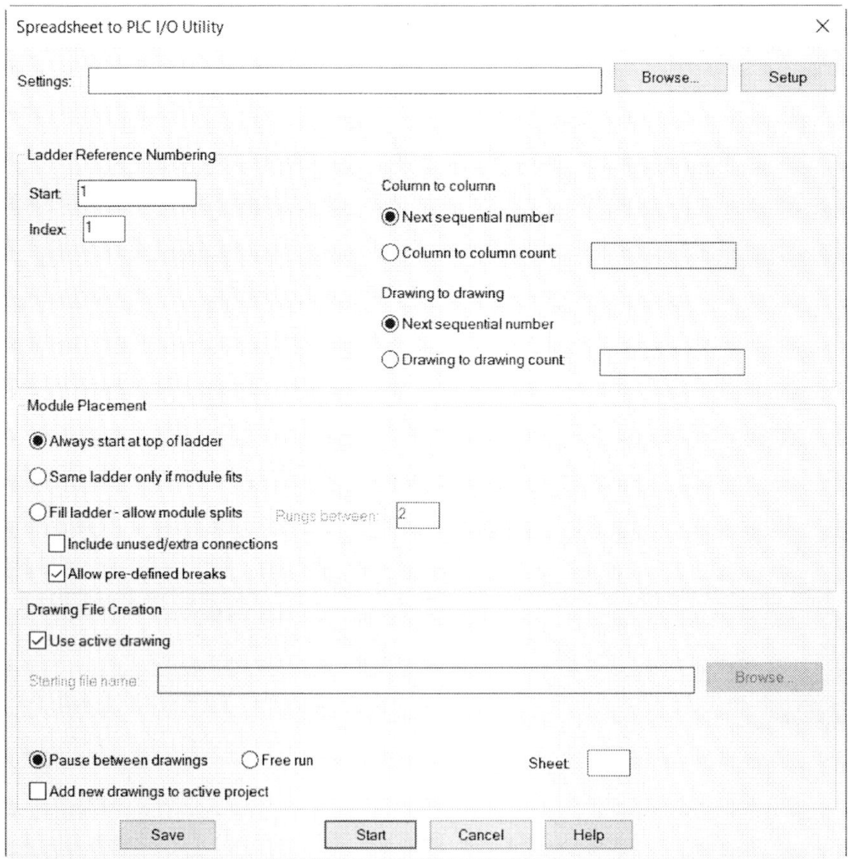


*Figure 10-36* The **Spreadsheet to PLC I/O Utility** *dialog box*

## Ladder Reference Numbering Area

This area is used to specify ladder reference numbers for the drawings to be created. The options in this area are discussed next.

### Start

The **Start** edit box is used to specify a value for the first line reference number of the first ladder of the first drawing. By default, 1 is displayed in this edit box.

### Index

The index edit box is used to increment the line reference number of a ladder. To do so, enter a value in the **Index** edit box. By default, 1 is displayed in this edit box.

### Next sequential number

The **Next sequential number** radio button under the **Column to column** field is selected by default. As a result, the next sequential number will be used for the first ladder on each successive column.

### Column to column count

When you select the **Column to column count** radio button that is under the **Column to column** field, the edit box on right of this radio button will be activated. By default, 30 is displayed in this edit box. You can enter the required value in this edit box to skip the first ladder reference of the next column.

### Next sequential number

The **Next sequential number** radio button under the **Drawing to drawing** field is selected by default and is used to specify the next sequential number to be used for the first ladder on each successive drawing.

### Drawing to drawing count

When you select the **Drawing to drawing count** radio button under the **Drawing to drawing** field, the edit box on right of this radio button will be activated. By default, 100 is displayed in this edit box. Enter a value in this edit box to skip the first ladder reference of the next drawing.

## Module Placement Area

The options in the **Module Placement** area are used to define the placement of a module. The different options in this area are discussed next.

### Always start at top of ladder

The **Always start at top of ladder** radio button is selected by default and is used to specify each I/O module to start at the top of a ladder.

### Same ladder only if module fits

The **Same ladder only if module fits** radio button is used to insert the module in a ladder on which previous module was inserted, only if it fits completely. On selecting the **Same ladder only if module fits** radio button, the **Rungs between** edit box will be activated. By default, 2 is displayed in this edit box.

### Fill ladder - allow module splits

This radio button is used to build the module in the same ladder even if it does not fit in it completely. The rest of the module continues in the next ladder or next drawing.

### Include unused/extra connections

Select the **Include unused/extra connections** check box to show the unused or extra connections on a PLC module.

### Allow pre-defined breaks

The **Allow pre-defined breaks** check box is selected by default and is used to break a PLC module at a point specified in the module's parametric data.

**Note**

*Correct PLC I/O drawings can be generated even if the spreadsheet used consists of a break.*

## Drawing File Creation Area

The options in the **Drawing File Creation** area are used to specify a drawing file for creation of PLC drawings. The options in this area are discussed next.

### Use active drawing

If the active drawing is included in the active project, the **Use active drawing** check box is selected by default. As a result, the active drawing file will be used for creating a PLC module drawing. If the active drawing is not included in the active project or if you clear this check box, the **Starting file name** edit box and the **Browse** button will become available.

### Starting file name

The **Starting file name** edit box is used to specify the drawing file for creating a PLC module drawing. To do so, enter the name of a drawing file in the **Starting file name** edit box. Alternatively, choose the **Browse** button on the right of this edit box to specify the starting file name.

### Pause between drawings

If the spreadsheet data file contains enough information to generate multiple drawings, you can use the **Pause between drawings** radio button. This radio button is selected by default. As a result, a dialog box opens which allows you to select between the two options: **Free run** and **Pause between drawings**.

### Free run

Select the **Free run** radio button to run a program uninterrupted till the end.

### Add new drawings to active project

The **Add new drawings to active project** check box is used to add the new drawings to the active project. These drawings will be added to the end of the active project's drawing list.

## Save

The **Save** button is used to save the settings to a *.wdi* file for later use.

## Start

Choose the **Start** button for creating a set of PLC I/O drawings based on the information carried in the selected PLC spreadsheet. Once the drawings are created, the **Spreadsheet to PLC I/O Utility** dialog box will be displayed again.

# Modifying and Saving the New Setting Configuration

To modify and save a new setting configuration, choose the **PLC I/O Utility** tool from the **Import** panel of the **Import/Export Data** tab; the **Select PLC I/O Spreadsheet Output File** dialog box will be displayed. Next, select the required spreadsheet file from this dialog box and choose the **Open** button; the **Spreadsheet to PLC I/O Utility** dialog box will be displayed. Choose the **Setup** button adjacent to the **Settings** edit box; the **Spreadsheet to PLC I/O Utility Setup** dialog box will be displayed, as shown in Figure 10-37. In this dialog box, you can define the settings for drawings. The different areas and options in this dialog box are discussed next.

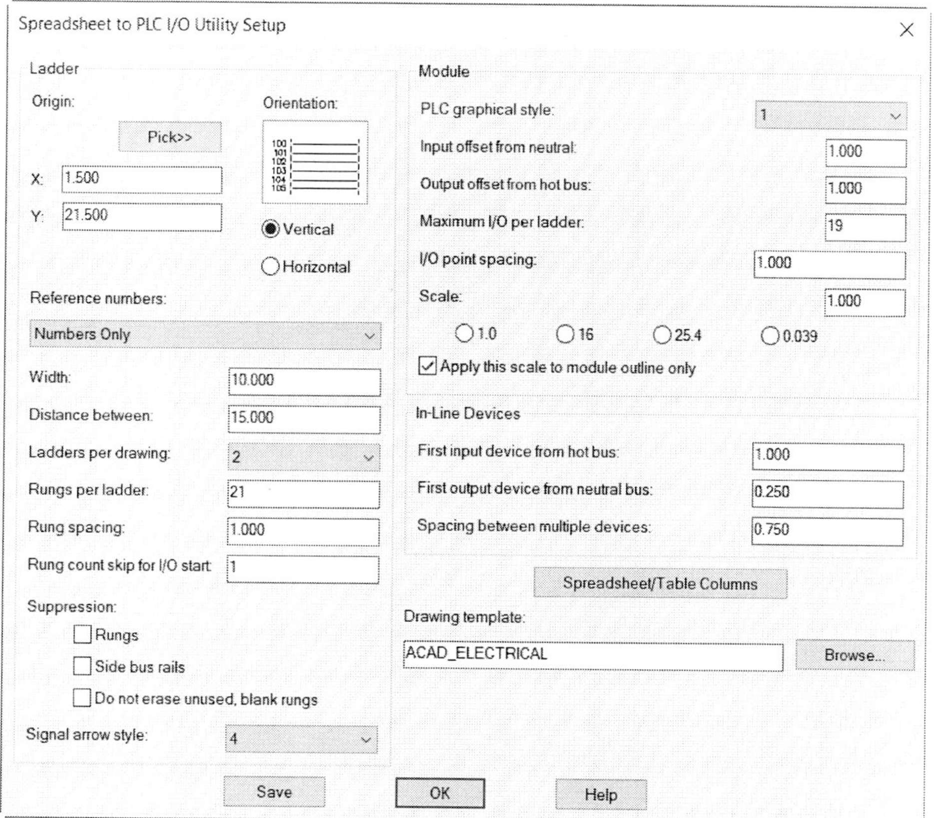


*Figure 10-37 The **Spreadsheet to PLC I/O Utility Setup** dialog box*

## Ladder Area

The options in the **Ladder** area are used to specify location and orientation of a ladder, number of ladders per drawing, rungs per ladder, spacing between rungs, and so on. The options in this area are discussed next.

### Origin
Specify the insertion point for a ladder in the **X** and **Y** edit boxes. Alternatively, choose the **Pick** button to select the location of a ladder manually.

### Orientation
You can select either the **Vertical** or **Horizontal** radio button to get the desired orientation of the bus ladder. You can see the preview of a ladder in the preview window, which is located above the **Vertical** radio button.

### Reference numbers
The **Reference numbers** drop-down list is used to specify reference numbers of a ladder. This drop-down list consists of five options: **Numbers Only**, **Numbers Ruling**, **User Blocks**, **X-Y Grid**, and **X Zones**.

### Width
The **Width** edit box is used to specify width between two vertical rails of a ladder.

### Distance between
The **Distance between** edit box is used to specify the distance between the insertion points of two ladders.

### Ladders per drawing
The **Ladders per drawing** drop-down list is used to select the number of ladders to be inserted into the drawing. Also, note that vertical ladders will be inserted from left to right, whereas horizontal ladders will be inserted from top to bottom.

### Rungs per ladder
The **Rungs per ladder** edit box is used to specify the number of rungs per ladder.

### Rung spacing
The **Rung spacing** edit box is used to specify the spacing between rungs of a ladder.

### Rung count skip for I/O start
The **Rung count skip for I/O start** edit box is used to specify the number of rungs to be skipped before inserting a PLC module.To do so, specify the number of rungs to be skipped. If you enter '0', no rung will be skipped.

### Suppression
In the **Suppression** area, the **Rungs**, **Side bus rails**, and **Do not erase unused, blank rungs** check boxes are available. All these check boxes are cleared by default. Select the **Rungs** check box to insert ladder without rungs. Select the **Side bus rails** check box to insert a ladder without bus rails. If you select the **Do not erase unused, blank rungs** check box, then the unused rungs will not be erased.

### Signal arrow style
The **Signal arrow style** drop-down list is used to select the wire signal arrow style.

## Module Area

The options in the **Module** area are used to specify graphical style for a PLC module, I/O point spacing, insertion scale of a PLC module, and so on.

### PLC graphical style

The **PLC graphical style** drop-down list is used to select the graphical style for the PLC.

### Input offset from neutral

The **Input offset from neutral** edit box is used to specify the distance between the insertion point of an input PLC module and neutral rail of a ladder. Note that if a vertical ladder is inserted, then the input offset from neutral distance will be measured from right-hand vertical bus upto the module's insertion point. If a horizontal ladder is inserted, then the input offset from neutral distance will be measured from lower horizontal bus upto module's insertion point.

### Output offset from hot bus

The **Output offset from hot bus** edit box is used to specify the distance between the insertion point of an output PLC module and hot bus (left vertical bus) of a ladder. Note that if a vertical ladder is inserted then the output offset from hot bus distance will be measured from left-hand vertical bus upto module's insertion point. If a horizontal ladder is inserted then the output offset from hot bus distance will be measured from upper horizontal bus upto the module's insertion point.

### Maximum I/O per ladder

The **Maximum I/O per ladder** edit box is used to specify maximum number of I/O points of a module to be inserted into each ladder.

### I/O point spacing

The **I/O point spacing** edit box is used to specify the insertion point distance between the in-line devices.

### Scale

The **Scale** edit box is used to specify scale for a PLC module. By default, 1.000 is displayed. In this edit box, you can enter the scale value for a PLC module manually or you can select any radio button located below the **Scale** edit box.

### Apply this scale to module outline only

The **Apply this scale to module outline only** check box is selected by default. As a result, the value entered in the **Scale** edit box will be applied only to the module's outline.

## In-Line Devices Area

The options in the **In-Line Devices** area are used to specify distance between the first input device and hot bus, first output device and neutral bus, and spacing between multiple devices. The **In-Line Devices** area is shown in Figure 10-38. The options in this area are discussed next.

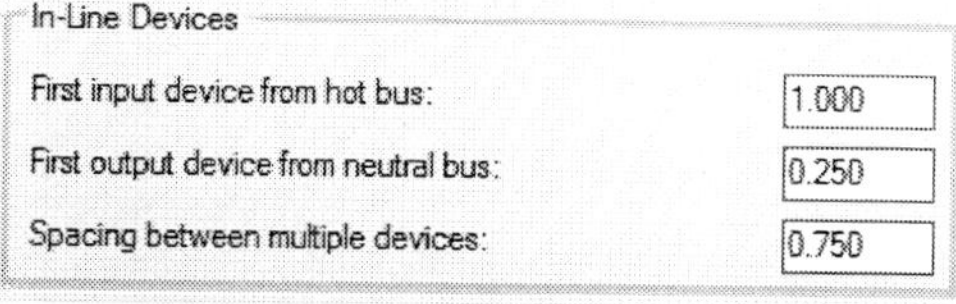


***Figure 10-38** The **In-Line Devices** area*

### First input device from hot bus

The **First input device from hot bus** edit box is used to specify the distance between the hot bus of a ladder and first input in-line device of I/O PLC module. Note that if a vertical ladder is inserted then the distance will be measured from the left-hand vertical bus and first input in-line device defined for each input module I/O point. However, if a horizontal ladder is inserted then the distance will be measured from the upper horizontal bus and first input in-line device defined for each input module I/O point.

### First output device from neutral bus

The **First output device from neutral bus** edit box is used to specify the distance between the neutral bus of a ladder and first output in-line device of I/O PLC module. Note that if a vertical ladder is inserted then the distance will be measured from the right-hand vertical bus and first output in-line device defined for each output module I/O point. However, if a horizontal ladder is inserted then the distance will be measured from the lower horizontal bus and first output in-line device defined for each output module I/O point.

### Spacing between multiple devices

The **Spacing between multiple devices** edit box is used to specify the distance between the in-line devices.

## Drawing template

The **Drawing template** edit box is used to specify template for new drawings. To do so, specify the template drawing file name and its path in the **Drawing template** edit box. Alternatively, choose the **Browse** button from the **Spreadsheet to PLC I/O Utility Setup** dialog box; the **Select Prototype/Template (.dwg or .dwt)** dialog box will be displayed, as shown in Figure 10-39. Next, select the required template from this dialog box and choose the **Open** button; the template drawing name will be displayed in the **Drawing template** edit box. Also, the path of the template drawing file will be displayed under the **Drawing template** edit box. Note that the template should not include any existing ladder.

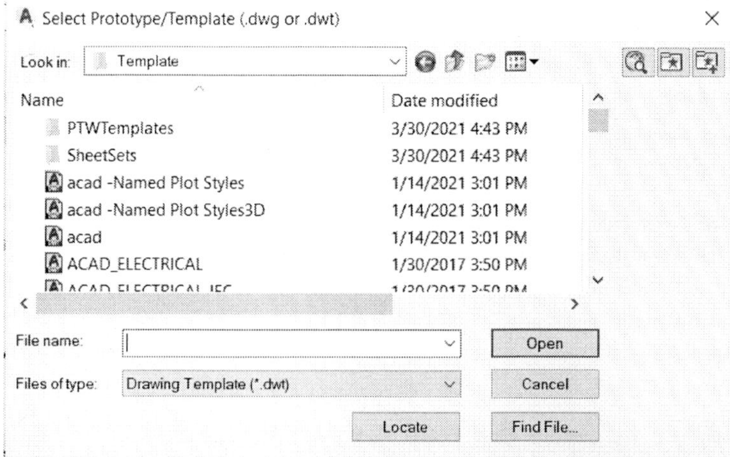


*Figure 10-39 The **Select Prototype/Template(.dwg or .dwt)** dialog box*

### Spreadsheet/Table Columns

The **Spreadsheet/Table Columns** button is used to map spreadsheet information to appropriate fields. To do so, choose the **Spreadsheet/Table Columns** button from the **Spreadsheet to PLC I/O Utility Setup** dialog box; the **Spreadsheet to PLC I/O Drawing Generator** dialog box will be displayed. The options in this dialog box are discussed in the next section.

### Save

The **Save** button is used to save the settings to a *.wdi* file. To do so, choose the **Save** button from the **Spreadsheet to PLC I/O Utility Setup** dialog box; the **Save Settings** dialog box will be displayed. In this dialog box, enter the file name in the **File name** edit box and choose the **Save** button; the spreadsheet information will be saved in the specified file for later use.

After specifying the required options in the **Spreadsheet to PLC I/O Utility Setup** dialog box, choose the **OK** button in this dialog box to save the changes made and to return to the **Spreadsheet to PLC I/O Utility** dialog box.

**Note**

*The devices for an input point of a PLC module are inserted from left to right or top to bottom and the devices for output point of a PLC module are inserted from right to left or bottom to top.*

## MAPPING THE SPREADSHEET INFORMATION

To map and review the spreadsheet information to the attributes of a PLC module, choose the **Spreadsheet/Table Columns** button from the **Spreadsheet to PLC I/O Utility Setup** dialog box; the **Spreadsheet to PLC I/O Drawing Generator** dialog box will be displayed, as shown in Figure 10-40. The areas and options in this dialog box are discussed next.



*Figure 10-40 The **Spreadsheet to PLC I/O Drawing Generator** dialog box*

## Spreadsheet data Area

The **Spreadsheet data** area displays the ASCII representation of a spreadsheet.

## Assign spreadsheet or table column numbers to data categories below Area

In this area, you can map the columns of a spreadsheet to component attributes by selecting the required value from the respective drop-down list in this area. For each attribute listed in this area, you need to use the associated column list to select a spreadsheet column.

## More

On choosing the **More** button, the **Connected device(s)** dialog box will be displayed, as shown in Figure 10-41. This dialog box is used to map the spreadsheet data to the connected devices. Also, the spreadsheet data can be defined upto nine series-connected devices on per input or output point basis. If you choose the **More** button from the **Connected device(s)** dialog box, the **Connected device(s)** dialog box will be displayed again. Next, assign the columns of the spreadsheet to the devices and choose **OK** to save the changes made.

After specifying the required options in the **Spreadsheet to PLC I/O Drawing Generator** dialog box, choose the **OK** button from this dialog box to save the changes made and to return to the **Spreadsheet to PLC I/O Utility Setup** dialog box.

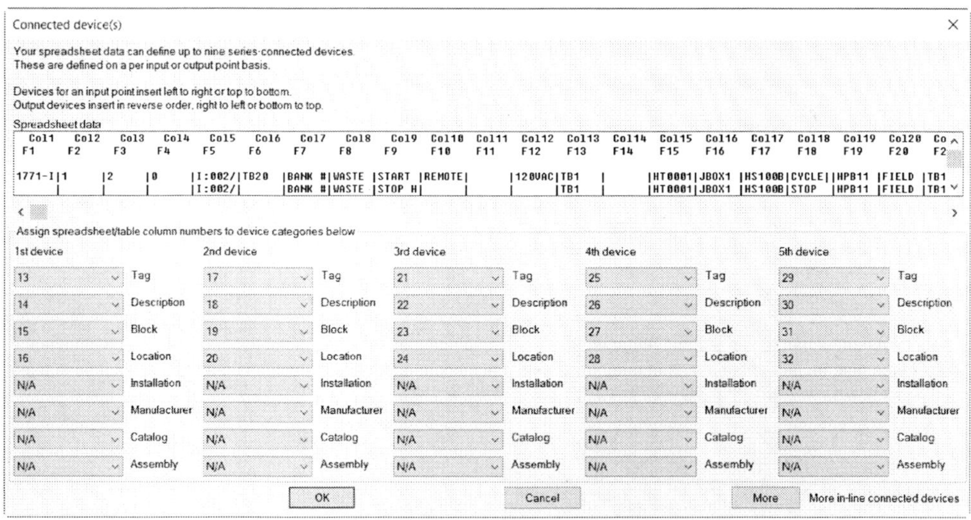


*Figure 10-41 The **Connected device(s)** dialog box*

# TAGGING BASED ON PLC I/O ADDRESS

The tags of a component and wire numbers can use PLC address instead of ladder reference number when inserted into a ladder. You can tag a component based on PLC address and then insert it into a drawing. Also, you can insert a wire number, which will use a PLC address. To use PLC address as the tags of a component and wire numbers, you need to set options in the **Drawing Properties** dialog box.

Right-click on the active drawing of an active project in the **PROJECT MANAGER**; a shortcut menu will be displayed. Choose **Properties > Drawing Properties** from the shortcut menu; the **Drawing Properties** dialog box will be displayed. Next, choose the **Components** tab from the **Drawing Properties** dialog box and select the **Search for PLC I/O address on insert** check box, as shown in Figure 10-42. Next, choose the **OK** button to close this dialog box.

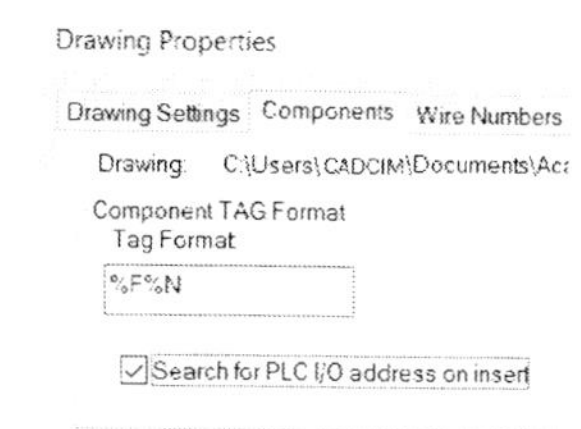


*Figure 10-42 Partial view of the* ***Components*** *tab of the* ***Drawing Properties*** *dialog box*

This check box is used to search for a PLC I/O address when you insert a component and then the tag of the inserted component will be based on the PLC I/O address. You can also tag individual components based on PLC I/O address while inserting or editing the component. To do so, choose the **Use PLC Address** button from the **Insert/Edit Component** dialog box; the I/O address of PLC attached to the component will be displayed in the edit box of the **Component Tag** area in the **Insert/Edit Component** dialog box, as shown in Figure 10-43. Note that if the components are already inserted into the ladder of a drawing, then you need to use the **Retag Component** tool for retagging all components present in a drawing.

To use PLC address as wire numbers, you need to select the **Search for PLC I/O address on insert** check box from the **Wire Numbers** tab of the **Drawing Properties** dialog box, as shown in Figure 10-44. Next, choose the **OK** button in this dialog box to exit. Now, if you insert wire numbers in the drawing, first the software will search the I/O address of a PLC. If the I/O address is found, the same will be used as a wire number. Note that if wire numbers are already inserted into the ladder of a drawing, then you need to use the **Wire Numbers** tool to assign the wire numbers based on the PLC I/O address.

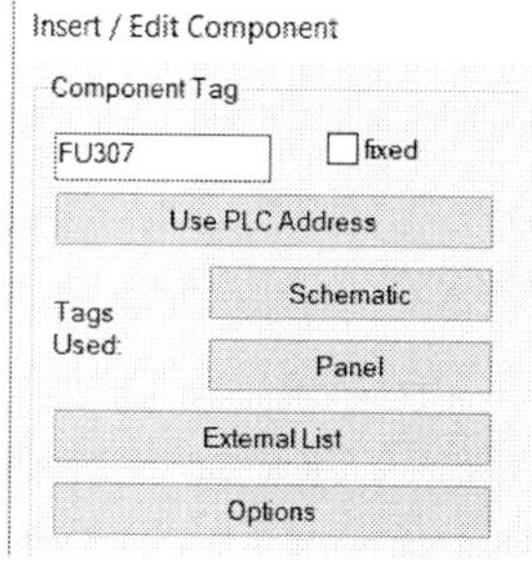


*Figure 10-43 The* ***Component Tag*** *area of the* ***Insert/Edit Component*** *dialog box*

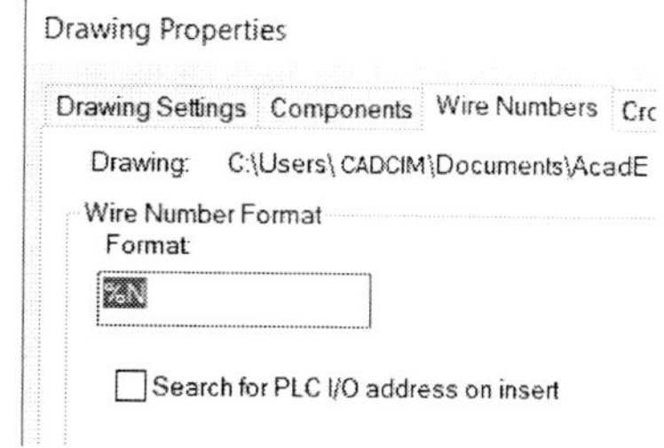


*Figure 10-44 The* ***Wire Numbers*** *tab of the* ***Drawing Properties*** *dialog box*

Figure 10-45 shows the tags of a component and the wire numbers inserted into a ladder based on PLC I/O address.

**Note**

*If a PLC I/O address is not found then the ladder reference number will be used as a component tag and wire number.*

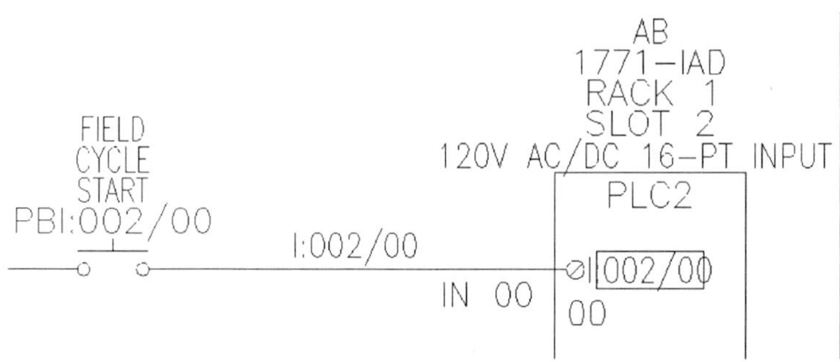


*Figure 10-45 Component tags and wire numbers inserted based on the PLC I/O address*

# TUTORIALS

## Tutorial 1

In this tutorial, you will first insert a ladder and then a parametric PLC module into the ladder. Also, you will add empty spaces in the PLC module and then break the module to continue inserting it a few rungs later. Next, you will continue inserting the remaining part of the module into a different ladder. **(Expected time: 20 min)**

The following steps are required to complete this tutorial:

a. Create a new drawing.
b. Insert a ladder into the drawing.
c. Insert the parametric PLC module into the drawing, add empty spaces, and break the module.
d. Save the drawing file.

### Creating a New Drawing

1. Create a new drawing with the name *C10_tut01* in the **CADCIM** project. Select the **ACAD_ELECTRICAL** template and enter **Parametric PLC** as description while creating the drawing.

2. Choose the **OK** button from the **Create New Drawing** dialog box; *C10_tut01.dwg* is created in the **CADCIM** project and displayed at the bottom of the drawing list in the **CADCIM** project. Next, move *C10_tut01.dwg* to the *TUTORIALS* subfolder of the **CADCIM** project.

### Inserting a Ladder into the Drawing

1. Choose the **Insert Ladder** tool from **Schematic > Insert Wires/Wire Numbers > Insert Ladder** drop-down; the **Insert Ladder** dialog box is displayed. 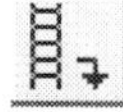

2. Set the following parameters in the **Insert Ladder** dialog box:

   Width: **10.000**
   Spacing: **1.000**
   1st Reference: **200**
   Rungs: **10**
   **1 Phase**: Select this radio button
   **Yes**: Select this radio button

3. Choose the **OK** button from the **Insert Ladder** dialog box; you are prompted to specify the start position of the first rung. Enter **4,19** at the Command prompt and press ENTER; a ladder is inserted into the drawing.

## Inserting the Parametric PLC Module into the Drawing

1. Choose the **Insert PLC (Parametric)** tool from **Schematic > Insert Components > Insert PLC** drop-down; the **PLC Parametric Selection** dialog box is displayed.

2. In the Manufacturer Catalog tree, click on the (+) sign beside **Allen-Bradley**; a list of series is displayed.

3. Click on the (+) sign beside the **1756** series; the **1756** series is expanded.

4. Double-click on the **Discrete Input** type from the Manufacturer Catalog tree; the list is expanded and the various modules of the discrete input type are displayed in the Manufacturer Catalog tree.

5. Select the **1756-IA16** module from the lower part of the **PLC Parametric Selection** dialog box.

6. From the **Graphics Style** area in the **PLC Parametric Selection** dialog box, make sure the **1** radio button is selected.

7. Choose the **OK** button from the **PLC Parametric Selection** dialog box; you are prompted to specify the insertion point for the PLC module.

8. Enter **11,19** at the Command prompt and press ENTER; the **Module Layout** dialog box is displayed.

9. In this dialog box, select the **Allow spacers/breaks** radio button and choose the **OK** button; the **I/O Point** dialog box is displayed.

10. In the **I/O Point** dialog box, enter **1** in the **RACK** edit box and **2** in the **SLOT** edit box.

11. Choose the **OK** button; the **I/O Address** dialog box is displayed. In this dialog box, select **I:12/00** from the **Quick picks** drop-down list; **1:12/00** is displayed in the **Beginning address** edit box.

12. Choose **OK** from the **I/O Address** dialog box; the **Custom Breaks/Spacing** dialog box is displayed.

13. Choose the **Add Spacer** button from this dialog box; a spacer is added to the selected PLC module.

14. Choose the **Insert Next I/O Point** button; an I/O point is inserted into the module.

15. Choose the **Insert Next I/O Point** button again; an I/O point is inserted into the module.

16. Choose the **Add Spacer** button; one more spacer is added to the PLC module.

17. Choose the **Insert Next I/O Point** button again; an I/O point is inserted into the selected module.

18. Next, choose the **Break Module Now** button; the inserted symbols are combined into a single module block and you are prompted to specify an insertion point for the rest of the PLC module.

19. Next, press ESC; the **Data Saved** message box is displayed. Choose the **OK** button from the message box; the I/O points of a Parametric PLC module are inserted into the ladder, as shown in Figure 10-46.

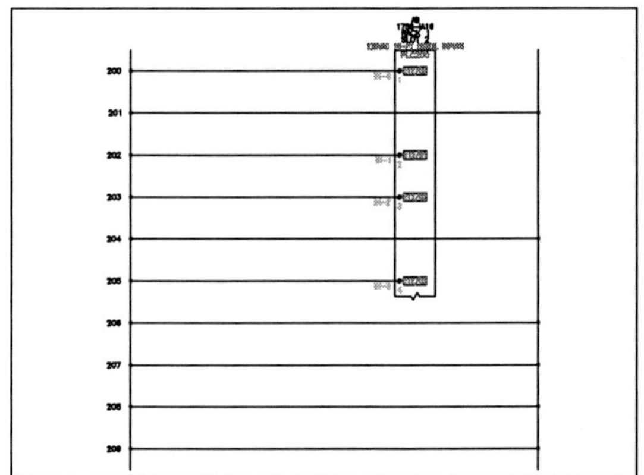

*Figure 10-46 A PLC module inserted into the ladder*

20. Choose the **Insert Ladder** tool from **Schematic> Insert Wires/Wire Numbers > Insert Ladder** drop-down; the **Insert Ladder** dialog box is displayed.

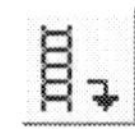

21. Set the following parameters in the **Insert Ladder** dialog box:

| | |
|---|---|
| Width: **10.000** | Spacing: **1.000** |
| 1st Reference: **210** | Rungs: **18** |
| **1 Phase**: Select this radio button | **Yes**: Select this radio button |

22. Choose the **OK** button from the **Insert Ladder** dialog box; you are prompted to specify the start position of first rung.

23. Enter **18,19** at the Command prompt and press ENTER; a ladder is inserted into the drawing, as shown in Figure 10-47.

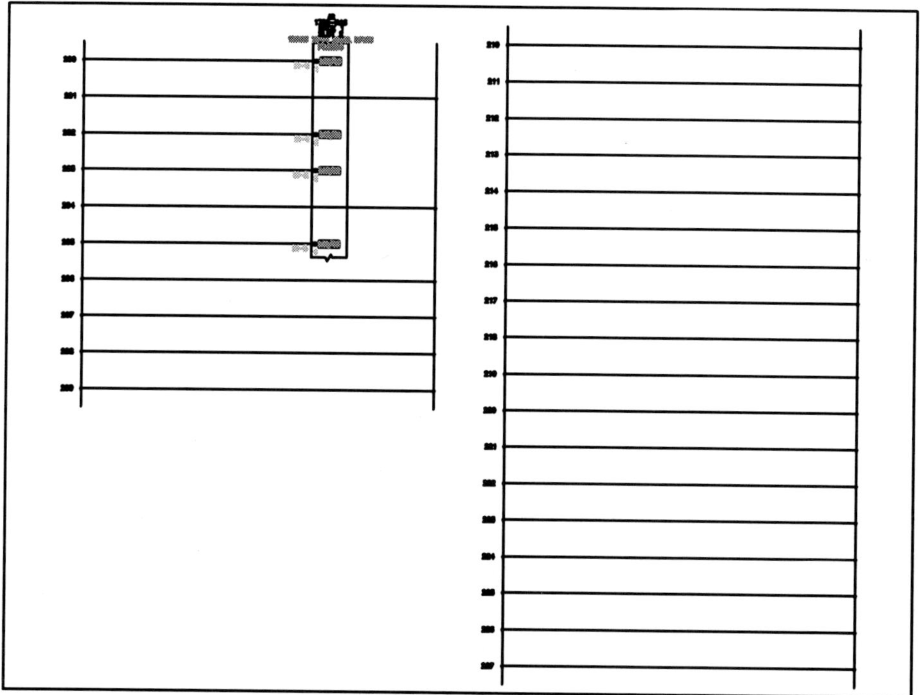

*Figure 10-47* *A ladder with 18 rungs inserted into the drawing*

24. Choose the **Insert PLC (Parametric)** tool from **Schematic > Insert Components > Insert PLC** drop-down; the **Continue "Broken" Module** dialog box is displayed. 

25. Choose the **Continue Module** button from the **Continue "Broken" Module** dialog box; you are prompted to specify an insertion point for the PLC module.

26. Enter **25,18** at the Command prompt and press ENTER; a PLC module is placed on the right of the ladder at rung 211 and the **Module Layout** dialog box is displayed simultaneously.

27. Select the **Insert all** radio button from the **I/O points** area of the **Module Layout** dialog box and choose **OK**; the **I/O Addressing** dialog box is displayed.

28. In this dialog box, choose the **Decimal** button; the remainder of the PLC module is inserted into the ladder, as shown in Figure 10-48.

## Saving the Drawing File

1. Choose **Save** from the **Application Menu** to save the drawing file *C10_tut01.dwg*.

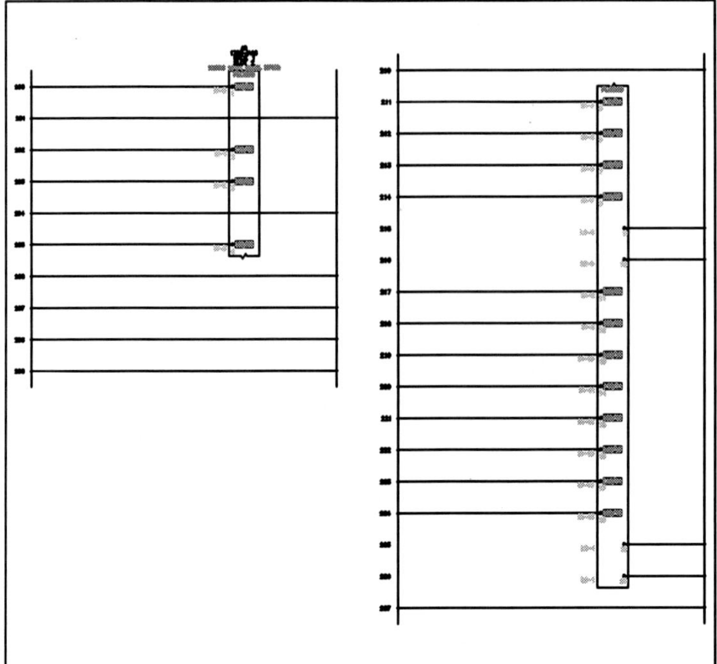

*Figure 10-48 The remaining PLC module inserted into the ladder*

## Tutorial 2

In this tutorial, you will insert a ladder into a drawing and then create a new PLC module using the **PLC Database File Editor** tool. Next, you will insert this new module into the ladder.

**(Expected time: 30 min)**

The following steps are required to complete this tutorial:

a. Create a new drawing.
b. Insert a ladder into the drawing.
c. Create and insert the PLC module using the **PLC Database File Editor** tool.
d. Save the drawing file.

### Creating a New Drawing

1. Create a new drawing with the name *C10_tut02* in the **CADCIM** project. Select the **ACAD_ELECTRICAL** template and enter **Parametric PLC** as description while creating the drawing. Next, move *C10_tut02.dwg* to the *TUTORIALS* subfolder of the **CADCIM** project.

### Inserting a Ladder into the Drawing

1. Choose the **Insert Ladder** tool from **Schematic** > **Insert Wires/Wire Numbers > Insert Ladder** drop-down; the **Insert Ladder** dialog box is displayed.

2. Set the following parameters in the **Insert Ladder** dialog box:

Width: **10.000**
1st Reference: **1**
**1 Phase**: Select this radio button
Spacing: **1.000**
Rungs: **10**
**Yes**: Select this radio button

3. Choose the **OK** button from the **Insert Ladder** dialog box; you are prompted to specify the start position of the first rung. Enter **10,19** at the Command prompt and press ENTER; a ladder is inserted into the drawing.

## Creating and Inserting a New PLC Module

1. Choose the **PLC Database File Editor** tool from the **Other Tools** panel of the **Schematic** tab; the **PLC Database File Editor** dialog box is displayed.

2. Choose the **New Module** button from the **PLC Database File Editor** dialog box; the **New Module** dialog box is displayed.

3. Set the following parameters in the **New Module** dialog box:

Manufacturer: **Automation Direct**
Series Type: **Discrete Input**
Description: **16-Point Input**
Base Addressing: **Prompt**
Terminals: **16**
Series: **DL205**
Code: **3456**
Module Type: **DC**
Rating: **4-20 mA**

4. Choose the **Module Prompts** button; the **Prompts at Module Insertion Time** dialog box is displayed.

5. Choose **%%1** from the **Prompt Number** area and enter **RACK** in the **New Prompt Text** edit box. Next, choose the **Change** button on the right of the **New Prompt Text** edit box; RACK is displayed in the **Prompt Text** area.

6. Choose **%%2** from the **Prompt Number** area and enter **SLOT** in the **New Prompt Text** edit box. Next, choose the **Change** button; SLOT is displayed in the **Prompt Text** area.

7. Choose the **OK** button from the **Prompts at Module Insertion Time** dialog box to save the changes and exit the dialog box.

8. Choose the **OK** button from the **New Module** dialog box to return to the **PLC Database File Editor** dialog box.

9. In the **Terminal Type** column, right-click on the first cell; a shortcut menu is displayed.

10. In the shortcut menu, choose the **Edit Terminal** option; the **Select Terminal Information** dialog box is displayed.

11. In this dialog box, select the **Top Input** category from the **Category** area and then choose the **Module info Input I/O Point Wire Left** type from the **Types for Category Top Input** area.

12. Choose the **OK** button from the **Select Terminal Information** dialog box; the **Module info Input I/O Point Wire Left** type is displayed in the first cell of the **Terminal Type** column.

13. Click on cell 1 of the **Show** column; the cell changes into a drop-down list. Select the **When Excluding Unused** option from the drop-down list.

14. Clear the **Break After** check box of the cell 1 if selected.

15. Right-click on cell 2 of the **Terminal Type** column; a shortcut menu is displayed. Choose the **Edit Terminal** option from the shortcut menu; the **Select Terminal Information** dialog box is displayed.

16. Select the **Top Terminal** category from the **Category** area. Next, choose the **Module Info Terminal Point Wire Left** type from the **Types for Category Top Terminal** area.

17. Choose the **OK** button; the **Module Info Terminal Point Wire Left** type is displayed in cell 2 of the **Terminal Type** column.

18. Click on cell 2 of the **Show** column; the cell changes into a drop-down list. Select **When Including Unused** from the drop-down list.

19. Similarly, right-click on cell 3 and choose the **Edit Terminal** option from the shortcut menu; the **Select Terminal Information** dialog box is displayed.

20. Select **Input** from the **Category** area and choose the **Input I/O Point Wire Left** category from the **Types for Category Input** area.

21. Choose **OK**; the **Input I/O Point Wire Left** is displayed in cell 3 of the **Terminal Type** column. Next, click on cell 3 of the **Show** column; the cell changes into a drop-down list. Now, select the **When Including Unused** option from the drop-down list.

22. Next, click on cell 4 of the **Terminal Type** column and then drag the cursor upto cell 10 of the **Terminal Type** column.

23. Right-click on cell 4; a shortcut menu is displayed. Choose the **Edit Terminal** option from the shortcut menu; the **Select Terminal Information** dialog box is displayed.

24. In this dialog box, select **Input** from the **Category** area and choose the **Input I/O Point Wire Left** category from the **Types for Category Input** area.

25. Choose **OK**; the **Input I/O Point Wire Left** option is displayed in cell 4 to cell 10 of the **Terminal Type** column.

26. Click on cell 4 of the **Show** column and select the **Always** option from the drop-down list. Similarly, select the **Always** option from cell 5 to cell 10 in the **Show** column, if it is not already selected.

27. Right-click on cell 11; a shortcut menu is displayed. Choose the **Edit Terminal** option from the shortcut menu; the **Select Terminal Information** dialog box is displayed.

28. In this dialog box, select **Terminal** from the **Category** area and choose the **Terminal Point Wire Rightx** type from the **Types for Category Terminal** area.

29. Choose **OK**; the **Terminal Point Wire Rightx** type is displayed in cell 11 of the **Terminal Type** column.

30. Choose the **Save Module** button from the **PLC Database File Editor** dialog box. Next, choose the **Done / Insert** button from the **PLC Database File Editor** dialog box; the **PLC Parametric Selection** dialog box is displayed.

31. Select **Automation Direct** from the Manufacturer Catalog tree of the **PLC Parametric Selection** dialog box and then click on it; a tree view of series is displayed. Next, select **3456** module from the lower part of the **PLC Parametric Selection** dialog box.

32. Choose the **OK** button from the **PLC Parametric Selection** dialog box; you are prompted to specify an insertion point for the 3456 module.

33. Enter **18,19** at the Command prompt and press ENTER; the **Module Layout** dialog box is displayed.

    The **Insert all** radio button in the **I/O points** area of the **Module Layout** dialog box is selected by default.

34. Choose the **OK** button from the **Module Layout** dialog box; the **I/O Point** dialog box is displayed. In this dialog box, enter **1** in the **RACK** edit box and **2** in the **SLOT** edit box and then choose the **OK** button; the **I/O Address** dialog box is displayed.

35. Select **1:12/00** from the **Quick picks** drop-down list; **1:12/00** is displayed in the **Beginning address** edit box.

36. Choose the **OK** button from the **I/O Address** dialog box; the Automation Direct-3456 PLC module is inserted into the ladder, as shown in Figure 10-49.

## Saving the Drawing File

1. Choose **Save** from the **Application Menu** to save the drawing file *C10_tut02.dwg*.

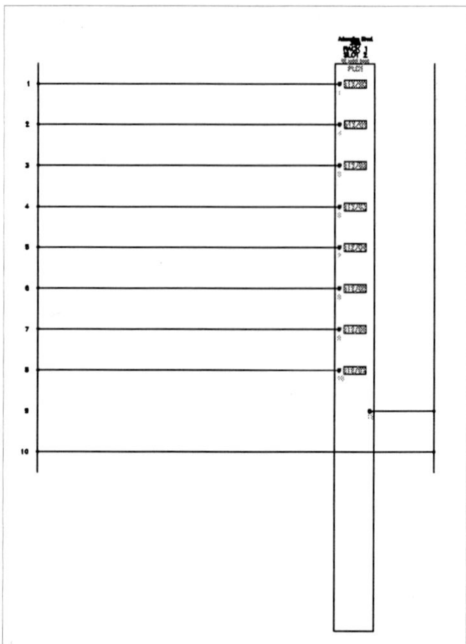

*Figure 10-49 The parametric PLC module inserted into the ladder*

## Tutorial 3

In this tutorial, you will generate PLC drawings using the **PLC I/O Utility** tool. Also, you will change the default settings and save the settings in a *.wdi* file. **(Expected time: 20 min)**

The following steps are required to complete this tutorial:

a. Create a new drawing.
b. Generate PLC drawings and save the settings.

### Creating a New Drawing

1. Create a new drawing with the name *C10_tut03* in the **CADCIM** project. Select the **ACAD_ELECTRICAL** template and enter **Parametric PLC** as description while creating the drawing. Next, move *C10_tut03.dwg* to the *TUTORIALS* subfolder of the **CADCIM** project.

### Generating PLC Drawings and Saving the Settings

1. Choose the **PLC I/O Utility** tool from the **Import** panel of the **Import/Export Data** tab; the **Select PLC I/O Spreadsheet Output File** dialog box is displayed. 

2. In this dialog box, select the *demoplc.xls* file and choose the **Open** button; the **Spreadsheet to PLC I/O Utility** dialog box is displayed.

3. Choose the **Setup** button; the **Spreadsheet to PLC I/O Utility Setup** dialog box is displayed.

4. Set the following parameters in the **Ladder** area of the **Spreadsheet to PLC I/O Utility Setup** dialog box.

   X : **2** Y: **21**

   Select **3** from the **PLC graphical style** drop-down list in the **Module** area.

5. Choose the **Save** button from the **Spreadsheet to PLC I/O Utility Setup** dialog box; the **Save Settings** dialog box is displayed.

6. Enter **PLC_Settings** in the **File name** edit box and select the **CADCIM** project folder (**Documents > Acade 2022 > AeData > Proj > CADCIM**) from the **Save in** drop-down list. Next, choose the **Save** button; the **Spreadsheet to PLC I/O Utility** dialog box is displayed again.

7. Set the following parameters in the **Spreadsheet to PLC I/O Utility** dialog box:

   **Ladder Reference Numbering** area
   Start: **100**

   **Drawing File Creation** area
   Select the **Use active drawing** check box, if it is not already selected.
   Make sure the **Free run** radio button is selected.
   Make sure the **Add new drawings to active project** check box is selected.

8. Choose the **Start** button in the **Spreadsheet to PLC I/O Utility** dialog box; the drawings are created. You will notice that the following three drawings are created and added to your **CADCIM** project: *C10_tut03.dwg*, *C10_tut04.dwg*, and *C10_tut05.dwg*.

---

## Self-Evaluation Test

**Answer the following questions and then compare them to those given at the end of this chapter:**

1. Which of the following dialog boxes is displayed on choosing the **More** button from the **Spreadsheet to PLC I/O Drawing Generator** dialog box?

   (a) **Connected device(s)** (b) **PLC Parametric Selection**
   (c) **Insert Component** (d) **Select PLC I/O Spreadsheet Output File**

2. The __________ tool is used to insert a complete PLC module into the drawing.

3. You can insert upto _________ inline connected devices per I/O point.

4. Components for input modules are inserted from ________ to ________ whereas components for output modules are inserted from ________ to ________.

5. The ________ tool is used to start the automatic drawing creation process.

6. You can tag components based on the PLC address by selecting the ________ check box in the ________ tab of the **Drawing Properties** dialog box.

7. A PLC module cannot be inserted as a single block. (T/F)

8. PLC modules can be built with a variety of graphical symbols. (T/F)

9. PLC modules can be oriented vertically or horizontally. (T/F)

10. The **PLC Database File Editor** tool is used only to create PLC modules. (T/F)

## Review Questions

**Answer the following questions:**

1. Which of the following commands is used to insert parametric PLC modules?

   (a) **AEPLC** (b) **AEPLCDB**
   (c) **AESS2PLC** (d) **AEPLCP**

2. Which of the following tools is used to copy an entire module into a new module?

   (a) **Spreadsheet to PLC I/O Utility** (b) **Insert PLC (Full Units)**
   (c) **PLC Database File Editor** (d) **Surfer**

3. Which of the following dialog boxes is used to set the outer box dimensions of a module?

   (a) **Module Prompts** (b) **Module Box Dimensions**
   (c) **Module Specifications** (d) **Style Box Dimensions**

4. Which of the following tools need to be chosen to display the **Edit PLC Module** dialog box?

   (a) **Move Component** (b) **Edit Attribute**
   (c) **Edit Component** (d) **Copy Component**

5. You can insert PLC I/O points as independent symbols or as a complete PLC module into a drawing. (T/F)

6. While inserting a parametric PLC module, you can break a module and restart it at a different location. (T/F)

7. In the **Terminal Block Settings** dialog box, you can add or update the symbols available for building a module. (T/F)

8. The **Spreadsheet to PLC I/O Utility** tool is used to read the Excel spreadsheet file only. (T/F)

9. You can insert individual PLC I/O points into a drawing using the **Insert Component** dialog box. (T/F)

# EXERCISES

## Exercise 1

Create a new drawing named *C10_exer01.dwg* in the **NEW_PROJECT** project and then insert a ladder into the drawing with the following specifications: Width = 6, Spacing =1, 1st Reference =1, and Rungs =12. Next, use the **Insert PLC (Parametric)** tool to insert PLC module with the following specifications: HONEYWELL, Discrete Input, 621-3550, 16 point input module. Next, break the module at rung 11 and then insert a new ladder with following specifications: Width = 6, Spacing =1, 1st Reference =1, Rungs = 12. Continue the previous PLC module by using the **Insert PLC (Parametric)** tool again. Figure 10-50 shows the complete parametric PLC module. **(Expected time: 20 min)**

## Exercise 2

Create a new drawing named *C10_exer02.dwg* in the **NEW_PROJECT** project and then insert a ladder into it. Also, insert a PLC module [L16-AWA 10in/out AC-DC/115AC-DC (3/4" spacing)] into a ladder using the **Insert PLC (Full Units)** tool. Figure 10-51 shows the values to be used for inserting the PLC module. Figure 10-52 shows the complete PLC module.

**(Expected time: 15 min)**

Hint: Accept the default values in the **Edit PLC Module** dialog box.

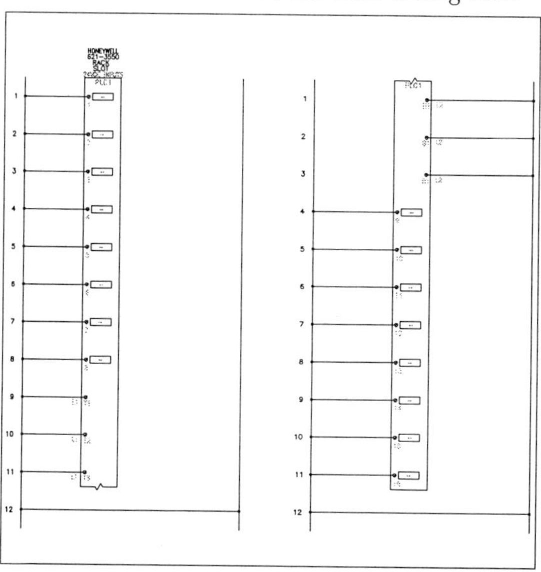


***Figure 10-50*** *Complete parametric PLC module*

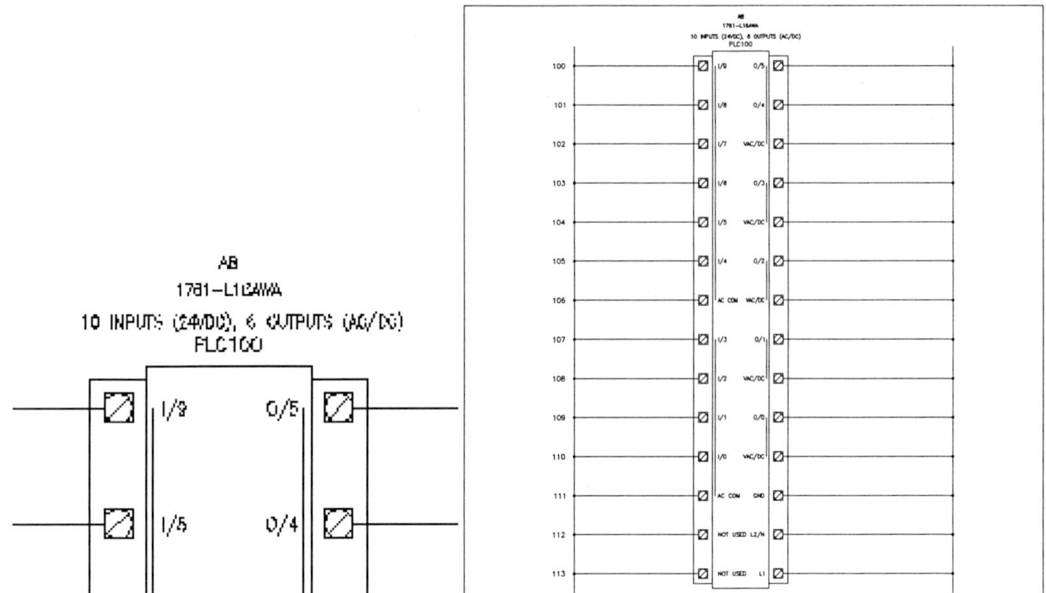


*Figure 10-51* Values for inserting the PLC module

*Figure 10-52* Complete PLC module

## Answers to Self-Evaluation Test

**1.** a, **2. Insert PLC (Full Units)**, **3.** nine, **4.** left, right, right, left, **5. Spreadsheet to PLC I/O Utility**, **6. Search for PLC I/O address on insert**, **Components**, **7.** F, **8.** T, **9.** T, **10.** F

# Chapter 11

# Terminals

## Learning Objectives

**After completing this chapter, you will be able to:**

- *Insert and edit terminal symbols*
- *Insert terminals from the schematic list and the panel list*
- *Insert terminals manually*
- *Select, create, edit, and insert terminal strips*
- *Configure the settings of a terminal strip table*
- *Generate a terminal strip table*
- *Edit and create the terminal properties database*
- *Resequence terminal numbers*
- *Copy the properties of a terminal block*
- *Insert and edit jumpers*

# INTRODUCTION

The terminals are used to connect wires together or to plug them into a component. In this chapter, you will learn to insert terminal symbols manually from the schematic list, or from the panel list. Also, you will come to know how to insert, edit, and create terminal strips. You will be able to insert jumpers, configure the settings, and generate terminal strip table. Further, you will learn about editing and creating a terminal properties database.

# INSERTING TERMINAL SYMBOLS

| | |
|---|---|
| **Ribbon:** | Schematic > Insert Components > Icon Menu drop-down > Icon Menu |
| **Toolbar:** | ACE:Main Electrical > Insert Component<br>or ACE:Insert Component > Insert Component |
| **Menu:** | Components > Insert Component |
| **Command:** | AECOMPONENT |

Terminal symbols are used to represent wire connection points on the schematic drawings. The function of terminal symbols is similar to source and destination signal arrows. Terminal symbols are schematic symbols that are linked by user-defined codes. To insert terminal symbol into a drawing, choose the **Icon Menu** tool from the **Insert Components** panel of the **Schematic** tab; the **Insert Component** dialog box will be displayed. Select the **Terminals/Connectors** icon from the **NFPA: Schematic Symbols** area of the **Insert Component** dialog box; the **NFPA: Terminals and Connectors** area will be displayed, as shown in Figure 11-1.

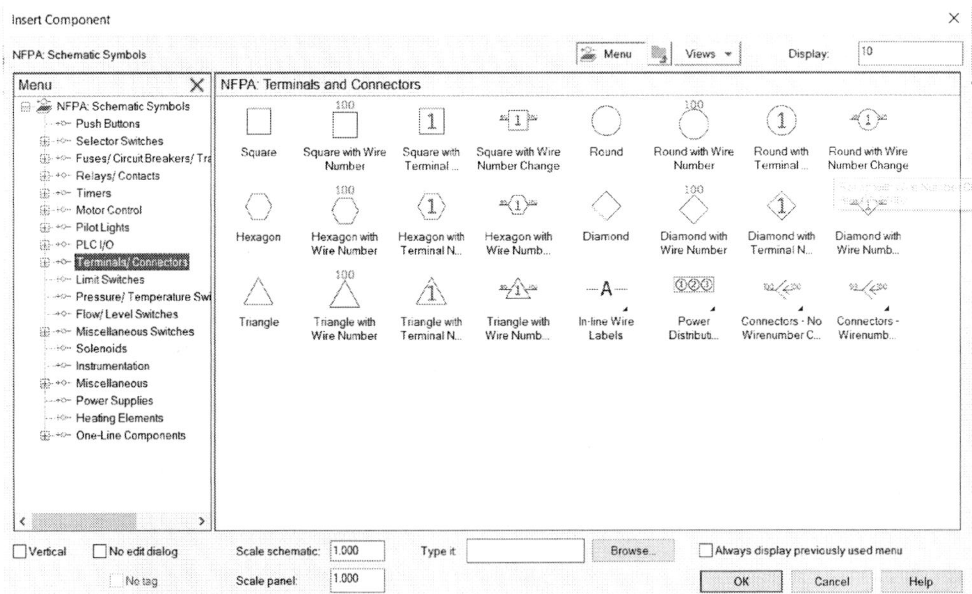


*Figure 11-1 The* ***Insert Component*** *dialog box showing the* ***NFPA: Terminals and Connectors*** *area*

AutoCAD Electrical has five types of terminal styles and four types of terminal behavior. The five types of terminal style are square, circle, hexagon, diamond, and triangle. The four types of terminal behavior along with their descriptions are shown in Figure 11-2. The terminals are connected together by the TAG-ID attribute.

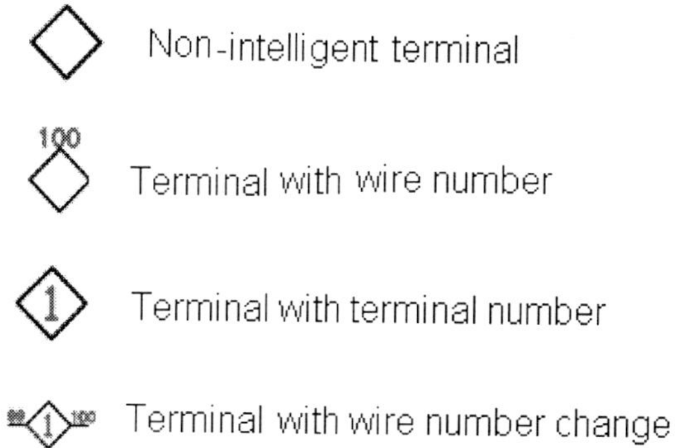


***Figure 11-2*** *The types of terminal behavior and their descriptions*

To insert a terminal symbol into a drawing, select the required terminal from the **NFPA: Terminals and Connectors** area of the **Insert Component** dialog box; the symbol attached to the cursor will be displayed and you will be prompted to specify the insertion point for the terminal symbol. Specify the insertion point; the **Insert/Edit Terminal Symbol** dialog box will be displayed. Enter the required information in this dialog box and choose **OK**; the terminal symbol will be inserted into the drawing. The options in the **Insert/Edit Terminal Symbol** dialog box are discussed next.

**Note**

*If you insert a non-intelligent terminal, the* ***Insert / Edit Terminal Symbol*** *dialog box will not be displayed.*

## Annotating and Editing Terminal Symbols

Enhanced

| | |
|---|---|
| **Ribbon:** | Schematic > Edit Components > Edit Components drop-down >Edit |
| **Toolbar:** | ACE:Main Electrical > Edit Component or ACE:Edit Component > Edit Component |
| **Menu:** | Components > Edit Component |
| **Command:** | AEEDITCOMPONENT |

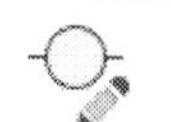

You can annotate and edit terminal symbols. To do so, choose the **Edit** tool from the **Edit Components** panel of the **Schematic** tab; you will be prompted to select the component. Select the terminal that you need to edit; the **Insert / Edit Terminal Symbol** dialog box will be displayed, as shown in Figure 11-3. Different options and areas in this dialog box are discussed next.

### Terminal Area

The options in the **Terminal** area are used to specify the installation code, location code, tag strip value, and terminal number. The symbol name is displayed above the **Installation** edit box in this area. The options in this area are discussed next.

You can specify installation and location codes in the **Installation** and **Location** edit boxes, respectively. Alternatively, choose the **Browse** button to select the installation and location codes that have been used in the active drawing, project, and external file. Note that the installation or location codes will be displayed in the **Drawing** and **Project** areas of the **Installation Codes** or **Location Codes** dialog box only if the installation and location codes are present in the active drawing and project.

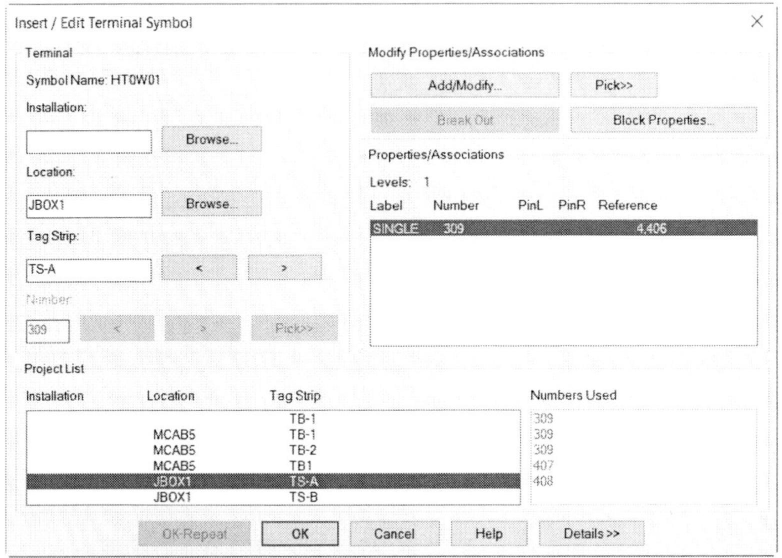


*Figure 11-3 The **Insert / Edit Terminal Symbol** dialog box*

**Note**

*1. To display the installation codes in the **External List** area of the **Installation Codes** dialog box, you need to create a default.inst file and add installation codes to it. For example, MAIN for main panel, JBOX for Junction box, MACHINE for devices located in the machine, and so on. The creation of a default.inst file will be discussed in the later chapters. Once you create this file, place it in the same folder where your project file is kept; the installation codes will be displayed in the **External List** area of the **Installation Codes** dialog box.*

*2. The same is the case with the location codes, but in this case you need to create a default.loc file. The creation of both the default.inst and default.loc files will be discussed in the next chapter.*

Enter the Tag ID for the terminal in the **Tag Strip** edit box. Choose the **<** or **>** buttons to decrease or increase the last digit of the Tag ID value. Note that if the terminal has already a Tag ID assigned to it, then it will appear in the **Tag Strip** edit box.

Enter the terminal number in the **Number** edit box. Choose the **<** or **>** buttons to decrease or increase the specified terminal number. Alternatively, choose the **Pick>>** button to select the text or attribute from the active drawing to use as a terminal number. The **Number** edit box will not be available if the terminal symbol does not have a TERM01 attribute or the terminal number and the wire number are same, refer to Figure 11-2.

## Modify Properties/Associations Area

The options in the **Modify Properties/Associations** area are used to modify the properties and associations of the terminal symbol, associate multiple terminal symbols, associate schematic terminal symbols and their panel terminal footprint, define block properties of a terminal, and so on. If the attributes are present in the terminal block, then the information about the terminal associations will be stored in it. Otherwise, the information will be stored in Xdata. The **Modify Properties/Associations** area is used to manage the linked terminals. Note that the options in this area will not be available if you insert one-line terminal symbol, if you insert a terminal symbol that is not a part of the active project, or if you are inserting terminals using the **Insert Terminal (Panel List)** and **Terminal Strip Editor** tools. The options in the **Modify Properties/ Associations** area are discussed next.

#### Add/Modify

The **Add/Modify** button is used to associate a terminal symbol to an existing terminal or association. Choose the **Add/Modify** button; the **Add/Modify Association** dialog box will be displayed. The options in this dialog box are discussed later in this chapter. Note that the **Add/Modify** button will be activated only if the active drawing is a part of an active project.

#### Pick>>

The **Pick>>** button is used to select the terminal symbol to be associated with the selected terminal symbol. Choose the **Pick>>** button; you will be prompted to select a single terminal symbol to associate. Also, the **Insert / Edit Terminal Symbol** dialog box will disappear. Next, select the terminal symbol; the **Insert / Edit Terminal Symbol** dialog box will be displayed again. In this way, the terminal symbol that you need to associate to the other terminal symbol can be selected. While selecting the terminal symbol, you can pan or zoom the drawing.

#### Break Out

The **Break Out** button is used to remove the selected terminal block from associations. However, the properties and levels of the terminal will be retained.

#### Block Properties

The **Block Properties** button is used to define the number of levels and maintain the properties of levels such as level description, wires per connection, pin left, pin right, and internal jumpers. To define terminal block properties, choose the **Block Properties** button; the **Terminal Block Properties** dialog box will be displayed, as shown in Figure 11-4.

The options in this dialog box will be discussed later in this chapter. Also, note that the **Block Properties** button will not be enabled if the active drawing is not from the active project.

**Note**

*In AutoCAD Electrical 2022, multiple catalog information is synced while editing or associating multilevel terminals.*

### Properties/Associations Area

The **Properties/Associations** area displays the associations of the terminal that you are editing or inserting. This area displays all the associated terminal symbols from the schematic and terminal panel footprints. The terminal that is to be edited will be highlighted in this area. Note that if you double-click on the highlighted entry displayed in the **Properties/Associations** area, the **Add / Modify Association** dialog box will be displayed. In this area, you can modify the terminal association. The options in the **Properties/Associations** area are discussed next.

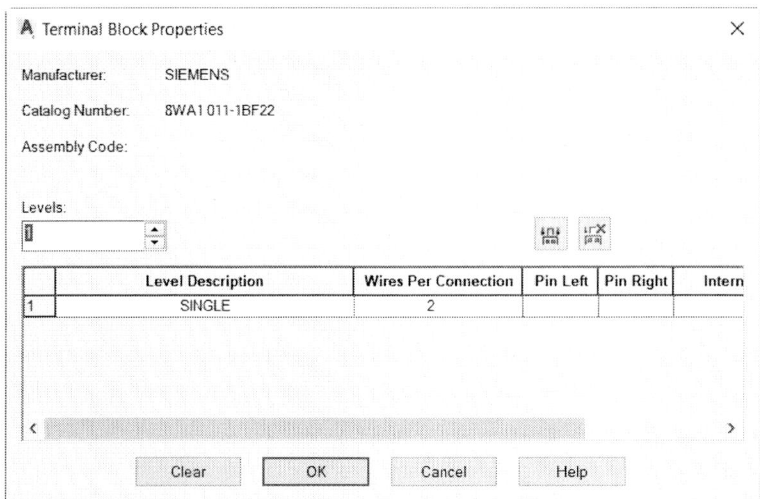


*Figure 11-4 The **Terminal Block Properties** dialog box*

### Levels

The number of levels defined in the **Terminal Block Properties** dialog box will be displayed on the right of the **Levels** in the **Properties/Associations** area.

### Label

The **Label** column displays the description of the level which has been defined in the **Level Description** column of the **Terminal Block Properties** dialog box.

### Number

The **Number** column displays the terminal numbers defined in the **Add / Modify Association** dialog box.

### PinL

The **PinL** column displays the pin numbers on the left side of the terminal block.

### PinR

The **PinR** column displays the pin numbers on the right side of the terminal block.

### Reference

The reference of the terminal symbol in the project is displayed under the **Reference** column. This column displays 'sheet, reference' based on the drawing settings.

## Project List Area

The **Project List** area displays the installation and location codes, tag strip, and terminal numbers that have been used in the active project.

The **Numbers Used** displays all the terminal numbers that are found in the active drawing or project, whose tag strip value matches the highlighted tag strip value.

## Details

Choose the **Details >>** button to expand the **Insert / Edit Terminal Symbol** dialog box, as shown in Figure 11-5. Note that when you choose the **Details>>** button, the **Catalog Data**, **Description**, and **Ratings** areas will be displayed in the **Insert / Edit Terminal Symbol** dialog box. The options in the expanded dialog box have already been discussed in the previous chapters.

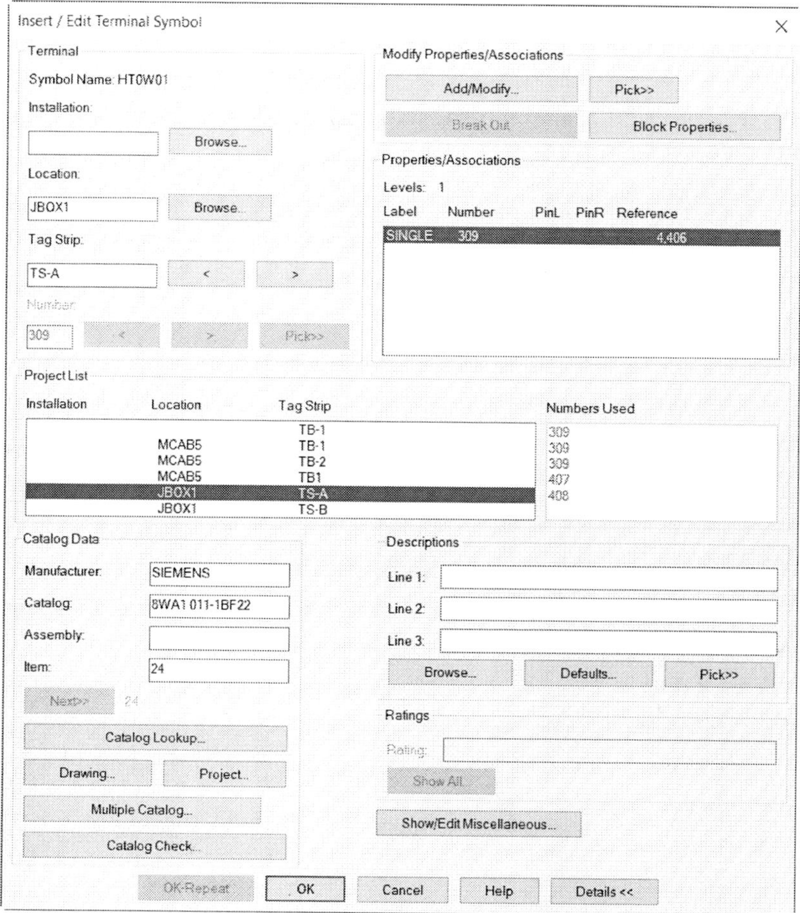


***Figure 11-5** The expanded **Insert / Edit Terminal Symbol** dialog box*

Enter the required information in the **Insert / Edit Terminal Symbol** dialog box and choose the **OK** button; the information of the terminal will be updated on the terminal symbol.

### Note

*1. When you insert a terminal symbol, the values of the previously inserted terminal symbol will be displayed in the **Insert / Edit Terminal Symbol** dialog box.*

*2. You can also insert multiple terminals together using the **Multiple Insert (Icon Menu)** tool and **Multiple Insert (Pick Master)** tools. There are options to hide tag, installation, and location code values of the terminals (excluding the first one) to be inserted using these two tools.*

# INSERTING TERMINAL FROM THE SCHEMATIC LIST

**Ribbon:** Panel > Terminal Footprints > Insert Terminals drop-down > Insert Terminal (Schematic List)
**Toolbar:** ACE:Panel Layout > Terminal Strip Editor > Insert Terminal (Schematic List)
ACE:Terminal Footprint > Insert Terminal (Schematic List)
**Menu:** Panel Layout > Insert Terminal (Schematic List)
**Command:** AEPANELTERMINALSCH

The **Insert Terminal (Schematic List)** tool is used to insert panel terminals from the schematic terminal list. Choose this tool from the **Insert Terminals** drop-down in the **Terminal Footprints** panel of the **Panel** tab, as shown in Figure 11-6; the **Schematic Terminals List --> Panel Layout Insert** dialog box will be displayed, as shown in Figure 11-7.

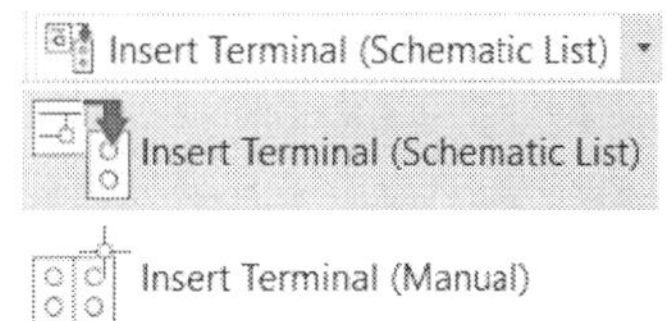


*Figure 11-6 The* ***Insert Terminals*** *drop-down*

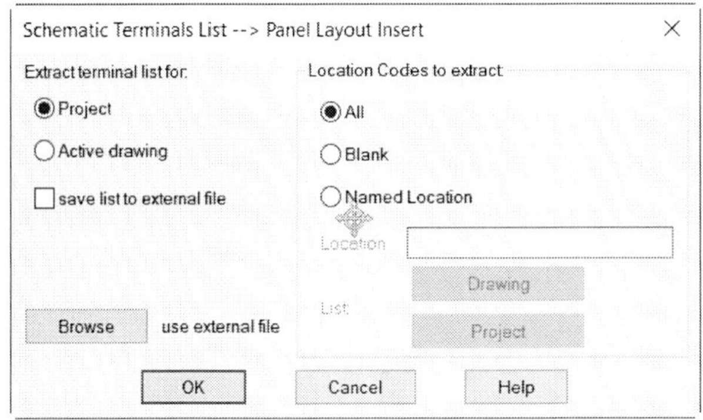


***Figure 11-7*** *The* ***Schematic Terminals List --> Panel Layout Insert*** *dialog box*

The options in this dialog box are the same as that of the **Schematic Components List --> Panel Layout Insert** dialog box and have been discussed in Chapter 8.

The **Project** radio button is selected by default. Choose the **OK** button in the **Schematic Terminals List --> Panel Layout Insert** dialog box; the **Select Drawings to Process** dialog box will be displayed. Select the required files and then choose the **Process** button; the drawings from the top list of the **Select Drawings to Process** dialog box will be transferred to the bottom list for processing. Next, choose the **OK** button in the **Select Drawings to Process** dialog box; the **Schematic Terminals (active project)** dialog box will be displayed, as shown in Figure 11-8. The options of the **Schematic Terminals (active project)** dialog box are the same as that of the **Schematic Components (active project)** dialog box that has been discussed in Chapter 8. Next, select the terminal from the **Schematic Terminals (active project)** dialog box; the **Insert** button will be activated. Note that the **Insert** button will be activated only if the selected terminal is not inserted into a drawing and if it has catalog data. Choose the **Insert** button; you will be prompted to specify the location point for the terminal. Specify the location point; you will be prompted to specify the rotation of the terminal. Move the cursor in the horizontal or vertical direction to place the terminal horizontally or vertically, respectively. Next, press ENTER; the

**Panel Layout - Terminal Insert/Edit** dialog box will be displayed. Enter the required information in this dialog box and choose the **OK** button; the terminal will be inserted in the drawing and the **Schematic Terminals (active project)** dialog box will be displayed again.

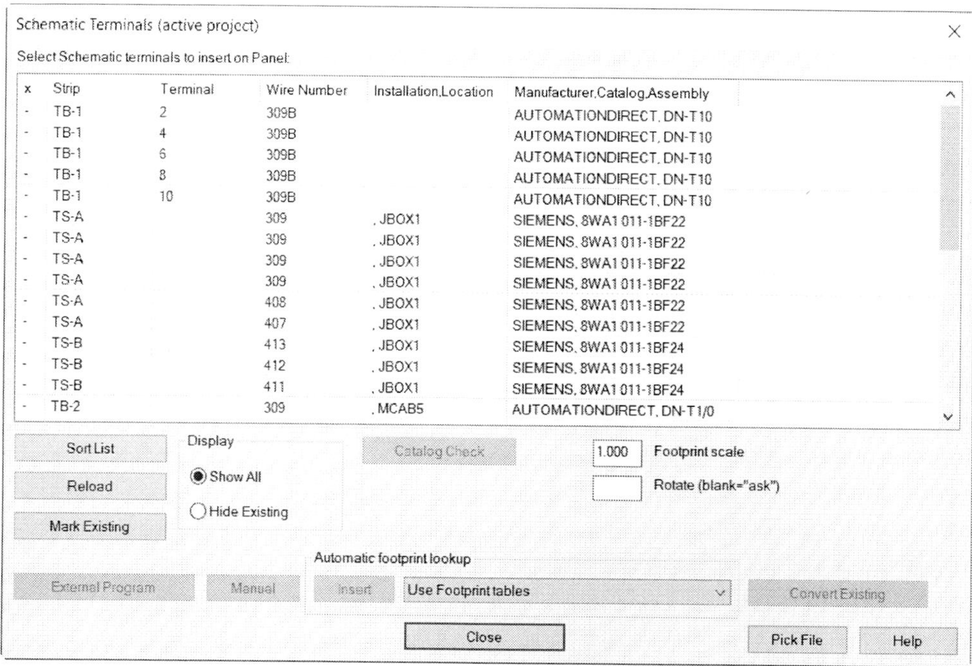


*Figure 11-8* ***The Schematic Terminals (active project)*** *dialog box*

Now, if you choose the **Pick File** button in the **Schematic Terminals (active project)** dialog box, the **Schematic Terminals List --> Panel Layout Insert** dialog box will be displayed again. Select the **Active drawing** radio button and choose the **OK** button in this dialog box; the **Schematic Terminals (active drawing)** dialog box will be displayed. Next, select the terminal from the list displayed and then insert the terminal symbol as discussed earlier.

If you insert panel terminals from the schematic terminal list, wire numbers will also be displayed with these panel terminals in the drawing. To further explain this, activate the **NFPADEMO** project. Next, open the *demo009.dwg* file from this project. Now, choose the **Insert Terminal (Schematic List)** tool from the **Insert Terminals** drop-down in the **Terminal Footprints** panel of the **Panel** tab; the **Schematic Terminals List --> Panel Layout Insert** dialog box will be displayed. In this dialog box, select the **Project** radio button and choose **OK**; the **Select Drawings to Process** dialog box will be displayed. Choose **Do All** and then the **OK** button in this dialog box; the **Schematic Terminals (active project)** dialog box will be displayed. In this dialog box, select the first terminal in the list and enter **3** in the **Footprint Scale** button. Next, choose the **Insert** button; you will be prompted to specify the location for the selected terminal. Next, specify the location, as shown in Figure 11-9 and then press ENTER twice; the **Panel Layout Insert/Edit** dialog box will be displayed. Choose the **OK** button in this dialog box. Figure 11-10 shows the wire number displayed along with the inserted panel terminal in the *demo009.dwg* file.

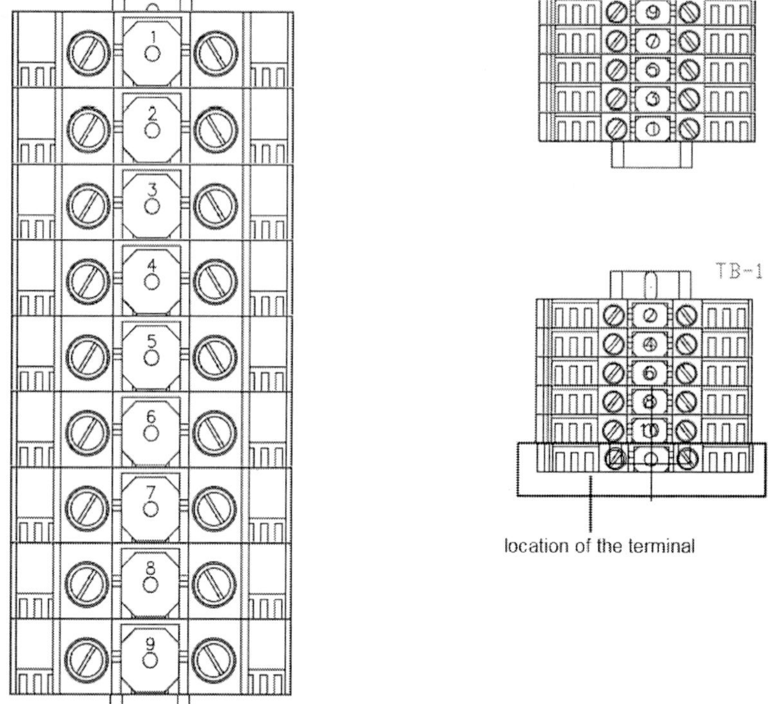


*Figure 11-9 Specifying the location of the terminal*

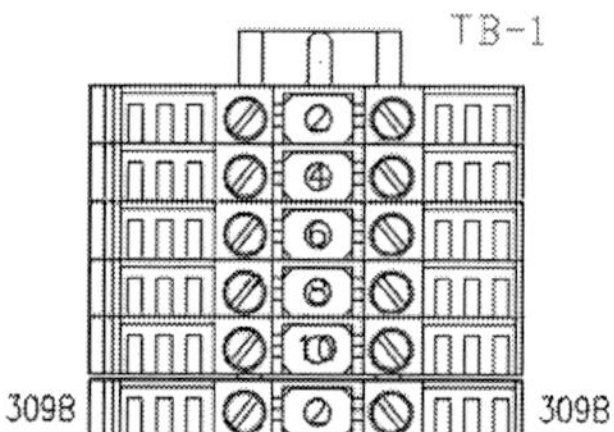


*Figure 11-10 Wire number displayed*

**Note**

*Refer to Chapter 8 for detailed description of the options in the* ***Schematic Components List -> Panel Layout Insert****, the* ***Schematic Terminals (active project)****, and the* ***Schematic Terminals (active drawing)*** *dialog boxes.*

# INSERTING TERMINALS MANUALLY

| | |
|---|---|
| **Ribbon:** | Panel > Terminal Footprints > Insert Terminals drop-down > Insert Terminal (Manual) |
| **Toolbar:** | ACE:Panel Layout > Terminal Strip Editor > Insert Terminal (Manual)<br>ACE:Terminal Footprint > Insert Terminal (Manual) |
| **Menu:** | Panel Layout > Insert Terminal (Manual) |
| **Command:** | AEPANELTERMINAL |

The **Insert Terminal (Manual)** tool is used to insert panel terminal footprints manually. To do so, choose the **Insert Terminal (Manual)** tool from the **Terminal Footprints** panel of the **Panel** tab; the **Insert Panel Terminal Footprint - Manual** dialog box will be displayed, as shown in Figure 11-11. The options in the **Insert Panel Terminal Footprint - Manual** dialog box are the same as that of the **Insert Component Footprint - Manual** dialog box that have been discussed in Chapter 8. The only difference is that in case of the **Insert Panel Terminal Footprint - Manual** dialog box, the **Terminal number preference** area is available.

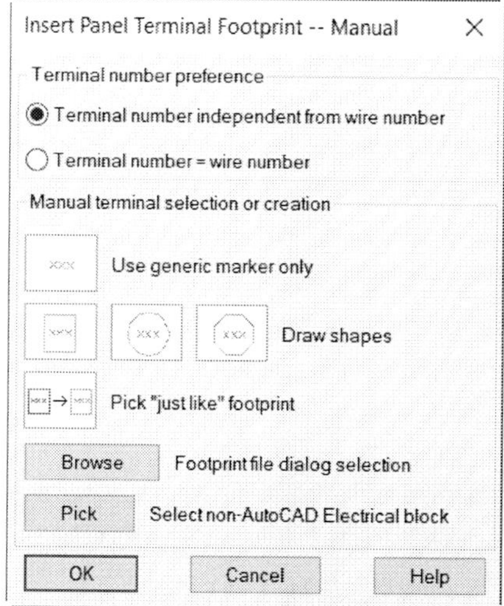


***Figure 11-11** The **Insert Panel Terminal Footprint - Manual** dialog box*

Next, select the required terminal from the **Manual terminal selection or creation** area and specify its position; the **Panel Layout - Terminal Insert/Edit** dialog box will be displayed. Enter the required information in this dialog box and choose **OK**; a terminal will be inserted into the drawing and information in the form of Xdata will be assigned to it automatically.

## INSERTING TERMINALS FROM THE PANEL LIST

| | |
|---|---|
| **Ribbon:** | Schematic > Insert Components > Icon Menu drop-down > Terminal (Panel List) |
| **Toolbar:** | ACE:Main Electrical > Insert Component > Insert Terminal (Panel List) or ACE:Insert Component > Insert Terminal (Panel List) |
| **Menu:** | Components > Insert Terminal (Panel List) |
| **Command:** | AETERMINALPNL |

The **Terminal (Panel List)** tool is used to insert a schematic terminal into a drawing using the panel list. Choose the **Terminal (Panel List)** tool from the **Insert Component** panel of the **Schematic** tab; the **Panel Terminal List --> Schematic Terminals Insert** dialog box will be displayed, as shown in Figure 11-12. The options in this dialog box are the same as that of the **Panel Layout List --> Schematic Components Insert** dialog box which have been discussed in Chapter 5.

The **Project** radio button is selected by default. Choose the **OK** button in the **Panel Terminal List -> Schematic Terminals Insert** dialog box; the **Select Drawings to Process** dialog box will be displayed. Select the required drawings and choose the **Process** button; the drawings will be transferred from the top list to the bottom list. Next, choose the **OK** button in the **Select Drawings to Process** dialog box; the **Panel Terminals** dialog box will be displayed, as shown in Figure 11-13. The options in the **Panel Terminals** dialog box are same as discussed for the **Schematic Terminals** dialog box, refer to Figure 11-8. The only difference in these two dialog boxes is that the **Panel Terminals** dialog box has the **Last symbol used** area. The **Last symbol used** area is discussed next.

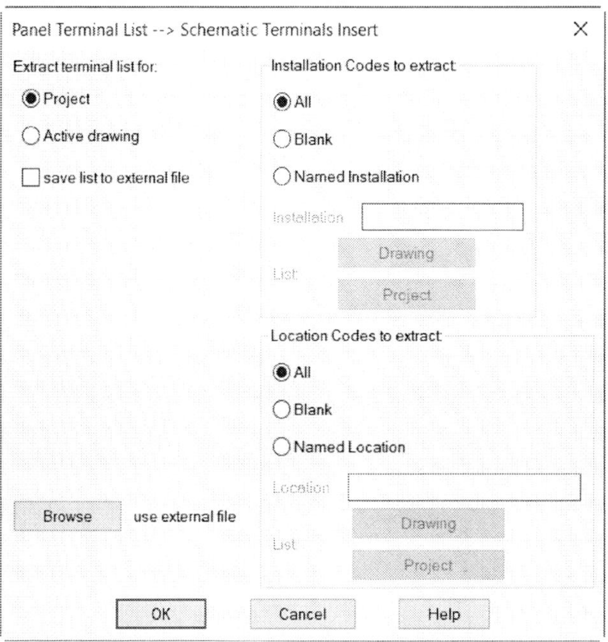


*Figure 11-12 The **Panel Terminal List --> Schematic Terminals Insert** dialog box*

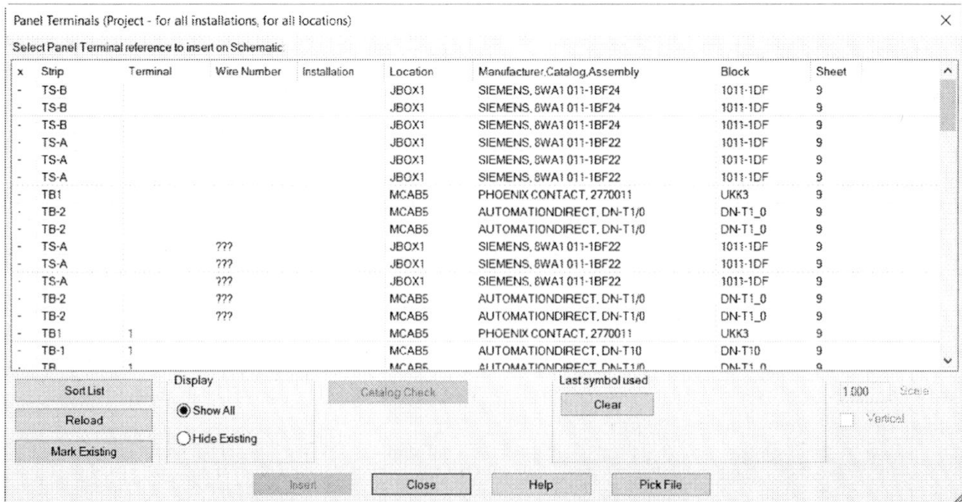


| x | Strip | Terminal | Wire Number | Installation | Location | Manufacturer,Catalog,Assembly | Block | Sheet |
|---|---|---|---|---|---|---|---|---|
| - | TS-B | | | | JBOX1 | SIEMENS, 8WA1 011-1BF24 | 1011-1DF | 9 |
| - | TS-B | | | | JBOX1 | SIEMENS, 8WA1 011-1BF24 | 1011-1DF | 9 |
| - | TS-B | | | | JBOX1 | SIEMENS, 8WA1 011-1BF24 | 1011-1DF | 9 |
| - | TS-A | | | | JBOX1 | SIEMENS, 8WA1 011-1BF22 | 1011-1DF | 9 |
| - | TS-A | | | | JBOX1 | SIEMENS, 8WA1 011-1BF22 | 1011-1DF | 9 |
| - | TS-A | | | | JBOX1 | SIEMENS, 8WA1 011-1BF22 | 1011-1DF | 9 |
| - | TB1 | | | | MCAB5 | PHOENIX CONTACT, 2770011 | UKK3 | 9 |
| - | TB-2 | | | | MCAB5 | AUTOMATIONDIRECT, DN-T1/0 | DN-T1_0 | 9 |
| - | TB-2 | | | | MCAB5 | AUTOMATIONDIRECT, DN-T1/0 | DN-T1_0 | 9 |
| - | TS-A | | ??? | | JBOX1 | SIEMENS, 8WA1 011-1BF22 | 1011-1DF | 9 |
| - | TS-A | | ??? | | JBOX1 | SIEMENS, 8WA1 011-1BF22 | 1011-1DF | 9 |
| - | TS-A | | ??? | | JBOX1 | SIEMENS, 8WA1 011-1BF22 | 1011-1DF | 9 |
| - | TB-2 | | ??? | | MCAB5 | AUTOMATIONDIRECT, DN-T1/0 | DN-T1_0 | 9 |
| - | TB-2 | | ??? | | MCAB5 | AUTOMATIONDIRECT, DN-T1/0 | DN-T1_0 | 9 |
| - | TB1 | 1 | | | MCAB5 | PHOENIX CONTACT, 2770011 | UKK3 | 9 |
| - | TB-1 | 1 | | | MCAB5 | AUTOMATIONDIRECT, DN-T10 | DN-T10 | 9 |

*Figure 11-13 The **Panel Terminals** dialog box*

The **Last symbol used** area displays the name and description of the previous symbol that was inserted in the drawing. Choose the **Clear** button to remove the name of the previously inserted symbol.

Next, select the panel terminal reference from the **Panel Terminals** dialog box; the **Insert** button, the **Catalog Check** button, the **Scale** edit box, and the **Vertical** check box will be activated. Choose the **Insert** button; the **Insert** dialog box will be displayed, as shown in Figure 11-14. Next, select the terminal from this dialog box; the **OK** button will be activated. Choose the **OK** button; you will be prompted to specify the insertion point. Specify the insertion point; the **Insert / Edit Terminal Symbol** dialog box will be displayed. Specify the required information in this dialog box. Choose the **OK** button; the terminal will be inserted in the drawing and the **Panel Terminals** dialog box will appear on the screen again. Choose the **Close** button to exit from this dialog box.

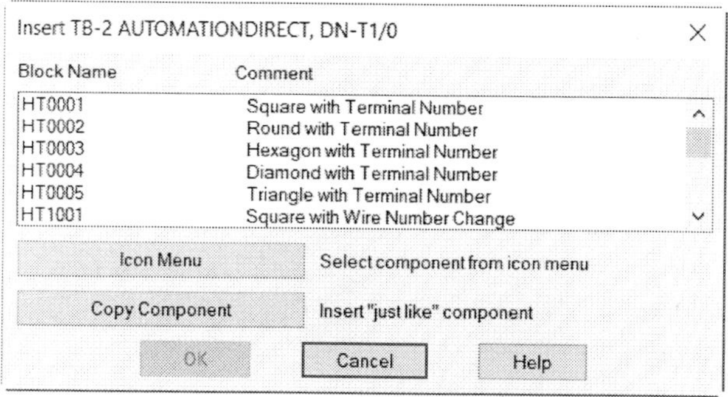


*Figure 11-14 The **Insert** dialog box*

**Note**

*1. The **Insert** dialog box will be displayed only when you are inserting the terminal symbol into the drawing for the first time.*

*2. If you select multiple terminals from the **Panel Terminals** dialog box and choose the **Insert** button, the **Spacing for Insertion** dialog box will be displayed. The options in this dialog box have already been discussed in the earlier chapters.*

# ADDING AND MODIFYING ASSOCIATIONS

In AutoCAD Electrical, you can add or modify a terminal association. You can also associate a terminal symbol to an existing association or terminal. To add or modify a terminal association, choose the **Add/Modify** button from the **Modify Properties/Associations** area of the **Insert / Edit Terminal Symbol** dialog box or of the **Panel Layout - Terminal Insert/Edit** dialog box; the **Add / Modify Association** dialog box will be displayed, as shown in Figure 11-15. The options in this dialog box are used to link the edited terminal to another terminal symbol for creating a multiple level terminal. Also, this dialog box displays the information of the active association of the edited terminal as well as all terminal strips present in the active project. Different areas and options in this dialog box are discussed next.

## Active Association Area

The **Active Association** area is used to modify the terminal number. This area displays the installation code, location code, tag strip, and terminal number of the terminal that is being edited.

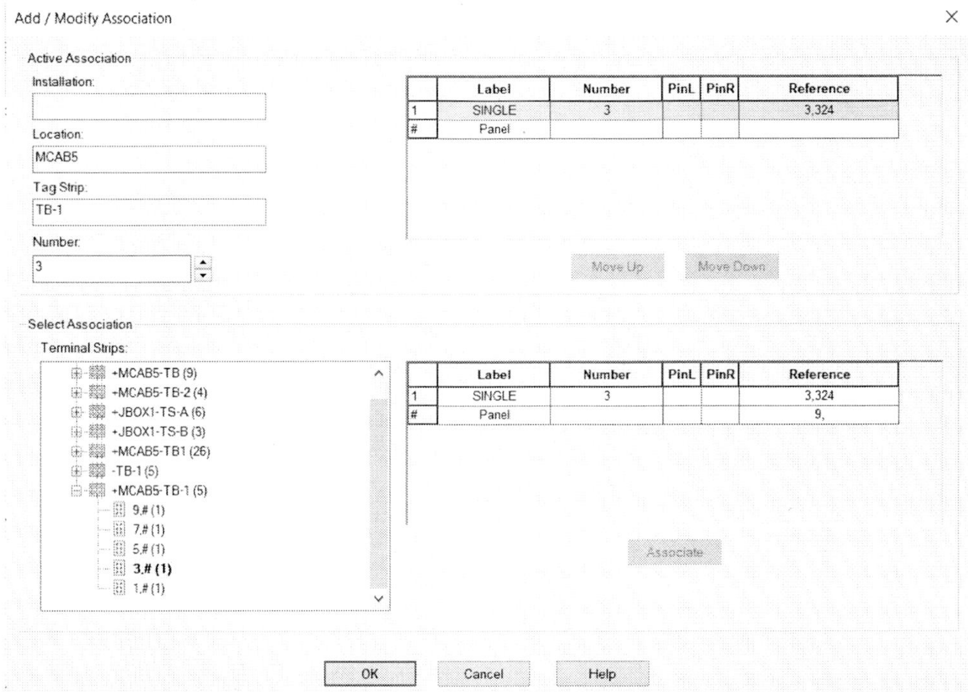


*Figure 11-15 The **Add / Modify Association** dialog box*

**Note**

*1. You cannot edit installation, location, and tag strip values in the **Add/Modify Association** dialog box.*

*2. If the terminal to be edited is from a drawing that is not a part of the active project, the **Add/Modify** and **Block Properties** buttons in the **Insert / Edit Terminal Symbol** will not be activated.*

## Number

The **Number** edit box displays the terminal number. Note that this edit box will not be available if you are editing a panel terminal.

## Active Association Grid

The Active Association Grid is shown in Figure 11-16. This grid displays the information of all the terminal symbols associated with the edited terminal. Note that if the schematic terminal is associated to a panel footprint, you will find a panel row added to the Active Association Grid. You cannot move this panel row up and down.

The row of the terminal symbol that you are editing will be highlighted in blue color. You can also move the edited terminal up or down. To move the row, right-click on the terminal symbol in the Active Association Grid; a shortcut menu will be displayed. Choose the **Move Up** option to move the terminal symbol one step up and choose the **Move Down** option from the shortcut menu to move it one step down. Alternatively, you can select the terminal symbol and drag it to the desired location. You can also choose the **Move Up** or **Move Down** button for moving the terminal symbol up or down. Note that while moving the terminal symbol, only the terminal number and reference will be moved but not the label, PinL, PinR information, as these are parts of terminal block property. You cannot move the panel terminal symbol. Note that it will always be displayed at the bottom of the Active Association Grid. The different columns in this grid have already been discussed.

Active Association
Installation:
Location: MCAB5
Tag Strip: TB
Number: 10

| | Label | Number | PinL | PinR | Reference |
|---|---|---|---|---|---|
| 1 | SINGLE | 10 | | | 4,428 |

Move Up Move Down

*Figure 11-16 The* ***Add / Modify Association*** *dialog box showing the Active Association Grid*

## Select Association Area

In the **Select Association** area, you can select the terminal for association. The options in this area are discussed next.

### Terminal Strips List Box

The **Terminal Strips** list box displays all the terminal strips present within an active project. This list box contains three nodes, shown in Figure 11-17, and they are discussed next. The active project node displays the name of an active project. If you click on this node, the list of all terminal strips present within an active project will be displayed. By default, this node is expanded.

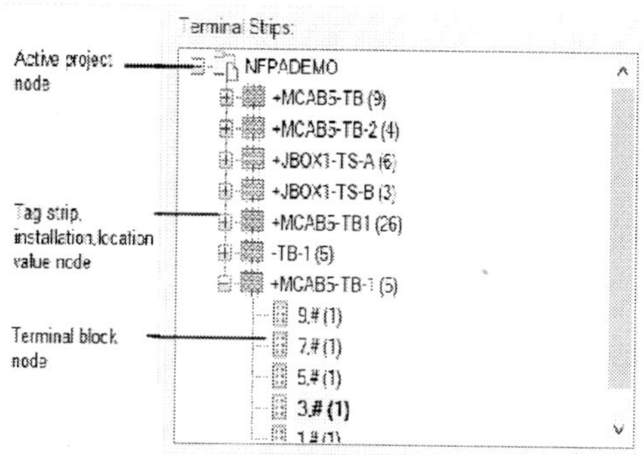


*Figure 11-17 The* ***Terminal Strips*** *list box showing different nodes*

The tag strip, installation, location value node displays the installation, location, and tag strip values of the terminal strips present within an active project. Now, if you click on the node of the terminal strip, a list of terminals linked to it will be displayed. The terminal block quantity will be displayed at the end of the node.

The terminal block node displays the terminal numbers and the number of levels in brackets defined for the terminal.

### Select Association Grid

The Select Association Grid displays all the information of the terminal that you have selected from the **Terminal Strips** list box. Select a row containing the terminal to be associated in this grid, right-click on it, and then choose the **Associate** option to associate the edited terminal to the selected terminal. Alternatively, you can choose the **Associate** button after selecting the row from the grid for associating the edited terminal to the selected terminal.

### Associate

This button will be activated only if you select a row from the Select Association Grid that does not have a terminal assigned to it. The **Associate** button is used to associate the active terminal to the selected terminal.

## TERMINAL BLOCK PROPERTIES

When you choose the **Block Properties** button from the **Insert / Edit Terminal Symbol** dialog box or from the **Panel Layout - Terminal Insert/Edit** dialog box, the **Terminal Block Properties** dialog box will be displayed, as shown in Figure 11-18. This dialog box is used to define and manage terminal block properties. This dialog box is also used to maintain the number of levels of the terminal being edited. Note that this button is disabled if the active drawing is not part of the active project. The options in this dialog box are discussed next.

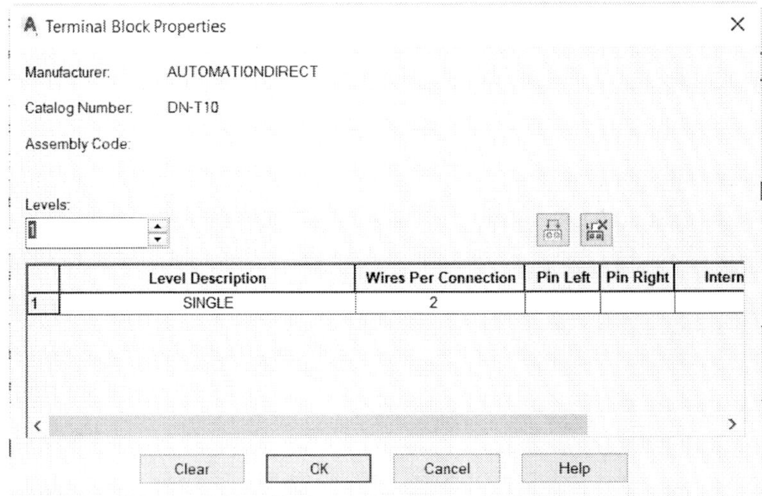


*Figure 11-18 The **Terminal Block Properties** dialog box*

### Manufacturer

The manufacturer of the edited terminal will be displayed on the right of the **Manufacturer** field.

### Catalog Number

The catalog number of the edited terminal will be displayed on the right of the **Catalog Number** field.

### Assembly Code

The assembly code of the edited terminal will be displayed on the right of the **Assembly Code** field. This code will be displayed if it is assigned to the terminal.

### Levels

Specify the number of levels for the terminal in the **Levels** spinner.

## Terminal Block Property Grid

The Terminal Block Property Grid displays the levels of the terminal. In this grid, you can edit and manage the properties of the terminal block. The different columns in this grid are discussed next.

### Level Description

Specify the description for the levels of the terminal block in the **Level Description** column. Also, this description will be displayed in the **Properties/Associations** area of the **Insert / Edit Terminal Symbol** dialog box.

### Wires Per Connection

Specify the number of wires per connection for the terminal connection point in the **Wires Per Connection** column.

### Pin Left

Specify the pin numbers for the left side of the terminal block in the **Pin Left** column.

### Pin Right

Specify the pin numbers for the right side of the terminal block in the **Pin Right** column.

### Internal Jumper

The **Internal Jumper** displays the jumper that has been assigned between the levels. This jumper will be displayed only after you assign it by using the **Assign Jumper** button.

## Assign Jumper

The **Assign Jumper** button is used to assign a jumper to the selected levels. Select the levels and then choose the **Assign Jumper** button; the jumper will be inserted between the levels and you can view it in the **Internal Jumper** column.

## Delete Jumper

The **Delete Jumper** button is used to delete the assigned jumper to the selected levels.

After specifying the required options in the **Terminal Block Properties** dialog box, choose the **OK** button to exit.

# SELECTING, CREATING, EDITING, AND INSERTING TERMINAL STRIPS

| | |
|---|---|
| **Ribbon:** | Panel > Terminal Footprints > Editor |
| **Toolbar:** | ACE:Panel Layout > Terminal Strip Editor<br>or ACE:Terminal Footprint > Terminal Strip Editor |
| **Menu:** | Panel Layout > Terminal Strip Editor |
| **Command:** | AETSE |

The **Editor** tool is used to search the project file for terminal symbols and groups them on the basis of tag strip, installation, and location. Using this tool, you can select, create, edit, and then insert a terminal strip into a drawing. Choose the **Editor** tool from the **Terminal Footprints** panel of the **Panel** tab; the **Terminal Strip Selection** dialog box will be displayed, refer to Figure 11-19.

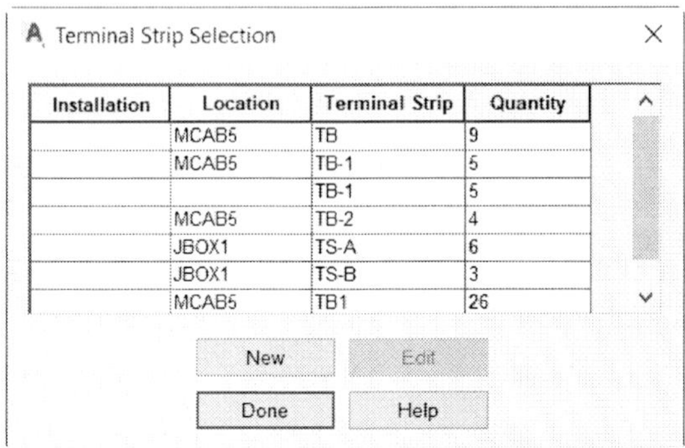


*Figure 11-19 The **Terminal Strip Selection** dialog box*

**Note**

*If the current drawing is not in the active project, the **Current Drawing is Not in the Active Project** message box will be displayed. Choose the **Yes** button in this message box to continue working in the same drawing.*

The **Terminal Strip Selection** dialog box displays the terminals that are present within the active project. This dialog box consists of the installation codes, location codes, terminal strip values, and the number of terminals associated with each terminal strip. The different options in this dialog box are discussed next.

## New

The **New** button is used to create a new terminal strip. Choose the **New** button; the **Terminal Strip Definition** dialog box will be displayed, as shown in Figure 11-20.

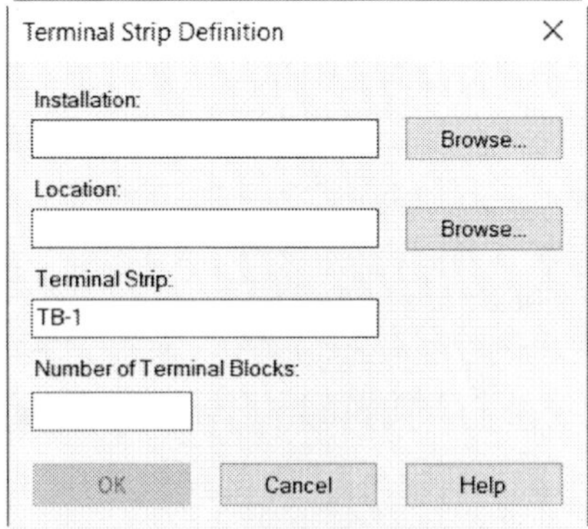


*Figure 11-20 The **Terminal Strip Definition** dialog box*

Specify the location code and the installation code for the new terminal in the respective edit boxes. Alternatively, you can choose the **Browse** button to specify the same.

Specify the tag name of the strip for the new terminal strip in the **Terminal Strip** edit box. Also, note that you cannot have duplicate terminal strip names in the active project.

Specify the number of blocks in the terminal strip in the **Number of Terminal Blocks** edit box.

Enter the values in the **Terminal Strip** and **Number of Terminal Blocks** edit boxes; the **OK** button of the **Terminal Strip Definition** dialog box will be activated. Choose the **OK** button;

the **Terminal strip editor** dialog box will be displayed. The options in this dialog box will be discussed in the next section.

### Edit

The **Edit** button will be activated only after selecting the terminal strip from the **Terminal Strip Selection** dialog box. This button is used to edit a terminal strip. Select the terminal strip from the **Terminal Strip Selection** dialog box and then choose the **Edit** button; the **Terminal Strip Editor** dialog box will be displayed. This dialog box displays the information of the selected terminal. The options in this dialog box will be discussed in the next section.

### Done

Choose the **Done** button to save the changes in the **Terminal Strip Selection** dialog box and exit from this dialog box.

**Note**

*You can create a new terminal strip by using an existing terminal strip. To do so, select the terminal strip from the* ***Terminal Strip Selection*** *dialog box and then choose the* ***New*** *button; the* ***Terminal Strip Definition*** *dialog box will be displayed. This dialog box displays the values of the existing terminal strip. Next, change the values according to your requirement and then choose the* ***OK*** *button to create a new terminal strip.*

*If you leave the* ***Installation*** *and* ***Location*** *edit boxes blank, only the terminal strip with the strip tag name will be created.*

## Editing the Terminal Strip

To edit the terminal strip, choose the **Editor** tool from the **Terminal Footprints** panel of the **Panel** tab; the **Terminal Strip Selection** dialog box will be displayed. Next, select the terminal strip; the **Edit** button will be available. Choose the **Edit** button; the **Terminal Strip Editor** dialog box will be displayed, refer to Figure 11-21. In this dialog box, you can make changes to the terminals before inserting the strip into the drawing. The **Terminal Strip Editor** dialog box consists of the **Terminal Strip**, **Catalog Code Assignment**, **Cable Information**, and **Layout Preview** tabs. These tabs are discussed next.

### Terminal Strip Tab

The **Terminal Strip** tab is chosen by default, refer to Figure 11-21. This tab displays the information of each terminal. In this tab, you can modify, copy, and paste terminal block properties, edit, reassign, renumber, and move terminals, destination settings, assign jumpers, associate terminals, and so on. Also, this tab displays the information of each terminal. These terminals can be sorted by selecting the column headings. The first click on the column heading sorts the column in ascending order and if you click again on the column heading, it will be sorted in the descending order. This sorting criterion applies to all tabs of this dialog box, so you do not need to sort again if you switch between the tabs such as **Catalog Code Assignment**, **Cable Information**, and **Layout Preview**. In this dialog box, the terminals will be displayed at the center of the list box with associated catalog information and the destinations on both sides. The terminals in this dialog box are separated by thick bold lines. Also, the column that is in the extreme left side of the grid indicates different levels for the multiple level terminal for example, L1, L2, L3, L4 and so on. This tab also consists of **Properties**, **Terminal**, **Spare**,

**Destinations**, **Jumpers**, and **Multi-Level** areas. These areas consist of various buttons. These buttons are used to reorder terminals, change information of a terminal, insert spare terminals, and so on. The different options in this tab are discussed next.

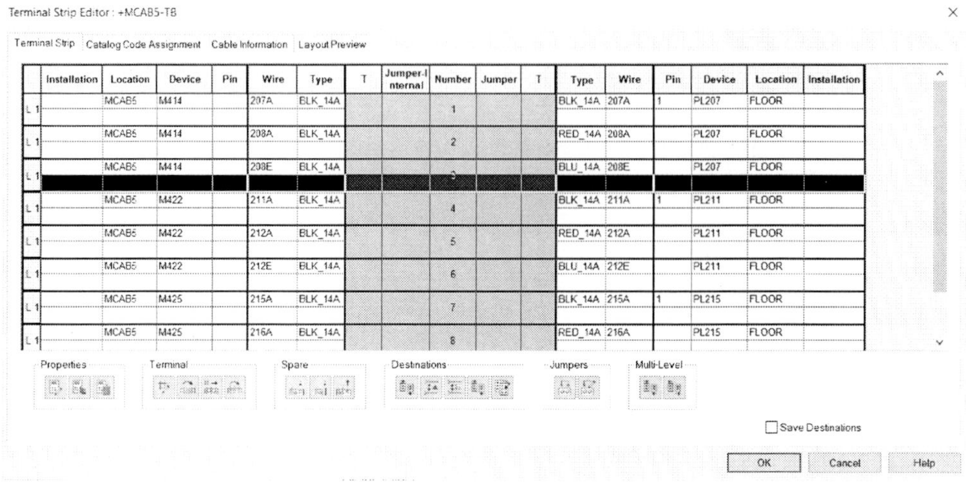

*Figure 11-21 The* ***Terminal Strip Editor*** *dialog box*

### Terminal Listing Area

The Terminal Listing area consists of three sections: the internal destination, terminal block information, and external destination. These three sections are easily identified by bold vertical lines. Similarly, bold horizontal lines distinguish between terminal blocks on the strip.

### Properties Area

The **Properties** area consists of the buttons that are used to edit, copy, and paste the terminal block properties. The buttons in this area are discussed next.

The **Edit Terminal Block Properties** button is used to define and edit the terminal block properties. To do so, select the terminal from the list displayed and then choose the **Edit Terminal Block Properties** button; the **Terminal Block Properties** dialog box will be displayed. The options in this dialog box have already been discussed in this chapter. In this dialog box, you can define or edit the terminal block properties. You can edit properties of a multi-level terminal block. Here, you can define up to 99 terminal levels.

The **Copy Terminal Block Properties** button is used to copy the terminal block properties. Select the terminal from the list displayed and then choose the **Copy Terminal Block Properties** button; the terminal block properties are copied.

The **Paste Terminal Block Properties** button is used to paste the copied terminal block properties into the selected terminals. Select the terminal from the list displayed and then choose the **Paste Terminal Block Properties** button; the terminal block properties will be pasted to the selected terminals.

### Terminal Area

The options in the **Terminal** area are used to edit the terminal attributes such as installation, location, tag strip, and number, reassign the terminal to another strip, renumber the terminal strip, and so on. The options in this area are discussed next.

The **Edit Terminal** button is used to edit the terminal block. Select the terminal block from the list displayed and then choose the **Edit Terminal** button; the **Edit Terminal** dialog box will be displayed, as shown in Figure 11-22. In this dialog box, you can modify information of the selected terminal block. Note that if you modify the information in the **Installation**, **Location**, and **Terminal Strip** edit boxes, the terminal block will be removed from its current terminal strip and moved to the modified or newly defined terminal strip. Next, enter the required information in this dialog box and choose **OK**; the information will get updated in the **Terminal Strip** tab of the **Terminal Strip Editor** dialog box.

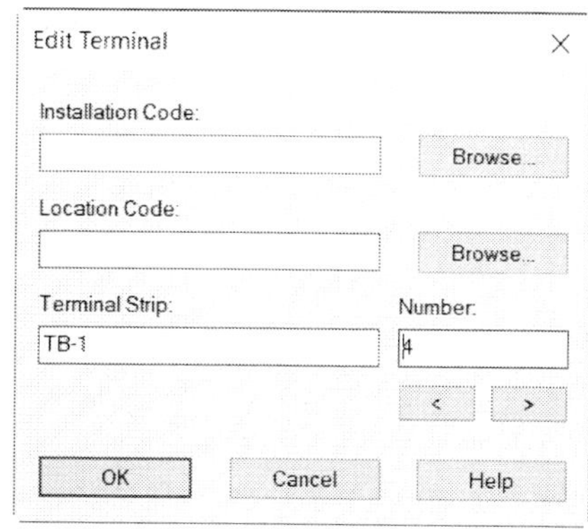


*Figure 11-22 The **Edit Terminal** dialog box*

The **Reassign Terminal** button is used to reassign one or more terminals to another terminal strip to create a new strip. It is also used to move the selected terminal block from an active terminal strip to the terminal strip that you will define in the **Reassign Terminal** dialog box. To reassign a terminal strip to a terminal block, select the terminal block from the list displayed and then choose the **Reassign Terminal** button; the **Reassign Terminal** dialog box will be displayed, as shown in Figure 11-23.

Next, specify the terminal block in the **Reassign Terminal** dialog box where you need to move the selected terminal and enter the required information in the **Terminal Strip** area. Choose the **OK** button; the selected terminal will be moved to the assigned terminal strip.

The **Renumber Terminal** button is used to renumber the entire or part of terminal blocks of the active terminal strip. To do so, select a terminal block from the list and then choose the **Renumber Terminal** button; the **Renumber Terminal Strip** dialog box will be displayed, as shown in Figure 11-24. The options in this dialog box are discussed next.

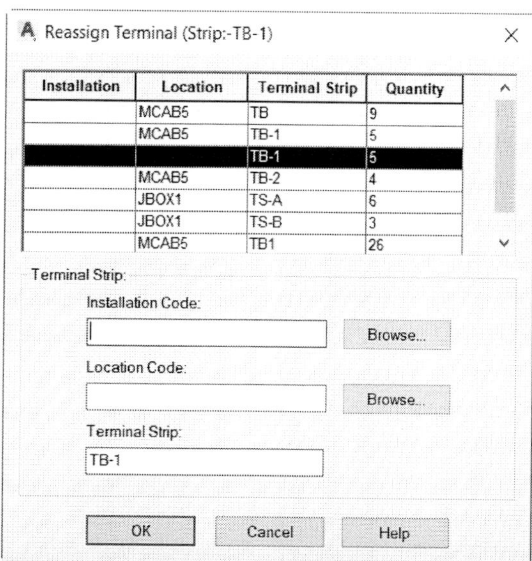

| Installation | Location | Terminal Strip | Quantity |
|---|---|---|---|
| | MCAB5 | TB | 9 |
| | MCAB5 | TB-1 | 5 |
| | | TB-1 | 5 |
| | MCAB5 | TB-2 | 4 |
| | JBOX1 | TS-A | 6 |
| | JBOX1 | TS-B | 3 |
| | MCAB5 | TB1 | 26 |



*Figure 11-23 The **Reassign Terminal** dialog box*

Specify the new starting number for the selected terminal block in the **Terminal Renumber starting with** edit box. This number can be numeric, alpha, or alphanumeric.

**Note**

*The terminal that uses a wire number as its terminal number cannot be renumbered.*

To renumber the selected terminal(s) from bottom level, select the **Start with Bottom Level** check box. By default, this check box is clear.

Select the **Ignore Alphanumeric Terminals** check box to ignore the terminals having alphanumeric value and process only the terminals having numeric value. By default, this check box is clear.

The **Ignore Accessories** check box is selected by default. As a result, the accessories associated with the terminal strip will be ignored.

The **Renumber** area consists of **Per Terminal** and **Per Level** radio buttons. In this area, you can specify whether you want to renumber the terminal based on terminal or level. The **Per Terminal** radio button is used to process the entire terminal at a time. The **Per Level** radio button is used to process each level at a time.

After specifying required options in the **Renumber Terminal Strip** dialog box, choose the **OK** button to save the changes and exit.

The **Move Terminal** button is used to move the entire terminal as well as its levels on the terminal strip to a specified location. Select the required terminal block and then choose the **Move Terminal** button; the **Move Terminal** dialog box will be displayed, as shown in Figure 11-25.

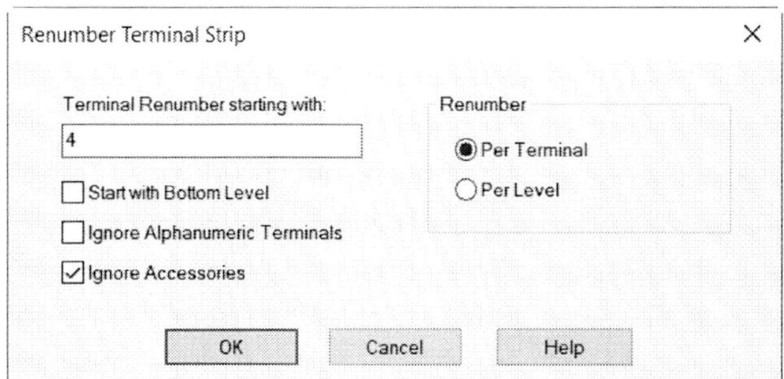


*Figure 11-24 The **Renumber Terminal Strip** dialog box*

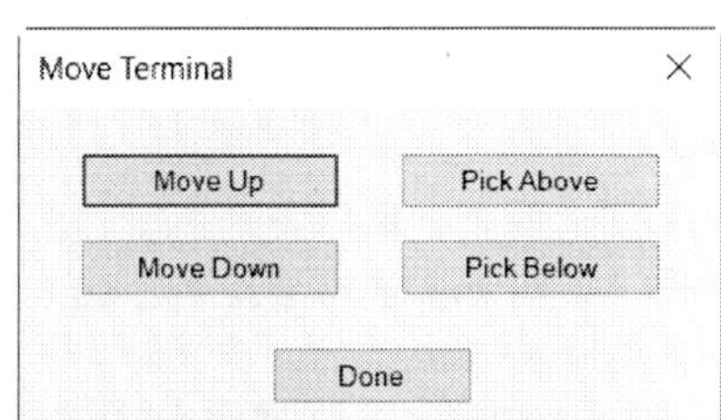


*Figure 11-25 The **Move Terminal** dialog box*

The options in this dialog box are used to move the terminal block up and down or to the position specified manually in the list displayed in the **Terminal Strip Editor** dialog box.

### Spare Area

The **Spare** area is used to insert and delete spare terminals, and insert accessories such as barriers, dividers, marker, jumper bars, and so on. The options in this area are discussed next.

The **Insert Spare Terminal** button is used to insert spare terminal blocks in an active terminal strip. To do so, select the terminal strip from the list displayed in the **Terminal Strip Editor** dialog box and then choose the **Insert Spare Terminal** button; the **Insert Spare Terminal** dialog box will be displayed, as shown in Figure 11-26.

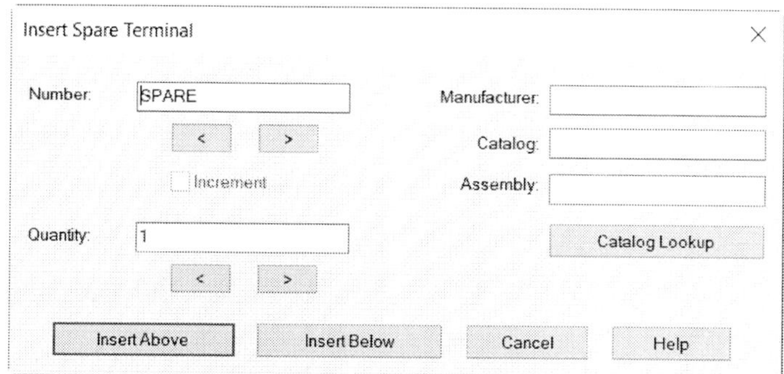


*Figure 11-26 The **Insert Spare Terminal** dialog box*

Specify the starting name or number for the spare terminal in the **Number** edit box. By default, **SPARE** is displayed in this edit box. To increase or decrease the value that you have entered in the **Number** edit box, choose **>** or **<** button. The **Increment** check box that is below the **Number** edit box will be activated only if the value in the **Quantity** edit box is more than 1. By default, the **Increment** check box is clear. If you select this check box, the terminal ID will be incremented when the spare terminal is inserted.

Specify the number of spare terminals that you need to insert in the **Quantity** edit box. To increase or decrease the value that you have entered in the **Quantity** edit box, choose **>** or **<** buttons.

Specify the manufacturer, catalog, and assembly values in the **Manufacturer**, **Catalog**, and **Assembly** edit boxes, respectively. Alternatively, you can use the **Catalog Lookup** button to specify the manufacturer, catalog, and assembly codes.

After specifying the required options in the **Insert Spare Terminal** dialog box, choose the **Insert Above** button; the spare terminal will be inserted above the selected terminal in the **Terminal Strip Editor** dialog box. If you choose the **Insert Below** button, the spare terminal will be inserted below the selected terminal in the **Terminal Strip Editor** dialog box.

**Note**

*If you choose the **Insert Above** or **Insert Below** button without entering the starting number of the spare terminal in the **Number** edit box, the **Spare Insert Warning** message box will be displayed, as shown in Figure 11-27.*

The **Insert Accessory** button is used to insert the accessories such as terminal end barriers, partitions, jumper bars, and so on into the selected terminal strip. Select the terminal block and then choose the **Insert Accessory** button; the **Insert Accessory** dialog box will be displayed, as shown in Figure 11-28.

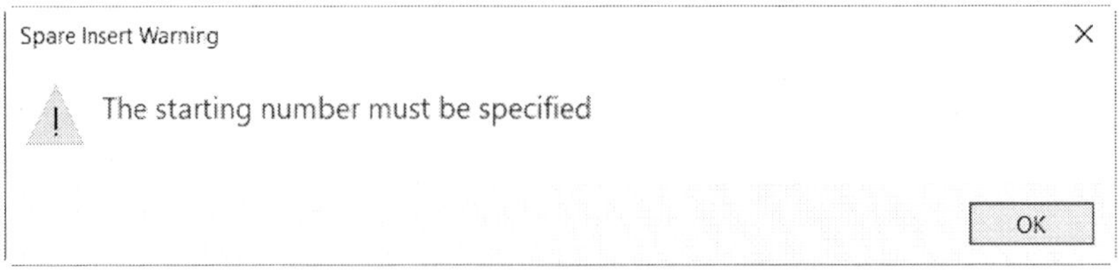

Spare Insert Warning

The starting number must be specified

OK

*Figure 11-27 The **Spare Insert Warning** message box*

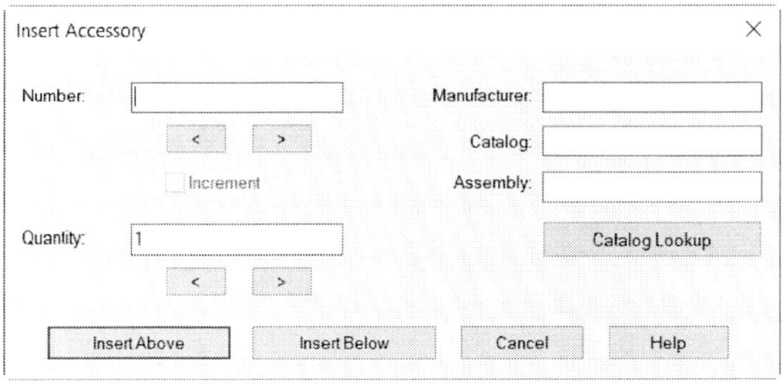

Insert Accessory

Number: Manufacturer: Catalog: Assembly: Increment Quantity: 1 Catalog Lookup Insert Above Insert Below Cancel Help

*Figure 11-28 The **Insert Accessory** dialog box*

The options in this dialog box are the same as those in the **Insert Spare Terminal** dialog box. Enter the required information in the **Insert Accessory** dialog box. Choose the **Insert Above** or **Insert Below** button to insert the accessory above or below the selected terminal block.

The **Delete Spare Terminals/Accessories** button is used to delete the spare terminal or accessories.

## Destinations Area

The buttons in this area are toggle buttons and are used to modify the installation and location codes. These buttons are discussed next.

The **Toggle Location** button is used to toggle the location codes from an external destination to an internal destination and vice versa. Choose the **Toggle Location** button; the **Toggle Location Codes** dialog box will be displayed, as shown in Figure 11-29.

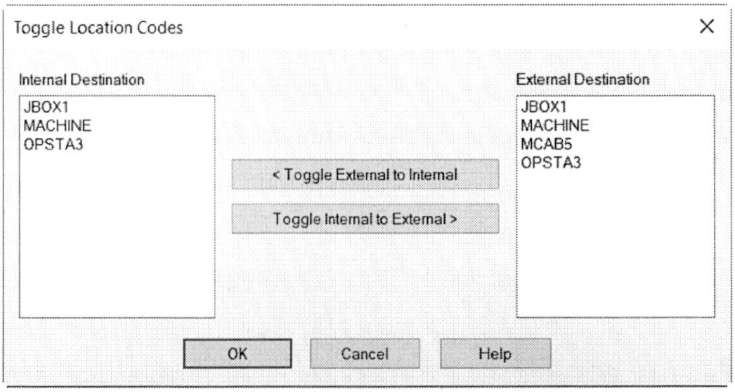

Toggle Location Codes

Internal Destination: JBOX1, MACHINE, OPSTA3

External Destination: JBOX1, MACHINE, MCAB5, OPSTA3

< Toggle External to Internal

Toggle Internal to External >

OK Cancel Help

*Figure 11-29 The **Toggle Location Codes** dialog box*

Choose the **< Toggle External to Internal** button to move the location code from the **External Destination** area to the **Internal Destination** area. Choose the **Toggle Internal to External >** button to move the location code from the **Internal Destination** area to the **External Destination** area. Choose the **OK** button; the location codes displayed in the list of the **Terminal Strip Editor** dialog box will be moved accordingly.

The **Toggle Installation** button is used to toggle the installation codes from an external destination to an internal destination and vice-versa. Note that the options in the **Toggle Installation Codes** dialog box are the same as those in the **Toggle Location Codes** dialog box.

**Note**

*If the components do not have location and installation codes, then question marks (??) will be displayed in both the **Toggle Location Codes** dialog box and the **Toggle Installation Codes** dialog box.*

The **Toggle Terminal Destinations** button is used to toggle the terminal destination from external to internal and vice-versa. To toggle the terminal destination, select the required terminal from the list displayed and then choose the **Toggle Terminal Destinations** button; the **Toggle Terminal Destinations** dialog box will be displayed, as shown in Figure 11-30.

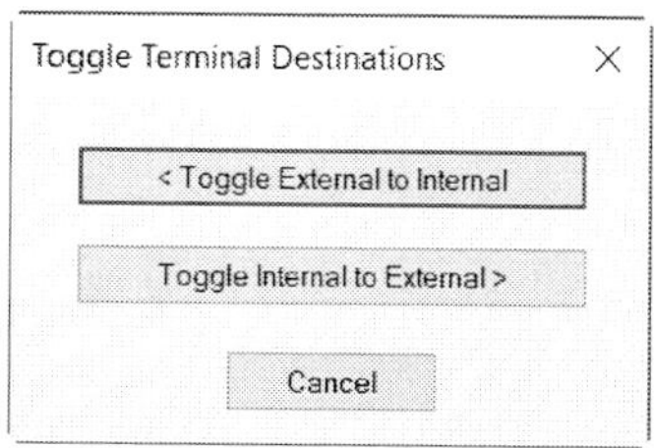


***Figure 11-30** The **Toggle Terminal Destinations** dialog box*

Choose the **<Toggle External to Internal** button to change the terminal destination from external (right) to internal (left). Choose the **Toggle Internal to External >** button to change the terminal destination from internal (left) to external (right). Choose the **Cancel** button to terminate the command.

The **Switch Terminal Destinations** button is used to exchange the internal and external destination values of the selected terminal. Select the terminal block and then choose the **Switch Terminal Destinations** button; the internal destination changes to the external (right) destination and vice versa.

The **Move Destination** button is used to move destination within terminal levels. Select a terminal block from the list displayed and then choose the **Move Destination** button; the **Destination Move** dialog box will be displayed, as shown in Figure 11-31.

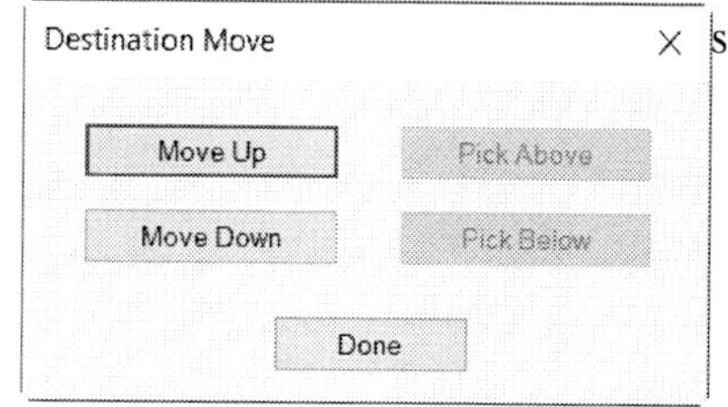


***Figure 11-31** The **Destination Move** dialog box*

Choose the **Move Up** or **Move down** button to move the selected destination up or down. Choose the **Done** button to exit this dialog box.

## Jumpers Area

The options in the **Jumpers** area are used to assign, edit, and delete the jumper. These options are discussed next.

The **Assign Jumper** button is used to assign a jumper to the selected terminals or levels. To assign a jumper, select the terminals from the same level or from different levels and then choose the **Assign Jumper** button; the **Edit/Delete Jumpers** dialog box will be displayed, as shown in Figure 11-32. In this dialog box, you can edit the jumper information, delete a jumper, remove terminals from a jumper, and edit catalog data. The different areas and options in this dialog box are discussed next.

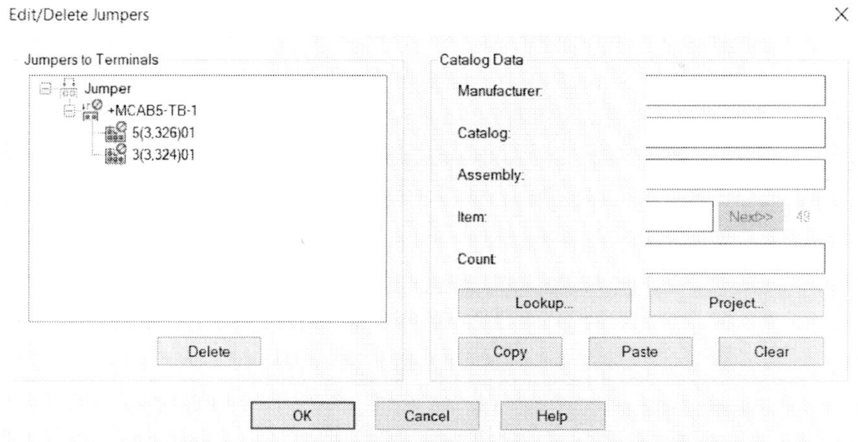

*Figure 11-32 The **Edit/Delete Jumpers** dialog box*

The **Jumpers to Terminals** area displays the jumpers of the selected terminal.

Choose the **Delete** button to delete jumpers from all terminals. In the **Catalog Data** area, you can specify the manufacturer, catalog, assembly, item, and count values for jumpers of the selected terminals. Alternatively, you can use the **Lookup** button to specify the catalog data.

You can also choose the **Project** button. On doing so, the **Jumper catalog values (this project)** dialog box will be displayed. Select the catalog value and choose the **OK** button; the respective values will be displayed in the **Catalog Data** area.

Choose the **Copy** button to copy the catalog values from the selected jumper. Choose the **Paste** button to paste the copied catalog values in the selected jumper. Choose the **Clear** button to clear the catalog values of the selected jumper.

After specifying the options in the **Edit/Delete Jumpers** dialog box, choose the **OK** button; the jumpers will be assigned to the selected terminals.

The **Edit/Delete Jumper** button of the **Jumpers** area in the **Terminal Strip Editor** dialog box is used to edit or delete one or more jumper definitions. Choose the **Edit/Delete Jumper** button; the **Edit/Delete Jumpers** dialog box will be displayed. The options in this dialog box have already been discussed in the previous section.

### Multi-Level Area

The options in the **Multi-Level** area are used to associate terminals and separate multi-level terminals. The buttons in this area are discussed next.

The **Associate Terminals** button is used to combine two or more terminal blocks into a single multiple level terminal block. Select the terminal blocks and then choose the **Associate Terminals** button; the **Associate Terminals** dialog box will be displayed, as shown in Figure 11-33. The options in this dialog box are discussed next.

**Note**

*If you select many levels of terminals from the list displayed to combine, the **Too Many Terminals Selected** message box will be displayed. This message box displays the message "**Currently, no terminal in the strip has enough available levels to support the selections you have made to associate**". Choose the **OK** button in this message box to exit.*

The **Selected** field displays the number of levels that you have selected to add to the association.

The **Terminals** area displays the terminals that contain enough levels to fit the number of levels you choose to associate. In this area, the level number for each level, which is defined in the **Terminal Block Properties** dialog box will be displayed. The level number of a panel symbol is represented by a symbol (#).

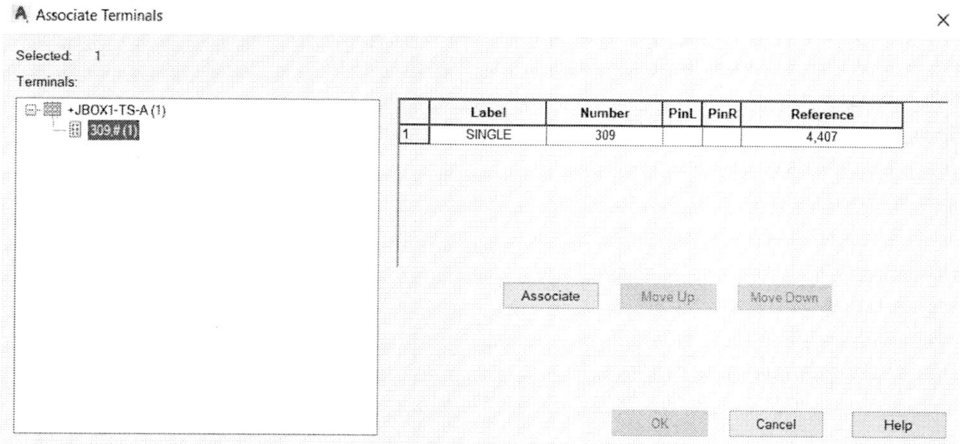


*Figure 11-33 The **Associate Terminals** dialog box*

The terminal grid, which is on the right of the **Associate Terminals** dialog box, displays the information of the terminal that you have selected from the **Terminals** area. The options in the Terminal grid are discussed next.

The **Label** column displays the description of level defined in the **Terminal Block Properties** dialog box.

The **Number** column displays the terminal numbers defined in the association. Note that the terminal numbers of panel terminal symbols will not be displayed. Also, if a terminal is not having a terminal number and the terminal levels are having assignment, question marks (???) will be displayed in this column.

The **PinL** column displays the pin numbers specified on the left of the terminal block.

The **PinR** column displays the pin numbers specified on the right of the terminal block.

The **Reference** column displays the reference location of the terminal symbol in the project.

The **Associate** button is used to add the selected terminal symbol to the terminal association selected in the **Terminal Strip Editor** dialog box.

Choose the **Move Up** button; the selected terminal will move one step up.

Choose the **Move Down** button; the selected terminal will move one step down.

After specifying the required options in the **Associate Terminals** dialog box, choose the **OK** button in the **Associate Terminals** dialog box to save the changes made in this dialog box and exit the dialog box.

The **Break Apart Terminal Associations** button is used to separate one or more levels from the multiple level terminal block into separate terminal blocks. To do so, select the required terminal from the list displayed and then choose the **Break Apart Terminal Associations** button; the **Break Apart Terminal Associations** dialog box will be displayed, as shown in Figure 11-34. The options in this dialog box are discussed next.

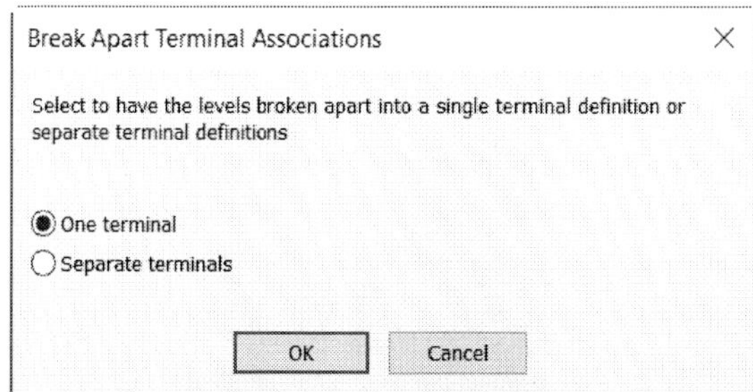


***Figure 11-34** The **Break Apart Terminal Associations** dialog box*

The **One terminal** radio button is selected by default and is used to break the selected levels from their original association and add them together into a new association.

Select the **Separate terminals** radio button to break the selected levels from their original association and add each level into a new individual association.

After specifying the required options in the **Break Apart Terminal Associations** dialog box, choose the **OK** button; the terminals will get separated accordingly.

### Save Destinations

This check box is used to save internal and external destination assignments. As a result, when you edit the terminal strip again, saved destination assignments will be displayed.

## Catalog Code Assignment Tab

The **Catalog Code Assignment** tab along with its options is shown in Figure 11-35. Using the options in this tab, you can modify the catalog data of the terminals. All the areas in this tab are the same as those in the **Terminal Strip** tab except that of the **Catalog** area. The options in the **Catalog** area are discussed next.

The options in the **Catalog** area are used to assign, delete, copy, and paste the catalog number to the selected terminal. These options are discussed next.

### Assign Catalog Number

The **Assign Catalog Number** button is used to assign the catalog number to the terminal blocks, spare terminals, and accessories. You can also edit the catalog number that has already been assigned to the terminal. To assign a catalog number to a terminal, select the terminal strip and then choose the **Assign Catalog Number** button; the **Catalog Browser** dialog box will be displayed. Next, select the catalog number and choose the **OK** button; the catalog number and manufacturer value will be displayed in the **Manufacturer** and **Catalog** columns in the **Terminal Strip Editor** dialog box.

**Note**

*The options in the **Catalog Browser** dialog box have already been discussed in Chapter 5.*

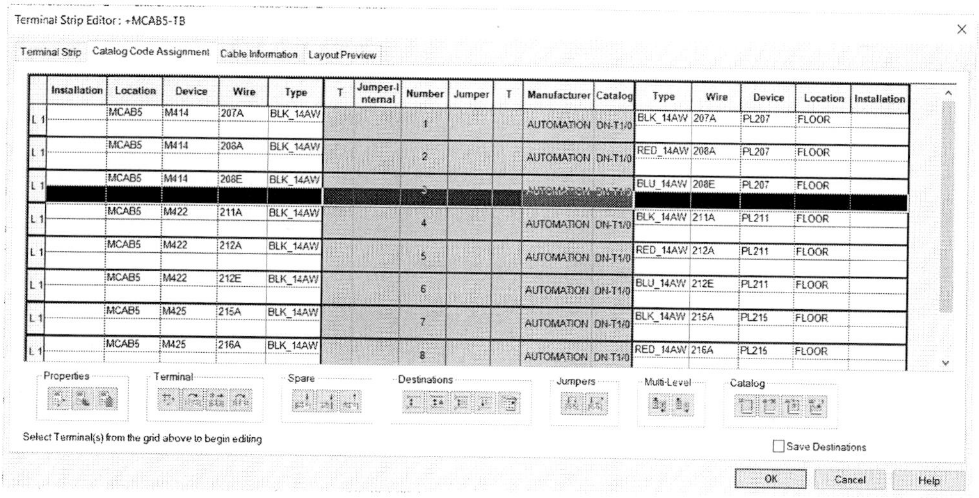

*Figure 11-35 The **Terminal Strip Editor** dialog box showing the **Catalog Code Assignment** tab*

The **Delete Catalog Number** button is used to delete the catalog number of the selected terminal blocks, spare terminal, and accessories that have been assigned to them.

The **Copy Catalog Number** button is used to copy the catalog number of the selected terminal block.

The **Paste Catalog Number** button is used to paste the copied catalog number to the selected terminal block.

## Cable Information Tab

The **Cable Information** tab and its options are shown in Figure 11-36. In this tab, the information of the cable associated to the terminals in the terminal strip is displayed. This tab displays terminal information at the center of the list, cable name, wire conductor information, and device destination information on both sides. The different areas in this tab have already been discussed earlier.

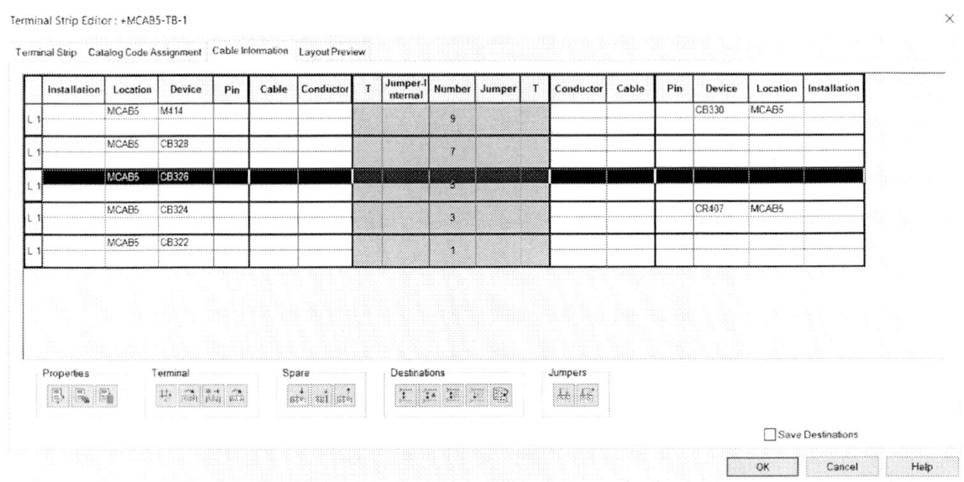


*Figure 11-36 The* ***Terminal Strip Editor*** *dialog box displaying the* ***Cable Information*** *tab*

## Layout Preview Tab

The **Layout Preview** tab is shown in Figure 11-37. In this tab, you can see the preview of the terminal strip and select the required format of the terminal strip to be inserted into a drawing. The **Layout Preview** tab consists of the **Graphical Terminal Strip**, **Tabular Terminal Strip (Table Object)**, and **Jumper Chart (Table Object)** radio buttons. These radio buttons are used to specify the type of terminal strip to be generated such as graphical, tabular, or jumper chart. The options in the **Layout Preview** tab will change according to the radio button that you select. Different areas and options in this tab are discussed next.

The **Graphical Terminal Strip** radio button is selected by default, refer to Figure 11-37, and is used to insert the AutoCAD blocks to represent the terminal strip. The options that are available on selecting this radio button are discussed next.

### Graphical Layout Area

In the **Graphical Layout** area, you can generate the graphical representation of a terminal strip that includes terminal footprints, terminal numbers, wiring information, and so on.

The total number of terminal block symbols needed to create the terminal strip layout is displayed on the right of the **Total Terminals** field.

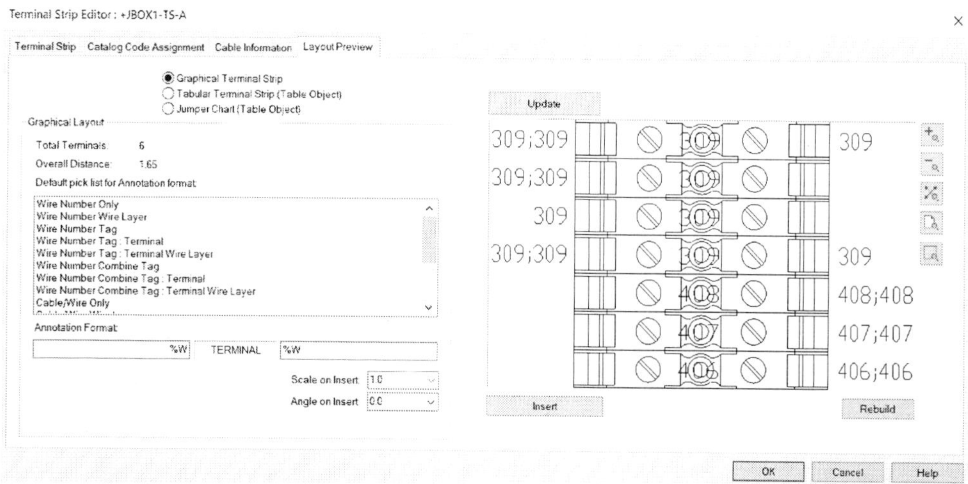


*Figure 11-37 The* ***Terminal Strip Editor*** *dialog box showing the* ***Layout Preview*** *tab*

On the right of the **Overall Distance** field, the overall distance of the terminal strip footprint will be displayed, when it is placed on the active drawing.

The **Default pick list for Annotation format** list box displays the type of annotation formats.

In the **Annotation Format** edit boxes, you can specify the format of the wiring information associated with the destination of the terminal. By default, %W is displayed in these edit boxes.

The **Scale on Insert** drop-down list is used to specify the scale of the graphical terminal strip when you insert it into a drawing. By default, 1.0 is displayed.

The **Angle on Insert** drop-down list is used to specify the angle for the graphical terminal strip when you insert it into a drawing. By default, 0.0 is displayed.

The **Update** button is used to update the preview of the terminal strip in the preview window, if you have made changes by using the different options of the **Layout Preview** tab. Also, you can zoom in, zoom out, and pan the preview displayed in the preview window by choosing the respective buttons that are displayed on the right side of the **Terminal Strip Editor** dialog box. Alternatively, you can zoom or pan inside the drawing by right-clicking in the preview window and then choosing the required option from the shortcut menu. The zoom tools are shown in Figure 11-38.

The **Insert** button is used to insert the terminal strip into a drawing. Choose the **Insert** button. Next, specify the insertion point for the terminal strip and press ENTER; the terminal strip will be inserted into a drawing.

The **Rebuild** button is used to update the terminal strip that you have inserted in a drawing. To update the already inserted terminal strip in an active project, choose the **Rebuild** button; the terminal strip will be updated accordingly. Note that if the terminal strip does not exist in the active project and you choose the **Rebuild** button, the **Terminal Strip Not Found** message box will be displayed, as shown in Figure 11-39.

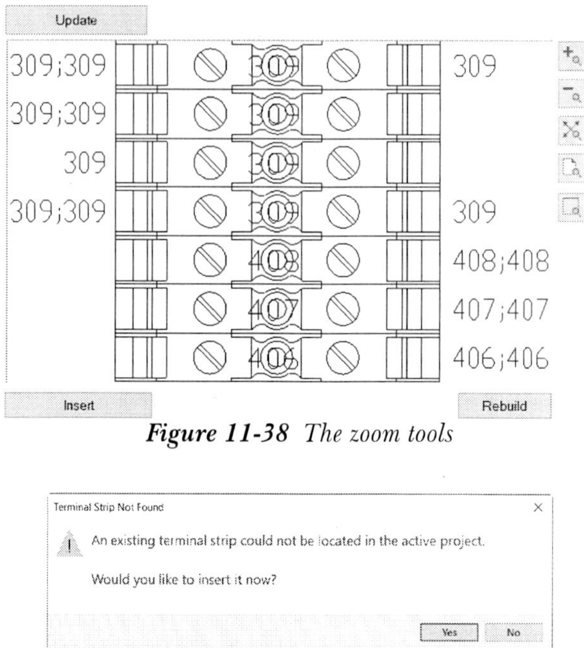


*Figure 11-38 The zoom tools*

*Figure 11-39 The **Terminal Strip Not Found** message box*

Choose the **Yes** button to insert the terminal strip. Choose the **No** button to exit from this message box. The **Tabular Terminal Strip (Table Object)** radio button is used to insert the terminal strip in a tabular format. Select the **Tabular Terminal Strip (Table Object)** radio button; the options in the **Layout Preview** tab will change accordingly, as shown in Figure 11-40. These options are discussed next.

## Tabular Layout Area

The options in the **Tabular Layout** area are used to specify table settings such as style, title, columns, row styles, and so on. The options in this area are discussed next.

Select the table style for the tabular report from the **Table Style** drop-down list. Alternatively, you can choose the **Browse** button on the right of the **Table Style** drop-down list; the **Select Drawing with Table style** dialog box will be displayed. Select the drawing from this dialog box and choose the **Open** button; the table style of the selected drawing will get added to the **Table Style** drop-down list.

The **Define Columns** button is used to define columns of the tabular report that includes headings, justification, order, jumper circles, internal jumper squares, and so on. Choose the **Define Columns** button; the **Terminal Strip Table Data Fields to Include** dialog box will be displayed, as shown in Figure 11-41. Specify the required options in this dialog box and choose the **OK** button to return to the **Terminal Strip Editor** dialog box.

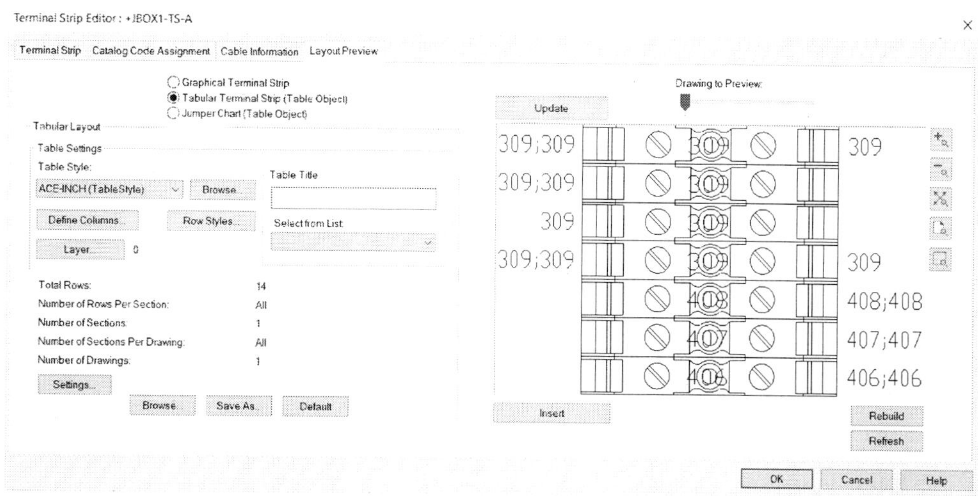


*Figure 11-40 The* ***LayoutPreview*** *tab when you select the* ***Tabular Terminal Strip (Table Object)*** *radio button*

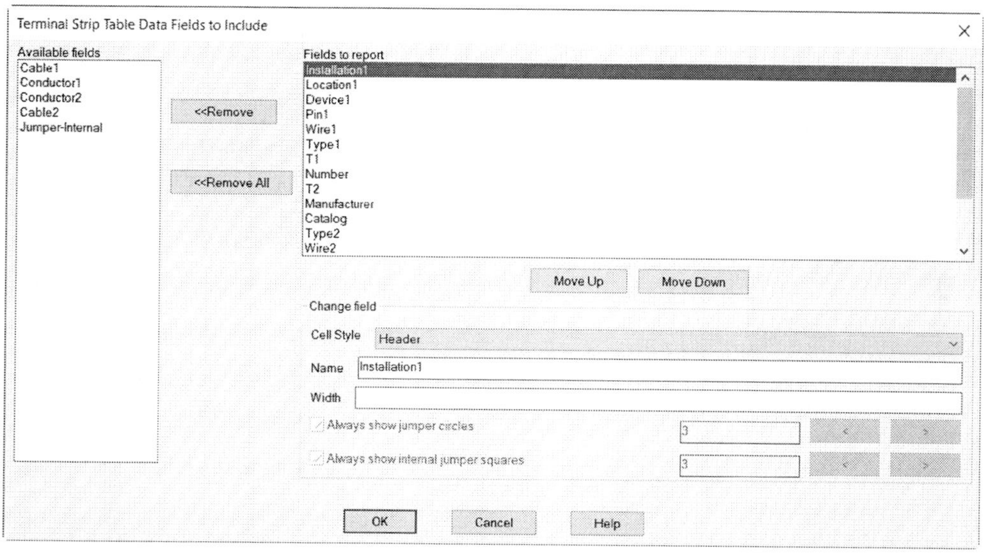


*Figure 11-41 The* ***Terminal Strip Table Data Fields to Include*** *dialog box*

The **Row Styles** button is used to define the row style to be used in the selected table style. Choose the **Row Styles** button; the **Select Row Cell Styles** dialog box will be displayed, as shown in Figure 11-42. Select the table style from the **Table Style** drop-down list. Next, select the row cell styles from the **Terminal** and **Accessory** drop-down lists. Choose the **OK** button to save the changes and exit from the dialog box.

The **Layer** button is used to define a layer for the tabular terminal strip. Choose the **Layer** button; the **Select Table Layer** dialog box will be displayed. Select the layer name from the list of layers. Alternatively, you can specify the name of the layer in the **Layer Name** edit box. Choose the **OK** button to save the changes and exit this dialog box.

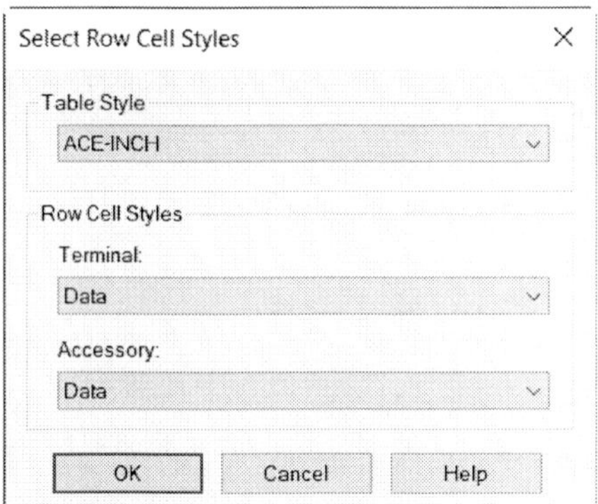


***Figure 11-42** The **Select Row Cell Styles** dialog box*

In the **Table Title** area, you can specify the title for the table. Specify the title for the table in the edit box. Alternatively, you can select the title for the table from the **Select from List** drop-down list. You can also use a combination of both.

The total number of rows, rows per section, number of sections, sections per drawing, and drawings of a terminal strip will be displayed below the **Layer** button in the **Layout Preview** tab of the **Terminal Strip Editor** dialog box.

The **Settings** button is used to define the tablesettings such as the number of rows per section, number of sections per drawing, table, and section placement, section offset, scale, angle, and so on. To define settings of a table, choose the **Settings** button; the **Terminal Strip Table Settings** dialog box will be displayed. The options in this dialog box will be discussed later in this chapter.

Choose the **Browse** button to browse for any saved table settings (*.tsl file).

The **Save As** button is used to save the settings of a table to an external file that can be used later.
Choose the **Default** button to create the tabular report with the default settings.

The **Drawing to Preview** slider is used to switch between the preview of drawings, if the table settings define a multi-section table that includes multiple drawings.

The **Refresh** button is used to update the data of the existing tabular terminal strip. This button is not used for inserting the new terminal strip but it just refreshes the already existing table inserted into the drawing. Choose the **Refresh** button; the drawing will be updated and the **Table Object Updated** message box will be displayed. Choose the **OK** button to exit from the **Table Object Updated** message box.

When you select the **Jumper Chart (Table Object)** radio button from the **Layout Preview** tab of the **Terminal Strip Editor** dialog box, the following options will be available:

### Tabular Layout Area

Most of the options in the **Table Settings** area are already discussed. The rest of the options in this area are discussed next.

The **Display all Accessories and Terminals** radio button is selected by default. As a result, all the terminals and the accessories of the terminal strip are displayed in the table.

Select the **Display Only Accessories and Jumpered Terminals** radio button to display only the accessories of a terminal and the terminals that are jumpered in a table.

Select the **Display Only Jumpered Terminals** radio button to display the terminals that are jumpered in the table.

If you select the **Show Unused Wire Connections in Table** check box, the rows of each terminal will be displayed even if no component is connected to terminal.

The **Save** button is used to save the settings to the *JumperChart.tjc* file. When you choose the **Save** button, the **Settings Saved Successfully** message box will be displayed.

After specifying the required options in the **Terminal Strip Editor** dialog box, choose the **OK** button; the **Graphical Terminal Strip Insert/Update Required** message box will be displayed, prompting you to rebuild or insert the updated terminal strip. Choose the desired option from this message box; you will return to the **Terminal Strip Selection** dialog box. Choose the **Done** button to exit from this dialog box.

## Defining the Settings of the Terminal Strip Table

You can define the settings of the terminal strip table in the **Terminal Strip Table Settings** dialog box. To do so, select the **Tabular Terminal Strip (Table Object)** radio button from the **Layout Preview** tab of the **Terminal Strip Editor** dialog box. Next, choose the **Settings** button from the **Tabular Layout** area; the **Terminal Strip Table Settings** dialog box will be displayed, as shown in Figure 11-43. The areas and options in this dialog box are discussed next.

### Rows Per Section Area

The **Rows Per Section** spinner is inactive by default. This spinner will become available only if you clear the **All Rows Same Section** check box. In this spinner, you can specify the number of rows for each table section.

### Insert All Sections on Active Drawing

The **Insert All Sections on Active Drawing** radio button is selected by default. As a result, all the sections will be inserted in the active drawing.

### Insert One Section Per Drawing

When you select the **Insert One Section Per Drawing** radio button, the **Section Placement** area, the **Drawing Information for Table Output** area, and the **Preview** button will become available. This radio button is used to insert a table with one section per drawing. You can specify the drawing name and template by using the options in the **Drawing Information for Table Output** area. These options will be discussed in detail later in this chapter.

## Insert All Sections on One Drawing

Select the **Insert All Sections on One Drawing** radio button to insert all the sections of a table in one drawing.

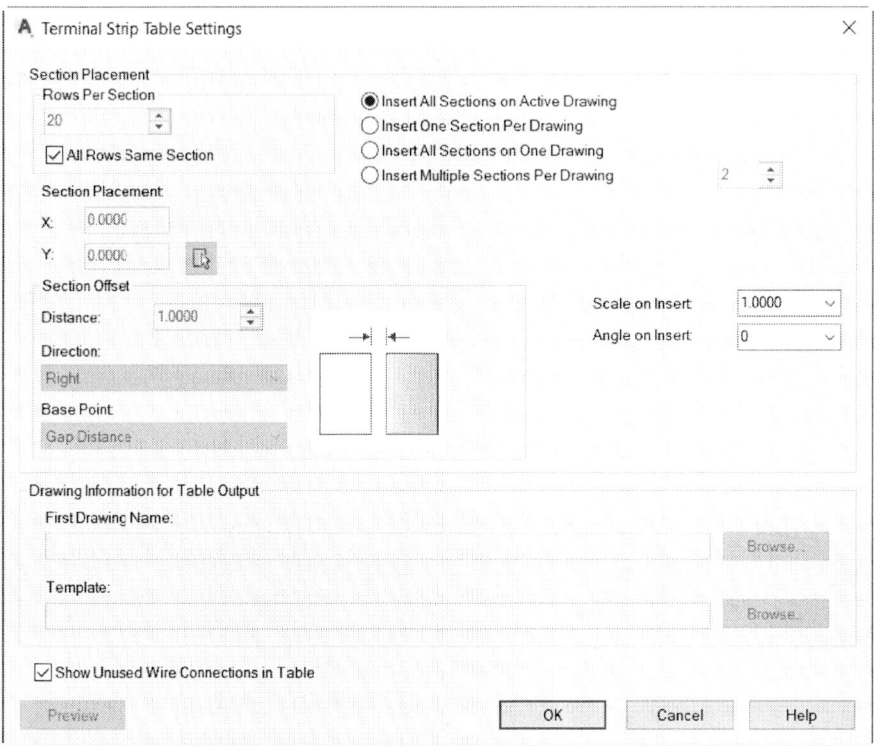


*Figure 11-43 The **Terminal Strip Table Settings** dialog box*

## Insert Multiple Sections Per Drawing

Select the **Insert Multiple Sections Per Drawing** radio button to insert multiple sections of a table per drawing. Also, note that the spinner adjacent to this radio button will become available. By default, 2 is displayed in the spinner.

## Section Placement Area

The **X** and **Y** edit boxes of the **Section Placement** area will be activated only when you select the **Insert One Section Per Drawing** radio button, the **Insert All Sections on One Drawing** radio button, or the **Insert Multiple Sections Per Drawing** radio button. In the **Section Placement** area, you can specify the co-ordinates for placing the table into the drawing. To do so, you need to specify the X and Y co-ordinates in the **X** and **Y** edit boxes. Alternatively, you can choose the **Pick Point** button. On doing so, you will be prompted to specify the first insertion point. The **Terminal Strip Table Settings** dialog box will disappear. Next, pick the point on the drawing; the **Terminal Strip Table Settings** dialog box will be displayed again and the X and Y coordinates will be displayed in the **X** and **Y** edit boxes.

## Section Offset Area

The **Section Offset** area will be activated only if you clear the **All Rows Same Section** check box and select any one of the following radio buttons: **Insert All Sections on Active Drawing**, **Insert All Sections on One Drawing**, or **Insert Multiple Sections Per Drawing**. In the **Section Offset** area, you can specify the distance between the sections, offset direction, and the base point. The options in this area are discussed next.

Specify the distance between the sections in the **Distance** spinner. By default, 1.000 is displayed in the **Distance** spinner.

Select the required option from the **Direction** drop-down list to specify the direction for the offset. By default, **Right** is displayed in this drop-down list.

Select the required option from the **Base Point** drop-down list to specify the base point for the distance measurement between the sections.

## Scale on Insert

Select the scale for the tabular section in the **Scale on Insert** drop-down list. By default, 1.000 is displayed.

## Angle on Insert

Select the angle for the tabular section in the **Angle on Insert** drop-down list. By default, 0 is displayed.

## Drawing Information for Table Output Area

The **Drawing Information for Table Output** area will become available only when you select any one of the following radio buttons: **Insert One Section Per Drawing**, **Insert All Sections on One Drawing**, or **Insert Multiple Sections Per Drawing**. The options in this area are discussed next.

In the **First Drawing Name** edit box, you can specify the starting drawing file name and location for creating the drawing files. These drawing files will automatically be added to the active project and will be displayed at the end of the drawing list in the **PROJECT MANAGER**. The last character of the drawing file name will be incremented for each drawing created. Alternatively, you can choose the **Browse** button on the right of the **First Drawing Name** edit box to specify the name of the first drawing.

Specify the template file to be used for new drawings in the **Template** edit box. Alternatively, choose the **Browse** button on the right of the **Template** edit box to select it.

## Show Unused Wire Connections in Table

If you select the **Show Unused Wire Connections in Table** check box, the rows of each terminal will be displayed even if no component is connected to it.

## Preview

Choose the **Preview** button; the **Preview** dialog box will be displayed. This dialog box displays the preview of the drawing. Choose the **Done** button to exit from this dialog box.

After specifying the required settings of the table in the **Terminal Strip Table Settings** dialog box, choose the **OK** button to save the changes and exit from this dialog box.

# GENERATING THE TERMINAL STRIP TABLE

| | |
|---|---|
| **Ribbon:** | Panel > Terminal Footprints > Table Generator |
| **Toolbar:** | ACE:Panel Layout > Terminal Strip Editor > Terminal Strip Table Generator<br>ACE:Terminal Footprint > Terminal Strip Table Generator |
| **Menu:** | Panel Layout > Terminal Strip Table Generator |
| **Command:** | AETSEGENERATOR |

The **Terminal Strip Table Generator** tool is used to create drawings along with a terminal strip table. This tool is also used to insert one or more than one terminal strip in the form of a table in a drawing. This tool is also used to rebuild and refresh the existing terminal strip tables present in an active project, and add the newly created drawings to the active project. To insert a tabular terminal strip, choose the **Table Generator** tool from the **Terminal Footprints** panel of the **Panel** tab; the **Terminal Strip Table Generator** dialog box will be displayed, as shown in Figure 11-44. You can insert a terminal strip as a single object or split it into multiple table objects. The new drawings will be created as needed and will automatically be added to the active project. Note that the terminal strip that you select will start in a new drawing.

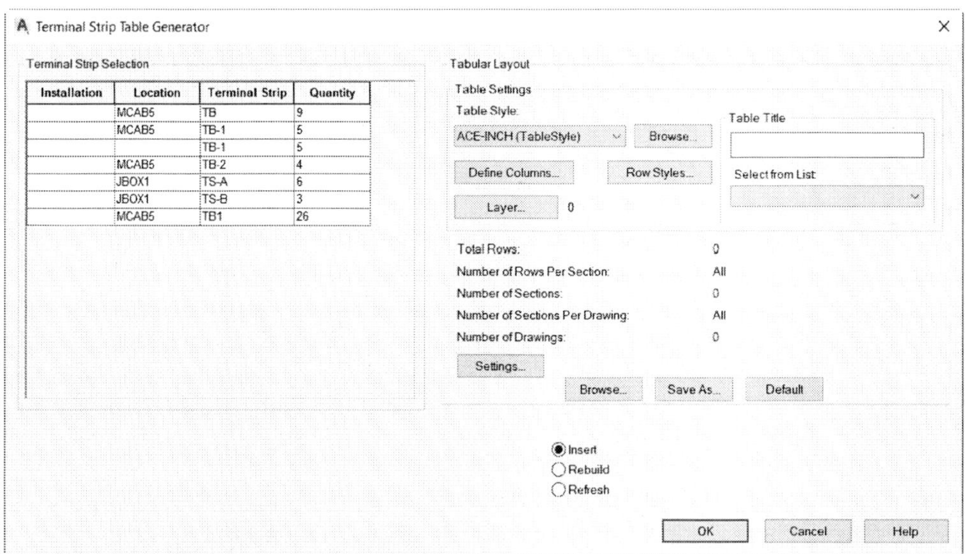


***Figure 11-44** The **Terminal Strip Table Generator** dialog box*

If you click on any of the column headers in the **Terminal Strip Selection** area, the terminal strips in this area will be sorted accordingly.

The options in this dialog box have already been discussed in the previous section.

Now, to insert a terminal strip table into a drawing, select the terminal strip from the **Terminal Strip Selection** area. Next, make the required changes in the **Tabular Layout** area and select the **Insert** radio button, if it is not already selected. Choose the **OK** button in the **Terminal Strip Table Generator** dialog box; the **Table(s) Inserted** message box will be displayed. This message box displays that table(s) has been inserted in the drawing. It also displays the path and location of the new drawing. Choose the **OK** button in the **Table(s) Inserted** message box to exit from the dialog box. You will notice that the new drawing is added at the end of the active project.

**Note**

*You can also select multiple terminal strips from the* ***Terminal Strip Selection*** *area by using the SHIFT or CTRL key or by clicking and dragging the mouse.*

# EDITING THE TERMINAL PROPERTIES DATABASE TABLE

**Ribbon:** Schematic > Insert Components > Icon Menu drop-down > Catalog Browser
**Command:** AECATALOGOPEN

The **Catalog Browser** tool is used to edit the existing entry or create a new entry in the terminal category list of the catalog database. To do so, choose the **Catalog Browser** tool from the **Icon Menu** drop-down in the **Insert Components** panel of the **Schematic** tab, refer to Figure 11-45; the **Catalog Browser** dialog box will be displayed. In this dialog box, select the **TRMS (Terminals)** category from the **Category** drop-down list. Next, delete the content from the **Search** field and choose the **Search** button; the catalog database of all the terminals (for all the manufacturers) will be displayed, refer to Figure 11-46. Scroll to the right in the Database grid. You will notice that there are some columns available in it. Now, choose the **Edit** button located below the **Search** field and again scroll to the right in the Database grid. On doing so, some more columns are added to this grid, namely **LEVELS, LEVELDESCRIPTION, INTERNALJUMPER, TPINL, TPINR, WIRESPERCONNECTION**, and so on, refer to Figure 11-47.

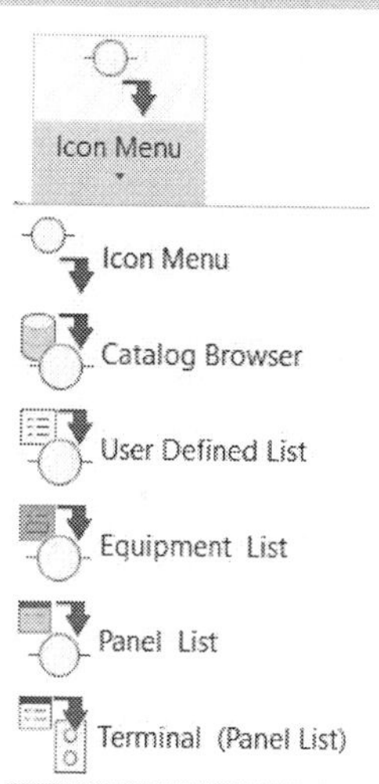


***Figure 11-45** The **Icon Menu** drop-down*

To edit the entry of a terminal, you need to click in the respective cell of the column and make the necessary changes. Also, you can right-click in the cell of the column and use the options in the shortcut menu displayed to edit it. Some of the major columns are discussed next.

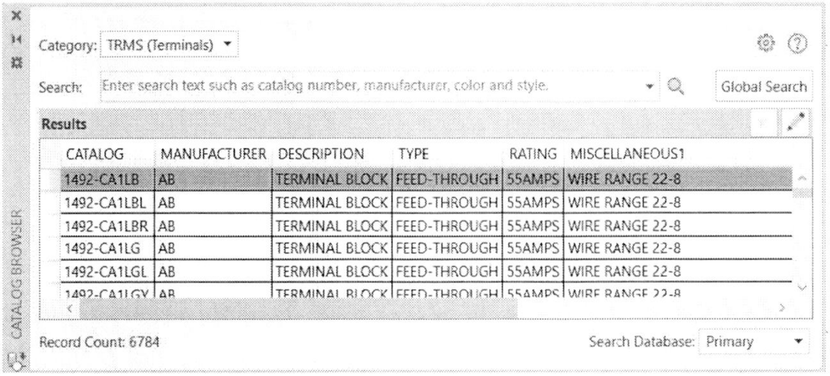

*Figure 11-46* *The* ***Catalog Browser*** *dialog box displaying all terminals in the database*

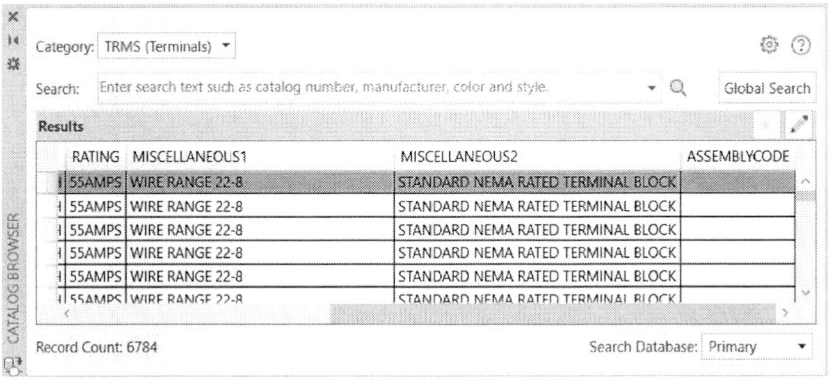

*Figure 11-47* *The columns added to the* ***Catalog Browser*** *dialog box*

If you double-click on a cell of the **SYMBOL2D** column, it will be converted into a field consisting of an edit box and a Browse button, as shown in Figure 11-48. You can enter the name of the 2D symbol in this edit box. If you click on the Browse button, the **2D Symbol** dialog box will be displayed, as shown in Figure 11-49. You can enter names for the 2D symbols in the edit boxes available in this dialog box. If you choose the **Icon menu** button from this dialog box, the **Insert Component** dialog box will be displayed. Now, you can select a symbol from this dialog box to be used as a 2D symbol for the corresponding terminal entry. Also, you can enter comments for this symbol in the **Comment** edit boxes. Note that a row is added at the bottom of the Database grid when you enter symbol name in the last row of this dialog box.

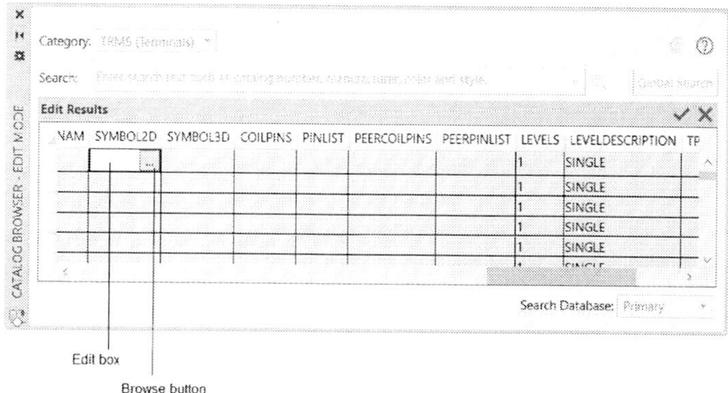


*Figure 11-48 The field with an edit box and the Browse button*

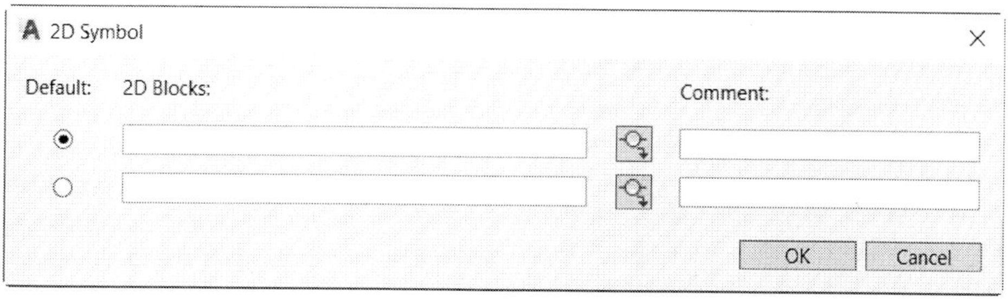

*Figure 11-49 The **2D Symbol** dialog box*

If you double-click on the cell of the **LEVELS**, **LEVELDESRIPTION**, **TPINL**, **TPINR**, or **WIRESPERCONNECTION** column, it will be converted into a field consisting of an edit box and a Browse button, refer to Figure 11-48. Choose the Browse button; the **Terminal Block Properties** dialog box will be displayed, as shown in Figure 11-50.

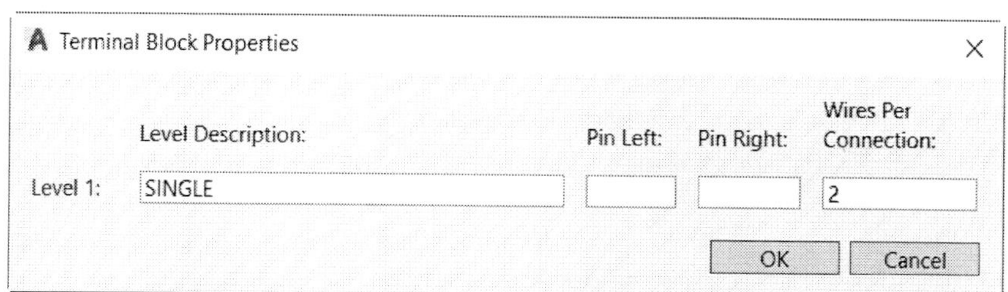


*Figure 11-50 The **Terminal Block Properties** dialog box*

Edit the values in this dialog box and choose the **OK** button; the values in the corresponding column of the **Catalog Browser** dialog box will change accordingly. Note that the number of rows in the **Terminal Block Properties** dialog box is equal to the number of levels in the corresponding terminal block.

If you double-click on the cell of the **INTERNALJUMPER** column, it will be converted into a field consisting of an edit box and a Browse button, refer to Figure 11-48. Click on the Browse button; the **Manage Internal Jumpers** dialog box will be displayed, as shown in Figure 11-51.

Note that the Browse button for this field will be activated only if the number of levels is more than one in the corresponding **LEVEL** column.

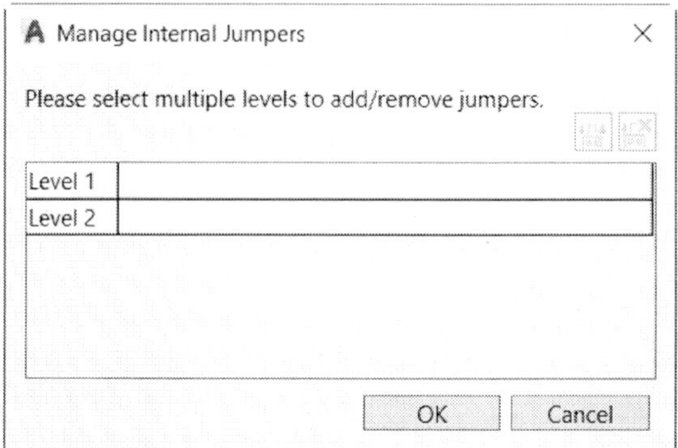


***Figure 11-51*** *The **Manage Internal Jumpers** dialog box*

There are two buttons in the **Manage Internal Jumpers** dialog box: **Assign Jumper** and **Delete Jumper**. The **Assign Jumper** button will be activated when you select more than one row, refer to Figure 11-52. If the jumper is assigned between any two levels of the terminal block, the **Delete Jumper** button will be activated.

To create a new entry in the Terminal category list, scroll down in the Database grid and then add details in the blank row available at the bottom.

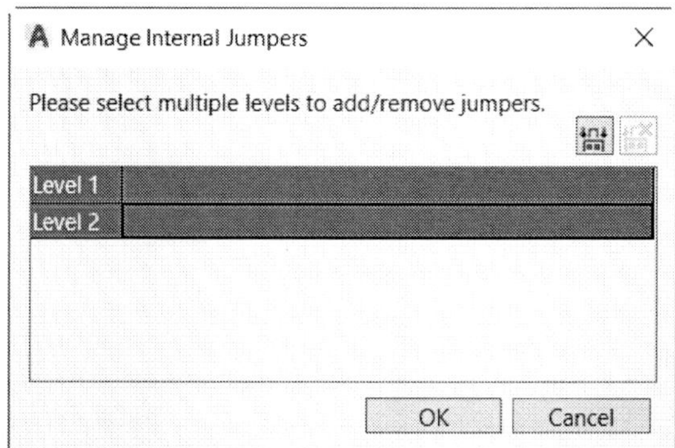


***Figure 11-52*** *The two rows selected*

Once you edit the entry or create a new entry, choose the **Accept Changes** button located below the **Search** field to save the changes made. If you want to cancel the changes made, choose the **Cancel Changes** button.

## RESEQUENCING TERMINAL NUMBERS

AutoCAD Electrical has some tools that help in resequencing terminal numbers in drawings. However, these tools do not resequence the terminals that use the wire number as a terminal number. The terminal strips can be resequenced by two methods and are discussed next.

**Note**

*The panel terminals cannot be renumbered using these tools. To resequence a terminal strip that has panel terminals, use the* ***Terminal Strip editor*** *tool.*

## First Method

| | |
|---|---|
| **Menu:** | Components > Terminals > Terminal Strip Utilities > Terminal Renumber (Pick Mode) |
| **Command:** | AETERMRENUMPICK |

To resequence the terminals by selecting them directly from the drawing, choose **Components > Terminals > Terminal Strip Utilities > Terminal Renumber (Pick Mode)** tool from the menu bar; you will be prompted to enter the start number. Enter the start number for the terminal number and then press ENTER. Alternatively, you can directly press ENTER to accept the default value. Next, you will be prompted to select the terminal symbol. Select the terminal symbols one by one from the drawing; the terminal number will get renumbered automatically and increment with each pick. Press ENTER to exit the command.

## Second Method

| | |
|---|---|
| **Menu:** | Components > Terminals > Terminal Strip Utilities > Terminal Renumber (Project-Wide) |
| **Command:** | AETERMRENUM |

To resequence the terminal numbers across the entire project, choose **Components > Terminals > Terminal Strip Utilities > Terminal Renumber (Project-Wide)** tool from the menu bar; the **Project-wide Schematic Terminal Renumber** dialog box will be displayed, as shown in Figure 11-53. The options in this dialog box are discussed next.

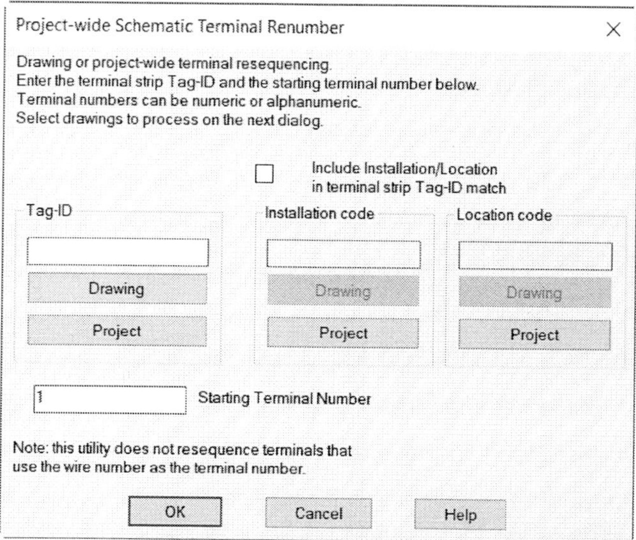


***Figure 11-53*** *The* ***Project-wide Schematic Terminal Renumber*** *dialog box*

The **Tag-ID** edit box is used to specify the Tag-ID of terminal that you need to resequence. Enter the terminal strip Tag-ID in the edit box in the **Tag-ID** area. Alternatively, you can choose the

**Drawing** or **Project** buttons to select the Tag-ID of the terminal strip to be renumbered from the active drawing or active project. Note that only the specified Tag-ID will be renumbered.

Select the **Include Installation/Location in terminal strip Tag-ID match** check box to include the installation and location codes in the terminal strip for the Tag-ID match. On selecting this check box, the **Installation code** and **Location code** areas will be activated. If you want to filter the search, enter the installation code and the location code in the **Installation code** and **Location code** areas, respectively. Alternatively, choose the **Drawing** or **Project** button to search for the installation and location codes in the active drawing or in the active project.

Note that the terminals will be renumbered only if they match with the specified Tag-ID, Installation code, and location code.

Next, enter the beginning number of terminal in the **Starting Terminal Number** edit box. After specifying the required options in the **Project-wide Schematic Terminal Renumber** dialog box, choose the **OK** button in this dialog box; the **Select Drawings to Process** dialog box will be displayed. Next, select the drawings that you need to process and choose the **Process** button; the selected drawings will be moved from the top list to the bottom list. Next, choose the **OK** button; the terminal numbers will be resequenced.

## COPYING TERMINAL BLOCK PROPERTIES

**Ribbon:** Schematic > Edit Components > Copy Terminal Block Properties
**Toolbar:** ACE:Main Electrical 2 > Symbol Builder > Copy Terminal Block Properties or ACE:Miscellaneous > Copy Terminal Block Properties
**Menu:** Components > Terminals > Copy Terminal Block Properties
**Command:** AECOPYTERMINALPROP

The **Copy Terminal Block Properties** tool is used to copy terminal properties of one terminal symbol and paste them into another terminal symbol. To do so, choose the **Copy Terminal Block Properties** tool from the **Edit Components** panel of the **Schematic** tab; you will be prompted to select the master terminal. Select the master terminal from which you need to copy the terminal properties; you will be prompted to select the target terminal(s). Select the terminal(s) to apply the terminal properties and press ENTER; the terminal properties will be applied to the target terminals. Press ENTER to exit the command. Now, if you want to view whether the terminal properties of the master terminal have been applied to the target terminal, right-click on it and choose the **Edit Component** option; the **Insert / Edit Terminal Symbol** dialog box will be displayed. In this dialog box, choose the **Block Properties** button to view the terminal properties of the target terminal.

## EDITING JUMPERS

**Ribbon:** Schematic > Edit Components > Edit Jumper
**Menu:** Components > Terminals > Edit Jumper
**Command:** AEJUMPER

The **Edit Jumper** tool is used to edit or delete jumper information on a terminal. This tool is also used to jumper two or more terminals together. To edit or delete a jumper on a terminal, choose the arrow on the right of the **Edit Components** panel of the **Schematic** tab; a flyout will be displayed. Choose the **Edit Jumper** tool from the flyout; you will be prompted to select a terminal symbol. Select the terminal symbol. The prompt sequence for this command is given next.

> Command: **AEJUMPER** Enter
> Select terminal <Browse>: *Select terminal symbol.*
> Select jumpered terminals [Browse/Edit/Show] <Edit>: *Enter any of the options or ESC to exit the command.*

The **AEJUMPER** command has the following three options.

**Browse** **Edit** **Show**

These options are discussed next.

## The Browse Option

If you enter **B** at the Command prompt, the **Select Terminals To Jumper** dialog box will be displayed, as shown in Figure 11-54. This dialog box displays a list of the terminals present within an active project in the **Schematic Terminals** area. In this dialog box, you can add terminals to the current jumper and view jumpers or terminals at the lower part of the dialog box by choosing the **View** button. The options in this dialog box are discussed next.

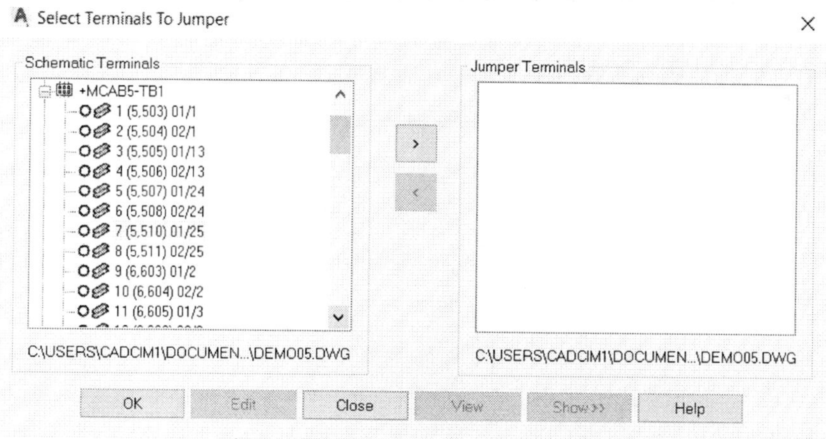


*Figure 11-54 The* ***Select Terminals To Jumper*** *dialog box*

### Schematic Terminals Area

The **Schematic Terminals** area displays the terminal strips and the terminals that are present in an active project. Click on the + sign of a terminal strip to expand it. Next, select the terminal that you want to jumper together from this area and choose the **>** button; the terminal will be added to the **Jumper Terminals** area. Also, you will notice that the terminals, which you transfer to the **Jumper Terminals** area become bold in the **Schematic Terminals** area. Note that when you select the terminal, the location and name of the drawing file are displayed at the bottom of the **Schematic Terminals** area. After you move the terminals from the **Schematic Terminals** area to the **Jumper Terminals** area, the **OK** and **Edit** buttons will be activated. Note that the empty circle on the left side of terminal node in the **Schematic Terminals** area indicates that the jumper is not attached to the terminal while a filled circle indicates that a jumper is attached.

### Jumper Terminals Area

The **Jumper Terminals** area displays the jumper and all associated terminals.

### > and <

Choose the **>** button to copy the selected terminal from the **Schematic Terminals** area to the **Jumper Terminals** area. Also, the selected terminals will become bold in the **Schematic Terminals** area. Choose the **<** button to remove the selected terminal from the **Jumper Terminals** area.

### Edit

The **Edit** button is used to create or edit the jumper across the selected terminals. To do so, choose the **Edit** button; the **Edit Terminal Jumpers** dialog box will be displayed. The options in this dialog box have already been discussed in this chapter.

### View

The **View** button is used to view the selected terminal. Choose the **View** button; the preview of the selected object will be displayed at the lower part of the dialog box. If you select a terminal, the terminal symbol will appear in the preview window, as shown in Figure 11-55.

If you select a terminal strip, the table having the information for terminals and a jumper column will be displayed in the preview window. By default, the preview window is hidden. To display this window, you can choose the **Show** button.

### Show>>

Choose the **Show>>** button to display the preview window at the bottom of the **Select Terminals to Jumper** dialog box. The preview window shows the preview of the selected terminal.

### << Hide

Choose the **<< Hide** button to hide the preview window that was displayed by choosing the **Show >>** or **View** button.

### Preview Window

The preview window displays the preview of the selected terminal. You can zoom or pan the image using the zoom tools and the pan tool available on the right side of the preview window.

### Close

Choose the **Close** button to close the **Select Terminals to Jumper** dialog box.

After closing this dialog box, you can continue with the rest of the options of the Command prompt. These options are discussed next.

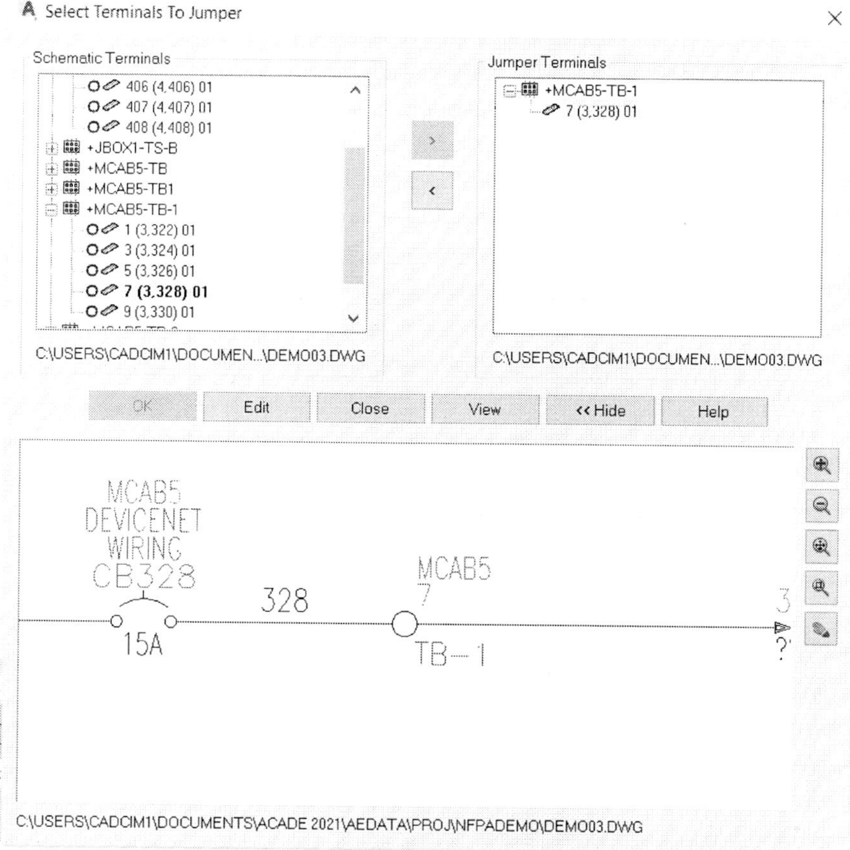


***Figure 11-55** The **Select Terminals To Jumper** dialog box displaying preview of the terminal symbol*

## The Edit Option

When you enter **E** at the Command prompt "*Select jumpered terminals [Browse/Edit/Show] <Edit>*", the **Edit Terminal Jumpers** dialog box will be displayed. The options in this dialog box have already been discussed in this chapter.

## The Show Option

When you enter **S** at the Command prompt "*Select jumpered terminals [Browse/Edit/Show] <Edit>*", a red dashed line which represents the jumper (temporary line), is drawn between the primary and secondary terminals within the same drawing, as shown in Figure 11-56. Choose **View > Redraw** from the menu bar to remove this red dashed line (temporary line).

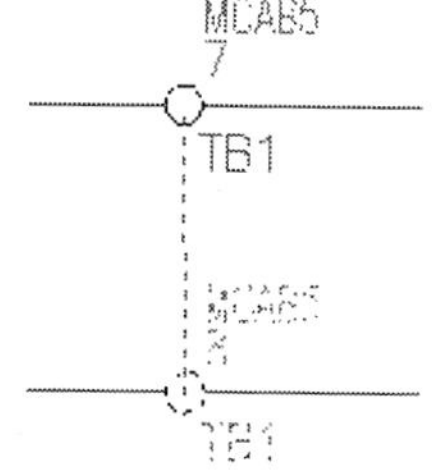


***Figure 11-56** Displaying jumper between terminals*

# TUTORIALS

## Tutorial 1

In this tutorial, you will create a ladder and then insert a terminal symbol in it. Also, you will enter required information in the **Insert / Edit Terminal Symbol** dialog box.

**(Expected time: 10 min)**

The following steps are required to complete this tutorial:

a. Create a new drawing.
b. Insert a ladder in the drawing.
c. Insert a terminal symbol into the drawing and enter the required information.
d. Save the drawing.

### Creating a New Drawing

1. Activate the **CADCIM** project. Next, click on the *TUTORIALS* subfolder and then create the *C11_tut01.dwg* drawing, as already discussed in the previous chapters.

### Inserting a Ladder into the Drawing

1. Choose the **Insert Ladder** tool from **Schematic > Insert Wires/Wire Numbers > Insert Ladder** drop-down; the **Insert Ladder** dialog box is displayed.

2. Set the following values in the edit boxes of the **Insert Ladder** dialog box:

   Width = **5.000**     Spacing = **1**
   1st Reference = **100**     Rungs = **5**

3. Choose the **OK** button in the **Insert Ladder** dialog box; you are prompted to specify the start position of the first rung.

4. Enter **9,11** at the Command prompt and press ENTER; the ladder is inserted in the drawing.

### Inserting Terminal Symbol and Entering Information

1. Choose the **Icon Menu** tool from **Schematic > Insert Components > Icon Menu** drop-down; the **Insert Component** dialog box is displayed.

2. Select the **Terminals/Connectors** icon from the **NFPA: Schematic Symbols** area; the **NFPA: Terminals and Connectors** area is displayed.

3. Select **Square with Terminal Number** located on the third column and first row of the **NFPA: Terminals and Connectors** area; you are prompted to specify the insertion point.

4. Enter **12.5,11** at the Command prompt and press ENTER; the **Insert / Edit Terminal Symbol** dialog box is displayed.

5. Enter **MACHINE** in the **Location** edit box, **TB1** in the **Tag Strip** edit box, and **1** in the **Number** edit box in the **Terminals** area.

6. Choose the **Details >>** button to expand the **Insert / Edit Terminal Symbol** dialog box if the dialog box is not already expanded.

7. Choose the **Catalog Lookup** button from the **Catalog Data** area; the **Catalog Browser** dialog box is displayed.

8. In this dialog box, enter **1492-WFB4** in the **Search** field and choose the **Search** button.

9. Select **1492-WFB4** catalog value from the list displayed in the **Catalog Browser** dialog box.

10. Choose the **OK** button in the **Catalog Browser** dialog box; the catalog values are displayed in the **Manufacturer** and **Catalog** edit boxes of the **Catalog Data** area.

11. Choose the **Block Properties** button in the **Modify Properties/Associations** area of the **Insert/Edit Terminal Symbol** dialog box; the **Terminal Block Properties** dialog box is displayed.

    By default, 1 is displayed in the **Levels** edit box, SINGLE is displayed under the **Level Description** column, and 2 is displayed under the **Wires Per Connection** column.

12. Enter **1** and **2** in the row under the **Pin Left** and **Pin Right** columns, respectively.

13. Choose the **OK** button from the **Terminal Block Properties** dialog box; the values you entered in this dialog box are displayed in the **Properties/Associations** area.

14. Choose the **OK** button from the **Insert / Edit Terminal Symbol** dialog box; the terminal symbol is inserted in the drawing, as shown in Figure 11-57.

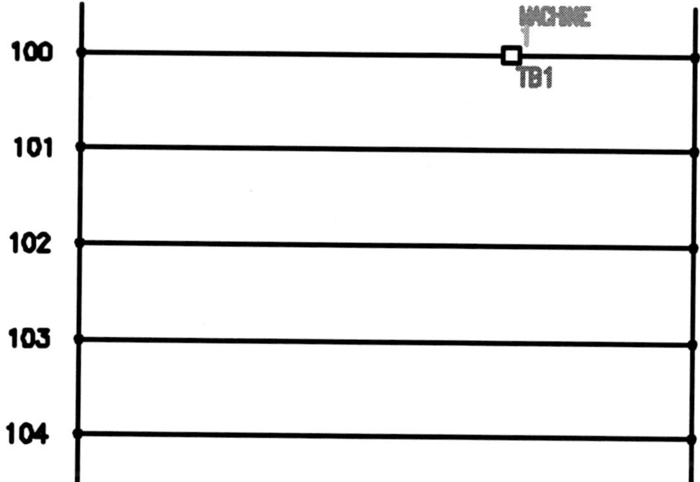


***Figure 11-57*** *Terminal symbol inserted in the ladder*

**Note**

*If the* ***Assign Symbol To Catalog Number*** *message box is displayed on choosing the* ***OK*** *button from the* ***Insert / Edit Terminal Symbol*** *dialog box, choose the* ***Map symbol to catalog number*** *option from this message box.*

## Saving the Drawing File

1. Choose **Save** from the **Application Menu** to save the drawing file *C11_tut01.dwg*.

# Tutorial 2

In this tutorial, you will insert DIN Rail in a drawing and then insert the terminal strip by extracting the terminal information from *Demo04.dwg* that you added to the **CADCIM** project in Tutorial 3 of Chapter 2. Also, you will add information to the terminal strip.

**(Expected time: 25 min)**

The following steps are required to complete this tutorial:

a. Create a new drawing.
b. Insert a DIN Rail into the drawing.
c. Insert a terminal strip into the drawing and add information to it.
d. Generate the terminal strip table.
e. Save the drawing.

## Creating a New Drawing

1. Activate the **CADCIM** project. Next, click on the *TUTORIALS* subfolder and then create the *C11_tut02.dwg* drawing as already discussed in the previous chapters.

## Inserting the DIN Rail into the Drawing

1. Choose the **Icon Menu** tool from **Panel > Insert Component Footprints > Icon Menu** drop-down; the **Alert** message box is displayed.

2. Choose the **OK** button in this message box; the non-visible 'WD_PNLM' block is inserted into the drawing and the **Insert Footprint** dialog box is displayed.

3. Choose the **DIN Rail** icon from the **Panel Layout Symbols** area of the **Insert Footprint** dialog box; the **Din Rail** dialog box is displayed.

4. Select **AB, 199-DR1, Symmetrical Rail 35mm x 7.5mm 1m Ion** from the drop-down list in the **Rail Type** area if it is not already selected.

5. Choose the **Pick Rail Information >>** button from the **Origin and Length** area; you are prompted to specify the insertion point for the rail.

6. Enter **13,17** at the Command prompt and press ENTER; you are prompted to specify the end point of rail.

7. Enter **13,7** at the Command prompt and press ENTER; the **Din Rail** dialog box is displayed again.

8. Select the **Vertical** radio button from the **Orientation** area and the **NC holes** radio button from the **Panel Mounting** area, if not already selected.

9. Make sure 1.0 is displayed in the **Scale** edit box.

10. Choose the **OK** button in the **Din Rail** dialog box; the **Panel Layout - Component Insert/Edit** dialog box is displayed.

11. Choose the **OK** button in this dialog box; DIN Rail is inserted into the drawing, as shown in Figure 11-58.

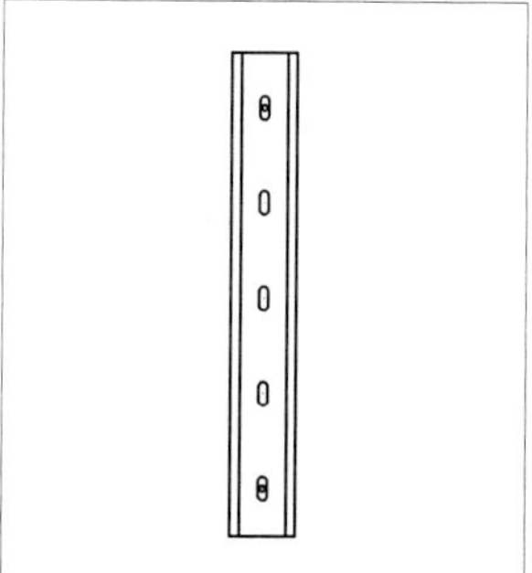

***Figure 11-58*** *DIN Rail inserted in the drawing*

## Inserting a Terminal Strip into the Drawing and Adding Information to it

1. Choose the **Editor** tool from the **Terminal Footprints** panel of the **Panel** tab; the **Terminal Strip Selection** dialog box is displayed.

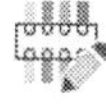

**Note**

*If the **QSAVE** message box is displayed after choosing the **Editor** tool from the **Terminal Footprints** panel of the **Panel** tab, choose the **OK** button in the **QSAVE** message box to display the **Terminal Strip Selection** dialog box.*

2. Select the **TS-A** terminal strip from this dialog box, refer to Figure 11-59.

3. Choose the **Edit** button; the **Terminal Strip Editor** dialog box is displayed.

**Note**

*After choosing the **Edit** button, if the **Defined Terminal Wiring Constraints Exceeded** message box is displayed, choose the **OK** button in this message box.*

4. Choose the **Catalog Code Assignment** tab from the **Terminal Strip Editor** dialog box and then select all the rows in this tab.

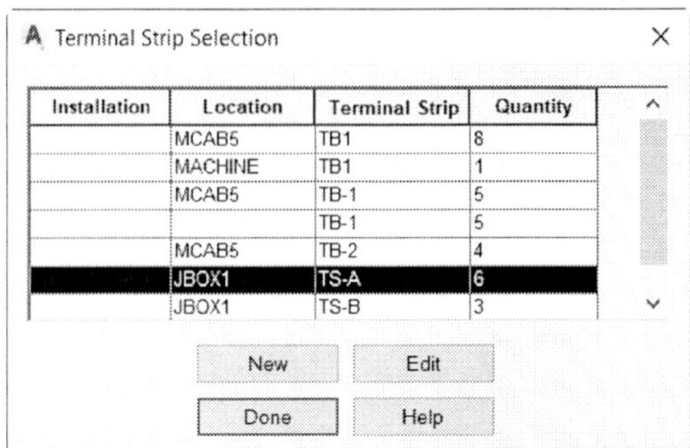


*Figure 11-59 The* ***Terminal Strip Selection*** *dialog box*

5. Choose the **Assign Catalog Number** button from the **Catalog** area; the **Catalog Browser** dialog box is displayed.

6. Enter **DN-T10** in the **Search** field of this dialog box and choose the **Search** button.

7. Next, select **DN-T10, GRAY, 18-10AWG, 50pcs/ft (166/m), TERMINAL BLOCK** from this dialog box and choose the **OK** button from this dialog box; the catalog data is added to the terminal strip.

8. Select the last row in the terminal list displayed in the **Catalog Code Assignment** tab and choose the **Insert Spare Terminal** button from the **Spare** area; the **Insert Spare Terminal** dialog box is displayed.

9. Enter **2** in the **Quantity** edit box and then choose the **Insert Below** button; the spare terminals are inserted below the last row of the terminal list in the **Catalog Code Assignment** tab.

10. Next, choose the **Layout Preview** tab and then select the **Graphical Terminal Strip** radio button from the **Terminal Strip Editor** dialog box, if not already selected.

11. Next, select the **Wire Number Tag** option from the **Default pick list for Annotation format** list box.

12. Make sure 1.0 is selected in the **Scale on Insert** drop-down list and 0.0 is selected in the **Angle on Insert** drop-down list. Next, choose the **Update** button; a preview of the terminal strip is displayed in the preview window.

13. Choose the **Insert** button and enter **13,16** at the Command prompt and then press ENTER; the terminal strip is inserted into the drawing and the **Terminal Strip Editor** dialog box is displayed again. Next, choose the **OK** button in this dialog box to return to the **Terminal Strip Selection** dialog box.

14. Choose the **Done** button in the **Terminal Strip Selection** dialog box to exit the dialog box. Figure 11-60 shows the terminal strip inserted in a DIN Rail. Figure 11-61 shows the zoomed view of the terminal strip.

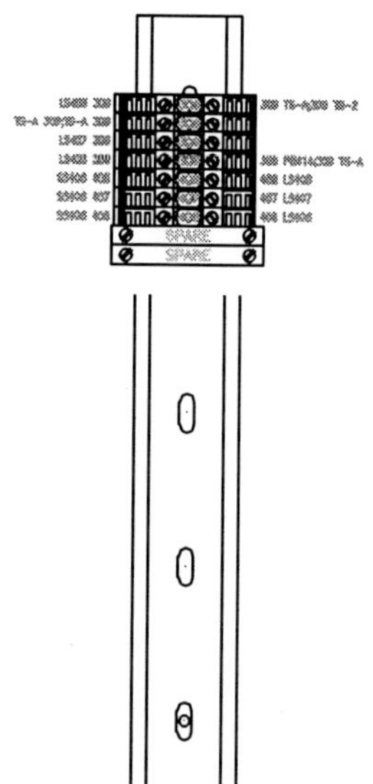

*Figure 11-60 Terminal strip inserted in a DIN Rail*

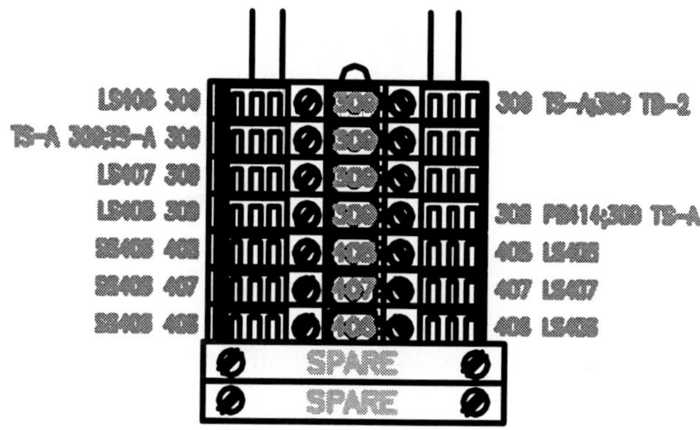


*Figure 11-61 The zoomed view of the terminal strip*

**Note**

*If the **QSAVE** message box is displayed, choose the **OK** button in this dialog box to save the drawing.*

## Generating the Terminal Strip Table

1. Choose the **Table Generator** tool from the **Terminal Footprints** panel of the **Panel** tab; the **Terminal Strip Table Generator** dialog box is displayed.

   The **Terminal Strip Selection** area in this dialog box displays the terminal strips used in the active Project.

2. Select the terminal strip named **TS-A** from the **Terminal Strip Selection** area. Next, choose the **Settings** button from the **Tabular Layout** area; the **Terminal Strip Table Settings** dialog box is displayed. Enter **1.5** in the **X** edit box and **10** in the **Y** edit box of the **Section Placement** area.

3. Choose the **Browse** button located next to the **First Drawing Name** edit box; the **First Drawing Name** dialog box is displayed. In this dialog box, browse to the location where *C11_tut02* is saved, select **C11_tut02** from this dialog box and choose **Save**; the path for the selected drawing file is displayed in the **First Drawing Name** edit box. Next, choose the **OK** button from the **Terminal Strip Table Settings** dialog box.

4. Choose **OK** from the **Terminal Strip Table Generator** dialog box; the **Table(s) Inserted** message box is displayed. Note that the terminal strip table is inserted in the new drawing *C11_tut03.dwg* as mentioned in this message box.

   The new drawing *C11_tut03.dwg* is automatically added to the active project at the bottom of the list. If it is not displayed, choose the **Refresh** button from the **PROJECT MANAGER** to display it.

### Saving the Drawing File

1. Choose **Save** from the **Application Menu** to save the drawing file *C11_tut02.dwg*.

---

## Self-Evaluation Test

**Answer the following questions and then compare them to those given at the end of this chapter:**

1. Which of the following dialog boxes will be displayed when you choose the **Editor** tool?

   (a) **Terminal Strip Selection** (b) **Terminal Strip Editor**
   (c) **Terminal Strip Table Generator** (d) None of these

2. Two or more terminal blocks from any drawing can be combined into a single multiple level terminal block using the __________ tool.

3. The __________ tool is used to insert a jumper between the terminals that belong to different terminal strips.

4. The __________ tool is used to copy terminal properties from one terminal symbol to another terminal symbol.

5 A terminal strip table can be added to the drawing using the __________ or __________ tool.

6. The __________ tool is used to annotate and edit terminal symbols.

7. There are four types of terminal behavior and five types of terminal styles. (T/F)

8. You can only modify the properties but not the associations of a terminal symbol. (T/F)

9. The settings of a terminal strip table can be defined in the **Terminal Strip Table Settings** dialog box. (T/F)

## Review Questions

**Answer the following questions:**

1. Which of the following attributes on terminal symbol is used to link individual symbols to a terminal strip?

   (a) Installation attributes (b) Location attributes
   (c) Tag Strip attributes (d) All of these

2. Which of the following dialog boxes will be displayed when you choose the **Define Columns** button in the **Terminal Strip Table Generator** dialog box?

   (a) **Terminal Strip Table Settings** (b) **Select Table Settings File**
   (c) **Terminal Strip Table Data Fields to Include** (d) **Select Table Layer**

3. If you click twice on the column heading in the **Terminal Strip Editor** dialog box, the terminals will be sorted in the descending order. (T/F)

4. The terminal that uses a wire number as its terminal number can be renumbered. (T/F)

5. The **Reassign Terminal** button is used to reassign one or more terminals to another terminal strip to create a new strip. (T/F)

6. Terminals are linked together by the Tag-ID attributes. (T/F)

7. You can generate the terminal strip information graphically but not in the table format. (T/F)

8. The **Terminal Strip Selection** dialog box displays the terminal strips present within all the projects. (T/F)

# EXERCISES

## Exercise 1

Create a new drawing as *C11_exer01.dwg* and then insert the ladder and terminal symbol in it, as shown in Figure 11-62. **(Expected time: 15 min)**

## Exercise 2

Create a new drawing as *C11_exer02.dwg*. You will insert a DIN Rail (AB, 1492-N22) in the drawing and specify the following information in the **Din Rail** dialog box: **Length** = 4, **X** = 13, **Y** = 17, **Orientation** = vertical. Also, you will assign item number 15 to this DIN Rail. The DIN Rail that you have inserted into a drawing is shown in Figure 11-63. Next, you will insert a terminal strip by using the **Editor** tool. You will select TS-B terminal strip from the **Terminal Strip Selection** dialog box. You will also add catalog information as AUTOMATIONDIRECT, FEED-THROUGH, 20AMPS (DN-T12) to the terminal list displayed in the **Terminal Strip Editor** dialog box. You will also insert two spare terminals after the last row in the **Catalog**

**Code Assignment** tab. The graphical terminal strip inserted into a drawing is shown in Figure 11-64. **(Expected time: 20 min)**

**Hint:** Select **Wire Number Tag : Terminal** from the **Default pick list for Annotation format** list box and **Scale on Insert** = 3.0.

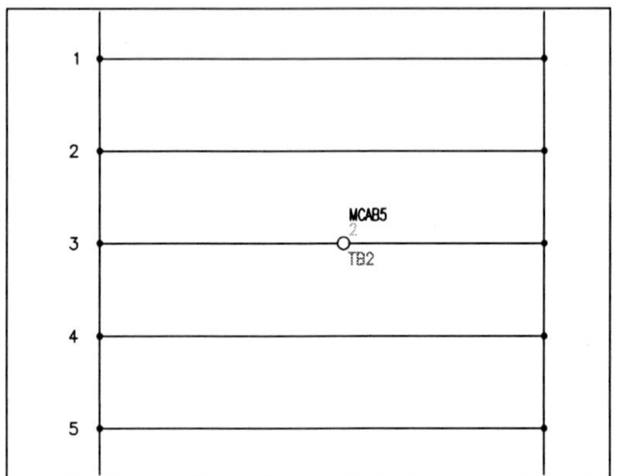


*Figure 11-62 Terminal symbol inserted in a ladder*

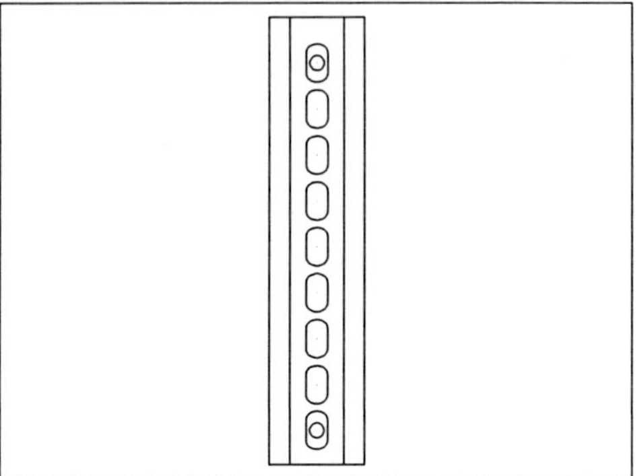

*Figure 11-63 DIN Rail inserted in a drawing*

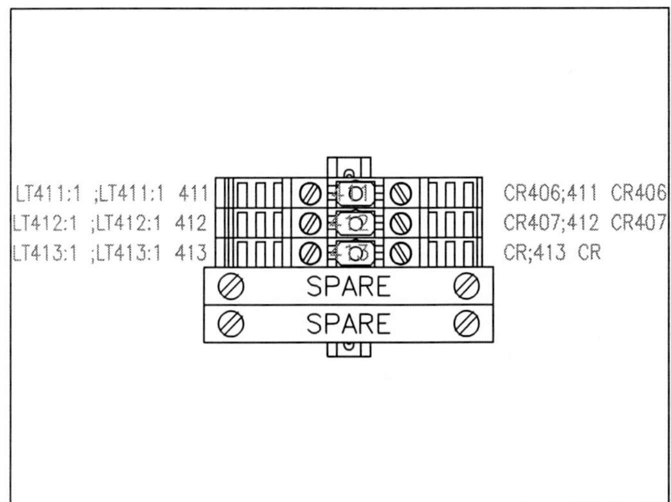


*Figure 11-64 Graphical terminal strip inserted in the drawing*

## Answers to Self-Evaluation Test

**1.** b, **2. Associate Terminals**, **3. Edit Jumper**, **4. Copy Terminal Block Properties**, **5. Terminal Strip Editor**, **Terminal Strip Table Generator**, **6. Edit**, **7.** T, **8.** F, **9.** T

# Chapter 12

# Settings, Configurations, Templates, and Plotting

## Learning Objectives

**After completing this chapter, you will be able to:**

- *Set the project and drawing properties*
- *Understand reference files*
- *Map a title block*
- *Update a title block*
- *Create template drawings*
- *Plot Projects*
- *Understand the project task list*

# INTRODUCTION

In this chapter, you will learn to set the project and drawings properties. You will also learn to use various reference files supported by AutoCAD Electrical, which will help you annotate drawings. Later in this chapter, you will learn about title blocks, creating template files, plotting drawings, and creating a project task list.

# SETTING PROJECT PROPERTIES

The Project properties organize the default settings and configuration of AutoCAD Electrical. These properties are used as the default properties when a new drawing is created for a project. You can apply the project settings to the drawing settings when you create or add a drawing to a project. To invoke the **Project Properties** dialog box, right-click on the active project in the **PROJECT MANAGER**, and then choose the **Properties** option from the shortcut menu; the **Project Properties** dialog box will be displayed, as shown in Figure 12-1. In this dialog box, you can define the settings for a new project and also use these settings for new drawings. In this dialog box, you can also edit and modify the properties for project settings, components, wire numbers, cross-references, styles, and drawing format.

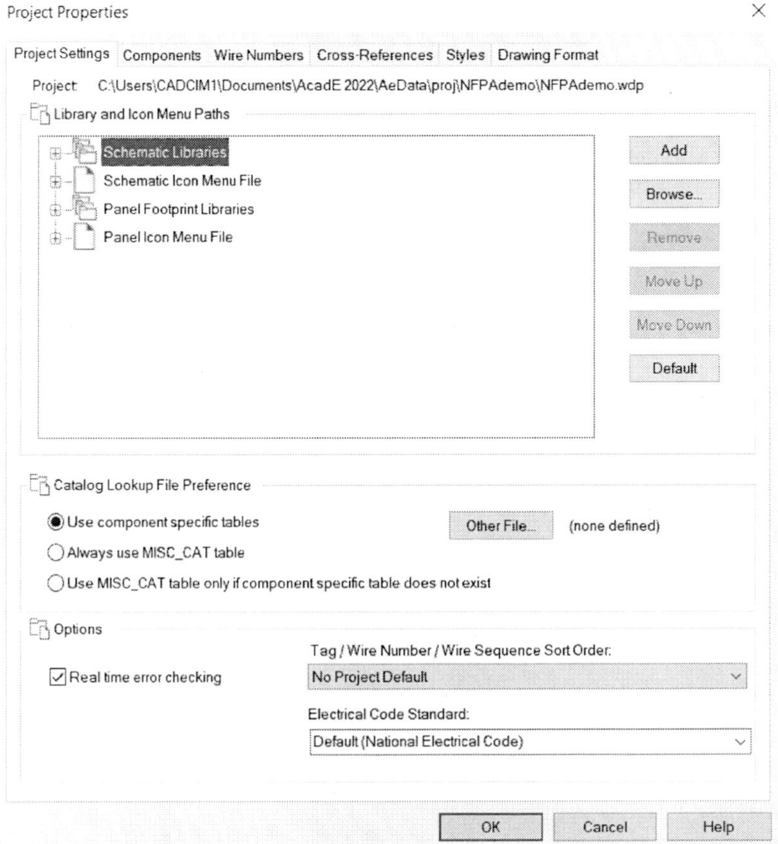


***Figure 12-1** The **Project Properties** dialog box*

The values that you define in this dialog box will be saved in the project file. The icons shown in Figure 12-2 indicate whether the settings will be applied to the project or the drawing. Different tabs and options in the **Project Properties** dialog box are discussed next.

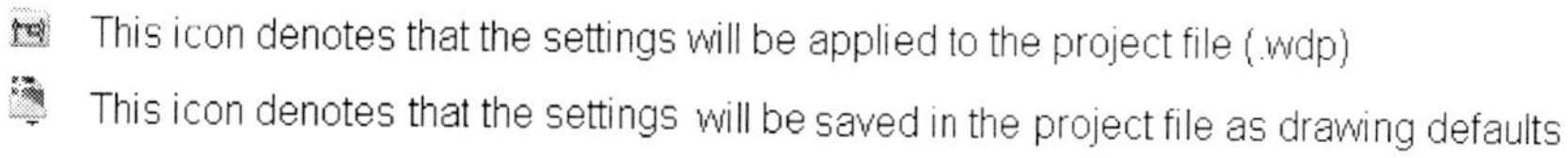

This icon denotes that the settings will be applied to the project file (.wdp)

This icon denotes that the settings will be saved in the project file as drawing defaults

***Figure 12-2*** *Icons indicating the settings for the project and drawing*

## Project Settings Tab

The **Project Settings** tab is chosen by default, refer to Figure 12-1. In this tab, you can modify the default settings of libraries and icon menu paths, catalog lookup files, and error checking. The information in this tab will be saved as default settings of the project in the project definition file (*.wdp*). Different areas in this tab are discussed next.

### Library and Icon Menu Paths Area

In this area, you can select the schematic library, panel footprint library, and icon menu files that you want to use. Different options in this area are discussed next.

#### Libraries

The Schematic Libraries and Panel Footprint Libraries are displayed in the **Library and Icon Menu Paths** area. When you click on the node of a library, the library will be expanded and its full name and path will be displayed. Select the library and then choose the **Browse** button; the **Browse For Folder** dialog box will be displayed. Select the library folder and choose the **OK** button; the library path will be changed.

**Note**

*In AutoCAD Electrical, metric panel library is also installed along with the inch panel library during installation. The path for this library is C:\Users\Public\Documents\Autodesk\Acade 2022\Libs\panel_mm.*

#### Icon Menu File

When you click on the node of an icon menu file, the icon menu file will get expanded and the name of the default icon menu file (.DAT) will be displayed. In order to change this default icon menu file, select the icon menu file and choose the **Browse** button; the **Select ".dat" AutoCAD Electrical icon menu file** dialog box will be displayed. Select the new icon menu file from this dialog box and then choose the **Open** button; the name of the selected file will be displayed in the **Library and Icon Menu Paths** area. This icon menu file will get saved in the *.wdp* file of the project.

#### Add

The **Add** button is used to add a new library in the **Library and Icon Menu Paths** area. To add a library, expand the tree structure. Next, select the library path and then choose the **Add** button; a text box for new entry of library path will be displayed. Enter the library path and notice that it will be added to the tree structure automatically. Also, note that the **Add** button will be activated only if you select the **Schematic Libraries** or **Panel Footprint Libraries**.

### Browse

The **Browse** button is used to browse or specify a path folder from where the symbol or icon menu files can be selected.

### Remove

The **Remove** button will be activated only if you select the library file (schematic or panel footprint file). This button is used to remove the selected library file from the library tree structure.

### Move Up

Choose the **Move Up** button to move the selected library path one step up in the library tree structure.

### Move Down

Choose the **Move Down** button to move the selected library path one step down in the library tree structure.

### Default

Choose the **Default** button to bring the default path from the environment file (WD.ENV) in the tree structure. Note that this button will not be activated if you select the library file.

## Catalog Lookup File Preference Area

In this area, you can control the preference for searching the bill of material catalog database. The options in this area are discussed next.

### Use component specific tables

The **Use component specific tables** radio button is selected by default. As a result, a component-specific table will be used while inserting a component in a drawing.

### Always use MISC_CAT table

Select the **Always use MISC_CAT table** radio button to search for the MISC_CAT catalog table.

### Use MISC_CAT table only if component specific table does not exist

Select the **Use MISC_CAT table only if component specific table does not exist** radio button to use the MISC_CAT table if the component or family tables do not exist in the catalog database file.

### Other File

The **Other File** button is used to select a secondary catalog look up file. To do so, choose the **Other File** button; the **Catalog Lookup File** dialog box will be displayed. In this dialog box, the **Single catalog lookup file(default)** radio button is selected by default. As a result, the default catalog lookup file is selected and used.

Select the **Optional: Define a secondary catalog lookup file for this project** radio button to select the secondary file. Enter the path and name of the catalog lookup file in the edit box given below this radio button. Alternatively, choose the **Browse** button to specify the secondary file.

## Options Area

The **Options** area is used to control the real-time error checking. The options in this area are discussed next.

### Real time error checking

The **Real time error checking** check box is selected by default and is used to check the real time error in the project. This helps in determining duplicate wire numbers or component tags in the project.

### Tag / Wire Number Sort Order

The options in the **Tag / Wire Number Sort Order** drop-down list are used to set the sort order for wire numbers and component tags in a project. Select the tag or wire number sort order option for the project from the **Tag / Wire Number Sort Order** drop-down list.

# Components Tab

In the **Components** tab, shown in Figure 12-3, you can modify the default settings of the components in the project. The information in this tab will be saved as default settings of the project in the project definition file (*.wdp*).

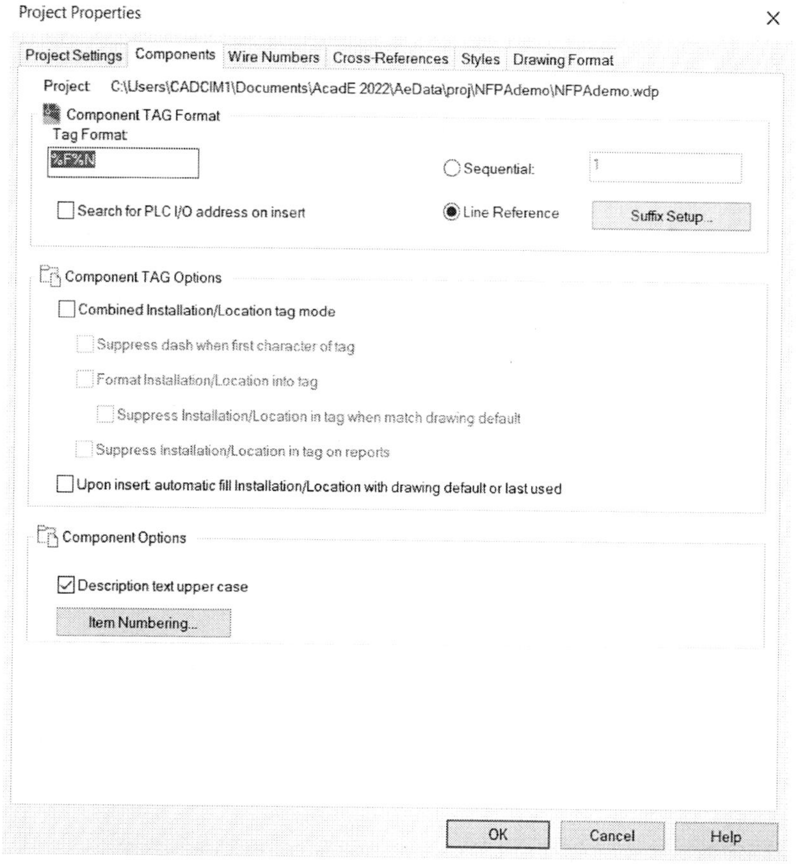

Project Properties

Project Settings | Components | Wire Numbers | Cross-References | Styles | Drawing Format

Project C:\Users\CADCIM1\Documents\AcadE 2022\AeData\proj\NFPAdemo\NFPAdemo.wdp

Component TAG Format

Tag Format

%F%N

Sequential: 1

Search for PLC I/O address on insert

Line Reference

Suffix Setup...

Component TAG Options

Combined Installation/Location tag mode

Suppress dash when first character of tag

Format Installation/Location into tag

Suppress Installation/Location in tag when match drawing default

Suppress Installation/Location in tag on reports

Upon insert automatic fill Installation/Location with drawing default or last used

Component Options

Description text upper case

Item Numbering...

OK Cancel Help

*Figure 12-3 The **Project Properties** dialog box showing the **Components** tab*

Different areas and options in this tab are discussed next.

## Component TAG Format Area

In the **Component TAG Format** area, you can specify the tag for the components in the project. The tag can be sequential or reference-based. The options in this area are discussed next.

### Tag Format

The **Tag Format** edit box is used to specify the tag format for the new components for the entire project. By default, %F%N is displayed in this edit box. You can define a new format by specifying the replaceable parameters in this edit box. These parameters are given next.

%F- Family code of the component string. For example, LS, PB, MOT, and so on.
%S- Sheet number of the drawing.
%D- Drawing number.
%G- Wire layer name.
%N- Sequential or Reference-based number applied to the component.
%X- Suffix character position for reference-based tagging (not present = end of tag).
%P- IEC-style project code (default for drawing).
%I- IEC-style installation code (default for drawing).
%L- IEC-style location code (default for drawing).
%A- Project drawing list's SEC value for the active drawing.
%B- Project drawing list's SUB-SEC value for the active drawing.

The tag format consists of two sets of information such as the family code and the alphanumeric reference number. For example, PB503 is an alphanumeric tag, where PB is the family code of the push button component and 503 is the line reference number of a component. Also, note that the %N parameter is compulsory for all tag formats.

Figure 12-4 shows the schematic drawing when you have defined %F%N as the tag format for the components.

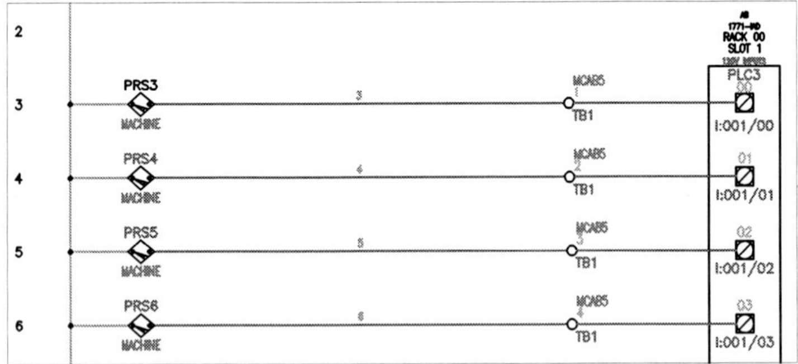


*Figure 12-4 The tag format set to %F%N*

**Note**

*1. After changing the format of the tags in the* ***Project Properties*** *dialog box, it is recommended to retag all the components.*

*2. After making changes in the* ***Project Properties*** *dialog box, if you are not able to see the changes in the current drawing, then you need to apply project settings to it. To do so, right-click on the active drawing; a shortcut menu will be displayed. Choose* ***Properties > Apply Project Defaults*** *from the shortcut menu; the project settings will be applied to the active drawing. The drawing properties override the properties defined for a project in the* ***Project Properties*** *dialog box. The* ***Drawing Properties*** *dialog box will be discussed in the next section.*

### Search for PLC I/O address on insert

By default, the **Search for PLC I/O address on insert** check box is clear. Select this check box to search for the PLC I/O module that is connected to the component. If the PLC I/O is found, then this value will be taken in place of %N part of the default component tag. Figure 12-5 shows the tags of the components after you have selected the **Search for PLC I/O address on insert** check box.

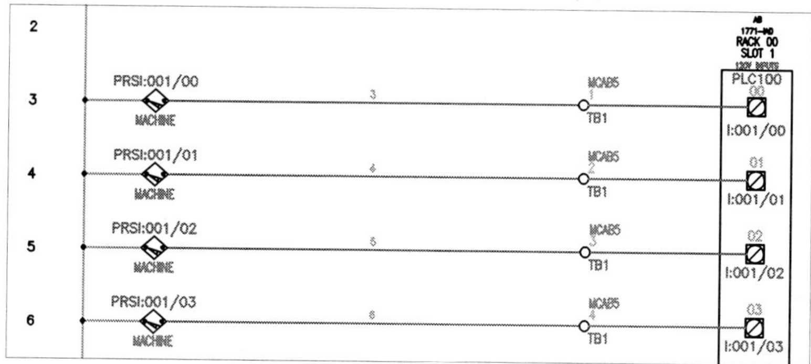


***Figure 12-5*** *The tags of components after selecting the* ***Search for PLC I/O address on insert*** *check box*

### Sequential

Select the **Sequential** radio button; the edit box adjacent to this radio button will be activated. In this edit box, you can enter the starting sequential number for the components of a drawing. Figure 12-6 shows the schematic drawing when 100 is specified in the edit box adjacent to the **Sequential** radio button.

### Line Reference

The **Line Reference** radio button is selected by default and is used to set the format of the tags based on their line reference.

Choose the **Suffix Setup** button on the right of the **Line Reference** radio button; the **Suffix List for Reference-Based Component Tags** dialog box will be displayed. This dialog box displays the suffix list. This list is used to create unique reference-based tag when multiple components of the same family are located in the same reference location. The component tag suffix automatically gets added at the end of the tag format.

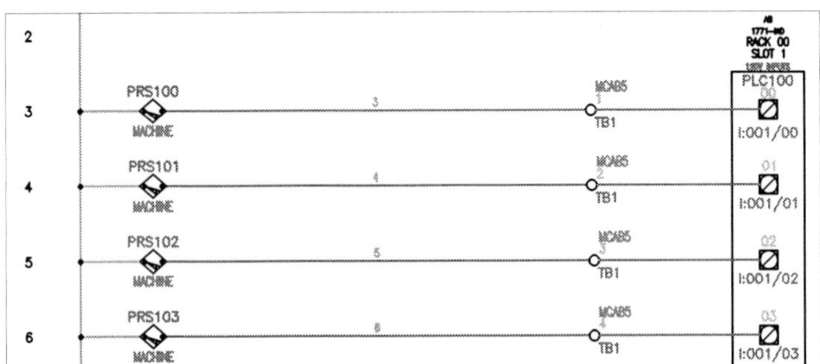


*Figure 12-6 The tags of components when the* ***Sequential*** *radio button is selected*

## Component TAG Options Area

The options in this area are used to set different options for component tags such as the combined installation/ location tag mode, suppressing dashes of tag, and so on. The options in this area are discussed next.

### Combined Installation/Location tag mode

Select the **Combined Installation/Location tag mode** check box to use the combined installation or location tag as the name of the component tag, as shown in Figure 12-7. Also, notice that all other check boxes in this area, except the **Suppress Installation/Location in tag when match drawing default** check box is activated. These check boxes are discussed next.

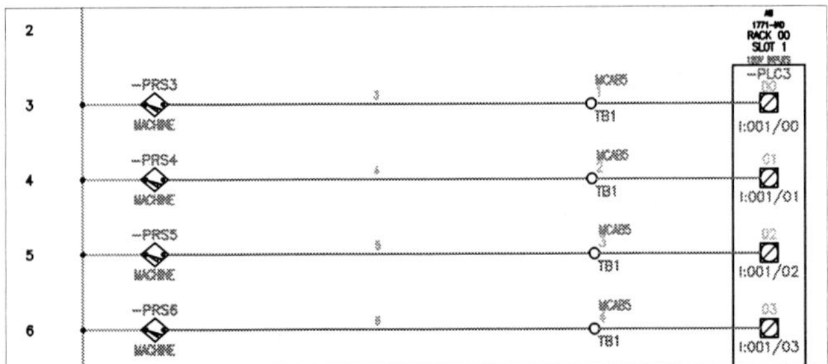


*Figure 12-7 The tags of the components when you select the* ***Combined Installation/Location tag mode*** *check box*

### Suppress dash when first character of tag

Select the **Suppress dash when first character of tag** check box to suppress the dash character if it is the first character of the tag, which does not have an installation/location prefix. By default, this check box is clear. Figure 12-8 shows the tags of the components in a schematic drawing when the **Suppress dash when first character of tag** check box is selected.

### Format Installation/Location into tag

Select the **Format Installation/Location into tag** check box to include the installation and location code values in the component tag.

### Suppress Installation/Location in tag when match drawing default

The **Suppress Installation/Location in tag when match drawing default** check box will be activated only if you select the **Format Installation/Location into tag** check box. Select the **Suppress Installation/Location in tag when match drawing default** check box to suppress the installation and location values of a component if they match with the drawing default values.

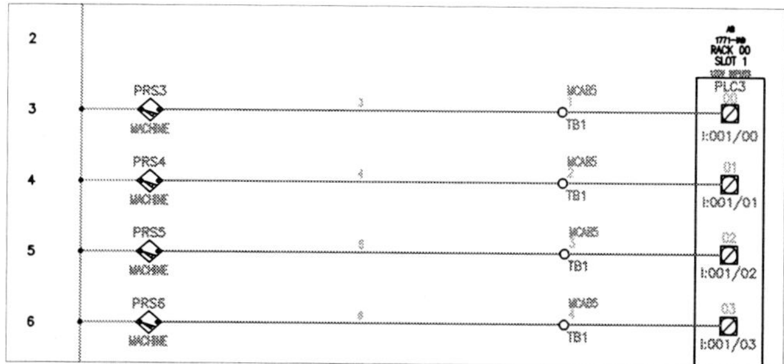


*Figure 12-8 The tags of the components when the* ***Suppress dash when first character of tag*** *check box is selected*

### Suppress Installation/Location in tag on reports

The **Suppress Installation/Location in tag on reports** check box will be activated only if you select the **Combined Installation/Location tag mode** check box. Select this check box to suppress the installation and location values as part of a component tag in reports. In other words, the installation and location values will not be included as part of the tag in the reports.

### Upon insert: automatic fill Installation/Location with drawing default or last used

If you select the **Upon insert: automatic fill Installation/Location with drawing default or last used** check box, the previously used installation and location values will be filled in automatically in the **Installation** and **Location** edit boxes of the **Insert/Edit Component** dialog box. Also, the attributes of the block will be filled with the drawing default or previously used values.

## Component Options Area

In the **Component Options** area, you can set the description of the text to upper case or lower case and the settings for item number of the panel component. The options in this area are discussed next.

### Description text upper case

The **Description text upper case** check box is selected by default. As a result, the description of the text will be in upper case.

### Item Numbering

Choose the **Item Numbering** button; the **Item Numbering Setup** dialog box will be displayed. In this dialog box, you can set the item number drawing wide or project wide. Also, you can set the item assignments on the basis of a component or part number.

## Wire Numbers Tab

In the **Wire Numbers** tab, shown in Figure 12-9, you can modify the default settings of the project for wire numbers. The information in this tab will be saved as default settings of the project in the project definition file (*.wdp*). Different areas and options in this tab are discussed next.

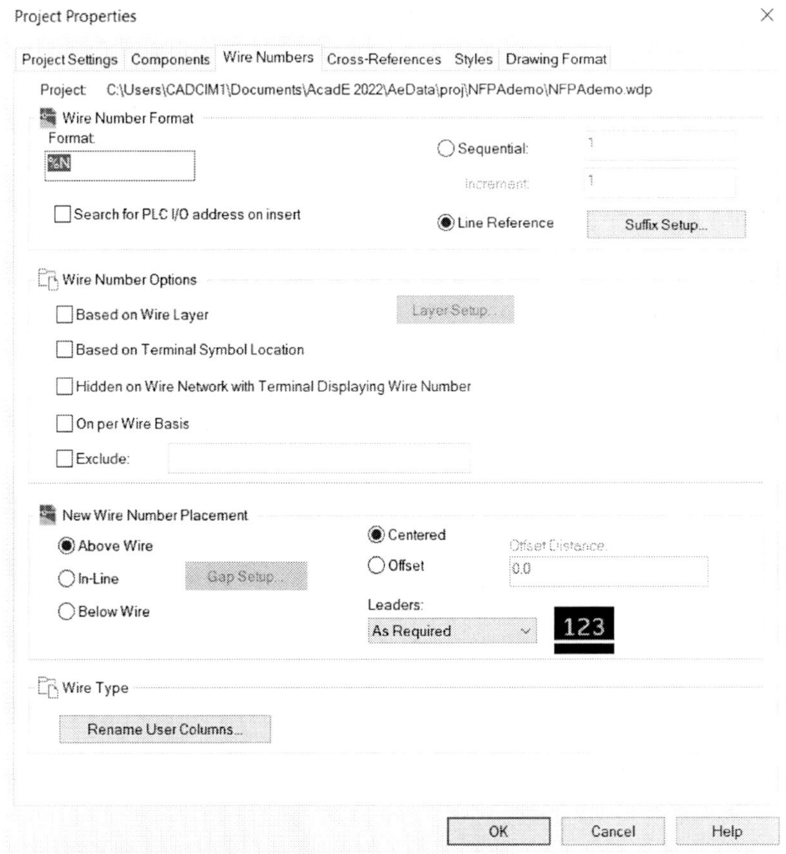


*Figure 12-9 The **Project Properties** dialog box showing the **Wire Numbers** tab*

## Wire Number Format Area

In the **Wire Number Format** area, you can specify the format for wire numbers. The options in this area are discussed next.

### Format

Specify the format for the new wire number in the **Format** edit box. By default, %N is displayed in this edit box.

### Search for PLC I/O address on insert

By default, the **Search for PLC I/O address on insert** check box is clear. Select this check box to search for the PLC I/O module that is connected to the wire. If the PLC I/O is found, the new wire numbers will be based on the I/O address of a PLC.

#### Sequential

The **Sequential** radio button is used to set the starting sequential number for the wire number. On selecting this radio button, the adjacent edit box and the **Increment** edit box will be activated. By default, 1 is displayed in both the edit boxes. Enter the starting sequential number for the wire number in the edit box. To increment this starting number, you need to enter the value in the **Increment** edit box.

#### Line Reference

By default, the **Line Reference** radio button is selected. This radio button is used to assign wire numbers to the wires based on their line reference number.

### Wire Number Options Area

The options in the **Wire Number Options** area are used to specify various options for the wire number. These options are discussed next.

#### Based on Wire Layer

The **Based on Wire Layer** check box is used to specify the format for wire number based on the wire layer. When you select the **Based on Wire Layer** check box, the **Layer Setup** button will be activated. Choose the **Layer Setup** button; the **Assign Wire Numbering Formats by Wire Layer** dialog box will be displayed. Enter the required information in this dialog box and choose the **OK** button. The options in this dialog box have already been discussed in Chapter 3. In this way, you can assign a different wire number format by using a wire layer.

#### Based on Terminal Symbol Location

The **Based on Terminal Symbol Location** check box is used to specify the format of wire numbers based on the location of the terminal symbol.

#### Hidden on Wire Network with Terminal Displaying Wire Numbers

Select this check box to hide the wire number of a wire network that has a wire number type terminal inserted into it.

#### On per Wire Basis

Select the **On per Wire Basis** check box for assigning the wire number to each wire.

#### Exclude

When you select the **Exclude** check box, the edit box next to it will be activated. Specify the wire number range that you want to exclude while inserting the wire numbers into the wires in this edit box.

### New Wire Number Placement Area

In the **New Wire Number Placement** area, you can specify the options for the placement of wire numbers such as above, in-line, or below with the wire. Note that the options in this area will show the results only if you are inserting the new wire numbers.

### Wire Type Area

In the **Wire Type** area, you can rename the column heading of the User1 to User20 fields. To do so, choose the **Rename User Columns** button in the **Wire Type** area; the **Rename User**

**Columns** dialog box will be displayed. Enter the name for the User1 to User20 fields; these changes will be reflected in the **Set Wire Type**, **Create/Edit Wire Type**, and **Change/Convert Wire Type** dialog boxes. In other words, the column headings of User1 to User 20 fields of the said dialog boxes will be automatically changed with the name that you have specified in the **Rename User Columns** dialog box.

## Cross-References Tab

In the **Cross-References** tab, shown in Figure 12-10, you can modify the default settings of the cross-references in the project. The new drawings that you create will be saved as default settings of the project in the project definition file (*.wdp*) for cross-referencing. The cross-reference tag indicates the location of the linked components within the project. Different areas in this tab are discussed next.

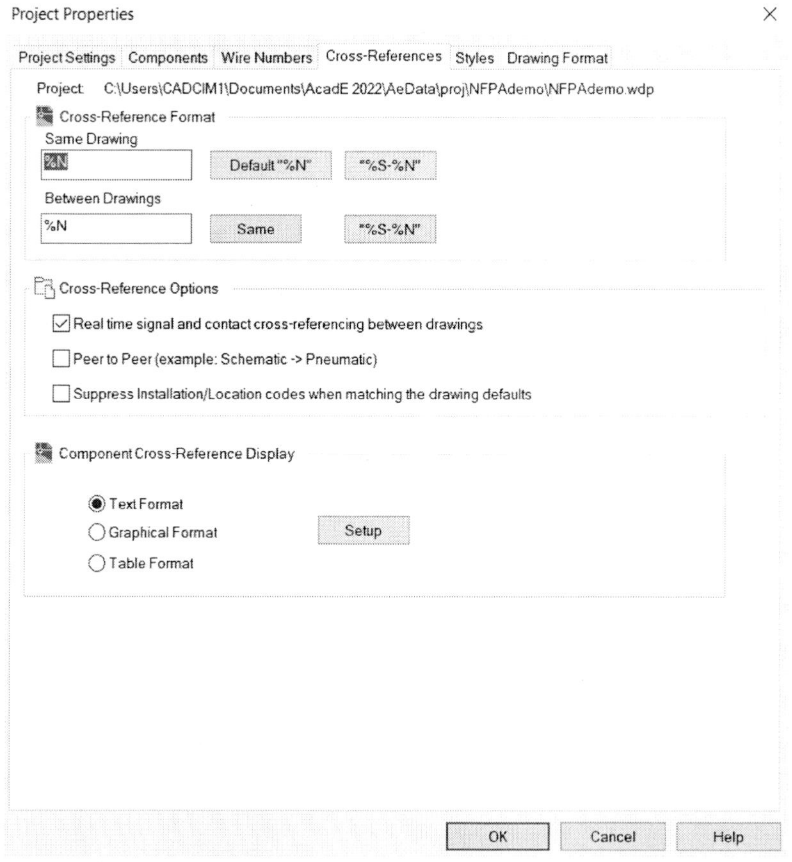


*Figure 12-10 The **Project Properties** dialog box showing the **Cross-References** tab*

### Cross-Reference Format Area

In the **Cross-Reference Format** area, you can set the format for cross-referencing in the same drawing and between the drawings. The options in this area are discussed next.

Enter the format for on-drawing references in the **Same Drawing** edit box. By default, %N parameter is displayed in it. Note that the cross-reference format should consist of the %N parameter. Next, choose the **Default "%N"** button to display the default %N parameter, which is the sequential or reference-based number applied to the component in the **Same Drawing** edit box. Choose the **"%S-%N"** button to apply the %S-%N format to the cross-reference. Also, the %S-%N will be displayed in the **Same Drawing** edit box.

Enter the format for off-drawing references in the **Between Drawings** edit box. By default, %N is displayed in it. Choose the **Same** button to display the same parameters that you have specified in the **Same Drawing** edit box in the **Between Drawings** edit box. Choose the **"%S-%N"** button to apply the %S-%N format to the cross-reference. Also, the %S-%N will be displayed in the **Between Drawings** edit box.

### Cross-Reference Options Area

In this area, the **Real time signal and contact cross-referencing between drawings** check box is selected by default. As a result, the cross-referencing of the relay and wire source and destination symbols will be updated across the drawings.

### Component Cross-Reference Display Area

In this area, you can specify the display format for cross-referencing. The display format for cross-referencing can be in the form of text, graphics, and table. By default, the **Text Format** radio button is selected. To change the display format, choose the **Setup** button; the **Text Cross reference Format Setup** dialog box will be displayed. Change the options in this dialog box to change the component cross reference display format. Note that the prefix of the name of the **Cross reference Format Setup** dialog box will be displayed based on the radio button selected in this area.

## Styles Tab

In the **Styles** tab, shown in Figure 12-11, you can modify the default settings for the component styles in the project. The information in this tab will be saved as default settings of the project in the project definition file (*.wdp*). Different areas and options in this tab are discussed next.

### Arrow Style Area

In the **Arrow Style** area, you can specify the style of the source and destination arrows. By default, **1** radio button is selected in this area. You can select the required arrow style from the four pre-defined styles or from the five user-defined styles. The preview of the selected arrow style will be displayed in the preview window.

### PLC Style Area

In the **PLC Style** area, you can specify the style of the PLC modules. By default, **1** radio button is selected in this area. You can select the PLC module style from the five pre-defined styles or from the four user-defined styles. In this area, the preview of the selected PLC style will be displayed in the preview window.

### Wiring Style Area

In the **Wiring Style** area, you can specify style for wires when they intersect. In this area, you can specify settings for wire crossings and wire tee connections. These settings are used while inserting a wire. The options in this area are discussed next.

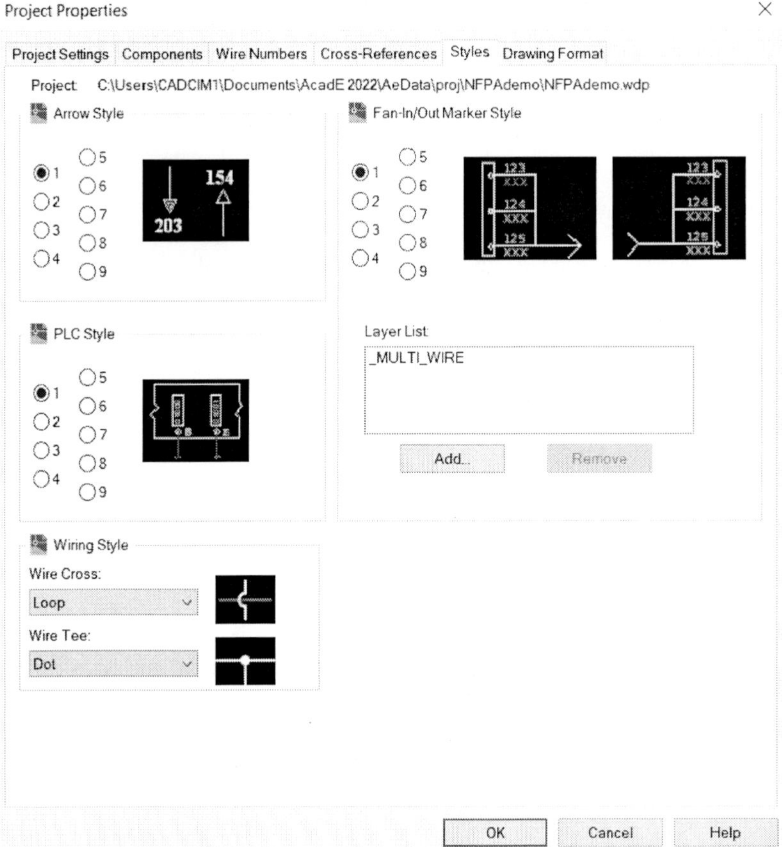


*Figure 12-11 The **Project Properties** dialog box showing the **Styles** tab*

## Wire Cross

From the **Wire Cross** drop-down list, select the style of the wires in which they intersect. By default, the **Loop** option is selected which implies that a loop will be formed when two wires intersect. Also, the preview of the selected option will be displayed in the preview window.

Select the **Gap** option from the **Wire Cross** drop-down list to insert a gap between the two wires when they intersect.

If you select the **Solid** option from the **Wire Cross** drop-down list, the wires will intersect without a gap.

## Wire Tee

Select a wire tee marker from the **Wire Tee** drop-down list. By default, the **Dot** option is selected, which implies that a dot will be formed when two wires meet (at tee point). Also, the preview of the selected option will be displayed in the preview window.

If you select the **None** option from the **Wire Tee** drop-down list, there will be no wire tee marker when two wires meet.

Select the **Angle 1** or **Angle 2** option from the **Wire Tee** drop-down list to create an angle between the wires when they meet.

## Fan-In/Out Marker Style Area

In the **Fan-In/Out Marker Style** area, you can specify the style for the fan in/out marker symbols. You can also specify the layer of the wires going out of **Fan In/Out Source** marker and coming into the **Fan In/Out Destination** marker. By default, **1** radio button is selected. You can select the style for the fan in/out marker from the four pre-defined styles and five user-defined styles. The preview of the selected option will also be displayed in the preview window. The options in this area are discussed next.

### Layer List

The **Layer List** displays the list of fan in/out layers. The **Add** button is used to add a layer to the **Layer List**. To do so, choose the **Add** button; the **Layers for Fan-In/Out Single-line Representations** dialog box will be displayed. Enter the Fan-In/Out layer name in the **Layer name** edit box. Alternatively, you can choose the **Pick** button to select the Fan-In/Out layer name from the **Select layer for Fan-In/Out single-line wire lines** dialog box.

The **Remove** button is used to remove the **Fan-In/Out** layer name from the **Layer List**.

**Note**

*The settings that you define in the **Styles** tab of the **Project Properties** dialog box will be overridden by the settings that you set in the **Drawing Properties** dialog box. In other words, if you set the style for the PLC module, wires, and so on, then it will not be reflected till you make similar settings in the **Drawing Properties** dialog box.*

# Drawing Format Tab

In the **Drawing Format** tab, shown in Figure 12-12, you can modify the project default settings for the drawings. Also, in this tab, you can set the defaults for ladder, format for cross-referencing, order of the tag and wire number, scale of drawing, and the layer for component. Also, the information in this tab will be saved as default settings of the project in the project definition file (*.wdp*). The different areas and options in this tab are discussed next.

## Ladder Defaults Area

In the **Ladder Defaults** area, you can set the default values of orientation and spacing for the ladder. The spacing values include spacing between the rungs, width, and the multi-wire spacing. The options in this area are discussed next.

The **Vertical** radio button is selected by default. As a result, the ladder will be created vertically.

Select the **Horizontal** radio button to create the horizontal ladder.

Specify the spacing between the rungs in the **Spacing** edit box. By default, 0.75 is displayed in this edit box.

Specify the width of the ladder in the **Width** edit box. By default, 4.5 is displayed in this edit box.

Specify the distance between each rung of multi-wire in the **Multi-wire Spacing** edit box. By default, 0.5 is displayed in this edit box.

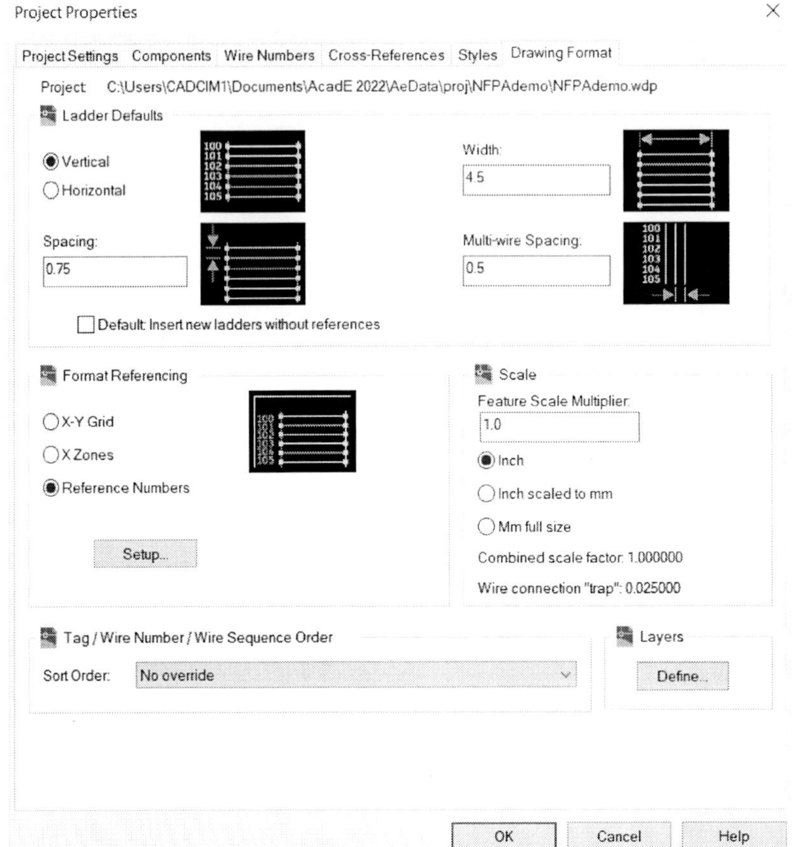


***Figure 12-12** The **Project Properties** dialog box showing the **Drawing Format** tab*

**Note**

*All options mentioned above, except the orientation of the ladder, can also be changed using the **Insert Ladder** tool.*

If you select the **Default: Insert new ladders without references** check box, then the new ladder that you insert in the drawing will be without references. By default, the **Default: Insert new ladders without references** check box is clear.

## Format Referencing Area

In the **Format Referencing** area, you can specify the format for the reference numbers of the ladder. The options in this area are discussed next.

The **X-Y Grid** radio button is used to insert the X-Y grid labels in the drawings. This referencing is commonly used with point-to-point wiring diagram style drawings. When you select the **X-Y Grid** radio button and choose the **Setup** button, the **X-Y Grid Setup** dialog box will be displayed. The options in this dialog box have already been discussed in Chapter 4. Enter the required information in this dialog box and choose the **OK** button to save the information and return to the **Project Properties** dialog box.

The **X Zones** button is used to insert the X grid labels for drawings. This format referencing is commonly used with IEC style drawings. When you choose the **Setup** button, the **X Zones Setup** dialog box will be displayed. The options in this dialog box have already been discussed in Chapter 4. Next, enter the required information in the **X Zones Setup** dialog box and choose the **OK** button to return to the **Project Properties** dialog box and to save the changes.

By default, the **Reference Numbers** radio button is selected. This radio button is used to change the display of reference numbers of a ladder in a drawing. Choose the **Setup** button; the **Line Reference Numbers** dialog box will be displayed, as shown in Figure 12-13. In this dialog box, you can define the style of line reference numbers of a ladder. By default, the **Numbers only** radio button is selected. Select the required radio button in this dialog box; the style of line reference numbers will be changed accordingly.

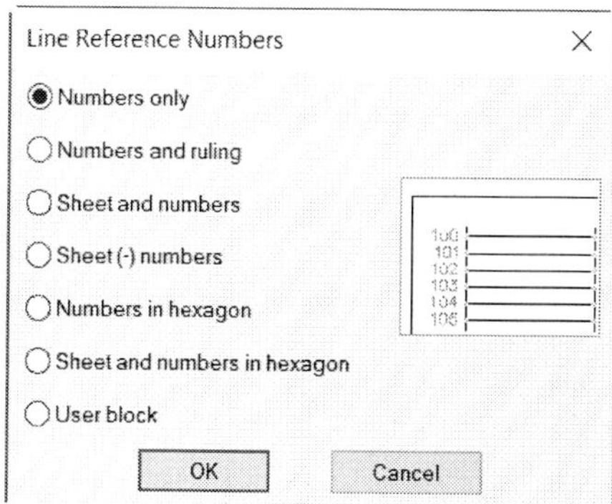


*Figure 12-13 The **Line Reference Numbers** dialog box*

Choose the **OK** button in the **Line Reference Numbers** dialog box to save the changes made and exit the dialog box.

## Tag / Wire Number / Wire Sequence Order Area

In the **Tag / Wire Number /Wire Sequence Order** area, you can set the default wire numbering, component tag, and wire sequence sort order for the active drawing. The sort order specified in this area is used for default wire sequencing of wire networks with multiple components. Your settings of sort order in this tab will override the settings that you have done in the **Project Settings** tab. Select the sort order from the **Sort Order** drop-down list. By default, the **No override** option is selected.

## Scale Area

In the **Scale** area, you can specify the scale for inserting the components and the wire numbers.

## Layers Area

In the **Layers** area, you can specify layers for wire and component. Also, in this case, wires will go to the wire layer and components will go to the component layer, irrespective of the current layer. To define layers for wires and components, choose the **Define** button; the **Define Layers** dialog box will be displayed, as shown in Figure 12-14. The options in this dialog box are discussed next.

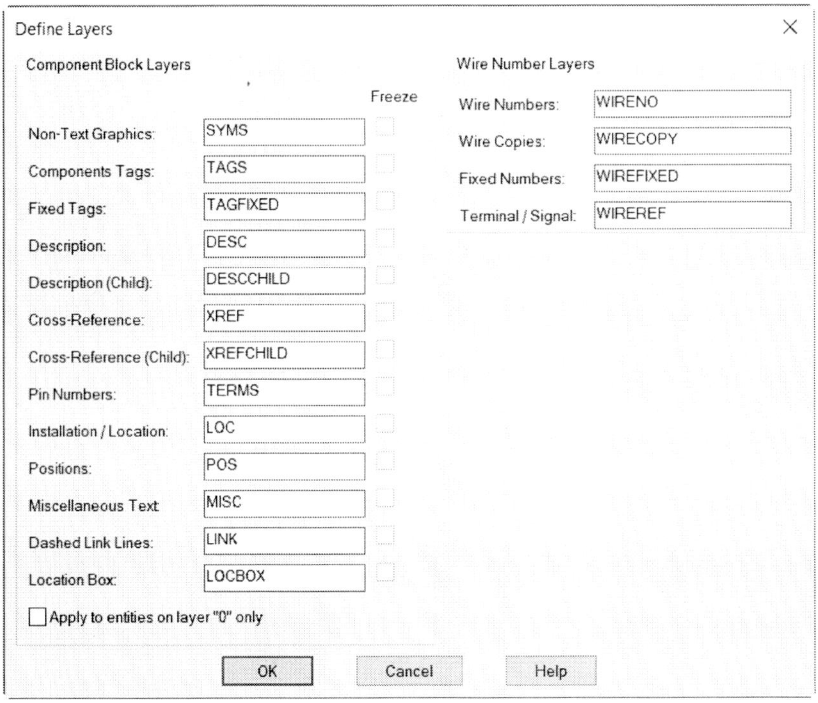

***Figure 12-14** The **Define Layers** dialog box*

## Component Block Layers

The **Component Block Layers** area displays the layer names corresponding to the components. Specify the layer names in the edit boxes of the corresponding components. If you do not enter the layer name in the edit box, then that component block will be placed on the current layer. You can also place multiple component blocks on the same layer by entering the same layer name in different edit boxes.

When you insert a schematic component, the graphics of a block will be inserted into a layer that is listed in the **Non-Text Graphics** edit box. The attribute text of a block will automatically be moved to the layers listed in the other edit boxes, depending on the function of the attribute.

The **Freeze** check box is used to hide all attributes present in that layer. You can also use the **LAYER** command of AutoCAD to perform the same operation.

## Wire Number Layers Area

The **Wire Number Layers** area displays the wire number layer name, wire copies layer name, fixed wire numbers name, and layer names for the wire numbers that are part of a terminal or signal arrow symbol in the respective edit boxes.

After specifying the required options in the **Define Layers** dialog box, choose the **OK** button to save the changes that you have made and return to the **Project Properties** dialog box. Next, choose the **OK** button in the **Project Properties** dialog box to save the changes and exit the dialog box.

# SETTING DRAWING PROPERTIES

| | |
|---|---|
| **Ribbon:** | Schematic > Other Tools > Drawing Properties drop-down > Drawing Properties |
| **Toolbar:** | ACE:Main Electrical 2 > Drawing Properties or ACE:Drawing Properties > Drawing Properties |
| **Menu:** | Projects> Drawing Properties |
| **Command:** | AEPROPERTIES |

Drawing properties are similar to the project properties. Each drawing has its own settings. To define settings for a drawing, choose the **Drawing Properties** tool from the **Other Tools** panel of the **Schematic** tab; the **Drawing Properties** dialog box will be displayed, as shown in Figure 12-15. Alternatively, to display the **Drawing Properties** dialog box, right-click on the drawing file name in the **PROJECT MANAGER**; a shortcut menu will be displayed. Choose the **Properties > Drawing Properties** option from the shortcut menu. In this dialog box, you can specify the settings for the new or selected drawing.

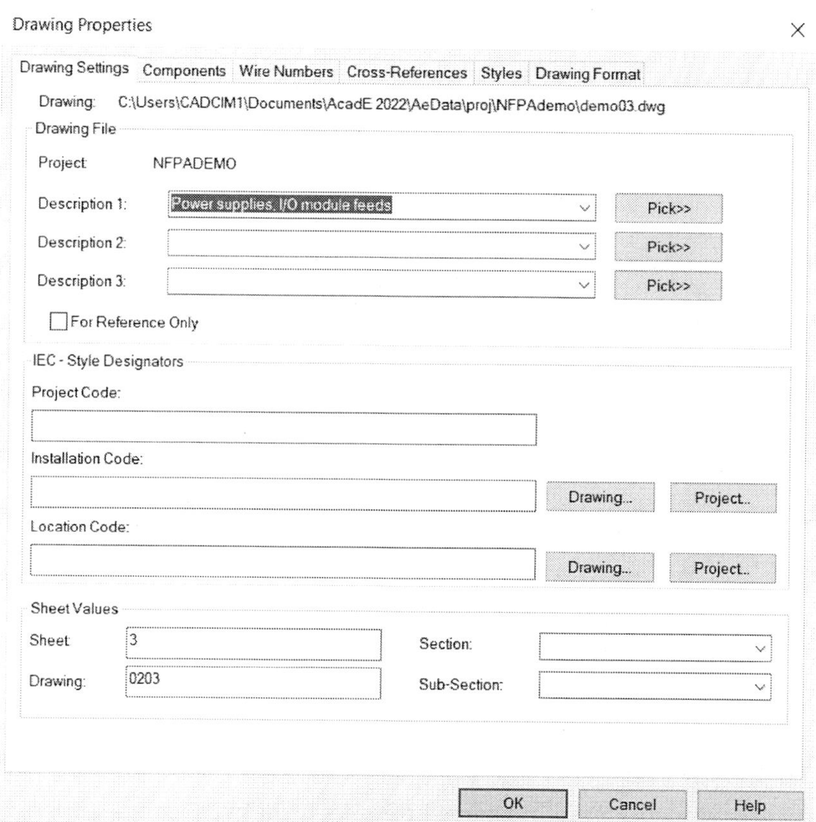


*Figure 12-15 The **Drawing Properties** dialog box*

The settings in the **Project Properties** dialog box will be overridden by the settings that you specify in the **Drawing Properties** dialog box. The settings that you specify in the **Drawing Properties** dialog box are saved in the WD_M block in the drawing file. Also, in this dialog box, you can edit and modify the properties for drawing settings, components, wire numbers, cross-references, styles, and drawing format. The options in the **Drawing Properties** dialog box are similar to that of the **Project Properties** dialog box, except in the **Drawing Settings** tab. Therefore, in the next section, only the **Drawing Settings** tab will be discussed.

**Note**

*If you open a drawing of a project that is not displayed in the **Projects** rollout of the **PROJECT MANAGER** and choose the **Drawing Properties** tool, the **Drawing Properties** dialog box will be displayed, as shown in Figure 12-16, with the text that the drawing is not available in the open project. Also, the drawing related edit fields that are saved in the .wdp file are not activated in this dialog box, refer to Figure 12-16. This text will not be displayed if the drawing is a part of the opened projects.*

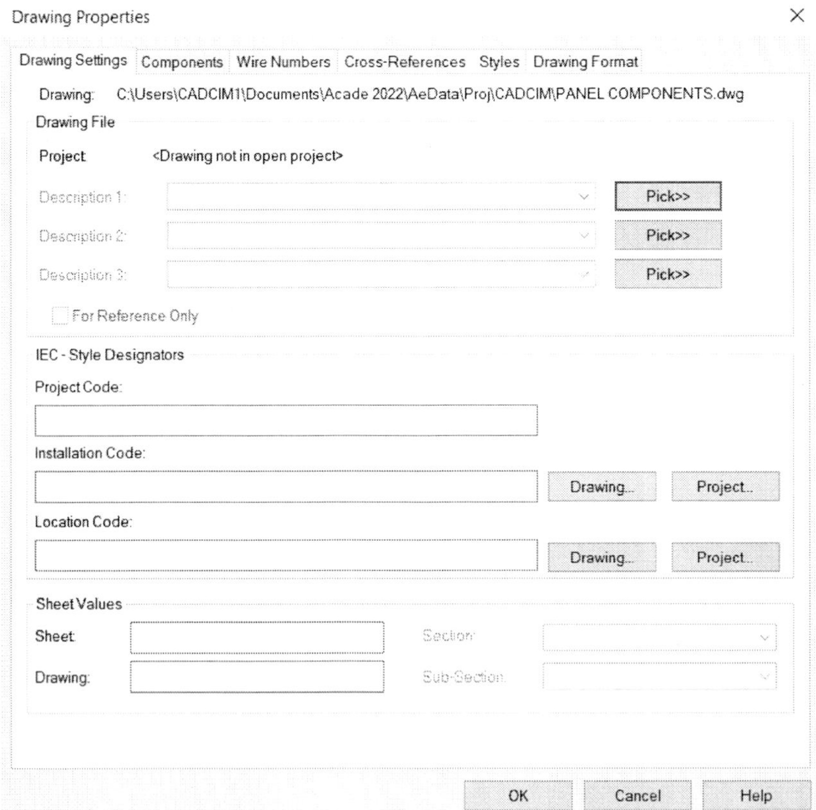


*Figure 12-16 The **Drawing Properties** dialog box*

## Drawing Settings Tab

In the **Drawing Settings** tab, shown in Figure 12-15, you can specify and edit the information of a drawing file. Also, you can add drawing specific descriptions and sheet values. Observe that the name and location of the drawing file is displayed above the **Drawing File** area. Different areas and options in this tab are discussed next.

## Drawing File Area

In the **Drawing File** area, you can edit the information of a drawing file. Also, you can add or edit the description of a drawing. The options in this area are discussed next.

### Project:

The name of the project will be displayed in front of the **Project:** of which the selected drawing is a part. Also, as already mentioned in the note above, if the drawing is not a part of the opened projects, then the name of the project will not be displayed.

### Description 1 to Description 3

Specify the description for the drawing in the **Description 1**, **Description 2**, and **Description 3** edit boxes. Alternatively, you can enter the pre-defined description for a drawing by selecting the down arrow on the right of these edit boxes. But this is possible only if you have entered the description in the earlier drawings of a project. You can also choose the **Pick** button to pick the description from the active drawing. These descriptions will be stored in the project file (*.wdp*) and will be displayed in the title blocks updates and custom drawing properties.

### For Reference Only

The **For Reference Only** check box is clear by default. Select this check box to exclude the drawing from tagging, cross-referencing, and reporting operations and include the drawing in project-wide plotting and title block operations. These changes will be saved in the project file (*.wdp*). The drawing will be used as a reference only.

## IEC - Style Designators Area

In the **IEC - Style Designators** area, you can specify the default value for the project code (%P), installation code (%I), and location code (%L). The code that you enter in this area will be stored in the drawing on the WD_M.dwg block file attributes.

## Sheet Values Area

In the **Sheet Values** area, you can set the sheet number, drawing numbers, section, and sub-section values. The values that you specify in this area will be saved in the drawing in the WD_M block file attributes. The options in this area are discussed next.

### Sheet

Specify the sheet number value for the drawing in the **Sheet** edit box. %S can be used as the replaceable parameter for this sheet value.

### Drawing

Specify the drawing number value for the drawing in the **Drawing** edit box. %D can be used as the replaceable parameter for this drawing value.

### Section

Section and sub-section codes are used to group drawings together. These groupings can be used as filters for reports, plotting, and so on. Specify the section value for the drawing file in the **Section** edit box. %A can be used as the replaceable parameter for the section.

### Sub-Section

Specify the sub-section value for the drawing value in the **Sub-Section** edit box. %B can be used as the replaceable parameter for the sub-section.

# UNDERSTANDING REFERENCE FILES

In this section, you will learn about various reference files that are supported by AutoCAD Electrical for annotating the drawings. The reference files are basically the ASCII text files, which are used for different purposes. You can edit these reference files using Notepad, Wordpad, and other word editors. These reference files can exist in multiple versions and are given as follows:

1. In the project folder, you will find the project's *.wdp* file. The name of the file will be the same as that of the project.

2. If the project-named file is not found, then AutoCAD Electrical will search the project directory for the default file.

3. If the project default file is not found, then AutoCAD Electrical will search for the default file that is present in the support directory.

By using these reference files, you can change the description of the drawing, update the title block attributes, and so on easily. Different reference files are discussed next.

## Project Files (.WDP File)

The project files application is a project-based system. These files are created and maintained using the **PROJECT MANAGER**. Each project is defined by an ASCII text file and has an extension *.wdp*. The project file, also called the *.wdp* file, consists of a list of project information, default settings of a project, drawing properties, and name of the drawing files. You can create unlimited number of projects but only one project can be active at a time. Also note that if the project contains a single wiring diagram drawing, the project file is not needed. The Notepad file of the **NFPADEMO** project is shown in Figure 12-17.

When you create or add new drawings to a project, the project settings that are stored in the project file are referenced for maintaining the same format throughout the project drawings. A single project file can find an unlimited number of drawings located in many different directories. If you add a drawing in a project that is stored in the same directory as the project file, then only the file name will be stored in the project file (*.wdp*) but if the drawing you add belongs to a different directory than the project file, then both the file name and complete location of the drawing will be stored in the project file(*.wdp*). The default path of the project file is *C:\User\User Name\My Documents\Acade 2022\AeData\Proj\'your project'*. The symbol libraries, settings of drawing files, and other reference files are stored in the project directory and by using them you can easily change the settings and configurations for different projects.

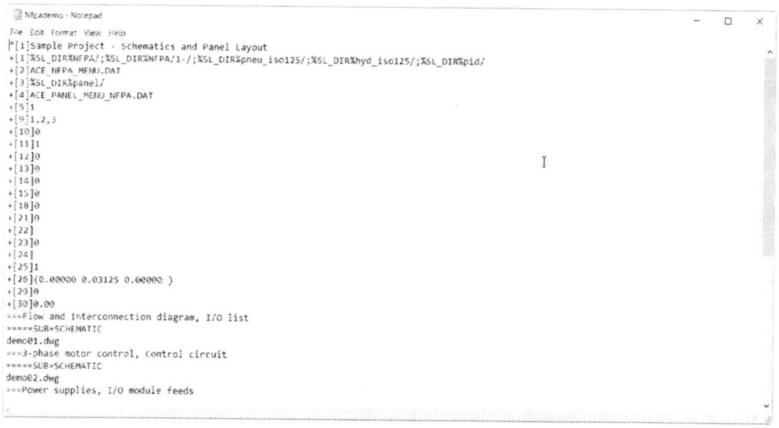

```
Nfpademo - Notepad
File Edit Format View Help
*[1]Sample Project - Schematics and Panel Layout
+[1]%SL_DIR%NFPA/;%SL_DIR%NFPA/1-/;%SL_DIR%pneu_iso125/;%SL_DIR%hyd_iso125/;%SL_DIR%pid/
+[2]ACE_NFPA_MENU.DAT
+[3]%SL_DIR%panel/
+[4]ACE_PANEL_MENU_NFPA.DAT
+[5]1
+[9]1,2,3
+[10]0
+[11]1
+[12]0
+[13]0
+[14]0
+[15]0
+[18]0
+[21]0
+[22]
+[23]0
+[24]
+[25]1
+[26](0.00000 0.03125 0.00000 )
+[29]0
+[30]0.00
===Flow and Interconnection diagram, I/O list
=====SUB=SCHEMATIC
demo01.dwg
===3-phase motor control, Control circuit
=====SUB=SCHEMATIC
demo02.dwg
===Power supplies, I/O module feeds
```

*Figure 12-17 The notepad file of the **NFPADEMO** project*

# Project Description Line Files (.WDL File)

When you right-click on a project name, a shortcut menu will be displayed. Next, choose the **Descriptions** option from the shortcut menu; the **Project Description** dialog box will be displayed, refer to Figure 12-18.

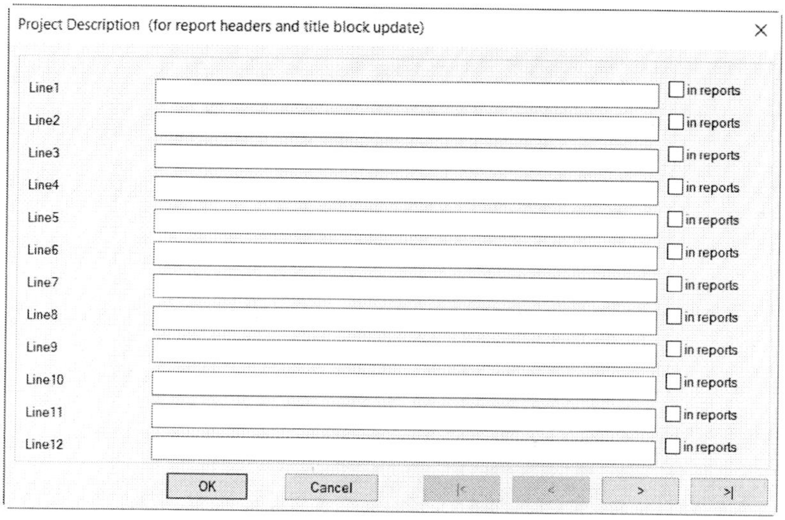

Project Description (for report headers and title block update)

| | | |
|---|---|---|
| Line1 | | in reports |
| Line2 | | in reports |
| Line3 | | in reports |
| Line4 | | in reports |
| Line5 | | in reports |
| Line6 | | in reports |
| Line7 | | in reports |
| Line8 | | in reports |
| Line9 | | in reports |
| Line10 | | in reports |
| Line11 | | in reports |
| Line12 | | in reports |

OK Cancel |< < > >|

*Figure 12-18 The **Project Description** dialog box*

You can customize the generic LINEx label description that is displayed in the **Project Description** dialog box by creating a *.wdl* file and then changing the values in it.

To create a *.wdl* file, open a Notepad file and then enter the values that you want to display in place of Line1, Line2, and so on. Next, save the Notepad file with extension *.wdl* in the project folder wherein you have stored all drawings of the project, project file, and other reference files. The naming convention for these files is *<projectname>_wdtitle.wdl* or *default_wdtitle.wdl*. The LINEx label values are changed to match the attribute values of the drawing title block but they can be used for different purposes such as drawing descriptions, report information, and so on. The *.wdl* file is shown in Figure 12-19.

Note that it is not necessary to have entries in order and also the line number can be skipped. You can store unlimited number of lines in the *.wdl* file but the file should consist of one line per label in the format LINEx = label, as shown in Figure 12-19. After you save the *.wdl* file in the respective project folder, right-click on the name of that project in the **PROJECT MANAGER**; a shortcut menu will be displayed. Next, choose the **Descriptions** option from the shortcut menu; the **Project Description** dialog box will be displayed, as shown in Figure 12-20. You will notice that on saving the *.wdl* file in the project folder, the **Project Description** dialog box will be modified. Also, select the **in reports** check box to include the information in the reports.

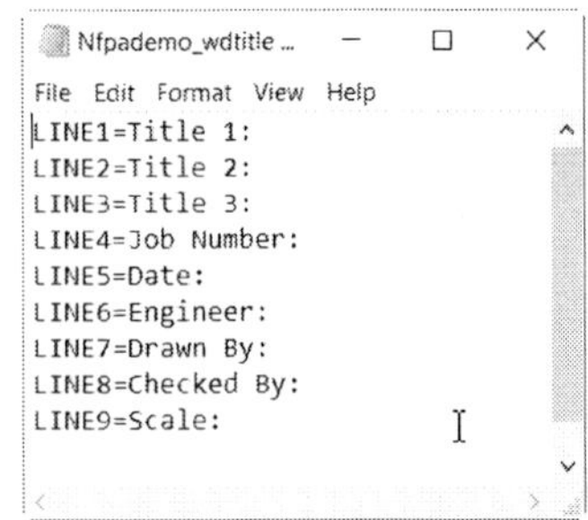


***Figure 12-19*** *The .wdl file of the **Nfpademo** project*

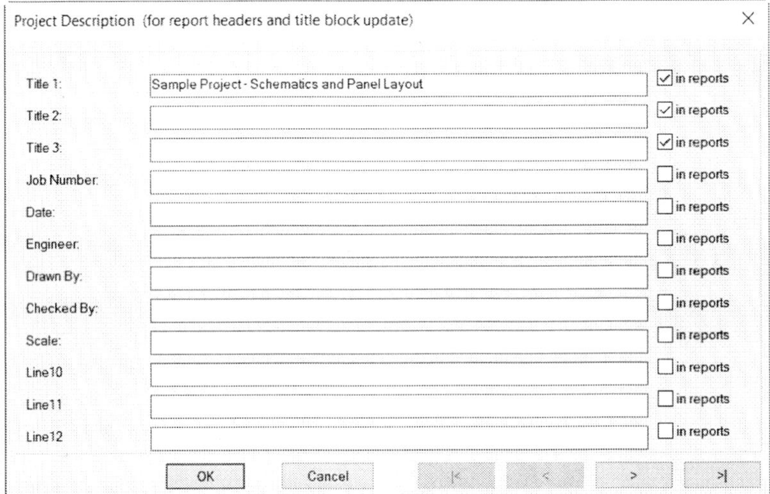


***Figure 12-20*** *The **Project Description** dialog box after saving the .wdl file in the respective project folder*

**Tip**

*It is advisable to save the project file and project drawings in the same directory.*

## Component Reference Files

In this topic, you will learn about various component reference files such as *.wdd, .loc, .inst* files. All these files are ASCII text files. These files save the time of the users as they can just select the values from the list, instead of entering the value every time. These files are discussed next.

### .WDD File

The generic description file is *wd_desc.wdd*. This file consists of the description of the components. The *.wdd* file can be accessed by choosing the **Defaults** button in the **Description** area of the **Insert / Edit Component** dialog box. When you choose the **Defaults** button, the **Descriptions** dialog box will be displayed. Now, from the **Descriptions** dialog box, you can select the description for the component. Choose the **OK** button to display the description in the **Description** area of the **Insert / Edit Component** dialog box. The *.wdd* file can be a family- specific ASCII text file, for example LS.WDD for family 'LS' limit switch. If family-specific file is not found, then it will search for project-specific file that is *<project>.wdd*.

If both family-specific and project-specific files are not found, then AutoCAD Electrical will search for the *WD_DESC.WDD* file, a general description file, in various AutoCAD Electrical search paths and AutoCAD support paths. If the AutoCAD Electrical does not find anything, you will be prompted to browse for a *.wdd* description file. The *.wdd* file can be edited using the Notepad file or Wordpad file. To create a new *.wdd* file, you need to open a Notepad or Wordpad file and then enter the values that you want to enter in the **Descriptions** area and save the file in the respective folder with an extension *.wdd*. The *wd_desc.wdd* file is shown in Figure 12-21. This file is saved at the *c:\Users\CADCIM \AppData\Roaming\Autodesk\AutoCAD Electrical 2022\R24.1\enu\Support* location.

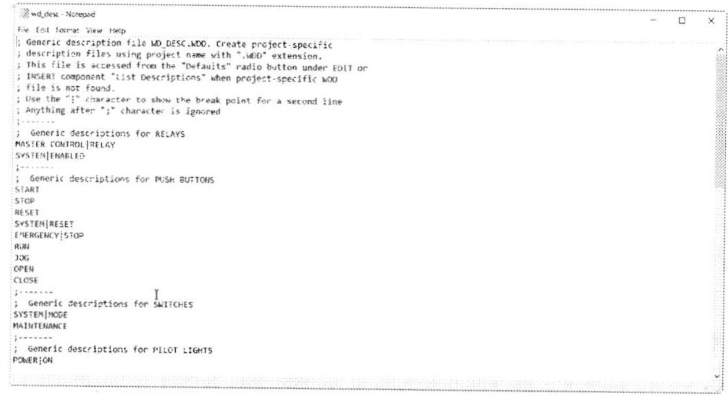


***Figure 12-21*** *The wd_desc.wdd file*

## .INST File

The installation codes file (default.inst) is an ASCII text file. This file contains installation codes. Now, to create the .inst file, open a Notepad or Wordpad file and then enter the installation codes that you want to use in the project and save the file in the respective folder as *Default.inst*. These installation codes will be displayed when you choose the **Project** button in the **Installation code** area of the **Insert / Edit Component** dialog box; the **All Installations - Project** dialog box will be displayed. Next, if you select the **Include external list** check box, the installation codes that you have saved in the *Default.inst* file will be displayed.

This way the *Default.inst* file is used for entering installation codes for components. This file can be named as *<projectname>.inst*. First, a file with the same path and name as the project and *.inst* extension will be searched. If the file is not found, the *Default.inst* file will be searched in the same directory as the project file and then in the subdirectory. The *Default.inst* file is shown in Figure 12-22.

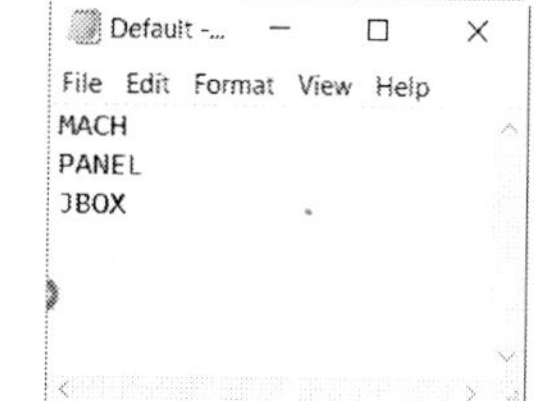


***Figure 12-22*** *The Default.inst file*

## .LOC File

The location codes file (*Default.loc*) is an ASCII text file. This file contains location codes. Now, to create the *.loc* file, open a Notepad or Wordpad file and enter the location codes that you want to use in the project. Next, save the file in the respective folder as *Default.loc*. These location codes will be displayed when you choose the **Project** button in the **Location code** area of the

**Insert / Edit Component** dialog box; the **All Locations - Project** dialog box will be displayed. Next, if you select the **Include external list** check box, the location codes that you have saved in the *Default.loc* file will be displayed. This way the *Default.loc* file is used for entering the location codes for components. Also, this file can be named as *<projectname>.loc*. First, a file with the same path and name as the project with the .loc extension will be searched. If the file is not found, then the *Default.loc* file will be searched in the same directory as the project file and then in the subdirectory. The *Default.loc* file is shown in Figure 12-23.

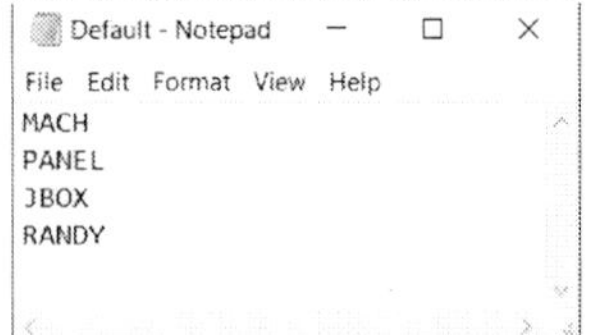

```
Default - Notepad
File Edit Format View Help
MACH
PANEL
JBOX
RANDY
```

***Figure 12-23*** *The Default.loc file*

# MAPPING THE TITLE BLOCK

You can update the values of the attributes in the title block with the properties of a project or drawing. The title block of a drawing consists of a block with attributes. The attributes can be mapped to the title block in the following ways: you can create the *default.wdt* ASCII text file using any text editor such as Notepad, Wordpad, or you can use **Title Block Setup** dialog box for creating the *.WDT* file and saving the mapping in an invisible WD_TB attribute on the title block. The *default.wdt* file defines each attribute's mapping. The *default.wdt* file is shown in Figure 12-24.

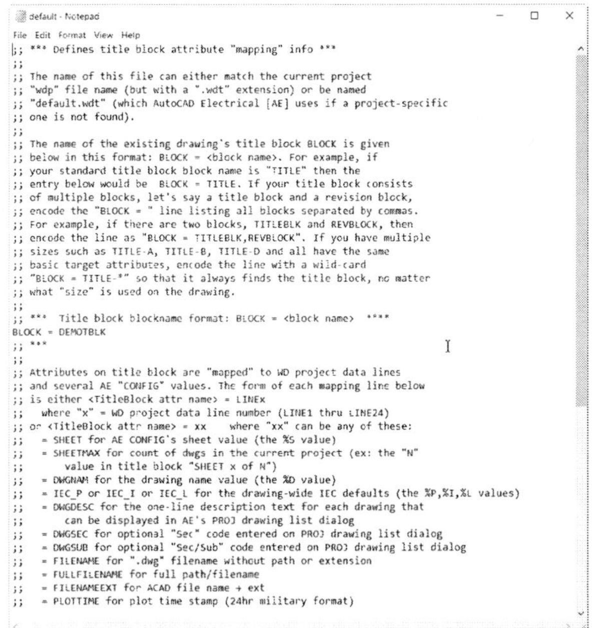

```
default - Notepad
File Edit Format View Help
;; *** Defines title block attribute "mapping" info ***
;;
;; The name of this file can either match the current project
;; "wdp" file name (but with a ".wdt" extension) or be named
;; "default.wdt" (which AutoCAD Electrical [AE] uses if a project-specific
;; one is not found).
;;
;; The name of the existing drawing's title block BLOCK is given
;; below in this format: BLOCK = <block name>. For example, if
;; your standard title block block name is "TITLE" then the
;; entry below would be  BLOCK = TITLE. If your title block consists
;; of multiple blocks, let's say a title block and a revision block,
;; encode the "BLOCK = " line listing all blocks separated by commas.
;; For example, if there are two blocks, TITLEBLK and REVBLOCK, then
;; encode the line as "BLOCK = TITLEBLK,REVBLOCK". If you have multiple
;; sizes such as TITLE-A, TITLE-B, TITLE-D and all have the same
;; basic target attributes, encode the line with a wild-card
;; "BLOCK = TITLE-*" so that it always finds the title block, no matter
;; what "size" is used on the drawing.
;;
;; ***  Title block blockname format: BLOCK = <block name>  ****
BLOCK = DEMOTBLK
;; ***
;;
;; Attributes on title block are "mapped" to WD project data lines
;; and several AE "CONFIG" values. The form of each mapping line below
;; is either <TitleBlock attr name> = LINEx
;;   where "x" = WD project data line number (LINE1 thru LINE24)
;; or <TitleBlock attr name> = xx    where "xx" can be any of these:
;;   = SHEET for AE CONFIG's sheet value (the %S value)
;;   = SHEETMAX for count of dwgs in the current project (ex: the "N"
;;       value in title block "SHEET x of N")
;;   = DWGNAM for the drawing name value (the %D value)
;;   = IEC_P or IEC_I or IEC_L for the drawing-wide IEC defaults (the %P,%I,%L values)
;;   = DWGDESC for the one-line description text for each drawing that
;;       can be displayed in AE's PROJ drawing list dialog
;;   = DWGSEC for optional "Sec" code entered on PROJ drawing list dialog
;;   = DWGSUB for optional "Sec/Sub" code entered on PROJ drawing list dialog
;;   = FILENAME for ".dwg" filename without path or extension
;;   = FULLFILENAME for full path/filename
;;   = FILENAMEEXT for ACAD file name + ext
;;   = PLOTTIME for plot time stamp (24hr military format)
```

***Figure 12-24*** *The default.wdt file*

Using this *.wdt* file, you can configure multiple blocks by separating block names with comma (,) or by creating multiple BLOCK =entries. Block names are followed by the attribute mappings.

The **Title Block Setup** tool is used to create title block mapping. Using this tool, you can pick blocks and attributes from the active drawing. To do so, choose the **Title Block Setup** tool from the **Other Tools** panel of the **Project** tab; the **Setup Title Block Update** dialog box will be displayed, as shown in Figure 12-25. Different areas and options in this dialog box are discussed next.

**Note**

*Before updating the title blocks of a project, you must define how the project and drawing data is mapped to the matching title block attributes.*

## Method 1 Area

In the **Method 1** area, you can use the *.wdt* file to save the mapping information. Also, in this area, different path and location of the *.wdt* files are displayed. The methods for creating mapping information using different *.wdt* files are discussed next.

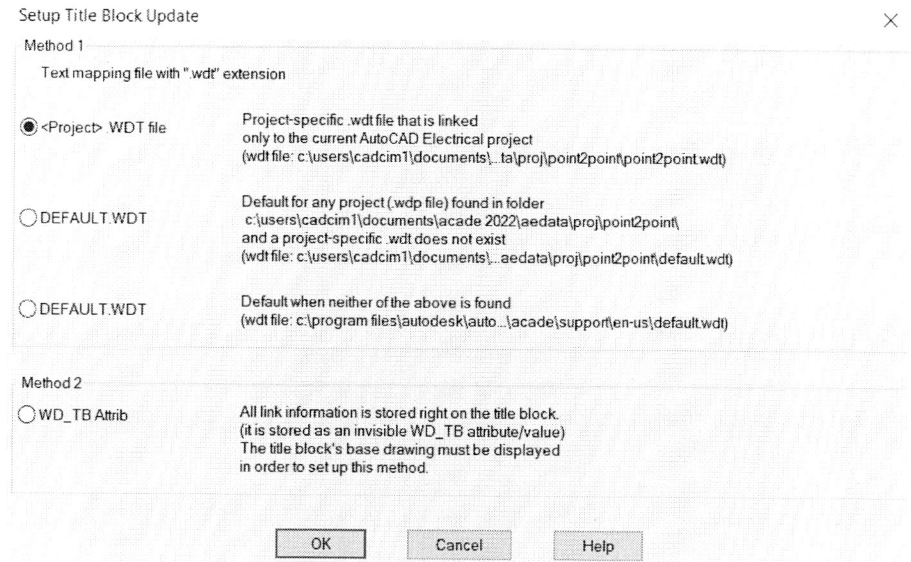


*Figure 12-25 The* ***Setup Title Block Update*** *dialog box*

### Case 1

If the **<Project>.WDT file** radio button is selected in the **Method 1** area and the *.wdt* file already exists and then you choose the **OK** button in the **Setup Title Block Update** dialog box, the **.WDT File Exists** dialog box will be displayed, as shown in Figure 12-26. The options in this dialog box are discussed next.

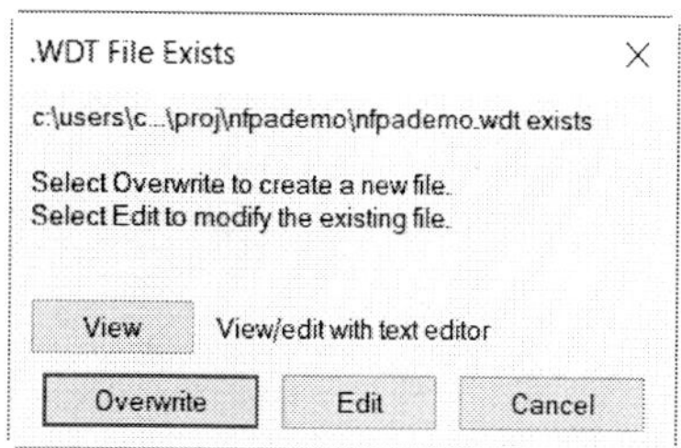


*Figure 12-26 The* ***.WDT File Exists*** *dialog box*

The **View** button is used to view the existing *.wdt* file. Choose the **View** button; the *.wdt* file will be opened using the default text editor.

The **Overwrite** button is used to overwrite the existing *.wdt* file and to create a new *.wdt* file. To do so, choose the **Overwrite** button; the **Enter Block Name** dialog box will be displayed. Specify the block name and choose the **OK** button in the **Enter Block Name** dialog box; the **Title Block Setup** dialog box will be displayed. The options in this dialog box will be discussed later in this chapter. Choose the **OK** button in the **Title Block Setup** dialog box for updating the *.wdt* file of a project.

The **Edit** button is used to edit the existing *.wdt* file.

Choose the **Cancel** button to exit the **.WDT File Exists** dialog box without saving the changes.

### Case 2

If the **<Project>.WDT file** radio button is selected in the **Method 1** area and the *.wdt* file does not exist and you choose the **OK** button in the **Setup Title Block Update** dialog box, the **Enter Block Name** dialog box will be displayed, as shown in Figure 12-27. The options in this dialog box are discussed next.

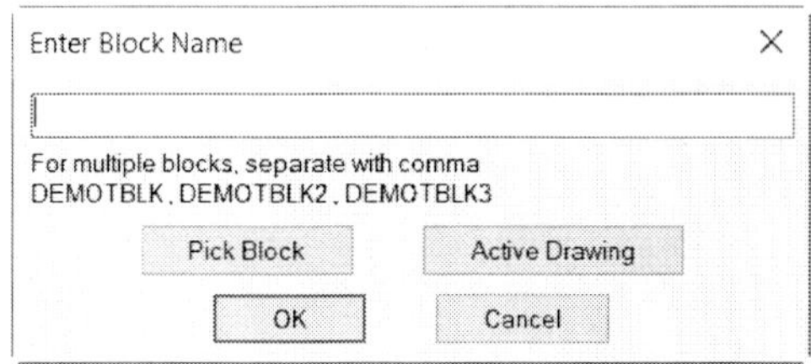


*Figure 12-27 The **Enter Block Name** dialog box*

Specify the block name in the edit box. Alternatively, you can choose the **Pick Block** button to select the block name from the drawing. Also, you can choose the **Active Drawing** button to use active drawing as the block name. If you want to enter multiple blocks in the edit box, separate block names with comma. Choose the **OK** button in the **Enter Block Name** dialog box; the **Title Block Setup** dialog box will be displayed. Specify the desired options and choose the **OK** button to save the changes and exit the **Title Block Setup** dialog box.

### DEFAULT.WDT

The **DEFAULT.WDT** radio button is used when the project-specific *.wdt* file such as *<Project>.WDT* file is not found in the current project folder. When you select the **DEFAULT.WDT** radio button, AutoCAD Electrical will search for *default.wdt* file and will use it for mapping the title block. Note that the *default.wdt* file is saved in the folder of the current project.

### DEFAULT.WDT

The **DEFAULT.WDT** radio button is used when the project-specific *.wdt* file *<Project>.WDT* file or *default.wdt* file is not found in the current project folder. When you select the **DEFAULT.WDT** radio button, AutoCAD Electrical will search for *default.wdt* file, which is saved at the *c:\program files\autodesk\acade 2022\support\default.wdt* location. AutoCAD Electrical will use this file for mapping the title block.

## Method 2 Area

In the **Method 2** area, you can save the mapping information in the WD_TB attribute. If you use the **Method 2** area, you need to open the base drawing for the title block in order to insert the attribute. To do so, enter **Explode** at the Command prompt; you will be prompted to select objects. Next, select the title block and press ENTER; the title block will be exploded. Now, you can see the WD_TB attribute at the bottom of the title block, as shown in Figure 12-28.

The WD_TB attribute helps in attribute mapping of a title block. Note that, if you double-click on the WD_TB attribute, the **Edit Attribute Definition** dialog box will be displayed. The values in the **Edit Attribute Definition** dialog box helps in mapping the AutoCAD Electrical properties to the attributes in the block. Press ESC to cancel the command.

Next, choose the **Title Block Setup** tool from the **Other Tools** panel of the **Project** tab; the **Setup Title Block Update** dialog box will be displayed. In this dialog box, select the **WD_TB attribute** radio button from the **Method 2** area; the **Title Block Setup** dialog box will be displayed. The options in this dialog box are discussed next. Specify the desired options in the **Title Block Setup** dialog box and choose the **OK** button to save the changes made and exit the dialog box.

***Figure 12-28*** *Lower right portion of the title block showing the WD_TB attribute*

## Setting up the Title Block

| | |
|---|---|
| **Ribbon:** | Project > Other Tools > Title Block Setup |
| **Menu:** | Projects> Drawing Properties |
| **Command:** | AESETUPTITLEBLOCK |

You can create attribute mapping files or map the existing attributes in the title block to the project, drawing, or user-defined values. To create an attribute mapping file, choose the **Title Block Setup** tool from the **Other Tools** panel of the **Project** tab; the **Setup Title Block Update** dialog box will be displayed. Select the required option from the **Method 1** area and choose the **OK** button; the **Enter Block Name** dialog box will be displayed. Specify the name of block in the edit box. Choose the **OK** button in the **Enter Block Name** dialog box; the **Title Block Setup** dialog box will be displayed, as shown in Figure 12-29. In this dialog box, you can use the **Project Values**, **Drawing Values**, and **User Defined** buttons to map the information to the title block attributes.

**Note**

*If the Project specific .wdt file is available for the active project, the* ***.WDT File Exists*** *message box will be displayed on selecting the* ***<Project> .WDT file*** *radio button from the* ***Method1*** *area of the* ***Setup Title Block Update*** *dialog box. Choose the* ***View*** *or* ***Edit*** *button to view and edit this file. Choose the* ***Overwrite*** *button to overwrite this file.*

By default, the **Title Block Setup** dialog box is set to map project descriptions to the title block attributes. The options in the **Title Block Setup** dialog box are discussed next.

Select the name for the title block from the drop-down list located on the left of the **Add New** button.

The **Add New** button is used to add new title blocks to the project.

The **Edit** button is used to edit the selected title block name.

*Figure 12-29 The **Title Block Setup** dialog box*

The **Remove** button will be available only if the drop-down list, which is on the left top portion of the **Title Block Setup** dialog box, consists of more than one title block name. This button is used to remove the selected title block from the *.wdt* file.

The **Pick on** column consists of the **Pick** button. The **Pick** button is used to select the attribute from the drawing. When you choose the **Pick** button, you will be prompted to select the attribute from the drawing. Next, select the attribute; the name of the attribute will be displayed under the **Attribute** column.

The **Attribute** column consists of various drop-down lists. You need to select the required attribute name from the corresponding drop-down list.

The **Project Value** column displays project descriptions. The values under the **Project Value** column can be changed by adding project descriptions to a project. This can be done by saving the *.wdl* file in the project folder, which has already been discussed in detail. So, when you add the project description (*.wdl* file) to a project, the values under the **Project Value** column are changed, as shown in Figure 12-30.

The **<** and **>** buttons are used to move to the previous page and next page of the project descriptions, respectively.

The **Drawing Values** button is used to map information from individual drawing to title block attributes. When you choose the **Drawing Values** button, the **Title Block Setup** dialog box will be changed, as shown in Figure 12-31. In this case, the title block will be updated with information only from the same drawing in which the title block is located. As the drawing parameters are displayed under the **Drawing Value** column, you need to select the drawing description from the respective drop-down list under the **Attribute** column. Also, under the **Plotting Value** column, the plotting value options are displayed.

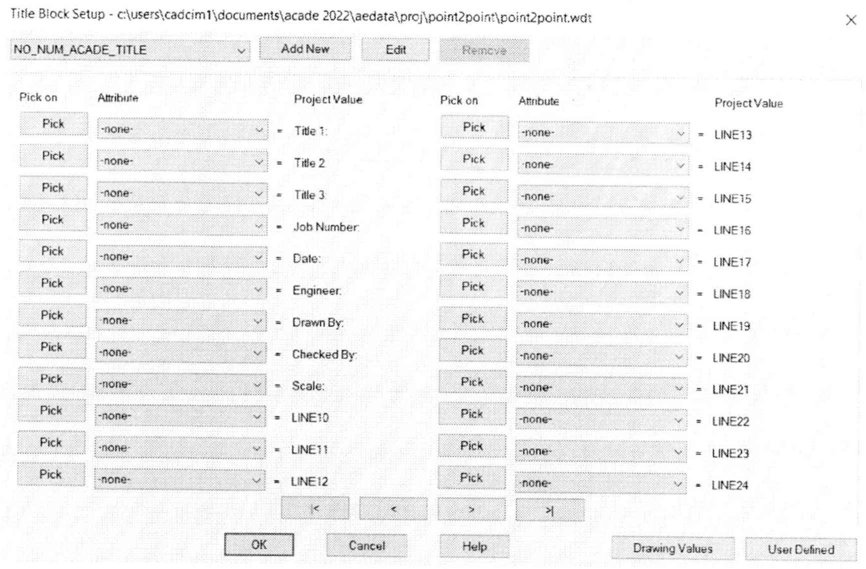

*Figure 12-30 The values under the **Project Value** column changed in the **Title Block Setup** dialog box*

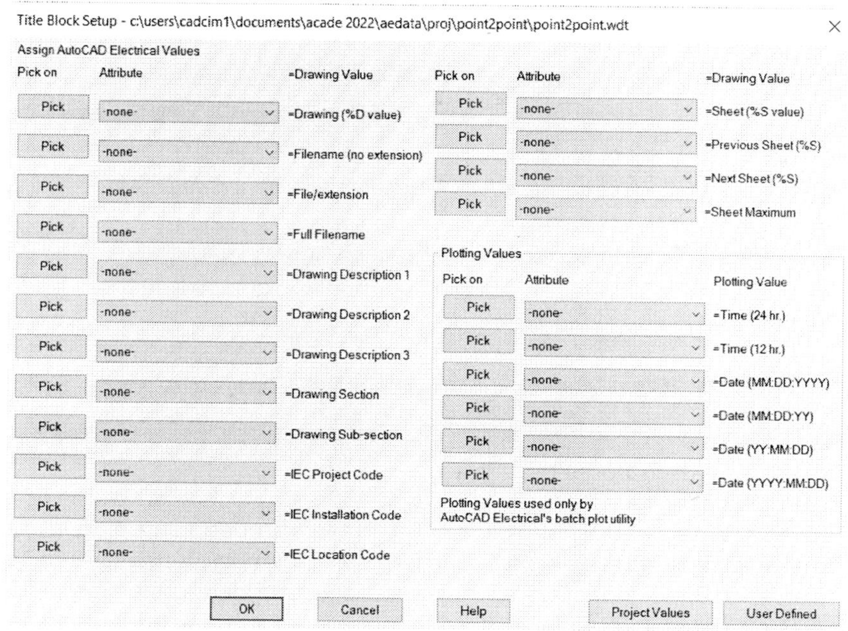

*Figure 12-31 The **Title Block Setup** dialog box after choosing the **Drawing Values** button*

The **User Defined** button is used to map attributes to text constants and Autolisp expression. Choose the **User Defined** button; the **Title Block Setup - User-Defined** dialog box will be displayed, as shown in Figure 12-32. The options in this dialog box are discussed next.

The **Current User-Defined Assignments** area displays the list of attributes and assigned text constant or Autolisp expression.

The **Attribute** drop-down list is used to modify an existing link, which is displayed in the **Current User-defined Assignments** area. By default, **none** is selected in this drop-down list.

The **Text Constant or Autolisp expression** edit box is used to specify a text constant or Autolisp expression that you want to assign to the attribute.

The **Update List** button is used to update the attribute list, which is displayed in the **Current User-defined Assignments** area.

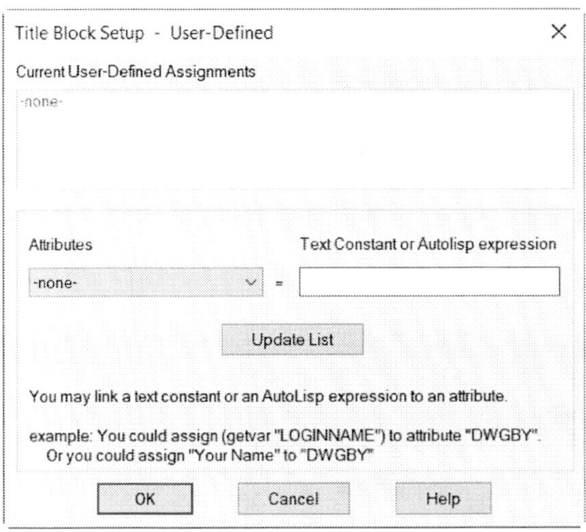


*Figure 12-32 The* ***Title Block Setup - User-Defined*** *dialog box*

After specifying the required options in the **Title Block Setup - User-Defined** dialog box, choose the **OK** button; you will return to the **Title Block Setup** dialog box. Now, choose the **OK** button in the **Title Block Setup** dialog box to save the changes and exit.

# UPDATING TITLE BLOCKS

| | |
|---|---|
| **Ribbon:** | Project > Other Tools > Title Block Update |
| **Command:** | AEUPDATETITLEBLOCK |

You can update the attribute values of title blocks for an active drawing or project. To update the information of a title block, right-click on the active project; a shortcut menu will be displayed. Next, choose the **Title Block Update** option from the shortcut menu; the **Update Title Block** dialog box will be displayed, refer to Figure 12-33. Alternatively, choose the **Title Block Update** tool from the **Other Tools** panel of the **Project** tab to display the **Update Title Block** dialog box.

Using the **Update Title Block** dialog box, you can update the information of the title block for an active drawing or project. Different areas and options in this dialog box are discussed next.

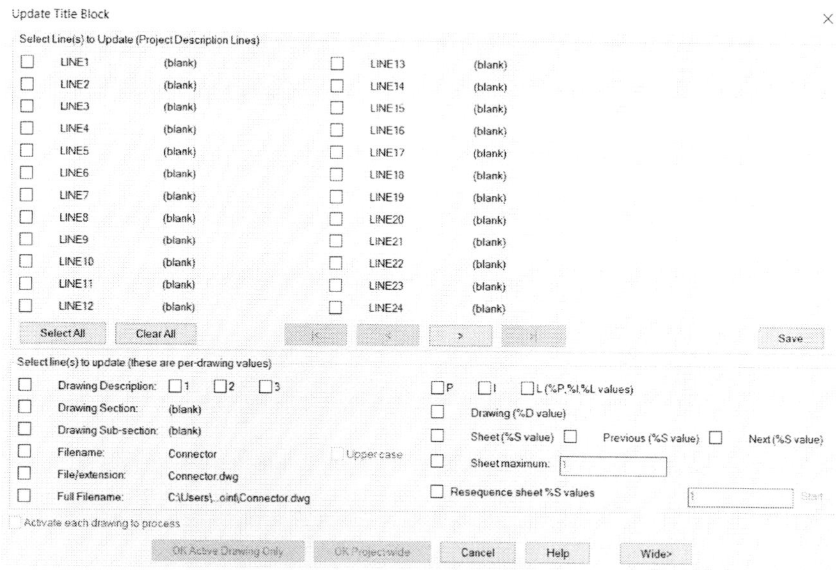

*Figure 12-33 The **Update Title Block** dialog box*

## Select Line(s) to Update (Project Description Lines) Area

This area is used to select the information for updating the title block attributes. This area displays the project description lines that were assigned by you while creating the project file. Note that the value for each line in this area is controlled by the *default_wdtitle.wdl* file or *<project name>_wdtitle.wdl* file, which is placed in the project folder. Note that if the *<project name>_wdtitle.wdl* file is not found in the project folder, then AutoCAD Electrical will search for the *default_wdtitle.wdl* file in the User folder. If you have already assigned the project description to the project, then the values of Line 1 to Line 9 in this area will be in the following format:

| | |
|---|---|
| LINE1 | Title 1 |
| LINE2 | Title 2 |
| LINE3 | Title 3 |
| LINE4 | Job Number |
| LINE5 | Date |
| LINE6 | Engineer |
| LINE7 | Drawn By |
| LINE8 | Checked By |
| LINE9 | Scale |

If you assign the project description to the project, the text values in this area will automatically be changed, as shown in Figure 12-34.

If you select the check box of any line from the **Select Line(s) to Update (Project Description Lines)** area, then only the parameter corresponding to that line will be updated in the title block. By default, all the check boxes in this area are clear.

Choose the **Select All** button to select all the check boxes in this area. Similarly, you can choose the **Clear All** button to clear all the check boxes in this area.

Update Title Block

Select Line(s) to Update (Project Description Lines)

| | | | |
|---|---|---|---|
| Title 1: | (blank) | LINE13 | (blank) |
| Title 2: | (blank) | LINE14 | (blank) |
| Title 3: | (blank) | LINE15 | (blank) |
| Job Number: | (blank) | LINE16 | (blank) |
| Date: | (blank) | LINE17 | (blank) |
| Engineer: | (blank) | LINE18 | (blank) |
| Drawn By: | (blank) | LINE19 | (blank) |
| Checked By: | (blank) | LINE20 | (blank) |
| Scale: | (blank) | LINE21 | (blank) |
| LINE10 | (blank) | LINE22 | (blank) |
| LINE11 | (blank) | LINE23 | (blank) |
| LINE12 | (blank) | LINE24 | (blank) |

Select All  Clear All  |<  <  >  >|  Save

Select line(s) to update (these are per-drawing values)

Drawing Description: 1 2 3  P I L (%P,%I,%L values)
Drawing Section: (blank)  Drawing (%D value)
Drawing Sub-section: (blank)  Sheet (%S value)  Previous (%S value)  Next (%S value)
Filename: Connector  Upper case  Sheet maximum: 1
File/extension: Connector.dwg  Resequence sheet %S values 1 Start
Full Filename: C:\Users\...oint\Connector.dwg

Activate each drawing to process

OK Active Drawing Only  OK Project-wide  Cancel  Help  Wide>

***Figure 12-34** The **Update Title Block** dialog box when the project description is assigned*

Choose the **>** and **<** buttons to move to the next and previous page of the project descriptions, respectively.

The **Save** button is used to save the changes made in this area. To do so, choose the **Save** button; the **AutoCAD Message** message box will be displayed, as shown in Figure 12-35. By default, the changes made in this dialog box will be saved in the *default.wdu* file. The location of this file is *C:\Users\User Name\AppData\Roaming\Autodesk\AutoCAD Electrical 2022\R24.1\enu\Support\User.*

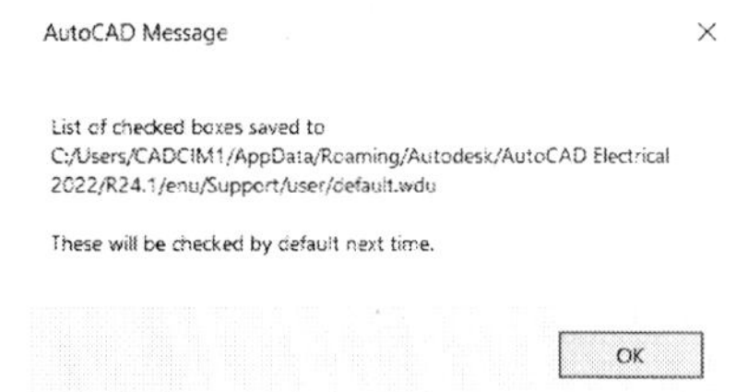


***Figure 12-35** The **AutoCAD Message** message box*

**Note**

*If you select the values that are indicated as blank in the **Select Line(s) to Update (Project Description Lines)** area or if an appropriate attribute is not found in the title block, then the mapping for that item will be ignored.*

## Select line(s) to update (these are per-drawing values) Area

This area displays the drawing specific values. The options in this area are discussed next.

### Drawing Description

By default, the **Drawing Description** check box is clear. Select this check box to include drawing description in the project. You can add three description lines to a drawing by selecting **1**, **2**, and **3** check boxes near this check box.

### Drawing Section
Select the **Drawing Section** check box to include the drawing sections in the project. By default, this check box is clear.

### Drawing Sub-section
Select the **Drawing Sub-section** check box to include the drawing sub-sections in the project. By default, this check box is clear.

### Filename
Select the **Filename** check box to include the filename in the project without extension. By default, this check box is clear.

### File/extension
Select the **File/extension** check box to include the file name along with the extension of the drawing file in the project. By default, this check box is clear.

### Full Filename
Select the **Full Filename** check box to include the full file name and location of the drawing file in the project. By default, this check box is clear.

### Upper case
The **Upper case** check box will be activated only if any of the following check boxes is selected: **Filename**, **File/extension**, and **Full Filename**. Select this check box to change the name and path of the drawing to upper case. By default, the **Upper case** check box is clear.

### P
Select the **P** check box to include the project value (%P) in the drawing. By default, this check box is clear.

### I
Select the **I** check box to include the installation value (%I) in the drawing. By default, this check box is clear.

### L
Select the **L** check box to include the location value (%L) in the drawing. By default, this check box is clear.

### Drawing(%D value)
Select the **Drawing(%D value)** check box to include the drawing number value of the drawing settings. By default, this check box is clear.

### Sheet(%S value)
Select the **Sheet(%S value)** check box to include the sheet number value of the drawing settings. By default, this check box is clear.

### Sheet maximum

When you select the **Sheet maximum** check box, the edit box adjacent to this check box will be activated. Enter the number of sheets in the edit box that you want to update. By default, the number of drawings in a project will be displayed in this edit box.

### Resequence sheet %S values

By default, the **Resequence sheet %S values** check box is clear. Select this check box to renumber the drawings of a project. After selecting this check box, the **Start** edit box will be activated. Enter the start value for the drawings in this edit box.

## Activate each drawing to process

By default, the **Activate each drawing to process** check box is clear. If you select this check box, then all drawings in a project will be processed and you will be able to update the title block lines on the selected drawings in the project.

## Wide> and Wide<

Choose the **Wide>** and **Wide<** buttons for widening and compressing the **Update Title Block** dialog box, respectively.

## OK Active Drawing Only

Choose the **OK Active Drawing Only** button to update the information of the selected lines of the title block of the active drawing only.

## OK Project-wide

The **OK Project-wide** button is used to update the information of the selected drawings in the project.

# CREATING TEMPLATES

One way to customize AutoCAD Electrical is to create template drawings that contain initial drawing setup information and if desired, visible objects and text. When the user starts a new drawing, the settings associated with the template drawing are automatically loaded. If you start a new drawing from scratch, AutoCAD Electrical will load default setup values such as the WD_M block, predefined standard AutoCAD Electrical layers, and so on.

In production drawings, most of the electrical drawing setup values remain the same. For example, the company title block, layers, schematic ladders already inserted, panel settings already configured, enclosure inserted, and other drawing setup values do not change. You will save considerable time if you save these values and reload them while starting a new drawing. You can do this by creating template drawings that contain the initial drawing setup information configured according to the company specifications.

With this template, when you start a new drawing, AutoCAD Electrical does not have to pause and ask permission to insert the non-visible block. These templates consist of title block information, layer information, and so on. The extension of the template file is *.dwt*.

In order to create a template file, you can open existing drawing file or you can create a new one. Now, to create a new drawing file, choose the **New Drawing** button from the **PROJECT MANAGER**; the **Create New Drawing** dialog box will be displayed. The options in the **Create New Drawing** dialog have been discussed earlier in Chapter 2. Specify the options in this dialog box as per your requirement and then choose the **OK** button; the drawing will be created and added in the active project.

Now, specify the settings for this drawing as per your requirement. For example, if you want to use this template drawing as a panel template, then you need to configure the panel settings. If you are creating a template drawing for schematic, then you need to insert ladders.

Next, choose **File > Save As** from the menu bar; the **Save Drawing As** dialog box will be displayed. Select the **AutoCAD Drawing Template (*.dwt)** option from the **Files of type** drop-down list; the **Template** folder will open automatically, where you need to save the template file. Alternatively, you can save the template file at the desired location. Next, enter the name of the template drawing in the **File name** edit box. Choose the **Save** button to save the template drawing; the **Template Options** dialog box will be displayed, as shown in Figure 12-36. The options in the **Template Options** dialog box are discussed next.

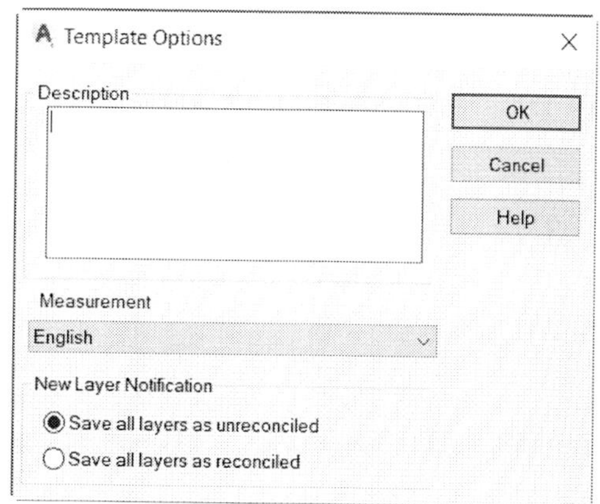


*Figure 12-36 The **Template Options** dialog box*

## Description Area

Specify the description for the template drawing in the **Description** area.

## Measurement

Select the measurement system for the template drawing from the **Measurement** drop-down list. By default, the **English** option is selected.

## New Layer Notification Area

This area is used to specify whether the template file is saved with reconciled layers or unreconciled layers. The options in this area are discussed next.

### Save all layers as unreconciled

The **Save all layers as unreconciled** radio button is selected by default and is used to save the template file with its layers set as unreconciled, which indicates the layer baseline is not created.

### Save all layers as reconciled

Select the **Save all layers as reconciled** radio button to save the template file with its layers set as reconciled, which indicates that the layer baseline is created.

Now, choose the **OK** button to save the changes and exit the **Template Options** dialog box. This way you can create the template drawing file.

**Note**

*To change the default template location, choose **Tools > Options** from the menu bar; the **Options** dialog box will be displayed. In the **Files** tab, click on the **Template Settings** node to expand it. Click on the **Drawing Template File Location** node. Here, you can change the default location of the template by choosing the **Browse** button; the **Browse For Folder** dialog box will be displayed. Specify the location and choose the **OK** button; the default location of the drawing template file will be changed.*

# PLOTTING THE PROJECT

The **Plot Project** option is used to plot full drawing set of a project or a group of drawings that you select. To plot full drawing set of a project, choose the **Publish/Plot** button from the **PROJECT MANAGER**; a flyout will be displayed, as shown in Figure 12-37. Choose the **Plot Project** option from this flyout; the **Select Drawings to Process** dialog box will be displayed, as shown in Figure 12-38. The options in this dialog box have already been discussed in the earlier chapters. Select the drawings that you need to plot using this dialog box.

*Figure 12-37 The flyout displayed on choosing the **Publish/Plot** button*

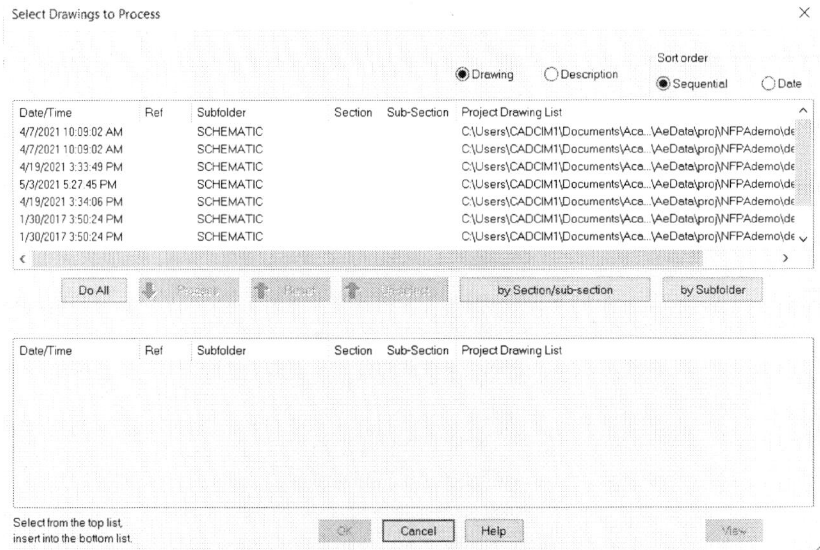


*Figure 12-38 The **Select Drawings to Process** dialog box*

If you choose the **Do All** button, all drawings will be moved to the bottom list of the **Select Drawings to Process** dialog box.

If you choose the **Process** button, the selected drawings will be moved to the bottom list of the **Select Drawings to Process** dialog box.

Choose the **OK** button from the **Select Drawings to Process** dialog box; the **Batch Plotting Options and Order** dialog box will be displayed, as shown in Figure 12-39. The options in this dialog box are discussed next.

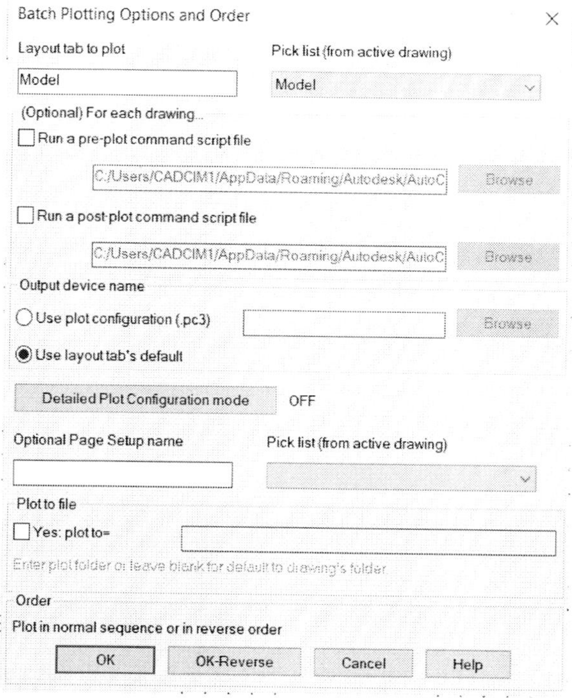


*Figure 12-39 The* ***Batch Plotting Options and Order*** *dialog box*

## Layout tab to plot

Specify the name of the layout, which you need to plot in the **Layout tab to plot** edit box. By default, **Model** is displayed in this edit box. Alternatively, select an option from the **Pick list (from active drawing)** drop-down list; it will be automatically displayed in the **Layout tab to plot** edit box.

## Pick list (from active drawing)

The **Pick list (from active drawing)** drop-down list consists of the layout tabs that are present in your active drawing. Select the layout that you need to plot from the **Pick list (from active drawing)** drop-down list; the layout tab to be plotted will be displayed in the **Layout tab to plot** edit box. Note that only one layout tab can be plotted during a single batch process. Also, in order to print multiple layout tabs at a time, you need to use the **Plot Project** option several times.

## (Optional) For each drawing Area

The options in the **(Optional) For each drawing** area are used to execute the command script file either before plotting a project, after plotting it, or in both conditions. The options in this area are discussed next.

The **Run a pre-plot command script file** check box is used to run an optional script file, which contains a list of commands that need to be executed before the plot command is used. To run a pre-plot script file, select this check box; the edit box and the **Browse** button will be activated. By default, the script file name *C:/Users/User Name/AppData/Roaming/Autodesk/AutoCAD Electrical 2022/R24.1/enu/Support/user/preplot.scr* is displayed in the edit box. You can either use the default script file or you can specify a new script file. To specify a new script file, choose the **Browse** button; the **Pre-plot script file(run before each drawing plots)** dialog box will be displayed. Select the script file and choose the **Open** button; the name and path of the pre-plot script file (.scr) will be displayed in the edit box.

The **Run a post-plot command script file** check box is used to run an optional script file, which contains a list of commands that need to be executed after the plot command has been used. This check box is used in a way similar to the **Run a pre-plot command script file** check box.

## Output device name Area

In the **Output device name** area, you can set options for the output devices. The **Output device name** area consists of the **Use plot configuration[.pc3]** and **Use layout tab's default** radio buttons, an edit box, and the **Browse** button. These options are discussed next.

The **Use plot configuration(.pc3)** radio button is used to select an existing plotter configuration file [.pc3]. When you select this radio button, the **Select Plot Device** dialog box will be displayed. Select the plotter file and choose the **Open** button; the name of the plotting device will be displayed in the edit box located on the right of the **Use plot configuration[.pc3]** radio button.

Select the **Use layout tab's default** radio button to use the default plotter configuration.

By default, the **Detailed Plot Configuration mode** button is set to OFF. As a result, the **Optional Page Setup name** edit box and the **Pick list (from active drawing)** drop-down list will be activated. You can enter the name of the optional page setup in the **Optional Page Setup name** edit box. Alternatively, you can select a page setup from the options available in the **Pick list (from active drawing)** drop-down list. When you choose the **Detailed Plot Configuration mode** button, the **Detailed Plot Configuration Option** dialog box will be displayed. In this dialog box, you can turn the detailed configuration mode on or off and can set the other options for the plot.

If you set the **Detailed Plot Configuration mode** button to ON, the **Optional Page Setup name** edit box and the **Pick list(from active drawing)** drop-down list in the **Batch Plotting Options and Order** dialog box will be disabled.

## Plot to file Area

In the **Plot to file** area, you can specify the location for a plot file. Plot files are saved with *.plt* extension. The options in this area are discussed next.

Select the **Yes: plot to=** check box; the **Yes: plot to=** edit box will be activated. Next, enter the plot folder for plotting the file in this edit box. By default, this edit box is blank, which indicates that it will use drawing's default folder.

## Order Area

In the **Order** area, you can specify whether the drawings that are listed in the project will be plotted in the order they appear in the project list or in the reverse order.

Choose the **OK-Reverse** button from the **Order** area to plot drawings in the reverse order.

After specifying the required options in the **Batch Plotting Options and Order** dialog box, choose the **OK** button from the **Order** area to plot the selected drawings in the order they appear in the project list displayed in the **PROJECT MANAGER**.

# PROJECT TASK LIST

Sometimes, while editing a component, you may be prompted to update the components related to it. Also, the **Update other drawings?** message box may be displayed, as shown in Figure 12-40. The options in this message box have already been discussed. You have the option to update the drawings immediately or add them to the task list. If you choose the **OK** button in this dialog box, the drawings will be updated immediately. Also, the current drawing will be saved and appropriate drawing will get opened, updated, saved, and closed and you will return to the drawing that you were editing.

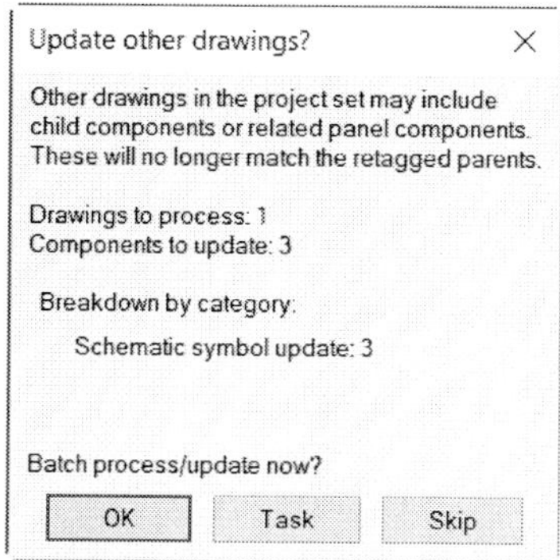


***Figure 12-40** The **Update other drawings?** message box*

Now, if you choose the **Task** button, the components will be added to the task list for updation. Also, the information will be saved to the project task list, which can be updated later. The **Project Task List** button in the **PROJECT MANAGER** is used to execute the pending updates on the modified drawing files of the active project. Choose the **Project Task List** button; the **Task List** dialog box will be displayed, as shown in Figure 12-41. This dialog box displays information of the saved tasks. Different options in this dialog box are discussed next.

The **By** column displays the login name of the user.

The **File Name** column displays the name of the drawing file that needs modification.

The **Installation** and **Location** columns display the installation and location codes of the components of a drawing that needs to be modified.

The **Tag** and **Type** columns display the tag and type of the component, respectively.

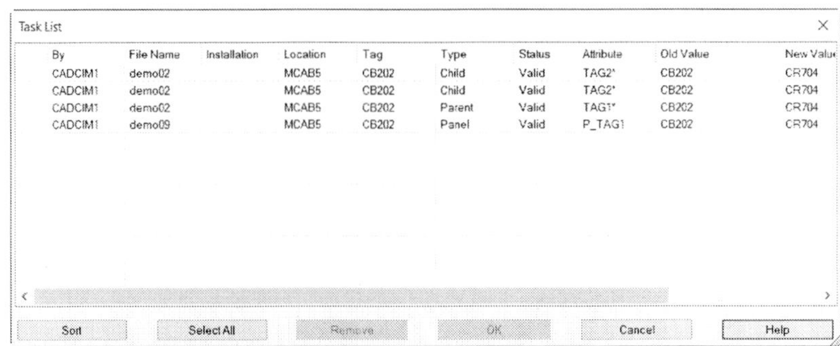


*Figure 12-41 The **Task List** dialog box*

The **Status** column displays **Valid**, if an attribute is up to date and **Stale**, if the attribute needs to be updated.

The **Attribute** column displays the attributes that need to be updated.

The **Old Value**, **New Value**, and **Current Value** columns display the previous, new, and current values of the attributes, respectively.

The **Sort** button is used to sort the task list. Choose the **Sort** button; the **Sort** dialog box will be displayed. Specify the options in this dialog box as per your requirement and choose the **OK** button; the task list will be sorted.

The **Select All** button is used to select all tasks in the list. Also, when you choose the **OK** button, all drawings will be updated.

Choose the **Remove** button to remove the selected task from the list displayed in the **Task List** dialog box.

When you select a task from the list displayed, the **Remove** and **OK** buttons will become available. Choose the **OK** button in this dialog box to perform the pending task.

# TUTORIALS

## Tutorial 1

In this tutorial, you will change the drawing properties for the wire numbers of a drawing and then update the wire numbers. **(Expected time: 15 min)**

The following steps are required to complete this tutorial:

a. Open and save the drawing.
b. Add the active drawing to the **CADCIM** project list.
c. Change format for wire numbers in the **Drawing Properties** dialog box.
d. Save the drawing.

## Opening and Saving the Drawing

1. Activate the **CADCIM** project and open the drawing *DEMO05.DWG*.

2. Save the drawing *DEMO05.DWG* with the name *C12_tut01.dwg*.

## Adding the Active Drawing to the CADCIM Project List

1. Add the drawing *C12_tut01.dwg* to the **CADCIM** project list, as discussed earlier. Next, move it to the *TUTORIALS* subfolder.

**Note**

*If the **Update Terminal Associations** message box is displayed, choose the **Yes** button in this message box; C12_tut01.dwg is added to the **CADCIM** project.*

2. Choose **Save** from the **Application Menu** to save the drawing.

## Changing Drawing Properties

1. Right-click on the *C12_tut01.dwg* drawing file in the **PROJECT MANAGER**; a shortcut menu is displayed. Choose **Properties > Drawing Properties** from the shortcut menu; the **Drawing Properties** dialog box is displayed.

2. By default, the **Drawing Settings** tab is chosen. Now, enter **01** in the **Sheet** edit box of the **Sheet Values** area.

3. Choose the **Wire Numbers** tab and enter **W-%S%N** in the **Format** edit box of the **Wire Number Format** area.

4. Choose the **OK** button in the **Drawing Properties** dialog box to save the changes and to exit from it.

5. Choose the **Wire Numbers** tool from the **Insert Wires/Wire Numbers** panel of the **Schematic** tab; the **Sheet01 - Wire Tagging** dialog box is displayed.

6. Accept the default values and then choose the **Drawing-wide** button; wire numbers are inserted in the wires throughout the drawing, as shown in Figure 12-42.

## Saving the Drawing File

1. Choose **Save** from the **Application Menu** to save the drawing file *C12_tut01.dwg*.

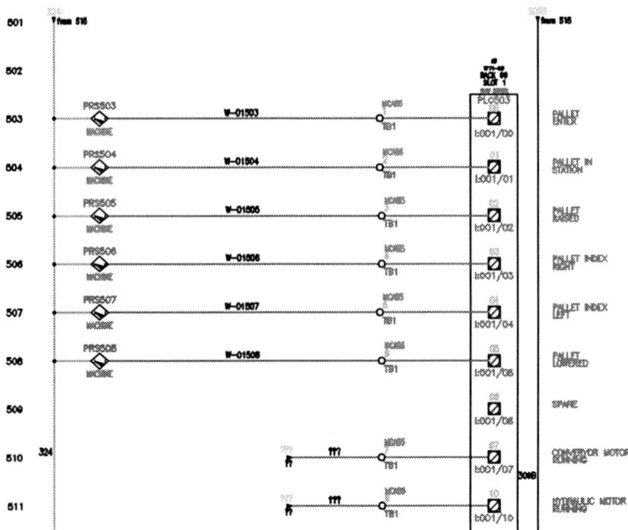


*Figure 12-42 Wire numbers inserted in the drawing after changing the drawing properties*

## Tutorial 2

In this tutorial, you will change the project properties and notice the changes taking place in the current drawing. **(Expected time: 15 min)**

The following steps are required to complete this tutorial:

a. Open and save the drawing.
b. Add drawing to the **CADCIM** project list.
c. Change the project properties.
d. Save the drawing.

### Opening and Saving the Drawing

1. Activate the **CADCIM** project and then open the *C12_tut01.dwg* drawing from it.

2. Save the drawing *C12_tut01.dwg* with the name *C12_tut02.dwg*.

### Adding Drawing to the CADCIM Project List

1. Add the drawing *C12_tut02.dwg* to the **CADCIM** project, as discussed earlier. Next, move it to the *TUTORIALS* subfolder.

**Note**

*If the* ***Update Terminal Associations*** *message box is displayed, choose the* ***Yes*** *button in it; C12_tut02.dwg is added to the TUTORIALS* subfolder of the **CADCIM** project.

2. Choose **Save** from the **Application Menu** to save the drawing.

## Changing Project Properties

1. To change the project properties, right-click on the **CADCIM** project; a shortcut menu is displayed. Choose the **Properties** option from the shortcut menu; the **Project Properties** dialog box is displayed.

2. Choose the **Components** tab and select the **Combined Installation/Location tag mode** and **Format Installation/Location into tag** check boxes from the **Component TAG Options** area. Also, clear all other check boxes in this area, if they are selected.

3. Choose the **OK** button in the **Project Properties** dialog box to save the changes made and to exit it; the **IEC Tag Mode Update** dialog box is displayed, as shown in Figure 12-43.

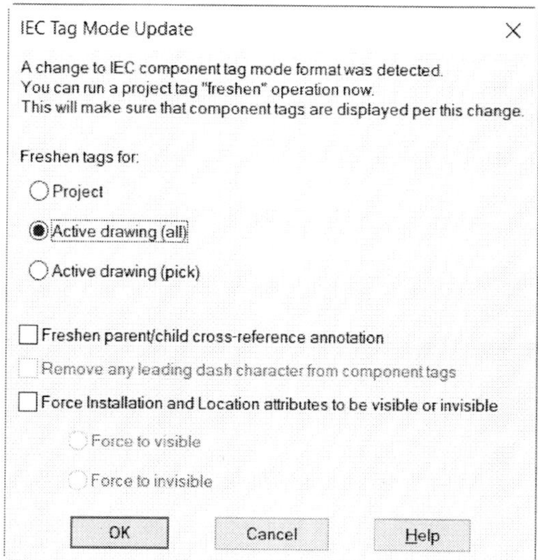


***Figure 12-43** The **IEC Tag Mode Update** dialog box*

4. Select the **Active drawing (all)** radio button and choose the **OK** button; the **QSAVE** message box is displayed.

5. Choose the **OK** button in the **QSAVE** message box and notice the changes in the drawing. Figure 12-44 shows the drawing *C12_tut02.dwg* after changing the project properties.

   Next, you need to revert back to the original settings again.

6. Right-click on the **CADCIM** project; a shortcut menu is displayed. Choose the **Properties** option from the shortcut menu; the **Project Properties** dialog box is displayed.

7. Choose the **Components** tab and then clear the **Combined Installation/Location tag mode** and **Format Installation/Location into tag** check boxes from the **Component TAG Options** area.

8. Choose the **OK** button in the **Project Properties** dialog box to save the changes made and to exit it.

## Saving the Drawing File

1. Choose **Save** from the **Application Menu** to save the drawing file *C12_tut02.dwg*.

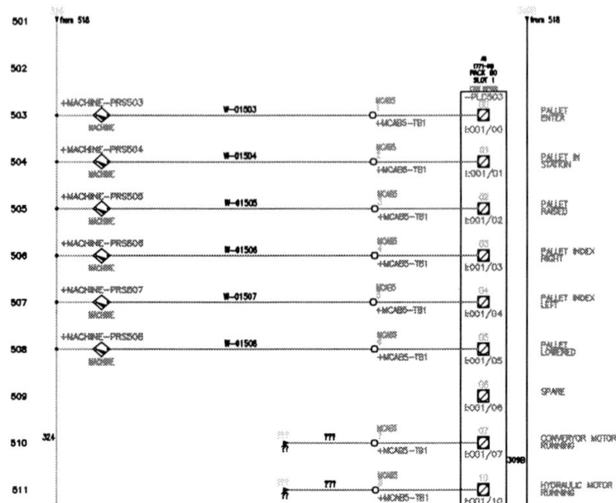

***Figure 12-44*** *Drawing after changing the project properties*

## Tutorial 3

In this tutorial, you will create a new drawing, set the schematic settings, insert a ladder, and save the drawing as a template file. Finally, you will create a new drawing using the template that has been created. **(Expected time: 20 min)**

The following steps are required to complete this tutorial:

a. Create a new drawing, define the schematic settings, and insert a ladder.
b. Save the drawing as *schematic_template.dwt* template.
c. Create the new drawing using the new template file.
d. Save the drawing.

## Creating a New Drawing, Defining Schematic Settings, and Inserting a Ladder

1. Activate the **CADCIM** project.

2. Create a drawing by choosing **New > Drawing** from the **Application Menu**; the **Select template** dialog box is displayed.

3. By default, the **ACAD_ELECTRICAL.dwt** is displayed in the **File name** edit box. If it is not displayed, select this template file from the **Select template** dialog box.

4. Choose the **Open** button; the drawing file is opened.

5. Choose the **Insert Ladder** tool from **Schematic > Insert Wires/Wire Numbers > Insert Ladder** drop-down; the **Alert** message box is displayed.

6. Choose the **OK** button in the **Alert** message box to insert the invisible wd_m block; the **Insert Ladder** dialog box is displayed.

7. Set the following parameters in this dialog box:

   **Width** = 5 **Spacing** = 1
   **1st Reference** = 1 **Rungs** = 6
   **Without reference numbers**: Clear this check box, if it is selected.
   **1 Phase**: Select this radio button **Yes**: Select this radio button

8. Choose the **OK** button in the **Insert Ladder** dialog box; you are prompted to specify the start position of the first rung.

9. Enter **10, 17.5** at the Command prompt and press ENTER; the ladder is inserted in the drawing.

## Saving the Template File

1. In order to save the drawing file as template, choose **Save** from the **Application Menu**; the **Save Drawing As** dialog box is displayed.

2. Select the **AutoCAD Drawing Template (.*dwt)** from the **Files of type** drop-down list and then enter **Schematic_Template** in the **File name** edit box.

3. Choose the **Save** button; the **Template Options** dialog box is displayed.

4. In this dialog box, enter **Schematic Template** in the **Description** area.

5. Choose the **OK** button in the **Template Options** dialog box; the drawing is saved as template drawing.

## Creating a New Drawing

1. Choose the **New Drawing** button from the **PROJECT MANAGER**; the **Create New Drawing** dialog box is displayed.

2. Enter **C12_tut03** in the **Name** edit box.

3. In order to specify the template drawing in the **Template** edit box, choose the **Browse** button on the right of the **Template** edit box; the **Select template** dialog box is displayed.

4. In this dialog box, select the **Schematic_Template** and choose the **Open** button, refer to Figure 12-45; the file name and location of template drawing is displayed in the **Template** edit box of the **Create New Drawing** dialog box.

5. Choose the **OK** button in the **Create New Drawing** dialog box; the **Apply Project Defaults to Drawing Settings** message box is displayed.

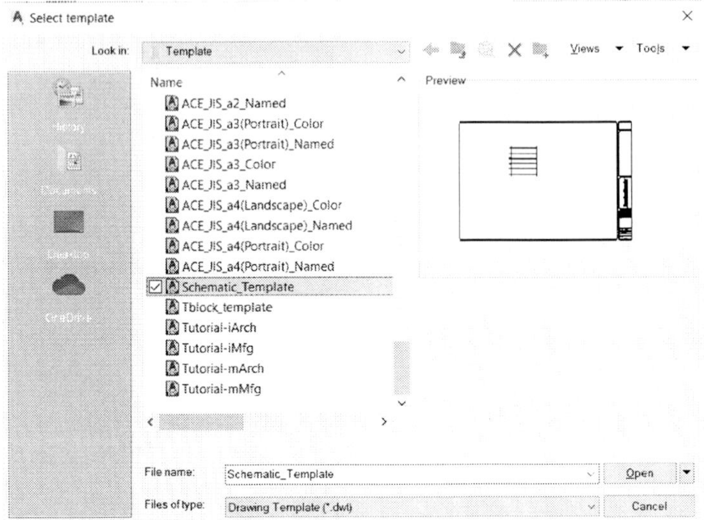


*Figure 12-45 The **Select template** dialog box*

6. Choose the **Yes** button in this dialog box; the *C12_tut03.dwg* file is created. Next, move it to the *TUTORIALS* subfolder.

## Saving the Drawing File

1. Choose **Save** from the **Application Menu** to save the drawing file *C12_tut03.dwg*.

# Tutorial 4

In this tutorial, you will create a project description line file (*.wdl*) and update the title block information of the given drawing accordingly. **(Expected time: 15 min)**

The following steps are required to complete this tutorial:

a. Open and save the drawing.
b. Add the active drawing to the **CADCIM** project list.
c. Change the LINEx values.
d. Update the title block information.
e. Save the drawing.

## Opening and Saving the Drawing

1. Open the *C12_tut01.dwg* drawing from the **CADCIM** project.

2. Save the drawing *C12_tut01.dwg* with the name *C12_tut04.dwg*, as discussed in the previous tutorials.

## Adding the Active Drawing to the CADCIM Project List

1. Add the drawing *C12_tut04.dwg* to the **CADCIM** project drawing list, as discussed.

**Note**

*If the **Update Terminal Associations** message box is displayed, choose the **Yes** button in it; C12_tut04.dwg is added to the TUTORIALS* subfolder of the **CADCIM** project.

2. Choose **Save** from the **Application Menu** to save the drawing.

## Changing the LINEx Values

1. To change the values of the lines of the **Project Description** dialog box, open a **Notepad** file and enter the following information in it:

   LINE1=Title 1:
   LINE2=Title 2:
   LINE3=Title 3:
   LINE4=Job Number:
   LINE5=Date:
   LINE6=Engineer:
   LINE7=Drawn By:
   LINE8=Checked By:
   LINE9=Scale:

2. Choose **File > Save As** from the menu bar; the **Save As** dialog box is displayed.

3. Browse to *C:\Users\User Name\Documents\Acade 2022\AeData\Proj\CADCIM* and enter **CADCIM_wdtitle.wdl** in the **File name** edit box and choose the **Save** button; the *CADCIM_wdtitle.wdl* file is saved in the respective project folder.

4. Right-click on the **CADCIM** project; a shortcut menu is displayed. Choose the **Descriptions** option from it; the **Project Description** dialog box is displayed, as shown in Figure 12-46. In this dialog box, notice that the line values have been changed to the specified values.

## Updating the Title Block

1. Right-click on the **CADCIM** project; a shortcut menu is displayed. Choose the **Title Block Update** option from it; the **Update Title Block** dialog box is displayed.

2. Select the check boxes shown in Figure 12-47.

3. Choose the **OK Active Drawing Only** button; the title block information is displayed in the title block of the drawing, as shown in Figure 12-48.

**Note**

*The **Project Description** dialog box displays the values shown in Figure 12-47 because you had specified these values in Tutorial 1 of Chapter 2. If these values are not displayed, you can enter the following information in the **Project Description** dialog box:*

*LINE1= CADCIM*
*LINE2= AutoCAD Electrical*
*LINE3= Sample Project*
*LINE4= 1*
*LINE5= 07/04/2021*
*LINE6= Sham*
*LINE7= John*
*LINE8= Crystal*
*LINE9= 1.00*

Project Description (for report headers and title block update)

| | | |
|---|---|---|
| Title 1: | CADCIM | ☑ in reports |
| Title 2: | AutoCAD Electrical | ☑ in reports |
| Title 3: | Sample Project | ☑ in reports |
| Job Number: | 1 | ☐ in reports |
| Date: | 07/04/2021 | ☐ in reports |
| Engineer: | Sham | ☐ in reports |
| Drawn By: | John | ☐ in reports |
| Checked By: | Crystal | ☐ in reports |
| Scale: | 1.00 | ☐ in reports |
| Line10 | | ☐ in reports |
| Line11 | | ☐ in reports |
| Line12 | | ☐ in reports |

OK | Cancel | |< | < | > | >|

***Figure 12-46** The **Project Description** dialog box*

Update Title Block

Select Line(s) to Update (Project Description Lines)

| | | |
|---|---|---|
| ☑ | Title 1: | CADCIM |
| ☑ | Title 2: | AutoCAD Electrical |
| ☑ | Title 3: | Sample Project |
| ☑ | Job Number: | 1 |
| ☑ | Date: | 25/4/2020 |
| ☑ | Engineer: | Sham |
| ☑ | Drawn By: | John |
| ☑ | Checked By: | Crystal |
| ☑ | Scale: | 1.00 |
| ☐ | LINE10 | (blank) |
| ☐ | LINE11 | (blank) |
| ☐ | LINE12 | (blank) |

Select All | Clear All

***Figure 12-47** Partial view of the **Update Title Block** dialog box*

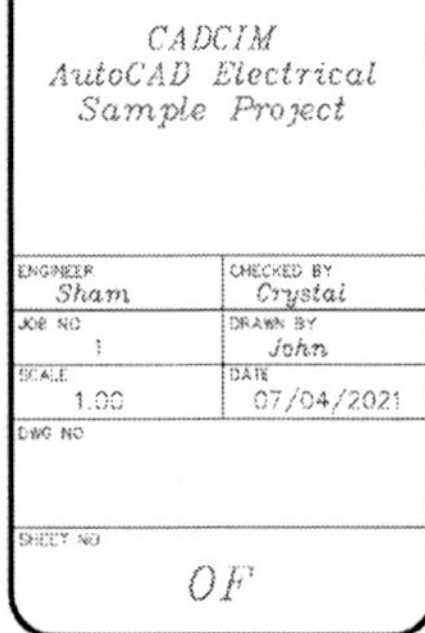


***Figure 12-48** The title block information*

## Saving the Drawing File

1. Choose **File > Save** from the menu bar to save the drawing file.

# Tutorial 5

In this tutorial, you will create a new block with attributes defined in it. Next, you will create a template using this block. You will also create a new drawing using this template and then set up the title block using method 1 and update the same for this drawing, refer to Figure 12-49.

**(Expected time: 30 min)**

***Figure 12-49*** *Updated title block*

The following steps are required to complete this tutorial:

a. Create a new block with attributes.
b. Create a new template file.
c. Create a new drawing.
d. Set up the title block.
e. Update the title block.
f. Save the drawing.

## Creating a New Block with Attributes

1. Make sure the CADCIM project is activated. Open any of the tutorial files in this project. (for ex: *c02tut01.dwg*)

2. Delete all the content, if any, and the title block from this drawing.

3. Choose the **Rectangle** tool from the **Draw** panel of the **Home** tab; you are prompted to specify the first corner point. Enter **F** at the Command prompt; you are prompted to specify the fillet radius. Enter **1** at the Command prompt. Next, you are prompted to specify the first corner point. Enter **0,0** at the Command prompt; you are prompted to specify the other corner point. Now, enter **30,22** at the Command Prompt; a rectangle is created with fillet corners, refer to Figure 12-50.

4. Similarly, draw two more rectangles with same fillet radius and corner points as mentioned below, refer to Figure 12-50.

| | First corner point | Second corner point |
|---|---|---|
| Rectangle 2 | 30.25,22 | 34,10 |
| Rectangle 3 | 30.25,9.75 | 34,0 |

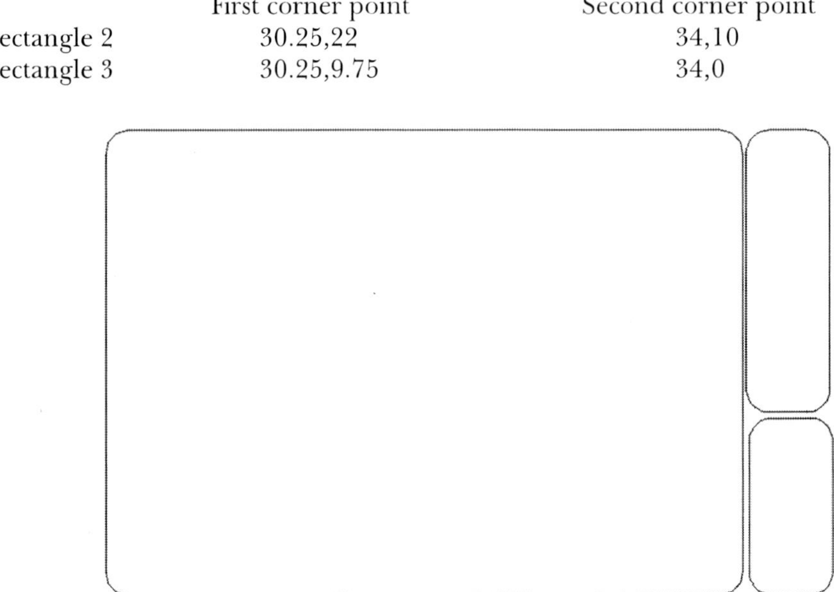

***Figure 12-50*** *Two more rectangles created*

5. Choose the **Multiline Text** tool from the **Text** drop-down in the **Annotation** panel of the **Home** tab; you are prompted to specify the first corner. Enter **32,11** at the Command Prompt and then enter **R** at the Command prompt; you are prompted to specify the rotation angle. Enter **90** at the Command prompt.

6. Enter **H** at the Command prompt; you are prompted to specify height. Enter **0.6** at the Command prompt; Now, you are prompted to specify the opposite corner. Enter **33,21** at the Command Prompt; a text box appears on the screen. Enter **CADCIM Technologies** in this text box.

7. Select **CADCIM Technologies** in the text box and then select **Times New Roman** from the **Text Style** drop-down list in the **Formatting** panel of the **Home** tab. Also, choose the **B** button from the **Formatting** panel. Now, click anywhere in the viewport; the text **CADCIM Technologies** is displayed vertically. Note that you may have to vary the text height as per the dimension of the upper rectangle. Next, choose the **Move** tool from the **Modify** panel and align it at the center in the upper rectangle, refer to Figure 12-51.

8. Choose the **Line** tool from the **Draw** panel of the **Home** tab and draw seven lines in the lower rectangle, as shown in Figure 12-52.

9. Choose the **Multiline Text** tool from the **Text** drop-down in the **Annotation** panel of the **Home** tab and enter **Engineer**, **Drawn By**, **Checked By**, **Scale**, **Drawing no**, **Sheet** in the lower rectangle, as shown in Figure 12-53.

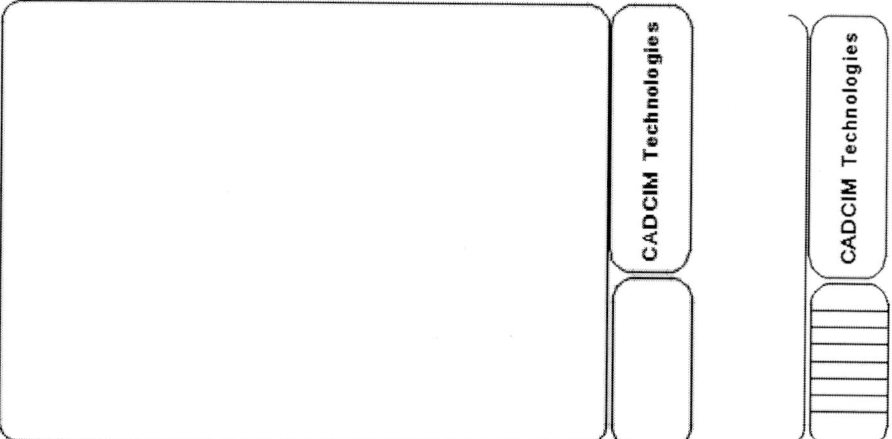


***Figure 12-51*** *Text aligned in the upper rectangle*

***Figure 12-52*** *Seven Lines drawn in the lower rectangle*

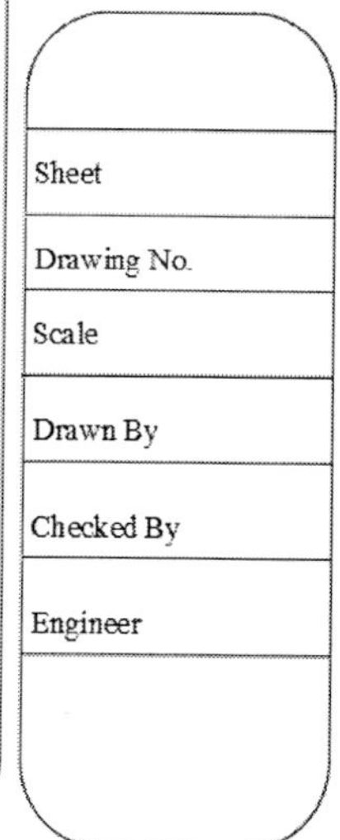


***Figure 12-53*** *Text entered in the lower rectangle*

Assume the text height as per the distance between the lines drawn.

Next, you need to define attributes for the block.

10. Choose the down arrow in the **Block** panel of the **Home** tab and then choose the **Define Attributes** tool; the **Attribute Definition** dialog box is displayed.

11. In this dialog box, make sure the **Invisible** check box is cleared in the **Mode** area. Enter **Engineer** in the **Tag** edit box of the **Attribute** area.

12. In the **Text Settings** area, select **ITALIC** from the **Text Style** drop-down list. Next, enter the text height as per the distance between the lines drawn in the **Text height** edit box. Also, make sure that the **Specify on-screen** check box is selected in the **Insertion Point** area and then choose **OK**; the *ENGINEER* attribute is attached to the cursor. Next, place the *ENGINEER* attribute next to the **Engineer** text, refer to Figure 12-54.

13. Similarly, add 7 more attributes to the block, as shown in Figure 12-54.

14. Choose the **Create** tool from the **Block** panel of the **Home** tab; the **Block Definition** dialog box is displayed. In this dialog box, enter **Tblock** in the **Name** edit box and choose the **Select objects** button; you are prompted to select the objects for the block. Select all the objects in the viewport (including attributes) and press ENTER. Next, choose **OK** from the dialog box; the selected objects are converted into a single block named **Tblock**.

## Creating a New Template File

1. Choose **Save As** from the **Application Menu**; the **Save Drawing As** dialog box is displayed.

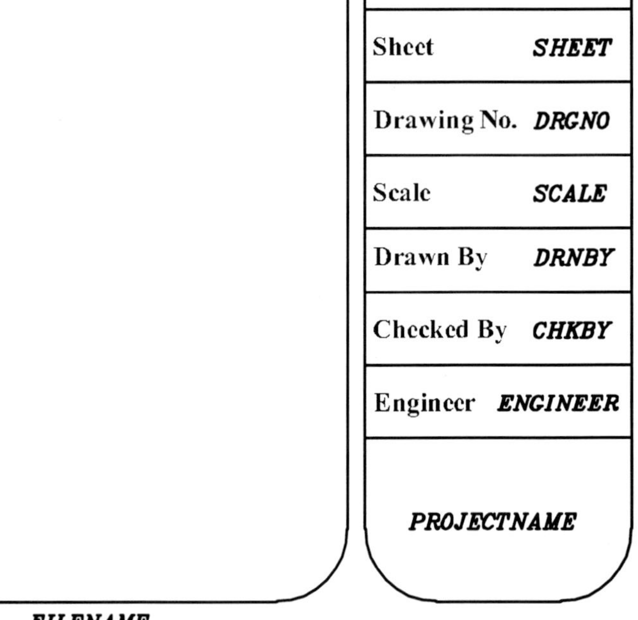


*Figure 12-54 Seven more attributes added*

2. Select **AutoCAD Drawing Template (*.dwt)** from the **Files of type** drop-down list and enter **Tblock_template** in the **File name** edit box. Next, choose **Save**; the **Template Options** dialog box is displayed. Enter **New CADCIM Template** in the **Description** area and choose **OK**; the drawing is saved as *TBlock_template.dwt* file.

## Creating a New Drawing File

1. Choose the **New Drawing** button from the **PROJECT MANAGER**; the **Create New Drawing** dialog box is displayed. In this dialog box, enter **C12_tut05** in the **Name** edit box.

2. Choose the **Browse** button next to the **Template** edit box; the **Select Template** dialog box is displayed. In this dialog box, select **Tblock_template** and then choose **Open** to close the dialog box.

3. In the **Sheet Values** area, enter **1205** in the **Drawing** edit box and enter **5** in the **Sheet** edit box. Next, choose **OK** from the **Create New Drawing** dialog box; the *C12_tut05.dwg* is created and the **Apply Project Defaults to Drawings** message box is displayed. Choose **Yes** from this message box; the **AutoCAD Message** message box is displayed, as shown in Figure 12-55. Choose **OK** in this message box.

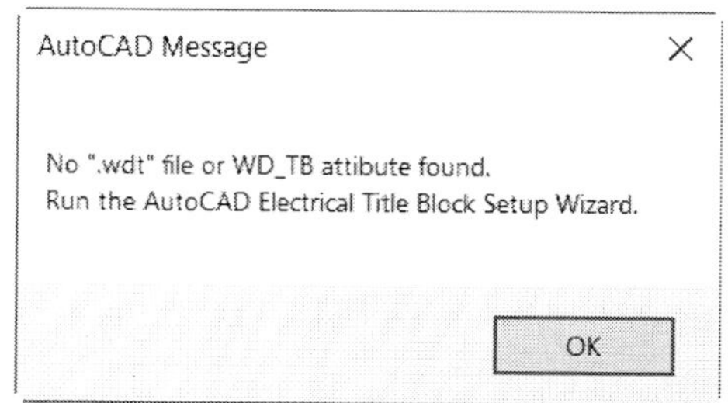


***Figure 12-55*** *The **AutoCAD Message** message box*

## Setting Up the Title Block

1. Choose the **Title Block Setup** tool from the **Other Tools** panel of the **Project** tab; the **Setup Title Block Update** dialog box is displayed. In this dialog box, make sure the **<Project>.WDT file** radio button is selected and then choose **OK**; the **Enter Block Name** dialog box is displayed.

2. In this dialog box, choose the **Pick Block** button; the **Enter Block Name** dialog box disappears temporarily and you are prompted to select objects.

3. Select the title block in the drawing and press ENTER; the **Enter Block Name** dialog box is displayed again and Tblock is displayed in the edit box, as shown in Figure 12-56. Next, choose **OK** in this dialog box; the **Title Block Setup** dialog box is displayed, as shown in Figure 12-57.

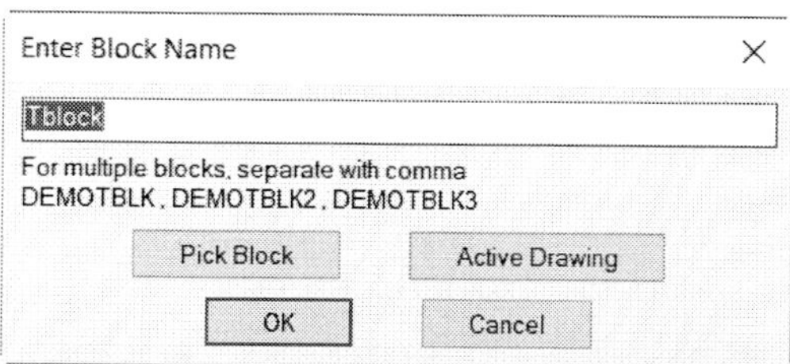


***Figure 12-56*** *The Tblock displayed in the edit box of the **Enter Block Name** dialog box*

4. In this dialog box, select **PROJECTNAME** from the **Attribute** drop-down list located at the left of the text **Line 1**, as shown in Figure 12-58.

*Figure 12-57 The **Title Block Setup** dialog box*

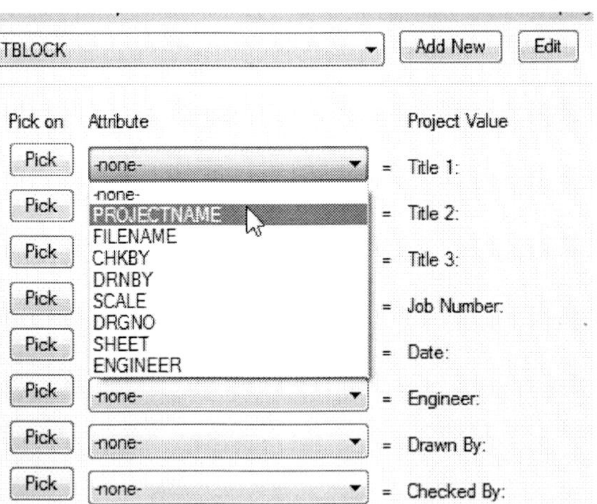


*Figure 12-58 Selecting **PROJECTNAME** from the **Attribute** drop-down list*

5. Similarly, select **ENGINEER** from the **Attribute** drop-down list located at the left of the text **Line 6**, select **DRNBY** from the **Attribute** drop-down list located at the left of the text **Line 7**, select **CHKBY** from the **Attribute** drop-down list located at the left of the text **Line 8**, and select **SCALE** from the **Attribute** drop-down list located at the left of the text **Line 9**, as shown in Figure 12-59.

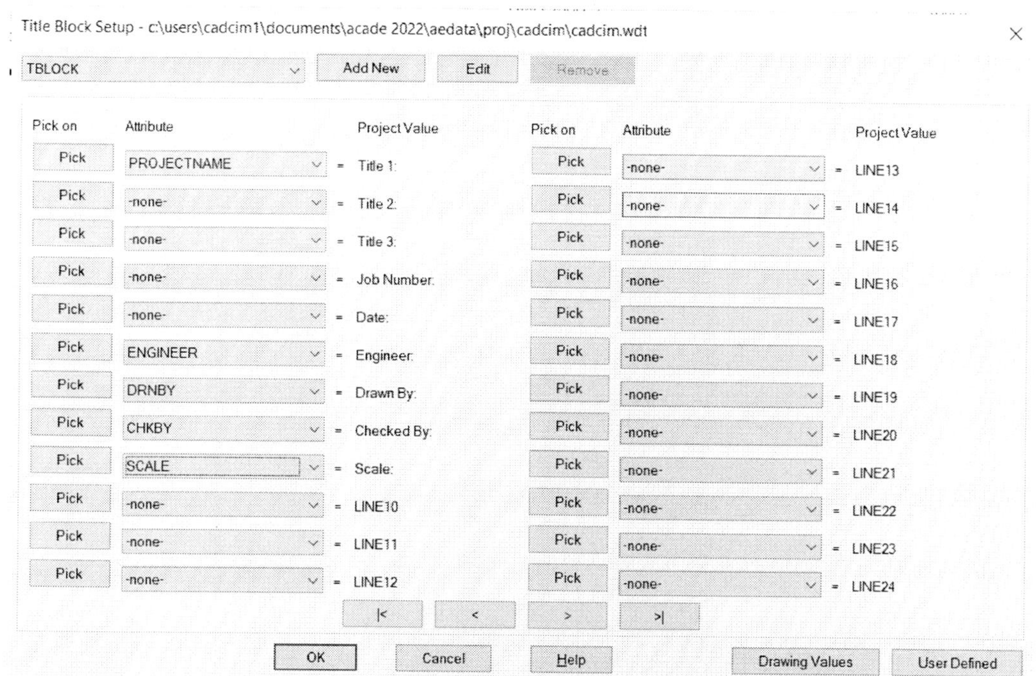


*Figure 12-59 Attributes selected from the **Attribute** drop-down list*

6. Choose the **Drawing Values** button; the modified **Title Block Setup** dialog box is displayed, as shown in Figure 12-60.

7. Select **DRGNO** from the **Attribute** drop-down list located at the left of **Drawing (% D value)**. Similarly, select **FILENAME** from the **Attribute** drop-down list located at the left of **Full Filename** and select **SHEET** from the **Attribute** drop-down list located at the left of **Sheet (%S value)**. Now, choose **OK** to close the dialog box.

## Updating the Title Block

1. Choose the **Title Block Update** tool from the **Other Tools** panel of the **Project** tab; the **Update Title Block** dialog box is displayed.

2. In this dialog box, select the **Title 1**, **Engineer**, **Drawn By**, **Checked By**, and **Scale** check boxes from the **Select Line(s) to Update (Project Description Lines)** area.

3. Select the **Full Filename**, **Drawing (% D Value)**, and **Sheet (%S Value)** check boxes from the **Select line(s) to update (these are per-drawing values)** area, as shown in Figure 12-61. Next, choose the **OK Active Drawing Only** button; the title block of the *C12_tut05.dwg* is modified, as shown in Figure 12-62.

## Saving the Drawing File

1. Choose **File > Save** from the menu bar to save the drawing file.

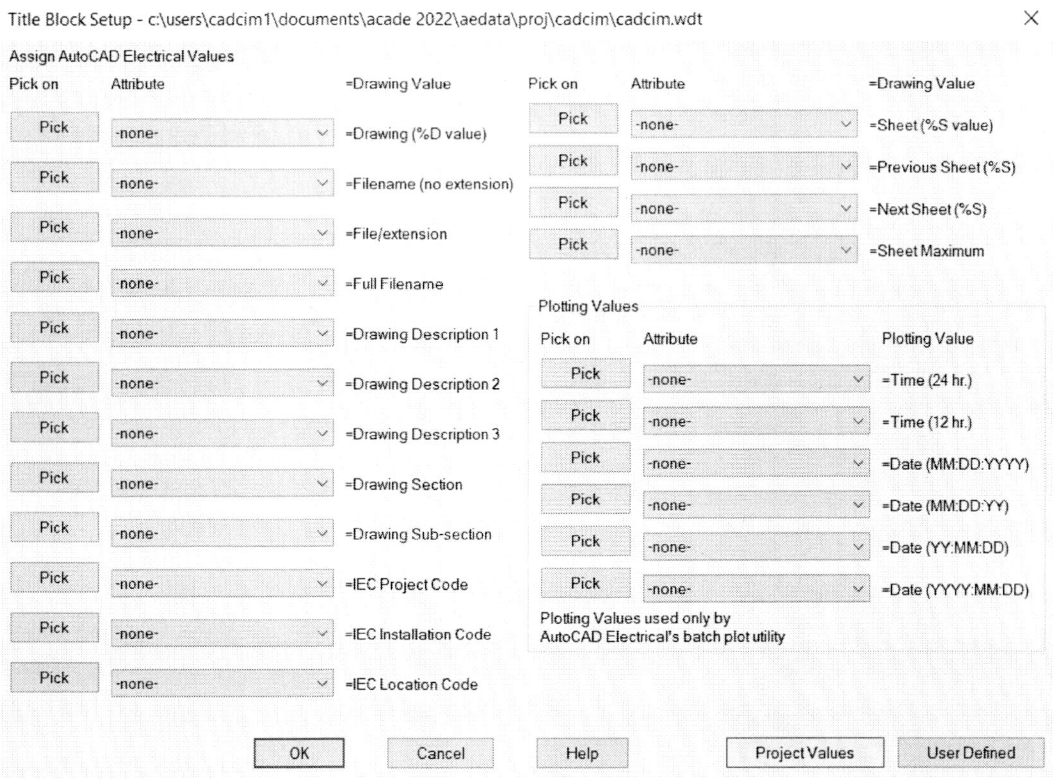

Title Block Setup - c:\users\cadcim1\documents\acade 2022\aedata\proj\cadcim\cadcim.wdt

Assign AutoCAD Electrical Values

| Pick on | Attribute | =Drawing Value |
|---|---|---|
| Pick | -none- | =Drawing (%D value) |
| Pick | -none- | =Filename (no extension) |
| Pick | -none- | =File/extension |
| Pick | -none- | =Full Filename |
| Pick | -none- | =Drawing Description 1 |
| Pick | -none- | =Drawing Description 2 |
| Pick | -none- | =Drawing Description 3 |
| Pick | -none- | =Drawing Section |
| Pick | -none- | =Drawing Sub-section |
| Pick | -none- | =IEC Project Code |
| Pick | -none- | =IEC Installation Code |
| Pick | -none- | =IEC Location Code |

| Pick on | Attribute | =Drawing Value |
|---|---|---|
| Pick | -none- | =Sheet (%S value) |
| Pick | -none- | =Previous Sheet (%S) |
| Pick | -none- | =Next Sheet (%S) |
| Pick | -none- | =Sheet Maximum |

Plotting Values

| Pick on | Attribute | Plotting Value |
|---|---|---|
| Pick | -none- | =Time (24 hr.) |
| Pick | -none- | =Time (12 hr.) |
| Pick | -none- | =Date (MM:DD:YYYY) |
| Pick | -none- | =Date (MM:DD:YY) |
| Pick | -none- | =Date (YY:MM:DD) |
| Pick | -none- | =Date (YYYY:MM:DD) |

Plotting Values used only by AutoCAD Electrical's batch plot utility

OK | Cancel | Help | Project Values | User Defined

*Figure 12-60 The modified* ***Title Block Setup*** *dialog box*

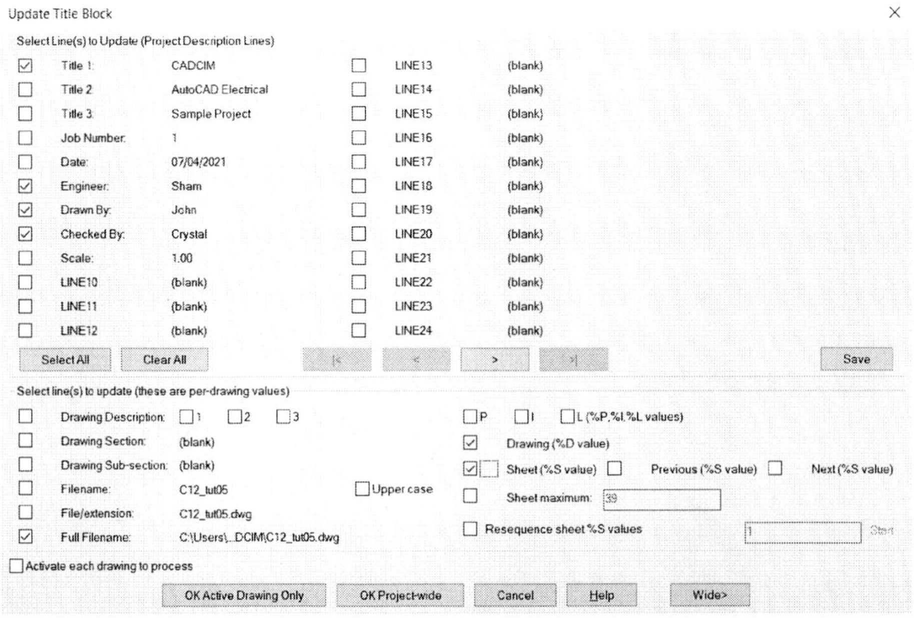

Update Title Block

Select Line(s) to Update (Project Description Lines)

| ☑ | Title 1: | CADCIM | ☐ | LINE13 | (blank) |
|---|---|---|---|---|---|
| ☐ | Title 2: | AutoCAD Electrical | ☐ | LINE14 | (blank) |
| ☐ | Title 3: | Sample Project | ☐ | LINE15 | (blank) |
| ☐ | Job Number: | 1 | ☐ | LINE16 | (blank) |
| ☐ | Date: | 07/04/2021 | ☐ | LINE17 | (blank) |
| ☑ | Engineer: | Sham | ☐ | LINE18 | (blank) |
| ☑ | Drawn By: | John | ☐ | LINE19 | (blank) |
| ☑ | Checked By: | Crystal | ☐ | LINE20 | (blank) |
| ☐ | Scale: | 1.00 | ☐ | LINE21 | (blank) |
| ☐ | LINE10 | (blank) | ☐ | LINE22 | (blank) |
| ☐ | LINE11 | (blank) | ☐ | LINE23 | (blank) |
| ☐ | LINE12 | (blank) | ☐ | LINE24 | (blank) |

Select All | Clear All | \|< | < | > | >\| | Save

Select line(s) to update (these are per-drawing values)

☐ Drawing Description: ☐1 ☐2 ☐3
☐ Drawing Section: (blank)
☐ Drawing Sub-section: (blank)
☐ Filename: C12_tut05 ☐Upper case
☐ File/extension: C12_tut05.dwg
☑ Full Filename: C:\Users\...DCIM\C12_tut05.dwg

☐P ☐I ☐L (%P,%I,%L values)
☑ Drawing (%D value)
☑☐ Sheet (%S value) ☐ Previous (%S value) ☐ Next (%S value)
☐ Sheet maximum: 39
☐ Resequence sheet %S values 1 Start

☐Activate each drawing to process

OK Active Drawing Only | OK Project-wide | Cancel | Help | Wide>

*Figure 12-61 The* ***Update Title Block*** *dialog box*

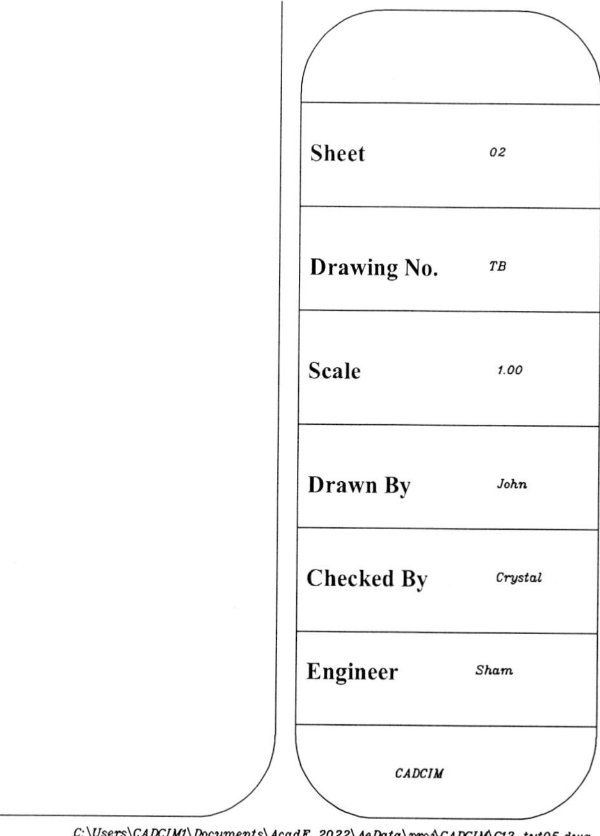


***Figure 12-62** The title Block updated*

## Self-Evaluation Test

**Answer the following questions and then compare them to those given at the end of this chapter:**

1. Which of the following dialog boxes is displayed when you right-click on an active project and then choose the **Properties** option from the shortcut menu?

   (a) **Drawing Properties** (b) **Project Properties**
   (c) **Properties** (d) None of these

2. The __________ option is used to plot the full drawing set of a project or the selected drawings.

3. The __________ button is used to execute the pending updates on the drawings of an active project.

4. The __________ can be edited by using **Wordpad** and **Notepad**.

5. In the __________ area of the **Project Properties** dialog box, you can specify format for the reference numbers of a ladder.

6. In the **Project Properties** dialog box, there are __________ different component cross-reference display format styles.

7. In the **Project Properties** dialog box, you can define the settings for a new project. (T/F)

8. In the **Drawing Properties** dialog box, you can define the settings for a new drawing and project. (T/F)

9. The project files are created and maintained using the **PROJECT MANAGER**. (T/F)

10. The **Title Block Update** option is used to update the attribute values of the title blocks. (T/F)

## Review Questions

**Answer the following questions:**

1. Which of the following reference files, if saved, in the project folder will change the LINEx label description of the **Project Description** dialog box?

   (a) .WDL (b) .LOC
   (c) .WDD (d) .INST

2. Which of the following dialog boxes is displayed when you right-click on an active project and choose the **Title Block Update** option from the shortcut menu displayed?

   (a) **Setup Title Block Update** (b) **Title Block Setup**
   (c) **Update Title Block** (d) None of these

3. Which of the following libraries is displayed in the **Library and Icon Menu Paths** area of the **Project Properties** dialog box?

   (a) Schematic (b) Footprint
   (c) Both (a) and (b) (d) Only (a)

4. Which of the following buttons, if chosen, in the **Update other drawings?** message box saves the required information in the project task list?

   (a) **OK** (b) **Skip**
   (c) **Task** (d) **All**

5. The **Project Task List** button is used to execute the pending updates on the drawing files of a project. (T/F)

6. The values of the drawing properties are not stored in the WD_M block in a drawing file. (T/F)

7. The template files have *.dwt* extension. (T/F)

8. The %S in the **Drawing Properties** or **Project Properties** dialog box represents the sheet value. (T/F)

9. You cannot change the settings of a drawing within a project. (T/F)

# EXERCISES

## Exercise 1

Open the *DEMO05.DWG* drawing file from the **CADCIM** project and save it as *C12_exer01.dwg*. Also, add this drawing file to the **NEW_PROJECT** project. Change the component tag format of the drawing as %N-%F. Also, update it using the **Update/Retag** tool.

**(Expected time: 15 min)**

## Exercise 2

Create a new drawing with the name *C12_exer02.dwg* in the **NEW_PROJECT** project and then change the default settings of the drawing in the **Drawing Properties** dialog box as: **Sheet:** = 1 in the **Sheet Values** area of the **Drawing Settings** tab; **Spacing** = 1; **Width** = 5 in the **Ladder Defaults** area of the **Drawing Format** tab. Also, change the line reference numbers of the ladder in the **Drawing Properties** dialog box and insert a ladder with 5 rungs with 1st reference number as 10, as shown in Figure 12-63. **(Expected time: 15 min)**

***Figure 12-63** Ladder diagram for Exercise 2*

## Exercise 3

Create a panel template as *Panel_Template.dwt*. Also, insert the following enclosures in it: MANUFACTURER = RITTAL, TYPE = OUTDOOR ENCLOSURES, STYLE = NEMA 3R, and catalog = 9783040. Figure 12-64 shows the *panel_template.dwt* template file.

**(Expected time: 20 min)**

**Hint**: Change the scale of the panel in the **Insert Footprint** dialog box to 0.2.

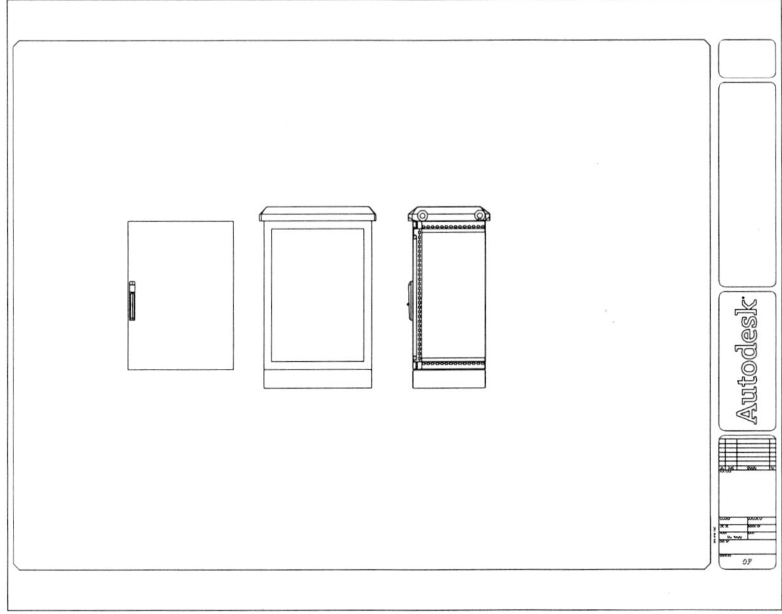


*Figure 12-64 Panel template for Exercise 3*

## Answers to Self-Evaluation Test

**1.** b, **2. Plot Project**, **3. Project Task List**, **4.** reference files, **5. Format Referencing**, **6.** three, **7.** T, **8.** F, **9.** T, **10.** T

# Chapter 13

# Creating Symbols

## Learning Objectives

**After completing this chapter, you will be able to:**

- *Create symbols*
- *Understand the naming convention of symbols*
- *Customize the icon menu*
- *Use the Mark/Verify, Export to Spreadsheet, and Update from Spreadsheet tools*

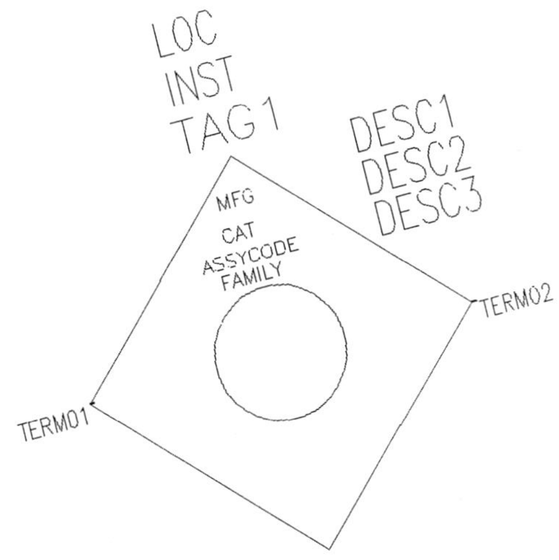

# INTRODUCTION

In this chapter, you will learn to create symbols for the components, terminals, panel components, and so on and also about their naming convention. You will also learn to customize the icon menu. Later in this chapter, you will learn about some miscellaneous tools such as **Mark/Verify**, **Export to Spreadsheet**, and **Update from Spreadsheet**.

# CREATING SYMBOLS

| | |
|---|---|
| **Ribbon:** | Schematic > Other Tools > Symbol Builder drop-down > Symbol Builder |
| **Toolbar:** | ACE:Main Electrical 2 > Symbol Builder<br>or ACE:Miscellaneous > Symbol Builder |
| **Menu:** | Components> Symbol Library > Symbol Builder |
| **Command:** | AESYMBUILDER |

The **Symbol Builder** tool is used to create new symbols such as filters, drives, controllers, and so on, or convert the existing symbols as per requirement. Using this tool, you can create the symbols easily and quickly. You can also create the electrical symbols using the AutoCAD tools but that takes more time. Also, this tool is used to convert the existing non-AutoCAD Electrical symbols to the AutoCAD Electrical symbols.

The symbols that you create using this tool will be compatible with AutoCAD Electrical and they will be displayed in the schematic reports. To create a symbol, choose the **Symbol Builder** tool from the **Symbol Builder** drop-down in the **Other Tools** panel of the **Schematic** tab, as shown in Figure 13-1; the **Select Symbol / Objects** dialog box will be displayed, as shown in Figure 13-2.

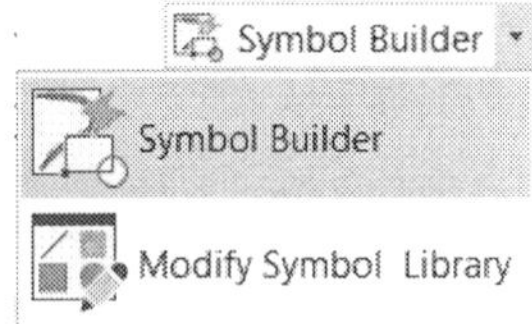


***Figure 13-1** The **Symbol Builder** drop-down*

Using this dialog box, you can create a new symbol or edit an existing symbol. Different areas and options in this dialog box are discussed next.

## Name

The **Name** drop-down list consists of the block definitions that are present within the active drawing. You can also specify the block or the drawing by choosing the **Browse** button. The preview of the selected drawing file will be displayed in the **Preview** area and the other options in the **Select from drawing** area of the dialog box will be deactivated.

## Objects Area

The options in this area are used to select the objects that you need to create or edit.

If you select the **Specify on screen** check box, you can select the objects after choosing the **OK** button in the dialog box. After selecting the objects, press ENTER; the **Symbol Builder Attribute Editor** palette, the **BLOCK AUTHORING PALETTES** palette, and the **Block Editor** environment will be displayed. However, if you choose the **Select objects** button, you can select the objects directly. Also, the preview of the selected object will be displayed in the **Preview** area. Note that the number of selected objects will be displayed under the **Select objects** button.

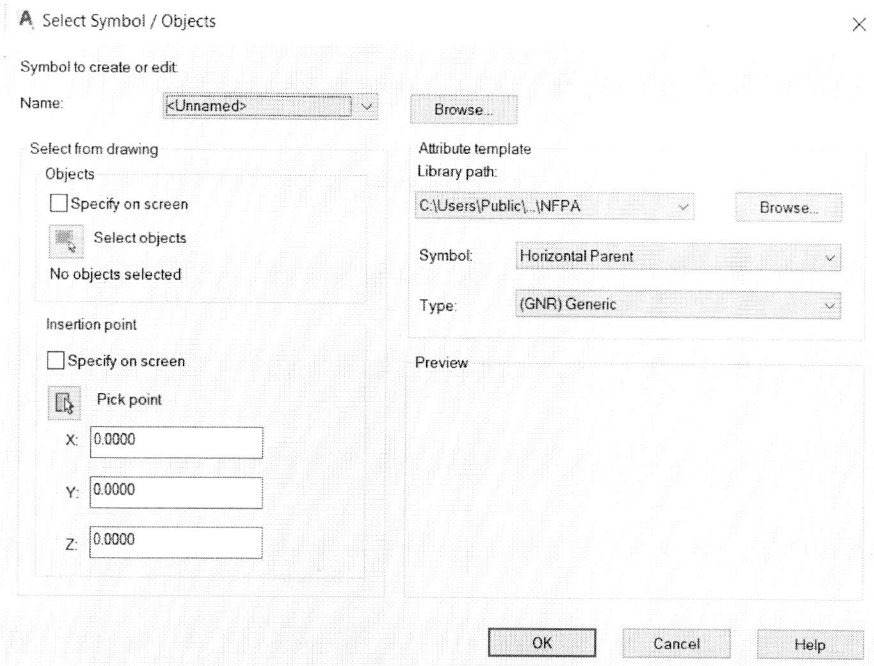


*Figure 13-2 The **Select Symbol / Objects** dialog box*

**Note**

*The objects can be attributes, existing block, attribute definitions, and any symbol graphics.*

## Insertion point Area

The options in this area are used to specify the insertion point for the symbol. Specify the insertion point for the symbol in the **X**, **Y**, **Z** edit boxes. Alternatively, you can specify the insertion point by choosing the **Pick point** button. You can also select the **Specify on screen** check box to specify the insertion point for the symbol on screen after choosing the **OK** button. Note that when you select the **Specify on screen** check box, the **Pick point** button and the **X**, **Y**, and **Z** edit boxes will be disabled.

## Attribute template Area

The options in this area are used to specify the library path, symbol category, and type for the attribute template. The options in this area are discussed next.

### Library path

You can select the library path for the attribute template from the **Library Path** drop-down list. This drop-down list consists of the list of location of the symbol builder attribute template. By default, the *C:\Users\Public\Doc...\NFPA* library path is selected. You can also specify the library path by choosing the **Browse** button displayed on the right of this drop-down list. Note that if you want to create one-line symbol, select the folder with the name '1-', which is under the schematic library folder.

### Symbol

The options in the **Symbol** drop-down list are used to specify the symbol category. From this drop-down list, you can select the orientation for the symbol and also specify whether it is schematic or panel. You can also select a category such as parent, child, terminal, footprint, nameplate, and so on for the symbol. By default, the Horizontal Parent is selected in this drop-down list.

### Type

The options in the **Type** drop-down list are used to specify the type of the attribute template. By default, the **GNR(Generic)** option is selected in this drop-down list.

## Preview Area

The **Preview** area is used to display the preview of the block that you have selected from the **Name** drop-down list or the preview of the objects that you have selected from the drawing.

After specifying the required options in the **Select Symbol/Objects** dialog box, choose the **OK** button; the **Symbol Builder** environment and the **Symbol Builder Attribute Editor** palette will be invoked. Next, choose the **Block Editor** tab; the **Block Editor** environment will be invoked, refer to Figure 13-3. The drawing area of the **Block Editor** environment has a dull background which is known as the authoring area. In addition to the authoring area, the **BLOCK AUTHORING PALETTES** is provided in the **Block Editor** environment.

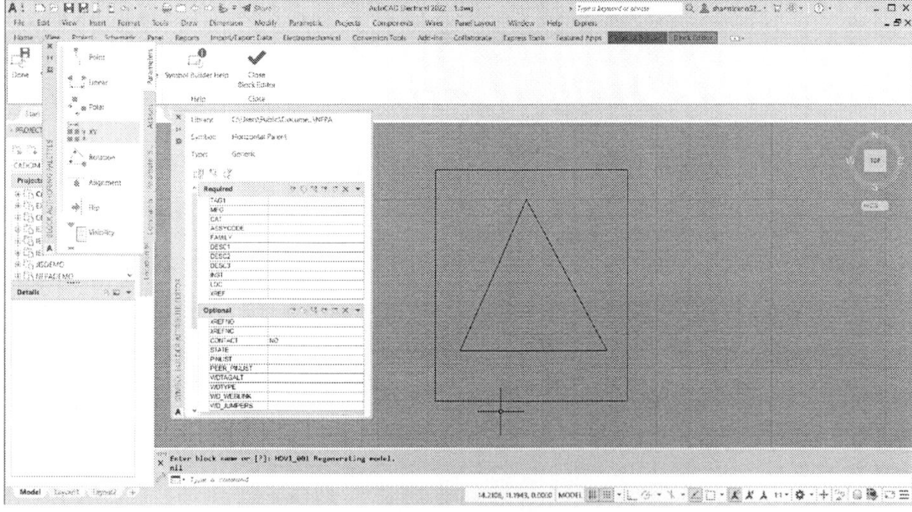

*Figure 13-3 The **Block Editor** environment*

**Note**

*In order to learn more about the AutoCAD **Block Editor** toolbar and **BLOCK AUTHORING Palettes**, refer to **AutoCAD 2022: A Problem-Solving Approach, Basic and Intermediate, 28th Edition** textbook by Prof. Sham Tickoo.*

The **Symbol Builder Attribute Editor** palette is shown in Figure 13-4. This palette is used to insert, add, modify, remove, and delete attributes. Notice that the library path of the attribute template, symbol category, and type of the attribute template are displayed on the upper left corner of the **Symbol Builder Attribute Editor** palette. Different tools and rollouts in this palette are discussed next.

## Common Tools

The **Symbol Builder Attribute Editor** palette consists of tools that are common to any symbol type. These tools are shown in Figure 13-5 and are discussed next.

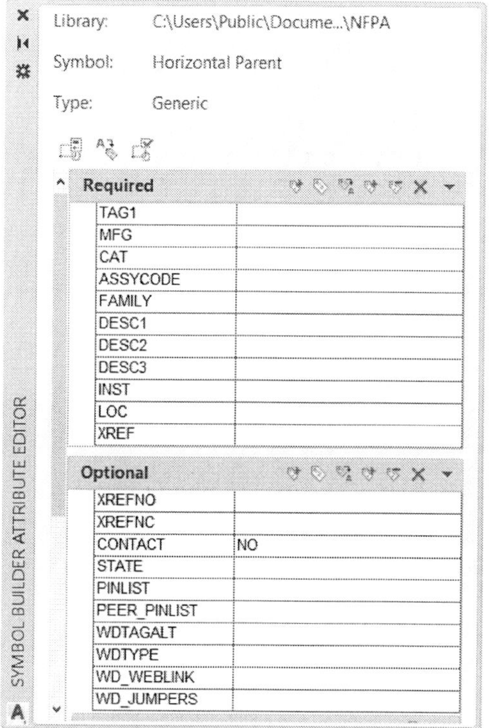


*Figure 13-4 The **Symbol Builder Attribute Editor** palette*

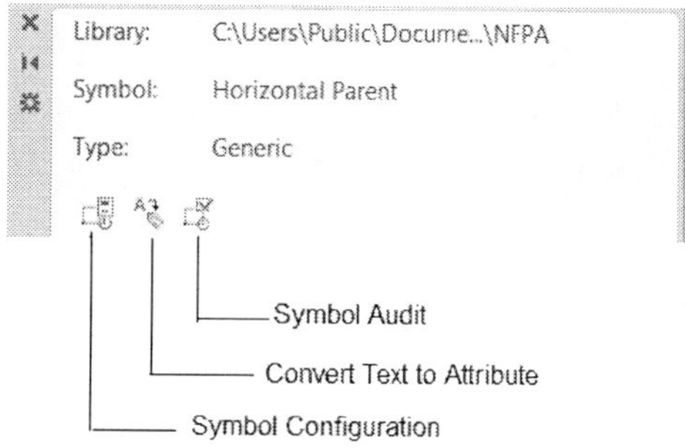


*Figure 13-5 The common tools of the **Symbol Builder Attribute Editor** palette*

### Symbol Configuration

The **Symbol Configuration** tool is used to redefine the attribute template library path, symbol category, symbol type, and insertion point. To define a new attribute template or insertion point, choose the **Symbol Configuration** tool from the **Symbol Builder Attribute Editor** palette; the **Symbol Configuration** dialog box will be displayed, as shown in Figure 13-6. The options in the **Symbol Configuration** dialog box are similar to that of the **Select Symbol / Objects** dialog box and have been discussed earlier in this chapter.

### Convert Text to Attribute

The **Convert Text to Attribute** tool is used to convert the existing text into the AutoCAD Electrical attribute. Using this tool, you can map the text to attributes of the selected symbol type. To convert the existing text into AutoCAD Electrical attribute, choose the **Convert Text to Attribute** button; the **Convert Text To Attribute** dialog box will be displayed, as shown in Figure 13-7. Note that this dialog box will be displayed only if there is an existing text available in the **Block Editor** environment. The options in the **Convert Text To Attribute** dialog box are discussed next.

*Figure 13-6 The **Symbol Configuration** dialog box*

*Figure 13-7 The **Convert Text To Attribute** dialog box*

The **Text** column displays the existing text present in the authoring area. The **Attribute** column displays only the list of attributes that are present in the **Required**, **Optional**, **POS**, and **RATING** rollouts of the **Symbol Builder Attribute Editor** palette such as TAG1, MFG, CAT, and so on, and are not present on the symbol.

Now, to convert the text into the attribute, select the text from the **Text** column and choose the **->** button, which points toward the attribute; the text present in the **Text** column will be greyed out and you will notice that it will automatically be displayed in the corresponding row of the **Symbol Builder Attribute Editor** palette. When you are finished with the conversion process, choose the **Done** button to exit the **Convert Text To Attribute** dialog box; the text present in the authoring area of the **Block Editor** environment will be changed to the selected attribute.

**Note**

*If the text present in the **Block Editor** environment has already been converted to the AutoCAD Electrical attributes or if there is no text that needs to be converted to the AutoCAD Electrical and you choose the **Convert Text to Attribute** button, the **Convert Text to Attribute - No Valid Text / Attribute** message box will be displayed. This message box depicts that "the drawing should have text entities or non-AutoCAD Electrical attributes and there should be at least one AutoCAD Electrical attribute which is not yet inserted in the drawing".*

## Symbol Audit

The **Symbol Audit** tool is used for auditing the symbol. The audit information includes the information of attributes and symbol name. The information of symbol auditing is based on the type of the symbol. Using this tool, you can check the errors found in a symbol. To audit a symbol, choose the **Symbol Audit** tool; the **Symbol Audit** dialog box will be displayed, as shown in Figure 13-8. This dialog box displays the number of errors that are found in the symbol in brackets in front of each category. If OK is displayed in front of the category, it implies that no errors have been found in the particular category. The categories present in the tree structure of the **Symbol Audit** dialog box are discussed next.

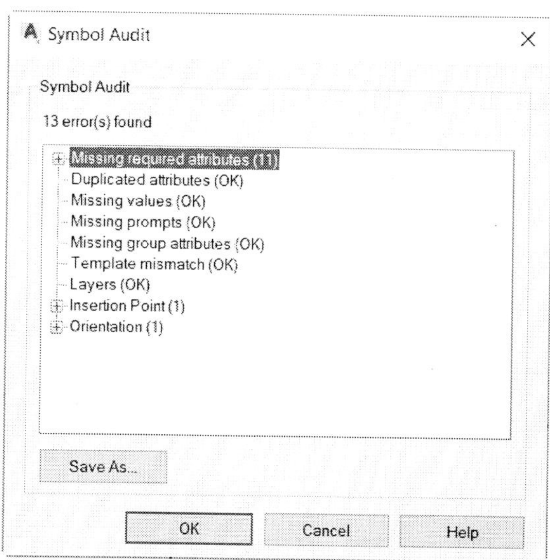

*Figure 13-8 The **Symbol Audit** dialog box*

The **Missing required attributes** category displays the attributes that are present in the **Required** rollout but are not present on the symbol.

The **Duplicated attributes** category displays the attributes that have duplicated tags and are present on the symbol.

The **Missing values** category displays the attributes with default values that are defined on the attribute template but are not present on the symbol.

The **Missing prompts** category displays the attributes with default prompts that are defined on the attribute template but are not present on the symbol.

The **Missing group attributes** category displays the attributes that are missing from common group such as MFG and CAT.

The **Template mismatch** category displays the list of attributes that exist on the attribute template but are removed from the list of attributes present in the **Symbol Builder Attribute Editor** palette.

The **Layers** category displays the layers other than the '0' layer.

The **Insertion Point** category displays the errors when the X or Y values of the insertion point do not match the insertion point of at least one of the wire connection attributes.

The **Orientation** category displays the errors when wire connection attributes of a horizontal or vertical symbol are not found.

**Note**

*If you create a panel symbol, the insertion point and orientation categories will not be included in the symbol auditing.*

The **Save As** button is used to save the symbol auditing report for reference. This report will be a .XML file.

## Required Rollout

The **Required** rollout consists of the attributes that are mandatory for a symbol. This rollout consists of the grid area and various tools. The tools and options in the **Required** rollout are shown in Figure 13-9 and are discussed next.

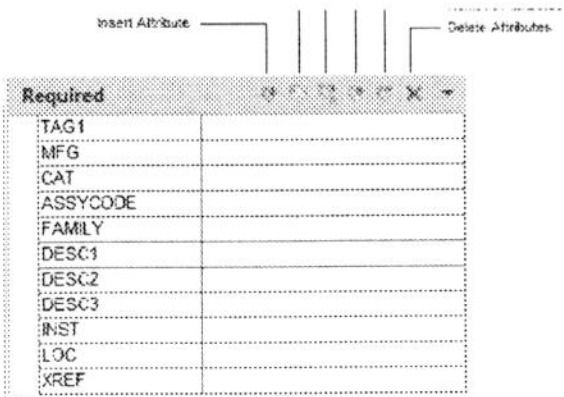


*Figure 13-9 The **Required** rollout*

### Insert Attribute

The **Insert Attribute** tool is used to insert the attribute that you select from the grid area of the **Required** rollout. Select the attribute from the grid area of the **Required** rollout and then choose the **Insert Attribute** tool; you will be prompted to specify the insertion base point. Specify the insertion point and press ENTER; the attribute will be inserted in the **Block Editor** environment and a check mark will be displayed on the left of the inserted attribute in the **Required** rollout. You can also insert multiple attributes at a time. To do so, select the attribute from the grid area and choose the **Insert Attribute** tool; you will be prompted to specify the insertion base point for all attributes. Specify the insertion base point; all attributes will be inserted in the **Block Editor** environment and a check mark will be displayed on the left of the inserted attributes, as shown in Figure 13-10. Figure 13-11 shows the attributes inserted into a symbol. Note that if you select the attribute that is already inserted in the **Block Editor** environment and choose the **Insert Attribute** tool, then the **Symbol Builder - Select Attributes** message box will be displayed informing that the selected attribute exists in the drawing.

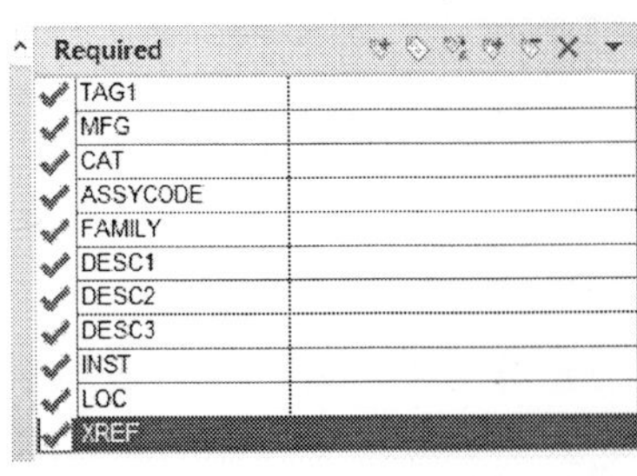


*Figure 13-10 The check marks displayed on the left of the attributes inserted*

*Figure 13-11 Attributes inserted into a symbol*

**Note**

*If you do not select any attribute from the grid area of the* ***Required*** *rollout and choose the* ***Insert Attribute*** *tool, the* ***Symbol Builder - Select Attributes*** *message box will be displayed. This message box displays the message "****Select attributes in the grid before invoking the command****". Choose the* ***Close*** *button to exit this dialog box.*

## Properties

The **Properties** tool is used to define the properties or modify the already assigned values of the selected attribute. To do so, select an attribute from the grid area of the **Required** rollout. Next, choose the **Properties** tool; the **Insert / Edit Attributes** dialog box will be displayed, as shown in Figure 13-12. This dialog box can also be invoked if you double-click on the selected attribute. Specify the values in this dialog box as per your requirement and choose the **OK** button; the values will be displayed in the respective attribute grid. Also, any changes that you made in this dialog box will be saved. Note that the **Insert** button in the **Insert / Edit Attributes** dialog box will be activated only if you add a new attribute to the grid area of the **Required** rollout. The new attribute can be added by using the **Add Attribute** tool. Figure 13-13 shows the attributes of a symbol after changing the height in the **Insert / Edit Attributes** dialog box.

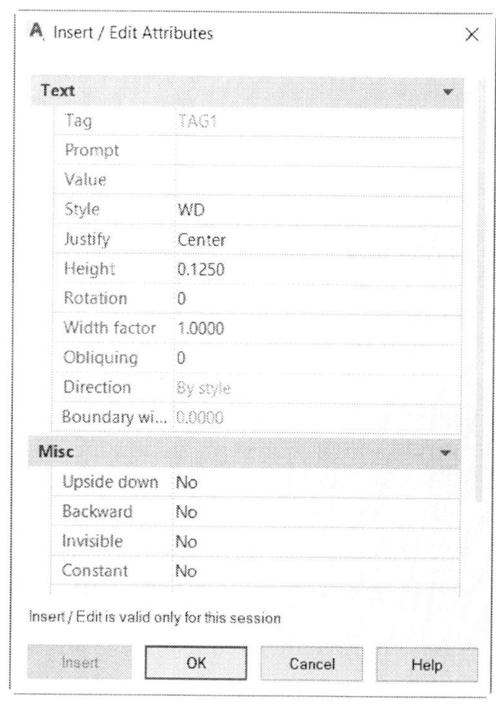


***Figure 13-12*** *The* ***Insert / Edit Attributes*** *dialog box*

***Figure 13-13*** *Attributes after changing their height*

### Convert Text

The **Convert Text** tool is used to convert the existing text objects to an attribute that you have selected from the grid area of the **Required** rollout. Select the attribute from the grid area and choose the **Convert Text** tool; you will be prompted to select the text for the selected attribute. Next, select the text; the text will be changed to the selected attribute and its name will be displayed in the row of the selected attribute of the grid area. Also, a check mark will be displayed on the left of the selected attribute. Note that this tool can be used only if there are text objects available in the **Block Editor** environment.

### Add Attribute

The **Add Attribute** tool is used to add an attribute to the grid area of the **Required** rollout. You can also define the properties of the attribute of the added attribute. To add an attribute, choose the **Add Attribute** tool; the **Insert / Edit Attribute** dialog box will be displayed. Specify the values in this dialog box as per your requirement. Choose the **OK** button; the new attribute will get added to the grid area. Choose the **Insert** button to add the attribute to the grid area as well as to insert the attribute in the **Block Editor** environment. Note that a check mark will be displayed on the left of the attribute that you have added and inserted in the environment.

### Remove Attribute

The **Remove Attribute** tool is used to remove the selected attribute from the grid area of the **Required** rollout. Select an attribute and then choose the **Remove Attribute** tool; the **Symbol Builder - Remove Attributes** dialog box will be displayed. Choose the **Remove** button to remove the selected attribute. Choose the **Cancel** button to cancel the command. Note that you cannot remove the attribute that has been inserted in the **Block Editor** environment.

### Delete Attributes

The **Delete Attributes** tool is used to delete the selected attributes from the symbol. To do so, select the attribute that has been inserted into the symbol. Next, choose the **Delete Attributes** tool; the **Symbol Builder - Delete Attributes** dialog box will be displayed. Choose the **Delete** button to delete the selected attribute from the symbol.

All the above options will also be available in the shortcut menu that will be displayed when you right click on an attribute in the **Required** rollout.

## Optional Rollout

The **Optional** rollout consists of the attributes that are not mandatory to be inserted into the symbol. The tools in the **Optional** rollout are similar to that of the **Required** rollout and have been discussed in the previous section.

## POS Rollout

Using the **POS** rollout, you can insert the position attributes into a symbol. You can insert upto 12 position attributes. This rollout consists of the **Add Next** button, which is used to insert the next available attribute in the symbol.

## RATING Rollout

Using the **RATING** rollout, you can insert the rating attributes into a symbol. You can insert up to 12 rating attributes. This rollout consists of the **Add Next** button, which is used to insert the next available attribute in the symbol.

## Wire Connection Rollout

The **Wire Connection** rollout is used to select the style and direction of the wire connection attributes. The options in the **Wire Connection** rollout are discussed next.

The **Direction/Style** field is used to select the direction and style for the wire connection attribute. To do so, choose the arrow opposite to the **Direction/Style** field; a drop-down list will be displayed, as shown in Figure 13-14. This drop-down list displays a list of styles and the direction for the wire connection. By default, the **Left / None** option is selected from this drop-down list.

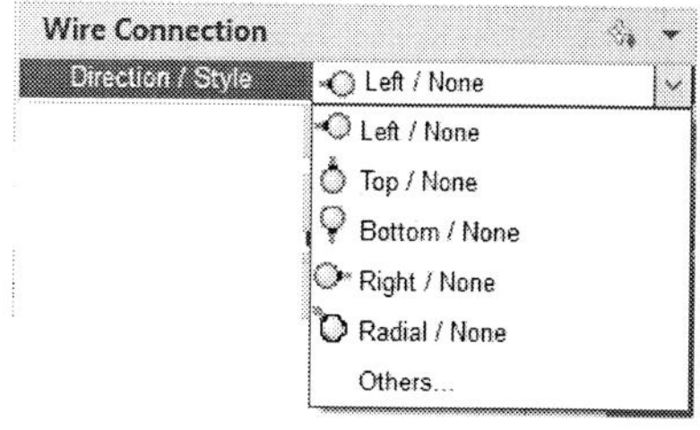


***Figure 13-14*** *The drop-down list displayed after choosing the arrow in the* ***Wire Connection*** *rollout*

Now, if you select the **Others** option from this drop-down list, the **Insert Wire Connections** dialog box will be displayed, as shown in Figure 13-15. The options in this dialog box are used to select the style, insert multiple wire connection attributes at a time, add pin information, and define the number and offset distance for the wire connection attributes. Specify the options in this dialog box as per your requirement. Next, choose the **Insert** button to insert the wire connection attributes into the symbol.

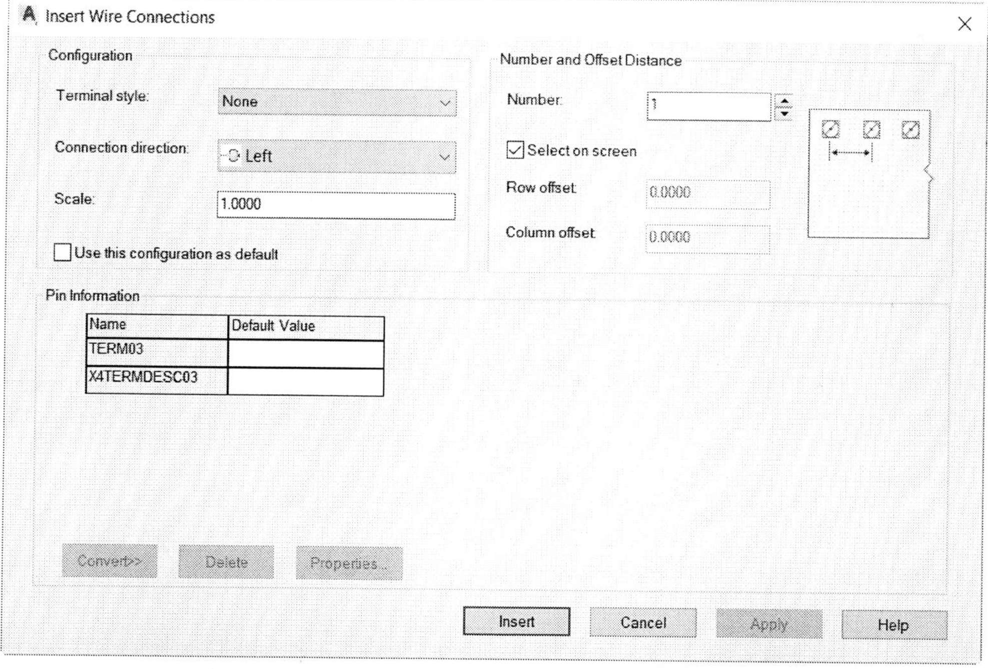


***Figure 13-15*** *The* ***Insert Wire Connections*** *dialog box*

The **Insert Wire Connection** tool is used to insert the selected wire connection to the attribute. To do so, you need to select the direction and style as discussed earlier and then choose the **Insert Wire Connection** tool; you will be prompted to select the direction. Specify the insertion point; the wire connection attribute will be inserted in the symbol. Press ESC to exit the command. Figure 13-16 shows the wire connection attribute inserted on the left of the symbol and Figure 13-17 shows the wire connection attribute inserted on the right of the symbol.

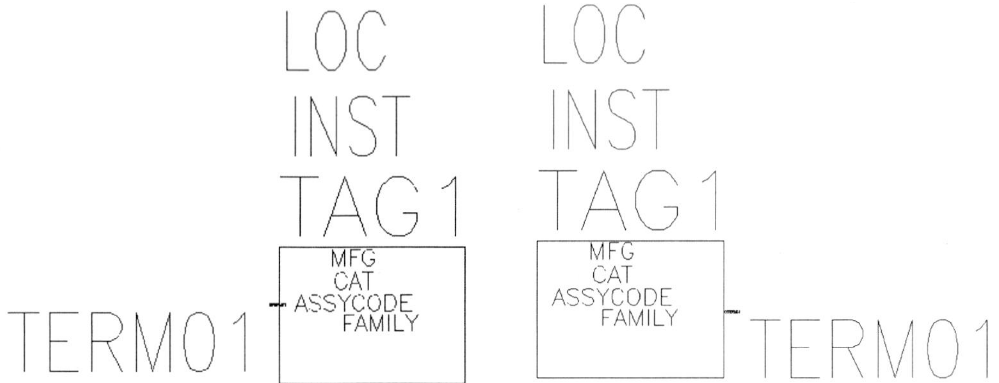


***Figure 13-16*** *Wire connection attribute inserted on the left of the symbol*

***Figure 13-17*** *Wire connection attribute inserted on the right of the symbol*

## Pins Rollout

The buttons in this rollout are used to add optional wire connection attributes, change attribute properties, move wire connection attribute, and so on. Note that the pins attributes will automatically be inserted in the symbol after the wire connection attributes are added to it.

## Link Lines Rollout

The **Link Lines** rollout consists of the **Direction** field and the **Insert Link Lines** tool. The options in this rollout are used to select the direction for the link line attributes and to insert the attribute on the symbol. To insert a link line attribute, click on the space in front of the **Direction** field; a drop-down list will be displayed, as shown in Figure 13-18.

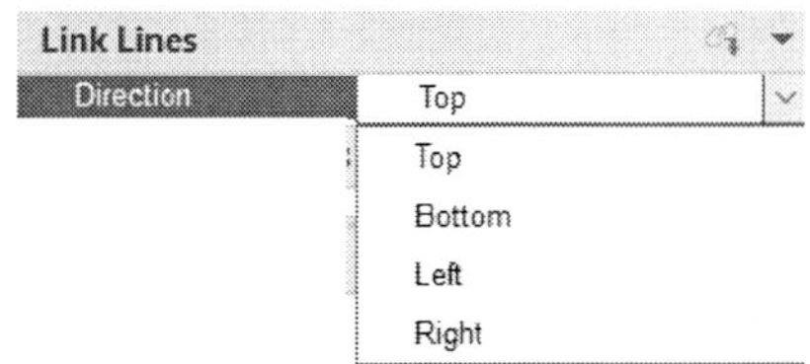


***Figure 13-18*** *A drop-down list displayed*

Select the direction from the drop-down list and then choose the **Insert Link Lines** tool; you will be prompted to specify the link line insertion point for the link line attributes. Specify the direction and insertion point for the link line attribute; the link line attribute will be inserted. Press ENTER to exit the command. Note that you can override the direction of link line attribute that you have selected from the drop-down list by entering an option while inserting the attribute at the Command prompt.

**Note**

*To delete the inserted link lines attribute from the symbol, choose the* ***Delete Link Lines*** *tool from the* ***Inserted Link Lines*** *rollout.*

Once you have added the attributes and completed the symbol graphics using the **Symbol Builder Attribute Editor** palette, choose the **Done** button from the **Edit** panel of the **Symbol Builder** tab, as shown in Figure 13-19; the **Close Block Editor: Save Symbol** dialog box will be displayed, as shown in Figure 13-20. Different areas and options in this dialog box are discussed next.

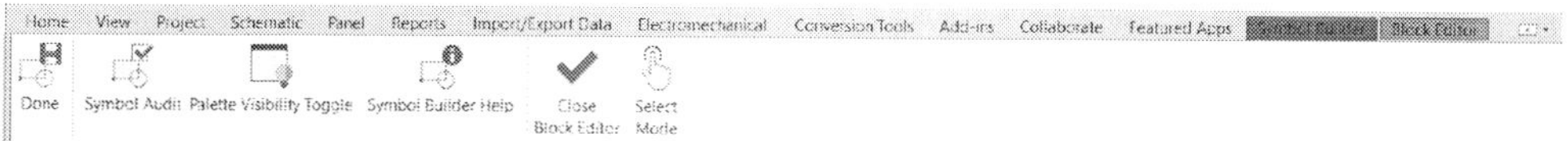


*Figure 13-19 The **Done** button in the **Edit** Panel*

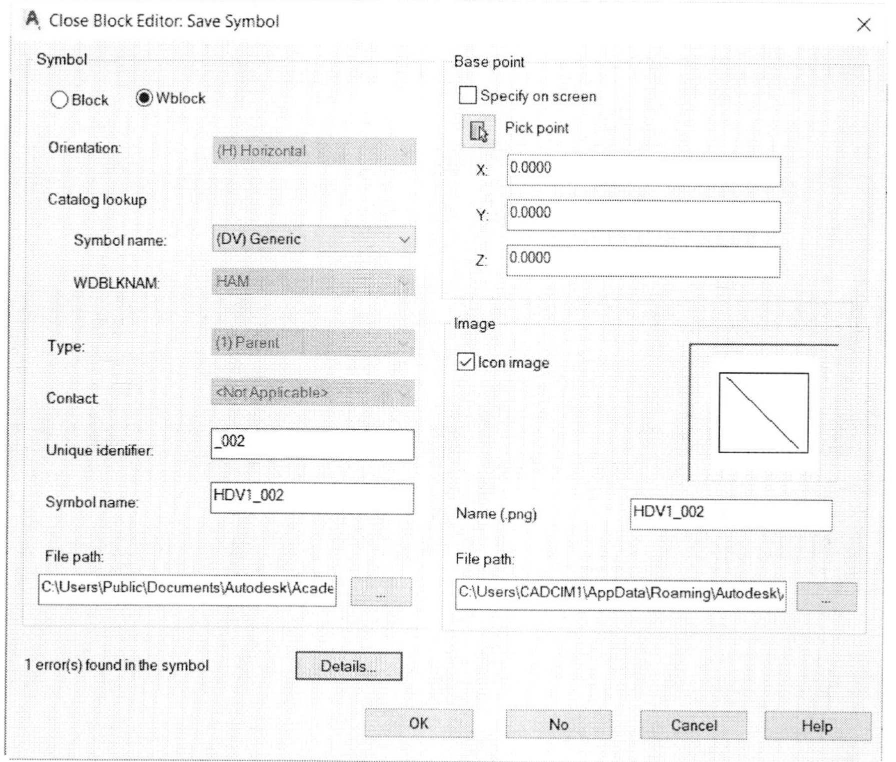


*Figure 13-20 The **Close Block Editor: Save Symbol** dialog box*

## Symbol Area

The options in the **Symbol** area are used to specify whether to save the symbol as block or Wblock, specify the symbol name, and so on. The options in this area are discussed next.

If you select the **Block** radio button, the symbols created can only be used in the drawing in which they were created. Note that when you select this radio button, the **File path** edit box will be disabled.

The **Wblock** radio button is selected by default and is used to export symbols by writing them to new drawing files that can then be inserted in any drawing. The drawing file will be saved to a location specified in the **Path** edit box.

The **Orientation** drop-down list displays the orientation of the symbol. This drop-down list displays the option that you have selected from the **Symbol** drop-down list of the **Symbol Configuration** dialog box. This drop-down list displays the first character of the symbol 'H', which implies the orientation of the block will be horizontal. On the other hand, if it is 'V' that means the symbol will be vertically oriented.

The **Symbol name** drop-down list displays the next two characters of the symbol name, which indicates the family type of a symbol.

The **Type** drop-down list displays the fourth character of the symbol name. The fourth character can be '1' or '2'. '1' for parent symbol, '2' for child symbol, and 'user-defined' for other symbol types.

The **Contact** drop-down list displays the fifth character, if the schematic symbol is child. If '1' is displayed in this drop-down list, then the schematic symbol will normally be open and if '2' is displayed, then the schematic symbol will normally be closed; otherwise, it will be user-defined.

In the **Unique identifier** edit box, you can enter some additional characters that will be added to the symbol for making it unique.

Based on the orientation, catalog lookup, type, contact, and unique identifier, the symbol builder automatically displays the name of the symbol in the **Symbol name** edit box. You can edit this symbol name as per your requirement.

The **File path** edit box displays the path of the symbol. If you want to save the symbol at different location, you can choose the **[...]** button placed next to this edit box and can specify the path.

The **Details** button is used to display the symbol audit report. On choosing this button, the **Symbol Audit** dialog box will be displayed. This dialog box displays the errors that are found in the symbol. The options in this dialog box have already been discussed. Note that the number of errors found in the symbol will be displayed on the left of the **Details** button.

## Base Point Area

In the **Base point** area, you can specify the base point co-ordinates for the symbol. The options in this area have already been discussed.

## Image Area

In the **Image** area, you can specify whether to create an image of the symbol, specify the name of the image and path of the image file.

The **Icon image** check box is used to create an image. This image will then be used for adding the new symbol to the icon menu. By default, this check box is selected. Also, you can preview the image in the preview window.

Specify the name for the image file in the **Name (.png)** edit box. By default, the name of the symbol that you have specified in the **Symbol name** edit box will be displayed as the name of the image in the **Name (.png)** edit box. Note that the format of the image file will be *.png*.

The **File path** edit box displays the path of the image file. You can also choose the Browse **[...]** button to specify the path of the image file.

After specifying the required options in the **Close Block Editor: Save Symbol** dialog box, choose the **OK** button; the **Close Block Editor** message box will be displayed. Choose the **Yes** button in this message box to insert the block or the **No** button to exit the **Block Editor** environment.

# NAMING CONVENTION OF SYMBOLS

In AutoCAD Electrical, a particular naming convention is used for naming symbols. Although following the naming convention is not compulsory but when you create a new AutoCAD Electrical symbol, you will be required to follow the naming convention. This naming is applicable to both the block name and drawing file name of the block in the library. The naming convention depends on the symbol type. The first four or five characters of the name are used to determine the type of the component (control relays, push buttons, limit switches etc.), orientation of the component (horizontal or vertical), whether the component is parent or child, or whether it is normally open or normally closed. The naming convention for all symbol types is given next.

## Schematic Symbols

The naming convention for schematic components such as push buttons, relays, pilot lights, switches, and so on is as follows:

First Character - The first character is 'H' for horizontal symbol or 'V' for vertical symbol. This indicates the orientation of the wire where the symbol is placed. The block name can be a maximum of 32 characters.

Second and Third Characters - The second and third characters indicate the family code for the symbol. For example, CR for control relays, PB for push button, LS for limit switches, and so on.

Fourth Character - The fourth character is '1' for everything else (parent or standalone components) and '2' for child contact.

Fifth Character - If the symbol is a contact, then '1' is used for normally open or '2' for normally closed as the fifth character.

The characters after the fifth characters are not specified in the naming convention; they are used to keep the drawing names unique. For example, Limit Switch, NO (HLS11) and Limit Switch NO Held Closed (HLS11H). The first five characters for both are HLS11. The Limit Switch NO Held Closed is having unique character 'H' as compared to the Limit Switch, NO.

Examples:
1. HPB12: Horizontal push button, parent, normally closed.
2. HPB21: Horizontal push button, child contact, normally open.
3. VPB11: Vertical push button, parent, normally open.
4. HCR21: Horizontal control relay, child contact, normally open.
5. HLS11: Horizontal limit switch, parent, normally open.
6. HSS123: Horizontal selector switch, parent, normally closed, 3 position NC
7. HPB11M: Horizontal push button, parent, normally open, mushroom head NO.

## Panel Layout Footprint Symbols

The panel layout footprint symbols do not follow any particular naming convention but the name of the block should be 32-characters only.

## Connector Symbols

The naming convention for connector symbols is as follows:

First Character - The first character is 'H' for horizontal orientation or 'V' for vertical orientation.

Second and Third Characters - The second and third characters are CN for connector.

Fourth Character - The fourth character is '1' for parent and '2' is for child.

Fifth Character - The fifth character is '_'.

Sixth Character - The sixth character is 1-9 for the style number.

Seventh Character - The seventh character is for plug or jack ID. In this character, 'P' is for plug and 'J' is for Jack (receptacle). Also, the seventh character is used for specifying the wire direction. '1' for right, '2' for top, '4' for left, and '8' for bottom.

Eighth Character - The eighth character is plug or jack. Here, 'P' is for plug and 'J' is for jack.

Examples:
1. HCN1_J: Horizontal, parent connector (receptacle).
2. HCN2_14J: Horizontal child connector (receptacle), wire connects from left or bottom.
3. VCN1_14P: Vertical parent connector (plug), wire connects from right or left.

## Plug / Jack Connector Pin Symbols

The naming convention for plug / jack connector pin symbols is as follows:

First Character - The first character is 'H' for horizontal wire insertion or 'V' for vertical wire insertion.

Second and Third Characters - The second and third characters are 'CO', if the connector does not change the wire number passing through it and 'CN', if the connector changes the wire number passing through it.

Fourth Character - The fourth character is '1' for parent marker and '2' is for the child marker.

The rest of the characters of the plug / jack connector pin symbols are not specified.

## Splice Symbol

The naming convention for splice symbols is as follows:

First Character to Fourth Character - The first four characters of a splice are 'HSP1' for horizontal splice or 'VSP1' for vertical splice.

Fifth to Seventh Character - The characters from fifth to seventh are '001', '002', '003' and so on.

Examples:
1. HSP1001: Horizontal splice #1
2. HSP1003: Horizontal splice #3
3. VSP1001: Vertical splice #1

## Parametric Twisted Pair Symbols

A parametrically twisted pair symbol does not have a parent and child version. This symbol must carry 'ACE_FLAG' attribute having a value '3'. The naming convention for this symbol is as follows:

First Character to Fourth Character - The first four characters of a parametric symbol are 'HT0_' for horizontal parametric symbol or 'VT0_' for parametric symbol.

The remaining characters can be anything. By default, 'TW' is set.

Examples:
1. HT0_TW: Horizontal parametric connector symbol.
2. VT0_TW: Vertical parametric connector symbol.

## Stand-alone PLC I/O Point Symbols

The stand-alone PLC I/O point symbols starts with 'PLCIO'. The symbol name, including the prefix 'PLCIO', can be up to maximum of 32 characters. There is no particular naming convention for this symbol except that you need to use the prefix 'PLCIO'.

Examples:
1. PLCIO50E1761-L16BBB: AB, 1761, Model: L16-BBB with 0.5 unit rung spacing.
2. PLCIOI1T: Standalone input point, single wire connection.

## PLC I/O Parametric Build Symbols

The PLC I/O parametric build symbol starts with 'HP' for horizontal rung or 'VP' for vertical rung. This is followed by a digit 1 through 9. Digits 1 through 5 are default PLC Module styles and 6 through 9 are user-defined PLC Module styles.

## Stand-alone Terminal Symbols

The naming convention for stand-alone terminal symbols is as follows:

First and Second Characters - The first and second characters of a standalone terminal symbol are 'HT'.

Third Character - If the wire number does not change through the terminal, the third character will be '0', or if the wire number changes through the terminal, the third character will be '1'.

Fourth Character - The fourth character is '_', if the terminal does not carry attributes for processing, otherwise fourth to eighth characters of the symbol are user-defined.

## Wire Number Symbols

The wire number symbol is a block consisting of a wire number attribute. The block's origin lies on its wire with the wire number lying above, below, or off to the side of the block.

Examples:
1. WD_WNH: Wire number for horizontal wire insertion.
2. WD_WNV: Wire number for vertical wire insertion.
3. WD_WCH: Extra wire number copy for horizontal wire.
4. WD_WCV: Extra wire number copy for vertical wire.

## Wire Dot Symbols

The naming convention for the wire dot symbol is WDDOT.

## Source / Destination Wire Signal Arrow Symbols

The naming convention for source / destination wire signal arrow symbols is as follows:

First Character to Fourth Character - The first four characters of this symbol are either 'HA?S' for source signal arrow or 'HA?D' for destination signal arrows. The '?' character is used for the style of the arrow. The first four styles are the default style in AutoCAD Electrical; from 5 to 9, the styles can be user-defined.

## Cable Marker Symbols

The naming convention for the cable marker symbols is as follows:

First Character - The first character is 'H' for horizontal wire insertion or 'V' for vertical wire insertion.

Second and Third characters - The second and third characters are 'W0'.

Fourth character - The fourth character is '1' for parent marker or '2' for child marker.

The rest of the characters are not specified.

Examples:
1. HW01: Horizontal wire insertion, parent cable conductor marker.
2. HW02: Horizontal wire insertion, child cable marker.
3. VW01: Vertical wire insertion, parent cable conductor marker.
4. VW02: Vertical wire insertion, child cable marker.

## Inline Wire Marker Symbols

The naming convention for inline wire marker symbols is as follows:

First Character - The first character is 'H' for horizontal wire insertion or 'V' for vertical wire insertion.

Second, third, and fourth characters - The next three characters are 'T0_'.
The rest of the characters are not defined.

Examples:
1. HT0_BLU: Horizontal wire insertion, blue inline marker.
2. HT0_ORG: Horizontal wire insertion, orange inline marker.
3. VT0_BLK: Vertical wire insertion, black inline marker.
4. VT0_GRY: Vertical wire insertion, grey inline marker.

## One-line Symbol

The one-line symbol follows the naming convention of schematic parent and child symbols. The one-line symbol block names have '1-' suffix.

# CUSTOMIZING THE ICON MENU

| | |
|---|---|
| **Ribbon:** | Schematic> Other Tools > Icon Menu Wizard |
| **Toolbar:** | ACE:Main Electrical 2 > Symbol Builder > Icon Menu Wizard<br>or ACE:Miscellaneous > Icon Menu Wizard |
| **Menu:** | Components> Symbol Library > Icon Menu Wizard |
| **Command:** | AEMENUWIZ |

You can customize the icon menu using the **Icon Menu Wizard** tool. The **Icon Menu Wizard** tool is used to modify or add icons of schematic symbol or panel symbol to the icon menu. Using this tool, you can create a new submenu, add icons that will be used for inserting the component or circuits, delete icons, cut, copy, and paste icons. To modify an icon menu, choose the **Icon Menu Wizard** tool from the **Other Tools** panel of the **Schematic** tab; the **Select Menu file** dialog box will be displayed, as shown in Figure 13-21. Using this dialog box, you can edit the default menu files such as *ace_nfpa_menu.dat* for schematic symbols and *ace_panel_menu.dat* for panel symbol. The options in this dialog box are discussed next.

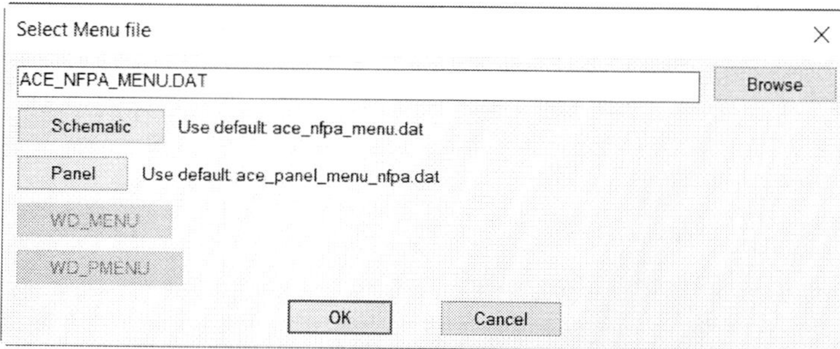


*Figure 13-21 The **Select Menu file** dialog box*

**Note**

*You can edit the icon menu files (.dat) using any text editor but if you use the* ***Icon Menu Wizard*** *tool, it will be easy for you to modify these files.*

Now, enter the name of the icon menu file that you need to edit in the edit box. Alternatively, you can choose the **Browse** button to select the icon menu file. When you choose this button, the **Select ".dat" icon menu file** dialog box will be displayed. Next, select the **.dat* file from this dialog box and choose the **Open** button; the name and path of the icon menu (*.dat*) file will be displayed in the edit box. You can also choose the **Schematic** button to display the default schematic icon menu file in the edit box. If you choose the **Panel** button, the default panel icon menu file will be displayed. By default, the *ACE_NFPA_MENU.DAT* file is displayed in the edit box. Next, choose the **OK** button in the **Select Menu file** dialog box; the **Icon Menu Wizard** dialog box will be displayed, as shown in Figure 13-22. The options in the **Icon Menu Wizard** dialog box are almost similar to those in the **Insert Component** or **Insert Footprint** dialog box, discussed in previous chapters, but the **Icon Menu Wizard** dialog box has an additional drop-down list, **Add**. This drop-down list is discussed next.

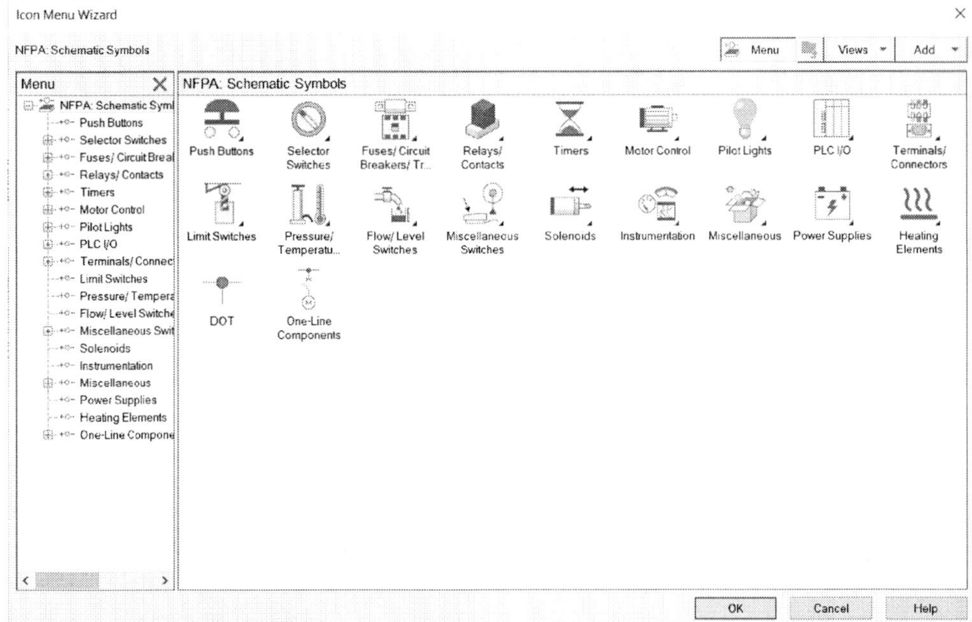


*Figure 13-22 The* ***Icon Menu Wizard*** *dialog box*

**Tip**

*In order to determine the active *.dat file, right-click on the active project; a shortcut menu will be displayed. Choose the* ***Properties*** *option from the shortcut menu; the* ***Project Properties*** *dialog box will be displayed. Next, in the* ***Project Settings*** *tab, expand the* ***Schematic Icon Menu File*** *node from the* ***Library and Icon Menu Paths*** *area; the schematic icon menu file is listed. Also, you can change the .dat file as per your requirement.*

**Note**

*You cannot insert the components using the **Icon Menu Wizard** dialog box.*

# Add

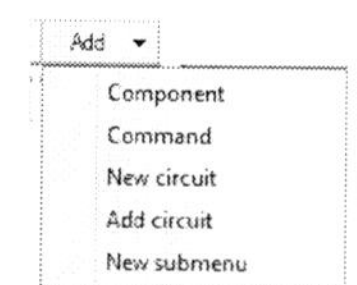


***Figure 13-23** The **Add** drop-down list displayed*

The options in the **Add** drop-down list are used to add a component, command, new circuit, existing circuit and submenu icon in the menu. Click on the **Add** drop-down list, various options will be displayed, as shown in Figure 13-23. You can also access the options present in this drop-down list by right-clicking in the symbol preview window (where icons are displayed) of the **Icon Menu Wizard** dialog box. The most commonly used options in this drop-down list are discussed next.

## Component

The **Component** option is used to add a component icon in the menu that can be used to insert a component in the drawing. To add an icon of a component, select the **Component** option from the **Add** drop-down list; the **Add Icon - Component** dialog box will be displayed, as shown in Figure 13-24. Also, if you right-click on the symbol preview window of the **Icon Menu Wizard** dialog box, a shortcut menu will be displayed. You can choose **Add icon > Component** from the shortcut menu to display the **Add Icon - Component** dialog box. Note that most of the options in this dialog box are similar to that of the **Create New Circuit** dialog box, which have been discussed in Chapter 7. The rest of the options in the **Block Name to Insert** area of the **Add Icon - Component** dialog box are discussed next.

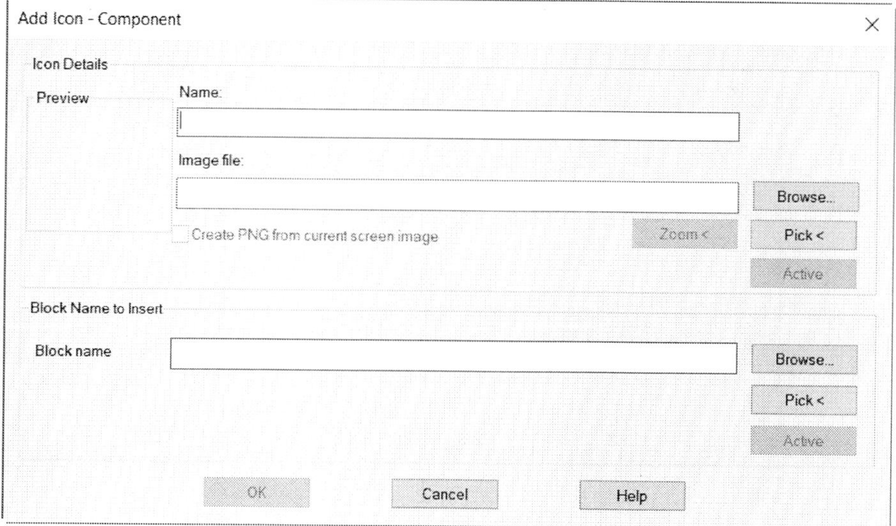


***Figure 13-24** The **Add Icon - Component** dialog box*

### Block Name to Insert Area

In the **Block Name to Insert** area, you can specify the block name of the symbol. The options in this area are discussed next.

Enter the symbol block name in the **Block name** edit box. You can also specify the block name by choosing the **Browse** or **Pick** button.

After specifying the options in the **Add Icon - Component** dialog box, the **OK** button will be activated. Choose the **OK** button; the icon will be created in the **Icon Menu Wizard** dialog box.

## New circuit

The **New circuit** option is used to create a new circuit and add an icon of the new circuit in the **Icon Menu Wizard** dialog box. To create a new circuit and add an icon, select the **New circuit** option from the **Add** drop-down list; the **Create New Circuit** dialog box will be displayed. The options in this dialog box have already been discussed in Chapter 7. Next, specify the options in the **Create New Circuit** dialog box as per your requirement. Choose the **OK** button; you will prompted to specify the base point of the circuit and the **Icon Menu Wizard** dialog box will disappear. Next, specify the base point; you will be prompted to select the objects. Select the objects and press ENTER; the **Icon Menu Wizard** dialog box will appear again and the icon of the circuit will be added in the **Icon Menu Wizard** dialog box. The preview of the icon will be displayed at the end of the existing icon images in the symbol preview window of this dialog box.

## Add circuit

The **Add circuit** option is used to add an icon of an existing circuit to the **Icon Menu Wizard** dialog box. To do so, select the **Add circuit** option from the **Add** drop-down list; the **Add Existing Circuit** dialog box will be displayed, as shown in Figure 13-25. The options in the **Add Existing Circuit** dialog box are almost similar to the **Create New Circuit** dialog box. The remaining options in the **Add Existing Circuit** dialog box are discussed next.

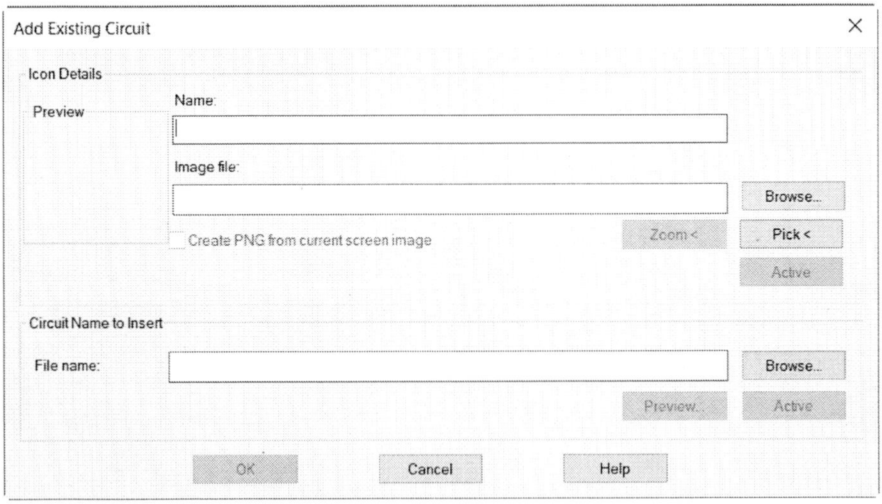

*Figure 13-25 The **Add Existing Circuit** dialog box*

### Circuit Name to Insert Area

The **Circuit Name to Insert** area is used to specify the name of the circuit to be inserted. Enter the file name in the **File name** edit box. Alternatively, you can choose the **Browse** button to specify the name and path of the drawing file. You can also choose the **Active** button to display and use the drawing name of the active drawing in this edit box. Choose the **Preview** button to preview the drawing file.

After specifying the required options in the **Add Existing Circuit** dialog box, choose the **OK** button; the icon of the circuit will be added in the **Icon Menu Wizard** dialog box and its preview will be displayed at the end of the existing icon images in the symbol preview window of this dialog box.

## New submenu

The **New submenu** option is used to add an icon for the submenu page. To do so, select the **New submenu** option from the **Add** drop-down list; the **Create New Submenu** dialog box will be displayed, as shown in Figure 13-26. The options in this dialog box are similar to the **Add Icon - Component** dialog box and have been discussed earlier. The remaining options in this dialog box are discussed next.

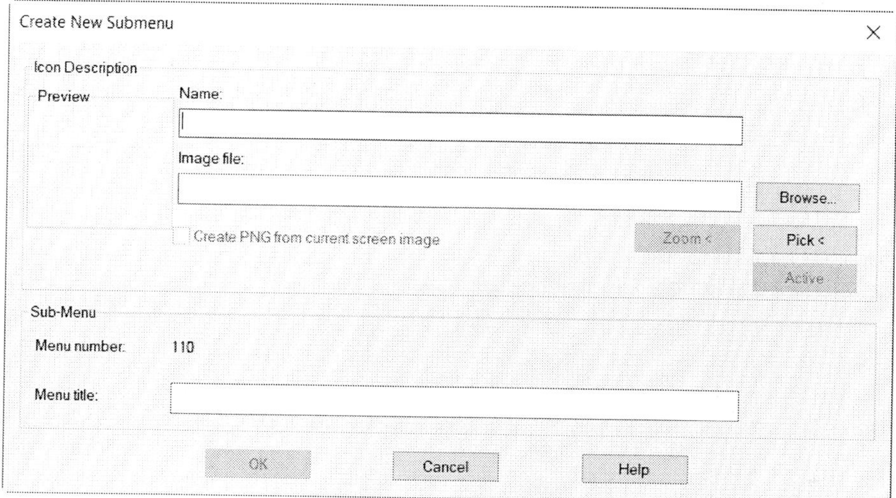


*Figure 13-26 The **Create New Submenu** dialog box*

### Sub-Menu Area

The **Sub-Menu** area is used to specify the title for the submenu. Also, this area displays the menu number of the submenu page.

The menu number of the submenu page will be displayed on the right of the **Menu number**. This number is for your reference only. Specify the title for the submenu, which will be used in the **Insert Component** dialog box later in the **Menu title** edit box.

After specifying the required options in the **Create New Submenu** dialog box, choose the **OK** button; the icon of the submenu page will be added in the **Icon Menu Wizard** dialog box and its preview will be displayed at the end of the existing icon images in the symbol preview window of this dialog box.

If you right-click on the symbol preview window or right-click on the selected icon in the **Icon Menu Wizard** dialog box, a shortcut menu will be displayed. The options in the shortcut menu are as follows:

1. View > Icon with text, Icon only, List view
2. Add icon > Component, Command, New circuit, Add circuit
3. New submenu
4. Cut
5. Copy
6. Paste
7. Delete
8. Properties

All the above options of the shortcut menu have already been discussed in the previous section. Note that the **View** option has been discussed in Chapter 5 in detail.

Also, if you right-click on the selected icon, a shortcut menu will be displayed. The options in the shortcut menu are as follows: **View**, **Add icon**, **New Submenu**, **Cut**, **Copy**, **Paste**, **Delete**, and **Properties**. Almost all options have been discussed earlier except the **Properties** option. Using the **Properties** option, you can modify the properties of the existing symbol icon like icon name, image, block names, and so on. Choose the **OK** button to overwrite the changes in the *.dat* file.

# MISCELLANEOUS TOOLS

In this topic, you will learn about the **Mark/Verify Drawings**, **Export to Spreadsheet**, **Update from Spreadsheet**, and **Utilities** tools. The usage of these tools is discussed next.

## Marking and Verifying Drawings

| | |
|---|---|
| **Ribbon:** | Project > Project Tools > Mark/Verify DWGs |
| **Toolbar:** | ACE:Main Electrical 2 > Project Manager > Mark/Verify Drawings or ACE:Project > Mark/Verify Drawings |
| **Menu:** | Projects > Mark/Verify Drawings |
| **Command:** | AEMARKVERIFY |

The **Mark/Verify DWGs** tool is used to add an invisible mark on the components, wires, wire numbers, and 1st reference of the ladder present into a drawing before sending it to the client for review or to the user to modify a drawing. When the drawings are returned, you can use the **Verify** option to generate a report of the changes. The report consists of a list of added, copied, changed, and deleted components and wire numbers. The changes made in the drawing using AutoCAD LT, AutoCAD, or AutoCAD Electrical will be indicated by the **Mark/Verify DWGs** tool.

### Marking Drawings

To mark drawing(s), choose the **Mark/Verify DWGs** tool from the **Project Tools** panel of the **Project** tab; the **Mark and Verify** dialog box will be displayed, as shown in Figure 13-27. Different areas and options in this dialog box are discussed next.

### Mark/Verify drawing or project Area

The **Mark/Verify drawing or project** area is used to specify whether to mark or verify the active drawing or the active project.

### What to do Area

The options in the **What to do** area are used to mark the electrical components, non-AutoCAD Electrical blocks, and lines/wires. The options are also used to verify the changes that have been made in the drawing and remove all AutoCAD Electrical marked data.

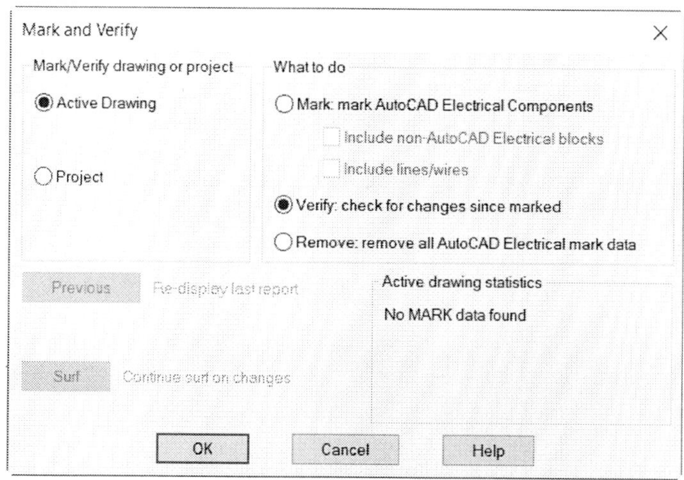


*Figure 13-27 The **Mark and Verify** dialog box*

Select the **Mark: mark AutoCAD Electrical Components** radio button to add some invisible information on the electrical components. Once you select this radio button, the **Include non-AutoCAD Electrical blocks** and **Include lines/wires** check boxes will become available. Select these check boxes to add a mark on the non-AutoCAD Electrical blocks and lines/wires.

By default, the **Verify: check for changes since marked** radio button is selected. This radio button is used to generate a list of changes that have been made in the marked drawing(s).

Select the **Remove: remove all AutoCAD Electrical mark data** radio button to remove the invisible mark data, which has been added to the drawings.

### Previous

The **Previous** button is used to display the previous report. To do so, choose the **Previous** button; the **REPORT: Changes made on this drawing since last Mark command** dialog box will be displayed. This dialog box displays the previous report.

### Active drawing statistics Area

The **Active drawing statistics** area displays the details of marked data found on the drawing such as date, time when the drawing was marked, the initials of the person by whom it was marked, and any comments that you have added.

You can mark active drawing and entire project in the following ways:

**Case - I**

By default, the **Active Drawing** radio button is selected in the **Mark and Verify** dialog box. Select the **Mark: mark AutoCAD Electrical Components** radio button and choose the **OK** button in the **Mark and Verify** dialog box; the **Enter Your Initials** dialog box will be displayed. Enter the initials of your name and the comments for the drawing, if required. The information that you enter in this dialog box will be displayed in the reports. Choose the **OK** button; the invisible marks will be added to the drawing.

**Case-II**

If you select the **Project** and the **Mark: mark AutoCAD Electrical Components** radio buttons in the **Mark and Verify** dialog box and then choose the **OK** button, the **Enter Your Initials** dialog box will be displayed. Enter the required information in this dialog box and choose the **OK** button; the **Select Drawings to Process** dialog box will be displayed. Select the drawings that you want to mark and choose the **Process** button; the drawings will be transferred from the top to bottom list. Next, choose the **OK** button; the invisible marks will be added to the selected drawings.

**Note**

*The invisible marks are added to the component tags and wire numbers. The appearance or functioning of the drawings will not be affected by these marks but the drawing size may increase by a small amount.*

## Verifying Drawings

You have learned to add the invisible marks to the drawing(s) before sending it to the client for review or before editing. Now, to verify the changes, which have been made by the client or after editing, choose the **Mark/Verify DWGs** tool from the **Project Tools** panel of the **Project** tab; the **Mark and Verify** dialog box will be displayed. The options in this dialog box have already been discussed in this chapter.

The **Verify: check for changes since marked** and the **Active Drawing** radio buttons are selected by default. Also, note that the marked components and wires status will be displayed in the **Active drawing statistics** area. Choose the **OK** button in the **Mark and Verify** dialog box; the **REPORT: Changes made on this drawing since last Mark command** dialog box will be displayed, as shown in Figure 13-28. This dialog box displays the changes that have been made to the drawings that were marked. The options in the **REPORT: Changes made on this drawing since last Mark command** dialog box are discussed next.

The **Save As** button is used to save the report. To do so, choose the **Save As** button; the **REPORT: Save As** dialog box will be displayed. Specify the location where you want to save the report and then choose the **Save** button; the **Optional Script File** dialog box will be displayed. The options in the **Optional Script File** dialog box have already been discussed in Chapter 9. Choose the **Close - No Script** button to exit the dialog box.

Choose the **Display: Report Format** button; the **Report Generator** dialog box will be displayed. The options in this dialog box have already been discussed in Chapter 9. Using this dialog box, you can edit the report, place it on the drawing, save it to a file, or print it.

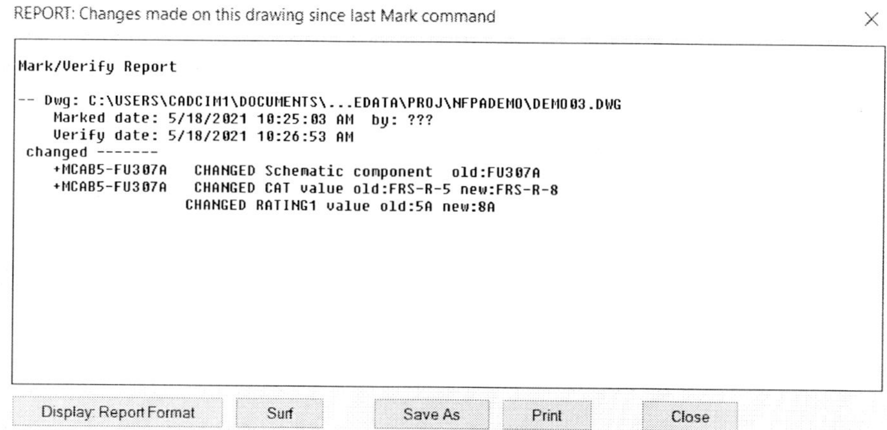


*Figure 13-28 The **REPORT: Changes made on this drawing since last Mark command** dialog box*

**Note**

*If you select the **Project** and **Verify: check for changes since marked** radio buttons and then choose the **OK** button in the **Mark and Verify** dialog box, the **Select Drawings to Process** dialog box will be displayed. Select the drawings that you want to process and choose the **OK** button; the **REPORT: Changes made on this drawing since last Mark command** dialog box will be displayed.*

## Exporting Data to the Spreadsheet

| | |
|---|---|
| **Ribbon:** | Import/Export Data > Export > To Spreadsheet |
| **Toolbar:** | ACE:Main Electrical 2 > Schematic Reports > Export to Spreadsheet or ACE:Schematic Reports > Export to Spreadsheet |
| **Menu:** | Projects> Export to Spreadsheet > Export to Spreadsheet |
| **Command:** | AEEXPORT2SS |

The **To Spreadsheet** tool is used to export the data from the active drawing or project to an external file. This file can be of different formats such as Excel file format (.xls), Access file format (.mdb), Tab - delimited ASCII, and comma-delimited ASCII. Note that the database will be automatically refreshed before it is exported to an output file. To export data, choose the **To Spreadsheet** tool from the **Export** panel of the **Import/Export Data** tab; the **Export to Spreadsheet** dialog box will be displayed, as shown in Figure 13-29. The options in this dialog box are discussed next.

### General (all * below)

The **General (all * below)** radio button is used for exporting all data categories to an Excel file (.xls) or Access file (.mdb) for editing. Using this radio button, you can generate the report for the categories that are marked with asterisk (*) in the **Export to Spreadsheet** dialog box.

### Components*

The **Components*** radio button is used for exporting components and related information such as component family, component tag, description, and so on to an output format file for editing.

**Note**

*The user defined attributes will also be included in the spreadsheet file that is created using the* ***To Spreadsheet*** *tool. The process of adding user defined attributes has already been discussed in detail in Chapter 9.*

## Components (parents only)

The **Components (parents only)** radio button is used for exporting data related to parent components to an output format file for editing. The information includes component family, component tag, description, and so on.

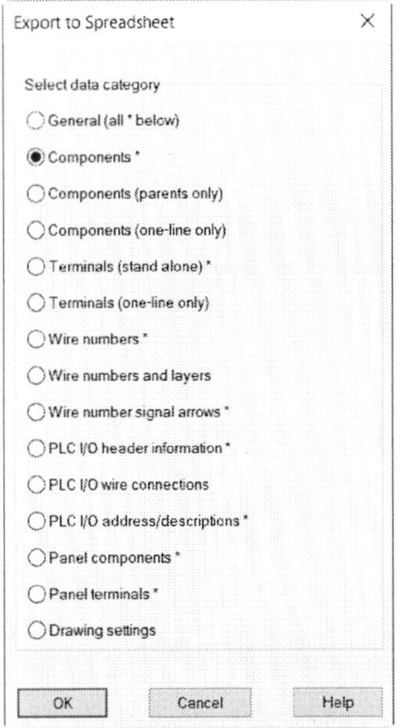


*Figure 13-29 The* ***Export to Spreadsheet*** *dialog box*

## Components (one-line only)

The **Components (one-line only)** radio button is used for exporting one-line components to an output format file for editing. This file includes information such as component family, component tag, description, reference number, catalog, manufacturer, location, attribute values, and so on.

## Terminals (stand alone)*

The **Terminals (stand alone)*** radio button is used for exporting the terminals to the output format file for editing. The output file includes information of tag strip, terminal number, installation code, location code, manufacturer, catalog, wire numbers, attribute values, and so on.

## Terminals (one-line only)

The **Terminals (one-line only)** radio button is used for exporting one-line terminals to an output format file for editing. The output file includes information of tag strip, terminal number, installation code, location code, manufacturer, catalog, wire numbers, attribute values, and so on.

## Wire numbers*

The **Wire numbers*** radio button is used for exporting the wire numbers to the output file for editing.

## Wire numbers and layers

The **Wire numbers and layers** radio button is used for exporting wire numbers and the related wire layers to the output file for editing.

## Wire number signal arrows*

The **Wire number signal arrows*** radio button is used for exporting all signal codes, source or destination information, and wire numbers to the output file for editing.

## PLC I/O header information*

The **PLC I/O header information*** radio button is used to export PLC I/O header information such as tag name, description, I/O address, manufacturer, catalog, and so on to the output file for editing.

## PLC I/O wire connections

The **PLC I/O wire connections** radio button is used to export the wire numbers for each I/O point for all PLC modules to the output file for editing. This file includes the information of tag name, I/O address, description, reference number, wire number, and so on.

## PLC I/O address/descriptions*

The **PLC I/O address/descriptions*** radio button is used to export PLC I/O address or description to the output file for editing.

## Panel components*

The **Panel components*** radio button is used to export the attribute values of the components in the panel drawings to the output file for editing.

## Panel terminals*

The **Panel terminals*** radio button is used to export the attribute information of the terminals in the panel drawings to the output file for editing.

Select the data category that you need to export from the **Select data category** area of the **Export to Spreadsheet** dialog box. Choose the **OK** button; the corresponding **Data Export** dialog box will be displayed, as shown in Figure 13-30. The options and the name of this dialog box depend on the option that you have selected from the **Export to Spreadsheet** dialog box. Different areas and options in the **Data Export** dialog box are discussed next.

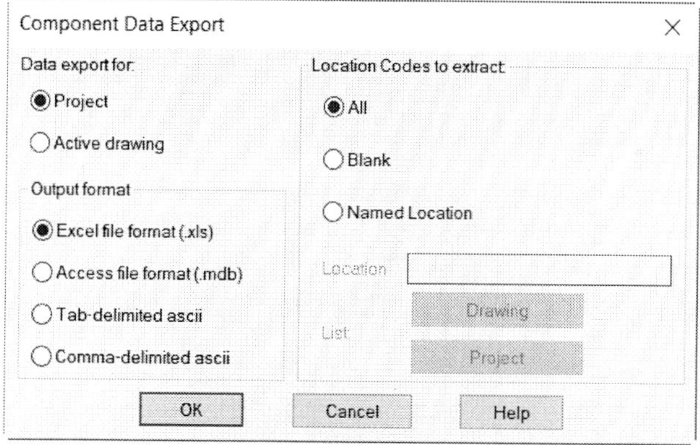


*Figure 13-30 The **Component Data Export** dialog box*

## Data export for Area

The **Data export for** area is used to specify whether to export the data from the entire project or an active drawing only. By default, the **Project** radio button is selected.

## Output format Area

The **Output format** area displays various formats for the output. The options in this area depend on the data category that you have selected from the **Select data category** area of the **Export to Spreadsheet** dialog box. The output format file can be of the following types: Excel file format

(.xls), Access file format (.mdb), Tab-delimited ascii, and Comma-delimited ascii. Select the format for the output. By default, the **Excel file format (.xls)** radio button is selected.

After specifying the options in the **Component Data Export** dialog box, choose the **OK** button; the **Select Drawings to Process** dialog box will be displayed, if the **Project** radio button is selected in the **Data export for** area. Next, select the drawings and choose the **Process** button. The options in this dialog box have already been discussed in the earlier chapters. Choose the **OK** button in the **Select Drawings to Process** dialog box; the **Select file name for Project-wide XLS output** dialog box will be displayed. If the **Active Drawing** radio button is selected in the **Data export for** area, then the **Select file name for drawing's XLS output** dialog box will be displayed. Next, specify the desired location for the exported data file and enter the name for the file in the **File name** edit box. Choose the **Save** button; the file will be saved at the specified location. Now, to view or edit this file, open it in the spreadsheet or database program.

## Drawing settings

The **Drawing settings** radio button is used to export drawing settings information of selected drawing(s) to the output file for editing. To export drawing settings information, select the **Drawing settings** radio button from the **Select Data Category** area and choose **OK**; the **Drawing Settings Data Export** dialog box will be displayed, as shown in Figure 13-31. The options in this dialog box are already discussed in the previous section. If you select the **Project** radio button from the **Data export for** area and choose **OK**, the **Select Drawings to Process** dialog box will be displayed. Select the drawings that you want to process and then choose the **Process** button. Next, choose **OK** from the **Select Drawings to Process** dialog box; the **Select file name for Project-wide XLS output** dialog box will be displayed. Enter the file name and path for the output file in this dialog box and choose **Save**; the drawing setting information for selected drawings will be saved in the output file with the specified file name at the specified location.

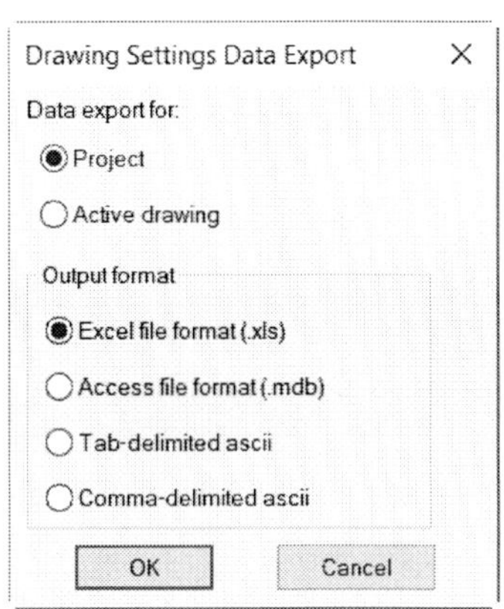


*Figure 13-31 The* ***Drawing Settings Data Export*** *dialog box*

If you select the **Active drawing** radio button from the **Data export for** area in the **Drawing Settings Data Export** dialog box and choose **OK**, the **Select File Name for drawing's XLS output** dialog box will be displayed. Enter the file name and path for the output file in this dialog box and then choose **Save**; the drawing setting information for selected drawing will be saved in the output file with the specified file name at the specified location. The output file consists of fields such as Section, Sub-section, Sheet (% S), and so on. Now, you can edit the output file based on your requirement and then import this edited file using the **From Spreadsheet** tool.

**Note**

*All reports consist of the HDL and FILENAME column headings. Do not change the values in these columns. The content in these columns is used to link the edited settings back to the correct drawing and correct block. Editing these columns may break the link or link the data to a wrong object.*

## Updating Data from the Spreadsheet

**Ribbon:** Import/Export Data > Import > From Spreadsheet
**Toolbar:** ACE:Main Electrical 2 > Schematic Reports > Update from Spreadsheet or ACE:Schematic Reports > Update from Spreadsheet
**Menu:** Projects> Export to Spreadsheet > Update from Spreadsheet
**Command:** AEIMPORTSS

The **From Spreadsheet** tool is used to import the data from an edited file and then modify the drawings within the active project according to the information present in the selected spreadsheet or database. Using this tool, you can only update the existing symbols but you cannot remove or add the symbols in the drawings. To update data, choose the **From Spreadsheet** tool from the **Import** panel of the **Import/Export Data** tab; the **Update Drawing from Spreadsheet File (xls, mdb, or csv Format)** dialog box will be displayed. Select the spreadsheet file to use as the source from the **Look in** drop-down list and choose the **Open** button; the **Update Drawings per Spreadsheet Data** dialog box will be displayed, as shown in Figure 13-32. Different options in this dialog box are discussed next.

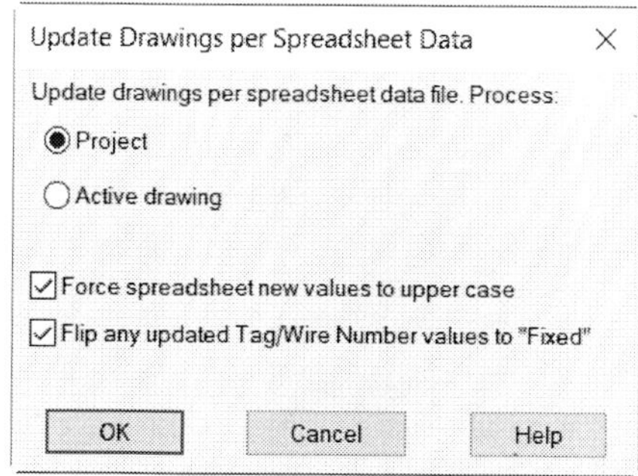


*Figure 13-32 The* ***Update Drawings per Spreadsheet Data*** *dialog box*

### Update drawings per spreadsheet data file. Process Area

This area is used to specify whether to import the spreadsheet data for the active project or active drawing. By default, the **Project** radio button is selected in this area.

### Force spreadsheet new values to upper case

The **Force spreadsheet new values to upper case** check box is used to change all new attribute values of a spreadsheet to upper case. By default, this check box is selected.

### Flip any updated Tag/Wire Number values to "Fixed"

The **Flip any updated Tag/Wire Number values to "Fixed"** check box is used to set any updated component tags or wire number values to fixed, so that they are not updated later.

After specifying the required options in the **Update Drawings per Spreadsheet Data** dialog box, choose the **OK** button; the **Select Drawings to Process** dialog box will be displayed.

Select the drawings that you need to process and choose the **OK** button; the **QSAVE** message box will be displayed. Choose the **OK** button in this message box; the selected drawings will be updated. Now, you can check whether the drawings have been updated with the data that you imported from the external file.

## Using Project-Wide Utilities

| | |
|---|---|
| **Ribbon:** | Project > Project Tools > Utilities |
| **Toolbar:** | ACE:Main Electrical 2 > Project Manager > Project-Wide Utilities or ACE:Project > Project-Wide Utilities |
| **Menu:** | Projects > Project-Wide Utilities |
| **Command:** | AEUTILITIES |

The **Utilities** tool is used to work on wire numbers, component tags, attribute text, wire types, and item numbers of an active project. This tool is also used to define script and run it for an active project. To work on these utilities, choose the **Utilities** tool from the **Project Tools** panel of the **Project** tab; the **Project-Wide Utilities** dialog box will be displayed, as shown in Figure 13-33. The areas and options in this dialog box are discussed next.

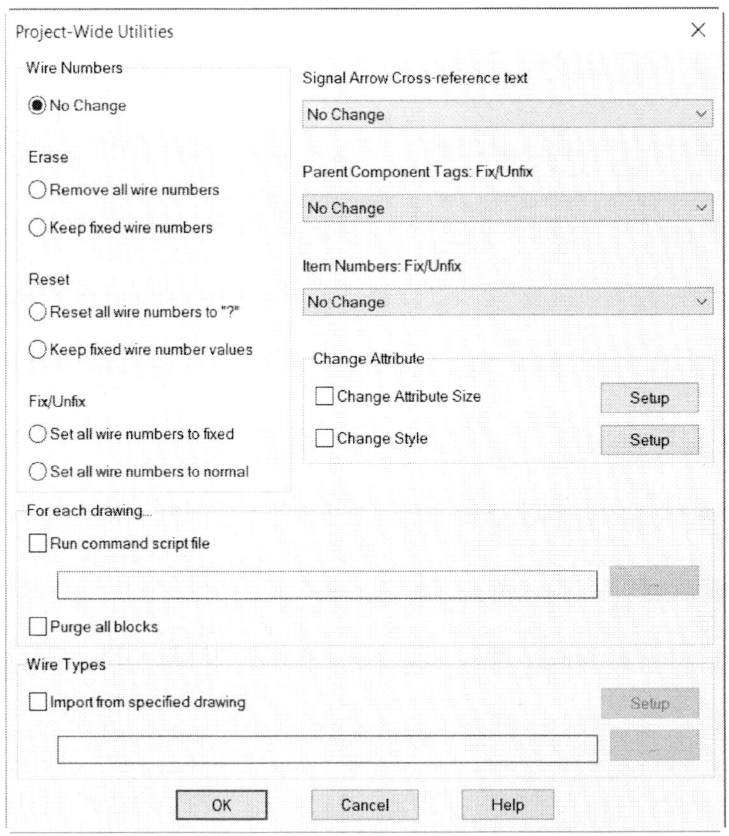


*Figure 13-33 The **Project-Wide Utilities** dialog box*

### Wire Numbers

The radio buttons in this area are used to work on wire numbers in the active project. Using these radio buttons, you can specify if you want to remove all wire numbers, retain fixed wire numbers, reset all wire numbers, set all wire numbers to fixed, and so on.

## Signal Arrow Cross-reference text

The options in this drop-down list are used to remove or retain all signal arrow cross reference texts in an active project.

## Parent Component Tags: Fix/Unfix

The options in this drop-down list are used to set all component tags in an active project to fixed or normal, or to retain them to their existing settings.

## Item Numbers: Fix/Unfix

The options in this drop-down list are used to set all item numbers in an active project to fixed or normal, or to retain them to their existing settings.

## Change Attribute

The options in this area are used to set the size and style of attributes in an active project. To set the size of attributes, select the **Change Attribute Size** check box. Next, choose the **Setup** button located next to it; the **Project-wide Attribute Size Change** dialog box will be displayed, as shown in Figure 13-34. Select the check boxes corresponding to the attributes that you want to change. Next, enter the required height and width in the **Height** and **width** edit boxes, respectively. After setting the options in this dialog box, choose the **OK** button to close the dialog box; the size of selected attributes will change accordingly.

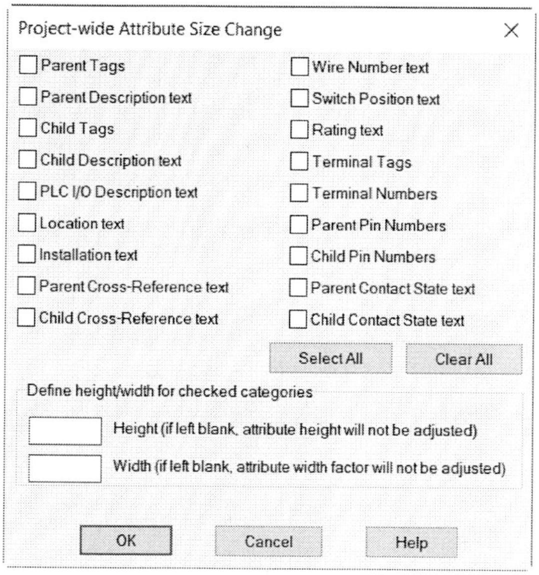

*Figure 13-34 The* ***Project-wide Attribute Size Change*** *dialog box*

To set the text style of the attributes, select the **Change Style** check box and choose the **Setup** button located next to it; the **Project-wide AutoCAD Electrical Style Change** dialog box will be displayed, as shown in Figure 13-35. In this dialog box, select the required style from the **Font Name** drop-down list and choose the **OK** button; the dialog box will be closed and the text style for the selected attributes will change accordingly.

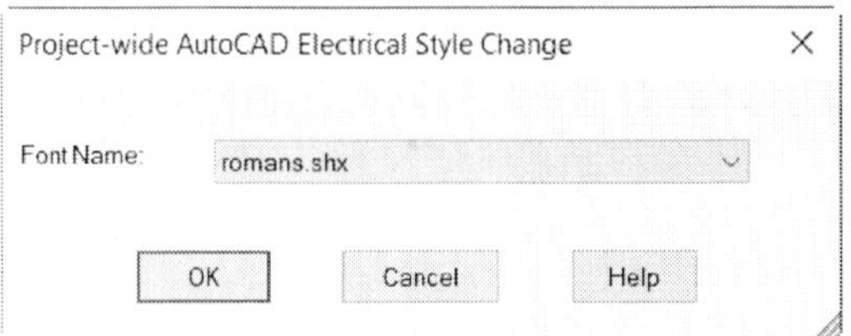


*Figure 13-35 The **Project-wide AutoCAD Electrical Style Change** dialog box*

## For each drawing

This area is used to define script and run it for an active project. To define script for an active project, select the **Run command script file** check box and then choose the browse button located next to it; the **Select Script File** dialog box will be displayed. Select the desired script from it and then choose the **Open** button; the path for the selected script will be displayed in the edit box. Now, when you choose the **OK** button in the **Project-Wide Utilities** dialog box, the corresponding script will run automatically for the active project. The **Purge all blocks** check box is selected to remove all unused blocks or symbols from the active project. Note that in AutoCAD Electrical 2022, all blocks in the selected drawings of the active project will be purged in the first attempt.

## Wire Types

This area is used to import wire types from the other drawings. To do so, select the **Import from specified drawing** check box and then choose the browse button located next to the edit box; the **Wire Type Import - Select Master Drawing** dialog box will be displayed. Select the desired drawing from it and choose the **Open** button; the path for the selected drawing will be displayed in the edit box. Now, choose the **Setup** button; the **Import Wire Types** dialog box will be displayed. This dialog box displays a list of wire types used in the selected drawing. Select the wire types to be imported and use the other options in this dialog box as per your requirement. Now, choose the **OK** button to close it. After specifying the desired options in the **Project-Wide Utilities** dialog box, choose the **OK** button; the **Batch Process Drawings** dialog box will be displayed. If you choose the **Project** button in this dialog box and choose **OK**, the **Select Drawings to Process** dialog box will be displayed. Select the drawings in which you want to make changes and choose **OK**; the selected drawings will be updated. Similarly, if you want to make changes in the active drawing only, select the **Active Drawing** radio button from the **Batch Process Drawings** dialog box and choose **OK**; the changes will be carried out in the active drawing only.

# TUTORIALS

## Tutorial 1

In this tutorial, you will create a symbol, insert attributes into it, and then save it. Next, you will insert the symbol created into the drawing. **(Expected time: 30 min)**

The following steps are required to complete this tutorial:

a. Create a new drawing.
b. Insert a ladder in the drawing.

c. Create a symbol, insert attributes, and insert wire connection attributes to the symbol.
d. Save and insert the symbol.
e. Save the drawing file.

## Creating a New Drawing

1. Create a new drawing *C13_tut01.dwg* in the **CADCIM** project with the *ACAD_ELECTRICAL.dwt* template and move it to the *TUTORIALS* subfolder, as already discussed in the previous chapters.

## Inserting a Ladder

1. Choose the **Insert Ladder** tool from **Schematic > Insert Wires/Wire Numbers > Insert Ladder** drop-down; the **Insert Ladder** dialog box is displayed. 

2. Set the following parameters in the **Insert Ladder** dialog box:

   Width: **12.000**
   Spacing: **5.000**
   1st Reference: **100**
   Rungs: **4**
   **1 Phase**: Select this radio button
   **Yes**: Select this radio button

   Keep the values in the rest of the edit boxes intact.

3. Choose the **OK** button in the **Insert Ladder** dialog box; you are prompted to specify the start position of the first rung. Enter **8,18** at the Command prompt and press ENTER; the ladder is inserted in the drawing.

## Creating a Symbol and Inserting Attributes in it

1. In order to create a symbol, first draw a circle in the drawing by choosing the **Center, Radius** tool from the **Circle** drop-down in the **Draw** panel of the **Home** tab or by choosing **Draw > Circle > Center, Radius** from the menu bar; you are prompted to specify the center point for the circle. Enter **7.5,30** at the Command prompt and press ENTER; you are prompted to specify the radius of the circle.

2. Enter **0.5** at the Command prompt and press ENTER; the circle is inserted in the drawing. Next, choose **Draw > Polygon** from the menu bar; you are prompted to specify the number of sides.

3. Enter **4** at the Command prompt and press ENTER; you are prompted to specify the center of the polygon.

4. Select the center of the circle as the center of the polygon; you are prompted to enter an option.

**Note**

*To snap the center of a circle, right-click on the **Object Snap** button in the Status Bar; a shortcut menu is displayed. Choose the **Object Snap Settings** options from the shortcut menu; the **Drafting Settings** dialog box is displayed. Select the **Center** check box from the **Object Snap** tab and choose the **OK** button to save the changes made in this dialog box. Press F3, if the object snap is off.*

5. Enter **I** at the Command prompt and press ENTER; you are prompted to specify the radius of the circle.

6. Enter **6,30** at the Command prompt and press ENTER; the polygon is inserted in the drawing, as shown in Figure 13-36.

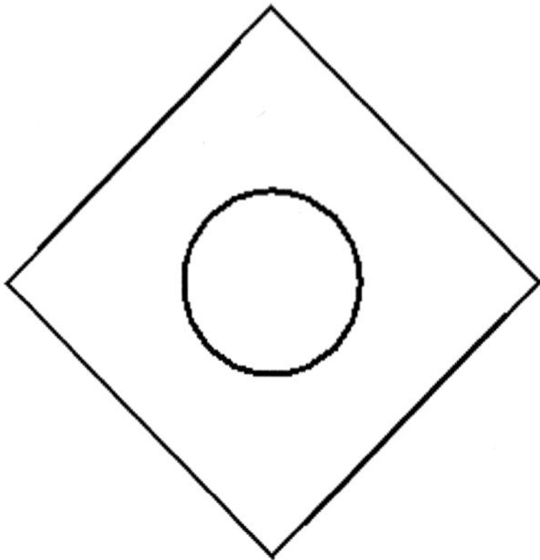

***Figure 13-36*** *The polygon inserted in the drawing*

7. Choose the **Symbol Builder** tool from **Schematic > Other Tools > Symbol Builder** drop-down; the **Select Symbol / Objects** dialog box is displayed.

8. By default, the **Unnamed** option is selected in the **Name** drop-down list. Do not change this option as this is used to create the symbol from scratch.

9. Choose the **Select objects** button from the **Select from drawing** area; you are prompted to select the objects. Select the circle and polygon and then press ENTER; the **Select Symbol / Objects** dialog box is displayed again and the preview of the polygon inscribed in circle is displayed in the **Preview** area of the **Select Symbol / Objects** dialog box.

10. In the **Attribute template** area, choose the **Browse** button located next to the **Library path** drop-down list; the **Browse For Folder** dialog box is displayed. In this dialog box, make sure the path *C:\users\public\ public doc...\NFPA* is displayed in the **Library path** drop-down list. Next, make sure **Horizontal Parent** is selected in the **Symbol** drop-down list, and **GNR (Generic)** is selected in the **Type** drop-down list. Keep rest of the values intact.

11. Choose the **OK** button in the **Select Symbol / Objects** dialog box; the **Block Editor** environment, the **Symbol Builder Attribute Editor** palette, the **Symbol Builder** and **Block Editor** tabs, and the **Block Authoring Palettes - All Palettes** palette are displayed. If the **Block Editor** environment is not invoked, choose the **Block Editor** tab to invoke it.

12. Select the **TAG1** row from the **Required** rollout of the **Symbol Builder Attribute Editor** palette and then choose the **Properties** button; the **Insert / Edit Attributes** dialog box is displayed. Enter **0.25** in the **Height** row of the **Text** area. Next, choose the **OK** button to save the changes made and exit the dialog box.

13. Choose the **Insert Attribute** button; you are prompted to specify the insertion base point of this tag. Also, notice that TAG1 attribute is attached to the cursor.

14. Enter **7.5,31.65** at the Command prompt and press ENTER; the TAG1 attribute for the symbol is inserted above the symbol, as shown in Figure 13-37.

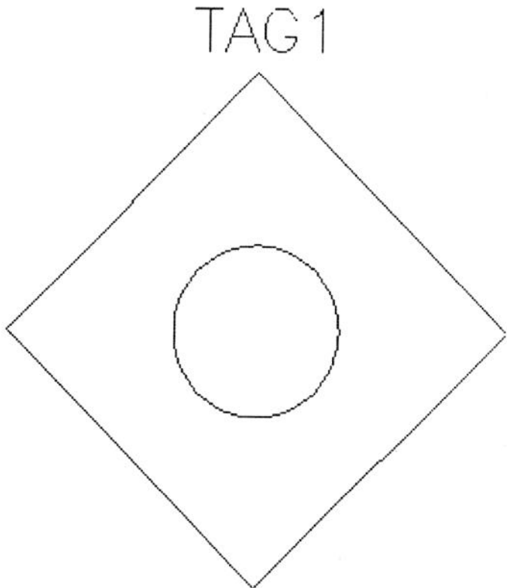


***Figure 13-37*** *The TAG1 attribute inserted into the symbol*

15. Select the **MFG** row from the **Symbol Builder Attribute Editor** palette and then choose the **Properties** button; the **Insert / Edit Attributes** dialog box is displayed. Enter **0.1** in the **Height** row. Choose the **OK** button to exit the dialog box.

16. Choose the **Insert Attribute** button; you are prompted to specify the insertion base point of the tag.

**Note**

*You can also insert an attribute to the symbol by right-clicking on the attribute and choosing the* ***Insert Attribute*** *option from the shortcut menu displayed.*

17. Insert MFG tag in the drawing, refer to Figure 13-38.

18. Change the height of the CAT, ASSYCODE, and FAMILY attributes to **0.1** in the **Insert / Edit Attributes** dialog box as discussed earlier and insert them into the symbol using the **Insert Attribute** button, refer to Figure 13-38. Make sure the **Snap Mode** button is deactivated to insert these attributes at desired places.

19. Similarly, change the height of the DESC1, DESC2, DESC3, INST, and LOC attributes to **0.25** using the **Properties** button in the **Required** rollout and then insert these attributes to the symbol using the **Insert Attribute** button, as shown in Figure 13-39.

20. To insert wire connections into the symbol, scroll down in the **Symbol Builder Attribute Editor** palette and make sure **Left/None** is selected in the **Direction/Style** row of the **Wire Connection** rollout.

21. Choose the **Insert Wire Connection** button from the **Wire Connection** rollout; you are prompted to select Left or (Top/Bottom/Right/rAdial).

22. Enter **6,30** at the Command prompt and press ENTER; the TERM01 attribute is inserted into the symbol and you are prompted to select the location for TERM02. Enter **R** at the Command prompt and press ENTER.

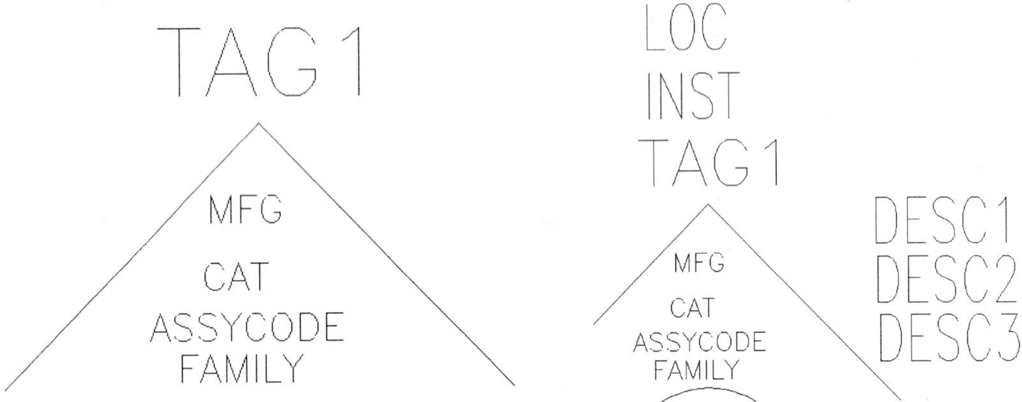


***Figure 13-38*** *Different attributes inserted into the symbol*

***Figure 13-39*** *Different attributes inserted into the symbol*

23. Enter **9,30** at the Command prompt and press ENTER; the TERM02 is inserted into the symbol. Figure 13-40 shows the TERM01 and TERM02 attributes inserted into the symbol.

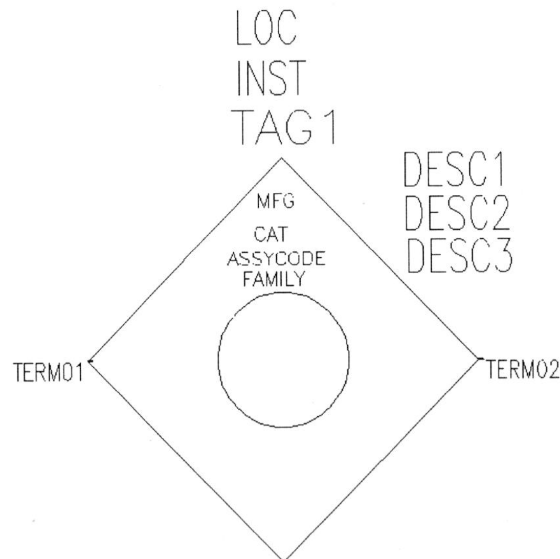


***Figure 13-40*** *TERM01 and TERM02 attributes inserted into the symbol*

24. Press ENTER to exit the command.

25. Select the **TERM01** attribute displayed in the **Pins** rollout and choose the **Properties** button; the **Insert / Edit Attribute** dialog box is displayed.

26. Enter **0.25** in the **Height** row and choose the **OK** button; the height of TERM01 is changed.

27. Similarly, change the height of the TERM02 attribute to **0.25**.

## Saving and Inserting the Symbol

1. To save the symbol, choose the **Done** button from the **Edit** panel of the **Symbol Builder** tab; the **Close Block Editor: Save Symbol** dialog box is displayed.

2. Select the **Wblock** radio button from the **Symbol** area, if it is not selected.

3. Choose the **Pick point** button from the **Base point** area; you are prompted to specify the insertion base point. Select the center of the circle as the base point.

4. Enter **_MY SYMBOL** in the **Unique identifier** edit box and click in the **Symbol name** edit box; the name of the symbol is displayed in the **Symbol name** edit box as HDV1_MY SYMBOL. Keep the rest of the values in this dialog box intact.

5. Choose the **OK** button in the **Close Block Editor: Save Symbol** dialog box; the **Close Block Editor** message box is displayed.

6. Choose the **Yes** button in the **Close Block Editor** message box for inserting the symbol; you are prompted to specify the insertion point for the symbol.

7. Enter **13.5,18** at the Command prompt and press ENTER; the **Insert / Edit Component** dialog box is displayed. Enter **100A** in the edit box of the **Component Tag** area and choose the **OK** button; the symbol is inserted into the ladder.

   You will notice that (-) symbol is displayed before the component tag. To remove this dash, follow the steps given next.

8. Right-click on the **CADCIM** project; a shortcut menu is displayed. Choose the **Properties** option from it; the **Project Properties** dialog box is displayed. In this dialog box, choose the **Components** tab. Next, select the **Suppress dash when first character of tag** check box and then choose **OK**; the **IEC Tag Mode Update** dialog box is displayed.

9. In this dialog box, select the **Active Drawing(Pick)** radio button and choose **OK**; you are prompted to select objects. Select the symbol that you have inserted and press ENTER; the **QSave** message box is displayed. Choose **Yes** in this message box. You will notice that dash is removed from the component tag of the symbol.

   Figure 13-41 shows the symbol inserted into the ladder. Figure 13-42 shows the zoomed view of the symbol inserted into the ladder.

## Saving the Drawing File

1. Choose **File > Save** from the menu bar or choose **Save** from the **Application Menu** to save the drawing file, *C13_tut01.dwg*.

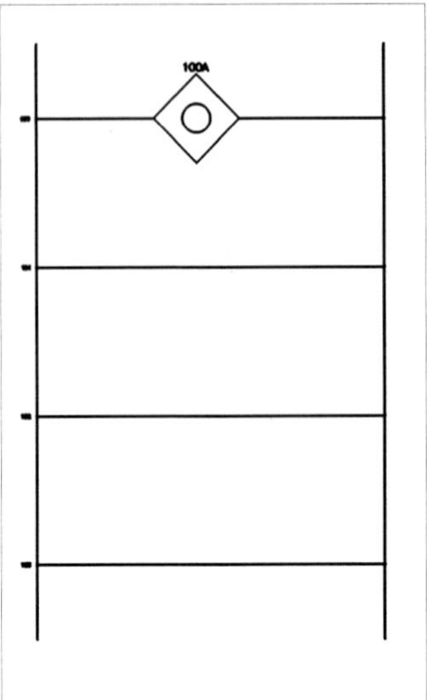


*Figure 13-41 Symbol inserted into the ladder*

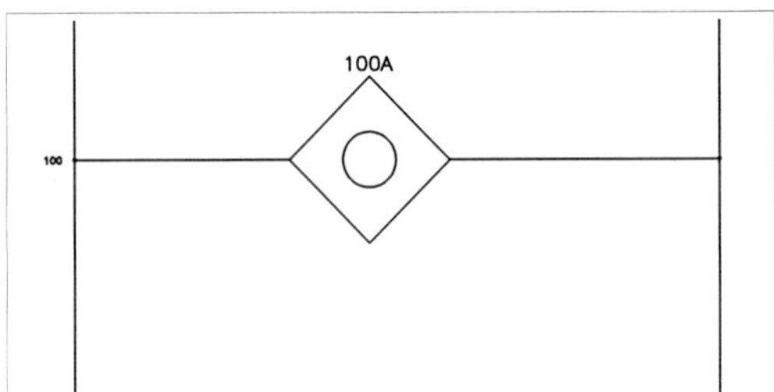


*Figure 13-42 The zoomed view of the symbol inserted into the ladder*

## Tutorial 2

In this tutorial, you will add the symbol that you created in Tutorial 1 of this chapter to the **Insert Component** dialog box using the **Icon Menu Wizard** tool. You will then insert the component into the drawing. **(Expected time: 20 min)**

The following steps are required to complete this tutorial:

a. Open, save, and add the drawing to the active project.
b. Add a new icon to the menu.
c. Insert the component.
d. Save the drawing.

### Opening, Saving, and Adding the Drawing to the Active Project

1. Open the *C13_tut01.dwg* from the **CADCIM** project and activate the CADCIM project.

2. Save the *C13_tut01.dwg* file with the name *C13_tut02.dwg*. You can also download this file from the CADCIM website. The path of the file is as follows:

   *Textbooks > CAD/CAM > AutoCAD Electrical > AutoCAD Electrical 2022 for Electrical Control Designers*

3. Add the drawing *C13_tut02.dwg* to the **CADCIM** project, as discussed in the previous chapters.

## Adding a New Icon to the Menu

1. To add the icon of the new symbol, choose the **Icon Menu Wizard** tool from the **Other Tools** panel of the **Schematic** tab; the **Select Menu file** dialog box is displayed.

2. Choose the **Schematic** button, if *ACE_NFPA_MENU.DAT* is not displayed in the edit box.

3. Next, choose the **OK** button; the **Icon Menu Wizard** dialog box is displayed.

4. Click on the **Add** drop-down list; various options are displayed. Select the **Component** option from the drop-down list; the **Add Icon - Component** dialog box is displayed.

5. Enter **MY SYMBOL** in the **Name** edit box of the **Icon Details** area.

6. Next, choose the **Pick <** button on the right of the **Image file** edit box; you are prompted to select the block.

7. Select the symbol you created in Tutorial 1 of this chapter; the name of block (HDVI_MY SYMBOL) is displayed in the **Image file** edit box.

8. Clear the **Create PNG from current screen image** check box, if it is selected.

9. Next, choose the **Browse** button on the right of the **Block name** edit box; the **Select File** dialog box is displayed. Browse to *"C:\Users\Public\Public Documents\Autodesk\Acade 2022\ Libs\NFPA"*. Enter **HDV1_MY SYMBOL** in the **File Name** edit box and choose the **Open** button; the path and location of *HDV1_MY SYMBOL.dwg* is displayed in the **Block name** edit box.

10. Choose the **OK** button in the **Add Icon - Component** dialog box; the icon is added to the **Icon Menu Wizard** dialog box, as shown in Figure 13-43.

11. Choose the **OK** button in the **Icon Menu Wizard** dialog box to save the changes made and exit the dialog box.

## Inserting the Component

1. In order to insert the component, choose the **Icon Menu** tool from **Schematic > Insert Components > Icon Menu** drop-down; the **Insert Component** dialog box is displayed.

2. Select **MY SYMBOL** from this dialog box; you are prompted to specify the insertion point.

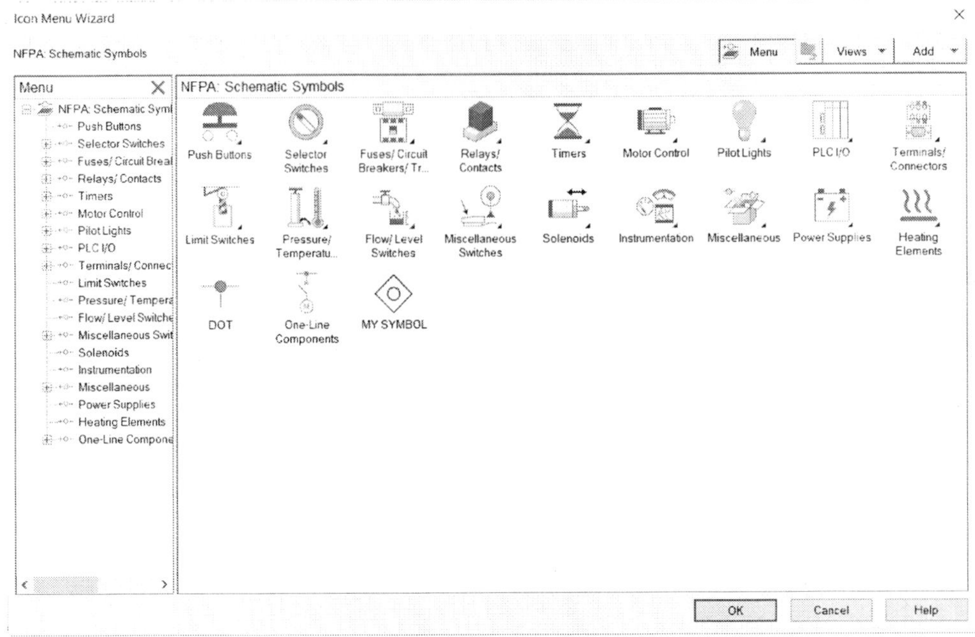


*Figure 13-43 The **Icon Menu Wizard** dialog box showing the icon of the symbol*

3. Enter **13,3** at the Command prompt and press ENTER; the **Insert / Edit Component** dialog box is displayed. Make sure **103** is displayed in the edit box of the **Component Tag** area and choose the **OK** button; the symbol is inserted in the rung 103 of the ladder, as shown in Figure 13-44. Figure 13-45 shows the zoomed view of the symbol inserted into the ladder.

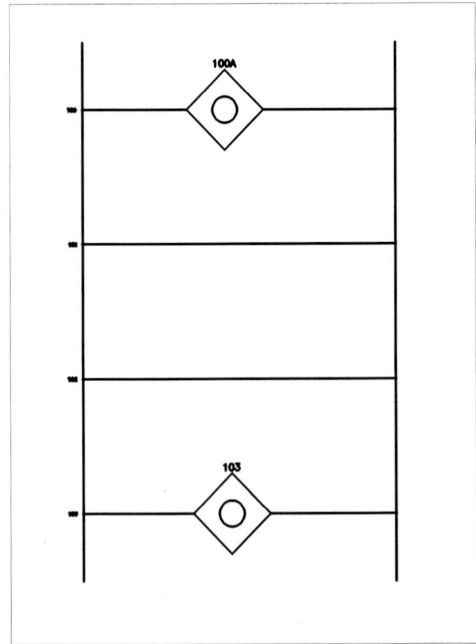


*Figure 13-44 Symbol inserted into the ladder*

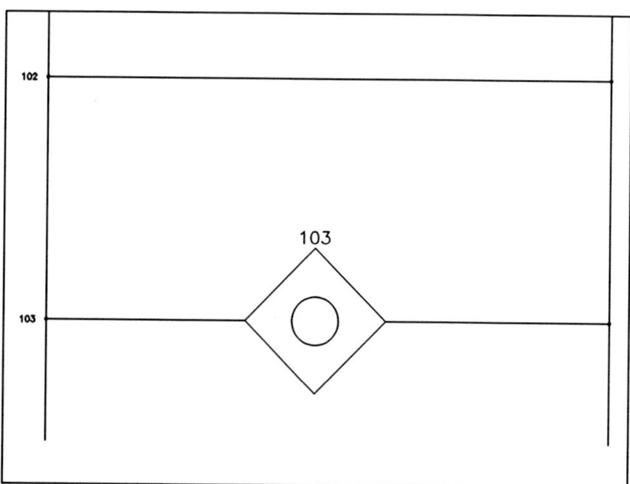


*Figure 13-45 The zoomed view of the symbol inserted into the ladder*

## Saving the Drawing File

1. Choose **Save** from the **Application Menu** or **File > Save** from the menu bar to save the drawing file.

# Tutorial 3

In this tutorial, you will export data from a drawing file to an excel sheet, make changes in that sheet, and then import the sheet data to the drawing file. **(Expected time: 15 min)**

The following steps are required to complete this tutorial:

a. Open, save, and add the drawing to the active project.
b. Export the data.
c. Modify the data.
d. Import the data.
e. Save the drawing.

## Opening, Saving, and Adding the Drawing to the Active Project

1. Open the *C05_tut01.dwg* from the **CADCIM** project and activate the **CADCIM** project.

2. Save the *C05_tut01.dwg* file with the name *C13_tut03.dwg*. You can also download this file from the CADCIM website. The path of the file is as follows:

   *Textbooks > CAD/CAM > AutoCAD Electrical > AutoCAD Electrical 2022 for Electrical Control Designers*

3. Add the drawing *C13_tut03.dwg* to the **CADCIM** project, as discussed in the previous chapters.

## Exporting the Data

1. Choose the **To Spreadsheet** tool from the **Export** panel of the **Import/Export Data** tab; the **Export to Spreadsheet** dialog box is displayed, as shown in Figure 13-46.

2. In this dialog box, make sure the **Components*** radio button is selected. Next, choose the **OK** button; the **Component Data Export** dialog box is displayed.

3. In this dialog box, select the **Active Drawing** radio button from the **Data export for** area. Next, select the **Excel file format (.xls)** radio button from the **Output format** area and then choose the **OK** button; the **Select file name for drawing's XLS output** dialog box is displayed.

4. In this dialog box, enter **C13_tut03_components** in the **File name** text box and select **C:\Users\User Name\Documents\AcadE 2022\AeData\Proj\CADCIM** from the **Save in** drop-down list, refer to Figure 13-47. Next, choose the **Save** button; an Excel file with the name *c13_tut03_components* is created at the specified location.

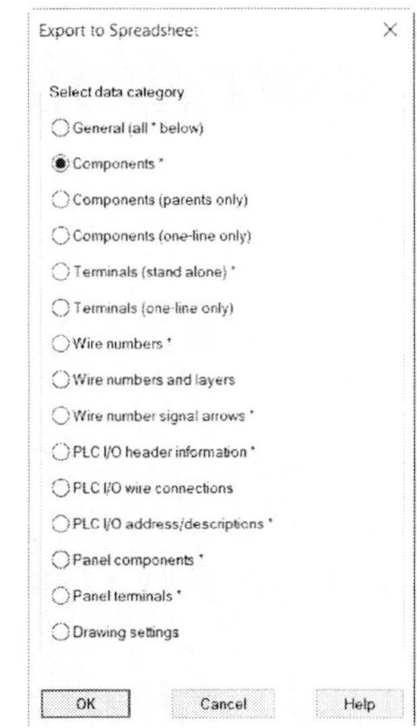


*Figure 13-46 The* ***Export to Spreadsheet*** *dialog box*

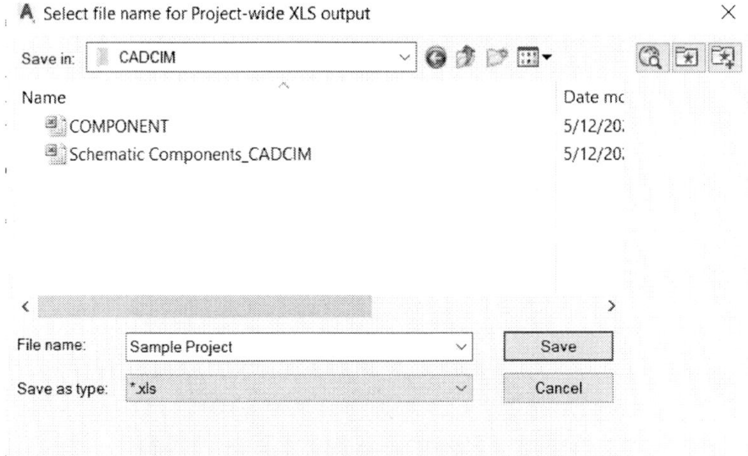


*Figure 13-47 The* ***Select file name for drawing's XLS output*** *dialog box*

5. Choose the **To Spreadsheet** tool again from the **Export** panel of the **Import/Export Data** tab; the **Export to Spreadsheet** dialog box is displayed.

6. In this dialog box, select the **Drawing settings** radio button and choose the **OK** button; the **Drawing Settings Data Export** dialog box is displayed. In this dialog box, make sure that the **Project** radio button is selected from the **Data export for** area and the **Excel file format [.xls]** is selected from the **Output format** area. Next, choose the **OK** button; the **Select Drawings to Process** dialog box is displayed.

7. In this dialog box, select all the tutorial files in the **CADCIM** project from the top list (Chapter 2 to Chapter 13) and then choose the **Process** button; all the tutorial files are shifted to the bottom part of the **Select Drawings to Process** dialog box. Next, choose the **OK** button; the **Select file name for Project-wide XLS output** dialog box is displayed.

8. In this dialog box, enter **CADCIM_drawing settings** in the **File name** text box and select the **C:\Users\User Name\Documents\AcadE 2022\AeData\Proj\CADCIM** from the **Save in** drop-down list. Next, choose the **Save** button; an Excel file with the name *CADCIM_drawing settings* is created at the specified location.

## Modifying the Data

1. Open the Windows Explorer and browse to the location *C:\ Users\User Name\Documents\AcadE 2022\AeData\Proj\CADCIM*. Next, open the *C13_tut03_components* file from this location.

2. Modify the data in the **DESC1** and **DESC2** columns of this file, refer to Figure 13-48. Next, save and close the file.

| | A | B | C | D | E | F | G |
|---|---|---|---|---|---|---|---|
| 1 | (PAR1 CH | FAMILY | TAGNAME | DESC1 | DESC2 | DESC3 | (REF) |
| 2 | 1 | PB | PB1 | NO | PUSH BUTTON | | 1 |
| 3 | 1 | PB | PB1A | NC | PUSH BUTTON | | 1 |
| 4 | 1 | CR | CR1 | CTRL RELAY | | | 1 |
| 5 | 2 | CR | CR1 | CTRL RELAY | NO | | 2 |
| 6 | 2 | CR | CR1 | CTRL RELAY | NC | | 3 |
| 7 | 1 | LT | LT3 | GREEN | OFF | | 3 |
| 8 | 2 | CR | CR1 | CTRL RELAY | NO | | 4 |
| 9 | 1 | LT | LT4 | RED | ON | | 4 |
| 10 | | | | | | | |
| 11 | | | | | | | |
| 12 | | | | | | | |

***Figure 13-48*** *The data changed in the* ***DESC1, DESC2*** *columns*

3. Open the *CADCIM_drawing settings* file from the *C:\ Users\User Name\Documents\AcadE 2022\AeData\Proj\CADCIM* location.

4. Change the data in the **SEC**, **SUBSEC**, and **SHDWGNAM** columns of this file, as shown in Figure 13-49. Next, save and close the file.

## Importing the Data

1. Make sure the *C13_tut03* file is open in AutoCAD Electrical. Next, choose the **From Spreadsheet** tool from the **Import** panel of the **Import/Export Data** tab; the **Update Drawing from Spreadsheet File** dialog box is displayed.

2. In this dialog box, browse to the *C:\Users\User Name\Documents\AcadE 2022\AeData\Proj\CADCIM* in the **Look in** drop-down list and then select the *c13_tut03_components* file from the list displayed. Next, choose the **Open** button; the **Update Drawings per Spreadsheet Data** dialog box is displayed.

| | A | B | C | D | E |
|---|---|---|---|---|---|
| 1 | (DWGNAM) | SEC | SUBSEC | SH | SHDWGNAM |
| 2 | C02_TUT01 | C2 | 1 | 01 | 201 |
| 3 | C03_TUT01 | C3 | 1 | 5 | 301 |
| 4 | C03_TUT02 | C3 | 2 | 5 | 302 |
| 5 | C03_TUT03 | C3 | 3 | 5 | 303 |
| 6 | C03_TUT04 | C3 | 4 | 5 | 304 |
| 7 | C04_TUT01 | C4 | 1 | 01 | 401 |
| 8 | C04_TUT03 | C4 | 3 | | 403 |
| 9 | C04_TUT04 | C4 | 4 | A | 404 |
| 10 | C05_TUT01 | C5 | 1 | | 501 |
| 11 | C05_TUT02 | C5 | 2 | | 502 |
| 12 | C05_TUT03 | C5 | 3 | | 503 |
| 13 | C05_TUT04 | C5 | 4 | | 504 |
| 14 | C06_TUT01 | C6 | 1 | | 601 |
| 15 | C06_TUT03 | C6 | 3 | | 603 |
| 16 | C06_TUT01_UPDATE | C6 | 1 | 01 | 601 |
| 17 | C06_TUT03_UPDATE | C6 | 3 | 02 | 603 |
| 18 | C07_TUT01 | C7 | 1 | | 701 |
| 19 | C07_TUT02 | C7 | 2 | | 702 |
| 20 | C07_TUT03 | C7 | 3 | | 703 |
| 21 | C07_TUT04 | C7 | 4 | | 704 |
| 22 | C08_TUT01 | C8 | 1 | | 801 |
| 23 | C08_TUT02 | C8 | 2 | | 802 |
| 24 | C08_TUT03 | C8 | 3 | | 803 |
| 25 | C08_TUT04 | C8 | 4 | | 804 |
| 26 | C09_TUT01 | C9 | 1 | | 901 |
| 27 | C09_TUT02 | C9 | 2 | | 902 |
| 28 | C10_TUT01 | C10 | 1 | | 1001 |
| 29 | C10_TUT2 | C10 | 2 | | 1002 |
| 30 | C10_TUT03 | C10 | 3 | 01 | 1003 |
| 31 | C10_TUT04 | C10 | 4 | 02 | 1004 |
| 32 | C10_TUT05 | C10 | 5 | 03 | 1005 |
| 33 | C11_TUT01 | C11 | 1 | | 1101 |
| 34 | C`11_TUT02 | C11 | 2 | | 1102 |
| 35 | C`11_TUT03 | C11 | 3 | | 1103 |
| 36 | C12_TUT01 | C12 | 1 | 01 | 1201 |
| 37 | C12_TUT02 | C12 | 2 | 01 | 1202 |
| 38 | C04_TUT02 | C4 | 2 | 01 | 402 |
| 39 | C12_TUT03 | C12 | 3 | | 1203 |
| 40 | C12_TUT04 | C12 | 4 | 01 | 1204 |
| 41 | C12_TUT05 | C12 | 5 | 5 | 1205 |
| 42 | C13_TUT01 | C13 | 1 | | 1301 |
| 43 | C13_TUT02 | C13 | 2 | | 1302 |
| 44 | C13_TUT03 | C13 | 3 | | 1303 |

***Figure 13-49*** *The data changed in the **SEC**, **SUBSEC**, and **SHDWGNAM** columns*

3. In this dialog box, select the **Active Drawing** radio button from the **Update drawings per spreadsheet data file. Process** area. Next, choose the **OK** button. You will notice that the description of components in the *C13_tut03* file is changed.

4. Choose the **From Spreadsheet** tool again from the **Import** panel of the **Import/Export Data** tab; the **Update Drawing from Spreadsheet File** dialog box is displayed.

5. In this dialog box, browse to the *C:\Users\User Name\Documents\AcadE 2022\AeData\Proj\CADCIM* in the **Look in** drop-down list and then select the *CADCIM_drawing settings* file from the list displayed. Next, choose the **Open** button; the **Update Drawings per Spreadsheet Data** dialog box is displayed.

6. In this dialog box, select the **Project** radio button from the **Update drawings per spreadsheet data file. Process** area. Next, choose the **OK** button; the **Select Drawings to Process** dialog box is displayed.

7. In this dialog box, select all the tutorial files in the **CADCIM** project from the top list (Chapter 2 to Chapter 13) and then choose the **Process** button; all the tutorial files are shifted to the bottom part of the **Select Drawings to Process** dialog box. Next, choose the **OK** button. If the **QSAVE** message box is displayed, choose the **OK** button in it.

You will notice that all the tutorial files are opened, changed, and then closed one by one.

To verify the changes in the drawing settings of the tutorial files, you need to follow the steps given next.

8. Right-click on any of the tutorial files in the **CADCIM** project; a shortcut menu is displayed. Choose **Properties > Drawing Properties** from this shortcut menu, refer to Figure 13-50; the **Drawing Properties** dialog box is displayed.

9. In this dialog box, the values in the **Drawing**, **Section**, **Sub-Section** edit boxes of the **Sheet Values** area are changed, refer to Figure 13-51.

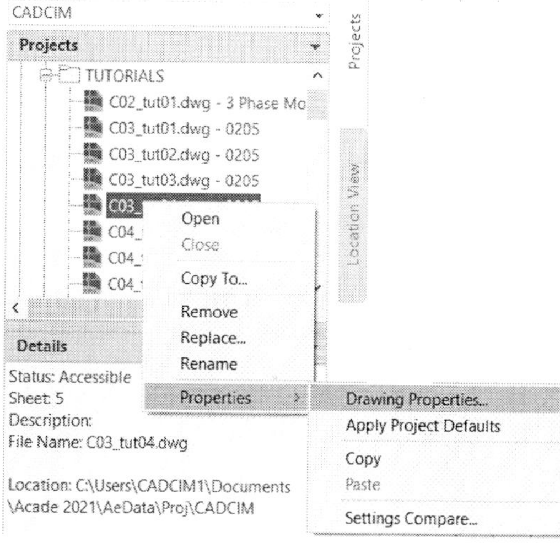


*Figure 13-50 Choosing **Properties > Drawing Properties** from the shortcut menu*

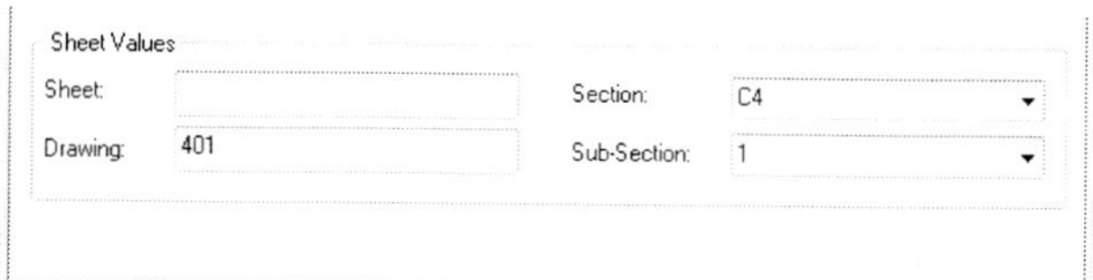


*Figure 13-51 Values changed in the **Drawing**, **Section**, **Sub-Section** edit boxes*

## Saving the Drawing File

1. Choose **Save** from the **Application Menu** or **File > Save** from the menu bar to save the drawing file.

# Tutorial 4

In this tutorial, you will mark a drawing in the **CADCIM** project, make changes in the drawing, and then verify the drawing using the **Mark/Verify DWGs** tool. **(Expected time: 15 min)**

The following steps are required to complete this tutorial:

a. Open, save, and add the drawing.
b. Mark the drawing.
c. Modify the drawing.
d. Verify the drawing.
e. Save the drawing.

## Opening, Saving, and Adding the Drawing to the Active Project

1. Open the *C13_tut03.dwg* from the **CADCIM** project and activate the **CADCIM** project.

2. Save the *C13_tut03.dwg* file with the name *C13_tut04.dwg*. You can also download this file from the CADCIM website. The path of the file is as follows:

   *Textbooks > CAD/CAM > AutoCAD Electrical > AutoCAD Electrical 2022 for Electrical Control Designers*

3. Add the drawing *C13_tut04.dwg* to the **CADCIM** project, as discussed in the previous chapters.

## Marking the Drawing

1. Choose the **Mark/Verify DWGs** tool from the **Project Tools** panel of the **Project** tab; the **Mark and Verify** dialog box is displayed, as shown in Figure 13-52.

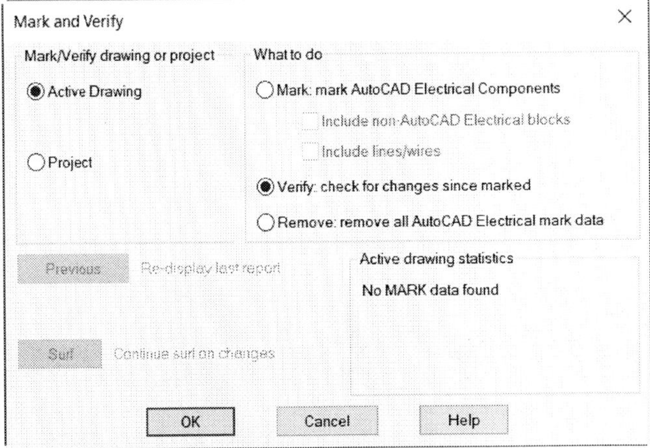


*Figure 13-52 The **Mark and Verify** dialog box*

2. In this dialog box, select the **Mark: mark AutoCAD Electrical Components** radio button from the **What to do** area and make sure that the **Active Drawing** radio button is selected in the **Mark/Verify drawing or project** area. Next, choose the **OK** button; the **Enter Your Initials** dialog box is displayed.

3. In this dialog box, enter the initials and the comments, if any, in the respective edit boxes and choose the **OK** button; the AutoCAD Electrical data is marked.

**Note**

*1. To include non-AutoCAD electrical blocks in the marked data, select the* ***include non-AutoCAD Electrical blocks*** *check box from the* ***What to do*** *area.*

*2. To include lines and wires in the marked data, select the* ***include lines/wires*** *check box from the* ***What to do*** *area.*

## Modifying the Data

1. Choose the **Edit** tool from **Schematic > Edit Components > Edit Components** drop-down; you are prompted to select the component to be edited. Select the PB1 push button; the **Insert/Edit Component** dialog box is displayed.

2. Choose the **Lookup** button in the **Catalog Data** area; the **Catalog Browser** dialog box is displayed. Select **800H-BR6D1** from this dialog box and choose the **OK** button; the catalog data is modified in the **Catalog Data** area of the **Insert/Edit Component** dialog box. Also, the **AutoCAD Message** message box is displayed. Choose the **OK** button from this message box. Next, choose the **OK** button from the **Insert/Edit Component** dialog box; the **Update other drawings** message box is displayed. Choose the **Task** button from this message box.

3. Choose the **Edit** tool from **Schematic > Edit Components > Edit Components** drop-down; you are prompted to select the component to be edited. Select the PB1A push button; the **Insert/Edit Component** dialog box is displayed.

4. Choose the **Lookup** button in the **Catalog Data** area; the **Catalog Browser** dialog box is displayed. In this dialog box, select **800H-BR6D2** from the **Catalog Browser** dialog box and choose the **OK** button; the catalog data is added in the **Catalog Data** area of the **Insert/Edit Component** dialog box. Next, choose the **OK** button from this dialog box; the **Update other drawings** message box is displayed. Choose the **Task** button from this message box.

## Verifying the Data

1. Choose the **Mark/Verify DWGs** tool from the **Project Tools** panel of the **Project** tab; the modified **Mark and Verify** dialog box is displayed, as shown in Figure 13-53.

   Notice that the **Active drawing statistics** area displays the date and time when the data was marked for the active drawing along with the initials entered in the **Enter Your Initials** dialog box.

2. Make sure that the **Verify: check for changes since marked** radio button is selected in the **What to do** area. Next, choose the **OK** button; the **REPORT: Changes made on this drawing since last Mark command** dialog box is displayed, as shown in Figure 13-54.

   You can use the **Display Report Format** button from this dialog box to display the changes in the **Report Generator** dialog box, refer to Figure 13-55. Using this dialog box, you can print the changes, save them to a file or can put them in the table format in a drawing, as discussed in detail in Chapter 9.

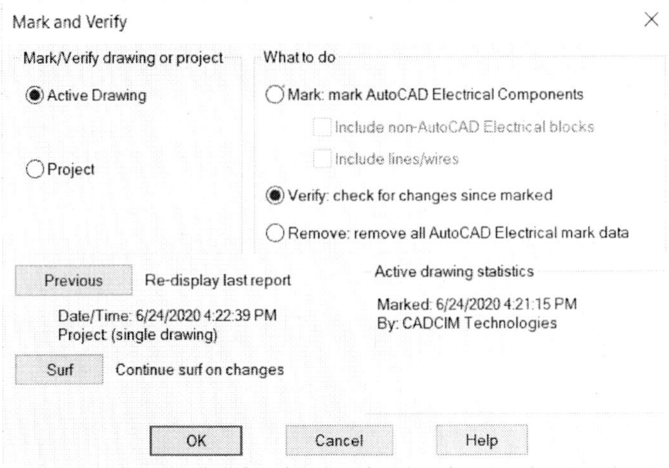

Mark and Verify

Mark/Verify drawing or project

- (•) Active Drawing
- ( ) Project

What to do

- ( ) Mark: mark AutoCAD Electrical Components
  - [ ] Include non-AutoCAD Electrical blocks
  - [ ] Include lines/wires
- (•) Verify: check for changes since marked
- ( ) Remove: remove all AutoCAD Electrical mark data

Previous — Re-display last report

Date/Time: 6/24/2020 4:22:39 PM
Project (single drawing)

Surf — Continue surf on changes

Active drawing statistics

Marked: 6/24/2020 4:21:15 PM
By: CADCIM Technologies

OK | Cancel | Help

*Figure 13-53 The modified **Mark and Verify** dialog box*

REPORT: Changes made on this drawing since last Mark command

```
Mark/Verify Report

-- Dwg: C:\USERS\CADCIM1\DOCUMENTS\...EDATA\PROJ\NFPADEMO\DEMO03.DWG
    Marked date: 5/18/2021 10:25:03 AM  by: ???
    Verify date: 5/18/2021 10:26:53 AM
 changed -------
    +MCAB5-FU307A   CHANGED Schematic component  old:FU307A
    +MCAB5-FU307A   CHANGED CAT value old:FRS-R-5 new:FRS-R-8
                   CHANGED RATING1 value old:5A new:8A
```

Display: Report Format | Surf | Save As | Print | Close

*Figure 13-54 The **REPORT: Changes made on this drawing since last Mark command** dialog box*

## Saving the Drawing File

1. Choose **Save** from the **Application Menu** or **File > Save** from the menu bar to save the drawing file.

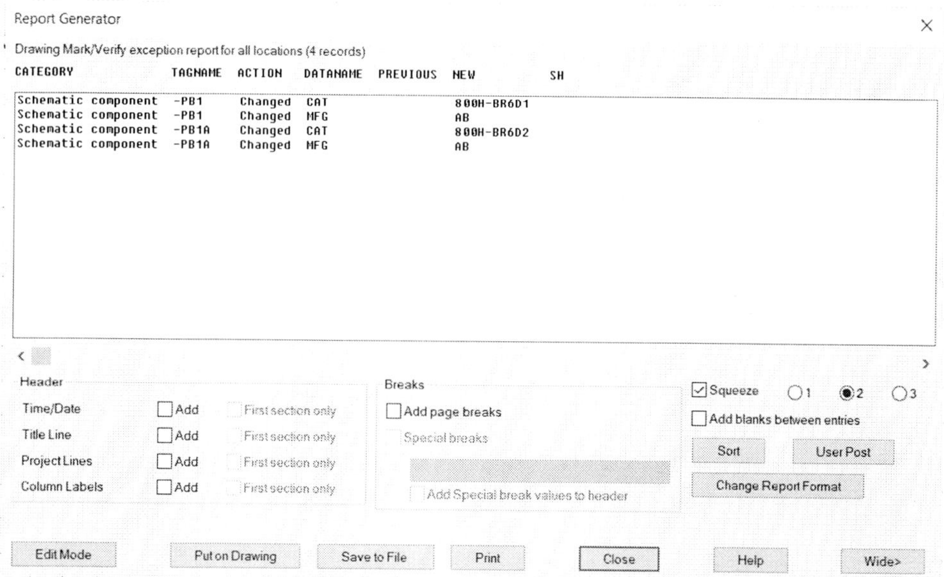


*Figure 13-55 The **Report Generator** dialog box*

## Self-Evaluation Test

**Answer the following questions and then compare them to those given at the end of this chapter:**

1. Which of the following dialog boxes will be displayed if you choose the **Symbol Builder** tool?

   (a) **Symbol Audit** (b) **Symbol Configuration**
   (c) **Select Symbol / Objects** (d) None of these

2. The **To Spreadsheet** tool is used to ______ data from the active drawing or project to an external file.

3. In AutoCAD Electrical, a symbol can be of any size and width. (T/F)

4. The **Icon Menu Wizard** tool is used to add or modify only the schematic symbol libraries. (T/F)

5. The AutoCAD blocks can be converted into AutoCAD Electrical intelligent symbols using the **Symbol Builder** tool. (T/F)

## Review Questions

**Answer the following questions:**

1. Which of the following rollouts is used to select the style and direction of the wire connection attributes?

   (a) **Wire Connection** (b) **Required**
   (c) **Optional** (d) All of these

2. The icon menus can be customized using the ________ tool.

3. The ________ option is used to create a new circuit.

4 The ________ tool is used to import data from an external file to an active drawing or project.

5. The **Mark/Verify** tool is used to add an invisible mark on the components and wire of a drawing before sending it to the client. (T/F)

# EXERCISES

## Exercise 1

Create a new drawing with the name *C13_exer01.dwg* and insert a single-phase ladder with width = 15, spacing between rungs as 3, and number of rungs = 4. Next, create the symbol and add the attributes to it, as shown in Figure 13-56 and then save it as HDV1_SYMBOL. You will also insert the symbol that you created into the ladder, as shown in Figure 13-57. Figure 13-58 shows the zoomed view of the symbol inserted into the ladder. **(Expected time: 25 min)**

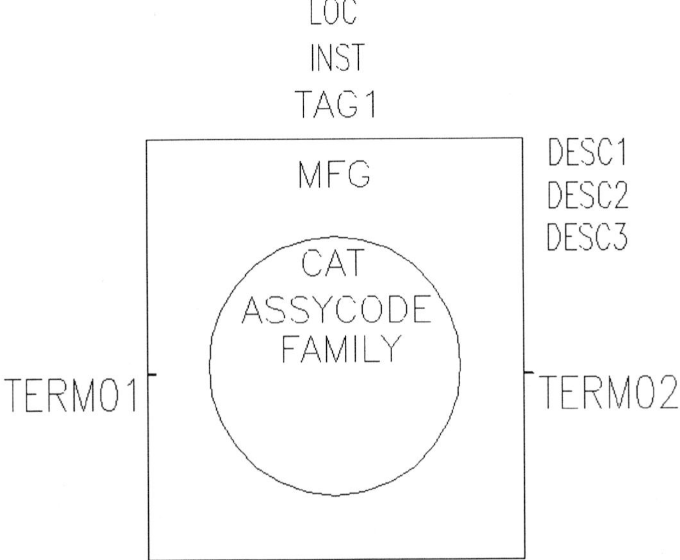


***Figure 13-56*** *Attributes added to the symbol*

**Hint:** Change the height of all attributes shown in Figure 13-56 to 0.1 in the **Symbol Builder Attribute Editor** palette. Also, insert TERM01 and TERM02 attributes at the mid-point of rectangle.

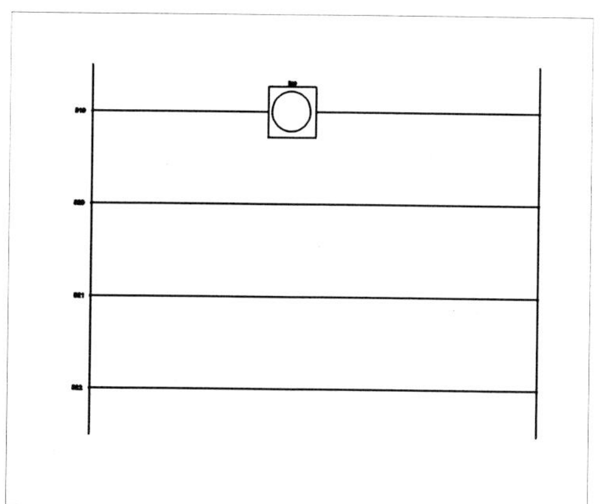

***Figure 13-57*** *Symbol inserted into the ladder*

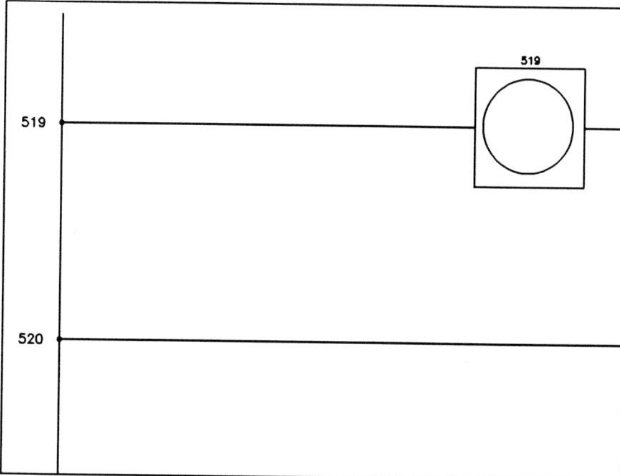


***Figure 13-58*** *The zoomed view of the symbol inserted into the ladder*

## Exercise 2

Open the *C13_exer01.dwg* drawing file. Use the **Icon Menu Wizard** tool to create a sub menu in the **Icon Menu Wizard** dialog box, as shown in Figure 13-59, and then add the icon of the symbol that you created in Exercise 1 to the **Miscellaneous** sub menu, as shown in Figure 13-60. Next, insert the symbol into the ladder, as shown in Figure 13-61. **(Expected time: 20 min)**

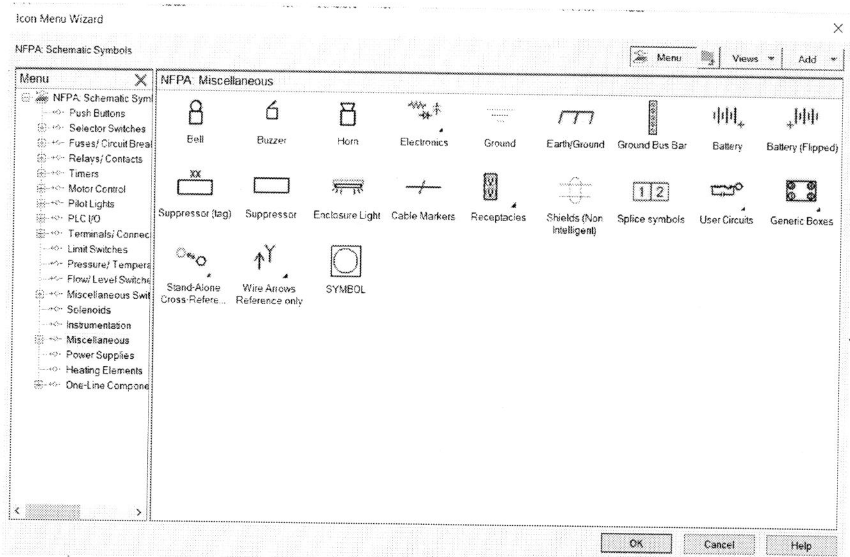


***Figure 13-59*** *Submenu created in the* ***Icon Menu Wizard*** *dialog box*

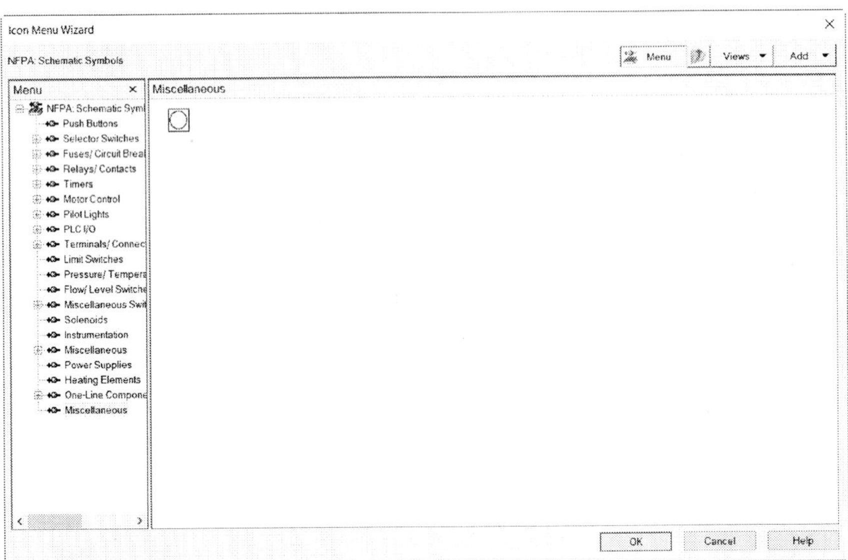


***Figure 13-60*** *The* ***Icon Menu Wizard*** *dialog box displaying the* ***Miscellaneous*** *submenu*

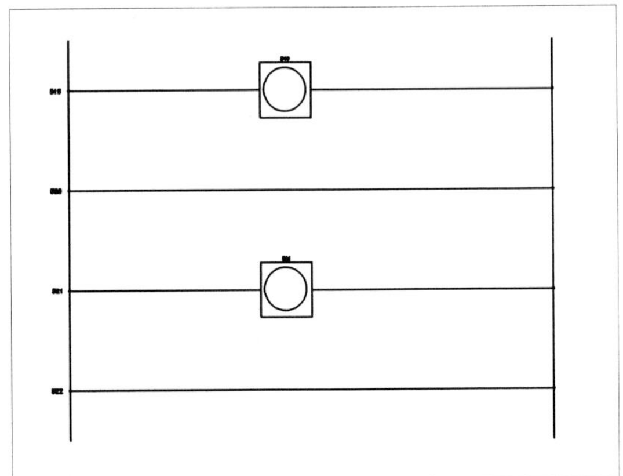

***Figure 13-61*** *Symbol inserted into the ladder*

## Answers to Self-Evaluation Test

**1.** c, **2.** export, **3.** T, **4.** F, **5.** T

# Project 1

# Schematic Drawing

## PROJECT DESCRIPTION

In this project, you will create a motor control circuit, as shown in Figure P1-1. This will be created by using ladder, multiple phase bus, and components such as 3 Phase Motor, 3 Pole Thermal Circuit Breaker, and terminals. Then, you will copy the circuit and save it in the icon menu. Next, you will insert the saved circuit in the drawing, audit the drawing, and save the auditing reports. Also, you will generate the **Wire From/To** report and place it in the new drawing.

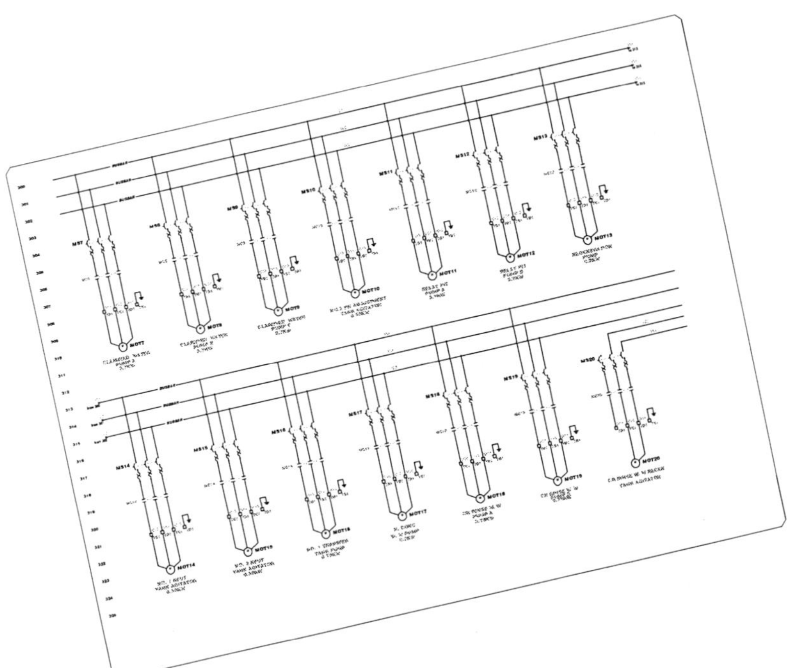

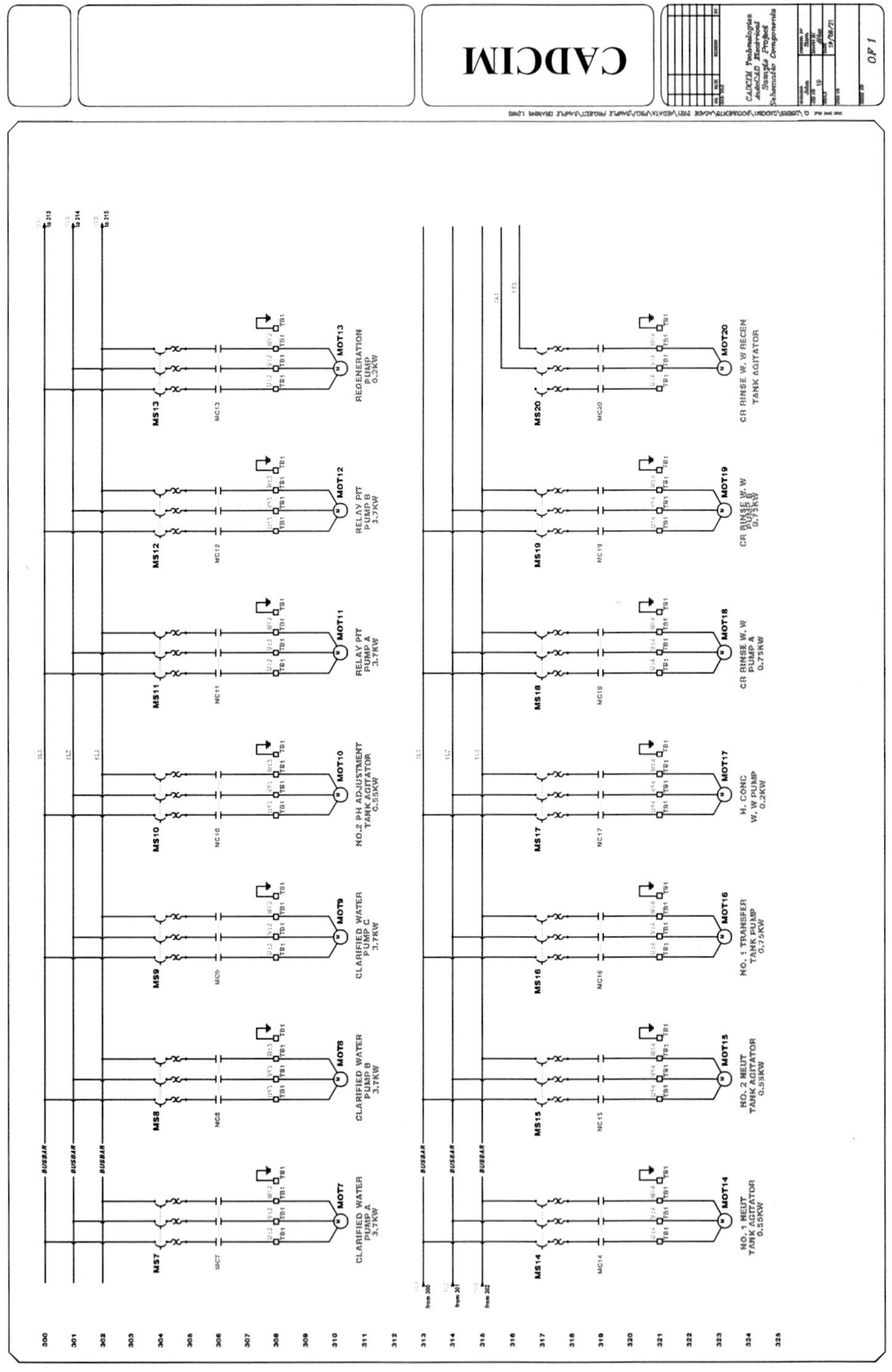


*Figure P1-1 Motor control circuit for Project 1*

## Creating a New Project

1. Choose the **New Project** button from the **PROJECT MANAGER**; the **Create New Project** dialog box is displayed.

2. In this dialog box, enter **Sample Project** in the **Name** edit box.

   By default, *C:\Users\User Name\Documents\Acade 2022\AeData\proj* is displayed in the **Location** edit box. Keep it as it is.

   Make sure that the **Create Folder with Project Name** check box is selected.

   By default, *C:\Users\User Name\Documents\Acade 2022\Aedata\Proj\NfpaDemo\Nfpademo.wdp* is displayed in the **Copy Settings from Project File** edit box.

3. Choose the **Descriptions** button; the **Project Description** dialog box is displayed.

4. Enter the following information in the **Project Description** dialog box:

   Line 1 = CADCIM Technologies
   Line 2 = AutoCAD Electrical
   Line 3 = Sample Project
   Line 4 = 10
   Line 5 = 19/05/21
   Line 6 = Tom
   Line 7 = Alice
   Line 8 = Sam
   Line 9 = 1.00

5. Make sure the **in reports** check box corresponding to all the lines mentioned in the previous step is selected.

6. Choose the **OK** button in the **Project Description** dialog box; the dialog box is closed and you return to the **Create New Project** dialog box.

7. Choose the **OK** button in the **Create New Project** dialog box; a new project is created and displayed in bold text at the top of the **Projects** rollout.

## Creating a Template Drawing File

1. Choose **New > Drawing** from the **Application Menu**; the **Select template** dialog box is displayed.

2. Select **ACAD_ELECTRICAL** from the list displayed and then choose the **Open** button; the drawing file is created.

3. Choose the **Edit** tool from the **Block** panel of the **Home** tab; the **Edit Block Definition** dialog box is displayed. Select **LOGO** from the list box displayed in this dialog box and choose the **OK** button; you switch to the **Block Editor** environment. Also, Autodesk logo is displayed in this environment.

4. Erase Autodesk from the **Block Editor** environment.Next, enter **MTEXT** at the Command prompt and press ENTER; you are prompted to specify the first corner.

5. Enter **18,38** at the Command prompt and press ENTER; you are prompted to specify the second corner.

6. Enter **234,0** at the Command prompt and press ENTER; you switch to the **Text Editor** environment and a text window is displayed in this environment. Type **CADCIM** in the text window and then select it.

7. Enter **30** in the **Annotative** drop-down list of the **Style** panel of the **Text Editor** tab and press ENTER.

8. Next, select **Times New Roman TUR** from the **Font** drop-down list in the **Formatting** panel of the **Text Editor** tab.

9. Next, choose the **B** button from the **Formatting** panel of the **Text Editor** tab and click anywhere outside the text window; CADCIM is displayed on the screen.

10. Choose the **Close Block Editor** button from the **Close** panel of the **Block Editor** tab; the **Block – Changes Not Saved** message box is displayed.

11. Choose the **Save the Changes to LOGO** button in this message box; the text of the template file is replaced with CADCIM. Next, choose **Save** from the **Application Menu**; the **Save Drawing As** dialog box is displayed.

12. In this dialog box, select **AutoCAD Drawing Template (*.dwt)** from the **Files of type** drop-down list and enter **CADCIM** in the **File name** edit box.

13. Choose the **Save** button; the **Template Options** dialog box is displayed. Enter **CADCIM Technologies** in the **Description** area and then choose the **OK** button; the template drawing is saved.

## Creating a New Drawing

1. Choose the **New Drawing** button from the **PROJECT MANAGER**; the **Create New Drawing** dialog box is displayed.

2. Enter **Sample Drawing 1** in the **Name** edit box. Next, choose the **Browse** button on the right of the **Template** edit box; the **Select template** dialog box is displayed.

3. Select **CADCIM** from this dialog box and choose the **Open** button; the name and path of the template file and its name is displayed in the **Template** edit box.

4. Enter **Schematic Components** in the **Description 1** edit box and **Wiring Diagram** in the **Description 2** edit box. Next, choose the **OK** button in the **Create New Drawing** dialog box; the drawing is created in the project and displayed in bold in the **Projects** rollout.

## Inserting the Ladder

1. Choose the **Insert Ladder** tool from **Schematic > Insert Wires/Wire Numbers > Insert Ladder** drop-down; the **Insert Ladder** dialog box is displayed.

2. In the **Insert Ladder** dialog box, set the parameters as follows:

   Select the **1 Phase** radio button
   Index = **1**
   1st Reference = **300**
   Rungs = **26**

   Select the **No Bus** radio button from the **Draw Rungs** area.

3. Choose the **OK** button; you are prompted to specify the start position of the first rung.

4. Enter **1,21.5** at the Command prompt and press ENTER; a ladder without vertical rails and rungs is inserted into the drawing, as shown in Figure P1-2.

***Figure P1-2** Ladder without vertical rails and rungs inserted into the drawing*

## Inserting a Multiple Phase Bus in the Drawing

1. Choose the **Multiple Bus** tool from the **Insert Wires/Wire Numbers** panel of the **Schematic** tab; the **Multiple Wire Bus** dialog box is displayed.

2. Select the **Empty Space, Go Horizontal** radio button from this dialog box.

3. Enter **3** in the **Number of Wires** edit box and **0.75** in the **Spacing** edit box of the **Horizontal** area. Next, choose the **OK** button in the **Multiple Wire Bus** dialog box; you are prompted to specify the start point for the 1st phase.

4. Enter **2,21.5** at the Command prompt and press ENTER; you are prompted to specify the end point of the 1st phase.

5. Enter **28,21.5** at the Command prompt and press ENTER; a three-phase wire is inserted into the drawing, as shown in Figure P1-3.

***Figure P1-3*** *A three-phase wire inserted into the drawing*

6. Repeat step 1. Select the **Another Bus (Multiple Wires)** radio button and enter **3** in the **Number of Wires** edit box. Next, choose the **OK** button in the **Multiple Wire Bus** dialog box; you are prompted to select the existing wire to begin the multi-phase bus connection.

7. Enter **3,21.5** at the Command prompt and press ENTER; you are prompted to specify the end point of the multi-phase bus.

8. Enter **3,14** at the Command prompt and press ENTER; the multiple wire bus is inserted into the drawing, as shown in Figure P1-4.

## Inserting Special Wire Numbers

1. Choose the **3 Phase** tool from **Schematic > Insert Wires/Wire Numbers** > **Insert Wire Numbers** drop-down; the **3 Phase Wire Numbering** dialog box is displayed.

2. In the **Base** area, make sure 1 is displayed in the edit box and the **hold** radio button is selected.

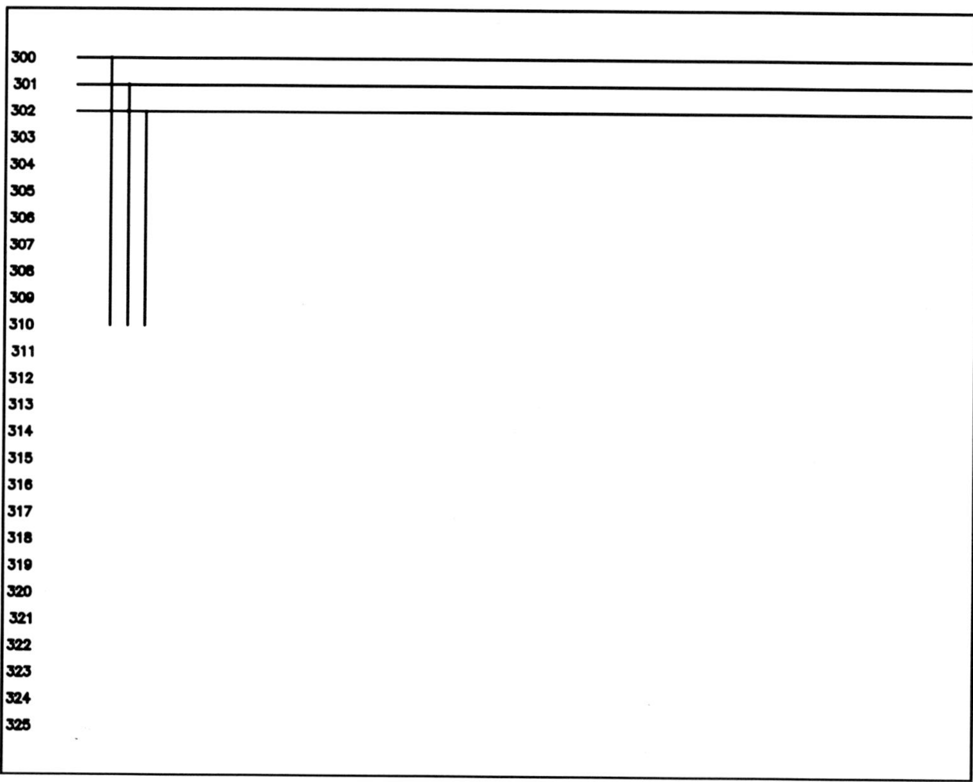


*Figure P1-4 Multiple wire bus inserted into the drawing*

3. In the **Suffix** area, make sure L1 is displayed in the edit box and the **increment** radio button is selected. Next, choose the **OK** button in this dialog box; you are prompted to select a wire.

4. Select the first wire that is on the right of the reference number 300; 1L1 is inserted into the wire.

5. Similarly, select the other two wires; the wire numbers 1L2 and 1L3 are inserted into the second and third wires, respectively, and the **3 Phase Wire Numbering** dialog box is displayed again. Choose the **Cancel** button in this dialog box to exit. Figure P1-5 shows the wire numbers inserted into the wires.

## Editing the Wire Numbers

1. Choose the **Edit Wire Number** tool from **Schematic > Edit Wires/Wire Numbers > Edit Wire Number** drop-down; you are prompted to select a wire.

2. Select the first wire that is on the right of the ladder reference number 300; the **Edit Wire Number/Attributes** dialog box is displayed.

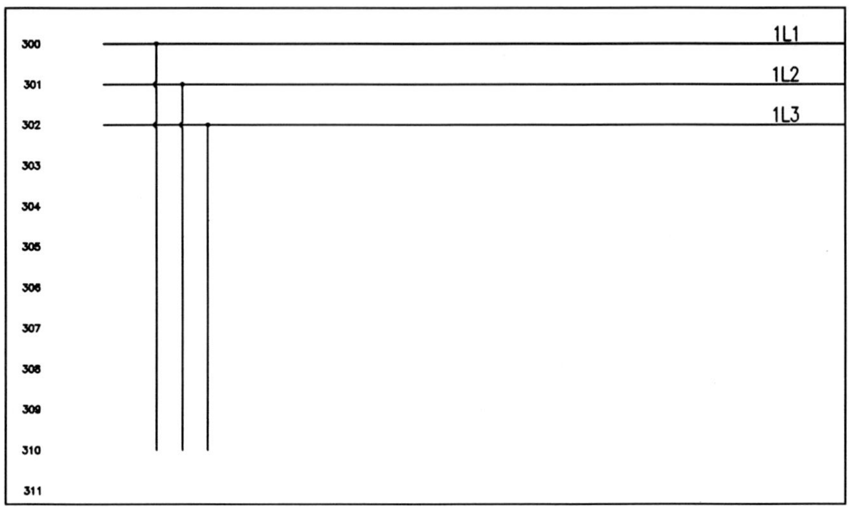


*Figure P1-5 Wire numbers inserted into the wires*

3. Clear the **Fixed** check box and choose the **OK** button in this dialog box; the wire number 1L1 is unfixed. Also, the color of the wire number is changed and you are prompted to select a wire.

4. Repeat the process performed in steps 2 and 3 for the second and third wires. Next, press ENTER to exit the command.

## Inserting Components in the Drawing

1. Choose the **Icon Menu** tool from **Schematic > Insert Components > Icon Menu** drop-down; the **Insert Component** dialog box is displayed.

2. Select the **Motor Control** icon from the **NFPA: Schematic Symbols** area; the **NFPA: Motor Control** area is displayed.

3. Select **3 Phase Motor** in the **NFPA: Motor Control** area; you are prompted to specify the insertion point.

4. Enter **3.5,13.85** at the Command prompt and press ENTER; the **Insert/Edit Component** dialog box is displayed.

5. Enter **CLARIFIED WATER** in the **Line 1** edit box of the **Description** area. Next, enter **PUMP A** in the **Line 2** edit box of the **Description** area.

6. Enter **3.7 KW** in the **Line 3** edit box of the **Description** area. Next, enter **M** in the **Rating** edit box of the **Ratings** area.

7. Choose the **OK** button in the **Insert/Edit Component** dialog box; a 3-phase motor is inserted into the drawing, as shown in Figure P1-6.

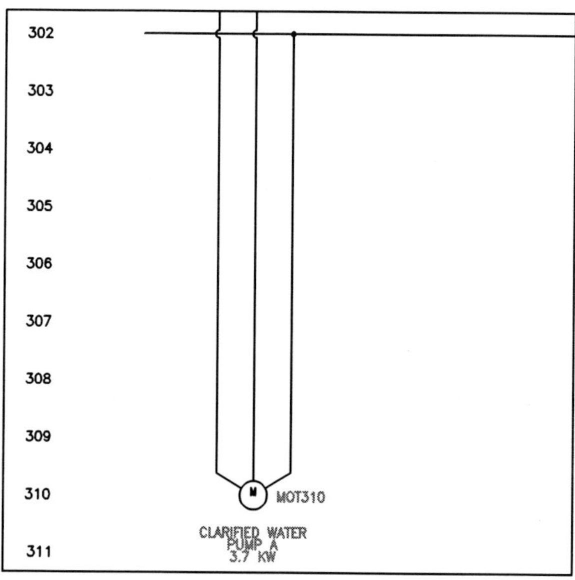


*Figure P1-6 A 3-phase motor inserted into the drawing*

8. Repeat step 1 and select the **Fuses/Circuit Breakers/Transformers** icon from the **NFPA: Schematic Symbols** area; the **NFPA: Fuses, Circuit Breakers and Transformers** area is displayed.

9. Select the **Circuit Breakers/Disconnects** icon from this area; the **NFPA: Disconnecting Means** area is displayed.

10. Select **3 Pole Thermal Circuit Breaker** from the **NFPA: Disconnecting Means** area; you are prompted to specify the insertion point. Make sure the **Object Snap** button in the Application Status Bar is deactivated.

11. Enter **3,18.5** at the Command prompt and press ENTER; the **Build to Left or Right?** dialog box is displayed.

12. Choose the **Right==>>** button; the **Insert/Edit Component** dialog box is displayed.

13. Accept the default values in this dialog box and choose the **OK** button; the 3 pole thermal circuit breaker is inserted into the drawing, as shown in Figure P1-7.

    After inserting the 3 pole thermal circuit breaker component into the drawing, the wire numbers 305, 305A and 305B are displayed. You need to hide these wire numbers.

14. To hide the wire number 305, right-click on it; a marking menu is displayed. Choose the **Edit Wire Number** option from it; the **Edit Wire Number/Attributes** dialog box is displayed. Select the **Hidden** radio button and choose the **OK** button in this dialog box; the wire number 305 gets hidden. Follow the same procedure for hiding the wire number 305A and 305B.

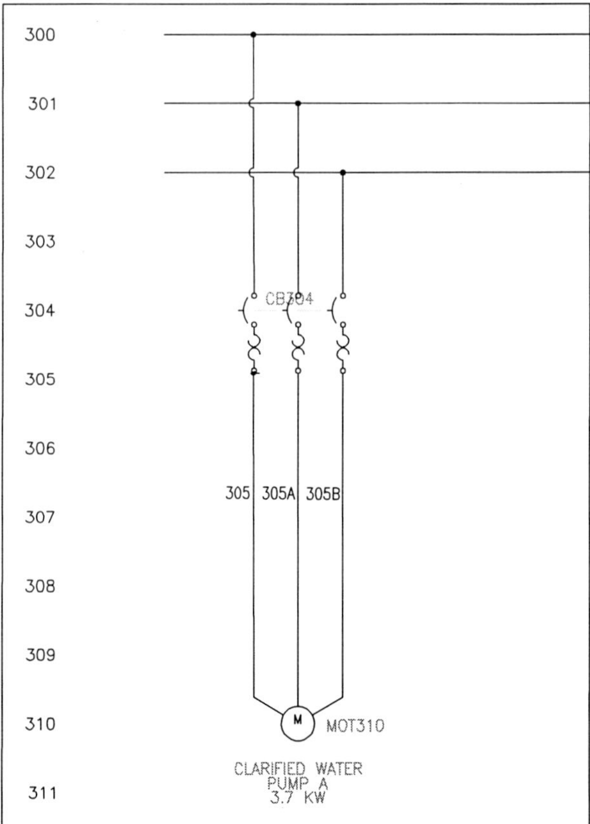


***Figure P1-7*** *The 3 pole thermal circuit breaker inserted into the drawing*

15. Repeat steps 1 and 2. Select the **3 Phase Starter Contacts NO** from the **NFPA: Motor Control** area; you are prompted to specify the insertion point.

16. Enter **3,17** at the Command prompt and press ENTER; the **Build to Left or Right?** dialog box is displayed. Choose the **Right==>>** button; the **Insert / Edit Child Component** dialog box is displayed.

17. Enter **MC7** in the **Tag** edit box in the **Component Tag** area of this dialog box. Next, choose the **OK** button in the **Insert / Edit Child Component** dialog box; the 3 Phase Starter Contacts NO component is inserted into the drawing, as shown in Figure P1-8.

    After inserting the 3 Phase Starter Contacts NO component into the drawing, the wire numbers 306, 306A and 306B are displayed. You need to hide these wire numbers.

18. Hide the wire numbers as discussed in step 14.

19. Repeat step 1 and then select the **Terminals/Connectors** icon from the **Insert Component** dialog box; the **NFPA: Terminals and Connectors** area is displayed.

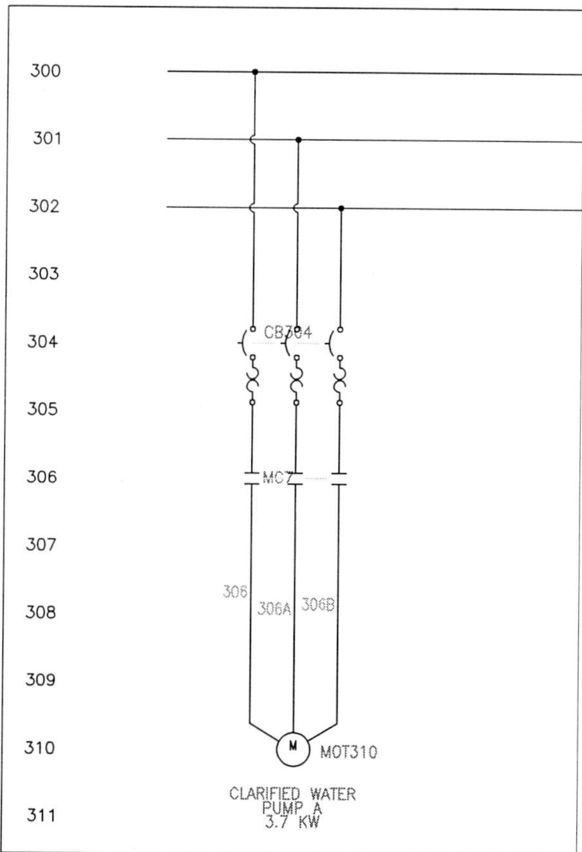


*Figure P1-8 The 3 Phase Starter Contacts NO component inserted into the drawing*

20. Select **Square with Terminal Number** from this area; you are prompted to specify the insertion point.

21. Enter **3,15.5** at the Command prompt and press ENTER; the **Insert Edit Terminal Symbol** dialog box is displayed.

22. Enter **TB1** in the **Tag Strip** edit box and **U7** in the **Number** edit box. Next, choose the **OK-Repeat** button in the **Insert / Edit Terminal Symbol** dialog box; you are prompted to specify the insertion point.

23. Enter **3.5,15.5** at the Command prompt and press ENTER; the **Insert/Edit Terminal Symbol** dialog box is displayed again. Enter **V7** in the **Number** edit box.

24. Choose the **OK-Repeat** button in the **Insert / Edit Terminal Symbol** dialog box; you are prompted to specify the insertion point.

25. Enter **4,15.5** at the Command prompt and press ENTER; the **Insert / Edit Terminal Symbol** dialog box is displayed again. Enter **W7** in the **Number** edit box and choose the **OK-Repeat** button in this dialog box; you are prompted to specify the insertion point.

26. Enter **4.5,15.5** at the Command prompt and press ENTER; the **Insert / Edit Terminal Symbol** dialog box is displayed. Remove the value from the **Number** edit box and choose the **OK** button; the terminal is inserted into the drawing. Figure P1-9 shows the terminals inserted into the drawing.

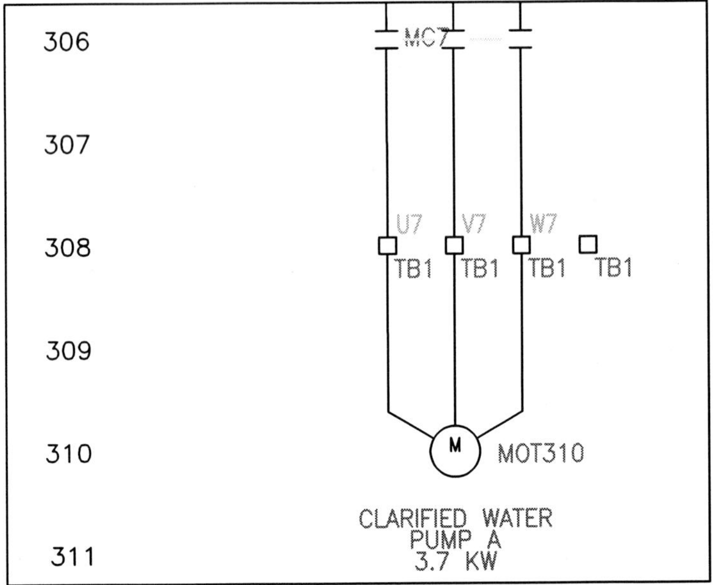


***Figure P1-9*** *Terminals inserted into the drawing*

Next, you need to insert a wire into the fourth terminal from the left.

27. Choose the **Wire** tool from **Schematic > Insert Wires/Wire Numbers > Wire** drop-down; you are prompted to specify the start point of the wire.

28. Enter **4.5,15.5** at the Command prompt and press ENTER; you are prompted to specify the end point of the wire.

29. Insert the wire in the terminal, as shown in Figure P1-10. Press ESC to exit the command.

30. Repeat step 1. Next, select the **Miscellaneous** icon from the **NFPA: Schematic Symbols** area; the **NFPA: Miscellaneous** area is displayed. Select **Ground** in this area; you are prompted to specify the insertion point.

31. Enter **4.7,15.7** at the Command Prompt and press ENTER; the ground symbol is placed in the drawing, refer to Figure P1-11. Also, the **Insert / Edit Component** dialog box is displayed. Delete **GND308** from the edit box in the **Component Tag** area and choose **OK** to close this dialog box.

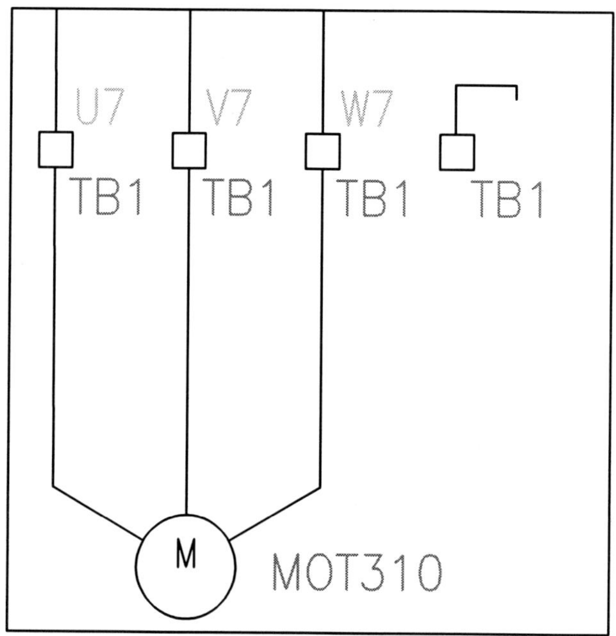


*Figure P1-10* *Inserting the wire in the terminal*

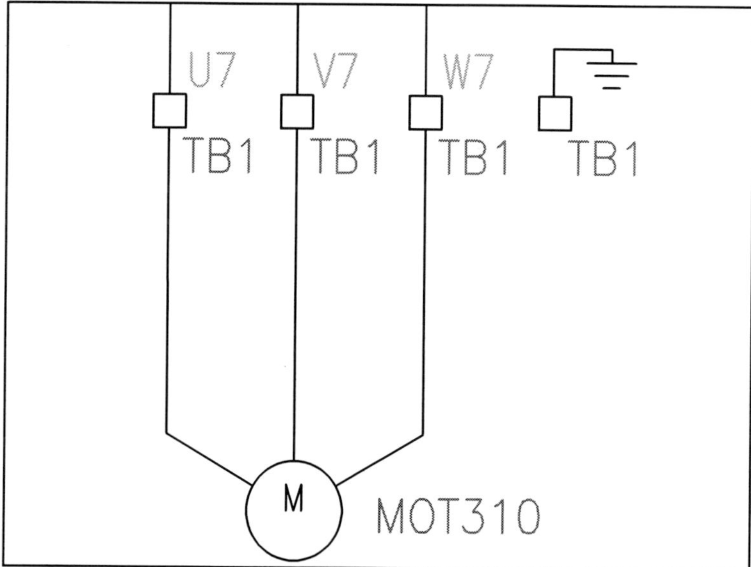


*Figure P1-11* *Ground symbol inserted into the drawing*

## Inserting the In-Line Wire Labels in the Drawing

1. Choose the **In-Line Wire Labels** tool from **Schematic > Insert Wires/Wire Numbers > Wire Number Leader** drop-down; the **Insert Component** dialog box is displayed. Select **You Type** from this dialog box; you are prompted to specify the insertion point.

2. Enter **5,21.5** at the Command prompt and press ENTER; the **Edit Attribute – COLOR** dialog box is displayed.

3. Enter **BUSBAR** in the edit box of this dialog box and choose the **OK** button; the specified in-line wire label is inserted in the wire and you are prompted to specify the insertion point.

**Note**

*You may need to move the wire ends at both sides of* ***BUSBAR*** *(on the right of the reference number 300) if* ***BUSBAR*** *and the wire ends are intersecting each other.*

4. Similarly, insert **BUSBAR** at the locations shown in Figure P1-12. Press ESC to exit the command; the in-line wire labels are inserted in the drawing.

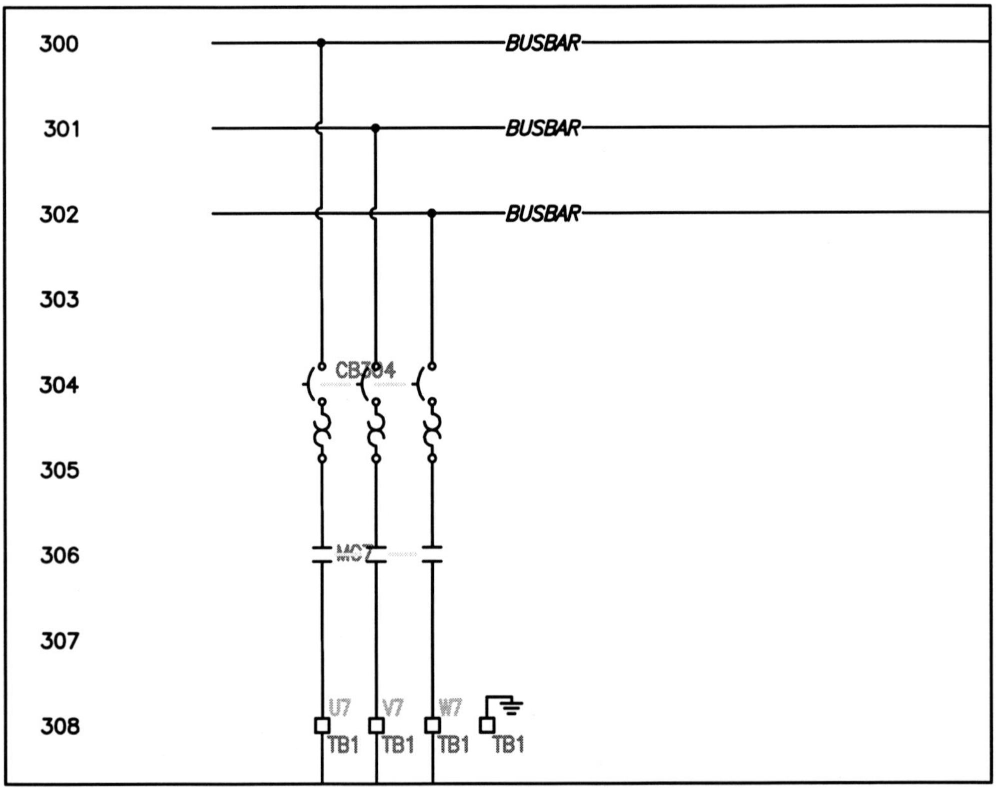

***Figure P1-12*** *In-line wire labels inserted in the drawing*

## Copying the Circuit

1. Choose the **Copy Circuit** tool from **Schematic > Edit Components > Circuit** drop-down; you are prompted to select the circuit to copy.

2. Select the circuit from left to right and press ENTER; you are prompted to specify the base point or displacement>/ multiple for the circuit.

3. Make sure that you have selected only the circuit, not the busbar. Next, enter **M** at the Command prompt for placing multiple circuits and press ENTER; you are prompted to specify the base point.

4. Enter **3,21.5** at the Command prompt and press ENTER; you are prompted to specify the second point of displacement.

5. Enter **6.5,21.5** at the Command prompt and press ENTER; a circuit is inserted at the specified location and you are prompted to specify the second point of displacement.

6. Enter **10,21.5** at the Command prompt and press ENTER; a circuit is inserted at the specified location and you are prompted to specify the second point of displacement.

7. Enter **13.5,21.5** at the Command prompt and press ENTER; a circuit is inserted at the specified location and you are prompted to specify the second point of displacement.

8. Enter **17,21.5** at the Command prompt and press ENTER; a circuit is inserted at the specified location and you are prompted to specify the second point of displacement.

9. Enter **20.5,21.5** at the Command prompt and press ENTER; a circuit is inserted at the specified location and you are prompted to specify the second point of displacement.

10. Enter **24,21.5** at the Command prompt and press ENTER; a circuit is inserted at the specified location and you are prompted to specify the second point of displacement.

11. Press ESC to exit the command. Figure P1-13 shows the copied circuits and Figure P1-14 shows the zoomed view of the copied circuits.

## Saving the Circuit to Icon Menu

1. Choose the **Save Circuit to Icon Menu** tool from **Schematic > Edit Components > Circuit** drop-down; the **Save Circuit to Icon Menu** dialog box is displayed.

2. Click on the **Add** drop-down located at the upper right corner of the **Save Circuit to Icon Menu** dialog box; different options are displayed. Choose the **New Circuit** option from it; the **Create New Circuit** dialog box is displayed.

3. Enter **Sample Circuit** in the **Name** edit box. Next, choose the **Active** button; the Sample Drawing 1 is displayed in the **Image file** edit box. Also, its preview is displayed in the **Preview** area.

4. Select the **Create PNG from current screen image** check box, if it is not selected.

5. Enter **Circuit Drawing** in the **File name** edit box. Next, choose the **OK** button in the **Create New Circuit** dialog box; you are prompted to specify the base point. Enter **2,21.5** at the Command prompt and press ENTER; you are prompted to select objects.

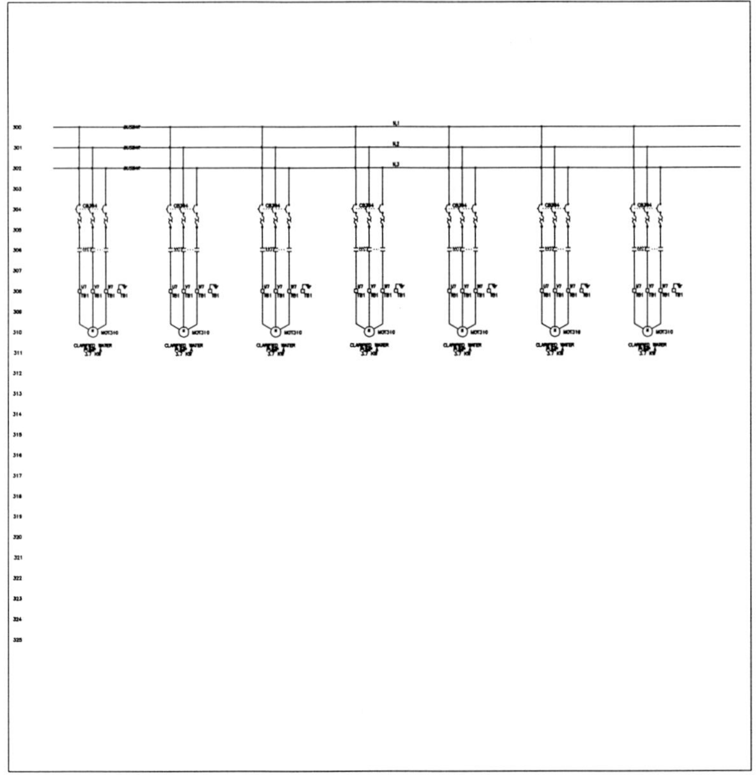

*Figure P1-13 Copied circuits*

6. Select all circuits by dragging the cursor from left to right, refer to Figure P1-15 and then press ENTER; the icon of the Sample Circuit is saved in the **Save Circuit to Icon Menu** dialog box. Next, choose the **OK** button in this dialog box to exit it.

## Inserting the Saved Circuit in the Drawing

1. Choose the **Insert Saved Circuit** tool from **Schematic > Insert Components > Insert Circuit** drop-down; the **Insert Component** dialog box is displayed. 

2. Select the **Sample Circuit** from the **NFPA: Saved User Circuits** dialog box; the **Circuit Scale** dialog box is displayed.

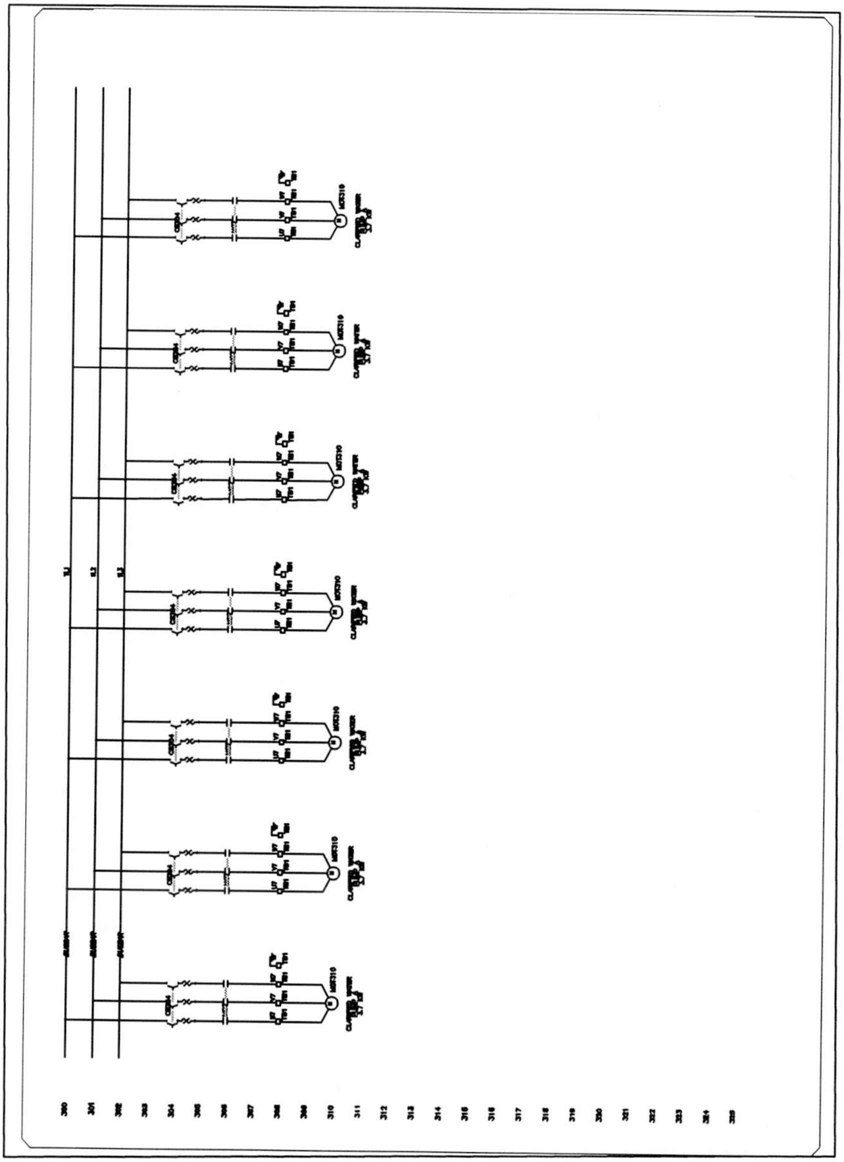

Figure P1-14 *Zoomed view of the copied circuits*

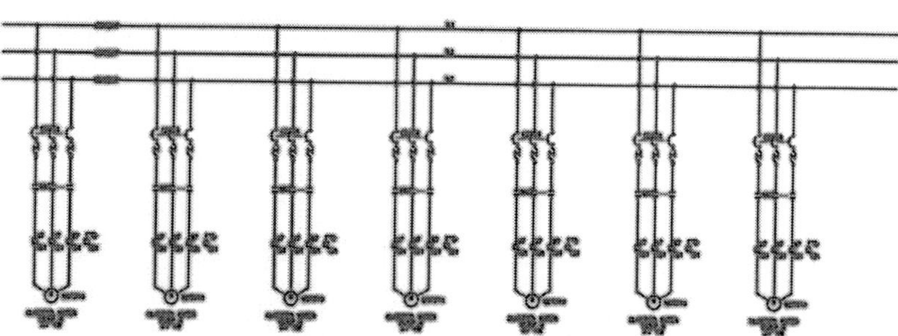

**Figure P1-15** *Selecting circuits*

3. Accept the default values in this dialog box and choose the **OK** button; you are prompted to specify the insertion point.

4. Enter **2,11.75** at the Command prompt and press ENTER; the circuit is inserted in the drawing, as shown in Figure P1-16. Figure P1-17 shows the zoomed view of Circuit 2.

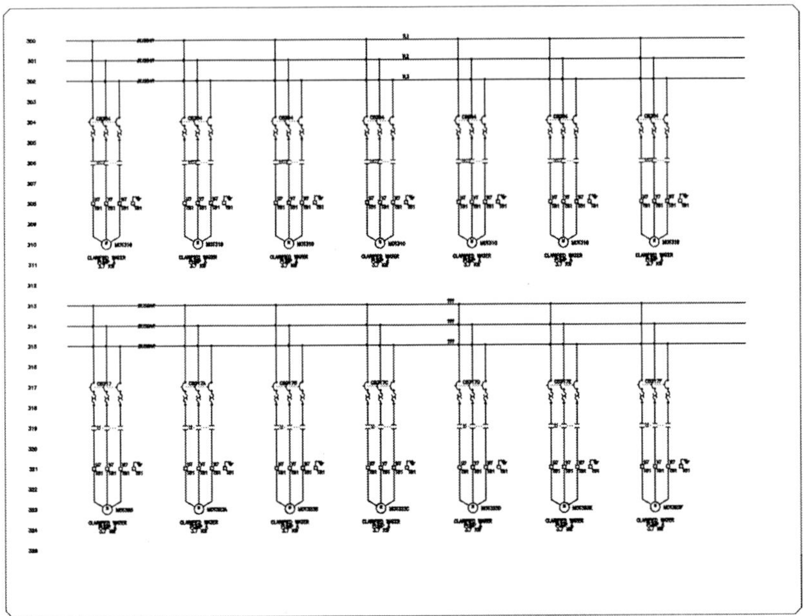

***Figure P1-16*** *Circuit 2 inserted in the drawing*

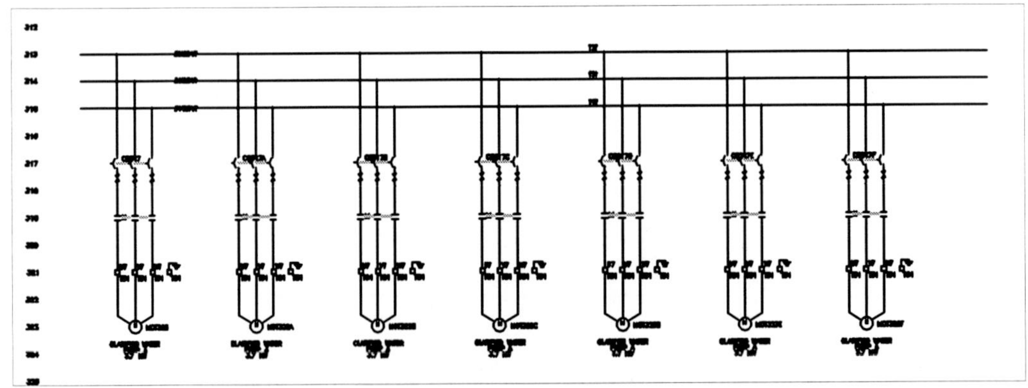

***Figure P1-17*** *Zoomed view of inserted circuit (Circuit 2)*

## Inserting the Special Wire Numbers in the Circuit 2

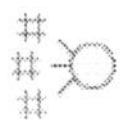

1. Choose the **3 Phase** tool from **Schematic > Insert Wires/Wire Numbers > Insert Wire Numbers** drop-down; the **3 Phase Wire Numbering** dialog box is displayed.

2. In the **Base** area, make sure 1 is displayed in the edit box and the **hold** radio button is selected. Also, in the **Suffix** area, make sure L1 is displayed in the edit box and the **increment** radio button is selected.

3. Choose the **OK** button in this dialog box; you are prompted to select the wire. Select the first wire that is on the right of the reference number 313; 1L1 is inserted into the wire.

4. Similarly, select the other two wires; the wire numbers 1L2 and 1L3 are inserted into the respective wires and the **3 Phase Wire Numbering** dialog box is displayed again. Choose the **Cancel** button in this dialog box to exit. Figure P1-18 shows wire numbers inserted into the wires.

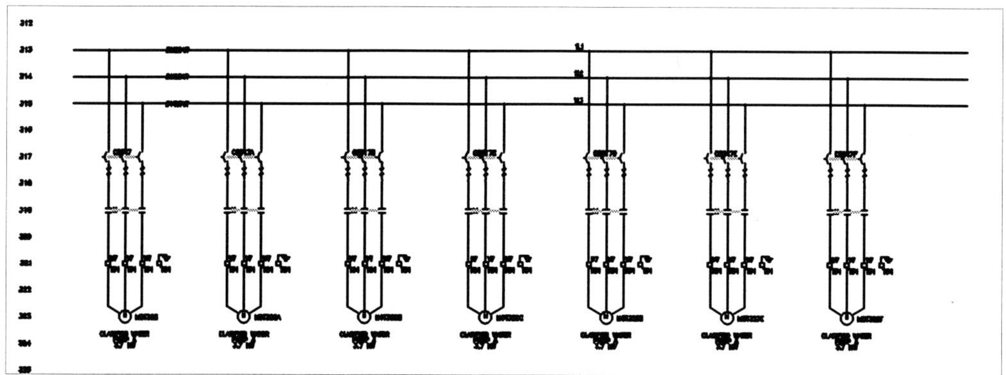

*Figure P1-18 Wire numbers inserted into the wires*

## Editing the Wire Numbers of the Circuit 2

1. Choose the **Edit Wire Number** tool from **Schematic > Edit Wires/Wire Numbers > Edit Wire Number** drop-down; you are prompted to select the wire.

2. Select the first wire that is on the right of the ladder reference number 313; the **Edit Wire Number/Attributes** dialog box is displayed.

3. Clear the **Fixed** check box and choose the **OK** button in this dialog box; the wire number 1L1 becomes unfixed and you are prompted to select the wire.

4. Select the second wire; the **Edit Wire Number/Attributes** dialog box is displayed. Clear the **Fixed** check box and choose the **OK** button in this dialog box; the wire number 1L2 becomes unfixed and you are prompted to select the wire.

5. Select the third wire; the **Edit Wire Number/Attributes** dialog box is displayed. Clear the **Fixed** check box and choose the **OK** button in this dialog box; the wire number 1L3 becomes unfixed. Next, press ENTER to exit the command.

## Editing the Components

1. Choose the **Edit** tool from **Schematic > Edit Components > Edit Components** drop-down; you are prompted to select the component.

   Make sure the **Snap Mode** button is deactivated.

2. Select the component and enter its details as follows:

   Circuit 1
   First Circuit
   a) Select **MOT310** (1st motor from left); the **Insert / Edit Component** dialog box is displayed.

   b) Enter **MOT7** in the edit box of the **Component Tag** area. Next, choose the **OK** button in this dialog box; the description of the selected component is changed.

**Note**
*After choosing the **OK** button in the **Insert / Edit Component** dialog box, if the **Update Related Components?** message box is displayed, choose the **Skip** button in this message box to skip the changes.*

   c) Repeat step1 and select **CB304** (3 Pole Thermal Circuit Breaker); the **Insert / Edit Component** dialog box is displayed.

   d) Enter **MS7** in the edit box of the **Component Tag** area.Next, choose the **OK** button in this dialog box; the description of the selected component is changed.

3. Similarly, edit other components as per the details provided in the table given next.

**Note**
*1. On choosing the **OK** button in the **Insert / Edit Component** dialog box, if the **Update Related Components?** message box is displayed, choose the **Skip** button in this message box to skip updating related components.*

*2. If the **Update linked components?** message box is displayed, choose the **Cancel** button in it.*

| **Component to be Selected** | **Tag to be entered in the edit box in the Component Tag area of the Insert/ Edit Component dialog box** | **Description to be entered** | **Terminal number to be entered in the Number edit box of Insert/Edit Terminal Symbol dialog box** |
|---|---|---|---|
| MOT310 (2nd motor from left) | MOT8 | Line 2: PUMP B | - |
| U7 connected to MOT310 | - | - | U8 |
| V7 connected to MOT310 | - | - | V8 |
| W7 connected to MOT310 | - | - | W8 |

| | | | |
|---|---|---|---|
| MC7 connected to MOT310 | MC8 | - | - |
| CB304 | MS8 | - | - |
| MOT310 (3rd motor from left) | MOT9 | Line 2: PUMP C | - |
| U7 connected to MOT310 | - | - | U9 |
| V7 connected to MOT310 | - | - | V9 |
| W7 connected to MOT310 | - | - | W9 |
| MC7 connected to MOT310 | MC9 | - | - |
| CB304 | MS9 | - | - |
| MOT310 (4th motor from left) | MOT10 | Line 1: No.2 PH ADJUSTMENT Line 2: TANK AGITATOR Line 3: 0.55KW | - |
| U7 connected to MOT310 | - | - | U10 |
| V7 connected to MOT310 | - | - | V10 |
| W7 connected to MOT310 | - | - | W10 |
| MC7 connected to MOT310 | MC10 | - | - |
| CB304 | MS10 | - | - |
| MOT310 (5th motor from left) | MOT11 | Line 1: RELAY PIT Line 2: PUMP A Line 3: 3.7KW | - |
| U7 connected to MOT310 | - | - | U11 |
| V7 connected to MOT310 | - | - | V11 |
| W7 connected to MOT310 | - | - | W11 |
| MC7 connected to MOT310 | MC11 | - | - |
| CB304 | MS11 | - | - |
| MOT310 (6th motor from left) | MOT12 | Line 1: RELAY PIT Line 2: PUMP B Line 3: 3.7KW | - |
| U7 connected to MOT310 | - | - | U12 |

| | | | |
|---|---|---|---|
| V7 connected to MOT310 | - | - | V12 |
| W7 connected to MOT310 | - | - | W12 |
| MC7 connected to MOT310 | MC12 | - | - |
| CB304 | MS12 | | |
| MOT310 (7th motor from left) | MOT13 | Line1: REGENERATION Line2:PUMP Line3:0.2KW | W.W |
| U7 connected to MOT310 | - | - | U13 |
| V7 connected to MOT310 | - | - | V13 |
| W7 connected to MOT310 | - | - | W13 |
| MC7 connected to MOT310 | MC13 | - | - |
| CB304 | MS13 | | |
| MOT323 | MOT14 | Line1: NO. 1 NEUT Line2: TANK AGITATOR Line3: 0.55KW | - |
| U7 connected to MOT323 | - | - | U14 |
| V7 connected to MOT323 | - | - | V14 |
| W7 connected to MOT323 | - | - | W14 |
| M connected to MOT323 | MC14 | - | - |
| CB317 | MS14 | - | - |
| MOT323A | MOT15 | Line1:NO.2 NEUT. Line2: TANK AGITATOR Line3: 0.55KW | - |
| U7 connected to MOT323A | - | - | U15 |
| V7 connected to MOT323A | - | - | V15 |
| W7 connected to MOT323A | - | - | W15 |
| M connected to MOT323A | MC15 | - | - |
| CB317A | MS15 | - | - |

| | | | |
|---|---|---|---|
| MOT323B | MOT16 | Line1:NO. 1 TRANSFER. Line2: TANK PUMP Line3: 0.75KW | - |
| U7 connected to MOT323B | - | - | U16 |
| V7 connected to MOT323B | - | - | V16 |
| W7 connected to MOT323B | - | - | W16 |
| M connected to MOT323B | MC16 | - | - |
| CB317B | MS16 | - | - |
| MOT323C | MOT17 | Line1: H. CONC Line2: W.W PUMP Line3: 0.2KW | - |
| U7 connected to MOT323C | - | - | U17 |
| V7 connected to MOT323C | - | - | V17 |
| W7 connected to MOT323C | - | - | W17 |
| M connected to MOT323C | MC17 | - | - |
| CB317C | MS17 | - | - |
| MOT323D | MOT18 | Line1: CR RINSE W.W Line2: PUMP A Line3: 0.75KW | - |
| U7 connected to MOT323D | - | - | U18 |
| V7 connected to MOT323D | - | - | V18 |
| W7 connected to MOT323D | - | - | W18 |
| M connected to MOT323D | MC18 | - | - |
| CB317D | MS18 | - | - |
| MOT323E | MOT19 | Line1: CR RINSE W.W Line2: PUMP B Line3: 0.75KW | - |
| U7 connected to MOT323E | - | - | U19 |
| V7 connected to MOT323E | - | - | V19 |
| W7 connected to MOT323E | - | - | W19 |
| M connected to MOT323E | MC19 | - | - |
| CB317E | MS19 | - | - |

| MOT323F | MOT20 | Line1: CR RINSE W.W RECEN Line2: TANK AGITATOR | - |
|---|---|---|---|
| U7 connected to MOT323F | - | - | U20 |
| V7 connected to MOT323F | - | - | V20 |
| W7 connected to MOT323F | - | - | W20 |
| CB317F | MS20 | - | - |
| M connected to MOT323F | MC20 | - | - |

4. Delete component tags for all the ground symbols located on the right of the reference number 321. Figure P1-19 shows the components after they have been edited.

## Inserting the Source and Destination Arrows

1. Choose the **Source Arrow** tool from **Schematic > Insert Wires/Wire Numbers > Signal Arrows** drop-down; you are prompted to select the wire end for the source.

2. Select the wire end of the first wire of the first circuit; the **Signal – Source Code** dialog box is displayed.

3. Enter **313** in the **Code** edit box and choose the **OK** button; the **Source/Destination Signal Arrows** message box is displayed. Choose the **OK** button in this message box; you are prompted to select the wire end for the destination.

4. Select the starting point of the wire on the right of the reference number 313; the source and destination arrows are inserted.

5. Repeat step 1 and insert the source and destination arrows into the wires, as shown in Figure P1-20.

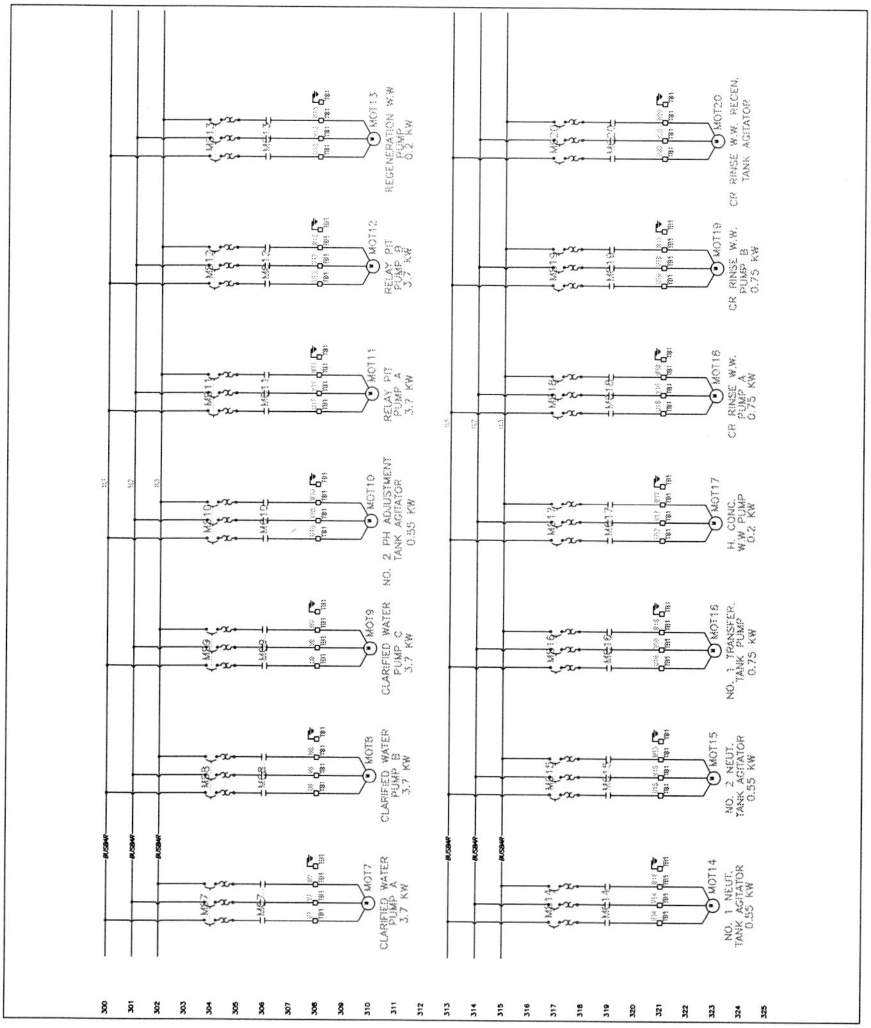

Figure P1-19 Components after editing

## Trimming the Wires

1. Choose the **Trim Wire** tool from the **Edit Wires/Wire Numbers** panel of the **Schematic** tab; you are prompted to select the wire to trim. 

2. Select the wires of the seventh circuit of Circuit 2, refer to Figure P1-21; the wires are trimmed, as shown in Figure P1-21. Figure P1-22 shows the zoomed view of the trimmed wires of a circuit.

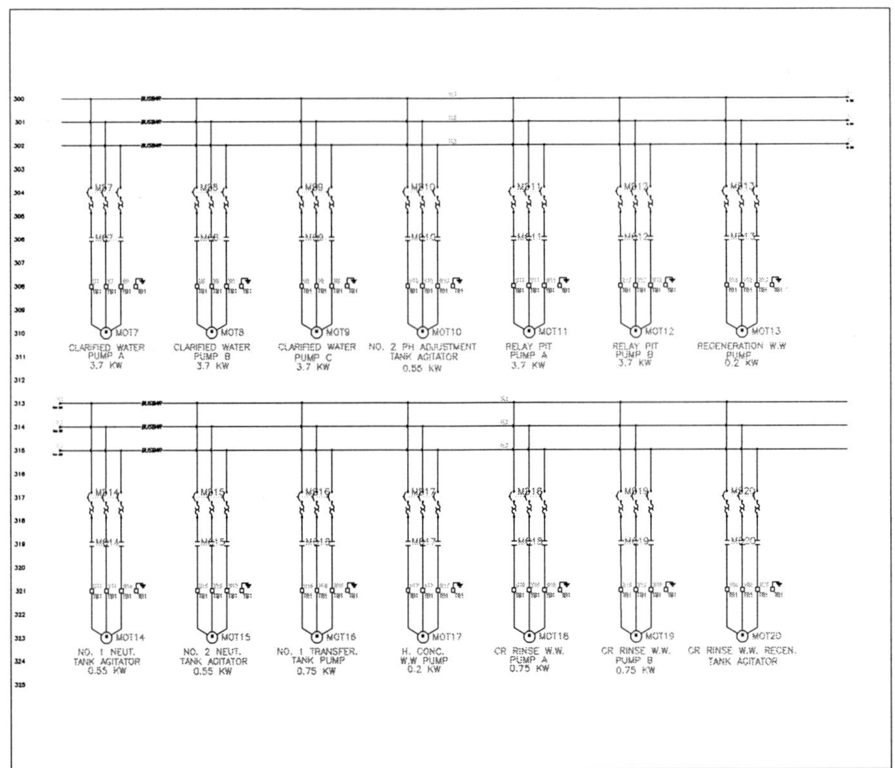


*Figure P1-20 The source and destination arrows inserted into the wires*

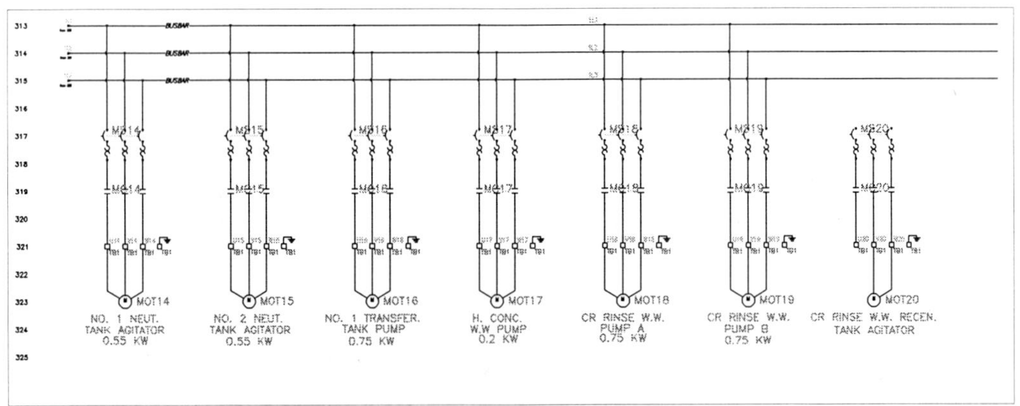


*Figure P1-21 The trimmed wires*

## Inserting Wires in the Drawing

1. To insert wires in the seventh circuit, which is connected to MOT20 of Circuit 2, choose the **Wire** tool from **Schematic > Insert Wires/Wire Numbers > Wire** drop-down; you are prompted to specify the starting point of the wire.

2. Enter **25,9** at the Command prompt and press ENTER; you are prompted to specify the wire end.

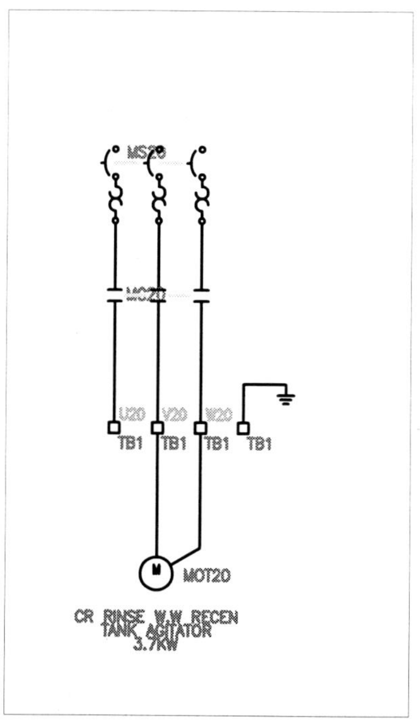


***Figure P1-22*** *Zoomed view of trimmed wires*

3. Insert wires in the seventh circuit, which is connected to MOT20 of Circuit 2, as shown in Figure P1-23.

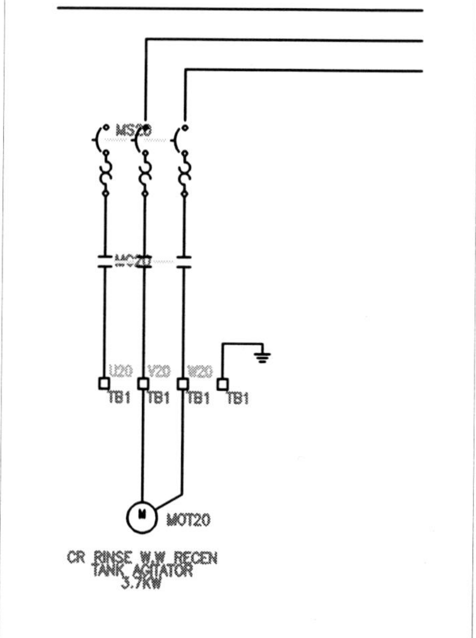


***Figure P1-23*** *Wires inserted in the circuit 2*

## Inserting the Wire Numbers in the Drawing

1. Choose the **3 Phase** tool from **Schematic > Insert Wires/Wire Numbers > Insert Wire Numbers** drop-down; the **3 Phase Wire Numbering** dialog box is displayed.

2. In the **Base** area, make sure **1** is displayed in the edit box and the **hold** radio button is selected.

3. In the **Suffix** area, enter **X1** in the edit box and select the **increment** radio button. Next, choose the **OK** button in this dialog box; you are prompted to select the wire.

4. Select the wire of the seventh circuit, which is connected to MOT20, as shown in Figure P1-24; 1X1 is inserted in the wire.

5. Select the other wire; the wire number 1X2 is inserted in the wire. Press ENTER; the **3 Phase Wire Numbering** dialog box is displayed again. Choose the **Cancel** button in this dialog box to exit. Figure P1-25 shows the wire numbers inserted into the wires.

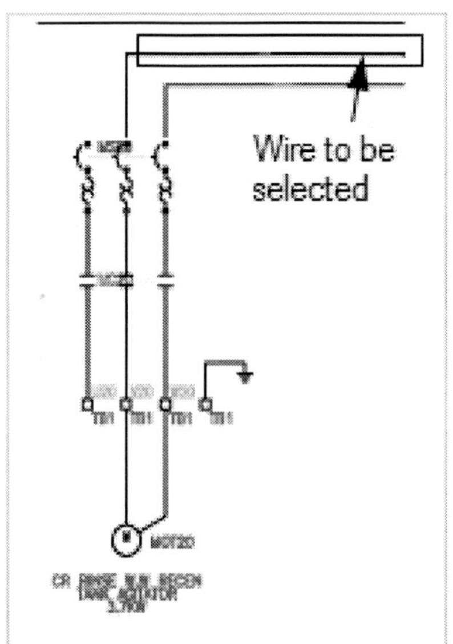


***Figure P1-24*** *Selection of the first wire*

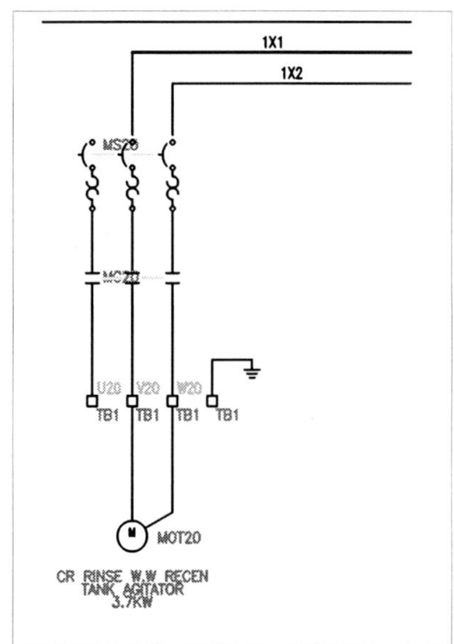


***Figure P1-25*** *Wire numbers inserted into the wires*

## Editing the Wire Numbers of the Seventh Circuit of Circuit 2

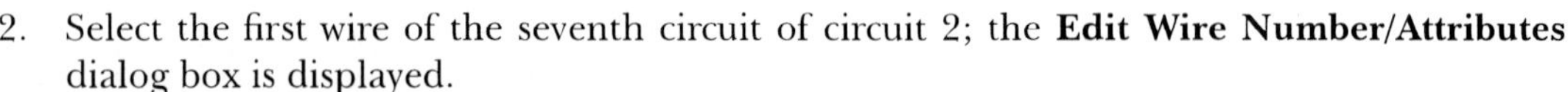

1. Choose the **Edit Wire Number** tool from **Schematic > Edit Wires/Wire Numbers > Edit Wire Number** drop-down; you are prompted to select the wire.

2. Select the first wire of the seventh circuit of circuit 2; the **Edit Wire Number/Attributes** dialog box is displayed.

3. Clear the **Fixed** check box and choose the **OK** button in this dialog box; the wire number 1X1 becomes unfixed and you are prompted to select the wire.

4. Select the second wire; the **Edit Wire Number/Attributes** dialog box is displayed. Clear the **Fixed** check box and choose the **OK** button in this dialog box; the wire number 1X2 becomes unfixed. Next, press ENTER to exit the command.

## Moving the Attributes

1. Choose the **Move/Show Attribute** tool from **Schematic > Edit Components > Modify Attributes** drop-down; you are prompted to select the attribute to be moved. 

2. Select MS7 from the first circuit of circuit 1 and press ENTER. Next, move it toward the left, if it is not already at the left, as shown in Figure P1-26.

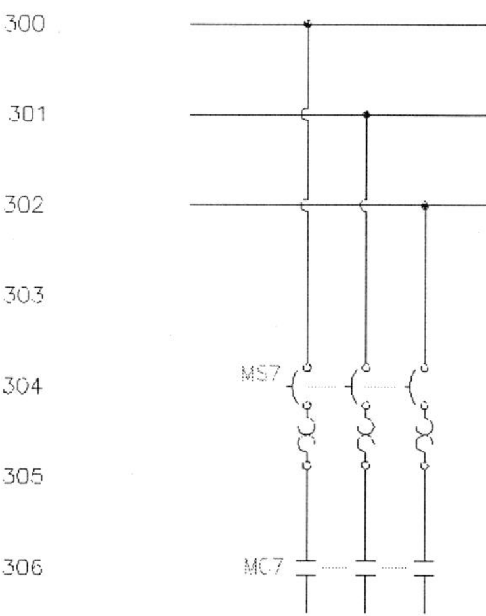


*Figure P1-26 MS7 moved to a new location*

3. Select MC7 from the first circuit and move it toward the left, if it is not already at the left.

4. Move attributes from MS8 to MS20 and MC8 to MC20 toward the left. Figure P1-27 shows the attributes moved to a new location.

## Showing the Wires in the Drawing

1. In order to highlight all wires present in the drawing, choose the **Show Wires** tool from **Schematic > Edit Wires/Wire Numbers > Modify Wires** drop-down; the **Show Wires and Wire Number Pointers** dialog box is displayed. 

2. Make sure the **Show wires (lines on wire layers)** check box is selected and choose the **OK** button; the **Drawing Audit** message box is displayed and all wires in the drawing are highlighted in red color, as shown in Figure P1-28. Choose the **OK** button in the **Drawing Audit** message box.

3. Choose **View > Redraw** from the menu bar to eliminate the wire indicators.

## Auditing the Drawing Using the DWG Audit Tool and Saving the Report

1. Choose the **DWG Audit** tool from the **Schematic** panel of the **Reports** tab; the **Drawing Audit** dialog box is displayed. 

2. In this dialog box, make sure the **Active drawing** radio button is selected and choose the **OK** button; the modified **Drawing Audit** dialog box is displayed. Select all check boxes in this dialog box.

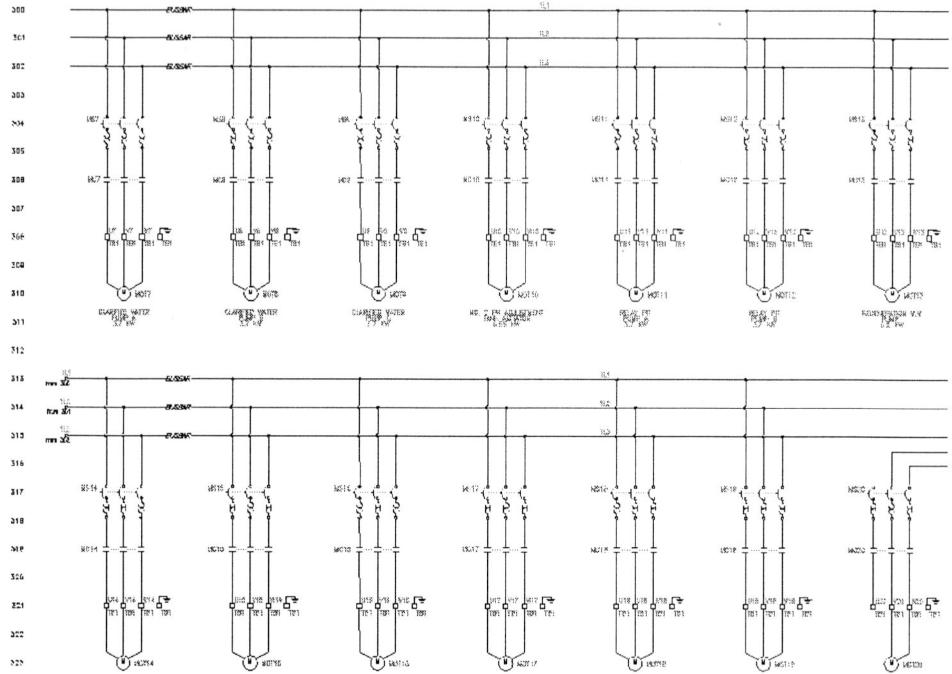

***Figure P1-27*** *Attributes moved to a new location*

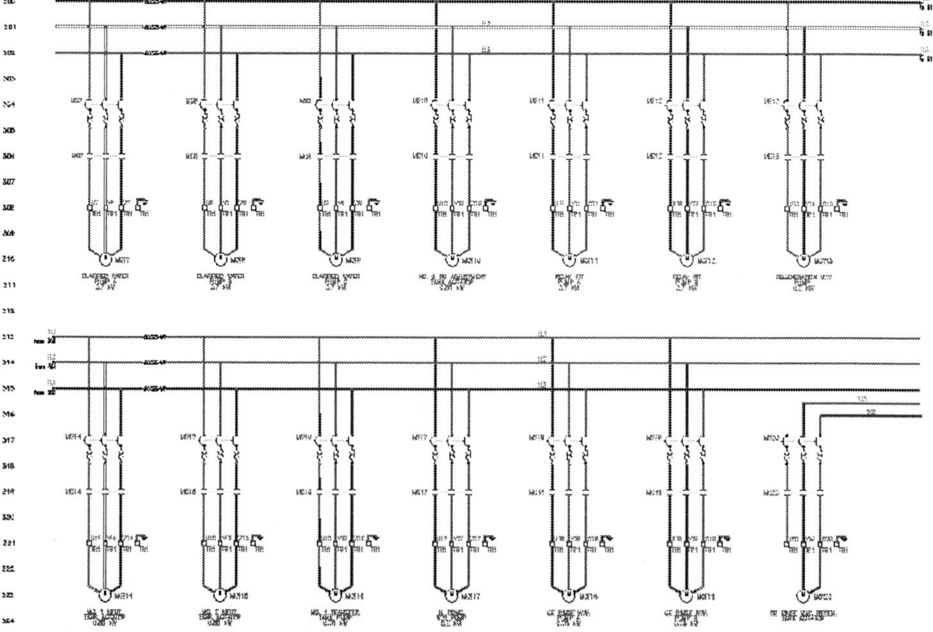

***Figure P1-28*** *Wires highlighted*

3. Choose the **OK** button in the **Drawing Audit** dialog box; the **Drawing Audit** message box is displayed and all wires in the drawing are highlighted in red color. Choose the **OK** button in the **Drawing Audit** message box; the **Report: Audit for this drawing** dialog box is displayed.

4. Choose the **Save As** button in this dialog box; the **REPORT: Save As** dialog box is displayed.

5. Browse to **Documents > Acade 2022 > AeData > Proj > Sample Project** from the **Save in** drop-down list. Next, enter **Drawing_Audit** in the **File name** edit box of the **REPORT: Save As** dialog box.

6. Choose the **Save** button; the **Optional Script File** dialog box is displayed. Choose the **Close – No Script** button; the **Report: Audit for this drawing** dialog box is displayed again.

7. Choose the **Close** button in the **Report: Audit for this drawing** dialog box.

   The wires in the drawing are highlighted in red color, as shown in Figure P1-29. These indicators represent wires in the drawing.

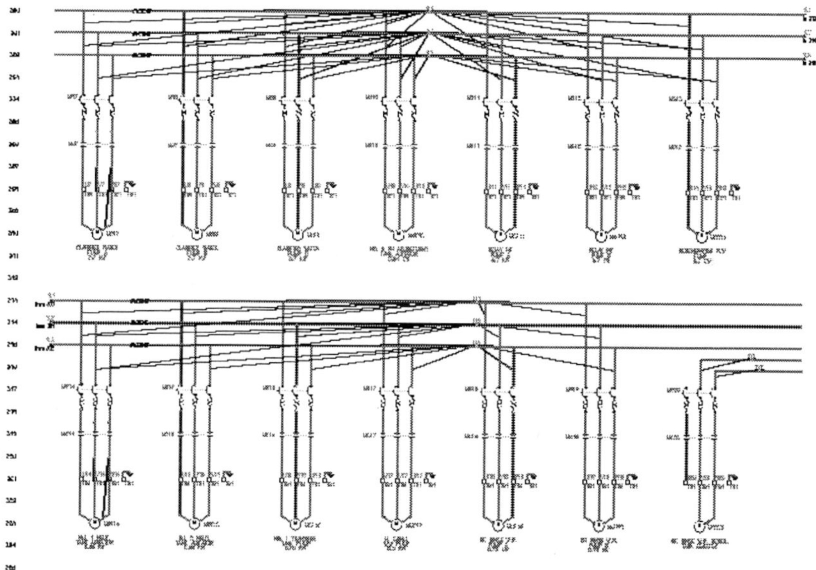

*Figure P1-29* *Wires highlighted in red*

8. Choose **View > Redraw** from the menu bar to remove the wire indicators.

## Auditing the Drawing Using the Electrical Audit Tool and Saving the Report

1. Choose the **Electrical Audit** tool from the **Schematic** panel of the **Reports** tab; the **Electrical Audit** dialog box is displayed.

2. Select the **Active Drawing** radio button; the number of errors are displayed in the edit box on the right of this radio button.

3. Choose the **Details** button; the **Electrical Audit** message box expands. In this expanded dialog box, you can view the errors found in the drawing.

4. Choose the **Export All** button in this dialog box; the **Create File** dialog box is displayed.

5. Browse to **Documents > Acade 2022 > AeData > Proj > Sample Project** from the **Save in** drop-down list.

6. Enter **Electrical_Audit** in the **File name** edit box and choose the **Save** button; the text file is saved and you return to the **Electrical Audit** dialog box. Next, close the **Electrical Audit** dialog box.

## Creating a .wdl File

1. To change the values of lines in the **Project Description** dialog box, open a Notepad file and enter the following information in it:
   Line 1 = **Title 1:**
   Line 2 = **Title 2:**
   Line 3 = **Title 3:**
   Line 4 = **Job Number:**
   Line 5 = **Date:**
   Line 6 = **Engineer:**
   Line 7 = **Drawn By:**
   Line 8 = **Checked By:**
   Line 9 = **Scale:**

2. Choose **File > Save As** from the menu bar; the **Save As** dialog box is displayed.

3. Browse to **Documents > Acade 2022 > AeData > Proj > Sample Project** from the **Save in** drop-down list.

4. Enter **Sample Project_wdtitle.wdl** in the **File name** edit box and then choose the **Save** button; the *Sample Project_wdtitle.wdl* file is saved in the respective project folder. Next, close the Notepad application.

5. Right-click on the **Sample Project** project; a shortcut menu is displayed. Choose the **Descriptions** option from it; the **Project Description** dialog box is displayed, as shown in Figure P1-30. In this dialog box, you will observe that the line values have changed to the specified values. Close this dialog box.

## Exporting Project Data to an Excel File

1. Choose the **To Spreadsheet** tool from the **Export** panel of the **Import/Export Data** tab; the **Export to Spreadsheet** dialog box is displayed. 

2. Make sure the **Components*** radio button is selected and choose the **OK** button; the **Component Data Export** dialog box is displayed.

3. Make sure the **Project** radio button from the **Data export for** area and the **Excel file format (.xls)** radio button from the **Output format** area are selected. Next, choose the **OK** button; the **Select Drawings to Process** dialog box is displayed.

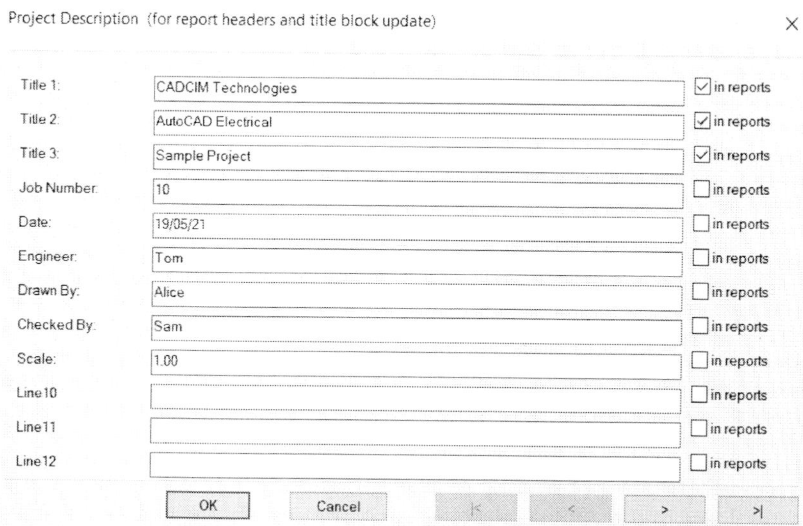


*Figure P1-30 The **Project Description** dialog box*

4. Choose the **Do All** button in this dialog box; the *Sample Drawing.dwg* drawing is transferred from the top list to the bottom list.

5. Choose the **OK** button in this dialog box; the **Select file name for Project-wide XLS output** dialog box is displayed.

6. Browse to **Documents > Acade 2022 > AeData > Proj > Sample Project** from the **Save in** drop-down list.

7. Enter **Sample Project 1** in the **File name** edit box.

8. Choose the **Save** button; the components present in the **Sample Project** are exported to an Excel sheet.

## Creating a New Drawing for Placing Schematic Reports

1. Choose the **New Drawing** button from the **PROJECT MANAGER**; the **Create New Drawing** dialog box is displayed.

2. Enter **Schematic Report** in the **Name** edit box.

3. Choose the **Browse** button on the right of the **Template** edit box; the **Select template** dialog box is displayed.

4. Select **CADCIM** from this dialog box and choose the **Open** button; the name and path of the template file is displayed in the **Template** edit box.

5. Enter **Wire From/To Report** in the **Description 1** edit box. Next, choose the **OK** button in the **Create New Drawing** dialog box; the drawing is created in the project and its name is displayed in bold in the **Projects** rollout.

6. Choose the **Reports** tool from the **Schematic** panel of the **Reports** tab; the **Schematic Reports** dialog box is displayed. Choose the **From/To** option in the **Report Name** area and select the **Project** radio button in the **From/To** area.

7. Choose the **OK** button in the **Schematic Reports** dialog box; the **Qsave** message box is displayed. Choose **OK**; the **Select Drawings to Process** dialog box is displayed. Choose the **Do All** button; the drawing is transferred from the top list to the bottom list. Choose the **OK** button; the **Location Code Selection for From/To Reporting** dialog box is displayed.

8. Choose the **All>>** and **All<<** buttons and then choose the **OK** button in this dialog box; the **Report Generator** dialog box is displayed.

9. Choose the **Put on Drawing** button in this dialog box; the **Table Generation Setup** dialog box is displayed.

10. Make sure the **Insert New** radio button is selected in the **Table** area.

11. Choose the **Pick** button from the **First New Section Placement** area; you are prompted to specify the insertion point.

12. Specify the upper left corner as the insertion point; you will return to the **Table Generation Setup** dialog box.

13. Enter **50** in the **End** edit box of the **Row Definition** area.

14. Choose the **OK** button; the table is inserted into the drawing and the **Report Generator** dialog box is displayed again. Choose the **Close** button; the **Location Code Selection for From/To Reporting** dialog box is displayed. Choose the **Cancel** button to exit the dialog box. Figure P1-31 shows the Wire From/To report.

## Using Project-wide Utilities

1. Choose the **Utilities** tools from the **Project Tools** panel of the **Project** tab; the **Project-Wide Utilities** dialog box is displayed.

2. Select the **Set all to fixed** option from the **Parent Component Tags: Fix/Unfix** drop-down list. Next, select the **Purge all blocks** check box from the **For each drawing** area.

3. Select the **Change Attribute Size** check box from the **Change Attribute** area and then choose the **Setup** button located next to it; the **Project-wide Attribute Size Change** dialog box is displayed, refer to Figure P1-32.

4. In this dialog box, select the **Parent Tags** and **Parent Description text** check boxes. Next, enter **0.15** in the **Height** edit box and **1** in the **Width** edit box of the **Define height /width for the checked categories** area. Next, choose the **OK** button to close the dialog box.

| WIRENO | LOC1 | CMP1 | PIN1 | LOC2 | CMP2 | PIN2 | WLAYR |
|---|---|---|---|---|---|---|---|
| | | MS7 | | | MC7 | | WIRES |
| | | MS8 | | | MC8 | | WIRES |
| | | C3 204 | | | MC8 | | WIRES |
| | | C3 304 | | | MC8 | | WIRES |
| | | MS9 | | | MC9 | | WIRES |
| | | C3 304 | | | MC9 | | WIRES |
| | | C3 504 | | | MC9 | | WIRES |
| | | MS10 | | | MC10 | | WIRES |
| | | C3 504 | | | MC10 | | WIRES |
| | | C3 304 | | | MC10 | | WIRES |
| | | MS11 | | | MC11 | | WIRES |
| | | C3 204 | | | MC11 | | WIRES |
| | | C3 204 | | | MC11 | | WIRES |
| | | MS12 | | | MC12 | | WIRES |
| | | C3 204 | | | MC12 | | WIRES |
| | | C3 204 | | | MC12 | | WIRES |
| | | MS13 | | | MC13 | | WIRES |
| | | C3 304 | | | MC13 | | WIRES |
| | | C3 304 | | | MC13 | | WIRES |
| | | MC7 | | | TBU | U7 | WIRES |
| | | MC8 | | | TBU | U8 | WIRES |
| | | MC8 | | | TBU | V8 | WIRES |
| | | MC8 | | | TBU | W8 | WIRES |
| | | MC9 | | | TBU | U9 | WIRES |
| | | MC9 | | | TBU | V9 | WIRES |
| | | MC9 | | | TBU | W9 | WIRES |
| | | MC10 | | | TBU | U10 | WIRES |
| | | MC10 | | | TBU | V10 | WIRES |
| | | MC10 | | | TBU | W10 | WIRES |
| | | MC11 | | | TBU | U11 | WIRES |
| | | MC11 | | | TBU | V11 | WIRES |
| | | MC11 | | | TBU | W11 | WIRES |
| | | MC12 | | | TBU | U12 | WIRES |
| | | MC12 | | | TBU | V12 | WIRES |
| | | MC12 | | | TBU | W12 | WIRES |
| | | MC13 | | | TBU | U13 | WIRES |
| | | MC13 | | | TBU | V13 | WIRES |
| | | MC13 | | | TBU | W13 | WIRES |
| | <1T> | | | | TBU | | WIRES |
| | <1T> | | | | TBU | | WIRES |
| | <1T> | | | | TBU | | WIRES |
| | <1T> | | | | TBU | | WIRES |
| | <1T> | | | | TBU | | WIRES |
| | <1T> | | | | TBU | | WIRES |
| | <1T> | | | | TBU | | WIRES |
| | | TBL | U7 | | MOT7 | | WIRES |
| | | TBL | U8 | | MOT8 | | WIRES |
| | | TBL | V8 | | MOT8 | | WIRES |
| | | TBL | W8 | | MOT8 | | WIRES |
| | | TBL | U9 | | MOT9 | | WIRES |
| | | TBL | V9 | | MOT9 | | WIRES |
| | | TBL | W9 | | MOT9 | | WIRES |
| | | TBL | U10 | | MOT10 | | WIRES |
| | | TBL | V10 | | MOT10 | | WIRES |
| | | TBL | W10 | | MOT10 | | WIRES |
| | | TBL | U11 | | MOT11 | | WIRES |
| | | TBL | V11 | | MOT11 | | WIRES |
| | | TBL | W11 | | MOT11 | | WIRES |
| | | TBL | U12 | | MOT12 | | WIRES |
| | | TBL | V12 | | MOT12 | | WIRES |
| | | TBL | W12 | | MOT12 | | WIRES |
| | | TBL | U13 | | MOT13 | | WIRES |
| | | TBL | V13 | | MOT13 | | WIRES |
| | | TBL | W13 | | MOT13 | | WIRES |
| | | MS14 | | | MC14 | | WIRES |
| | | MS15 | | | MC15 | | WIRES |
| | | C3 207 | | | MC15 | | WIRES |
| | | C3 207 | | | MC15 | | WIRES |
| | | MS16 | | | MC16 | | WIRES |
| | | C3 307 | | | MC16 | | WIRES |
| | | C3 307 | | | MC16 | | WIRES |
| | | MS17 | | | MC17 | | WIRES |
| | | C3 507 | | | MC17 | | WIRES |

***Figure P1-31*** *The partial view of Wire From/To report*

5. Select the **Change Style** check box from the **Change Attribute** area and then choose the **Setup** button located next to it; the **Project-wide AutoCAD Electrical Style Change** dialog box is displayed.

6. In this dialog box, select the **Swiss 721 BT (True Type)** option from the **Font Name** drop-down list and then choose the **OK** button to close the dialog box. Next, choose the **OK** button from the **Project-Wide Utilities** dialog box; the **Batch Process Drawings** dialog box is displayed. In this dialog box, select the **Active Drawing** radio button and then choose the **OK** button. You will notice that the font style for all attributes has changed.

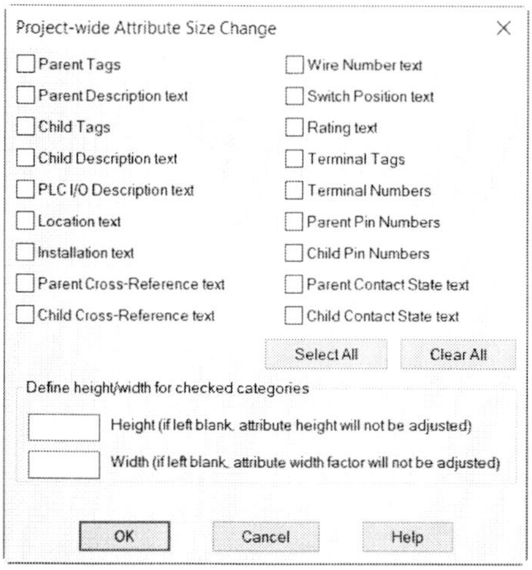

*Figure P1-32 The **Project-wide Attribute Size Change** dialog box*

# Project 2

# Panel Layout Drawing

## PROJECT DESCRIPTION

In this project, you will create a drawing and insert the footprints such as DIN Rail, control relay, PLCs, and so on in it. Then, you will copy and edit these footprints. Next, you will add balloons to these footprints and make their Xdata visible. Figure P2-1 shows the complete panel layout drawing.

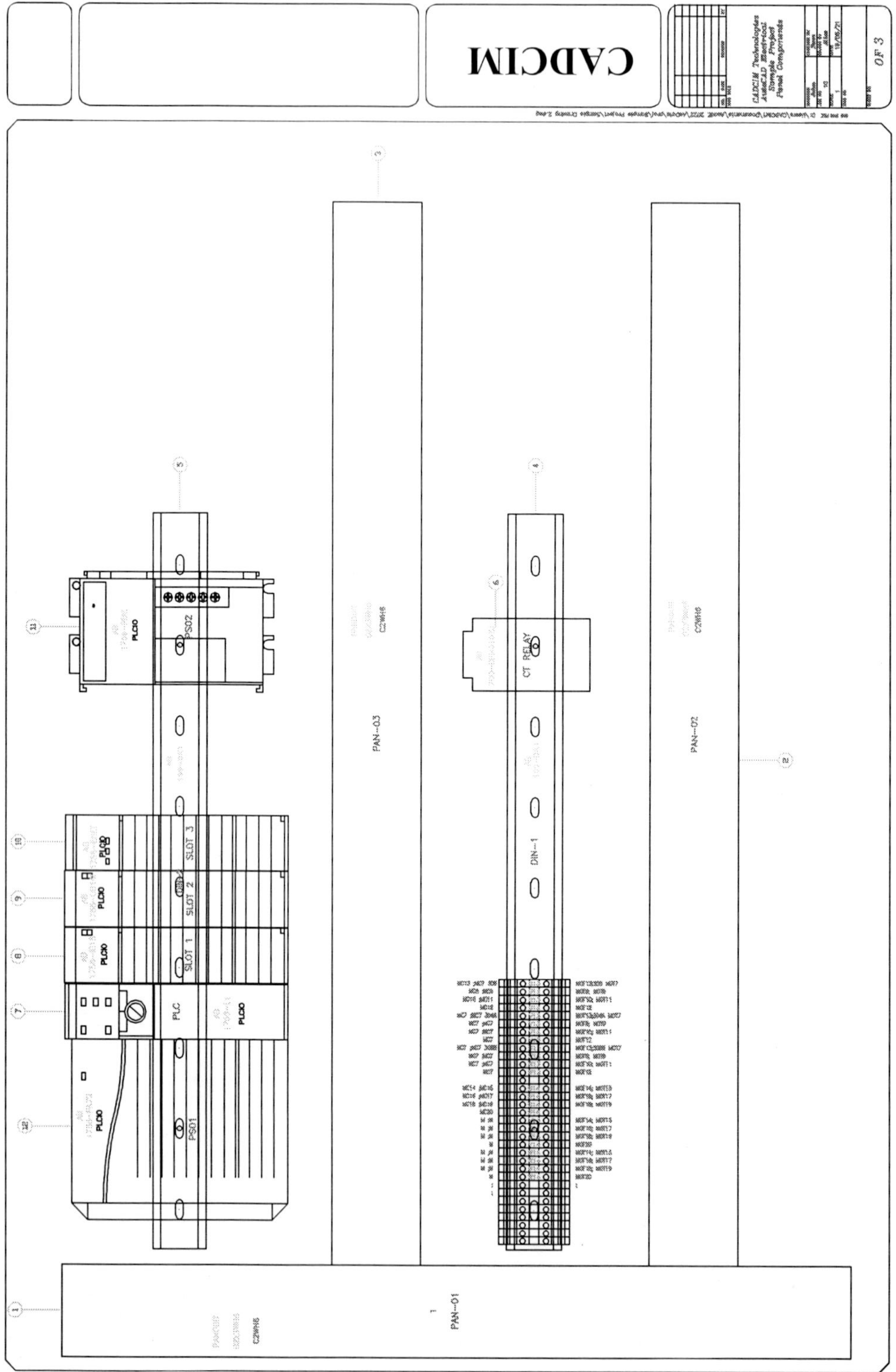


***Figure P2-1** Panel layout drawing for Project 2*

## Creating a New Drawing

1. Make sure **Sample Project** is activated. Next, choose the **New Drawing** button from the **PROJECT MANAGER**; the **Create New Drawing** dialog box is displayed.

2. Enter **Sample Drawing 2** in the **Name** edit box.

3. Choose the **Browse** button on the right of the **Template** edit box; the **Select template** dialog box is displayed.

4. Select **CADCIM** in this dialog box and choose the **Open** button; the name and path of the template file is displayed in the **Template** edit box.

5. Enter **Panel Components** in the **Description 1** edit box.

6. Enter **Panel Layout diagram** in the **Description 2** edit box.

7. Choose the **OK** button in the **Create New Drawing** dialog box; the drawing is created in the project and its name is displayed in bold in the **Projects** rollout.

## Inserting and Copying the DIN Rail

1. Choose the **Icon Menu** tool from **Panel > Insert Component Footprints > Insert Footprints** drop-down; the **Alert** message box is displayed.

2. Choose the **OK** button in this message box; the **Insert Footprint** dialog box is displayed.

3. Select the **DIN Rail** icon from the **Panel Layout Symbols** area; the **Din Rail** dialog box is displayed.

4. Select **PANDUIT, G2X3WH6, Wire duct, 2.25"x3" tall, white, slotted** from the drop-down list in the **Rail Type** area of the **Din Rail** dialog box.

5. Choose the **Pick Rail Information >>** button from the **Origin and Length** area; you are prompted to specify the insertion point of the rail.

6. Enter **1.5,21** at the Command prompt and press ENTER; you are prompted to specify the end point of the rail.

7. Enter **1.5,1** at the Command prompt and press ENTER; the **Din Rail** dialog box is displayed again.

8. Make sure the **Vertical** radio button is selected in the **Orientation** area of the **Din Rail** dialog box and make sure the **NC holes** radio button is selected in the **Panel Mounting** area.

9. Choose the **OK** button in the **Din Rail** dialog box; the **Panel Layout - Component Insert/Edit** dialog box is displayed.

10. Enter **PAN-01** in the **Tag** edit box of the **Component Tag** area.

11. Choose the **OK** button in this dialog box; the PAN-01 DIN Rail is inserted in the drawing, as shown in Figure P2-2.

***Figure P2-2*** *PAN-01 DIN Rail inserted in the drawing*

12. Choose the **Icon Menu** tool from **Panel > Insert Component Footprints > Insert Footprints** drop-down; the **Insert Footprint** dialog box is displayed.

13. Select the **DIN Rail** icon in the **Panel Layout Symbols** area; the **Din Rail** dialog box is displayed.

14. In the **Din Rail** dialog box, select **PANDUIT, G2X3WH6, Wire duct, 2.25"x3" tall, white, slotted** from the drop-down list in the **Rail Type** area.

15. Choose the **Pick Rail Information >>** button in the **Origin and Length** area; you are prompted to specify the insertion point of the rail.

16. Enter **2.625**,**5** at the Command prompt and press ENTER; you are prompted to specify the end point of the rail.

17. Enter **28.625,13** at the Command prompt and press ENTER; the **Din Rail** dialog box is displayed again.

18. In the **Din Rail** dialog box, make sure the **Horizontal** radio button is selected in the **Orientation** area and the **NC holes** radio button is selected in the **Panel Mounting** area.

19. Choose the **OK** button from the **Din Rail** dialog box; the **Panel Layout - Component Insert/Edit** dialog box is displayed.

20. In the **Panel Layout - Component Insert/Edit** dialog box, enter **PAN-02** in the **Tag** edit box of the **Component Tag** area.

21. Choose the **OK** button in this dialog box; the PAN-02 DIN Rail is inserted in the drawing, as shown in Figure P2-3.

22. Choose the **Copy Footprint** tool from the **Edit Footprints** panel of the **Panel** tab; you are prompted to select "just like" component. Select PAN-02 DIN Rail.

23. Enter **2.625,13** at the Command prompt and press ENTER; the **Panel Layout - Component Insert/Edit** dialog box is displayed.

24. Enter **PAN-03** in the **Tag** edit box in the **Component Tag** area of this dialog box.

25. Choose the **OK** button in this dialog box; the PAN-03 DIN Rail is inserted in the drawing, as shown in Figure P2-4.

***Figure P2-3*** *PAN-02 DIN Rail inserted in the drawing*

26. Choose the **Icon Menu** tool from **Panel > Insert Component Footprints > Insert Footprints** drop-down; the **Insert Footprint** dialog box is displayed.

27. Select the **DIN Rail** icon in the **Panel Layout Symbols** area; the **Din Rail** dialog box is displayed.

28. Select **AB, 199-DR1 Symmetrical Rail 35mm x 7.5mm 1m Ion** from the drop-down list in the **Rail Type** area of the **Din Rail** dialog box.

29. Choose the **Pick Rail Information >>** button from the **Origin and Length** area; you are prompted to specify the insertion point of the rail.

30. Enter **3,9** at the Command prompt and press ENTER; you are prompted to specify the end point of the rail.

***Figure P2-4*** *PAN-03 DIN Rail inserted in the drawing*

31. Enter **21,9** at the Command prompt and press ENTER; the **Din Rail** dialog box is displayed again.

32. Make sure the **Horizontal** radio button is selected in the **Orientation** area and make sure the **NC holes** radio button is selected in the **Panel Mounting** area.

33. Choose the **OK** button in the **Din Rail** dialog box; the **Panel Layout - Component Insert/ Edit** dialog box is displayed.

34. Enter **DIN-1** in the **Tag** edit box of the **Component Tag** area.

35. Choose the **OK** button; the DIN-1 DIN Rail is inserted in the drawing, as shown in Figure P2-5.

36. Choose the **Copy Footprint** tool from the **Edit Footprints** panel of the **Panel** tab; you are prompted to select "just like" component. Select DIN-1 DIN Rail.

37. Enter **3,18** at the Command prompt and press ENTER; the **Panel Layout - Component**

**Insert/Edit** dialog box is displayed.

38. Enter **DIN-2** in the **Tag** edit box of the **Component Tag** area.

39. Choose the **OK** button; the DIN-2 DIN Rail is inserted in the drawing, as shown in Figure P2-6.

## Inserting Relay in the Drawing

1. Choose the **Icon Menu** tool from **Panel > Insert Component Footprints > Insert Footprints** drop-down; the **Insert Footprint** dialog box is displayed.

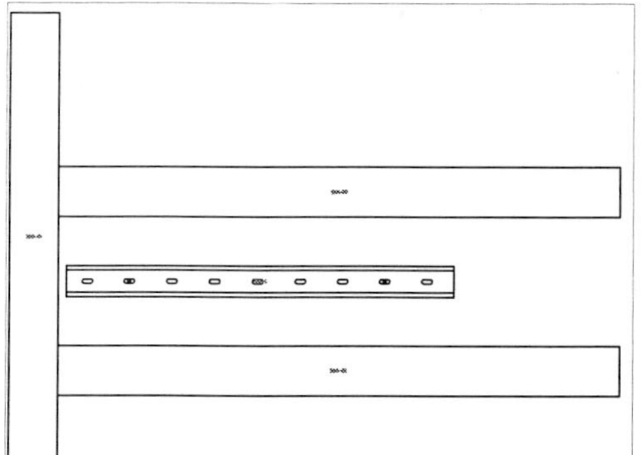

*Figure P2-5 DIN-1 DIN Rail inserted in the drawing*

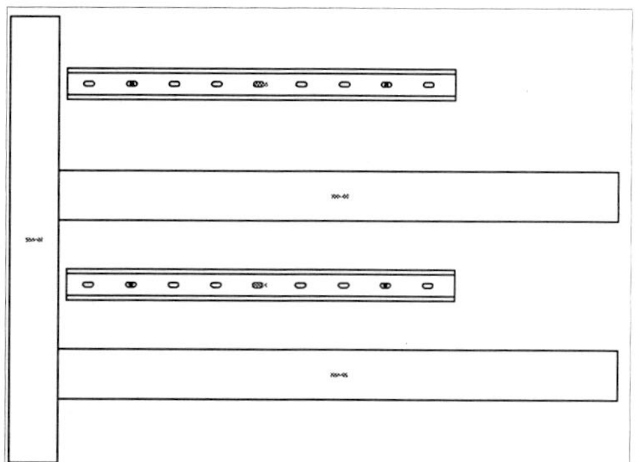

*Figure P2-6 DIN-2 DIN Rail inserted in the drawing*

2. Select the **Relays** icon in the **Panel Layout Symbols** area; the **Panel: Relays and Latches** area is displayed.

3. Select **Relay Coil** from this area; the **Footprint** dialog box is displayed.

4. Choose the **Catalog lookup** button in the **Choice A** area of this dialog box; the **Catalog Browser** dialog box is displayed.

5. In this dialog box, erase the content from the **Search** field and enter **700-CFM310ZJ** in this field. Next, choose the **Search** button.

6. Select the row with **700-CFM310ZJ** in the **Catalog** column of the **Catalog Browser** dialog box and choose the **OK** button; the catalog is displayed in the **Choice A** area of the **Footprint** dialog box.

7. Choose the **OK** button in the **Footprint** dialog box; you are prompted to specify the location for AB/CR-CONTROL RELAYS/abcrcf.dwg.

8. Enter **16.375,7.625** at the Command prompt and press ENTER; you are prompted to select rotation.

9. Move the cursor toward the right in the horizontal direction and click on the screen; the

**Panel Layout - Component Insert/Edit** dialog box is displayed.

10. Enter **CR300** in the **Tag** edit box of the **Component Tag** area.

11. Choose the **OK** button; the CR300 relay is inserted in the drawing, as shown in Figure P2-7.

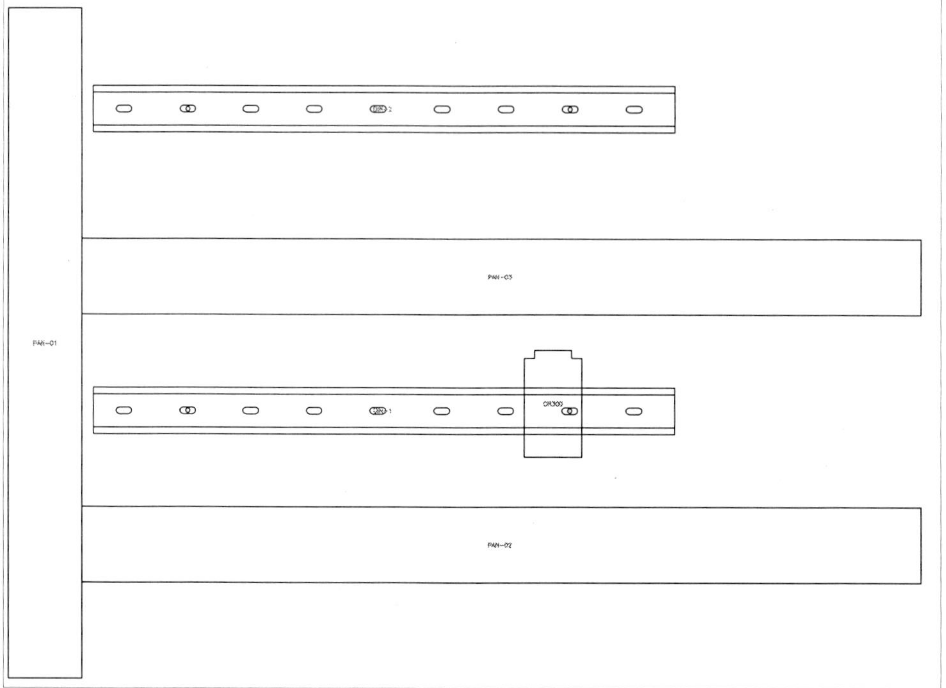

*Figure P2-7 The CR300 relay inserted in the drawing*

## Inserting PLCS in the Drawing

1. Choose the **Icon Menu** tool from **Panel > Insert Component Footprints > Insert Footprints** drop-down; the **Insert Footprint** dialog box is displayed.

2. Select the **PLC I/O** icon in the **Panel Layout Symbols** area; the **Footprint** dialog box is displayed.

3. Choose the **Catalog lookup** button from the **Choice A** area of the **Footprint** dialog box; the **Catalog Browser** dialog box is displayed.

4. In this dialog box, erase the content from the **Search** field and enter **1756-L1** in this field. Next, choose the **Search** button.

5. Select the row with **1756-L1** in the **Catalog** column of the **Catalog Browser** dialog box and then choose the **OK** button; the selected catalog is displayed in the **Choice A** area of the **Footprint** dialog box.

6. Choose the **OK** button in this dialog box; you are prompted to specify the location for AB/

PLCIO-PLCS/ABIPA140.dwg.

7. Enter **8.125,15.25** at the Command prompt and press ENTER; you are prompted to select rotation.

8. Move the cursor toward right in the horizontal direction and click on the screen; the **Panel Layout - Component Insert/Edit** dialog box is displayed.

9. Enter **PLC** in the **Tag** edit box of the **Component Tag** area.

10. Choose the **OK** button; the PLC is inserted in the drawing, as shown in Figure P2-8.

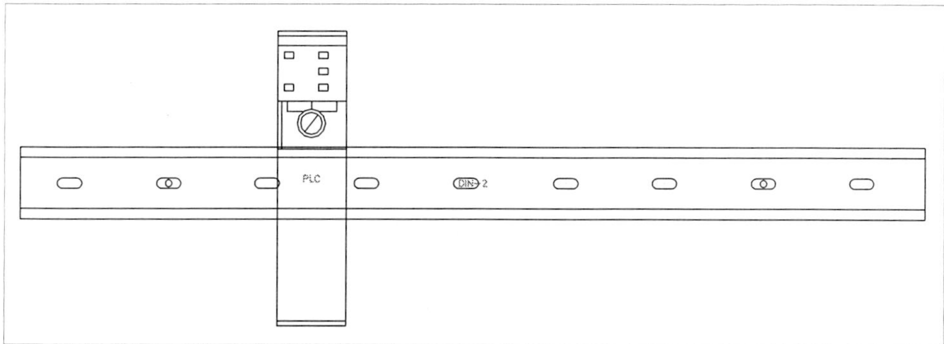


***Figure P2-8*** *PLC inserted in the drawing*

11. Repeat step 1 and select the **PLC I/O** icon in the **Panel Layout Symbols** area; the **Footprint** dialog box is displayed.

12. Choose the **Catalog lookup** button from the **Choice A** area of this dialog box; the **Catalog Browser** dialog box is displayed.

13. In this dialog box, erase the content from the **Search** field and enter **1756** in this field. Next, choose the **Search** button.

14. Select the row with **1756-IB16** in the **Catalog** column of the **Catalog Browser** dialog box and then choose the **OK** button; the catalog is displayed in the **Choice A** area of the **Footprint** dialog box.

15. Choose the **OK** button in the **Footprint** dialog box; you are prompted to specify the location for AB/PLCIO-PLCS/ABIOM130.dwg.

16. Enter **9.5,15.25** at the Command prompt and press ENTER; you are prompted to select rotation.

17. Move the cursor toward right in the horizontal direction and click on the screen; the **Panel**

**Layout - Component Insert/Edit** dialog box is displayed.

18. Enter **SLOT 1** in the **Tag** edit box of the **Component Tag** area.

19. Choose the **OK** button; the SLOT 1 is inserted in the drawing, as shown in Figure P2-9.

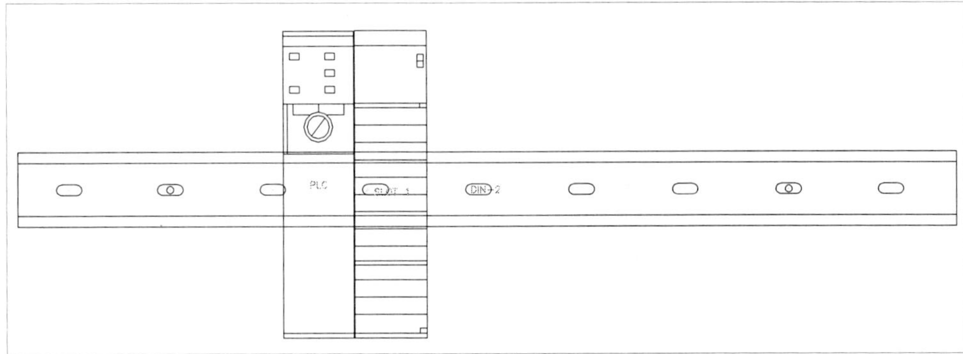


*Figure P2-9 The SLOT 1 inserted in the drawing*

20. Repeat step 1 and select the **PLC I/O** icon in the **Panel Layout Symbols** area; the **Footprint** dialog box is displayed.

21. Choose the **Catalog lookup** button from the **Choice A** area of this dialog box; the **Catalog Browser** dialog box is displayed.

22. In this dialog box, erase the content from the **Search** field and enter **1756** in this field. Next, choose the **Search** button.

23. Select the row having **1756-OB16I** in the **Catalog** column of the **Catalog Browser** dialog box and then choose the **OK** button; the catalog is displayed in the **Choice A** area of the **Footprint** dialog box.

24. Choose the **OK** button in this dialog box; you are prompted to specify the location for AB/PLCIO-PLCS/ABIOM020.dwg.

25. Enter **10.875,15.25** at the Command prompt and press ENTER; you are prompted to select rotation.

26. Move the cursor toward the right in the horizontal direction and click on the screen; the **Panel Layout - Component Insert/Edit** dialog box is displayed.

27. Enter **SLOT 2** in the **Tag** edit box of the **Component Tag** area.

28. Choose the **OK** button in this dialog box; the SLOT 2 is inserted in the drawing, as shown in Figure P2-10.

29. Repeat step 1 and select the **PLC I/O** icon in the **Panel Layout Symbols** area; the

**Footprint** dialog box is displayed.

30. Choose the **Catalog lookup** button from the **Choice A** area of this dialog box; the **Catalog Browser** dialog box is displayed.

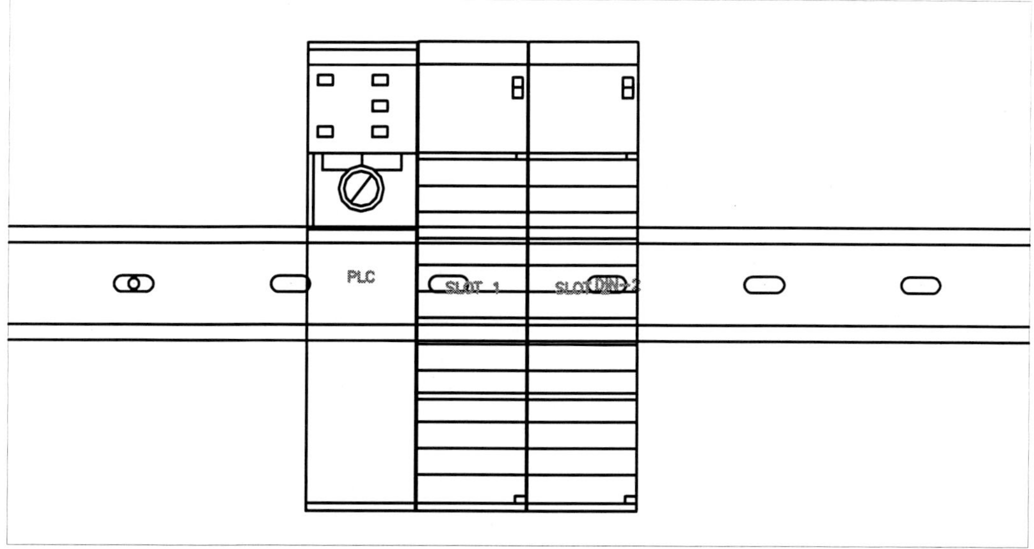


*Figure P2-10 The SLOT 2 inserted in the drawing*

31. In this dialog box, erase the content from the **Search** field and enter **1756** in this field. Next, choose the **Search** button.

32. Select the row with **1756-ENET** in the **Catalog** column of the **Catalog Browser** dialog box and then choose the **OK** button; the catalog is displayed in the **Choice A** area of the **Footprint** dialog box.

33. Choose the **OK** button in this dialog box; you are prompted to specify location for AB/PLCIO-PLCS/ABCMA230.dwg.

34. Enter **12.25,15.25** at the Command prompt and press ENTER; you are prompted to select rotation.

35. Move the cursor toward right in the horizontal direction and click on the screen; the **Panel Layout - Component Insert/Edit** dialog box is displayed.

36. Enter **SLOT 3** in the **Tag** edit box of the **Component Tag** area.

37. Choose the **OK** button; the SLOT 3 is inserted in the drawing, as shown in Figure P2-11.

38. Repeat step 1 and select the **PLC I/O** icon from the **Panel Layout Symbols** area of the **Insert Footprint** dialog box; the **Footprint** dialog box is displayed.

39. Choose the **Catalog lookup** button from the **Choice A** area of this dialog box; the **Catalog Browser** dialog box is displayed.

40. In this dialog box, erase the content from the **Search** field and enter **1769** in this field. Next, choose the **Search** button.

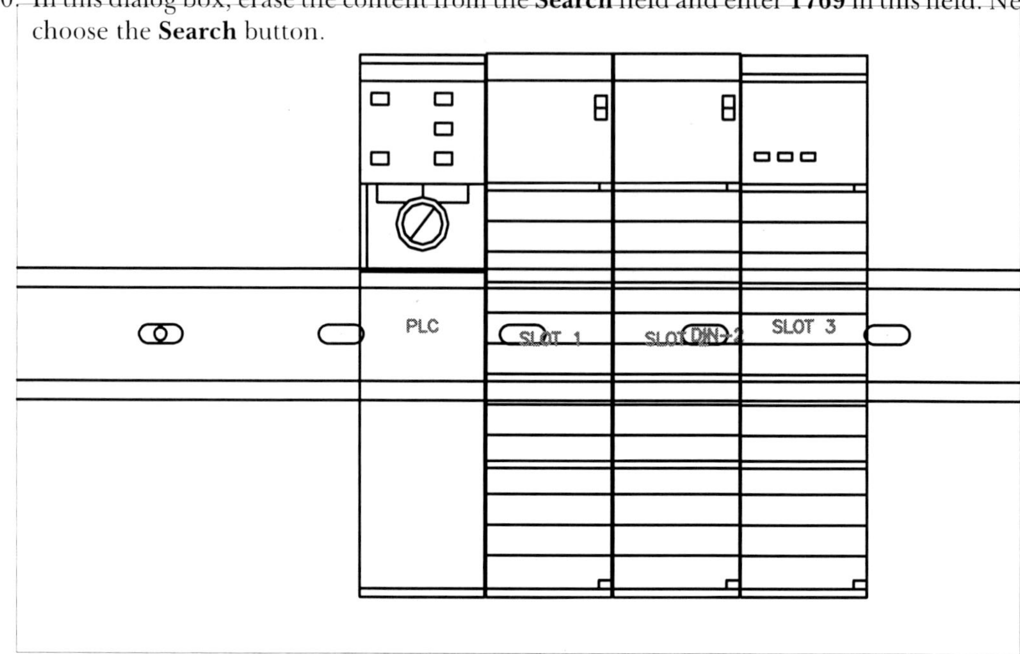


*Figure P2-11 The SLOT 3 inserted in the drawing*

41. Select the row with **1769-PB2** in the **Catalog** column of the **Catalog Browser** dialog box and then choose the **OK** button; the catalog is displayed in the **Choice A** area of the **Footprint** dialog box.

42. Choose the **OK** button in the **Footprint** dialog box; you are prompted to specify the location for AB/PLCIO-PLCS/1769-PS.dwg.

43. Enter **16.625,15.625** at the Command prompt and press ENTER; you are prompted to select rotation.

44. Move the cursor toward right in the horizontal direction and click on the screen; the **Panel Layout - Component Insert/Edit** dialog box is displayed.

45. Enter **PS01** in the **Tag** edit box of the **Component Tag** area.

46. Choose the **OK** button; the PS01 power supply is inserted in the drawing, as shown in Figure P2-12.

47. Repeat step 1 and select the **PLC I/O** icon in the **Panel Layout Symbols** area; the **Footprint** dialog box is displayed.

48. Choose the **Catalog lookup** button from the **Choice A** area of this dialog box; the **Catalog Browser** dialog box is displayed.

49. In this dialog box, erase the content from the **Search** field and enter **1756** in this field. Next,

choose the **Search** button.

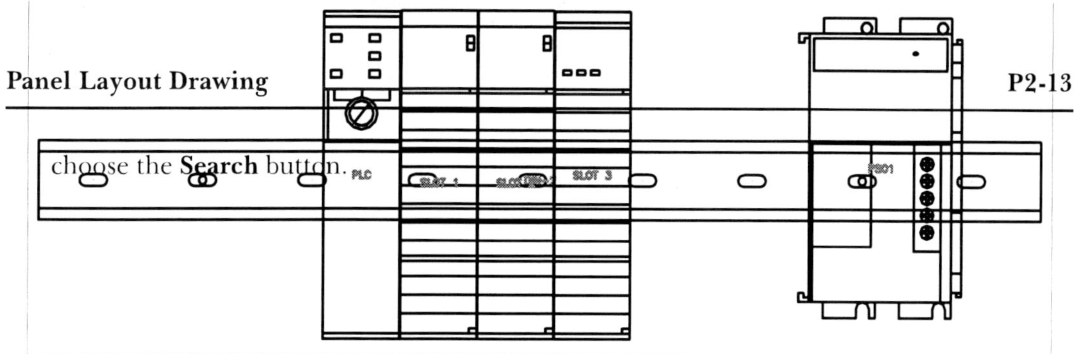


*Figure P2-12 The PS01 power supply inserted in the drawing*

50. Select the row with **1756-PA72** in the **Catalog** column of the **Catalog Browser** dialog box and then choose the **OK** button; the catalog is displayed in the **Choice A** area of the **Footprint** dialog box.

51. Choose the **OK** button in the **Footprint** dialog box; you are prompted to specify the location for AB/PLCIO-PLCS/ABCMA180.dwg.

52. Enter **8.125,15.25** at the Command prompt and press ENTER; you are prompted to select rotation.

53. Move the cursor toward right in the horizontal direction and click on the screen; the **Panel Layout - Component Insert/Edit** dialog box is displayed.

54. Enter **PS01** in the **Tag** edit box of the **Component Tag** area. Next, choose the **OK** button in this dialog box; the **Duplicate Panel Layout Tag** message box is displayed. Choose the **Continue** button from it and then choose the **OK** button from the **Panel Layout - Component Insert/Edit** dialog box; PS01 power supply is inserted in the drawing, as shown in Figure P2-13. Figure P2-14 shows all footprints inserted in the drawing.

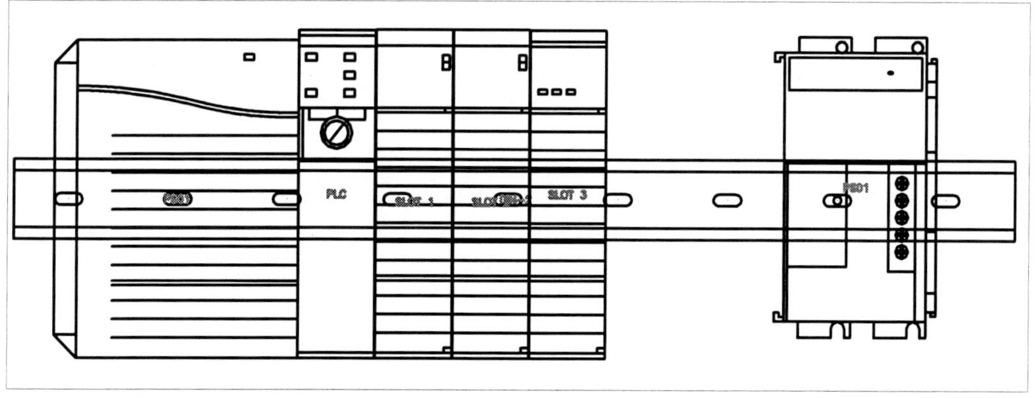


*Figure P2-13 The PS01 power supply inserted in the drawing*

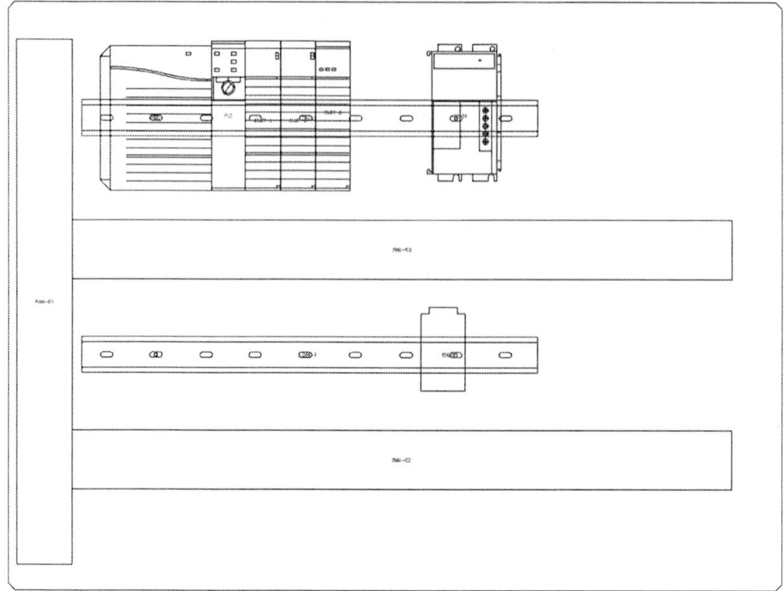

*Figure P2-14 All footprints inserted in the drawing*

## Inserting the Terminal Strip

1. Choose the **Editor** tool from the **Terminal Footprints** panel of the **Panel** tab; the **Terminal Strip Selection** dialog box is displayed.

**Note**

*If the **QSAVE** message box is displayed, choose the **OK** button in it to save the drawing.*

2. In this dialog box, select the **TB1** terminal strip and choose the **Edit** button; the **Terminal Strip Editor** dialog box is displayed. If the **Defined Terminal Wiring Constraints Exceeded** message box is displayed, choose the **OK** button in this message box to close it.

3. Choose the **Catalog Code Assignment** tab and then select all terminal strips by using the SHIFT key. Next, choose the **Assign Catalog Number** button in the **Catalog** area; the **Catalog Browser** dialog box is displayed.

4. In this dialog box, erase the content from the **Search** field and enter **1492** in this field, if any. Next, choose the **Search** button.

5. Select the row having **1492-W3** in the **Catalog** column of the **Catalog Browser** dialog box and then choose the **OK** button; the catalog is displayed in the **Catalog Code Assignment** tab.

6. Choose the **Layout Preview** tab and make sure the **Graphical Terminal Strip** radio button is selected.

7. Select **Wire Number Tag : Terminal** from the **Default pick list for Annotation format** list box.

8. Make sure **1.0** is selected in the **Scale on Insert** drop-down list and then select **270.0** from the **Angle on Insert** drop-down list.

9. Choose the **Insert** button. Next, enter **11.25,9** at the Command prompt and press ENTER; the **Terminal Strip Editor** dialog box is displayed again. Choose the **OK** button in this dialog box; the **Terminal Strip Selection** dialog box is displayed. Choose the **Done** button in this dialog box; the terminal strip is inserted in the drawing, as shown in Figure P2-15.

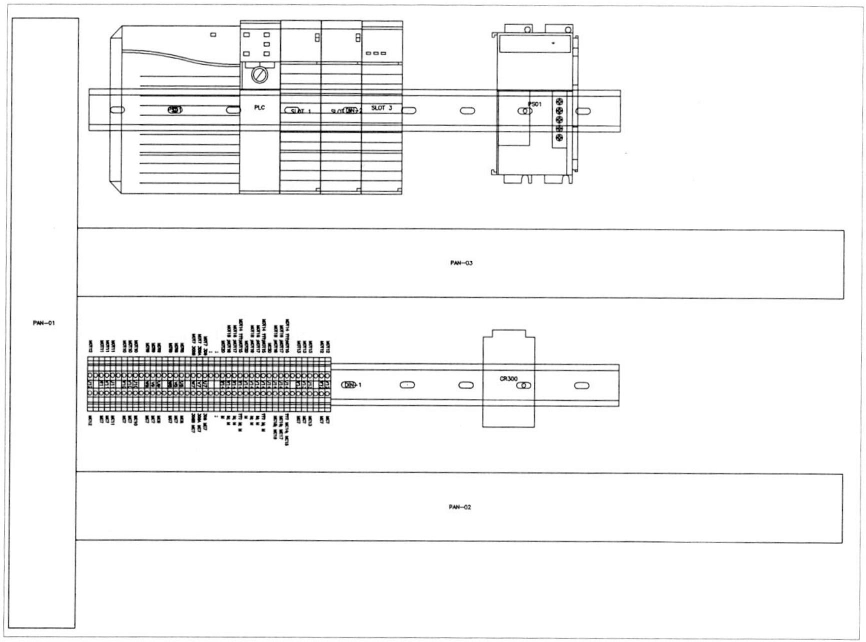


***Figure P2-15*** *Terminal strip inserted in the drawing*

**Note**

*If the **QSAVE** message box is displayed, choose the **OK** button in it to save the drawing.*

## Editing Footprints

1. Choose the **Edit** tool from the **Edit Footprints** panel of the **Panel** tab; you are prompted to select the component.

2. Select **PAN-01** DIN Rail; the **Panel Layout - Component Insert/Edit** dialog box is displayed.

3. Enter **1** in the **Item Number** edit box and choose the **OK** button.

4. Similarly, select the following components and give them the item number in the **Item Number** edit box of the **Panel Layout - Component Insert/Edit** dialog box.

**Note**

*1. If the* ***Mismatch Item Number Found*** *message box is displayed, choose the* ***OK*** *button in it.*

*2. If the* ***Update Related Components*** *message box is displayed, choose the* ***Skip*** *button in it.*

a) PAN-02 = 2
b) PAN-03 = 3
c) DIN-1 = 4
d) DIN-2 = 5
e) CR300 = 6
f) PLC = 7
g) SLOT 1= 8
h) SLOT 2= 9
i) SLOT 3= 10
j) PS01 mounted on the right of DIN Rail DIN-2 = 11
k) PS01 mounted on the left of DIN Rail DIN-2 = 12

## Adding Balloons to Footprints

1. Choose the **Balloon** tool from the **Insert Component Footprints** panel of the **Panel** tab; you are prompted to select the component to add balloon.

2. Select **PAN-01** DIN Rail; you are prompted to specify the leader start or the balloon insert point.

3. Enter **1.5,21** at the Command prompt and press ENTER; you are prompted to specify the end point.

4. Enter **1.5,22** at the Command prompt and press ENTER.

5. Press ENTER; the balloon is inserted in the **PAN-01** DIN Rail, as shown in Figure P2-16; you are prompted to select the component to add balloon.

6. Select **PAN-02** DIN Rail; you are prompted to specify the leader start or the balloon insert point.

7. Enter **15,3.875** at the Command prompt and press ENTER; you are prompted to specify the end point.

8. Enter **15,2.875** at the Command prompt and press ENTER; the balloon is inserted in the **PAN-02** DIN Rail.

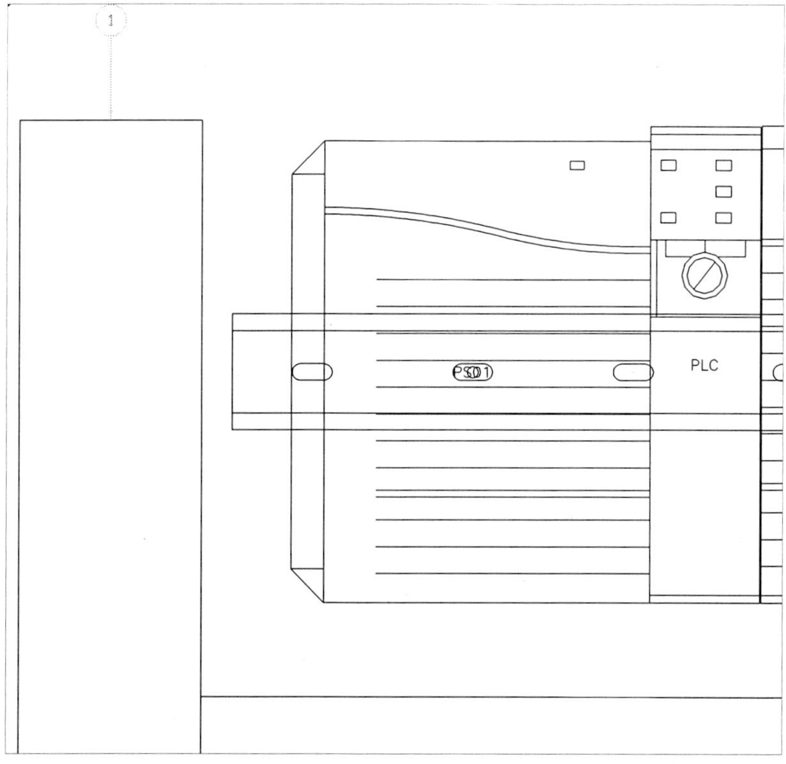


***Figure P2-16*** *The balloon inserted in the **PAN-01** DIN Rail*

9. Similarly, select and add the balloons to the following components at the given coordinates:

| Component | Start Point | End Point |
|---|---|---|
| PAN-03 | 28.625,13 | 29.625,13 |
| DIN-1 | 21,9 | 22,9 |
| DIN-2 | 21,18 | 22,18 |
| CR300 | 18.15,10 | 19.15,10 |
| PLC | 8.8,20.92 | 8.8,21.92 |
| SLOT 1 | 10.15,20.93 | 10.15,21.93 |
| SLOT 2 | 11.55,20.93 | 11.55,21.93 |
| SLOT 3 | 12.95,20.93 | 12.95,21.93 |
| PS01 mounted on the right of DIN Rail DIN-2 | 18.20,20.56 | 18.20,21.56 |
| PS01 mounted on the left of DIN Rail DIN-2 | 6,20.75 | 6,21.75 |

10. When you complete adding balloons to the components, press ENTER to exit the command. Figure P2-17 shows the balloons inserted in all components.

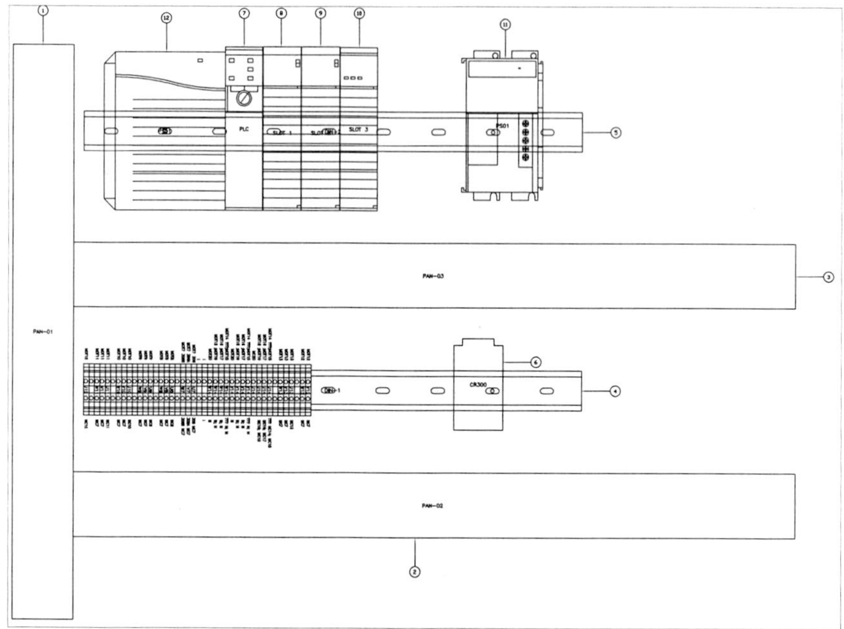

*Figure P2-17 Balloons added to all components*

## Making Xdata of the Footprints Visible

1. Choose the **Make Xdata Visible** tool from **Panel > Other Tools > Panel Configuration** drop-down; you are prompted to select the footprint. 

2. Select **PAN-01** DIN Rail; the **Select XData to Change to a Block Attribute** dialog box is displayed.

3. Select the radio button on the left of the **MFG** drop-down list and choose the **Insert** button; you are prompted to specify the location for inserting attribute.

4. Enter **1,17** at the Command prompt and press ENTER; the **Select XData to Change to a Block Attribute** dialog box appears again.

5. Select the radio button on the left of the **CAT** drop-down list and choose the **Insert** button; you are prompted to specify the location for inserting attribute.

6. Enter **1,16.5** at the Command prompt and press ENTER; the **Select XData to Change to a Block Attribute** dialog box appears again.

7. Select the radio button on the left of the **ASSYCODE** drop-down list and choose the **Insert** button; you are prompted to specify the location for inserting attribute.

8. Enter **1,16** at the Command prompt and press ENTER; the **Select XData to Change to a Block Attribute** dialog box is displayed again.

9. Choose the **Done** button to exit the dialog box. Figure P2-18 shows the attributes inserted in the footprint.

10. Similarly, you need to make Xdata of the rest of the footprints visible. To do so, repeat step 1, select the remaining footprints, and then place the attributes in the footprints, as shown in Figures P2-19 and P2-20. Figure P2-21 shows the panel layout drawing after inserting the attributes.

*Figure P2-18 Attributes inserted in the footprint*

## Moving the Attributes and Changing their Size

1. Choose the **Move/Show Attribute** tool from **Schematic > Edit Components > Modify Attributes** drop-down; you are prompted to select the attribute to move.

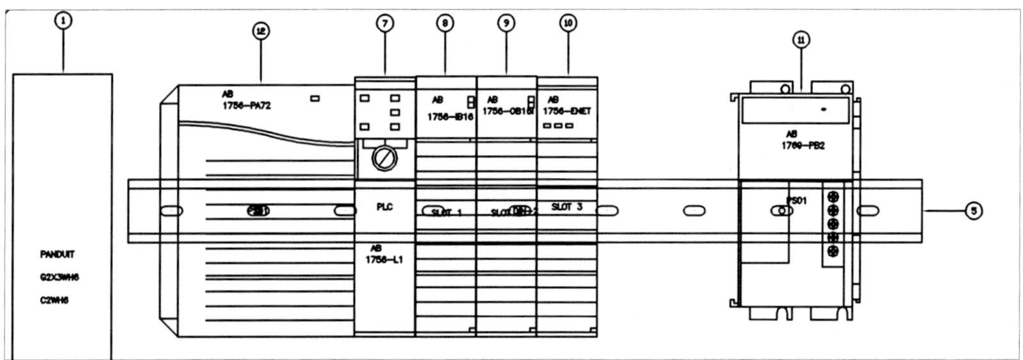


*Figure P2-19 Attributes inserted in the upper part of the panel layout drawing*

2. Select DIN-1 attribute and move it to a new location, as shown in Figure P2-22.

3. Similarly, select the following attributes and move them to new locations:

a) PS01 mounted on the left of DIN-2
b) SLOT 1
c) SLOT 2
d) DIN-2
e) PS01 mounted on the right of DIN-2

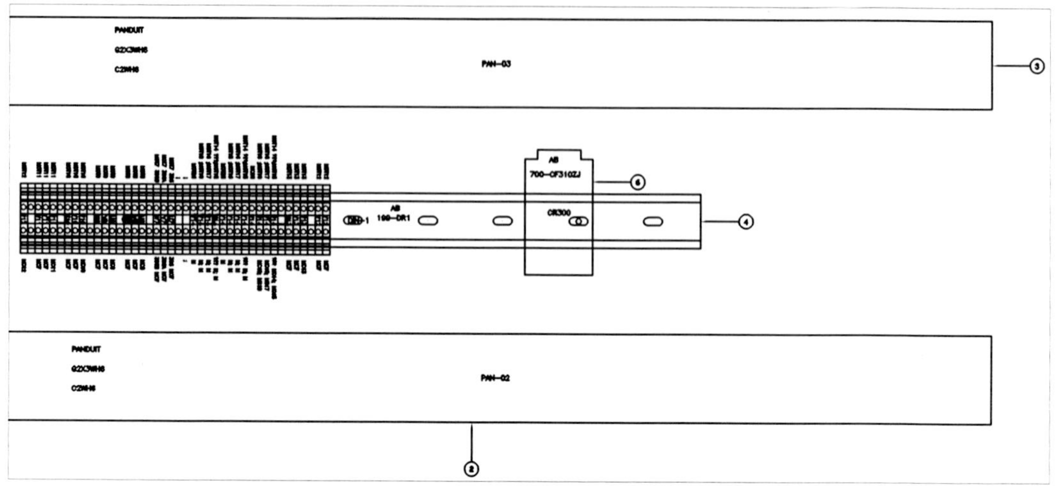


*Figure P2-20 Attributes inserted in the lower part of the panel layout drawing*

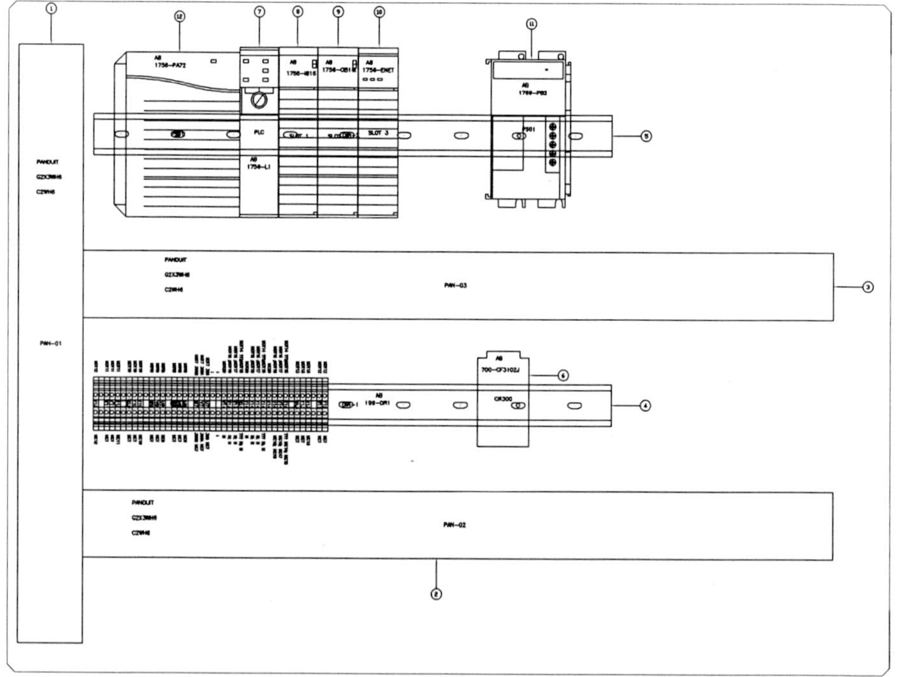


*Figure P2-21 Panel layout drawing after inserting the attributes*

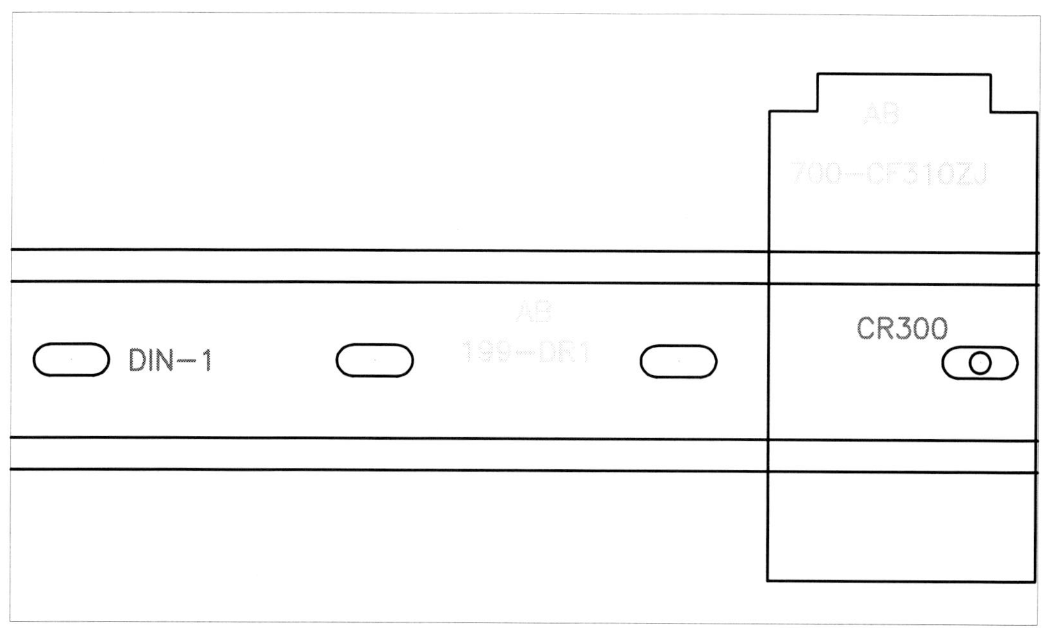


*Figure P2-22 DIN-1 attribute moved*

Figure P2-23 shows the attributes moved to new locations.

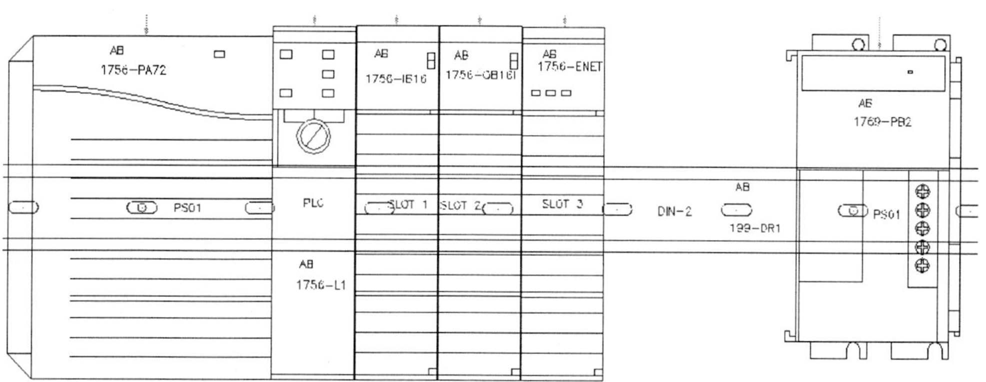


*Figure P2-23 Attributes moved to new locations*

4. To change the size of the attributes, choose the **Change Attribute Size** tool from **Schematic > Edit Components > Modify Attributes** drop-down; the **Change Attribute Size** dialog box is displayed. 

5. Enter **0.15** in the **Size** edit box and make sure 1.0 is displayed in the **Width** edit box. Next, select the **Apply** check box.

6. Choose the **Single** button and select the following attributes to change their size:

   PAN-01
   PAN-02
   DIN-1
   PAN-03
   PS01 mounted on the left of DIN-2
   PLC
   SLOT 1
   SLOT 2
   SLOT 3
   DIN-2
   PS01 mounted on the right of DIN-2

7. Press ENTER to exit the command.

## Exporting Drawing Data to an Excel File

1. Choose the **To Spreadsheet** tool from the **Export** panel of the **Import/Export Data** tab; the **Export to Spreadsheet** dialog box is displayed.

2. In this dialog box, select the **Panel Components*** radio button and choose the **OK** button; the **Panel Layout Data Export** dialog box is displayed, as shown in Figure P2-24.

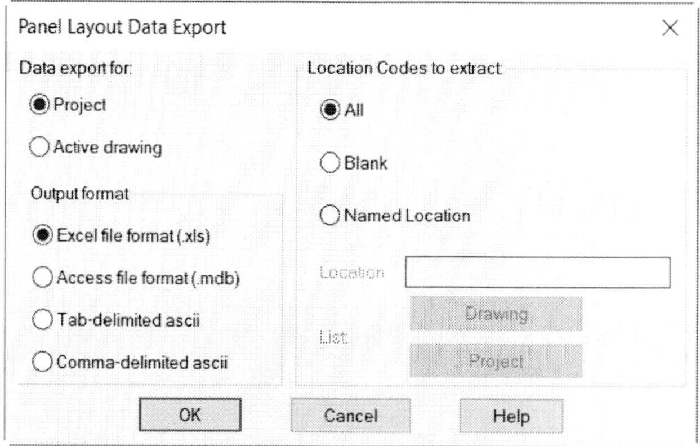


*Figure P2-24 The **Panel Layout Data Export** dialog box*

3. Select the **Active Drawing** radio button from the **Data export for** area and the **Excel file format (.xls)** radio button from the **Output format** area. Next, choose the **OK** button; the **Select file name for drawing's XLS output** dialog box is displayed.

4. Browse to **Documents > Acade 2022 > AeData > Proj > Sample Project** in the **Save in** drop-down list.

5. Enter **Panel Components** in the **File name** edit box.

6. Choose the **Save** button; the components present in the *Sample Drawing 2.dwg* file are exported to an Excel sheet.

## Changing Data in an Excel File

1. Open the Windows Explorer and browse to **Documents > Acade 2022 > AeData > Proj > Sample Project**. Next, open the *Panel Components.xls* file.

2. In this file, change the tag of the power supply corresponding to catalog number 1769-PB2 to **PS02** under the **TAGNAME** column, as shown in Figure P2-25. Next, save and close this file.

## Importing Drawing Data from an Excel File

1. Choose the **From Spreadsheet** tool from the **Import** panel of the **Import/Export Data** tab; the **Update Drawings from Spreadsheet File (xls, mdb, csv Format)** dialog box is displayed.

2. In this dialog box, select **Panel Components** from the list displayed and choose **Open**; the **Update Drawing per Spreadsheet Data** dialog box is displayed. In this dialog box, select the **Active Drawing** radio button and choose the **OK** button; the tagname of the power supply on the right of DIN-2 is changed to PS02, as shown in Figure P2-26.

| (PAR1_CH | TAGNAME | DESC1 | DESC2 | DESC3 | (REF) | MFG | CAT | ASSYCOD | CNT | UM | INST | LOC | MOUNT | GROUPW | WDBLKNA | R |
|---|---|---|---|---|---|---|---|---|---|---|---|---|---|---|---|---|
| 1 | PAN-01 | | | | | PANDUIT | G2X3WH6 | C2WH6 | | | | | | | WW | |
| 1 | PS01 | | | | | AB | 1756-PA72 | | | | | | | | PLCIO | |
| 1 | PLC | | | | | AB | 1756-L1 | | | | | | | | PLCIO | |
| 1 | SLOT 1 | | | | | AB | 1756-IB16 | | | | | | | | PLCIO | |
| 1 | SLOT 2 | | | | | AB | 1756-OB16I | | | | | | | | PLCIO | |
| 1 | SLOT 3 | | | | | AB | 1756-ENET | | | | | | | | PLCIO | |
| 1 | PS02 | | | | | AB | 1769-PB2 | | | | | | | | PLCIO | |
| 1 | PAN-03 | | | | | PANDUIT | G2X3WH6 | C2WH6 | | | | | | | WW | |
| 1 | DIN-1 | | | | | AB | 199-DR1 | | | | | | | | DIN | |
| 1 | CR300 | | | | | AB | 700-CF310ZJ | | | | | | | | CR | |
| 1 | PAN-02 | | | | | PANDUIT | G2X3WH6 | C2WH6 | | | | | | | WW | |
| 1 | DIN-2 | | | | | AB | 199-DR1 | | | | | | | | DIN | |

***Figure P2-25*** *The value of tag of the power supply under the TAGNAME column changed*

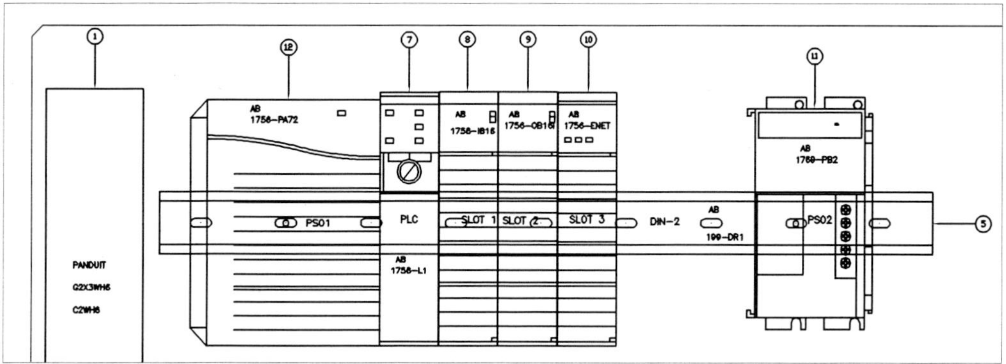


***Figure P2-26*** *The tagname of power supply changed to PS02*

## Creating a New Drawing and Placing the Panel Bill of Material Report in it

1. Choose the **New Drawing** button from the **PROJECT MANAGER**; the **Create New Drawing** dialog box is displayed.

2. Enter **Panel Report** in the **Name** edit box.

3. Choose the **Browse** button on the right of the **Template** edit box; the **Select template** dialog box is displayed.

4. Select **CADCIM** from this dialog box and choose the **Open** button; the name and path of the template file is displayed in the **Template** edit box.

5. Enter **Panel Bill of Material Report** in the **Description 1** edit box.

6. Choose the **OK** button in the **Create New Drawing** dialog box; the drawing is created in the project and its name is displayed in bold in the **Projects** rollout.

7. Choose the **Reports** tool from the **Panel** panel of the **Reports** tab; the **Panel Reports** dialog box is displayed.

8. Select the **Bill of Material** in the **Report Name** area and make sure the **Project** radio button is selected in the **Panel Bill of Material** area.

9. Choose the **OK** button from the **Panel Reports** dialog box; the **Select Drawings to Process** dialog box is displayed. Choose the **Do All** button; the drawings are transferred from the top list to the bottom list. Choose the **OK** button; the **Qsave** message box is displayed. Choose **OK**; the **Report Generator** dialog box is displayed.

10. Choose the **Put on Drawing** button from this dialog box; the **Table Generation Setup** dialog box is displayed.

11. Make sure the **Insert New** radio button is selected in the **Table** area.

12. Choose the **Pick** button from the **First New Section Placement** area; you are prompted to specify the insertion point.

13. Click on the upper left corner of the title block; you will return to the **Table Generation Setup** dialog box.

14. Choose the **OK** button; the table is inserted into the drawing and the **Report Generator** dialog box is displayed again. Choose the **Close** button to exit the dialog box. Figure P2-27 shows the panel Bill of Material report.

| ITEM | TAGS | QTY | SUB | CATALOG | MFG | DESCRIPTION |
|---|---|---|---|---|---|---|
| | TB1 | 42 | | 1492-W3 | AB | TERMINAL BLOCK/STRIP<br>FEED-THROUGH<br>20AMPS<br>600V, #14-#22 WIRE RANGE<br>GRAY COLOUR |
| 1 | PAN-01 | 1 | | G2X3WH6 | PANDUIT | WIDE FINGER, SLOTTED WIRING DUCT<br>2.25 x 3.12<br>SLOTTED<br>WHITE<br>LEAD-FREE PVC, STANDARD MOUNTING HOLES |
| 2 | PAN-02 | 1 | | G2X3WH6 | PANDUIT | WIDE FINGER, SLOTTED WIRING DUCT<br>2.25 x 3.12<br>SLOTTED<br>WHITE<br>LEAD-FREE PVC, STANDARD MOUNTING HOLES |
| 3 | PAN-03 | 1 | | G2X3WH6 | PANDUIT | WIDE FINGER, SLOTTED WIRING DUCT<br>2.25 x 3.12<br>SLOTTED<br>WHITE<br>LEAD-FREE PVC, STANDARD MOUNTING HOLES |
| 4 | DIN-1 | 1 | | 199-DR1 | AB | ZINC/STEEL DIN RAIL EN 50022 (35mm x 7.5mm x 1m)<br>35mm x 7.5mm<br>SLOTTED |
| 5 | DIN-2 | 1 | | 199-DR1 | AB | ZINC/STEEL DIN RAIL EN 50022 (35mm x 7.5mm x 1m)<br>35mm x 7.5mm<br>SLOTTED |
| 6 | CR300 | 1 | | 700-CF310ZJ | AB | CF TYPE RELAY, 4 POLE, DC COIL, STANDARD CONTACTS<br>TYPE CF<br>24VDC<br>3 NO 1 NC<br>24VDC, STANDARD, RATING: 5A |
| 7 | PLC | 1 | | 1756-L1 | AB | 1756 CONTROL LOGIX PROCESSORS LOGIX5550<br>1756<br>PROCESSOR<br>CONTROL LOGIX LOGIX5550 PROCESSOR |
| 8 | SLOT 1 | 1 | | 1756-IB16 | AB | 1756 CONTROL LOGIX PLC DIGITAL DC INPUT MODULE<br>1756<br>DISCRETE INPUT<br>24 VDC 16 INPUTS (2 SETS OF 8); 24 SOURCE LOAD<br>RTB: 1756-TBNH; 1756-TBSH |
| 9 | SLOT 2 | 1 | | 1756-OB16I | AB | 1756 CONTROL LOGIX PLC DIGITAL DC OUTPUT MODULE<br>1756<br>DISCRETE OUTPUT<br>12/24 VDC 16 INDIVIDUALLY ISOLATED OUTPUTS; 12/24 SOURCE<br>RTB: 1756-TBCH; 1756-TBS6H |
| 10 | SLOT 3 | 1 | | 1756-ENET | AB | 1756 CONTROL LOGIX COMMUNICATION INTERFACE MODULE<br>1756<br>COMMUNICATION<br>I/O COMMUNICATION MODULE ETHERNET |
| 11 | PS02 | 1 | | 1769-PB2 | AB | 1769 MICRO LOGIX 1500 COMPACT I/O MODULE<br>1769<br>POWER SUPPLY<br>24VDC<br>POWER SUPPLY |
| 12 | PS01 | 1 | | 1756-PA72 | AB | 1756 CONTROL LOGIX POWER SUPPLY<br>1756<br>POWER SUPPLY<br>INPUT VOLTAGE: 120 VAC OR 220 VAC |

***Figure P2-27*** *The panel Bill of Material report*

**This page is intentionally left blank**

# Index

## Symbols



## A



## B



## C

## Q



## R



## S

## X



## Z

# Other Titles of Interest - BPB/TICKOO SERIES

## Publication by BPB/TICKOO SERIES

The following is the list of some of the publications by BPB/TICKOO series:

### AutoCAD Electrical Textbooks

- AutoCAD Electrical 2021 for Engineers and Designers
- AutoCAD Electrical 2019 for Engineers and`Designers
- AutoCAD Electrical 2018 for Electrical Control Designers, 9th Edition
- AutoCAD Electrical 2021: Atutorial Approach for Engineers and Designers
- AutoCAD Electrical 2020: Atutorial Approach for Engineers and Designers

### AutoCAD Textbooks

- AutoCAD 2022 for Engineers and Designers - Basic and Intermediate
- AutoCAD 2021 for Engineers and Designers - Basic and Intermediate
- AutoCAD 2021(3D and Advanced) for Engineers and Designers
- AutoCAD 2020 for Engineers and Designers - Basic and Intermediate
- AutoCAD 2019: A Problem-Solving Approach, Basic and Intermediate, 25th Edition
- AutoCAD 2020 Workbook

### Autodesk Inventor Textbooks

- Autodesk Inventor Professional 2022 for Engineers and Designers
- Autodesk Inventor Professional 2020 for Engineers and Designers
- Autodesk Inventor Professional 2019 for Designers, 19th Edition
- Inventor 2020 Workbook

### Autodesk Fusion 360

Autodesk Fusion 360: A Tutorial Approach
Autodesk Fusion 360: A Learner's Guide, 2nd Edition

### AutoCAD MEP Textbooks

- AutoCAD MEP 2020 for Engineers and Designers
- AutoCAD MEP 2018 for Designers, 4th Edition

### AutoCAD Plant 3D Textbook

- AutoCAD Plant 3D 2018 for Designers, 4th Edition

### NX Textbooks

- Siemens NX 2021 for Engineers and Designers
- Siemens NX 2020 for Engineers and Designers
- Siemens NX 2019 for Engineers and Designers
- Siemens NX 12.0 for Designers, 11th Edition
- Seimens NX 2019 Workbook

## NX Mold Textbook
- Mold Design Using NX 11.0: A Tutorial Approach

## AutoCAD LT Textbooks
- AutoCAD LT 2022 for Engineers and Designers
- AutoCAD LT 2020 for Engineers and Designers
- AutoCAD LT 2017 for Designers, 12th Edition

## Solid Edge Textbooks
- Solid Edge 2021 for Engineers and Designers
- Solid Edge 2019 for Engineers and Designers
- Solid Edge ST 10 for Designers, 15th Edition

## SOLIDWORKS Textbooks
- SOLIDWORKS 2021 for Engineers and Designers
- SOLIDWORKS 2020 for Engineers and Designers
- SOLIDWORKS 2019 for Engineers and Designers
- SOLIDWORKS 2018 for Designers, 16th Edition

## SOLIDWORKS Simulation Textbooks
- SOLIDWORKS Simulation 2018: A Tutorial Approach
- SOLIDWORKS Simulation 2016: A Tutorial Approach

## Creo Parametric Textbooks
- Creo Parametric 6.0 for Engineers and Designers
- Creo Parametric 5.0 for Designers, 5th Edition
- Creo Parametric 6.0 Workbook

## CATIA Textbooks
- CATIA V5-6R2020 for Engineers and Designers
- CATIA V5-6R2019 for Engineers and Designers
- CATIA V5-6R2018 for Engineers and Designers

## Autodesk Revit Architecture Textbooks
- Exploring Autodesk Revit 2021 for Architects and Building Designers
- Exploring Autodesk Revit 2020 for Architects and Building Designers
- Exploring Autodesk Revit 2019 for Architecture, 15th Edition

## Autodesk Revit Structure Textbooks
- Exploring Autodesk Revit 2021 for Structural Engineers
- Exploring Autodesk Revit 2019 for Structure, 9th Edition
- Exploring Autodesk Revit 2018 for Structure, 8th Edition

## Autodesk Revit MEP Textbooks
- Exploring Autodesk Revit 2019 for MEP, 6th Edition
- Exploring Autodesk Revit 2018 for MEP, 5th Edition

## RISA-3D Textbook
- Exploring RISA-3D 14.0

## Bentley STAAD.Pro Textbooks
- Exploring Bentley STAAD.Pro (CONNECT Edition), 3rd Edition
- Exploring Bentley STAAD.Pro V8i (SELECT series 6)

## AutoCAD Civil 3D Textbooks
- Exploring AutoCAD Civil 3D 2020 for Engineers and Designers
- Exploring AutoCAD Civil 3D 2019 for Engineers and Designers
- Exploring AutoCAD Civil 3D 2018, 8th Edition

## AutoCAD Map 3D Textbooks
- Exploring AutoCAD Map 3D 2018, 8th Edition
- Exploring AutoCAD Map 3D 2017, 7th Edition

## Autodesk Navisworks Textbooks
- Exploring Autodesk Navisworks 2019 for BIM
- Exploring Autodesk Navisworks 2017, 4th Edition

## Oracle Primavera Textbooks
- Exploring Oracle Primavera P6 Professional 18 for Planners and Engineers
- Exploring Oracle Primavera P6 R8.4

## AutoCAD Raster Design Textbook
- Exploring AutoCAD Raster Design 2017

## CINEMA 4D Textbooks
- MAXON CINEMA 4D Studio R20 Studio for Digital Artists
- MAXON CINEMA 4D Studio R19: A Tutorial Approach, 6th Edition
- MAXON CINEMA 4D Studio R18: A Tutorial Approach, 5th Edition

## Autodesk 3ds Max Textbooks
- Autodesk 3ds Max 2021 for 3D Designers
- Autodesk 3ds Max 2020: A Comprehensive Guide, 20th Edition
- Autodesk 3ds Max 2019: A Comprehensive Guide, 19th Edition
- Autodesk 3ds Max 2018: A Comprehensive Guide, 18th Edition
- Autodesk 3ds Max 2021: A Beginners Guide
- Autodesk 3ds Max 2020: A Beginners Guide

## Autodesk Maya Textbooks
- Autodesk Maya 2020 for 3D Artists
- Autodesk Maya 2019 for 3D Artists
- Autodesk Maya 2018: A Comprehensive Guide, 10th Edition

## ZBrush Textbooks

- Pixologic ZBrush 2021 for Digital Artists
- Pixologic ZBrush 2020 for Digital Artists
- Pixologic ZBrush 2018 for Digital Artists
- Pixologic ZBrush 4R8: A Comprehensive Guide, 4th Edition